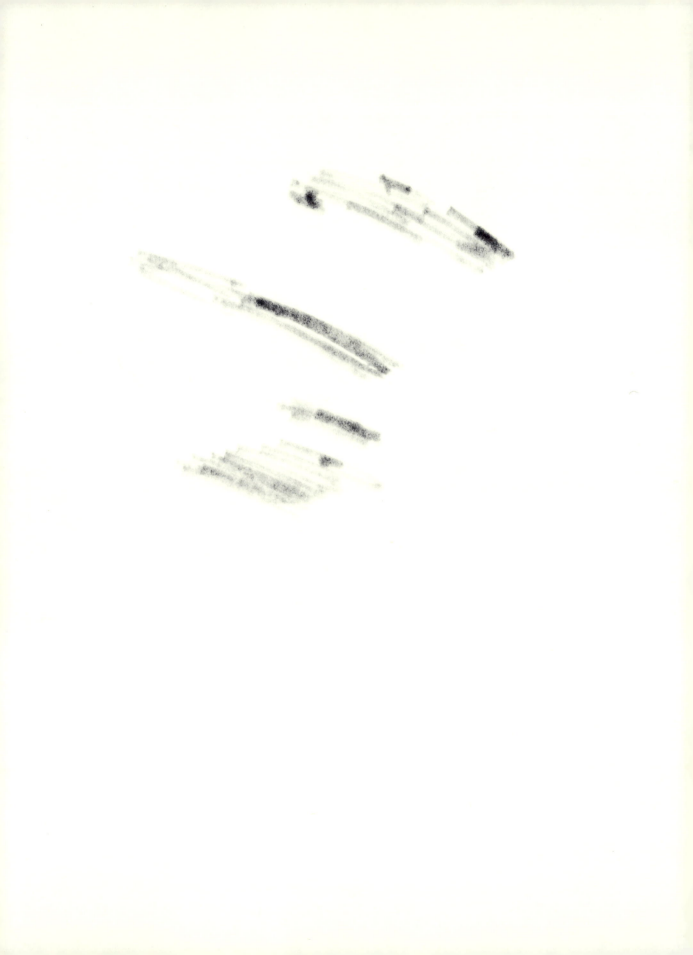

International Trade Law

ASPEN CASEBOOK SERIES

International Trade Law

Problems, Cases, and Materials

Second Edition

Daniel C.K. Chow

Joseph S. Platt-Porter Wright Morris & Arthur Professor of Law,
The Ohio State University Michael E. Moritz College of Law

Thomas J. Schoenbaum

Research Professor of Law,
George Washington University, Washington, DC

Wolters Kluwer
Law & Business

Printed in the United States of America.

1 2 3 4 5 6 7 8 9 0

ISBN 978-1-4548-0686-8

Library of Congress Cataloging-in-Publication Data

Chow, Daniel C. K.
  International trade law : problems, cases, and materials / Daniel C.K. Chow, Joseph S. Platt-Porter Wright Morris & Arthur Professor of Law, the Ohio State University, Michael E. Moritz College of Law, Thomas J. Schoenbaum, research professor of law, George Washington University, Washington, DC. — Second edition.
       pages cm. — (Aspen casebook series)
  Includes bibliographical references and index.
  ISBN 978-1-4548-0686-8
  1. Foreign trade regulation—United States—Cases. 2. Foreign trade regulation—Cases. 3. Foreign trade regulation—United States—Problems, exercises, etc. 4. Foreign trade regulation—Problems, exercises, etc. I. Schoenbaum, Thomas J. II. Title.
  KF1976.C455 2012
  343.7308'7—dc23

                                                                    2012037668

SUSTAINABLE FORESTRY INITIATIVE

Certified Sourcing
www.sfiprogram.org
SFI-01234

SFI label applies to the text stock

About Wolters Kluwer Law & Business

Wolters Kluwer Law & Business is a leading global provider of intelligent information and digital solutions for legal and business professionals in key specialty areas, and respected educational resources for professors and law students. Wolters Kluwer Law & Business connects legal and business professionals as well as those in the education market with timely, specialized authoritative content and information-enabled solutions to support success through productivity, accuracy and mobility.

Serving customers worldwide, Wolters Kluwer Law & Business products include those under the Aspen Publishers, CCH, Kluwer Law International, Loislaw, Best Case, ftwilliam.com and MediRegs family of products.

CCH products have been a trusted resource since 1913, and are highly regarded resources for legal, securities, antitrust and trade regulation, government contracting, banking, pension, payroll, employment and labor, and healthcare reimbursement and compliance professionals.

Aspen Publishers products provide essential information to attorneys, business professionals and law students. Written by preeminent authorities, the product line offers analytical and practical information in a range of specialty practice areas from securities law and intellectual property to mergers and acquisitions and pension/benefits. Aspen's trusted legal education resources provide professors and students with high-quality, up-to-date and effective resources for successful instruction and study in all areas of the law.

Kluwer Law International products provide the global business community with reliable international legal information in English. Legal practitioners, corporate counsel and business executives around the world rely on Kluwer Law journals, looseleafs, books, and electronic products for comprehensive information in many areas of international legal practice.

Loislaw is a comprehensive online legal research product providing legal content to law firm practitioners of various specializations. Loislaw provides attorneys with the ability to quickly and efficiently find the necessary legal information they need, when and where they need it, by facilitating access to primary law as well as state-specific law, records, forms and treatises.

Best Case Solutions is the leading bankruptcy software product to the bankruptcy industry. It provides software and workflow tools to flawlessly streamline petition preparation and the electronic filing process, while timely incorporating ever-changing court requirements.

ftwilliam.com offers employee benefits professionals the highest quality plan documents (retirement, welfare and non-qualified) and government forms (5500/PBGC, 1099 and IRS) software at highly competitive prices.

MediRegs products provide integrated health care compliance content and software solutions for professionals in healthcare, higher education and life sciences, including professionals in accounting, law and consulting.

Wolters Kluwer Law & Business, a division of Wolters Kluwer, is headquartered in New York. Wolters Kluwer is a market-leading global information services company focused on professionals.

To my wife Ching and our son Alan.

DC

To three inspirational teachers and scholars of this subject: John H. Jackson, Eric Stein, and Mitsuo Matsushita.

TJS

Summary of Contents

Contents

2   *Dispute Settlement Within the WTO*   63

3 *The Implementation of International Trade Obligations in the Domestic Legal Order* **95**

4 The Core Principles of the WTO: Most Favored Nation and National Treatment   **129**

5   *Trade in Goods: Customs and Tariff Law*   179

6   *Non-Tariff Trade Barriers*   245

7   *General Exceptions: Trade and Civil Society*   **299**

9   *Developing Countries*   **403**

13   *Intellectual Property and TRIPS*   **587**

14 *Export Controls* — 641

Preface

Over two years in the making, this edition reflects the many comments of users as well as our own experiences teaching the subject. Several new ideas have dominated our approach to this new edition.

First, we have reorganized the book to emphasize the most important of the global trade agreements administered by the World Trade Organization (WTO) — that is, the General Agreement on Tariffs and Trade (GATT). This casebook is purposely constructed to cover every GATT article, even those of only historical significance; we believe this comprehensive approach improves understanding of the whole. Of course, not all GATT provisions are given "equal time." We single out the most important provisions for extensive treatment.

Second, we have improved the coherence of the book by systematic coverage of all the GATT articles, integrating coverage of specialized WTO trade agreements with those GATT articles on which they depend or elaborate. For example, we cover the WTO Government Procurement Agreement (GPA) in conjunction with GATT Article III on national treatment because government procurement is excluded from national treatment except for those WTO members accepting the GPA.

Third, we have revised our approach to provide systematic coverage of the GATT and closely related WTO specialized agreements before tackling the WTO agreements that are more independent of the GATT, such as the General Agreement on Trade in Services (GATS) and the Agreement on Trade-Related Aspects of Intellectual Property Rights (TRIPS). We believe this approach improves student understanding.

Fourth, we cover in this edition every one of the many trade agreements administered by the WTO, given that all are now regularly in play and relevant to trade disputes and negotiations. Whereas in the past certain agreements could be virtually ignored, now all are relevant—although, of course, not to the same degree.

In preparing this new edition, we retain the salient characteristics of the first edition:

We are convinced of the pedagogical necessity to separate the teaching and study of International Trade Law and International Business Transactions. While the traditional approach is to cover these subjects together, we believe that this is confusing and unwise for several reasons. International Trade Law is now primarily a specialized branch of public international law, while International Business Transactions is largely private law with an important smattering of public and private international law. Moreover, the jurisprudence in both subjects is now enormous, and we think that, although the practitioner may handle both subjects in an integrated fashion, the student can best learn these two complex areas in different courses. Accordingly, we have designed this book to be a companion book to our own IBT book, Chow and Schoenbaum, *International Business Transactions* (Aspen 2d ed. 2010). Although each of these two books can be used independently, we have carefully designed each book to complement the other with virtually no overlap of coverage. We believe that these two compact books together provide an excellent coverage of the entire field of international business/economic law.

We continue to believe that students studying international trade law must study the primary materials of the law: the texts of the WTO agreements and the jurisprudence, as well as trade law cases decided by the WTO panels and Appellate Body. Accordingly, we have kept use of secondary materials to the absolute minimum. Our second edition is up to date, including some 70 principal cases as well as scores of cases discussed in the notes. We have, of course, edited the principal cases extensively to keep the book a manageable size. We publish herewith a Documents Supplement containing the text of the WTO trade agreement and other relevant materials.

Since International Trade Law is international economic law, the student must understand the basics of the economics of international trade and the economic basis and impacts of trade law provisions. We have included enough materials on economics throughout the text so that, in our experience, this need is served.

We believe that solving short problems is an excellent pedagogical aid to learning the law, and we have included many new problems in this edition. The problems are designed to be used selectively by professors and students: the teacher may wish to announce in advance the problems he or she wishes to cover in class.

We also retain the "channels" approach to international trade law as in the first edition. Although trade in goods is the most important channel of international business, three other "channels" are very important as well: trade in services, trade in technology, and foreign direct investment. Although we have revised this edition to reflect the overriding importance of trade in goods, this is not to downgrade the importance of the other three channels and the WTO agreements relevant to them.

The new edition of this book also reflects the growing importance of China and emerging-market and developing-member countries of the WTO. We emphasize as well the growing importance of preferential trade agreements and their sometimes uneasy fit with the law of the WTO. We have expanded our coverage of "linkage" issues, such as trade and environment and human rights. At the same time, we have carefully pruned outdated materials from the first edition and have developed a concise teaching tool of 670 pages that can be covered in a one-semester, three- or four-hour course in law school or business school.

We enjoy hearing comments and criticisms on our work. We hope that teachers who use this book will share their experiences teaching the subject with us and let us know what techniques and problems work best for them. We promise to consider all comments carefully and to adapt as many as we can.

Our colleagues Cinnamon Carlarne, Steve Charnovitz, Susan Karamanian, Robert Lutz, Alison Peck, and Maria Pereyra provided helpful comments and suggestions for this edition. Our students, Cindy Bi, Adam Colegrove, Ruxton McClure, and Adam Okuley provided tireless research assistance. Matt Cooper, research librarian at the Moritz College of Law, was able to find the most obscure materials.

Daniel C.K. Chow
chow.1@osu.edu

Thomas J. Schoenbaum
tschoen@law.gwu.edu

September 2012

Acknowledgments

Irwin, Douglas A., *Free Trade Under Fire*, pp. 21-26, 29-30, 32-33, 35-36, 45-46, 70-72, 83-85, 87-94, 98-99 (2004). Reprinted with the permission of the Princeton University Press.

International Trade Law

1

The Law of International Trade and the Multilateral Trading System

We begin by discussing the subject matter, scope, and approach of this book. We then provide an overview of the main international economic institutions and the multilateral trading systems that govern and make possible world trade and investment. This Chapter also covers some topics that are at the heart of the international system of economic relations: (1) the evaluation of arguments for and against "free" trade; (2) the conduct of international trade negotiations; and (3) an introduction to free trade areas and other preferential trading regimes.

I. Some Background Considerations

A. What Is the Law of International Trade?

For the purposes of this book, the law of international trade refers to the public international law treaties and legal institutions that constitute the multilateral trading system. Our primary focus will be the World Trade Organization (WTO) and the implementation of its obligations into U.S. domestic law. The role of the WTO is to reduce barriers to international trade in order to promote and foster trade, business, and economic development.

To understand the field of international trade and to give it some background and context, we draw some distinctions between two related but distinct fields of study: the law of international trade (sometimes also called international economic law)[1] and the law of international business transactions (commonly called IBT). Because both of these fields concern the legal aspects of international trade and business, we begin with a general economic definition of international trade and business below.

International trade refers broadly to economic and commercial activities that cross national boundaries or that have an effect across national boundaries. In the modern world, there are four major channels of international trade: (1) trade in goods, (2) trade in services, (3) technology transfer, and (4) foreign direct investment. Trade in goods is the most basic and oldest channel of international trade, but the other channels are rapidly gaining in importance. An obvious example of the international trade in goods occurs when a buyer in the United

---

1. *See* Steve Charnovitz, *What Is International Economic Law?* 14 J. Int'l Econ. L. 3 (2011).

States purchases a product from a seller in Japan. An example of the trade in services occurs when a lawyer or accountant residing in the United States provides legal or financial advice to a client in France via e-mail, fax, or phone. Technology transfer refers to access provided by the owner of technology, usually in the form of intellectual property, to another business entity in the form of an assignment or a license. An international transfer of technology occurs, for example, when a U.S. owner of a patent, trademark, or copyright assigns or licenses the rights to use these intellectual property rights in Germany to a German corporation. Foreign direct investment (commonly called FDI) occurs when an entity resident in one nation obtains a lasting ownership interest in an entity resident in another nation for business purposes involving some form of management control. For example, a U.S. parent company may establish a wholly or partially owned subsidiary in China.

These four channels often represent a progression by which a business entity does international business today. Many business entities begin with the international sale of goods or services, then progress to technology transfer and finally to FDI. Each progression involves a higher commitment of resources, promising higher returns in exchange for higher risk. All international business in the world today falls into one or some combination of these four channels.

The law of international trade and the law of IBT concern different legal aspects of these four channels. We elaborate more fully on these different legal aspects in the next section. Below we first explain the approach of this casebook.

This book responds to the foregoing definition of international trade both in its organization and its content:

- We employ a "channels of trade" approach to learning the law of international trade, covering in turn the law relating to trade in goods, services trade, trade in technology, and investment and trade.
- Our emphasis is on the international law of trade: the agreements of the WTO and the multilateral trading systems that relate to each of these four channels of trade as well as the important decisions rendered under the WTO dispute settlement system that interpret this international law.
- We cover in detail the principal national laws that lawyers use to serve clients in international trade. In many cases, these national laws are the domestic law implementations of WTO obligations. Our focus in this regard is the law of the United States. We cover to some extent the law of the European Union, an economic and political union of twenty-seven European states. We also cover in as much detail as space allows trade with China and developing countries.
- In this book we do not cover the law of international business transactions (IBT). We believe that these two bodies of law are conceptually distinct, and, while the practicing lawyer will combine them, the best approach for a student is to learn them one at a time. We have authored a companion book, Chow and Schoenbaum, *International Business Transactions: Problems, Cases, and Materials* (Aspen 2d ed. 2010) that examines the IBT dimensions of each of the four channels of trade and is designed as the IBT counterpart to this book.
- Our methodology in this book as well as in our IBT book is to provide a concise teaching tool that employs short problems as the best way for students to work their way through the law with the help of a teacher.

This book is organized to present in a systematic fashion the law and the most important jurisprudence of the WTO as well as the salient features of certain regional free trade agreements. We take special care to cover every provision of the General Agreement on Tariffs and Trade (GATT), the oldest and still most important global trade agreement. We also cover every additional international trade agreement presently administered by the WTO, although we give more attention to some than to others.

B. Distinguishing the Law of International Business Transactions and the Law of International Trade

The international business lawyer faces two sets of related, but fundamentally different, questions with regard to a client's legal problems. The first set of questions has to do with the structure of the transactions involved; this is primarily a matter of private law to be worked out with the parties involved. The second set of legal questions has to do with how the transactions involved may be regulated or benefited by the public law of international trade. We emphasize that these two sets of questions are discrete, but related, as the following discussion will clarify.

1. The Law of International Business Transactions

The first set of questions relate to the structuring and implementation of the trade transaction itself. For example, how does a buyer in the United States go about setting up the international sales transaction with a seller in Japan so that the buyer can both complete the transaction in a timely manner and receive the goods? How can the Japanese seller make sure that it will be paid expeditiously and not left to try to compel a payment from a buyer located in the United States? Who will pay for arranging the shipment of the goods from Japan to the United States? Who will be responsible for insurance and for bearing the risk of loss should the goods be damaged or lost in transit? Even in a simple sale of goods, there are a number of risks, and many ways in which things can go wrong. We use the sales transaction to illustrate some of these planning, structuring, and implementation issues, but the same questions arise (and can be even more complex) in trade in services, technology transfer, and FDI.

In structuring this sales transaction, the international business lawyer will need to take into account the law of the United States and the law of Japan relating to the major issues underlying the transaction. For example, the U.S. buyer may wish to have the transaction governed by the contract law of the state in which the buyer resides (most likely a version of the Uniform Commercial Code). On the other hand, the seller in Japan might wish to have the transaction governed by Japanese contract law.[2] In this context, we refer to these national laws as private law because they are the laws that derive from some single nation that purports to govern commercial activity conducted by persons or business entities resident in that nation. The law applicable to an IBT is private law because it is the law of a single

---

2. A contract for the international sale of goods between parties in the United States and in a foreign country may also be subject to an international treaty, the United Nations Convention on Contracts for the International Sale of Goods (CISG). S. Treaty Doc. No. 9, 98th Cong., 1st Sess. 22 (1983), 19 I.L.M., reprinted at 15 U.S.C. App. 52 (1997).

nation (or a combination of the laws of both nations involved) that is intended to govern a transaction between parties. These laws, such as contract law, deal with the interests of private parties and do not, for the most part, concern third parties or the public. The choice between the laws of the United States and of Japan will most likely be decided by a court in one of these two countries if and when a dispute arises. In making a decision on which law to apply, the court is engaged in an application of "private" international law; i.e., a choice of law between two private domestic laws in an international context.[3]

We categorize the planning, structure, and implementation of these private transactions as part of the field of IBT. We do not deal with the law of IBT in this book, except as background or as needed.

2. *The Law of International Trade*

While the international sale of goods transaction involves primarily the private interests of the buyer and seller, the sale might also involve public law issues of international trade law. Every international sale of goods is both an export from the country of the seller and an import into the country of the buyer. What might be the public law issues that are involved in such a sale?

From the perspective of the exporting country, there are usually fewer issues than on the importing side because most countries are less concerned about what leaves their borders than what comes in. Nevertheless, an exporting country might restrict exports if the goods had a military use or were dual-use goods that included advanced technologies that might be converted to military uses. A country may also wish to restrict or limit exports to certain countries that are considered to be hostile.

From the importing country's perspective, there are a number of issues that might affect the national interest. An importing country might wish to restrict the influx of goods that might harm an important domestic industry, such as agriculture, or an infant industry that might not be able to withstand foreign competition. Some countries might consider inexpensive imports to lead to the loss of jobs in industries that are unable to compete with the foreign goods. Common methods that importing countries have used to restrict imports are through the imposition of a customs duty or tariff on imports or through a numerical restriction called a quota. Our purpose in introducing these issues is to illustrate that the international sale of goods—indeed, all international transactions—have a public law dimension, as they involve the interests of a nation in its trading relationship with other nations.

It is readily apparent that international trade would be impossible if each nation were left to its own devices in dealing with the public law issues arising from international trade. In order to bring a modicum of order to this system, a remarkable and growing body of law has developed to provide the basis for the way nations deal with each other in trade and economic matters. This legal system, known as

---

3. Thus, the term "private" international law is actually a misnomer since the result of the application of a private international law analysis is national or domestic law; i.e., the law of one of the nations to the private business transaction or sometimes a combination of national laws. Private international law is sometimes also referred to as the international choice of laws. We introduce this concept to contrast it with the concept of public international law introduced later in this section.

the multilateral trading system, was begun in the 1940s and includes significant international economic institutions. A highlight was the establishment in 1947 of GATT, the precursor of the modern WTO. One of the major roles played by GATT and the WTO was to establish a legal framework and a set of rules and guidelines that concerns the conduct of international trade as well as the resolution of disputes between members using the system.

The WTO legal framework (as well as other aspects of international economic law) is part of what is commonly termed public international law. A full discussion of the meaning of this term is impossible here, but since the major source of public international law is treaties, the multilateral trading system, which was created over the last sixty years by concluding such agreements, qualifies as a preeminent example of this field of law. But while the multilateral trading system has been established as a matter of public international law through a series of treaties, these treaties generally do not have direct legal effect within the nations themselves. Rather, the treaties of the multilateral trading system create obligations on the part of nations to implement these treaties in national law. In the United States, the WTO treaties are implemented into U.S. law through federal (and certain state) statutes and regulations. It is primarily through their national implementations that the law of international trade affects private business; nevertheless, the public international law of international trade (and the international economic institutions involved) exercise great influence not only over economic policies between states but also, derivatively, over IBT.

3.   *Three Levels of Analysis*

As the preceding discussion indicates, three levels of analysis must be considered by the international business lawyer. The first level is private law regulation through domestic or national law. In our example, we have used an international sales transaction as an illustration because it is the most fundamental and common type of international transaction; but the same would hold true for the other channels of trade, such as trade in services, technology transfer, and to some extent, FDI. The first and most basic level concerns the national laws that apply to the interests of the private parties to the transaction. At this level, the concern is primarily with complying with applicable national (or private) laws in planning, structuring, and implementing the transaction. At the risk of being redundant, we consider this to be the field of study called international business transactions. For most lawyers interested in international business, IBT is the first and most basic field of study.

Second, IBTs occur against the background of international rules established by the multilateral trading system. Thus, the international business lawyer must be intimately familiar with the public international law of international trade. This involves the study of the corpus of international trade law: the treaties, agreements, and understandings entered into at the international level. This body of law is extensive—the treaties alone involve thousands of provisions—and there is a growing body of important jurisprudence created by international tribunals, especially the Appellate Body of the WTO, which functions as a busy high court of international trade.

The third and perhaps most important level of analysis that must be undertaken by the international business lawyer is public law regulation at the national level. For example, a seller and a buyer in an international sale of goods must comply with any applicable laws that apply to exports in the country of the seller and imports in the country of the buyer. These can range from tariffs and quotas to anti-dumping regulations and export controls. It is important to realize, however, that the national laws regulating trade in most cases are *implementations of international obligations that have their origins on the international level.* This also means that conflicts can (and frequently do) arise between the international obligations undertaken and their national law counterparts. The identification and resolution of these conflicts are also the work of the international business lawyer.

The subject matter of this book concerns the second and third levels of analysis of international business and trade: the law of international trade as public international law and its transformation into the domestic law of primarily one jurisdiction, the United States. Our methodology will be to present the applicable public international law rules and processes that govern a subject matter, and then to present the way the U.S. trade laws implement and apply these international norms.

In our view, the fields of IBT and international trade law are two separate fields and should be the subject of different courses of study in the law school curriculum. The two fields are too vast and complicated to combine in a single course or casebook. A sophisticated international business lawyer, of course, will need to understand both the law of IBT and the law of international trade. But learning the two subjects is best done one at a time. Thus, students interested in international business law should first complete a course in IBT to learn the basic transactional law applicable to the four main channels of trade. That course should be followed by a course in the law of international trade that examines the international and national regulatory frameworks within which trade and international business must operate. This casebook is intended as a text for the second course of study, and it is a companion work to our book, *International Business Transactions: Problems, Cases, and Materials* (Aspen 2d ed. 2010). We believe that these two compact volumes offer a complete and concise package for the student interested in international business and trade, at least insofar as these vast, complicated, and important subjects can be studied in law schools.

NOTES AND QUESTIONS

1. In our discussion above, we referred to *treaties* as a source of public international law. The term "treaty" in international law and as used in this book refers very broadly to any kind of agreement (whether called a convention, charter, agreement, protocol, or understanding) between states and between or among other international actors, such as intergovernmental organizations. The public international law rules governing the creation, operation, and enforcement of treaties may be found in the Vienna Convention on the Law of Treaties, May 23, 1969, 1155 U.N.T.S. 331. Currently, 110 states (but not the United States) are parties to this Convention, which is literally a "treaty on treaties." The United States accepts the Vienna Convention as expressive of the customary international law of treaties. For a concise analysis of public international law, see Sean D. Murphy, *Principles of Public International Law* (2006).

2. A second source of public international law is known as "custom." While states can bind themselves through treaties (considered to be a type of contract), states may also become legally bound through *customary international law*, the second major source of public international law. The basic reason that custom can be transformed into law is that states are considered to consent to the creation of legal

obligations if their behavior (known as "state practice") manifests an intention (known by the Latin phrase *opinio juris*) to be bound. Most of our attention in this book will be focused on multilateral treaties as the source of public international law because such treaties are the primary source of the law of international trade. Other recognized sources of international law include *general principles of law* common to most states (such as equity), *decisions of international tribunals,* and the *writings of legal experts and scholars.*

3. It has long been settled — at least as a "black letter" legal rule — that public international law is part of the law of the United States. The Supremacy Clause of the U.S. Constitution provides that treaties entered into by the United States, as well as the Constitution and the laws of the United States, shall be "the Supreme Law of the Land." U.S. Const. art. VI. In addition, the United States Supreme Court has stated that "international law is part of our law." *The Paquete Habana,* 175 U.S. 677, 700 (1900). Both treaties and customary international law are generally considered to be forms of federal law, equivalent in rank to federal statutes, and supreme over the law of the states. *See Ware v. Hylton,* 3 U.S. (3 Dall.) 199, 326 (1796). Where applicable, international law must be applied in federal or state courts without the need for any further action by the President or Congress. In *Foster v. Neilson,* 27 U.S. 253 (1829), however, Chief Justice Marshall drew an important distinction between self-executing and non-self-executing treaties that is now followed by many countries in addition to the United States. A self-executing treaty has direct effect and force within the United States. Such a treaty must be applied directly by federal or state courts whenever applicable. A non-self-executing treaty does not have a direct effect in the United States but must be implemented through domestic legislation. The treaties of the multilateral trading system that we will be considering in this book are considered to be non-self-executing treaties. The United States has implemented its WTO obligations by enacting new federal statutes or by amending existing statutes, both scattered throughout the United States Code. Note that where a non-self-executing treaty has been implemented through federal legislation, it is the domestic implementing law that is given effect in a federal or state court, not the treaty itself. However, as a treaty creates a legal obligation on the part of the state to implement its contents through domestic legislation, the issue of whether the domestic implementing legislation fully implements the treaty obligations is an important one that is sometimes contested in the WTO.

PROBLEM 1-1

A French company believes that a new tax on foreign goods issued by the State of Ohio is discriminatory and in violation of the WTO General Agreement on Tariffs and Trade. The French company files a lawsuit in federal district court on the theory that the WTO treaties are part of the federal law of the United States and that the new state statute violates the basic principles contained in the GATT. Will the case be dismissed or be allowed to go forward. Why?

PROBLEM 1-2

You represent Advanced Encryption Devices (AED), a manufacturer of automated teller machines (ATMs) and other sophisticated devices for use by banks.

The ATMs use state-of-the-art encryption techniques and also enable linkages to numerous financial and information networks used by banks. You have been approached by a private distributor of electronic goods located in Country Z, a newly democratic regime that at one time had a repressive military government that was hostile to the United States. The distributor wishes to purchase a large quantity of the ATMs for sale in Country Z but wants your assurances that the machines are compatible for use with Country Z's telecommunications system. Country Z is also developing its own fledgling electronics industry that wants to compete with AED. What private law issues involving IBT, and what public law issues involving international trade law, may arise out of this transaction?

II.   International Trade Flows

We present a summary picture of international trade in the world economy. The rapid growth of all channels of international trade has been a hallmark of the world economy since the end of the Second World War. As Figure 1-1 indicates, the trade in goods has more than doubled in the past two decades.

Although merchandise trade has traditionally been and remains the fundamental channel of international trade, in the past several decades the growth in the trade in services, FDI, and technology transfer have all exceeded the growth in the trade in goods. For example, among developed countries the export of commercial services (such as financial, insurance, legal, and business services) has grown at a rate of 8.6 percent for the period from 1985 to 2000, which is slightly higher than the 8.3 percent growth rate for those same countries for the export of goods. *See United Nations Conference on Trade and Development (UNCTAD) World Investment Report 2001*, 300-315. Trade in services often occurs through FDI, as a great deal of new investment and cross-border mergers and acquisitions involve business entities that provide services, such as financial services and research and development. In 2004, over 63 percent of all cross-border mergers and acquisitions involved the

FIGURE 1-1
Growth of World Merchandise Exports in the Past Two Decades
and Percentage Share

	World	Developed Countries	EU	USA	Developing Countries
1980	1,932	65.5	36.4	11.7	34.5
1985	1,875	68.4	35.6	11.7	31.6
1990	3,423	71.7	40.5	11.5	28.3
1995	5,104	68.0	40.4	11.5	32.0
1999	5,577	66.9	39.1	12.6	33.1
2001	5,984	75.1	37.7	13.6	20.3
2005	8,975	63.1	40.4	9.1	33.5
2010	15,230	53.9	33.8	12.1	41.9

Sources: IMF and UNCTADSTAT (2011) available at http://unctadstat.unctad.org.

services sector. *See UNCTAD World Investment Report 2005*, 8. All forms of FDI have increased in the past two decades by 780 percent for an annual growth rate of 9.5 percent, outpacing both the growth in exports and the trade in services. Of all of the channels of international trade, technology transfer has enjoyed the highest rate of growth, at least by some measures. One measure of the international volume of technology transfer can be ascertained by the increase in the payment of royalty and licensing fees. An owner of technology in the form of patents, copyrights, and trademarks usually makes this technology available to another party in exchange for the payment of a fee. In a span of less than two decades, technology payments increased nearly sevenfold, from $12 billion in 1983 to $80 billion in 1999. *See* Jon Kleinert, *The Role of Multinational Enterprises in Globalization* 9 (2001). As shown in Figure 1-5 (see page 15), the growth of technology transfer in world trade is one indication that knowledge and advanced technology in the form of intellectual property have never been more important to economic development.

In the present century, both trade and economic activity continue to grow at a record pace. Between 2001 and 2011 the world economy expanded by more than 20 percent. World trade (both exports and imports) rose by over 30 percent; and outstanding international debt securities have jumped by almost 90 percent to more than $14 trillion. We now present more recent figures of the four channels of world trade.

PROBLEM 1-3

You are a consultant for Citizens for Responsible Economic Development, a nonprofit organization monitoring global economic development and the problems that can arise. You have been asked to review trends in the charts (Figures 1-2, 1-3, 1-4, 1-5) and to write a memorandum discussing the following issues. For these purposes, you are to divide countries into two groups: developed countries (i.e., wealthy states such as the United States, Japan, and many European nations) and developing countries (i.e., poorer countries in Africa, South America, and Asia).

(1) Which group of nations dominates in the area of international trade in goods in terms of revenues earned and share of global trade? (For the moment, leave out China, which, although a developing nation, has an enormous export trade, and consider all other developing countries. Due to its huge impact on trade, we focus specifically on China later in this Chapter.)

(2) Which group of nations dominates in the area of technology innovation and creation? One indication of dominance is the amount of royalties that these nations receive for licensing their technology. Which group of nations are recipients of technology transfer from the innovator countries?

(3) If certain nations dominate international trade, would you expect the rules of the multilateral trading system, at least historically, to reflect the interests of these nations? Why? Does this create a concern?

A.   Trade in Goods

In 2010, total world merchandise trade totaled U.S. $15.3 trillion, a growth of 22 percent over the previous year, but down 6 percent from a high in 2008. Figure 1-2 shows the levels of trade by regions.

FIGURE 1-2
World Merchandise Trade by Region and Selected Country, 2010 (USD Billion and Percentage)

	Exports					Imports				
	Value	Annual Percentage Change				Value	Annual Percentage Change			
	2010	2005-2010	2008	2009	2010	2010	2005-2010	2008	2009	2010
World	15,230	6.15	15.15	−22.56	22.00	15,262	5.70	15.55	−23.20	20.98
North America	1,962					2,676				
United States	1,278	5.51	11.88	−18.78	20.90	1,968	0.48	7.38	−26.01	22.60
Canada	386	−0.54	8.52	−30.10	22.14	391	1.89	7.20	−20.95	18.60
Mexico	298	4.29	7.27	−21.29	29.80	317	4.06	9.64	−24.31	28.63
South and Central America	847					837				
Brazil	202	9.53	23.21	−22.71	31.97	191	18.28	44.01	−26.71	43.23
Europe	5,481					5,494				
European Union	5,149	3.71	10.45	−22.42	12.52	5,234	3.56	11.80	−24.89	13.05
Germany	1,268	4.22	9.16	−22.55	13.64	1,066	5.13	12.02	−21.83	15.52
France	521	1.72	9.75	−21.32	7.85	605	3.28	13.11	−21.72	8.52
United Kingdom	405	−1.19	4.40	−23.23	15.34	558	−0.67	1.34	−23.71	16.09
Italy	448	2.63	8.28	−25.02	10.42	484	3.00	9.52	−26.12	16.98
CIS	584	9.24	35.28	−35.80	29.53	427	11.98	32.05	−33.60	22.87
Russian Federation	400	8.19	33.12	−35.69	31.85	273	12.56	30.64	−34.31	29.49
Africa	503					449				
South Africa	85	6.68	12.67	−22.73	28.99	76	1.97	6.36	−22.28	2.70
Asia	5,838					5,331				
Japan	770	3.02	9.50	−25.74	32.57	692	4.48	23.06	−27.81	25.78
China	1,578	13.54	17.32	−15.88	31.33	1,395	14.11	18.34	−11.26	38.89
Four East Asian Traders	1,483	9.32	9.21	−19.44	28.55	1,480	10.54	6.38	−17.77	35.72

	Exports					Imports				
	Value	Annual Percentage Change				Value	Annual Percentage Change			
	2010	2005-2010	2008	2009	2010	2010	2005-2010	2008	2009	2010
India	217	15.55	29.73	–15.22	31.50	324	17.10	40.27	–19.83	25.83
Memorandum Items:										
MERCOSUR (4)	282	9.99	24.89	–22.11	29.41	267	16.93	40.90	–27.87	43.37
ASEAN (10)	1,051	8.00	15.40	–18.54	29.21	951	8.00	22.16	–23.44	31.30
Developing Economies	6,395	9.08	19.17	–21.28	29.20	5,932	10.19	21.69	–19.22	28.47
Developing Asia	5010	9.67	18.50	–19.70	29.73	4,577	10.25	21.04	–18.68	30.68

Source: UNCTADSTAT (2011) available at http://unctadstat.unctad.org.

Notes: CIS refers to Commonwealth and Independent States; Four East Asian traders (sometimes referred to as the "Four Asian Tigers") are Taiwan, Hong Kong, South Korea, and Singapore; MERCOSUR (Market of the South) consists of four countries: Argentina, Brazil, Paraguay, and Uruguay; ASEAN (Association of South East Asian Nations) consists of ten countries: Brunei Darussalam, Cambodia, Indonesia, Lao People's Democratic Republic, Malaysia, Myanmar, Philippines, Singapore, Thailand, and Vietnam.

FIGURE 1-3
World Trade of Commercial Services by Region and Selected Country, 2010 (USD Billion)

	Exports Value						Imports Value					
	2005	2006	2007	2008	2009	2010	2005	2006	2007	2008	2009	2010
World	2,564	2,903	3,477	3,928	3,468	3,745	2,466	2,754	3,244	3,699	3,302	3,560
North America	457	508	584	632	579	624	401	445	482	520	473	509
United States	385	432	501	546	505	541	314	349	375	405	370	393
Canada	56	60	65	68	59	68	66	73	83	89	79	91
Mexico	16	16	18	18	15	15	21	23	24	26	24	26
South and Central America	66	75	88	103	92	105	87	97	117	139	129	156
Brazil	16	19	24	30	28	33	24	29	37	47	47	63
Europe	1,270	1,434	1,733	1,938	1,673	1,575	1,125	1,235	1,465	1,635	1,432	1,446
European Union	1,188	1,344	1,811	1,624	1,557	1,576	1,068	1,173	1,390	1,550	1,352	1,363
Germany	167	195	229	261	233	238	212	226	261	292	257	263
United Kingdom	208	237	288	289	240	238	163	176	203	204	167	169
France	122	129	150	168	143	143	107	113	130	142	127	130
Italy	89	99	112	120	103	98	90	101	122	131	117	110
CIS	43	53	67	86	71	79	62	73	95	119	97	112
Russian Federation	25	31	39	51	42	44	39	73	83	89	79	72
Africa	60	67	79	90	82	92	77	93	120	154	137	155
South Africa	11	12	14	13	12	14	12	14	16	17	15	18
Asia	605	696	841	985	884	1,048	675	768	912	1,066	979	1,117
Japan	110	117	129	149	128	141	134	136	150	170	149	158
China	74	92	122	147	130	158	84	101	130	159	159	183

| | Exports | | | | | | Imports | | | | | |
| | Value | | | | | | Value | | | | | |
	2005	2006	2007	2008	2009	2010	2005	2006	2007	2008	2009	2010
Four East Asian traders	190	218	266	321	283	340	180	205	236	265	237	283
India	53	70	87	104	91	116	47	59	71	88	81	109
Memorandum Items:												
MERCOSUR (4)	25	30	37	46	42	50	33	39	50	62	61	79
ASEAN (10)	119	138	176	200	183	215	139	157	184	212	195	226
Developing Economies	628	727	887	1,035	937	1,110	704	823	996	1,187	1,094	1,270
Developing Asia	477	559	691	812	734	882	527	618	744	877	813	941

Source: UNCTADSTAT (2011) available at http://unctadstat.unctad.org.

FIGURE 1-4
Foreign Direct Investment By Region (USD Billion and Percentage)

	FDI Inflow			FDI Outflow		
	1970	*2000*	*2010*	*1970*	*2000*	*2010*
Value ($bn)						
Developed Nations	9.5	1,138.0	601.9	14.1	1,094.7	935.2
High-Income Developing Nations	1.5	156.9	277.2	0.0	129.0	209.1
Middle-Income Developing Nations	1.5	92.3	209.0	0.0	3.6	97.3
Low-Income Developing Nations	0.8	8.4	87.4	0.0	1.7	21.1
Sub-Saharan States	0.8	8.1	39.7	0.0	1.3	3.3
Shares (%)						
Developed Nations	71.1	81.1	48.4	99.6	88.8	70.7
High-Income Developing Nations	11.0	11.2	22.3	0.0	10.5	15.8
Middle-Income Developing Nations	11.3	6.6	16.8	0.3	0.3	7.4
Low-Income Developing Nations	6.5	0.6	7.0	0.0	0.1	1.6
Sub-Saharan States	6.2	0.6	3.2	0.1	0.1	0.3

Source: UNCTADSTAT (2011) available at http://unctadstat.unctad.org.

B.   Services Trade

Trade in services rose by 11 percent in 2011 to reach U.S. $4.2 trillion. Figure 1-3 shows the levels of services trade by regions.

C.   Foreign Direct Investment

In 2011, world FDI rose by 17 percent to a total of U.S. $1.5 trillion. Cross-border mergers and acquisitions amounting to $716 billion accounted for the bulk of this figure. Major FDI investors were not only from developed countries; companies based in China (including Hong Kong), Russia, and Brazil were major players. Companies from developing countries invested $117 billion abroad. Figure 1-4 provides an overview of world FDI.

Most FDI recipients were developed countries, which received $542 billion. Investment into western Asia and Africa totaled $34 billion and $31 billion, respectively. South and East Asia received a new high of $164 billion. The largest recipients of FDI were the United Kingdom ($165 billion), China ($99 billion), and the United States ($72 billion).

D.   Technology Trade

The value of technology trade can be measured by compiling information on international transactions involving royalties and license fee payments (R & LF payments). Figure 1-5 is a summary of the payment and receipt of global R & LF payments:

FIGURE 1-5
Receipts and Payments of Royalties and License Fees of Selected Countries, 2000-2010 (USD Billion)

	2000	2005	2006	2007	2009	2010
Payments						
United States	16.6	25.6	25.0	26.5	29.8	33.4
Japan	11.0	14.7	15.5	16.7	16.8	18.8
Canada	3.8	6.9	7.0	8.2	8.1	8.7
Singapore	5.0	9.3	9.0	9.0	11.6	15.9
South Korea	3.2	4.6	4.7	5.1	7.2	9.0
China	1.3	5.3	6.6	8.2	11.1	13.0
Taiwan	1.8	1.8	2.3	2.6	3.4	4.9
Australia	1.1	2.0	2.2	2.8	3.0	N/A
Thailand	0.7	1.7	2.0	2.3	2.3	3.1
Receipts						
United States	43.2	64.4	70.7	84.5	93.9	89.8
Japan	10.2	17.7	20.1	23.2	21.7	26.7
Canada	2.3	2.8	3.2	3.5	3.4	3.8
Singapore	0.1	0.9	1.0	1.2	1.3	1.9
South Korea	0.7	1.9	2.0	1.7	3.2	3.1
China	0.1	0.2	0.2	0.3	0.4	0.8
Taiwan	0.4	0.2	0.2	0.2	0.2	0.5
Australia	0.4	0.6	0.6	0.7	0.7	N/A
Thailand	0.0	0.0	0.0	0.1	0.1	0.2

Source: UNCTADSTAT (2011) available at http://unctadstat.unctad.org.

PROBLEM 1-4

In the span of about two decades, China has risen from an Original Equipment Manufacturer (OEM) of plasma television sets for multinational companies (that then placed their own brand names on the sets) to become the leading manufacturer of plasma television sets in the world with its own brand names. Note that as an OEM, China was given access by the multinationals to technology in the form of patents, know-how, and other information in order to manufacture the televisions for its multinational clients; China would not have been able to manufacture the products for its clients without access to such know-how and technology.

(1) How did China rise so quickly to dominate the global market for plasma televisions and beat out the multinationals that once occupied the industry? Where did China acquire the know-how to do so?

(2) Can China replicate this process in other industries (such as in computers, automobiles, and telecommunications) where many multinationals are also heavily investing in China? If so, what will be the result for China over the long term?

NOTES AND QUESTIONS

1. All nations seek economic development. For developed nations, economic development means greater productivity and a higher standard of living for their

citizens. For developing nations, economic development means modernization and industrialization that will help them overcome poverty and backwardness. For several decades after the Second World War, many developing nations were wary of international trade with their former colonial masters and pursued a policy of isolationism and self-sufficiency. Based on the table statistics above, which policy leads to greater economic development, isolationism or engagement in international trade?

2. Until the middle of the last century, developed nations dominated the world both politically and economically. The nations of Europe, Japan, and the United States obtained colonial concessions throughout what is now the developing world. South and East Asia, West Asia, and most of Africa were subjected to colonial rule, often backed by the point of a gun. Developing countries in Africa and Asia gained their independence from their former colonial masters only after the Second World War. How might this history be relevant in explaining the causes of poverty and lack of economic development that continue to exist in many developing countries? Does this history create any special obligations on the part of developed countries?

The picture of the world economy in 2012 looks very different from the past. We now live in a multipolar, multispeed economy. The developed world—North America, Europe, and Japan—is experiencing sluggish economic growth and sovereign debt problems, while many developing countries and especially the BRICS (Brazil, Russia, India, China, and South Africa) are growing between 4 and 10 percent annually. Some predict a future economic transformation that will shift significant economic and political power to so-called emerging market countries. *See* Antoine van Agtmael, *The Emerging Markets Century* (2007).

3. All aspects of international trade have greatly increased since the end of the Second World War, especially during the last several decades. What accounts for this? One reason is political reform. During the Cold War the world was divided into opposing camps with the United States, the champion of democracy and free market capitalism, leading one side, and the Soviet Union and China, the leading proponents of communism, leading the other. Deep mistrust and hostility prevented the two camps from engaging in meaningful levels of international trade. A new era of international trade began when the disintegration of the Soviet Union and its satellite countries marked the end of the Cold War. In 1978, the People's Republic of China opened its doors to the world and has emerged as one of the world's most vibrant economies. In addition, many developing countries that initially viewed the multilateral trading system with mistrust shifted their priorities to economic development and are actively pursuing trade opportunities. These developments have allowed international trade to become truly global

4. International trade is a key aspect of the process of change known as "globalization," which in economic terms can be defined as the relatively free movement of goods, services, capital, technology, information, and people all over the world. *See generally*, Thomas L. Friedman, *The World is Flat* (2007). In our time the scope and pace of globalization is unique in human history. International economic institutions such as the International Monetary Fund (IMF), discussed in the next section, and the WTO are regarded with great suspicion by many people, especially so-called antiglobalists, who accuse these institutions of promoting unchecked globalization and economic development at the cost of social and human values. The complex issues of the globalization controversy are largely outside the scope of this book, but we believe that the impact of international trade on civil society presents an important set of policy questions. We address the major issues in various

places throughout this book as well as in Chapter 7, which is devoted entirely to this subject.

PROBLEM 1-5

Not everyone applauds the growth of international trade. Many believe that the expansion of international trade and globalization have created many harmful effects on the world that are disproportionately borne by poor countries. These critics argue that the WTO is the not-so-secret tool of multinational enterprises (MNEs), large corporations that are able to organize their structures (usually consisting of a holding or parent company and many foreign subsidiaries) to evade their legal and social responsibilities. In this view, the growth of international trade, new opportunities for market access, and the elimination of trade barriers—all attributable in some significant part to the WTO—have led to harmful effects such as:

- Permanent damage to the environment, including deforestation, destruction of natural habitats, extinction of species, damage to the earth's atmosphere, and global warming;
- Exploitation of workers in low-wage countries;
- Increasing disparity in wealth between developed and developing countries.

Can you explain how globalization has allowed MNEs to exploit the advantages of trade to create these harmful effects? If an MNE had dangerous operations, where would it likely set them up? How does an increase in trade lead to these harmful effects? Why do some critics blame the WTO?

PROBLEM 1-6

A central concept closely related to the issues discussed in Problem 1-5 above is the economic concept of "externalities." An externality is a cost (or benefit) that falls not on the actor whose conduct creates the cost, but on some third party.[4] Externalities tend to lead to inefficiencies because an actor will not take into full account the costs (or benefits) of its actions since these costs are not borne by the actor. The classic example is environmental pollution. Suppose that an MNE pollutes the environment in Country B, a developing economy. The MNE reaps the economic rewards from its conduct but the costs (i.e., damage to the environment) fall upon others. You might believe that the costs fall upon the population of Country B, but that might also be a more complex issue than it first appears, which explains why externalities can be so difficult to control.

(1) Why might Country B's leaders and population welcome the MNE into its borders and be totally unconcerned about the harmful effects of its activities? Hint: Many environmental problems, such as global warming or extinction of species, do not manifest their damaging effects on the ecosystem for decades.

---

4. *See* Daniel Chow, *Counterfeiting as an Externality Imposed by Multinational Companies on Developing Countries*, 51 Va. J. Int'l L. 785, 789 (2011).

(2) Economists often emphasize what appears to be a truism: There is no externality that is external to the world—in other words, someone must bear the cost imposed by the externality. But this statement is also more nuanced than it might first appear. In this problem, neither the MNE nor the present population of Country B will bear the full cost, but someone will. Who? Do these parties have a say at the table? Who will represent these parties?

(3) Why are environmental issues now a major concern for countries and international organizations, including the WTO?

III.   The Principal Global Economic Institutions

The principal organization that we will study in this book is the WTO, but the student should also be familiar with its affiliated institutions, the World Bank, and the IMF. All three organizations work closely together.

The modern multilateral trading system has its origins in the period immediately following the Second World War when a group of nations, led by the United States, held a conference in Bretton Woods, New Hampshire, for the purpose of establishing a set of international institutions that would help avoid the disastrous economic policies that contributed to the war.

In the early part of the twentieth century, after the First World War, many nations erected protectionist trade barriers. In 1930, the U.S. Congress passed the Smoot-Hawley Tariff Act, which established tariffs that averaged over 53 percent of the value of the products imported into the United States. Many other nations followed suit with similarly draconian tariffs. The purpose of these tariffs was to prevent trade. During this period, as economic tensions continued to rise, many nations viewed each other with mistrust and hostility, which eventually led to the Second World War. Where economic conflict exists, military conflict often soon erupts.

To establish a basis for international economic cooperation, the nations who assembled at Bretton Woods sought to create three international institutions—the World Bank, the IMF, and the International Trade Organization (ITO)—to serve as the pillars of world trade and finance. The ITO was to reduce trade barriers and to provide rules for international trade. The World Bank and the IMF, both further discussed below, were quickly approved, but the ITO failed to win approval due primarily to opposition in the Congress of the United States.

Two other global international organizations play key roles in trade matters and will be mentioned in this book from time to time. The Organization of Economic Cooperation and Development (OECD),[5] based in Paris, is an organization of thirty leading developed countries that deals with economic and social issues of concern to its members. The United Nations Conference on Trade and Development (UNCTAD)[6] is an organization of 192 member countries (mostly developing countries). UNCTAD seeks to help developing countries in global trade and economic development. Both OECD and UNCTAD work closely—and sometimes at cross-purposes—with the WTO, the World Bank, and the IMF.

---

5. *See* http://www.oecd.org.
6. *See* http://www.unctad.org.

A.   The World Bank

The primary mission of the World Bank[7] is to alleviate poverty by providing loans with favorable conditions and outright grants to poor countries. The World Bank is funded primarily by monetary subscriptions from its 187 member governments and through loans from private banks that are backed by government bonds issued by its members.

The World Bank currently provides over $44 billion annually in development loans and grants to the developing world. Day-to-day duties are delegated to twenty-four executive directors who work on-site at the Bank. Five of the executive directors are permanently allocated to the five largest shareholders of the Bank: the United States, Japan, Germany, the United Kingdom, and France. Since voting power in the Bank is allocated according to each member's "quota" or contribution, the United States, as the largest contributor, is the largest shareholder with 16.36 percent of the total voting power.

The World Bank consists of five closely affiliated groups. The International Bank for Reconstruction and Development (IBRD) provides loans to middle-income and poor countries while the International Development Association (IDA) provides loans to the least developed and poorest countries of the world to assist in economic development. The International Finance Corporation (IFC) promotes economic development in poor countries by providing financing in markets that investors would otherwise find too risky; and the Multilateral Investment Guarantee Agency (MIGA) helps promote FDI in developing countries by insuring against political risk, such as expropriation, war, and disturbance. The International Center for the Settlement of Investment Disputes (ICSID) provides facilities for the conciliation and arbitration of investment disputes between foreign investors and national governments (and their affiliated political entities).

Each of the three World Bank lending institutions plays a distinct role. The IBRD lends at favorable rates to governments of middle-income and credit-worthy low-income countries. In 2010, outstanding loans totaled $120,103 billion. The IDA provides long-term interest-free loans known as "credits," with repayment terms of thirty-five to forty years, as well as outright grants to seventy-nine of the world's poorest countries. As of 2010, the outstanding credits of the IDA totaled $113,474 billion. The IFC provides capital to private companies and individuals to invest in developing countries, totaling about $18 billion each year.

World Bank institutions also offer analytic and general advisory services as well as technical assistance networks around the world. The World Bank adopts and implements poverty reduction strategies (with varying and controversial effects) on regional and member-country levels.

B.   The International Monetary Fund

The IMF[8] was founded to ensure stability in the flow of currency (money) across national borders. One of the original goals of the IMF was to control the vicious cycle of currency devaluations that gave rise to the Great Depression of the 1930s.

---

7. *See* http://www.worldbank.org.

8. *See* http://www.imf.org.

If Country B is holding large amounts of Country A's currency and Country A suddenly devalues its currency by 50 percent, Country B's holdings of A's currency immediately decrease in value by one-half and B may feel cheated.[9] Today, the IMF ensures stability by discouraging devaluations and encouraging countries to allow for free convertibility of currencies through the use of stable exchange rates. The IMF also assists countries with balance of payment obligations; i.e., the need to repay loans or other monetary obligations in foreign currency. To achieve these objectives, the IMF provides loans as well as technical assistance. Membership in the IMF (187 states) overlaps with membership in the World Bank and both institutions work closely together. Like the World Bank, voting in the IMF is determined by the monetary contributions of its members.

What are some of the balance of payment issues that the IMF seeks to address? Suppose that Country A has purchased a large quantity of imports from Country B and is due to pay B a sum in B's national currency. Or A has borrowed a loan from B and must repay B. Due to domestic problems, A may lack sufficient amounts of foreign exchange reserves (i.e., B's currency) to pay B. For example, a sudden drop in the price of a key export from A, imprudent domestic fiscal policies, high levels of external debt, and natural disasters can all contribute to A's balance of payment problems. Or A may be living beyond its means by buying goods from B without having earned sufficient foreign currency reserves to pay B. In this case, A may seek to repay B using A's own currency. If B balks at accepting A's currency, the IMF will encourage, but cannot require, B to convert A's currency into B's currency and thus allow A to pay in A's own currency. The free convertibility of currencies is a key component of international trade; one of the IMF's roles is to encourage all of its members to allow for free convertibility.

Suppose, however, that due to mismanagement, A does not even have enough of its own currency to convert into B's currency. At this point, A is faced with several difficult alternatives. It could reduce its spending, attempt to raise money by selling government bonds, or print more money. It may find, however, that reducing spending could lead to hardship, selling its bonds are impossible because there are no buyers, and printing more money will lead to hyper-inflation. These events might trigger a financial and political crisis. The IMF can provide a loan to A to give it breathing room. Such loans are usually conditioned on A's agreement to an appropriate IMF program of economic policies to create fiscal discipline.

The IMF encourages the convertibility of its member currencies and generally supervises (but has no power to control) the international system of rates of currency exchange. Since the breakdown of the system of fixed currency exchange rates in the 1970s, major world currencies are allowed to "float," which means their value is determined by world supply and demand. The IMF and its members have pledged to keep currency exchange rates stable despite this "float." However, exchange rates are still affected in important respects sometimes by massive interventions of central banks that attempt to manipulate currency valuations. Moreover, many currencies—most notably the Chinese Renminbi (RMB)—are

---

9. Assume that the original exchange rate for A's currency in B's currency is 1:1 so that one unit of A's currency can be exchanged for one unit of B's currency. If A devalues its currency by 50 percent, the exchange rate for A's currency becomes 2:1 so that two units of A's currency must now be exchanged for one unit of B's currency. Country B's holdings of A's currency have just decreased in value by one-half.

"pegged," which means they are tied, sometimes artificially, to other currencies for various political and financial reasons. The artificial valuation of the RMB is currently one of the world's most controversial trade issues that we will further explore in this Chapter.

The funds of the IMF are contributed by members in the form of assigned quotas, which vary with the size of each member's economy. The largest quota is accorded to the United States. As of January 2011 the total quotas amounted to $340 billion and loans committed amounted to $254 billion. The biggest borrowers are Ukraine, Greece, and Romania.

The IMF also (1) provides advice based on a formal system known as surveillance, which reviews monetary policy as well as national, regional, and global economic and financial developments; and (2) provides technical assistance and training in the areas of tax policy and administration, expenditure management, monetary and exchange rate policies, bank and financial system regulation and management, legislative work, and statistical analysis.

NOTES AND QUESTIONS

1. Alleviating world poverty (the work of the World Bank) and ensuring stability of money flows (the work of the IMF) are critical in assisting the WTO to promote global trade. A truly global trading system cannot exist if some nations are too poor to participate or participate effectively. Trade cannot occur if transnational payments for goods, services, and technology are not made or are made on an unpredictable basis with currencies that have been devalued.

2. The headquarters of the World Bank and the IMF are located in Washington, D.C. on opposite sides of the same street. Both institutions were at one time in the same building. By tradition, the President of the World Bank is an American and the chief of the IMF is a European. This practice continues today. Why? The U.S. Treasury Secretary works closely with both leaders. How do you think developing countries view these traditions?

3. Both the World Bank and the IMF in 2010-11 significantly realigned quota shares and voting powers of members. The United States continues to wield the most power in these organizations with a 16.36 percent voting share in the World Bank and 17 percent quota share in the IMF, but U.S. influence and power has waned. China has moved up to number three just behind Japan in both organizations. Emerging market and developing countries (so-called EMDCs) are gaining influence in both the IMF and the World Bank. These trends are expected to continue.

3. Perhaps the single most frequent criticism leveled against both the IMF and the World Bank is that both organizations promote as conditions to their loans and as technical advice—a combination of carrots and sticks—the so-called "Washington Consensus," a term coined in the 1990s to refer to economic policies that promote the following:

- Fiscal discipline
- Redirection of public expenditures towards fields that offer potential for economic return, such as primary health care, primary education, and infrastructure
- Tax reforms (lower marginal rates and broadened tax base)

- Interest rate liberalization
- A competitive rate of currency exchange
- Trade liberalization
- Privatization
- Deregulation
- Secure property rights
- Control of government corruption

Critics of the Washington Consensus are legion. Perhaps the most prominent is Joseph Stiglitz, who served as Chairman of the President's Council of Economic Advisors from 1993 to 1997, and as Chief Economist of the World Bank from 1997 to 2000. In 2001 he was awarded the Nobel Prize in Economics. Stiglitz's criticism may be found in his influential book, *Globalization and its Discontents* (2003). Stiglitz maintains that IMF and World Bank policies contributed to the crisis experienced by Russia in the 1990s, as well as the East Asia financial crisis of 1998 and the Argentine financial collapse of 1999-2001. He opposes the neo-liberal ideas that markets always work well and that there should be a minimal role for government and argues that Washington Consensus policies were unthinkingly and rigidly applied and were too quickly implemented without regard to a country's individual characteristics. Stiglitz argues in favor of the necessity of social safety nets, government financial regulation, job creation policies, selective government interventions, and adjustment intervals when adopting new economic policies. *See also Challenging the Washington Consensus: An Interview with Joseph Stiglitz*, The Brown Journal of World Affairs, Vol. IX, Winter/Spring 2003, p. 33. What is your opinion of the Washington Consensus? Why might some countries resent or object to the Washington Consensus? What additional policies and ideas are necessary or appropriate?

4. In the aftermath of the global economic recession that began in 2007 (further discussed in note 5 below), at the Seoul Summit in November 2010, the G-20, a group of leading developed and developing nations, adopted the Seoul Development Consensus for Shared Growth, which might be viewed as an alternative to the Washington Consensus.[10] The key points from the G-20's Declaration of the Seoul Development Consensus are: (1) narrowing of the wealth gap between developed and developing countries; (2) engaging developing and low-income countries as equal partners while respecting each country's own development policy; (3) integrating developing countries more effectively into global or regional trade; (4) promoting private sector involvement and access to private capital; and (5) developing yardsticks and accountability standards that measure progress in overcoming problems that block economic growth for developing countries.[11] The Seoul Development Consensus also identified nine key pillars where action and reform are most needed to assist developing countries: infrastructure, private investment and job creation, human resource development, trade, financial inclu-

---

10. The G-20 consists of the following members: Argentina, Australia, Brazil, Canada, China, European Union, France, Germany, India, Indonesia, Italy, Japan, Mexico, Russia, Saudi Arabia, South Africa, Republic of Korea, Turkey, United Kingdom, and the United States.

11. *The G20 Seoul Summit Declaration*, G20, p. 1-2 (November 11-12, 2010) available at http://www.economicsummits.info/2010/11/g20-seoul-summit-final-declaration.

sion, growth with resilience, food security, domestic resource mobilization, and knowledge sharing.[12]

How does the Seoul Consensus differ from the Washington Consensus? Which view appears to be designed to impose a certain set of policies on other countries? Which view shows more respect for the views of developing and least developed countries?

5. In 1996 the WTO and the IMF entered into an Agreement, under which they will keep each other informed of their work so far as it relates to currency issues, send representatives to each other's meetings, and work collaboratively. *See* Agreement between the IMF and the WTO, ¶¶2-9. This Agreement is clearly insufficient, but what additional ideas would you propose to deal with the trade imbalances problem and the related issue that some countries keep their currency artificially low in order to stimulate exports? At the G-20 meeting in November 2010, Secretary of the Treasury Timothy Geithner proposed that nations agree on a cap for how large a trade surplus or deficit a country can run relative to the size of its economy. He proposed the figure of 4 percent of GDP be accepted as to the size of such a cap, beginning in 2015. His proposal was not accepted. What else can be done? Should nations maintain closer international coordination of monetary and fiscal policies? What can the IMF do to promote exchange rate realism and stability?

Article IV:1 of the Articles of Agreement of the IMF states that members "should avoid manipulating [currency] exchanges in order to gain an unfair competitive advantage over other members." But no IMF member has ever been found in breach of this obligation. *See* Claus D. Zimmermann, *Exchange Rate Misalignment and International Law*, 105 Am. J. Int'l L. 423 (2011) (currency exchange rate obligations constitute "soft law" in the international economic legal system).

NOTE ON THE GLOBAL FINANCIAL CRISIS AND THE ROLE OF THE WORLD BANK, IMF, AND THE WTO

In 2007 began what is now called the Global Financial Crisis and the Great Recession, the worst economic downturn in seventy-five years. Unlike most other economic crises, the Global Economic Crisis was centered in the United States and was characterized by the collapse of major financial institutions rather than a contraction of economic output. In 2009, world trade dropped by 11.6 percent, and private investment in emerging market countries plunged from $928 billion in 2007 to $466 billion in 2008 and just $165 billion in 2009. In 2010, trade and investment rebounded significantly, but the Crises produced profound changes in the international economic system as summarized in the following excerpt, Thomas J. Schoenbaum, *Saving the Global Financial System: International Financial Reforms and United States Financial Reform, Will They Do the Job?* 43 UCC L.J. 479, 514-523 (2010):

> The Global Financial Crisis exposed the unpreparedness and inadequacy of international financial institutions. The IMF and the World Bank neither foresaw nor had the funds to ameliorate the Crisis. National governments not international institutions took the lead in combating the Crisis. Nevertheless, international institutions played a key role in coordinating the national responses, and governments, seeing the

---

12. *Id.* at p. 3.

impotence of international institutions, have taken significant steps to provide them with the means to be better prepared in the future.

The G-20. The most important international body to deal with the Crisis was the G-20. During the Crisis the G-20 has so far held four Summit meetings, in November 2008, in April and September 2009, and in June 2010. Perhaps more importantly, working groups of the G-20 met many times and were in constant touch during the Crisis. [T]he real story of the G-20 is the remarkable concord, cooperation and coordination there has been over the past three years, probably the single biggest reason why the world has not plunged into a Great Depression similar to the 1930s. The G-20 has successfully coordinated massive fiscal stimulus measures in member countries as well as monetary measures in most major economy countries that have reduced policy interest rates close to the zero interest floor. The G-20 also took important decisions to make more money available to international financial institutions: (1) $750 billion for IMF; (2) $350 billion in capital increases for the Multilateral Development Banks; and (3) $250 billion for trade finance. In addition, the G-20 decided to increase the voting power of developing and transition countries in the World Bank by 4.59%, giving them a total voting power of 47.19%. The G-20 also committed to move over time towards even more equitable World Bank voting power. These reforms will increase the voice of China, South Korea, Mexico, and Turkey and will revise many other countries' quotas as well, giving developing and emerging-market countries more power at the IMF.

The International Monetary Fund. At the outset of the Crisis the IMF extended $50 billion in loans to 15 countries: the amounts were relatively small, ranging from $1.2 billion to Iceland to $16.7 billion to Ukraine. The Crisis exposed the weaknesses of the IMF, in that these loans largely exhausted its available lending capacity. Now, largely because of the G-20 initiative described above, the IMF enjoys reinvigoration and new respect. IMF lending programs will be greatly expanded as a result of $750 billion of new capital, $500 billion coming from sales of bonds to the public and $250 billion coming from additional quota pledges from members. With its lending capacity now quadrupled, the IMF now once again plays a central role in providing liquidity to support the world economy.

The World Bank. Like the IMF, the World Bank has gone through a historic transformation as a result of the Global Financial Crisis. Members have agreed to support a $5.1 billion increase in the operating capital of the Bank and to give developing economies a greater voice in running the anti-poverty institution. The Bank's lending is at a record's pace: $105 billion in financial commitments were concluded between July 2008 and April 2010, including a new Global Food Crisis Response Program for 21 African countries. In its lending the World Bank has focused on maintaining long-term infrastructure and sustaining private sector growth and job creation. In addition to high lending volume, the Bank has changed the quotas of members: the US retains the highest share at 16%, but Japan is reduced to 6.84% while China will rise to 4.42%, a level above Germany, Britain, and France. The quota shares (and voting power) of emerging and developing countries will rise by 3.13%, a cumulative shift of 4.59 percent, the greatest realignment of the Bank since 1988.

World Trade Organization. The G-20 has joined WTO Director General Pascal Lamy in calling for completion of the long stalled WTO trade negotiations known as the Doha Development Agenda. The G-20 has also called for continuation of Aid for Trade, an initiative to increase the export capacity of developing countries through technical assistance, building trade-related infrastructure, and addressing supply-side obstacles to trade. The WTO Working Group on Debt, Trade and Finance has also discussed problems of increasing sources of trade finance during the Global Financial Crisis. During the Crisis Pascal Lamy warned against trade protectionism, and the G-20 at the Washington Summit in November 2008 pledged that "we will refrain from raising new barriers in investment or to trade in goods and services, imposing export restrictions or implementing World Trade Organization-inconsistent measures to stimulate exports." By and large this pledge was honored.

Additional reforms include new standards for liquidity and minimum capital requirements for banks (since one of the key causes of the financial crisis was that banks and other financial institutions took on too much leverage). *See id.* at 519. The global financial crisis appears to have strengthened the role of some developing countries, particularly China, which has massive foreign currency reserves and did not invest in the risky financial instruments that led to the collapse of banks in the United States and Europe. China's growing economic power may lead it to demand even more of a voice and a leading role in institutions such as the IMF, the World Bank, and the WTO. *See generally,* Daniel Chow, *China's Response to the Global Financial Crisis: Implications for the U.S.-China Economic Relations,* 1 Global Bus. L. Rev. 47 (2010).

PROBLEM 1-7

World trade has grown exponentially in recent years but massive trade imbalances exist among members of the IMF. For example, the United States in 2011 was running a trade deficit at an annual rate of $560 billion, while other countries (such as China) were racking up large surpluses. The United States finances its trade deficit through borrowing and is now soaking up roughly two-thirds of all global net savings used by other countries to lend money to the United States. This raises the specter of a precipitous realignment of economic power resulting in massive dollar depreciation that might spark a global economic slowdown or even a devastating world financial crisis. In theory, the IMF has the power to deal with and discipline these problems and practices set forth below. Can you explain how? What must occur for a country to be subject to the discipline of the IMF?

- Countries such as the United States that incur massive trade and budget deficits;
- Countries like Japan and Germany that are contemplating ill-timed tax increases that may impair economic growth;
- Countries whose financial systems are rife with corruption;
- Countries that pursue bad fiscal and monetary policies;
- Countries such as China that maintain currency controls so that their currency is arguably greatly undervalued;
- Countries such as Japan that sometimes intervene in international currency markets to secure a favorable international exchange rate; and
- Countries that borrow massively in international financial markets, building up debts many times in excess of GDP.

C.   The World Trade Organization

Read the Agreement Establishing the World Trade Organization (WTO Agreement) in the Documents Supplement and GATT Articles XXV-XXXV, which this Agreement is intended to supplement.

The WTO, located in Geneva, Switzerland, is a multilateral organization that is designed to reduce barriers to trade in goods, services, and technology (intellectual property) for the purposes of promoting international trade and business.

The origins of the WTO can also be traced to the Bretton Woods conference, discussed earlier. As previously noted, the ITO was never established due to the opposition of the U.S. Congress, which believed that its agenda was too ambitious. While the ITO was still being negotiated, a number of countries led by the United States decided to move ahead with a multilateral treaty to reduce tariff barriers, the General Agreement on Tariffs and Trade (GATT), which received provisional approval in 1947. The GATT was intended to be administered by the ITO, but when the latter did not win approval, the GATT 1947 became a *de facto* international organization in Geneva until the WTO was established in 1995. When the WTO was approved, a new GATT 1994 was adopted. GATT 1994 consists of GATT 1947 plus a number of Understandings interpreting various provisions of GATT 1947 that were adopted during the decades between the first adoption of the GATT 1947 and the formation of the WTO in 1995. Although GATT 1947 no longer exists as a separate agreement, it is part of GATT 1994.

Before we study the WTO, we examine briefly the history of the GATT 1947 and its evolution through the first fifty years of its existence.

1. GATT 1947

The overarching purpose of GATT 1947 and the Havana Charter (1948) was to create the ITO and to liberalize trade in goods among members by instituting non-discriminatory tariff-treatment among members, prohibiting most import quotas, and requiring national treatment of imported products once they had cleared customs at the border. Although the relatively high tariffs (i.e., taxes imposed on goods at the customs port of entry) of the time were to remain, the GATT and the ITO were conceived as a mechanism for negotiations that could progressively reduce high tariffs. Despite the failure of the Havana Charter, the GATT came into effect on January 1, 1948 as both an international agreement and an international organization through the Protocol of Provisional Application signed in 1947. The GATT functioned until January 1, 1995 when it was replaced by the WTO (1994). At the same time, a new GATT entered into force as GATT 1994. The GATT 1994 consists of the provisions of GATT 1947 as amended and modified before the entry into force of the Marrakesh Agreement; certain Understandings on various GATT articles; and the Marrakesh Protocol, some 22,500 pages of trade concessions and schedules agreed among WTO members.

Tariffs were the focus of the early GATT as provided in Article 17 of the Havana Charter:

> Each Member shall, upon the request of any other Member or Members, and subject to procedural arrangements established by the Organization, enter into and carry out with such other Member or Members negotiations directed to the substantial reduction of general levels of tariffs and other charges on imports and exports, and to the elimination of . . . preferences . . . on a reciprocal and mutually advantageous basis.

This general obligation was implemented through GATT Article XXV (Joint Action by the Contracting Parties), which sets the first meeting of the "contracting parties" (the GATT was not permitted to have "members") for March 1, 1948. This article also provides that each contracting party is entitled to one vote and that decisions shall be taken by a majority of the votes cast. Article XXV also provides for waivers of GATT obligations by two-thirds majority of the votes cast. Article XXV is now superseded by Article IX of the WTO Agreement. The topic of waivers is also addressed in the Separate Understanding in Respect of Waivers of Obligations under GATT 1994, which specifies that, in principle, waivers in effect on the date of the entry into force of the WTO Agreement were to expire within two years.

GATT Article XXVI (Acceptance, Entry into Force and Registration) specifies that GATT 1947 entered into force October 30, 1947. Of course this date was superseded by the GATT Protocol of Provisional Application (1947) and now by Article XIV of the WTO Agreement and the GATT 1994, both of which entered into force on January 1, 1995.

GATT Article XXVII (Withholding or Withdrawal of Concessions) affirms that any contracting party may withdraw trade concessions from any party who has ceased to be a contracting party. This provision still holds as part of GATT 1994, but no member has withdrawn since the creation of the WTO.

In order to facilitate multilateral tariff negotiations, GATT Article XXVIII bis (Tariff Negotiations) was added in 1954-55 to enter into force October 7, 1957. This Article confirms that the Ministerial Conference of the parties may from time to time sponsor trade negotiations to expand international trade. Trade negotiations are to take into account the diverse needs of the contracting parties, including the needs of developing countries. Participation in the negotiating "rounds" is not mandatory, but the parties recognize that the success of multilateral trade negotiations depends upon the broad participation of the parties.

In the early days of the GATT before Article XXVIII bis was adopted, negotiations for tariff concessions were commonly commenced whenever two or more of the GATT contracting parties decided to convene trade talks. With the approval of Article XXVIII bis, multilateral trade negotiations became the norm and that is the case in the WTO. The modalities of trade negotiations have also changed: the first five rounds of trade negotiations proceeded on a product-by-product basis; beginning with the Kennedy Round, negotiations have proceeded on a linear, across-the-board tariff reduction basis.

Article XXVIII (Modification of Schedules) concerns the complex topic of modification of trade concessions. Modification or withdrawal of a trade concession may be initiated by a WTO member (the applicant) (1) on the first day of each three-year period that began on January 1, 1958; or (2) the first day of any other period specified by two-thirds vote of members' votes cast. The applicant, however, is first required to negotiate with the member(s) with which the concession was originally negotiated and with any member who is determined to have a "principal supplying interest" in the product involved. In addition, consultations must be made with all members having a "substantial interest" in the concession. These modification negotiations will be successful only if the applicant agrees to provide interested parties with other trade concessions that are "not less favorable" than the concessions being withdrawn. If no agreement is reached, the applicant is free to unilaterally make the requested modification, but in that case affected members may in turn withdraw "substantially equivalent" concessions against the applicant. This procedure is designed to make modification of trade concessions difficult and rare.

GATT Article XXIX (The Relation of this Agreement to the Havana Charter), Article XXX (Amendments), Article XXXI (Withdrawal), Article XXXII (Contracting Parties), and Article XXXIII (Accession) are obsolete, replaced by the 1994 WTO Agreement. Article XXXIV (Annexes) simply provides that the GATT annexes are an integral part of the GATT.

GATT Article XXXV (Non-application of the Agreement between Particular Contracting Parties) is virtually obsolete: This provision can be invoked only between original members of the WTO that were contracting parties to GATT 1947, and only where Article XXXV of that Agreement had been invoked earlier and was effective between those contracting parties at the time of entry into force of the WTO Agreement. This Article was invoked by GATT members a total of seventy-nine times; mainly against Japan, and in some cases against Portugal and South Africa. Virtually all of these invocations have been removed.

2. *The WTO*

The WTO assumes the role that was originally intended for the ITO; namely, to administer the GATT 1947, although the WTO has many other powers as well. The structure of the WTO is organized around the three major agreements, each administered by a WTO authority: (1) the GATT 1994, which governs the trade in goods; (2) the General Agreement on Trade in Services (GATS), which governs the trade in services; and (3) the Agreement on Trade-Related Intellectual Property Rights (TRIPS), which governs trade in technology. The WTO also administers a fourth major agreement, the Dispute Settlement Understanding (DSU) governing the WTO dispute settlement system, which we take up in detail in a later section.

The highest authority in the WTO is the Ministerial Conference, a meeting of all of its members that occurs every two years. Just below the Ministerial Conference is the General Council, a permanent body of representatives from WTO members, which meets regularly. The General Council also sits as the Dispute Settlement Body (DSB) and the Trade Policy Review Body. The members of the General Council simply put on a different hat when they meet as the DSB or as the Trade Policy Review Body. The DSB settles disputes by adopting decisions made by WTO panels or the Appellate Body. The Trade Policy Review Body examines the internal laws and policies of its members to determine whether any potential WTO trade issues exist. Decisions in the General Council are made by consensus, although the General Council has the authority in some cases to act by majority vote.

The General Council has established bodies below it to do the day-to-day work of the WTO. The General Council has established a Council for Trade in Goods that administers the GATT, a Council for Trade in Services that administers the GATS, and a Council for Trade-Related Intellectual Property Rights that administers TRIPS. These councils have the power to establish committees that deal with specific issues under any of the major agreements. The General Council has also established committees to deal with emerging or controversial issues, such as trade and the environment, and trade and development. The General Council also oversees the plurilateral agreements, which are optional agreements only upon those members that voluntarily chose to adopt them, such as the Government Procurement Agreement, which governs the purchase of goods and services by governments from private vendors.

The structure of the WTO is set forth schematically in Figure 1-6:

FIGURE 1-6
Organization Chart of the WTO

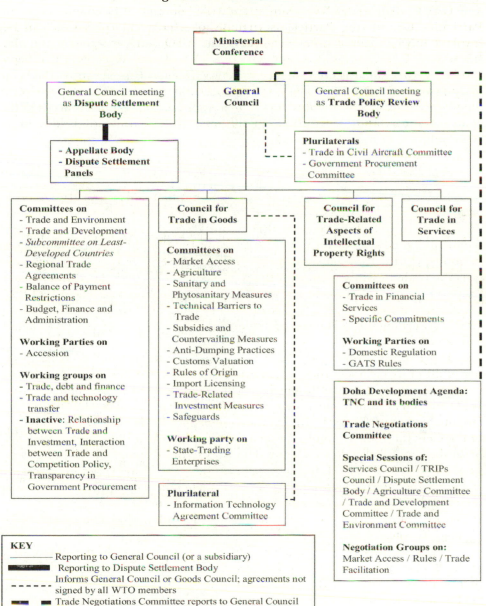

IV.   *The Case For and Against Free Trade: A Brief Look at International Economics*

The WTO and other international organizations were established for the express purpose of promoting free trade on a global basis. The basic assumption behind this goal is that free trade is beneficial, but not everyone agrees with this proposition. In this section, we present both sides of the argument: for and against free trade.

The case for free trade is that it increases economic welfare for the world as a whole and for each nation. The argument against free trade is that, at least for some countries, the harmful effects of free trade outweigh its benefits.

To better understand this debate and the materials that follow, you will need to master a few basic economic terms and concepts often used in international trade:

- A *trade balance* is the relationship between a country's exports of goods (or services and a few smaller categories) and its imports. Most all of the time when experts or the media refer to a trade balance, the reference is to the trade in goods, still the most important channel of trade. In the discussion below, we focus on the trade in goods, but the same concepts apply to the other channels.
- A *trade surplus* exists when a nation's exports of goods to a trading partner exceed its imports from that partner. The exporting nation is selling more than it is buying and is earning more than it is spending from the trade in goods.
- A *trade deficit* exists when a nation's imports of goods from a trading partner exceed its exports to that partner. The importing country is buying more than it is selling so it is spending more than it is earning from the trade in goods.
- When a nation has an overall trade surplus with its trading partners, that nation becomes wealthier over time because it receives revenue or earnings from the sale of goods. The exporting nation might, as in the case of China below, become flush with export earnings and experience rapid economic growth. Most nations in the world would rather be net exporters than net importers.
- When a nation has an overall trade deficit with its trading partners, that nation begins to experience a decline in wealth unless other growth factors are present. The nation is spending more than it is earning and is living beyond its means. Unless the nation is able to earn revenue and generate economic growth through other means (i.e., by selling services, by innovation in technology, by attracting inward foreign capital investment, or by borrowing money) the nation's economy will begin to shrink.

Economists often refer to the trade balance as the *current account*. When a nation has a trade surplus, the nation has a *positive* current account. Conversely, when a nation has a trade deficit, it has a *negative* current account. We introduce some additional economic concepts in the materials below.

A.   Arguments in Favor of and Against Free Trade

A key concept in free trade is comparative advantage, explored in the problem below and in the excerpt. The excerpt also discusses the traditional economic arguments in favor of trade and the arguments against trade.

PROBLEM 1-8

The following is a hypothetical breakdown of the production capacities of two countries, the United States and China, in two different economic sectors.

U.S.-China Hypothetical Production of One Person in One Week
(U.S. Production Rate: 1 bushel soybeans/1.67 yard textiles)

Product	United States	China
Soybeans	9 bushels	3 bushels
Textiles	15 yards	9 yards

One person in the United States can produce either (1) a total of nine bushels of soybeans (and zero textiles) or (2) a total ,of fifteen yards of textiles used to make clothing (and zero soybeans) or (3) some combination of both along a production possibility curve that plots one bushel of soybeans for every 1.67 yards of textiles.

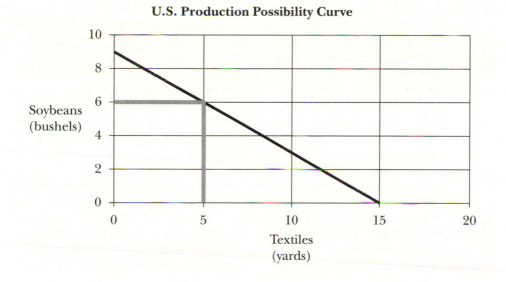

U.S. Production Possibility Curve

Suppose further that the current demand in the United States is now six bushels of soybeans and nine yards of textiles per week, but the production possibility curve will only allow the United States to produce six bushels of soybeans and five yards of textiles per week. In China, three bushels of soybeans will buy nine yards of textiles. The United States has an absolute advantage over China in both soybeans and textiles but the advantage that the United States enjoys in soybean production is comparatively greater than the advantage in textiles. In soybeans, the efficiency advantage of the United States is 3:1 whereas the efficiency advantage in textiles is 1.67:1. This is determined by comparing the efficiency of one person in soybean production (nine bushels) to production in China (three bushels) and the same is done for textiles.

How should the United States arrange its internal affairs and its trade with China to make it possible to consume six bushels of soybeans and nine yards of textiles per week? Even though the United States has an absolute advantage in both soybeans and textiles, is the United States better off if it trades? Consult the following excerpt.

Douglas Irwin, Free Trade Under Fire (2004)
21-26, 29-30, 32-33, 35-36, 45-46, 70-72, 83-85, 87-94, 98-99

SPECIALIZATION AND TRADE

The traditional case for free trade is based on the gains from specialization and exchange. These gains are easily understood at the level of the individual. Most people do not produce for themselves even a fraction of the goods they consume. Rather, we earn an income by specializing in certain activities and then using our earnings to purchase various goods and services—food, clothing, shelter, health care—produced by others. In essence, we "export" the goods and services that we produce with our own labor and "import" the goods and services produced by others that we wish to consume. This division of labor enables us to increase our consumption beyond that which would be possible if we tried to be self-sufficient and produce everything for ourselves. Specialization allows us to enjoy a much higher standard of living than otherwise and gives us access to a greater variety and better quality of goods and services.

Trade between nations is simply the international extension of this division of labor. For example, the United States has specialized in the production of aircraft, industrial machinery, and agricultural commodities (particularly corn, soybeans, and wheat). In exchange for exports of these products, the United States purchases, among other things, imports of crude oil, clothing, and iron and steel mill products. Like individuals, countries benefit immensely from this division of labor and enjoy a higher real income than countries that forgo such trade. Just as there seems no obvious reason to limit the free exchange of goods within a country without a specific justification, there is no obvious reason why trade between countries should be limited in the absence of a compelling reason for doing so. (Popular arguments for limiting trade will be examined later to see if they are persuasive.)

Adam Smith, whose magnificent work *The Wealth of Nations* was first published in 1776, set out the case for free trade with a persuasive flair that still resonates today. Smith advocated the "obvious and simple system of natural liberty" in which individuals would be free to pursue their own interests, while the government provided the legal framework within which commerce would take place. With the government enforcing a system of justice and providing certain public goods (such as roads, in Smith's view), the private interests of individuals could be turned toward productive activities, namely, meeting the demands of the public as expressed in the marketplace. Smith envisioned a system that would give people the incentive to better themselves through economic activities, where they would create wealth by serving others through market exchange, rather than through political activities, where they might seek to redistribute existing wealth through, for example, legal restraints on competition. Under such a system, the powerful motivating force of self-interest could be channeled toward socially beneficial activities that would serve the general interest rather than socially unproductive activities that might advance the interests of a select few but would come at the expense of society as a whole.

Free trade is an important component of this system of economic liberty. Under a system of natural liberty in which domestic commerce is largely free from restraints on competition, though not necessarily free from government regulation, commerce would also be permitted to operate freely between countries. According to Smith, free trade would increase competition in the home market and curtail the power of domestic firms by checking their ability to exploit consumers through high prices and poor service. Moreover, the country would gain by exchanging exports of goods that are dear on the world market for imports of goods that are cheap on the world market. As Smith put it:

> What is prudence in the conduct of every family can scarce be folly in that of a great kingdom. If a foreign country can supply us with a commodity cheaper than we ourselves can make it, better buy it off them with some part of the produce of our own industry, employed in a way in which we have some advantage. The general industry of the country . . . will not thereby be diminished . . . but only left to find out the way in which it can be employed to the greatest advantage. It is certainly not employed to the greatest advantage when it is thus directed towards an object it can buy cheaper than it can make.

Smith believed that the benefits of trade went well beyond this simple arbitrage exchange of what is abundant in the home market for what is scarce on the world market. The wealth of any society depends upon the division of labor. The division of labor, the degree to which individuals specialize in certain tasks, enhances productivity. And productivity, the ability to produce more goods with the same resources, is the basis for rising living standards. But, as he put it, the division of labor is limited by the extent of the market. Smaller, more isolated markets cannot support a high degree of specialization among their population and therefore tend to be relatively poor. Free trade enables all countries, but particularly small countries, to extend the effective size of their market. Trade allows such countries to achieve a more refined division of labor, and therefore reap a higher real income, than if international exchange were artificially limited by government policies.

Smith also issued a scathing attack on the contemporary mercantilist policies that restricted trade for the ostensible purpose of promoting national wealth.

COMPARATIVE ADVANTAGE

In 1799, a successful London stockbroker named David Ricardo came across a copy of *The Wealth of Nations* while on vacation and quickly became engrossed in the book. Ricardo admired Smith's great achievement, but thought that many of the topics deserved further investigation. For example, Smith believed that a country would export goods that it produces most efficiently and import goods that other countries produce most efficiently. In this way, trade is a mutually beneficial way of increasing total world output and thus the consumption of every country. But, Ricardo asked, what if one country was the most efficient at producing everything? Would that country still benefit from trade? Would disadvantaged countries find themselves unable to export anything?

To overcome this problem, Ricardo arrived at a brilliant deduction that became known as the theory of comparative advantage. Comparative advantage implies that a country could find it advantageous to import some goods even if it could produce those same goods more efficiently than other countries. Conversely, a country would be able to export some goods even if other countries could produce them more efficiently. In either case, countries would be able to benefit from trade.

At first, the principle of comparative advantage seems counterintuitive. Why would a country ever import a good that it could produce more efficiently than another country? Yet comparative advantage is the key to understanding the pattern of international trade.

According to Ricardo and the other classical economists of the early nineteenth century, international trade is not driven by the *absolute* costs of production, but by the *opportunity* costs of production. The country most efficient at producing textiles might be even more efficient than other countries at producing other goods, such as shoes. In that case, the country would be best served by directing its labor to producing shoes, in which its margin of productive advantage is even greater than in textiles. As a result, despite its productivity advantage in textiles, the country would export shoes in exchange for imports of textiles. In the absence of other information, the absolute efficiency of one country's textile producers in comparison to another country's is insufficient to determine whether that country produces all of the textiles it consumes or imports some of them.

Put differently, a country can obtain textiles either directly through domestic production, or indirectly by producing something else and exporting it in exchange for imports of textiles. The most efficient way of getting textiles is whichever way yields the country the greatest quantity of such goods at the least cost. So when looking at the textile question, our consultants must first recognize that the real choice facing a country is whether it should devote its resources to producing textiles, or to producing other goods that can be exported in exchange for textiles. The efficiency of domestic and foreign textile producers alone is not the sole determining factor.

Although the concept of comparative advantage can be counterintuitive when applied to countries, individuals base their actions on it every day. The neighborhood teenager may take three hours to mow your lawn when you could do it in one, but given the amount you have to pay the teenager for the chore, you might have a much better way to spend your time. Without information on alternative activities, your absolute efficiency in this one activity should not determine where you choose to direct your (scarce) labor time.

ARGUMENTS IN FAVOR OF TRADE

While the idea that all countries can benefit from international trade goes back to Smith and Ricardo, subsequent research has described the gains from trade in much greater detail. In the *Principles of Political Economy* (1848), John Stuart Mill, one of the leading economists of the nineteenth century, pointed to three principal gains from trade. First, there are what Mill called the "direct economical advantages of foreign trade." Second, there are "indirect effects" of trade, "which must be counted as benefits of a higher order." Finally, Mill argued that "the economical benefits of commerce are surpassed in importance by those effects which are intellectual and moral." What, specially, are these three advantages of trade?

[1] DIRECT ECONOMIC ADVANTAGES

The[se] are the standard gains that arise from specialization, as described by Smith and Ricardo. By exporting some of its domestically produced goods in exchange for imports, a country engages in mutually advantageous trade that enables it to use its limited productive resources (such as land, labor, and capital) more efficiently and therefore achieve a higher real national income than it could in the absence of trade. A higher real income translates into an ability to afford more of all goods and services than would be possible without trade.

These gains from specialization are sizable. The classic illustration of the direct gains from trade comes from Japan's opening to the world economy. In 1858, as a result of American pressure, Japan opened its ports to international trade after decades of autarky (economic isolation). The gains from trade can be summarized by examining the prices of goods in Japan before and after the opening of trade. For example, the price of silk and tea was much higher on world markets than in Japan prior to the opening of trade, while the price of cotton and woolen goods was much lower on world markets. Japan therefore exported silk and tea in exchange for imports of clothing and other goods. With the introduction of trade, prices of those goods in Japan converged to the prices on the world market. Japan's terms of trade—the prices of the goods it exported relative to the prices of the goods it imported—improved by a factor of more than three and increased Japan's real income by as much as 65 percent.

More importantly, the reallocation of resources across industries as calculated in the simulation models does not take into account the other channels by which trade can improve economic performance. What are these other channels? One view is that greater openness to trade allows firms to sell in a potentially larger market, and that firms are able to reduce their average costs of production by expanding the size of their output. The lower production costs resulting from these economies of scale are passed on to consumers and thereby generate additional gains from trade. In evaluating the impact of NAFTA through general equilibrium simulations, for example, moving from the assumption of constant returns to scale to increasing returns to scale boosted the calculated U.S. welfare gain from 1.67 percent to 2.55 percent of its GDP, Canadian welfare gain from 4.87 percent to 6.75 percent of its GDP, and Mexican welfare gain from 2.28 percent to 3.29 percent to its GDP, according to one study.

These numbers are more impressive, but there are also reasons to be skeptical. Evidence from both developed and developing economics suggests that economies of scale at the plant level for most manufacturing firms tend to be small relative to the size of the market. As a result, most plants have attained their minimum efficient scale. Average costs seem to be relatively unaffected by changes in output, so that a big increase in a firm's output does not lead to lower costs, and a big reduction in output does not lead to higher costs. For example, many firms are forced to reduce output as a result of competition from imports, but these firms' production costs rarely rise significantly. This suggests that the importance of scale economies may be overstated, and yet the simulation models sometimes include them.

There is much better, indeed overwhelming, evidence that free trade improves economic performance by increasing competition in the domestic market. This competition diminishes the market power of domestic firms and leads to a more efficient economic outcome. This benefit does not arise because foreign competition changes a domestic firm's costs through changes in the scale of output, as just noted. Rather, it comes through a change in the pricing behavior of imperfectly competitive domestic firms. Firms with market power tend to restrict output and raise prices, thereby harming consumers while increasing their own profits. With international competition, firms cannot get away with such conduct and are forced to behave more competitively. After Turkey's trade liberalization in the mid-1980s, for example, price-cost margins fell for most industries, consistent with a more competitive outcome. Numerous studies confirm this finding in other countries, providing powerful evidence that trade disciplines domestic firms with market power. Yet the beneficial effects of increasing competition are not always taken into account in simulation models because they frequently assume that perfect competition already exists.

Another problem with the standard estimates of the gains from trade is that they largely overlook the benefits to consumers from exposure to a greater variety of goods. This neglect comes from the traditional emphasis on the easily calculated effects of trade on production, whereas the gains to consumers from choice among a wider variety of goods are more difficult to quantify. (Consumer utility is an amorphous concept, and detailed product-level data are difficult to come by.)

[2]   PRODUCTIVITY GAINS

Trade improves economic performance not only by allocating a country's resources to their most efficient use, but by making those resources more productive in what they are doing. This is the second [of] John Stuart Mill's three gains from trade, the one he called "indirect effects." These indirect effects include "the tendency of every extension of the market to improve the processes of production. A country which produces for a larger market than its own can introduce a more extended division of labour, can make greater use of machinery, and is more likely to make inventions and improvements in the processes of production."

In other words, trade promotes productivity growth. The higher is an economy's productivity level, the higher is that country's standard of living. International trade contributes to productivity growth in at least two ways: it serves as a conduit for the transfer of foreign technologies that enhance productivity, and it increases competition in a way that stimulates industries to become more efficient and improve their productivity, often by forcing less productive firms out of business and allowing more productive firms to expand. After neglecting them for many decades, economists are finally beginning to study these productivity gains from trade more systematically.

[3]   ADDITIONAL BENEFITS OF TRADE

The economic gains from trade are substantial, but they are not the only benefits that come to countries with a policy of open trade. John Stuart Mill's third and final claim was that "the economical advantages of commerce are surpassed in importance by those of its effects which are intellectual and moral." Mill did not elaborate, but he may have been referring to the idea of *deux commerce*, exemplified by Montesquieu's observation in *The Spirit of the Laws* (1748) that "commerce cures destructive prejudices." Trade brings people into contact with one another and, according to this view, breaks down the narrow prejudices that come with insularity. Commerce can also force merchants to be more responsive to customers, as greater competition gives consumers a wider choice. This may be one margin on which producers compete for the patronage of consumers.

There is also a long-standing idea that trade promotes peace among nations. Many Enlightenment philosophers in the eighteenth century and classical liberals in the nineteenth century expressed this view. Montesquieu argued that "the natural effect of commerce is to lead to peace" because "two nations that trade with each other become reciprocally dependent." In his essay "Perpetual Peace," Immanuel Kant suggested that durable peace could be built upon the tripod of representative democracy, international organizations, and economic interdependence. A burgeoning political science literature now examines whether economic interdependence mitigates conflict between nations. Most of that work affirms that there is indeed a positive link between trade and peace.

[ARGUMENTS AGAINST FREE TRADE

After setting forth the arguments in favor of free trade, Professor Irwin then examines some of the more popular arguments against free trade in the excerpted materials below.

[1]   FREE TRADE NEGATIVELY AFFECTS EMPLOYMENT]

The claim that trade should be limited because imports destroy jobs has been trotted out since the sixteenth century. And imports do indeed destroy jobs in certain industries: for example, employment in the Maine shoe industry and in the South Carolina apparel industry is lower to the extent that both industries face competition from imports. So we can understand why the plant owners and workers and the politicians who represent them prefer to avoid this foreign competition.

But just because imports destroy some jobs does not mean that trade reduces overall employment or harms the economy. After all, imports are not free: in order to acquire them, a country must sell something in return. Imports are usually paid for in one of two ways: the sale of goods and services or the sale of assets to foreign countries. In other words, all of the dollars that U.S. consumers hand over to other countries in purchasing imports do not accumulate there, but eventually return to purchase either U.S. goods (exports) or U.S. assets (foreign investment). Both exports and foreign investment create new jobs: employment in export-oriented sectors such as farming and aircraft production is higher because of those foreign sales, and foreign investment either contributes directly to the national capital stock with new plants and equipment or facilitates domestic capital accumulation by reducing the cost of capital.

Thus, the claim that imports destroy jobs is misleading because it ignores the creation of jobs elsewhere in the economy as a result of trade. Similarly, while trade proponents like to note that exports create jobs, which is true, they generally fail to note that this comes at the expense of employment elsewhere. Export industries will certainly employ more workers because of the foreign demand for their products, but exports are used to purchase the very imports that diminish employment in other domestic industries.

Since trade both creates and destroys jobs, the pertinent question is whether trade has a *net* effect on employment. The public debate over NAFTA consisted largely of claims and counterclaims about whether it would add to or subtract from total employment. NAFTA opponents claim that free trade with Mexico would destroy jobs: the Economic Policy Institute put the number at 480,000. NAFTA proponents countered with the claim that it would create jobs: the Institute for International Economics suggested that 170,000 jobs would be created.

In fact, the overall effect of trade on the number of jobs in an economy is best approximated as zero. Total employment is not a function of international trade, but the number of people in the labor force. As Figure 1-7 shows, employment in the United States since 1950 has closely traced the number of people in the labor force. And while there is always some unemployment, represented by the gap between the two series, this is determined by the business cycle, demographics, and labor market policies rather than changes in trade flows or trade policy. For example, unemployment rose in the early 1980s and the early 1990s because the economy fell into a recession, not because of the behavior of imports.

How can we be sure that the number of jobs destroyed by imports is matched by the number of jobs created by exports and foreign investment? The enormous turnover in the American labor market makes it impossible to identify the precise reasons for changes in an individual's job status. But Figure 1-8 shows us that, in the aggregate, the process of job creation and of job destruction is roughly matched over time.

FIGURE 1-7
Civilian Labor Force and Civilian Employment in the
United States, 1950-2000

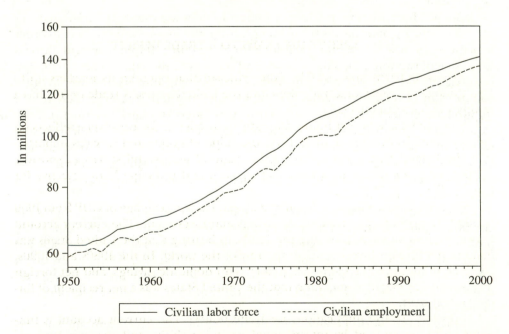

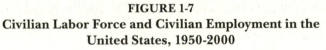

Source: Data from Council of Economic Advisers 2001, table B-35.

FIGURE 1-8
Balance of Payments and the Trade Deficit, 1960-2000

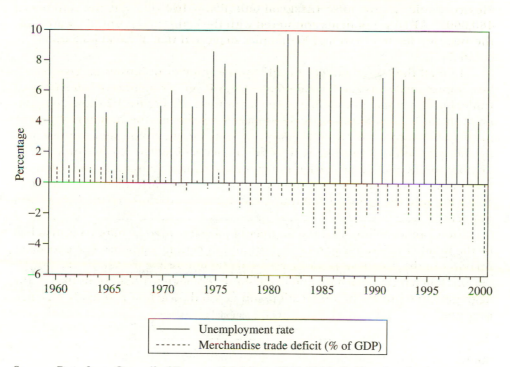

Source: Data from Council of Economic Advisers 2001, Table B-42 and author's sources.

[[2] FREE TRADE LEADS TO A TRADE DEFICIT

Professor Irwin now considers the criticism that opening its markets up to free trade is the cause of a trade deficit in the United States. A trade deficit has a number of harmful effects.]

Does the trade deficit injure domestic industries and have adverse effects on employment? In every year since 1976, the value of goods and services imported into the United States has exceeded the value of goods and services exported. Should the trade deficit be a matter of concern and reversing it an objective for trade policy?

Figure 1-9 presents the U.S. current account as a percentage of GDP from 1950 to 1999, along with the evolution of savings and investment. The current account registered a slight surplus during the 1960s, indicating that the United States was making net foreign investments in the rest of the world. In the 1980s and 1990s, however, domestic investment was greater than domestic savings, and net foreign investment was negative, meaning that the United States was a net recipient of foreign investment.

So what are the implications for trade policy? The current account is fundamentally determined by international capital mobility and the gap between domestic savings and investment. Current account imbalances have nothing to do

FIGURE 1-9
Savings and Investment in the United States as a
Percentage of GDP, 1960-1999

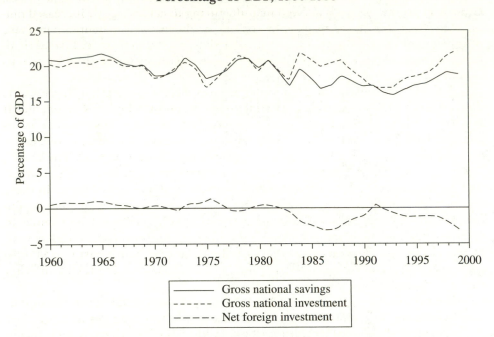

Source: Data from Council of Economic Advisers 2001, Table B-32.

with whether a country is open or closed to foreign goods, engages in unfair trade practices or not, or is more "competitive" than other countries. If net capital flows are zero, the current account will be balanced. Japan's $11 billion current account deficit in 1980 grew to an $87 billion current account surplus in 1987 not because it closed its market, or because the United States opened its market, or because Japanese manufacturers suddenly become more competitive on international markets. The surplus emerged because of financial and macroeconomic reasons in Japan and the United States.

Trade policy cannot directly affect the current account deficit because trade policy has little influence on the underlying determinants of domestic savings and investment, the ultimate sources of the current account. If a country wishes to reduce its trade deficit, then it must undertake macroeconomic measures to reduce the gap between domestic savings and investment.

[[3]   TRADE LEADS TO A SHIFT FROM HIGH PAYING TO LOW PAYING JOBS]

Even those who agree that the overall effect of trade on employment is essentially zero may oppose free trade because they believe that it shifts jobs into less desirable sectors.

The gravest of such concerns is that in the last three decades good jobs in manufacturing have been traded for bad jobs in services. In the United States, employment in manufacturing fell from 19.4 million workers in 1970 to 18.5 million in 1999. Manufacturing's share of total employment fell even more sharply, from 27 percent in 1970 to 14 percent in 1999. At the same time, real manufacturing output has increased significantly, by nearly 40 percent in the 1990s alone, and has declined only slightly as a share of GDP when measured at constant prices. Growth in productivity has allowed manufacturing to achieve vastly increased output with roughly the same number of workers, or alternatively to maintain its share of constant-dollar GDP with a much smaller share of the workforce. Like agriculture starting in the mid-nineteenth century, manufacturing has been a victim of its own improving productivity.

But an even more basic point must be stressed: the perception that imports destroy good, high-wage jobs in manufacturing is almost completely erroneous. It is closer to the truth to say that imports destroy bad, low-wage jobs in manufacturing. This is because wages in industries that compete against imports are well below average, whereas wages in exporting industries are well above average. The United States tends to import labor-intensive products, such as apparel, footwear, leather, and goods assembled from components. Comparable domestic industries in these labor-intensive sectors tend to employ workers who have a lower than average educational attainment, and who therefore earn a relatively low wage. For example, in 1999 average hourly earnings of Americans working in the apparel industry were 36 percent less than in manufacturing as a whole. Average hourly earnings were 30 percent lower in the leather industry and 23 percent lower in the textile industry than in the average manufacturing industry.

By contrast, the United States tends to export more skill-intensive manufactured products, such as aircraft, construction machinery, engines and turbines, and industrial chemicals. Workers in these industries earn relatively high wages. For example, in 1999 average hourly earnings in the aircraft industry were 42 percent above the average in manufacturing, 8 percent higher in industrial machinery, and 24 percent higher in pharmaceuticals.

As a result, any policy that limits overall trade by reducing both exports and imports tends to increase employment in low-wage industries and reduce employment in high-wage industries. Restricting trade would shift American workers away from things that they produce relatively well (and hence export and earn relatively high wages in producing) and toward things that they do not produce so well (and hence import and earn relatively low wages in producing) in comparison to other countries. Employment gains for the low-wage textile machine operators in the factory mills would be offset by employment losses for the high-wage engineers in aircraft and pharmaceutical plants.

This general finding—industries that compete against imports tend to be low-wage—has two important exceptions: steel and automobiles. Wages are high in these two industries, and yet they confront competition from imports and are relatively unsuccessful in exporting. Not coincidentally, they also have strong labor unions. Could protecting these unionized manufacturing industries be justified on the basis of preserving high-wages jobs? Some researchers suggest yes, arguing that the existence of wage premiums in such industries justifies government support.

But the case for protecting these industries to preserve the wage premiums is extremely dubious. First, it's not even clear that these wage premiums, which are the large unexplained variation in the inter-industry wage structure and which some economists attribute to labor market rents, should be explained on that basis. If the variation is unexplained, we cannot be certain of what it represents, which makes it a questionable target for intervention. Second, even if workers in certain industries earn a wage premium, the case for promoting those industries depends on those premiums being taken as given. If instead the wage premium is determined by the behavior of labor unions, then using protection to promote the industry might enhance the union's ability to raise wages above the competitive level and exacerbate the wage premium without significantly increasing employment.

NOTES AND QUESTIONS

The common criticisms of free trade are: (1) jobs are lost in domestic industries subject to import competition; (2) trade deficits are created when countries open up their markets to foreign competition; and (3) good high-paying jobs are replaced by bad low-paying jobs. How does Professor Irwin respond to each of these arguments? Do you agree? Can you think of any other arguments? These issues are also further explored in the problems below.

PROBLEM 1-9

Professor Irwin states the position of orthodox economics that the net effect on jobs (jobs created minus jobs lost) is far more important than just focusing on the loss of jobs due to trade. As a result of free trade, jobs will be lost in less competitive sectors but jobs will be created in more competitive sectors as resources will be shifted in each nation to its areas of comparative advantage. For example, in the United States jobs are lost in the lower-paying manufacturing industries but are created in higher-paying advanced technology industries. The overall net effect is an increase in U.S. wealth production.

A criticism of this position is that it ignores the social and political costs of the redistributive effects of trade on the labor market. What are these effects? Consider:

(1) You are a U.S. elected official at a town meeting with angry residents of a working class industrial town in Ohio that is now in decline. Joe, a married fifty-two-year-old worker with three school-aged children, has just lost his job in the steel manufacturing industry due to cheap steel imports from Brazil. You explain Professor Irwin's argument to Joe that although free trade has caused the loss of his job, new jobs are being created in high-technology industries in Silicon Valley that will more than make up for the wages Joe has lost. Over the long term, the wealth effects will "trickle down" to Joe and his family. What will Joe's reaction be to your argument?

(2) Joe says that it not just about losing his wages, but also about self-respect and dignity. What is he referring to? Is this figured into the economic analysis?

(3) You offer to provide unemployment benefits to Joe for the short term and training programs to learn new skills for the long term so that he can get a job in a high-technology industry. Will this appease Joe?

(4) Your opponent for the next election arrives in town the next day decrying the harmful effects of free trade on the United States and promises to impose new high tariffs on steel imports in order to restore all jobs in the steel industry in town. Will his argument be popular and win favor with

Joe and his coworkers? Is the argument for free trade, even if one accepts the economic arguments, complicated by political "realities"?

PROBLEM 1-10

Suppose that a study by a graduate student in statistics at Ohio State University shows that for every three jobs lost in steel manufacturing in Ohio, one new job is created in Silicon Valley but that the new job earns more than all three lost jobs together. Does this create any additional issues caused by the redistributive effects of trade? Is there not only a redistributive effect on the job market but on wealth? Is this a concern?

B.   United States-China Economic Relations

The arguments both for and against free trade might seem rather abstract to you but this is far from an academic debate. These arguments play a prominent role in the current controversy concerning the United States' trade deficit with China.

PROBLEM 1-11

You are part of the U.S. government's trade negotiation team with China. After the formal sessions are over, you attend a closing dinner during which one of your counterparts from China says in an unguarded moment, "You know, all this China bashing is getting out of hand. We're really not at fault at all for this trade imbalance. No one is forcing the U.S. consumer to buy goods from China. We're just meeting the huge appetite of the U.S. consumer for Chinese goods so we're actually helping you."

(1) Is there any merit to this comment? Can you explain China's side of the debate? Now, how do you respond?

(2) Many critics argue that China is not playing by the rules by unfairly "hoarding" its earnings from its export sales to the United States. What does this mean? Why is China "hoarding" its wealth and what is China's long-term plan?

(3) Is the growing trade deficit with China harming the United States? Consult the discussion below.

1.   The Growing U.S. Trade Deficit with China

The classic theory of free trade is that everyone benefits. For this to occur, however, some economists argue that spending must be circular. Developing countries, such as China, sell labor-intensive goods such as toys, clothes, furniture, and shoes to developed countries, such as the United States. China should then use its earnings from its exports to buy technology-intensive goods from the United States, such as airplanes, power generators, and pharmaceuticals. Circular spending leads to trade balances with each country excelling in its area of comparative advantage. Living standards in all countries rise. Some workers and industries might suffer in the short term but in the long term resources are shifted from less competitive industries and most workers are re-employed in more efficient industries. The classic theory that everyone benefits from free trade assumes that countries that sell then buy with their earnings. But what if countries that sell, such as China, do not buy with their earnings but instead hoard their excess export earnings and create a permanent expanding trade surplus with the United States? If the United States incurs a permanent trade deficit as a result of trading with China, is the United States being harmed by trading with China? If free trade is harming the United States, then is the United States justified in imposing protectionist measures against China?

Every year since 1985 the United States has maintained a deficit in the trade in goods with China. (For recent trends in the U.S.-China trade balance, see Figure 1-10.) In 1985, the trade deficit was $6 billion but began to grow steadily and spectacularly since then. By 2011, the United States had a trade deficit with China of approximately $301.5 billion dollars. These trends indicate that it is unlikely that the United States will be able to eliminate its trade deficit with China anytime in the near future. The continuing and mounting U.S. trade deficit with China is in tension with some basic principles of international trade theory.

Under classic trade theory, nations that sell also have an incentive to buy, and trade imbalances should naturally self-correct. Why does this occur? In our earlier examples of trade, we assumed a barter system in which nations exchange goods in kind; i.e., soybeans for textiles. In practice, of course, nations trade using money to purchase goods, and the value of money varies depending upon exchange rates. The theory of international trade posits that trading between nations using money

FIGURE 1-10
U.S.-China Trade Deficit

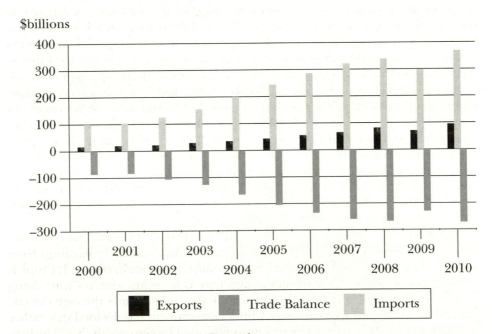

Source: U.S. Int'l Trade Commission Dataweb.

tends to adjust itself toward equilibrium and that both nations will gain from trade. For example, suppose that China sells goods to the United States. The United States will use U.S. dollars to purchase Chinese currency (Renminbi (RMB) or "people's currency") in order to pay for the goods. Let us assume for the moment that the RMB exchange rate is allowed to float; i.e., adjust itself in the market in relation to the U.S. dollar and other currencies. (In fact, the RMB is fixed by the PRC government within very narrow ranges.) The demand for Chinese imports will increase demand for RMB (in exchange for U.S. dollars), and this increase in demand should increase the value of the RMB versus the dollar, assuming that the exchange rate is allowed to float in the currency market. The increase in the value of the RMB versus the dollar will require more dollars to be exchanged for the same quantity of RMB. On the flip side, fewer RMB can be used to purchase U.S. dollars. The adjustment in the exchange rate means that U.S. goods now become cheaper to the Chinese consumer as fewer RMB can be used to purchase equivalent goods. At the same time, Chinese goods become more expensive to the U.S. consumer. In response to increasing demand for U.S. goods, China begins to use its U.S. currency that it has received from the United States to purchase U.S. goods. China begins to import more U.S. goods and the United States begins to import fewer Chinese goods. Over time, the trade imbalance between the United States and China will tend to balance out and both countries should be better off. There should be a trade equilibrium with each nation selling goods in areas where each has a comparative advantage. This self-correction of the trade imbalance encourages circular spending.

2.   *Currency Valuation Issues and "Hoarding" by China*

Although economic theory indicates that a trade imbalance should correct itself, in the real world there are a number of reasons why this might not occur. Recall that in our example, we assumed that the applicable currency exchange rate would be allowed to float and to adjust itself in accordance with market conditions. China, however, has not historically allowed its currency exchange rate to float but has fixed its rate to the U.S. dollar. As a result, although the demand for Chinese currency should result in a devaluation of the U.S. dollar, there is little or no devaluation of the dollar as against the RMB that would make U.S. goods less expensive to the Chinese consumer. There is in turn no (or very little) increase in demand by Chinese consumers for U.S. goods as they do not become less expensive. A number of politicians and other advocates in the United States believe that China's practice of not allowing the RMB to float harms the interests of the United States by sustaining the U.S.-China trade deficit. China has recently responded to pressure from the United States by allowing its currency to vary slightly within a very narrow range as against the U.S. dollar. However, the United States is continuing to apply pressure on China to make additional changes.

A second and related reason that the U.S. trade deficit with China continues to increase is that China has decided that it has a better use for its earnings from selling goods to the United States than to consume U.S. goods in return. If China is not using its reserves of U.S. currency to purchase U.S. goods, what is China doing with all of its U.S. dollars that it has earned from the United States through the sale of goods? China is saving its earnings. China's government has decided that rather than allow its own citizens to increase consumption of foreign goods, it will instead save and invest the surplus mostly in the form of very safe instruments, such as U.S.

Treasury bonds. This saving is what many have described as China "hoarding" its cash. Many U.S. groups criticize China for saving its money instead of choosing to increase its consumption of U.S. imports. These critics charge that China is not reciprocating in the trade relationship with the United States. But there is no legal obligation on the part of China to spend its money (earned selling its goods to the United States) instead of saving and investing the funds instead.

China's trade practices have allowed it to quickly accumulate massive reserves of U.S. currency (see Figure 1-11). As of January 2012, China has accumulated a total of $3.18 trillion in foreign currency reserves. Chinese central bank governor Zhou Xiaochuan has admitted that "foreign exchange reserves have exceeded the reasonable level that our country actually needs."[13] Yet China remains a developing country with per capita annual income of about $3,000. This is a first in world history—a low-income country that has become a global economic powerhouse. The foreign exchange accumulation cannot be spent inside China without causing inflation. However, the money could be used to buy imports from the United States or for foreign investment in the United States. At present, however, most of China's cash is invested in relatively low-yield U.S. Treasury bonds and other foreign government debt obligations.

FIGURE 1-11
China Holdings of U.S. Securities in $Billions

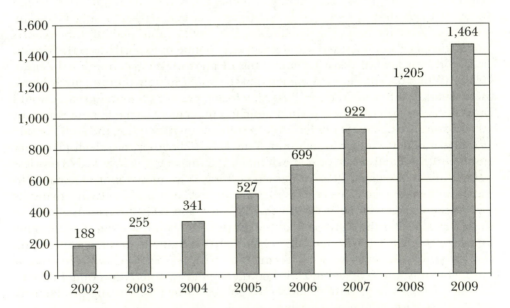

Source: U.S. Treasury Department. Includes short-term and long-term debt, Treasury securities, U.S. government securities, U.S. corporate securities, U.S. equities.

---

13. *See* Howard Schneider, *Beijing Blues: How to Handle All Those Trillions of Dollars,* Washington Post, Apr. 20, 2011, at A12.

China has followed a very conservative currency exchange policy. Between 2005 and February 2012, China allowed the RMB to appreciate by over 40 percent.[14] During the Global Financial Crisis, the RMB was held steady at about 6.83 to the dollar. Then, partially in response to international pressure, the Bank of China announced on June 20, 2010 that "China will improve foreign exchange management and keep the renminbi exchange rate at a reasonable and balanced level of basic stability and safeguard macroeconomic and financial market stability."[15] In the one year since this announcement, the RMB has appreciated 6 percent against the U.S. dollar and 10 percent on a trade-weighted basis. Is this sufficient? Should Beijing change its policy to allow a large and immediate jump in the value of the RMB? In 1985, Japan in response to international pressure adopted the Plaza Accord and the value of the Japanese yen appreciated against the dollar by 85 percent in less than two years. This, however, did not end the United States' and other countries' trade deficits with Japan and contributed to the Japanese bubble economy and the collapse of this bubble in 1990-91. What should China do?

3.   Risks Created by the Trade Deficit with China

Is the current trade deficit with China harmful to the United States? This is the most complex question of all. Many economists would argue that the best case scenario is not for the United States to purchase fewer imports from China but for China to use its earnings to purchase more U.S. goods. But even the argument that China may be harming U.S. interests by purchasing claims to U.S. capital assets instead of U.S. imports is not free from debate. On the one hand, some would argue that hoarding does harm U.S. interests because by purchasing U.S. capital assets, China increases the demand for U.S. dollars, thus making U.S. exports more expensive and further driving down the volume of exports from the United States to China. This process appears to create an endless cycle in which the trade deficit with China continues to increase, with no end in sight. On the other hand, by purchasing U.S. capital assets, China is giving the U.S. resources that it would not otherwise have to fuel its consumption and investment in the United States. In other words, the United States is supplementing its own spending through the sale of capital assets to foreign purchasers. When the U.S. government sells Treasury bonds to China and other countries, the U.S. government is able to borrow less from its own citizens and able to tax less, giving U.S. citizens more resources to use for either consumption or savings. Of course, China is not actually giving its cash to the U.S. government. The sale of Treasury bonds to China means that the United States is borrowing money from China as the bonds are debt instruments that require interest payments and full payment upon maturity. China is lending cash to the United States, which is going into further debt with China. However, if China did not help finance the U.S. deficit, then U.S. consumption would have to fall or U.S. investment and capital formation would be less, hurting productivity and economic growth in the United States.

The additional resources from China are available to U.S. citizens to use to save and invest or to consume even more. Many people in the United States are

---

14. *See Renminbi (Yuan)* available at http://topics.nytimes.com/top/reference/timestopics/subjects/c/currency/yuan/index.html.

15. *See Beijing Vows Slow Pace for Rise of Its Currency,* International Herald Tribune, Jun. 21, 2010, at 1.

choosing to consume more cheap Chinese imports rather than to save and invest. Satisfying demand, of course, benefits U.S. consumers who have greater access to cheap toys, shoes, furniture, and electronic goods, but consuming the additional resources, rather than saving and investing them in U.S. manufacturing and industry, deprives the U.S. economy of capital investment that leads to increased productivity and growth.

What about the popular argument that China needs to allow its currency, the RMB, to appreciate against the U.S. dollar in order to reduce China's large and growing trade surplus? Some economists also reject this argument, noting that in the long term the trade imbalance is caused by China's tendency to save rather than consume, combined with the opposite tendency in the United States, neither of which will be predictably affected by a change in the formal RMB-dollar exchange rate. If consumers in China and the United States had similar consumption and savings habits, then a change in the exchange rate might predictably affect the trade balance. But consumers in China and the U.S. have different, even opposite tendencies. The savings rate in China is about 40 percent of income whereas the savings rate is negligible (or negative) in the United States. For example, suppose that the RMB is allowed to appreciate against the dollar. In the short term, this change will make U.S. goods cheaper in China and Chinese goods more expensive in the United States. For U.S. consumers, if goods become cheaper, it is predictable that consumption will increase. However, while there might be a rise in the consumption of U.S. goods in China, Chinese consumers whose tendency is to save will not automatically consume more, and many U.S. goods will remain on the shelves in China. In the United States, an increase in the price of Chinese goods may lead in the short term to a decrease in consumption, but U.S. consumers (who have a tendency to spend and consume) are not likely to start saving instead just because there is an increase in the price of goods. Rather, the tendency is to borrow more to consume just as much. In addition, U.S. merchants who find that more expensive Chinese goods are not selling as well but who are aware of the high demand will tend to cut the prices of such goods, which move them off the shelves very quickly. In China, a much smaller increase in demand for U.S. goods might have the opposite effect, leading merchants to raise prices for U.S. goods. Thus, it is far from clear that changes in the nominal exchange rate will reduce China's trade surplus as these changes may be offset by changes in the actual price of the goods in response to supply and demand in the marketplace. Whatever the nominal exchange rate, the "real" price of the goods might still make Chinese goods cheaper to the U.S. consumer and U.S. goods more expensive to the Chinese consumer. A change in the nominal exchange rate may do little to alter the trade balance in the long term between the U.S. and China if more fundamental issues, like consumption and savings habits, do not change.

Finally, if the trade deficit with China results in China providing more resources to the United States to use and consume, then what exactly is the downside? According to some critics, the risk is that as China owns more and more of the U.S. economy, China will become more bold and assertive in its dealings with the United States on trade issues, such as intellectual property, and political issues, such as human rights. China might aggressively expand its sphere of influence in other parts of Asia, Africa, and the Middle East. China's implicit threat is that at some point it might require the United States to repay all of its debt; i.e., rather than reinvesting its money by buying more Treasury bonds when the bonds mature, China may choose to cash them all in. At this point, the United States might have to engage in painful measures such as curbing consumption, raising taxes, or print-ing more money, which might lead to inflation or hyper-inflation. To avoid these consequences, the United States might have to be willing to make concessions to China in political and economic matters.

NOTES AND QUESTIONS

To decrease the trade deficit with China, isn't the most simple solution for the United States to just tell China to consume more and save less? How would China react to such a "request"? Why is China saving rather than spending? Another effective way is for U.S. consumers to buy fewer Chinese made goods; i.e., to spend less and save more. Why are U.S. politicians hesitant to tell Americans to live within their means?

PROBLEM 1-12

You are part of a delegation led by the United States Trade Representative and are in a meeting with the Minister of Commerce in China. Your team lectures the Chinese delegation on how China, by hoarding its cash instead of buying more U.S. imports (which would decrease the U.S. trade deficit), is not playing by the rules. The China delegation responds, "We are puzzled. We have heard this criticism many times from you. Yet, we have scoured all legal instruments and have found that there is no obligation contained in the WTO, any other treaty, or any rule of customary international law that requires us to reciprocate by buying goods from the United States instead of saving our earned cash. Since you argue that China is not playing by the rules, whose 'rules' are you referring to?"

———————————

China's growing economic power means that we will return to a discussion of China throughout this book, but our treatment is not meant to be comprehensive. For a detailed treatment, see Daniel C.K. Chow and Anna M. Han, *Doing Business in China: Problems, Cases, and Materials* (West 2012).

V.   Negotiating Trade Concessions

Read again the GATT Articles XXV to XXVIII bis.

Prior to the creation of the WTO in 1995, the GATT operated between 1948 and 1994 to facilitate the negotiations of trade concessions. The authority for these negotiations is found principally in the GATT itself in Articles XXV-XXVIII bis. The main purpose of the early negotiations during this period was to agree on reducing trade barriers. In the early phases, the focus was on trade barriers cre-ated by high tariffs on goods. Mutual reduction of these tariffs would facilitate the international trade in goods. These negotiations occurred in "rounds" named after the place in which the negotiation took place or the person who initiated them.

Beginning with the Geneva Round in the 1960s, GATT countries moved beyond reductions in tariffs and began to consider other trade topics. The Tokyo Round in the 1970s was the first to consider trade barriers not in the form of tariffs. The Uruguay Round was the most ambitious round at the time as it established the new WTO and led to a new set of agreements covering issues such as the trade in services, intellectual property, and dispute settlement. See Figure 1-12.

A.   The Doha Development Agenda of 2001

In 2001 the WTO Ministerial Conference formally opened a new and ongoing negotiation, which is known as the Doha Development Agenda; its focus of concern is not only on tariff and trade barrier reductions but also on the need to address specifically the trade problems encountered by developing countries that now make up the majority of WTO members. The Work Program of the Doha Development Agenda is very complex. The negotiations have lasted many years and are still ongoing. The negotiation agenda includes agriculture, services, market access for non-agricultural products, intellectual property rights and access to medicines, the relationship between trade and investment, the relationship between trade and competition policy, government procurement, trade facilitation, dispute settlement, trade and the environment, electronic commerce, small economies, technology transfer, technical cooperation and capacity building, least developed countries, and special and differential treatment for countries under the WTO agreements. The agenda items are set forth in *Doha WTO Ministerial 2001: Ministerial Declaration*, WT/MIN(01)/Dec/1 (Nov. 20, 2001), available at http://www.wto.org.

At the WTO Ministerial Conference in Geneva in December 2011, no Ministerial Declaration was forthcoming, an admission that the Doha negotiations are effectively suspended. The Conference chairman, Olusegun Aganga, Trade

FIGURE 1-12
The GATT and WTO Trade Rounds, 1947-1994

Year	Place/name	Subjects Covered	Countries
1947	Geneva	Tariffs	23
1949	Annecy	Tariffs	13
1951	Torquay	Tariffs	38
1956	Geneva	Tariffs	26
1960-1961	Geneva Dillon Round	Tariffs	26
1964-1967	Geneva Kennedy Round	Tariffs and anti-dumping measures	62
1973-1979	Geneva Tokyo Round	Tariffs, non-tariff measures, "framework" agreements	102
1986-1994	Geneva Uruguay Round	Tariffs, non-tariff measures, rules, services, intellectual property, dispute settlement, textiles, agriculture, creation of WTO and other issues.	123

Source: Public Domain Materials

Minister from Nigeria, stated that WTO members had agreed only to "more fully explore different negotiating approaches" and "intensify their efforts to look into ways" to overcome the stalemate.

NOTES AND QUESTIONS

For most of its existence the GATT/WTO was concerned with barriers to the trade in goods in the form of tariffs. Why are the current negotiations so multi-faceted and complex? Is the agenda too ambitious? Why do you think that WTO countries have moved beyond trade in goods to cover other trade issues, such as intellectual property?

VI. *Preferential Trade Agreements*

A. Introduction

Preferential trade agreements (PTAs) create voluntary associations of countries that allow their members to enjoy preferential trade benefits that generally exceed those available under the WTO. For example, under the North American Free Trade Agreement (NAFTA), the three members (the United States, Canada, and Mexico) trade goods subject to zero tariffs. These preferences, agreed to by members of NAFTA, are not available to goods of WTO members who are not part of NAFTA; these non-NAFTA goods are subject to normal tariffs. The result is that NAFTA members enjoy "WTO plus" treatment in their trade relations. This differential treatment is inconsistent with the basic rule that all members of the WTO must enjoy equal treatment as set forth in the Most Favored Nation principle contained in GATT Article I. Although PTAs are undertakings outside of the WTO framework, the WTO recognizes and encourages them because they help achieve the ultimate goal of liberalizing trade. Under the WTO, PTAs are exempt from a number of WTO obligations (such as equal treatment) so long as they qualify under the conditions set forth in GATT XXIV.

PTAs are proliferating all over the world, and trade among preference partners has emerged as a new force in international economic relations. As of this writing, 195 PTAs have been concluded by WTO members and notified to the WTO. With the deadlock in negotiations in the WTO Doha Development Agenda and general unrest over globalization, more members of the WTO have turned to PTAs with politically compatible partners as an alternative to greater global economic integration. This trend has in fact accelerated greatly in the early twenty-first century. This trend raises serious policy questions as to whether the proliferation of PTAs is compatible with the multinational trading system. The compatibility question can be analyzed on many levels:

- Are PTAs politically compatible with the multilateral trading system?
- Are PTAs economically compatible?
- Are PTAs legally compatible?

Read GATT Article XXIV in the Documents Supplement. Compare Article V of the GATS.

Complete answers to the first two questions are beyond the scope of this book. An introduction to the main issues must suffice. Political and economic compatibility are related and can only be determined through extensive analysis of the economic and political effects of each particular PTA. It is evident that PTAs have two primary effects: (1) They increase trade and political cooperation between the parties, and (2) they divert trade (and perhaps political cooperation) away from the rest of the world. The most important question to be answered with respect to the compatibility issue in each case is how the balance is struck between these two effects. A PTA that is open to the rest of the world economically and politically may actually benefit the multilateral trading system even though the PTA creates special privileges amongst its members. This was the idea implicit in Article XXIV of the GATT, which permits qualifying PTAs as legally compatible with the global trading system.

What conditions are necessary to comply with Article XXIV? In general, Article XXIV requires that the PTA does not create greater burdens for non-members than existed prior to the formation of the PTA. Under Article XXIV, the most important condition is that the WTO is to be given an opportunity to review plans for a PTA and to make recommendations before the PTA is established. However, in practice, members first form a PTA and then notify the WTO, sometimes years later, and no PTA has ever been declared illegal under this Article. In 1994, however, at the conclusion of the Uruguay Round, negotiators concluded an Understanding on the Interpretation of Article XXIV as follows:

> The provisions of Articles XXII and XXIII of GATT 1994 as elaborated and applied by the Dispute Settlement Understanding may be invoked with respect to any matters arising from the application of those provisions of Article XXIV relating to customs unions, free trade areas, or interim agreements leading to the formation of a customs union or a free trade area.

What is the impact of this Understanding? Why do you think it was concluded? To date, no WTO case has directly challenged a PTA; but several cases have ruled against members that tried to justify GATT-inconsistent practices by citing Article XXIV. In the *European Communities—Regime for the Importation, Sale and Distribution of Bananas*, DS 38/R, GATT Panel Report, unadopted (Feb. 11, 1994), a GATT panel ruled (¶¶159-164) that the Lomé Convention between the European Community (EC) and African-Pacific-Caribbean countries (former colonies of the EC) did not qualify as an FTA under GATT Article XXIV and that this article could not be used to justify the EC's discriminatory import regime for bananas. Thus, while GATT Article XXIV has not been successfully used to strike down PTAs, attempts to use it to defend actions of PTAs have also failed.

The landscape of PTAs is vast: PTAs exist in every part of the globe, and every member of the WTO has concluded multiple PTAs with favored partners. Not only economic but also political considerations dictate the choice of a PTA. For example, the United States is organizing a Middle East Free Trade Area to supplement its influence in that volatile region. PTAs are frequently organized on a regional basis to provide economic and political regional coherence, but many PTAs are also between states on opposite sides of the globe.

Consider the following case in which Turkey attempted to justify a quantitative restriction (a quota), a trade measure prohibited by GATT Article XI, on the ground that the quota was justified by Article XXIV because the quota was necessary to establish a customs union.

Turkey — Restrictions on Imports of Textile and Clothing Products
Report of the Appellate Body, adopted on November 19, 1999
WT/DS34/AB/R

[As part of the final phase of joining the EU, Turkey adopted the existing EU commercial policy allowing for zero tariffs on goods from other EU countries, but imposed quotas on 19 categories of textiles (clothing) from India. Quotas are prohibited by Articles XI and XIII of the GATT, but Turkey argued that the quotas were justified under Article XXIV, which creates exceptions to GATT obligations when necessary to create a customs union. Turkey argued that the quotas were necessary because Turkey resold textiles from India to EU countries. The EU treated the textiles from Turkey as originating from a non-EU country (i.e., India) and subjected them to normal tariffs and not the duty free treatment granted to goods sold from an EU country; the EU considered the textiles to originate from India even though they passed through Turkey into the EU. The EU appears to have treated all textiles from Turkey as originating in India and did not or could not distinguish between textiles originating in Turkey and textiles originating in India and resold through Turkey. Thus, all textiles from Turkey (even those of Turkish origin) were subject to normal tariffs. Turkey argued that since textiles comprised 40 percent of exports from Turkey to the EU, subjecting the textiles to a normal tariff would subject a large portion of trade from Turkey to normal tariffs, undermining the creation of a customs union between Turkey and the EU. In order to protect a large portion of its trade (i.e. textiles), Turkey imposed a quota — a numerical restriction — on the amount of textiles allowed to be imported into Turkey from India. This quota would allow Turkey to take the position that any textiles from Turkey that were subject to the quota could not be of Indian origin and so should be given duty free treatment.

India challenged Turkey's actions as a quota inconsistent with Articles XI and XIII of the GATT prohibiting the imposition of quotas. Turkey attempted to justify the restriction based upon Article XXIV permitting PTAs. The panel ruled in favour of India and Turkey appealed to the Appellate Body, which issued the decision below.]

58. [O]n the basis of the text and the context of the chapeau of paragraph 5 of Article XXIV, we are of the view that Article XXIV may justify a measure which is inconsistent with certain other GATT provisions. However, in a case involving the formation of a customs union, this "defence" is available only when two conditions are fulfilled. First, the party claiming the benefit of this defence must demonstrate that the measure at issue is introduced upon the formation of a customs union that fully meets the requirements of sub-paragraphs 8(a) and 5(a) of Article XXIV. And, second, that party must demonstrate that the formation of that customs union would be prevented if it were not allowed to introduce the measure at issue. Again, *both* these conditions must be met to have the benefit of the defence under Article XXIV.

60. More specifically, with respect to the first condition, the Panel, in this case, did not address the question of whether the regional trade arrangement between Turkey and the European Communities is, in fact, a "customs union" which meets the requirements of paragraphs 8(a) and 5(a) of Article XXIV. The assumption by the Panel that the agreement between Turkey and the European Communities is a "customs union" within the meaning of Article XXIV was not appealed. Therefore, the issue of whether this arrangement meets the requirements of paragraphs 8(a) and 5(a) of Article XXIV is not before us.

61. With respect to the second condition that must be met to have the benefit of the defence under Article XXIV, Turkey asserts that had it not introduced the quantitative restrictions on textile and clothing products from India that are at issue, the European Communities would have "exclud[ed] these products from free trade within the Turkey/EC customs union". According to Turkey, the European Communities would have done so in order to prevent trade diversion. Turkey's exports of these products accounted for 40 per cent of Turkey's total exports to the European Communities. Turkey expresses strong doubts about whether the requirement of Article XXIV:8(a)(i) that duties and other restrictive regulations of commerce be eliminated with respect to "substantially all trade" between Turkey and the European Communities could be met if 40 per cent of Turkey's total exports to the European Communities were excluded. In this way, Turkey argues that, unless it is allowed to introduce quantitative restrictions on textile and clothing products from India, it would be prevented from meeting the requirements of Article XXIV:8(a)(i) and, thus, would be prevented from forming a customs union with the European Communities.

62. We agree with the Panel that had Turkey not adopted the same quantitative restrictions that are applied by the European Communities, this would not have prevented Turkey and the European Communities from meeting the requirements of sub-paragraph 8(a)(i) of Article XXIV, and consequently from forming a customs union. We recall our conclusion that the terms of sub-paragraph 8(a)(i) offer some—though limited—flexibility to the constituent members of a customs union when liberalizing their internal trade. As the Panel observed, there are other alternatives available to Turkey and the European Communities to prevent any possible diversion of trade, while at the same time meeting the requirements of sub-paragraph 8(a)(i). For example, Turkey could adopt rules of origin for textile and clothing products that would allow the European Communities to distinguish between those textile and clothing products originating in Turkey, which would enjoy free access to the European Communities under the terms of the customs union, *and* those textile and clothing products originating in third countries, including India. In fact, we note that Turkey and the European Communities themselves appear to have recognized that rules of origin could be applied to deal with any possible trade diversion. Article 12(3) of Decision 1/95 of the EC-Turkey Association Council, which sets out the rules for implementing the final phase of the customs union between Turkey and the European Communities, specifically provides for the possibility of applying a system of certificates of origin. A system of certificates of origin would have been a reasonable alternative until the quantitative restrictions applied by the European Communities are required to be terminated under the provisions of the *ATC*. Yet no use was made of this possibility to avoid trade diversion. Turkey preferred instead to introduce the quantitative restrictions at issue.

63. For this reason, we conclude that Turkey was not, in fact, required to apply the quantitative restrictions at issue in this appeal in order to form a customs union with the European Communities. Article XXIV does not justify the adoption by Turkey of these quantitative restrictions.

NOTES AND QUESTIONS

1. The EU imposed tariffs on all textiles from Turkey, even those of Turkish origin, because it was not possible to distinguish between those textiles that originated in India and those that did not. Turkey believed that the best way to avoid the tariff was to impose a quota on textiles from India. The Appellate Body ruled that it was not necessary for Turkey to impose a quota because there was a less restrictive method to achieve the same result. What was this method?

2. The *Turkey — Textiles* case shows that, while preferential trade areas may happily coexist with the WTO rules by fulfilling the GATT Article XXIV conditions, WTO members may not use Article XXIV to justify trade barriers they wish to erect against third-party states. However, the legal tests that justify preferential trade agreements are relatively loose. Should these tests be tightened up to ensure that the trade creation aspect of such agreements outweighs the trade diversion they cause? Is this politically possible in the WTO?

B.   Customs Unions and Free Trade Areas: Two Types of Preferential Trade Areas

There are two basic types of preferential trade areas: free trade areas and customs unions. The EU, consisting of twenty-seven states as of this writing, is a customs union whereas NAFTA, consisting of three states, establishes a free trade area. Both entities are similar in that they allow for free trade within their member states. The difference between a customs union and a free trade area is that the former maintains a common tariff structure for external economic relations with non-members whereas the latter allows each member to maintain its own tariff system in accordance with its national laws. For example, all twenty-seven members of the EU maintain a single unified tariff system for dealing with goods from non-member states as part of the EU's common commercial policy. Goods from non-member states will be subject to the same tariffs no matter where the goods enter among any of the twenty-seven states. For tariff purposes, it makes no difference to a U.S. seller whether the goods clear customs in Germany, France, or Belgium — the goods are subject to the same rates. Once the goods lawfully enter the EU, the goods then enjoy free movement throughout the entire EU. By contrast, while goods also move freely within NAFTA, the United States, Canada, and Mexico are entitled to maintain their own tariff system under their own national laws with respect to goods from non-NAFTA states. As tariff rates may vary significantly among the members of a free trade area for any given product, it becomes possible to forum shop for the lowest tariff rates for the point of entry for the goods from which point the goods can then travel duty-free to the desired final country of sale. A non-member state, such as Japan or Korea, might import cars into Mexico; the cars can then be shipped to the United States duty-free where they are finally sold.

To discourage this result, free trade areas, such as NAFTA, apply complex rules of origin tests to determine whether the goods should be deemed to originate within the free trade area and be entitled to duty-free status. To return to our example, cars that are shipped to Mexico from a non-member state will be treated as of Mexican origin only if they meet certain tests, such as whether a certain percentage of the value of the goods can be attributed to Mexico. Goods from a non-member state might also qualify as of NAFTA origin if they have undergone additional work or transformation in Mexico. In general, manual assembly or packaging will not satisfy NAFTA rules of origin. If the NAFTA rules of origin are not met, then the goods are subject to tariffs as if they were shipped from the originating country. In our example above, the U.S. would apply tariffs to the automobiles as if they were shipped from Japan. NAFTA rules of origin are very important and are examined in detail in Chapter 5.

The formation of a customs union requires each partner to give up sovereign control of many matters, so it is not a popular choice among WTO members. The leading example is the EC, but the EC is more than just a customs union. The EC is also a political union (the EU) as well as a monetary union and a single market for the free movement of goods, services, capital, and people (i.e., the famous four freedoms). The EC as a separate legal entity is a WTO member in addition to its member states. Another example of a successful customs union is the Southern African Customs Union (SACU), which consists of South Africa, Botswana, Swaziland, Lesotho, and Namibia.

The most popular form of the PTA is the free trade area (FTA). Examples of functioning FTAs exist all over the world. In Africa, we find the Economic Community of West African States (ECOWAS) and the Common Market for Eastern and Southern Africa (COMESA). In South America, there is the Market of the South (MERCOSUR), consisting of Brazil, Argentina, Uruguay, and Paraguay with several more associated South American states. In North America there is the NAFTA between Mexico, Canada, and the United States. Australia, New Zealand, and ten Asian nations have formed the Association of Southeast Asian Nations (ASEAN). Japan has concluded bilateral FTAs with Singapore, Mexico, Thailand, and Malaysia. China has preferential trade agreements with ASEAN. In the near future, Asian nations are expected to create one giant FTA to include China, South Korea, and Japan (to be known as ASEAN plus 3). There are many more FTAs as well, too many to list here.

The United States has been particularly active in creating FTAs that have increased and reshaped the patterns of American trade. NAFTA (1994) was followed by another multilateral FTA that took effect in 2005, the Central American-Dominican Republic-United States FTA (known as CAFTA-DR). The United States also concluded bilateral FTAs with the following: Australia, Jordan, Morocco, Bahrain, Chile, Israel, Oman, Panama, SACU, Singapore, South Korea. Several more are in the works, including FTAs with Thailand, Malaysia, and New Zealand. The United States has also concluded Trade Promotion Agreements (TPAs)—a little less extensive than a full FTA—with Peru and Colombia. The United States has proposed a Free Trade Agreement of the Americas (FTAA) that would encompass the entire Western Hemisphere (leaving out Cuba). In recent years, influential voices also called for a Japan-U.S. FTA as well as an EU-U.S. FTA. Thus, the pace of creation of FTAs is quickening and, statistically at least, preferential trading dominates world trade.

Two additional types of trade agreements merit mention as well. First, the United States and twenty other nations participate in the Asia Pacific Economic Cooperation Forum (APEC), which is a discussion forum on trade, meeting periodically to consider common trade and security issues. (In 2006, the United States proposed that APEC be transformed into a vast Free Trade Area of the Asia Pacific.)[16] Second, important preferential trade also takes place between developed countries and developing countries under the Generalized System of Preferences. We cover the latter type of PTA in Chapter 9 on developing countries.

Instead of devoting a chapter to PTAs, we treat them pervasively throughout this book. In this introductory section, however, we provide a summary of what an FTA looks like and how it operates, using NAFTA as an example. The provisions of NAFTA have been used as models for the conclusion of other FTAs around the world. Thus, NAFTA can be regarded as typical of the FTA phenomenon.

PROBLEM 1-13

Lucky Electronics, a Taiwanese manufacturer of flat screen plasma televisions, exports parts, such as the screen and electronic components, to Mexico City, where the components are assembled by workers in a factory and then exported to the United States. The assembly work is tedious but is manual labor that requires no education. Will the televisions enter the United States duty-free under NAFTA? What is the country of origin of the goods? What rate of duty will be applied?

PROBLEM 1-14

Yamamoto Zipper Co. is a Japanese company that exports zippers from Japan to many countries in Asia. Yamamoto Zipper is now contemplating exporting its zippers to Europe as well. The company has received requests for information from potential buyers in seven countries, all member states of the EU. If Yamamoto Co. establishes a sales office and central warehouse in Frankfurt, Germany, can shipments of zippers be made duty-free to other member states of the EU, or will duties have to be paid at the border of those countries?

Yamamoto also plans to sell its zippers in North America. If it opens a sales office in Kansas City, can shipments be made duty-free to buyers in Mexico and Canada? To answer this problem, review the discussion distinguishing between free trade areas and customs unions.

PROBLEM 1-15

In 2007, several incidents in the United States (and other countries) involving the safety of imported foods and products from China garnered media attention around the world. With the proliferation of free trade agreements, concerns about product safety are also on the rise. China might export to a country with an FTA

---

16. In 2010, the leaders of APEC agreed to form an APEC Community. *See The APEC Leaders' Declaration: "The Yokohama Vision — Bogor and Beyond,"* http://www.apec.org.

with the United States, and for the goods to then be re-exported to the United States under the FTA, which uses simplified customs procedures. The U.S. Food and Drug Administration is considering new rules that require labeling whether food products such as meat have a purely U.S. origin; have a mixed origin (a cow born in Mexico and slaughtered in the United States); or have a purely foreign origin. Is labeling an adequate response to the food and product safety problem? Does the GATT allow food and product labeling and food inspection? *See* GATT Articles IX and XX. We cover these articles more extensively in later chapters.

PROBLEM 1-16

Suppose that the U.S. Congress believes that more drastic steps are necessary in light of continuing food safety and quality problems with Chinese products that continue to be transshipped through FTAs into the United States. Congress passes a law that all products containing dairy ingredients from China must be marked "DAIRY INGREDIENTS FROM CHINA." Dairy products from other countries, which have not had food safety issues, do not need to be marked. China argues that this labeling requirement is unlawful. Who is right? In addition to GATT Articles IX and XX, see also GATT I:1.

C.   The North American Free Trade Agreement: An Overview

Taking effect on January 1, 1994, NAFTA is a comprehensive trade agreement that eliminates virtually all tariffs between the three member countries, the United States, Canada, and Mexico. As a result of NAFTA, trade has tripled between the United States and Mexico, and Canada increased its standing as the largest trading partner of the United States.

Chapters One and Two of NAFTA set out the objectives of the agreement and provide general definitions.

The heart of NAFTA is contained in Chapters Three to Five of the agreement. Chapter Three provides for tariff elimination, National Treatment (i.e., non-discriminatory treatment further discussed in Chapter 4 of this book), and market access for goods. Chapter Five standardizes customs procedures of the three countries. Chapter Four contains complex and important requirements on rules of origin to implement the basic premise of a free trade agreement to extend preferential (duty-free) treatment only to goods that qualify as the product of the countries involved. Only those items deemed under the NAFTA rules of origin to originate from Mexico, the United States, or Canada will be eligible for duty-free treatment when exported from one NAFTA country into another. All non-NAFTA originating items will be fully dutiable at ordinary rates agreed under the WTO for members or at possibly higher rates for non-WTO members. Thus, PTAs affect products from third countries in various ways; we consider these issues in more depth in Chapter 7 of this book.

Here is a summary of the other NAFTA chapters:

Chapter Six has special rules for energy because of the sensitivity and importance of this sector.

Chapter Seven deals with agriculture and sanitary and phytosanitary standards (SPS) dealing with food safety. Both of these topics are covered by the WTO as well. NAFTA avoids any discipline for agricultural subsidies but generally abolishes border restrictions on trade in agricultural products. SPS standards are similar to those of the WTO.

Chapter Eight allows NAFTA members to impose emergency safeguard actions (such as the imposition of higher tariffs or quotas on imports) to offset market disruptions caused by trade concessions. Safeguards available under NAFTA are similar to those available under the WTO agreements.

Chapter Nine requires closer cooperation than does the WTO, on developing technical product standards to be enforced at the border. Technical standards relating to the characteristics of products serve legitimate national interests in health and safety but can also operate as a trade barrier or a disguised protectionist measure if the standards are very difficult to satisfy. Companies and interested parties can participate directly in the development of standards. The aim of NAFTA is to create compatible standards.

Chapter Ten deals with government procurement (i.e., the purchase of goods and services by governments). Governments have traditionally preferred to purchase goods and services from domestic suppliers, no matter what the market efficiencies might dictate. Going further than the WTO, NAFTA requires virtually all federal government agencies in the three countries, and a significant number of other government enterprises, to open competition to foreign suppliers by making purchasing decisions based on market factors. NAFTA requires covered entities to follow procedures with respect to awarding contracts, bidding, challenging, qualification of suppliers, time limits for tendering, as well as submission, receipt, and opening of tenders.

Chapter Eleven provides for National Treatment for foreign direct investment and creates significant protections against the mistreatment of foreign investors, as well as remedies in the form of a claim for arbitration for investors. Chapter Eleven arbitration is patterned after investor-state dispute settlement mechanisms contained in standard Bilateral Investment Treaties.

Chapter Twelve covers cross-border service trade, covering virtually all services except financial, aviation, maritime, and telecommunications. NAFTA goes beyond the WTO by providing for a general opening of services markets subject to exceptions under a "negative list" approach (i.e., market access is required for all services sectors unless the sector is explicitly proscribed) instead of a "positive list" approach (i.e., market access is provided only for the committed or listed services sector) as provided in the WTO. Licensing and certification requirements for service providers are retained.

Chapter Thirteen contains special rules for telecommunications services.

Chapter Fourteen contains special rules for financial services.

Chapter Fifteen requires exchanges of information and cooperation, including a Trilateral Working Group, concerning competition policy and enforcement.

Chapter Sixteen liberalizes immigration laws for the business entry of persons. Temporary entry is allowed for (1) business visitors; (2) traders and investors; (3) intra-company transferees; and (4) professionals.

Chapter Seventeen addresses protection of intellectual property, reaffirming the WTO TRIPS Agreement and other international agreements.

Chapter Eighteen ensures the prompt publication of laws and regulations.

Chapter Nineteen establishes a special procedure for dispute settlement in anti-dumping and countervailing duty proceedings (discussed further in Chapter 10 of this book). Such determinations made by government agencies in the NAFTA countries may be appealed to ad hoc panels of private individuals drawn from the importing and exporting countries, rather than reviewed by national courts. The binational panels are required to review agency determinations on the basis of their consistency with the national law of the importing country. Panel decisions are final and binding although an extraordinary challenge procedure is available.

Chapter Twenty sets out detailed procedures for the resolution of disputes that may arise between NAFTA governments over the provisions of NAFTA. If a dispute concerns both NAFTA and the WTO agreements, the parties can choose to resolve the dispute in either forum.

NAFTA parties have also entered into two side agreements; the North American Agreement on Labor Cooperation, which aims to improve conditions for workers by requiring the parties to enforce their own national laws,[17] and the North American Agreement on Environmental Cooperation, which provides for the enforcement of national laws on environmental protection.[18]

PROBLEM 1-17

Japan and Mexico entered into an agreement to form a free trade area in 2005. Under this agreement, tariffs on all imports (except for a few agricultural products) will be reduced to zero. You are a lawyer specializing in international trade law. You receive a telephone call from Mr. Aoki, the President of Doko Manufacturing, a Japanese company that makes hoses that hook up deep-fat kitchen fryers and other cooking appliances to gas outlets. Mr. Aoki has heard from the Japanese Ministry of Economy, Trade and Industry that the hoses manufactured by Doko may now enter Mexico duty-free under the Japan-Mexico Free Trade Agreement. Doko also exports to both United States and Canada but all these hoses are subject to ordinary duties under U.S. and Canadian law. Mr. Aoki knows that under NAFTA, goods from Mexico enter into the United States and Canada duty-free.

Mr. Aoki would like to know whether Doko hoses that transit through Mexico (i.e., are processed as a pass-through by Mexican customs but never enter Mexican commerce) will be allowed to enter duty-free into the United States or Canada. What do you tell him? Mr. Aoki asks, "What can be done, if anything, that will also produce tariff-free entry of the Doko hoses into the United States and Canada?"

NOTE ON LABOR AND ENVIRONMENTAL STANDARDS IN PREFERENTIAL TRADE AGREEMENTS

We have seen that NAFTA contains path-breaking side agreements on Labor and on Environmental Protection, the first time these topics had been addressed in an important trade agreement. Although these Side Agreements have so far had minimal impact, they established an important principle—that nations that open their markets to trade must also take concrete steps to protect the rights of workers and to safeguard the environment.

---

17. *See* http://www.cec.org.
18. *See* http://www.naalc.org.

A major test of this principle came in 2007 when, for the first time, the Republican Administration of President George W. Bush had to submit important free trade agreements for approval by a Congress under the control of the Democratic Party. The political clash came to a boil over the U.S.-South Korean Free Trade Agreement (known as KORUS); South Korea is the world's tenth-ranking economy. After prolonged negotiations, the Bush Administration and congressional leaders announced agreement on a new bipartisan policy on international trade on May 10, 2007. KORUS commits the parties to effectively enforce their own domestic environmental laws and to fulfill obligations under the seven covered multilateral environmental agreements. KORUS also includes an enforceable reciprocal obligation to adopt and maintain basic rights of workers as set forth in the 1998 International Labor Organization Declaration on Fundamental Principles and Rights at Work. KORUS was approved by the U.S. Congress on October 12, 2011. The policy that free trade agreements should routinely provide protections for the rights of workers and the environment seems to be embedded in the United States.

NOTE ON DISPUTE SETTLEMENT AND PREFERENTIAL TRADE AGREEMENTS

Preferential trade agreements typically include provisions for dispute settlement. NAFTA creates five separate dispute settlement procedures: Chapter Eleven, investor-state arbitrations; Chapter Nineteen, binational panels for anti-dumping and countervailing duty cases; Chapter Twenty, general disputes; and environmental and labor party-to-party proceedings under the two NAFTA side agreements. Of these procedures, Chapter Eleven and Chapter Nineteen have been frequently used, while only three cases have been completed under Chapter Twenty, and very few cases have been filed and none completed under the two side agreements.

When a dispute arises between parties to a free trade agreement such as NAFTA, if the dispute also implicates a provision of a WTO agreement, which dispute system has jurisdiction? NAFTA Article 2005 provides that if a dispute arises under both NAFTA and a WTO agreement, the dispute "may be settled in either forum at the discretion of the complaining party." This article further states that, once the dispute settlement has been initiated, "the forum selected shall be used to the exclusion of the other." This system was tested in a dispute between the United States and Mexico over U.S. quota restrictions on Mexican sugar imports and Mexican duties on U.S. imports of high fructose corn syrup.

In *Mexico—Tax Measures on Soft Drinks and Other Beverages*, WT/DS308/AB/R, Report of the Appellate Body, adopted on March 24, 2006, the WTO Appellate Body considered the complaint of the United States that Mexico had imposed a series of tax measures on soft drinks and other beverages that use a sweetener other than cane sugar. The United States alleged that these taxes were inconsistent with GATT Article III in that they were in excess of taxes imposed on like domestic products from Mexico and discriminated against U.S. sugar. Mexico asked the panel to decline to exercise jurisdiction in favor of an arbitral panel under Chapter Twenty of NAFTA and stated that the dispute was "inextricably linked to a broader dispute regarding access of Mexican sugar to the United States market under NAFTA." (¶92). The Appellate Body ruled on Mexico's request as follows:

51. Article 11 of the DSU [the WTO Dispute Settlement Understanding] states that panels *should* make an objective assessment of the matter before them. The Appellate Body has previously held that the word "should" can be used not only "to imply an exhortation, or to state a preference", but also "to express a duty [or] obligation".

52. Article 23 of the DSU states that Members of the WTO *shall* have recourse to the rules and procedures of the DSU when they "seek the redress of a violation of obligations . . . under the covered agreements". The fact that a Member may initiate a WTO dispute whenever it considers that "any benefits accruing to [that Member] are being impaired by measures taken by another Member" implies that that Member is *entitled* to a ruling by a WTO panel.

54. [W]e express no view as to whether there may be other circumstances in which legal impediments could exist that would preclude a panel from ruling on the merits of the claims that are before it. In the present case, Mexico argues that the United States' claims under Article III of the GATT 1994 are inextricably linked to a broader dispute, and that only a NAFTA panel could resolve the dispute as a whole. [N]o NAFTA panel as yet has decided the "broader dispute" to which Mexico has alluded. We do not express any view on whether a legal impediment to the exercise of a panel's jurisdiction would exist in the event that features such as those mentioned above were present. In any event, we see no legal impediments applicable in this case.

NOTES AND QUESTIONS

1. Suppose a NAFTA Article 20 dispute had been pending between Mexico and the United States. Would the Appellate Body have deferred to NAFTA Article 2005 providing that disputes involving both WTO and NAFTA obligations can be settled in either body? The Appellate Body further observed (¶80) that adjudicating non-WTO disputes "is not the function of panels and the Appellate Body as intended by the DSU."

2. After the Appellate Body's decision, a deadline was agreed upon by the United States and Mexico for compliance with the WTO panel's recommendation to remove the offending tax measures. On July 27, 2006, Mexico and the United States concluded a NAFTA Sugar Agreement ending their twelve-year dispute. Mexico received partial duty-free access to the U.S. sugar market in return for eliminating the tax measures.

2 *Dispute Settlement Within the WTO*

In this Chapter, we turn to the topic of dispute settlement in the WTO. An examination of this topic will introduce the student to how WTO opinions are created and their status within the WTO and U.S. legal system. Dispute settlement is central to the work of the WTO.

Read GATT Articles XXII and XXIII and the WTO Understanding on Rules and Procedures Governing the Settlement of Disputes (DSU) in the Documents Supplement.

I. General Considerations

One of the major achievements of the Uruguay Round was the Dispute Settlement Understanding (DSU). By establishing an effective legal mechanism for the settlement of trade disputes, the DSU has addressed one of the basic problems that historically plagued all forms of public international law: the lack of an effective enforcement system. The WTO's Dispute Settlement mechanism is largely responsible for establishing a "rule of law" in international trade.

The WTO's dispute settlement mechanism differs markedly from most international tribunals. In general, the jurisdiction of international tribunals is based on consent. A sovereign state cannot be brought before an international tribunal without its prior consent. For example, members of the United Nations (UN) are not subject to suit before the International Court of Justice (ICJ), which functions as the UN's court, unless they separately agree to at least one of the types of contentious jurisdictions of the ICJ. *See* the Statute of the ICJ Article 36 (1945). In addition, the ICJ has no power to enforce its judgments. In contrast, when a state becomes a member of the WTO, it automatically submits to the jurisdiction of the WTO dispute settlement system. The WTO system also carries automatic penalties that apply if the WTO member does not comply with a final ruling under the WTO dispute settlement system.

Before we study the process under the DSU, we discuss briefly the GATT under which dispute settlement was conducted until 1994. Dispute settlement under the GATT proceeded on the basis of two articles, GATT Article XXII and GATT Article XXIII. Under Article XXIII, the complainant had to demonstrate a "nullification or impairment" of a trade benefit. The DSU continues to operate under this approach and we will shortly examine the meaning of this provision. The GATT established panels, composed of experts, to resolve disputes.

The DSU now supplements the original GATT provisions with a more structured, rule-oriented process with flexible deadlines, but also with mandatory requirements. Three institutions administer the DSU. The DSB establishes panels, adopts panel reports, is responsible for the implementation of rulings and recommendations, and authorizes sanctions for failure to comply with decisions. *See* DSU Article 2.1. The DSB is composed of the same membership as the WTO General Council, the standing body of the WTO, although the DSB follows its own procedures and has its own chair. Panels, first used in the GATT system, are composed of three persons who serve in their individual capacities and not as representatives of their governments. The DSB has established an Appellate Body to review the decisions of the panels. The Appellate Body is a standing institution of the WTO consisting of seven persons who sit for cases in divisions of three. *See* DSU Articles 17.1 and 17.3.

At the preliminary stages of the dispute settlement process, the parties have an opportunity to settle the dispute informally through consultation and mediation. *See* DSU Articles 4-5. Once a party decides to move forward with the formal dispute settlement process, the DSB will establish a panel, which consists of three to five persons, and will set forth a timetable for proceedings, including the submission of written statements and "meetings" (the WTO eschews the more adversarial-sounding "hearings"). At these closed sessions both parties are allowed to present their case. At the close of the first session, the parties are allowed to make a second written submission, which can serve to rebut arguments made at the first session. At the request of the parties, the panel can hold a second meeting. This is usually the last opportunity for the parties to make their case before the panel.

The panel then issues a draft report to the parties, who have an opportunity to submit written comments. *See* DSU Article 15.1. The panel then issues an interim report with its findings and conclusions. *See* DSU Article 15.2. The parties are allowed to comment on the interim report and to request a meeting with the panel to discuss the report. *See* DSU Article 15.2. If no comments are received during the comment period, the interim report becomes the panel's final report. *See* DSU Article 15.2. A final report is normally issued within six months of the establishment of the panel, although in urgent cases the panel will strive to issue a report in three months. *See* DSU Article 12.8.

Within sixty days after the submission of a final report by the panel the DSB must adopt the report unless there is a consensus not to adopt the report or there is a formal notice of appeal. *See* DSU Article 16.4. A decision of the panel can be appealed to the Appellate Body, which has the authority to uphold, modify, or reverse the findings of the panel. *See* DSU Article 17.13. However, the Appellate Body lacks the authority to remand a case to the panel with instructions. This means that the legal issue involved can only be resolved if the Appellate Body completes the analysis itself with respect to the issue. The Appellate Body must normally issue its decision within sixty days of the filing of the notice of appeal and the decision can in no event exceed ninety days. *See* DSU Article 17.5.

An Appellate Body report must be adopted by the DSB within thirty days unless the DSB decides by consensus not to adopt the report. *See* DSU Article 17.14. If the report finds that a measure is not consistent with a covered WTO agreement, the report will recommend the member bring the measure into conformity. See Figure 2-1.

FIGURE 2-1
The Panel and Appellate Body Process

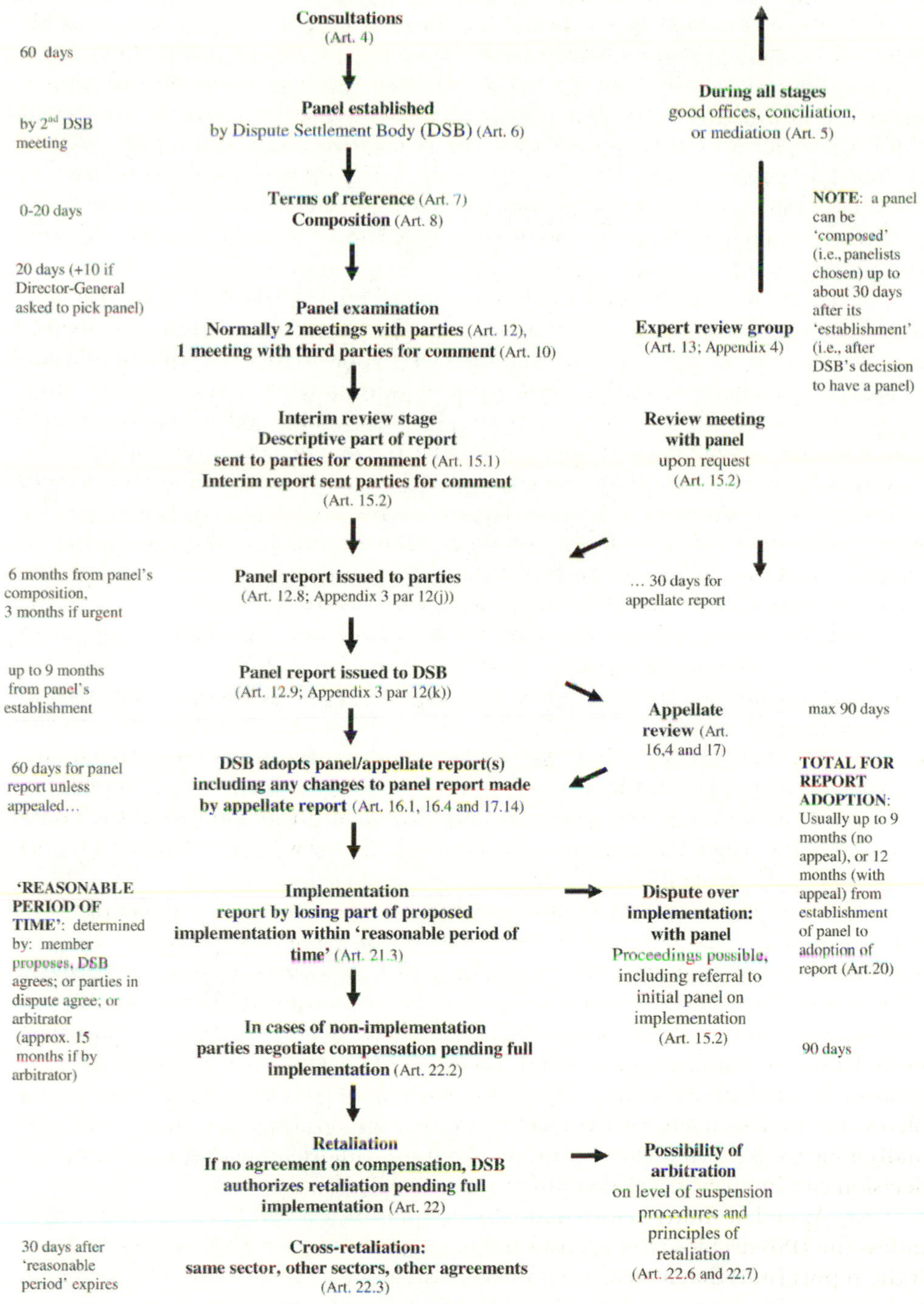

Consultations
(Art. 4)

60 days

Panel established
by Dispute Settlement Body (DSB) (Art. 6)

by 2ⁿᵈ DSB
meeting

During all stages
good offices, conciliation,
or mediation (Art. 5)

Terms of reference (Art. 7)
Composition (Art. 8)

0-20 days

NOTE: a panel
can be
'composed'
(i.e., panelists
chosen) up to
about 30 days
after its
'establishment'
(i.e., after
DSB's decision
to have a panel)

20 days (+10 if
Director-General
asked to pick panel)

Panel examination
Normally 2 meetings with parties (Art. 12),
1 meeting with third parties for comment (Art. 10)

Expert review group
(Art. 13; Appendix 4)

Interim review stage
Descriptive part of report
sent to parties for comment (Art. 15.1)
Interim report sent parties for comment
(Art. 15.2)

Review meeting
with panel
upon request
(Art. 15.2)

6 months from panel's
composition,
3 months if urgent

Panel report issued to parties
(Art. 12.8; Appendix 3 par 12(j))

… 30 days for
appellate report

up to 9 months
from panel's
establishment

Panel report issued to DSB
(Art. 12.9; Appendix 3 par 12(k))

Appellate
review (Art.
16,4 and 17)

max 90 days

60 days for panel
report unless
appealed…

DSB adopts panel/appellate report(s)
including any changes to panel report made
by appellate report (Art. 16.1, 16.4 and 17.14)

TOTAL FOR
REPORT
ADOPTION:
Usually up to 9
months (no
appeal), or 12
months (with
appeal) from
establishment
of panel to
adoption of
report (Art.20)

'REASONABLE
PERIOD OF
TIME': determined
by: member
proposes, DSB
agrees; or parties in
dispute agree; or
arbitrator
(approx. 15
months if by
arbitrator)

Implementation
report by losing part of proposed
implementation within 'reasonable period of
time' (Art. 21.3)

Dispute over
implementation:
with panel
Proceedings possible,
including referral to
initial panel on
implementation
(Art. 15.2)

In cases of non-implementation
parties negotiate compensation pending full
implementation (Art. 22.2)

90 days

Retaliation
If no agreement on compensation, DSB
authorizes retaliation pending full
implementation (Art. 22)

Possibility of
arbitration
on level of suspension
procedures and
principles of
retaliation
(Art. 22.6 and 22.7)

30 days after
'reasonable
period' expires

Cross-retaliation:
same sector, other sectors, other agreements
(Art. 22.3)

NOTES AND QUESTIONS

1. Must a complaining member be prepared to demonstrate its legal interest as a precondition to bringing a case? In *European Communities—Regime for the Importation, Sale and Distribution of Bananas*, WT/DS27/AB/R, Report of the Appellate Body, adopted on September 25, 1997, the EC questioned the legal interest of the United States to bring a case concerning bananas since U.S. banana production is minimal and the United States does not export bananas. The Appellate Body ruled (¶132) that "We do not accept that the need for a legal interest is implied in the DSU." This ruling might be read to imply that all WTO members have an interest in the other members' compliance with the WTO agreements. This could give standing to all members to challenge a violation of the WTO agreements, subject to other requirements (such as an injury discussed in the next section).

2. What must be alleged in the complaint? *See* Article 6.2 of the DSU. In *European Communities—Selected Customs Matters*, WR/DS315/AB/R, Report of the Appellate Body, adopted on December 11, 2006, the Appellate Body stated (¶132) that the two requirements of this provision must be kept separate: "These two requirements are conceptually different and they should not be confused." The Appellate Body interpreted (¶130) Article 6.2 to "relate to different aspects of the complainant's challenge to measures taken by another Member. The 'specific measure' to be identified in a panel request is the object of the challenge, namely, the measure that is alleged to be causing the violation of an obligation contained in a covered agreement. In contrast, the legal basis of the complaint, namely the 'claim,' pertains to the specific provision of the covered agreement that contains the obligation alleged to be violated. A brief summary of the legal basis of the complaint required by Article 6.2 of the DSU aims to explain succinctly *how* or *why* the measure at issue is considered by the complaining Member to be violating the WTO obligation in question."

3. What kind of "measures" may be the object of dispute settlement? *See* DSU Article 3.3. In the *EC—Customs* case, *supra*, the Appellate Body stated (¶133) that "[a]s long as the specificity requirements of Article 6.2 are met, we see no reason why a Member should be precluded from setting out in a panel request 'any act or omission' attributable to another Member as the measure at issue."

4. The Appellate Body has interpreted DSU Articles 3.7 and 12.7 as importing the requirements of good faith, fundamental fairness, and due process as concepts that must be adhered to by WTO members in dealing with each other, as well as by WTO panels in handling cases. *See, e.g., Mexico—Anti-Dumping Investigation of High Fructose Corn Syrup (HFCS) from the United States, Recourse to Article 21.5 of the DSU by the United States*, WT/DS132/AB/RW, Report of the Appellate Body, adopted on November 21, 2001. In that case, Mexico raised an objection to the panel's authority before the Appellate Body that had not been raised before the panel. The Appellate Body cited (¶¶46-48) good faith in stating that Mexico's objection was out of line.

PROBLEM 2-1

In a dispute between the United States and Norway, the United States loses both in the Panel and on appeal before the Appellate Body. Assume that the report of the Appellate Body has now been circulated before the DSB, which must adopt the report within thirty days. The United States would like to block the adoption of the report, but Norway acting on its own has the ability to ensure the adoption of the Appellate Body report. Can you explain how? *See* DSU Article 17.14.

NOTES ON IMPLEMENTATION AND REMEDIES

What are the steps to be taken to implement decisions of the DSB and what remedies are available?

- *Notification of intentions on implementation of DSB recommendations (DSU Article 21.3).* Within thirty days after the adoption of a panel or Appellate Body report, the member concerned shall appear at a meeting and inform the DSB of the intentions of that member concerning the recommendation of the report.
- *Determination of a reasonable period of time under Article 21.3 of the DSU.* The member concerned has a reasonable period of time in which to comply with the recommendations of the report adopted by the DSB. The reasonable period of time can be determined by mutual agreement of the parties or by arbitration. In *Canada—Patent Protection of Pharmaceutical Products, Recourse to Arbitration under DSU Article 21.3,* WT/DS114/13/DSR 2002:I (2000), the arbitrator ruled that the burden of proof (under Article 21.3) falls on the implementing member to justify the duration of the proposed "reasonable period of time."
- *Surveillance by the DSB pursuant to Article 21.6.* The DSB will monitor the implementation of the recommendations by the member concerned. Within six months following the establishment of the reasonable period of time, the DSB will put the matter of implementation on its agenda and will monitor the matter until the issue is resolved.
- *Recourse to Article 21.5.* In some cases, the parties will disagree whether the measures taken by the offending member comply with the recommendations of the DSB. In this case, a "compliance" panel can be instituted to decide whether the adopted measures cure the violation. In most cases the matter will be submitted to the original panel, whose decision can be appealed to the Appellate Body. It is possible to have multiple recourses to Article 21.5. *See, e.g., Canada—Measures Affecting the Importation of Milk and the Exportation of Dairy Products, Second Recourse to Article 21.5 of the DSU,* WT/DS103/AB/RW2, Report of the Appellate Body, adopted on January 17, 2002.
- *Recourse to Article 22.2.* If a member fails to bring an offending measure into conformity or fails to follow the recommendations of the DSB, the aggrieved party can seek compensation, which is voluntary on the part of the offending party. Compensation does not consist of a monetary payment but the granting of additional concessions that benefit the aggrieved party. For example, the offending party might agree to zero tariffs on certain imports from the aggrieved party, which would provide a financial benefit or compensation to the aggrieved party. However, like retaliation, compensation is viewed as a temporary measure to induce the offending member to bring its measures into compliance with the WTO. Recourse to compensation has been very infrequent.

- *Recourse to Article 22.3.* If the parties cannot agree on compensation and the reasonable period of time has lapsed, the WTO may authorize the aggrieved party to retaliate; i.e., suspend trade concessions given to the offending party. Countermeasures must be undertaken in the following order: (1) in the same sector(s) in which the violation occurs (e.g., if certain goods from the aggrieved member are subject to the non-conforming measure by the offending member, the aggrieved member imposes countermeasures on imports of the same type of goods from the offending member); (2) in a different sector covered by the same agreement (e.g., the aggrieved member is allowed to impose countermeasures on a different type of goods than the goods subject to the non-conforming measure by the offending member); and (3) in a different sector covered by another agreement or "cross retaliation" (e.g., an aggrieved member takes countermeasures in the area of intellectual property against the offending member, which has enacted non-conforming measures affecting goods from the aggrieved member). The preferred course is imposing countermeasures in the same sector. Countermeasures in a different sector are permitted only when countermeasures in the same sector are not practicable. Cross retaliation must be justified by the aggrieved member. In *European Communities—Regime for the Importation, Sale and Distribution of Bananas, Recourse to Arbitration under DSU Article 22.6,* WT/DS27/ARB/ECU (2000), Ecuador's level of nullification or impairment caused by the EC's restrictions on banana imports from Ecuador was set at U.S. $201 million per year; however, Ecuador's remedies would be very limited, if not illusory, if Ecuador was to enforce restrictions on bananas from the EU. Rather, Ecuador was authorized to suspend obligations under both the GATS and TRIPS agreements.
- *Request for Arbitration under Article 22.6 of the DSU.* If the offending member that is subject to the authorized countermeasures objects to the level of the suspensions, the offending member can challenge the level of suspensions through arbitration. The arbitrator(s), often the original panel, must determine whether the level of suspensions is equivalent to the injury; i.e., the level of nullification or impairment suffered by the aggrieved party. The burden of proof in an Article 22.6 proceeding is on the party challenging the conformity of the proposed suspension with Article 22. Under Article 25 of the DSU the level of benefits that are being nullified or impaired may be up to an arbitrator. *See United States—Section 110(5) of the US Copyright Act, Recourse to Arbitration under DSU Article 25,* WT/DS160/ARB25/1 (2001).
- *Lifting countermeasures.* Countermeasures are lifted when the inconsistent measure has been brought into conformity with the WTO or the parties have reached a mutually satisfactory solution. *See* Article 22.8.

As of this writing, the WTO has handled over 400 complaints, but countermeasures have been authorized in only eight cases. More typically, implementation and compliance proceeds more or less according to a set schedule. Below is an actual schedule:

**United States — Standards for Reformulated and Conventional Gasoline
Report of the Appellate Body, adopted on April 29, 1996
WT/DS2/AB/R
Step-by-Step Schedule**

Time (0 = start of case)	Target/actual period	Date	Action
−5 years		1990	U.S. Clean Air Act amended
−4 months		September 1994	U.S. restricts gasoline imports under Clear Air Act
0	"60 days"	23 January 1995	Venezuela complains to Dispute Settlement Body, asks for consultation with U.S.
+1 month		24 February 1995	Consultations take place. Fail.
+2 months		25 March 1995	Venezuela asks Dispute Settlement Body for a panel
+2½ months	"30 days"	10 April 1995	Dispute Settlement Body agrees to appoint panel. U.S. does not block. (Brazil starts complaint, requests consultation with U.S.)
+3 months	9 months (target is 6-9)	28 April 1995	Panel appointed. (31 May, panel assigned to Brazilian complaint as well)
+6 months		10-12 July and 13-15 July 1995	Panel meets
+11 months		11 December 1995	Panel gives interim report to U.S., Venezuela, and Brazil for comment
+1 year		29 January 1996	Panel circulates final report to Dispute Settlement Body
+1 year, 1 month	"60 days"	21 February 1996	U.S. appeals
+1 year, 3 months		29 April 1996	Appellate Body submits report
+1 year, 4 months	"30 days"	20 May 1996	Dispute Settlement Body adopts panel and appeal reports

Time (0 = start of case)	Target/actual period	Date	Action
+1 year, 10 months		3 December 1996	U.S. and Venezuela agree on what U.S. should do (implementation period is 15 months from 20 May)
+1 year, 11½ months		9 January 1997	U.S. makes first of monthly reports to Dispute Settlement Body on status of implementation
+2 years, 7 months		19-20 August 1997	U.S. signs new regulation (19th). End of agreed implementation period (20th)

PROBLEM 2-2

Assume that the United States and China have just resolved a WTO dispute concerning claims by the United States that China is not adequately protecting intellectual property rights. China has stated its intentions that it will, of course, fully comply with the panel's recommendations. In fact, China intends to set up a new committee to undertake an extensive review of all current intellectual property laws and a survey of current attitudes among consumers, foreign and local businesses, and government agencies concerning intellectual property. The committee will then issue a comprehensive report with suggestions to address these concerns and seek comments from the public and interested parties. Should the United States be concerned with China's response? *See* DSU Article 21.3. What steps are available? Consider DSU Article 21.5.

PROBLEM 2-3

Suppose that in the WTO dispute above, the United States asks the DSB to recommend that China adopt a term of protection for patents for twenty-five years instead of the twenty-year minimum term required by TRIPS Article 33 and several other "WTO plus" commitments. The United States explains that these additional protections are necessary given the current rampant piracy problem. Is this permitted? *See* DSU Article 19.2.

PROBLEM 2-4

Country X and Country Z are both members of the WTO. Country X is a developed country and an innovator of high-technology audio-visual media products that are exported to Country Z, a developing country. Country Z's main exports are agricultural products, including bananas and pineapples, that are exported in large quantities to Country X. Country X believes that Country Z is violating its intellectual property rights by condoning piracy of its audio-visual media products in violation of the WTO Agreement on Trade-Related Intellectual Property Rights. A government official from X comes to your law office and says, "We want to bring a WTO action against Country Z, but we are concerned that there isn't going to be any bite in any decisions reached by the DSB. After all, the ultimate threat is retaliation but it would be useless for us to threaten to suspend trade concessions and impose higher tariffs on technology imports from Z, because Z does not produce any high-technology products. What can be done?" What do you tell the trade official?

NOTE ON TRADE REMEDIES

The issue of retaliation as a sanction or trade remedy in the WTO is controversial. Some commentators have argued that retaliation is the weakest part of the WTO dispute settlement system because it: (1) creates an additional departure from negotiated trade concessions in the form of the sanction and (2) creates the possibility that some nations will refuse to comply for many years because they can choose to live with retaliation. More effective alternatives might be to make compensation mandatory, impose a fine, or progressively remove a member's right to participate in the WTO system. *See* Mitsuo Matsushita, Thomas J. Schoenbaum, and Petros C. Mavroidis, *The World Trade Organization: Law, Practice and Policy*, 94-95 (2003). *See also* Rachel Brewster, *The Remedy Gap: Institutional Design, Retaliation, and Trade Law Enforcement*, 80 Geo. Wash. L. Rev. 102, 150 (2011) (suggesting a procedure whereby WTO panels would have the power to issue preliminary injunctions); Steve Charnovitz, *Rethinking WTO Trade Sanctions*, 95 Am. J. Int'l L. 792, 808 (2001) (arguing that the disadvantages of trade sanctions as a WTO remedy outweigh the advantages, and proposing reforms).

II.   Nullification or Impairment

What is the standard for determining when a member can assert a claim in the WTO? Under GATT Article XXIII, a complaining party must show a "nullification or impairment" of a trade benefit in order to assert a viable claim against a responding party. One can view this as a requirement that a complaining member must be able to show an injury. This is also the standard adopted in the DSU. *See* DSU Article 3.

GATT Article XXIII Nullification or Impairment

1. If any contracting party should consider that any benefit accruing to it directly or indirectly under this Agreement is being nullified or impaired or that the attainment of any objective of the Agreement is being impeded as the result of

    (a) the failure of another contracting party to carry out its obligations under this Agreement, or

(b) the application by another contracting party of any measure, whether or not it conflicts with the provisions of this Agreement, or

(c) the existence of any other situation,

the contracting party may, with a view to the satisfactory adjustment of the matter, make written representations or proposals to the other contracting party or parties which it considers to be concerned. Any contracting party thus approached shall give sympathetic consideration to the representations or proposals made to it.

Article XXIII:1(a) is commonly referred to as a "violation" case because the responding member is accused of enacting a measure that is inconsistent with its WTO obligations. Article XXIII:1(b) is referred to as a "non-violation" case because while the measure is not itself in violation of the WTO, the measure might undermine or conflict with a member's WTO obligations. No case has arisen under Article XXIII:1(c).

PROBLEM 2-5

Suppose that Russia passes a law that provides for a fifteen-year term of protection for patents. Under TRIPS Article 33, members are required to provide for a twenty-year term of protection. The United States wishes to challenge Russia's new law. Is this a violation or non-violation case under Article XXIII? See the case below.

PROBLEM 2-6

Country F and Country G are both WTO members. Companies from Country F sell high-end sophisticated business and entertainment software to buyers in Country G. Country F's products are entitled to protection in Country G under G's patent and copyright law. Under pressure from local industries, G now amends its patent and copyright laws to offer less protection in a manner that is inconsistent with TRIPS. Country F brings a WTO dispute settlement proceeding and argues that because its products will receive less protection under G's amended laws in violation of TRIPS, a nullification or impairment of a trade benefit has occurred.

Country G responds that there is no nullification or impairment because companies from Country F have not suffered any actual harm. Due to the popularity of Country F's products, the volume of exports from F to G has actually increased significantly despite the enactment of the new revisions to Country G's patent and copyright laws. In addition, Country G points out that there is no evidence of any infringement of intellectual property rights in Country G. What is the result? Consult the case below.

United States — Taxes on Petroleum and Certain Imported Substances
Report of the GATT Panel, adopted on June 17, 1987
GATT B.I.S.D. (34th Supp.) 136

[In 1980, the U.S. Congress passed legislation known as the Superfund Act (the Comprehensive Environmental Response, Compensation and Liability Act,

42 U.S.C. §9601 *et seq.*) for the purpose of funding the clean-up of properties contaminated with petroleum and other hazardous chemicals. As a funding mechanism, the Act levied a tax of 8.2 cents per barrel on domestic crude oil received at a U.S. refinery and a tax of 11.7 cents per barrel on imported petroleum products. Canada, the European Economic Community, and Mexico contested this tax as a violation of the National Treatment principle contained in GATT Article III, which prohibits a country from discriminating against foreign imports in favor of its domestic products. The complaining countries argued that a violation of the National Treatment principle occurred because the United States charged a higher tax on foreign crude oil than on U.S. crude oil. The United States, while admitting the violation, argued that there was no nullification or impairment of a trade benefit.]

5.1.6. The Panel examined how the CONTRACTING PARTIES have reacted in previous cases to claims that a measure inconsistent with the General Agreement had no adverse impact and therefore did not nullify or impair benefits accruing under the General Agreement to the contracting party that had brought the complaint. The Panel noted such claims had been made in a number of cases but that there was no case in the history of the GATT in which a contracting party had successfully rebutted the presumption that a measure infringing obligations causes nullification and impairment.

5.1.7. The Panel concluded from its review of the above and other cases that, while the CONTRACTING PARTIES had not explicitly decided whether the presumption that illegal measures cause nullification or impairment could be rebutted, the presumption had in practice operated as an irrefutable presumption.

5.1.8. The Panel then examined whether—even assuming that the presumption could be regarded as rebuttable in the present case—a demonstration that the trade effects of the tax differential were insignificant would constitute a proof that the benefits accruing to Canada, the EEC and Mexico under Article III:2, first sentence, had not been nullified or impaired.

5.1.9. An acceptance of the argument that measures which have only an insignificant effect on the volume of exports do not nullify or impair benefits accruing under Article III:2, first sentence, implies that the basic rationale of this provision—the benefit it generates for the contracting parties—is to protect expectations on export volumes. That, however, is not the case. Article III:2, first sentence, obliges contracting parties to establish certain competitive conditions for imported products in relation to domestic products. Unlike some other provisions in the General Agreement, it does not refer to trade effects. The majority of the members of the Working Party on the "Brazilian Internal Taxes" therefore correctly concluded that the provisions of Article III:2, first sentence, "were equally applicable, whether imports from other contracting parties were substantial, small or non-existent" (BISD Vol. II/185). The Working Party also concluded that "a contracting party was bound by the provisions of Article III whether or not the contracting party in question had undertaken tariff commitments in respect of the goods concerned" (BISD Vol. II/182), in other words, the benefits under Article III accrue independent of whether there is a negotiated expectation of market access or not. Moreover, it is conceivable that a tax consistent with the national treatment principle (for instance, a high but non-discriminatory excise tax) has a more severe impact on the exports of other contracting parties than a tax that violates that principle (for instance a very low but discriminatory tax). The case before the panel illustrates this point: the United States could bring the tax on petroleum in conformity with Article III:2, first sentence, by raising the tax on domestic products, by lowering the tax on imported products or by fixing a new common tax rate for both imported and domestic products. Each of these solutions would have different trade results, and it is therefore logically not possible to determine the difference in trade impact between the present tax and one consistent with Article III:2, first sentence, and hence to determine the trade impact resulting from the non-observance of that provision. For these reasons, Article III:2, first sentence, cannot be interpreted to protect expectations on export volumes; it protects expectations on the competitive relationship between imported and domestic products. A change in the competitive relationship contrary to that provision must consequently be regarded *ipso facto* as a nullification or impairment of benefits accruing under the General Agreement. A demonstration that a measure inconsistent with Article III:2, first sentence, has no or insignificant effects would therefore in the view of the Panel not be a sufficient demonstration that the benefits accruing under that provision had not been nullified or impaired even if such a rebuttal were in principle permitted.

PROBLEM 2-7

Country H and Country J are both members of the WTO. Country H's domestic law currently provides for a uniform tariff of 4 percent on most imports. Country H's trade concessions negotiated in the last round of WTO trade negotiations contain tariff schedules that substantially exceed 4 percent for certain products. As a result, H is permitted under the WTO ceilings to impose tariffs that are higher than the 4 percent tariff that H would normally apply under its domestic law to imports. Country H has recently decided to raise the tariff rate on imports to the maximum allowed under its WTO ceilings. This means that with respect to many products exported by Country J to Country H, the tariff rate will suddenly and unexpectedly be raised, in some cases substantially. In order to demonstrate a violation of GATT XXIII, Country J must show that a benefit under the WTO has been subject to nullification or impairment. Does Country J have a legitimate claim that it has a benefit under the WTO that has been compromised by Country H? Is this a violation or non-violation case? Consult Article XXIII and the two cases that follow.

EEC — Payments and Subsidies Paid to Processors and Producers of Oilseeds and Related Animal-Feed Proteins
Report of the GATT Panel, adopted on January 25, 1990
GATT B.I.S.D. (37th Supp.) 86

[This case involves a "non-violation" claim under Article XXIII:1(b). The United States claimed that the European Economic Community, after binding the duty on oilseeds at zero in 1962, undermined that binding by providing government subsidies (e.g., payments) to EC oilseed producers. The zero tariffs on oilseeds imported from the United States allow importers to pass on the savings to consumers by charging a lower price for the U.S. imports. However, the United States claimed that the effect of the zero tariff was negated by the government payments to the EC oilseed producers, which can also charge a lower price as a result of the government-provided subsidies. The EEC countered that GATT Article

III:8(b) states that "[T]he provisions of this Article shall not prevent the payment of subsidies exclusively to domestic producers . . ."; therefore, the payment of subsidies to domestic oilseed producers (and not to foreign producers of oilseeds) was perfectly legal and was not in violation of any GATT obligations. The GATT panel considered the U.S. claim as a non-violation matter.]

147. The Panel carefully analyzed the price mechanism established in the framework of the Community's market organization for oilseeds and found that the production subsidy schemes of the Community protect Community producers completely from the movement of prices for imports and hence prevent the lowering of import duties from having any impact on the competitive relationship between domestic and imported oilseeds. The Panel examined whether it was reasonable for the United States to expect that the Community would not introduce subsidy schemes systematically counteracting the price effect of the tariff concessions. The essential argument of the United States on this point was that the CONTRACTING PARTIES had already recognized in 1955 the legitimacy of such expectations when they decided that: "a contracting party which has negotiated a concession under Article II may be assumed, for the purpose of Article XXIII, to have a reasonable expectation, failing evidence to the contrary, that the value of the concession will not be nullified or impaired by the contracting party which granted the concession by the subsequent introduction or increase of a domestic subsidy . . . ."

148. The Panel examined in detail the implications of these arguments and found the following: the case before it does not require the Panel to address the question of whether the assumption created by the 1955 decision of the CONTRACTING PARTIES applies to all production subsidies, including generally available subsidies serving broad policy objectives of the kind mentioned in Article 11:1 of the Subsidies Code. At issue in the case before it are product-specific subsidies that protect producers completely from the movement of prices for imports and thereby prevent tariff concessions from having any impact on the competitive relationship between domestic and imported oilseeds. The Panel considered that the main value of a tariff concession is that it provides an assurance of better market access through improved price competition. Contracting parties negotiate tariff concessions primarily to obtain that advantage. They must therefore be assumed to base their tariff negotiations on the expectation that the price effect of the tariff concessions will not be systematically offset. If no right of redress were given to them in such a case they would be reluctant to make tariff concessions and the General Agreement would no longer be useful as a legal framework for incorporating the results of trade negotiations. The Panel does not share the view of the Community that the recognition of the legitimacy of such expectations would amount to a re-writing of the rules of the General Agreement. The CONTRACTING PARTIES have decided that a finding of impairment does not authorize them to request the impairing contracting party to remove a measure not inconsistent with the General Agreement; such a finding merely allows the contracting party frustrated in its expectation to request, in accordance with Article XXIII:2, an authorization to suspend the application of concessions or other obligations under the General Agreement. The recognition of the legitimacy of an expectation thus essentially means the recognition of the legitimacy of such a request. The recognition of the legitimacy of an expectation relating to the use of production subsidies therefore in no way prevents a contracting party from using production subsidies consistently with the General Agreement; it merely delineates the scope of the protection of a negotiated balance of concessions. For these reasons the Panel found that the United States may be assumed not to have anticipated the introduction of subsidies

which protect Community producers of oilseeds completely from the movement of prices for imports and thereby prevent tariff concessions from having any impact on the competitive relationship between domestic and imported oilseeds, and which have as one consequence that all domestically-produced oilseeds are disposed of in the internal market notwithstanding the availability of imports.

150. The Community claims that the subsidy schemes for oilseeds, even if they could not reasonably have been anticipated, did not actually impair the concessions because they did not displace or impede imports, as imports of rapeseed, sunflower seed and soybeans had risen from 4.5 million tones in 1966 to 20.4 million tones in 1988 on a meal equivalent basis. The United States' view is that they did impair the tariff concessions because they upset the competitive relationship between domestic and imported oilseeds. These arguments of the parties raise the question of the nature of the benefit accruing under Article II: does that benefit consist of the protection of expectations on competitive conditions or on trade flows? The Panel noted that the CONTRACTING PARTIES have consistently interpreted the basic provisions of the General Agreement on restrictive trade measures as provisions establishing conditions of competition. Thus they decided that an import quota constitutes an import restriction within the meaning of Article XI:1 whether or not it actually impeded imports and that an internal tax on imported products does not meet the national treatment requirement of Article III whether or not the tax is actually applied to imports. A previous panel pointed out that Articles III and XI are "to protect expectations of the contracting parties as to the competitive relationship between their products and those of other contracting parties. Both articles are not only to protect current trade but also create the predictability needed to plan future trade." In the past Article XXIII:1(b) cases, the CONTRACTING PARTIES have adopted the same approach: their findings of nullification or impairment were based on a finding that the products for which a tariff concession had been granted were subjected to an adverse change in competitive conditions. In none of these cases did they consider the trade impact of the change in competitive conditions to be determining. In one case they specifically rejected the relevance of statistics on trade flows for a finding on nullification and impairment. It is of course true that, in the tariff negotiations in the framework of GATT, contracting parties seek tariff concessions in the hope of expanding their exports, but the commitments they exchange in such negotiations are commitments on conditions of competition for trade, not on volumes of trade.

152. For these reasons the Panel found that benefits accruing to the United States under Article II of the General Agreement in respect of the zero tariff bindings for oilseeds in the Community Schedule of Concessions were impaired as a result of subsidy schemes which operate to protect Community producers of oilseeds completely from the movement of prices of imports and thereby prevent the oilseeds tariff concessions from having any impact on the competitive relationship between domestic and imported oilseeds.

Japan — Measures Affecting Consumer Photographic Film and Paper
Report of the WTO Panel, adopted on April 22, 1998
WT/DS44/R

[At the behest of the Kodak Company, the United States brought a complaint against Japan, charging that various practices condoned by the Japanese government prevented the sale and distribution of more than token amounts of imported photographic film and paper. The practices favoring domestic photographic film and paper included (1) a complex distribution system making import penetration difficult; (2) restrictions on the opening of large retail stores that are more likely to carry imported film and other imported products; and (3) promotion methods that favor domestic film-makers. The United States charged violations of various provisions of the GATT, but in the main the case was a non-violation case under GATT Article XXIII.]

10.36. The text of Article XXIII:1(b) establishes three elements that a complaining party must demonstrate in order to make out a cognizable claim under Article XXIII:1(b): (1) application of a measure by a WTO Member; (2) a benefit accruing under the relevant agreement; and (3) nullification or impairment of the benefit as the result of the application of the measure. We shall proceed with our analysis by considering in turn each of these three elements.

(A) APPLICATION OF A MEASURE

10.43. The ordinary meaning of *measure* as it is used in Article XXIII:1(b) certainly encompasses a law or regulation enacted by a government. But in our view, it is broader than that and includes other governmental actions short of legally enforceable enactments.

10.49. In our view, a government policy or action need not necessarily have a substantially binding or compulsory nature for it to entail a likelihood of compliance by private actors in a way so as to nullify or impair legitimately expected benefits within the purview of Article XXIII:1(b). Indeed, it is clear that non-binding actions, which include sufficient incentives or disincentives for private parties to act in a particular manner, can potentially have adverse effects on competitive conditions of market access. For example, a number of non-violation cases have involved subsidies, receipt of which requires only voluntary compliance with eligibility criteria. Moreover, we also consider it conceivable, in cases where there is a high degree of cooperation and collaboration between government and business, e.g., where there is substantial reliance on administrative guidance and other more informal forms of government-business cooperation, that even non-binding, hortatory wording in a government statement of policy could have a similar effect on private actors to a legally binding *measure* or what Japan refers to as regulatory administrative guidance. Consequently, we believe we should be open to a broad definition of the term measure for purposes of Article XXIII:1(b), which considers whether or not a non-binding government action has an effect similar to a binding one.

(B) BENEFIT ACCRUING UNDER THE GATT

10.61. The second required element which must be considered to establish a case of non-violation nullification or impairment under Article XXIII:1(b) is the existence of a benefit accruing to a WTO Member under the relevant agreement (in this case, GATT 1994). In all but one of the past GATT cases dealing with Article XXIII:1(b) claims, the claimed benefit has been that of legitimate expectations of improved market-access opportunities arising out of relevant tariff concessions.

10.79. We consider that the issue of reasonable anticipation should be approached in respect of specific "measures" in light of the following guidelines. First, in the case of measures shown by the United States to have been introduced subsequent to the conclusion of the tariff negotiations at issue, it is our view that the United States has raised a presumption that it should not be held to have anticipated these measures and it is then for Japan to rebut that presumption. Such a rebuttal might be made, for example, by establishing that the measure at issue is so clearly contemplated in an earlier measure that the United States should be held to have anticipated it. However, there must be a clear connection shown. In our view, it is not sufficient to claim that a *specific* measure should have been anticipated because it is consistent with or a continuation of a past *general* government policy. As in the *EEC—Oilseeds* case, we do not believe that it would be appropriate to charge the United States with having reasonably anticipated all GATT-consistent measures, such as "measures" to improve what Japan describes as the inefficient Japanese distribution sector. Indeed, if a Member were held to anticipate all GATT-consistent measures, a non-violation claim would not be possible. Nor do we consider that as a general rule the United States should have reasonably anticipated Japanese measures that are similar to measures in other Members' markets. In each such instance, the issue of reasonable anticipation needs to be addressed on a case-by-case basis.

10.80 Second, in the case of measures shown by Japan to have been introduced prior to the conclusion of the tariff negotiations at issue, it is our view that Japan has raised a presumption that the United States should be held to have anticipated those measures and it is for the United States to rebut that presumption. In this connection, it is our view that the United States is charged with knowledge of Japanese government measures as of the date of their publication. We realize that knowledge of a measure's existence is not equivalent to understanding the impact of the measure on a specific product market. For example, a vague measure could be given substance through enforcement policies that are initially unexpected or later changed significantly. However, where the United States claims that it did not know of a measure's relevance to market access conditions in respect of film or paper, we would expect the United States to clearly demonstrate why initially it could not have reasonably anticipated the effect of an existing measure on the film or paper market and when it did realize the effect. Such a showing will need to be tied to the relevant points in time (i.e., the conclusions of the Kennedy, Tokyo and Uruguay Rounds) in order to assess the extent of the United States' legitimate expectations of benefits from these three Rounds. A simple statement that a Member's measures were so opaque and informal that their impact could not be assessed is not sufficient.

(C) Nullification or Impairment of Benefit: Causality

10.82. The third required element of a non-violation claim under Article XXIII:1(b) is that the benefit accruing to the WTO Member (e.g., improved market access from tariff concessions) is *nullified or impaired as the result of* the application of a measure by another WTO Member. In other words, it must be demonstrated that the competitive position of the imported products subject to and benefiting from a relevant market access (tariff) concession is being *upset by* ("nullified or

impaired . . . as the result of") the application of a measure not reasonably anticipated. The equation of "nullification or impairment" with "upsetting the competitive relationship" established between domestic and imported products as a result
of tariff concessions has been consistently used by GATT panels examining non-
violation complaints. For example, the *EEC—Oilseeds* panel, in describing its findings, stated that it had "found . . . that the subsidies concerned had impaired the
tariff concession because they *upset the competitive relationship between domestic and
imported oilseeds,* not because of any effect on trade flows." The same language was
used in the *Australian Subsidy* and *Germany—Sardines* cases. Thus, in this case, it is
up to the United States to prove that the governmental measures that it cites have
upset the competitive relationship between domestic and imported photographic
film and paper in Japan to the detriment of imports. In other words, the United
States must show a clear correlation between the measures and the adverse effect
on the relevant competitive relationships.

10.83. We consider that this third element—causality—may be one of the
more factually complex areas of our examination. In this connection, we note that
in the three prior non-violation cases in which panels found that the complaining
parties had failed to provide a detailed justification to support their claims, the
issue turned primarily on the lack of evidence of causality. Four issues related to
causation merit general discussion. First, the question of the degree of causation
that must be shown—"but for" or less. Second, the relevance of the origin-neutral
nature of a measure to causation of nullification or impairment. Third, the relevance of intent to causality. And fourth, the extent to which measures may be
considered collectively in an analysis of causation.

10.84. As to the first issue, Japan should be responsible for what is caused
by measures attributable to the Japanese Government as opposed, for example,
to what is caused by restrictive business conduct attributable to private economic
actors. At this stage of the proceeding, the issue is whether such a measure has
caused nullification or impairment, i.e., whether it has made more than a *de minimis* contribution to nullification or impairment.

10.85. In respect of the second issue, [i]n our view, even in the absence of
de jure discrimination (measures which on their face discriminate as to origin),
it may be possible for the United States to show *de facto* discrimination (measures which have a disparate impact on imports). However, in such circumstances, the complaining party is called upon to make a detailed showing of any
claimed disproportionate impact on imports resulting from the origin-neutral
measure.

10.87. The third issue is the relevance of intent to causality. Article XXIII:1(b)
does not require a proof of intent of nullification or impairment of benefits by a
government adopting a measure. What matters for purposes of establishing causality is the impact of a measure, i.e. whether it upsets competitive relationships.
Nonetheless, intent may not be irrelevant. In our view, if a measure that appears
on its face to be origin-neutral in its effect on domestic and imported products
is nevertheless shown to have been intended to restrict imports, we may be more
inclined to find a causal relationship in specific cases, bearing in mind that intent
is not determinative where it in fact exists.

10.88. Finally, as for the US position that the Panel should examine the impact
of the measures *in combination* as well as individually (a position contested by Japan),
we do not reject the possibility of such an impact.

DISTRIBUTION MEASURES

10.90. The US case against distribution "measures" may best be understood in the context of the general theme advanced by the United States to the effect that there exists in Japan a unique relationship between government and industry. The US argument is that for Japan to develop and implement its industrial policy, the government relies heavily on different types of quasi-governmental entities, including, *inter alia*, fair trade councils, advisory committees, study groups, research institutes, and chambers of commerce. The US position is that the participation of these entities in the "concerted adjustment" process increases the "peer pressure" on these entities to comply with the industrial policies adopted by the government.

10.204. The essence of the US claim in respect of distribution "countermeasures" is that Japan created vertical integration and single-brand distribution in the Japanese film and paper market. In the US view, this was done through standardization of transaction terms, systemization and limitations on premiums to businesses. As we have found above, the United States has not been able to show that the various "measures" it cites have upset competitive relationships between domestic and US film and paper in Japan, principally because single-brand distribution appears to have occurred before and independently of those "measures," but also because the United States has not demonstrated that these "measures" are directed at promoting vertical integration or single-brand distribution. In answering the timing problem, the United States has provided no convincing evidence or arguments that the cited "measures" in fact had the effect of reinforcing single-brand distribution. Equally, the United States has not explained why the vertically integrated, single-brand distribution structure of the film sector in Japan—a state of affairs that the evidence suggests is similar to that occurring elsewhere in the world (including in the United States)—would have broken down in the absence of continuing government intervention.

NOTES AND QUESTIONS

1. Can you explain why the *EEC—Oilseeds* case was a non-violation case? The United States argued that the EEC provided a trade concession with one hand (i.e., zero tariffs) but took it away with the other hand (i.e., the government subsidies). How?

2. While WTO agreements are "treaties" as that term is defined in the Vienna Convention on the Law of Treaties (1969) (VCLT), WTO law employs concepts and terminology that are different from those applied to treaties under the VCLT. One of the most significant of such departures in terminology is that, while the VCLT uses the term "breach" to describe a treaty violation (VCLT art. 60), WTO law uses the concept of "nullification or impairment." Under the GATT, a non-violation situation can be a nullification or impairment. Is this necessary or desirable? In the case of the WTO Agreement on Trade-Related Intellectual Property Rights (TRIPS), TRIPS Article 64.2 declares a "moratorium" on the filing of non-violation complaints for five years (1995-1999); this moratorium has been extended since then by the TRIPS Council, over the opposition of the United States. Do you agree with the moratorium? Are non-violation complaints possible under the GATS? *See* GATS Article XXIII.

III. Burden of Proof

The allocation of the burden of proof in a WTO case, as in national litigation, is crucial and may determine the outcome in a given situation. Burden of proof has two principal aspects: It determines which of the parties (1) has the burden of going forward with the presentation of the evidence and (2) will win with respect to the particular issue when insufficient evidence is presented to the court. Burden of proof applies only to issues of fact; issues of law are determined by the court (in this case the WTO panels and the Appellate Body) according to applicable rules of interpretation, a matter that is covered in the next section of this book. In WTO cases, the rules on evidence and burdens of proof are often complex because of the structure and wording of the various WTO agreements. Consider the following case, but first read GATT Article II in the Documents Supplement.

India — Additional and Extra-Additional Duties on Imports from the United States
Report of the Appellate Body, adopted on November 17, 2008
WT/DS360/AB/R

[This case concerned additional and extra duties imposed by India on alcoholic beverages and certain other products imported from the United States. The United States brought a complaint against India that charged a violation of GATT Article II, which deals with tariff concessions. The United States complaint charged India with violating Article II:1(a) and (b), the provisions that make trade concessions contained in WTO members' Schedules of Concessions binding. Members pledge not to charge a tariff on imports that is greater than the tariff contained in its Schedule. But Article II:2(a) provides that "[n]othing in this Article shall prevent any Member from imposing at any time" additional charges that are equivalent to a valid internal tax, as opposed to a tariff (which is imposed at the border rather than internally). India accordingly maintained that the additional charges were justified under Article II:2(a). The Appellate Body reversed the Panel's findings on the principal substantive issues and found that the additional duties imposed by India would not be justified under Article II:2(a) insofar as they resulted in the imposition of charges on U.S. products in excess of those applied on like domestic products, in violation of the National Treatment Principle contained in Article III:2. However, the Appellate Body made no recommendation to the Dispute Settlement Body under DSU Article 19.1 because it could not complete the analysis to determine whether in fact the duties were in excess of those applied on like domestic products. A "recommendation" in WTO jurisprudence is in essence a ruling or disposition of the case. The United States thus won the principal legal point of the case, but was unable to obtain a ruling in its favor. The reason for this was a failure on the part of the United States to correctly interpret the WTO law on burden of proof.]

BURDEN OF PROOF

183. The United States claims that the Panel erred in finding that, in the circumstances of this case, it was "incumbent upon the United States to make a *prima facie* case that the measures at issue fall outside the scope of Article II:2(a)."

According to the United States, "although Article II:2 is an exception that may be invoked in defence of a measure that would otherwise be inconsistent with Article II, it is not an affirmative defence in the sense that the responding party bears the ultimate burden of proof." Rather, if a responding party asserts that the measure does not breach Article II:1(b) because it is a measure described in Article II:2 and "substantiates that assertion, then the complaining party would bear the burden of proving the measure falls outside the scope of Article II:2 and, therefore, cannot be justified by way of Article II:2." The United States emphasizes, however, that the fact that the complaining party would bear the burden of proof in this case does not relieve the responding party of its burden of substantiating its own assertions. According to the United States, "[t]his is consistent with the responsibility that either party has to support the facts and arguments it puts forward."

184. India criticizes the United States' contention that Article II:2(a) represents an exception but not an affirmative defence; asserts that there is no support for the United States' contentions; and supports the reasoning of the Panel by noting that it "adequately defined the contours of what is required of a complaining party" to establish a *prima facie* case. India argues that the Panel "was correct in ruling that the burden of proof must be squarely borne by the United States to make out a *prima facie* case" that the Additional Duty and Extra-Additional Duty violate Article II:1(b) and are not charges falling within the scope of Article II:2(a).

185. In examining the United States' claims concerning the elements required to establish a *prima facie* showing in this case, we first recall certain features of the Appellate Body's approach to the burden of proof in WTO dispute settlement proceedings. Although the DSU contains no express rules with respect to allocation of the burden of proof in dispute settlement, the Appellate Body has recognized that generally accepted legal principles provide "that the burden of proof rests upon the party, whether complaining or defending, who asserts the affirmative of a particular claim or defence".[1] Where the complaining party has met the burden of making its *prima facie* case, it is then for the responding party to rebut that showing.

186. With respect to legal argumentation and the production of evidence, the Appellate Body has explained that "[t]he party asserting that another party's municipal law, as such, is inconsistent with relevant treaty obligations bears the burden of introducing evidence as to the scope and meaning of such law to substantiate that assertion."[2] The nature and scope of arguments and evidence required to establish a *prima facie* case "will necessarily vary from measure to measure, provision to provision, and case to case".[3]

187. Importantly, the Appellate Body has also recognized that the principle that a complainant must establish a *prima facie* case of inconsistency does not resolve the question of who bears the burden of proving each specific fact alleged in a dispute. In *Japan — Apples*, the Appellate Body pointed out that "[i]t is important to distinguish, on the one hand, the principle that the complainant must establish a *prima facie* case of inconsistency with a provision of a covered agreement from, on the other hand, the principle that the party that asserts a fact is responsible

1. Appellate Body Report, *US—Wool Shirts and Blouses*, p. 14, DSR 1997:1, 323, at 335.

2. Appellate Body Report, *US—Carbon Steel*, para. 157 (referring to Appellate Body Report, *US—Wool Shirts and Blouses*, p. 14, DSR 1997:1, 323, at 335).

3. Appellate Body Report, *Chile—Price Band System (Article 21.5—Argentina)*, para. 134 (referring to Appellate Body Report, *US—Wool Shirts and Blouses*, p. 14, DSR 1997:1, 323, at 335).

for providing proof thereof."[4] The Appellate Body went on to find that, although the complainant must establish the *prima facie* case in support of its complaint, the respondent bears the burden of proving the facts that it asserts in its defence.

188. We recall that, in the context of this dispute, the United States in the first instance sought to establish that the Additional Duty and Extra-Additional Duty are inconsistent with Article II:1(b) as in excess of those set out in India's Schedule of Concessions. The United States made no reference to Article II:2 in its first written submission to the Panel, nor, it contends, did it need to do so. Rather, the United States considers that all it was required to show in order to establish a *prima facie* case of violation of Article II:1(b) was that the Additional Duty and Extra-Additional Duty are duties or charges falling within Article II:1(b), and that they are in excess of India's bound rates. In the United States' view, it was up to India to show that the charges fall within the scope of Article II:2 as part of its refutation of the United States' *prima facie* case.

190. Not every challenge under Article II:1(b) will require a showing with respect to Article II:2(a). In the circumstances of this dispute, however, where the potential for application of Article II:2(a) is clear from the face of the challenged measures, and in the light of our conclusions above concerning the need to read Articles II:1(b) and II:2(a) together as closely inter-related provisions, we consider that, in order to establish a *prima facie* case of a violation of Article II:1(b), the United States was also required to present arguments and evidence that the Additional Duty and the Extra-Additional Duty are not justified under Article II:2(a).

191. We note that, in any event, India responded in its first written submission to the Panel that the Additional Duty and Extra-Additional Duty are not in violation of Article II:1(b) because they are charges justified under Article II:2(a). Consequently, India was required to adduce arguments and evidence in support of that assertion. Once the responding party seeks to rebut arguments and evidence offered by the complaining party, the complaining party, depending on the nature and content of the rebuttal submission, may need to present additional arguments and evidence in order to prevail on its claim. In this case, following India's rebuttal submission, the United States presented further argumentation concerning the issue of whether the Additional Duty and Extra-Additional Duty are justified under Article II:2(a). At that point, it was for the Panel to decide the issues before it based on the arguments and evidence of the parties. We note, in this respect, the statement of the United States that, once a responding party asserts and supports a defence under Article II:2(a), "the ultimate burden would rest with the complaining party to rebut and ultimately disprove that evidence and argument."

192. The United States contends that, if the Panel's *prima facie* standard were accepted, complaining parties alleging a violation of Article II:1(b) would have to prove, first, that the challenged duty or charge falls outside the scope of each of the subparagraphs of Article II:2 (even when the relevance of Article II:2 is not evident), and, secondly, that the measure is not some *other* type of duty or charge not covered by Article II:2. We do not consider that a complaining party alleging a violation of Article II:1(b) must also disprove in all cases that the challenged charge is justified under Article II:2, much less some other hypothetical category of charges.

---

4. Appellate Body Report, *Japan—Apples*, para. 157 (referring to Appellate Body Report, *US—Wool Shirts and Blouses*, p. 14, DSR 1997:1, 323 at 335; Appellate Body Report, *EC—Hormones*, para. 98).

We do consider, however, that if, due to the characteristics of the measures at issue or the arguments presented by the responding party, there is a reasonable basis to understand that the challenged measure may not result in a violation of Article II:1(b) because it satisfies the requirements of Article II:2(a), then the complaining party bears some burden in establishing that the conditions of Article II:2(a) are not met.

193. We do not find unduly burdensome the complaining party's responsibility to establish a *prima facie* showing by adducing evidence and arguments also with respect to Article II:2(a). Consistent with what we have said above, the showing required by the complaining party that the conditions for the application of Article II:2(a) are not met will to some extent vary, depending upon the particular substance of the challenged measure and the extent to which a relationship between the border charge and the corresponding internal taxes is identifiable. In the circumstances of this case, both parties had a responsibility, in our view, to adduce relevant evidence at their disposal, both with respect to Article II:1(b) and Article II:2(a). Failure of a party to prove the facts it asserts leaves that party at risk of losing the case.

[Despite affirming the Panel's findings on the burden of proof, the Appellate Body reversed the Panel's findings on its substantive interpretations of Articles II:1(a) and (b) and Article II:2(a), ruling that the Panel had erroneously interpreted these articles as prohibiting only duties that inherently discriminate against imports. The Appellate Body then considered whether it could "complete the analysis" by applying the correct rule—that Article II:2(a) protects only internal charges that are not in excess of the internal charges applied on like domestic products. However the Appellate Body, after examining the evidence, was unable to complete the analysis and made no recommendation to the Dispute Settlement Body concerning the United States complaint.]

NOTES AND QUESTIONS

1. In the *India—Extra Duties* case, the issue of burden of proof was determinative. Do you fault the United States for not correctly interpreting the burden of proof question? What should the United States have done to gain a favorable recommendation by the Appellate Body? Was the Appellate Body's ruling on burden of proof unfair and unrealistic? After all, the necessary information regarding the applicability of Article II:2(a) was more accessible to the government of India than it was to the government of the United States. Was it possible for the United States to fulfill its duty to make a prima facie case under this provision?

2. This case also highlights one of the glaring flaws of the WTO Dispute Settlement mechanism—the lack of remand authority on the part of the Appellate Body. The DSU Article 17.13 states that the Appellate Body may "uphold, modify, or reverse" the legal findings and conclusions of panels. In a national court system, the appellate court in a case such as this would state the law—as was done by the Appellate Body—and remand to the trial court to conduct further proceedings and to hear further evidence that would be necessary to apply the law. But because of the lack of remand authority, the Appellate Body in this case determined that it could not "complete the analysis" due to lack of evidence and therefore no recommendation was made to the DSB in this case.

3. The Appellate Body has not always been consistent in its rulings on burden of proof. For example, in *European Communities—Conditions for Granting Tariff Preferences to Developing Countries*, WT/DS246/AB/R, Report of the Appellate Body, adopted on April 20, 2004, the Appellate Body ruled (¶90) that the Enabling Clause, a WTO agreement allowing tariff preferences to developing countries, was an exception to the general rule of Most Favored Nation treatment (mandated by GATT Article I) and that consequently, although India as the complaining country had the duty of identifying the issue of the Enabling Clause and making a written submission in support of the Enabling Clause, the respondent European Communities "must prove" that its challenged measure is in compliance with the conditions of the Enabling Clause (¶104). This ruling seems inconsistent with the *India—Extra Duties* case. One commentator has stated that the "jurisprudence on the allocation of the burden of proof is in a confused state." *See* Michelle T. Grando, *Allocating the Burden of Proof in WTO Disputes: A Critical Analysis*, 9 J. Int'l Econ. L. 615, 655 (2006).

4. In rare cases a relevant WTO agreement may speak expressly to the issue of burden of proof. Such a situation arose in *Canada—Measures Affecting the Importation of Milk and the Exportation of Dairy Products*, WT/DS103, 113/AB/R, Report of the Appellate Body, adopted on December 20, 2002, in which Article 10.3 of the Agreement on Agriculture (AoA) was interpreted to shift the burden of proof from the complaining member to the responding member. Article 10.3 concerns prevention of circumvention of export subsidies, which are prohibited beyond a certain amount under the AoA. Article 10.3 states that "any member which claims that any quantity exported in excess of a reduction commitment level must establish that no export subsidy . . . has been granted."

5. Read GATT Article XX, which is the important provision that establishes "general exceptions" to GATT obligations. A similar general exception provision is in the GATS Article XIV. Does the complaining member or responding member have the burden of proof to prove a qualified exception? In the Appellate Body cases dealing with the issue, the burden of proof of the elements of a general exception is placed on the responding member. *See, e.g., China—Measures Affecting Trading Rights and Distribution Services for Certain Publications and Audiovisual Entertainment Products*, WT/DS363/AB/R, Report of the Appellate Body, adopted on January 19, 2010, ¶289; *United States—Measures Affecting the Cross-Border Supply of Gambling and Betting Services*, WT/DS285/AB/R, Report of the Appellate Body, adopted on April 20, 2005, ¶¶309-311. Is this correct? Should the general rule apply, namely that the burden of proof is on the complaining member?

IV.   Principles of Interpretation and Status of Adopted Reports

The following materials deal with principles of interpretation and sources of law in WTO cases.

PROBLEM 2-8

Assume that the U.S. Chamber of Commerce, a nonprofit group of industry representatives, has led an effort to compile an "Authoritative Document and Instrument of Interpretation and Source of Law for WTO Cases." The U.S. Chamber has assembled an impressive array of practicing lawyers, academicians, former judges, and government trade officials from countries around the world. The group has carefully assembled and edited a document containing discussion and analysis of the WTO treaty provisions based on textual exegesis and legislative history. The document also discusses all GATT/WTO cases and a number of federal court cases in the United States relating to international trade and the WTO. The analysis contained in the document distills many important principles of WTO law from its sources. The document has been endorsed by many counterparts of the U.S. Chamber in other countries and has also received the endorsement of many government trade officials, several of whom were involved in WTO negotiations. What is the status of this document in the WTO? Is it an authoritative instrument or does it merit any consideration at all? What can be done, if anything, to make it authoritative?

Japan — Taxes on Alcoholic Beverages
Report of the WTO Appellate Body, adopted on November 1, 1996
WT/DS8, 10, 11/AB/R

TREATY INTERPRETATION

Article 3.2 of the DSU directs the Appellate Body to clarify the provisions of GATT 1994 and the other "covered agreements" of the *WTO Agreement* "in accordance with customary rules of interpretation of public international law". Following this mandate, in *United States — Standards for Reformulated and Conventional Gasoline*, we stressed the need to achieve such clarification by reference to the fundamental rule of treaty interpretation set out in Article 31(1) of the *Vienna Convention*. We stressed there that this general rule of interpretation "has attained the status of a rule of customary or general international law". There can be no doubt that Article 32 of the *Vienna Convention*, dealing with the role of supplementary means of interpretation, has also attained the same status.

Article 31, as a whole, and Article 32 are each highly pertinent to the present appeal. They provide as follows:

Article 31 General rule of interpretation

1. A treaty shall be interpreted in good faith in accordance with the ordinary meaning to be given to the terms of the treaty in their context and in the light of its object and purpose.

2. The context for the purpose of the interpretation of a treaty shall comprise, in addition to the text, including its preamble and annexes:

(a) any agreement relating to the treaty which was made between all the parties in connexion with the conclusion of the treaty;

(b) any instrument which was made by one or more parties in connexion with the conclusion of the treaty and accepted by the other parties as an instrument related to the treaty.

3. There shall be taken into account together with the context:

    (a) any subsequent agreement between the parties regarding the interpretation of the treaty or the application of its provisions;

    (b) any subsequent practice in the application of the treaty which establishes the agreement of the parties regarding its interpretation;

    (c) any relevant rules of international law applicable in the relations between the parties.

4. A special meaning shall be given to a term if it is established that the parties so intended.

Article 32 Supplementary means of interpretation

Recourse may be had to supplementary means of interpretation, including the preparatory work of the treaty and the circumstances of its conclusion, in order to confirm the meaning resulting from the application of Article 31, or to determine the meaning when the interpretation according to Article 31:

    (a) leaves the meaning ambiguous or obscure; or

    (b) leads to a result which is manifestly absurd or unreasonable.

Article 31 of the *Vienna Convention* provides that the words of the treaty form the foundation for the interpretive process: "interpretation must be based above all upon the text of the treaty". The provisions of the treaty are to be given their ordinary meaning in their context. The object and purpose of the treaty are also to be taken into account in determining the meaning of its provisions. A fundamental tenet of treaty interpretation flowing from the general rule of interpretation set out in Article 31 is the principle of effectiveness (*ut res magis valeat quam pereat*). In *United States—Standards for Reformulated and Conventional Gasoline*, we noted that "[o]ne of the corollaries of the 'general rule of interpretation' in the *Vienna Convention* is that interpretation must give meaning and effect to all the terms of the treaty. An interpreter is not free to adopt a reading that would result in reducing whole clauses or paragraphs of a treaty to redundancy or inutility".

STATUS OF ADOPTED PANEL REPORTS

In this case, the Panel concluded that,

> . . . panel reports adopted by the GATT CONTRACTING PARTIES and the WTO Dispute Settlement Body constitute subsequent practice in a specific case by virtue of the decision to adopt them. Article 1(b)(iv) of GATT 1994 provides institutional recognition that adopted panel reports constitute subsequent practice. Such reports are an integral part of GATT 1994, since they constitute "other decisions of the CONTRACTING PARTIES to GATT 1947."

Article 31(3)(b) of the *Vienna Convention* states that "any subsequent practice in the application of the treaty which establishes the agreement of the parties regarding its interpretation" is to be "taken into account together with the context" in interpreting the terms of the treaty. Generally, in international law, the essence of subsequent practice in interpreting a treaty has been recognized as a "concordant, common and consistent" sequence of acts or pronouncements which is sufficient to establish a discernable pattern implying the agreement of the parties regarding its interpretation. An isolated act is generally not sufficient to establish subsequent practice; it is a sequence of acts establishing the agreement of the parties that is relevant.

Although GATT 1947 panel reports were adopted by decisions of the CONTRACTING PARTIES, a decision to adopt a panel report did not under GATT 1947 constitute agreement by the CONTRACTING PARTIES on the legal reasoning in that panel report. The generally-accepted view under GATT 1947 was that the conclusions and recommendations in an adopted panel report bound the parties to the dispute in that particular case, but subsequent panels did not feel legally bound by the details and reasoning of a previous panel report.

We do not believe that the CONTRACTING PARTIES, in deciding to adopt a panel report, intended that their decision would constitute a definitive interpretation of the relevant provisions of GATT 1947. Nor do we believe that this is contemplated under GATT 1994. There is specific cause for this conclusion in the *WTO Agreement*. Article IX:2 of the *WTO Agreement* provides: "The Ministerial Conference and the General Council shall have the exclusive authority to adopt interpretations of this Agreement and of the Multilateral Trade Agreements". Article IX:2 provides further that such decisions "shall be taken by a three-fourths majority of the Members". The fact that such an "exclusive authority" in interpreting the treaty has been established so specifically in the *WTO Agreement* is reason enough to conclude that such authority does not exist by implication or by inadvertence elsewhere.

Historically, the decisions to adopt panel reports under Article XXIII of the GATT 1947 were different from joint action by the CONTRACTING PARTIES under Article XXV of the GATT 1947. Today, their nature continues to differ from interpretations of the GATT 1994 and the other Multilateral Trade Agreements under the WTO Agreement by the WTO Ministerial Conference or the General Council. This is clear from a reading of Article 3.9 of the DSU, which states:

> The provisions of this Understanding are without prejudice to the rights of Members to seek authoritative interpretation of provisions of a covered agreement through decision-making under the WTO Agreement or a covered agreement which is a Plurilateral Trade Agreement.

Article XVI:1 of the *WTO Agreement* and paragraph 1(b)(iv) of the language of Annex 1A incorporating the GATT 1994 into the *WTO Agreement* bring the legal history and experience under the GATT 1947 into the new realm of the WTO in a way that ensures continuity and consistency in a smooth transition from the GATT 1947 system. This affirms the importance to the Members of the WTO of the experience acquired by the CONTRACTING PARTIES to the GATT 1947—and acknowledges the continuing relevance of that experience to the new trading system served by the WTO. Adopted panel reports are an important part of the GATT *acquis*. They are often considered by subsequent panels. They create legitimate expectations among WTO Members, and, therefore, should be taken into account where they are relevant to any dispute. However, they are not binding, except with respect to resolving the particular dispute between the parties to that dispute. In short, their character and their legal status have not been changed by the coming into force of the *WTO Agreement*.

For these reasons, we do not agree with the Panel's conclusion in paragraph 6.10 of the Panel Report that "panel reports adopted by the GATT CONTRACTING PARTIES and the WTO Dispute Settlement Body constitute subsequent practice in a specific case" as the phrase "subsequent practice" is used in Article 31 of the *Vienna Convention*. Further, we do not agree with the Panel's conclusion in the same paragraph of the Panel Report that adopted panel reports in themselves constitute "other decisions of the CONTRACTING PARTIES to GATT 1947" for the purposes of paragraph 1(b)(iv) of the language of Annex 1A incorporating the GATT 1994 into the *WTO Agreement*.

However, we agree with the Panel's conclusion in that same paragraph of the Panel Report that *unadopted* panel reports "have no legal status in the GATT or WTO system since they have not been endorsed through decisions by the CONTRACTING PARTIES to GATT or WTO Members." Likewise, we agree that "a panel could nevertheless find useful guidance in the reasoning of an unadopted panel report that it considered to be relevant."

NOTES AND QUESTIONS

1. Consider Vienna Convention Article 31(3)(c). Does this open the way for WTO panels and the Appellate Body to decide legal questions outside the scope of the WTO agreements? The precise scope of the relevance of non-WTO international law is unclear, but we will see in the following chapters of this book that the Appellate Body has discussed and even decided issues of non-WTO international customary and treaty law. WTO law is not, therefore, a self-contained regime. But the Appellate Body seems to draw a line by refusing to decide actual disputes involving non-WTO treaties. In *Mexico—Tax Measures on Soft Drinks and Like Beverages*, WT/DS308/AB/R, Report of the Appellate Body, adopted on March 24, 2006, the Appellate Body dealt with a case brought by the United States against Mexico concerning certain discriminatory taxes on U.S. soft drinks and related U.S. services. Mexico asked the Appellate Body to decline jurisdiction on the basis that the dispute was in reality a bilateral trade issue arising under the North American Free Trade Agreement (NAFTA). Mexico further alleged that the United States, by an illegal act, namely refusing to nominate panelists to the NAFTA panel, was preventing Mexico from having recourse to the appropriate NAFTA dispute settlement panel. The Appellate Body ruled that it had to accept jurisdiction in the WTO case and that declining to accept the case would in effect be a determination that the United States had acted inconsistently with its NAFTA obligations. The Appellate Body further stated (¶55) that there is "no basis in the DSU for Panels and the Appellate Body to adjudicate non-WTO disputes." The Appellate Body agreed with the panel that, since WTO jurisdiction over the dispute was uncontested, the panel had no discretion under the DSU to decline to hear the case.

2. In the case of *United States—Final Anti-Dumping Measures on Stainless Steel from Mexico*, WT/DS344/AB/R, Report of the Panel, adopted on May 20, 2008, the WTO panel, relying on the Appellate Body's statements in *Japan—Alcoholic Beverages*, decided not to follow the Appellate Body's legal interpretations of the GATT Article VI:2 and Article 9.3 of the WTO Anti-Dumping Agreement. Instead, the Panel relied upon findings in panel reports that the Appellate Body had reversed. Mexico challenged the panel's ruling as contrary to DSU Article 11, which stipulates that the function of panels is to assist the DSB in discharging its responsibilities, as well as DSU Articles 3.2 and 3.3 on the effective functioning of the dispute settlement system. The Appellate Body, while avoiding a ruling directly based on Article 11 of the DSU, stated (¶160) that "[e]nsuring the 'security and

predictability' in the dispute settlement system, as contemplated in Article 3.2 of the DSU, implies that, absent cogent reasons, an adjudicatory body will resolve the same legal question in the same way in a subsequent case." The Appellate Body went on to say it was "deeply concerned" by the panel's decision, termed the panel's ruling "misguided," and reversed all of the panel's findings and conclusions that were appealed (¶162).

V. Trade Retaliation Under National Laws

Prior to the establishment of the WTO, the United States, the EU, and several other nations had legislation that might permit unilateral retaliation under their own laws for trade disputes. These nations continue to maintain these remedies and so the issue arises of whether these remedies are consistent with the WTO. In the United States, Section 301 of the Trade Act of 1974, Pub. L. No. 93-618, 88 Stat. 1978, (also known as Super 301, or Special 301) and its variants permit the United States to use unilateral trade remedies against its trading partners. In some cases, Section 301 mandates trade sanctions, such as increased tariffs or quotas, on goods from U.S. trading partners, as well as other forms of retaliation for violations of U.S. rights.

The United States has a long history of using these trade remedies that predate the WTO. Once the WTO came into existence, U.S. trading partners now had a legal argument that Section 301, allowing for unilateral trade sanctions, was inconsistent with the WTO dispute settlement system. Note carefully that Section 301 and its variants allow the United States to unilaterally resolve many types of trade disputes, including disputes that fall outside of the WTO agreements, which are of no concern to the WTO. However, there is an area of overlap in which Section 301 might permit the United States to take unilateral action for violations of the WTO agreements. To deal with this criticism, the United States continued to maintain Section 301 but modified its procedures. Private parties are still allowed to initiate an action under Section 301 but when the complaint concerns the violation of a WTO agreement, the United States Trade Representative (USTR) is required to launch a parallel action in the WTO. As a result, Section 301 now allows private parties to enlist the aid of the USTR in initiating a suit in the WTO. For example, in September 2010, the United Steelworkers Union filed a Section 301 petition alleging that China's green-technology practices violate the rules of the WTO. *See* http://assets.usw.org/releases. In October 2010, the USTR accepted the petition and opened an investigation. In March 2011, after consultations with the Chinese government, the United States launched a formal complaint against China in the WTO, alleging that China's special fund for wind power manufacturing constitutes an illegal subsidy under international trade law. As of this writing, this complaint is ongoing as a pending WTO dispute.

In the following case, the specific legal issue is whether Section 301 requires the United States to make a unilateral decision that its rights under a WTO agreement were being violated, before the DSB of the WTO can reach a decision on the same issue. If so, is this form of unilateralism on the part of the United States consistent with the WTO? The EC challenged Section 301 on these grounds with the following result.

Read Sections 301-310 of the U.S. Trade Act of 1974 (19 U.S.C. §§2411-2420) in the Documents Supplement.

PROBLEM 2-9

A senator from a state that has lost a large number of jobs due to import competition sponsors a bill to create a special federal appeals court to review decisions of the WTO. The court will have the authority to reverse decisions involving the rights of the United States under the WTO agreements if the WTO decision is inconsistent with U.S. law. Is this permitted under the WTO? *See* DSU Article 23.2(a) and the case below.

United States — Sections 301-310 of the Trade Act of 1974
Report of the WTO Panel, adopted on January 27, 2000
WT/DS152/R

7.2 The EC claims that by adopting, maintaining on its statute book and applying Sections 301-310 of the 1974 Trade Act after the entry into force of the Uruguay Round Agreements, the US has breached the historical deal that was struck in Marrakech between the US and the other Uruguay Round participants. According to the EC, this deal consists of a trade-off between, on the one hand, the practical certainty of adoption by the Dispute Settlement Body ("DSB") of panel and Appellate Body reports and of authorization for Members to suspend concessions — in the EC's view, an explicit US request — and, on the other hand, the complete and definitive abandoning by the US of its long-standing policy of unilateral action. The EC submits that the second leg of this deal, which is, in its view, the core of the present Panel procedure, has been enshrined in the following WTO provisions: Articles 3, 21, 22 and, most importantly, 23 of the DSU and Article XVI:4 of the WTO Agreement.

7.29 The EC claims that Section 304 mandates the USTR to make a "unilateral" determination on whether another WTO Member has violated US rights under the WTO. The EC submits that this determination by the USTR has to be made within 18 months after the initiation of an investigation under Section 302, a date that normally coincides with the request for consultations under the DSU. According to the EC, DSU procedures can, however, be assumed to take 19½ months. The EC submits that, as a result of the 18 months deadline, the determination under Section 304 is required even if the DSB has not yet adopted a report with findings on the matter, contrary to Article 23.2(a) of the DSU.

7.30 The US responds that nothing in Section 304 compels the USTR to make a specific determination that US rights have been denied in the absence of panel or Appellate Body findings, adopted by the DSB. In its second submission, the US goes even further and submits that since Section 304 determinations have to be made on the basis of WTO dispute settlement proceedings pursuant to Section 304(a)(1), a determination that US rights have been denied before the adoption of DSB findings is *precluded*. According to the US, Section 304 only requires the USTR to "determine *whether*" — not to determine *that* — US rights have been denied. In the US view, the USTR has the discretion to determine that no violation has occurred, that no violation has been confirmed by the DSB, that a violation will be confirmed on the date the DSB adopts panel or Appellate Body findings or that the ongoing investigation must terminate. The US also argues that the relevant period for DSU procedures to be completed—from the request for consultations to the adoption of reports by the DSB—is not 19 months, as claimed by the EC, but 16 months and 20 days.

7.32 [The Panel then examined the language of Section 304 in detail and reached the following conclusion.] [T]he statutory language of Section 304 *mandates* the USTR in certain cases to make a unilateral determination on whether US rights have been denied even *before* the adoption by the DSB of its findings on the matter. However, the statutory language of Section 304 neither *mandates* the USTR to make a determination of inconsistency nor *precludes* him or her from making such a determination.

7.96 Consequently, the statutory language of Section 304 must be considered presumptively to be inconsistent with the obligations in Article 23.2(a). The discretion given to the USTR to make a determination of inconsistency creates a real risk or threat for both Members and individual economic operators that determinations prohibited under Article 23.2(a) will be imposed. The USTR's discretion effectively to make such determinations removes the guarantee which Article 23 is intended to give not only to Members but indirectly also to individuals and the market place. In this sense, the USTR's discretion under Section 304 does not—as the US argued—ensure the consistency of Section 304. On the contrary, it is the core element of the *prima facie* inconsistency of the statutory language of Section 304.

7.98 In the previous analysis we have deliberately referred to the "statutory language" of Section 304 and likewise we have deliberately concluded that the statutory language creates a *prima facie* violation. We did not conclude that a violation has been confirmed. This is so because of the special nature of the Measure in question. The Measure in question includes statutory language as well as other institutional and administrative elements. To evaluate its overall WTO conformity we have to assess all of these elements together.

7.101 One can imagine different ways to remove the *prima facie* violation. If, for example, the statutory language itself were modified so that the USTR were not under an obligation to make a determination within the 18 months time-frame, but could, for example, await the making of any determination until such time as DSU procedures were completed the guarantee that Article 23 was intended to create would remain intact and the *prima facie* inconsistency would not exist.

7.102 Changing the statute is not the only way to remove the *prima facie* inconsistency. If the possibility of the USTR making a determination of inconsistency prior to exhaustion of DSU proceedings were lawfully curtailed in a different manner, the same legal effect would be achieved. The obligation on Members to bring their laws into conformity with WTO obligations is a fundamental feature of the system and, despite the fact that it affects the internal legal system of a State, has to be applied rigorously. At the same time, enforcement of this obligation must be done in the least intrusive way possible. The Member concerned must be allowed the maximum autonomy in ensuring such conformity and, if there is more than one lawful way to achieve this, should have the freedom to choose that way which suits it best.

7.103 Critically, the offending discretionary element has to be *lawfully* curtailed since, as found in WTO case law, conformity with WTO obligations cannot be obtained by an administrative promise to disregard its own binding internal legislation, i.e. by an administrative undertaking to act illegally.

7.104 For the following reasons we find that the *prima facie* violation has in fact in this case been lawfully removed and no longer exists.

7.108 The language of Section 304 allows the existence of multilateral dispute resolution proceedings to be taken into account. It also allows for determinations of inconsistency to be postponed until after the exhaustion of DSU proceedings. This language surely permits the Administration to limit the discretion of the USTR so that no determination of inconsistency would be made before the exhaustion of DSU proceedings. The wide discretion granted as to the content of the determination to be made should be interpreted as including the power of the US Administration to adopt an administrative decision limiting the USTR's discretion in a manner consistent with US international obligations.

7.109 For reasons we explain below, we find that this is precisely the situation in the present case. Briefly, the US Administration has carved out WTO covered situations from the general application of the Trade Act. It did this in a most authoritative way, *inter alia*, through a Statement of Administrative Action ("SAA") submitted by the President to, and approved by, Congress. Under the SAA so approved " . . . it is the expectation of the Congress that future administrations would observe and apply the [undertakings given in the SAA]". One of these undertakings was to "base any section 301 determination that there has been a violation or denial of US rights . . . on the panel or Appellate Body findings adopted by the DSB". This limitation of discretion would effectively preclude a determination of inconsistency prior to exhaustion of DSU proceedings. The exercise of discretion under the statutory scheme is in the hands of the Administration and it is the Administration which has given this undertaking. We recognize of course that an undertaking given by one Administration can be repealed by that Administration or by another Administration. But this is no different from the possibility that statutory language under examination by a panel be amended subsequently by the same or another Legislator. The critical question is whether the curtailment of discretion is lawful and effective. This Panel finds that it is.

7.112 In the SAA the US Administration indicated its interpretation of Sections 301-310 as well as the manner in which it intends to use its discretion under Sections 301-310, as follows (emphases added):

> "Although it will enhance the effectiveness of section 301, the DSU does not require any significant change in section 301 *for investigations that involve an alleged violation of a Uruguay Round agreement or the impairment of US benefits under such an agreement.* In such cases, *the Trade Representative will:*
>
> - invoke DSU dispute settlement procedures, as required under current law;
> - base any section 301 determination that there has been a violation or denial of US rights under the relevant agreement on the panel or Appellate Body findings adopted by the DSB;
> - following adoption of a favourable panel or Appellate Body report, allow the defending party a reasonable period of time to implement the report's recommendations; and
> - if the matter cannot be resolved during that period, seek authority from the DSB to retaliate" (emphasis added).

This official statement in the SAA—in particular, the commitment undertaken in the second bullet point—approved by the US Congress in the expectation that it will be followed by future US Administrations, is a major element in our conclusion that the discretion created by the statutory language permitting a determination of inconsistency prior to exhaustion of DSU proceeding has effectively been curtailed. We find that this decision of the US Administration on the manner in which it plans to exercise its discretion, namely to curtail it in such a way so as never to adopt a determination of inconsistency prior to the adoption of DSB findings, was lawfully made under the statutory language of Section 304.

NOTES AND QUESTIONS

1. The EU has its own version of a unilateral trade remedy, the Trade Barriers Regulation (TBR), Council Regulation No. 3286/94 as amended in 1995 and 2008. *See* http://www.ec.europa.eu/trade/tackling.unfair-trade. Under the TBR, however, it is clear that the EU cannot act unilaterally before the WTO has come to a decision, and that the EU must abide by whatever decision is reached by the WTO. Like Section 301, the TBR is designed so that private companies, although they are not permitted to directly access the WTO dispute settlement mechanism, may obtain the aid of a government to bring a complaint on their behalf. The EU Commission provides a Model TBR Complaint that provides guidance on what a company must file with the EU Trade Commissioner. The complaint should contain information about the identity of the complainant; the product or products at issue; a description of the market; a description of the obstacle to trade; the right of action under international trade law rules; the adverse trade effects and injury suffered; and a request that the EU Commission open an investigation. Examples of successful use of the TBR are (1) a complaint by Volkswagen AG that Colombian tax law discriminates against imported motor vehicles; (2) a complaint by the European Association of Pharmaceutical Industries concerning the lack of transparency and discrimination in the Turkish pharmaceuticals market; and (3) a complaint by the Conseil Interprofessionel du Vin de Bordeaux about the lack of protection in Canada of Bordeaux and Medoc (two names for wines) as geographical indications. *See* http://www.ec.europa.eu/trade.

2. As a political matter, why might the possibility of unilateral action by the United States be necessary to gain support from private industry for U.S. participation in the WTO? The SAA discussed in the *Sections 301-310* case can always be revoked by the U.S. government. Is there an argument that the threat (or possibility) of unilateral action by the United States, rather than its actual implementation, serves a useful purpose?

3. Is unilateralism (or taking the law into one's own hands) inconsistent with both the letter and spirit of the WTO? Explain.

PROBLEM 2-10

El Salvador and Peru enter into an agreement that all WTO disputes between the two members will be decided by binding arbitration before an ad hoc arbitration tribunal to be established in a third South American country. Both countries cite the ease of travel and the use of Spanish in the proceedings as reasons. Is this permitted? *See* DSU Article 23.1.

3 The Implementation of International Trade Obligations in the Domestic Legal Order

I. Introduction

Chapter 1 examined how the law of international trade is in large part an extensive body of public international law created through international negotiations over the last sixty-five years. This Chapter deals with how this international law becomes embedded in the domestic legal orders of the states that constitute the international actors of the world. When states that are members of international trade organizations such as the WTO consent to a negotiation, they become legally bound to carry through or implement the obligations undertaken, but this legal constraint operates only on the international level. Members must take further steps to incorporate these international obligations into their individual domestic laws. How this is done and the consequences for domestic law are the subjects of this Chapter.

Three sets of interrelated issues are explored in this Chapter:

First, we address questions relating to how international obligations are transformed into domestic law. The technical term for this is *implementation*: An international obligation must be implemented in domestic law in order that the state undertaking the obligation may fulfill its duty of compliance under international law. Related to this first issue are issues concerning the authority or competence of government actors within a state (or a confederation of states) to deal with external relations, including international trade. Often more than one government entity has authority to deal with foreign relations, giving rise to issues of shared, overlapping, and conflicting authority.

Second, we address questions related to the effect of international agreements (and decisions of international tribunals) in the domestic legal order of states. International trade agreements are "treaties" under international law. Some treaties have a direct legal effect within a domestic legal order; these treaties do not need to be implemented into domestic law. Other types of treaties do not have a direct legal effect but can be given effect only through implementation by domestic legislation.

Third, we consider questions relating to conflicting legal obligations. If a conflict or inconsistency arises between international trade law and domestic law, what is the impact? How is the conflict resolved, and which legal norm prevails?

Not only are these complex questions, but the answers can only be provided in the context of each individual state's constitutional and domestic legal order. Each state will approach each of these questions differently, in accordance with its own laws and legal traditions. There are 195 states in the world, and the WTO has 154 members (at this writing); obviously, we do not have space to consider how these questions play out in each state.

Fortunately, despite the complexity of the matters and the number of states, these sets of questions are handled relatively simply in most cases in a straightforward manner by the governments involved, according to certain general principles. The next section covers these general principles, but we give extensive consideration to the United States and the EU, not only because these two entities have particular importance in international trade, but also because both exhibit special and unique characteristics.

II.   Domestic Implementation of International Trade Obligations

Each member of the WTO that undertakes an international trade obligation has a duty to implement that obligation in its domestic legal order. This is normally done by each individual member in accordance with its existing legal and constitutional structure. In most cases this implementation is carried out quickly and simply by the government in power. In many states, the government that negotiated the trade agreement normally controls not only the relevant ministries, but also the legislative or other governing apparatus of the state. Accordingly, implementation of an agreed international trade obligation can be carried out by straightforward administrative and political actions. For example, the prime minister of the WTO member that has negotiated a trade agreement can call a meeting of the relevant ministers, and call on each of them to adopt necessary administrative regulations; a project of law can be introduced and passed in the national assembly or parliament if legal changes are required. This is normally done without controversy because the government that negotiated the international agreement controls all the domestic levers of power. Many countries, such as China, follow this general model of implementation.

Two major exceptions stand out from this general pattern: the United States and the EU. Both have complex domestic implementation processes that we must take up in detail.

A.   The United States

The United States has a complex constitutional and administrative structure that governs international trade. There are two unique aspects of this system that contribute to its complexity. First, the United States has a federal system consisting of a dual system of government: the federal government and individual states. Both share competence in international trade. Second, the U.S. federal government follows a system of separation of powers in which separate branches of government have exclusive or shared areas of authority. All three branches of the U.S. government have competence in foreign trade, although their sphere of authority is markedly different.

We first turn to an overview of the various important actors in the U.S. constitutional scheme; then we will consider how these actors interact and the conflicts that can arise.

1.   The Executive Branch

- *The President.* Although the U.S. Constitution does not give the President any special power over international trade, Article II vests the President with particular responsibilities over foreign affairs and the power to negotiate and make treaties and international agreements. These powers allow the President to exercise substantial authority over international trade. The President is, of course, part of the Executive Branch and not a member of the Legislative Branch of the U.S. government, but he can also exercise legislative power delegated by Congress and participate in the formulation and passage of legislation by reason of his political status and his constitutional power to veto congressional legislation.

- *The United States Trade Representative (USTR).* Appointed by the President with cabinet rank, the USTR is the chief official of the Executive Branch with respect to international trade. He or she has the assigned duties to develop and coordinate U.S. international trade policy. The USTR is the principal advisor to the President on trade law and policy matters and is the principal trade spokesperson and negotiator on trade matters with other countries and within the multilateral trading system. The USTR took the lead in the negotiations in the Uruguay Round leading to the establishment of the WTO and also plays a primary role in negotiating bilateral trade treaties with countries. In addition, the USTR plays a primary role in resolving trade disputes both within the WTO system and on a bilateral basis. The USTR also works closely with other agencies and Congress. He or she chairs the Trade Policy Review Group and the Trade Policy Committee, two interagency bodies consisting of representatives from the USTR and other important federal agencies. The purpose of both of these bodies is to ensure coordination among federal agencies on international trade matters and to avoid conflict. Conflicts among federal governmental bodies are resolved by the cabinet-level Trade Policy Committee or, ultimately, by the President. The Office of the USTR is organized as shown in Figure 3-1:

FIGURE 3-1
The Office of the United States Trade Representative

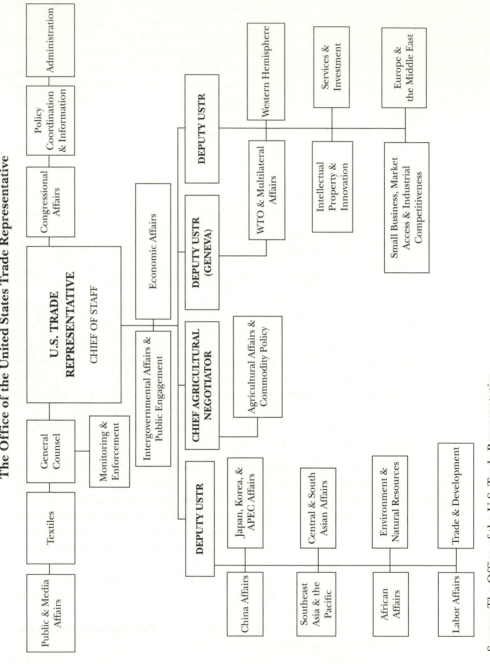

Source: The Office of the U.S. Trade Representative.

- *Other Departments of the U.S. Government.* Many departments of the U.S. government are involved with trade policy or administration in addition to their responsibilities over domestic matters.
  (1) The Department of State works to implement U.S. trade policy and influences trade policy through its regional and functional bureaus;
  (2) The Department of Agriculture has responsibility for developing and expanding markets abroad for U.S. agricultural products;
  (3) The Department of Homeland Security operates the U.S. Customs Service, which has primary responsibility for regulating imports from other countries into the United States and the assessment and collection of tariffs and import duties;
  (4) The Department of the Treasury deals with matters relating to international finance and international fiscal and monetary policy. The Department of the Treasury works closely with the World Bank and the IMF, both of which have their headquarters in Washington, D.C.;
  (5) The Department of Justice is involved with international antitrust and competition matters and certain other major international trade issues, such as corruption in international business. The Department of Justice enforces the Foreign Corrupt Practices Act, 15 U.S.C. §78dd-1 *et seq.*, which prohibits the making of bribes and other illegal payments to foreign government officials for the purpose of obtaining or retaining business;
  (6) The Department of Commerce is the agency that has primary responsibility for promoting and regulating international trade under the laws passed by Congress. While the U.S. Customs Service regulates imports, the Department of Commerce regulates exports through an elaborate bureaucratic mechanism that governs approval and licensing requirements. The Department of Commerce also has many responsibilities related to promoting the trade of the United States with other countries, including providing assistance for individual entrepreneurs and companies that seek to do business abroad. See Figure 3-2.

- *Independent Agencies.* Several independent agencies (in the sense that they are not directly subject to presidential control) of the U.S. government have responsibility for certain trade policy matters. Most importantly:
  (1) The U.S. International Trade Commission helps administer federal trade laws relating to dumping, countervailing duties, and safeguard actions, to protect domestic industries from suffering injury due to international trade.
  (2) The Overseas Private Investment Corporation (OPIC) promotes economic development by encouraging and guaranteeing certain private international investment projects.
  (3) The U.S. Export-Import Bank finances and facilitates exports, especially by small businesses.

2.   *The Legislative Branch*

The Congress of the United States, composed of the House of Representatives and the Senate, constitutes the Legislative Branch of the U.S. federal government. Article 1, section 8 of the U.S. Constitution grants Congress the power to "regulate commerce with foreign nations." Thus, Congress has the final say as to legislation concerning U.S. trade law and policy.

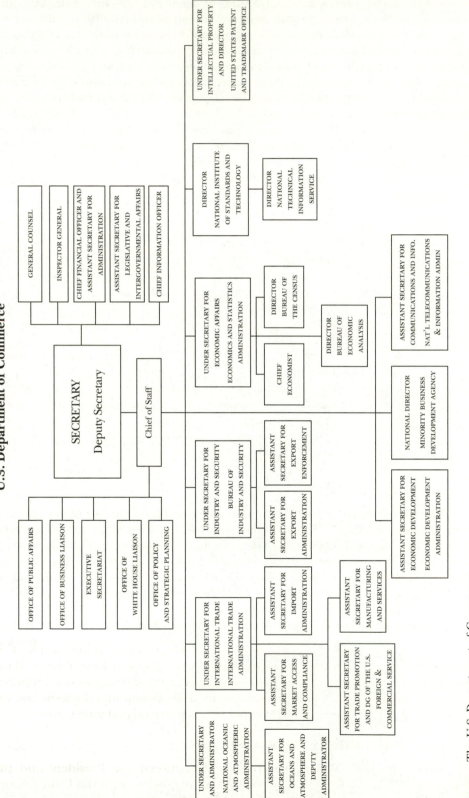

FIGURE 3-2
U.S. Department of Commerce

Source: The U.S. Department of Commerce.

Congress not only exercises legislative power over trade, but the Senate must also approve all ambassadors and high-level executive branch officials such as the USTR. As discussed further below, treaties and other international agreements concerning trade must be approved by Congress. In addition, certain treaties and international agreements must be implemented into law through domestic legislation, which is subject to the control of Congress. Congress also exercises oversight and investigative power and controls the funding of all government activities, including those related to trade.

3. *The Judicial Branch*

Under the U.S. constitutional scheme, federal and state courts play only a minor role over matters of international trade, but their powers can be substantial in a given case. The judicial power over trade comes through the courts' role of exercising judicial review over administrative actions and through the power to declare a law or even a presidential action unconstitutional.

The most important court for our subject matter is the United States Court of International Trade (CIT), a national court established under Article III of the Constitution, which sits in New York City and plays a special role in the judicial system. The CIT consists of nine judges appointed by the President with the advice and consent of the Senate. The CIT was established under the Custom Courts Act of 1980 (Pub. L. No. 96-417; 94 Stat. 1727) to create a comprehensive system for judicial review of civil actions arising out of import transactions and federal statutes affecting international trade. The CIT's organization is established by 28 U.S.C. §§251-258; the jurisdiction of the court is stated at 28 U.S.C. §§1581-1585; and the court's procedures are stated at 28 U.S.C. §§2631-2647. All appeals from the CIT are heard by the United States Court of Appeals for the Federal Circuit, which has nationwide jurisdiction to hear appeals in specialized cases, such as those involving patent laws and appeals from the CIT and the Court of Federal Claims. Decisions of the Federal Circuit can be appealed to the U.S. Supreme Court.

4. *State and Local Government*

States and local governments enjoy considerable autonomy under the U.S. constitutional scheme. Although states and local governments cannot exercise direct power over foreign affairs, they can pass legislation that affects international trade. However, due to the supremacy of federal law, a state or local law that conflicts with a federal statute or encroaches upon a federal power will not be given effect; questions of this nature are normally decided by the courts.

5. *Problems in the Allocation of Power over Trade*

The complex allocation of powers over international trade in the U.S. Constitution causes unique problems to arise. We concentrate on four of these: (1) the process of negotiating an international trade agreement; (2) congressional approval of an international trade agreement and its implementation into domestic law; (3) the power of the President; and (4) clashes between federal and state power.

a. NEGOTIATING A TRADE AGREEMENT

Given the split in authority over trade between the President and the Congress, how can a foreign government that negotiates with the United States be assured that an agreement reached will not be changed or even rejected by

Congress? For example, after the Executive Branch (through the President or the USTR) negotiates a treaty with a foreign government, the treaty must receive approval by at least two-thirds of the Senate. The Senate might reject the treaty or require revisions to the treaty that will require starting the lengthy negotiation process all over again. Treaties might never be concluded if this process of revision were to occur on a regular basis, and foreign countries might become reluctant to negotiate with the United States. How can these difficulties be avoided?

The answer to this question is the so-called Fast Track Procedure, also now called "Trade Promotion Authority." Under this procedure, Congress accords the President authority, limited in time, to negotiate an international trade agreement, and the President agrees to involve key members of Congress in the negotiations as they progress. The approval of the agreement occurs under a special legislative process. The same basic elements of the Fast Track Procedure have been used for all international trade agreements since 1974, including the WTO agreements.[1] These elements are as follows:

- Notification by the President of intent to negotiate;
- Continuous contemporaneous consultations with the key congressional committees;
- Notification of intent to conclude an agreement;
- Expedited congressional action by both the House of Representatives and the Senate, and a vote in both Houses on the agreement in question, without amendment or reservations, within a limited period (usually sixty legislative days).

b.   TREATY VERSUS EXECUTIVE AGREEMENT

Although all binding international agreements are "treaties" under international law and are a source of public international law, the U.S. Constitution reserves the term "treaty" only for international agreements that the President chooses to submit to the Senate for what is termed "advice and consent," which requires approval of at least two-thirds of the Senate.

Under well-established U.S. constitutional practice, the President can also enter into an "executive agreement" with another state, and this is also considered to be a "treaty" in international law. *See United States v. Belmont*, 301 U.S. 324, 331 (1937). However, unlike a treaty, an executive agreement does not require Senate approval. Rather, an executive agreement is implemented in U.S. domestic law through the usual legislative process that requires a majority vote in both the House and the Senate. International agreements under the Fast Track Procedure are treated as executive agreements and not as treaties. Not all executive agreements, however, are entitled to the Fast Track Procedure. Only those executive agreements entitled to invoke the Fast Track Procedure enjoy expedited approval in Congress.

There is sometimes disagreement between the President and key members of Congress about which procedure to use in a given case. For all recent international trade agreements, the President has chosen the executive agreement process. The Department of State has issued the following guidelines for choosing between the treaty and executive agreement processes:

---

1. The Fast Track Procedure expired on June 30, 2007 but President Obama is expected to seek renewal of the Fast Track Procedure in 2012.

United States Department of State, Foreign Affairs Manual
Circular No. 175 (2d ed. 1985)

SECTION 721.3 CONSIDERATIONS FOR SELECTING AMONG CONSTITUTIONALLY AUTHORIZED PROCEDURES

In determining a question as to the procedure which should be followed for any particular international agreement, due consideration is given to the following factors along with [constitutional requirements]:

(a) The extent to which the agreement involves commitments or risks affecting the nation as a whole;

(b) Whether the agreement is intended to affect State laws;

(c) Whether the agreement can be given effect without the enactment of subsequent legislation by the Congress;

(d) Past U.S. practice as to similar agreements;

(e) The preference of the Congress as to a particular type of agreement;

(f) The degree of formality desired for an agreement;

(g) The proposed duration of the agreement, the need for prompt conclusion of an agreement, and the desirability of concluding a routine or short-term agreement; and

(h) The general international practice as to similar agreements.

NOTES AND QUESTIONS

Review the State Department circular above.

How much restraint does it place upon the Executive Branch in deciding whether to proceed by treaty or executive agreement? Who makes the initial decision on whether to proceed by treaty or executive agreement? Why has the Executive Branch consistently chosen to go the route of the executive agreement for international trade agreements?

PROBLEM 3-1

The United States has just finished negotiating a complex trade agreement with Vietnam that includes an increase in the importation of Vietnamese-grown sugar cane. The treaty is submitted to Congress under the "Fast Track Procedure" discussed above. A delegation of senators from southern states with large sugar industries will not vote for the treaty unless a provision is inserted into the treaty, subjecting the imports to a duty surcharge of 20 percent if harvested under improper working conditions, or by workers paid at extremely low wages. Is this possible?

c.   PRESIDENTIAL POWER OVER INTERNATIONAL TRADE

Unlike the power that Congress exercises with respect to trade, the President's constitutional power is unclear and ill-defined. The President is able to claim three sources of power: (1) explicit power under Article II of the U.S. Constitution; (2) inherent power; and (3) power delegated by Congress.

PROBLEM 3-2

Assume that Congress has passed a law entitled the "Law for Promoting Global Democracy and Protection of the Environment." The law requires the United States to impose economic sanctions on Country J, a repressive authoritarian regime headed by a military government. Under the law, the USTR is required to make a report to Congress on an annual basis on the progress that Country J is making in the areas of human rights and the environment; if the USTR and Congress determine that Country J is making substantial progress, then Country J is to be rewarded with a trade agreement giving preferential trading rights with the United States. In a chance meeting with the Prime Minister of Country J at an international conference, the USTR is so encouraged by documented evidence of important progress that, under directions from the President, the USTR enters into an executive agreement with Country J providing for trade.

The President believes that Country J needs immediate encouragement to make further progress, and the yearly review process will be too slow and cumbersome to be effective. The President believes that the existence of the WTO agreements indicates a long pattern of congressional acquiescence in the power of the Executive to enter into trade agreements with other countries. Is the new agreement a lawful exercise of executive power? See *Capps* and *Dames & Moore* below.

United States v. Capps, Inc.
United States Court of Appeals, Fourth Circuit, 1953
204 F.2d 655, *aff'd*, 348 U.S. 296 (1955)

PARKER, Chief Judge:

[In 1948, the U.S. government entered into a program to protect American potato farmers. The government agreed to purchase all potatoes grown by eligible American farmers that could not be sold at commercial prices. To protect the U.S. market from foreign competition, the Acting Secretary of State of the United States entered into an executive agreement with the Canadian government. Under the executive agreement, Canada agreed, in exchange for certain trade benefits, to require export permits for all Canadian grown potatoes. The export permits were then to be granted only to Canadian potatoes to be used for seed and not for food. All sales contracts with U.S. purchasers were required to include a clause that the potatoes would not be diverted for table stock purposes. The defendant, a U.S. company, purchased Canadian potatoes pursuant to a sales contract with a clause prohibiting resale of the potatoes for table stock purposes. However, the defendant then sold the potatoes without restrictions to retail grocery establishments. The U.S. government brought an action for breach of contract against the defendant. The district court entered judgment for the defendant and the U.S. government now appeals.]

Defendant, a corporation engaged in business in Norfolk, Virginia, entered into a contract in December 1948 with H. B. Willis, Inc., a Canadian exporter, to purchase 48,544 sacks of Canadian seed potatoes, containing 100 lbs. each, to be shipped on the S.S. Empire Gangway docking in Jacksonville, Florida, in January 1949. Defendant's officers admittedly knew of the agreement with Canada and stated in a telegram to an official of the United States Department of Agriculture that the potatoes were being brought in for seed purposes. Defendant sent a telegram to the exporter in Canada on the same day that the potatoes were billed stating that they were for planting in Florida and Georgia. Defendant sold the potatoes while in shipment to the Atlantic Commission Company, a wholly owned agency of Great Atlantic & Pacific Tea Company, a retail grocery organization. No attempt was made to restrict their sale so that they would be used for seed and not for food, and there is evidence from which the jury could properly have drawn the conclusion that they were sold on the market as food displacing potatoes grown in this country and causing damage to the United States by requiring greater purchases of American grown potatoes in aid of the price support program than would have been necessary in the absence of their importation.

On these facts we think that judgment was properly entered for the defendant, but for reasons other than those given by the District Court. We have little difficulty in seeing in the evidence breach of contract on the part of defendant and damage resulting to the United States from the breach. We think, however, that the executive agreement was void because it was not authorized by Congress and contravened provisions of a statute dealing with the very matter to which it related and that the contract relied on, which was based on the executive agreement, was unenforceable in the courts of the United States for like reason. We think, also, that no action can be maintained by the government to recover damages on account of what is essentially a breach of a trade regulation, in the absence of express authorization by Congress. The power to regulate foreign commerce is vested in Congress, not in the executive or the courts; and the executive may not exercise the power by entering into executive agreements and suing in the courts for damages resulting from breaches of contracts made on the basis of such agreements.

In the Agricultural Act of 1948, Congress had legislated specifically with respect to the limitations which might be imposed on imports if it was thought that they would render ineffective or materially interfere with any program or operation undertaken pursuant to that act. Section 3 of the act, which amended prior statutes, provided in the portion here pertinent, 62 Stat. 1248-1250, 7 U.S.C.A. §624:

> "(a) Whenever the President has reason to believe that any article or articles are being or are practically certain to be imported into the United States under such conditions and in such quantities as to render or tend to render ineffective, or materially interfere with, any program or operation undertaken under this title he shall cause an immediate investigation to be made by the United States Tariff Commission. . . .
>
> "(b) If, on the basis of such investigation and report to him of findings and recommendations made in connection therewith, the President finds the existence of such facts, he shall by proclamation impose such quantitative limitations on any article or articles which may be entered for consumption as he finds and declares shown by such investigation to be necessary. . . ."

There was no pretense of complying with the requirements of this statute. The President did not cause an investigation to be made by the Tariff Commission, the Commission did not conduct an investigation or make findings or recommendations, and the President made no findings of fact and issued no proclamation imposing quantitative limitations. All that occurred in the making of this executive agreement, the effect of which was to exclude entirely a food product of a foreign country from importation into the United States, was an exchange of correspondence between the Acting Secretary of State and the Canadian Ambassador. Since the purpose of the agreement as well as its effect was to bar imports which would interfere with the Agricultural Adjustment program, it was necessary that the provisions of this statute be complied with and an executive agreement excluding such imports which failed to comply with it was void.

It is argued, however, that the validity of the executive agreement was not dependent upon the Act of Congress but was made pursuant to the inherent powers of the President under the Constitution. The answer is that while the President has certain inherent powers under the Constitution such as the power pertaining to his position as Commander in Chief of Army and Navy and the power necessary to see that the laws are faithfully executed, the power to regulate interstate and foreign commerce is not among the powers incident to the Presidential office, but is expressly vested by the Constitution in the Congress.

We think that whatever the power of the executive with respect to making executive trade agreements regulating foreign commerce in the absence of action by Congress, it is clear that the executive may not, through entering into such an agreement, avoid complying with a regulation prescribed by Congress. Imports from a foreign country are foreign commerce subject to regulation, so far as this country is concerned, by Congress alone. The executive may not by-pass congressional limitations regulating such commerce by entering into an agreement with the foreign country that the regulation be exercised by that country through its control over exports. Even though the regulation prescribed by the executive agreement be more desirable than that prescribed by Congressional action, it is the latter which must be accepted as the expression of national policy.

It is argued that irrespective of the validity of the executive agreement, the contract sued on was a valid contract between defendant and the Canadian exporter and that since the contract was made for the benefit of the United States, this country may maintain action upon it. The answer is that the contract was but the carrying out of the executive agreement entered into in contravention of the policy declared by Congress; and the courts of the United States will not lend their aid to enforcing it against the public policy of the country so declared. As stated, the regulation of imports from foreign countries is a matter for Congress and, when Congress has acted, the executive may not enforce different regulations by suing on contracts made with reference thereto.

Dames & Moore v. Regan
Supreme Court of the United States, 1981
453 U.S. 654

Justice REHNQUIST delivered the opinion of the Court.

[In 1979, the American Embassy in Teheran was seized, and U.S. personnel were held hostage. In response, President Carter declared a national emergency pursuant to the International Emergency Economic Powers Act (IEEPA), 50 U.S.C. §§1701-1706 (1976) and ordered that all Iranian assets in the United States were to be blocked, but allowed certain lawsuits to be brought against Iranian defendants. In 1981, as part of an Agreement to release the U.S. hostages, the United States agreed to set up an Iran-U.S. Claims Tribunal to resolve all existing claims by arbitration. President Carter then issued a series of executive orders to implement the Agreement. The orders required the transfer of all blocked assets, nullified all attachments, and suspended all existing claims in federal courts. Shortly after the seizure of the U.S. Embassy, petitioner Dames & Moore had brought a breach of contract action against several Iranian defendants. Pursuant to the executive orders above, the district court suspended execution of the judgment awarded to Dames

& Moore, vacated the pre-judgment attachment that Dames & Moore had obtained against the Iranian defendants, and stayed all further proceedings. Petitioner challenged the executive orders of the President as beyond his constitutional power. Several lower courts had upheld the President's power before the Supreme Court granted Petitioner's writ of certiorari.]

In nullifying post-November 14, 1979, attachments and directing those persons holding blocked Iranian funds and securities to transfer them to the Federal Reserve Bank of New York for ultimate transfer to Iran, President Carter cited five sources of express or inherent power. The Government, however, has principally relied on §203 of the IEEPA, 91 Stat. 1626, 50 U.S.C. §1702(a)(1) (1976 ed., Supp. III), as authorization for these actions. Section 1702(a)(1) provides in part:

> "At the times and to the extent specified in section 1701 of this title, the President may, under such regulations as he may prescribe, by means of instructions, licenses, or otherwise—
> "(A) investigate, regulate, or prohibit—
> "(i) any transactions in foreign exchange,
> "(ii) transfers of credit or payments between, by, through, or to any banking institution, to the extent that such transfers or payments involve any interest of any foreign country or a national thereof,
> "(iii) the importing or exporting of currency or securities, and
> "(B) investigate, regulate, direct and compel, nullify, void, prevent or prohibit, any acquisition, holding, withholding, use, transfer, withdrawal, transportation, importation or exportation of, or dealing in, or exercising any right, power, or privilege with respect to, or transactions involving, any property in which any foreign country or a national thereof has any interest;
> "by any person, or with respect to any property, subject to the jurisdiction of the United States."

The Government contends that the acts of "nullifying" the attachments and ordering the "transfer" of the frozen assets are specifically authorized by the plain language of the above statute. The two Courts of Appeals that have considered the issue agreed with this contention. In *Chas. T. Main Int'l, Inc. v. Khuzestan Water & Power Authority*, the Court of Appeals for the First Circuit explained:

> "The President relied on his IEEPA powers in November 1979, when he 'blocked' all Iranian assets in this country, and again in January 1981, when he 'nullified' interests acquired in blocked property, and ordered that property's transfer. The President's actions, in this regard, are in keeping with the language of IEEPA: initially he 'prevent[ed] and prohibit[ed]' 'transfers' of Iranian assets; later he 'direct[ed] and compel[led]' the 'transfer' and 'withdrawal' of the assets, 'nullify[ing]' certain 'rights' and 'privileges' acquired in them."
>
> "Main argues that IEEPA does not supply the President with power to override judicial remedies, such as attachments and injunctions, or to extinguish 'interests' in foreign assets held by United States citizens. But we can find no such limitation in IEEPA's terms. The language of IEEPA is sweeping and unqualified. It provides broadly that the President may void or nullify the 'exercising [by *any* person of] *any* right, power or privilege with respect to . . . *any* property in which any foreign country has any interest. . . .' 50 U.S.C. §1702(a)(1)(B)." 651 F.2d, at 806-807 (emphasis in original).

Petitioner contends that we should ignore the plain language of this statute because an examination of its legislative history as well as the history of §5(b) of the Trading With the Enemy Act (hereinafter TWEA), 40 Stat. 411, as amended, 50 U.S.C. App. §5(b) (1976 ed. and Supp. III), from which the pertinent language of §1702 is directly drawn, reveals that the statute was not intended to give the President such extensive power over the assets of a foreign state during times of national emergency. According to petitioner, once the President instituted the November 14, 1979, blocking order, §1702 authorized him "only to continue the freeze or to discontinue controls." Brief for Petitioner 32.

We do not agree and refuse to read out of §1702 all meaning to the words "transfer," "compel," or "nullify." Nothing in the legislative history of either §1702 or §5(b) of the TWEA requires such a result. To the contrary, we think both the legislative history and cases interpreting the TWEA fully sustain the broad authority of the Executive when acting under this congressional grant of power.

Although we have concluded that the IEEPA constitutes specific congressional authorization to the President to nullify the attachments and order the transfer of Iranian assets, there remains the question of the President's authority to suspend claims pending in American courts. Such claims have, of course, an existence apart from the attachments which accompanied them. In terminating these claims through Executive Order No. 12294 the President purported to act under authority of both the IEEPA and 22 U.S.C. §1732, the so-called "Hostage Act." 46 Fed. Reg. 14111 (1981).

We conclude that although the IEEPA authorized the nullification of the attachments, it cannot be read to authorize the suspension of the claims. The claims of American citizens against Iran are not in themselves transactions involving Iranian property or efforts to exercise any rights with respect to such property. An *in personam* lawsuit, although it might eventually be reduced to judgment and that judgment might be executed upon, is an effort to establish liability and fix damages and does not focus on any particular property within the jurisdiction. The terms of the IEEPA therefore do not authorize the President to suspend claims in American courts.

Although the broad language of the Hostage Act suggests it may cover this case, there are several difficulties with such a view. The legislative history indicates that the Act was passed in response to a situation unlike the recent Iranian crisis. Congress in 1868 was concerned with the activity of certain countries refusing to recognize the citizenship of naturalized Americans traveling abroad, and repatriating such citizens against their will. These countries were not interested in returning the citizens in exchange for any sort of ransom. This also explains the reference in the Act to imprisonment "in violation of the rights of American citizenship." Although the Iranian hostage-taking violated international law and common decency, the hostages were not seized out of any refusal to recognize their American citizenship—they were seized precisely *because of* their American citizenship. The legislative history is also somewhat ambiguous on the question whether Congress contemplated Presidential action such as that involved here or rather simply reprisals directed against the offending foreign country and *its* citizens.

Concluding that neither the IEEPA nor the Hostage Act constitutes specific authorization of the President's action suspending claims, however, is not to say that these statutory provisions are entirely irrelevant to the question of the validity of the President's action. We think both statutes highly relevant in the looser sense of indicating congressional acceptance of a broad scope for executive action in circumstances such as those presented in this case.

Although we have declined to conclude that the IEEPA or the Hostage Act directly authorizes the President's suspension of claims for the reasons noted, we cannot ignore the general tenor of Congress' legislation in this area in trying to determine whether the President is acting alone or at least with the acceptance of Congress. As we have noted, Congress cannot anticipate and legislate with regard to every possible action the President may find it necessary to take or every possible situation in which he might act. Such failure of Congress specifically to delegate authority does not, "especially . . . in the areas of foreign policy and national security," imply "congressional disapproval" of action taken by the Executive. *Haig v. Agee*, 453 U.S. 280, 291, 101 S. Ct. 2766, 2774, 69 L.Ed.2d 640. On the contrary, the enactment of legislation closely related to the question of the President's authority in a particular case which evinces legislative intent to accord the President broad discretion may be considered to "invite" "measures on independent presidential responsibility," *Youngstown*, 343 U.S., at 637, 72 S. Ct., at 871 (Jackson, J., concurring). At least this is so where there is no contrary indication of legislative intent and when, as here, there is a history of congressional acquiescence in conduct of the sort engaged in by the President. It is to that history which we now turn.

Not infrequently in affairs between nations, outstanding claims by nationals of one country against the government of another country are "sources of friction" between the two sovereigns. *United States v. Pink*, 315 U.S. 203, 225, 62 S. Ct. 552, 563, 86 L. Ed. 796 (1942). To resolve these difficulties, nations have often entered into agreements settling the claims of their respective nationals. [T]he United States has repeatedly exercised its sovereign authority to settle the claims of its nationals against foreign countries. Though those settlements have sometimes been made by treaty, there has also been a longstanding practice of settling such claims by executive agreement without the advice and consent of the Senate. Under such agreements, the President has agreed to renounce or extinguish claims of United States nationals against foreign governments in return for lump-sum payments or the establishment of arbitration procedures. It is clear that the practice of settling claims continues today. Since 1952, the President has entered into at least 10 binding settlements with foreign nations, including an $80 million settlement with the People's Republic of China.

Crucial to our decision today is the conclusion that Congress has implicitly approved the practice of claim settlement by executive agreement. This is best demonstrated by Congress' enactment of the International Claims Settlement Act of 1949, 64 Stat. 13, as amended, 22 U.S.C. §1621 *et seq.* (1976 ed. and Supp. IV). The Act had two purposes: (1) to allocate to United States nationals funds received in the course of an executive claims settlement with Yugoslavia, and (2) to provide a procedure whereby funds resulting from future settlements could be distributed. To achieve these ends Congress created the International Claims Commission, now the Foreign Claims Settlement Commission, and gave it jurisdiction to make final and binding decisions with respect to claims by United States nationals against settlement funds. 22 U.S.C. §1623(a). By creating a procedure to implement future settlement agreements, Congress placed its stamp of approval on such agreements. Indeed, the legislative history of the Act observed that the United States was seeking settlements with countries other than Yugoslavia and that the bill contemplated settlements of a similar nature in the future. H.R. Rep. No. 770, 81st Cong., 1st Sess., 4, 8 (1949).

Over the years Congress has frequently amended the International Claims Settlement Act to provide for particular problems arising out of settlement agreements, thus demonstrating Congress' continuing acceptance of the President's claim settlement authority. With respect to the Executive Agreement with the People's Republic of China, for example, Congress established an allocation formula for distribution of the funds received pursuant to the Agreement. 22 U.S.C. §1627(f) (1976 ed. and Supp. IV). As with legislation involving other executive agreements, Congress did not question the fact of the settlement or the power of the President to have concluded it. In 1976, Congress authorized the Foreign Claims Settlement Commission to adjudicate the merits of claims by United States nationals against East Germany, prior to any settlement with East Germany, so that the Executive would "be in a better position to negotiate an adequate settlement . . . of these claims." S. Rep. No. 94-1188, p. 2 (1976), U.S. Code Cong. & Admin. News, 1976, pp. 5582, 5583; 22 U.S.C. §1644b. Similarly, Congress recently amended the International Claims Settlement Act to facilitate the settlement of claims against Vietnam. 22 U.S.C. §§1645, 1645a(5) (1976 ed., Supp. IV). The House Report stated that the purpose of the legislation was to establish an official inventory of losses of private United States property in Vietnam so that recovery could be achieved "through future direct Government-to-Government negotiation of private property claims." H.R. Rep. No. 96-915, pp. 2-3, U.S. Code Cong. & Admin. News, 1980, pp. 7328, 7329-7330. Finally, the legislative history of the IEEPA further reveals that Congress has accepted the authority of the Executive to enter into settlement agreements. Though the IEEPA was enacted to provide for some limitation on the President's emergency powers, Congress stressed that "[n]othing in this act is intended . . . to interfere with the authority of the President to [block assets], or to impede the settlement of claims of U.S. citizens against foreign countries." S. Rep. No. 95-466, p. 6 (1977), U.S. Code Cong. & Admin. News, 1977, pp. 4540, 4544; 50 U.S.C. §1706(a)(1) (1976 ed., Supp. III).

In addition to congressional acquiescence in the President's power to settle claims, prior cases of this Court have also recognized that the President does have some measure of power to enter into executive agreements without obtaining the advice and consent of the Senate. In *United States v. Pink*, 315 U.S. 203, 62 S. Ct. 552, 86 L.Ed. 796 (1942), for example, the Court upheld the validity of the Litvinov Assignment, which was part of an Executive Agreement whereby the Soviet Union assigned to the United States amounts owed to it by American nationals so that outstanding claims of other American nationals could be paid. The Court explained that the resolution of such claims was integrally connected with normalizing United States' relations with a foreign state:

> "Power to remove such obstacles to full recognition as settlement of claims of our nationals . . . certainly is a modest implied power of the President. . . . No such obstacle can be placed in the way of rehabilitation of relations between this country and another nation, unless the historic conception of the powers and responsibilities . . . is to be drastically revised." *Id.*, at 229-230, 62 S. Ct., at 565-566.

In light of all of the foregoing—the inferences to be drawn from the character of the legislation Congress has enacted in the area, such as the IEEPA and the Hostage Act, and from the history of acquiescence in executive claims settlement—we conclude that the President was authorized to suspend pending claims pursuant to Executive Order No. 12294.

Just as importantly, Congress has not disapproved of the action taken here. Though Congress has held hearings on the Iranian Agreement itself, Congress has not enacted legislation, or even passed a resolution, indicating its displeasure with the Agreement. Quite the contrary, the relevant Senate Committee has stated that the establishment of the Tribunal is "of vital importance to the United States." S. Rep. No.97-71, p. 5 (1981). We are thus clearly not confronted with a situation in which Congress has in some way resisted the exercise of Presidential authority.

The judgment of the District Court is accordingly affirmed, and the mandate shall issue forthwith.

NOTES AND QUESTIONS

In *United States v. Capps*, why did the United States permit the importation of Canadian potatoes to be used for seed (i.e., planting) but not for table stock (i.e., food)? Can you explain how the entry of Canadian potatoes used for table stock would undermine the U.S. potato program?

d. THE CLASH BETWEEN STATE AND FEDERAL POWER

In the United States, the individual states exercise considerable power under the federal form of government set forth in the U.S. Constitution. In certain cases, the exercise of state power over international trade may conflict with federal interests.

PROBLEM 3-3

The State of Ohio is seeking to enter directly into several international agreements with several foreign countries for the purpose of promoting trade. The governor seeks to promote all Ohio industries, but is particularly concerned with promoting Ohio's corn and wheat industries, which have been struggling. You are chief counsel to the governor, who asks you whether there might be any limits under the U.S. constitutional scheme, on Ohio's authority to enter into agreements with the following countries:

(1) L, a developing country with a repressive government that is subject to a broad set of economic sanctions under legislation passed by Congress;
(2) M, a developed country that has entered into a framework trade agreement with the United States concerning trade in a wide range of agricultural commodities, but no specific mention is made in the agreement of the trade in corn or wheat;
(3) N, a middle-income country that currently has trade agreements with a number of countries but has yet to enter into any international agreements with the United States.

The governor says, "Look, I realize that this is pretty sketchy and there are many facts you don't have. I'm not asking for a definitive answer—just your initial assessment on the basis of these facts. Will the exercise of state power in these cases be in conflict with the power of the federal government over foreign relations and trade?" Consider *Crosby* below.

PROBLEM 3-4

You are the chief legal advisor to the Treasurer of the State of Illinois, which operates a public employees' retirement system with many billions of dollars in assets. The Treasurer invests these assets in the United States and in foreign countries to provide the returns necessary to pay the retirement pensions for state employees enrolled in the plan.

Your boss, the State Treasurer, has decided to adopt politically motivated investment guidelines to govern the retirement system's investments in emerging markets. The guidelines would rule out investment in nations found lacking in political freedom and essential civil liberties, including workers' rights and a free press. These guidelines would rule out many countries with which the United States has friendly diplomatic relations and common political interests, such as Egypt and Singapore, due to the autocratic control exercised by their governments over their citizens. If Illinois adopts these guidelines as legally binding criteria, would they be vulnerable to attack as an unconstitutional intrusion on the foreign affairs power of the federal government? See *Crosby* below.

Crosby v. National Foreign Trade Council
Supreme Court of the United States, 2000
530 U.S. 363

Justice SOUTER delivered the opinion of the Court.

In June 1996, Massachusetts adopted "An Act Regulating State Contracts with Companies Doing Business with or in Burma (Myanmar)," 1996 Mass. Acts 239, ch. 130 (codified at Mass. Gen. Laws §§7:22G-7:22M, 40 F. 1/2 (1997)). The statute generally bars state entities from buying goods or services from any person (defined to include a business organization) identified on a "restricted purchase list" of those doing business with Burma.

[Three months later,] Congress passed a statute imposing a set of mandatory and conditional sanctions on Burma. *See* Foreign Operations, Export Financing, and Related Programs Appropriations Act, 1997, §570, 110 Stat. 3009-166 to 3009-167 (enacted by the Omnibus Consolidated Appropriations Act, 1997, §101(c), 110 Stat. 3009-121 to 3009-172).

[The federal Act] imposes three sanctions directly on Burma. [First,] it bans all aid to the Burmese Government except for humanitarian assistance, counternarcotics efforts, and promotion of human rights and democracy. The statute instructs United States representatives to international financial institutions to vote against loans or other assistance to or for Burma, and it provides that no entry visa shall be issued to any Burmese Government official unless required by treaty or to staff the Burmese mission to the United Nations. These restrictions are to remain in effect "[u]ntil such time as the President determines and certifies to Congress that Burma has made measurable and substantial progress in improving human rights practices and implementing democratic government." Sec. 570(a).

Second, the federal Act authorizes the President to impose further sanctions subject to certain conditions. Sec. 570(b).

Third, the statute directs the President to work to develop "a comprehensive, multilateral strategy to bring democracy to and improve human rights practices and the quality of life in Burma." Sec. 570(c).

[A] fourth section requires the President to report periodically to certain congressional committee chairmen on the progress toward democratization and better living conditions in Burma as well as on the development of the required strategy. Sec. 570(d). And [a] fifth part authorizes the President "to waive, temporarily or permanently, any sanction [under the federal Act] . . . if he determines and certifies to Congress that the application of such sanction would be contrary to the national security interests of the United States." Sec. 570(e).

Respondent National Foreign Trade Council is a nonprofit corporation representing companies engaged in foreign commerce; 34 of its members were on the Massachusetts restricted purchase list in 1998. Three withdrew from Burma after the passage of the state Act, and one member had its bid for a procurement contract increased by 10 percent under the provision of the state law allowing acceptance of a low bid from a listed bidder only if the next-to-lowest bid is more than 10 percent higher.

[Previously,] the Council filed suit in the United States District Court for the District of Massachusetts, seeking declaratory and injunctive relief against the petitioner state officials charged with administering and enforcing the state Act (whom we will refer to simply as the State). The Council argued that the state law unconstitutionally infringed on the federal foreign affairs power, violated the Foreign Commerce Clause, and was preempted by the federal Act. [T]he District Court permanently enjoined enforcement of the state Act, holding that it "unconstitutionally impinge[d] on the federal government's exclusive authority to regulate foreign affairs."

A fundamental principle of the Constitution is that Congress has the power to preempt state law. Even without an express provision for preemption, we have found that state law must yield to a congressional Act in at least two circumstances. When Congress intends federal law to "occupy the field," state law in that area is preempted. And even if Congress has not occupied the field, state law is naturally preempted to the extent of any conflict with a federal statute. We will find preemption where it is impossible for a private party to comply with both state and federal law, and where "under the circumstances of [a] particular case, [the challenged state law] stands as an obstacle to the accomplishment and execution of the full purposes and objectives of Congress." *Hines v. Davidowitz*, 312 U.S. 52, at 67, 61 S. Ct. 399, 85 L. Ed. 581 (1941). What is a sufficient obstacle is a matter of judgment, to be informed by examining the federal statute as a whole and identifying its purpose and intended effects.

[W]e see the state Burma law as an obstacle to the accomplishment of Congress's full objectives under the federal Act. We find that the state law undermines the intended purpose and "natural effect" of at least three provisions of the federal Act.

First, Congress clearly intended the federal Act to provide the President with flexible and effective authority over economic sanctions against Burma. Although Congress immediately put in place a set of initial sanctions, it authorized the President to terminate any and all of those measures upon determining and certifying that there had been progress in human rights and democracy in Burma. It invested the President with the further power to ban new investment by United States persons, dependent only on specific Presidential findings of repression in Burma. And, most significantly, Congress empowered the President "to waive, temporarily or permanently, any sanction [under the federal Act] . . . if he determines and certifies to Congress that the application of such sanction would be contrary to the national security interests of the United States."

[T]he statute has placed the President in a position with as much discretion to exercise economic leverage against Burma, with an eye toward national security, as our law will admit. And it is just this plenitude of Executive authority that we think controls the issue of preemption here. The President has been given this authority not merely to make a political statement but to achieve a political result, and the fullness of his authority shows the importance in the congressional mind of reaching that result. It is simply implausible that Congress would have gone to such lengths to empower the President if it had been willing to compromise his effectiveness by deference to every provision of state statute or local ordinance that might, if enforced, blunt the consequences of discretionary Presidential action.

And that is just what the Massachusetts Burma law would do in imposing a different, state system of economic pressure against the Burmese political regime. [T]he state statute penalizes some private action that the federal Act may allow, and pulls levers of influence that the federal Act does not reach. But the point here is that the state sanctions are immediate and perpetual, there being no termination provision. This unyielding application undermines the President's intended statutory authority by making it impossible for him to restrain fully the coercive power of the national economy when he may choose to take the discretionary action open to him. Quite simply, if the Massachusetts law is enforceable the President has less to offer and less economic and diplomatic leverage as a consequence. It thus "stands as an obstacle to the accomplishment and execution of the full purposes and objectives of Congress."

[Second,] Congress manifestly intended to limit economic pressure against the Burmese Government to a specific range. Congress's calibrated Burma policy is a deliberate effort "to steer a middle path."

The State has set a different course, and its statute conflicts with federal law at a number of points by penalizing individuals and conduct that Congress has explicitly exempted or excluded from sanctions. [The Court furthermore points out differences in the scope of subject matter addressed by the ban and the class of companies at which the acts are aimed.]

[Third], the state Act is at odds with the President's intended authority to speak for the United States among the world's nations in developing a "comprehensive, multilateral strategy to bring democracy to and improve human rights practices and the quality of life in Burma." As with Congress's explicit delegation to the President of power over economic sanctions, Congress's express command to the President to take the initiative for the United States among the international community invested him with the maximum authority of the National Government, cf. *Youngstown Sheet & Tube Co.*, 343 U.S. at 635, 72 S. Ct. 863, in harmony with the President's own constitutional powers. Again, the state Act undermines the President's capacity, in this instance for effective diplomacy. It is not merely that the differences between the state and federal Acts in scope and type of sanctions threaten to complicate discussions; they compromise the very capacity of the President to speak for the Nation with one voice in dealing with other governments.

B. The European Union

The European Union (EU) is an economic, political union of twenty-seven sovereign states, seventeen of which use the euro as a common currency. (The EU will have twenty-eight members as of July 1, 2013, when Croatia is due to join.) With a population of about 503 million and a $17.5 trillion economy, the EU is, along with the United States and China, one of the cornerstones of the world economy, responsible for about 25 percent of world gross domestic product and about 20 percent of world trade.

From its beginning in the 1950s, the EU and its predecessor entities sought to use economic integration to enhance European peace and security. To this end the EU today is first and foremost a customs union within which four freedoms flourish: the freedoms of movement of goods, services, capital, and workers. The EU maintains a common commercial policy with a common customs tariff and common trade rules: Regulation (EC) 2609/69 establishes common rules on exports and Regulation (EC) 3285/94 establishes a common legal regime on imports. The common commercial policy means that every EU country applies the same tariffs and export restrictions on goods.

The EU was established by a series of treaties, most importantly the European Economic Community Treaty of Rome in 1957 and the Treaty on European Union (Maastricht Treaty) of 1993. To further the ambitious goals of the EU, a series of additional treaties were approved by EU members, culminating in the Treaty of Lisbon (2009), which gives the EU formal international legal status and endows the EU with a full-time President (who serves a renewable term of two and one-half years), a High Representative in charge of foreign affairs, and increased power for the European Parliament. The Treaty of Lisbon consolidates the EU's powers into a Treaty on the Functioning of the European Union (TFEU), which has replaced the founding treaty, the European Economic Community Treaty, or EC Treaty. The treaties that today form the "constitution" of the EU are the Consolidated Versions of the Treaty on European Union and the Treaty on the Functioning of the European Union, O.J. 2010/C 83/01 (March 30, 2010), available at http://eur-lex.europa.eu. The EU institutions pass legislation (termed "regulations" and "directives") through a complex procedure known as "co-decision" because the process involves three separate institutions: the European Commission, which has the authority to propose legislation; the Council of the European Union, which consists of representatives of member states; and the European Parliament, which is the only popularly elected EU body.

The EU also has a powerful court, officially named the Court of Justice, but commonly called the European Court of Justice, or ECJ. The ECJ consists of a General Court (formerly the Court of First Instance) and the Court of Justice, which acts as a supreme court. The ECJ has the sole authority to provide interpretations of the EU treaties and EU legislative acts; EU law (the treaties as well as secondary laws) is superior to the laws of EU member states.

The EU has been a WTO member in its own right since January 1, 1995, although for legal reasons until November 30, 2009, the WTO membership was in the name of the European Communities. The EU is a single customs union with a single trade policy and a single tariff. The EU Commission as the executive arm of the EU speaks for all EU members at virtually all WTO meetings, although all twenty-seven EU member states are also members of the WTO.

The legal basis for the EU and the Commission's authority over trade is Article 207 of the TFEU (ex TEC Art. 133), which reads in relevant part as follows:

Article 207

1. The common commercial policy shall be based on uniform principles, particularly with regard to changes in tariff rates, the conclusion of tariff and trade agreements relating to trade in goods and services, and the commercial aspects of

intellectual property, foreign direct investment, the achievement of uniformity in measures of liberalisation, export policy and measures to protect trade such as those to be taken in the event of dumping or subsidies. The common commercial policy shall be conducted in the context of the principles and objectives of the Union's external action. ***

3. Where agreements with one or more third countries or international organisations need to be negotiated and concluded, Article 218 shall apply, subject to the special provisions of this Article.

The Commission shall make recommendations to the Council, which shall authorise it to open the necessary negotiations. The Council and the Commission shall be responsible for ensuring that the agreements negotiated are compatible with internal Union policies and rules.

TFEU Article 218 (ex TEC Art. 300), referenced in Article 207, provides as follows:

Article 218

1. Without prejudice to the specific provisions laid down in Article 207, agreements between the Union and third countries or international organisations shall be negotiated and concluded in accordance with the following procedure.

2. The Council shall authorise the opening of negotiations, adopt negotiating directives, authorise the signing of agreements and conclude them.

3. The Commission, or the High Representative of the Union for Foreign Affairs and Security Policy where the agreement envisaged relates exclusively or principally to the common foreign and security policy, shall submit recommendations to the Council, which shall adopt a decision authorising the opening of negotiations and, depending on the subject of the agreement envisaged, nominating the Union negotiator or the head of the Union's negotiating team.

The ECJ has interpreted TEC Article 183, the predecessor article to the current TFEU Article 207, to give wide powers to negotiate and conclude agreements with respect to the common commercial policy. *See Opinion 1/75, Opinion of the Court Given Pursuant to Article 228 of the EEC Treaty* [1975] ECR 1355. Under Article 207, the EU has sole competence to negotiate agreements falling within the common commercial policy to the exclusion of member states. Member states are also constrained from acting, even when the EU has not yet acted, as long as the subject matter is assigned to the EU by treaty. *See Joined Cases 3, 4 & 6/76, In re Kramer* [1976] ECR 1279. If an agreement involves costs that are to be borne directly by the member states, however, they can participate in the negotiations with the EU. *See* Opinion 1/78, *International Agreement on Rubber* [1979] ECR 2871. Such agreements may be termed "mixed agreements."

NOTES AND QUESTIONS

1. What are the implications of this broad allocation of powers for the member states of the EU? Do member states have any authority over trade matters? In a case dealing with the competence of the EU Commission to negotiate and implement the WTO Uruguay Round agreements, the ECJ ruled that, although the Common Commercial Policy gave the EU and the Commission exclusive competence over

trade in goods, competence over trade in services and intellectual property was not exclusive but was shared with the member states. Opinion 1/94, *Competence of the Community to Conclude International Agreements Concerning Services and the Protection of Intellectual Property,* of November 15, 1994 (ECR 1994 I-5267). Investment has also been regarded as a matter of shared competence since EU member states have concluded about 1,000 bilateral investment treaties with non-EU states.

2. Read carefully TFEU Article 207. Does the EU now have exclusive competence over the fields of services, intellectual property, and investment insofar as WTO agreements are concerned? Will there be any more mixed agreements over international trade matters? But does the EU Commission now have exclusive power over these fields?

III.   *The Effect of International Trade Agreements on Domestic Law and Resolving Conflicts Between International and Domestic Law*

A.   The United States

Under U.S. constitutional practice, international obligations undertaken in international agreements do not necessarily become part of domestic law. A distinction is drawn between agreements that are "self-executing" and those that are "non-self-executing." A treaty is self-executing when its provisions exhibit the intent to prescribe rules enforceable in court. This is ascertained by examining the language of the treaty and the circumstances of its execution. *See, e.g., Diggs v. Richardson,* 555 F.2d 848, 851 (D.C. Cir. 1976). A self-executing agreement has immediate effect on U.S. domestic law; its provisions prevail over prior federal law and are superior to both prior and future state law. *See, e.g., United States v. Belmont,* 301 U.S. 324, 331 (1937). A non-self-executing treaty has no direct effect but must be implemented through domestic legislation.

With this in mind, consider the effect of the WTO agreements on U.S. domestic law under the law passed by Congress to implement those agreements, the Uruguay Round Agreements Act (URAA).

PROBLEM 3-5

In order to protect the domestic peanut industry, the State of Arkansas has passed a law that requires all vendors to display the following sign in a conspicuous place, in letters at least three inches high, "WE SELL FOREIGN PEANUTS." The sign is to be placed over imported peanuts or peanut butter made from foreign peanuts. An association of retail establishments believes that this law discriminates against foreign peanuts and would like to bring an action in state court in Arkansas seeking to declare the law to be invalid because it is in conflict with the GATT, which prohibits discrimination against foreign goods. The state attorney general's office is also thinking of joining the lawsuit or taking the lead in suing on behalf of the retailers. Can either of these entities bring an action in state court? What about in a federal court? What result under the URAA below?

PROBLEM 3-6

Assume that the United States Patent and Trademark Office, under pressure from consumer groups and advocates for senior citizens, amends the Patent Law to reduce the term of patent protection for drugs, from its current term of twenty years, to fifteen years for all new patents. Article 33 of TRIPS requires a minimum term of protection of twenty years for all patents. You are general counsel to EuroPharma, a multinational company based in Germany, that has a number of existing patents (that are not affected) in the United States as well as many pending patent applications in the United States for its drugs that it would like to sell through its foreign subsidiaries and distributors in the United States. Under the amendment, however, all new patents for EuroPharma's drugs will be limited to fifteen years. You bring an action in federal district court seeking to invalidate the amendment on the grounds that it is in violation of TRIPS. What result under the URAA below? What course of action should you take to challenge the law?

The Uruguay Round Agreements Act (1994)
Title I—Approval of, and General Provisions Relating to, the Uruguay Round Agreements

19 U.S.C. §3511

SEC. 101.   APPROVAL AND ENTRY INTO FORCE OF THE URUGUAY ROUND AGREEMENTS

(a) Approval of Agreements and Statement of Administrative Action.— Pursuant to section 1103 of the Omnibus Trade and Competitiveness Act of 1988 (19 U.S.C. 2903) and section 151 of the Trade Act of 1974 (19 U.S.C. 2191), the Congress approves

(1) the trade agreements described in subsection (d) of this section resulting from the Uruguay Round of multilateral trade negotiations under the auspices of the General Agreement on Tariffs and Trade, entered into on April 15, 1994, and submitted to the Congress on September 27, 1994; and

(2) the statement of administrative action proposed to implement the agreements that was submitted to the Congress on September 27, 1994.

(b) Entry Into Force.—At such time as the President determines that a sufficient number of foreign countries are accepting the obligations of the Uruguay Round Agreements, in accordance with article XIV of the WTO Agreement, to ensure the effective operation of, and adequate benefits for the United States under, those Agreements, the President may accept the Uruguay Round Agreements and implement article VIII of the WTO Agreement.

(c) Authorization of Appropriations.—There are authorized to be appropriated annually such sums as may be necessary for the payment by the United States of its share of the expenses of the WTO.

(d) Trade Agreements to Which This Act Applies.—Subsection (a) of this section applies to the WTO Agreement and to the following agreements annexed to that Agreement:

(1) The General Agreement on Tariffs and Trade 1994.

(2) The Agreement on Agriculture.

(3) The Agreement on the Application of Sanitary and Phytosanitary Measures.

(4) The Agreement on Textiles and Clothing.

(5) The Agreement on Technical Barriers to Trade.

(6) The Agreement on Trade-Related Investment Measures.

(7) The Agreement on Implementation of Article VI of the General Agreement on Tariffs and Trade 1994.

(8) The Agreement on Implementation of Article VII of the General Agreement on Tariffs and Trade 1994.

(9) The Agreement on Preshipment Inspection.

(10) The Agreement on Rules of Origin.

(11) The Agreement on Import Licensing Procedures.

(12) The Agreement on Subsidies and Countervailing Measures.

(13) The Agreement on Safeguards.

(14) The General Agreement on Trade in Services.

(15) The Agreement on Trade-Related Aspects of Intellectual Property Rights.

(16) The Understanding on Rules and Procedures Governing the Settlement of Disputes.

(17) The Agreement on Government Procurement.

(18) The International Bovine Meat Agreement.

19 U.S.C. §3512

SEC. 102.   RELATIONSHIP OF THE AGREEMENTS TO UNITED STATES LAW AND STATE LAW

(a) Relationship of Agreements to United States Law.

(1) United States law to prevail in conflict.—No provision of any of the Uruguay Round Agreements, nor the application of any such provision to any person or circumstance, that is inconsistent with any law of the United States shall have effect.

(2) Construction.—Nothing in this Act shall be construed

(A) to amend or modify any law of the United States, including any law relating to

(i) the protection of human, animal, or plant life or health,

(ii) the protection of the environment, or

(iii) worker safety, or

(B) to limit any authority conferred under any law of the United States, including section 301 of the Trade Act of 1974, unless specifically provided for in this Act.

(b) Relationship of Agreements to State Law.

(1) Federal-State consultation.

(A) In general.—Upon enactment of this Act, the President shall, through the intergovernmental policy advisory committees on trade established under section 306(c)(2)(A) of the Trade and Tariff Act of 1984 (19 U.S.C. 2114c(2)(A)), consult with the States for the purpose of achieving conformity of State laws and practices with the Uruguay Round Agreements.

(B) Federal-State consultation process.—The Trade Representative shall establish within the Office of the United States Trade Representative a Federal-State consultation process for addressing issues relating to the Uruguay Round Agreements that directly relate to, or will potentially have a direct effect on, the States.

(2) Legal challenge.

(A) In general.—No State law, or the application of such a State law, may be declared invalid as to any person or circumstance on the ground that the provision or application is inconsistent with any of the Uruguay Round Agreements, except in an action brought by the United States for the purpose of declaring such law or application invalid.

(B) Procedures governing action.—In any action described in subparagraph (A) that is brought by the United States against a State or any subdivision thereof—

(i) a report of a dispute settlement panel or the Appellate Body convened under the Dispute Settlement Understanding regarding the State law, or the law of any political subdivision thereof, shall not be considered as binding or otherwise accorded deference;

(ii) the United States shall have the burden of proving that the law that is the subject of the action, or the application of that law, is inconsistent with the agreement in question;

(iii) any State whose interests may be impaired or impeded in the action shall have the unconditional right to intervene in the action as a party, and the United States shall be entitled to amend its complaint to include a claim or cross-claim concerning the law of a State that so intervenes; and

(iv) any State law that is declared invalid shall not be deemed to have been invalid in its application during any period before the court's judgment becomes final and all timely appeals, including discretionary review, of such judgment are exhausted.

(c) Effect of Agreement With Respect to Private Remedies.

(1) Limitations.—No person other than the United States

(A) shall have any cause of action or defense under any of the Uruguay Round Agreements or by virtue of congressional approval of such an agreement, or

(B) may challenge, in any action brought under any provision of law, any action or inaction by any department, agency, or other instrumentality of the United States, any State, or any political subdivision of a State on the ground that such action or inaction is inconsistent with such agreement.

(2) Intent of Congress.—It is the intention of the Congress through paragraph (1) to occupy the field with respect to any cause of action or defense under or in connection with any of the Uruguay Round Agreements, including by precluding any person other than the United States from bringing

any action against any State or political subdivision thereof or raising any defense to the application of State law under or in connection with any of the Uruguay Round Agreements

>   (A) on the basis of a judgment obtained by the United States in an action brought under any such agreement; or

>   (B) on any other basis.

PROBLEM 3-7

Country R and Country T have just joined the WTO. Suppose that:

(1) Country R's highest court has just held that the WTO agreements are self-executing treaties, and are a form of international law that prevails over domestic law.

(2) Country T's highest court has just held that the WTO agreements are non-self-executing treaties.

What must Countries R and T do to fulfill their obligations to make WTO obligations part of their domestic legal order?

PROBLEM 3-8

In each of the following scenarios, which is the proper court or forum in which to resolve the dispute?

(1) A law passed by the State of Alabama is inconsistent with a WTO agreement;

(2) A law passed by the State of Oregon is inconsistent with a federal statute that implements a WTO agreement;

(3) A federal implementing statute is inconsistent with the WTO obligation that the statute is designed to implement.

NOTES AND QUESTIONS

1. No WTO agreement has been held to be self-executing under U.S. law, and leading scholars prior to the conclusion of the WTO agreements considered the GATT to be non-self-executing. For a discussion, see Ronald Brand, *The Status of the General Agreement on Tariffs and Trade in United States Domestic Law*, 26 Stan. J. Int'l L. 479 (1990).

2. Is a provision of a WTO agreement superior to state law? How are conflicts between state law and the agreements resolved? Special difficulties in implementing the WTO agreements may arise in federal states such as the United States. The GATT Article XXIV:12 is a very brief provision that requires WTO members to take "such reasonable measures as may be available to it to ensure such observance [of the provisions of this Agreement] by regional and local governments and authorities within its territory." How should this language be interpreted? Can a WTO member evade an obligation on the ground that its constitution does not provide any way to compel compliance by sub-units of government?

Article XXIV:12 was construed by a GATT Panel in a case brought by South Africa against Canada in the 1980s. South Africa complained about the application of a special retail sales tax levied by the provincial government of Ontario that afforded protection to domestically produced gold coins and discriminated against foreign coins in violation of the National Treatment principle contained in GATT Article III, which prohibits such discriminatory treatment. The GATT panel interpreted Article XXIV:12 to mean that the non-observance of Article III by Ontario "constituted a *prima facie* case of nullification or impairment of benefits accruing to South Africa under the General Agreement. Canada's obligations to ensure the observance of Article III:2 by Ontario are limited to those set out in Article XXIV:12 but, until its efforts . . . have secured the withdrawal of the measure, Canada is obliged to compensate South Africa for the competitive opportunities lost as a result of the Ontario measure." *Canada—Measures Affecting the Sale of Gold Coins,* Report of the Panel, L/5863, September 17, 1985, at 65. Will this ruling carry over to the WTO?

3. What is the effect of a WTO dispute settlement report on U.S. domestic law? The U.S. Court of International Trade has concluded that even when adopted by the DSB of the WTO, dispute settlement reports have no binding effect within the U.S. legal system. *See Hyundai Electronics Co. v. United States,* 53 F. Supp. 2d 1334, 1343 (CIT 1999). This echoes the view of the courts under the GATT. In *Footwear Distributors and Retailers of America v. United States,* 852 F. Supp. 1078, 1096 (CIT 1994), the court concluded, "However cogent the reasoning [of] the GATT panels, it cannot lead to the precise domestic, judicial relief for which the plaintiff prays." Why not?

PROBLEM 3-9

In the case of *Murray v. The Charming Betsy,* 6 U.S. (2 Cranch) 64, 118 (1804), the Supreme Court stated that "an Act of Congress ought never be construed to violate the law of nations if any other possible construction remains." To what extent is this dictum applicable to conflicts between U.S. trade law and the WTO agreements? In *Mississippi Poultry Association v. Madigan,* 992 F.2d 1359 (5th Cir. 1993), the court considered a poultry inspection law. The court construed the law in a manner so that the law was in violation of the GATT. The court considered but rejected the argument that it should construe the law so as not to violate the GATT. The court reasoned that there was "no supporting authority that the GATT—or for that matter any multilateral trade agreement—falls under the rubric of the law of nations." *Id.* at 1367. Based on the readings in this Chapter, was the court correct?

B. The European Union

The European Court of Justice has held that certain provisions of international agreements, especially the constituent treaties of the EU, can have direct effect within its member states in the sense that they become part of the domestic legal order of the member states without the necessity of implementing legislation. *See Van Gend en Loos v. Nederlandse Administratie der Belastingen,* Case 26/62 [1963] ECR 1. The "direct effects" doctrine under EU law is analogous to the concept of a self-executing treaty under U.S. law. However, it is broader in that regulations as well as some directives (the main form of EU legislation) also have direct effect. In addition, under the EU doctrine, certain international agreements can have direct effect in the sense that they create rights in favor of individuals that may be directly asserted by individuals before member state courts and EU institutions.

In *International Fruit Company v. Produktschap voor Groenten en Fruit*, Cases 21-24/72 [1972] ECR 1219, the ECJ considered the issue of whether the GATT conferred rights on individual citizens of the Community that they could directly invoke before the courts. The ECJ concluded from various aspects of the GATT, including the "great flexibility of its provisions," the possibilities of derogation, and the power of unilateral withdrawal from its obligations, that it was "not capable of conferring on citizens of the Community rights which they can invoke before the courts." *Id.* at 27. In other words, in terms of the criteria for direct effect laid down in earlier cases, the provisions of GATT were insufficiently precise and unconditional in the sense that they permitted the obligations contained therein to be modified, and they allowed for too great a degree of flexibility. What about the status of the WTO agreements? Do they have direct effect? Consider the following.

PROBLEM 3-10

The EU Council passes a regulation that implements new criminal penalties to combat trademark counterfeiting on a commercial scale. The preamble to the statute provides that "the purpose of this law is to comply with Article 61 of TRIPS dealing with criminal enforcement." A private citizen group brings a lawsuit in the ECJ seeking to set aside the EU Regulation on the grounds that it is inconsistent with the WTO agreements. The ECJ can rule on this issue only if TRIPS has direct effect in the EU. What result in this case? See the case below and the accompanying notes.

Portuguese Republic v. Council
European Court of Justice, 1998
Case C-149/96, ECR I-7379

[Portugal sought to annul an EC Council of Ministers' decision providing market access (i.e., lower tariffs) for textile products originating in India and Pakistan. The ECJ rejected Portugal's argument that WTO Agreements could serve as the legal grounds for invalidating a Council decision.]

35) It should also be remembered that according to the general rules of international law there must be bona fide performance of every agreement. Although each contracting party is responsible for executing fully the commitments which it has undertaken it is nevertheless free to determine the legal means appropriate for attaining that end in its legal system, unless the agreement, interpreted in the light of its subject-matter and purpose, itself specifies those means.

36) While it is true that the WTO agreements, as the Portuguese Government observes, differ significantly from the provisions of GATT 1947, in particular by reason of the strengthening of the system of safeguards and the mechanism for resolving disputes, the system resulting from those agreements nevertheless accords considerable importance to negotiation between the parties.

37) Although the main purpose of the mechanism for resolving disputes is in principle, according to Article 3(7) of the Understanding on Rules and Procedures Governing the Settlement of Disputes (Annex 2 to the WTO), to secure the

withdrawal of the measures in question if they are found to be inconsistent with the WTO rules, that understanding provides that where the immediate withdrawal of the measures is impracticable compensation may be granted on an interim basis pending the withdrawal of the inconsistent measure.

38) According to Article 22(1) of that Understanding, compensation is a temporary measure available in the event that the recommendations and rulings of the dispute settlement body provided for in Article 2(1) of that Understanding are not implemented within a reasonable period of time, and Article 22(1) shows a preference for full implementation of a recommendation to bring a measure into conformity with the WTO agreements in question.

39) However, Article 22(2) provides that if the member concerned fails to fulfill its obligation to implement the said recommendations and rulings within a reasonable period of time, it is, if so requested, and on the expiry of a reasonable period at the latest, to enter into negotiations with any party having invoked the dispute settlement procedures, with a view to finding mutually acceptable compensation.

40) Consequently, to require the judicial organs to refrain from applying the rules of domestic law which are inconsistent with the WTO agreements would have the consequence of depriving the legislative or executive organs of the contracting parties of the possibility afforded by Article 22 of that memorandum of entering into negotiated arrangements even on a temporary basis.

41) It follows that the WTO agreements, interpreted in the light of their subject-matter and purpose, do not determine the appropriate legal means of ensuring that they are applied in good faith in the legal order of the contracting parties.

42) As regards, more particularly, the application of the WTO agreements in the Community legal order, it must be noted that, according to its preamble, the agreement establishing the WTO, including the annexes, is still founded, like GATT 1947, on the principle of negotiations with a view to 'entering into reciprocal and mutually advantageous arrangements' and is thus distinguished, from the viewpoint of the Community, from the agreements concluded between the Community and non-member countries which introduce a certain asymmetry of obligations, or create special relations of integration with the Community, such as the agreement which the Court was required to interpret in *Kupferberg*.

43) It is common ground, moreover, that some of the contracting parties, which are among the most important commercial partners of the Community, have concluded from the subject-matter and purpose of the WTO agreements that they are not among the rules applicable by their judicial organs when reviewing the legality of their rules of domestic law.

44) Admittedly, the fact that the courts of one of the parties consider that some of the provisions of the agreement concluded by the Community are of direct application whereas the courts of the other party do not recognize such direct application is not in itself such as to constitute a lack of reciprocity in the implementation of the agreement.

45) However, the lack of reciprocity in that regard on the part of the Community's trading partners, in relation to the WTO agreements which are based on 'reciprocal and mutually advantageous arrangements' and which must ipso facto be distinguished from agreements concluded by the Community, referred to in paragraph 42 of the present judgment, may lead to disuniform application of the WTO rules.

46) To accept that the role of ensuring that Community law complies with those rules devolves directly on the Community judicature would deprive the legislative or executive organs of the Community of the scope for manoeuvre enjoyed by their counterparts in the Community's trading partners.

47) It follows from all those considerations that, having regard to their nature and structure, the WTO agreements are not in principle among the rules in the light of which the Court is to review the legality of measures adopted by the Community institutions.

48) That interpretation corresponds, moreover, to what is stated in the final recital in the preamble to Decision 94/800, according to which 'by its nature, the Agreement establishing the World Trade Organization, including the Annexes thereto, is not susceptible to being directly invoked in Community or Member State courts'.

49) It is only where the Community intended to implement a particular obligation assumed in the context of the WTO, or where the Community measure refers expressly to the precise provisions of the WTO agreements, that it is for the Court to review the legality of the Community measure in question in the light of the WTO rules (*see*, as regards GATT 1947, Fediol, paragraphs 19 to 22, and Nakajima, paragraph 31).

50) It is therefore necessary to examine whether, as the Portuguese Government claims, that is so in the present case.

51) The answer must be in the negative. The contested decision is not designed to ensure the implementation in the Community legal order of a particular obligation assumed in the context of the WTO, nor does it make express reference to any specific provisions of the WTO agreements. Its purpose is merely to approve the Memoranda of Understanding negotiated by the Community with Pakistan and India.

52) It follows from all the foregoing that the claim of the Portuguese Republic that the contested decision was adopted in breach of certain rules and fundamental principles of the WTO is unfounded.

NOTES AND QUESTIONS

1. *Portuguese Republic v. Council* states the general rule on direct effect of the WTO agreements in the EU. In *Brazil—Measures Affecting Desiccated Coconut*, WT/DS22/AB/R, Report of the Appellate Body, adopted on March 20, 1997, the WTO Appellate Body stated (¶¶11-13) that the WTO Agreement is fundamentally different from the GATT 1947 because the WTO agreement is a single-treaty instrument and is therefore an "integrated system" of law. In *Portuguese Republic v. Council*, the ECJ accepted this idea, but still came to the conclusion that as a general rule the WTO agreements do not have direct effect. What reasons did the court give for this conclusion?

2. *Portuguese Republic v. Council* refers to two well-established exceptions to the general rule. The first is where the EU measure in question refers expressly to the precise provisions of a WTO agreement. This is called the *Fediol* doctrine from the case of *Federation de l'Industrie de l' Huilerie de la CEE (Fediol) v. Commission*, Case C-70/87, [1989] ECR I-1781. In this case the court held that it may review the legality of an EC application of countervailing duties in the light of WTO rules. The second exception is where the EU measure in question was intended to implement

a specific WTO obligation. This exception is known as the *Nakajima* doctrine from the case of *Nakajima All Precision Co. v. Council*, Case C-69/89, [1991] ECR-I-2069. In this case, the court ruled that it may review the application of anti-dumping duties in the light of WTO rules. On what grounds did the court reject the application of these exceptions? Do you agree?

3. How easy is it to apply the *Fediol* and *Nakajima* exceptions? What about a case in which the WTO Appellate Body has found that a particular measure of EU law is inconsistent with a WTO agreement and the EU adopts corrective legislation. Can a private company sue to annul the corrective legislation on the basis that it too is inconsistent with a WTO obligation? This was the question in *Leon Van Parys NV v. Belgisch Interventie- en Restitutiebureau (BIRB)*, Case C-377/02, Court of Justice of the European Communities (Grand Chamber), March 1, 2005, available at http://www.curia.eu.int. This case involved the EU regime on the importation of bananas. The ECJ ruled that the *Nakajima* exception did not apply even though the DSB had adopted a decision of the Appellate Body that the corrective legislation was incompatible with WTO rules since the WTO system gives considerable importance and scope to negotiation between the parties to find a solution to specific trade disputes.

4. The ECJ has developed a distinctive doctrine on direct effect in connection with the WTO Agreement on Trade-Related Intellectual Property Rights (TRIPS). First, as stated in Part II of this Chapter, the ECJ ruled in the case, Opinion I/94, [1994] ECR I-5267, that the EC and the member states had joint competence to negotiate and conclude the TRIPS agreement. TRIPS, therefore, was a "mixed" agreement, not one within the exclusive competence of the EC. The problem of direct effect of TRIPS arose when Dior SA, the owner of various trademarks for perfumery products, brought an action in the District Court of the Netherlands alleging that Tuk BV had infringed its trademarks by selling perfumes bearing Dior marks. When the District Court granted Dior provisional relief, the issue arose whether the provisions of TRIPS Article 50.6, which places time and other limits on the granting of provisional measures, had direct effect, and the case was referred to the ECJ for an answer. The ECJ, in *Parfums Dior SA v. Tuk Consultancy BV* and the related case of *Asseco Geruste GmbH, Rob van Dijk and Wilhelm Layher GmbH & Co.*, Joined Cases C-300/98 and C-392/98, [2000] ECJ I-11307, ruled that (1) the ECJ has jurisdiction to interpret the TRIPS agreement; (2) TRIPS does not grant individuals rights upon which they may rely directly before the courts under EU law; and (3) EU law neither requires nor forbids that the legal orders of member states accord rights to individuals under TRIPS upon which they may rely directly in the legal order of the member states. Thus TRIPS does not have direct effect under EU law, but a member state may grant TRIPS direct effect under its own law. This rather clumsy doctrine involves a danger that the different member states may interpret TRIPS differently. But in *Hermes International v. FHT Marketing Choice BV*, Case C-53/96, [1998] ECR I-3603, the ECJ ruled that TRIPS provisions that fall within the competence of both national law and EU law should be interpreted "uniformly," thus ensuring that the ECJ will have the last word. This doctrine is known as the principle of consistent interpretation of trade agreements, an important principle of EU law.

5. In *FIAMM (Fabbrica italiana accumulatori motocarri Montecchio SpA) and Giorgio Fedon*, Joined Cases C-120/06 P and C-121/06 P, the ECJ, Grand Chamber, dismissed appeals by two companies seeking compensation from the EU for damages suffered because the DSB of the WTO in 1999 authorized the United States to levy USD

191.4 million in customs duties on EU imports in the United States in retaliation for the fact that the EU did not comply with a ruling of the WTO Appellate Body in the case *European Communities—Regime for the Importation, Sale and Distribution of Bananas*, WT/DS27/AB/R, Report of the Appellate Body, adopted on September 25, 1997. The United States imposed 100 percent ad valorem import duties on a variety of products produced by FIAMM and Fedon, including batteries, bed linen, and bath products. The ECJ rejected this claim (¶111) for compensation on the grounds that neither WTO agreements nor a decision of the DSB "are in principle among the rules in the light of which the Court is to review the legality of measures adopted by Community institutions." The ECJ cited *Portugal v. Council* in support of this ruling. The Court also stated (¶119) as justification for its ruling that "to accept that Community courts have the direct responsibility for ensuring that Community law complies with the WTO rules would effectively deprive the Community's legislative or executive organs of the scope for manoeuvre enjoyed by their counterparts in the Community's trading partners." Do you agree? Would a business be able to recover damages from the U.S. government for failure to implement a WTO ruling?

NOTE ON THE RELATIONSHIP BETWEEN THE INTERNATIONAL AND DOMESTIC LEGAL ORDERS

We have examined in this Chapter the relationship between international law and domestic law. An important related issue is the relationship between the international and domestic (sometimes called "municipal") legal orders. Are these two separate legal orders or systems, and what is their relationship? A full examination of this issue is beyond the scope of this book but we touch upon it briefly here. Legal theory commonly uses two basic solutions to explain the relationship involved. The first solution, called monism, holds that international law and domestic law are part of the same legal order, and, therefore, international law should be directly applicable in the domestic legal order and, as higher law, should prevail over inconsistent domestic laws. The second solution, known as dualism, holds that international and domestic law are separate systems of law, stem from different sources, and have different subject matters, and each system is independent and supreme in its own sphere, so a national court must apply domestic law in case of a conflict between the two systems.[2]

Most states apply a mixture of these two theories each according to its own particular constitutional structure. In this Chapter we have presented the constitutional structures of the United States and the European Union in this regard, because these two WTO members are very important and because each exhibits particularly complex legal doctrines to explain the relationship between the international law of the WTO agreements and their domestic legal orders.

Most WTO members have considerably less complex legal doctrines to explain the relationship between their domestic law and WTO law. In most states, the government controls the domestic lawmaking process, so the implementation of WTO agreements is virtually automatic once the government of the state accedes to the

---

2. For a more complete explanation, see Ian Brownlie, *Principles of Public International Law* 31-51 (7th ed. 2008) (Oxford University Press 2008).

WTO or the particular international agreement. Whether a WTO agreement has direct effect or supersedes existing domestic law, however, is quite another matter. As we have seen in this Chapter, neither the United States nor the EU (with certain exceptions) gives direct effect to WTO agreements or WTO dispute settlement decisions.

Does this reluctance to give direct effect hold true in other states? This would, of course, depend on the constitutional law of the particular state involved.

Some WTO members, in notable contrast to the United States and the EU, provide in their national constitutions that international agreements and international law prevail over inconsistent national laws. The Constitution of Costa Rica (1949, as amended) Article 7, provides, for example, that "Public treaties, international agreements, and concordats duly approved by the Legislative Assembly have a higher authority than the laws upon their enactment or from the day that they designate." Despite this and similar provisions, we are skeptical that any WTO member would give direct effect to WTO agreements or decisions. A case in point is Japan, which has a constitutional provision that holds that treaties and customary international law are supreme,[3] so that international agreements automatically prevail over inconsistent domestic law. This provision was tested in the *Kyoto Necktie* case,[4] which involved a provision of the 1976 Japan Raw Silk Stabilization Law that established a price stabilization scheme for domestically produced raw silk. This law restricted the import of raw silk and designated a government agency, the Silk Business Agency, as the sole importer of raw silk. Japanese fabric producers challenged this law as inconsistent with GATT Article XVII:1(a), which requires state-trading agencies to operate on the basis of commercial considerations only in terms of price, quality, and availability. The Japan fabric producers argued that since the Silk Business Agency was a state-trading agency, the import and sales price restrictions of this agency were in violation of the GATT. The Kyoto District Court, however, refused to grant direct effect or to recognize the supremacy of the GATT rule, stating that "it cannot be held that the legislation in question is contrary to the GATT and null and void."[5] The Kyoto court's decision was appealed both to the Osaka High Court and to the Supreme Court of Japan. In both instances the appeal was summarily dismissed.[6] Thus, as a general rule, despite any legal provisions to the contrary, all WTO members can be expected to apply a dualist approach to the relationship between WTO law and domestic laws—that is, WTO and domestic laws are separate legal orders with domestic law prevailing in a domestic legal system in case of conflict.

---

3. Kenpo (Constitution) of Japan Article 98(2).

4. *Endo v. Japan*, 530 Hanrei Taimuzu 265 (Kyoto District Court, June 29, 1984).

5. *Id.*

6. Osaka High Court, Judgment of Nov. 25, 1986, 634 Hanrei 186; Supreme Court, Judgment of Feb. 6, 1990, 36 Shomu Geppo 2242.

4 The Core Principles of the WTO: Most Favored Nation and National Treatment

I. Introduction

One of the principal goals of the WTO is to promote a fair and neutral system of multilateral trade. In this Chapter we examine two important principles of non-discriminatory treatment that are central to achieving this goal.

The first is the well-known but widely misunderstood "Most Favored Nation" (MFN) principle. This is sometimes taken as a principle of favoritism, but rather it is a principle of non-discrimination. MFN in the context of the WTO requires that a WTO member must give equal treatment concerning trade advantages to all other members; no WTO member can discriminate in favor of or against any other WTO member. The second core principle is "National Treatment," which prohibits a member from discriminating against other members in favor of its own domestic industry. MFN is a rule of external non-discrimination whereas National Treatment is a rule of internal non-discrimination. Together, these two principles form two of the most important pillars of the modern multilateral trading system.

These two principles were first expressed in the GATT 1947, but with the establishment of the WTO, they are now also featured not only in the GATT 1994, but also in the General Agreement on Trade in Services (Articles II and XVII) and in the Agreement on Trade-Related Intellectual Property Rights (Articles 3 and 4). However, a great deal of the jurisprudence concerning these principles was developed in connection with the GATT in the nearly fifty years prior to the establishment of the WTO. As a result, most of the cases that we examine in this Chapter concern trade in goods, but the learning in these cases is immediately transferable to the other areas of trade.

II. The Most Favored Nation Principle

The MFN principle was first enshrined in Article I of the GATT 1947:

Article I General Most-Favoured-Nation Treatment

1. With respect to customs duties and charges of any kind imposed on or in connection with importation or exportation or imposed on the international transfer of payments for imports or exports, and with respect to the method of levying such duties and charges, and with respect to all rules and formalities in connection with importation and exportation, and with respect to all matters referred to in paragraphs 2 and 4 of Article III, any advantage, favour, privilege or immunity granted by any contracting party to any product originating in or destined for any other country shall be accorded immediately and unconditionally to the like product originating in for destined or the territories of all other contracting parties.

Under Article I:1, the scope of application of MFN encompasses

- border measures applied at a point of entry that are fiscal (e.g., customs duties) or non-fiscal (e.g., methods for levying duties, rules, and formalities);
- internal measures that are fiscal (e.g., internal taxes) or non-fiscal (e.g., internal laws and regulations).

Internal measures apply to imported goods once they have cleared customs and have entered the internal market. The application of MFN to internal measures is made clear by the reference above to "all matters referred to in paragraphs 2 and 4 of Article III." GATT Article III:2 refers to internal taxation and Article III:4 refers to internal regulations. Although Article III sets forth the National Treatment principle, the references in Article I to Article III:2 and III:4 have been interpreted to mean that MFN applies to internal measures.

Turning to the substantive aspects of MFN, we can see that there are four separate elements: (1) a*ny* trade advantage given by a contracting party to a product originating in (2) *any other country* must be (3) *immediately and unconditionally* given to (4) *like products* originating in WTO member states.

As an example of how Article I operates, suppose that Country A grants Country B an advantage related to the trade in goods. The advantage can be in the form of a border measure or an internal regulation that is fiscal or non-fiscal in nature. If A and C are both WTO members, then under Article I, A must immediately and unconditionally grant the same advantage to C.

The advantages of MFN to the multilateral trading system are several: (1) It protects the value of trade concessions against gradual erosion through the granting of special favors; (2) it engenders and promotes free and fair competition; (3) it guards against corruption of the multilateral trading system (through the ability of members to buy special favors or to single out nations for less than equal treatment); (4) it respects the idea of the sovereign equality of nations; (5) it multiplies the effects of trade concessions by spreading them automatically to all members; and (6) it fosters simplicity of administration.

The disadvantages are that (1) MFN encourages and even fosters free riders, and (2) there is no way to guarantee strict reciprocity of concessions—to ensure that a party is not giving up more than it is getting in return. In order to counter these disadvantages, some have called for making MFN conditional on approximately equal concessions by all members. But this would turn the WTO into a complex structure of thousands of interlocking bilateral agreements whose administration would be impossible.

PROBLEM 4-1

The United States has entered into a bilateral trading agreement with Country Z, which is not a member of the WTO. Under the agreement, the United States agrees to provide a 50 percent rebate of all U.S. customs duties and tariffs paid on a popular type of tropical fruit for the first five years of the trade agreement. Led by Brazil, a group of South American countries, all WTO members, now approaches the USTR for the same treatment. The USTR says, "Wait a minute, Z is not even a member of the WTO. What obligation do we have to extend benefits given to Z to you?" Review GATT Article I:1 above. How might this application of the MFN principle serve as an inducement to join the WTO?

PROBLEM 4-2

Several developing nations in Africa have entered into a free trade agreement to provide "WTO plus" treatment to all members of the group. The members will enjoy zero tariffs for intra-group trade but all goods from members outside the group (such as the United States) will be subject to regular GATT bound tariffs of each nation. Do these nations have an obligation under the MFN principle to extend the "WTO plus" treatment of zero tariffs to all other WTO members? *See* GATT Article XXIV(5).

PROBLEM 4-3

France passes a new law providing that all exports of caviar to Russia must be processed through the Port of Marseilles in Southern France. Exports of caviar to other countries can proceed through regular channels. The new law causes a delay in shipments of exports to Russia of up to three weeks due to additional paperwork and other delays due to insufficient capacity in Marseilles. Is the new law consistent with GATT Article I:1?

PROBLEM 4-4

You are an advocate for developing countries and believe that your clients deserve special and preferential treatment within the WTO to compensate for their lower level of economic development. However, the MFN principle might operate as a barrier to the WTO aim of preferential treatment for developing countries. How so? This was true early in the history of the GATT. What must be done to obtain preferential treatment for developing countries?

A.   Scope of the MFN Obligations

One of the most important issues concerning the MFN principle is the scope of its application. The materials below explore this issue.

PROBLEM 4-5

Assume that South Africa has instituted a special trade program with
Germany, the United Kingdom, and France concerning the sale of fiber optic
wire used for high-speed telecommunications and Internet transmissions. Fiber
optic wire imported into South Africa from all countries is subject to the same
tariffs and duties under rates required by South Africa's GATT commitments.
However, once all customs duties are paid, fiber optic wire from only these three
countries are entitled to a rebate of 50 percent on all sales and excise taxes paid
when sold to various local Internet and technology companies for installation.
The United States argues that this tax rebate law is a violation of the MFN principle. South Africa replies that the MFN principle deals with differential treatment in the imposition of tariffs at the border and that this program, imposing
sales and excise taxes after the goods have cleared customs, has nothing to do
with border measures. What is the result? To answer this problem, see GATT
Article I, Article III:2, and Article III:4, and *Belgian Family Allowances* below.

Belgian Family Allowances (Allocations Familiales)
Report of the GATT Panel, adopted on November 7, 1952
GATT B.I.S.D. (1st Supp.) 59

1. The Panel on Complaints examined the legal issues involved in the complaint submitted by the Norwegian and Danish delegations regarding the application of the Belgian law on the levy of a charge on foreign goods purchased by
public bodies when these goods originated in a country whose system of family
allowances did not meet specific requirements.

2. After examining the legal provisions regarding the methods of collection of that charge, the Panel came to the conclusion that the 7.5 percent levy
was collected only on products purchased by public bodies for their own use
and not on imports as such, and that the levy was charged, not at the time of
importation, but when the purchase price was paid by the public body. In those
circumstances, it would appear that the levy was to be treated as an "internal charge" within the meaning of paragraph 2 of Article III of the General
Agreement, and not as an import charge within the meaning of paragraph 2 of
Article II.

3. According to the provisions of paragraph 1 of Article I of the General
Agreement, any advantage, favor, privilege or immunity granted by Belgium to
any product originating in the territory of any country with respect to all matters referred to in paragraph 2 of Article III shall be granted immediately and
unconditionally to the like product originating in the territories of all contracting parties. Belgium has granted exemptions from the levy under consideration to
products purchased by public bodies when they originate in Luxemburg and the
Netherlands, as well as in France, Italy, Sweden and the United Kingdom. If the
General Agreement were definitively in force in accordance with Article XXVI, it
is clear that that exemption would have to be granted unconditionally to all other
contracting parties (including Denmark and Norway). The consistency or otherwise
of the system of family allowances in force in the territory of a given contracting
party with the requirements of the Belgian law would be irrelevant in this respect,
and the Belgian legislation would have to be amended insofar as it introduced a
discrimination between countries having a given system of family allowances and

those which had a different system or no system at all, and made the granting of the exemption dependent on certain conditions.

[The Panel concluded that Belgium's tax treatment was inconsistent with GATT Article I:1.]

NOTES AND QUESTIONS

1. *Belgian Family Allowances* helped to establish two basic principles of GATT jurisprudence: MFN applies to internal measures (in this case the 7.5 percent levy), and the same treatment extended to France and others (foregoing of the levy) must be extended unconditionally to all other WTO members. The unconditional extension of MFN must occur even if Norway or Denmark did not have a system of family allowances. While *Belgian Family Allowances* interprets the unconditional extension of MFN to mean without *any* conditions, it is also possible to interpret this requirement to prohibit any *additional* conditions beyond what is required of the original recipient of the benefit or privilege. *See* Matsushita, Schoenbaum, and Mavroidis *The World Trade Organization: Law, Practice and Policy* 214-225 (2d ed. 2006).

2. Can the MFN obligation be satisfied by separate but equal treatment? In the case of *European Communities—Regime for the Importation, Sale and Distribution of Bananas*, WT/DS27/AB/R, Report of the Appellate Body, adopted on September 25, 1997, the EC was operating two different import regimes for bananas: one for banana imports for so-called ACP countries (African-Caribbean-Pacific countries, mainly former colonies of EC countries) and another for banana imports from other WTO members. The EC argued that the first regime was operated on an MFN basis as required by the WTO Licensing Agreement, while the other regime was operated on an MFN basis with respect to the GATT. In effect, the EC argument was that MFN treatment applies separately to each of the WTO agreements. The Appellate Body rejected this argument as follows:

> The issue here is not whether the European Communities is correct in stating that two separate import regimes exist for bananas, but whether the existence of two, or more, separate EC import regimes is of any relevance for the application of the non-discrimination provisions of the GATT 1994. The essence of the non-discrimination obligations is that like products should be treated equally, irrespective of their origin. If, by choosing a different legal basis for imposing import restrictions, or by applying different tariff rates, a Member could avoid the application of the non-discrimination provisions to the imports of like products from different Members, the object and purpose of the non-discrimination provisions would be defeated.

Id. at ¶191.

3. In the *United States—Denial of Most-Favoured-Nation Treatment as to Non-Rubber Footwear from Brazil*, GATT B.I.S.D. (39th Supp.) 128, Report of the GATT Panel, adopted on June 19, 1992, the GATT panel ruled that the United States was in violation of Article I with respect to the method of revoking countervailing duties levied on the imports of subsidized products. (A countervailing duty is a tax levied to offset the effect of a subsidy or grant provided by the government to the exporter.) The United States employed two different methods: Certain WTO developing countries benefited from automatic backdating of revocation orders, while this was not extended to revocation orders involving other countries that

were WTO members. What is the lesson here about the scope of Article I? Can an "advantage" be purely procedural?

PROBLEM 4-6

Assume that China enters into a bilateral trading agreement with Germany, covering technology transfer and trade in high-technology goods. One of the provisions of the China-Germany agreement provides that in exchange for Germany's entry into the agreement, China will provide a heightened level of enforcement for all intellectual property rights in China owned by German companies or citizens, through the new China-Germany Intellectual Property Enforcement Task Force. You are the Assistant USTR for China Affairs. You see your counterpart from China at a WTO conference in Geneva and you say, "U.S. companies are complaining to me all the time about rampant piracy of their intellectual property rights. You must extend the same level of increased protection immediately and unconditionally to us." China's Assistant Trade Minister replies, "Of course. Just sign a bilateral agreement covering technology with us." Does the United States have to sign an agreement to get increased enforcement or must China provide the same enforcement without any agreement? This turns on the meaning of the MFN requirement that a benefit must be extended immediately and *unconditionally* to other WTO members. Does "unconditionally" mean that China must extend the same treatment without the signing of a trade agreement by the United States? *See* TRIPS, Article 4. Also review note 1 above.

B. The "Like Product" Issue

The MFN obligation applies only to "like" products. If two products are not "like," then differential treatment may be lawful.

Treatment by Germany of Imports of Sardines
Report of the GATT Panel, adopted October 31, 1952
GATT B.I.S.D. (1st Supp.) 53

I. INTRODUCTION

1. The Panel examined the factual situation resulting from (a) the imposition, as from October 1, 1951, of an import duty of 14 percent on preparations of clupea pilchardus [European sardines] as compared with a duty of 20 percent for clupea harengus [Atlantic Herring] and 25 percent for clupea sprattus [European Sprat], (b) the application as from November 16, 1951, of a charge equivalent to the German turnover tax at a rate of 4 percent on preparations of clupea pilchardus and of 6 percent on preparations of clupea sprattus and clupea harengus, and (c) the removal of quantitative restrictions on preparations of clupea pilchardus while these restrictions were maintained on the preparations of the other varieties. It then considered whether the aforementioned measures taken by the Government of the Federal Republic of Germany constituted, within the terms of Article XXIII:1(a), a failure by that Government to carry out its obligations under the Agreement. Having come to the conclusion that the evidence produced by the parties was not

such as to warrant a finding that the measures taken by the Government of the Federal Republic of Germany were in conflict with the provisions of Article I:1 or of Article XIII:1 of the General Agreement, the Panel then examined whether those measures had nullified or impaired the tariff concessions granted by Germany to Norway on sub-items 1604 C 1 (d)-sprats (clupea sprattus) and 1604 C 1 (e) herring, and agreed on the text of a recommendation which, in its opinion, would best assist the German and Norwegian Governments to arrive at a satisfactory adjustment of the question submitted by Norway to the CONTRACTING PARTIES.

II.   FACTS OF THE CASE

2. Prior to the tariff negotiations conducted at Torquay between Germany and Norway within the framework of the General Agreement, canned products of clupea sprattus and clupea harengus enjoyed the same customs treatment in Germany as the canned products of clupea pilchardus. This equality of treatment had been guaranteed by notes exchanged between the two Governments in 1925 and 1927.

3. The Torquay negotiations were conducted on the basis of the draft of a new German Customs Tariff, following the nomenclature elaborated in 1949 by the European Customs Union Study Group. The canned products of clupea pilchardus, clupea sprattus and clupea harengus were classified under separate sub-items of item 1604 C 1, but the duties proposed were uniformly at 30 percent *ad valorem*.

III.   CONSISTENCY OF THE GERMAN MEASURES WITH THE PROVISIONS OF ARTICLE I:1 AND ARTICLE XIII:1

10. The Panel considered whether, by failing to extend to particular preparations of the clupeoid family, of interest to Norway, the advantages, favors and privileges granted by Germany to other preparations of the same family, which are of interest to Portugal, Germany had acted inconsistently with the provisions of paragraph 1 of Article I and of paragraph 1 of Article XIII of the General Agreement.

11. The Panel noted that the difference of treatment was not based on the origin of the goods but on the assumption that preparations of clupea pilchardus, clupea sprattus and clupea harengus are not "like products" within the terms of Article I and Article XIII.

12. The Panel did not feel that it was called upon to give a definition of "like products" or that it was necessary for the consideration of the Norwegian complaint to decide whether the preparations of clupea pilchardus, clupea sprattus and clupea harengus had to be generally treated as "like products". Although the Norwegian complaint rested to a large extent on the concept of "like products" as set out in the Agreement and the German reply addressed itself also to that concept, the Panel was satisfied that it would be sufficient to consider whether in the conduct of the negotiations at Torquay the two parties agreed expressly or tacitly to treat these preparations as if they were "like products" for the purposes of the General Agreement.

13. The evidence produced before the Panel shows that in the course of the Torquay negotiations the German delegation had consistently treated the preparation of the various types of clupeae as if they were separate products; the wording of item 1604 and its sub-items was not objected to by other delegations and separate

negotiations were in effect conducted on the various sub-items. The Norwegian delegation tried without success to obtain that preparations of sprats and herrings should be treated as sardines for marketing purposes and, failing that, was content with assurances that equality of treatment in customs matters would be continued. It would seem, therefore, that the Norwegian Government, in order to secure the extension of advantages or privileges granted to preparations of clupea pilchardus to preparations of clupea sprattus and clupea harengus, relied on assurances which it considered it had obtained in the course of the negotiation rather than on the automatic operation of the most-favoured-nation clause.

15. The examination of the evidence submitted to the Panel drew the conclusion that no sufficient evidence had been presented to show that the German Government had failed to carry out its obligations under Article I:1 and Article XIII:1.

IV.   Nullification or Impairment of the Concessions Granted to Norway on Preparations of Clupea Sprattus and Clupea Harengus

16. The Panel next considered whether the injury which the Government of Norway claimed it had suffered represented a nullification or an impairment of a benefit accruing to Norway directly or indirectly under the General Agreement and was therefore subject to the provisions of Article XXIII. It agreed that such impairment would exist if the action of the German Government, which resulted in upsetting the competitive relationship between preparations of clupea pilchardus and preparations of the other varieties of the clupeoid family could not reasonably have been anticipated by the Norwegian Government at the time it negotiated for tariff reductions on preparations of clupea sprattus and clupea harengus. The Panel concluded that the Government of Norway had reason to assume, during these negotiations that preparations of the type of clupeae in which they were interested would not be less favorably treated than other preparations of the same family and that this situation would not be modified by unilateral action of the German Government. In reaching this conclusion, the Panel was influenced in particular by the following circumstances:

(a) the products of the various varieties of clupeae are closely related and are considered by many interested parties as directly competitive;

(b) that both parties agreed that the question of the equality of treatment was discussed in the course of the Torquay negotiations; and

(c) although no conclusive evidence was produced as to the scope and tenor of the assurances or statements which may have been given or made in the course of these discussions, it is reasonable to assume that the Norwegian delegation, in assessing the value of the concessions offered by Germany regarding preparations of clupeae and in offering counter concessions, had taken into account the advantages resulting from the continuation of the system of equality which had prevailed ever since 1925.

18. In the light of the considerations set out above, the Panel suggests to the CONTRACTING PARTIES that it would be appropriate for the CONTRACTING

PARTIES to make a recommendation to Germany and Norway in accordance with the first sentence of paragraph 2 of Article XXIII. This recommendation should aim at restoring, as far as practicable, the competitive relationship which existed at the time when the Norwegian Government negotiated at Torquay and which that Government could reasonably expect to be continued.

NOTES AND QUESTIONS

1. *Germany Sardines* establishes the basic GATT approach that in determining "like" products in Article I cases, the principal criterion is tariff classification. If two products are classified under the same tariff line, then they are "like" products. *See* ¶13 of the Report. Germany, however, consistently treated the different products under different tariff lines, see *id.*, and so no like products were involved. *See* ¶15.

2. If the fish were not "like" products, differential tariff and quota treatment are permitted. Why then did the panel rule against Germany? What was the basis of the decision? *See* ¶16.

PROBLEM 4-7

Two goods, A and B, have virtually identical physical characteristics. However, A is produced in developing countries using a costly low-technology method with high physical-labor inputs while B is produced in developed countries using a cost efficient high-technology method with little physical labor. Can these products be differentiated based on the "like product" test on the basis that the production processes are different? Review the *Belgian Family Allowances* case above.

C.   De Facto Discrimination

Suppose that a law, as written, is neutral and non-discriminatory on its face. As applied, however, the law has discriminatory effects. Is such a law in violation of the MFN principle in the GATT?

Canada — Certain Measures Affecting the Automotive Industry
Report of the WTO Appellate Body, adopted on June 19, 2000
WT/DS139, 142/AB/R

[Canada imposed a tariff of 6.1 percent on imported automobiles but waived this tax under certain conditions set forth in the Motor Vehicles Tariff Order of 1998 (MVTO) and the Special Remission Orders (SROs). These conditions all pertained to certain performance requirements of the manufacturers, such as a ratio of net sales of automobiles manufactured in Canada to net sales of all automobiles, produced locally or imported, sold in Canada in a year. The conditions also applied to local content value requirements, i.e., a certain percentage of the inputs of automobiles manufactured had to be of Canadian origin. In order to meet the conditions for the waiver of the tariff, a manufacturer had to set up a manufacturing facility in Canada. Canada designated certain manufacturers as eligible to receive duty free treatment but closed the list of eligible manufacturers as of January 1, 1998. Several member countries challenged this scheme as inconsistent with the MFN principle contained in GATT Article I:1. The panel found a violation of Article I:1, which Canada appealed to the Appellate Body, which in turn issued the opinion below.]

70. In examining the measure in issue, we note that the import duty exemption is afforded by Canada to imports of some, but not all, motor vehicles. We observe, first of all, that the Canadian Customs Tariff provides that a motor vehicle normally enters Canada at an MFN tariff rate of 6.1 percent. This is also the bound *ad valorem* rate in Canada's WTO Schedule of Concessions. The MVTO 1998 and the SROs modify this rate by providing the import duty exemption for motor vehicles imported by certain manufacturers meeting certain ratio requirements and CVA requirements. The MVTO 1998 accords the import duty exemption in the form of a "reduced rate of customs duty", established in the amended Canadian Customs Tariff as "free". The SROs accord the import duty exemption in the form of a full duty "remission".

71. Although the measure on its face imposes no formal restriction on the *origin* of the imported motor vehicle, the Panel found that, in practice, major automotive firms in Canada import only their own make of motor vehicle and those of related companies. Thus, according to the Panel,

> General Motors in Canada imports only GM motor vehicles and those of its affiliates; Ford in Canada imports only Ford motor vehicles and those of its affiliates; the same is true of Chrysler and of Volvo. These four companies all have qualified as beneficiaries of the import duty exemption. In contrast, other motor vehicle companies in Canada, such as Toyota, Nissan, Honda, Mazda, Subaru, Hyundai, Volkswagen and BMW, all of which also import motor vehicles only from related companies, do not benefit from the import duty exemption.

72. Therefore, the Panel considered that, in practice, a motor vehicle imported into Canada is granted the "advantage" of the import duty exemption only if it originates in one of a small number of countries in which an exporter of motor vehicles is affiliated with a manufacturer/importer in Canada that has been designated as eligible to import motor vehicles duty-free under the MVTO 1998 or under an SRO.

73. Since 1989, no manufacturer not already benefiting from the import duty exemption on motor vehicles has been able to qualify under the MVTO 1998 or under an SRO. The list of manufacturers eligible for the import duty exemption was closed by Canada in 1989 in fulfillment of Canada's obligations under the Canada-United States Free Trade Agreement.

74. In sum, while the Canadian Customs Tariff normally allows a motor vehicle to enter Canada at the MFN duty rate of 6.1 percent, the same motor vehicle has the "advantage" of entering Canada duty-free when imported by a designated manufacturer under the MVTO 1998 or under the SROs.

75. In determining whether this measure is consistent with Article I:1 of the GATT 1994, we begin our analysis, as always, by examining the words of the treaty. Article I:1 states, in pertinent part:

> With respect to customs duties and charges of any kind imposed on or in connection with importation or exportation . . . *any* advantage, favour, privilege or immunity granted by any Member to any product originating in or destined for any other country shall be accorded *immediately* and *unconditionally* to the *like product* originating in or destined for the territories of *all other Members.* (emphasis added)

76. The applicability of certain elements of Article I:1 is not in dispute in this case. First, the parties do not dispute that the import duty exemption is an "advantage, favour, privilege or immunity granted by any Member to any product". Second, it is not disputed that some, but not all, motor vehicles imported from certain Members are accorded the import duty exemption, while some, but not all, like motor vehicles imported from certain other Members are not. Third, the Panel's interpretation that the term "unconditionally" refers to advantages conditioned on the "situation or conduct" of exporting countries has not been appealed.

77. One main issue remains in dispute: has the import duty exemption, accorded by the measure to motor vehicles originating in some countries, in which affiliates of certain designated manufacturers under the measure are present, also been accorded to like motor vehicles from all other Members, in accordance with Article I:1 of the GATT 1994?

78. In approaching this question, we observe first that the words of Article I:1 do not restrict its scope only to cases in which the failure to accord an "advantage" to like products of all other Members appears on the face of the measure, or can be demonstrated on the basis of the words of the measure. Neither the words "*de jure*" nor "*de facto*" appear in Article I:1. Nevertheless, we observe that Article I:1 does not cover only "in law", or *de jure*, discrimination. As several GATT panel reports confirmed, Article I:1 covers also "in fact", or *de facto*, discrimination. Like the Panel, we cannot accept Canada's argument that Article I:1 does not apply to measures which, on their face, are "origin-neutral".

79. We note next that Article I:1 requires that "*any advantage*, favour, privilege or immunity granted by any Member to *any product* originating in or destined for any other country shall be accorded immediately and unconditionally to the like product originating in or destined for the territories of *all other Members.*" (emphasis added) The words of Article I:1 refer not to some advantages granted "with respect to" the subjects that fall within the defined scope of the Article, but to "*any advantage*"; not to some products, but to "*any product*"; and not to like products from some other Members, but to like products originating in or destined for "*all other*" Members.

80. We note also the Panel's conclusion that, in practice, a motor vehicle imported into Canada is granted the "advantage" of the import duty exemption only if it originates in one of a small number of countries in which an exporter of motor vehicles is affiliated with a manufacturer/importer in Canada that has been designated as eligible to import motor vehicles duty-free under the MVTO 1998 or under an SRO.

81. Thus, from both the text of the measure and the Panel's conclusions about the practical operation of the measure, it is apparent to us that "[w]ith respect to customs duties . . . imposed on or in connection with importation . . . ," Canada has granted an "advantage" to some products from some Members that Canada has not "accorded immediately and unconditionally" to "like" products "originating in or destined for the territories of *all other Members.*" (emphasis added) And

this, we conclude, is not consistent with Canada's obligations under Article I:1 of the GATT 1994.

82. The context of Article I:1 within the GATT 1994 supports this conclusion. Apart from Article I:1, several "MFN-type" clauses dealing with varied matters are contained in the GATT 1994. The very existence of these other clauses demonstrates the pervasive character of the MFN principle of non-discrimination.

84. The object and purpose of Article I:1 supports our interpretation. The object and purpose is to prohibit discrimination among like products originating in or destined for different countries. The prohibition of discrimination in Article I:1 also serves as an incentive for concessions, negotiated reciprocally, to be extended to all other Members on an MFN basis.

85. The measure maintained by Canada accords the import duty exemption to certain motor vehicles entering Canada from certain countries. These privileged motor vehicles are imported by a limited number of designated manufacturers who are required to meet certain performance conditions. In practice, this measure does not accord the same import duty exemption immediately and unconditionally to like motor vehicles of *all* other Members, as required under Article I:1 of the GATT 1994. The advantage of the import duty exemption is accorded to some motor vehicles originating in certain countries without being accorded to like motor vehicles from *all* other Members. Accordingly, we find that this measure is not consistent with Canada's obligations under Article I:1 of the GATT 1994.

NOTES AND QUESTIONS

1. What was the essence of the violation in *Canada—Autos*? In a similar case, *Indonesia—Certain Measures Affecting the Automotive Industry*, WT/DS 54, 55, 59, 64/R, Report of the Panel, adopted on July 23, 1998, a WTO panel considered the legality of certain exemptions from Indonesian customs duties and internal taxes that were conditional and de facto available only to imports of motor vehicles (so-called National Cars made with Indonesian components) from a Korean company that was a joint venture partner with the Indonesian auto industry. The issue was whether the measure violated the MFN obligation in Article I. The panel found a violation ruling as follows:

14.143 The GATT case law is clear to the effect that any such advantage (here tax and customs duty benefits) cannot be made conditional on any criteria that is not related to the imported product itself.

14.145 [I]t appears that the design and structure of the June 1996 car programme is such as to allow situations where another Member's like product to a National Car imported by PT PTN from Korea will be subject to much higher duties and sales taxes than those imposed on such National Cars. For example, customs duties as high as 200 percent can be imposed on finished motor vehicles while an imported National Car benefits from a 0 percent customs duty. No taxes are imposed on a National Car while an imported like motor vehicle from another Member would be subject to a 35 percent sales tax. The distinction depends on whether or not PT TPN had made a "deal" with that exporting company to produce that National Car, and is covered by the authorization of June 1996 with specifications that correspond to those of the Kia car produced only in Korea. In the GATT/WTO, the right of Members cannot be made dependent upon, conditional on or even affected by, any private contractual obligations in place. The existence of these conditions is inconsistent with the provisions of Article I:1 which provides that tax and customs duty benefits accorded to products of one Member (here on Korean products) be accorded to imported like products from other Members "immediately and unconditionally".

What was the basis of the violation in *Indonesia—Autos*? Does the difference in the reasoning in this case compared to *Canada—Autos* depend on the interpretation of the word "unconditional" in Article I? Does the term "unconditional" mean that the availability of a tariff rate cannot be made subject to conditions, on the one hand, or simply that such conditions, although permissible, cannot result in de facto discrimination? If the latter interpretation is correct, can you think of any conditions that would not be de facto discriminatory?

2. On the issue of discrimination, two possible elements may be used to establish a violation: (1) evidence of intent (aim or purpose) to discriminate and (2) evidence of discriminatory effect (differential impact). In interpreting Article I, the Appellate Body appears to focus on discriminatory effect. Should intent also play a role? With respect to discrimination on the face of a measure, both effect and intent are clear. For example, a measure may provide for a 20 percent tariff on a category of products from Country A, while the same category of products from Country B is subject only to a tariff of 5 percent. Facial discrimination is relatively easy to spot. De facto discrimination may occur, however, with respect to a measure that is origin-neutral on its face. How should effect be evaluated in such a case? What approach was used in the *Canada Autos* case? Read ¶¶79 and 80 closely. Do they reflect slightly different approaches to the problem? Does not ¶79 focus on individual product discrimination, while ¶80 keys on the discriminatory effect as a whole?

D.   Exceptions to MFN Obligations

The MFN obligation is subject to several important exceptions under the GATT. Anti-dumping or countervailing duties under GATT Article VI may be levied only on goods from certain targeted countries, when warranted, without regard to Article I. Discrimination is permitted, allowing some targeting in connection with applying safeguard trade restrictions under Article XIX and balance of payments trade restrictions under Article XIV. National security trade restrictions under Article XXI may also be targeted. Article IX of the Agreement Establishing the WTO permits members to request authorization for a waiver, on a temporary basis, of WTO obligations, including the MFN obligation.

GATT Article I:2, I:3, and I:4 allow special treatment for trade with certain current and former colonies and associated states, but these preferences have largely given way to two important exceptions: (1) preferences for developing countries under the Enabling Clause and (2) preferences for customs unions and free trade areas. The Enabling Clause allows countries to give preferential treatment to developing countries without having to extend the same treatment to all other WTO members. Treatment of developing countries under the Enabling Clause is an important topic that we cover in detail in Chapter 9.

The exceptions for Preferential Trade Areas merit special discussion. Both customs unions and free trade areas permit the free movement of goods, without the payment of tariffs, among their members. Other areas of trade, such as intellectual property rights, services, and capital are often also included within the scope of these free trade arrangements. Countries establish a customs union or free trade area with a special level of trade preferences for the mutual benefit of their members, which usually have friendly political relations and share common economic goals. However, the benefits of free trade among the members of a customs union or free trade area would be lost if the members had to extend the same treatment to all WTO members under the MFN principle. For this reason, a series of special exceptions were created to the MFN principle. Under GATT Article XXIV, it is possible for countries to establish a customs union or free trade area without extending the same trading benefits to non-members. GATS Article V contains a similar exception to MFN for services for customs unions and free trade areas. TRIPS does not contain an explicit exception to MFN for intellectual property rights. However, under footnote 1 of TRIPS, it is possible for members to form a "separate customs area" and to treat all nationals in the customs area effectively as one group of nationals for National Treatment purposes. This would allow the European Union, itself a member of the WTO, to provide a certain level of treatment for intellectual property rights to all nationals from all EU member states without being required to extend the same treatment to all other WTO members. *See European Communities—Protection of Trademarks and Geographical Indications for Agricultural Products and Foodstuffs*, WT/DS174/R, Report of the Panel, adopted on March 15, 2005, at ¶7.725.

III. National Treatment

Tariff concessions that ease trade barriers created by high tariffs at the borders can be easily undermined if the imports were subject to discriminatory treatment once they had cleared customs and entered the domestic market. To deal with this issue, the GATT imposed an obligation of non-discrimination between imported and domestic goods in the use of internal measures. The National Treatment principle requires that once goods have cleared customs and tariffs have been collected, all WTO members must treat the foreign goods no less favorably than domestic goods.

GATT Article III provides in part as follows:

Article III National Treatment on Internal Taxation and Regulation

1. The contracting parties recognize that internal taxes and other internal charges, and laws, regulations and requirements affecting the internal sale, offering for sale, purchase, transportation, distribution or use of products, and internal quantitative regulations requiring the mixture, processing or use of products in specified amounts or proportions, should not be applied to imported or domestic products so as to afford protection to domestic production.

2. The products of the territory of any contracting party imported into the territory of any other contracting party shall not be subject, directly or indirectly, to internal taxes or other internal charges of any kind in excess of those applied, directly or indirectly, to like domestic products. Moreover, no contracting party shall otherwise apply internal taxes or other internal charges to imported or domestic products in a manner contrary to the principles set forth in paragraph 1.

* * *

4. The products of the territory of any contracting party imported into the territory of any other contracting party shall be accorded treatment no less favourable than that accorded to like products of national origin in respect of all laws, regulations and requirements affecting their internal sale, offering for sale, purchase, transportation, distribution or use. The provisions of this paragraph shall not prevent the application of differential internal transportation charges which are based exclusively on the economic operation of the means of transport and not on the nationality of the product.

The main policy of Article III is that no law, regulation, or pattern of taxation should be allowed to adversely modify the conditions of competition between like imported and domestic products in the domestic market of a WTO member. Note that the test is not one of trade effects but discrimination in the conditions of completion; a measure can violate Article III even if it does not result in any adverse trade effects. The jurisprudence under Article III specifies that favoring domestic products is inconsistent with the National Treatment obligation whether actual or potential, direct or indirect, *de jure* or *de facto*. Article III therefore holds that once an imported product has been legally cleared at the border, there must be an equal competitive relationship between the import and like domestic products. Article III is one of the most important and most litigated GATT provisions.

Article III:1 is a statement of policy and considered to provide a context against which the remaining paragraphs of Article III are to be interpreted. We will see a further explanation of this relationship in *Japan—Alcoholic Beverages* below. Article III:2 prohibits discriminatory fiscal internal measures (taxes or other charges) while Article III:4 prohibits discriminatory non-fiscal internal measures (laws, regulations, and requirements) applied to imported goods.

Article III:2 consists of two sentences. A considerable jurisprudence has developed that interprets these two sentences, as exemplified by *Japan—Alcoholic Beverages* below. Both sentences refer explicitly or implicitly to "like" products, but the meaning of this term is different in each sentence. Article III:2 second sentence is the subject of an interpretive note *Ad* Article III:2, which has equal status as the treaty language. *Ad* Article III:2 is critical to understanding the meaning of "like" products in Article III:2 second sentence. You should now review *Ad* Article III:2, which is contained in an Appendix to the GATT in the Documents Supplement.

PROBLEM 4-8

Assume that as part of its recent commitment to developing its economy, and to assume a leading role in Asia, India seeks to enter into a trade agreement with the United States covering high-technology medical devices. The agreement promises some exclusive benefits to the United States as an inducement. For example, all local manufacturers of medical devices in India must obtain a certification from government laboratories that the equipment meets certain national standards, but this certification requirement is waived for U.S. imports. U.S. rights holders enjoy a patent term of thirty years, instead of the standard twenty-year term available to domestic companies. Analyze the following issues in light of the National Treatment principle:

(1) Does the waiver of the certification requirement for U.S. imports violate the National Treatment principle contained in GATT Article III?

(2) Does the extended patent term violate the National Treatment principle contained in TRIPS Article 3, which provides as follows: "Each member shall accord to the nationals of other Members treatment no less favourable than it accords to its own nationals with regard to the protection of intellectual property."

(3) What about MFN? *See* GATT Article I and TRIPS Article 4.

PROBLEM 4-9

The United States is providing a subsidy of $3 billion to all companies engaged in the research and development of cars that run only on electric power. The U.S. subsidy program is available only to companies owned by U.S. citizens or entities. Gen-X Cars, a California-based wholly owned subsidiary of a Japanese parent company, has applied for a grant and has been denied. Japan claims that this program discriminates against foreign companies and is in violation of the National Treatment principle. What result? *See* GATT III:8(b).

NOTES AND QUESTIONS

Paragraph 8 of Article III (not reproduced above) specifies two important exceptions to National Treatment. Article III:8(a) provides an exception for government procurement (i.e., the purchase by governments of goods or services), and Article III:8(b) provides an exception for government subsidies provided exclusively to domestic producers. These exceptions allow governments to discriminate in favor of local industries in the purchase of goods and services and in providing government payments or subsidies. The scope of the exception in Article III:8(b) is discussed in *Canada — Certain Measures Concerning Periodicals* set forth in this section below. What is the purpose of these exceptions?

PROBLEM 4-10

Article IX of the GATT allows WTO countries to require that imported products disclose their country of origin. Article IX provides an explicit exception to the National Treatment principle, so WTO countries can lawfully require country of origin markings for imported products only and can lawfully exempt domestically produced goods from the same disclosure requirement. The basic justification for this differential treatment is that consumers have a legitimate interest in knowing the country of origin of a product because this will affect their purchasing decisions.

Suppose that France, a member of the WTO, has passed a law requiring that the country of origin for all imports must be physically marked on the product itself in a conspicuous manner. Locally produced goods do not have to be marked. Is this law valid under the GATT Article IX:4? What would you recommend to France?

PROBLEM 4-11

Italy requires all imported sausage and meat products from China and Japan to be marked with their country of origin on the package. Imports from France do not need to be marked. Is this law valid under the GATT Article IX?

A.   Internal Taxes and Charges

GATT Article III requires that "internal taxes and charges" be applied in a non-discriminatory manner to both foreign and domestic products. The meaning of this term, along with several related key concepts, is explored in the principal case below.

PROBLEM 4-12

The State of Kentucky charges a 35 percent sales tax on retail sales of *mao tai*, a potent liquor imported from China, and on vodka imported from Russia. Kentucky charges a 20 percent tax on bourbon made in Kentucky. China and Russia argue that this tax is a blatantly protectionist measure as all three products contain the same level of alcohol and potency. Both nations argue that the Kentucky tax violates the National Treatment principle. Suppose that consumers in Kentucky who order bourbon at a bar or restaurant will accept vodka if no bourbon is available but most consumers have never heard of *mao tai*, which is only offered for sale at some local Chinese restaurants and supermarkets. Is the Kentucky tax in violation of the National Treatment principle? Consider the following case.

Japan — Taxes on Alcoholic Beverages
Report of the WTO Appellate Body, adopted on November 1, 1996
WT/DS8, 10, 11/AB/R

INTRODUCTION

Japan and the United States appeal from certain issues of law and legal interpretations in the Panel Report, *Japan—Taxes on Alcoholic Beverages* (the "Panel Report"). That Panel (the "Panel") was established to consider complaints by the European Communities, Canada and the United States against Japan relating to the Japanese Liquor Tax Law (Shuzeiho), Law No. 6 of 1953 as amended (the "Liquor Tax Law").

The Panel Report was circulated to the Members of the World Trade Organization (the "WTO") on July 11, 1996. It contains the following conclusions:

(i) Shochu and vodka are like products and Japan, by taxing the latter in excess of the former, is in violation of its obligation under Article III:2, first sentence, of the General Agreement on Tariffs and Trade 1994.

(ii) Shochu, whisky, brandy, rum, gin, genever, and liqueurs are "directly competitive or substitutable products" and Japan, by not taxing them similarly, is in violation of its obligation under Article III:2, second sentence, of the General Agreement on Tariffs and Trade 1994.

ARTICLE III:1

The terms of Article III must be given their ordinary meaning—in their context and in the light of the overall object and purpose of the *WTO Agreement*. Thus, the words actually used in the Article provide the basis for an interpretation that must give meaning and effect to all its terms. The proper interpretation of the Article is, first of all, a textual interpretation. Consequently, the Panel is correct in seeing a distinction between Article III:1, which "contains general principles", and Article III:2, which "provides for specific obligations regarding internal taxes and internal charges". Article III:1 articulates a general principle that internal measures should not be applied so as to afford protection to domestic production. This general principle informs the rest of Article III. The purpose of Article III:1 is to establish this general principle as a guide to understanding and interpreting the specific obligations contained in Article III:2 and in the other paragraphs of Article III, while respecting, and not diminishing in any way, the meaning of the words actually used in the texts of those other paragraphs. In short, Article III:1 constitutes part of the context of Article III:2, in the same way that it constitutes part of the context of each of the other paragraphs in Article III. Any other reading of Article III would have the effect of rendering the words of Article III:1 meaningless, thereby violating the fundamental principle of effectiveness in treaty interpretation. Consistent with this principle of effectiveness, and with the textual differences in the two sentences, we believe that Article III:1 informs the first sentence and the second sentence of Article III:2 in different ways.

ARTICLE III:2

1.   FIRST SENTENCE

Article III:1 informs Article III:2, first sentence, by establishing that if imported products are taxed in excess of like domestic products, then that tax measure is inconsistent with Article III. Article III:2, first sentence does not refer specifically to Article III:1. There is no specific invocation in this first sentence of the general principle in Article III:1 that admonishes Members of the WTO not to apply measures "so as to afford protection". This omission must have some meaning. We believe the meaning is simply that the presence of a protective application need not be established separately from the specific requirements that are included in the first sentence in order to show that a tax measure is inconsistent with the general principle set out in the first sentence. However, this does not mean that the general principle of Article III:1 does not apply to this sentence. To the contrary, we believe the first sentence of Article III:2 is, in effect, an application of this general principle. The ordinary meaning of the words of Article III:2, first sentence leads inevitably to this conclusion. Read in their context and in the light of the overall object and purpose of the *WTO Agreement*, the words of the first sentence require an examination of the conformity of an internal tax measure with Article III by determining, first, whether the taxed imported and domestic products are "like" and, second, whether the taxes applied to the imported products are "in excess of" those applied to the like domestic products. If the imported and domestic products are "like products", and if the taxes applied to the imported products are "in excess of" those applied to the like domestic products, then the measure is inconsistent with Article III:2, first sentence.

(a)   *"Like Products"*

Because the second sentence of Article III:2 provides for a separate and distinctive consideration of the protective aspect of a measure in examining its application to a broader category of products that are not "like products" as contemplated by the first sentence, we agree with the Panel that the first sentence of Article III:2 must be construed narrowly so as not to condemn measures that its strict terms are not meant to condemn. Consequently, we agree with the Panel also that the definition of "like products" in Article III:2, first sentence, should be construed narrowly.

How narrowly is a matter that should be determined separately for each tax measure in each case. We agree with the practice under the GATT 1947 of determining whether imported and domestic products are "like" on a case-by-case basis. The Report of the Working Party on *Border Tax Adjustments*, adopted by the CONTRACTING PARTIES in 1970, set out the basic approach for interpreting "like or similar products" generally in the various provisions of the GATT 1947:

> . . . the interpretation of the term should be examined on a case-by-case basis. This would allow a fair assessment in each case of the different elements that constitute a "similar" product. Some criteria were suggested for determining, on a case-by-case basis, whether a product is "similar": the product's end-uses in a given market; consumers' tastes and habits, which change from country to country; the product's properties, nature and quality.

This approach was followed in almost all adopted panel reports after *Border Tax Adjustments*. This approach should be helpful in identifying on a case-by-case basis the range of "like products" that fall within the narrow limits of Article III:2, first sentence in the GATT 1994. Yet this approach will be most helpful if decision makers keep ever in mind how narrow the range of "like products" in Article III:2, first sentence is meant to be as opposed to the range of "like" products contemplated in some other provisions of the GATT 1994 and other Multilateral Trade Agreements of the *WTO Agreement*. In applying the criteria cited in *Border Tax Adjustments* to the facts of any particular case, and in considering other criteria that may also be relevant in certain cases, panels can only apply their best judgement in determining whether in fact products are "like". This will always involve an unavoidable element of individual, discretionary judgement.

The Panel [correctly] determined in this case that shochu and vodka are "like products" for the purposes of Article III:2, first sentence. We note that the determination of whether vodka is a "like product" to shochu under Article III:2, first sentence, or a "directly competitive or substitutable product" to shochu under Article III:2, second sentence, does not materially affect the outcome of this case.

(b)   *"In Excess Of"*

The only remaining issue under Article III:2, first sentence, is whether the taxes on imported products are "in excess of" those on like domestic products. If so, then the Member that has imposed the tax is not in compliance with Article III.

Even the smallest amount of "excess" is too much. "The prohibition of discriminatory taxes in Article III:2, first sentence, is not conditional on a 'trade effects test' nor is it qualified by a *de minimis* standard." We agree with the Panel's legal reasoning and with its conclusions on this aspect of the interpretation and application of Article III:2, first sentence.

2.   SECOND SENTENCE

Article III:1 informs Article III:2, second sentence, through specific reference. Article III:2, second sentence, contains a general prohibition against "internal taxes or other internal charges" applied to "imported or domestic products in a manner contrary to the principles set forth in paragraph 1". As mentioned before, Article III:1 states that internal taxes and other internal charges "should not be applied to imported or domestic products so as to afford protection to domestic production". Again, *Ad* Article III:2 states as follows:

> A tax conforming to the requirements of the first sentence of paragraph 2 would be considered to be inconsistent with the provisions of the second sentence only in cases where competition was involved between, on the one hand, the taxed product and, on the other hand, a directly competitive or substitutable product which was not similarly taxed.

Article III:2, second sentence, and the accompanying *Ad* Article have equivalent legal status in that both are treaty language which was negotiated and agreed at the same time. The *Ad* Article does not replace or modify the language contained in Article III:2, second sentence, but, in fact, clarifies its meaning. Accordingly, the language of the second sentence and the *Ad* Article must be read together in order to give them their proper meaning.

Unlike that of Article III:2, first sentence, the language of Article III:2, second sentence, specifically invokes Article III:1. The significance of this distinction lies in the fact that whereas Article III:1 acts implicitly in addressing the two issues that must be considered in applying the first sentence, it acts explicitly as an entirely separate issue that must be addressed along with two other issues that are raised in applying the second sentence. Giving full meaning to the text and to its context, three separate issues must be addressed to determine whether an internal tax measure is inconsistent with Article III:2, second sentence. These three issues are whether:

(1)   the imported products and the domestic products *are "directly competitive or substitutable products" which are in competition with each other;*

(2)   the directly competitive or substitutable imported and domestic products *are "not similarly taxed";* and

(3)   the dissimilar taxation of the directly competitive or substitutable imported domestic products *is "applied . . . so as to afford protection to domestic production".*

Again, these are three separate issues. Each must be established separately by the complainant for a panel to find that a tax measure imposed by a Member of the WTO is inconsistent with Article III:2, second sentence.

(a) "Directly Competitive or Substitutable Products"

If imported and domestic products are not "like products" for the narrow purposes of Article III:2, first sentence, then they are not subject to the strictures of that sentence and there is no inconsistency with the requirements of that sentence. However, depending on their nature, and depending on the competitive conditions in the relevant market, those same products may well be among the broader category of "directly competitive or substitutable products" that fall within the domain of Article III:2, second sentence. How much broader that category of "directly competitive or substitutable products" may be in any given case is a matter for the panel to determine based on all the relevant facts in that case. As with "like products" under the first sentence, the determination of the appropriate range of "directly competitive or substitutable products" under the second sentence must be made on a case-by-case basis.

In this case, the Panel emphasized the need to look not only at such matters as physical characteristics, common end-uses, and tariff classifications, but also at the "market place". This seems appropriate. The GATT 1994 is a commercial agreement, and the WTO is concerned, after all, with markets. It does not seem inappropriate to look at competition in the relevant markets as one among a number of means of identifying the broader category of products that might be described as "directly competitive or substitutable".

Nor does it seem inappropriate to examine elasticity of substitution as one means of examining those relevant markets. The Panel did not say that cross-price elasticity of demand is "*the* decisive criterion" for determining whether products are "directly competitive or substitutable". The Panel stated the following:

> In the Panel's view, the decisive criterion in order to determine whether two products are directly competitive or substitutable is whether they have common end-uses, *inter alia,* as shown by elasticity of substitution.

We agree. And, we find the Panel's legal analysis of whether the products are "directly competitive or substitutable products" to be correct.

(b) "Not Similarly Taxed"

To give due meaning to the distinctions in the wording of Article III:2, first sentence, and Article III:2, second sentence, the phrase "not similarly taxed" in the *Ad* Article to the second sentence must not be construed so as to mean the same thing as the phrase "in excess of" in the first sentence. On its face, the phrase "in excess of" in the first sentence means *any* amount of tax on imported products "in excess of" the tax on domestic "like products". The phrase "not similarly taxed" in the *Ad* Article to the second sentence must therefore mean something else. It requires a different standard, just as "directly competitive or substitutable products" requires a different standard as compared to "like products" for these same interpretive purposes.

To interpret "in excess of" and "not similarly taxed" identically would deny any distinction between the first and second sentences of Article III:2. Thus, in any given case, there may be some amount of taxation on imported products that may well be "in excess of" the tax on domestic "like products" but may not be so much as to compel a conclusion that "directly competitive or substitutable" imported and domestic products are "not similarly taxed" for the purposes of the *Ad* Article to

Article III:2, second sentence. In other words, there may be an amount of excess taxation that may well be more of a burden on imported products than on domestic "directly competitive or substitutable products" but may nevertheless not be enough to justify a conclusion that such products are "not similarly taxed" for the purposes of Article III:2, second sentence. We agree with the Panel that this amount of differential taxation must be more than *de minimis* to be deemed "not similarly taxed" in any given case. And, like the Panel, we believe that whether any particular differential amount of taxation is *de minimis* or is not *de minimis* must, here too, be determined on a case-by-case basis. Thus, to be "not similarly taxed", the tax burden on imported products must be heavier than on "directly competitive or substitutable" domestic products, and that burden must be more than *de minimis* in any given case.

In this case, the Panel applied the correct legal reasoning in determining whether "directly competitive or substitutable" imported and domestic products were "not similarly taxed". However, the Panel erred in blurring the distinction between that issue and the entirely separate issue of whether the tax measure in question was applied "so as to afford protection". Again, these are separate issues that must be addressed individually. If "directly competitive or substitutable products" are *not* "not similarly taxed", then there is neither need nor justification under Article III:2, second sentence, for inquiring further as to whether the tax has been applied "so as to afford protection". But if such products are "not similarly taxed", a further inquiry must necessarily be made.

(c)   *"So As To Afford Protection"*

This third inquiry under Article III:2, second sentence, must determine whether "directly competitive or substitutable products" are "not similarly taxed" in a way that affords protection. This is not an issue of intent. It is not necessary for a panel to sort through the many reasons legislators and regulators often have for what they do and weigh the relative significance of those reasons to establish legislative or regulatory intent. If the measure is applied to imported or domestic products so as to afford protection to domestic production, then it does not matter that there may not have been any desire to engage in protectionism in the minds of the legislators or the regulators who imposed the measure. It is irrelevant that protectionism was not an intended objective if the particular tax measure in question is nevertheless, to echo Article III:1, "*applied* to imported or domestic products so as to afford protection to domestic production". This is an issue of how the measure in question is *applied*.

Although it is true that the aim of a measure may not be easily ascertained, nevertheless its protective application can most often be discerned from the design, the architecture, and the revealing structure of a measure. The very magnitude of the dissimilar taxation in a particular case may be evidence of such a protective application, as the Panel rightly concluded in this case. Most often, there will be other factors to be considered as well. In conducting this inquiry, panels should give full consideration to all the relevant facts and all the relevant circumstances in any given case.

We have reviewed the Panel's reasoning in this case as well as its conclusions on the issue of "so as to afford protection" in paragraphs 6.33-6.35 of the Panel Report. We find cause for thorough examination. The Panel began in paragraph 6.33 by describing its approach as follows:

. . . if directly competitive or substitutable products are not "similarly taxed", and if it were found that the tax favours domestic products, then protection would be afforded to such products, and Article III:2, second sentence, is violated.

This statement of the reasoning required under Article III:2, second sentence is correct.

In paragraph 6.34, the Panel added:

(i) The benchmark in Article III:2, second sentence, is whether internal taxes operate "so as to afford protection to domestic production", a term which has been further interpreted in the Interpretative Note ad Article III:2, paragraph 2, to mean dissimilar taxation of domestic and foreign directly competitive or substitutable products.

And, furthermore, in its conclusions, in paragraph 7.1(ii), the Panel concluded that:

(ii) Shochu, whisky, brandy, rum, gin, genever, and liqueurs are "directly competitive or substitutable products" and Japan, by not taxing them similarly, is in violation of its obligation under Article III:2, second sentence, of the General Agreement on Tariffs and Trade 1994.

Thus, having stated the correct legal approach to apply with respect to Article III:2, second sentence, the Panel then equated dissimilar taxation above a *de minimis* level with the separate and distinct requirement of demonstrating that the tax measure "affords protection to domestic production". As previously stated, a finding that "directly competitive or substitutable products" are "not similarly taxed" is necessary to find a violation of Article III:2, second sentence. Yet this is not enough. The dissimilar taxation must be more than *de minimis*. It may be so much more that it will be clear from that very differential that the dissimilar taxation was applied "so as to afford protection". In some cases, that may be enough to show a violation. In this case, the Panel concluded that it was enough. Yet in other cases, there may be other factors that will be just as relevant or more relevant to demonstrating that the dissimilar taxation at issue was applied "so as to afford protection". In any case, the three issues that must be addressed in determining whether there is such a violation must be addressed clearly and separately in each case and on a case-by-case basis. And, in every case, a careful, objective analysis, must be done of each and all relevant facts and all the relevant circumstances in order to determine "the existence of protective taxation". Although the Panel blurred its legal reasoning in this respect, nevertheless we conclude that it reasoned correctly that in this case, the Liquor Tax Law is not in compliance with Article III:2. As the Panel did, we note that:

. . . the combination of customs duties and internal taxation in Japan has the following impact: on the one hand, it makes it difficult for foreign-produced shochu to penetrate the Japanese market and, on the other, it does not guarantee equality of competitive conditions between shochu and the rest of 'white' and 'brown' spirits. Thus, through a combination of high import duties and differentiated internal taxes, Japan manages to "isolate" domestically produced shochu from foreign competition, be it foreign produced shochu or any other of the mentioned white and brown spirits.

NOTE ON PHILIPPINES—TAXES ON DISTILLED SPIRITS

In *Philippines—Taxes on Distilled Spirits*, WT/DS396/403/AB/R, Report of the Appellate Body, adopted on January 20, 2012, the Appellate Body reiterated the analysis of the *Japan—Alcoholic Beverages* case, ruling that the Philippines acted inconsistently with Article III:2 by applying dissimilar internal taxation rates to imported and domestic distilled spirits, such as gin, brandy, whiskey, vodka, and rum. This case is especially important, however, because the Appellate Body discussed and clarified somewhat the "like product" issue in Article III:2 cases. The Philippines justified the different tax rates on the basis that different raw materials are used to make different varieties of distilled spirits. Most of the distilled spirits made in the Philippines are made from sugar cane molasses, while most imported distilled spirits are made from other raw materials, such as cereals, potatoes, coconut, cassava, and buri palm. On appeal the Philippines challenged the WTO panel's ruling that all distilled spirits are "like products" irrespective of the raw materials from which they are made.

With respect to Article III:2, first sentence, the Appellate Body upheld the panel's consideration of evidence on the "like product" issue with respect to (1) the products' physical characteristics, nature, and quality; (2) end uses of the products in the Philippines; (3) Philippine consumers' tastes and habits; (4) tariff classifications; and (5) relevant Philippine regulations. Concerning the most important factor in this case, physical characteristics, the Appellate Body stated (¶128) that, as the panel had determined, "even where the products are made from different raw materials and may, as a consequence, present some physical differences that are not eliminated in the production process, they can be in a sufficiently close competitive relationship to be considered like products within the meaning of Article III:2, first sentence." With respect to the panel's consideration of tariff classification, the Appellate Body found (¶¶163-164) that the panel had erred by attributing relevance to the classification of the spirits under the same general four digit heading because the heading in question was not sufficiently detailed. (Tariffs are usually assessed at the six or eight digit subheading levels.) Even so, the Appellate Body upheld the panel's ruling that each type of imported distilled spirit made from non-designated raw materials is "like" the same type of domestic distilled spirit made from designated raw materials within the meaning of Article III:2, first sentence, because tariff classification is only one relevant criterion. Furthermore, the panel's conclusion was also supported by the balance of the evidence with respect to the other criteria of "likeness."

With respect to Article III:2, second sentence, the panel had ruled that all distilled spirits whether imported or domestic and irrespective of their raw material base are "like products." The Appellate Body, in reviewing this finding, examined evidence (in the form of "substitutability studies") that the imported and domestic distilled spirits are directly competitive and substitutable in the Philippines market. The Appellate Body agreed (¶¶242-243) with the panel that "all the distilled spirits at issue in the present dispute, whether imported or domestic, and irrespective of the raw materials from which they are made, are directly competitive and substitutable" and are therefore "like products" within the meaning of Article III:2, second sentence of the GATT.

Applying these "like product" rulings, the Appellate Body concluded that by applying different rates of internal taxation to like products, the Philippines acted inconsistently with Article III:2, first sentence; and by imposing different rates of internal taxation so as to afford protection to Philippine production of distilled spirits, the Philippines acted inconsistently with Article III:2, second sentence.

Compare the Appellate Body's treatment of the "like product" issue in the first and second sentences of Article III:2. What are the similarities and differences of interpretation?

Canada—Certain Measures Concerning Periodicals
Report of the WTO Appellate Body, adopted on June 30, 1997
WT/DS31/AB/R

[The United States challenged three measures used by Canada in connection with split-run editions of periodicals from the United States. A split-run edition is an edition of a periodical originally produced for the U.S. market but that is then also shipped to the Canadian market with advertising targeted specifically at Canada. The measures involved were (1) Canadian Tariff Code 9958, which prohibits the importation into Canada of split-run editions; (2) Part V.1 of the Canadian Excise Tax Act, which imposes a tax on split-run periodicals; and (3) special favorable postage rates provided to Canadian periodicals but not to split-run periodicals. The panel found that Tariff Code 9958 was an import prohibition and inconsistent with GATT Article XI, which prohibits import quotas. Canada did not appeal this finding. The panel also found that the excise tax was inconsistent with the GATT National Treatment principle. This finding was appealed by Canada. Finally, the panel found that the favorable postage rates enjoyed by Canadian periodicals were justified under GATT Article III:8(b), recognizing certain exceptions to the National Treatment principle for subsidies. This finding was appealed by the United States. In the opinion below, the Appellate Body first turns to a consideration of the excise tax and then to the subsidies issue concerning postage rates.]

IV.   APPLICABILITY OF THE GATT 1994

An examination of Part V.1 of the Excise Tax Act demonstrates that it is an excise tax which is applied on a good, a split-run edition of a periodical, on a "per issue" basis. By its very structure and design, it is a tax on a periodical. It is the publisher, or in the absence of a publisher resident in Canada, the distributor, the printer or the wholesaler, who is liable to pay the tax, not the advertiser.

Based on the above analysis of the measure, which is essentially an excise tax imposed on split run editions of periodicals, we cannot agree with Canada's argument that this internal tax does not "indirectly" affect imported products. It is a well-established principle that the trade effects of a difference in tax treatment between imported and domestic products do not have to be demonstrated for a measure to be found to be inconsistent with Article III. The fundamental purpose of Article III of the GATT 1994 is to ensure equality of competitive conditions between imported and like domestic products. We do not find it necessary to look to Article III:1 or Article III:4 of the GATT 1994 to give meaning to Article III:2, first sentence, in this respect. In *Japan—Alcoholic Beverages*, the Appellate Body stated that "Article III:1 articulates a general principle" which "informs the rest of Article III". However, we also said that it informs the different sentences in Article III:2 in different ways. With respect to Article III:2, second sentence, we held that "Article III:1 informs Article III:2, second sentence, through specific reference".

Article III:2, first sentence, uses the words "directly or indirectly" in two different contexts: one in relation to the application of a tax to imported products and the other in relation to the application of a tax to like domestic products. Any measure that indirectly affects the conditions of competition between imported and like domestic products would come within the provisions of Article III:2, first sentence, or by implication, second sentence, given the broader application of the latter.

V. ARTICLE III:2, FIRST SENTENCE, OF THE GATT 1994

With respect to the application of Article III:2, first sentence, we agree with the Panel that:

> . . . the following two questions need to be answered to determine whether there is a violation of Article III:2 of GATT 1994: *(a)* Are imported "split-run" periodicals and domestic non "split-run" periodicals like products?; and *(b)* Are imported "split-run" periodicals subject to an internal tax in excess of that applied to domestic non "split-run" periodicals? If the answers to both questions are affirmative, there is a violation of Article III:2, first sentence. If the answer to the first question is negative, we need to examine further whether there is a violation of Article III:2, second sentence.

A. LIKE PRODUCTS

[The Appellate Body found that in order to determine whether "like" products were involved within the meaning of Article III:2 first sentence, it was necessary to compare imports with domestic products. Due to the import ban, however, there were no imports to compare to domestic products. (The import ban was held by the Panel to be in violation of GATT Article XI, which prohibits quotas.) The Panel then attempted to construct a hypothetical import, but the Appellate Body found fault with the Panel's methodology. The Appellate Body concluded that without a comparison of imports and domestic goods in order to determine whether "like" products were involved, it was not possible to find a violation of Article III:2 first sentence.]

VI. ARTICLE III:2, SECOND SENTENCE, OF THE GATT 1994

We will proceed to examine the consistency of Part V.1 of the Excise Tax Act with the second sentence of Article III:2 of the GATT 1994. In our Report in *Japan—Alcoholic Beverages*, we held that:

> . . . three separate issues must be addressed to determine whether an internal tax measure is inconsistent with Article III:2, second sentence. These three issues are whether:
>
> (1) the imported products and the domestic products *are "directly competitive or substitutable products" which are in competition with each other;*
>
> (2) the directly competitive or substitutable imported and domestic products *are "not similarly taxed";* and
>
> (3) the dissimilar taxation of the directly competitive or substitutable imported domestic products is *"applied . . . so as to afford protection to domestic production".*

1.   "Directly Competitive or Substitutable Products"

According to the Panel Report, Canada considers that split-run periodicals are not "directly competitive or substitutable" for periodicals with editorial content developed for the Canadian market. Although they may be substitutable advertising vehicles, they are not competitive or substitutable information vehicles. Substitution implies interchangeability. Once the content is accepted as relevant, it seems obvious that magazines created for different markets are not interchangeable. They serve different end-uses. Canada draws attention to a study by the economist, Leigh Anderson, on which the *Task Force Report* was at least partially-based, which notes:

> US magazines can probably provide a reasonable substitute for Canadian magazines in their capacity as an advertising medium, although some advertisers may be better served by a Canadian vehicle. In many instances however, they would provide a very poor substitute as an entertainment and communication medium.

Canada submits that the *Task Force Report* characterizes the relationship as one of "imperfect substitutability"—far from the direct substitutability required by this provision. The market share of imported and domestic magazines in Canada has remained remarkably constant over the last 30-plus years. If competitive forces had been in play to the degree necessary to meet the standard of "directly competitive" goods, one would have expected some variations. All this casts serious doubt on whether the competition or substitutability between imported split-run periodicals and domestic non-split-run periodicals is sufficiently "direct" to meet the standard of *Ad* Article III.

According to the United States, the very existence of the tax is itself proof of competition between split-run periodicals and non-split-run periodicals in the Canadian market. As Canada itself has acknowledged, split-run periodicals compete with wholly domestically-produced periodicals for advertising revenue, which demonstrates that they compete for the same readers. The only reason firms place advertisements in magazines is to reach readers. A firm would consider split-run periodicals to be an acceptable advertising alternative to non-split-run periodicals only if that firm had reason to believe that the split-run periodicals themselves would be an acceptable alternative to non-split-run periodicals in the eyes of consumers. According to the United States, Canada acknowledges that "[r]eaders attract advertisers" and that, ". . . Canadian publishers are ready to compete with magazines published all over the world in order to keep their readers, but the competition is fierce".

According to the United States, the *Task Force Report* together with statements made by the Minister of Canadian Heritage and Canadian officials, provide further acknowledgment of the substitutability of imported split-run periodicals and domestic non-split-run periodicals in the Canadian market.

We find the United States' position convincing, while Canada's assertions do not seem to us to be compatible with its own description of the Canadian market for periodicals.

According to the Panel:

> Canada explained that there is a direct correlation between circulation, advertising revenue and editorial content. The larger the circulation, the more advertising a magazine can attract. With greater advertising revenue, a publisher can afford more to spend on editorial content. The more a publisher spends, the more attractive the

magazine is likely to be to its readers, resulting in circulation growth. Similarly, a loss of advertising revenue will produce a "downward spiral". Less advertising entails less editorial, a reduction in readership and circulation and a diminished ability to attract advertising. Magazines can be sold on newsstands, or through subscriptions, or distributed at no cost to selected consumers . . . . Canadian English-language publications face tough competition on newsstands; they account for only 18.5 percent of English-language periodicals distributed on newsstands, where space is dominated by foreign publications . . . .

. . . Canadian periodical publishers face a major competitive challenge in their business environment that is not common to their counterparts in countries with a larger population to serve. The pivotal fact is the penetration of the Canadian market by foreign magazines. Canadian readers have unrestricted access to imported magazines. At the same time, Canadian readers have demonstrated that they value magazines that address their distinct interests and perspectives. However, foreign magazines dominate the Canadian market. They account for 81.4 percent of all newsstand circulation and slightly more than half (50.4 percent) of the entire circulation of English-language magazines destined for the general public in Canada.

This description corresponds also to the statement made by the then Minister of Canadian Heritage, the Honourable Michel Dupuy:

Canadians are much more interested in American daily life, be it political or sports life or any other kind, than vice versa. Therefore, the reality of the situation is that we must protect ourselves against split-runs coming from foreign countries and, in particular, from the United States.

Our conclusion that imported split-run periodicals and domestic non-split-run periodicals are "directly competitive or substitutable" does not mean that all periodicals belong to the same relevant market, whatever their editorial content. A periodical containing mainly current news is not directly competitive or substitutable with a periodical dedicated to gardening, chess, sports, music or cuisine. But newsmagazines, like TIME, TIME Canada and Maclean's, are directly competitive or substitutable in spite of the "Canadian" content of Maclean's. The competitive relationship is even closer in the case of more specialized magazines, like Pulp & Paper as compared with Pulp & Paper Canada, two trade magazines presented to the Panel by the United States.

We, therefore, conclude that imported split-run periodicals and domestic non-split-run periodicals are directly competitive or substitutable products in so far as they are part of the same segment of the Canadian market for periodicals.

2.   *"Not Similarly Taxed"*

Having found that imported split-run and domestic non-split-run periodicals of the same type are directly competitive or substitutable, we must examine whether the imported products and the directly competitive or substitutable domestic products are not similarly taxed. Part V.1 of the Excise Tax Act taxes split-run editions of periodicals in an amount equivalent to 80 per cent of the value of all advertisements in a split-run edition. In contrast, domestic non-split-run periodicals are not subject to Part V.1 of the Excise Tax Act. Following the reasoning of the Appellate Body in *Japan—Alcoholic Beverages*, dissimilar taxation of even some imported products as compared to directly competitive or substitutable domestic products is inconsistent with the provisions of the second sentence of Article III:2. In *United States—Section 337*, the panel found:

> . . . that the "no less favourable" treatment requirement of Article III:4 has to be understood as applicable to each individual case of imported products. The Panel rejected any notion of balancing more favourable treatment of some imported products against less favourable treatment of other imported products.

With respect to Part V.1 of the Excise Tax Act, we find that the amount of the taxation is far above the *de minimis* threshold required by the Appellate Body Report in *Japan—Alcoholic Beverages*. The magnitude of this tax is sufficient to prevent the production and sale of split-run periodicals in Canada.

3.   *"So as to Afford Protection"*

The Appellate Body established the following approach in *Japan—Alcoholic Beverages* for determining whether dissimilar taxation of directly competitive or substitutable products has been applied so as to afford protection:

> . . . we believe that an examination in any case of whether dissimilar taxation has been applied so as to afford protection requires a comprehensive and objective analysis of the structure and application of the measure in question on domestic as compared to imported products. We believe it is possible to examine objectively the underlying criteria used in a particular tax measure, its structure, and its overall application to ascertain whether it is applied in a way that affords protection to domestic products.
>
> Although it is true that the aim of a measure may not be easily ascertained, nevertheless its protective application can most often be discerned from the design, the architecture, and the revealing structure of a measure. The very magnitude of the dissimilar taxation in a particular case may be evidence of such a protective application, . . . Most often, there will be other factors to be considered as well. In conducting this inquiry, panels should give full consideration to all the relevant facts and all the relevant circumstances in any given case.

With respect to Part V.1 of the Excise Tax Act, we note that the magnitude of the dissimilar taxation between imported split-run periodicals and domestic non-split-run periodicals is beyond excessive, indeed, it is prohibitive. There is also ample evidence that the very design and structure of the measure is such as to afford protection to domestic periodicals.

During the debate of Bill C-103, An Act to Amend the Excise Tax Act and the Income Tax Act, the Minister of Canadian Heritage, the Honourable Michel Dupuy, stated the following:

> . . . the reality of the situation is that we must protect ourselves against split-runs coming from foreign countries and, in particular, from the United States.

Canada also admitted that the objective and structure of the tax is to insulate Canadian magazines from competition in the advertising sector, thus leaving significant Canadian advertising revenues for the production of editorial material created for the Canadian market. With respect to the actual application of the tax to date, it has resulted in one split-run magazine, *Sports Illustrated*, to move its production for the Canadian market out of Canada and back to the United States. Also,

Harrowsmith Country Life, a Canadian-owned split-run periodical, has ceased production of its United States' edition as a consequence of the imposition of the tax.

We therefore conclude on the basis of the above reasons, including the magnitude of the differential taxation, the several statements of the Government of Canada's explicit policy objectives in introducing the measure and the demonstrated actual protective effect of the measure, that the design and structure of Part V.1 of the Excise Tax Act is clearly to afford protection to the production of Canadian periodicals.

VII.   ARTICLE III:8(B) OF THE GATT 1994

Article III:8(b) of the GATT 1994 reads as follows:

(b) The provisions of this Article shall not prevent the payment of subsidies exclusively to domestic producers, including payments to domestic producers derived from the proceeds of internal taxes or charges applied consistently with the provisions of this Article and subsidies effected through governmental purchases of domestic products.

Both participants agree that Canada's "funded" postal rates involve "a payment of subsidies". The appellant, the United States, argues, however, that the "funded" postal rates programme involves a transfer of funds from one government entity to another, i.e. from Canadian Heritage to Canada Post, and not from the Canadian government to domestic producers as required by Article III:8(b).

As we understand it, through the Publications Assistance Program (PAP), Canadian Heritage provides Canada Post, a wholly-owned Crown corporation, with financial assistance to support special rates of postage for eligible publications, including certain designated domestic periodicals mailed and distributed in Canada. This programme has been implemented through a series of agreements, the MOA, between Canadian Heritage and Canada Post, which provide that in consideration of the payments made to it by Canadian Heritage, Canada Post will accept for distribution, at special "funded" rates, all publications designated by Canadian Heritage to be eligible under the PAP. The MOA provides that while Canadian Heritage will administer the eligibility requirements for the PAP based on criteria specified in the MOA, Canada Post will accept for distribution all publications that are eligible under the PAP at the "funded" rates.

A proper interpretation of Article III:8(b) must be made on the basis of a careful examination of the text, context and object and purpose of that provision. In examining the text of Article III:8(b), we believe that the phrase, "including payments to domestic producers derived from the proceeds of internal taxes or charges applied consistently with the provisions of this Article and subsidies effected through governmental purchases of domestic products" helps to elucidate the types of subsidies covered by Article III:8(b) of the GATT 1994. It is not an exhaustive list of the kinds of programmes that would qualify as "the payment of subsidies exclusively to domestic producers", but those words exemplify the kinds of programmes which are exempted from the obligations of Articles III:2 and III:4 of the GATT 1994.

Our textual interpretation is supported by the context of Article III:8(b) examined in relation to Articles III:2 and III:4 of the GATT 1994. Furthermore, the object and purpose of Article III:8(b) is confirmed by the drafting history of Article III. In this context, we refer to the following discussion in the Reports of the Committees and Principal Sub-Committees of the Interim Commission for the International Trade Organization concerning the provision of the Havana Charter for an International Trade Organization that corresponds to Article III:8(b) of the GATT 1994:

> This sub-paragraph was redrafted in order to make it clear that nothing in Article 18 could be construed to sanction the exemption of domestic products from internal taxes imposed on like imported products or the remission of such taxes. At the same time the Sub-Committee recorded its view that nothing in this sub-paragraph or elsewhere in Article 18 would override the provisions of Section C of Chapter IV.

We do not see a reason to distinguish a reduction of tax rates on a product from a reduction in transportation or postal rates. Indeed, an examination of the text, context, and object and purpose of Article III:8(b) suggests that it was intended to exempt from the obligations of Article III only the payment of subsidies which involves the expenditure of revenue by a government.

As a result of our analysis of the text, context, and object and purpose of Article III:8(b), we conclude that the Panel incorrectly interpreted this provision. For these reasons, we reverse the Panel's findings and conclusions that Canada's "funded" postal rates scheme for periodicals is justified under Article III:8(b) of the GATT 1994.

VIII.   FINDINGS AND CONCLUSIONS

For the reasons set out in this Report, the Appellate Body:

(a) upholds the Panel's findings and conclusions on the applicability of the GATT 1994 to Part V.1 of the Excise Tax Act;

(b) reverses the Panel's findings and conclusions on Part V.1 of the Excise Tax Act relating to "like products" within the context of Article III:2, first sentence, thereby reversing the Panel's conclusions on Article III:2, first sentence, of the GATT 1994;

(c) modifies the Panel's findings and conclusions on Article III:2 of the GATT 1994, by concluding that Part V.1 of the Excise Tax Act is inconsistent with Canada's obligations under Article III:2, second sentence, of the GATT 1994; and

(d) reverses the Panel's findings and conclusions that the maintenance by Canada Post of the "funded" postal rates scheme is justified by Article III:8(b) of the GATT 1994, and concludes that the "funded" postal rates scheme is not justified by Article III:8(b) of the GATT 1994.

NOTES AND QUESTIONS

1. In the *Canadian Periodicals* case, the import prohibition contained in Tariff Code 9958 did not involve GATT Article III. Why not? Import bans are prohibited by GATT Article XI, which we cover in Chapter 6.

2. In the *Canadian Periodicals* case, the Appellate Body refused to apply the "like products" test of Article III:2, first sentence. Why? If you apply this test, how does the case turn out?

3. What do you think of the Appellate Body's formulation of legal tests for the "like products" issue under Article III:1 first and second sentences? Are these tests overly technical? Do they count the trees but miss the forest?

B. Government Regulation

Governments have sovereignty to regulate their own internal economic affairs, but when government regulation over internal affairs also affects international trade, a clash may arise. Government regulations that treat domestic products differently from imports might be subject to a claim that the regulations violate the National Treatment principle under GATT Article III:4.

PROBLEM 4-13

To ease dependence on foreign oil, the United States has set aside a $25 billion energy fund to assist in finding alternatives sources of energy. Creative Energy Technologies (CET) has developed an alternative fuel based on ethanol, which is derived from corn. However, to recoup its research and development costs, CET will need to charge a retail price for ethanol that is so high that it will not be competitive with regular gasoline. Senator Jones from Iowa is in favor of using the U.S. energy fund to give hefty rebates to consumers who purchase ethanol from CET. The rebates will allow CET to compete effectively with gasoline.

Brazil would like to export its ethanol to the United States, but consumers will get rebates only if they purchase the ethanol from U.S. companies. Brazil argues that the rebate program violates the National Treatment principle. Senator Jones says, "That's outrageous. The WTO can't interfere with our ability to regulate the energy sector, which is vital to our national interests." Is Senator Jones right? What course of action would you recommend to accomplish his objective? Consider the *Italian Discrimination* case below.

Italian Discrimination Against Imported Agricultural Machinery
Report of the GATT Panel, adopted on October 23, 1958
L/833—7S/60

I. INTRODUCTION

1. The Panel examined the complaint of the United Kingdom Government that certain provisions of chapter III of Italian Law No. 949 of 25 July 1952, which provides special credit facilities to some categories of farmers or farmers' co-operatives for the purchase of agricultural machinery produced in Italy, were inconsistent with the obligations of Italy under Article III of the General Agreement.

II.   Facts of the Case

2. In accordance with the Law of 25 July 1952, the Italian Government established a revolving fund which enabled the Ministry of Agriculture and Forestry to grant special credit terms *inter alia* for the purchase of Italian agricultural machinery. To this fund are allocated by budgetary appropriations 25 thousand million lire a year for five fiscal years starting with the year 1952-53; out of these 25 thousand million lire, the Law provides that 7.5 thousand million would be assigned for the purchase of agricultural machinery, an amount which may be modified by the Italian authorities. The loans are granted at 3 per cent, including fees to the Credit Institute, for a period of five years to finance up to 75 per cent of the cost of the machinery. The interest and repayments of the loans are paid into the revolving fund and may be used for further loans. The revolving fund will remain in existence until 1964. Eligible purchasers may benefit from these favourable terms when they buy Italian agricultural machinery; if, on the other hand, they wish to buy foreign machinery on credit, the terms would be less favourable. The United Kingdom delegation indicated that loans on commercial terms were presently available at the rate of about 10 per cent while the Italian delegation stated that farmers could obtain from agricultural credit institutions five-year loans on terms substantially more favourable than 10 per cent.

3. The Italian delegation estimated that during the period 1952-1957 the purchasers of about half of the Italian tractors sold in Italy (i.e. about one-third of all tractors sold in the country) benefitted from the credit facilities provided under Law No. 949.

III.   Alleged Inconsistency of the Effects of the Provisions of the Italian Law with the Provisions of Paragraph 4 of Article III

5. The United Kingdom delegation noted that Article III:4 of the General Agreement provided that products imported into the territory of any contracting party "shall be accorded treatment no less favourable than that accorded to like products of national origin in respect of all laws, regulations and requirements affecting their internal sale, offering for sale, purchase, transportation . . ." etc. As the credit facilities provided under the Italian Law were not available to the purchasers of imported tractors and other agricultural machinery these products did not enjoy the equality of treatment which should be accorded to them. The fact that these credit facilities were reserved exclusively to the purchasers of Italian tractors and other agricultural machinery represented a discrimination and the operation of the Law involved an inconsistency with the provisions of Article III of the General Agreement which provides that laws, regulations and requirements affecting internal sale should not be applied to imported products so as to afford protection to domestic producers. The United Kingdom would not challenge the consistency with the General Agreement of subsidies which the Italian Government might wish to grant to domestic producers of tractors and other agricultural machinery in accordance with the terms of paragraph 8 (b) of Article III. However, in the case of the Italian Law the assistance by the State was not given to producers but to the purchasers of agricultural machinery, a case which is not covered by the provisions of paragraph 8 (b).

Even in the case of subsidies granted to producers, the rights of the United Kingdom under Article XXIII of the General Agreement would be safeguarded as was recognized by the CONTRACTING PARTIES in paragraph 13 of the report on other barriers to trade which they approved during the course of the Review Session.

6. The Italian delegation considered that the General Agreement was a trade agreement and its scope was limited to measures governing trade; thus the text of paragraph 4 of Article III applied only to such laws, regulations and requirements which were concerned with the actual conditions for sale, transportation, etc., of the commodity in question and should not be interpreted in an extensive way. In particular, the Italian delegation stated that the commitment undertaken by the CONTRACTING PARTIES under that paragraph was limited to qualitative and quantitative regulations to which goods were subjected, with respect to their sale or purchase on the domestic market.

7. It was clear in their view that Law No. 949 which concerned the development of the Italian economy and the improvement in the employment of labour was not related to the questions of sale, purchase or transportation of imported and domestically produced products which were the only matters dealt with in Article III.

8. Moreover the Italian delegation considered that the text of Article III:4 could not be construed in such a way as to prevent the Italian Government from taking the necessary measures to assist the economic development of the country and to improve the conditions of employment in Italy.

9. Finally, the Italian delegation, noting that the United Kingdom delegation recognized that the Italian Government would be entitled to grant subsidies exclusively to domestic producers, stressed it would not be logical to exclude this possibility in the case of credit facilities which had a far less pronounced effect on the terms of competition.

10. In the view of the Italian delegation it would be inappropriate for the CONTRACTING PARTIES to construe the provisions of Article III in a broad way since this would limit the rights of contracting parties in the formulation of their domestic economic policies in a way which was not contemplated when they accepted the terms of the General Agreement.

13. The Italian delegation alleged that the provisions of paragraph 8 (b) which exempted the granting of subsidies to producers from the operation of this Article showed that the intention of the drafters of the Agreement was to limit the scope of Article III to laws and regulations directly related to the conditions of sale, purchase, etc. On the other hand, the Panel considered that if the Italian contention were correct and if the scope of Article III was limited in this way (which would, of course, not include any measure of subsidization) it would have been unnecessary to include the provisions contained in paragraph 8 (b) since they would be excluded *ipso facto* from the scope of Article III. The fact that the drafters of Article III thought it necessary to include this exemption for production subsidies would indicate that the intent of the drafters was to provide equal conditions of competition once goods had been cleared through customs.

14. Moreover, the Panel agreed with the contention of the United Kingdom delegation that in any case the provisions of paragraph 8 (b) would not be applicable to this particular case since the credit facilities provided under the Law were granted to the purchasers of agricultural machinery and could not be considered as subsidies accorded to the producers of agricultural machinery.

15. The Panel also noted that if the Italian contention were correct, and if the scope of Article III were limited in the way the Italian delegation suggested

to a specific type of laws and regulations, the value of the bindings under Article II of the Agreement and of the general rules of non-discrimination as between imported and domestic products could be easily evaded.

16. The Panel recognized—and the United Kingdom delegation agreed with this view—that it was not the intention of the General Agreement to limit the right of a contracting party to adopt measures which appeared to it necessary to foster its economic development or to protect a domestic industry, provided that such measures were permitted by the terms of the General Agreement. The GATT offered a number of possibilities to achieve these purposes through tariff measures or otherwise. The Panel did not appreciate why the extension of the credit facilities in question to the purchasers of imported tractors as well as domestically produced tractors would detract from the attainment of the objectives of the Law, which aimed at stimulating the purchase of tractors mainly by small farmers and co-operatives in the interests of economic development. If, on the other hand, the objective of the Law, although not specifically stated in the text thereof, were to protect the Italian agricultural machinery industry, the Panel considered that such protection should be given in ways permissible under the General Agreement rather than by the extension of credit exclusively for purchases of domestically produced agricultural machinery. [The panel concluded that the Italian Law No. 949 was inconsistent with Article III:4.]

PROBLEM 4-14

Assume that the United States Patent and Trademark Office (USPTO) is considering the following changes to accommodate the recent increase of foreign patent applications:

(1)   The USPTO will be divided into two different divisions. A new foreign division will be established within the USPTO for the purpose of handling all foreign applications; all U.S. applications will be handled in the new domestic division.

(2)   Foreign applicants have the choice of finding a U.S. citizen or corporation to serve as the official patent applicant, in which case the application can proceed through the domestic division.

(3)   New guidelines indicate that the average processing and examination period for a foreign application will require an additional six months over a national application but all foreign patents, once approved, will be given an additional six-month period of protection as an offset.

Are each of these changes consistent with the National Treatment principle? *See* TRIPS Article 3 and the *Korea—Chilled Beef* case and notes below.

Korea—Measures Affecting Imports of Fresh, Chilled and Frozen Beef
Report of the Appellate Body, adopted on December 11, 2000
WT/DS161, 169/AB/R

[The United States and Australia claimed that Korea's dual retail distribution system for beef was a violation of the National Treatment principle. The system required one set of retail establishments for domestic beef and a separate set of

establishments for imported beef. The panel found that the system was in violation of the National Treatment principle contained in GATT Article III:4, based
upon its view that any measure based exclusively on criteria relating to the origin
of the goods was in violation of Article III. Korea then appealed this finding. The
Appellate Body reasoned that in order to establish a violation of Article III:4 three
elements had to be satisfied: (1) The imported and domestic products must be
"like products"; (2) the measure in question must be a law, regulation, or requirement affecting their internal sale, offering for sale, purchase, transportation, distribution, or use; and (3) the imported products must be accorded treatment that
is "less favorable" than treatment accorded to domestic products. Only this last
element (3) was contested by the parties in the panel proceedings and on appeal.
The opinion of the Appellate Body on this issue follows.]

VI. DUAL RETAIL SYSTEM

A. ARTICLE III:4 OF THE GATT 1994

134. The Panel began its analysis of the phrase "treatment no less favourable"
by reviewing past GATT and WTO cases. It found that "treatment no less favourable" under Article III:4 requires that a Member accord to imported products
"effective equality of opportunities" with like domestic products in respect of the
application of laws, regulations and requirements. The Panel concluded its review
of the case law by stating:

> Any regulatory distinction that is based exclusively on criteria relating to the nation-
> ality or the origin of the products is incompatible with Article III and this conclu-
> sion can be reached even in the absence of any imports (as hypothetical imports can
> be used to reach this conclusion) confirming that there is no need to demonstrate
> the actual and specific trade effects of a measure for it to be found in violation of
> Article III. The object of Article III:4 is, thus, to guarantee effective market access to
> imported products and to ensure that the latter are offered the same market oppor-
> tunities as domestic products.

135. The Panel stated that "any regulatory distinction that is based exclusively on criteria relating to the nationality or origin" of products is incompatible
with Article III:4. We observe, however, that Article III:4 requires only that a measure accord treatment to imported products that is "no less favourable" than that
accorded to like domestic products. A measure that provides treatment to imported
products that is *different* from that accorded to like domestic products is not necessarily inconsistent with Article III:4, as long as the treatment provided by the
measure is "no less favourable". According "treatment no less favourable" means, as
we have previously said, according *conditions of competition* no less favourable to the
imported product than to the like domestic product. In *Japan — Taxes on Alcoholic
Beverages*, we described the legal standard in Article III as follows:

> The broad and fundamental purpose of Article III is to avoid protectionism in the
> application of internal tax and regulatory measures. More specifically, the purpose
> of Article III "is to ensure that internal measures 'not be applied to imported or
> domestic products so as to afford protection to domestic production'". Toward this

end, Article III obliges Members of the WTO to provide *equality of competitive conditions* for imported products in relation to domestic products. "[T]he intention of the drafters of the Agreement was clearly to treat the imported products in the same way as the like domestic products once they had been cleared through customs. Otherwise indirect protection could be given".[1] (emphasis added)

136. This interpretation, which focuses on the *conditions of competition* between imported and domestic like products, implies that a measure according formally *different* treatment to imported products does not *per se*, that is, necessarily, violate Article III:4.

138. We conclude that the Panel erred in its general interpretation that "[a]ny regulatory distinction that is based exclusively on criteria relating to the nationality or the origin of the products is incompatible with Article III."

142. We believe that a more direct, and perhaps simpler, approach to the dual retail system of Korea may be usefully followed in the present case. In the following paragraphs, we seek to focus on what appears to us to be the fundamental thrust and effect of the measure itself.

143. Korean law in effect requires the existence of two distinct retail distribution systems so far as beef is concerned: one system for the retail sale of domestic beef and another system for the retail sale of imported beef. A small retailer (that is, a non-supermarket or non-department store) which is a "Specialized Imported Beef Store" may sell any meat *except domestic beef*; any other small retailer may sell any meat *except imported beef*. A large retailer (that is, a supermarket or department store) may sell both imported and domestic beef, as long as the imported beef and domestic beef are sold in separate sales areas. A retailer selling imported beef is required to display a sign reading "Specialized Imported Beef Store".

144. Thus, the Korean measure formally separates the selling of imported beef and domestic beef. However, that formal separation, *in and of itself*, does not necessarily compel the conclusion that the treatment thus accorded to imported beef is less favourable than the treatment accorded to domestic beef. To determine whether the treatment given to imported beef is less favourable than that given to domestic beef, we must, as earlier indicated, inquire into whether or not the Korean dual retail system for beef modifies the *conditions of competition* in the Korean beef market to the disadvantage of the imported product.

145. When beef was first imported into Korea in 1988, the new product simply entered into the pre-existing distribution system that had been handling domestic beef. The beef retail system was a unitary one, and the conditions of competition affecting the sale of beef were the same for both the domestic and the imported product. In 1990, Korea promulgated its dual retail system for beef. Accordingly, the existing small retailers had to choose between, on the one hand, continuing to sell domestic beef and renouncing the sale of imported beef or, on the other hand, ceasing to sell domestic beef in order to be allowed to sell the imported product. Apparently, the vast majority of the small meat retailers chose the first option. The result was the virtual exclusion of imported beef from the retail distribution channels through which domestic beef (and until then, imported beef, too) was distributed to Korean households and other consumers throughout the country. Accordingly, a new and separate retail system had to be established and gradually

---

1. Appellate Body Report, WT/DS8/AB/R, WT/DS10/AB/R, WT/DS11/AB/R, adopted [on] November 1,1996, pp. 16-17.

built from the ground up for bringing the imported product to the same house-holds and other consumers if the imported product was to compete at all with the domestic product. Put in slightly different terms, the putting into legal effect of the dual retail system for beef meant, in direct practical effect, so far as imported beef was concerned, the sudden cutting off of access to the normal, that is, the previously existing, distribution outlets through which the domestic product continued to flow to consumers in the urban centers and countryside that make up the Korean national territory. The central consequence of the dual retail system can only be reasonably construed, in our view, as the imposition of a drastic reduction of commercial opportunity to reach, and hence to generate sales to, the same consumers served by the traditional retail channels for domestic beef. In 1998, when this case began, eight years after the dual retail system was first prescribed, the consequent reduction of commercial opportunity was reflected in the much smaller number of specialized imported beef shops (approximately 5,000 shops) as compared with the number of retailers (approximately 45,000 shops) selling domestic beef.

146. We are aware that the dramatic reduction in number of retail outlets for imported beef followed from the decisions of individual retailers who could choose freely to sell the domestic product or the imported product. The legal necessity of making a choice was, however, imposed by the measure itself. The restricted nature of that choice should be noted. The choice given to the meat retailers was *not* an option between remaining with the pre-existing unified distribution set-up or going to a dual retail system. The choice was limited to selling domestic beef only or imported beef only. Thus, the reduction of access to normal retail channels is, in legal contemplation, the effect of that measure. In these circumstances, the intervention of some element of private choice does not relieve Korea of responsibility under the GATT 1994 for the resulting establishment of competitive conditions less favourable for the imported product than for the domestic product.

148. We believe, and so hold, that the treatment accorded to imported beef, as a consequence of the dual retail system established for beef by Korean law and regulation, is less favourable than the treatment given to like domestic beef and is, accordingly, not consistent with the requirements of Article III:4 of the GATT 1994.

B.   ARTICLE XX(D) OF THE GATT 1994

152. The Panel went on to conclude that the dual retail system, which it found to be inconsistent with Article III:4, could *not* be justified pursuant to Article XX(d) of the GATT 1994. The Panel found that the dual retail system is a disproportionate measure not necessary to secure compliance with the Korean law against deceptive practices.

155. Article XX(d), together with the introductory clause of Article XX, reads as follows:

Article XX General Exceptions

Subject to the requirement that such measures are not applied in a manner which would constitute a means of arbitrary or unjustifiable discrimination between countries where the same conditions prevail, or a disguised restriction on international trade, nothing in this Agreement shall be construed to prevent the adoption or enforcement by any Member of measures: . . .

>   (d)   necessary to secure compliance with laws or regulations which are not incon-
>   sistent with the provisions of this Agreement, including those relating to
>   customs enforcement, the enforcement of monopolies operated under para-
>   graph 4 of Article II and Article XVII, the protection of patents, trade marks
>   and copyrights, and the prevention of deceptive practices;

157. For a measure, otherwise inconsistent with GATT 1994, to be justified provisionally under paragraph (d) of Article XX, two elements must be shown. First, the measure must be one designed to "secure compliance" with laws or regulations that are not themselves inconsistent with some provision of the GATT 1994. Second, the measure must be "necessary" to secure such compliance. A Member who invokes Article XX(d) as a justification has the burden of demonstrating that these two requirements are met.

158. The Panel examined these two aspects one after the other. The Panel found, "despite . . . troublesome aspects, . . . that the dual retail system was put in place, at least in part, in order to secure compliance with the Korean legislation against deceptive practices to the extent that it serves to prevent acts inconsistent with the *Unfair Competition Act*."[2] It recognized that the system was established at a time when acts of misrepresentation of origin were widespread in the beef sector. It also acknowledged that the dual retail system "does appear to reduce the oppor-tunities and thus the temptations for butchers to misrepresent [less expensive] for-eign beef for [more expensive] domestic beef".[3] The parties did not appeal these findings of the Panel.

159. We turn, therefore, to the question of whether the dual retail system is "necessary" to secure compliance with the *Unfair Competition Act*. Once again, we look first to the ordinary meaning of the word "necessary", in its context and in the light of the object and purpose of Article XX, in accordance with Article 31(1) of the *Vienna Convention*.

160. The word "necessary" normally denotes something "that cannot be dis-pensed with or done without, requisite, essential, needful".[4] We note, however, that a standard law dictionary cautions that:

> "[t]his word must be considered in the connection in which it is used, as it is a word
> susceptible of various meanings. It may import absolute physical necessity or inevi-
> tability, or it may import that which is only convenient, useful, appropriate, suitable,
> proper, or conducive to the end sought. It is an adjective expressing degrees, and
> may express mere convenience or that which is indispensable or an absolute physical
> necessity".[5]

161. We believe that, as used in the context of Article XX(d), the reach of the word "necessary" is not limited to that which is "indispensable" or "of absolute necessity" or "inevitable". Measures which are indispensable or of absolute neces-sity or inevitable to secure compliance certainly fulfill the requirements of Article

---

2. Panel Report, para. 658.
3. *Ibid.*
4. *The New Shorter Oxford English Dictionary*, (Clarendon Press, 1993), Vol. II, p. 1895.
5. *Black's Law Dictionary*, (West Publishing, 1995), p. 1029.

XX(d). But other measures, too, may fall within the ambit of this exception. As used in Article XX(d), the term "necessary" refers, in our view, to a range of degrees of necessity. At one end of this continuum lies "necessary" understood as "indispensable"; at the other end, is "necessary" taken to mean as "making a contribution to." We consider that a "necessary" measure is, in this continuum, located significantly closer to the pole of "indispensable" than to the opposite pole of simply "making a contribution to".

162. In appraising the "necessity" of a measure in these terms, it is useful to bear in mind the context in which "necessary" is found in Article XX(d). The measure at stake has to be "necessary to ensure compliance with laws and regulations . . . , *including* those relating to customs enforcement, the enforcement of [lawful] monopolies . . . , the protection of patents, trademarks and copyrights, and the prevention of deceptive practices". (emphasis added) Clearly, Article XX(d) is susceptible of application in respect of a wide variety of "laws and regulations" to be enforced. It seems to us that a treaty interpreter assessing a measure claimed to be necessary to secure compliance of a WTO-consistent law or regulation may, in appropriate cases, take into account the relative importance of the common interests or values that the law or regulation to be enforced is intended to protect. The more vital or important those common interests or values are, the easier it would be to accept as "necessary" a measure designed as an enforcement instrument.

164. In sum, determination of whether a measure, which is not "indispensable", may nevertheless be "necessary" within the contemplation of Article XX(d), involves in every case a process of weighing and balancing a series of factors which prominently include the contribution made by the compliance measure to the enforcement of the law or regulation at issue, the importance of the common interests or values protected by that law or regulation, and the accompanying impact of the law or regulation on imports or exports.

165. The panel in *United States — Section 337* described the applicable standard for evaluating whether a measure is "necessary" under Article XX(d) in the following terms:

> It was clear to the Panel that a contracting party cannot justify a measure inconsistent with another GATT provision as "necessary" in terms of Article XX(d) if an alternative measure which it could reasonably be expected to employ and which is not inconsistent with other GATT provisions is available to it. By the same token, in cases where a measure consistent with other GATT provisions is not reasonably available, a contracting party is bound to use, among the measures reasonably available to it, that which entails the least degree of inconsistency with other GATT provisions.[6]

166. The standard described by the panel in *United States — Section 337* encapsulates the general considerations we have adverted to above. In our view, the weighing and balancing process we have outlined is comprehended in the determination of whether a WTO-consistent alternative measure which the Member concerned could "reasonably be expected to employ" is available, or whether a less WTO-inconsistent measure is "reasonably available".

167. The Panel followed the standard identified by the panel in *United States — Section 337*. It started scrutinizing whether the dual retail system is "necessary" under paragraph (d) of Article XX by stating:

---

6. Panel Report, *United States — Section 337, supra*, footnote 69, para. 5.26.

Korea has to convince the Panel that, contrary to what was alleged by Australia and the United States, no alternative measure consistent with the WTO Agreement is reasonably available at present in order to deal with misrepresentation in the retail market as to the origin of beef.[7]

168. The Panel first considered a range of possible alternative measures, by examining measures taken by Korea with respect to situations involving, or which could involve, deceptive practices similar to those which in 1989-1990 had affected the retail sale of foreign beef. The Panel found that Korea does not require a dual retail system in *related product areas*, but relies instead on traditional enforcement procedures. There is no requirement, for example, for a dual retail system separating domestic Hanwoo beef from domestic dairy cattle beef. Nor is there a requirement for a dual retail system for any other meat or food product, such as pork or seafood. Finally, there is no requirement for a system of separate restaurants, depending on whether they serve domestic or imported beef, even though approximately 45 percent of the beef imported into Korea is sold in restaurants. Yet, in all of these cases, the Panel found that there were numerous cases of fraudulent misrepresentation. For the Panel, these examples indicated that misrepresentation of origin could, in principle, be dealt with "on the basis of basic methods . . . such as normal policing under the Korean *Unfair Competition Act*."

171. The enforcement measures that the Panel examined were measures taken to enforce the same law, the *Unfair Competition Act*. This law provides for penal and other sanctions against any "unfair competitive act", which includes any:

> *Act misleading the public to understand the place of origin of any goods* either by falsely marking that place on any commercial document or communication, in said goods or any advertisement thereof *or in any manner of misleading the general public*, or by selling, distributing, importing or exporting goods bearing such mark; (emphasis added)

The language used in this law to define an "unfair competitive act" — "any manner of misleading the general public" — is broad. It applies to all the examples raised by the Panel — domestic dairy beef sold as Hanwoo beef, foreign pork or seafood sold as domestic product, as well as to imported beef served as domestic beef in restaurants.

173. Having found that possible alternative enforcement measures, consistent with the *WTO Agreement*, existed in other related product areas, the Panel went on to state that:

> . . . it is for Korea to demonstrate that such an alternative measure is not reasonably available or is unreasonably burdensome, financially or technically, taking into account a variety of factors including the domestic costs of such alternative measure, to ensure that consumers are not misled as to the origin of beef.

174. The Panel proceeded to examine whether the alternative measures or "basic methods" — investigations, prosecutions, fines, and record-keeping — which were used in related product areas, were "reasonably available" to Korea to secure compliance with the *Unfair Competition Act*. The Panel concluded "that Korea has not demonstrated to the satisfaction of the Panel that alternative measures consistent

---

7. Panel Report, para. 659.

with the WTO Agreement were not reasonably available". Thus, as noted at the outset, the Panel found that the dual retail system was "a disproportionate measure not necessary to secure compliance with the Korean law against deceptive practices". The dual retail system was, therefore, not justified under Article XX(d).

180. We share the Panel's conclusion. We are not persuaded that Korea could not achieve its desired level of enforcement of the *Unfair Competition Act* with respect to the origin of beef sold by retailers by using conventional WTO-consistent enforcement measures, if Korea would devote more resources to its enforcement efforts on the beef sector. It might also be added that Korea's argument about the lack of resources to police thousands of shops on a round-the-clock basis is, in the end, not sufficiently persuasive. Violations of laws and regulations like the Korean *Unfair Competition Act* can be expected to be routinely investigated and detected through selective, but well-targeted, controls of potential wrongdoers. The control of records will assist in selecting the shops to which the police could pay particular attention.

185. In sum, we uphold the Panel's conclusion that the dual retail system, which is inconsistent with Article III:4, is not justified under Article XX(d) of the GATT 1994.

NOTES AND QUESTIONS

1. *General Scope of Article III:4.* The famous decision in *Italian Discrimination Against Imported Agricultural Machinery* established several important interpretations of Article III:4. First, Article III:4 requires equal conditions of competition once foreign goods have been cleared through customs. Second, Article III:4 covers not only laws affecting the sale and purchase of domestic and foreign goods but also laws concerning the conditions of competition, such as credit terms, between domestic and foreign goods. While the panel recognized that the Italian government had a legitimate interest in fostering the nation's economic development, such development must be consistent with the GATT.

Can governments satisfy their National Treatment obligation by providing for a scheme in which less favorable treatment for imports in some instances is balanced out by more favorable treatment in others? A GATT panel rejected this argument, noting that National Treatment requires "effective equality of opportunities for imported products." *See United States—Section 337 of the Tariff Act of 1930*, GATT B.I.S.D. (36th Supp.) 345, Report of the GATT Panel, adopted on November 7, 1989 at ¶¶5.11, 5.14. Differences in treatment for imports and domestic products are not conclusively in violation of Article III:4, but the WTO member applying differential treatment has the burden of showing that the "no less favourable" standard is satisfied. *See id.* at ¶5.11.

Article III:4 has been found applicable in a wide variety of contexts. For example, the European Community successfully challenged Section 337 of the U.S. Tariff Act of 1930, which allows parties to obtain remedies against certain unfair methods of competition, including barring the importation of products found to infringe intellectual property rights. The panel found that Section 337 violated Article III:4 of the GATT because it was easier to sustain a claim of unfair competition against goods of foreign origin than against U.S. domestic "like products." *See United States—Section 337 of the Tariff Act of 1930, supra*, at ¶5.10.

2. *De Facto Discrimination.* Beginning in 1987 with *Japan — Customs, Duties, Taxes, and Labeling Practices on Imported Wines and Alcoholic Beverages*, GATT B.I.S.D. (34th Supp.) 83, Report of the GATT Panel, adopted on November 10, 1987, GATT/WTO panels have consistently found that de facto discrimination violates the National Treatment principle. This approach is important because nations could otherwise enact facially neutral laws but apply them in a discriminatory manner. For example, in *United States — Measures Affecting Alcoholic and Malt Beverages*, GATT B.I.S.D. (39th Supp.) 206, Report of the GATT Panel, adopted on June 19, 1992, a GATT panel found that a lower excise tax enacted by Mississippi for certain types of grapes was discriminatory because the type of grapes eligible for favorable tax treatment were found only in Mississippi and a few other U.S. regions. In *Canada — Import, Distribution, and Sale of Certain Alcoholic Drinks by Provincial Marketing Agencies*, GATT B.I.S.D. (39th Supp.) 27, Report of the GATT Panel, adopted on February 18, 1992, a GATT panel found (¶5.31) that a law requiring certain minimum prices for domestic and imported beer was applied in practice to discriminate in favor of domestic beer.

3. *The "Like Products" Issue.* The leading case on the "like products" issue under Article III:4 is *European Communities — Measure Affecting Asbestos and Asbestos-Containing Products*, WT/DS135/AB/R, Report of the Appellate Body, adopted on April 5, 2001. This case concerned a ban by the EC on the importation of all asbestos and asbestos-containing products. Canada, the complaining member, argued, and the WTO panel agreed, that chrysotile asbestos fibre products are like products to non-asbestos PVA, cellulose, and glass (PCG) fibre products because they serve the same functions and are in a competitive relationship. The issue was important because asbestos products were banned because of their danger to human health, while the non-asbestos-containing products did not pose such dangers and could be freely made and sold, whether imported or domestic. The Appellate Body stated (¶99) that the meaning of "like product" in Article III:4 was somewhat wider than "like product" under Article III:2, first sentence, but not wider than the combined "like products" scope of Article III:2, first and second sentences. In addition, Article III:4 requires a showing that the imported product is accorded "less favorable treatment" than the domestic like product. The Appellate Body noted (¶101) that four general (and non-exhaustive) criteria are relevant to determine likeness: (1) the physical properties, nature, and quality of the products; (2) the end uses; (3) consumer tastes and habits; and (4) tariff classifications of the products. These four and any other considerations should be weighed separately on a case-by-case basis to determine likeness. Turning to the evidence, the Appellate Body stated that carcinogenicity (or toxicity) is an important aspect of the physical properties of chrysotile asbestos fibres. In such a case criteria (2) and (3) are particularly important since these involve the competitive relationship of products in the marketplace. The Appellate Body first faulted the panel for not adequately considering the four criteria, particularly the question of the risk of the products as part of a consideration of criteria (1), (2), and (3). Then the Appellate Body sought to complete the analysis by applying the requisite criteria itself. The Appellate Body noted that since chrysotile asbestos products and PCG products are very different physically, there is a "high burden" on the complaining party to show there is a competitive relationship between the products. Since the two types of products share only a small number of end uses and because no evidence was shown as to consumer preferences, and because the products have different

tariff classifications, the Appellate Body ruled (¶141) that Canada had not met the burden of showing that the products were "like."

How does the interpretation of the "like product" issue under Article III:4 compare with that under Article III:2? Does *EC—Asbestos* open the door to differentiating between products that pose risks to health or the environment and similar products that do not?

4. *Exceptions to National Treatment.* In *European Communities—Measures Affecting Trade in Commercial Vessels*, WT/DS301/R, Report of the Panel, adopted on June 20, 2005, the Republic of Korea challenged direct aid granted to European shipbuilders by the EC and its member states. The panel concluded (¶7.75) that "the state aid provided . . . is covered by [the exception to National Treatment for government subsidies to domestic industries contained in] Article III:8(b) of the GATT 1994 and that, as a consequence . . . is not inconsistent with Article III:4."

5. Additional exceptions to Article III include Article XX (General Exceptions); Article XXI (National Security); government procurement (GATT Article III:8(a)); and the balance of payment exception and temporary application of quantitative restrictions in a discriminatory manner (GATT Articles XII, XVII.B, and XIV).

PROBLEM 4-15

Graham, a third-year law student at a law school in the United States, is eager to move to China to work as a lawyer in its booming economy. However, Graham has just discovered that China's national lawyer's examination has a low passage rate and is given exclusively in Chinese. As a result, very few foreign takers ever pass the exam, and those who do are inevitably from another Chinese-speaking country, such as Taiwan. Foreign citizens are allowed to qualify and work as foreign lawyers in China although they cannot appear in court unless they have passed the national lawyer's examination. Graham says, "China joined the WTO in 2001. The exam is already hard enough but I also need to spend five years to learn Chinese first to take it! This is de facto discrimination in violation of the National Treatment principle in the General Agreement on Trade in Services (GATS). China needs to offer the bar exam in English." Assume for this problem that China has made an unqualified and unconditional market access commitment for legal services. Is Graham correct? Consult GATS Article XVII n.10.

C. Government Procurement

Read the Agreement on Government Procurement in the Documents Supplement.

PROBLEM 4-16

China is seeking bids for a $10 billion new airport to be built in Chengdu, a city in its western region, as a measure to spur economic development in this region, which is lagging behind the coastal areas. China has stated that it will consider bids from U.S. suppliers under certain conditions: (1) All bids must be at least 25 percent lower than bids by Chinese vendors for the airport; and (2) all U.S.

suppliers must transfer any intellectual property rights contained in their products to the PRC government. No such restrictions apply to domestic bidders. The United States Chamber of Commerce cries foul and states that these conditions are blatantly discriminatory in violation of the National Treatment principle. Is the Chamber right?

What should the United States do? Assuming that no exceptions or exclusions to its commitments apply, can the United States impose similar restrictions on China? To solve this problem, read GATT Article III:8(a) and the discussion below.

Government procurement refers to the purchase by national governments of goods (and services) from private vendors and has emerged as a significant trade issue. Today, in most countries government procurement accounts for 15-20 percent of Gross Domestic Product (GDP). In some countries, such as India, government procurement represents over 30 percent of GDP.

Due to political concerns, government procurement was largely excluded from the original GATT 1947 through an explicit exception to the National Treatment principle contained in Article III:8(a). This exclusion meant that governments that purchase goods were entirely free to discriminate against foreign goods in favor of domestic goods.

In 1979, efforts were made to adopt some standards for government procurement in the GATT. At the end of the Uruguay Round, the WTO adopted the 1994 WTO Agreement on Government Procurement (1994 GPA), which requires all member states to extend national treatment to include foreign goods in government procurement. Unlike the GATT, GATS, and TRIPS, which are automatically binding on all members upon entry into the WTO, the GPA is a "plurilateral" agreement, meaning that it is binding only on WTO members who voluntarily agree to accept it. As of this writing there are fifteen parties composed of forty-two WTO members (the EU has joined on behalf of twenty-seven members), and virtually all developed countries (including the United States). Many developing countries, such as China, are not members of the 1994 GPA. Moreover, not all government procurement is within the scope of the 1994 GPA. Every signatory has excluded certain government agencies altogether, and only larger procurement transactions are covered (generally goods and services procurement by the central government in excess of SDR 130,000[8] and in excess of SDR 200,000 for local governments). Construction contracts are not covered unless they exceed SDR 5 million.

A new Government Procurement Agreement was adopted by WTO members on December 15, 2011, and became effective in 2012. The 2011 GPA expands market access commitments in government procurement by an estimated $100 billion per year. The 2011 GPA was designed to speed up membership for countries that are currently negotiating to become GPA members, such as China. The 2011 GPA opens more government entities to international competition in procurement, and now all goods are covered in principle (for instance, medicines, machinery,

---

8. The SDR (Special Drawing Right) is used by the International Monetary Fund as a neutral unit based on a basket of major currencies in international trade. The SDR varies daily with the values of the underlying currencies. On March 23, 2012, 1 SDR = US$1.54.

fuels, and textiles) as well as a broad range of services and construction services, including such matters as transport infrastructure (highways, ports, and airports), telecommunication services, computer and related services, financial services, and management consulting services.

The 2011 GPA provides extended government procurement opportunities as follows:

- Over 150 additional central government entities are covered, particularly in EU member countries.
- GPA parties such as Japan and Korea have added a significant number of sub-central government entities. U.S. companies can compete for Canadian provincial procurement since 2010 when a bilateral agreement was signed with Canada.
- New government enterprises are covered in many countries, such as the Environmental Services Company in Israel.
- More than fifty new categories of services are added.
- Electronic methods of procurement are advanced.

The 2011 GPA contains five annexes as follows:

- Central government entities
- Sub-central government entities
- All other entities that procure in accordance with the GPA
- Services that each party covers under the GPA
- Construction services that each party covers under the GPA

Each of the parties to the 2011 GPA—from Armenia to the United States—has filed a separate Annex corresponding with these five categories. To determine if any particular project is covered by the GPA in any member country, you must consult the relevant Annex in the particular country. The annexes are available on the WTO web site, http://www.wto.org.

In addition to the WTO GPA, the United States and several other countries have bilateral government procurement agreements with other countries, and most free trade agreements contain government procurement provisions.

Norway—Procurement of Toll Collection Equipment for the City of Trondheim
GATT Panel Report, adopted on May 13, 1992
GATT Doc. GPR.DS2/R (April 28, 1992)

[This case involved an interpretation of Article V:16(e) of the 1979 Government Procurement Agreement, set forth in the opinion below, which allows certain exceptions to MFN requirements. Article V:16(e) is identical to Article XV.1(e) of the 2011 GPA.]

IV.   FINDINGS

4.1 The basic facts of the case before the Panel are that in March 1991 the Norwegian Public Roads Administration awarded a contract relating to electronic toll collection equipment for a toll system around the city of Trondheim to a Norwegian company, Micro Design, after single tendering the procurement with that company. The central point of difference between the two parties to the dispute was whether, in single tendering the procurement, Norway had met the requirements of Article V:16(e) of the Agreement. Norway maintained that the single tendering of the contract was justifiable under these provisions, since the contract was for research and development and the part of the contract which it considered was covered by the Agreement was for the procurement of prototypes which had been developed in the course of and for that research and development contract. The United States maintained that Article V:16(e) was not applicable since, in its view, the objective of the contract was not research and development but the procurement of toll collection equipment.

4.4 The Panel noted that it was not in dispute that the procurement had been single tendered and that therefore it would have to meet the requirements of Article V:16 if it were to be in conformity with the Agreement. Only sub-paragraph (e) had been invoked by Norway in this regard. Article V:16(e) reads as follows:

> The provisions of paragraphs 1-15 above governing open and selective tendering procedures need not apply in the following conditions, provided that single tendering is not used with a view to avoiding maximum possible competition or in a manner which would constitute a means of discrimination among foreign suppliers or protection to domestic producers: . . .
>
> (e) when an entity procures prototypes or a first product which are developed at its request in the course of, and for, a particular contract for research, experiment, study or original development. When such contracts have been fulfilled, subsequent procurements of products shall be subject to paragraphs 1-15 of this Article.

There is a footnote to sub-paragraph (e) which reads as follows:

> Original development of a first product may include limited production in order to incorporate the results of field testing and to demonstrate that the product is suitable for production in quantity to acceptable quality standards. It does not extend to quantity production to establish commercial viability or to recover research and development costs.

4.6 The Panel first examined the conformity of the procurement with the conditions contained in the text of sub-paragraph (e) of Article V:16. The Panel noted that there was a basic difference of interpretation of this sub-paragraph between the parties to the dispute. The United States understood the words "contract for research . . . or original development" to mean that the objective of the contract must be the procurement of the results of research and/or development. In this view, the mere fact that a good deal of research and/or development was necessary in order to produce a product would not be sufficient to meet this standard, if it was the product rather than the results of the research and/or development that was the object of the procurement. For Norway, this phrase meant that the basic task required under the contract must be the conduct of research and/or development. In this interpretation, there was no requirement that the principal purpose of the procurement must be the acquisition of research and/or development results as such, as opposed to the products developed through such research and/or development (provided that the products were prototypes or a first product).

4.7 In examining this issue, the Panel first noted that, while the provision referred to "research, experiment, study or original development", the parties to the dispute had referred only to research and development. Furthermore, although the provision relates to "prototypes or a first product", only prototypes had been referred to. The Panel therefore limited its examination to these aspects. The question therefore before the Panel was whether, under the contract, the Norwegian Public Roads Administration had procured prototypes which had been developed at its request in the course of, and for, a particular contract for research or original development. The Panel then proceeded to examine the different interpretations of Norway and the United States of the phrase "contract for research . . . or original development", bearing in mind the general rule for the interpretation of treaties that a treaty be interpreted in accordance with the ordinary meaning to be given to the terms of the treaty in their context and in the light of its object and purpose.

4.8 Given the above, it was clear to the Panel that the words "contract for research . . . or original development" in Article V:16(e) had to be interpreted from the perspective of the procuring entity. What was relevant at this point in the Agreement, as at others, was what the procuring entity was procuring, not the nature of the work that would have to be undertaken by the supplier to supply the goods and/or services being procured. It was the output of suppliers that the Agreement dealt with and that procuring entities were interested in purchasing, not the input of factors of production necessary to produce such output. For example, if most of the cost of producing a product that was being procured were to consist of payments for labour required to produce it, this would clearly not constitute a ground for claiming that that procurement was excluded from the coverage of the Agreement. The same reasoning must also apply if research and/or development were to constitute an input into the production of products being procured and were not itself the object of the procurement. For these reasons the Panel concluded that the phrase "contract for research . . . or original development" had to be understood as referring to a contract for the purpose of the procurement by the procuring entity of the results of research and/or original development, i.e. knowledge.

4.11 All the information provided by Norway to the Panel indicated that the principal purpose of the contract of the Norwegian Public Roads Administration with Micro Design had been the procurement of operational toll collection equipment for a functioning toll ring system. Norway had emphasised to the Panel the importance that the procuring entity attached to a speedy establishment of the toll ring as a fully operational system, for financial reasons in particular. The Panel further noted that Norway had said:

> What the procuring entity had needed from the contract was not the research and development results *as such*, but, with regard to matters before the Panel, prototypes as part of the solutions constituting an entire integrated payment system. The Public Roads Administration had accordingly been provided with what it had requested, an *operational* toll ring and a national and European test area. (Norway's emphases)

4.12 Given that the Panel had found that Norway had not met the conditions of Article V:16(e), the Panel did not consider it necessary to examine whether in fact Micro Design had had to perform research and/or development in order to fulfil the terms of the contract. The Panel did not wish to contest that original development and possibly applied research may have been required. The Panel also wished to make it clear that the mere fact that prototypes might be put to operational use did not in itself mean that Article V:16(e) could not be invoked, provided nonetheless that the principal purpose governing their procurement was research and/or development.

5.1 On the basis of the findings set out above, the Panel concluded that Norway had not complied with its obligations under the Agreement on Government Procurement in its conduct of the procurement of toll collection equipment for the city of Trondheim in that the single tendering of this procurement could not be justified under Article V:16(e) or under other provisions of the Agreement.

NOTES AND QUESTIONS

1. The GPA takes a "positive list" approach following the GATT. Only those entities that are covered by a member's commitment under the GPA are subject to the obligations set forth in the GPA. The issue of whether an entity is covered under the GPA can frequently arise because large government projects are often under the authority of several government entities, and authority for the project might shift from one entity to another. In *Korea — Measures Affecting Government Procurement*, WT/DS163/R, Report of the WTO Panel, adopted on May 1, 2000, the United States argued that the Korean Airport Authority (KAA), which was responsible for government procurement for the Inchon International Airport (IIA), was a covered entity. The Ministry of Construction and Transportation (MOCT) had originally been granted authority under Korean law over construction of the IIA, but the Seoul Airport Act later shifted responsibility to the KAA. The United States argued that the KAA established bid deadlines, qualification, and domestic partnership requirements that discriminated against U.S. companies interested in selling goods and services for the construction of the IIA. Korea argued that while the MOCT was listed in Korea's Schedule of Commitments under the GPA and was therefore a covered entity, the KAA was not listed and had no GPA obligations. The panel agreed with Korea that the KAA itself was not listed, but went on to consider two other issues:

> Our view is that the relevant questions are: (1) Whether an entity (KAA, in this case) is essentially a part of a listed central government entity (MOCT) — in other words, are the entities, legally unified? and (2) Whether KAA and its successors have been acting on behalf of MOCT. The first test is appropriate because if entities that are essentially a part of, or legally unified with, listed central government entities [that] are not considered covered, it could lead to great uncertainty as to what was actually covered because coverage would be dependent on the internal structure of an entity which may be unknown to the other negotiating parties. The second test is appropriate because procurements that are genuinely undertaken on behalf of a listed entity (as, for example, in the case where a principal/agent relationship exists between the listed entity and another entity) should properly be covered because they would be considered legally as procurements by MOCT.

Id. at ¶759.

The panel found (¶¶761, 768) no evidence to indicate that the KAA was under the control of the MOCT or acted as an agent on behalf of the MOCT in procurement for the airport. *Id.*

2. While a number of developed countries have joined the GPA, many developing countries are reluctant to join. Why should any country voluntarily join the GPA?

5   *Trade in Goods: Customs and Tariff Law*

I.   Introduction

This Chapter and the next four Chapters examine extensively the law of the GATT applicable to the trade in goods. In this Chapter and the next, we examine the GATT law applicable to the reduction or elimination of barriers to the trade in goods. Or put conversely, both Chapters deal with the WTO law of market access: the removal of barriers to trade in order to promote market access for imports.

Countries typically use two types of measures that act as barriers to the trade in goods. The most common is the tariff; i.e., a duty (tax) imposed on goods at the point of entry. This is the main subject of this Chapter, which considers the law of tariffs and associated problems. A second method of blocking imports is to use so called non-tariff barriers, which are a catch-all category comprising the myriad ways of limiting imports other than by using tariffs. Non-tariff barriers are the subject of the next Chapter. Both the tariff and non-trade barriers that we will examine are for the most part border measures applied at the point of entry.

This Chapter continues our intensive study of the GATT, the most important WTO trade agreement. We have already covered GATT Articles XXV-XXXV inclusive and Articles XXII, XXIII, and XXIV (Chapter 1), as well as Articles I and III (Chapter 4). Now we turn to the GATT Article II on Tariffs and associated Articles V, VII, VIII, IX, and X.

Read the following GATT Articles in the Documents Supplement:

     Article II—Schedules of Concessions
     Article V—Freedom of Transit
     Article VII—Valuation for Customs Purposes
     Article VIII—Fees and Formalities Connected with Importation and Exportation
     Article IX—Marks of Origin
     Article X—Publication and Administration of Trade Regulations

A.   Tariff Concessions

All WTO members have agreed to tariff concessions; i.e., lower tariffs on goods imported from other WTO members. These tariffs are "bound" or limited to ceilings. Developed country members of the WTO have agreed to bind 99 percent of their tariffs; developing countries have bound 73 percent. Thus, most of world trade benefits from bound tariff rates, which are very low by comparison to historical rates from the early twentieth century.

1.   Types of Tariffs

A tariff is a tax paid upon an import. To understand how tariffs are calculated, it is first necessary to understand that tariffs generally come in four varieties:

(1)   An *ad valorem* tariff is a charge that is expressed as a percentage of the value of the product in question; e.g., 5 percent of the value—this is the most common type of tariff;

(2)   A specific tariff is a flat charge on a quantity of the good in question; e.g., $10 per item, $3 per kilogram, $2 per pair;

(3)   A mixed tariff combines aspects of the *ad valorem* and specific tariff; e.g., $5 per kilogram plus 10 percent of value;

(4)   A tariff rate quota (TRQ) is a sliding scale tariff; e.g., a 10 percent *ad valorem* tariff imposed on the first 10,000 tons of the imported product (the in-quota amount), then an 80 percent *ad valorem* tariff imposed on all quantities above the quota limit (the out-of-quota amount).

2.   Calculation of Tariffs Under U.S. Law

Most tariffs in the United States are *ad valorem* tariffs. The calculation of the amount of duty owed under an *ad valorem* tariff, the most common tariff in the United States, depends on the resolution of three issues:

(1)   classification (discussed at pages 201-209)
(2)   valuation (discussed at pages 213-222); and
(3)   origin of the goods (discussed at pages 224-232).

Read the following Agreements in the Documents Supplement:

WTO Agreement on Implementation of Article VII of the General Agreement on Tariffs and Trade 1994 (Valuation Agreement)
WTO Agreement on Rules of Origin

From reading the relevant GATT/WTO documents you will observe that, with respect to the basic issues involved in determining the tariff set forth above, only valuation, the second issue, is covered in detail.

With respect to classification, however, most WTO members, including the United States, adhere to the Harmonized System Convention (entered into force in 1988), which features the Harmonized System of Classification (HSC) developed by the World Customs Organization (WCO) and administered by the Harmonized System Committee of that body. The GATT contracting parties made decisions in

1983 and in 1991 to facilitate adoption of the Harmonized System of Classification, and many WTO Agreements are now linked to the HSC.

The third issue, rules of origin, is the subject of the WTO Agreement on Rules of Origin agreed to in the Uruguay Round. However, the WTO has not yet completed its work program under the Agreement to develop detailed rules of origin. Until this work program is complete, rules of origin will continue to be determined largely by national law, subject only to the general constraints contained in the WTO Agreement.

We will examine each of these issues in detail in separate sections in this Chapter but first we will examine the policy debate over tariffs and WTO rules.

PROBLEM 5-1

In order to protect sugar farmers from foreign competition, the United States has imposed a tariff rate quota (TRQ) on sugar as well as certain sugary products, such as syrups with a high sugar content that are readily accepted as a substitute for sugar by consumers. Assume that any syrup with a sugar content above 35 percent will be subject to the out-of-quota rate under the sugar TRQ, but that syrups with a sugar content of less than 35 percent are subject to much lower tariffs for ordinary syrups. You represent a consortium of U.S. sugar farmers and have discovered a company in Canada that produces a syrup with a content of 30 percent sugar and 70 percent molasses and other non-sugar substances. Once the syrup clears U.S. customs and all duties are paid, however, the company's U.S. subsidiary then extracts the molasses and the non-sugar substances from the syrup before it is sold to consumers. The molasses is then shipped back to Canada where it is reused. Can you explain why the Canadian company might be using this practice? Is it lawful? *Cf. Heartland By-Products, Inc. v. United States*, 264 F.3d 1126 (Fed. Cir. 2001).

B. Economic and Social Policy Implications of Tariffs

We summarize the economic effects of tariffs as follows:

- Imports will generally be reduced;
- Consumers will generally reduce their purchases because of higher prices;
- Domestic producers may be able to increase production;
- Revenue will accrue to the importing state;
- Consumers will pay higher prices not only for imports but also for competing domestic goods. Higher consumer prices constitute a "subsidy" to all domestic producers (not only to high-cost, inefficient producers but also to low-cost, efficient producers who can raise their prices). On imported goods, the effect of a tariff is to impose a consumer "tax" in the form of a higher consumer price. The excess will accrue to the government imposing the tariff, to the extent that the tariff is passed on to consumers in the price of the good.

When a tariff is imposed, the gain in producer surplus and the revenue gain to the importing country will generally be less than the losses suffered by consumers as a result of increased prices. Thus, the net economic effect of a tariff is negative. This net amount is termed the "dead-weight loss" of the tariff by economists.

A tariff also has a negative impact on the seller and exporting country since it reduces demand for their products. The negative impact on exporters is a form of trade protection that creates a competitive advantage for domestic sellers in the importing country.

Although the aggregate effect of a tariff is often a dead-weight loss for the importing country, some sectors, such as domestic industries that compete with imports, will benefit directly. Industries that receive protection can raise prices and maintain or increase jobs. If these industries are in obvious economic distress, the beneficial effect of a tariff can be highly visible. Conversely, the harm caused by the tariff is far more diffuse and less visible because consumers as a whole bear the cost in the form of a tax on consumption. The differences in the visibility of these effects may account in part for the continuing popularity of the tariff as a policy measure despite its overall negative economic effect.

II.   GATT Rules on Tariffs and Customs

GATT Article II requires each WTO member to bind or commit to ceilings on the tariffs that the member is allowed to impose on specific products from other WTO members. These commitments are set forth in each member's tariff schedule, which is attached as an annex to GATT 1994. These tariff schedules are usually reached after lengthy negotiations with all other WTO members. Each member has its own schedule so tariffs vary from member to member.

GATT Article II:1(a) and II:1(b) provide that a member cannot impose a tariff that is higher than provided for in its tariff schedule. A member is also prohibited from circumventing its GATT commitments through changes in methods for assessing dutiable value, or changes in the way currencies are converted. *See* Article II:3. In addition, no WTO member may act unilaterally to change its tariff bindings, but must follow a complicated procedure. *See* Articles XXVII and XXVIII.

PROBLEM 5-2

Assume that Argentina has bound its tariffs for textiles (clothing) at 25 percent, but that Argentina imposes a 10 percent tariff on textiles from India. Is this permitted? In other words, is Argentina allowed to use a tariff that is lower than its GATT bound rate? *See* GATT Article II:1(a). If Argentina is allowed to impose a tariff of 10 percent on textiles from India, can Argentina impose a 25 percent tariff on textiles from China? *See* GATT Article I.

PROBLEM 5-3

Assume that Brazil's GATT bound rate for a new type of handheld tablet is 10 percent *ad valorem*. Brazil now implements a new tariff law that imposes a tariff of 10 percent *ad valorem* or a flat duty of $100 for all tablets $1,000 or less. Is this law consistent with GATT Article II? See the case below.

Argentina—Measures Affecting Imports of Footwear, Textiles, Apparel and Other Items
Report of the Appellate Body, adopted on April 22, 1998
WT/DS56/AB/R

[This dispute involved minimum specific import duties (known as DIEM) at flat rates maintained by Argentina on footwear and certain other products. However, Argentina's GATT Schedule provided for *ad valorem* duty rates. The Appellate Body examined whether this DIEM system was a violation of GATT Article II.]

44. The legal issue before us here is whether the application by a Member of a type of duty other than that provided for in its Schedule is, in itself, inconsistent with Article II of the GATT 1994. We now turn to an examination of this question, first, in the light of the terms of Article II:1 of the GATT 1994 and, second, in the context of Argentina's DIEM system at issue in this case.

45. The terms of Article II:1(a) require that a Member "accord to the commerce of the other Members treatment no less favourable than that provided for" in that Member's Schedule. Article II:1(b), first sentence, states, in part: "The products described in Part I of the Schedule . . . shall, on their importation into the territory to which the Schedule relates, . . . be exempt from ordinary customs duties in excess of those set forth and provided therein." Paragraph (a) of Article II:1 contains a general prohibition against according treatment less favourable to imports than that provided for in a Member's Schedule. Paragraph (b) prohibits a specific kind of practice that will always be inconsistent with paragraph (a): that is, the application of ordinary customs duties in excess of those provided for in the Schedule. Because the language of Article II:1(b), first sentence, is more specific and germane to the case at hand, our interpretative analysis begins with, and focuses on, that provision.

46. A tariff binding in a Member's Schedule provides an upper limit on the amount of duty that may be imposed, and a Member is permitted to impose a duty that is less than that provided for in its Schedule. The principal obligation in the first sentence of Article II:1(b), as we have noted above, requires a Member to refrain from imposing ordinary customs duties in excess of those provided for in that Member's Schedule. However, the text of Article II:1(b), first sentence, does not address whether applying a type of duty different from the type provided for in a Member's Schedule is inconsistent, in itself, with that provision.

49. As we understand it, the Argentine methodology of determining the DIEM is, first, to identify a representative international price for each relevant tariff category of textile and apparel products. Once this representative international price has been established, Argentina then multiplies that price by the bound rate of 35 per cent, or by the actually applied rate of less than 35 per cent, to arrive at the DIEM for the products in that category. Customs officials are directed, in a specific transaction, to collect the higher of the two values: the applied ad valorem rate or the DIEM.

50. To grasp the meaning and implications of the Argentine system, it is important to keep in mind that for any specific duty, there is an ad valorem equivalent deduced from the ratio of the absolute amount collected to the price of the imported product. Thus, the ad valorem equivalent of a specific duty varies with the variation in the price of imports. It is higher for low-priced products than for high-priced products. To illustrate, a specific duty of $10 collected on all imported products in a certain tariff category, is equivalent to 10 per cent ad valorem if the

price of the imported product is $100; however, it is equivalent to 20 per cent ad valorem if the price is only $50.

51. Thus, under the Argentine system, whenever the amount of the specific duty is determined by applying the bound rate of 35 per cent to the representative international price in a certain tariff category, the ad valorem equivalent of the specific duty is greater than 35 per cent for all imports at prices below the representative international price; it is less than 35 per cent for all imports at prices above the representative international price. Therefore, collecting the higher of the two values means applying the bound tariff rate of 35 per cent ad valorem to the range of prices above the representative international price, and applying the minimum specific import duty with an ad valorem equivalent of more than 35 per cent to the range of prices below the representative international price.

52. In cases where the amount of the DIEM is determined by applying a rate of less than 35 per cent—for example, 20 per cent—to the representative international price in a certain tariff category, the result would be as follows. For the range of prices above the representative international price, the ad valorem equivalent of the specific duty would be less than 20 per cent. With respect to the range of prices below the representative international price, a distinction should be made between two zones. As to a certain zone of prices immediately below the representative international price, the ad valorem equivalent of the specific duty would be greater than 20 per cent but less than 35 per cent. However, for products at prices below that zone, the ad valorem equivalent of the specific duty would be greater than 35 per cent.

53. In the light of this analysis, we may generalize that under the Argentine system, whether the amount of the DIEM is determined by applying 35 per cent, or a rate less than 35 per cent, to the representative international price, there will remain the possibility of a price that is sufficiently low to produce an ad valorem equivalent of the DIEM that is greater than 35 per cent. In other words, the structure and design of the Argentine system is such that for any DIEM, no matter what ad valorem rate is used as the multiplier of the representative international price, the possibility remains that there is a "break-even" price below which the ad valorem equivalent of the customs duty collected is in excess of the bound ad valorem rate of 35 per cent.

55. We conclude that the application of a type of duty different from the type provided for in a Member's Schedule is inconsistent with Article II:1(b), first sentence, of the GATT 1994 to the extent that it results in ordinary customs duties being levied in excess of those provided for in that Member's Schedule. In this case, we find that Argentina has acted inconsistently with its obligations under Article II:1(b), first sentence, of the GATT 1994, because the DIEM regime, by its structure and design, results, with respect to a certain range of import prices in any relevant tariff category to which it applies, in the levying of customs duties in excess of the bound rate of 35 per cent ad valorem in Argentina's Schedule.

PROBLEM 5-4

Country F's GATT bound rate for certain agricultural products is 10 percent *ad valorem*, but Country F's customs authorities also add a 1 percent administrative charge for all shipments over a certain size to cover expenses by its customs authorities. Country F argues that the products will spoil if not processed rapidly and extra charges must be made to cover the additional paperwork, processing, and handling charges for the expeditious liquidation of large shipments. Is this practice lawful? *See* GATT Article II:1(a) and II:2(c).

PROBLEM 5-5

Country A, a WTO member, operates a major port that is important in international trade. Imported products arrive regularly at this port by ship and are loaded onto trucks and rail cars for shipment inland, not only to destinations in Country A, but also to cities in neighboring Country B, which is also a WTO member. Products that have a final destination in Country A must pay a tariff under the bindings contained in A's GATT tariff schedule. Products that pass through Country A and have a final destination in Country B, however, are not subject to A's tariffs, but are subject to tariffs when they clear customs in Country B.

Country A's port authority has recently approved a requirement that all imported products processed by Country A and ultimately destined for Country B must pay an extra charge of U.S. $1 per product unit. Products destined for Country A itself are exempt from this charge. Country A justifies this charge on the basis that the products destined for Country B, which incur an expense when they are processed by A's customs service, do not have to pay its GATT bound tariff, while goods imported into Country A must pay the tariff. Is this extra charge valid? *See* GATT Article V and Article XXIV:12.

PROBLEM 5-6

Country K, a member of the WTO, has a national customs service that prides itself on careful and competent administration of the WTO rules. Country K is a relatively poor developing country and does not permit any independent review of its customs decisions because of the high cost of maintaining such a reviewing body. As a result, the decisions of the customs authority of Country K are final. Is Country K in violation of any GATT requirement? *See* GATT Article X.

NOTES AND QUESTIONS

1. The European Union (formerly the European Communities) does not maintain its own separate customs service, but instead administers customs matters through the customs authorities of the member states, which must follow applicable EC regulations. The United States brought a claim against the EC alleging that the non-uniform administration of EC customs laws violates Article X:3(a) of the GATT. In *European Communities — Selected Customs Matters*, WT/DS315/AB/R, Report of the Appellate Body, adopted on December 11, 2006, the Appellate Body ruled on the specific charges made by the United States as follows:

- The practice by some EU states of classifying liquid crystal display flat monitors as computer monitors (duty-free) and others of classifying them as video monitors (14 percent duty) amounts to non-uniform administration in violation of GATT Article X:3(a). *Id.* at ¶260.

- Differences in penalty provisions, in and of themselves, do not necessarily lead to a violation of Article X:3(a); no evidence was produced by the United States on "the impact of such differences in the enforcement of European Communities customs law." *Id*. at ¶211.
- Differences in audit procedures among member states are not sufficient to show a violation of Article X:3(a); the United States did not supply any concrete example of the application of audit procedures that led to non-uniform customs administration. *Id*. at ¶216.
- Article X:3(a) "does not require uniformity of administrative processes" in order to show a violation based on features of an administrative process; the complainant must show "how and why" those features necessarily lead to a lack of uniform, impartial, or reasonable administration. *Id*. at ¶227.
- Article X:3(b) does not contain any requirement that the authorities, and the tribunal charged with the review of customs administrative action must be entrusted with administrative enforcement throughout the territory of the WTO member. *Id*. at ¶304.

The Appellate Body also ruled that under Article X, a complaining member can challenge a responding member's system of customs administration "as a whole," but held that because of an inadequate foundation of undisputed facts, it was "unable to complete this analysis." *Id*. at ¶287.

2. The Information Technology Agreement (ITA) is a plurilateral (or optional) WTO agreement that requires participants to eliminate tariffs on a specific list of information technology products. These products include computer hardware and peripherals, telecommunications equipment, computer software, semi-conductor manufacturing equipment, analytical instruments, semi-conductors, and other electronic products. The ITA covers over 95 percent of world trade in information technology products. Ninety-five WTO members have accepted the ITA; most world trade in information technology products is tariff-free. The ITA foreshadows future plurilateral agreements that may eliminate tariffs in other sectors, such as green technology products.

NOTE ON FREEDOM OF TRANSIT IN INTERNATIONAL TRADE

In *Colombia—Indicative Prices and Restrictions on Ports of Entry*, WT/DS366/R, Report of the Panel, adopted on May 20, 2009, the Panel rendered an important opinion on the meaning of GATT Article V on freedom of transit in international trade. The case involved restrictions on ports of entry for imported goods adopted in 2007 by Colombia. A regulation issued by Colombia restricted the entry of textile, apparel, and footwear imports to eleven ports out of a total of twenty-six ports for international trade. In addition, imports of textiles, apparel, and footwear from Panama that originate in the Colon Free Trade Zone (CFZ) were limited to two ports of entry. However, textiles, apparel, and footwear arriving from Panama that were being trans-shipped were exempt from the port of entry restrictions. Trans-shipment occurs when goods are transferred from one mode of transport to another. A common method of trans-shipment in international trade is when goods are transported by ocean carriage on a ship to a port of entry and then are reloaded onto trucks that travel to a final destination. In this case, if goods from

Panama arrived in Colombia by rail but were then loaded onto trucks for delivery to their final destination, the goods could enter any of the twenty-six ports and could not be restricted. Panama argued that the Colombia regulation violated the freedom of transit guaranteed in GATT Article V. Colombia argued that no restrictions applied to goods from Panama that were trans-shipped. Colombia also stated that the purpose of these customs measures was to strengthen and improve customs control of these kinds of products.

The Panel determined that Colombia's restrictions were in violation of GATT Article V, which requires "freedom of transit through the territory of each contracting party . . . for traffic in transit to or from the territory of other contracting parties." The Panel ruled as follows:

> 7.413 The issue before the Panel is therefore whether freedom of transit is extended to subject textiles, apparel and footwear arriving from Panama in international transit.
>
> 7.414 The Panel concluded above that the provision of "freedom of transit" requires extending *unrestricted* access via the most convenient routes for the passage of goods in international transit whether or not the goods have been trans-shipped, warehoused, break-bulked, or have changed modes of transport. While a Member is not required to guarantee transport on necessarily any or all routes in its territory, transit must be provided on those routes "most convenient" for transport through its territory.
>
> 7.415 Article 4 of Resolution No. 7373 indicates that exemption from the measure imposing the ports of entry restriction arises where goods are "subjected to trans-shipment".
>
> 7.416 Based on the Panel's earlier interpretation that freedom of transit under Article V:2 must be extended to goods in international transit regardless of whether the goods have been trans-shipped or have changed modes of transport, the Panel preliminarily finds that the language in Article 4, paragraph 3, when considered in light of the definition of "trans-shipment" as it appears in applicable Colombian legislation, *denies* freedom of transit to *all* textiles, apparel and footwear that are traffic in transit arriving from Panama or the CFZ.

The Panel also found (¶7.430) that the Colombian regulation violated Article V:2, second sentence, because only goods arriving from Panama and the CFZ were subject to the port restrictions whereas goods arriving from any other WTO member were not subject to those restrictions. In addition, the Panel found a violation of GATT Article V:6, which requires "treatment no less favorable" for goods arriving from Panama and the CFZ in comparison to the same goods had they been transported from a different WTO member. The Colombian regulation subjected all goods, regardless of their country of origin to the restrictions on goods from Panama and the CFZ, so long as they traveled through those territories. *See id.* at ¶7.481.

PROBLEM 5-7

Russia passes a law that all goods from Japan that transit through Russian territory to reach Europe must be transported by truck. Transport by truck is more expensive than by rail because the route is more circuitous and must cross rough terrain. Truck transport is also subject in winter months to the vicissitudes of weather that might cause long delays. Russia argues that this law is intended to support the trucking industry, which is depressed, while transport by rail is robust. Is this law consistent with GATT Article V:2?

III. The Harmonized Tariff System

In assessing tariffs, the initial step is to classify a product under a country's tariff schedule. As noted previously, most WTO members have adopted the so-called Harmonized Tariff System (HTS) developed by the World Customs Organization (WCO), formerly the Customs Cooperation Council, located in Brussels. The WCO works in close collaboration with the WTO to develop agreed-upon customs rules and procedures and to provide assistance to national customs services.

The HTS classifies goods into twenty-two different categories called Sections, which are further subdivided into chapters. Note that the HTS is a classification system only; nothing in the HTS concerns the rate of duty that must be imposed upon any particular classification. This decision is up to each nation, consistent with its GATT obligations. The HTS itself does not have the direct force of law within national legal systems. Each WTO member adopting the HTS will transform it into its own law, and it is the domestic implementation, not the HTS itself, which has legal force. For example, the United States has adopted the HTS (with some inevitable variations) as the Harmonized Tariff Schedule of the United States (HTSUS).

A Harmonized Tariff classification under this system is an eight-digit number used to identify a specific product. The first two digits refer to the appropriate chapter; the first four digits combined identify the article's heading within that chapter; the first six digits break that heading down into subheadings. A country adopting the HTS may freely adapt the last four digits as it sees fit; this means that WTO nations have agreed to be consistent for chapters, headings, and subheadings up to the six-digit level but allow for national differences beyond this point. In the United States, tariffs are assessed at the eight-digit level. The United States uses a ten-digit classification; the last two digits of the ten-digit number are used by the United States for information-gathering purposes.

In the excerpt from the HTSUS that follows, note the application of this scheme. Three rates of duty are provided for in two columns. The applicable tariff rate depends upon the origin of the goods, a topic that we take up later in this Chapter. Column 1 is divided into "General" and "Special" rates. "General" is the applicable GATT-bound rate. These are the rates that the United States applies under the Most Favored Nation principle to goods from all WTO members. Other nations that are non-WTO members may also be entitled to this rate under bilateral or multilateral trade agreements with the United States. "Special" is the rate that applies to countries that enjoy preferences, either as a member of a free trade agreement with the United States or as a beneficiary of a special program of preferences for developing countries. Countries are identified by codes in the Column 1 Special rates: A refers to Beneficiary Developing Countries under the General System of Preferences; AU is Australia; CA is Canada; CL is Chile; E applies to beneficiaries of the Caribbean Basin Economic Recovery Act; J refers to beneficiaries of the Andean Trade Preferences Act; JO is Jordan; MX is Mexico; and SG is Singapore. A new category under "Special" will soon be added for the members of the new Dominican Republic-Central American Free Trade Agreement (CAFTA) and for other countries that the United States takes on as partners of free trade agreements. Recall that under an exception to the Most Favored Nation principle contained in GATT Article XXIV, the United States is not required to extend preferences and trade benefits created under free trade agreements to other WTO members.

Column 2 is the rate for non-WTO members. This is also referred to as the "statutory rate" and is the tariff rate imposed by the Smoot-Hawley Tariff Act of 1930, which set the prevailing rates in the United States prior to the GATT 1947. A comparison between Column 2 rates and the General rates under Column 1 provides evidence of how extensive tariff reductions have been in the United States under the GATT/WTO. The vast majority of the United States' trading partners enjoy the General or Special rates under Column 1.

PROBLEM 5-8

An importer based in New York City seeks a supply of a compact combination washer and dryer machine in order to supply the luxury condominium market in Manhattan, where space is at a premium. The importer has found a high-end model with a washer that conserves water stacked on top of a high-speed centrifugal dryer. The machine must be purchased as mounted on an attractive cherry wooden base with a storage area for detergent and fabric softener. The importer is considering models from suppliers from Country X ($1,200 for the machine and $300 for the base), Y ($1,220 for the machine and $305 for the base), and Z ($950 for the machine and $200 for the base). Assume that these prices do not include transportation costs to New York City (the U.S. Customs Service does not include transportation costs in assessing dutiable value). The importer has done extensive research and has found that all of the models are about equal in quality. Where should the importer purchase the set if X is an EU country, Y is a member of the Andean Trade Preferences Act, and Z is a non-WTO member without a trade agreement with the United States? Besides the tariff, are there any other cost concerns? Consult the HTSUS below.

PROBLEM 5-9

The importer is also interested in a compact ironing and press machine for busy New Yorkers to touch up clothes taken out of the dryer. The importer has the following proposed prices from the same suppliers: X ($800), Y ($810), and Z ($650). Where should the importer buy the presses? How important is MFN or preferential treatment to exporters to the U.S. market?

NOTES AND QUESTIONS

The number of countries entitled to the Column 1 Special rate of duty has grown steadily in recent years. Since 2000, the United States has followed a policy that pursues free trade agreements (FTAs) that it considers in its interest, all over the world. These are concluded not only for economic reasons but also for political considerations, because the United States believes that free trade will help spread democracy. In addition to the countries listed in Column 1, FTAs are now in force with Morocco (2006), Bahrain (2007), Oman (2009), Peru (2009), and South Korea (2012). The Central American-Caribbean Free Trade Agreement, covering Costa Rica, Dominican Republic, El Salvador, Guatemala, Honduras, and Nicaragua, was approved by Congress in 2005. FTAs with Colombia and Panama have been concluded and are pending before the Congress. Negotiations are proceeding with

Harmonized Tariff Schedule of the United States

Heading/ Subheading	Stat. Suffix	Article Description	Unit of Quantity	Rates of Duty 1 General	Rates of Duty 1 Special	Rates of Duty 2
8449.00		Machinery for the manufacture of finishing of felt or nonwovens in the piece or in shapes, including machinery for making felt hats; blocks for making hats; parts thereof				
8449.00.10	00	Finishing machinery and parts thereof	X......	2.6%	Free (A, AU, CA, CL, E, IL, J, JO, MX, SG)	40%
8449.00.50	00	Other	X......	Free		40%
8450		Household- or laundry-type washing machines, including machines which both wash and dry; parts thereof:				
		Machines, each of a dry linen capacity not exceeding 10kg:				
8450.11.00		Fully automatic machines	No......	1.4%	Free (A, AU, CA, CL, E, IL, J, JO, MX, SG)	35%
	10	Coin operated				
		Other:				
	40	Top Loading	No......			
	80	Other	No......			
8450.12.00	00	Other Machines with built-in centrifugal dryer	No......	2.6%	Free (A, AU, CA, CL, E, IL, J, JO, MX, SG)	40%
8450.19.00	00	Other	No......	1.8%	Free (A, AU, CA, CL, E, IL, J, JO, MX, SG)	35%
8450.20.00		Machines, each of a dry linen capacity exceeding 10 kg.		1%	Free (A, AU, CA, CL, E, IL, J, JO, MX, SG)	35%
	10	Coin operated	No......			

Heading/ Subheading	Stat. Suffix	Article Description	Unit of Quantity	General	Special	2
	90	Other	No.			
8450.90		Parts:				
8450.90.20	00	Tubs and tub assemblies	X	2.6%	Free (A, AU, CA, CL, E, IL, J, JO, MX, SG)	40%
8450.90.40	00	Furniture designed to receive the machines of subheadings 8450.11 through 8450.20, inclusive	X	2.6%	Free (A, AU, CA, CL, E, IL, J, JO, MX, SG)	40%
8450.90.60	00	Other	X	2.6%	Free (A, AU, CA, CL, E, IL, J, JO, MX, SG)	40%
8451		Machinery (other than machines of heading 8450) for washing, cleaning, wringing, drying, ironing, pressing (including fusing presses), bleaching, dyeing, dressing, finishing, coating or impregnating textile yarns, fabrics or made up textile articles and machines for applying the paste to the base fabric or other support used in the manufacture of floor coverings such as linoleum; machines for reeling, unreeling, folding, cutting or pinking textile fabrics; parts thereof:				
8451.10.00	00	Dry-cleaning machines	No.	Free		35%
		Drying machines:				
8451.21.00		Each of a dry linen capacity not exceeding 10kg		3.4%	Free (A, AU, CA, CL, E, IL, J, JO, MX, SG)	40%
	10	Coin operated	No.			
	90	Other	No.			
8451.29.00		Other		2.6%	Free (A, AU, CA, CL, E, IL, J, JO, MX, SG)	40%
	10	For drying made up articles	No.			
	90	Other	No.			

Heading/ Subheading	Stat. Suffix	Article Description	Unit of Quantity	Rates of Duty 1 General	Rates of Duty 1 Special	2
8451.30.00	00	Ironing machines and presses (including fusing presses)	No.	Free		35%
8451.40.00	00	Washing, bleaching or dyeing machines.	No.	3.5%	Free (A, AU, CA, CL, E, IL, J, JO, MX, SG)	40%
8451.50.00	00	Machines for reeling, unreeling, folding, cutting or pinking textile fabrics.	No.	Free		40%
8451.80.00	00	Other machinery	No.	3.5%	Free (A, AU, CA, CL, E, IL, J, JO, MX, SG)	40%
8451.90		Parts:				
8451.90.30		Drying chambers for the drying machines of subheading 8451.21 or 8451.29, and other parts of drying machines incorporating drying chambers.	X.	3.5%	Free (A, AU, CA, CL, E, IL, J, JO, MX, SG)	40%
8451.90.60	00	Furniture designed to receive the drying machines subheading 8451.21 or 8451.23.	X.	3.5%	Free (A, AU, CA, CL, E, IL, J, JO, MX, SG)	40%
8451.90.90		Other.	X.	3.5%	Free (A, AU, CA, CL, E, IL, J, JO, MX, SG)	40%
	10	Of machines for washing, dry-cleaning, ironing pressing or drying made up textile articles or of other household or laundry type machines.	X.			
	20	Other.				
		Of machines for bleaching, dyeing, washing or cleaning.	X.			
	90	Other.	X.			

many other states, including Ecuador, Malaysia, the Southern African Customs Union, Thailand, and the United Arab Emirates. These developments portend a higher number of FTAs for the future.

IV.   *Customs Procedures*

An international sale of goods inevitably requires either the exporter or the importer to undergo procedures at the applicable port of entry to clear customs and to pay the applicable tariff that is assessed, if any. Under most international sales transactions, the obligations of the exporter usually end with the delivery of the goods for transport at the port of departure, so it is usually the importer (or more frequently, a professional customs broker hired by the importer) who clears customs in the port of arrival.

The GATT does not contain detailed rules on customs procedures. Rather, the GATT generally requires (1) transparency; (2) uniform and impartial application of laws; and (3) the availability of judicial, arbitral, or administrative tribunals to correct erroneous administrative actions relating to customs and trade. *See* GATT Article X; *see also* 2003 Guide to WTO Law and Practice, pp. 264-269. Detailed rules that harmonize rules for the clearance of goods are contained in the Kyoto Convention,[1] for those countries that have accepted the Convention. The description below sets forth procedures, within the framework of the Kyoto Convention, that are common to many countries.

In the simplest case a product that arrives at a port of entry by ship, air, or land transport will immediately be processed and cleared by a customs official who will assess the duty—tariff—to be paid. The final computation and assessment of duty is termed "liquidation"—an invoice that must be paid by the importer. The goods are released after full payment of this invoice; the goods may also be released subject to periodic payments or released after the posting of a bond. Most countries, like the United States, permit customs brokers to file an Entry Summary Form at the time of entry of merchandise and to post a bond in order to obtain immediate release of imported merchandise before liquidation. *See* 19 C.F.R. §142. The use of the Entry Summary Form relies on an accurate statement of the product information by importers or customs brokers.

In many cases, however, goods are not immediately cleared for entry. This may occur in the following situations. First, a product may be imported into a foreign trade zone (FTZ). An FTZ is a specifically designated area, usually near an airport or ocean port, where imported goods may be landed without paying an import duty. The FTZ can be a place of assembly of finished goods (a finished good may carry a lesser duty than its component parts; or the goods may be re-exported and escape duty altogether). Second, the imported good may be entered into a bonded facility. This is a duty-free customs area used for storage, repacking, clearing, or sorting of imported merchandise. The duty must be paid only when the goods are withdrawn. Third, an importer can do a temporary importation under bond, avoiding the payment of duty for up to one year by posting a bond equal to twice the

---

1. *See* International Convention on the Simplification and Harmonization of Customs Procedures, done at Kyoto, May 18, 1973 (entered into force September 25, 1974).

amount of the estimated duty. This can give the importer a chance to inspect the goods before acceptance or rejection.

If goods on which duty has been paid are re-exported, the importer/exporter may apply for a duty drawback, a refund of the duty paid, less a small administrative fee of about 1 percent. Eligibility for a duty drawback depends, however, on each jurisdiction's rules and standards of proof. The U.S. law on drawbacks may be found in 19 U.S.C. §1313(a)-(j) and the regulations are contained in 19 C.F.R. §191. In a 2006 opinion, the Court of International Trade criticized §1313 as "inartfully drafted." *See Merck & Co. v. United States*, 435 F. Supp. 2d 1253, 1260 (CIT 2006) (case denying drawback for exports to NAFTA countries where fungible merchandise imported duty-free was substituted for imported merchandise on which duty had been paid).

Fraud or deception on the part of importers, such as smuggling, misrepresenting the nature of goods imported, or importing goods that violate intellectual property rights, will lead to stiff penalties in the form of customs fines and forfeitures of merchandise. Criminal penalties are also possible. The United States is granted wide enforcement power under 19 U.S.C. §1592 to conduct any necessary investigations, to recoup any unpaid duties, and to assess monetary penalties for fraud or negligence in customs matters.

If an importer disagrees with a decision of a customs official, the first step is to file a "protest" that details the reasons for the disagreement. A protest will trigger an administrative proceeding within the customs service that will either confirm or change the official's ruling. The protest procedure under U.S. law is contained in 19 U.S.C. §1514. Under paragraph (c)(3) of this section, such a protest must be filed within 180 days after the notice of liquidation, or the date of the decision, that is the subject of the protest.

Except for the EU, all WTO members have a national customs service that carries out the functions of entering merchandise and collecting duties. In the United States, this function is conducted by the Bureau of Customs and Border Protection (BCBP), part of the United States Department of Homeland Security. The EU, while a member of the WTO in its own right, does not have a separate customs service; rather, customs functions are handled by officials of the twenty-seven member states of the EU.

WTO members typically allow judicial review of decisions of the national customs service. The United States Court of International Trade (CIT) is a specialized federal court located in New York City that has jurisdiction over determinations made by the BCBP, as well as anti-dumping and countervailing duty decisions made by the U.S. International Trade Administration and the U.S. International Trade Commission. The Customs and International Trade Bar Association is a specialized bar for lawyers practicing before that court. Appeals from the CIT are heard by the United States Court of Appeals for the Federal Circuit, located in Washington, D.C. The United States Supreme Court has authority to hear customs cases on appeal from the Federal Circuit on writ of certiorari.

Under U.S. law, a timely protest is necessary to invoke the jurisdiction of the CIT. *See* 28 U.S.C. §1581(a). For a case denying jurisdiction because the importer failed to file a timely protest, see *Ford Motor Co. v. United States*, 435 F. Supp. 2d 1324 (CIT 2006).

An importer may typically request an advance ruling from a customs service. In the United States, a ruling letter may be requested from a BCBP field office regarding a prospective customs entry. *See* 19 C.F.R. §177.9(a). A customs field office may refer the request for a Customs Headquarters Ruling. *See id.* at §177.11(a). Under 28

U.S.C. §1581(h), the CIT may exercise jurisdiction over a pre-importation customs ruling if a party demonstrates that it would be irreparably harmed unless given an opportunity to obtain judicial review prior to importation.

Judicial review of a determination by a customs service of one of the EU member states can be obtained by requesting a referral of the case to the European Court of Justice (ECJ) for a preliminary ruling under Article 234 of the European Economic Community Treaty of 1957, as amended. Only the ECJ has jurisdiction to rule on a disputed question of EU law. Due to the Common Commercial Policy set forth in the EEC Treaty, customs law is EU law, not the law of the member states.

Most customs disputes concern the amount of the duty or tariff that must be paid on the importation of a product.

As we noted earlier, the calculation of a tariff depends on three variables: (1) the classification of the product, (2) the valuation, and (3) its origin. We now consider each of these issues in turn under the WTO system, and their implementation into the law of the United States and the EU.

V. Product Classification

A. The WTO Rules

As we have already noted, the WTO does not contain a detailed tariff classification system; rather, many countries adopt the Harmonized Tariff System. However, issues of classification arise before the WTO under GATT articles that are subject to principles of interpretation under international law.

PROBLEM 5-10

Assume that Vietnam is concerned about the possible impact of lower tariffs on its rice industry. Before WTO accession, Vietnam imposed a tariff of 40 percent on all rice imports. Vietnam's GATT Schedule now provides for a duty on rice of 8 percent.

Vietnam has discovered that many forms of rice that are produced in developed countries are genetically altered and that rice produced in developing countries now typically use organic (non-chemical) fertilizers. Vietnam decides to add two new tariff lines to its domestic tariff classification to cover these two items. Under the revised schedule, a tariff of 40 percent now applies to genetically altered rice and rice grown with organic fertilizer. All other rice is subject to Vietnam's GATT bound rate of 8 percent. Are these new classifications (or reclassifications) valid? Consider the *EC—Frozen Boneless Chicken* case below.

European Communities — Customs Classification of Frozen Boneless Chicken Cuts
Report of the Appellate Body, adopted on September 27, 2005
WT/DS269, 286/AB/R

[The EC classified imported chicken cuts under line 02.10.90.20, which applies to certain types of "salted" meat including chicken. In 2002, the EC reclassified the chicken cuts under tariff line 02.07.41.10, which applies to chilled or frozen bone-less chicken cuts. The GATT bound duty rate for this line is 1024 euros or 102.4 euros/100kg/net. In addition, Article 5 of the WTO Agreement on Agriculture creates a special safeguard that permits much higher tariffs to be imposed on items in this tariff line. The EC had invoked Article 5, so the tariff actually in effect for items in this line was about 60 percent. The reclassification of chicken cuts from 02.10.90.20 to 02.07.41.10 resulted in the application of the much higher 60 percent tariffs to frozen boneless chicken cuts.

The complainants, Brazil and Thailand, argued that this reclassification vio-lated Articles II:1(a) and II:1(b) of the GATT. The key issue involved was the mean-ing of the term: "salted." In the panel proceeding, the EC argued that the term "salted" in tariff line 02.10 carries the meaning that salt is added for the purpose of preservation; since the chicken cuts in question are not salted for this purpose, they are appropriately and validly reclassified under tariff line 02.07. The complainants argued that the products had been validly classified as "salted" meat under 02.10 from 1996 to 2002, and that the reclassification, due to the simple addition of salt to the product, was not warranted and was a violation of the GATT.]

DOES A CRITERION OF "PRESERVATION" UNDERMINE THE SECURITY AND PREDICTABILITY OF TARIFF CONCESSIONS?

244. The European Communities appeals the Panel finding that:

> . . . the lack of certainty associated with the application of the criterion of long-term preservation with respect to the concession contained in heading 02.10 of the EC Schedule . . . could undermine the object and purpose of security and predictabil-ity [of the reciprocal and mutually advantageous arrangements [that] must be pre-served], which lie . . . at the heart of the WTO Agreement and the GATT 1994.

245. The European Communities contends that the Panel misrepresented the criterion of preservation, because EC Regulation 1223/2002 and EC Decision 2003/97/EC do not, in fact, apply a "criterion of long-term preservation" but, instead, treat chicken cuts with a salt content of up to 3 per cent as falling under heading 02.07 rather than heading 02.10.

246. We agree with the Panel that, in characterizing a product for purposes of tariff classification, it is necessary to look exclusively at the "objective charac-teristics" of the product in question when presented for classification at the bor-der. At the same time, we note that the European Communities provides examples indicating that product descriptions including a criterion of "preservation" may qualify as "objective characteristics" under the Harmonized System. The European Communities considers that, accordingly, the criterion of preservation is not intrin-sically uncertain, given its use in other parts of the Harmonized System. In this sense, we consider that the Harmonized System does not preclude the use of a cri-terion of preservation, as such. Therefore, the application of such a criterion would not necessarily be in conflict with the objectives of security and predictability of the *WTO Agreement* and the GATT 1994 (including Schedules of tariff commitments).

247. Turning to the facts of this case, we recall the Panel's statement that the European Communities had never explained what it meant exactly, for purposes of heading 02.10, by " 'long-term preservation' in practice". The Panel was satisfied

that it could be ascertained through laboratory analyses whether a salted and frozen product was preserved for the long-term. However, it was unclear to the Panel
whether preservation for the long-term had to be the result of salting, or freezing,
or a combination of the two. The European Communities submits on appeal that
there are no such practical problems, either with respect to the products at issue
(which have not been claimed to be preserved) or for a customs official with access
to tools of analysis and for whom the highly traditional products under heading
02.10 are recognizable and familiar. According to the European Communities, if a
product has been "frozen" within the meaning of heading 02.07, it will still be classified under heading 02.10 of the EC Schedule as a "salted" product, provided that
the salting ensures "preservation" within the meaning of EC Regulation 1223/2002
and EC Decision 2003/97/EC.

248. Although the European Communities clarifies that, for purposes of
heading 02.10 of the EC Schedule, preservation has to be the result of the processes mentioned in that heading and not of the processes listed under heading
02.07 (namely, chilling, freezing), it does not explain how, in respect of frozen and
salted meat, the preservation effect of the processes listed in heading 02.10 could
be distinguished from the processes listed in heading 02.07. Therefore, we share
the Panel's concern about the lack of certainty in the application of the preservation criterion used by the European Communities regarding the tariff commitment under heading 02.10 of the EC Schedule.

249. In the light of these considerations, we see no reason to disturb the Panel's
finding, in paragraph 7.328 of the Panel Reports, that "the lack of certainty associated with the application of the criterion of long-term preservation with respect
to the concession contained in heading 02.10 of the EC Schedule . . . could undermine the object and purpose of security and predictability, which [underlie] both
the WTO Agreement and the GATT 1994."

NOTES AND QUESTIONS

1. Doesn't every change of a tariff classification undermine the security and
predictability of tariff concessions? Under *EC—Chicken Cuts*, what types of reclassifications are not subject to challenge? Are countries now taking the risk that any
reclassifications resulting in a higher duty will be challenged at the WTO?

2. There are no specific, detailed WTO rules on tariff classifications or reclas-
sifications, but the WTO has created some guidelines and constraints through
its decisions on the ability of members to make classifications. In addition to
EC—Chicken Cuts, an important case on the subject matter of classification is
*European Communities and Its Member States—Tariff Treatment of Certain Information
Technology Products*, WT/DS375, 376, 377/R, Report of the Panel, adopted on
September 21, 2010. In the case, the panel considered a complaint by the United
States, Japan, and Chinese Taipei that the EC, which is a party to the Information
Technology Agreement (ITA), an agreement among certain WTO members to
maintain duty-free concessions on products related to information technology, had
nevertheless assigned high-tariff classifications for certain new products developed
after the ITA, on the grounds that they were outside the scope of the ITA commitments. The products involved were flat panel displays using LCD technology, set-top
boxes with a communication function, and multifunctional digital machines. The
EC argued that these products were new, multifunctional products for which there

was no specifically applicable classification heading and that it was free to assign them new classifications outside the scope of the ITA on a case-by-case basis. The panel, in an opinion in excess of 300 pages, parsed the factual evidence with regard to the products at issue, and concluded that the EC could not classify new products outside the scope of the ITA if such products possessed objective characteristics so that they came within the scope of the ITA. The panel further observed that the ITA has no express limitation on technical characteristics of covered products and that the ITA covers products not only by specific tariff headings, but also through a narrative listing of products covered wherever they may fall into a particular classification scheme. *EC—IT Products* and *EC—Chicken Cuts* together constrain WTO members both from reclassifications that move products into higher tariff categories and from automatically generating, high-tariff classification for new products.

PROBLEM 5-11

Country M's GATT tariff schedule does not include any bindings for salted preserved fish, a delicacy in many Asian countries. Country M imposes a tariff of 5 percent on salted mackerel imported from Japan based on a subheading for preserved meats. Country M imposes a tariff of 9.5 percent on salted mackerel imported from China based on a subheading for fish. Country M argues that because salted fish is not even on M's GATT tariff schedule, M is free to impose any tariff that it wishes and that its classification of the fish is its own business. Is Country M correct? Consider the *Japan—Lumber* and *Spain—Unroasted Coffee* cases below.

Canada/Japan—Tariff on Import of Spruce, Pine, Fir (SPF) Dimension Lumber
Report of the GATT Panel, adopted on July 19, 1989
GATT B.I.S.D. (36th Supp.) 167

[Canada complained that Japan's tariffs on certain lumber cut to specified dimensions (SPF dimension lumber) violated the MFN clause of GATT Article I. Canada claimed that SPF Lumber was a "like product" entitled to tariff-free treatment in Japan given to lumber of some species of coniferous trees from countries other than Canada.]

5.4 According to Canada, Article I:1 required Japan to accord also to SPF dimension lumber the advantage of the zero tariff granted by Japan, under sub-position 4407.10-320 of its Tariff, to planed and sanded lumber of "other" coniferous trees, including the genera cedar and other Chamaecyparis, hemlock (Tsuga), and douglas-fir (Pseudotsuga), and five species excluded from sub-position No. 4407.10-110.

5.5 The Panel noted that the tariff classification for 4407.10-110 had been established autonomously by Japan, without negotiation.

5.7 In substance, Canada complains of the fact that Japan had arranged its tariff classification in such a way that a considerable part of Canadian exports of SPF dimension lumber to Japan was submitted to a customs duty of 8 per cent, whereas other comparable types of dimension lumber enjoy the advantage of a zero-tariff duty. The Panel considered it impossible to appreciate fully the Canadian complaint if it had not in a preliminary way clarified the bearing of some principles of the GATT-system in relation to tariff structure and tariff classification.

5.8 The Panel noted in this respect that the General Agreement left wide discretion to the contracting parties in relation to the structure of national tariffs and the classification of goods in the framework of such structure. The adoption of the Harmonized System, to which both Canada and Japan have adhered, had brought about a large measure of harmonization in the field of customs classification of goods, but this system did not entail any obligation as to the ultimate detail in the respective tariff classifications. Indeed, this nomenclature has been on purpose structured in such a way that it leaves room for further specifications.

5.9 The Panel was of the opinion that, under these conditions, a tariff classification going beyond the Harmonized System's structure is a legitimate means of adapting the tariff scheme to each contracting party's trade policy interests, comprising both its protection needs and its requirements for the purposes of tariff and trade negotiations. It must however be borne in mind that such differentiations may lend themselves to abuse, insofar as they may serve to circumscribe tariff advantages in such a way that they are conducive to discrimination among like products originating in different contracting parties. A contracting party prejudiced by such action may request therefore that its own exports be treated as "like products" in spite of the fact that they might find themselves excluded by the differentiations retained in the importing country's tariff.

5.11 "Dimension lumber" as understood by Canada is defined by its presentation in a standard form of measurements, quality-grading and finishing. It appears from the information provided by Canada that this type of lumber is largely used in platform-house construction in Canada as well as in the United States and that it has found also widespread use in Japan, as is testified by the existence of a Japanese technical standard known under the name of "JAS 600".

5.12 Japan objected to this claim on different grounds. Japan explained that dimension lumber was only one particular type of lumber among many other possible presentations and that house-building is only one of the many possible uses of this particular kind of lumber. From the legal point of view, Japan contended that the concept of "dimension lumber" is not used either in any internationally accepted tariff classification, or in the Japanese tariff classification. In accordance with the Harmonized System, position No. 4407.10 embraces all types of coniferous wood "sawn or chipped lengthwise . . . exceeding 6 mm". Apart from the thickness and the grade of finishing, customs treatment of lumber according to the Japanese Tariff was determined exclusively on the basis of a distinction established between certain biological genera or species. Dimension lumber was therefore not identified as a particular category in the framework of the Japanese tariff classification.

5.13 The Panel considered that the tariffs referred to by the General Agreement are, quite evidently, those of the individual contracting parties. This was inherent in the system of the Agreement and appeared also in the current practice of tariff negotiations, the subject matter of which were the national tariffs of the individual contracting parties. It followed that, if a claim of likeness was raised by a contracting party in relation to the tariff treatment of its goods on importation by some other contracting party, such a claim should be based on the classification of the latter, i.e. the importing country's tariff.

5.14 The Panel noted in this respect that "dimension lumber" as defined by Canada was a concept extraneous to the Japanese Tariff. It was a standard applied by the Canadian industry which appeared to have some equivalent in the United States and in Japan itself, but it could not be considered for that reason alone as a category for tariff classification purposes, nor did it belong to any internationally accepted customs classification. The Panel concluded therefore that reliance by Canada on the concept of dimension lumber was not an appropriate basis for establishing "likeness" of products under Article I:1 of the General Agreement.

Spain — Tariff Treatment of Unroasted Coffee
Report of the GATT Panel, adopted on June 11, 1981
GATT B.I.S.D. (28th Supp.) 102

[Prior to 1979, Spain had classified all unroasted, non-decaffeinated coffee under one tariff heading. In 1979, Spain subdivided its classification for such coffee into five parts, three of which had a 7 percent duty applied and two of which had a zero rate of duty applied. Brazil, which was the principal supplier of the type of coffee subjected to duty, brought a complaint under the GATT, and a panel was established to consider the dispute. The Spanish tariff was not bound under GATT Article II.]

4.6 The Panel examined all arguments that had been advanced during the proceedings for the justification of a different tariff treatment for various groups and types of unroasted coffee. It noted that these arguments mainly related to organoleptic differences resulting from geographical factors, cultivation methods, the processing of the beans, and the genetic factor. The Panel did not consider that such differences were sufficient reason to allow for a different tariff treatment. It pointed out that it was not unusual in the case of agricultural products that the taste and aroma of the end-product would differ because of one or several of the above-mentioned factors.

4.7 The Panel furthermore found relevant to its examination of the matter that unroasted coffee was mainly, if not exclusively, sold in the form of blends, combining various types of coffee, and that coffee in its end-use, was universally regarded as a well-defined and single product intended for drinking.

4.8 The Panel noted that no other contracting party applied its tariff régime in respect of unroasted, non-decaffeinated coffee in such a way that different types of coffee were subject to different tariff rates.

4.9 In the light of the foregoing, the Panel concluded that unroasted, non-decaffeinated coffee beans listed in the Spanish Customs Tariffs under CCCN 09.01 A.1a, as amended by the Royal Decree 1764/79, should be considered as "like products" within the meaning of Article I:1.

4.10 The Panel further noted that Brazil exported to Spain mainly "unwashed Arabica" and also Robusta coffee which were both presently charged with higher duties than that applied to "mild" coffee. Since these were considered to be "like products", the Panel concluded that the tariff regime as presently applied by Spain was discriminatory vis-à-vis unroasted coffee originating in Brazil.

NOTES AND QUESTIONS

1. Since the Spanish tariff for coffee was unbound, doesn't Spain have the right to set the tariff at any level? Or does the MFN principle still apply to unbound tariffs? Why does the MFN principle require extending duty-free treatment to coffee from Brazil even though the tariff is unbound?

2. In applying the GATT and other WTO agreements, many other agreements outside of the WTO system may be relevant. The customs practices of particular states might be relevant as well. Is this practice justified, or does this make classification unnecessarily complex and difficult?

B. The United States

As we have already noted, the United States has adopted the HTS as its tariff classification system. The HTSUS contains some 8,500 eight-digit tariff classification lines (and many ten-digit lines), so the task of customs officials in making the correct classification can be complex. The U.S. Customs Service has promulgated the General Rules of Interpretation (GRI) to assist in classifications. To summarize:

(1) goods must be classified first in accordance with the headings of the HTSUS using common sense and commercial meanings; only four-digit headings are comparable. No consideration should be given to the terms of any subheading within any four-digit heading when considering the proper classification of the item at the four-digit heading level;

(2) when goods can be classified under two or more headings, the goods should be classified in accordance with the heading that is most specific, unless the headings refer to only a part of the goods, in which case they are classified by the component that gives the goods their essential character;

(3) when goods cannot be classified under either of the preceding approaches, they should be classified in accordance with the heading that occurs last in numerical order among the headings that merit equal consideration; and

(4) when goods cannot be classified under any of the preceding methods, they should be classified under the heading for goods to which they are most akin.

See GRI 1-4.

The following problems and cases examine some of the issues that arise in interpreting this system.

PROBLEM 5-12

Sam imports electric shavers from Denmark. The possible classifications under the HTSUS are as follows:

Heading 8467	Electro-mechanical tools for working in the hand with self-contained electric motor
Heading 8509	Electro-mechanical domestic appliances with self-contained electric motor
Heading 8510	Shavers and hair clippers with self-contained electric motor

Which is the proper classification? Why?

PROBLEM 5-13

In the case below, there are two potential classifications for the item in question, an electric toothbrush: heading 8509, as an electromechanical domestic appliance with self-contained motor, and heading 9603 as a brush. Within 9603, the heading for a brush, subheading 9603.21 provides for "toothbrushes." The importer argued that subheading 9603.21 for toothbrushes was clearly the most applicable. The importer also argued that when a good can be classified under two or more headings, the good should be classified in accordance with the heading that is most specific. However, the court rejected this argument. In this case, classifying the electric toothbrushes under subheading 9603.21 for "toothbrushes" would violate a fundamental principle of classification under the HTSUS. This case affirms this basic principle. What is this basic principle (see GRI (1) above), and how does this case vindicate it? Read the case below and review the summary of the GRIs above.

Bausch & Lomb, Inc. v. United States
United States Court of Appeals, Federal Circuit, 1998
148 F.3d 1363

PLAGER, Circuit Judge.

This case requires us to answer the question of whether an electric toothbrush is properly classified under the Harmonized Tariff Schedule of the United States ("HTSUS") as a "toothbrush" or as an "electromechanical domestic appliance."

The merchandise at issue in this classification case is a battery-operated electric toothbrush sold under the trademark "Interplak." Appellant, Bausch & Lomb, Inc. ("Bausch & Lomb"), imports several different models of this product. For purposes of the present appeal it is sufficient to focus on the common elements of each. [T]he Interplak comprises three basic elements:

one to four interchangeable plastic toothbrush heads;
a detachable plastic handle containing a battery-operated motor and a compartment for two rechargeable batteries; and
a stand that incorporates a battery recharger.

Bausch & Lomb imported the subject merchandise into the United States between January 8, 1991 and August 12, 1992. Until February 6, 1991, the merchandise was classified by Customs as "[t]oothbrushes" under HTSUS Subheading 9603.21.00. On that date, however, Customs issued a Notice of Action reclassifying the Interplak as "[o]ther [electromechanical domestic] appliances" under HTSUS Subheading 8509.80.00. Despite their prior treatment as toothbrushes, Customs liquidated the subject merchandise as "[o]ther appliances." Bausch & Lomb filed a protest, claiming that the entries should continue to be classified as "[t]oothbrushes." Customs denied the protest, and Bausch & Lomb filed the present suit in the Court of International Trade.

Before that court, both parties moved for summary judgment. Finding no genuine issue of material fact, the trial court granted the Government's motion and denied Bausch & Lomb's, holding that, as a matter of law, the Interplak was properly classified as an appliance under 8509.80.00 of the HTSUS. Bausch & Lomb now appeals from that decision.

We start first with the competing tariff headings. Customs classified the Interplak electric toothbrushes as "Other appliances" under Subheading 8509.80.00 of the HTSUS, which provides:

8509   Electromechanical domestic appliances, with self-contained
                               electric motor; parts thereof:

                                         * * *

8509.80.00   Other appliances . . . [duty rate of 4.2% *ad valorem*]

The plain language of Subheading 8509.80.00 covers electromechanical domestic appliances with self-contained electric motors—of which an electric tooth-brush is undoubtedly one. This interpretation is supported by the *Explanatory Notes* under Heading 8509, which specifically classify "Electric tooth brushes" under that Heading, rather than under Heading 9603, as well as the *Explanatory Notes* under Heading 9603, which appear to limit that Heading to brushes "for" appliances, and not the appliances themselves. *See Lonza Inc. v. United States*, 46 F.3d 1098, 1109 (Fed. Cir. 1995) ("While the *Explanatory Notes* do not constitute controlling legislative history, they do offer guidance in interpreting HTS subheadings.").

Bausch & Lomb does not dispute that this provision literally covers the Interplak. Instead, it contends that electric toothbrushes are more specifically provided for under HTSUS Subheading 9603.21.00 in light of the legislative history and prior case law of this court and its predecessor. Under General Rule of Interpretation ("GRI") 3(a) of the Harmonized Tariff System, according to Bausch & Lomb, the more specific *eo nomine* description "brush" in Heading 9603 is preferred to the more general description "electromechanical appliance with self-contained motor" contained in Heading 8509. Thus, even though the Interplak could literally fall within Heading 8509, the preferred classification is under Heading 9603, argues Bausch & Lomb. We must therefore construe Heading 9603.

The relevant provisions in Heading 9603 provide:

9603   Brooms, brushes (including brushes constituting parts of
          machines, appliances or vehicles) . . .

                              * * *

Toothbrushes . . . for use on the person, including such brushes constituting parts of appliances:

9603.21.00   Toothbrushes . . . [duty rate of 0.2 ¢ each plus 3.4% *ad valorem*]

Bausch & Lomb advances the following definition for "brush"—

brush: a hand-operated or power-driven tool or device composed of bristles set into a back or handle or attached to a roller and designed or adapted for such uses as sweeping, scrubbing, painting or smoothing.

Brief of Plaintiff-Appellant 29 (quoting *Webster's Third New International Dictionary* 286 (1981)). Without deciding whether this is the correct definition of brush, it is not inconsistent with definitions in prior opinions.

The word brush, however, does not appear alone in Heading 9603; brush is limited by the parenthetical "including brushes constituting parts of machines, appliances or vehicles." We interpret this phrase to cover only brushes that are a part of a machine, appliance or vehicle that [is] imported separately. To interpret this phrase otherwise would require all "machines, appliances or vehicles" that include a brush such as a street sweeper to fall within this heading. Under our reading, only if the brush is separately imported would it fall under this provision. This interpretation is consistent with treating "appliances" separately under Heading 9603.

Bausch & Lomb argues that its interpretation does not require a street sweeper to be classified under Heading 9603 because a street sweeper cannot reasonably be considered a "power driven tool or device composed of bristles." We disagree. It is quite possible that a street sweeper could accurately be described as a "power-driven tool or device composed of bristles . . . designed or adapted for such uses as sweeping. . . ." Obviously, under Bausch & Lomb's definition the device does not have to be composed entirely of bristles or its own Interplak would fail to satisfy this definition. Even assuming Bausch & Lomb is correct, however, we can certainly think of other electromechanical devices composed of bristles that would, improperly in our view, be classified under Heading 9603 — shoe polishers, vacuum cleaners, car buffers, etc. — and Bausch & Lomb conceded as much at oral argument. As a result, we must reject Bausch & Lomb's construction.

Bausch & Lomb argues that the legislative history of Heading 9603 and prior case law compel a contrary result. We disagree. The predecessor to Subheading 9603.21 was Item 750.40 in the Tariff Schedule of the United States ("TSUS"). That item covered "Other brooms and brushes: Tooth brushes. . . ." Noticeably absent from this provision is the "including" parenthetical currently present in Subheading 9603.21.00. We can safely assume that Congress changed the language for a reason. "A change in the language of a statute is generally construed to import a change in meaning. . . ." Ruth F. Sturm, *Customs Laws and Administration* §51.7 at 57 (1995); *see also Schott Optical Glass, Inc. v. United States,* 678 F. Supp. 882, 887-88 (1987), *aff'd,* 862 F.2d 866 (Fed. Cir.1988). Moreover, we should construe the statute, if at all possible, to give effect and meaning to all the terms. To construe Heading 9603.21 as coextensive with Item 750.40 in the manner advocated by Bausch & Lomb would, in effect, read the "including" parenthetical right out of the Heading. Our reading of Heading 9603 gives effect to the "including" language by ensuring that, *inter alia,* brushes that are part of appliances, but which are imported separately, are properly classified under Heading 9603, even though they could arguably be considered merely a part of the appliance.

It is true, as Bausch & Lomb points out, that electric toothbrushes have long been classified under the toothbrush provision. *See E.R. Squibb & Sons, Inc. v. United States,* 65 C.C.P.A. 61, 576 F.2d 921, 925 (CCPA 1978) (noting that the legislative history of TSUS 750.40 does "evince a clear Congressional intent that electric toothbrushes *qua* electric toothbrushes be classified under item 750.40"); *see also Kaysons,* 56 Cust. Ct. at 152 (holding that, an electric toothbrush, "being known in common speech and to commerce as a toothbrush, is properly classifiable as such."). The government does not argue to the contrary. In none of those cases, however, did the brush or toothbrush provision have the "including" parenthetical that now appears. As a result, Bausch & Lomb's reliance on those decisions, while not without merit, misses the mark because the Heading has been substantially changed.

Affirmed.

Mead Corporation v. United States
United States Court of Appeals, Federal Circuit, 2002
283 F.3d 1342

RADER, Circuit Judge.

I.

At issue are five models of Mead's day planners (model nos. 47192, 47062, 47124, 47104, and 47102). The day planners differ from each other only stylistically based on size (ranging from 7½" × 4⅜" to 12" × 10⅝"), outer jacket cover material, and type of closure. The basic model contains a calendar, a section for daily notes, a section for telephone numbers and addresses, and a notepad. The larger models contain the features of the basic model with additional items such as a daily planner section, plastic ruler, plastic pouch, credit card holder, and computer diskette holder. A loose-leaf ringed binder holds the contents of the day planner, except for the notepad, which fits into the rear flap of the day planner's outer cover.

In a January 11, 1993 ruling, Customs classified the subject planners as bound diaries under subheading 4820.10.20 (emphasis added):

4820	Registers, account books, notebooks, order books, receipt books, letter pads, memorandum pads, *diaries and similar articles*, exercise books, blotting pads, binders (loose-leaf or other), folders, file covers, manifold business forms, interleaved carbon sets and other articles of stationery, of paper or paperboard; albums for sample or for collections and book covers (including cover boards and book jackets) of paper or paperboard:
4820.10	Registers, account books, notebooks, order books, receipt books, letters pads, memorandum pads, *diaries and similar articles*:
4820.10.20	*Diaries*, notebooks and address books, *bound*; memorandum pads, letter pads and similar articles

Customs' original 1993 ruling offered little explanation for classifying Mead's day planners as bound diaries. After Mead protested, Customs issued a new ruling on October 21, 1994, with more detailed reasoning about the classification under subheading 4820.10.20. This 1994 ruling is at issue in this case.

Moving for summary judgment in the trial court, Mead asserted both that its imports were not diaries and were not bound. Either contention, if accepted, compels classification under the "other" provision of subheading 4820.10.40. Under that subheading, Mead would owe no tariff on the imported articles, in contrast with the 4.0% tariff assessed in Customs' 1993 ruling. In support of its motion, Mead submitted dictionary definitions of the terms at issue, affidavits from seven individuals from the U.S. stationery goods industry, and affidavits from two bookbinding experts. The Government cross-moved for summary judgment in support of Customs' classification, offering its own definitions of "diary" and "bound," and submitting supporting affidavits.

In a July 14, 1998 opinion (No. 98-101), the trial court granted the Government's motion. The Court of International Trade broadly defined "diaries" as "articles whose principle purpose is to allow a person to make daily notations concerning events of importance." Under that definition, the trial court decided that Mead's day planners qualify as diaries even though they admittedly contain "supplementary material"—non-diary elements such as a section for addresses and telephone numbers. With respect to the term "bound," the trial court opined: "The common meaning of 'bound' is fastened. The irrevocability of the fastening is not important so long as it goes beyond the transitory role of packaging." The trial court thus found that Mead's day planners, whose contents fit in a loose-leaf ringed binder, fall within that broad definition of "bound."

Mead argued for a different definition of "diaries": "A book for recording a person's observations, thoughts and/or events." Mead further contended that "bound" applies only when pages are "permanently secured along one edge between covers in a manner traditionally performed by a bookbinder." Reversing the Court of International Trade, this court held that Mead's day planners were neither "diaries" nor "bound." *Mead II,* 185 F.3d at 1311. Thus, this court concluded that the day planners required classification under the "other" provision of subheading 4820.10.40. In reaching its conclusion, this court did not accord ordinary classification rulings the deference described in *Chevron U.S.A., Inc. v. Natural Resources Def. Council, Inc.,* 467 U.S. 837, 844, 104 S. Ct. 2778, 81 L. Ed. 2d 694 (1984).

II.

[The U.S. government appealed the decision to the U.S. Supreme Court, which remanded the case. The Supreme Court held that although the more expansive *Chevron* deference did not apply, customs decisions merited deference under *Skidmore,* which should receive deference proportional to its "power to persuade," which in turn depends on the thoroughness, validity of reasoning, consistency with earlier and later pronouncements, and formality attendant to the particular ruling. Customs' expertise should also be considered. Following these instructions, the court of appeals ruled as follows.]

III.

This court construes a tariff term according to its common and commercial meanings, which it presumes are the same. To discern the common meaning of a tariff term, this court consults dictionaries, scientific authorities, and other reliable information sources.

A. DIARIES

The *Oxford English Dictionary,* at 612 (1989), defines a diary as: "1. A daily record of events or transactions, a journal; specifically, a daily record of matters affecting the writer personally, or which come under his personal observation." This definition largely comports with the definition cited in *Baumgarten* and with other dictionary definitions. The *American Heritage Dictionary of the English Language,* at 516 (3d ed. 1992), for example, defines a diary as: "1. A daily record, especially a personal record of events, experiences, and observations, a journal." *See also Webster's*

New Twentieth Century Dictionary of the English Language at 504 (2d ed. 1961) ("1. a daily written record, especially of the writer's own experiences, thoughts, etc.")

These definitions reflect two key aspects of a diary. A diary provides space for a record, especially, as the Court of International Trade recognized, "concerning events of importance." Thus, a diary facilitates recording more than the mere date or time of events, but also more detailed observations, thoughts, or feelings about those events. This court, however, would not expand a diary record to embrace a broad range of writings embraced by the term "notations." To the contrary, the term "notations" encompasses the use of only a word or a brief phrase—writings too brief to include details about events, observations, thoughts, or feelings. To constitute a diary record at all, then, notations must be relatively extensive. In the words of *Charles Scribner's Sons,* a diary must have space for "more than a sentence or two." 6 CIT at 175, 574 F. Supp. 1058.

In addition, a diary is a "record" in the sense that it "recalls or relates *past* events." *Webster's Ninth New Collegiate Dictionary* at 984 (1990) (emphasis added). A diarist records events, observations, feelings, or thoughts after they happen. A diary is retrospective, not prospective. A diary is not a place to jot down the date and time of a distant dentist appointment, regardless of whether that appointment would constitute an "event of importance."

Applying these aspects of the definition of a diary, the imports are articles similar to diaries (encompassed by "other" in subheading 4820.10.40), rather than diaries themselves under subheading 4820.10.20. With regard to the question of sufficient space to record detailed observations, this court notes that the Government's brief does not identify which part of the imports constitutes the diary portion. The record suggests that the trial court below focused on the "daily planner" section, which all five imported models have in common. The daily planner section includes a series of pages allocated to days and numbered with the hours of the day along the left hand side of the page. Two blank lines (four shorter lines in the largest model) extend to the right of each hour. The very limited space provided by these blank lines would not permit a diarist to record detailed notations about events, observations, feelings, or thoughts. This limited space permits only the briefest notations. Space for only a word or phrase disqualifies these articles as diaries.

Moreover, an examination of the articles shows that the few lines for recording events does not envision recording of past events. The caption "Daily Planner" appears at the top of each page. The word "Appointments" appears above the blank lines. These pages facilitate advance planning and scheduling. As noted above, however, a diary is not a planning tool. Instead, a diary receives a retrospective record of events, observations, thoughts, or feelings. Mead markets its entire article as a "Day *Planner,*" further buttressing the distinction between this prospective scheduling article and a diary. While the importer's marketing of the goods will not dictate the classification, such evidence is relevant to the determination and, in this case, weighs against classifying the articles as diaries.

B. BOUND

Reasoning that the tariff provisions at issue cover a "wide variety of book and non-book articles," the trial court eschewed the meaning of "bound" as used in the trade of book manufacturing. While heading 4820 covers book and non-book articles, the term "bound" does not appear in that heading. Rather, the term appears for the first time in subheading 4820.10.20 where it modifies "Diaries, notebooks and address books." These three items, the parties agree, are all books. Thus, the proper context to ascertain the meaning of "bound" is in the context of the manufacture of books. The trial court interpreted the term "bound" more broadly because it applied the term to non-book articles as well. In proper context, however, the HTSUS subheading uses "bound" in connection with types of books. Therefore, anchored to this correct context, this court seeks the meaning of that term.

The Dictionary of Publishing, at 43-44 (1982), defines the term "bound book" as: "Books that have been cased in, usually referring to books that have been sewn, glued, or stapled into permanent bindings." *Webster's Ninth New Collegiate Dictionary* defines "bound" as "4. *of a book:* secured to the covers by cords, tapes, or glue." These definitions within the proper context describe binding methods and materials as permanent. Thus, this court concludes that the term "bound," when used with reference to books as in subheading 4820.10.20, means permanently secured or fastened. In addition, affidavits from bookbinding and stationery goods experts in the record confirmed this meaning of the term "bound" in its proper context.

Customs' definition of "bound," in contrast, essentially disregards the bookbinder's meaning of the term. The HTSUS specifies a "bound diary." This specificity contemplates the existence of an "unbound diary." The Customs definition, however, would make the meaning of "bound" (fastened regardless of the permanency) so broad that it leaves no room for an "unbound diary." The Government argues that a stack of loose-leaf pages could constitute an unbound diary. While such a stack would certainly be unbound, the record as a whole does not suggest that this stack would qualify as a diary. The definition adopted in this opinion, however, leaves room for a class of goods to qualify as unbound diaries, namely, those not permanently fastened. In sum, the imported articles are not "bound" because they are in loose-leaf binders.

IV.

Despite Customs' relative expertise and the reasoning in its classification ruling, for the reasons stated above, this court holds that Mead's day planners are neither "diaries" nor "bound." The classification ruling at issue here lacks the power to persuade under the principles set forth in *Skidmore.* Because the imported articles are properly classified under the "other" provision of subheading 4820.10.40, this court reverses the decision of the Court of International Trade.

PROBLEM 5-14

Maria imports a high-powered portable flashlight that is popular among police units and private security services. The flashlight can project a high beam for clear vision for up to thirty yards. This level of vision is essential in night-time security and police work. The flashlight also comes with a radio that can receive public transmissions (such as news and music) that police officers and security guards use in their spare time. HTSUS heading 8513 refers to "flashlights" and heading 8527 refers to "radios"; however, there is no heading for a combination article that contains both a flashlight and a radio. Which is the proper classification? Why? Review the summary of the GRIs.

PROBLEM 5-15

Agra Foods imports a product called "Barley-Oats Mix." The product consists of 50 percent barley and 50 percent oats. Agra considers this breakdown to be perfect for its customers, who have large farms. Under the HTSUS, heading 1003 refers to barley, and heading 1004 refers to oats. However, there is no heading for a mixture of barley and oats. Which is the proper classification?

C. The European Union

The EU has adopted the HTS as its tariff classification system, which is called the Community Customs Code (CCC). Under the Treaty Establishing the European Economic Community (1957) (now the Treaty on the Functioning of the European Union), the EU is a customs union. By establishing a customs union, all of the members of the EU agreed to forgo their own national customs services in favor of a single common customs tariff (CCT) pursuant to Articles 18-29 of the EEC Treaty. Accordingly, imported goods are subject to a tariff determination under the CCC, no matter where the goods enter among any of the EU member states. Once the goods have lawfully cleared customs, they enjoy freedom of movement (i.e., without tariffs) throughout the territory of the EU. Although the EU establishes the rules on customs procedures contained in the CCC, the EU has no separate customs service, so customs officials from each member state apply the CCC at ports of entry. The EU has also adopted rules of interpretation, set forth below, to guide the application of the CCC.

Council Regulation 2658/87 of July 23, 1987
2000 O.J. (L 256/1), 15-16, as amended in 2001 O.J. (L 264)

GENERAL RULES FOR THE INTERPRETATION OF THE
COMBINED NOMENCLATURE

1. The titles of sections, chapters and sub-chapters are provided for ease of reference only; for legal purposes, classification shall be determined according to the terms of the headings and any relative section or chapter notes.

2. (a) Any reference in a heading to an article shall be taken to include a reference to that article incomplete or unfinished, provided that, the incomplete or unfinished article has the essential character of the complete or finished article.

(b) Any reference in a heading to a material or substance shall be taken to include a reference to mixtures or combinations of that material or substance with other materials or substances.

3. When by application of rule 2(b) or for any other reason, goods are *prima facie* classifiable under two or more headings:

(a) the heading which provides the most specific description shall be preferred to headings providing a more general description. However, when two or more headings each refer to part only of the materials or to part only of the items, those headings are to be regarded as equally specific in relation to those goods;

(b) goods which cannot be classified by reference to 3(a), shall be classified as if they consisted of the material or component which gives them their essential character;

(c) when goods cannot be classified by reference to 3(a) or (b), they shall be classified under the heading which occurs last in numerical order.

4. Goods which cannot be classified in accordance with the above rules shall be classified under the heading appropriate to the goods to which they are most akin.

E. I. DuPont deNemours, Inc. v. Commissioners of Customs and Excise
European Court of Justice, 1982
Case 234/81, [1982] ECR 3515

[This case concerns the classification of the DuPont product "corian," which is used for kitchen countertops and tables. Corian looks like marble but is about two-thirds aluminum hydroxide and one-third polymethyl methacrylate plus trace amounts of catalytic and curing agents. The case was referred to the European Court of Justice by a domestic court in the United Kingdom under Article 234 of the EEC Treaty for a preliminary ruling on an issue of EC law.]

4. In order to determine the correct tariff classification of corian regard must be had, first, to rule 2 (b) of the rules for the interpretation of the nomenclature of the common customs tariff, which provides that: "any reference in a heading to a material or substance shall be taken to include a reference to mixtures or combinations of that material or substance with other materials or substances. Any reference to goods of a given material or substance shall be taken to include a reference to goods consisting wholly or partly of such material or substance. The classification of goods consisting of more than one material or substance shall be according to the principles of rule 3."

5. Inasmuch as corian contains a material, namely polymethyl methacrylate, which comes under subheadings 39.02 c XII and 39.07 b V (d), it is prima facie classifiable under those subheadings pursuant to rule 2 (b).

6. By contrast, the presence of the other component, aluminum hydroxide, is not a reason for considering heading 26.01, which covers metallic ores, even if that substance is regarded as gibbsite, and therefore an ore. That is because, according to note 2 to chapter 26, that heading includes only metallic ores which have not been "submitted to processes not normal to the metallurgical industry", which is manifestly not true of the gibbsite present in corian since it is in fact obtained by means of a chemical process. Heading 28.20, which covers inter alia aluminum oxide and aluminum hydroxide, must likewise be rejected on the basis of note 1 to chapter 28, according to which the chapter covers only "separate chemical elements and separate chemically defined compounds", a description not satisfied by the aluminum hydroxide present in corian.

7. The other tariff heading which might be considered for the classification of corian is heading 68.11, provided, however, that that product may be regarded as "artificial stone".

8. There is no universally accepted interpretation of that concept in either trade or scientific circles, although the prevailing view is that "artificial stone contains natural stone". That approach was adopted in the explanatory notes of the customs cooperation Council, to which reference may be made in order to

interpret headings in the common customs tariff. According to those notes, "artificial stone is an imitation of natural stone usually obtained by agglomerating pieces of natural stone, crushed or powdered natural stone (limestone, marble, granite, porphyry, serpentine, etc.) with lime or cement or other binders (e.g., artificial plastic material)".

9. It was submitted by Dupont that the word "usually," which was used in the notes, implies that there may be exceptions and thus allows even products which do not contain natural stone to be regarded as "artificial stone". That argument cannot be accepted, however, for the position of the word "usually", which precedes the words "by agglomerating" and not the words "powdered natural stone", indicates in fact than an exception might be made at most to allow for the possibility of using a manufacturing process other than the agglomeration of binders with powdered natural stone, but not for the case where no natural stone is used.

10. It follows that the only headings of the common customs tariff which may be considered for the classification of corian are subheadings 39.02 c XII and 39.07 b V (d).

NOTES AND QUESTIONS

In the *EC—Corian* case, General Rule 2(b) would give corian a *prima facie* classification as a methacrylic polymer (heading 39.02). But why was this not definitive? What about an artificial stone classification under heading 68.11?

VI.   Valuation

A.   The WTO Rules

Most states use an *ad valorem* tariff that expresses a duty as a percentage of the value of the goods. Valuation is therefore necessary to establish the dutiable basis of the customs transaction. Tariff duties can vary greatly due to differences in valuation methods used by different states. For this reason, the GATT contracting parties adopted a Customs Valuation Code negotiated in the Tokyo Round in 1979. With the establishment of the WTO, the WTO adopted a Customs Valuation Agreement called the Agreement on Implementation of Article VII of the GATT 1994, which did not significantly change the 1979 Valuation Code.

Read the WTO Agreement on Customs Valuation in the Documents Supplement.

A summary of the valuation methods set forth in the 1994 Customs Valuation Agreement is as follows: In the first place, tariffs are to be based on the transaction valuation of the goods; i.e., the price actually paid for the goods with adjustments (increases or additions) for certain specified costs incurred but not reflected in the price of the goods (such as selling commissions, container costs, packing costs, royalties, and licensing fees). Deductions from transaction value are also permitted under some circumstances. Transaction value as outlined in Article 1 of the Valuation Agreement covers over 90 percent of world trade. If transaction value cannot be used (because, for example, the sale is not an arm's length sale but is between related parties) then the following methods are used in order: (1) transaction value of identical goods; (2) transaction value of similar goods; (3) deductive value, which is defined as the price at which the imported goods, identical, or similar goods are sold in the greatest aggregate quantity to unrelated persons in the country of importation with deductions for commissions, profit, general expenses, transportation, insurance, customs duties, and other costs incurred as a result of selling the goods; and (4) computed value, which is determined by summing the cost of producing the goods in the country of export, including an amount for general expenses, profit, and other expenses. Customs Valuation Agreement Articles 1-6. What if none of these methods can be used? *See* Article 7.

The dispute *Colombia—Indicative Prices and Restrictions on Ports of Entry*, WT/DS366/R, Report of Panel, adopted on May 20, 2009, concerned so-called indicative prices on imports. Colombian customs authorities valued certain imported products based upon the average production price of imported goods, when data was available, or on the lowest price actually negotiated or offered for exportation of the product into Colombia. The panel ruled that this indicative price requirement violated the WTO Customs Valuation Agreement because the system precluded Colombian customs authorities from sequentially applying the customs valuation methods provided in Articles 1-6 of the Agreement.

PROBLEM 5-16

Article 8.1(b) of the 1994 Valuation Agreement lists what are called "assists." The basic premise behind Article 8.1(b) is that an importer should not be allowed to circumvent payment of a duty on the full value of the import by providing certain materials on a cost-free basis to a foreign-based manufacturer. If the costs of these materials are excluded from dutiable value, the importer might be able to avoid payment of duties that are lawfully due. Article 8.1 allows customs officials to recapture these costs and to include them in dutiable value.

Suppose that an importer of garments in WTO member Country W sources fabric from abroad, pays for it, and supplies it directly from the sourcing country to the overseas manufacturer in Country V free of charge. Once the garments are produced, the manufacturer in Country V sells them to the importer in W. The finished garments are then shipped from the manufacturer in Country V and imported into Country W where a tariff must be assessed based on transaction value. The invoice or contract price paid by the importer in Country W to the manufacturer for the garments does not include the cost of the fabric (which was supplied free of charge).

Must the reported customs value of the garments include the full value of the fabric supplied by the importer from Country W in addition to any other costs that occurred prior to the importation of the product into Country W? *See* Article 8.1(b).

PROBLEM 5-17

An importer of garments in Country W buys fabric from a supplier in Country W. The importer then ships the fabric overseas and supplies it at no charge to a manufacturer in Country X, who makes a garment for import into Country W. The manufacturer in Country X never paid for the fabric but, unlike in the previous problem, the fabric was sourced in Country W. Does this make a difference? Should the purchase price of the fabric be included in the import transaction value of the garment as it clears customs in Country W?

B.   United States Law

The 1979 Valuation Code was implemented into U.S. law by the Trade Agreements Act of 1979, 19 U.S.C. §1401a, which has been amended most recently in 1999. Issues arising under this provision and other U.S. valuation laws are discussed in the cases and materials below.

Century Importers, Inc. v. United States
United States Court of Appeals, Federal Circuit, 2000
205 F.3d 1308

RADER, Circuit Judge.

[Century, a wholly owned subsidiary of the Miller Brewing Company of Milwaukee, Wisconsin, entered into an agreement on January 14, 1993 (the Beer Agreement) with Molson Breweries of Toronto, Canada. Under the Beer Agreement, Molson agreed to reimburse Century for the duties that Century would pay to U.S. Customs. Under their arrangement, Century would pay the duties and then separately send an invoice to Molson, which would reimburse Century. The sales invoices that Molson used to bill Century for the beer, however, made no mention about subsequent duty reimbursements. U.S. Customs assessed the duty at the then prevailing *ad valorem* rate of 50 percent using the transaction value method on the basis of the sales invoices. Century paid the duty and then Miller later billed Molson for the duty. Molson subsequently reimbursed Miller and Century. Century brought an action in the Court of International Trade seeking a refund of part of the duties paid on the ground that Customs should have deducted the amount of the reimbursed duties from the sales invoices. Century argued that the sales invoices represented the nominal price for the beer but that the real or actual price was the nominal price minus the amount of the reimbursed duties. In the trial court, the United States argued that Molson's reimbursement was actually a rebate and that rebates are to be disregarded in calculating the transaction value of the products. The Court of International Trade found that Customs should have deducted the reimbursed duties before assessing the duty, that the reimbursement was not a rebate, and that Century's failure to separately identify the duties at the time of importation was a ministerial error that Century was entitled to correct. The United States appealed this decision.]

Title 19 authorizes Customs to determine the value of imported merchandise. *See* 19 U.S.C. §1500(a) (1999). According to title 19, Customs appraises imports "on the basis of . . . (A) The transaction value provided for under subsection (b) of this section." §1401a(a)(1). Transaction value is the "price actually paid or payable for the merchandise." §1401a(b)(1). Two further provisions inform the meaning of the "price actually paid or payable." Title 19 uses that phrase again in excluding rebates from the transaction value: "[a]ny rebate of, or other decrease in, the *price actually paid or payable* that is made or otherwise effected between the buyer and seller after the date of the importation . . . shall be disregarded in determining the transaction value. . . ." §1401a(b)(4)(B) (emphasis supplied). Again, title 19 uses the phrase in excluding from transaction value several items when identified separately from the price: "[t]he transaction value . . . does not include any of the following, if identified separately from the *price actually paid or payable*. . . . (B) The customs duties . . . currently payable on the imported merchandise by reason of its importation. . . ." §1401a(b)(3)(B) (emphasis supplied).

These provisions show that title 19 makes the transaction value a touchstone for valuation of imports. Transaction value or "the price actually paid or payable" is "the total payment . . . made, or to be made, for imported merchandise by the buyer to . . . the seller." §1401a(b)(4)(A). From this touchstone, title 19 authorizes deductions "for transportation, insurance, and related services incident to the international shipment of the merchandise." *Id.* Those deductions are not at issue in this case. Title 19 also enumerates other costs that Customs must exclude from transaction value, but only if they were identified separately from the price actually paid or payable. These costs include "[t]he customs duties and other Federal taxes currently payable on the imported merchandise." §1401a(b)(3)(B). According to title 19, the transaction value, the touchstone of duty calculation, does not include customs duties payable upon importation, if identified separately from the price actually paid.

Applying the statutory formula to this case, §1401a(b)(3) explicitly excludes customs duties from the transaction value if identified separately to Customs. Therefore, because the record shows that the parties did not identify these duties separately, Customs has no authorization to deduct them from the price calculation. Beyond this straightforward application of the statute to this case, title 19 supplies further confirmation for Customs' refusal to deduct the duties from the transactional value. Because Molson reimbursed the duties after the date of importation, that post-importation action was in fact a rebate. *See Black's Law Dictionary* 1266 (6th ed. 1990). Section 1401a(b)(4)(B) directs Customs to disregard rebates after the date of importation. Thus Customs properly appraised the merchandise at the invoiced unit prices.

In the declaration of its Import Specialist, Customs acknowledges that it might well have reached a different appraisal if it had been informed of the duty rebates at the time of importation. The Court of International Trade considered this omitted notice a simple error in the preparation of the entry papers and thus considered it remediable under 19 U.S.C. §1520(c)(1) (1994), which states:

> [A] clerical error, mistake of fact, or other inadvertence . . . not amounting to an error in the construction of a law, adverse to the importer and manifest from the record or established by documentary evidence, in any entry, liquidation, or other customs transaction, [may give rise to a refund] when the error, mistake, or inadvertence is brought to the attention of the Customs Service within one year after the date of liquidation.

The Court of International Trade read §1520 to give Miller a year to correct its failure to identify the "duty paid" invoice at the time of importation. To the contrary, §1520 does not apply to this case.

Century's repeated failure to mark its documents "duty paid" falls outside the allowance for correction under §1520(c)(1). Section 1520 extends a correction chance to "a clerical error, mistake of fact, or *other inadvertence*." (Emphasis supplied.) A correctable inadvertence under §1520(c)(1) is easy to recognize because it is commensurate with, as the statute states, a "clerical error" or a "mistake of fact." In *Aviall of Texas, Inc. v. United States*, 70 F.3d 1248 (Fed. Cir. 1995) this court acknowledged a correctable inadvertence when the importer did not file certifications for duty-free import for one year. Because the importer had correctly filed these certifications for the eight previous years, and rectified his error for the ninth year immediately upon notification, this court concluded that the importer's error in the ninth year was a correctable "mistake which occurred through inadvertence." *Id.* at 1251. This court discerned in *Aviall* that a fact that was thought to exist (the certification) did not, in reality, exist.

The facts in *Executone Information Systems v. United States*, 96 F.3d 1383 (Fed. Cir. 1996) illustrate an uncorrectable inadvertence. In that case, this court found that the importer had repeatedly failed to file documentation required for duty-free import, and also failed to show that this failure was due to a "mistake of fact or inadvertence," rather than "intentional or negligent inaction." *Executone*, 96 F.3d at 1389. *Century* is similar to *Executone* in that the importer repeatedly did not properly document its imports as "duty-paid." None of the four invoices of July 29, 1993, were marked duty-paid. Moreover, Century did not mark invoices over the entire period from April, 1993 (when the Miller-Molson agreement went into effect) to August 5, 1993 (when the fifty per cent duty was removed). Also, in its appeal to this court, Century did not demonstrate that this failure was due to a mistake of fact or inadvertence. Therefore *Century* falls within the rule of *Executone*.

Century's course of conduct with respect to the entries that occurred both before and after the entries at issue is relevant in demonstrating that its error is one of law. *See Executone*, 96 F.3d at 1390. The repetition of "inadvertence" may indicate an advertent misunderstanding of the law. In this case, Century's repeated failures to provide notice of the duty arrangements over a period of at least four months do not qualify as inadvertent clerical errors or as inadvertent mistakes of fact. Century might well have known that it was not marking its import documents "duty paid," but not have known it was operating under a misapprehension of the law. To use an alternative label, Century acted negligently. "[I]nadvertence does not stretch so far as to encompass intentional or negligent inaction." *Ford Motor Co. v. United States*, 157 F.3d 849, 860 (Fed. Cir. 1998) (citing *Aviall*, 70 F.3d at 1250 and *Executone*, 96 F.3d at 1389-90). Century's failure to provide notice falls outside the scope of inadvertence correctable under 19 U.S.C. §1520(c)(1).

Correction is not possible if the error is one in the construction of law. *See Aviall*, 70 F.3d at 1250; *see also*, 19 C.F.R. §173.4 ("Correction pursuant to . . . 19 U.S.C. [§]1520(c)(1), may be made . . . if the clerical error, mistake of fact, or other inadvertence . . . [d]oes not amount to an error in the construction of a law."). Mistakes of law occur where the facts are known but their legal consequences are not, or are believed to be different than they really are. *See Executone*, 96 F.3d at 1387. Thus, misunderstanding or ignorance of the law does not qualify as a correctable inadvertence under §1520.

Because the Court of International Trade mistakenly interpreted the Century's import transactions to be duty-paid imports, improperly assessed by Customs due to remediable error on the part of the importer, it erred in its grant of summary judgment. This court therefore vacates the grant of summary judgment to Century and reverses the denial of summary judgment to the United States.

VACATED and REVERSED.

Luigi Bormioli Corp., Inc. v. United States
United States Court of Appeals, Federal Circuit, 2002
304 F.3d 1362

ARCHER, Senior Circuit Judge.

Luigi Bormioli Corp. ("Bormioli") appeals the judgment of the United States Court of International Trade granting summary judgment to the United States that the appraised transaction value of certain entries of Bormioli's imported glassware includes a charge of 1.25 percent of its invoice price. *See Luigi Bormioli Corp. v. United States,* 118 F. Supp. 2d 1345 (CIT 2000). The court held that Bormioli did not demonstrate that the 1.25 percent charge was a *bona fide* interest charge excludable from the transaction value of the merchandise pursuant to *Treatment of Interest Charges in the Customs Value of Imported Merchandise,* 19 Cust. B. & Dec. 258 (1985), 50 Fed. Reg. 27,886 (July 8, 1985) ("TD 85-111"). Because we agree with the Court of International Trade that the United States Customs Service ("Customs") correctly determined that Bormioli did not demonstrate that the 1.25 percent charge should be excluded from transaction value, we affirm.

FACTUAL BACKGROUND

This case arises from certain favorable payment terms extended to Bormioli by its Italian parent company, Luigi Bormioli S.p.A. ("Bormioli Italy"). Bormioli imports into the United States glassware it purchases from Bormioli Italy. Typically, Bormioli Italy requires payment from its customers within 60 days of the date of its invoice for the subject merchandise. However, in a January 8, 1987 letter, Bormioli Italy granted Bormioli an extension of the payment deadline from 60 to 180 days.

Under the terms of the agreement, if Bormioli elected to delay payment to Bormioli Italy beyond the normal 60-day deadline, Bormioli would be required to pay interest on the balance to Bormioli Italy at the then-prevailing Italian prime rate. Bormioli was required to make any such interest payments to Bormioli Italy at the end of each quarter. Of course, Bormioli still was required to pay the principal balance on the merchandise to Bormioli Italy within 180 days of the invoice.

Over time, Bormioli Italy reduced the term of the payment extensions. In a December 11, 1987 letter, Bormioli Italy shortened the payment deadline to 120 days effective January 1, 1988, and in a June 8, 1989 letter, it further shortened the payment deadline to 90 days effective August 1, 1989. The remainder of the terms of the original letter were unchanged. Bormioli states that these decreases in the length of the payment extensions reflected its increasing financial viability.

The glassware merchandise entries at issue in this case were imported in 1996, when the 90-day payment deadline was in effect. Using a "corporate charge invoice," Bormioli Italy billed Bormioli a 15 percent annual interest charge (1.25 percent per month) for delayed payment of one month (i.e., the difference between 90 and 60 days) for the imported merchandise. Bormioli recorded the charges in its books as "corporate charges," denominated "special [payment] terms 15% interest charges." Bormioli Italy's invoices to Bormioli for the glassware itself did not include an "interest" listing for the subject charges.

In practice, Bormioli's payment of these "interest" charges deviated from the terms of its letter agreement with Bormioli Italy in several ways. First, Bormioli made payments on six to twelve months worth of accrued charges, rather than quarterly. Second, Bormioli made the payments on the basis of a 15 percent interest rate (1.25 percent per month), rather than the roughly 11.1 percent prime rate in effect in Italy in 1996. Finally, it frequently paid the outstanding invoices after the 90-day deadline (up to 22 days later).

In 1996, Customs appraised the Bormioli imported merchandise on the basis of transaction value pursuant to 19 U.S.C. §1401a(b). It determined that the value of the goods was the invoice price, plus an additional 1.25 percent of the invoice price based on the payments Bormioli made to Bormioli Italy. Customs made this determination based on its policy set forth in TD 85-111, which provides in relevant part:

> [I]nterest payments, whether or not included in the price actually paid or payable for merchandise, should not be considered part of dutiable value provided the following criteria are satisfied:
>
> I.   The interest charges are identified separately from the price actually paid or payable for the goods;
> II. The financing arrangement in question was made in writing;
> III. Where required by Customs, the buyer can demonstrate that
>   — The goods undergoing appraisement are actually sold at the price declared as the price paid or payable, and
>   — The claimed rate of interest does not exceed the level for such transaction prevailing in the country where, and at the time, when the financing was provided.

TD 85-111.

The criteria in paragraph "C" are considered satisfied if the claimed charges for interest and principal are "consistent with those usually reflected in sales of identical or similar merchandise." *Id.*

Bormioli filed suit in the Court of International Trade to challenge the inclusion of the 1.25 percent charge. Bormioli argued that TD 85-111 did not "apply" to its interest payments, or, alternatively, that its payments satisfied TD 85-111's test for excludable interest. The Court of International Trade granted summary judgment to the United States.

DISCUSSION
I.

We begin by a review of the statutory framework. In 1979, the parties to the GATT agreed to a comprehensive Customs Valuation Code. The Code established that the preferred method of calculating the appraised value of imported merchandise would be "transaction value," based on the "price actually paid or payable" for the merchandise.

The United States adopted the transaction valuation method of appraisal in 19 U.S.C. §1401a(b) (codifying section 402(b) of the Trade Agreements Act of 1930, amended by the Trade Agreements Act of 1979). Paragraph (b)(1) of that section provides: "The transaction value of imported merchandise is *the price actually paid or payable for the merchandise* when sold for exportation to the United States, plus [certain additional] amounts . . ." 19 U.S.C. §1401a(b)(1) (1994) (emphasis added).[7] These additional amounts (set forth in sub-paragraphs (A)-(E) of the statute) are to be added to the "price actually paid or payable" only if they are not otherwise included in that price, and if they are based on sufficient information. *Id.* Congress also expressly excluded certain charges from transaction value (such as certain taxes and post-importation costs).[8] Section 1401a(b)(3) specifies that these enumerated excluded costs are not included in transaction value if they are identified separately from the "price actually paid or payable" and from any cost or other item referred to in section (b)(1). 19 U.S.C. §1401a(b)(3) (1994).

"Interest" is not one of the specifically statutorily mandated inclusions or one of the exclusions. Nonetheless, Congress provided a flexible definition for the "price actually paid or payable":

> The term "price actually paid or payable" means *the total payment* (whether direct or indirect, and exclusive of any costs, charges, or expenses incurred for transportation, insurance, and related services incident to the international shipment of the merchandise from the country of exportation to the place of importation in the United States) *made, or to be made, for imported merchandise* by the buyer to, or for the benefit of, the seller.

19 U.S.C. §1401a(b)(4)(A) (emphases added).

We have interpreted the term "total payment" in the "price actually paid or payable" definition to be "all-inclusive." *Generra Sportswear Co. v. United States,* 905 F.2d 377, 379 (Fed. Cir. 1990) Therefore, we have held that the "price actually paid or payable" includes payments made by the buyer to the seller in exchange for merchandise even if the payment "represents something other than the *per se* value

---

7. These additional amounts are

    (A) the packing costs incurred by the buyer with respect to the imported merchandise;

    (B) any selling commission incurred by the buyer with respect to the imported merchandise;

    (C) the value, apportioned as appropriate, of any assist;

    (D) any royalty or license fee related to the imported merchandise that the buyer is required to pay, directly or indirectly, as a condition of the sale of the imported merchandise for exportation to the United States; and

    (E) the proceeds of any subsequent resale, disposal, or use of the imported merchandise that accrue, directly or indirectly, to the seller.

19 U.S.C. §1401a(b)(3)(1994).

8. These excluded charges are

    (A) Any reasonable cost or charge that is incurred for—

        (i) the construction, erection, assembly, or maintenance of, or the technical assistant provided with respect to, the merchandise after its importation into the United States; or

        (ii) the transportation of the merchandise after such importation.

    (B) The customs duties and other Federal taxes currently payable on the imported merchandise by reason of its importation, and any Federal excise tax on, or measured by the value of, such merchandise for which vendors in the United States are ordinarily liable.

19 U.S.C. §1401a(b)(3) (1994).

of the goods." *Id.* at 379-80 (holding that quota payments were properly included in the "price actually paid or payable") This interpretation is consistent with the broad definition of "price actually paid or payable" adopted by the GATT.[2]

In 1985, Customs promulgated TD 85-111 in order to implement an April 26, 1984 decision on the treatment of interest charges made by the Committee on Customs Valuation of the GATT. TD 85-111 closely mirrors the operative language of the GATT Committee's "Decision of the Treatment of Interest Charges in the Customs Value of Imported Goods."

> Charges for interest under a financing arrangement entered into by the buyer and relating to the purchase of imported goods shall not be regarded as part of the customs value provided that:
>   (a) the charges are distinguished from the price actually paid or payable for the goods;
>   (b) the financing arrangement was made in writing;
>   (c) where required, the buyer can demonstrate that
>   Such goods are actually sold at the price declared as the price actually paid or payable, and
>   The claimed rate of interest does not exceed the level for such transactions prevailing in the country where, and at the time when the finance was provided.

Decision of the Treatment of Interest Charges in the Customs Value of Imported Goods, GATT Committee on Customs Valuation, April 26, 1984, *reprinted in* TD 85-111, Annex A—General Agreement on Tariffs and Trade (hereinafter "1984 GATT Committee decision").

* * *

We must first consider whether TD 85-111 is consistent with the statute. Although all the detailed criteria of TD 85-111 cannot be found in the explicit language of the statute, we think that the statute must be interpreted to be consistent with GATT obligations, absent contrary indications in the statutory language or its legislative history. Here there are no such contrary indications. The GATT approach is quite consistent with the statute. Like 19 U.S.C. §1401a(b)(4)(A), the GATT broadly defines "price actually paid or payable." *See* 1994 GATT Interpretive Note. GATT is also consistent with the policy of the statute. The GATT parameters not only provide a uniform method to evaluate when "interest" charges are included in transaction value, but they also serve to prevent importers from manipulating the amount of duties assessed on particular merchandise by simply designating part of the payment made for that merchandise as "interest." Without a policy that requires both sufficient documentation of the transaction, and evidence of comparable prevailing rates and sales, an importer could easily reduce the "price actually paid or payable" of the goods by denominating charges that actually represented

---

2. "The price actually paid or payable is *the total payment made or to be made by the buyer to or for the benefit of the seller for the imported goods.* The payment need not necessarily take the form of a transfer of money. . . . Payment may be made directly or indirectly . . . ." Agreement on Implementation of Article VI of the General Agreement on Tariffs and Trade 1994, Annex I, Interpretive Notes, Note to Article 1, "Price Actually Paid or Payable," 1994 WL 761483 (GATT) (emphasis added) (hereinafter "1994 GATT Interpretive Note").

a portion of the price of the goods as "interest." Thus, we construe the statute to make it consistent with GATT.

Under that construction, TD 85-111 is consistent with the statute because it is the same as GATT. Like the 1984 GATT Committee decision on the treatment of interest charges, TD 85-111 does not only apply to "unitary prices." *See* 1984 GATT Committee decision. Rather, it serves as a tool to evaluate all "[c]harges for interest under a financing arrangement entered into by the buyer and relating to the purchase of imported goods." *Id.* TD 85-111, like the 1984 GATT Committee decision, includes a criterion that the charges be separately documented from "the price actually paid or payable for the goods." *Id.* (stating the criterion that "[t]he charges are distinguished from the price actually paid or payable for goods."). TD 85-111 and the 1984 GATT Committee decision are otherwise identical. Both include the requirements that the financing arrangement be made in writing; the buyer can demonstrate that the goods are actually sold at the price declared as the price paid or payable; and the buyer can demonstrate that the claimed rate of interest does not exceed the rate for such transactions prevailing in the country where and at the time when the financing was provided. *Id.;* TD 85-11. Thus, in all relevant respects, TD 85-111 and the 1984 GATT Committee decision set forth the same criteria.

II.

[T]he Court of International Trade did not err in granting the United States summary judgment that Bormioli's interest payments did not satisfy the TD 85-111 criteria.

There is no dispute that Bormioli's payments meet the first criteria of TD 85-111: that the charges be "identified separately from the price actually paid or payable for the goods." Bormioli Italy billed the 15 percent annual interest charge (1.25 percent per month) on a "corporate charge invoice" separate from Bormioli Italy's invoices to Bormioli for the glassware itself. However, each of the remaining criteria is disputed. For the reasons set forth below, Bormioli's attempt to create a factual dispute sufficient to negate summary judgment fails.

Bormioli argues first that it satisfied the criterion that "the financing arrangement in question was made in writing." *See* TD 85-111. It contends that the January 8, 1987, December 11, 1987, and June 8, 1989 letters from Bormioli Italy to Bormioli constitute the written financing agreement required by TD 85-111. Bormioli acknowledges that the parties departed from the terms of these letters. However, it argues that these departures at most mean that the parties modified a term of the contract through course of conduct or that there was a breach of the agreement—not that the agreement did not exist.

We agree that the parties to a written financing arrangement may contractually modify the terms of their agreement. However, for the financing arrangement to comport with TD 85-111, the modifications also must be in writing. Further, while Customs may choose to ignore a de minimis variation from the terms of a written financing arrangement, the parties' repeated violation of the salient terms of the arrangement must remove it from coverage under TD 85-111. TD 85-111 does not merely require that the parties have a written financing arrangement, but that the written financing arrangement actually govern the payments at issue. *See* TD 85-111 (requiring that the financing arrangement "in question" be in writing); *see also* 1984 GATT Committee decision (referring to "[c]harges for interest under a financing arrangement entered into by the buyer and relating to the purchase of imported goods. . . ." and requiring such financing arrangement to be in writing). Were it otherwise, the parties could manipulate the transaction by setting up a "written financing arrangement" without adhering to any of its terms.

Bormioli Italy's letter agreement with Bormioli had only three essential terms: (1) the rate of interest to be charged (the prime rate in Italy in effect at the time), (2) the frequency of billing for interest charges (quarterly), and (3) the deadlines for payment of principal (within 180/120/90 days of invoice). The record reflects that Bormioli and Bormioli Italy did not adhere to any of these terms. While the average prime rate in Italy in 1996 was 11.1 percent, the rate for Bormioli's interest payments was 15 percent. Rather than making its interest payments quarterly, Bormioli made payments on six to twelve months of accrued charges. Finally, Bormioli frequently paid its outstanding invoices after the 90-day deadline (from one to 22 days later). We conclude that the Court of International Trade correctly held that Bormioli did not demonstrate that it met TD 85-111's criterion that its financing arrangement with Bormioli Italy for the subject charges was in writing.

For these reasons, the judgment of the Court of International Trade is AFFIRMED.

NOTES AND QUESTIONS

1. In *Century Importers*, a simple procedure was available for Century, the importer, to have the paid tariff excluded from dutiable value. How is this done? Why did Century fail to carry out this simple task?

2. In *Luigi Bormioli*, the court of appeals refused to treat the payments from the buyer-importer to the seller-exporter as excludable interest not subject to duty. What then was the true purpose of the "interest" payments by the buyer-importer?

PROBLEM 5-18

Deluxe is in the business of selling motor vehicles. In connection with the development of a new model of car, the Standard, Deluxe enters into a contract with a Japanese company, Soria, to develop prototype engines of an advanced design for a total price of $20 million. While many of the prototype engines remained in Japan, a number of prototype engines were imported into the United States with full payment of the applicable duties.

Deluxe now contracts with Soria for the purchase and importation of production engines for installation into its new Standard model cars that will be sold to consumers. Must the $20 million paid to Soria for the design and development of the prototype engines be included in the transaction value of the imported production engines? Since duties were already paid on many of the prototypes (those that were imported into the United States), would not adding the $20 million cost be double counting?

Under U.S. law, 19 U.S.C. §1401a(h)(1)(A), an "assist" is defined as a good or service that is "supplied directly or indirectly, and free of charge or at reduced cost, by the buyer of imported merchandise for use in connection with the production or the sale for export to the United States of the [imported] merchandise." Is the $20 million cost in the foregoing transaction an assist? Even if it is not an assist, should the cost be included in transaction value? *See Ford Motor Co. v. United States*, 435 F. Supp. 2d 1324, 1327-1328 (CIT 2006).

C. European Union Law

The EU has implemented the WTO Valuation Agreement into the Community Customs Code. Consider the following case:

Hans Sommer GmbH v. Hauptzollamt Bremen
Case C-15/99 [2000] ECR I-8989

[This case involved the valuation of honey imported into Germany from Russia. The initial export contract was a sale to Kessler Co., which resold the honey to the importer, Hans Sommer, a German corporation. Kessler separately invoiced Sommer for its additional costs of ensuring that the honey complied with German regulations calculated at a flat rate per ton of honey. Sommer ignored these costs in declaring the value of the honey in order to clear customs. The German court sought the opinion of the European Court of Justice on whether these additional costs incurred by Kessler and billed separately to Sommer should be included in the transaction value of the honey for the purpose of assessing customs duties. The opinion of the ECJ follows.]

3. Article 3 of Regulation No. 1224/80 [now Article 29 of the Community Customs Code] provides:

> (1) The customs value of imported goods determined under this article shall be the transaction value, that is, the price actually paid or payable for the goods when sold for export to the customs territory of the Community adjusted in accordance with Article 8 . . .
> . . .
> (3) (a) The price actually paid or payable is the total payment made or to be made by the buyer to or for the benefit of the seller for the imported goods and includes all payments made or to be made as a condition of sale of the imported goods by the buyer to the seller or by the buyer to a third party to satisfy an obligation of the seller. . . .

19. By this question the national court is asking essentially whether the costs of analyses designed to establish the conformity of the imported goods with the national legislation of the importing Member State, which the importer invoices to the buyer in addition to the price of goods, must be regarded as an integral part of their transaction value within the meaning of Article 3(1) of Regulation No. 1224/80.

20. Sommer submits that the question should be answered in the negative. It argues that those costs are in respect of services supplied in the Community by undertakings established there and relate to goods which have already been sold for export to the Community customs territory. It is therefore necessary to apply the case-law of the Court to the effect that, subject to the adjustments provided for in Article 8 of Regulation No. 1224/80, payment for services provided to the buyer on the purchase of imported goods is not included in the customs value of the goods.

21. The national court and the Commission observe that the seller undertook to deliver honey of a quality specified in the contract of sale by reference to a detailed analysis made by the seller in accordance with the applicable German legislation. The analysis costs should therefore be regarded as pertaining to a condition of sale of the imported goods and, accordingly, are part of the customs value of those goods in accordance with Article 3(3)(a) of Regulation No. 1224/80.

22. In answering the first question, it should be borne in mind that under the system established by Regulation No. 1224/80 the concept of transaction value, that is to say, as a general rule, the price actually paid or payable for the goods, forms the basis for calculating the customs value. That calculation must therefore be made on the basis of the conditions on which the individual sale was made (Case 65/85 *Hauptzollamt Hamburg-Ericus v Van Houten* [1986] ECR 447, paragraph 13).

23. It is apparent from the national court's findings that in the contracts of sale Kessler undertook to deliver to Sommer honey satisfying the quality requirements laid down by German legislation. It follows that the analyses performed after importation in order to establish the quality of the honey were necessary in order for the goods to be delivered in accordance with the provisions of the contracts.

24. The costs pertaining to those analyses must therefore be regarded as part of the payments made or to be made as a condition of sale of the imported goods by the buyer to the seller to satisfy an obligation of the seller within the meaning of Article 3(3)(a) of Regulation No. 1224/80 and, accordingly, as an integral part of the customs value.

NOTES AND QUESTIONS

Compare the approaches to valuation of the United States and the EU. Both are implementations of the WTO rules. Are the approaches similar?

VII.   *Rules of Origin*

Read the WTO Agreement on Rules of Origin in the Documents Supplement.

A.   WTO Standards

Once classification and valuation determinations are made, the last step in the tariff calculation is to determine the origin of the goods. Goods entering the United States from other WTO members are subject to GATT rates, but the same goods may be duty-free if they trace their origins to countries with which the United States has a free trade agreement or preferential trade program. If the goods are from a non-WTO member, they may be subject in the United States to the pre-GATT statutory rate set forth in the Smoot-Hawley Tariff Act.

An attempt at international harmonization of origin determinations is contained in the Kyoto Convention, which provides that rules of origin requirements may not be overly burdensome. This provision has limited effect in harmonizing rules. The WTO Agreement on Rules of Origin, entered into during the

Uruguay Round, sets forth a work program in cooperation with the World Customs Organization to develop detailed rules of origin. To date, the WTO work program is proceeding very slowly. In general, the "last substantial transformation" test must be used to determine origin. *See* Agreement on Rules of Origin Article 3(b). This test is based upon the practice of the United States and the EU, both of which currently use a substantial transformation test.

Until the work program is completed, rules of origin are determined by nations under domestic law, although they are required to apply their current rules under the GATT principles of non-discrimination and transparency. Other requirements are fairness and neutrality. *See* Agreement on Rules of Origin Article 2.

Determinations of origin are also relevant to non-tariff trade laws, such as laws pertaining to origin marking requirements, anti-dumping and countervailing duties, and quota administration. Determinations of origin under these laws serve different policy goals. For example, GATT allows countries to maintain statutes requiring marks of origin to protect consumers from false and misleading information. The GATT/WTO also recognizes that consumers have a legitimate interest in knowing the origin of the goods because this information may affect their purchasing decisions. Laws governing anti-dumping duties, countervailing duties, and quotas impose restrictions on goods from certain countries, so it becomes necessary to determine the origin of the goods.

B. United States Law

Consistent with the general guidelines of the WTO Agreement on Rules of Origin, the United States applies a substantial transformation test in deciding origin questions. The test is based on U.S. law, however, because the WTO Agreement has not yet set forth detailed rules of its own.

In *Koru*, the principal case below, the court applied a rule for determining the country of origin for marking purposes. Under the federal marking statute, 19 U.S.C. §1304(a), the country of origin must be conspicuously displayed on the product. Marking is required to inform consumers of the origin of the product and is not related to tariff issues, but the courts use the same approach, the substantial transformation test used in *Koru*, for determining country of origin for tariff purposes.

PROBLEM 5-19

Paddlefish eggs are obtained in the Ukraine by a Ukrainian affiliate of Le Haut, a French company. The raw eggs are then shipped frozen to Poland, where the eggs are cooked and prepared into paddlefish caviar by a Polish subsidiary of Le Haut; finally, the caviar is sent to France, where it is packaged into attractive gourmet cans, which are labeled by Le Haut as the "Product of France."

When the goods arrive at U.S. Customs in New Orleans, the importer declares the caviar to be a product of France and subject to tariff rates applicable to France. However, a customs official decides the caviar is subject to tariffs that apply to the Ukraine because the eggs were obtained there and orders that must be relabeled accordingly. Is the official correct? What about Poland? Consider the *Koru* and *SDI* cases below.

Koru North America v. United States
United States Court of International Trade, 1988
701 F. Supp. 229

Tsoucalas, Judge:

Plaintiff, Koru North America, brings this action to contest the United States Customs Service's (Customs) exclusion of frozen Hoki fillets that entered through the port of Seattle under entry # 110-0659025-8 on February 23, 1988. Upon determining that plaintiff improperly marked the subject merchandise as a "Product of New Zealand," rather than as a "Product of the Soviet Union," for country of origin purposes, Customs issued a Notice of Redelivery with respect to these goods. Plaintiff claims that since the product was correctly marked, Customs improperly issued the Notice of Redelivery.

The fish, known as the "New Zealand Hoki," were caught off the shores of New Zealand within its Exclusive Economic Zone (EEZ).[3] They were caught by ships chartered by Fletcher Fishing, Ltd. (Fletcher), the largest fishing company in New Zealand, while flying the flags of New Zealand, Japan and the Union of Soviet Socialist Republic. The fish were beheaded, de-tailed, eviscerated and frozen aboard the ships within New Zealand's EEZ, then landed and offloaded in New Zealand where they were commingled and stored under Fletcher's control. The initial processing aboard the vessel had to conform with all of New Zealand's fishing laws and regulations.

Once ashore, the fish were inspected and certified by the New Zealand Ministry of Agriculture and Fisheries as being of New Zealand origin, fit for human consumption and caught in conformity with the requirements imposed by New Zealand.

The fish were then sent to Korea for further processing; they were thawed, skinned, boned, trimmed, glazed, refrozen and packaged for exportation to the United States.

The merchandise arrived in the United States in cartons marked "Product of New Zealand." Customs issued a Notice of Redelivery against the merchandise in its condition marked as imported. Customs' position is that the fish caught and commingled should be labeled "Product of the Soviet Union, Japan and New Zealand," based on the doctrine of the Law of the Flag. It reasons that since the EEZ is outside the territorial waters of a country, it is the high seas, and that fish caught on the high seas are products of the country of the flag of the catching vessel. Plaintiff, on the other hand, claims that the fish are products of New Zealand since they were caught within New Zealand's EEZ on behalf of a New Zealand company, and were at all times owned by that company.

At the hearing of this action and in their briefs, the parties presented arguments as to whether the fish are a product of New Zealand or a product of the Soviet Union, but sought to reserve judgment on the issue of whether the product

---

3. New Zealand defines its EEZ as those areas of sea, beyond and adjacent to the territorial sea, having as their outer limits a line measured seaward from the defined baseline every point of which is 200 nautical miles from the nearest point of the baseline. *Id.* at 7. New Zealand's definition is in accordance with the definition provided in the United Nations Convention on the Law of the Sea, A/Conf. 62/122, U.N. Sales No. E.83.V.5, Articles 55, 57 (1983).

was substantially transformed in South Korea, thereby rendering it a product of South Korea for country of origin purposes.

At the direction of the Court at oral argument, the parties briefed the issue pertaining to substantial transformation and agreed that the fish were substantially transformed in South Korea. The following discussion sets forth the Court's rationale for finding that substantial transformation occurred in South Korea.

DISCUSSION

A.   THE LAW OF THE FLAG

On the high seas, the country of origin of fish is determined by the flag of the catching vessel. In international law, a ship on the high seas is considered foreign territory, functionally, "a floating island of the country to which [it] belongs." *Thompson v. Lucas,* 252 U.S. 358, 361, 40 S. Ct. 353, 64 L. Ed. 612 (1920).

Plaintiff maintains that "the maritime principle that the nationality of a vessel on the 'high seas' is determined by the flag it flies, is of no relevance to this particular controversy, because the fish in question were caught in the EEZ by registered New Zealand fishing vessels on behalf of the New Zealand industry and against its share of the total allowable catch." *Plaintiff's Reply* at 18. Plaintiff additionally claims that the foreign ships became *de facto* "New Zealand fishing vessels" despite being foreign owned and flagged because: (1) the fish were caught by vessels under charter to the New Zealand company, Fletcher, for the specific purpose of enabling Fletcher to exhaust its Hoki quota allocation; (2) the vessels were controlled by Fletcher and New Zealand laws; Fletcher owned all the fish caught and processed by the vessels; the vessels, which were temporarily imported for home consumption whereby Fletcher entered into a deed of covenant of NZ $700,000.00 for each vessel, were thought of as New Zealand fishing vessels by the New Zealand Ministry of Agriculture; and (3) the Director General consented to registration of the vessels as "New Zealand fishing vessels." *Plaintiff's Brief* at 24-27. Thus, plaintiff asserts that the proper country of origin is New Zealand.

However, plaintiff's fiction of "*de facto* New Zealand vessels" ignores that even though the ships were registered in New Zealand for purposes of fishing within the EEZ, the ships maintained their Soviet registry, meaning, they flew the flag of the Soviet Union, applied Soviet law on board ship, and remained part of the sovereignty of the Soviet Union. The law of the flag has been found to "supersede[ ] the territorial principle . . . because [the ship] 'is deemed to be a part of the territory of that sovereignty [whose flag it flies], and not to lose that character when in navigable waters within the territorial limits of another sovereignty,'" *Lauritzen v. Larsen,* 345 U.S. 571, 585. Therefore, since the subject merchandise was caught and initially processed on Soviet territory, it originates from that country.

Plaintiff misinterprets the application of rights conveyed through the establishment of an EEZ. The authority for establishing an EEZ derives from the United Nations Convention on the Law of the Sea (LOS Convention) where each country is provided with certain sovereign rights within its EEZ, specifically "sovereign rights for the purpose of exploring and exploiting, conserving and managing the natural resources, whether living or nonliving. . . ." Article 56 of the LOS Convention. These rights need not be claimed by a coastal State to exist. *See* Art. 55, LOS Convention.

Even though plaintiff would like this Court to equate the EEZ with the territorial sea, such a conclusion would be clearly improper, as certain elements of the high seas are retained in an EEZ. Specifically, the "freedoms . . . of navigation and overflight and of the laying of submarine cables and pipelines, and other internationally lawful uses of the sea related to these freedoms. . . ." Art. 58 of the LOS. In addition, a State is free in its territorial sea to prohibit fishing by foreigners, monopolize the fishing resources and the exploitation thereof, and fully control those waters. Within an EEZ, however, the State retains control of the fishing resources only for the purpose of optimum utilization and to prevent the unnecessary exhaustion of resources. In this regard, although the State retains the exclusive right to determine the amount of allowable catch, it is obligated to allocate the surplus among the other States. Art. 62 of the LOS. Consequently, it would be improper to characterize fish caught within a country's EEZ as originating from that country on the basis of their being caught within the EEZ.

The extra grant of jurisdiction to a State through its EEZ must be considered in light of the purposes of the marking statute. In ascertaining what constitutes the country of origin under the marking statute, a court must look at the sense in which the term is used in the statute, giving reference to the purpose of the particular legislation involved.

The purpose of the marking statute is outlined in *United States v. Friedlaender & Co.*, 27 CCPA 297, 302, C.A.D. 104 (1940), where the court stated that:

> Congress intended that the ultimate purchaser should be able to know by an inspection of the marking on imported goods the country of which the goods is the product. The evident purpose is to mark the goods so that at the time of purchase the ultimate purchaser may, by knowing where the goods were produced, be able to buy or refuse to buy them, if such marking should influence his will.

This purpose would be best served in the instant action by finding the fish to be products of the Soviet Union, Japan and New Zealand since the catching and initial processing occurred on the vessels of these countries.

The fish in the instant action were caught beyond the boundaries of the mother country (New Zealand), i.e., in an area which is not within the sovereignty of New Zealand but where New Zealand merely possesses preferential fishing rights. Therefore, the fish are a product of the Soviet Union, Japan and New Zealand, provided they have not been substantially transformed in South Korea.

B.   SUBSTANTIAL TRANSFORMATION

The marking statute, section 304 of the Tariff Act of 1930, as amended, 19 U.S.C. §1304 (1982 & Supp. III 1985) requires all articles imported into the United States to "be marked in a conspicuous place as legibly, indelibly, and permanently [as possible] . . . to indicate to an ultimate purchaser in the United States the English name of the country of origin of the article." 19 U.S.C. §1304(a). The country of origin of an article is defined as "the country of manufacture, production, or growth of any article of foreign origin entering the United States." 19 C.F.R. §134.1(b). In the instant action, that country would be either New Zealand, because the fish were caught in its claimed EEZ, or the Soviet Union, since the catches were made on board a Soviet-flag vessel. However, an important exception exists to the marking statute. When "[f]urther work or material added to an article in another country [would] effect a substantial transformation", such other country will be the "country of origin" within the meaning of the statute. *Id.* The Court finds the procedures performed upon the fish in South Korea to constitute a "substantial transformation" within the meaning of the statute.

Courts have developed several tests in determining whether substantial transformation has occurred. The most significant is the "name, character or use" test. A substantial transformation occurs where articles "lose their identity as such, and become new articles having . . . a new name, character, and use. . . ." *United States v. Gibson-Thomsen Co.*, 27 CCPA 267, 270, C.A.D. 98 (1940)

The Customs Service has incorporated the name, character or use test of *Gibson-Thomsen* in its regulations. *See* 19 C.F.R. §134.35. A processor who converts an imported article into a different article having a new name, character or use has substantially transformed the imported article, thereby requiring the markings on the product to reflect this change. *Id.*

The article need not experience a change in name, character *and* use to be substantially transformed. Only one of the three prongs needs to be satisfied for a product to achieve substantial transformation. The name element, however, has received less weight and is considered "the weakest evidence of substantial transformation." *National Juice Products*, 10 CIT at 59, 628 F. Supp. at 989

In the present action, the criteria for substantial transformation have been satisfied. The fish's name has been changed as the result of the processing method which occurred in Korea. When the fish arrive in Korea they are known as "headed and gutted" Hoki, as they have been beheaded, de-tailed and eviscerated.

The fish's character, after its journey through Korea, is also vastly different from what it was upon departure from New Zealand. The fish arrive in Korea, with the look of a whole fish, albeit without heads, tails or viscera, *see id.* at 9 (citing Easton Reply Affidavit, paras. 5(e) and (g)), whereas the fish that are exported from Korea have no skin or bones, "no longer possess the essential shape of the fish . . . have been trimmed of jagged edges, fat lines and impurities, glazed to preserve their moisture and thereby enhance their shelf life, frozen to protect the fish from spoilage and finally, packaged." *Id.* at 9. Additionally, the fillets are considered discrete commercial goods and are sold in separate areas and markets. *Id.* at 10. Unlike the product in *National Juice Products*, the fresh article here (the headed and gutted fish) undergoes its transformation into a processed retail product (fillet) in the second country (Korea). These changes go to the fundamental nature and character of the fish; the fish have been transformed, both in name and in character. Therefore, a new article of commerce has been created.

SDI Technologies, Inc. v. United States
United States Court of International Trade, 1997
977 F. Supp. 1235

GOLDBERG, Judge.

Plaintiff, SDI Technologies, Inc. ("SDI"), claims that defendant, the United States Customs Service ("Customs"), improperly declined to classify articles imported from Mexico to the United States as exempt from duty under the Generalized System of Preferences ("GSP"), 19 U.S.C. §2463(b) (Supp. II 1990). At issue is whether the goods imported from Mexico are "products of" Mexico for GSP purposes. To make this determination, the Court must decide if goods imported into Mexico from China were substantially transformed in Mexico before being exported to the United States. This Court finds that the goods were not substantially transformed in Mexico, and therefore holds that Customs correctly denied GSP status to the articles when they were imported to the United States.

SDI, formerly known as "Soundesign," is a consumer electronic manufacturer and distributor, whose major production in the past has included audio rack systems, CD players, "boom boxes," clock radios, telephones, and VCRs. Oral Test. of Mr. Edward Kurowski (expert witness for SDI) (Nov. 19, 1996) ("Kurowski Test."). The subject goods, model numbers 46C46M1 and 63R63M, are imported into the United States from Mexico, and sold by SDI as "rack stereo systems." Legal Mem. Supp. Pl.'s Claims at 1. The subject goods consist of a center console, which houses the electronic equipment, and two speakers. The major difference between models is that the speakers for model 46C46M1 are attached to the console by hinges, while the speakers for model 63R63M are free standing.

SDI's manufacturing operation in Juarez, Mexico consisted of laminating imported raw particle board, cutting and grooving this board, molding plastic components, cutting and painting imported foam, and finally joining these parts "with other components that did not require additional processing prior to the assembly of the rack stereo systems." Legal Mem. Supp. Pl.'s Claims at 3; *accord* Kurowski Test. Components that did not require "additional processing" included the audio electronics for each system, "*i.e.,* unhoused printed circuit board assemblies with face-plate incorporating components for radio receivers [and] duel cassette decks," and the raw speaker cones. Legal Mem. Supp. Pl.'s Claims at 3. Both the former elements, which SDI terms a "chassis," and the raw speaker cones were imported from China. Kurowski Test. The audio electronics were complete and fully functional when they were imported into Mexico. At the end of the process, the fully assembled subject goods were packaged in boxes marked "Stereo Music Center," and imported into the United States.

The subject goods were imported to the United States between 1990 and 1992. Customs withheld liquidation of the entries while awaiting a ruling on whether the goods were eligible for duty-free entry under the GSP. Customs Ruling HQ 556699 denied duty-free status to the goods pursuant to the GSP, 19 U.S.C. §2463(b), and Customs accordingly assessed a duty of 3.7% *ad valorem.* SDI filed a timely protest which Customs denied. SDI then initiated this case, claiming that Customs improperly denied duty-free status to the subject goods. This Court finds that Customs acted correctly.

DISCUSSION

Congress originally enacted the GSP program "to extend preferential tariff treatment to the exports of less-developed countries to encourage economic diversification and export development within the developing world." S. Rep. No. 93-1298, at 5 (1974), *reprinted in* 1974 U.S.C.C.A.N. 7186, 7187. The GSP provides that certain "eligible articles" may be imported into the United States duty-free if they meet three requirements. First, the article must be the "growth, product or manufacture" of a beneficiary developing country ("BDC"). 19 U.S.C. §2463(b)(1); *see also* 19 U.S.C. §2463 (b)(2). Second, the article must be imported directly from a BDC into the customs territory of the United States. *Id.* §2463(b)(1)(A). Third, the sum of the cost or value of the material produced in the BDC plus the direct costs of processing operations performed in the BDC must not be less than thirty-five percent of the appraised value of such article at the time of its entry into the customs territory of the United States. *Id.* §2463(b)(1)(B).

Both parties agree that for the purposes of the GSP, Mexico was a BDC for the years 1990, 1991, and 1992, and that for these years, the stereo rack systems were eligible articles for duty-free treatment. Likewise, both parties have stipulated that the subject goods were imported directly from a BDC into the customs territory of the United States, and that the thirty-five percent requirement is met. [T]he only issue in this case is whether the subject goods are the growth, product, or manufacture of Mexico.

To be considered the growth, product, or manufacture of a BDC for GSP purposes, goods imported into the BDC from a third, non-BDC country must undergo a "substantial transformation" in the BDC before they are imported to the United States. *Zuniga,* 996 F.2d at 1206. "[S]ubstantial transformation occurs when an article emerges from a manufacturing process with a name, character, or use which differs from those of the original material subjected to the process." *Torrington v. United States,* 764 F.2d 1563, 1568 (1985). However, because "[t]he article need not experience a change in name, character, *and* use to be substantially transformed," all three of these elements need not be met before a court may find substantial transformation. *Koru North America v. United States,* 701 F. Supp. 229, 234 (1988).

A. THE SUBJECT GOODS HAVE NOT UNDERGONE A CHANGE IN CHARACTER

SDI first asserts that when an article has been refined from a producers' good to a consumers' good, the article *a fortiori* has undergone a change in character. SDI then attempts to characterize the chassis as imported into Mexico as producers' goods, and the stereo rack systems as exported from Mexico into the United States as consumers' goods. Yet the court has never held that the producer/consumer shift alone is dispositive. Quite simply, it proves too much: by SDI's argument, virtually any unfinished product that is finished by a producer before it is sold to a consumer would have undergone substantial transformation.

Nevertheless, the Court still recognizes that the producer/consumer shift does have some evidentiary value. Here, however, the chassis imported into Mexico from China were the fully-functional electronic components of the stereo rack systems, capable of use by the consumer in the state in which they arrived in Mexico. Indeed, the chassis underwent no changes before they were housed, paired with speakers, and renamed "stereo rack systems."

SDI next claims that the subject goods have undergone a change in character because the chassis have been transformed from items that are "fragile," "unsafe," and low in value, to "completed products" with "a finished appearance" which are durable and "entirely safe" with a value roughly double that of the value of the chassis. Legal Mem. Supp. Pl.'s Claims at 15-16. However, SDI does not offer the Court any support for the proposition that these changes are proof of a change in character, and the Court declines to expand our formulation of the name, character, and use test to include these elements.

Additionally, the Court finds that, because the essence of the chassis remains the same, its character has not changed. While the Court acknowledges that a change in essence is not always a necessary prerequisite to a change in character, a lack of a change in essence evidences a lack of a change in character. The relation between essence and character is apparent in *Webster's New World Dictionary* which defines "character" as "a distinctive trait, quality, or attribute; characteristic" or "essential quality." This Court finds no evidence of a change in essence of the goods during the process in which the chassis became a stereo rack system. When it was imported into Mexico, the chassis contained all of the electronics in the rack system, and were completely functional. The essence of the goods, stereo receivers and tape players, did not change when the chassis were housed in the wood-laminate cabinets.

B.   THE SUBJECT GOODS HAVE NOT UNDERGONE A CHANGE
IN USE

SDI also argues that the chassis have undergone a substantial transformation because their use has changed in three distinct manners. First, SDI asserts that before it completed the assembly process, the chassis functioned only as an audio recording and reproduction device, yet after the addition of two speakers, the chassis were transformed, gaining the ability to produce sound, and thus became capable of "audio entertainment." Legal Mem. Supp. Pl.'s Claims at 16. [U]nder this analysis *any* stereo system without speakers would be considered only an audio recording and reproduction device. Indeed, if SDI's analysis were carried to its logical conclusion, a stereo system could be substantially transformed by simply adding or removing speakers, or even headphones. However, such ease of transformation is clearly ruled out by 19 U.S.C. §2463(b)(2) which states that "no article or material of a beneficiary developing country shall be eligible for GSP treatment by virtue of having merely undergone [ ][a] simple combining or packaging operation[ ]."

Second, SDI contends that it has transformed the chassis into furniture. However, SDI's commitment to this argument is belied both by the packaging insert it includes with the system, and by the manual provided to the repair personnel. The former congratulates the owners on their purchase of electronics, and the latter lays out how to fix the electronics—neither mentions the wood-laminate housing.

Third and finally, SDI claims that there has been a change in use because when the chassis were imported into Mexico, they were capable of being used for a number of products, but that after they "were subjected to the Plaintiff's manufacturing process, they were dedicated to only one use, i.e., as integral parts of the center console of the subject rack stereo systems." Legal Mem. Supp. Pl.'s Claims at 17. However, in the present case, the end use of the chassis remains the same. Before its incorporation into the stereo rack system, the chassis was a recording and receiving device with the ability to produce sound once speakers were attached. After it was incorporated into the stereo rack system, its use was exactly the same.

C.   THE COURT'S FINDING IS CONSISTENT WITH THE
STATUTE'S PURPOSE

Finally, the Court notes that its holding is fully consistent with the statutory purpose of the GSP. As noted previously, the GSP program was designed to encourage BDCs to produce goods for export, thereby fostering economic diversification and industrialization.

Previous courts have evaluated several factors to determine whether the production operation at issue promotes the purposes of the GSP. One such factor is the number of employees that require technical training to perform their jobs, and whether this technical training will "lay[ ] the groundwork for the acquisition of even higher skills and more self-sufficiency." *See, e.g., Texas Instruments Inc. v. United States,* 69 C.C.P.A. 151, 160, 681 F.2d 778, 785 (1982). The GSP program, therefore, is not meant to encourage an increase in the number of simple labor intensive jobs within a BDC.

In the instant case the complex manufacturing took place in China. Moreover, the majority of the operations in SDI's plant in Juarez, Mexico only required a skill level of a first to sixth grade education. Accordingly, this Court finds that the purpose of the GSP is not met through the jobs that SDI created.

NOTES AND QUESTIONS

1. *SDI Technologies* arose prior to the establishment of NAFTA. If the case arose today, a court would apply NAFTA rules of origin for goods shipped from Mexico. These rules are very technical and specific and deserve special attention, so we will examine them at the end of this Chapter. Although the specific situation in *SDI Technologies* would be decided under NAFTA rules of origin today, the court's analysis continues to be relevant to any case involving processing operations in a Beneficiary Developing Country under the Generalized System of Preferences.

2. Do you agree with the court's assessment in *Koru* that the "character" of the fish was changed by the processing operations in Korea? How predictable is the substantial transformation test as applied in these cases?

3. In *Koru*, aside from tariff issues, why would an importer be concerned about marking the fish fillets as from the Soviet Union as opposed to New Zealand? Do consumers really care?

C.   European Union Law

Like the United States, the EU also applies a substantial transformation test. In *SDI*, the court held that mere assembly is not a substantial transformation. Can assembly ever constitute a substantial transformation? See the case below.

Brother International GmbH v. Hauptzollamt Giessen
European Court of Justice, 1989
Case 26/88, [1989] ECR 4253

[Germany had imposed anti-dumping duties on typewriters imported from Japan. Anti-dumping duties are extra tariffs imposed on imports that are sold at artificially low prices in order to obtain market share. After Germany imposed the anti-dumping duties, the Japanese company sent typewriter parts to Taiwan to be assembled into typewriters that were then exported to Germany. The issue was whether Taiwan or Japan was the country of origin of the typewriters. If Taiwan is the country of origin then the typewriters are outside the scope of the antidumping order, which applied only to typewriters from Japan. If Japan was the country of origin of the typewriters assembled in Taiwan, then they were subject to antidumping duties. The issued turned on whether there was a substantial transformation through the assembly in Taiwan. The German court referred this case to the ECJ.]

THE INTERPRETATION OF ARTICLE 5 OF REGULATION (EEC) NO. 802/68

11. In its first question the national court is essentially asking under what conditions the mere assembly of previously manufactured parts originating in a country other than that of assembly suffices to confer on the resulting product the origin of the country where the assembly took place.

13. Brother considers that the conditions set out in Article 5 are of a technical nature and that an assembly constitutes a classic processing operation for the purposes of that provision in so far as it consists, as in the present case, of assembling a large number of parts to form a new coherent whole. An implementing regulation adopted under Article 14 of Regulation No. 802/68 laying down the conditions for conferring origin might define the economic criteria of an assembly but not criteria in relation to its intellectual content.

14. The Commission considers on the other hand that the mere assembly of previously manufactured parts should not be regarded as a substantial process or operation within the meaning of Article 5 of the regulation where, in view of the work involved and the expenditure on materials on the one hand and the value added on the other, the operation is clearly less important than other processes or operations carried out in another country or countries.

15. It is clear from Article 5 as interpreted in previous judgments of the Court that the decisive criterion is that of the last substantial process or operation. That view is moreover confirmed by Rule 3 of Annex D.1 to the International Convention on the simplification and harmonization of customs procedures (the Kyoto Convention), which was accepted on behalf of the Community by Council Decision 77/415/EEC of 3 June 1977 (Official Journal 1977, L 166, pp. 1 and 3). Rule 3 reads "Where two or more countries have taken part in the production of the goods, the origin of the goods shall be determined according to the substantial transformation criterion".

16. Article 5 of Regulation No. 802/68 does not specify to what extent assembly operations may be regarded as a substantial process or operation. Rule 6 of the Kyoto Convention states that

> "operations which do not contribute or which contribute to only a small extent to the essential characteristics or properties of the goods, and in particular operations confined to one or more of those listed below, shall not be regarded as constituting substantial manufacturing or processing:
>
> . . . (c) simple assembly operations . . . ".

17. "Simple assembly operations" means operations which do not require staff with special qualifications for the work in question or sophisticated tools or

specially equipped factories for the purposes of assembly. Such operations cannot be held to be such as to contribute to the essential characteristics or properties of the goods in question.

18. The Kyoto Convention confines itself to excluding from the concept of substantial process or operation simple assembly operations without specifying the conditions under which other types of assembly may constitute a substantial process or operation. For such other types of assembly it is necessary to determine in each case and on the basis of objective criteria whether or not they represent a substantial process or operation.

19. An assembly operation may be regarded as conferring origin where it represents from a technical point of view and having regard to the definition of the goods in question the decisive production stage during which the use to which the component parts are to be put becomes definite and the goods in question are given their specific qualities.

20. In view however of the variety of operations which may be described as assembly there are situations where consideration on the basis of technical criteria may not be decisive in determining the origin of goods. In such cases it is necessary to take account of the value added by the assembly as an ancillary criterion.

21. The relevance of that criterion is moreover confirmed by the Kyoto Convention the notes of which in relation to Rule 3 of Annex D.1 state that in practice the substantial transformation criterion can be expressed by the *ad valorem* percentage rule, where either the percentage value of the materials utilized or the percentage of the value added reaches a specified level.

22. As regards the application of that criterion and in particular the question of the amount of value added which is necessary to determine the origin of the goods in question, the basis should be that the assembly operations as a whole must involve an appreciable increase in the commercial value of the finished product at the ex-factory stage. In that respect it is necessary to consider in each particular case whether the amount of the value added in the country of assembly in comparison with the value added in other countries justifies conferring the origin of the country of assembly.

23. Where only two countries are concerned in the production of goods and examination of technical criteria proves insufficient to determine the origin, the mere assembly of those goods in one country from previously manufactured parts originating in the other is not sufficient to confer on the resulting product the origin of the country of assembly if the value added there is appreciably less than the value imparted in the other country. It should be stated that in such a situation value added of less than 10%, which corresponds to the estimate put forward by the Commission in its observations, cannot in any event be regarded as sufficient to confer on the finished product the origin of the country of assembly.

25. [T]he answer to the first question must be that the mere assembly of previously manufactured parts originating in a country different from that in which they were assembled is sufficient to confer on the resulting product the origin of the country in which assembly took place, provided that from a technical point of view and having regard to the definition of the goods in question such assembly represents the decisive production stage during which the use to which the component parts are to be put becomes definite and the goods in question are given their specific qualities; if the application of that criterion is not conclusive, it is necessary to examine whether all the assembly operations in question result in an appreciable increase in the commercial, ex-factory value of the finished product.

THE INTERPRETATION OF ARTICLE 6 OF REGULATION
(EEC) NO. 802/68

26. In its second question the national court is asking whether the transfer of the assembly from the country of manufacture of the component parts to a country where use is made of already existing factories in itself justifies the presumption that the sole object of the transfer was to circumvent the applicable provisions, and in particular the application of anti-dumping duties, within the meaning of Article 6 of the Regulation.

27. Article 6 provides that

> "any process or work in respect of which it is established, or in respect of which the facts as ascertained justify the presumption, that its *sole* object was to circumvent the provisions applicable in the Community or the Member States to goods from specific countries shall in no case be considered, under Article 5, as conferring on the goods thus produced the origin of the country where it is carried out". [emphasis added]

29. The answer to the second question must be that the transfer of assembly from the country in which the parts were manufactured to another country in which use is made of existing factories does not in itself justify the presumption that the sole object of the transfer was to circumvent the applicable provisions unless the transfer of assembly coincides with the entry into force of the relevant regulations. In that case, the manufacturer concerned must prove that there were reasonable grounds, other than avoiding the consequences of the provisions in question, for carrying out the assembly operations in the country from which the goods were exported.

VIII. *Customs and Free Trade Areas*

Chapter 1 introduced the important topic of preferential trade agreements (PTAs) and the criteria for their compatibility with WTO norms under GATT Article XXIV. Free Trade Areas (FTAs), the most common type of PTA, commonly reduce tariffs to zero for intra-FTA trade, but each FTA member retains complete autonomy to set tariffs and commercial policy with respect to trade with non-FTA members.

With the proliferation of free trade areas and customs unions, determinations of origin have taken on a greater importance. These issues are especially acute in NAFTA. Under NAFTA, all tariffs and non-tariff barriers with respect to trade within North America have been abolished. Thus, there is free trade between the territories of the United States, Canada, and Mexico. But the United States, Canada, and Mexico have retained their separate national tariffs with respect to third-party trade. This system potentially allows a third party to enter goods in the country that allows for the lowest tariff rate on the goods and then ship them duty-free to its final destination, such as the United States, for sale. To prevent this type of abuse, tariffs for intra-NAFTA trade were abolished only on goods that "originate" in one or more of the three NAFTA countries. Thus, determining the origin of the goods becomes very important under NAFTA; to deal with this issue, NAFTA has promulgated its own set of rules to determine origin. In this section we cover the most important of these "rules of origin" issues under NAFTA (which presents some of the most complex and frequently litigated rules of origin questions) but the principles discussed carry over to other FTAs as well.

While *Koru* and *SDI Technologies*, discussed in a previous section, involved the substantial transformation test to determine the origin of the goods, NAFTA employs a different approach. The primary test employed when goods come from a non-NAFTA country, but are worked on in a NAFTA country, is the "tariff shift" test. Under this test, U.S. Customs officials will determine (1) how the goods would have been classified under the HTSUS (the U.S. customs classification scheme) when they first entered a NAFTA country (e.g., Mexico) and (2) whether the goods would be classified under a different tariff line under the HTSUS when they enter the United States. If such a tariff shift is found, then the article will be considered to be of NAFTA origin for purposes of U.S. customs. Note that the tariff shift rules often contain specific conditions on what type of shift must occur within a group of tariff lines. NAFTA rules of origin may also require, in addition to a tariff shift, a minimum content attributable to NAFTA countries. We explore minimum content issues at the end of this Chapter.

Cummins Inc. v. United States
United States Court of Appeals, Federal Circuit, 2006
454 F.3d 1361

MAYER, Circuit Judge.

Cummins Inc. appeals the United States Court of International Trade's grant of summary judgment, which held that the crankshafts imported by Cummins into the United States did not originate in Mexico and were not entitled to preferential treatment under the North American Free Trade Agreement ("NAFTA"). *Cummins Inc. v. United States*, 377 F. Supp. 2d 1365 (Ct. Int'l Trade 2005). We affirm.

BACKGROUND

Under the United States' tariff laws, products that "originate in the territory of a NAFTA party" are entitled to preferential duty treatment. General Note 12(a)(ii), Harmonized Tariff Schedule of the United States ("HTSUS"); *see also* 19 U.S.C. §3332 (2000). One way a product may so originate is if it is "transformed in the territory" of a NAFTA party. General Notes 12(b)(i)-(iv), HTSUS. One manner in which a good can be transformed, as is relevant to this case, is by undergoing a "change in tariff classification" "to subheading 8483.10 from any other heading." General Notes 12(b)(ii)(A), 12(t)/84.243(A), HTSUS. Here, Cummins contends that the crankshafts it imports into the United States undergo such a tariff shift in Mexico from heading 7224 to subheading 8483.10.30, and are thereby entitled to preferential duty treatment.

The facts surrounding the production of the crankshafts are undisputed. Production begins in Brazil, where Krupp Metalurgica Campo Limpo creates a forging having the general shape of a crankshaft. This forging is created from a closed-die forging process, which involves forging alloy steel between matrices. After forging, the excess material that was squeezed out of the matrices, called "flash," is removed by a process called trimming. The trimming is done on a

separate machine within approximately ten seconds of the forging press operation. Because the process of trimming can distort the forging, the forging is then
coined. Coining involves applying pressure to the forging, which is still hot and
malleable, in a closed die. After coining, the forging is subjected to shot blasting.
Shot blasting uses abrasive particles to strike the surface of the forging to remove
dirt and oxide from its surface. The forging is then cooled, and its ends are milled
so that it can be securely clamped into machines in Mexico for final machining
operations. The last manufacturing process performed in Brazil is mass centering,
in which the forging's center of balance is determined and locator center points are
machined into each end.

After these processes are performed in Brazil, the forging is imported into
Mexico by Cummins de Mexico, S.A. ("CUMMSA"), a wholly owned subsidiary
of Cummins. As imported, the forging has the general shape of, but cannot yet
function as, a crankshaft. After importation into Mexico, CUMMSA performs at
least fourteen different steps on the forging that cover over 95% of its surface area
resulting in a useable crankshaft, which Cummins imports into the United States.
It is undisputed that the crankshaft imported into the United States is classifiable
under subheading 8483.10.30 of the HTSUS, which covers "[t]ransmission shafts
(including camshafts and crankshafts) and cranks. . . ."

DISCUSSION

We review the trial court's grant of summary judgment on tariff classifications
de novo. A classification decision involves two underlying steps: determining the
proper meaning of the tariff provisions, which is a question of law; and then determining which heading the disputed goods fall within, which is a question of fact.

It is undisputed that the crankshafts imported into the United States are
properly classified under subheading 8483.10.30. The disputed issue is whether
the crankshafts undergo a tariff shift in Mexico. That is, do the crankshafts enter
Mexico under a different tariff heading than they leave Mexico? The trial court
concluded that the crankshafts do not undergo a tariff shift as they are classified under subheading 8483.10.30 upon import into and export out of Mexico.
Cummins contends that this classification was error, and the proper classification of the product upon import into Mexico is under heading 7224, which covers
"[o]ther alloy steel in ingots or other primary forms; semifinished products of
other alloy steel."

"The General Rules of Interpretation (GRI) govern the classification of goods
within the HTSUS." *Hewlett-Packard Co. v. United States*, 189 F.3d 1346, 1348 (Fed.
Cir. 1999). Under GRI 1, the classification "shall be determined according to the
terms of the headings and any relevant section or chapter notes." As noted above,
Cummins contends that the goods imported into Mexico are properly classified
as "semifinished products of other alloy steel" under heading 7224. Chapter 72's
notes expressly define "semifinished," in pertinent part, as "products of solid section, which have not been further worked than . . . roughly shaped by forging,
including blanks for angles, shapes or sections." Chapter 72, Note 1(ij), HTSUS.
Thus, if the product imported into Mexico has been further worked beyond being
roughly shaped by forging, it does not fall within heading 7224. The parties dispute
the meaning of the term "further worked."

Cummins relies on Additional U.S. Note 2 to Chapter 72, which defines "further worked" as subjecting the product to one of several expressly listed surface treatments.[4] It is undisputed that none of these surface treatments are performed in Brazil, and Cummins contends that so long as none of these specific operations are performed prior to importation into Mexico, the product has not been "further worked." The trial court rejected this argument in *Cummins I,* and we do so now.

The definition of "further worked" in Chapter 72 is expressly inapplicable where "the context provides otherwise." Here, to read the term "further worked" as referring to only these specific treatments would lead to a nonsensical result. In particular, this definition would render the phrase "than . . . roughly shaped by forging" meaningless and contravene the well-established principle that a statute should be construed "if at all possible, to give effect and meaning to all the terms." *Bausch,* 148 F.3d at 1367.

Absent an applicable express definition or contrary legislative intent, we must construe the term "further worked" "according to [its] common and commercial meanings, which are presumed to be the same." *Carl Zeiss, Inc. v. United States,* 195 F.3d 1375, 1379 (Fed. Cir. 1999) Here, the plain meaning of "further worked," when read in context, means working the product beyond the point of roughly shaping it by forging. The trial court defined "further worked" more precisely as "to form, fashion, or shape an existing product to a greater extent." We agree that this definition is suitable in the context before us.

Here, the product was forged and then trimmed, coined, shot blasted, milled, and mass centered in Brazil. Cummins suggests that these are steps within the "forging process." However, the relevant language is not "further worked beyond the forging process" but "further worked than roughly shaped by forging." The government cites evidence that the act of forging is understood in the industry as being distinct from the additional operations performed by Cummins in Brazil. In particular, the *Forging Handbook* provides that trimming occurs "[u]pon completion of the forging operation." Forging Handbook Forging Industry Association, *Forging Handbook* 153 (Thomas G. Byrer 1985). This handbook also describes coining as a "finishing operation." Significantly, Cummins agreed that trimming (and hence every step thereafter) takes place "after forging." Moreover, milling the ends of the forging product is outside of the forging process and constitutes working the product beyond roughly shaping it by forging, namely forming, fashioning, or shaping it to a greater extent. Thus, the product imported into Mexico from Brazil cannot be classified under heading 7224.

We agree with the trial court that the forging is properly classified under heading 8483 upon importation into Mexico. GRI 2(a) provides that "[a]ny reference in a heading to an article shall be taken to include a reference to that article incomplete or unfinished, provided that, as entered, the incomplete or unfinished article has the essential character of the complete or finished article." GRI 2(a), HTSUS. In addition, the Explanatory Notes to GRI 2(a) provide that this rule applies "to

---

4. Additional U.S. Note 2 to Chapter 72, HTSUS provides:

For the purposes of this Chapter, unless the context provides other wise, the term, "further worked" refers to products subjected to any of the following surface treatments: polishing and burnishing; artificial oxidation; chemical surface treatments such as [sic] phosphatizing, oxalating and borating; coating with metal; coating with non-metallic substances (e.g., enameling, varnishing, lacquering, painting, coating with plastics materials); or cladding.

blanks unless these are specified in a particular heading. The term 'blank' means an article, not ready for direct use, having the approximate shape or outline of the finished article or part, and which can only be used, other than in exceptional circumstances, for completion into the finished article. . . ." Explanatory Note II to GRI 2(a). Here, the product imported into Mexico had the general shape of a crankshaft and was intended for use only in producing a finished crankshaft. In fact, certain operations done in Brazil, such as milling the forgings' ends, were done solely to simplify the operations in Mexico in completing the crankshaft. As such, the forged product imported into Mexico was properly classified under subheading 8483.10.30. Accordingly, it did not undergo a tariff shift and was not entitled to preferential treatment under NAFTA when imported into the United States.

PROBLEM 5-20

Apex Home Appliances Co. imports sewing machines from Indonesia for sale throughout North America. Should Apex set up three separate importing operations, one in each of the NAFTA countries, or should the company establish one import point in Long Beach, California from which it can fill orders anywhere in the NAFTA region? Why?

PROBLEM 5-21

A South Korea company manufactures goods in Russia using local labor and materials and then sends the goods to Mexico where the goods are put into packages labeled "Product of Mexico." The goods then transit through Toronto (so that no customs duties are paid) and enter U.S. Customs in Detroit. Based on the readings so far, answer the following:

(1)   What is the country of origin of the goods? What tariff is due?
(2)   Assume that Canadian authorities treat the goods as of Mexican origin so that they enter Canada duty-free. What tariff, if any, is due when the goods enter the United States?
(3)   Assume instead that Canadian customs authorities fully tax the goods as non-NAFTA goods. Now the goods enter the United States. What tariff is due?

PROBLEM 5-22

Real Wood Furniture located in Atlanta, Georgia seeks to import wooden furniture from Mexico duty-free under NAFTA into the United States. The furniture is assembled in Mexico from parts imported from China into Mexico. The parts are shipped to Mexico where a local factory assembles the parts into finished pieces of furniture. The pieces are then sold to Real Wood and shipped to the United States.

The furniture is produced in Mexico at a cost of $182 for each piece. The parts from China have a value of $90. The cost of labor in Mexico to assemble each piece is $92. Each piece is sold with an invoice price of $200 to Real Wood Furniture.

Real Wood would like to import the furniture duty-free into the United States.

Chapter 94 of the Harmonized Tariff Schedule of the United States (HTSUS) refers to "Furniture and Bedding." Under Chapter 94, the relevant headings are

9403.50 Wooden Furniture
9403.90 Parts of Furniture

The applicable NAFTA rule of origin is as follows:

(1) A change to subheading 9403.10 through 9403.80 from any other chapter; or
(2) A change to subheading 9403.10 through 9403.80 from subheading 9403.90 provided there is a regional value-content of not less than:
    a) 60 percent where the transaction value is used; or
    b) 50 percent where the net cost method is used.

Can Real Wood import the furniture duty-free under NAFTA into the United States?

NOTE ON DETERMINING ORIGIN UNDER NAFTA

Article 401 of NAFTA sets out the rules of origin that determine when goods "originate" in NAFTA, which will entitle goods to duty-free treatment when entering any NAFTA country. Article 401 of NAFTA defines "originating goods" in four ways:

(1) Goods wholly obtained or produced in NAFTA.
(2) Goods meeting the tariff shift rules of origin or other applicable rules of origin where no tariff shift is required (such as regional value content);
(3) Unassembled goods that do not meet tariff shift rules of origin but which contain a regional value content of 60 or 50 percent depending on the method used (further explained below);
(4) Goods produced in NAFTA wholly from originating materials;

See NAFTA Article 401.

The following excerpt from the U.S. government further explains how these tests are met.

NAFTA: A Guide to Customs Procedures
United States Department of Commerce Guidelines

(1) GOODS WHOLLY OBTAINED OR PRODUCED IN CANADA

Goods wholly obtained or produced entirely in Canada, Mexico or the United States contain no foreign materials or parts from outside the NAFTA territory. Article 415 defines goods wholly produced in the NAFTA region as:

(a)   mineral goods extracted in Canada, Mexico or the United States;
   — Silver mined in Mexico is originating because it is extracted in the terri-
      tory of one of the Parties.
(b)   vegetable goods, as such goods are defined in the Harmonized System, har-
      vested in Canada, Mexico or the United States;
   — Wheat grown in Canada is originating because it is harvested in the ter-
      ritory of one of the Parties.
(c)   live animals born and raised in Canada, Mexico or the United States;
(d)   goods obtained from hunting, trapping or fishing in Canada, Mexico or
      the United States;
(e)   goods (fish, shellfish and other marine life) taken from the sea by vessels
      registered or recorded with Canada, Mexico or the United States and flying
      its flag;
(f)   goods produced on board factory ships from the goods referred to in sub-
      paragraph (e) provided such factory ships are registered or recorded with
      that country and fly its flag;
(g)   goods taken by Canada, Mexico or the United States or a person of these
      countries from the seabed or beneath the seabed outside territorial waters,
      provided that Canada, Mexico or the United States has rights to exploit
      such seabed;
(h)   goods taken from outer space, provided they are obtained by Canada,
      Mexico or the United States or by a person of these countries and not pro-
      cessed in a non-NAFTA country;
(i)   waste and scrap derived from
   •   production in Canada, Mexico and/or the United States, or
   •   used goods collected in Canada, Mexico and/or the United States, pro-
       vided such goods are fit only for the recovery of raw materials; and,
   •   Copper wire recovered in Canada from scrap telephone or electrical
       wires is wholly obtained or produced in Canada regardless of where it
       was originally produced.
(j)   goods produced in Canada, Mexico or the United States exclusively from
      goods referred to in subparagraphs (a) through (i), or from their deriva-
      tives, at any stage of production.
   — Silver jewelry made in the United States from silver mined in Mexico is
      wholly obtained or produced in the NAFTA territory because it is made
      exclusively of a mineral good extracted in Mexico.

(2) TARIFF SHIFT

   Article 401 indicates that goods may "originate" in Canada, Mexico or the
United States, even if they contain non-originating materials, if the materials satisfy the rule of origin based on a change in tariff classification, a regional value-
content requirement or both. Annex 401 is organized by Harmonized Tariff
Schedule (HTS) numbers, so one must know the HTS number of a good and the
HTS numbers of all the non-NAFTA materials used to produce the good to find its
specific rule of origin and determine if the rule has been met. Annex 401 gives the
applicable rule of origin opposite the HTS number.
   When a rule of origin is based on a change in tariff classification, each of
the non-originating materials used in the production of the goods must undergo
the applicable change as a result of production occurring entirely in the NAFTA
region. This means that the non-originating materials are classified under one tariff provision prior to processing and classified under another upon completion of

processing. The specific rule of origin in Annex 401 defines exactly what change in tariff classification must occur for the goods to be considered "originating."

Frozen pork meat (HTS 02.03) is imported into the United States from Hungary and combined with spices imported from the Caribbean (HTS 09.07-9.10) and cereals grown and produced in the U.S. to make pork sausage (HTS 16.01). The Annex 401 rule of origin for HTS 16.01 states:

A change to heading 16.01 through 16.05 from any other chapter.

Since the imported frozen meat is classified in Chapter 2 and the spices are classified in Chapter 9, these non-originating materials meet the required tariff change. One does not consider whether the cereal meets the applicable tariff change since it is originating—only non-originating materials must undergo the tariff change.

---

(3) REGIONAL VALUE CONTENT

Some specific NAFTA rules of origin require that a good have a minimum regional value content, meaning that a certain percentage of the value of the goods must be from North America. Article 402 gives two formulas for calculating the regional value content. In general, the exporter or producer may choose between these two formulas: the "transaction value" method or the "net cost" method. Having two methods gives producers more than one way of demonstrating that the rule of origin has been satisfied. The transaction value method is generally simpler to use but a producer may choose whichever method is most advantageous.

The *transaction value method* calculates the value of the non-originating materials as a percentage of the GATT transaction value of the good, which is the total price paid for the good, with certain adjustments for packing and other items, and is based on principles of the GATT Customs Valuation Code. The essence of this method is that the value of non-originating materials can be calculated as a percentage of the invoice price which is usually the price actually paid for them. Because the transaction value method permits the producer to count all of its costs and profit as territorial, the required percentage of regional value content under this method is higher than under the net cost method.

However, there are a number of situations where the transaction value method cannot be used, and the *net cost method* is the only alternative. The net cost method must be used when there is no transaction value, in some related party transactions, for certain motor vehicles and parts and for some special cases involving minimum regional content value. The producer may also revert to the net cost method if the result using the transaction value method is unfavorable.

The formula for calculating the regional value content using the transaction value method is:

$$RVC = \frac{TV - VNM}{TV} \times 100$$

where

RVC   is the regional value content, expressed as a percentage;
TV   is the transaction value of the good; and
VNM   is the value of non-originating materials used by the producer in the
           production of the good.

The net cost method calculates the regional value content as a percentage of the net cost to produce the good. Net cost represents all of the costs incurred by the producer minus expenses for sales promotion (including marketing and after-sales service), royalties, shipping and packing costs, and non-allowable interest costs. The percentage content required for the net cost method is lower than the percentage content required under the transaction value method because of the exclusion of certain costs from the net cost calculation.

The formula for calculating the regional value content using the net cost method is:

$$RVC = \frac{NC - VNM}{NC} \times 100$$

where

RVC   is the regional value content, expressed as a percentage;
NC   is the net cost of the good; and
VNM   is the value of non-originating materials used by the producer in the
           production of the good.

An electric hair curling iron (HTS 8516.32) is made in Mexico from Japanese hair curler parts (HTS 8516.90). Each hair curling iron is sold for US$4.40; the value of the non-originating hair curler parts is US$1.80. The Annex 401 rule of origin for HTS 8516.32 states:

A change to subheading 8516.32 from subheading 8516.80 or any other heading; or
   A change to subheading 8516.32 from subheading 8516.90, whether or not there is also a change from subheading 8516.80 or any other heading, provided there is a regional value content of not less than:

(a)   60 percent where the transaction value method is used, or
(b)   50 percent where the net cost method is used.

The first of these two rules is not met since there is no heading change; therefore the producer must verify whether the curling irons can qualify under the second rule. In the second rule the required subheading change is met (from HTS 8516.90 to 8516.32), so one proceeds to calculate the regional value content. The regional value content under the transaction value method is:

$$\frac{(4.40 - 1.80)}{4.40} \times 100 = 59.1\%$$

The hair curler is not considered an originating good under this method, since the required regional value content is 60 percent where the transaction value is used.

Instead, the producer uses the net cost method. The total cost of the hair curler is US$3.90, which includes US$0.25 for shipping and packing costs. There are no costs for royalties, sales promotion or non-allowable interest. The net cost is therefore US$3.65. The regional value content under the net cost method is:

$$\frac{(3.65 - 1.80)}{3.65} \times 100 \ = \ 50.1\%$$

The hair curler would be considered originating, since the required regional value content is 50 percent where the net cost method is used.

(4) GOODS PRODUCED IN NAFTA FROM WHOLLY ORIGINATING MATERIALS

Goods also originate if they are produced entirely in Canada, Mexico, and/or the United States exclusively from materials that are considered to be originating according to the terms of the Agreement.

Company A imports whole raw bovine skins (HTS 41.01) into Mexico from Argentina and processes them into finished leather (HTS 41.04). The finished leather is then purchased by Company B to make leather eyeglass cases (HTS 4202.31). The rule of origin for HTS 41.04 states:

A change to heading 41.04 from any other heading, except from heading 41.05 through 41.11.

The finished leather originates in Mexico because it meets the Annex 401 criterion. Assuming the eyeglass cases do not contain any non-originating materials, they originate since they are made wholly of a material that is originating (because the finished leather satisfied the Annex 401 criterion).

NOTES AND QUESTIONS

1. Compare NAFTA rules of origin to the substantial transformation test. What are the differences between the two? Which is a subjective test and which is an objective test?

2. The key to any value-based method of determining origin is the manufacturing or processing costs. Do these costs include both costs that are directly incurred in the manufacture of the product and costs that can be reasonably allocated to the manufacturing process, such as costs related to distribution, sales, and marketing costs? What about such costs as the telephone system at the plant? What about expenses for computer training and environmental, health, and safety concerns? Where does one draw the line?

6   *Non-Tariff Trade Barriers*

I. *Introduction*

This Chapter examines the principal non-tariff barriers to trade in goods. We concentrate mainly on four types of non-tariff trade barriers that are applied at the border or have the effect of a border measure:

- quotas (also known as quantitative restrictions)
- agricultural trade barriers
- technical regulations and product standards; and
- state trading enterprises

As in the case of tariffs, the WTO considers non-tariff barriers to be protectionist and seeks to reduce or eliminate them to the greatest extent possible. We reserve for separate treatment in Chapter 7 other non-tariff trade restrictions on trade, such as health, safety, and environmental requirements. These restrictions are treated as general exceptions, not illegal protectionist measures, which are justified by GATT Article XX.

II. *Quotas*

A. **Background**

Tariffs are the most popular form of trade barrier of any kind while the most common type of non-tariff barrier is the import quota or quantitative restriction. A quota is a government-imposed limit on the quantity or value of goods traded between countries. For example, a government may mandate that no more than one million imported vehicles may be imported into its domestic market during a given period. Such a quota can be imposed and enforced by the importing country. The exporting country can also impose and enforce such a restriction (usually as a result of political pressure by the importing country). In the latter case, the restriction is called a voluntary export restraint (VER).

Quotas are popular politically for two reasons: They present clear and (usually) immediate import relief, and they can target a putative trade emergency. The economic and political effect of a quota is much more visible than the effect of a tariff. Nevertheless, these advantages mask many economic and political difficulties:

- Is the quota set at the "correct" or "optimal" level? A quota is a blunter instrument than a tariff; if set too low or too high, the economic impact may backfire. For example, too stringent a quota may raise prices precipitously; if set too low, its purpose may not be met.
- Should the quota be applied to limit all imports of a category of products from all suppliers from all countries, or should imports only from certain countries or suppliers be targeted? For example, the United States and the European Union administered quotas for many years against Japanese light trucks and cars only. A quota of this type raises questions of discrimination.
- How is the quota to be allocated among trading partners? Many different countries might be suppliers of the product that is subject to the quota. Administering the quota requires making choices about how to apply the quota in restricting trade with various trading partners. An obvious choice is to impose the same quantitative restriction on all trading partners, but there are other alternatives that can be considered.
- How should the nations whose exports are subject to the quota allocate the quota among their own domestic manufacturers producing the goods for export? Should all of the producers be restricted on equal terms or is there a better alternative?
- Are antitrust and competition issues implicated? The administration of a quota inevitably requires some agreement to divide markets among competing supplier nations, and even among private producers of imported products themselves. Division of markets is a classic restraint of trade that is a per se antitrust violation if done by private companies, but this must be tolerated and even encouraged in the administration of an international trade quota by a government authority.

What is the economic impact of a quota? Consider Figure 6-1.

In Figure 6-1, D and S represent the respective domestic demand and supply curves for a product. Assume that with no trade restrictions the domestic price

FIGURE 6-1
The Revenue Effect of a Quota

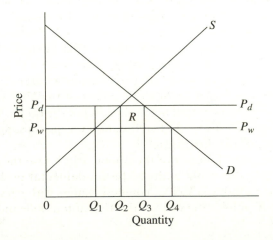

would be Pw and domestic consumption would be Q_4, of which domestic producers would supply Q_1. A quota limiting imports would cause the price to rise to Pd, reducing consumption to Q_3 and increasing the domestic suppliers share to Q_2, and the import share to Q_3 minus Q_2. No tariff is paid, so who gets the additional revenue (R in the diagram) that is the result of the quota? How does this revenue effect compare with that of a tariff?

PROBLEM 6-1

A classic case of a quota was the VER imposed as a result of U.S. pressure on the import of Japanese-manufactured motor vehicles between 1981 and 1994. In 1981, after informal talks, Japan "voluntarily" agreed to restrict the export of passenger automobiles to the United States to 1.68 million vehicles per year. Consider the following in connection with this quota:

It is 1981 and the quota on Japanese passenger cars has just been announced.

(1) You are the CEO of one of the major U.S. auto companies; your inventories have been stagnant or rising and sales have been sluggish before the quota. What are your plans after the quota becomes operational? Will you raise, lower, or keep your prices the same?

(2) You are the CEO of a major Japanese auto company, one of six companies that currently export into the U.S. market. What strategies will you adopt? Will you change the make-up of your exports? Will you raise, lower, or keep your prices the same? Will you consider investing in the United States by setting up a factory to manufacture cars, which, of course, would not be subject to the quota? Are you worried that your profits from sales in the United States will seriously fall?

(3) You are a consumer thinking of buying a new car. What do you expect will happen to the prices and availability of new domestic and imported cars? Will the prices go up, down, or remain the same?

(4) You are a high official of the Japanese Ministry of Trade and Industry in charge of implementing the VER. You will need to ensure that Japanese automobile companies "voluntarily" restrain their exports. How will you do this? What measures will be necessary? What decisions will you have to make concerning the implementation of the quota?

(5) You are the Assistant Attorney General of the U.S. Department of Justice in charge of antitrust matters. You learn that Japanese automobile companies will voluntarily agree to limit their exports to certain quantities. What will be your concern? Will you take any action?

(6) By 1991, the immediate economic impact of the VER was zero because Japanese imports were well below the level of the quota. Why? If Japanese imports were well below quota levels, how was Japan supplying cars to the U.S. market? Is this surprising?

(7) What is the overall impact of the quota? Did it save the U.S. automobile industry? Did the quota address the fundamental problem in the U.S. automobile industry: a lack of competitiveness with cars from Japan? Or did the quota add to the woes of the U.S. automobile industry?

To answer these questions, review the introductory materials and Figure 6-1.

At the height of the VER in 1984, one economist measured the "quota premium" (the rise in price due to the quota) at $2,400 per car. The total welfare cost of the quota for that year was estimated to be $15.5 billion.[1] Who bore this cost?

B. GATT Rules on Quotas

1. Overview

Read the following GATT provisions in the Supplement:

> Article XI—General Elimination of Quantitative Restrictions
> Article IV—Special Provisions Relating to Cinematograph Films

The GATT rules on quotas are complex. The fundamental policy thrust of the rules is to abolish quotas, but there are numerous and complex exceptions. Before analyzing the rules and the cases, it is useful to have an overview.

The point of departure is GATT Article XI, which embodies a general rule eliminating import and export quotas:

GATT Article XI
General Elimination of Quantitative Restrictions

1. No prohibitions or restrictions other than duties, taxes or other charges, whether made effective through quotas, import or export licenses or other measures, shall be instituted or maintained by any contracting party on the importation of any product of the territory of any other contracting party or on the exportation or sale for export of any product destined for the territory of any other contracting party.

This title is misleading in two ways: First, this elimination provision concerns more than just "quantitative restrictions"; it applies to "restrictions" and "other measures" as well; and second, the term "general elimination" is too broad. Paragraph 2 of Article XI immediately sets forth a number of exceptions that specifically permit certain quotas and quantitative restrictions. In the materials that follow we will examine the meaning and scope of Article XI:1 and the three exceptions contained in Article XI:2.

Another exception to the "no quotas" rule is GATT Article IV, which concerns a specific economic sector, cinematographic films. GATT Article IV(a) permits WTO members to maintain quotas on films in the form of "screen quotas" under certain conditions. Article IV(d) provides that these screen quotas "shall be subject to negotiation for their limitation, liberalization or elimination." This article is self-explanatory and has been a source of controversy, particularly between the United States, the nation with the world's leading film industry, and certain other WTO members, especially France, the EU, Canada, and China. Despite Article IV's importance, we only mention it in passing here. This GATT article is bound up

---

1. *See The Economic Effects of Significant U.S. Import Restraints,* U.S. International Trade Commission Publication 2699 at 25 (November 1993).

primarily with the more general question of trade exceptions and restrictions for the purpose of preserving national cultural autonomy.

The GATT quota rules also cannot be understood without considering two additional controversial economic sectors where quotas were once common: (1) agriculture and (2) clothing and textiles. The WTO agreements that govern trade in these specialized areas, the Agreement on Agriculture (AoA) and the Agreement on Textiles and Clothing, were both concluded at the end of the Uruguay Round in 1994. The importance of these two agreements is that quotas are now generally prohibited in these two economic sectors. The WTO Agreement on Textiles and Clothing was a transitional agreement, which ended the special quotas regime and integrated textile and clothing trade into the rules of the GATT 1994 and is now terminated. The AoA, however, still singles out agricultural trade for special treatment. Under the AoA, quotas are now prohibited, but tariff rate quotas (TRQ), which are now generally used to restrict imports of agricultural products, are permitted and present problems analogous to the quotas that they replaced.

GATT Article XIII, entitled "Non-discriminatory Administration of Quantitative Restrictions," applies where quotas are exceptionally permitted. This article operates as a complement to Article I, the general Most Favored Nation principle. Article XIII requires that quotas, where permitted, and other import restrictions must be applied on a non-discriminatory basis among foreign trading partners. No single partner can be favored or disadvantaged concerning a quota without the same treatment being extended to all other trading partners. Article XIII:5 applies this rule to TRQs as well. We cover Article XIII in this Chapter, but it also comes up in connection with safeguards covered in Chapter 8.

The use of safeguards is another important exception to the GATT "no quotas" rule. Safeguards are temporary trade restrictions (including quotas) that WTO members may impose if the restrictions are needed to protect domestic industries threatened by a surge in imports or if the restrictions are needed because of balance of payments issues (i.e., a member may be permitted to restrict imports if paying for the imports will threaten its currency supply). GATT Articles XII, XIV, XV, XVIII, and XIX contain complex rules on these issues, and we treat this topic separately in Chapter 8.

Finally, GATT Article XX allows "General Exceptions" to the GATT rules, including the "no quota" rule. Since the imposition of trade bans (which are a type of quota) under this general exceptions provision is a large and important topic that concerns civil society and policies related to globalization, we treat these types of "quotas" separately in Chapter 7. Another area where trade bans are permitted is GATT Article XXI—"Security Exceptions." This topic is also treated in Chapter 7.

With this overview, we return to the central provision on quotas, GATT Article XI, which embodies a general rule of eliminating quotas.

2. Article XI: The "General Elimination" Rule

Article XI prohibits import and export quotas, subject to a number of exceptions. An import quota has been discussed above, but what constitutes an export quota? Can the voluntary actions of a country in restricting its exports through a VER constitute an export quota in violation of Article XI? Consider the following problem and case.

PROBLEM 6-2

At the request of the U.S. electronics industry, U.S. government officials have held informal talks with South Korea concerning the export of South Korean household electronic goods, such as fifty-inch flat screen plasma televisions, portable DVD players, and combination televisions with recording and playback capabilities. The United States is concerned that a recent surge in imports of these products from South Korea is threatening the U.S. electronics industry. At the informal talks, South Korean officials expressed their understanding and sympathy for the U.S. industry and have agreed to voluntarily limit their exports. To implement this "understanding" with the United States, South Korean officials have issued several non-binding administrative notices to local industries asking for their cooperation. Under South Korean practice, the government often wishes to persuade private industry to cooperate voluntarily. However, the South Korean government has the legal authority and means to issue binding legal orders if voluntary cooperation is not successful. One option available to the Korean government is to require an export license issued by the government before a company can lawfully export its products.

To implement the voluntary program, South Korea companies are asked to submit a quarterly report to the South Korean government detailing the amount of their proposed exports to the United States. The South Korean government will then examine the reports to see if they are consistent with proposed export targets. Once the government gives an informal approval of the reports, the shipments to the United States can go forward. As a practical matter, the South Korean companies wait until the approval of the report to make all of their export shipments, including to other countries, since the companies cannot be sure of how much they can sell until the shipments to the United States, its largest market, have been approved. This procedure results in a delay of two months for all exports. Japan has brought a complaint against South Korea alleging that this program violates GATT Article XI. South Korea replies that the program is outside the scope of GATT Article XI because (1) the program has nothing to do with imports, and (2) the program is not the result of government action but is the result of voluntary action on the part of the South Korean electronics industry. In addition, there is no formal trade agreement with the United States but just an informal understanding. What result? See the case below.

Japan — Trade in Semi-Conductors
Report of the GATT Panel, adopted on May 4, 1988
GATT B.I.S.D. (35th Supp.) 116

[The U.S. semi-conductor industry complained that Japan was dumping its products in the U.S. market, i.e., selling them at artificially low prices. Such a low price might benefit U.S. consumers in the short term, but might also harm U.S. producers. Faced with the threat of U.S. trade sanctions, Japan agreed to restrict exports of semi-conductors to the United States and to other foreign markets, such as the European Community. Dumping of Japanese semi-conductors in the EC would harm U.S. exports of semi-conductors to the same market and the dumped chips may be transshipped to the United States. To ensure that Japan would no longer dump its semi-conductors, Japan monitored exports through an export licensing system, which caused long delays in exports to the EC. The EC argued that this arrangement amounted to an export quota in violation of GATT Article XI.]

99. The Panel considered the following facts as central to its examination of this part of the EEC's complaint. After having concluded the Arrangement with the United States concerning Trade in Semi-Conductors, the Japanese Government:

— requested Japanese producers and exporters of semi-conductors covered by the Arrangement not to export semi-conductors at prices below company-specific costs;
— collected data on company and product-specific costs from producers; introduced a statutory requirement, reinforced by penal servitude not exceeding six months or a fine not exceeding ¥ 200,000, for exporters of semi-conductors to report data on export prices;
— systematically monitored company and product-specific cost and export price data on semi-conductors which were sold for export to certain contracting parties other than the United States;
— instituted quarterly supply and demand forecasts and communicated to manufacturers its concern about the need to accommodate their production levels to the forecasts as compiled by MITI.

102. The Panel understood the main contentions of the parties to the dispute on the consistency of the measures set out in [the above] paragraph with Article XI:1 of the General Agreement to be the following. The EEC considered that such measures constituted restrictions on the sale for export of semi-conductors at prices below company-specific costs through measures other than duties, taxes or charges within the meaning of Article XI:1. Japan contended that there were no governmental measures limiting the right of Japanese producers and exporters to export semi-conductors at any price they wished. The Government's measures to avoid sales at dumping prices were not legally binding and therefore did not fall under Article XI:1. Exports were limited by private enterprises in their own self-interest and such private action was outside the purview of Article XI:1.

103. As for the export approval system, the EEC [asked] the Panel to examine the delays in the issuing of export licenses [for products destined for the EEC] resulting from the monitoring of costs and export prices. The EEC considered that these delays constituted restrictions on exportation made effective through export licences within the meaning of Article XI:1. Japan maintained that the delays in the granting of export licences resulting from the monitoring of costs and export prices had occurred for purely administrative reasons and did not constitute restrictions within the meaning of Article XI:1, since no export licence had ever been denied for reasons related to export pricing.

104. The Panel examined the parties' contentions in the light of Article XI:1, the relevant part of which stated that:

"No prohibitions or restrictions other than duties, taxes or other charges, whether made effective through quotas . . . , export licenses or other measures, shall be instituted or maintained by any contracting party . . . on the exportation or sale for export of any product destined for the territory of any other contracting party".

The Panel noted that this wording was comprehensive: it applied to all measures instituted or maintained by a contracting party prohibiting or restricting the importation, exportation or sale for export of products other than measures that take the form of duties, taxes or other charges.

106. The Panel then examined the contention of the Japanese Government that the measures complained of were not restrictions within the meaning of Article XI:1 because they were not legally binding or mandatory. In this respect the Panel noted that Article XI:1, unlike other provisions of the General Agreement, did not refer to laws or regulations but more broadly to measures. This wording indicated clearly that any measure instituted or maintained by a contracting party which restricted the exportation or sale for export of products was covered by this provision, irrespective of the legal status of the measure.

108. The Panel recognized that not all non-mandatory requests could be regarded as measures within the meaning of Article XI:1. Government-industry relations varied from country to country, from industry to industry, and from case to case and were influenced by many factors. There was thus a wide spectrum of government involvement ranging from, for instance, direct government orders to occasional government consultations with advisory committees. The task of the Panel was to determine whether the measures taken in this case would be such as to constitute a contravention of Article XI.

109. In order to determine this, the Panel considered that it needed to be satisfied on two essential criteria. First, there were reasonable grounds to believe that sufficient incentives or disincentives existed for non-mandatory measures to take effect. Second, the operation of the measures to restrict export of semi-conductors at prices below company-specific costs was essentially dependent on Government action or intervention.

110. On the first criterion, the Panel considered the background against which the measures operated. The Panel noted that the Government of Japan had formally concluded in September 1986 an Arrangement with the Government of the United States, one of the main provisions of which was for the Japanese Government to monitor costs and export prices to third country markets in order to prevent dumping. Following bilateral consultations, the Government of Japan assured the United States in April 1987 that it had taken "appropriate action to ensure that Japanese semi-conductor exports are being sold at not less than their costs in third country markets". In the light of this, the Panel considered that at least by April 1987, there would certainly have been no doubt in the minds of relevant Japanese producers and exporters that the Japanese Government had made an undertaking to the United States to ensure that a certain class of sales did not take place. They would also have known that any such action would have led to the Government of Japan being unable to fulfil a commitment which it had given to the United States, and therefore would have adverse consequences for Japan. They would also have been aware that the Government had the fullest information available to identify any producers or exporters selling at prices below costs.

111. The Panel considered that, in the above circumstances, the Japanese Government's measures did not need to be legally binding to take effect, as there were reasonable grounds to believe that there were sufficient incentives or disincentives for Japanese producers and exporters to conform.

115. The Panel then considered whether the operation of the measures was essentially dependent on Government action. The complex of measures was, in the Panel's view, so dependent. The period between September 1986 and January 1987 gave an interesting indication of how Japanese firms were disposed to

operate where they were subject to less constraint. It was apparent that they had been prepared to produce and sell up to a quantity which included what was later termed "false demand" in the context of the revised supply or demand forecast in February 1987. The Panel considered that the disposition to produce and sell was what the Government of Japan by its complex of measures intended to control, by the strengthening of the monitoring measures, lowering of the minimum export amount requiring an export licence to 50,000 yen, requests to producers not to export at prices below company-specific costs, and the revisions of the supply and demand forecasts.

117. All these factors led the Panel to conclude that an administrative structure had been created by the Government of Japan which operated to exert maximum possible pressure on the private sector to cease exporting at prices below company-specific costs. The Panel considered that the complex of measures exhibited the rationale as well as the essential elements of a formal system of export control.

118. The Panel then reverted to the issue raised by the EEC concerning the delays of up to three months in the issuing of export licenses that had resulted from the monitoring of costs and export prices of semi-conductors destined for contracting parties other than the United States. It examined whether the measures taken by Japan constituted restrictions on exportation or sale for export within the meaning of Article XI:1. It noted that the CONTRACTING PARTIES had found in a previous case that automatic licensing did not constitute a restriction within the meaning of Article XI:1 and that an import license issued on the fifth working day following the day on which the license application was lodged could be deemed to have been automatically granted (BISD 25S/95). The Panel recognized that the above applied to import licences but it considered that the standard applicable to import licenses should, by analogy, be applied also to export licenses because it saw no reason that would justify the application of a different standard. The Panel therefore found that export licensing practices by Japan, leading to delays of up to three months in the issuing of licenses for semi-conductors destined for contracting parties other than the United States, had been non-automatic and constituted restrictions on the exportation of such products inconsistent with Article XI:1.

130. The Japanese measures relating to exports of semi-conductors to third country markets had been found to be inconsistent with Article XI:1. They were therefore, according to GATT practice, presumed to have nullified or impaired the benefits accruing to the EEC under the General Agreement (BISD 26S/216).

PROBLEM 6-3

In *Japan—Semi-conductors* and Problem 6-1, concerning the Japanese automobile VER, the United States pressured Japan into accepting a VER. The United States could have chosen to impose an import quota but did not. Why not? *See* GATT Article XI:1. Can you explain why, from the United States perspective, a VER is a more much desirable arrangement than an import quota? If the actions of a government will be challenged as inconsistent with the GATT, who will be subject to litigation if a quota is imposed? What if a VER is imposed? Is allowing a country to pressure another country into adopting a VER a circumvention of the "no quotas" rule?

PROBLEM 6-4

France has decided that the number of Japanese-made high-definition television (HDTV) sets being sold within its borders is too high and is threatening the financial health of domestic producers of HDTV receivers. France has announced that HDTV imports require special handling by customs officials, and all non-EU imports of HDTV receivers into France must be entered through Perpignan, a small port on the coast of France bordering the Mediterranean Sea. Is this inconsistent with GATT Article XI? See *Columbia—Ports of Entry* discussed in note 2 below.

PROBLEM 6-5

Brazil has instituted a requirement that all imports to the port of Rio de Janeiro must be shipped in high-technology super-lightweight shipping containers (a metal box for transporting goods that is loaded on a truck and that can be directly lifted onto a ship at the port of export and then reloaded directly on a truck at the port of entry). Brazil states that the light weight of the containers saves on fuel during transport. Brazil is a leading manufacturer of the containers and, because there is a limited supply, the use of the new containers will add 25 percent to the costs of shipping goods by ocean carriage to Brazil. Is this measure consistent with Article XI?

NOTES AND QUESTIONS

1. Was the EC complaint in *Japan—Semi-conductors* really directed against the United States, rather than Japan? Why didn't the EC file a complaint against the United States instead? Did Japan really "voluntarily" agree to limit exports to the United States? Which country had a stronger incentive to defend the agreement limiting the exports of semi-conductors?

2. In *Colombia—Indicative Prices and Restrictions on Ports of Entry*, WT/DS366/R, Report of the Panel, adopted on May 20, 2009, the Panel interpreted Article XI to prohibit a measure enacted by Colombia to limit certain imports from Panama to two ports of entry out of a total of twenty-six ports in Columbia. The Panel stated in relevant part as follows:

> 7.227 WTO panels have also concluded that the language "other measures" in Article XI:1 is meant to encompass a "broad residual category", and that the concept of a restriction on importation covers any measures that result in "any form of limitation imposed *on, or in relation to* importation".
>
> 7.229 In order to determine whether the ports of entry measure violates Article XI:1, the Panel must establish whether the measure imposes a "restriction" within the meaning of Article XI:1.
>
> 7.234 The panel in *India—Autos* subsequently endorsed the view set forth in *India—Quantitative Restrictions* that a measure which imposes a "limiting condition" or imposes a "limitation on action" constitutes a "restriction" within the meaning of Article XI:1:
>
>> "The question of whether [the] measure can appropriately be described a restriction on importation turns on the issue of whether Article XI can be considered to cover situations where products are technically allowed into the

market without an express formal quantitative restriction, but are only allowed under certain conditions which make the importation more onerous than if the condition had not existed, thus generating a disincentive to import. [A] 'restriction' need not be a blanket prohibition or a precise numerical limit. Indeed, the term 'restriction' cannot mean merely 'prohibitions' on importation, since Article XI:1 expressly covers both 'prohibition or restriction'. Furthermore, the Panel considers that the expression '*limiting condition*' used by the *India—Quantitative Restrictions* panel to define the term 'restriction' and which this Panel endorses, is helpful in identifying the scope of the notion in the context of the facts before it. That phrase suggests the need to identify not merely a condition placed on importation, but a condition that is limiting, i.e. that has a limiting effect. In the context of Article XI, that limiting effect must be on importation itself."[2]

7.240 [A] number of GATT and WTO panels have recognized the applicability of Article XI:1 to measures which create uncertainties and affect investment plans, restrict market access for imports or make importation prohibitively costly, all of which have implications on the competitive situation of an importer.

PROBLEM 6-6

Portugal limits the importation of bananas from South America to three months of the year: June, July, and August. Portugal argues that this measure is not a quota because there is no restriction on the quantity of bananas that can be imported during this period. Is Portugal right? See GATT Article XI and *Columbia—Ports of Entry* discussed above.

PROBLEM 6-7

The U.S. Department of Agriculture has instituted a domestic sugar program imposing restrictions on the production of sugar in the United States in order to avoid an oversupply of sugar that would cause prices to fall. The United States has supplemented this program with payments of subsidies to U.S. sugar farmers to limit domestic production.

To support the domestic sugar program, the United States has also instituted (1) a ban on the importation of raw sugar and (2) a quota system limiting imports of various products made from sugar, such as sugar syrup used as a sweetener in soft drinks and other beverages. The United States believes that the imports of these sugar-containing products will displace the use of sugar produced in the United States that otherwise would have been used to make these products. For example, U.S. producers of sugar syrup will no longer use as much U.S.-produced sugar to make syrup because consumers will purchase some quantities of imported sugar syrup instead. Imports of sugar syrup might lead to an oversupply of sugar in the United States and would undermine the U.S. sugar program by causing prices to drop.

Brazil now challenges the U.S. program as a violation of the GATT Article XI. The United States argues that these restrictions are permitted under Article XI:2

---

2. Panel Report, *India—Autos*, WT/DS146/R, ¶¶7.269-7.270 (Dec 21, 2001).

because they are necessary to support the domestic sugar program. What result? Consult the case below and GATT Article XI:2.

Canada — Import Restrictions on Ice Cream and Yoghurt
GATT B.I.S.D. (36th Supp.) 68
Report of the GATT Panel, adopted on December 4, 1989

[The United States complained that Canadian import restrictions on ice cream and yogurt were quotas in violation of Article XI:1. Canada conceded that the restrictions were quotas, but argued that the restrictions were justified under an exception contained in Article XI:2(c)(i).]

58. The Panel proceeded to examine whether Canada's import restrictions on ice cream and yoghurt could be justified under Article XI:2(c)(i). The text of this paragraph provides that:

> "2. The provisions of paragraph 1 of this Article shall not extend to the following: . . .
>> (c) Import restrictions on any agricultural or fisheries product, imported in any form, necessary to the enforcement of governmental measures which operate:
>>> (i) to restrict the quantities of the like domestic product permitted to be marketed or produced, or, if there is no substantial domestic production of the like product, of a domestic product for which the imported product can be directly substituted;"

and further (in last sub-paragraph) that:

> "[A]ny restrictions applied under (i) above shall not be such as will reduce the total of imports relative to the total of domestic production, as compared with the proportion which might reasonably be expected to rule between the two in the absence of restrictions. In determining this proportion, the contracting party shall pay due regard to the proportion prevailing during a previous representative period and to any special factors which may have affected or may be affecting the trade in the product concerned."

62. As the party invoking an exception, it was incumbent upon Canada to demonstrate that the measures applied to imports of ice cream and yoghurt met each of the conditions under Article XI:2(c)(i) and XI:2(c) last sub-paragraph. These conditions are:

— the measure on importation must constitute an import restriction (and not a prohibition);
— the import restriction must be on an agricultural or fisheries product;
— the import restriction and the domestic marketing or production restriction must apply to "like" products in any form (or directly substitutable products if there is no substantial production of the like product);
— there must be governmental measures which operate to restrict the quantities of the domestic product permitted to be marketed or produced;
— the import restriction must be necessary to the enforcement of the domestic supply restriction;

— the contracting party applying restrictions on importation must give public notice of the total quantity or value of the product permitted to be imported during a specified future period; and

— the restrictions applied must not reduce the proportion of total imports relative to total domestic production, as compared with the proportion which might reasonably be expected to rule between the two in the absence of restrictions.

[The Panel found that the first two conditions had been met. The Canadian measures constituted a restriction and not a prohibition of trade. The Panel also found that under longstanding GATT practice, ice cream and yogurt were agricultural products within the meaning of Article XI:2(c).]

LIKE PRODUCTS IMPORTED IN ANY FORM

67. The Panel next considered whether ice cream and yoghurt were "like" products to raw milk. In the drafting of this provision it had been stated that the words "like products" in Article XI:2(c) ". . . definitely do not mean what they mean in other contexts—merely a competing product" (EPCT/C.II/PV.12). The Japanese Agriculture Panel had observed that Article XI:2(c)(i) and the note supplementary to it regarding "in any form" established different requirements for (a) restrictions on the importation of products that are "like" the product subject to domestic supply restrictions and (b) restrictions on the importation of products that are processed from a product that is "like" the product subject to domestic supply restrictions. The Japanese Agriculture Panel had considered that this differentiation would be lost if a product in its original form and a product processed from the original one were to be considered to be "like" products within the meaning of Article XI:2(c). This Panel concurred with that observation. It further noted that there was virtually no international trade in raw milk.

70. In light of these considerations, the Panel examined whether ice cream and yoghurt met all the conditions for "like" products "in any form": that they were in an "early stage of processing", "still perishable", "directly competitive" with raw milk and if freely imported would "make the restriction on the fresh product ineffective". The exception to Article XI:1 could be applied only to those processed products which met all of these conditions.

[The Panel decided that it was not necessary to make a finding on products that were in an "early stage of process" or "still perishable" in light of its disposition of the following issues.]

DIRECTLY COMPETITIVE

73. The Panel then proceeded to examine whether ice cream and yoghurt "compete directly" with fresh raw milk. Canada argued that imported ice cream and yoghurt competed directly with Canadian produced ice cream and yoghurt and thus displaced the raw milk which would have been processed into these products. The United States argued that ice cream and yoghurt were neither substitutable for nor destined for the same markets as raw milk. The Panel considered that the

term "compete *directly* with . . ." imposed a more limiting requirement than merely "compete with". As stated in the US arguments, the concept of "displacement" was apparently not intended by this provision. The essence of direct competition was that a buyer was basically indifferent if faced with the choice between one product or the other and viewed them as substitutable in terms of their use. Only limited competition existed between raw milk and ice cream and yoghurt. The Panel thus found that imports of ice cream and yoghurt did not compete directly with raw milk in terms of Article XI:2(c)(i).

WOULD MAKE THE RESTRICTIONS INEFFECTIVE

74. The exception to Article XI:1 is further limited by its application only to those processed products whose free importation would render ineffective the restrictions on the fresh product. The drafters agreed that the exception "should not be construed as permitting the use of quantitative restrictions as a method of protecting the industrial processing of agricultural or fisheries products" (Havana Reports, p. 94). Canada argued that developments in the United States dairy situation encouraged the expansion of US exports. Uncontrolled imports of these products could displace close to 11 per cent of its industrial milk production (on a butterfat basis). As the United States had pointed out, the current Canadian dairy restriction programme had been in force since 1976, and although many other dairy products had been subject to quotas since that time, it had not previously been considered necessary to restrict imports of ice cream and yoghurt. Unrestricted imports of ice cream and yoghurt in the five years previous to the 1988 imposition of restrictions averaged, respectively, two-tenths of one per cent and three-tenths of one per cent of Canadian production of these products. Their impact upon total raw milk production in Canada could only be considered as minuscule.

GOVERNMENTAL MEASURES TO RESTRICT DOMESTIC PRODUCTION

77. The *raison d'être* of Article XI:2(c)(i) is to permit the operation of governmental measures that restrict the quantity of some fresh agricultural product permitted to be produced or marketed. The drafters indicated that "to restrict" means to ". . . keep output below the level which it would have attained in the absence of restrictions". Proposals to make the *regulation* of production, through price stabilization programmes, an accepted criterion were rejected. The Panel further observed that other than requiring a governmental measure, Article XI:2(c)(i) did not specify how the production or marketing restriction was to be imposed.

NECESSARY

80. A further requirement of Article XI:2(c)(i) is that the import restrictions be "necessary to the enforcement" of the supply-restricting governmental measures.

81. The Panel recognized the merits of Canada's argument that for a product which is traded almost exclusively in its processed forms, such as milk, restrictions

on the imports of the processed products might in some sense be "necessary" to ensure that the restriction on the production of the raw material was not undermined. At this time, however, there was not sufficient evidence to believe that future imports of ice cream and yoghurt would achieve such levels as to significantly affect Canadian producers ability to market raw milk. In the past, unrestricted imports had gained less than a half a percent share of the Canadian ice cream and yoghurt market, and accounted for less than ten one-thousandths of one per cent of total raw milk production. Against this background and in the absence of an imminent threat to the Canadian dairy system, the Panel found that the criterion of "necessary" to the operation of the governmental restrictions could *not* be met.

CONCLUSIONS

84. In light of the considerations set out in paragraphs 57 to 81 above, the Panel concluded that Canada's restrictions on the importation of ice cream and yoghurt are inconsistent with Article XI:1 and cannot be justified under the provisions of Article XI:2(c)(i).

NOTES AND QUESTIONS

1. In *Canada—Ice Cream and Yoghurt*, Canada had a national program restricting the production of milk. Canada also imposed quotas on imported ice cream and yogurt. Canada argued that the restrictions were necessary to support the milk program. What was Canada's argument? Did the panel agree?

2. The United States successfully used Article XI against Japan to challenge quotas maintained on twelve product categories of agricultural products in *Japan—Restrictions on Imports of Certain Agricultural Products*, GATT B.I.S.D. (35th Supp.) 163, Report of the GATT Panel, adopted on February 2, 1988, 163, 220. Japan attempted unsuccessfully to justify the restrictions based upon the exceptions in Article XI:2(c). The panel rejected Japan's argument. *Id.* at 6.4-6.8.

3. What is the purpose of the exceptions contained in Article XI:2(c)? Is there any possibility of formulating a quota that meets the standards of these exceptions?

4. In the WTO AoA, which became effective on January 1, 1995, Article 4.2 prohibits "quantitative restrictions" (see footnote 1) for imports of agricultural products as defined in Annex 1 of that agreement. Fish and fisheries products are not covered in the AoA. If a WTO member imposes a quota on the import of an agricultural product that is consistent with GATT Article XI:2(c), but the product is one that is covered by the AoA, which agreement controls, the GATT or the AoA? The answer to this question is supplied by the General Interpretative Note to Annex 1A of the WTO Agreement Establishing the World Trade Organization (Marrakesh Agreement), which states as follows:

> In the event of a conflict between a provision of the General Agreement on Tariffs and Trade 1994 and a provision of another agreement . . . , the provision of the other agreement shall prevail to the extent of the conflict.

Does this further narrow the scope of the GATT Article XI:2(c) exception?

3. The Administration of Quotas

As we have seen, certain types of quotas are permitted under the GATT Article XI:2 exceptions as well as under certain other GATT provisions. However, even if a quota falls within a permitted exception, it must be administered in accordance with the following:

GATT Article XIII
Non-Discriminatory Administration of Quantitative Restrictions

1. No prohibition or restriction shall be applied by any contracting party on the importation of any product of the territory of any other contracting party or on the exportation of any product destined for the territory of any other contracting party, unless the importation of the like product of all third countries or the exportation of the like product to all third countries is similarly prohibited or restricted.
2. In applying import restrictions to any product, contracting parties shall aim at a distribution of trade in such product approaching as closely as possible the shares which the various contracting parties might be expected to obtain in the absence of such restrictions.

The interpretation of these provisions was the issue in the following case. This case also deals with the usual way of administering quotas through a licensing system. Import licensing is the subject of a separate WTO Uruguay Round agreement, which also comes up in the *EC—Bananas* case.

European Communities — Regime for the Importation, Sale and Distribution of Bananas
Report of the Appellate Body, adopted on September 25, 1997
WT/DS27/AB/R

[This case, known as the *Banana Dispute*, was brought by the United States, a non-producer of bananas, and several Latin American countries that are banana exporters, for the purpose of establishing free trade in bananas. This dispute focused on the treatment the EU/EC gave to the import of bananas from African, Caribbean, and Pacific (ACP) countries in preference to bananas from Latin America. Prior to July 1, 1993, each EU member state maintained its own banana import regime, but on that date a new EU-wide banana import regime came into effect that favored ACP countries. Under the applicable EC regulation, up to 857,700 tons of bananas could enter duty-free from twelve African, Caribbean, and Pacific (ACP) countries, all former European colonies, which were traditional suppliers. This duty-free treatment was accorded by the EC pursuant to a special agreement—the Lomé Convention—designed to benefit developing countries and former colonies. Other bananas from ACP countries, although not entitled to duty-free treatment, were given a preferential tariff rate. The EC asked for and received a special GATT waiver of the Most Favored National principle to allow the operation of the Lomé Convention. The waiver of the MFN obligation was necessary because otherwise the EC might have been required to extend the same benefits given to the ACP countries to all other WTO members.

While the first 857,700 tons of ACP bananas were allowed entry duty-free, all additional ACP bananas, as well as bananas from other WTO members, were allowed entry into the EU under a complex tariff-rate quota system set forth in the Banana Framework Agreement (BFA). Under a tariff-rate quota, there is one lower tariff rate for "in quota" bananas (i.e., all bananas up to a stated quantity) and a second higher tariff rate for "out of quota" bananas (i.e., all bananas above the stated quantity). The amount within the quota was allocated in a highly discriminatory fashion that favored ACP countries over additional producer countries from South America, such as Guatemala, Nicaragua, and Venezuela. Since ACP countries were allowed much higher in quota amounts, ACP countries benefited from a lower tariff rate for these bananas. Certain Latin American countries were also major banana producers, but because they were allocated higher out-of-quota amounts, their imports to the EU were subject to much higher tariffs. Multinational U.S. companies, such as Dole and Chiquita Brands, had invested heavily in some of these countries, allowing them to produce bananas more efficiently and at a much lower cost than the ACP countries. The United States believed that imports from the South American countries were subject to unfair discrimination in favor of bananas from ACP countries.

The issues in the portion of the opinion below concern three sets of issues. Of these, the issue most directly related to quotas is (2) below but this issue cannot be understood without examining the others. The issues were:

(1) What type of preferential treatment was required by the Lomé Convention for ACP countries? Did the Convention require duty-free treatment for some ACP bananas and preferential in-quota amounts for other ACP bananas? If the treatment was not required, then the EU could simply change it practices with no consequences under Lomé.

(2) What was the scope of the Lomé Waiver obtained by the EC? The parties all acknowledged that the Lomé Waiver exempted the EC from the MFN obligation under the GATT, but did the Waiver also explicitly or implicitly exempt the EC from having to comply with GATT Article XIII in its administration of TRQs that discriminated in favor of the ACP countries? If the Lomé Waiver did not exempt the EC from Article XIII, then the discriminatory administration of import preferences in favor of the ACP countries was a violation of Article XIII.

(3) Was the EC import licensing scheme for bananas consistent with the WTO Licensing Agreement?]

THE SCOPE OF THE LOMÉ WAIVER

164. On 9 December 1994, at the request of the European Communities and of the 49 ACP States that were also GATT contracting parties, the CONTRACTING PARTIES granted the European Communities a waiver from certain of its obligations under the GATT 1947 with respect to the Lomé Convention.[3] The operative paragraph of this Decision of the CONTRACTING PARTIES reads as follows:

> Subject to the terms and conditions set out hereunder, the provisions of paragraph 1 of Article I of the General Agreement shall be waived, until 29 February 2000, to the extent necessary to permit the European Communities to provide preferential treatment for products originating in ACP States as required by the relevant provisions of

---

3. The Fourth ACP-EEC Convention of Lomé, Decision of the CONTRACTING PARTIES of 9 December 1994, L/7604, December 19, 1994.

the Fourth Lomé Convention, without being required to extend the same preferential treatment to like products of any other contracting party.

This is the Lomé Waiver. The WTO General Council, acting pursuant to paragraphs 3 and 4 of Article IX of the *WTO Agreement* and the provisions of the *Understanding in Respect of Waivers of Obligations under the General Agreement on Tariffs and Trade 1994*, decided on 14 October 1996 to extend this waiver until 29 February 2000.[4]

WHAT IS "REQUIRED" BY THE LOMÉ CONVENTION?

167. The European Communities asserts that the Panel should not have conducted an objective examination of the requirements of the Lomé Convention, but instead should have deferred to the "common" EC and ACP views on the appropriate interpretation of the Lomé Convention. This assertion is without merit. The Panel was correct in stating:

> We note that since the GATT CONTRACTING PARTIES incorporated a reference to the Lomé Convention into the Lomé waiver, the meaning of the Lomé Convention became a GATT/WTO issue, at least to that extent. Thus, we have no alternative but to examine the provisions of the Lomé Convention ourselves in so far as it is necessary to interpret the Lomé waiver.

We, too, have no alternative.

[The Appellate Body then parsed through the Lomé Convention and concluded as follows:]

178. Thus, of the relevant provisions of the measures at issue in this appeal, we conclude that the European Communities is "required" under the relevant provisions of the Lomé Convention to: provide duty-free access for all traditional ACP bananas; provide duty-free access for 90,000 tonnes of non-traditional ACP bananas; provide a margin of tariff preference in the amount of 100 ECU/tonne for all other non-traditional ACP bananas; and allocate tariff quota shares to the traditional ACP States that supplied bananas to the European Communities before 1991 in the amount of their pre-1991 best-ever export volumes. We conclude also that the European Communities is *not* "required" under the relevant provisions of the Lomé Convention to: allocate tariff quota shares to some traditional ACP States in excess of their pre-1991 best-ever export volumes; allocate tariff quota shares to ACP States exporting non-traditional ACP bananas; or maintain the import licensing procedures that are applied to third country and non-traditional ACP bananas. We therefore uphold the findings of the Panel in paragraphs 7.103, 7.204 and 7.136 of the Panel Reports.

WHAT IS COVERED BY THE LOMÉ WAIVER?

179. Having determined what is "required" by the Lomé Convention, we must next determine what is covered by the Lomé Waiver.

---

4. EC—The Fourth ACP-EC Convention of Lomé, Extension of Waiver, Decision of the WTO General Council of 14 October 1996, WT/L/186, October 18, 1996.

180. Specifically, we must determine whether the Lomé Waiver applies not only to breaches of Article I:1 of the GATT 1994, but also to breaches of Article XIII of the GATT 1994, with respect to the EC's country-specific tariff quota allocations for traditional ACP States.

181. The operative paragraph of the Lomé Waiver reads in relevant part:

> Subject to the terms and conditions set out hereunder, the provisions of *paragraph 1 of Article I* of the General Agreement shall be waived, until 29 February 2000, to the extent necessary to permit the European Communities to provide preferential treatment for products originating in ACP States as required by the relevant provisions of the Fourth Lomé Convention, . . . (emphasis added)

182. The Panel, nevertheless, concluded that the Lomé Waiver should be interpreted so as to waive not only compliance with the obligations of Article I:1, but also compliance with the obligations of Article XIII of the GATT 1994. The Panel based its conclusion on the need to give "real effect" to the Lomé Waiver and on the "close relationship" between Articles I and XIII:1.

183. We disagree with the Panel's conclusion. The wording of the Lomé Waiver is clear and unambiguous. By its precise terms, it waives only "the provisions of paragraph 1 of Article I of the *General Agreement* . . . to the extent necessary" to do what is "required" by the relevant provisions of the Lomé Convention. The Lomé Waiver does not refer to, or mention in any way, any other provision of the GATT 1994 or of any other covered agreement. Neither the circumstances surrounding the negotiation of the Lomé Waiver, nor the need to interpret it so as to permit it to achieve its objectives, allow us to disregard the clear and plain wording of the Lomé Waiver by extending its scope to include a waiver from the obligations under Article XIII. Moreover, although Articles I and XIII of the GATT 1994 are both non-discrimination provisions, their relationship is not such that a waiver from the obligations under Article I implies a waiver from the obligations under Article XIII.

LICENSING AGREEMENT

192. The appeal by the European Communities raises two legal issues relating to the interpretation and application of the *Licensing Agreement*. The first is whether the *Licensing Agreement* applies to import licensing procedures for tariff quotas. The second is whether the requirement of "neutrality in application" in Article 1.3 of the *Licensing Agreement* precludes the imposition of different import licensing systems on like products when imported from different Members.

193. With respect to the first issue, "import licensing" is defined in Article 1.1 of the *Licensing Agreement* as follows:

> For the purpose of this Agreement, import licensing is defined as *administrative procedures used for the operation of import licensing régimes* requiring the submission of an application or other documentation (other than that required for customs purposes) to the relevant administrative body *as a prior condition* for importation into the customs territory of the importing Member. (emphasis added)

Although the precise terms of Article 1.1 do not say explicitly that licensing procedures for tariff quotas are within the scope of the *Licensing Agreement*, a careful reading of that provision leads inescapably to that conclusion. The EC import licensing procedures require "the submission of an application" for import licences as "a prior condition for importation" of a product at the lower, in-quota tariff rate. The fact that the importation of that product is possible at a high out-of-quota tariff rate without a licence does not alter the fact that a licence is required for importation at the lower in-quota tariff rate.

194. We note that Article 3.2 of the *Licensing Agreement* provides that:

> Non-automatic licensing shall not have trade-restrictive or -distortive effects on imports additional to those caused by the imposition of *the restriction*. (emphasis added)

We note also that Article 3.3 of the *Licensing Agreement* reads:

> In the case of licensing requirements for purposes *other than the implementation of quantitative restrictions,* Members shall publish sufficient information for other Members and traders to know the basis for granting and/or allocating licences. (emphasis added)

We see no reason to exclude import licensing procedures for the administration of tariff quotas from the scope of the *Licensing Agreement* on the basis of the use of the term "restriction" in Article 3.2. We agree with the Panel that, in the light of the language of Article 3.3 of the *Licensing Agreement* and the introductory words of Article XI of the GATT 1994, the term "restriction" as used in Article 3.2 should not be interpreted to encompass only quantitative restrictions, but should be read also to include tariff quotas.

195. For these reasons, we agree with the Panel that import licensing procedures for tariff quotas are within the scope of the *Licensing Agreement.*

196. With respect to the second issue, the Panel found that Article 1.3 of the *Licensing Agreement* "preclude[s] the imposition of one system of import licensing procedures in respect of a product originating in certain Members and a different system of import licensing procedures on the same product originating in other Members".

197. Article 1.3 of the *Licensing Agreement* reads as follows:

> The rules for import licensing procedures shall be *neutral in application* and *administered* in a fair and equitable manner. (emphasis added)

By its very terms, Article 1.3 of the *Licensing Agreement* clearly applies to the *application* and *administration* of import licensing procedures, and requires that this application and administration be "neutral . . . fair and equitable". Article 1.3 of the *Licensing Agreement* does not require the import licensing *rules*, as such, to be neutral, fair and equitable. Furthermore, the context of Article 1.3—including the preamble, Article 1.1 and, in particular, Article 1.2 of the *Licensing Agreement*—supports the conclusion that Article 1.3 does not apply to import licensing *rules*. Article 1.2 provides, in relevant part, as follows:

> Members shall ensure that the administrative procedures used to implement import licensing régimes are in conformity with the relevant provisions of GATT 1994 . . . as interpreted by this Agreement, . . .

As a matter of fact, none of the provisions of the *Licensing Agreement* concerns import licensing *rules, per se.* As is made clear by the title of the *Licensing Agreement*, it concerns import licensing *procedures.* The preamble of the *Licensing Agreement* indicates clearly that this agreement relates to import licensing procedures and their administration, not to import licensing rules. Article 1.1 of the *Licensing Agreement* defines its scope as the *administrative procedures* used for the operation of import licensing regimes.

198. We conclude, therefore, that the Panel erred in finding that Article 1.3 of the *Licensing Agreement* precludes the imposition of different import licensing systems on like products when imported from different Members.

NOTES AND QUESTIONS

1. The *EC—Bananas* case, decided by the WTO Appellate Body in 1997, was the key decision that ultimately led to the EU adoption of a non-discriminatory, tariff-only regime for the import of bananas. The EU is the world's largest buyer of foreign bananas, which is the world's fourth most valuable food crop after wheat, rice, and corn, with world banana exports valued at over $16 billion annually. Ecuador is the largest exporter of bananas. The most significant rulings in this case were as follows:

- There is no requirement under the Dispute Settlement Understanding Article 3.7 that a complaining party have a "legal interest" to have standing to complain. WTO members have "broad discretion" in deciding whether to bring a claim (¶¶132-138). The United States was criticized by many ACP states in that the United States is not a producer or exporter of bananas. The U.S. interest was rather that large banana producers, Dole Foods and Chiquita Brands, have corporate offices in the United States. ACP countries charged that the United States was threatening the livelihood of millions of poor people in ACP countries.
- The Appellate Body reversed (¶¶179-188) the panel's ruling and found that the Lomé Waiver does not apply to violations of GATT Article XIII. The Appellate Body also ruled (¶¶160-162) that the allocation of tariff quota shares to some WTO members, but not to others, was a violation of Article XIII:1. Moreover, EC allocation rules under which a portion of a tariff quota share not used by one ACP country can be reallocated exclusively to other ACP countries, was inconsistent with GATT Article XIII:1 and XIII:2, chapeau (¶163).
- Although the Appellate Body upheld the panel's ruling that import licensing procedures for tariff quotas are within the scope of the Licensing Agreement, the Appellate Body ruled that the panel erred in concluding that Licensing Agreement Article 1.3 precludes the imposition of different import licensing systems on like products when imported from different members, since the Licensing Agreement applies only to administrative procedures, not to the system itself (¶198).
- The Appellate Body ruled that WTO members may consult and rely upon private counsel during the oral hearing of a WTO dispute (¶¶10-12).

2. The *Banana Dispute* was one of the longest-running trade disputes in history. During the course of this dispute, WTO panels and the Appellate Body handed down several significant rulings, and two arbitrations were held at the WTO. For a complete chronology of the dispute, see *Lamy Hails Accord Ending Long-running Banana Dispute*, December 15, 2009, available at http://www.wto.org. Ultimately the *Banana Dispute* was settled by the good offices of the WTO Director General, Pascal Lamy, employing his authority under Article 3.12 of the WTO Dispute Settlement Understanding. Director Lamy held both formal and informal meetings with the parties beginning in 2007, and the dispute was finally resolved by two agreements: (1) the Geneva Agreement on Trade in Bananas, WT/L/784, of December 15, 2009, and (2) an agreement between the EC and the United States, initialed on December 15, 2009, and signed June 8, 2010. *See* http://geneva.usmission.gov/2010/06/08. These two agreements require the EU to progressively lower tariffs on imports of bananas from Latin American exporters, and the EU pledged to eliminate measures that discriminate among banana distributors based on the ownership or control of the distributors or the source of the bananas, and to maintain a non-discriminatory tariff-only regime for the importation of bananas. To placate ACP countries the EU will provide 200 million euros in additional aid to those countries.

The accord is predicted to expand Latin American exports of bananas to the EU by 17 percent, while ACP exports will fall about 14 percent. The price of bananas in the EU will decline about 11 percent. *See International Center for Trade and Sustainable Development*, Dec. 15, 2009, http://www.ictsd.org/i/press, accessed March 4, 2012.

3. Read the WTO Agreement on Import Licensing Procedures. There are generally two kinds of licensing that states employ; automatic and non-automatic licensing. What is the purpose of licensing imports? Licensing is not commonly used now, but it was very common at one time. What are the criteria for licensing procedures that must be observed by WTO members? What is the time limit for acting on a licensing application?

4. Another non-tariff barrier addressed by a special WTO agreement is pre-shipment inspection (PSI). PSI is a service used primarily by developing countries to monitor the quality and quantity of their imports and to verify shipment details. PSI is commonly done by private firms before the products in question are permitted to depart from the country of exportation. A major purpose of PSI is to fight corruption in developing countries, but sometimes PSI leads to corruption by facilitating payments to government members. The WTO Agreement on Pre-Shipment Inspection establishes both rules and obligations. What obligations are imposed on user governments? What are the obligations of exporting contracting parties?

III.   Agricultural Trade

Trade in agricultural products is the area of international trade most subject to intervention through government measures that distort free trade. These government measures fall into three general categories:

(1) quotas and other non-tariff barriers (NTBs) applied at the border;

(2) domestic support programs; and

(3) export subsidies.

Quotas and other customs measures deny market access by restricting imports of agricultural products. Market access is a major concern for all countries, but especially for developing countries that seek to increase their exports of agricultural products to developed countries. The use of quotas and other non-tariff barriers to trade in agriculture is the subject of this Chapter.

Domestic support programs include government payments to farmers as income support. These payments distort trade because they allow farmers to charge lower prices for their agricultural products that create a competitive advantage over imports in the domestic market. Domestic support is very high, especially in the United States, the EU, and Japan. In 2010, government payments constituted 10 percent of farm income in the United States; 24 percent in the EU; and 36 percent in Japan.[5]

Export subsidies are payments by a government to farmers contingent upon export of the agricultural product. The export subsidy allows the exporter to charge a lower price for the export, creating a competitive advantage in the import market and a trade distortion. Export subsidies are still employed, especially by the EU, which has pledged to remove them by 2013 if an agreement can be reached in the Doha Development Agenda (DDA) trade negotiations.

Some of these practices, such as quotas and export subsidies, were clearly illegal under the GATT, but although agriculture was subject to the GATT from the very beginning, many rules were not enforced. The collapse of world agricultural prices during the Great Depression of the 1930s and the need to support domestic food production in the aftermath of the Second World War meant that agriculture was singled out for special treatment. GATT rules were ignored, often without any justification, resulting in many trade distortions.

The 1994 Agreement on Agriculture (AoA), signed as part of the Uruguay Round, subjects trade in agriculture to special rules and reforms. The goal of the AoA is to gradually eliminate these trade distortions. The AoA is much litigated. As of this writing, there are over forty Appellate Body and panel reports dealing with the AoA. Since the beginning of the Doha Development Agenda of trade negotiations in 2001, negotiations over protection of agriculture have taken center stage. Reform of the AoA is a major topic at the DDA, but members are far from agreement. For a discussion of the issues, see Thomas J. Schoenbaum, *Fashioning a New Regime for Agricultural Trade: New Issues and the Global Food Crisis*, 14 J. Int'l Econ. L. 593 (2011).

Read the WTO Agreement on Agriculture in the Documents Supplement.

The matter of agricultural trade is quite complex. In this Chapter, we treat issues of the elimination or reduction of non-tariff barriers to trade (e.g., market access) for agricultural products. This is category (1) of barriers to trade in agriculture set forth above.

---

5. *See* http://www.oecd.org/agriculture.

In Chapter 9 on developing countries, we deal with issues related to domestic and export subsidies for agriculture, which are of intense concern to developing countries. Chapter 9 deals with categories (2) and (3) of trade barriers to agricultural trade set forth above.

In this Chapter and in Chapter 8 (on safeguards), we also deal briefly with the special safeguard rules, permitting trade restrictions that apply to agricultural trade. In addition, agricultural trade is involved in many other areas of trade law, such as product standards and health and safety standards.

A. Overview of the AoA

We begin with a brief overview of the AoA and its general approach to eliminating and reducing all of the three categories of trade barriers. The basic obligations under the AoA concerning all three categories of trade distortions are as follows:

1. Quotas and NTBs

The AoA takes a two-step approach to eliminating or reducing non-tariff trade barriers in agriculture: (1) convert all NTBs into tariffs and (2) reduce tariffs by fiat and through further negotiations.

Article 4.2 of the AoA requires that all customs access barriers on agricultural products be "converted into ordinary customs duties." All types of trade barriers concerning agriculture, such as quotas, must be converted into ordinary tariffs and incorporated into the schedules required under GATT Article II. This process required under Article 4.2 of the AoA is called "tariffication." The rationale is that tariffs are widely understood and transparent. Countries that would otherwise impose all types of ingenuous, confusing, and non-transparent measures must convert them to tariffs. Note that a TRQ is considered to be a tariff for the purposes of the AoA and is permitted. A TRQ imposes a lower tariff for imports up to a certain quantity and a higher rate above the quantity. Most countries have chosen to convert their quotas and other border measures (such as variable import levies discussed in *Chile—Price Band* below) into TRQs.

Once tariffication has occurred, the AoA then requires tariff rates to be reduced during an implementation period by an average of 36 percent over six years for developed countries and 24 percent over ten years for developing countries. Minimum tariff cuts per product were also agreed upon: 15 percent for developed and 10 percent for developing countries. Further tariff reductions can be achieved through tariff negotiations under the AoA/GATT.

Tariffication, however, is subject to two exceptions: (a) special safeguard measures (explained below) and (b) special treatment for designated products singled out by a WTO member. (For example, Japan designated rice for special treatment until 1998; under this special designation, Japan was allowed to impose quotas on rice imports.)

Article 5 of the AoA allows special emergency actions to restrict imports of agricultural products in cases of import surges (i.e., when imports exceed certain trigger levels) and falling prices (i.e., when the price of a domestic agricultural product falls below a certain trigger level). In such cases, an additional duty may be temporarily levied on imports of the agricultural product in question to protect the domestic agricultural industry.

2. Domestic Support

The AoA distinguishes between two categories of domestic support programs: (1) support with no or minimal trade distorting effect, or exempt domestic support programs; and (2) support that distorts trade, or non-exempt support programs. An example of the former is government-provided agricultural research or training while an example of the latter is the government purchase of an agricultural product at a minimum price. Articles 3, 6, and 7 require WTO members to reduce non-exempt domestic support programs. WTO members are not required to reduce exempt domestic support programs but can give as much support through these programs as they wish.

The following are exempt domestic support programs (and therefore not subject to any reduction commitments under the AoA):

a. GREEN BOX SUBSIDIES

Annex 2 of the AoA defines these as domestic payments that do not distort trade, or cause only minimal distortion. Green Box subsidies are government programs that do not provide direct payments or price support to agricultural producers. Examples of green box subsidies are programs for research, pest and disease control, training, extension and advisory services, marketing and promotional services, domestic food aid, insurance schemes, regional assistance, environmental programs, structural adjustment assistance, and income support payments not linked to agricultural production.

b. BLUE BOX SUBSIDIES

Article 6.5 of the AoA exempts domestic payments to producers that are required to place limits on production. Such payments must be for production limits on crops based upon fixing the area or yields. Limits for livestock are based on a fixed number of heads.

c. DE MINIMIS EXCEPTIONS

Article 6.4 exempts product-specific domestic support that does not exceed 5 percent of the total value of production of that product, or non-product specific domestic support that does not exceed 5 percent of the value of the member's total agricultural production. For developing country members, the allowed percentage for each of these exceptions is 10 percent.

d. SPECIAL AND DIFFERENTIAL TREATMENT BOX SUBSIDIES

Article 6.2 of the AoA exempts government measures used to encourage agricultural and rural development and also exempts subsidies to encourage investment in low-income areas or areas with a concentration of resource-poor producers.

e. AMBER BOX SUBSIDIES

The residue of domestic support subsidies remaining outside the foregoing boxes and exceptions is termed the Amber Box. These subsidy programs are non-exempt; i.e., they are subject to reductions. All members must make a reduction commitment for Amber Box subsidies that are set forth in their schedules annexed to the GATT. The reduction commitments are expressed in terms of a "Total Aggregate Measurement of Support" (total AMS), which includes all domestic support (product specific or non-product specific) in one single number. Any country with a total AMS has non-exempt domestic support programs; countries with only exempt domestic support programs do not have an AMS. Members with an AMS have to reduce base period support by 20 percent over six years (developed countries) or by 13 percent over ten years (developing countries). In any year of the implementation period, the current total AMS cannot exceed the scheduled total AMS for that year. In other words, the maximum level of non-exempt domestic support is bound by the WTO for that particular year. These maximum levels are then subject to mandatory reductions. Twenty-eight members (counting the EU as one) had non-exempt domestic support programs during the base period.

3. Export Subsidies

AoA Articles 8 and 9 define and place limits on export subsidies for agricultural products. Export subsidies must be reduced by developed WTO members by an average of 36 percent by value (financial outlay) and 21 percent by volume (subsidized quantities); developing country members must reduce by an average of 24 percent by value and 14 percent by volume.

NOTES AND QUESTIONS

1. *Food security.* Food security—access to adequate supplies of food at affordable prices—has emerged as a significant global issue. As of December 2010 food prices have hit a thirty-year high. In 2008 United Nations' Secretary General Ban Ki-moon established a High-Level Task Force on the Global Security Crisis, which has since recommended a Global Framework for Action (2008) calling for more investment and international stability of food supplies.[6] What is the impact of agricultural trade and the AoA on food security? On the one hand, international trade is essential to move supplies to those to whom food is needed and to ensure adequate supplies for food-deficit countries. Thus, free trade in agriculture, by removing trade distortions, will create greater market access that benefits developing countries, by giving them greater access to food supplies. On the other hand, there is an argument that the AoA and promoting trade will not enhance food security. The most crucial food security issue is not greater access to food supplies that come from developed nations. Such access still creates dependence on food produced by other nations. Real security in food supplies is created when developing countries are able to produce their own food to meet their needs. In this light, the AoA may actually work against the interests of developing nations; the availability of cheap imports created by the AoA reduces the incentive for developing nations to improve their capacity to produce their own food. To help promote their own food production capacity, developing countries call for a three-prong approach: (1) dramatically lower tariffs to be adopted by developed countries and (2) elimination of export subsidies and domestic support by developed countries. The reduction of tariffs will allow food produced by developing countries greater

---

6. *See* http://un.org/issues/food.

access to markets in developed countries and create incentives for developed countries to produce greater supplies of food for export; the elimination of export subsidies in developed countries will reduce the competitive advantage that the exports enjoy when they are sold in developing countries, giving developing countries a greater chance to produce their own food supplies that can compete with the foreign imports from developed countries. These demands are not new, but developing countries have inserted a third demand that proved to be a deal breaker: developing countries argue that they must be allowed to protect their domestic markets from imports from developed countries, and call for (3) a strong special safeguard provision that would allow only developing countries to adopt high tariffs against cheap imports from developed countries.[7] Is this negotiating position realistic? This demand for a special safeguard led to the breakdown in the 2008 meeting of the DDA negotiators.

2. *Non-trade concerns.* Article 20(c) of the AoA mandates consideration for "non-trade concerns" in agricultural trade. This is the idea that domestic subsidy programs have purposes in addition to increasing agricultural production. Domestic subsidies to farmers are made for the purposes of rural development, environmental protection, and enhancing food security. Can subsidies be ended while preserving these values?

3. *Export restrictions.* Article 12 of the AoA calls for discipline on export bans and restrictions of foodstuffs. Is this adequate? In 2008-2010, many countries adopted restrictions on food exports, causing difficulties for some WTO members such as Japan. We deal in depth with export restrictions in Chapter 14.

4. *Food safety.* Food safety is a growing concern. The AoA Article 14 delegates this important matter to the WTO Agreement on Sanitary and Phytosanitary Measures (SPS Agreement). We cover this important matter in Chapter 7.

5. *Subsidies.* The WTO Appellate Body has decided several cases involving complaints by members that the anti-subsidy provisions of the AoA were violated. Three of the most celebrated cases are:

(1) *Canada—Measures Affecting the Importation of Milk and the Exportation of Dairy Products*, WT/DS103, 113/AB/R, Report of the Appellate Body, adopted on October 27, 1999. In this case, the United States and New Zealand successfully challenged Canada's so-called Special Milk Classes scheme through which the Canadian government set government price supports tied to production quotas. Milk produced in excess of the quotas could only be sold for export. The Appellate Body ruled that the scheme amounted to a subsidy for the low-priced exported milk, violating Articles 9 and 10 of the AoA.

(2) *United States—Subsidies on Upland Cotton*, WT/DS267/AB/R, Report of the Appellate Body, adopted on March 21, 2005. In this case the Appellate Body ruled that certain domestic subsidies provided to cotton producers were not green box measures exempt from the subsidy reduction commitments by virtue of Annex 2 of the AoA. In addition, the export credit guarantee programs operated by the U.S. are export subsidies in violation of Article 3.1 of the AoA. This case is addressed in more detail in Chapter 9.

---

7. *See* The WTO Agreement on Agriculture (2003), http://www.actionaid.org.

(3) *European Communities—Export Subsidies on Sugar*, WT/DS265, 266, 283/
AB/R, Report of the Appellate Body, adopted on May 19, 2005. In this
case, the EC was ruled in violation of Article 9 of the AoA through cross-
subsidization that transferred financial resources resulting from the
operation of the EC sugar regime. This case is discussed in more detail in
Chapter 9.

PROBLEM 6-8

As part of its commitments under the AoA, Country Z, a developed country,
has agreed to limit its domestic support of agricultural products to the ceiling
established by its AMS. Country Z has also agreed to convert all quotas into tariffs
as required by the AoA. Which of the following domestic subsidies are exempt from
inclusion in Country Z's annual AMS? In addition, has Country Z complied with
the tariffication requirement?

(1) Farmers receive government-provided fertilizer, soil, chemicals, and other
materials used to grow crops;
(2) Farmers receive government payments to be used for pest control and
spraying;
(3) Government-sponsored training programs on marketing and sales are
provided free of charge to farmers;
(4) Imports are subject to the GATT bound tariff of 37.5 percent, calculated
based upon the current market price of the same domestically grown agricultural product, or the actual transaction value of the import, whichever
is higher.

Review the summary of the AoA above and consider the *Chile—Price Band* case
below.

PROBLEM 6-9

You are a trade lawyer asked by a client to explain why a TRQ is permissible under the AoA, whereas the use of a variable import levy in *Chile—Price Band*
below, is not. A TRQ and the Chile price band system both involve variable tariffs;
i.e., tariff rates that can vary due to an internal mechanism of the tariff. What is
the difference?

Chile—Price Band System and Safeguard Measures
Relating to Certain Agricultural Products
Report of the Appellate Body, adopted on October 23, 2002
WT/DS207/AB/R

[The issue in this case was the legality of Chile's price band system employed to
calculate tariffs on certain imported agricultural products. Under the price band
system, an upper and a lower price threshold are designated for a product using

international market prices. These price bands are set once per year by decree. In addition, weekly "reference prices" are set for each product based on prices in certain foreign markets. When a product subject to the price band was imported, the standard *ad valorem* duty is first applied, but the final duty would depend on a comparison of the price band to the reference price. If the reference price was below the lower threshold of the band, the duty was increased in the amount of this difference. If the reference price was within the price band, only the *ad valorem* duty was charged. If the reference price was higher than the upper threshold of the price band, a rebate would be granted equal to this difference. Chile's WTO bound tariff rate on products subject to the price band was 31.5 percent. In 2001, Chile amended the price band system to provide that the duties charged could in no case exceed the WTO bound tariff. Argentina challenged Chile's price band system before a WTO panel on the grounds that the system was a measure "of the kind which has been required to be converted into ordinary customs duties" and which, under Article 4.2 of the AoA, members are required not to maintain. Chile replied that the price band system was not such a measure. Chile argued that the duties resulting from its price band system were "ordinary customs duties" and consistent with the AoA. The panel agreed with Argentina, and Chile brought this appeal to the Appellate Body.]

ASSESSMENT OF CHILE'S PRICE BAND SYSTEM IN THE LIGHT OF ARTICLE 4.2 AND FOOTNOTE 1

218. We turn now to the Panel's finding that Chile's price band system is a border measure similar to a variable import levy and a minimum import price within the meaning of footnote 1 to Article 4.2 of the *Agreement on Agriculture*.

219. Footnote 1 lists six categories of border measures and a residual category of such measures that are *included* in "measures of the kind which have been required to be converted into ordinary customs duties" within the meaning of Article 4.2. The list is illustrative, and includes "quantitative import restrictions, variable import levies, minimum import prices, discretionary import licensing, non-tariff measures maintained through state-trading enterprises, voluntary export restraints, and similar border measures other than ordinary customs duties".

221. A plain reading of Article 4.2 and footnote 1 makes clear that, if Chile's price band system falls within any *one* of the categories of measures listed in footnote 1, it is among the "measures of the kind which have been required to be converted into ordinary customs duties", and thus must not be maintained, resorted to, or reverted to, as of the date of entry into force of the WTO *Agreement*.

232. We begin with the interpretation of "variable import levies". In examining the ordinary meaning of the term "*variable import levies*" as it appears in footnote 1, we note that a "levy" is a duty, tax, charge, or other exaction usually imposed or raised by legal execution or process. An "import" levy is, of course, a duty assessed upon importation. A levy is "variable" when it is "liable to vary". This feature alone, however, is not conclusive as to what constitutes a "variable import levy" within the meaning of footnote 1. An "ordinary customs duty" could also fit this description. A Member may, fully in accordance with Article II of the GATT 1994, exact a duty upon importation and periodically change the rate at which it applies that duty (provided the changed rates remain *below* the tariff rates bound in the Member's

Schedule). This change in the *applied* rate of duty could be made, for example, through an act of a Member's legislature or executive at any time. Moreover, it is clear that the term "variable import levies" as used in footnote 1 must have a meaning different from "ordinary customs duties", because "variable import levies" must be *converted into* "ordinary customs duties". Thus, the mere fact that an import duty can be varied cannot, alone, bring that duty within the category of "variable import levies" for purposes of footnote 1.

233. To determine *what kind* of variability makes an import levy a "variable import levy", we turn to the immediate context of the other words in footnote 1. The term "variable import levies" appears after the introductory phrase "[t]hese *measures* include". Article 4.2—to which the footnote is attached—also speaks of "*measures*". This suggests that at least one feature of "variable import levies" is the fact that the *measure* itself—as a mechanism—must impose the *variability* of the duties. Variability is inherent in a measure if the measure incorporates a scheme or formula that causes and ensures that levies change automatically and continuously. Ordinary customs duties, by contrast, are subject to discrete changes in applied tariff rates that occur independently, and unrelated to such an underlying scheme or formula. The level at which ordinary customs duties are applied can be *varied* by a legislature, but such duties will not be automatically and continuously *variable*. To vary the applied rate of duty in the case of ordinary customs duties will always require *separate* legislative or administrative action, whereas the ordinary meaning of the term "variable" implies that *no* such action is required.

234. However, in our view, the presence of a formula causing automatic and continuous variability of duties is a *necessary*, but by no means a *sufficient*, condition for a particular measure to be a "variable import levy" within the meaning of footnote 1. "Variable import levies" have additional features that undermine the object and purpose of Article 4, which is to achieve improved market access conditions for imports of agricultural products by permitting only the application of ordinary customs duties. These additional features include a lack of transparency and a lack of predictability in the level of duties that will result from such measures. This lack of transparency and this lack of predictability are liable to restrict the volume of imports. As Argentina points out, an exporter is less likely to ship to a market if that exporter does not know and cannot reasonably predict what the amount of duties will be. This lack of transparency and predictability will also contribute to distorting the prices of imports by impeding the transmission of international prices to the domestic market.

253. However, Chile argues that, in making its finding, the Panel failed to take proper account of the fact that the total amount of duties that may be levied as a result of Chile's price band system is "capped" at the level of the tariff rate of 31.5 per cent *ad valorem* bound in Chile's Schedule. According to Chile, the existence of this cap differentiates Chile's price band system from a "variable import levy". Chile argues that Chile's price band system enables imports to enter Chile's market below the lower thresholds of Chile's price bands when world market prices drop below a certain level, while allowing imports to enter at duty rates that can be as low as zero when the weekly reference prices rise above the upper thresholds of Chile's price bands. Chile submits that the cap makes Chile's price band system less distortive and less insulating than if Chile simply levied duties at its bound tariff level.

254. This argument by Chile compels us to consider whether Chile's price band system ceases to be similar to a "variable import levy" because it is subject to a cap. In doing so, we find nothing in Article 4.2 to suggest that a measure prohibited

by that provision would be rendered consistent with it if applied with a cap. Before the conclusion of the Uruguay Round, a measure could be recognized as a "variable import levy" even if the products to which the measure applied were subject to tariff bindings. And, there is nothing in the text of Article 4.2 to indicate that a measure, which was recognized as a "variable import levy" before the Uruguay Round, is exempt from the requirements of Article 4.2 simply because tariffs on some, or all, of the products to which that measure *now* applies were bound as a result of the Uruguay Round.

259. The fact that duties resulting from Chile's price band system are "capped" at 31.5 per cent *ad valorem* merely reduces the extent of the trade distortions in that system by reducing the extent to which those duties fluctuate. It does not, however, eliminate those distortions. Moreover, the cap does not *eliminate* the lack of transparency, or the lack of predictability, in the fluctuation of the duties resulting from Chile's price band system. Thus, the fact that Chile's price band system is subject to a "cap" may be said to make this system *less* inconsistent with Article 4.2. But this is not enough. Article 4.2 not only prohibits "similar border measures" from being applied to *some* products, or to *some* shipments of *some* products with low transaction values, or the imposition of duties on *some* products in an amount *beyond* the level of a bound tariff rate. Article 4.2 prohibits the application of such "similar border measures" to *all* products in *all* cases.

262. We, therefore, uphold the Panel's finding that Chile's price band system is a "border measure similar to 'variable import levies' and 'minimum import prices'" within the meaning of footnote 1 and Article 4.2 of the *Agreement on Agriculture*.

NOTES AND QUESTIONS

1. Most WTO members now employ TRQs to imports of agricultural products. For example, Japan's TRQ on rice is 292 Japanese yen per kilogram for the first 767,000 tons to enter Japan and 341 Japanese yen plus a tariff of 490 percent for all imports of rice in excess of this quota.

2. Turkey maintained a TRQ for imports of rice, and, in addition, importers of rice had to obtain a certificate of control from the Turkish government. The United States complained against Turkey that certificates of control were rejected by the Turkish government for rice shipments unless they would be subject to the highest MFN duty applicable to rice outside the TRQ. Turkey denied the charges and said that the issuance of a certificate of control was simply an administrative matter. However, Turkey refused to provide evidence to support its claims of automatic approval. In *Turkey—Measures Affecting the Importation of Rice*, WT/DS334/R, Report of the Panel, adopted on October 22, 2007, the panel stated (¶7.106) that it would draw the appropriate inferences against Turkey and ruled (¶7.138) that Turkey was in violation of AoA Article 2.4 in two respects, characterizing Turkey's measure as both a quantitative import restriction and as discretionary import licensing.

3. GATT Article XIII requires that quotas, where they are permitted, must be administered on a non-discriminatory basis. Does this rule apply to TRQs or can some countries be granted privileged access? In *European Communities—Measures Affecting the Importation of Certain Poultry Products*, WT/DS69/AB/R, Report of the Appellate Body, adopted on July 23, 1998, the Appellate Body considered whether the TRQ adopted by the EC for frozen poultry had to be allocated on an MFN basis. Brazil, the complaining member, argued that the TRQ had been negotiated

as a modification of the EC's GATT Article II Schedule pursuant to GATT Article XXVIII as compensation and that by agreement the entire TRQ was reserved for Brazil so that poultry from other countries were not subject to the TRQ. The Appellate Body found (¶¶93-94) no evidence supporting the creation of country-specific TRQs through bilateral agreements under Article XIII:2(d) and ruled that the general rule of Article XIII requires that a TRQ, even one negotiated under Article XXVIII, cannot be limited to one country (Brazil) but must be administered on a non-discriminatory basis.

IV. *Technical Regulations and Product Standards*

Under the WTO, *technical regulations* are requirements to which the characteristics of products must conform before they can clear customs and enter the domestic market. A regulation is a mandatory law that is usually based upon a *standard*. The standard can be either a national or an international standard. We elaborate on these definitions below.

Technical regulations can create non-tariff trade barriers when the regulations are burdensome, overly complex, opaque, or impose requirements that create competitive disadvantages for imports. Of course, technical regulations can also serve legitimate purposes in assuring the quality and usefulness of products so a balance must be struck.

Technical regulations and standards are the subject of binding international norms under the WTO Agreement on Technical Barriers to Trade, known as the TBT Agreement. The WTO's basic approach toward technical regulations is as follows:

(1) Technical regulations must not discriminate — no less favorable treatment can be accorded than that accorded to like products of national origin or to like products originating in other countries (Art. 2.1).

(2) If international standards exist or are being developed, members must use them as a basis for their national technical regulations except when the international standards would be "ineffective or inappropriate means" for the fulfillment of the "legitimate objectives pursued" by the member (Art. 2.4).

(3) Technical regulations must not create "unnecessary obstacles to international trade" and must not be "more trade-restrictive than necessary to fulfill a legitimate objective." Legitimate objectives include national security; prevention of deceptive practices; protection of human health or safety, animal or plant life or health or the environment (Art.2.2).

The most basic of the TBT Agreement's obligations is contained in Article 2.1, which forbids discrimination. Article 2.1 was the subject of the Report of the Appellate Body in *United States — Measures Affecting the Production and Sale of Clove Cigarettes*, WT/DS406/AB/R, Report of the Appellate Body, adopted on April 24, 2012. In this case Indonesia challenged section 907(a)(1)(A) of the U.S. Food, Drug, and Cosmetic Act, 21 U.S.C. §387g(a)(1)(A), which provides as follows:

> [A] cigarette or any of its components . . . shall not contain, as a constituent . . . or additive, an artificial or natural flavor (other than tobacco or menthol) or herb or spice, including strawberry, grape, orange, clove, cinnamon, pineapple, vanilla, coconut, liquorice, cocoa, chocolate, cherry, or coffee, that is a characterizing flavor of the tobacco product or tobacco smoke.

The purpose of this law is to protect public health by banning cigarettes that have particular appeal to young people. *See* H.R. Rep. No. 111-58, Pt. 1 (2009). Indonesia argued that this law, which permits the sale of menthol cigarettes, which are primarily domestic-made, discriminates against clove cigarettes, which are imported.

The Appellate Body in considering this case first observed (¶87) that Article 2.1 "contains both a national treatment and a most-favoured nation treatment obligation." But Article 2.1 is devoid of any general exceptions clause analogous to GATT Article XX (¶101). The Appellate Body noted (¶100) that there is an overlap between the TBT Agreement Article 2.1 and GATT Article III:4, which requires National Treatment for laws and regulations affecting products.

As a threshold matter the Appellate Body considered whether clove cigarettes and menthol cigarettes are like products within the meaning of Article 2.1. The Appellate Body disagreed with the panel on the criteria for determining the "like product" issue. The Appellate Body ruled it was error for the panel to focus on the regulatory objective of the measure—public health of young people. Rather what is important for the purpose of answering the "like product" question under Article 2.1 is similar to the "like product" issue under GATT Article III:4; namely, the competitive relationship between and among the products in question. The Appellate Body focused upon two aspects of the competitive relationship: end uses and consumer tastes and habits. With respect to the latter point, rather than considering especially young people as the principal consumers, the "panel should have assessed the tastes and habits of all relevant consumers of the products at issue" (¶137). Despite the errors of the panel, the Appellate Body agreed (¶160) with the panel that clove cigarettes and menthol cigarettes are like products.

To establish a violation of Article 2.1 of the TBT Agreement the Appellate Body stated (¶168) that three elements must be satisfied: (1) the measure at issue must be a technical regulation; (2) the imported and domestic products at issue must be like products; and (3) the imported products must be accorded less favorable treatment than the like domestic product. With respect to the "less favorable treatment" issue, the Appellate Body ruled (¶175) that Article 2.1 prohibits both de jure and de facto discrimination, "while at the same time permitting detrimental impact on competitive opportunities for imports that stems exclusively from legitimate regulatory distinctions."

Applying this analysis, the Appellate Body ruled that the mere existence of a detrimental impact on competitive opportunities for imported products versus domestic like products is not enough to establish a violation of Article 2.1. A panel must further analyze whether the detrimental impact stems exclusively from a legitimate regulatory distinction, considering "the design, architecture, revealing structure, operation, and application of the technical regulation at issue" (¶182). The Appellate Body further ruled (¶225) that "we are not persuaded that the detrimental impact of Section 907(a)(1)(A) on competitive opportunities for imported clove cigarettes does stem from a legitimate regulatory distinction [because] menthol cigarettes have the same product characteristic that, from the stated objective of Section 907(a)(1)(A), justified the prohibition of clove cigarettes."

Thus the Appellate Body affirmed that the U.S. law was inconsistent with TBT Article 2.1. The Appellate Body recommended that the DSB of the WTO request the United States to bring its measure into conformity with its obligations under the TBT Agreement.

Read the WTO Agreement on Technical Barriers to Trade in the Documents Supplement.

Annex 1 of the TBT Agreement defines the term "technical regulation" as a "[d]ocument which lays down product characteristics or their related processes and production methods, including the applicable administrative provisions, with which compliance is mandatory." A "standard" is defined as a "[d]ocument approved by a recognized body that provides for common and repeated use of rules, guidelines or characteristics for products of related processes or production methods, with which compliance is not mandatory." These terms include terminology, symbols, packaging, and labeling requirements as well.

PROBLEM 6-10

You are a senior fellow at a think tank in Washington, D.C. You are asked why the WTO prefers international standards in the TBT over national standards as a basis for national technical regulations. The WTO favors objectivity and harmonization in technical standards and avoids subjectivity and local variation. How does the approach of the WTO address these concerns?

PROBLEM 6-11

Country M has recently passed a new customs regulation concerning cotton fabrics and clothing. The new regulation requires, as part of customs clearance, the completion of a fifty-page questionnaire. The purpose of the documentation is to ensure that the cotton fabrics meet certain technical standards for durability and comfort. The questionnaire is highly detailed and requires five business days to complete by one full-time clerk. Is this regulation consistent with the TBT? *See* Article 2.2.

PROBLEM 6-12

Colombia is considering a challenge to a national technical regulation imposed by Peru for certain types of dairy products. Colombia's trade minister believes that Peru's technical regulation, based on a national standard, has the effect of restricting trade and that there is an applicable international standard for dairy products Peru should use instead, as the basis of its national regulations. On the burden of proof, the trade minister argues that it should be sufficient to demonstrate a *prima facie* case to simply show the existence of a relevant international standard for dairy products. At this point, the burden should shift to the defending member to explain why it did not adopt the international standard. If the defending member cannot explain then it loses the case. Do you agree? Consult *EC — Sardines* below.

PROBLEM 6-13

India takes great national pride in basmati rice, an indigenous crop that is popular because of its resistance to disease. Several years ago, scientists from the United States cross-bred basmati rice sourced in India with other varieties, producing a superior product, and have obtained a U.S. patent for the new basmati variety. Many people in India are outraged when they learn that the United States has patented "their" national product. India has recently passed a technical regulation providing that only rice grown in India, Malaysia, Indonesia, and a few other southeast Asian countries can use word "basmati" in its label.

U.S. producers and exporters of basmati rice are concerned about this new law and come to your law firm for advice:

(1) Are U.S. producers prohibited by the new law from exporting their U.S.-produced basmati rice to India? What exactly does the law require?

(2) Does this law operate as a protectionist trade measure? If so, how?

(3) A specialized agency of the United Nations has passed the following standard: "Developing countries are entitled to pass technical regulations that require that the unqualified name of indigenous agricultural products be used only in connection with agricultural products actually produced in those countries. Agricultural crops indigenous to developing countries but produced in other countries cannot use the name of the indigenous crop unless the name is qualified by the country where the crop is actually produced." What is the effect of this law on the Indian law relating to basmati rice? What are American producers of basmati rice allowed to do under this law? Will this law satisfy your clients? Consult *EC—Sardines.*

European Communities—Trade Description of Sardines
Report of the Appellate Body, adopted on October 23, 2002
WT/DS231/AB/R

[This dispute concerns the marketing of "preserved sardines" in the European Communities. At issue are the trade descriptions of two small fish species—*Sardina pilchardus walbaum (Sardina pilchardus)* and *Sardinops sagax sagax (Sardinops sagax).* Both species belong to the *Clupeinae* subfamily of the *Clupeidae* family, while the former belongs to the genus Sardina and the latter belongs to the genus Sardinops. *Sardina pilchardus* is found mainly around the coasts of the Eastern North Atlantic, the Mediterranean Sea, and the Black Sea, while *Sardinops sagax* is found mainly in the Eastern Pacific along the coasts of Peru and Chile (Peru exports preserved products prepared from *Sardinops sagax).* While morphological differences can be observed between the two species (e.g., head and length, type and number of gill-rakes or bone striae, and size and weight), the two species also display similar characteristics (e.g., they live in a coastal pelagic environment, form schools, engage in vertical migration, feed on plankton and have similar breeding seasons). Both species are used in the preparation of preserved and canned fish products, packed in water, oil, or other suitable medium.

On June 21, 1989, the European Communities adopted Council Regulation (EEC) No. 2136/89 (the EC Regulation), which establishes common marketing standards for preserved sardines. Article 2 of the EC Regulation provides, *inter alia,* that only products prepared from *Sardina pilchardus* may be marketed as preserved sardines. In other words, only products of this species may have the word "sardines" as part of the name on the container.

International standards for sardines and sardine-type products played a central role in the dispute. In 1978, the Codex Alimentarius Commission of the United Nations Food and Agriculture Organization and the World Health Organization (the Codex Alimentarius Commission) adopted a standard for these products, Codex Stan 94. Article 2.1 of Codex Stan 94 provides that canned sardines or sardine-type products are prepared from fresh or frozen fish from a list of twenty-one species, including *Sardina pilchardus* and *Sardinops sagax*. Article 6 of Codex Stan 94 sets forth specific labeling provisions for these products, as follows:

> 6. LABELLING
> In addition to the provisions of the Codex General Standard for the Labelling of Prepackaged Foods (CODEX STAN 1-1985, Rev. 3-1999) the following specific provisions shall apply:
> 6.1 NAME OF THE FOOD
> The name of the products shall be:
> 6.1.1(i) "Sardines" (to be reserved exclusively for *Sardina pilchardus* (Walbaum)); or
>   (ii) "X sardines" of a country, a geographic area, the species, or the common name of the species in accordance with the law and custom of the country in which the product is sold, and in a manner not to mislead the consumer.

Under Codex Stan 94 Article 2.1, a label with the unqualified term "sardines" could only be used for *Sardina pilchardus*, but it would be possible for *Sardinops sagax* from Peru to be labelled "Peruvian Sardines" or "South American Sardines" along with the other type of options involving use of the name of the species or its common name. Under the EC Regulation, the word sardines, whether qualified or not, could be used only for *Sardina pilchardus*. Thus, Peru would not be able to use the word "sardines" anywhere in the label for *Sardinops sagax* under the EC Regulation. Before the Panel, Peru challenged the EC Regulation under TBT Agreement Articles 2.1, 2.2, and 2.4. The Panel found that the EC Regulation was a technical regulation, that a relevant international standard (Codex Stan 94) existed, and that the regulation was not based on the standard in violation of TBT Article 2.4. The Appellate Body considered whether the Panel correctly ruled on these issues.]

The Characterization of the EC Regulation as a "Technical Regulation"

171. We now turn to whether the Panel erred by finding that the EC Regulation is a "technical regulation" for purposes of Article 2.4 of the *TBT Agreement*.

176. We interpreted [the definition of a technical regulation in the TBT Agreement] in *EC—Asbestos*. In doing so, we set out *three criteria* that a document must meet to fall within the definition of "technical regulation" in the *TBT Agreement*. *First*, the document must apply to an identifiable product or group of products. The *identifiable* product or group of products need not, however, be expressly *identified* in the document. *Second*, the document must lay down one or more characteristics of the product. These product characteristics may be intrinsic, or they may be related to the product. They may be prescribed or imposed in either

a positive or a negative form. *Third*, compliance with the product characteristics must be mandatory.

178. We begin with the European Communities' contention that the EC Regulation is a "technical regulation" only for preserved *Sardina pilchardus*, and that preserved *Sardinops sagax* is not an identifiable product under the EC Regulation.

185. As we explained in *EC—Asbestos*, the requirement that a "technical regulation" be applicable to *identifiable* products relates to aspects of compliance and enforcement, because it would be impossible to comply with or enforce a "technical regulation" without knowing to what the regulation applied. As the Panel record shows, the EC Regulation has been enforced against preserved fish products imported into Germany containing *Sardinops sagax*. This confirms that the EC Regulation is applicable to preserved *Sardinops sagax*, and demonstrates that preserved *Sardinops sagax* is an *identifiable product* for purposes of the EC Regulation. Indeed, the European Communities admits that the EC Regulation is applicable to *Sardinops sagax*, when it states in its appellant's submission that "[t]he only legal consequence of the [EC] Regulation for preserved *Sardinops sagax* is that they may not be called 'preserved sardines'."

187. Next, we examine whether the EC Regulation meets the second criterion of a "technical regulation", which is that it must be a document that lays down product characteristics. According to the European Communities, Article 2 of the EC Regulation does not lay down product characteristics; rather, it sets out a "naming" rule. The European Communities argues that, although the definition of "technical regulation" in the *TBT Agreement* covers labelling requirements, it does not extend to "naming" rules. Therefore, the European Communities asserts that Article 2 of the EC Regulation is not a "technical regulation".

190. We do not find it necessary, in this case, to decide whether the definition of "technical regulation" in the *TBT Agreement* makes a distinction between "naming" and labelling. This question is irrelevant to the issue before us. As we stated earlier, the EC Regulation expressly identifies a product, namely "preserved sardines". Further, Article 2 of the EC Regulation provides that, to be marketed as "preserved sardines", products must be prepared exclusively from fish of the species *Sardina pilchardus*. We are of the view that this requirement—to be prepared exclusively from fish of the species *Sardina pilchardus*—is a product characteristic "intrinsic to" preserved sardines that is laid down by the EC Regulation. Thus, we agree with the Panel's finding in this regard that:

> . . . one product characteristic required by Article 2 of the EC Regulation is that preserved sardines must be prepared exclusively from fish of the species *Sardina pilchardus*. This product characteristic must be met for the product to be "marketed as preserved sardines and under the trade description referred to in Article 7" of the EC Regulation. We consider that the requirement to use exclusively *Sardina pilchardus* is a product characteristic as it objectively defines features and qualities of preserved sardines for the purposes of their "market[ing] as preserved sardines and under the trade description referred to in Article 7" of the EC Regulation.

194. The third and final criterion that a document must fulfil to meet the definition of "technical regulation" in the *TBT Agreement* is that compliance must be mandatory. The European Communities does not contest that compliance with the EC Regulation is mandatory. We also find that it is mandatory.

195. We, therefore, uphold the Panel's finding, in paragraph 7.35 of the Panel Report, that the EC Regulation is a "technical regulation" for purposes of the *TBT Agreement*.

THE CHARACTERIZATION OF CODEX STAN 94 AS A "RELEVANT INTERNATIONAL STANDARD"

217. We proceed to the European Communities' claim that the Panel erred in finding that Codex Stan 94 is a "relevant international standard" within the meaning of Article 2.4 of the *TBT Agreement*.

THE EUROPEAN COMMUNITIES' ARGUMENT THAT CONSENSUS IS REQUIRED

219. The European Communities argues that only standards that have been adopted by an international body by consensus can be *relevant* for purposes of Article 2.4. The European Communities contends that the Panel did not verify that Codex Stan 94 was not adopted by consensus, and that, therefore, it cannot be a "relevant international standard".

220. However, in our view, the European Communities' contention is essentially related to whether Codex Stan 94 meets the definition of a "standard" in Annex 1.2 of the *TBT Agreement*. The term "standard", is defined in Annex 1.2 as follows:

2.   Standard

Document approved by a recognized body, that provides, for common and repeated use, rules, guidelines or characteristics for products or related processes and production methods, with which compliance is not mandatory. It may also include or deal exclusively with terminology, symbols, packaging, marking or labelling requirements as they apply to a product, process or production method.

Explanatory note

The terms as defined in ISO/IEC Guide 2 cover products, processes and services. This Agreement deals only with technical regulations, standards and conformity assessment procedures related to products or processes and production methods. Standards as defined by ISO/IEC Guide 2 may be mandatory or voluntary. For the purpose of this Agreement standards are defined as voluntary and technical regulations as mandatory documents. *Standards prepared by the international standardization community are based on consensus. This Agreement covers also documents that are not based on consensus.* (emphasis added)

221. The European Communities does not contest that the Codex Commission is an international standardization body, and that it is a "recognized body" for purposes of the definition of a "standard" in Annex 1.2. The issue before us, rather, is one of *approval*. The definition of a "standard" refers to documents *approved* by a recognized body. Whether approval takes place by consensus, or by other methods, is not addressed in the definition, but it is addressed in the last two sentences of the Explanatory note.

227. Therefore, we uphold the Panel's conclusion, in paragraph 7.90 of the Panel Report, that the definition of a "standard" in Annex 1.2 to the *TBT Agreement* does not require approval by consensus for standards adopted by a "recognized body" of the international standardization community.

THE EUROPEAN COMMUNITIES' ARGUMENT ON THE PRODUCT COVERAGE OF CODEX STAN 94

228. We turn now to examine the European Communities' argument that Codex Stan 94 is not a "*relevant* international standard" because its product coverage is different from that of the EC Regulation.

229. In analyzing the merits of this argument, the Panel first noted that the ordinary meaning of the term "relevant" is "bearing upon or relating to the matter in hand; pertinent". The Panel reasoned that, to be a "relevant international standard", Codex Stan 94 would have to bear upon, relate to, or be pertinent to the EC Regulation.

230. [T]he European Communities argues that, although the EC Regulation deals *only* with preserved sardines—understood to mean exclusively preserved *Sardina pilchardus*—Codex Stan 94 *also covers* other preserved fish that are "sardine-type".

231. We are not persuaded by this argument. First, even if we accepted that the EC Regulation relates only to preserved *Sardina pilchardus*, which we do not, the fact remains that section 6.1.1(i) of Codex Stan 94 also relates to preserved *Sardina pilchardus*. Therefore, Codex Stan 94 can be said to bear upon, relate to, or be pertinent to the EC Regulation because both refer to preserved *Sardina pilchardus*.

232. Second, we have already concluded that, although the EC Regulation expressly mentions only *Sardina pilchardus*, it has legal consequences for other fish species that could be sold as preserved sardines, including preserved *Sardinops sagax*. Codex Stan 94 covers 20 fish species in addition to *Sardina pilchardus*. These other species also are legally affected by the exclusion in the EC Regulation. Therefore, we conclude that Codex Stan 94 bears upon, relates to, or is pertinent to the EC Regulation.

WHETHER CODEX STAN 94 WAS USED "AS A BASIS FOR" THE EC REGULATION

234. We turn now to whether Codex Stan 94 has been used "as a basis for" the EC Regulation. It will be recalled that Article 2.4 of the *TBT Agreement* requires Members to use relevant international standards "as a basis for" their technical regulations under certain circumstances. The Panel found that "the relevant international standard, i.e., Codex Stan 94, was not used as a basis for the EC Regulation". The European Communities appeals this finding.

235. The starting point of the Panel's analysis was the interpretation of section 6.1.1(ii) of Codex Stan 94, which reads as follows:

> The name of the product shall be . . .
>> (ii) "X sardines" of a country, a geographic area, the species, or the common name of the species in accordance with the law and custom of the country in which the product is sold, and in a manner not to mislead the consumer.

236. Two interpretations of section 6.1.1(ii) of Codex Stan 94 were submitted to the Panel. The European Communities argued that the phrase "the common name of the species in accordance with the law and custom of the country in which the product is sold", found in section 6.1.1(ii) of Codex Stan 94, is intended as a self-standing option for "naming", independent of the formula "X sardines", and that, under this section, "each country has the option of choosing between 'X sardines' and the common name of the species".

237. For its part, Peru contended that, under section 6.1.1(ii), the species other than *Sardina pilchardus* to which Codex Stan 94 refers may be marketed as "X sardines" where "X" is one of the four following alternatives: (1) a country; (2) a geographic area; (3) the species; or (4) the common name of the species. Thus, in Peru's view, "the common name of the species" is not a stand-alone option for naming, but rather is one of the qualifiers for naming sardines that are not *Sardina pilchardus*. Further, Peru argued that prohibiting the marketing in the European Communities of *Sardinops sagax* imported from Peru as, for example, "Peruvian sardines" would run counter to the first of the four options in section 6.1.1(ii).

238. The Panel was of the view that a textual reading of section 6.1.1(ii) favoured the interpretation advocated by Peru, adding that:

> We consider that paragraph 6.1.1(ii) of Codex Stan 94 contains four alternatives and each alternative envisages the use of the term "sardines" combined with the name of a country, name of a geographic area, name of the species or the common name of the species in accordance with the law and custom of the country in which the product is sold.

239. We agree with Peru and with the Panel that section 6.1.1(ii) permits the marketing of non-*Sardina pilchardus* as "sardines" with one of four qualifiers.

240. With this understanding of this international standard in mind, we turn to the requirement that relevant international standards must be used "as a basis for" technical regulations. We note that the Panel interpreted the word "basis" to mean "the principal constituent of anything, the fundamental principle or theory, as of a system of knowledge". In applying this interpretation of "basis" to the measure in this dispute, the Panel contrasted its interpretation of section 6.1.1(ii) of Codex Stan 94 as setting forth "four alternatives for labelling species other than *Sardina pilchardus*" that all "require the use of the term 'sardines' with a qualification", with the fact that, under the EC Regulation, "species such as *Sardinops sagax* cannot be called 'sardines' even when . . . combined with the name of a country, name of a geographic area, name of the species or the common name in accordance with the law and custom of the country in which the product is sold." In the light of this contrast, the Panel concluded that Codex Stan 94 was *not* used "as a basis for" the EC Regulation.

248. We see no need here to define in general the nature of the relationship that must exist for an international standard to serve "as a basis for" a technical regulation. Here we need only examine this measure to determine if it fulfils this obligation. In our view, it can certainly be said—at a minimum—that something cannot be considered a "basis" for something else if the two are *contradictory*. Therefore, under Article 2.4, if the technical regulation and the international standard *contradict* each other, it cannot properly be concluded that the international standard has been used "as a basis for" the technical regulation.

257. The effect of Article 2 of the EC Regulation is to prohibit preserved fish products prepared from the 20 species of fish other than *Sardina pilchardus* to which Codex Stan 94 refers—including *Sardinops sagax*—from being identified and marketed under the appellation "sardines", even with one of the four qualifiers set out in the standard. Codex Stan 94, by contrast, permits the use of the term "sardines" with any one of four qualifiers for the identification and marketing of preserved fish products prepared from 20 species of fish other than *Sardina pilchardus*. Thus, the EC Regulation and Codex Stan 94 are manifestly contradictory. To us, the existence of this contradiction confirms that Codex Stan 94 was not used "as a basis for" the EC Regulation.

THE QUESTION OF THE "INEFFECTIVENESS OR INAPPROPRIATENESS" OF CODEX STAN 94

259. We turn now to the second part of Article 2.4 of the *TBT Agreement*, which provides that Members need not use international standards as a basis for their technical regulations "when such international standards or relevant parts would be an ineffective or inappropriate means for the fulfillment of the legitimate objectives pursued".

A.   THE BURDEN OF PROOF

269. Before the Panel, the European Communities asserted that Codex Stan 94 is "ineffective or inappropriate" to fulfil the "legitimate objectives" of the EC Regulation. The Panel was of the view that the European Communities was thus asserting the affirmative of a particular claim or defence, and, therefore, that the burden of proof rests with the European Communities to demonstrate that claim. The Panel justified its position as follows: first, it reasoned that the complainant is not in a position to "spell out" the "legitimate objectives" pursued by a Member through a technical regulation; and, second, it reasoned "that the assessment of whether a relevant international standard is 'inappropriate' . . . may extend to considerations which are proper to the Member adopting or applying a technical regulation."

270. We recall that, in *United States—Measure Affecting Imports of Woven Wool Shirts and Blouses from India*, we said the following about the burden of proof:

> . . . the burden of proof rests upon the party, whether complaining or defending, who asserts the affirmative of a particular claim or defence. If that party adduces evidence sufficient to raise a presumption that what is claimed is true, the burden then shifts to the other party, who will fail unless it adduces sufficient evidence to rebut the presumption.
>
> In the context of the GATT 1994 and the *WTO Agreement*, precisely how much and precisely what kind of evidence will be required to establish such a presumption will necessarily vary from measure to measure, provision to provision, and case to case. (footnote omitted)

271. In *EC—Hormones*, we stated that characterizing a treaty provision as an "exception" does not, by itself, place the burden of proof on the respondent Member. That case concerned, among other issues, the allocation of the burden

of proof under Articles 3.1 and 3.3 of the *SPS Agreement*. Those Articles read as follows:

Article 3
Harmonization

1. To harmonize sanitary and phytosanitary measures on as wide a basis as possible, Members shall base their sanitary or phytosanitary measures on international standards, guidelines or recommendations, where they exist, except as otherwise provided for in this Agreement, and in particular in paragraph 3.

. . .

3. Members may introduce or maintain sanitary or phytosanitary measures which result in a higher level of sanitary or phytosanitary protection than would be achieved by measures based on the relevant international standards, guidelines or recommendations, if there is a scientific justification, or as a consequence of the level of sanitary or phytosanitary protection a Member determines to be appropriate in accordance with the relevant provisions of paragraphs 1 through 8 of Article 5.

272. In *EC—Hormones*, the panel assigned the burden of showing that the measure there was justified under Article 3.3 to the respondent, reasoning that Article 3.3 provides an exception to the general obligation contained in Article 3.1. The panel there was of the view that it was the *defending* party that was asserting the *affirmative* of that particular defence. We reversed the panel's finding. In particular, we stated:

The general rule in a dispute settlement proceeding requiring a complaining party to establish a *prima facie* case of inconsistency with a provision of the *SPS Agreement* before the burden of showing consistency with that provision is taken on by the defending party, is *not* avoided by simply describing that same provision as an "exception". In much the same way, merely characterizing a treaty provision as an "exception" does not by itself justify a "stricter" or "narrower" interpretation of that provision than would be warranted by examination of the ordinary meaning of the actual treaty words, viewed in context and in the light of the treaty's object and purpose, or, in other words, by applying the normal rules of treaty interpretation. (original emphasis)

275. Given the conceptual similarities between, on the one hand, Articles 3.1 and 3.3 of the *SPS Agreement* and, on the other hand, Article 2.4 of the *TBT Agreement*, we see no reason why the Panel should not have relied on the principle we articulated in *EC—Hormones* to determine the allocation of the burden of proof under Article 2.4 of the *TBT Agreement*. In *EC—Hormones*, we found that a "general rule-exception" relationship between Articles 3.1 and 3.3 of the *SPS Agreement* does not exist, with the consequence that the complainant had to establish a case of inconsistency with *both* Articles 3.1 and 3.3. We reached this conclusion as a consequence of our finding there that "Article 3.1 of the *SPS Agreement* simply excludes from its scope of application the kinds of situations covered by Article 3.3 of that Agreement". Similarly, the circumstances envisaged in the second part of Article 2.4 are excluded from the scope of application of the first part of Article 2.4. Accordingly, as with Articles 3.1 and 3.3 of the *SPS Agreement*, there is no "general rule-exception" relationship between the first and the second parts of Article 2.4. Hence, in this case, it is for Peru—as the complaining Member seeking a ruling on the inconsistency with Article 2.4 of the *TBT Agreement* of the measure applied

by the European Communities—to bear the burden of proving its claim. This burden includes establishing that Codex Stan 94 has not been used "as a basis for" the EC Regulation, as well as establishing that Codex Stan 94 is effective and appropriate to fulfil the "legitimate objectives" pursued by the European Communities through the EC Regulation.

283. We turn now to consider whether Peru effectively discharged its burden of proof under the second part of Article 2.4 of the *TBT Agreement*.

B.   WHETHER CODEX STAN 94 IS AN EFFECTIVE AND APPROPRIATE MEANS TO FULFILL THE "LEGITIMATE OBJECTIVES" PURSUED BY THE EUROPEAN COMMUNITIES THROUGH THE EC REGULATION

284. We recall that the second part of Article 2.4 of the *TBT Agreement* reads as follows:

> . . . except when such international standards or relevant parts would be an ineffective or inappropriate means for the fulfilment of the legitimate objectives pursued . . .

Before ruling on whether Peru met its burden of proof in this case, we must address, successively, the interpretation and the application of the second part of Article 2.4.

1.   *The Interpretation of the Second Part of Article 2.4*

285. The interpretation of the second part of Article 2.4 raises two questions: first, the meaning of the term "ineffective or inappropriate means"; and, second, the meaning of the term "legitimate objectives". As to the first question, we noted earlier the Panel's view that the term "ineffective or inappropriate means" refers to two questions—the question of the *effectiveness* of the measure and the question of the *appropriateness* of the measure—and that these two questions, although closely related, are different in nature. The Panel pointed out that the term "ineffective" "refers to something which is not 'having the function of accomplishing', 'having a result', or 'brought to bear', whereas [the term] 'inappropriate' refers to something which is not specially suitable', 'proper', or 'fitting'". The Panel also stated that:

> Thus, in the context of Article 2.4, an ineffective means is a means which does not have the function of accomplishing the legitimate objective pursued, whereas an inappropriate means is a means which is not specially suitable for the fulfilment of the legitimate objective pursued . . . . The question of effectiveness bears upon the *results* of the means employed, whereas the question of appropriateness relates more to the *nature* of the means employed. (original emphasis)

We agree with the Panel's interpretation.

286. As to the second question, we are of the view that the Panel was also correct in concluding that "the 'legitimate objectives' referred to in Article 2.4 must be interpreted in the context of Article 2.2", which refers also to "legitimate objectives", and includes a description of what the nature of some such objectives can be.

Two implications flow from the Panel's interpretation. First, the term "legitimate objectives" in Article 2.4, as the Panel concluded, must cover the objectives explicitly mentioned in Article 2.2, namely: "national security requirements; the prevention of deceptive practices; protection of human health or safety, animal or plant life or health, or the environment." Second, given the use of the term "*inter alia*" in Article 2.2, the objectives covered by the term "legitimate objectives" in Article 2.4 extend beyond the list of the objectives specifically mentioned in Article 2.2. Furthermore, we share the view of the Panel that the second part of Article 2.4 implies that there must be an examination and a determination on the legitimacy of the objectives of the measure.

2.   The Application of the Second Part of Article 2.4

287. With respect to the application of the second part of Article 2.4, we begin by recalling that Peru has the burden of establishing that Codex Stan 94 is an effective *and* appropriate means for the fulfillment of the "legitimate objectives" pursued by the European Communities through the EC Regulation. Those "legitimate objectives" are market transparency, consumer protection, and fair competition. To satisfy this burden of proof, Peru must, at least, have established a *prima facie* case of this claim. If Peru has succeeded in doing so, then a presumption will have been raised which the European Communities must have rebutted in order to succeed in its defense. If Peru has established a *prima facie* case, and if the European Communities has failed to rebut Peru's case effectively, then Peru will have discharged its burden of proof under Article 2.4. In such an event, Codex Stan 94 must, consistent with the European Communities' obligation under the *TBT Agreement*, be used "as a basis for" any European Communities regulation on the marketing of preserved sardines, because Codex Stan 94 will have been shown to be both effective and appropriate to fulfill the "legitimate objectives" pursued by the European Communities. Further, in such an event, as we have already determined that Codex Stan 94 was not used "as a basis for" the EC Regulation, we would then have to find as a consequence that the European Communities has acted inconsistently with Article 2.4 of the *TBT Agreement*.

288. This being so, our task is to assess whether Peru discharged its burden of showing that Codex Stan 94 is appropriate and effective to fulfil these same three "legitimate objectives". In the light of our reasoning thus far, Codex Stan 94 would be *effective* if it had the capacity to accomplish all three of these objectives, and it would be *appropriate* if it were suitable for the fulfillment of all three of these objectives.

289. We share the Panel's view that the terms "ineffective" and "inappropriate" have different meanings, and that it is conceptually possible that a measure could be effective but inappropriate, or appropriate but ineffective. This is why Peru has the burden of showing that Codex Stan 94 is both *effective* and *appropriate*. We note, however, that, in this case, a consideration of the *appropriateness* of Codex Stan 94 and a consideration of the *effectiveness* of Codex Stan 94 are interrelated—as a consequence of the nature of the objectives of the EC Regulation. The capacity of a measure to accomplish the stated objectives—its *effectiveness*—and the suitability of a measure for the fulfillment of the stated objectives—its *appropriateness*—are *both* decisively influenced by the perceptions and expectations of consumers in the European Communities relating to preserved sardine products.

290. We note that the Panel concluded that "Peru has adduced sufficient evidence and legal arguments to demonstrate that Codex Stan 94 is not ineffective or inappropriate to fulfill the legitimate objectives pursued by the EC Regulation." We have examined the analysis which led the Panel to this conclusion. We note, in particular, that the Panel made the factual finding that "it has not been established that consumers in most member States of the European Communities have always associated the common name 'sardines' exclusively with *Sardina pilchardus*". We also note that the Panel gave consideration to the contentions of Peru that, under Codex Stan 94, fish from the species *Sardinops sagax* bear a denomination that is distinct from that of *Sardina pilchardus*, and that "the very purpose of the labeling regulations set out in Codex Stan 94 for sardines of species other than *Sardina pilchardus* is to ensure market transparency". We agree with the analysis made by the Panel. Accordingly, we see no reason to interfere with the Panel's finding that Peru has adduced sufficient evidence and legal arguments to demonstrate that Codex Stan 94 meets the legal requirements of effectiveness and appropriateness set out in Article 2.4 of the *TBT Agreement*.

291. We, therefore, uphold the finding of the Panel, in paragraph 7.138 of the Panel Report, that Peru has adduced sufficient evidence and legal arguments to demonstrate that Codex Stan 94 is not "ineffective or inappropriate" to fulfil the "legitimate objectives" of the EC Regulation.

PROBLEM 6-14

France passes a law that all liqueurs must contain a minimum content of 25 percent alcohol. A French importer wishes to import a product labeled "liqueur" from Italy, which has an alcohol content of 15-20 percent, but the product is denied entry under the description as "liqueur." France argues that the purpose of the law is to protect public health as permitted under TBT Article 2.2. France argues the law will prevent a proliferation of alcohol beverages with low alcoholic content, which might induce a tolerance for alcohol among the public and lead to higher levels of alcohol consumption, resulting in various health and social problems. Is the French law consistent with Article 2.2? How else might France accomplish its objective?

PROBLEM 6-15

China passes a regulation that requires that all imported computers and handheld electronic devices that contain encryption capabilities must use encryption software that complies with China's national encryption code. Encryption software can, for example, send an e-mail message in code that can be read only with a key. China's encryption code differs from that presently used by the United States, which is based on standards now used on a worldwide basis. However, China is the midst of an all-out effort to promulgate its encryption code among its many trading partners conditioning access to the China market on the use of the code and is obtaining many adoptions. A U.S. manufacturer complains that this measure will add significant costs as new software must be developed or purchased. Is China's law consistent with TBT Article 2.1-2.5?

NOTE ON THE TBT AGREEMENT AND FOOD AND
PRODUCT LABELING STANDARDS

At this writing United States' food and product labeling requirements are under challenge in the following WTO cases.

(1) *United States—Measures Concerning the Importation, Marketing and Sale of Tuna and Tuna Products*, WT/DS381/R, Report of the Panel, Final Report circulated on September 15, 2011. Mexico challenged the U.S. labeling standards for "dolphin safe" tuna, which are specified by the Dolphin Protection Consumer Information Act, 16 U.S.C. §1385 and 50 C.F.R. §216.91. U.S. requirements for labels on tuna that assure consumers that the tuna was caught consistent with protecting dolphins do not permit "dolphin safe" labeling for tuna caught using purse seine nets set on dolphins, a common Mexican fishing method. Mexico argued that modern equipment and methods have vastly reduced dolphin mortality so that setting purse seine nets on dolphins to catch tuna is dolphin safe and in compliance with the stringent requirements of the Agreement on International Dolphin Conservation Program (AIDCP). The WTO panel ruled (one panelist dissenting) that the U.S. dolphin safe labeling requirements are technical regulations within the meaning of the TBT Agreement. The panel then ruled that Mexico had not demonstrated that the dolphin safe labeling provisions were inconsistent with TBT Article 2.1 (MFN and National Treatment) since the U.S. requirements apply the same origin-neutral requirements to all tuna products, and the U.S. provisions depend on a number of factors not related to the nationality of the product. With regard to TBT Article 2.2, the panel ruled that the objectives of the dolphin safe provisions are "legitimate," but that Mexico had demonstrated that the U.S. provisions are more restrictive than necessary by identifying a less restrictive alternative (AIDCP Certification, which the panel found to be a "relevant" international standard under TBT Article 2.4) that would achieve an equivalent level of protection to the U.S. measures. Finally, the panel ruled that the U.S. labeling provisions were lawful under TBT Article 2.4 because the proposed alternative, the AIDCP labeling standards, would not achieve U.S. objectives of protecting consumers and ensuring enhanced protection of dolphins.

On appeal the WTO Appellate Body substantially modified the panel's determinations in Appellate Body Report, *United States—Measures Concerning the Importation, Marketing and Sale of Tuna and Tuna Products*, WT/DS381/AB/R, Report of the Appellate Body, adopted on June 13, 2012. First, the Appellate Body agreed with the panel that the U.S. labeling measure under the Dolphin Protection Consumer Information Act is a technical regulation subject to the TBT Agreement. The Appellate Body stated (¶199) that, "the measure at issue sets out a single and legally mandated definition of a 'dolphin safe' tuna product and disallows the use of other labels on tuna products that do not satisfy this definition. In doing so, the US measure prescribes in a broad and exhaustive manner the conditions that apply for making any assertion on a tuna product as to its 'dolphin safety', regardless of what 'dolphin safe' means in relation to tuna products."

Second, the Appellate Body reversed the finding of the panel that the U.S. labeling measure was not inconsistent with TBT Agreement Article 2.1. Since the parties did not appeal the issue of "like product" under Article 2.1, the Appellate Body focused on the issue of whether the U.S. measure infringed the "treatment no less favourable" requirement of Article 2.1. As to the meaning of this term, the

Appellate Body stated (¶221) that the crucial inquiry is "an analysis of whether the contested measure modifies the conditions of competition to the detriment of imported products." The Appellate Body noted (¶216) that the burden of proof "rests upon the party who asserts the affirmative of a particular claim or defence." Applying this analysis, the Appellate Body cited (¶239) the panel's findings that the U.S. labeling measure has modified the conditions of competition in the market to the detriment of Mexican tuna, and that the detrimental impact flowed from the measure at issue. The Appellate Body therefore ruled (¶284) that Mexico had carried its burden of showing *prima facie* that the labeling results in less favourable treatment for Mexican tuna, and that "the question before us is . . . whether the United States has demonstrated that this difference in labeling conditions is a legitimate regulatory distinction, and hence whether the detrimental impact of the measure stems exclusively from such a distinction rather than reflecting discrimination." The Appellate Body concluded (¶298) that the United States had not met its burden to show that the labeling difference requirements applicable to tuna caught by setting on dolphins (the Mexican fishing method) as opposed to labeling requirements for tuna caught by other fishing methods is sufficiently "calibrated" to the risks to dolphins arising from different fishing methods. Thus the U.S. labeling requirements were inconsistent with TBT Article 2.1.

Third, the Appellate Body considered the panel's determination as to TBT Article 2.2. An assessment whether a technical regulation is "more trade restrictive than necessary" under this article involves, according to the Appellate Body (¶322), "(1) the degree of contribution made by the measure to the legitimate objective at issue; (2) the trade restrictiveness of the measure; and (3) the nature of the risks at issue and the gravity of the consequences that would arise from non-fulfillment of the objective(s) pursued." The Appellate Body found (¶323) that to show that a technical regulation is inconsistent with Article 2.2 "the complainant must prove its claim that the challenged measure constitutes an unnecessary obstacle to international trade. In order to make a prima facie case, the complainant must establish that the challenged measure is more trade restrictive than necessary to achieve the contribution it makes to the legitimate objectives. In making its prima facie case, a complainant may also seek to identify a possible alternative measure that is less trade restrictive, makes an equivalent contribution to the legitimate objective, and is reasonably available. It is then for the respondent to rebut the complainant's prima facie case." Applying this analysis, the Appellate Body ruled (¶330) that the less trade-restrictive alternative identified by Mexico—the AIDCP label—would be confusing to consumers and "would allow more tuna harvested in conditions that adversely affect dolphins to be labeled 'dolphin safe.'" Thus the Appellate Body ruled that the U.S. labeling measure was not inconsistent with TBT Article 2.2.

Fourth, the Appellate Body handed down a significant interpretation of Article 2.4 of the TBT Agreement. The Appellate Body agreed (¶401) with the argument of the United States that the AIDCP dolphin safe definition and certification does not qualify as a relevant international standard for purposes of Article 2.4. The Appellate Body emphasized (¶382) that to be a relevant international standard the standard setting body must be open to all WTO members on a non-discriminatory basis. Because the AIDCP operated on an invitation basis, this body did not qualify as "open" and therefore did not qualify as an "international standardizing organization" under Article 2.4. Thus the Appellate Body affirmed (¶407) the panel's finding that the U.S. labeling measure was not inconsistent with Article 2.4, but on different grounds.

The Appellate Body (¶408) recommended that the United States bring its labeling measure into compliance with the TBT Agreement.

(2) *United States—Certain Country of Origin Labelling (COOL) Requirements,* WT/DS384, 386/R, Report of the Panel, Final Report circulated on November 18, 2011. Canada and Mexico challenged labeling provisions in the U.S. Farm Bill, 2008, which sets out country-of-origin labeling requirements for muscle cuts of meat. For a cut of meat to be labeled "product of the U.S." the animal must have been born, raised, and slaughtered in the United States, a requirement that creates problems for ranchers in the United States and abroad—if an animal is born in Mexico, for example, and raised and slaughtered in the United States, it must be labeled "product of the U.S. and Mexico." In 2010, some 2.3 million head of cattle and 5.7 million head of hogs were imported but raised in the United States. Such animals must be processed separately from U.S. cattle, raising costs for slaughterhouse owners who then seek lower prices from ranchers selling the animals. The panel concluded first that the COOL regulation is a technical regulation under TBT Annex 1.1. The panel then ruled that COOL (1) is inconsistent with TBT Article 2.1 in that it creates an incentive in favor of processing exclusively domestic livestock and a disincentive against handling imported livestock; and (2) is inconsistent with TBT Article 2.2 in that it fails to convey meaningful origin information.

In *United States—Certain Country of Origin Labelling (COOL) Requirements,* WT/DS384/AB/R and WT/DS386/AB/R (adopted July 23, 2012), the Appellate Body upheld the panel's finding of less favorable treatment under TBT Article 2.1, the National Treatment obligation. But the Appellate Body stated that "Article 2.1 should not be read to mean that any distinctions, in particular ones that are based exclusively on such particular product characteristics or on particular process and production methods, would per se constitute less favorable treatment under Article 2.1." The Appellate Body ruled (¶¶267-269) that guidance for interpreting the phrase "less favorable treatment" may be found in the GATT Article III:4 jurisprudence. The complaining party has the burden of proof of showing less favorable treatment. The Appellate Body then upheld (¶349) the panel's finding on the different ground that the COOL measure modifies the conditions of competition to the detriment of imported livestock, and this detrimental impact does not stem from any legitimate regulatory distinction. With regard to TBT Article 2.2, the Appellate Body said that some trade restrictiveness is allowed, and the question of inconsistency involves a weighing and balancing process: a comparison of the trade restrictiveness and the degree of achievement of the objective by the measure at issue in comparison with possible alternative measures that are reasonably available. Again, the complaining party has the burden of proof on this issue. The Appellate Body upheld the panel's finding that consumer information on origin is a legitimate objective. But the Appellate Body found that the panel had erred in finding that the COOL measure did not fulfill the identified objective because it failed to convey meaningful information to consumers. Accordingly, the Appellate Body reversed (¶491) the panel's ruling under TBT Article 2.2 and was unable to complete the analysis as to whether there was an inconsistency between the COOL measure and Article 2.2.

———————

National labeling standards are no longer immune from scrutiny under international law. Is this a salutary development?

V. State Trading Enterprises

State trading enterprises refer to enterprises that benefit from special or exclusive privileges. *See* GATT Article XVII:1(a). One example of such special privileges is monopoly control over an entire sector of goods. A state trading enterprise can be an entity that is wholly or partially owned by a government or can even be a private enterprise. State ownership is not the decisive element. The decisive factor is whether the state gives the enterprise privileges that can distort the market.

State trading enterprises are most often found in state-controlled economies, but not exclusively so. In China, there are over 1,000 state-owned enterprises, but there are also many state-owned enterprises in South Korea and Japan and in other countries. Because state trading enterprises might be given monopoly control over an entire sector of goods, they can easily distort trade and create barriers to trade.

The barriers created by the state trading enterprise differ from the other non-tariff trade barriers that we have considered in this Chapter. All of the other non-tariff trade barriers are enforced by customs at the border. State trading enterprises, however, can create trade barriers that are similar to measures enforced at the border. For example, a state trading enterprise might refuse to purchase any foreign goods at all, creating what is a de facto total ban on imports, or to purchase only a certain amount of goods, creating a de facto quota. We have chosen to study state enterprises in this Chapter because they are among the most common form of non-tariff trade barriers.

Read GATT Article XVII—State Trading Enterprises in the Documents Supplement.

The basic approach of the GATT/WTO toward state trading companies is to accept their existence but to require them to behave as private companies would in the international trade in goods. State trading enterprises are held to three overriding substantive norms in the GATT/WTO system: (1) to act in a manner consistent with the general principles of non-discrimination prescribed in the GATT for governmental measures concerning imports and exports (Article XVII:1(a)); (2) to make purchases or sales solely in accordance with commercial considerations (Article XVII:1(b)); and (3) to afford other enterprises adequate opportunity to compete for such purchases or sales (Article XVII:1(b)).

PROBLEM 6-16

China's State Tobacco Monopoly (STM) controls the wholesale distribution of cigarettes, among other aspects of the trade. Wholesale distribution channels, under the control of the STM, sell cigarettes to large and small retailers all over the country. American tobacco companies, which export their cigarettes to China, find that counterfeit cigarettes are able to infiltrate these wholesale distribution channels through various means (such as bribes paid to STM officials). Once inside the wholesale distribution chain, the counterfeits are sold (along with genuine American-made cigarettes) to retailers who sell them to consumers. U.S. tobacco companies are very concerned because the sale of counterfeit cigarettes in China (and on a global scale) is a major business problem. A number of U.S. tobacco companies believe that a key strategy in controlling the trade in counterfeit cigarettes in China is to control the wholesale distribution channels on their own in order to prevent the infiltration of counterfeits.

An industry group of U.S. tobacco companies believes that now that China has joined the WTO, China is bound by GATT Article XVII, which applies to all state trading enterprises, including the STM. The tobacco companies argue that Article XVII requires all state enterprises to behave as commercial actors. Under GATT Article XVII:1(b), China's STM "shall afford the enterprises of the other Members adequate opportunity, in accordance with customary business practice, to compete for participation in such purchases or sales." The U.S. tobacco companies argue that this provision requires China to allow them to set up their own wholesale distribution channels, which would help prevent the penetration of counterfeits into the distribution channels from which the counterfeits will ultimately reach consumers. Assume that China is under no other WTO obligations to open up the distribution sector for cigarettes. Is this a good argument? Read the following case.

Canada — Measures Relating to Exports of Wheat and Treatment of Imported Grain
Report of the Appellate Body, adopted on September 27, 2004
WT/DS276/AB/R

[The United States filed this complaint concerning Canada's state trading enterprise relating to wheat, the Canadian Wheat Board (CWB). Under its governing law, the CWB has (1) the exclusive right to purchase and sell Western Canadian wheat for export and domestic human consumption; (2) the right to set the initial price payable for such wheat; and (3) the right to guarantee payment to producers of such wheat. The CWB benefited from a government guarantee of its borrowing and from government-guaranteed credit sales to foreign buyers. The United States maintained that this regime was inconsistent with GATT Article XVII. On these points, the Panel held for Canada.]

RELATIONSHIP BETWEEN SUBPARAGRAPHS (a) AND (b) OF ARTICLE XVII:1 OF THE GATT 1994

77. The United States' appeal relates to the Panel's *interpretation of subparagraph (b)* of Article XVII:1; to the Panel's *application* of this interpretation *to the CWB Export Regime*; and to the Panel's ultimate finding that the United States had not established any inconsistency with the principles of subparagraphs (a) or (b) of Article XVII:1 of the GATT 1994.

84. Before assessing the approach taken by the Panel in this case, we consider the relationship between the first two subparagraphs of Article XVII:1, which provide:

(*a*) Each Member undertakes that if it establishes or maintains a State enterprise, wherever located, or grants to any enterprise, formally or in effect, exclusive or special privileges, such enterprise shall, in its purchases or sales involving either imports or exports, act in a manner consistent with the general principles of non-discriminatory treatment prescribed in this Agreement for governmental measures affecting imports or exports by private traders.

(*b*) The provisions of subparagraph (*a*) of this paragraph shall be understood to require that such enterprises shall, having due regard to the other provisions of this Agreement, make any such purchases or sales solely in accordance with commercial considerations, including price, quality, availability, marketability, transportation and other conditions of purchase or sale, and shall afford the enterprises of the other Members adequate opportunity, in accordance with customary business practice, to compete for participation in such purchases or sales.

85. Subparagraph (a) of Article XVII:1 contains a number of different elements, including both an acknowledgement and an obligation. It recognizes that Members may establish or maintain State enterprises or grant exclusive or special privileges to private enterprises, but requires that, *if they do so*, such enterprises must, when they are involved in certain types of transactions ("purchases or sales involving either imports or exports"), comply with a specific requirement. That requirement is to act consistently with certain principles contained in the GATT 1994 ("general principles of non-discriminatory treatment . . . for governmental measures affecting imports or exports by private traders"). Subparagraph (a) seeks to ensure that a Member cannot, through the creation or maintenance of a State enterprise or the grant of exclusive or special privileges to any enterprise, engage in or facilitate conduct that would be condemned as discriminatory under the GATT 1994 if such conduct were undertaken directly by the Member itself. In other words, subparagraph (a) is an "anti-circumvention" provision.

86. Each of the elements of subparagraph (a) raises, in turn, a number of interpretative questions, including: (i) *which enterprises* are subject to the requirement set forth in subparagraph (a); (ii) *what transactions* qualify as "purchases or sales involving either imports or exports"; and (iii) *which principles* of the GATT 1994 fall under the "general principles of non-discriminatory treatment prescribed in this Agreement for governmental measures affecting imports or exports by private traders". The first two of these interpretative questions define the scope of application of the requirement in subparagraph (a). The third question goes to the nature of the requirement itself.

88. In this case, the Panel did not consider which types of discrimination are covered by the reference to "the principles of non-discriminatory treatment" in Article XVII:1(a). Nor has any participant in this appeal asked us to do so.

89. Instead, the question we are asked to consider is how subparagraph (a) relates to subparagraph (b) of Article XVII:1. In our view, the answer to that inquiry is not found in the text of subparagraph (a). Rather, the words that bear most directly on the relationship between the first two paragraphs of Article XVII:1 are found in the opening phrase of subparagraph (b), which states that the "provisions of subparagraph (*a*) of this paragraph *shall be understood to require* that such enterprises shall . . .". (emphasis added) This phrase makes it abundantly clear that the remainder of subparagraph (b) is dependent upon the content of subparagraph (a), and operates to clarify the scope of the requirement not to discriminate in subparagraph (a). We note, particularly, the use of the words "shall be understood". Elsewhere in the GATT 1994, and throughout the covered agreements, these words are used, together with the verb "to mean", to define the scope or to clarify the *meaning* of the term that precedes it. In our view, the words "shall be understood" serve the same purpose when used together with the verb "to require", that is, to

define the scope of or to clarify the *requirement* in the preceding provision. Thus, the opening phrase in subparagraph (b) of Article XVII:1 supports Canada's view that the *principal source* of the relevant obligation(s) in Article XVII:1(a) and (b) is, indeed, found in "[t]he provisions of subparagraph (*a*)".

90. Subparagraph (b) also refers to "*such* enterprises", which can mean only the STEs defined in subparagraph (a). In addition, subparagraph (b) twice refers to "*such* purchases or sales". It is clear that the word "such" in this phrase must refer to the purchases and sales identified in subparagraph (a), namely the "purchases or sales [of STEs] involving either imports or exports". Thus, the word "such" in subparagraph (b) confirms the link between the two subparagraphs, and ties the content of subparagraph (b) back to subparagraph (a).

91. Having examined the text of subparagraphs (a) and (b) of Article XVII:1, it is our view that subparagraph (b), by defining and clarifying the requirement in subparagraph (a), is dependent upon, rather than separate and independent from, subparagraph (a).

106. Our conclusions regarding the relationship between subparagraphs (a) and (b) imply that a panel confronted with a claim that an STE has acted inconsistently with Article XVII:1 will need to begin its analysis of that claim under subparagraph (a), because it is that provision which contains the principal obligation of Article XVII:1, namely the requirement not to act in a manner contrary to the "general principles of non-discriminatory treatment prescribed in [the GATT 1994] for governmental measures affecting imports or exports by private traders." At the same time, because both subparagraphs (a) and (b) define the scope of that non-discrimination obligation, we would expect that panels, in most if not all cases, would not be in a position to make any finding of violation of Article XVII:1 until they have properly interpreted and applied both provisions.

Affording Other Members' Enterprises Adequate Opportunity to Compete for Participation in Purchases or Sales

152. Before the Panel, the United States argued that the second clause of subparagraph (b), which requires STEs to "afford the enterprises of the other Members adequate opportunity . . . to compete for participation in such purchases or sales" should in this case be interpreted to mean that the CWB must offer the requisite opportunity to "any enterprise that is competing for participation in CWB wheat sales, including enterprises competing to purchase wheat from the CWB (*i.e.*, wheat buyers) and those enterprises selling wheat in the same market as the CWB (*i.e.*, wheat sellers)." The Panel, however, was:

> . . . unable to accept the United States' view that, in the case of an export STE, the "enterprises of the other [Members]" may include enterprises selling the same product as that offered for sale by the export STE in question (*i.e.*, the competitors of the export STE).

153. The United States appeals this finding by the Panel. According to the United States, the Panel failed to interpret the term "enterprises" according to its ordinary meaning, read in its context and in the light of the object and purpose of the GATT 1994. The United States asserts that the Panel's incorrect interpretative

approach led it to the erroneous conclusion that this term referred to enterprises that wish to *buy* from an STE, but not to enterprises that wish to *sell* in competition with an STE. In so finding, the Panel adopted an interpretation that, according to the United States, "impermissibly narrows the reach of Article XVII's disciplines". The United States requests us to reverse this interpretation and to find that the term "enterprises" in the second clause of subparagraph (b) includes both buyers and sellers.

154. The second clause of Article XVII:1(b) provides:

> [the provisions of subparagraph (a) are to be understood to require that STEs] shall afford the enterprises of the other Members adequate opportunity, in accordance with customary business practice, to compete for participation in such purchases or sales.

155. The United States correctly points out that the ordinary meaning of the word "enterprises", which is used in this phrase, includes both enterprises that buy and enterprises that sell. This observation alone, however, does not resolve the interpretative question raised. The meaning of the word must also be examined within its context, particularly the phrase "compete for participation in such purchases or sales".

156. In the abstract, competition to participate in purchases and sales could include competition to participate as a buyer, as a seller, or both. However, the clause under examination does not refer, in the abstract, to *any* purchases and sales. Rather, it refers to "*such* purchases or sales", repeating the phrase found in the first clause of subparagraph (b). As discussed in our analysis above, this phrase in subparagraph (b) of Article XVII:1 refers back to the activities identified in subparagraph (a), namely the purchases and sales of an STE involving imports or exports.

157. In other words, the second clause of subparagraph (b) refers to purchases and sales transactions where: (i) one of the parties involved in the transaction is an STE; and (ii) the transaction involves imports to or exports from the Member maintaining the STE. Thus, the requirement to afford an adequate opportunity to compete for participation (*i.e.*, taking part with others) in "such" purchases and sales (import or export transactions involving an STE) must refer to the opportunity to become the STE's counterpart in the transaction, *not* to an opportunity to replace the STE as a participant in the transaction. If it were otherwise, the transaction would no longer be the type of transaction described by the phrase "*such* purchases or sales" in the second clause of Article XVII:1(b), because it would not involve an STE as a party. Thus, in transactions involving two parties, one of whom is an STE seller, the word "enterprises" in the second clause of Article XVII:1(b) can refer *only* to buyers.

[The Appellate Body upheld the Panel's ruling that Canada complied with Article XVII.]

NOTES AND QUESTIONS

State trading enterprises that are subject to Article XVII are also subject to: (1) the MFN principle in GATT Article I; (2) the National Treatment principle contained in GATT Article III; (3) the general prohibition on quotas contained in GATT XI; and (4) the general norms applicable to subsidies and dumping, which we consider in Chapter 10.

7 General Exceptions: Trade and Civil Society

I. Introduction

The previous two Chapters considered barriers to trade in goods in the form of tariffs (Chapter 5) and non-tariff barriers (Chapter 6) and their discipline under the GATT. This Chapter considers exceptions to the trade in goods and their treatment under the GATT. Both barriers and exceptions limit trade, but they are viewed differently. The WTO recognizes that tariffs and non-tariff barriers generally serve unjustified and illegitimate purposes—trade protectionism—and that such barriers are to be reduced or eliminated to the fullest extent possible. By contrast, exceptions to trade serve legitimate purposes and are justified because they protect other core instrumental values, including protection of the environment, human health and safety, and food safety. As trade becomes linked more frequently with civil society issues, some exceptions are being expanded through WTO decisions recognizing their growing importance.

In this Chapter we consider the most important exceptions to trade justified by social and civil society issues. Non-trade concerns creating exceptions have arisen most often in cases involving the trade in goods under the GATT, which is our concern here. After a brief look at GATT XXI, the security exception article, we read important cases involving GATT Article XX, which contains general exceptions to the GATT obligations. We consider in turn the following linkage issues under GATT Article XX:

- Environmental protection
- Product safety
- Food safety
- Waste minimization and disposal
- Culture
- Climate change
- Workers' rights and human rights

We begin by setting out the provisions of GATT Article XX, the central focus of this Chapter.

Article XX
General Exceptions

Subject to the requirement that such measures are not applied in a manner which would constitute a means of arbitrary or unjustifiable discrimination between countries where the same conditions prevail, or a disguised restriction on international trade, nothing in this Agreement shall be construed to prevent the adoption or enforcement by any contracting party of measures:

(a)   necessary to protect public morals;
(b)   necessary to protect human, animal or plant life or health;
(c)   relating to the importations or exportations of gold or silver;
(d)   necessary to secure compliance with laws or regulations which are not inconsistent with the provisions of this Agreement, including those relating to customs enforcement, the enforcement of monopolies operated under paragraph 4 of Article II and Article XVII, the protection of patents, trade marks and copyrights, and the prevention of deceptive practices;
(e)   relating to the products of prison labour;
(f)   imposed for the protection of national treasures of artistic, historic or archaeological value;
(g)   relating to the conservation of exhaustible natural resources if such measures are made effective in conjunction with restrictions on domestic production or consumption.

Article XX requires a two-step analysis: The measure must (1) fall within one of the enumerated exceptions (a)-(g) and (2) satisfy the introductory section of Article XX known as the "chapeau." While the chapeau looks like boilerplate that is too general to have any effect, we will find that this is not the case.

NOTES AND QUESTIONS

1. The items listed in Article XX were initially agreed in 1947. Which were the most important at that time? Which have become important only recently?

2. The term "necessary" appears in subsections (a), (b), and (d) of Article XX. We will see that the term has different meanings in each of these subsections.

NOTE ON GATT ARTICLE XXI ON SECURITY EXCEPTIONS

Many of the WTO agreements contain exceptions for national security: GATT Article XXI; TRIPS Article 72; and GATS Article XIV, for example. These exceptions mean, in theory, that trade in goods, technology, and services can be limited for reasons of national security. However, the scope of these exceptions is unclear, as is the matter of whether an issue of national security is even justiciable in the WTO dispute resolution system. The only cases filed on this matter were under the GATT Article XXI, and each time definitive interpretations were avoided. For a detailed review, see Michael J. Hahn, *Vital Interests and the Law of GATT: An Analysis of GATT's Security Exception*, 12 Mich. J. Int'l L. 558 (1991); Matsushita et al., *The World Trade Organization: Law, Practice and Policy* 594-598 (2d ed. 2006).

GATT Article XXI contains three subsections: Article XXI(a) is phrased subjectively and appears to be open-ended. Article XXI(c) is the clearest since it depends on objective action, an obligation imposed by the United Nations Charter. Article XXI(b) is the most controversial and is really three separate exceptions. But the chapeau of Article XXI(b) is phrased in subjective terms similar to the open-ended Article XXI(a) — "which it considers necessary." The most important subparagraph in the Article is undoubtedly Article XXI(b)(iii), which permits actions taken "in time of war or other emergency in international relations." These two concepts—war and emergency in international relations—have some objective content. This provision was obliquely involved in two cases— *United States and Nicaragua: United States—Import of Sugar from Nicaragua,* GATT B.I.S.D. (31st Supp.) 67, Report of the GATT Panel, adopted on March 13, 1984; and *United States—Trade Measures Affecting Nicaragua,* GATT Doc. L/6053, GATT Panel Report, unadopted, October 13, 1986—but in each case the United States maintained that its dispute was outside the purview of the GATT, and the GATT panels did not deal directly with the issue.

The most important national security case filed under GATT Article XXI was an EU complaint against the United States to challenge the Cuban Liberty and Democratic Solidarity Act of 1996, commonly known as the Helms-Burton Act, 22 U.S.C. §§6021 *et seq.,* which imposed additional trade restrictions that tightened the longstanding U.S. embargo of trade with Cuba. The EU complaint in May 1996 alleged that U.S. trade restrictions on goods of Cuban origin and other measures violated various provisions of the GATT. The DSB of the WTO established a panel to hear the EU complaint on November 20, 1996, but after President Clinton used his authority to suspend applicable provisions of the act, the EU requested that the panel suspend its work. The panel's authority lapsed on April 22, 1998, pursuant to Article 12.12 of the DSU.

Why does it appear that the GATT/WTO appears reluctant to decide issues concerning the national security exception under Article XXI?

II. *Environmental Protection*

When the WTO was created in 1994, the members adopted, in the first paragraph to the Preamble to the Agreement Establishing the World Trade Organization, a recital that world trade rules should foster "the optimal use of the world's resources in accordance with the objective of sustainable development, seeking both to protect and preserve the environment and enhance the means for doing so." In addition, the members approved the creation of a WTO Committee on Trade and Environment. The Work Program of the Committee focuses on examining a number of linkages between trade and the environment including (1) the relationship between the WTO agreements and Multilateral Environmental Agreements; (2) environmental requirements for products, including packaging, labeling, recycling standards, and regulations; (3) trade rules requiring transparency (i.e., disclosure of trade measures with environmental impacts and environmental measures with trade impacts); (4) barriers created by environmental measures to market access for exports from developing countries and the potential environmental benefits of removing trade restrictions and distortions; (5) the relationship between the environment and trade in technology and in services; and (7) the WTO's relationship with non-governmental and intergovernmental organizations. As of this writing, the Trade and Environment Committee has not come to any agreement on any of these issues.

The WTO's explicit acknowledgement of the linkage between environment and trade contrasts sharply with that of the GATT, which was not much concerned with environmental issues. The GATT Working Group on Environmental Measures and International Trade, established in 1971, did not even meet for over twenty years. Beginning in 1993, however, two infamous GATT decisions ignited a storm of controversy over the GATT's treatment of environmental concerns. In *United States—Restrictions on Imports of Tuna*, GATT B.I.S.D. (39th Supp.) 155, GATT Panel Report, unadopted, September 3, 1991 (*Tuna/Dolphin I*), a GATT panel declared a U.S. embargo on tuna caught by fishing methods causing high dolphin mortality to be illegal. The United States had unilaterally instituted an import ban against yellowfin tuna that were caught using methods that also killed dolphins, a species protected under the federal Marine Mammal Protection Act (MMPA). Mexico challenged the ban before the GATT on the ground that the ban violated GATT Article XI:1, the provision calling for the general elimination of quotas or import bans. The United States sought to justify the ban under the National Treatment principle set forth in GATT Article III:1 and III:4. The United States argued that nothing in Article III precludes trade restrictions targeted at production, process, and methods (PPMs) for obtaining products so long as the restrictions were applied equally to imports and domestic products. The GATT panel rejected the U.S. argument on the grounds that Article III:1 and Article III:4 permit only regulations relating to products as such and not to PPMs. The MMPA regulations concerned harvesting techniques that could not possibly affect the physical characteristics of tuna as a product; therefore, the ban on tuna could not be justified. This holding was reiterated by a second GATT panel in *United States—Restrictions on Imports of Tuna*, DS29/R, GATT Panel Report, unadopted, June 16, 1994 (*Tuna/Dolphin II*), which involved the legality of a secondary embargo of tuna products from countries that processed tuna caught by the offending countries. The *Tuna Dolphin II* panel rejected the ban in even stronger terms.

Both *Tuna/Dolphin* panels also concluded that the exceptions contained in GATT Article XX(b) and XX(g) could not justify the U.S. ban. As to Article XX(b), both panels held that the ban failed the "necessary" test. They rejected the U.S. argument that "necessary" means "needed." The panel stated that "necessary" means that no other reasonable alternative exists and that a contracting party is bound to use, among any available measures, that which entails the least degree of inconsistency with the meaning of Article XX(b). *See Tuna/Dolphin I* at ¶¶5.26-5.29 and *Tuna/Dolphin II* at ¶¶5.34-5.39. Both panels concluded that Article XX(g) was not applicable; they found that the terms "relating to" and "in conjunction with" in Article XX(g) meant "primarily aimed at" and held that unilateral measures to force other countries to change conservation policies cannot satisfy the "primarily aimed at" standard. *See Tuna/Dolphin I* at ¶¶5.30-5.34 and *Tuna/Dolphin II at* ¶¶5.21-5.27.

The *Tuna/Dolphin* reports were never adopted by the GATT contracting parties, so neither has official standing today, but, even without official status they outraged environmentalists at the time. The *Tuna/Dolphin* cases suggested that the GATT/WTO is concerned with products, but not with PPMs, the way a product is produced, manufactured, harvested, or obtained. However, the environment can be damaged either if (1) certain products (i.e., animals, plants, and other parts of the environment) are destroyed through capture and consumption or if (2) certain PPMs that are used to capture animals, plants, or other products have the side effect of harming the environment, even if the PPMs do not harm the animals, plants, or products themselves. Environmentalists argued that by excluding PPMs, the WTO had left the door open to destruction of everything from dolphins to rain forests. Trade specialists countered that allowing the regulation of PPMs would open the door to any trade restriction that any country wanted to employ because it objected to the policies of another country. For example, Country E might be opposed to eating beef for religious reasons and place trade sanctions on Country F for permitting the slaughter of cattle using techniques that Country E found objectionable. But a second group of trade specialists found a reason to support the regulation of PPMs for competition reasons. This group argued that countries that disregard environmental standards, health and safety laws, and workers' rights are able to cut costs to gain a competitive advantage. This group argued that countries should be able to prohibit imports from any country that does not have standards similar to that of the importing country in order to level the playing field.

The GATT rule taking a hard line against all PPM import restrictions not based on product characteristics has been modified under recent WTO cases. The WTO has reshaped the scope of the exception contained in GATT Article XX(g) especially in two cases we now consider, the *U.S. — Gasoline* case and the *U.S. Shrimp/Turtle* case. In conjunction with reading these cases, consider the following problems.

PROBLEM 7-1

To protect the limited supply of yellow fin tuna, in high demand by Japanese consumers, the Japanese government encourages the establishment of domestic tuna farms, imposes a restriction on the domestic fishing industry limiting the fishing season to three months, and institutes a ban on all imports. Is this lawful under Article XX?

PROBLEM 7-2

The people of Country J have a long cultural tradition of showing great respect for animal life. Country J has strict domestic laws that regulate the killing of animals for food. The methods are complex and designed to alleviate suffering as much as possible. Country J has strict penalties for anyone who violates these laws. Country J has also banned all meat products that do not follow their own methods of killing animals. The practical result of J's laws is a complete ban on all imported meat. Based on the readings so far, is this lawful under Article XX?

———————

The cases that follow below involve the use of environmental restrictions on trade in goods under Article XX(g): the exception "relating to the conservation of natural resources if such measures are made effective in conjunction with restrictions on domestic production or consumption."

United States—Standards for Reformulated and Conventional Gasoline
Report of the Appellate Body, adopted on May 20, 1996
WT/DS2/AB/R

[This case concerned the 1990 amendments to the U.S. Clean Air Act, which directed the U.S. Environmental Protection Agency (EPA) to promulgate new regulations concerning the composition of gasoline. The new regulations were adopted to reduce vehicle emissions of toxic air pollutants and ozone-forming volatile organic compounds in order to improve air quality. The 1990 amendments directed the EPA to use the quality of 1990 gasoline as a baseline to set standards for both future reformulated and conventional gasoline. The EPA's final rule establishing the 1990 baselines was the subject of this dispute. The issue concerned whether the EPA guidelines, which applied to both domestic refiners and foreign refiners of gasoline discriminated against gasoline imported from foreign refiners.

In respect of both reformulated gasoline and conventional gasoline, the 1990 baselines established a two tier system for domestic refiners: (1) domestic refiners were permitted to use an individual baseline representing the quality of gasoline produced by that refiner in 1990 or (2) a statutory baseline established by the EPA. All foreign refiners, however, were required to use the EPA statutory baselines. Ultimately, the EPA's May 1994 proposal never entered into force, as the United States Congress enacted legislation in September 1994 denying the funding necessary for its implementation. However, in the meantime, Brazil and Venezuela, the complaining parties, claimed that the Gasoline Rule was discriminatory against foreign oil refiners. The WTO panel agreed, finding that the Rule was inconsistent with the National Treatment Principle contained in GATT Article III:4 and not justified under GATT Article XX(g). On appeal, the Appellate Body first considered whether the EPA regulations satisfied Article XX(g) and then whether the EPA regulations also satisfied the chapeau of Article XX.]

ARTICLE XX(g)

[The Appellate Body began by parsing the language of Article XX(g) set forth above.] The ordinary or natural meaning of "made effective" when used in connection with a measure—a governmental act or regulation—may be seen to refer to such measure being "operative", as "in force", or as having "come into effect." Similarly, the phrase "in conjunction with" may be read quite plainly as "together with" or "jointly with." Taken together, the second clause of Article XX(g) appears to us to refer to governmental measures like the baseline establishment rules being promulgated or brought into effect together with restrictions on domestic production or consumption of natural resources. Put in a slightly different manner, we believe that the clause "if such measures are made effective in conjunction with restrictions on domestic product or consumption" is appropriately read as a requirement that the measures concerned impose restrictions, not just in respect of imported gasoline but also with respect to domestic gasoline. The clause is a requirement of *even-handedness* in the imposition of restrictions, in the name of conservation, upon the production or consumption of exhaustible natural resources.

There is, of course, no textual basis for requiring identical treatment of domestic and imported products. Indeed, where there is identity of treatment—constituting real, not merely formal, equality of treatment—it is difficult to see how inconsistency with Article III:4 would have arisen in the first place. On the other hand, if no restrictions on domestically-produced like products are imposed at all, and all limitations are placed upon imported products alone, the measure cannot be accepted as primarily or even substantially designed for implementing conservationist goals. The measure would simply be naked discrimination for protecting locally-produced goods.

In the present appeal, the baseline establishment rules affect both domestic gasoline and imported gasoline, providing for—generally speaking—individual baselines for domestic refiners and blenders and statutory baselines for importers. Thus, restrictions on the consumption or depletion of clean air by regulating the domestic production of "dirty" gasoline are established jointly with corresponding restrictions with respect to imported gasoline. That imported gasoline has been determined to have been accorded "less favourable treatment" than the domestic gasoline in terms of Article III:4, is not material for purposes of analysis under Article XX(g). It might also be noted that the second clause of Article XX(g) speaks disjunctively of "domestic production *or* consumption."

THE INTRODUCTORY PROVISIONS OF ARTICLE XX OF THE GENERAL AGREEMENT: APPLYING THE CHAPEAU OF THE GENERAL EXCEPTIONS

Having concluded, in the preceding section, that the baseline establishment rules of the Gasoline Rule fall within the terms of Article XX(g), we come to the question of whether those rules also meet the requirements of the chapeau of Article XX. In order that the justifying protection of Article XX may be extended to it, the measure at issue must not only come under one or another of the particular exceptions—paragraphs (a) to (j)—listed under Article XX; it must also satisfy the requirements imposed by the opening clauses of Article XX. The analysis is, in other words, two-tiered: first, provisional justification by reason of characterization of the measure under XX(g); second, further appraisal of the same measure under the introductory clauses of Article XX.

The chapeau by its express terms addresses, not so much the questioned measure or its specific contents as such, but rather the manner in which that measure is applied. The chapeau is animated by the principle that while the exceptions of Article XX may be invoked as a matter of legal right, they should not be so applied as to frustrate or defeat the legal obligations of the holder of the right under the substantive rules of the *General Agreement*. If those exceptions are not to be abused or misused, the measures falling within the particular exceptions must be applied reasonably, with due regard both to the legal duties of the party claiming the exception and the legal rights of the other parties concerned.

The burden of demonstrating that a measure provisionally justified as being within one of the exceptions set out in the individual paragraphs of Article XX rests on the party invoking the exception. That is, of necessity, a heavier task than that involved in showing that an exception, such as Article XX(g), encompasses the measure at issue.

The chapeau, it will be seen, prohibits such application of a measure at issue (otherwise falling within the scope of Article XX(g)) as would constitute

(a) "arbitrary discrimination" (between countries where the same conditions prevail);
(b) "unjustifiable discrimination" (with the same qualifier); or
(c) "disguised restriction" on international trade.

"Arbitrary discrimination", "unjustifiable discrimination" and "disguised restriction" on international trade may be read side-by-side; they impart meaning to one another. It is clear to us that "disguised restriction" includes disguised *discrimination* in international trade. It is equally clear that *concealed* or *unannounced* restriction or discrimination in international trade does *not* exhaust the meaning of "disguised restriction." We consider that "disguised restriction", whatever else it covers, may properly be read as embracing restrictions amounting to arbitrary or unjustifiable discrimination in international trade taken under the guise of a measure formally within the terms of an exception listed in Article XX. Put in a somewhat different manner, the kinds of considerations pertinent in deciding whether the application of a particular measure amounts to "arbitrary or unjustifiable discrimination", may also be taken into account in determining the presence of a "disguised restriction" on international trade. The fundamental theme is to be found in the purpose and object of avoiding abuse or illegitimate use of the exceptions to substantive rules available in Article XX.

There was more than one alternative course of action available to the United States in promulgating regulations implementing the CAA. These included the imposition of statutory baselines without differentiation as between domestic and imported gasoline. This approach, if properly implemented, could have avoided any discrimination at all. Among the other options open to the United States was to make available individual baselines to foreign refiners as well as domestic refiners. The United States has put forward a series of reasons why either of these courses was not, in its view, realistically open to it and why, instead, it had to devise and apply the baseline establishment rules contained in the Gasoline Rule.

In explaining why individual baselines for foreign refiners had not been put in place, the United States laid heavy stress upon the difficulties which the EPA would have had to face. These difficulties related to anticipated administrative problems that individual baselines for foreign refiners would have generated. This argument was made succinctly by the United States in the following terms:

> Verification on foreign soil of foreign baselines, and subsequent enforcement actions, present substantial difficulties relating to problems arising whenever a country exercises enforcement jurisdiction over foreign persons. In addition, even if individual baselines were established for several foreign refiners, the importer would be tempted to claim the refinery of origin that presented the most benefits in terms of baseline restrictions, and tracking the refinery or origin would be very difficult because gasoline is a fungible commodity. The United States should not have to prove that it cannot verify information and enforce its regulations in every instance in order to show that the same enforcement conditions do not prevail in the United States and other countries . . . The impracticability of verification and enforcement of foreign refiner baselines in this instance shows that the "discrimination" is based on serious,

not arbitrary or unjustifiable, concerns stemming from different conditions between enforcement of its laws in the United States and abroad.

Thus, according to the United States, imported gasoline was relegated to the more exacting statutory baseline requirement because of these difficulties of verification and enforcement. The United States stated that verification and enforcement of the Gasoline Rule's requirements for imported gasoline are "much easier when the statutory baseline is used" and that there would be a "dramatic difference" in the burden of administering requirements for imported gasoline if individual baselines were allowed.

In its submissions, the United States also explained why the statutory baseline requirement was not imposed on domestic refiners as well. Here, the United States stressed the problems that domestic refineries would have faced had they been required to comply with the statutory baseline. The Panel Report summarized the United States' argument in the following terms:

> The United States concluded that, contrary to Venezuela's and Brazil's claim, Article XX did not require adoption of the statutory baseline as a national standard even if the difficulties associated with the establishment of individual baselines for importers were insurmountable. Application of the statutory baseline to domestic producers of reformulated and conventional gasoline in 1995 would have been *physically and financially impossible because of the magnitude of the changes required in almost all US refineries; it thus would have caused a substantial delay in the programme.* Weighing the feasibility of policy options in economic or technical terms in order to meet an environmental objective was a legitimate consideration, and did not, in itself, constitute protectionism, as alleged by Venezuela and Brazil. Article XX did not require a government to choose the most expensive possible way to regulate its environment. (emphasis added)

Clearly, the United States did not feel it feasible to require its domestic refiners to incur the physical and financial costs and burdens entailed by immediate compliance with a statutory baseline. The United States wished to give domestic refiners time to restructure their operations and adjust to the requirements in the Gasoline Rule. This may very well have constituted sound domestic policy from the viewpoint of the EPA and U.S. refiners. At the same time we are bound to note that, while the United States counted the costs for its domestic refiners of statutory baselines, there is nothing in the record to indicate that it did other than disregard that kind of consideration when it came to foreign refiners.

We have above located two omissions on the part of the United States: to explore adequately means, including in particular cooperation with the governments of Venezuela and Brazil, of mitigating the administrative problems relied on as justification by the United States for rejecting individual baselines for foreign refiners; and to count the costs for foreign refiners that would result from the imposition of statutory baselines. In our view, these two omissions go well beyond what was necessary for the Panel to determine that a violation of Article III:4 had occurred in the first place. The resulting discrimination must have been foreseen, and was not merely inadvertent or unavoidable. In the light of the foregoing, our conclusion is that the baseline establishment rules in the Gasoline Rule, in their application, constitute "unjustifiable discrimination" and a "disguised restriction on international trade." We hold, in sum, that the baseline establishment rules, although within the terms of Article XX(g), are not entitled to the justifying protection afforded by Article XX as a whole.

PROBLEM 7-3

The United States passes a law imposing a ban on fruit imported from
Colombia because the fruit was grown using pesticides containing a locally produced chemical that harms the environment. The United States law provides that
the imports can be admitted only if Colombia uses a new chemical pesticide, developed by the subsidiary of a U.S. chemicals company located in Brazil. Is this lawful?
Read the case below.

United States — Import Prohibition of Certain Shrimp and Shrimp Products (Shrimp/Turtle Case)
Report of the Appellate Body, adopted on November 6, 1998
WT/DS58/AB/R

[Pursuant to the Endangered Species Act of 1973, the federal government
required all U.S. shrimp trawling vessels to use Turtle Excluder Devices (TEDs) in
order to protect an endangered species of sea turtle. Section 609 [of Public Law
101-162], enacted on November 21, 1989, imposed a ban on imports of shrimp
captured without the use of TEDs. In order for shrimp imports to enter the United
States, Section 609 required that the exporting nation receive a certification from
the United States. The certification process was elaborated in regulatory guidelines
issued in 1991, 1993, and 1996. The United States could grant a certification to (1)
countries with a fishing environment that did not pose a threat to sea turtles; or (2)
countries with a regulatory program that governed the taking of sea turtles in the
course of shrimp trawling and was comparable to that of the United States, and to
places with similar average rates of incidental capture of sea turtles. The original
1991 guidelines for Section 609 limited its application to the wider Caribbean/
Western Atlantic region and granted those countries a three-year phase-in period.
On December 29, 1995, the Court of International Trade held that the ban had to
be imposed worldwide by May 1, 1996. On April 10, 1996, the United States issued
the 1996 guidelines, which extended the ban to all countries worldwide. Malaysia,
India, and Thailand challenged the U.S. import ban. The United States argued
that Section 609 was justified by Article XX(g) as a measure "relating to the conservation of exhaustible natural resources."]

ARTICLE XX(g): PROVISIONAL JUSTIFICATION OF SECTION 609 "EXHAUSTIBLE NATURAL RESOURCES"

127. We begin with the threshold question of whether Section 609 is a measure concerned with the conservation of "exhaustible natural resources" within the
meaning of Article XX(g). The Panel, of course, with its "chapeau-down" approach,
did not make a finding on whether the sea turtles that Section 609 is designed to
conserve constitute "exhaustible natural resources" for purposes of Article XX(g).
In the proceedings before the Panel, however, the parties to the dispute argued
this issue vigorously and extensively. India, Pakistan and Thailand contended that
a "reasonable interpretation" of the term "exhaustible" is that the term refers to
"finite resources such as minerals, rather than biological or renewable resources."
In their view, such finite resources were exhaustible "because there was a limited

supply which could and would be depleted unit for unit as the resources were consumed." Moreover, they argued, if "all" natural resources were considered to be exhaustible, the term "exhaustible" would become superfluous. They also referred to the drafting history of Article XX(g), and, in particular, to the mention of minerals, such as manganese, in the context of arguments made by some delegations that "export restrictions" should be permitted for the preservation of scarce natural resources. For its part, Malaysia added that sea turtles, being living creatures, could only be considered under Article XX(b), since Article XX(g) was meant for "nonliving exhaustible natural resources". It followed, according to Malaysia, that the United States cannot invoke both the Article XX(b) and the Article XX(g) exceptions simultaneously.

128. We are not convinced by these arguments. Textually, Article XX(g) is *not* limited to the conservation of "mineral" or "non-living" natural resources. The complainants' principal argument is rooted in the notion that "living" natural resources are "renewable" and therefore cannot be "exhaustible" natural resources. We do not believe that "exhaustible" natural resources and "renewable" natural resources are mutually exclusive. One lesson that modern biological sciences teach us is that living species, though in principle, capable of reproduction and, in that sense, "renewable", are in certain circumstances indeed susceptible of depletion, exhaustion and extinction, frequently because of human activities. Living resources are just as "finite" as petroleum, iron ore and other non-living resources.

132. We turn next to the issue of whether the living natural resources sought to be conserved by the measure are "exhaustible" under Article XX(g). That this element is present in respect of the five species of sea turtles here involved appears to be conceded by all the participants and third participants in this case. The exhaustibility of sea turtles would in fact have been very difficult to controvert since all of the seven recognized species of sea turtles are today listed in Appendix 1 of the Convention on International Trade in Endangered Species of Wild Fauna and Flora ("CITES"). The list in Appendix 1 includes "all species *threatened with extinction* which are or may be affected by trade." (emphasis added)

134. For all the foregoing reasons, we find that the sea turtles here involved constitute "exhaustible natural resources" for purposes of Article XX(g) of the GATT 1994.

"RELATING TO THE CONSERVATION OF [EXHAUSTIBLE NATURAL RESOURCES]"

135. Article XX(g) requires that the measure sought to be justified be one which "relat[es] to" the conservation of exhaustible natural resources. In making this determination, the treaty interpreter essentially looks into the relationship between the measure at stake and the legitimate policy of conserving exhaustible natural resources.

137. In the present case, we must examine the relationship between the general structure and design of the measure here at stake, Section 609, and the policy goal it purports to serve, that is, the conservation of sea turtles.

138. Section 609(b)(1) imposes an import ban on shrimp that have been harvested with commercial fishing technology which may adversely affect sea turtles. This provision is designed to influence countries to adopt national regulatory programs requiring the use of TEDs by their shrimp fishermen. In this connection,

it is important to note that the general structure and design of Section 609 *cum* implementing guidelines is fairly narrowly focused. There are two basic exemptions from the import ban, both of which relate clearly and directly to the policy goal of conserving sea turtles. First, Section 609, as elaborated in the 1996 Guidelines, excludes from the import ban shrimp harvested "under conditions that do not adversely affect sea turtles". Thus, the measure, by its terms, excludes from the import ban: aquaculture shrimp; shrimp species (such as *pandalid* shrimp) harvested in water areas where sea turtles do not normally occur; and shrimp harvested exclusively by artisanal methods, even from non-certified countries. The harvesting of such shrimp clearly does not affect sea turtles. Second, under Section 609(b)(2), the measure exempts from the import ban shrimp caught in waters subject to the jurisdiction of certified countries.

139. There are two types of certification for countries under Section 609(b) (2). First, under Section 609(b)(2)(C), a country may be certified as having a fishing environment that does not pose a threat of incidental taking of sea turtles in the course of commercial shrimp trawl harvesting. There is no risk, or only a negligible risk, that sea turtles will be harmed by shrimp trawling in such an environment.

140. The second type of certification is provided by Section 609(b)(2)(A) and (B). Under these provisions, as further elaborated in the 1996 Guidelines, a country wishing to export shrimp to the United States is required to adopt a regulatory program that is comparable to that of the United States program and to have a rate of incidental take of sea turtles that is comparable to the average rate of United States' vessels. This is, essentially, a requirement that a country adopt a regulatory program requiring the use of TEDs by commercial shrimp trawling vessels in areas where there is a likelihood of intercepting sea turtles. This requirement is, in our view, directly connected with the policy of conservation of sea turtles. It is undisputed among the participants, and recognized by the experts consulted by the Panel, that the harvesting of shrimp by commercial shrimp trawling vessels with mechanical retrieval devices in waters where shrimp and sea turtles coincide is a significant cause of sea turtle mortality. Moreover, the Panel did "not question . . . the fact generally acknowledged by the experts that TEDs, when properly installed and adapted to the local area, would be an effective tool for the preservation of sea turtles."

141. In its general design and structure, therefore, Section 609 is not a simple, blanket prohibition of the importation of shrimp imposed without regard to the consequences (or lack thereof) of the mode of harvesting employed upon the incidental capture and mortality of sea turtles. Focusing on the design of the measure here at stake, it appears to us that Section 609, *cum* implementing guidelines, is not disproportionately wide in its scope and reach in relation to the policy objective of protection and conservation of sea turtle species. The means are, in principle, reasonably related to the ends. The means and ends relationship between Section 609 and the legitimate policy of conserving an exhaustible, and, in fact, endangered species, is observably a close and real one, a relationship that is every bit as substantial as that which we found in *United States — Gasoline* between the EPA baseline establishment rules and the conservation of clean air in the United States.

142. In our view, therefore, Section 609 is a measure "relating to" the conservation of an exhaustible natural resource within the meaning of Article XX(g) of the GATT 1994.

C. The Introductory Clauses of Article XX: Characterizing Section 609 Under the Chapeau's Standards

147. Although provisionally justified under Article XX(g), Section 609, if it is ultimately to be justified as an exception under Article XX, must also satisfy the requirements of the introductory clauses—the "chapeau"—of Article XX, that is,

Article XX
General Exceptions

Subject to the requirement that such measures are *not applied in a manner which would constitute a means of arbitrary or unjustifiable discrimination between countries where the same conditions prevail*, or *a disguised restriction on international trade*, nothing in this Agreement shall be construed to prevent the adoption or enforcement by any Member of measures: (emphasis added)

150. There are three standards contained in the chapeau: first, arbitrary discrimination between countries where the same conditions prevail; second, unjustifiable discrimination between countries where the same conditions prevail; and third, a disguised restriction on international trade. In order for a measure to be applied in a manner which would constitute "arbitrary or unjustifiable discrimination between countries where the same conditions prevail", three elements must exist. First, the application of the measure must result in *discrimination*. As we stated in *United States—Gasoline*, the nature and quality of this discrimination is different from the discrimination in the treatment of products which was already found to be inconsistent with one of the substantive obligations of the GATT 1994, such as Articles I, III or XI. Second, the discrimination must be *arbitrary* or *unjustifiable* in character. We will examine this element of *arbitrariness* or *unjustifiability* in detail below. Third, this discrimination must occur *between countries where the same conditions prevail*. In *United States—Gasoline*, we accepted the assumption of the participants in that appeal that such discrimination could occur not only between different exporting Members, but also between exporting Members and the importing Member concerned. Thus, the standards embodied in the language of the chapeau are not only different from the requirements of Article XX(g); they are also different from the standard used in determining that Section 609 is violative of the substantive rules of Article XI:1 of the GATT 1994.

"Unjustifiable Discrimination"

161. We scrutinize first whether Section 609 has been applied in a manner constituting "unjustifiable discrimination between countries where the same conditions prevail". Perhaps the most conspicuous flaw in this measure's application relates to its intended and actual coercive effect on the specific policy decisions made by foreign governments, Members of the WTO. Section 609, in its application, is, in effect, an economic embargo which requires *all other exporting Members*, if they wish to exercise their GATT rights, to adopt *essentially the same* policy (together with an approved enforcement program) as that applied to, and enforced on, United States domestic shrimp trawlers.

163. The actual *application* of the measure, through the implementation of the 1996 Guidelines and the regulatory practice of administrators, *requires* other WTO Members to adopt a regulatory program that is not merely *comparable*, but rather *essentially the same*, as that applied to the United States shrimp trawl vessels. Thus, the effect of the application of Section 609 is to establish a rigid and unbending standard by which United States officials determine whether or not countries will be certified, thus granting or refusing other countries the right to export shrimp to the United States. Other specific policies and measures that an exporting country may have adopted for the protection and conservation of sea turtles are not taken into account, in practice, by the administrators making the comparability determination.

164. It may be quite acceptable for a government, in adopting and implementing a domestic policy, to adopt a single standard applicable to all its citizens throughout that country. However, it is not acceptable, in international trade relations, for one WTO Member to use an economic embargo to *require* other Members to adopt essentially the same comprehensive regulatory program, to achieve a certain policy goal, as that in force within that Member's territory, *without* taking into consideration different conditions which may occur in the territories of those other Members.

165. This suggests to us that this measure, in its application, is more concerned with effectively influencing WTO Members to adopt essentially the same comprehensive regulatory regime as that applied by the United States to its domestic shrimp trawlers, even though many of those Members may be differently situated. We believe that discrimination results not only when countries in which the same conditions prevail are differently treated, but also when the application of the measure at issue does not allow for any inquiry into the appropriateness of the regulatory program for the conditions prevailing in those exporting countries.

166. Another aspect of the application of Section 609 that bears heavily in any appraisal of justifiable or unjustifiable discrimination is the failure of the United States to engage the appellees, as well as other Members exporting shrimp to the United States, in serious, across-the-board negotiations with the objective of concluding bilateral or multilateral agreements for the protection and conservation of sea turtles, before enforcing the import prohibition against the shrimp exports of those other Members.

167. *A propos* this failure to have prior consistent recourse to diplomacy as an instrument of environmental protection policy, which produces discriminatory impacts on countries exporting shrimp to the United States with which no international agreements are reached or even seriously attempted, a number of points must be made. First, the Congress of the United States expressly recognized the importance of securing international agreements for the protection and conservation of the sea turtle species in enacting this law. Apart from the negotiation of the Inter-American Convention for the Protection and Conservation of Sea Turtles (the "Inter-American Convention") which concluded in 1996, the record before the Panel does not indicate any serious, substantial efforts to carry out these express directions of Congress.

168. Second, the protection and conservation of highly migratory species of sea turtles, that is, the very policy objective of the measure, demands concerted and cooperative efforts on the part of the many countries whose waters are traversed in the course of recurrent sea turtle migrations. The need for, and the appropriateness

of, such efforts have been recognized in the WTO itself as well as in a significant number of other international instruments and declarations.

169. Third, the United States did negotiate and conclude one regional international agreement for the protection and conservation of sea turtles: The Inter-American Convention. This Convention was opened for signature on 1 December 1996 and has been signed by five countries, in addition to the United States, and four of these countries are currently certified under Section 609. This Convention has not yet been ratified by any of its signatories. The Inter-American Convention provides that each party shall take "appropriate and necessary measures" for the protection, conservation and recovery of sea turtle populations and their habitats within such party's land territory and in maritime areas with respect to which it exercises sovereign rights or jurisdiction.

171. The Inter-American Convention thus provides convincing demonstration that an alternative course of action was reasonably open to the United States for securing the legitimate policy goal of its measure, a course of action other than the unilateral and non-consensual procedures of the import prohibition under Section 609. It is relevant to observe that an import prohibition is, ordinarily, the heaviest "weapon" in a Member's armoury of trade measures. The record does not, however, show that serious efforts were made by the United States to negotiate similar agreements with any other country or group of countries before (and, as far as the record shows, after) Section 609 was enforced on a world-wide basis on 1 May 1996. Finally, the record also does not show that the appellant, the United States, attempted to have recourse to such international mechanisms as exist to achieve cooperative efforts to protect and conserve sea turtles before imposing the import ban.

172. Clearly, the United States negotiated seriously with some, but not with other Members (including the appellees), that export shrimp to the United States. The effect is plainly discriminatory and, in our view, unjustifiable. The unjustifiable nature of this discrimination emerges clearly when we consider the cumulative effects of the failure of the United States to pursue negotiations for establishing consensual means of protection and conservation of the living marine resources here involved, notwithstanding the explicit statutory direction in Section 609 itself to initiate negotiations as soon as possible for the development of bilateral and multilateral agreements. The principal consequence of this failure may be seen in the resulting unilateralism evident in the application of Section 609.

173. The application of Section 609, through the implementing guidelines together with administrative practice, also resulted in other differential treatment among various countries desiring certification. Under the 1991 and 1993 Guidelines, to be certifiable, fourteen countries in the wider Caribbean/western Atlantic region had to commit themselves to require the use of TEDs on all commercial shrimp trawling vessels by 1 May 1994. These fourteen countries had a "phase-in" period of three years during which their respective shrimp trawling sectors could adjust to the requirement of the use of TEDs. With respect to all other countries exporting shrimp to the United States (including the appellees, India, Malaysia, Pakistan and Thailand), on 29 December 1995, the United States Court of International Trade directed the Department of State to apply the import ban on a world-wide basis not later than 1 May 1996.[1] On 19 April 1996, the 1996 Guidelines were issued by the Department of State bringing shrimp harvested in

---

1. *Earth Island Institute v. Warren Christopher*, 913 F. Supp. 559 (CIT 1995).

all foreign countries within the scope of Section 609, effective 1 May 1996. Thus, all countries that were not among the fourteen in the wider Caribbean/western Atlantic region had only four months to implement the requirement of compulsory use of TEDs.

175. Differing treatment of different countries desiring certification is also observable in the differences in the levels of effort made by the United States in transferring the required TED technology to specific countries. Far greater efforts to transfer that technology successfully were made to certain exporting countries—basically the fourteen wider Caribbean/western Atlantic countries cited earlier—than to other exporting countries, including the appellees. The level of these efforts is probably related to the length of the "phase-in" periods granted—the longer the "phase-in" period, the higher the possible level of efforts at technology transfer. Because compliance with the requirements of certification realistically assumes successful TED technology transfer, low or merely nominal efforts at achieving that transfer will, in all probability, result in fewer countries being able to satisfy the certification requirements under Section 609, within the very limited "phase-in" periods allowed them.

176. When the foregoing differences in the means of application of Section 609 to various shrimp exporting countries are considered in their cumulative effect, we find, and so hold, that those differences in treatment constitute "unjustifiable discrimination" between exporting countries desiring certification in order to gain access to the United States shrimp market within the meaning of the chapeau of Article XX.

[The Appellate Body also found that Section 609 violated the chapeau because it was a form of "arbitrary discrimination between countries where the same conditions prevail." The Appellate Body concluded that this violation occurred because Section 609 is an application by the United States of a rigid standard that requires countries to adopt the same regulatory program as that of the United States without any inquiry into the appropriateness of the program for the conditions in the exporting countries. The Appellate Body concluded that Section 609 was not entitled to the exception contained in Article XX(g).]

United States—Import Prohibition of Certain Shrimp and Shrimp Products Recourse to Article 21.5 by Malaysia
Report of the Appellate Body, adopted on November 21, 2001
WT/DS58/AB/RW

[Following the 1998 WTO Appellate Body decision, the United States issued new, more flexible regulations that allow a country's shrimp products to be certified for importation on the basis of several ways of precluding threats to sea turtles: the use of turtle excluder devices, the use of artisanal harvesting techniques, and harvesting exclusively in waters where sea turtles do not inhabit. The regulations also inserted due process procedures into the import certification process. Malaysia brought a challenge to the revised U.S. program under Article 21.5 of the WTO Dispute Settlement Understanding. A WTO panel convened under Article 21.5 found that the United States had made adequate efforts to negotiate agreements to preserve turtles with Southeast Asian nations. The panel also found that the United States had cured the problems of unjustifiable and arbitrary discrimination in the previous program. The panel's conclusions were reviewed by the Appellate Body.]

The Nature and Extent of the Duty of the United States to Pursue International Cooperation in the Protection and Conservation of Sea Turtles

122. We concluded in *United States — Shrimp* that, to avoid "arbitrary or unjustifiable discrimination", the United States had to provide all exporting countries "similar opportunities to negotiate" an international agreement. Given the specific mandate contained in Section 609, and given the decided preference for multilateral approaches voiced by WTO Members and others in the international community in various international agreements for the protection and conservation of endangered sea turtles that were cited in our previous Report, the United States, in our view, would be expected to make good faith efforts to reach international agreements that are comparable from one forum of negotiation to the other. The negotiations need not be identical. Indeed, no two negotiations can ever be identical, or lead to identical results. Yet the negotiations must be *comparable* in the sense that comparable efforts are made, comparable resources are invested, and comparable energies are devoted to securing an international agreement.

123. Under the chapeau of Article XX, an importing Member may not treat its trading partners in a manner that would constitute "arbitrary or unjustifiable discrimination". With respect to this measure, the United States could conceivably respect this obligation, and the conclusion of an international agreement might nevertheless not be possible despite the serious, good faith efforts of the United States. Requiring that a multilateral agreement be *concluded* by the United States in order to avoid "arbitrary or unjustifiable discrimination" in applying its measure would mean that any country party to the negotiations with the United States, whether a WTO Member or not, would have, in effect, a veto over whether the United States could fulfill its WTO obligations. Such a requirement would not be reasonable.

130. The Panel compared the efforts of the United States to negotiate the Inter-American Convention with one group of exporting WTO Members with the efforts made by the United States to negotiate a similar agreement with another group of exporting WTO Members. The Panel rightly used the Inter-American Convention as a factual reference in this exercise of comparison. It was all the more relevant to do so given that the Inter-American Convention was the only international agreement that the Panel could have used in such a comparison. As we read the Panel Report, it is clear to us that the Panel attached a relative value to the Inter-American Convention in making this comparison, but did not view the Inter-American Convention in any way as an absolute standard. Thus, we disagree with Malaysia's submission that the Panel raised the Inter-American Convention to the rank of a "legal standard".

131. The Panel noted that while "factual circumstances may influence the duration of the process or the end result, . . . any effort alleged to be a 'serious good faith effort' must be assessed against the efforts made in relation to the conclusion of the Inter-American Convention." Such a comparison is a central element of the exercise to determine whether there is "unjustifiable discrimination". The Panel then analyzed the negotiation process in the Indian Ocean and South-East Asia region to determine whether the efforts made by the United States in those negotiations were serious, good faith efforts comparable to those made in relation with the Inter-American Convention.

132. On this basis and, in particular, on the basis of the "contribution of the United States to the steps that led to the Kuantan meeting and its contribution to the Kuantan meeting itself", the Panel concluded that the United States had made serious, good faith efforts that met the "standard set by the Inter-American Convention." In the view of the Panel, whether or not the South-East Asian MOU is a legally binding document does not affect this comparative assessment because differences in "factual circumstances have to be kept in mind". Furthermore, the Panel did not consider as decisive the fact that the final agreement in the Indian Ocean and South-East Asia region, unlike the Inter-American Convention, had not been concluded at the time of the Panel proceedings. According to the Panel, "at least until the Conservation and Management Plan to be attached to the MOU is completed, the United States efforts should be judged on the basis of its active participation and its financial support to the negotiations, as well as on the basis of its previous efforts since 1998, having regard to the likelihood of a conclusion of the negotiations in the course of 2001."

134. In sum, Malaysia is incorrect in its contention that avoiding "arbitrary and unjustifiable discrimination" under the chapeau of Article XX requires the *conclusion* of an international agreement on the protection and conservation of sea turtles. Therefore, we uphold the Panel's finding that, in view of the serious, good faith efforts made by the United States to negotiate an international agreement, "Section 609 is now applied in a manner that no longer constitutes a means of unjustifiable or arbitrary discrimination, as identified by the Appellate Body in its Report".

THE FLEXIBILITY OF THE REVISED GUIDELINES

136. Malaysia disagrees with the Panel that a measure can meet the requirements of the chapeau of Article XX if it is flexible enough, both in design and application, to permit certification of an exporting country with a sea turtle protection and conservation programme "comparable" to that of the United States. According to Malaysia, even if the measure at issue allows certification of countries having regulatory programs "comparable" to that of the United States, and even if the measure is applied in such a manner, it results in "arbitrary or unjustifiable discrimination" because it conditions access to the United States market on compliance with policies and standards "unilaterally" prescribed by the United States.

140. In *United States—Shrimp*, we concluded that the measure at issue there did not meet the requirements of the chapeau of Article XX relating to "arbitrary or unjustifiable discrimination" because, through the application of the measure, the exporting members were faced with "a single, rigid and unbending requirement" to adopt *essentially the same* policies and enforcement practices as those applied to, and enforced on, domestic shrimp trawlers in the United States. In contrast, in this dispute, the Panel found that this new measure is more flexible than the original measure and has been applied more flexibly than was the original measure. In the light of the evidence brought by the United States, the Panel satisfied itself that this new measure, in design and application, does *not* condition access to the United States market on the adoption by an exporting Member of a regulatory programme aimed at the protection and the conservation of sea turtles that is *essentially the same* as that of the United States.

143. Given that the original measure in that dispute required "essentially the same" practices and procedures as those required in the United States, we found it necessary in that appeal to rule only that Article XX did not allow such inflexibility. Given the Panel's findings with respect to the flexibility of the new measure in this dispute, we find it necessary in this appeal to add to what we ruled in our original Report. The question raised by Malaysia in this appeal is whether the Panel erred in inferring from our previous Report, and thereby finding, that the chapeau of Article XX permits a measure which requires only "comparable effectiveness".

144. In our view, there is an important difference between conditioning market access on the adoption of essentially the same programme, and conditioning market access on the adoption of a programme *comparable in effectiveness*. Authorizing an importing Member to condition market access on exporting Members putting in place regulatory programmes *comparable in effectiveness* to that of the importing Member gives sufficient latitude to the exporting Member with respect to the programme it may adopt to achieve the level of effectiveness required. It allows the exporting Member to adopt a regulatory programme that is suitable to the specific conditions prevailing in its territory. As we see it, the Panel correctly reasoned and concluded that conditioning market access on the adoption of a programme *comparable in effectiveness*, allows for sufficient flexibility in the application of the measure so as to avoid "arbitrary or unjustifiable discrimination". We, therefore, agree with the conclusion of the Panel on "comparable effectiveness".

146. We note that the Revised Guidelines contain provisions that permit the United States authorities to take into account the specific conditions of Malaysian shrimp production, and of the Malaysian sea turtle conservation programme, should Malaysia decide to apply for certification. The Revised Guidelines explicitly state that "[if] the government of a harvesting nation demonstrates that it has implemented and is enforcing a comparably effective regulatory program to protect sea turtles in the course of shrimp trawl fishing without the use of TEDs, that nation will also be eligible for certification." Likewise, the Revised Guidelines provide that the "Department of State will take fully into account any demonstrated differences between the shrimp fishing conditions in the United States and those in other nations as well as information available from other sources."

147. Further, the Revised Guidelines provide that the import prohibitions that can be imposed under Section 609 do not apply to shrimp or products of shrimp "harvested in any other manner or under any other circumstances that the Department of State may determine, following consultations with the [United States National Marine Fisheries Services], does not pose a threat of the incidental taking of sea turtles." Section II.B(c)(iii) states that "[i]n making certification determinations, the Department shall also take fully into account other measures the harvesting nation undertakes to protect sea turtles, including national programmes to protect nesting beaches and other habitat, prohibitions on the direct take of sea turtles, national enforcement and compliance programmes, and participation in any international agreement for the protection and conservation of sea turtles."

148. These provisions of the Revised Guidelines, on their face, permit a degree of flexibility that, in our view, will enable the United States to consider the particular conditions prevailing in Malaysia if, and when, Malaysia applies for certification. As Malaysia has not applied for certification, any consideration of whether Malaysia would be certified would be speculation.

[The Appellate Body upheld the panel's decision that the revised Section 609 guidelines were justified as a trade restriction by Article XX(g).]

NOTES AND QUESTIONS

1. The *U.S. — Shrimp/Turtle* case did not rely on the National Treatment principle contained in GATT Article III to justify the trade ban and thus avoided the whole issue of whether PPMs can ever be justified under the National Treatment principle. Instead, *U.S. — Shrimp/Turtle* crafted a tailored exception based on GATT Article XX for environmental PPMs. Accordingly, a ban based on a PPM (such as requiring turtle excluder devices when fishing for shrimp) will be permitted if it meets the tests for the application of Article XX. Has the WTO opened the door too wide? How easy will it be in the future to adopt trade-restricting measures to protect the environment?

2. What does the *U.S. — Shrimp/Turtle* case mean for international environmental agreements that adopt trade restrictions to induce compliance or to punish states that do not adequately observe international environmental norms? For example, the Montreal Protocol on Substances that Deplete the Ozone Layer (1987) requires parties to the Protocol to ban the import and export of all "controlled substances" (designated ozone-layer-destroying substances) from all non-parties. Would such a trade ban be permitted under Article XX? What if the parties to the Kyoto Protocol of 1998, which mandates reductions in greenhouse gas emissions, decide to place a mandatory trade ban on non-party states? The United States, the world's largest producer of greenhouse gas emissions, is not a party to the Kyoto Protocol. Could the United States object to the use of environmental issues to limit trade?

3. Under the Kyoto Protocol to the UN Convention on Climate Change, thirty-five countries and the European Union are obligated to reduce emissions of so-called greenhouse gases, such as carbon dioxide, by required percentages from 1990 levels by the year 2012. The United States and Australia are the only developed countries that have rejected the mandatory requirements of the Kyoto Protocol. In November 2006, Prime Minister Dominique de Villepin of France proposed to introduce special "carbon taxes" on products imported from certain countries that reject the Kyoto Protocol. He is quoted by Reuters News Service as saying, "I would like us to study now with our European partners the principle of a carbon tax on the import of industrial products from countries which refuse to commit themselves to the Kyoto Protocol after 2012. Europe has to use all its weight to stand up to this sort of environmental dumping." Would such a tax be valid under the standards in GATT Article XX? We consider this issue in more detail in Section VII of this Chapter.

III.   Product Safety

GATT Article XX(b) contains an exception that permits trade restrictions on imported goods when such measures are "necessary to protect human, animal or plant life or health." The interpretation of this provision is involved in the famous case below.

European Communities — Measures Affecting Asbestos and Asbestos-Containing Products
Report of the Appellate Body, adopted on April 5, 2001
WT/DS135/AB/R

1. Canada appeals certain issues of law and legal interpretations developed in the Panel Report in *European Communities — Measures Affecting Asbestos and Asbestos-Containing Products* (the "Panel Report"). The Panel was established to consider claims made by Canada regarding French Decree No. 96-1133 concerning asbestos and products containing asbestos ("the Decree"), which entered into force on 1 January 1997.

2. Articles 1 and 2 of the Decree set forth prohibitions on asbestos and on products containing asbestos fibres, followed by certain limited and temporary exceptions from those prohibitions:

Article 1

I. For the purpose of protecting workers, and pursuant to Article L. 231-7 of the Labour Code, the manufacture, processing, sale, import, placing on the domestic market and transfer under any title whatsoever of all varieties of asbestos fibres shall be prohibited, regardless of whether these substances have been incorporated into materials, products or devices.

II. For the purpose of protecting consumers, and pursuant to Article L. 221.3 of the Consumer Code, the manufacture, import, domestic marketing, exportation, possession for sale, offer, sale and transfer under any title whatsoever of all varieties of asbestos fibres or any product containing asbestos fibres shall be prohibited.

III. The bans instituted under Articles I and II shall not prevent fulfillment of the obligations arising from legislation on the elimination of wastes.

Article 2

I. On an exceptional and temporary basis, the bans instituted under Article 1 shall not apply to certain existing materials, products or devices containing chrysotile fibre when, to perform an equivalent function, no substitute for that fibre is available which:

— On the one hand, in the present state of scientific knowledge, poses a lesser occupational health risk than chrysotile fibre to workers handling those materials, products or devices;

— on the other, provides all technical guarantees of safety corresponding to the ultimate purpose of the use thereof.

ARTICLE XX(B) OF THE GATT 1994 AND ARTICLE 11 OF THE DSU

155. Under Article XX(b) of the GATT 1994, the Panel examined, first, whether the use of chrysotile-cement products poses a risk to human health and, second, whether the measure at issue is "necessary to protect human . . . life or health". Canada contends that the Panel erred in law in its findings on both these issues.

156. We recall that Article XX(b) of the GATT 1994 reads:

Subject to the requirement that such measures are not applied in a manner which would constitute a means of arbitrary or unjustifiable discrimination between countries where the same conditions prevail, or a disguised restriction on international trade, nothing in this Agreement shall be construed to prevent the adoption or enforcement by any Member of *measures*:

. . .

(b) necessary to protect human, animal or plant *life or health*; (emphasis added)

. . .

A. "TO PROTECT HUMAN LIFE OR HEALTH"

157. On the issue of whether the use of chrysotile-cement products poses a risk to human health sufficient to enable the measure to fall within the scope of application of the phrase "to protect human . . . life or health" in Article XX(b), the Panel stated that it "considers that the evidence before it *tends to show* that handling chrysotile-cement products constitutes a risk to health rather than the opposite." (emphasis added) On the basis of this assessment of the evidence, the Panel concluded that:

. . . the EC has made a prima facie case for the existence of a health risk in connection with the use of chrysotile, in particular as regards lung cancer and mesothelioma in the occupational sectors downstream of production and processing and for the public in general in relation to chrysotile-cement products. This prima facie case has not been rebutted by Canada. Moreover, the Panel considers that the comments by the experts confirm the health risk associated with exposure to chrysotile in its various uses. *The Panel therefore considers that the EC have shown that the policy of prohibiting chrysotile asbestos implemented by the Decree falls within the range of policies designed to protect human life or health.* . . . (emphasis added)

Thus, the Panel found that the measure falls within the category of measures embraced by Article XX(b) of the GATT 1994.

158. According to Canada, the Panel deduced that there was a risk to human life or health associated with manipulation of chrysotile-cement products from seven factors. These seven factors all relate to the scientific evidence which was before the Panel, including the opinion of the scientific experts. Canada argues that the Panel erred in law by deducing from these seven factors that chrysotile-cement products pose a risk to human life or health.

159. Although Canada does not base its arguments about these seven factors on Article 11 of the DSU, we bear in mind the discretion that is enjoyed by panels as the trier of facts. In *United States—Wheat Gluten*, we said:

. . . in view of the distinction between the respective roles of the Appellate Body and panels, we have taken care to emphasize that a panel's appreciation of the evidence falls, in principle, "within the *scope of the panel's discretion as the trier of facts*". (emphasis added) In assessing the panel's appreciation of the evidence, we cannot base a finding of inconsistency under Article 11 simply on the conclusion that we might have reached a different factual finding from the one the panel reached. Rather, we must be satisfied that the panel has exceeded the bounds of its discretion, as the trier of facts, in its appreciation of the evidence. As is clear from previous appeals, we will not interfere lightly with the panel's exercise of its discretion.

162. With this in mind, we have examined the seven factors on which Canada relies in asserting that the Panel erred in concluding that there exists a human health risk associated with the manipulation of chrysotile-cement products. We see Canada's appeal on this point as, in reality, a challenge to the Panel's assessment of the credibility and weight to be ascribed to the scientific evidence before it. Canada contests the conclusions that the Panel drew both from the evidence of the scientific experts and from scientific reports before it. As we have noted, we will interfere with the Panel's appreciation of the evidence only when we are "satisfied that the panel has *exceeded the bounds of its discretion, as the trier of facts, in its appreciation of the evidence.*" (emphasis added) In this case, nothing suggests that the Panel exceeded the bounds of its lawful discretion. To the contrary, all four of the scientific experts consulted by the Panel concurred that chrysotile asbestos fibres, and chrysotile-cement products, constitute a risk to human health, and the Panel's conclusions on this point are faithful to the views expressed by the four scientists. In addition, the Panel noted that the carcinogenic nature of chrysotile asbestos fibres has been acknowledged since 1977 by international bodies, such as the International Agency for Research on Cancer and the World Health Organization. In these circumstances, we find that the Panel remained well within the bounds of its discretion in finding that chrysotile-cement products pose a risk to human life or health.

163. Accordingly, we uphold the Panel's finding, in paragraph 8.194 of the Panel Report, that the measure "protect[s] human . . . life or health", within the meaning of Article XX(b) of the GATT 1994.

B.   "NECESSARY"

164. On the issue of whether the measure at issue is "necessary" to protect public health within the meaning of Article XX(b), the Panel stated:

> In the light of France's public health objectives as presented by the European Communities, the Panel concludes that the EC has made a prima facie case for the non-existence of a reasonably available alternative to the banning of chrysotile and chrysotile-cement products and recourse to substitute products. Canada has not rebutted the presumption established by the EC. We also consider that the EC's position is confirmed by the comments of the experts consulted in the course of this proceeding.

165. Canada argues that the Panel erred in applying the "necessity" test under Article XX(b) of the GATT 1994 "by stating that there is a high enough risk associated with the manipulation of chrysotile-cement products that it could in principle justify strict measures such as the Decree." Canada advances four arguments in support of this part of its appeal. First, Canada argues that the Panel erred in finding, on the basis of the scientific evidence before it, that chrysotile-cement products pose a risk to human health. Second, Canada contends that the Panel had an obligation to "quantify" itself the risk associated with chrysotile-cement products and that it could not simply "rely" on the "hypotheses" of the French authorities. Third,

Canada asserts that the Panel erred by postulating that the level of protection of health inherent in the Decree is a halt to the spread of asbestos-related health risks. According to Canada, this "premise is false because it does not take into account the risk associated with the use of substitute products without a framework for controlled use." Fourth, and finally, Canada claims that the Panel erred in finding that "controlled use" is not a reasonably available alternative to the Decree.

166. With respect to Canada's first argument, we note simply that we have already dismissed Canada's contention that the evidence before the Panel did not support the Panel's findings.

167. As for Canada's second argument, relating to "quantification" of the risk, we consider that, as with the *SPS Agreement*, there is no requirement under Article XX(b) of the GATT 1994 to *quantify*, as such, the risk to human life or health. A risk may be evaluated either in quantitative or qualitative terms. In this case, contrary to what is suggested by Canada, the Panel assessed the nature and the character of the risk posed by chrysotile-cement products. The Panel found, on the basis of the scientific evidence, that "no minimum threshold of level of exposure or duration of exposure has been identified with regard to the risk of pathologies associated with chrysotile, except for asbestosis." The pathologies which the Panel identified as being associated with chrysotile are of a very serious nature, namely lung cancer and mesothelioma, which is also a form of cancer. Therefore, we do not agree with Canada that the Panel merely relied on the French authorities' "hypotheses" of the risk.

168. As to Canada's third argument, relating to the level of protection, we note that it is undisputed that WTO Members have the right to determine the level of protection of health that they consider appropriate in a given situation. France has determined, and the Panel accepted, that the chosen level of health protection by France is a "halt" to the spread of *asbestos*-related health risks. By prohibiting all forms of amphibole asbestos, and by severely restricting the use of chrysotile asbestos, the measure at issue is clearly designed and apt to achieve that level of health protection.

169. In its fourth argument, Canada asserts that the Panel erred in finding that "controlled use" is not a reasonably available alternative to the Decree. This last argument is based on Canada's assertion that, in *United States—Gasoline*, both we and the panel held that an alternative measure "can only be ruled out if it is shown to be impossible to implement." We understand Canada to mean by this that an alternative measure is only excluded as a "reasonably available" alternative if implementation of that measure is "impossible". We certainly agree with Canada that an alternative measure which is impossible to implement is not "reasonably available". But we do not agree with Canada's reading of either the panel report or our report in *United States—Gasoline*. In *United States—Gasoline*, the panel held, in essence, that an alternative measure did not *cease* to be "reasonably" available simply because the alternative measure involved *administrative difficulties* for a Member. The panel's findings on this point were not appealed, and, thus, we did not address this issue in that case.

171. In our Report in *Korea—Beef*, we addressed the issue of "necessity" under Article XX(d) of the GATT 1994. In that appeal, we found that the panel was correct in following the standard set forth by the panel in *United States—Section 337 of the Tariff Act of 1930*:

It was clear to the Panel that a contracting party cannot justify a measure inconsistent with another GATT provision as "necessary" in terms of Article XX(d) if an alternative measure which it could reasonably be expected to employ and which is not inconsistent with other GATT provisions is available to it. By the same token, in cases where a measure consistent with other GATT provisions is not reasonably available, a contracting party is bound to use, among the measures reasonably available to it, that which entails the least degree of inconsistency with other GATT provisions.

172. We indicated in *Korea—Beef* that one aspect of the "weighing and balancing process . . . comprehended in the determination of whether a WTO-consistent alternative measure" is reasonably available is the extent to which the alternative measure "contributes to the realization of the end pursued". In addition, we observed, in that case, that "[t]he more vital or important [the] common interests or values" pursued, the easier it would be to accept as "necessary" measures designed to achieve those ends. In this case, the objective pursued by the measure is the preservation of human life and health through the elimination, or reduction, of the well-known, and life-threatening, health risks posed by asbestos fibres. The value pursued is both vital and important in the highest degree. The remaining question, then, is whether there is an alternative measure that would achieve the same end and that is less restrictive of trade than a prohibition.

173. Canada asserts that "controlled use" represents a "reasonably available" measure that would serve the same end. The issue is, thus, whether France could reasonably be expected to employ "controlled use" practices to achieve its chosen level of health protection—a halt in the spread of asbestos-related health risks.

174. In our view, France could not reasonably be expected to employ *any* alternative measure if that measure would involve a continuation of the very risk that the Decree seeks to "halt". Such an alternative measure would, in effect, prevent France from achieving its chosen level of health protection. On the basis of the scientific evidence before it, the Panel found that, in general, the efficacy of "controlled use" remains to be demonstrated. Moreover, even in cases where "controlled use" practices are applied "with greater certainty", the scientific evidence suggests that the level of exposure can, in some circumstances, still be high enough for there to be a "significant residual risk of developing asbestos-related diseases." The Panel found too that the efficacy of "controlled use" is particularly doubtful for the building industry and for DIY enthusiasts, which are the most important users of cement-based products containing chrysotile asbestos. Given these factual findings by the Panel, we believe that "controlled use" would not allow France to achieve its chosen level of health protection by halting the spread of asbestos-related health risks. "Controlled use" would, thus, not be an alternative measure that would achieve the end sought by France.

175. For these reasons, we uphold the Panel's finding that the European Communities has demonstrated a *prima facie* case that there was no "reasonably available alternative" to the prohibition inherent in the Decree. As a result, we also uphold the Panel's conclusion that the Decree is "necessary to protect human . . . life or health" within the meaning of Article XX(b) of the GATT 1994.

NOTE ON THE "NECESSARY" REQUIREMENT IN GATT ARTICLE XX

Under Article XX, the concept "necessary" is critical because this word qualifies three major Article XX exceptions: measures "(a) necessary to protect public morals; (b) necessary to protect human, animal or plant life or health; [and] (d) necessary to secure compliance with laws or regulations."

Prior to the establishment of the WTO in 1995, GATT panels interpreted the word "necessary" in Article XX in a rigid and strict way:

> [A] contracting party cannot justify a measure . . . as "necessary" . . . if an alternative measure which it could reasonably be expected to employ and which is not inconsistent with other GATT provisions is available to it.
>
> [A] contracting party is bound to use, among the measures reasonably available to it, that which entails the least degree of inconsistency with other GATT provisions.[2]

This strict interpretation of "necessary" was one reason why a U.S. measure designed to protect dolphins was rejected in the notorious *Tuna/Dolphin* cases discussed earlier. However, this rigid interpretation of "necessary" set such a high threshold that it became untenable under the WTO. Even on its face, a strict view of what is "necessary" seems to be inconsistent with the object and purpose of Article XX. This is so because exceptional measures under Article XX(b) to protect human health are permitted only if they are "necessary," whereas exceptional measures to conserve natural resources under Article XX(g) are permitted without being "necessary." A strict interpretation of "necessary" would require a higher standard to protect human health than to protect resources.

The solution to this dilemma in the WTO was to keep the GATT formulation of the test for "necessary," but to adopt a balancing approach based on a continuum in which both a strict and a flexible interpretation of "necessary" would be possible, depending on the context and the values and interests at stake. In the *Korea—Beef* case, the Appellate Body considered the exception under Article XX(d) for measures that are necessary to comply with laws and regulations. Korea had sought to protect a separate distribution system for imported beef, but the Appellate Body did not find that this interest justified a flexible interpretation of "necessary." In the context of Article XX(d) the word "necessary" has a relatively strict meaning. *See Korea—Measures Affecting Imports of Fresh, Chilled and Frozen Beef*, WT/DS161, 169/AB/R, Report of the Appellate Body, adopted on December 11, 2000, at ¶162. The Appellate Body held (¶¶167-168) that Korea had not shown that a separate distribution system for imported beef products was "necessary" in the sense that no alternative measure to deal with misrepresentation in the retail market for beef (such as ordinary police measures against fraud) was reasonably available. In contrast, in the *EC—Asbestos* case (above), decided a few months later, the Appellate Body considered an exception under Article XX(b) for the protection of public health. In this context, the Appellate Body upheld the measure, a ban on asbestos-containing products, using a very flexible meaning of "necessary." The Appellate Body found (¶172) the value at stake, the protection of public health, to be "both vital and important in the highest degree." As a result, it was relatively easy for the EC to prove that there was no reasonably available alternative.

---

2. *Thailand—Restrictions on Importation of and Internal Taxes on Cigarettes*, WT/DS122/R, Report of the Panel, adopted on April 5, 2001, at ¶75; *United States—Section 337 of the Tariff Act of 1930*, GATT B.I.S.D. (36th Supp.) 345, Report of the GATT Panel, adopted on November 7, 1989, at ¶5.26.

Additional WTO Appellate Body decisions indicate that a flexible "necessary" test applies not only in the context of Article XX but in other WTO agreements as well. *United States—Measures Affecting the Cross Border Supply of Gambling and Betting Services*, WT/DS285/AB/R, Report of the Appellate Body, adopted on April 7, 2005, considered the issue in the context of the general exceptions provision of the GATS Article XIV. The Appellate Body stated that the determination of necessity involves weighing and balancing the relative importance of the interests or values furthered by the challenged measure, assessing how the measure realizes the ends pursued, and judging its restrictive effect on commerce. In *Dominican Republic—Measures Affecting the Importation and Internal Sale of Cigarettes*, WT/DS302/AB/R, Report of the Appellate Body, adopted on April 25, 2005, the Appellate Body emphasized weighing a fourth factor, whether an alternative to the measure is reasonably available. These cases indicate that the WTO has now evolved a method of applying the "necessary" test based on a balancing approach and a continuum of meanings based upon the value that is being protected.

NOTES AND QUESTIONS

1. In the *EC—Asbestos* case, the Appellate Body also considered the argument made by Canada that the French decree was a "technical regulation" and was not consistent with the requirements of the TBT Agreement. Canada appealed from the ruling of the panel and stated that the decree and the ban were not technical regulations. The Appellate Body reversed the panel on this point and ruled (¶¶75-76) that, considering the EC measure as an "integrated whole," it meets the criteria of a technical regulation under Annex 1.1 of the TBT Agreement. Do you agree? The Appellate Body also ruled (¶83) that since the panel had not made findings on the substantive claims under the TBT Agreement, it did not have an "adequate basis" to rule on the matter.

2. An alternative ground of the Appellate Body's ruling upholding the French decree in the *EC—Asbestos* case was that asbestos- and non-asbestos-containing products are not "like products" for purposes of GATT Article III. The French decree had banned imports of asbestos but did not prohibit the sale of domestic non-asbestos products used for insulation. Why does this make a crucial difference? If the two products were "like" products then the differential treatment could be found to be discrimination in violation of the National Treatment principle in Article III:4. The Appellate Body found that the products were not "like" products and so no violation of Article III:4 had occurred. The holding of the Appellate Body was important. Consider the following excerpt from Mitsuo Matsushita, Thomas J. Schoenbaum, and Petros C. Mavroidis, *The World Trade Organization: Law, Practice and Policy*, 490-491 (2003):

> The Appellate Body reasoned that health risks could differentiate products. Health risks may be considered in assessing whether products are "like" because (1) they are important in the competitive relationship between the products in the marketplace; and (2) they influence consumers' tastes and habits. Thus, the national treatment obligation of Article III:4 did not prevent France from banning asbestos-containing products.
>
> The Appellate Body's decision established the proposition that objective health or safety factors associated with a product may be sufficient to distinguish it from otherwise closely associated products such that the two products are not "like" under

GATT Article III:4. If so, imports of the dangerous product may be banned under GATT rules. Of course, this determination must be made on a case-by-case basis, and the dangerous product must be banned domestically as well.

NOTE ON DOMESTICALLY PROHIBITED GOODS AND DANGEROUS PRODUCTS IN INTERNATIONAL TRADE

The *EC—Asbestos* case provides the legal framework for import and export prohibitions on dangerous products. In many countries chemicals that are banned domestically may be legally exported. For example, the U.S. Toxic Substance Control Act permits exports of pesticides that are illegal in the U.S. as long as the government of the importing country is informed in advance and the foreign purchaser or government signs a statement acknowledging that the chemical cannot be sold in the United States.[3] Two international conventions place constraints on the import and export of a wide variety of hazardous chemicals. The Rotterdam Convention for the Application of Prior Informed Consent Procedure for Certain Chemicals and Pesticides in International Trade (1998) requires consent of the importing country as a condition for permitting certain pesticide and chemical exports. In addition the Stockholm Convention on Persistent Organic Pollutants (2001) singles out certain dangerous organic chemicals and requires parties to reduce or eliminate their release into the environment. The *EC—Asbestos* case would seem to pose no problems for these efforts under WTO rules.

IV. Food Safety: Sanitary and Phytosanitary Measures

A. Introduction

Read the WTO Sanitary and Phytosanitary Measures (SPS) Agreement.

Although members are permitted under GATT Article XX to use measures to restrict trade to ensure food safety (i.e., to protect human and animal health), WTO members considered it important to develop more specific criteria on this important issue. Accordingly, a separate Agreement on the Application of Sanitary and Phytosanitary Measures was concluded in 1994. This SPS Agreement, as it is called, is specifically intended to "elaborate rules for the application of the provisions of GATT 1994[,] in particular the provisions of Article XX(b)." *See* SPS Agreement, Preamble ¶8. The SPS Agreement is also intended to complement its close cousin, the Agreement on Technical Barriers to Trade (TBT).

Annex A, paragraph 1 of the SPS Agreement defines sanitary and phytosanitary measures to include any measure applied to protect animal or plant life and health, arising from risks associated with

---

3. *See* 15 U.S.C. §2611 (1976).

- the entry, establishment, or spread of pests, diseases, disease-carrying organisms, or disease-causing organisms;
- additives, contaminants, toxins or disease-causing organisms in foods, beverages, or feedstuffs;
- animals, plants or products thereof, or from the entry, establishment, or spread of pests.

The basic approach of the SPS Agreement is similar to that of the TBT Agreement, which we have already studied in Chapter 6 on non-tariff trade barriers. The SPS requires the following basic approach:

(1) WTO members must base all national SPS measures on international standards, guidelines, or recommendations (where they exist) (Article 3.1);

(2) WTO members are, however, allowed to use national measures implementing levels of protection that exceed existing international standards (Article 3.3) if the member conducts a risk assessment that justifies the use of the national measure. A risk assessment must be based on (a) scientific evidence and (b) economic factors such as the loss of production or sales due to the entry of the imports, costs of control or eradication of pests arising from imports, and the cost effectiveness of alternative approaches to limiting risks (Article 5.2). If no scientific evidence exists due to the incomplete state of knowledge, a member is still allowed to impose a national measure with a higher standard of protection on a provisional basis (Article 5.7). This is considered to be an expression of the precautionary principle under international law.

The following materials deal with the major issues that arise under the SPS Agreement.

PROBLEM 7-4

Chile has a national measure restricting imports of certain industrial products on the grounds that contact with the products increase risks for a certain type of skin cancer. There is a current debate in the international scientific community about this type of risk but no consensus. Can Chile impose such a measure? Must the measure be based on scientific evidence? What can Chile do given the current controversy? *See* SPS Article 2.2. Must Chile conduct a risk assessment? *See* SPS Article 5.1.

PROBLEM 7-5

Italy wants to prohibit the import of certain fruits because they can serve as breeding grounds for disease-carrying mosquitoes. The measure is based on several preliminary studies conducted as part of an ongoing research project at the University of Florence but no conclusive scientific proof exists. Is this possible? *See* SPS Article 5.7.

PROBLEM 7-6

France has a law that all imported cheese must contain sterilized milk. Domestically produced cheeses do not need to meet this requirement because of high safety standards used in French farms. Is this law permitted? *See* SPS Article 2.3.

PROBLEM 7-7

Belgium is considering a national measure restricting imports of certain food products containing additives, based on its recent research that such additives cause an unhealthy increase in blood pressure. The existing international standard does not require such a high level of protection. Belgium has not conducted a risk assessment but claims that it is not required to conduct such an assessment under Article 3.3 because it is written in the disjunctive: a national measure affording higher levels of protection can be adopted if it is supported by a "scientific justification" *or* a risk assessment under Article 5. A risk assessment includes taking into account economic factors. Is Belgium correct? See *EC—Hormones* below.

PROBLEM 7-8

Based upon its reading of the SPS Agreement, Country G is considering a law that would impose one of the highest food and safety standards in the world: a requirement that all crops used for domestic consumption must be organically produced. The law would impose a ban on all domestic and imported crops treated with chemical fertilizers, additives, and pesticides. Health officials in Country G decided to propose the law based upon a risk assessment study done by Professor Turban Bey, a renowned scientist at the country's leading university.

Professor Bey conducted a comprehensive five-year risk assessment study in the field, complete with scientific and medical data indicating that if improperly applied, chemical fertilizers and pesticides leave residues that cause serious long-term harm to human health and safety. A second study by Professor Bey contains scientific evidence, widely accepted by the international scientific community, that shows organically grown crops provide great health benefits. Is the law completed by Country G consistent with the SPS? Consult SPS Article 3 and the *EC—Hormones* case below.

European Communities—Measures Concerning
Meat and Meat Products (Hormones Case)
Report of the Appellate Body, adopted on February 13, 1998
WT/DS26, 48/AB/R

[The United States and Canada challenged an EC prohibition of imports of meat derived from cattle to which either certain natural hormones (oestradiol-17β, progesterone, or testosterone) or synthetic hormones (trenbolone acetate, zeranol, or melengestrol acetate (MGA)) had been administered to promote growth. The panel found that the prohibition was inconsistent with the SPS Agreement and was therefore an unjustified trade restriction that had to be removed. The EC, the United States, and Canada appeal from certain issues in the Panel Report. The panel found that since the EC promulgated a national regulation that provided a level of protection beyond that required by relevant international standards, the EC was required by Article 3.3 to justify its measure through a risk assessment. The panel found that the EC had failed to perform a proper risk assessment. The Appellate Body reviewed this finding below.]

RELATIONSHIP BETWEEN ARTICLES 3.1, 3.2 AND 3.3 OF THE SPS AGREEMENT

169. We turn to the relationship between Articles 3.1, 3.2 and 3.3 of the *SPS Agreement.*

170. Under Article 3.2 of the *SPS Agreement,* a Member may decide to promulgate an SPS measure that conforms to an international standard. Such a measure would embody the international standard completely and, for practical purposes, converts it into a municipal standard. Such a measure enjoys the benefit of a presumption (albeit a rebuttable one) that it is consistent with the relevant provisions of the *SPS Agreement* and of the GATT 1994.

171. Under Article 3.1 of the *SPS Agreement,* a Member may choose to establish an SPS measure that is based on the existing relevant international standard, guideline or recommendation. Such a measure may adopt some, not necessarily all, of the elements of the international standard. The Member imposing this measure does not benefit from the presumption of consistency set up in Article 3.2; but, as earlier observed, the Member is not penalized by exemption of a complaining Member from the normal burden of showing a *prima facie* case of inconsistency with Article 3.1 or any other relevant article of the *SPS Agreement* or of the GATT 1994.

172. Under Article 3.3 of the *SPS Agreement,* a Member may decide to set for itself a level of protection different from that implicit in the international standard, and to implement or embody that level of protection in a measure not "based on" the international standard. The Member's appropriate level of protection may be higher than that implied in the international standard. The right of a Member to determine its own appropriate level of sanitary protection is an important right.

C.   THE REQUIREMENTS OF ARTICLE 3.3 OF THE SPS AGREEMENT

173. The right of a Member to define its appropriate level of protection is not, however, an absolute or unqualified right.

174. The European Communities argues that there are two situations covered by Article 3.3 and that its SPS measures are within the first of these situations. It is claimed that the European Communities has maintained SPS measures "which result in a higher level of . . . protection than would be achieved by measures based on the relevant" Codex standard, guideline or recommendation, for which measures "there is a scientific justification". It is also, accordingly, argued that the requirement of a risk assessment under Article 5.1 does not apply to the European Communities. At the same time, it is emphasized that the EC measures have satisfied the requirements of Article 2.2.

175. Article 3.3 is evidently not a model of clarity in drafting and communication. The use of the disjunctive "or" does indicate that two situations are intended to be covered. These are the introduction or maintenance of SPS measures which result in a higher level of protection:

(a) "if there is a scientific justification" ; or
(b) "as a consequence of the level of . . . protection a Member determines to be appropriate in accordance with the relevant provisions of paragraphs 1 through 8 of Article 5".

It is true that situation (a) does not speak of Articles 5.1 through 5.8. Nevertheless, two points need to be noted. First, the last sentence of Article 3.3 requires that "all measures which result in a [higher] level of . . . protection", that is to say, measures falling within situation (a) as well as those falling within situation (b), be "not inconsistent with any other provision of [the SPS] Agreement". "Any other provision of this Agreement" textually includes Article 5. Secondly, the footnote to Article 3.3, while attached to the end of the first sentence, defines "scientific justification" as an "examination and evaluation of available scientific information in conformity with relevant provisions of this Agreement . . .". This examination and evaluation would appear to partake of the nature of the risk assessment required in Article 5.1 and defined in paragraph 4 of Annex A of the *SPS Agreement.*

176. On balance, we agree with the Panel's finding that although the European Communities has established for itself a level of protection higher, or more exacting, than the level of protection implied in the relevant Codex standards, guidelines or recommendations, the European Communities was bound to comply with the requirements established in Article 5.1.

THE READING OF ARTICLES 5.1 AND 5.2 OF THE SPS AGREEMENT: BASING SPS MEASURES ON A RISK ASSESSMENT

179. Article 5.1 of the *SPS Agreement* provides:

Members shall ensure that their sanitary or phytosanitary measures are *based on an assessment, as appropriate to the circumstances, of the risks to human,* animal or plant *life or health,* taking into account risk assessment techniques developed by the relevant international organizations. ([emphasis] added)

A.　THE INTERPRETATION OF RISK ASSESSMENT

180. At the outset, two preliminary considerations need to be brought out. The first is that the Panel considered that Article 5.1 may be viewed as a specific application of the basic obligations contained in Article 2.2 of the *SPS Agreement,* which reads as follows:

Members shall ensure that any sanitary or phytosanitary measure is applied only *to the extent necessary to protect* human, animal or plant life or health, is *based on scientific principles* and is not maintained without *sufficient scientific evidence,* except as provided for in paragraph 7 of Article 5. [emphasis added]

We agree with this general consideration and would also stress that Articles 2.2 and 5.1 should constantly be read together. Article 2.2 informs Article 5.1: the elements that define the basic obligation set out in Article 2.2 impart meaning to Article 5.1.

1.   Risk Assessment and the Notion of "Risk"

182. Paragraph 4 of Annex A of the *SPS Agreement* sets out the treaty definition of risk assessment: This definition, to the extent pertinent to the present appeal, speaks of:

> . . . the evaluation of the *potential for adverse effects on human* or animal *health* arising from the presence of additives, contaminants, toxins or disease-causing organisms in food, beverages or feedstuffs. [emphasis added]

183. Interpreting the above definition, the Panel elaborates risk assessment as a two-step process that "should (i) *identify* the *adverse effects* on human health (if any) arising from the presence of the hormones at issue when used as growth promoters *in meat* . . . , and (ii) if any such adverse effects exist, *evaluate* the *potential* or probability of occurrence of such effects".

184. The European Communities appeals from the above interpretation as involving an erroneous notion of risk and risk assessment. Although the utility of a two-step analysis may be debated, it does not appear to us to be substantially wrong. What needs to be pointed out at this stage is that the Panel's use of "probability" as an alternative term for "potential" creates a significant concern. The ordinary meaning of "potential" relates to "possibility" and is different from the ordinary meaning of "probability". "Probability" implies a higher degree or a threshold of potentiality or possibility. It thus appears that here the Panel introduces a quantitative dimension to the notion of risk.

186. To the extent that the Panel purported to require a risk assessment to establish a minimum magnitude of risk, we must note that imposition of such a quantitative requirement finds no basis in the *SPS Agreement.* A panel is authorized only to determine whether a given SPS measure is "based on" a risk assessment. As will be elaborated below, this means that a panel has to determine whether an SPS measure is sufficiently supported or reasonably warranted by the risk assessment.

2.   Factors to Be Considered in Carrying Out a Risk Assessment

187. Article 5.2 of the *SPS Agreement* provides an indication of the factors that should be taken into account in the assessment of risk. Article 5.2 states that:

> In the assessment of risks, Members shall take into account available scientific evidence; relevant processes and production methods; relevant inspection, sampling and testing methods; prevalence of specific diseases or pests; existence of pest- or disease-free areas; relevant ecological and environmental conditions; and quarantine or other treatment.

The listing in Article 5.2 begins with "available scientific evidence"; this, however, is only the beginning. We note in this connection that the Panel states that, for purposes of the EC measures in dispute, a risk assessment required by Article 5.1 is "a *scientific* process aimed at establishing the *scientific* basis for the sanitary measure a Member intends to take". To the extent that the Panel intended to refer to a process characterized by systematic, disciplined and objective enquiry and analysis, that is, a mode of studying and sorting out facts and opinions, the Panel's statement is unexceptionable. However, to the extent that the Panel purports to exclude from the scope of a risk assessment in the sense of Article 5.1, all matters not susceptible of quantitative analysis by the empirical or experimental laboratory methods commonly associated with the physical sciences, we believe that the Panel is in error. Furthermore, there is nothing to indicate that the listing of factors that may be taken into account in a risk assessment of Article 5.2 was intended to be a closed list. It is essential to bear in mind that the risk that is to be evaluated in a risk assessment under Article 5.1 is not only risk ascertainable in a science laboratory operating under strictly controlled conditions, but also risk in human societies as they actually exist, in other words, the actual potential for adverse effects on human health in the real world where people live and work and die.

B.   THE INTERPRETATION OF "BASED ON"

188. Although it expressly recognizes that Article 5.1 does *not* contain any specific procedural requirements for a Member to base its sanitary measures on a risk assessment, the Panel nevertheless proceeds to declare that "there is a minimum procedural requirement contained in Article 5.1". That requirement is that "the Member imposing a sanitary measure needs to submit evidence that at least it actually *took into account* a risk assessment when it enacted or maintained its sanitary measure in order for that measure to be considered as *based on* a risk assessment". The Panel goes on to state that the European Communities did not provide any evidence that the studies it referred to or the scientific conclusions reached therein "*have actually been taken into account by the competent EC institutions* either when it *enacted* those measures (in 1981 and 1988) or *at any later point in time*". (emphasis added) Thereupon, the Panel holds that such studies could not be considered as part of a risk assessment on which the European Communities based its measures in dispute. Concluding that the European Communities had not met its burden of proving that it had satisfied the "minimum procedural requirement" it had found in Article 5.1, the Panel holds the EC measures as inconsistent with the requirements of Article 5.1.

189. We are bound to note that, as the Panel itself acknowledges, no textual basis exists in Article 5 of the *SPS Agreement* for such a "minimum procedural requirement". The term "based on", when applied as a "minimum procedural requirement" by the Panel, may be seen to refer to a human action, such as particular human individuals "taking into account" a document described as a risk assessment. Thus, "take into account" is apparently used by the Panel to refer to some subjectivity which, at some time, may be present in particular individuals but that, in the end, may be totally rejected by those individuals. We believe that "based on" is appropriately taken to refer to a certain *objective relationship* between two elements, that is to say, to an *objective situation* that persists and is observable between an SPS measure and a risk assessment. Such a reference is certainly embraced in the ordinary meaning of the words "based on" and, when considered in context

and in the light of the object and purpose of Article 5.1 of the *SPS Agreement*, may be seen to be more appropriate than "taking into account". We do not share the Panel's interpretative construction and believe it is unnecessary and an error of law as well.

190. Article 5.1 does not insist that a Member that adopts a sanitary measure shall have carried out its own risk assessment. It only requires that the SPS measures be "based on an assessment, as appropriate for the circumstances . . . ". The SPS measure might well find its objective justification in a risk assessment carried out by another Member, or an international organization. The "minimum procedural requirement" constructed by the Panel, could well lead to the elimination or disregard of available scientific evidence that rationally supports the SPS measure being examined. This risk of exclusion of available scientific evidence may be particularly significant for the bulk of SPS measures which were put in place before the effective date of the *WTO Agreement* and that have been simply maintained thereafter.

192. Having posited a "minimum procedural requirement" of Article 5.1, the Panel turns to the "substantive requirements" of Article 5.1 to determine whether the EC measures at issue are "based on" a risk assessment. In the Panel's view, those "substantive requirements" involve two kinds of operations: first, identifying the scientific conclusions reached in the risk assessment and the scientific conclusions implicit in the SPS measures; and secondly, examining those scientific conclusions to determine whether or not one set of conclusions matches, i.e. conforms with, the second set of conclusions. Applying the "substantive requirements" it finds in Article 5.1, the Panel holds that the scientific conclusions implicit in the EC measures do not conform with any of the scientific conclusions reached in the scientific studies the European Communities had submitted as evidence.

193. We consider that, in principle, the Panel's approach of examining the scientific conclusions implicit in the SPS measure under consideration and the scientific conclusion yielded by a risk assessment is a useful approach. We believe that Article 5.1, when contextually read as it should be, in conjunction with and as informed by Article 2.2 of the *SPS Agreement*, requires that the results of the risk assessment must sufficiently warrant—that is to say, reasonably support—the SPS measure at stake. The requirement that an SPS measure be "based on" a risk assessment is a substantive requirement that there be a rational relationship between the measure and the risk assessment.

195. We turn now to the application by the Panel of the substantive requirements of Article 5.1 to the EC measures at stake in the present case. The Panel lists the following scientific material to which the European Communities referred in respect of the hormones here involved (except MGA):

— the 1982 Report of the EC Scientific Veterinary Committee, Scientific Committee for Animal Nutrition and the Scientific Committee for Food on the basis of the Report of the Scientific Group on Anabolic Agents in Animal Production ("Lamming Report");

— the 1983 Symposium on Anabolics in Animal Production of the *Office international des epizooties* ("OIE") ("1983 OIE Symposium");

— the 1987 Monographs of the International Agency for Research on Cancer ("IARC") on the Evaluation of Carcinogenic Risks to Humans, Supplement 7 ("1987 IARC Monographs");

— the 1988 and 1989 JECFA Reports;

— the 1995 European Communities Scientific Conference on Growth
Promotion in Meat Production ("1995 EC Scientific Conference");

— articles and opinions by individual scientists relevant to the use of hormones (three articles in the journal Science, one article in the International
Journal of Health Service, one report in The Veterinary Record and separate scientific opinions of Dr. H. Adlercreutz, Dr. E. Cavalieri, Dr. S.S.
Epstein, Dr. J.G. Liehr, Dr. M. Metzler, Dr. Perez-Comas and Dr. A. Pinter,
all of whom were part of the EC delegation at [the] joint meeting with
experts).

196. The Panel states:

. . . none of the scientific evidence referred to by the European Communities which
specifically addresses the safety of some or all of the hormones in dispute when used
for growth promotion, indicates that an identifiable risk arises for human health
from such use of these hormones if good practice is followed. All of the scientific
studies outlined above came to the conclusion that the use of the hormones at issue
(all but MGA, for which no evidence was submitted) for growth promotion purposes
is safe; most of these studies adding that this conclusion assumes that good practice
is followed.

197. Prescinding from the difficulty raised by the Panel's use of the term
"identifiable risk", we agree that the scientific reports listed above do not rationally
support the EC import prohibition.

199. The European Communities laid particular emphasis on the 1987 IARC
Monographs and the articles and opinions of individual scientists referred to above.
The Panel notes, however, that the scientific evidence set out in these Monographs
and these articles and opinions relates to the carcinogenic potential of entire
categories of hormones, or of the hormones at issue *in general*. The Monographs
and the articles and opinions are, in other words, in the nature of general studies of or statements on the carcinogenic potential of the named hormones. The
Monographs and the articles and opinions of individual scientists have not evaluated the carcinogenic potential of those hormones when used specifically *for growth
promotion purposes*. Moreover, they do not evaluate the specific potential for carcinogenic effects arising from the presence *in "food"*, more specifically, "meat or meat
products" of residues of the hormones in dispute. The Panel concludes that these
Monographs and these articles and opinions are insufficient to support the EC
measures at issue in this case.

200. We believe that the above findings of the Panel are justified. Those general studies, are in other words, relevant but do not appear to be sufficiently specific to the case at hand.

[Turning to the risk assessment concerning MGA, the Appellate Body noted
that there was evidence submitted by the European Communities related to hormones (progestins) used in treating meat but none submitted that directly related
to MGA. The European Communities argued that MGA mimicked the actions of
the hormones that were the subject of the study but none of the evidence, consisting of monographs and opinions of individual scientists, indicated a chemical or pharmacological connection between MGA and the hormones that were
studied. In addition, finding a lack of evidence of a connection between MGA

and the hormones studied, the Appellate Body also found that the studies could not be accepted as a risk assessment of MGA for the additional reason set forth as follows.]

206. Most, if not all, of the scientific studies referred to by the European Communities, in respect of the five hormones involved here, concluded that their use for growth promotion purposes is "safe", if the hormones are administered in accordance with the requirements of good veterinary practice. Where the condition of observance of good veterinary practice (which is much the same condition attached to the standards, guidelines and recommendations of Codex with respect to the use of the five hormones for growth promotion) is *not* followed, the logical inference is that the use of such hormones for growth promotion purposes may or may not be "safe".

207. The question that arises, therefore, is whether the European Communities did, in fact, submit a risk assessment demonstrating and evaluating the existence and level of risk arising in the present case from abusive use of hormones and the difficulties of control of the administration of hormones for growth promotion purposes, within the United States and Canada as exporting countries, and at the frontiers of the European Communities as an importing country. Here, we must agree with the finding of the Panel that the European Communities in fact restricted itself to pointing out the condition of administration of hormones "in accordance with good practice" "without further providing an assessment of the potential adverse effects related to non compliance with such practice". The record of the panel proceedings shows that the risk arising from abusive use of hormones for growth promotion combined with control problems for the hormones at issue, may have been examined on two occasions in a scientific manner. The first occasion may have occurred at the proceedings before the Committee of Inquiry into the Problem of Quality in the Meat Sector established by the European Parliament, the results of which constituted the basis of the Pimenta Report of 1989. However, none of the original studies and evidence put before the Committee of Inquiry was submitted to the Panel. The second occasion could have been the 1995 EC Scientific Conference on Growth Promotion in Meat Production. One of the three workshops of this Conference examined specifically the problems of "detection and control". However, only one of the studies presented to the workshop discussed systematically some of the problems arising from the combination of potential abuse and problems of control of hormones and other substances. The study presented a theoretical framework for the systematic analysis of such problems, but did not itself investigate and evaluate the actual problems that have arisen at the borders of the European Communities or within the United States, Canada and other countries exporting meat and meat products to the European Communities. At best, this study may represent the beginning of an assessment of such risks.

208. We affirm, therefore, the ultimate conclusion of the Panel that the EC import prohibition is not based on a risk assessment within the meaning of Articles 5.1 and 5.2 of the *SPS Agreement* and is, therefore, inconsistent with the requirements of Article 5.1.

209. Since we have concluded above that an SPS measure, to be consistent with Article 3.3, has to comply with, *inter alia*, the requirements contained in Article 5.1, it follows that the EC measures at issue, by failing to comply with Article 5.1, are also inconsistent with Article 3.3 of the *SPS Agreement*.

NOTES AND QUESTIONS

1. The panel in the *EC—Hormones* case found also that the EC violated Article 5.5 of the SPS Agreement by making an arbitrary or unjustifiable distinction because the EC had banned the use of growth hormones in meat production but had not addressed or regulated their natural occurrence in meat and foods generally. The Appellate Body reversed (¶221) this finding on the basis that "there is a fundamental distinction between added hormones (natural or synthetic) and naturally occurring hormones in meat and other foods." Thus, the EC was justified in not regulating naturally occurring hormones in meat and foods. Do you agree? In the case of *Australia—Measures Affecting the Importation of Salmon*, WT/DS18/AB/R, Report of the Appellate Body, adopted on November 6, 1998, the Appellate Body upheld the finding (¶177) of an Article 5.5 violation based upon what the panel had called "warning signals" and "other factors" considered "cumulatively." The warning signals and other factors included the absence of measures to control the movement of salmon products within Australia and a change in the conclusions drawn in draft and final risk assessment reports.

2. What role should expert witnesses play in SPS cases? Review Articles 11.2 and 13 of the DSU. Can WTO adjudicating bodies seek outside expert advice? In the *EC—Hormones* case, the panel sought expert advice on the carcinogenic effect of hormones. The panel first asked each of the parties to name one outside expert. The panel then named three experts; two selected from a list prepared by the Codex Alimentarius Commission and the International Agency for Research on Cancer, and one additional expert.

3. A key finding in the *EC—Hormones* case was that the EC measures were not based on a risk assessment in violation of SPS Article 5.1. In *Australia—Measures Affecting the Importation of Salmon*, WT/DS18/AB/R, Report of the Appellate Body, adopted on November 6, 1998, the Appellate Body ruled (¶¶120-124) that the definition of risk assessment in SPS Agreement, Annex A, requires that a risk assessment within the meaning of Article 5.1 must do the following:

(1) identify the diseases whose entry, establishment, or spread a member wants to prevent, as well as the potential biological and economic consequences associated with the disease in question;

(2) evaluate the likelihood of entry, establishment, or spread of the disease in question, as well as the associated biological and economic consequences; and

(3) evaluate the likelihood of entry, establishment, or spread of the disease in the light of the SPS measures which might be applied.

In *Japan—Measures Affecting Agricultural Products*, WT/DS76/AB/R, Report of the Appellate Body, adopted on March 19, 1999, the Appellate Body ruled (¶112):

> The job of the WTO panels and Appellate Body is not to perform a risk assessment, but rather to review whether a risk assessment has been performed by the trade restricting member.

In *Australia—Measures Affecting the Importation of Apples from New Zealand*, WT/DS367/AB/R, Report of the Appellate Body, adopted on December 17, 2010, the Appellate Body examined sixteen measures taken by Australia relating to the importation of apples from New Zealand to keep the disease "fire blight" from spreading to Australian apples. Applying the test of risk assessment to each measure, the Appellate Body upheld (¶¶261-262) the panel's findings that the Australian measures were inconsistent with SPS Articles 5.1 and 5.2 as well as by implication Article 2.2 (improper risk assessment and failure to take into account relevant scientific evidence).

4. The *EC—Hormones* Panel and Appellate Body Reports were adopted by the DSB on February 13, 1998. When the EC did not comply with the ruling to bring its measures into compliance within a reasonable time, an arbitrator acting under DSU Article 22.6 determined the level of nullification and authorized Canada to suspend trade concessions amounting to Canadian dollars 11.3 million per year and authorized the United States to suspend trade concessions amounting to $116.8 million per year. *European Communities—Measures Concerning Meat and Meat Products (Hormones)*, WT/DS26, 48/AB/R, Report of the Appellate Body, adopted on February 13, 1998. The United States and Canada responded by imposing 100 percent *ad valorem* duties on a selected number of EU imports. The EU meanwhile commissioned further studies of the consequences of hormones in meat products, and on October 27, 2003 issued Directive 2003/73/EC, amending the original offending Directive 96/22/EC by incorporating the new studies and prohibiting one growth hormone, oestradiol-17 beta, based on evidence that this hormone was both carcinogenic and genotoxic. The other five hormones in question (progesterone, testosterone, zeranol, trenbolene acetate, and melengestrol) were prohibited on a provisional basis since research showed the existence of risks, but information necessary for a complete risk assessment was incomplete. When the United States and Canada refused to lift the retaliatory tariffs, the EC brought a complaint against both nations at the WTO. This complaint produced the decision in *Canada/United States—Continued Suspension of Obligations in the EC—Hormones Dispute*, WT/DS320/AB/R, Report of the Appellate Body, adopted on November 14, 2008. In this case the Appellate Body faulted (¶590) the panel below for applying an incorrect standard of review of the EC risk assessment for the hormone oestradiol-17 beta, ruling that "the review power of a panel is not to determine whether the risk assessment undertaken by a WTO Member is correct, but rather to determine whether that risk assessment is supported by coherent reasoning and respectable scientific evidence and is, in this sense, objectively justifiable." But the Appellate Body refused to complete the analysis, leaving undecided the question of whether the EC's risk assessment was consistent with Article 5.1. As to the provisional ban on meat treated with the five other hormones, the Appellate Body reviewed the four requirements of Article 5.7: (1) The measure is imposed in respect of a situation where relevant scientific information is insufficient; (2) the measure is adopted on the basis of pertinent information; (3) the member seeks to obtain additional information necessary for a more objective assessment of risk; and (4) the member will review the information within a reasonable period of time. Although the Appellate Body again found numerous flaws in the panel's analysis, it again was impossible to complete the analysis. Thus, the Appellate Body stated (¶737) that the recommendations and rulings adopted by the DSB in the *EC—Hormones* case "remain operative."

Despite the refusal of the Appellate Body to accept the EU/EC's new information, the opinion of the Appellate Body in the *U.S.—Continued Suspension* case sheds some light on three difficult issues that are especially relevant where a WTO member seeks to implement a higher level of protection than permitted by relevant international standards. First, the Appellate Body advised that risk assessment under SPS Article 5.1 as well as Article 5.7 must take into account risk management considerations. The Appellate Body agreed (¶¶537-542) with the EC's argument that risk assessment and risk management partly overlap in the SPS Agreement. Thus it follows that "the fact that the WTO member has chosen to set a higher level of protection may require it to perform certain research as part of its risk assessment that is different from the parameters considered and the research carried out in the risk assessment underlying the international standard" (¶685). Second, the Appellate Body approved (¶590) a deferential standard of review of WTO members' SPS measures: "the review power of a panel is not to determine whether the risk assessment undertaken by a WTO member is correct, but rather to determine whether that risk assessment is supported by coherent reasoning and respectable scientific evidence and is, in that sense, objectively justifiable." Third, the Appellate Body clarified (¶703) when a WTO member is justified in relying upon SPS Article 5.7: "Limiting the application of Article 5.7 to situations where scientific advances lead to a paradigm shift would be too inflexible an approach. WTO members should be permitted to take a provisional measure where new evidence from a qualified and respected source puts into question the relationship between the pre-existing body of scientific evidence and the conclusions regarding the risks." Does the *U.S. — Continued Suspension* case inject new flexibility into the SPS Agreement, making it easier for national authorities to fashion SPS measures based upon local situations and concerns? For analysis, see Alison Peck, *Nation-Specific Risk Tolerance in the WTO: US — Continued Suspension of Obligations in the EC-Hormones Dispute,* available at http://www.NationalAgLawCenter.org (July 2009) (concluding that the Appellate Body's opinion "will likely result in less harmonization of SPS measures" and "higher costs in international trade").

The question of whether the new EU Directive cures the defects in the *EC — Hormones* case must await the filing of a new dispute settlement complaint by one of the parties under DSU Article 21.5.

PROBLEM 7-9

The following facts are taken from the case *United States — Certain Measures Affecting Imports of Poultry from China,* WT/DS392/R, Report of the Panel, adopted on October 25, 2010. The United States has a food safety inspection regime that applies to both domestic and imported poultry products. In the years 2008 and 2009 there were numerous instances of contaminated food exported from China. After several such incidents, an agricultural appropriation measure passed the U.S. Congress stating that "none of the funds made available in this Act may be used to establish or implement a rule allowing poultry products to be imported into the United States from the People's Republic of China." The effect of this provision was to cut off imports of poultry from China since funds could not be expended for inspections. The United States explained this as congressional oversight of the relevant governmental agencies. China brought a complaint against the United States at the WTO.

(1) Does the provision violate any GATT article? Consider GATT Articles I:1 and XI:1.

(2) Does the U.S. measure violate AoA Article 4.2?

(3) Does the GATT exception Article XX(b) apply?

(4) Does the U.S. "measure" fit the definition of an SPS measure so that it comes within the scope of the SPS Agreement? *See* SPS Annex A(I).

(5) If the SPS Agreement applies, does the U.S. measure comply with Articles 5.1, 5.2, and 2.2?

(6) Does the measure violate SPS Article 5.5?

(7) Does the measure violate SPS Article 2.3?

(8) Does the measure violate SPS Article 5.6?

The United States tried without success to justify the measure as an equivalency measure under SPS Article 4.1.

NOTE ON THE EC BIOTECH PRODUCTS CASE

In 2003, the United States, Australia, and Canada brought cases in the WTO against the EC to challenge EC policies on biotechnology products that have been produced through recombinant DNA technology. The EC had adopted several measures: EC Directive 2001/18 deals with the problem of "deliberate release into the environment of genetically modified organisms (GMOs)" while EC Regulation 258/97 regulates "novel foods and novel food ingredients." The EC under this legislation evaluates on a case-by-case basis the potential risks of biotechnology products. EC law also permits any member state to adopt a safeguard measure to provisionally restrict or prohibit the importation, use, or sale of a biotechnology product that has received EC approval.

The complainants challenged in particular an EC moratorium on biotechnology approvals in effect from 1998 to 2003, as well as the member state safeguard provision.

The panel report was finally released on September 29, 2006. *See European Communities—Measures Affecting the Approval and Marketing of Biotech Products*, WT/DS291, 292, 293/R, Report of the Panel, adopted on November 21, 2006. Although the opinion was over 1,000 pages in length, the case was decided on very narrow grounds, and there was no ruling on either the issue of the safety of GMOs or the legality of the EC approval process. The panel rejected most of the claims made against the EC approval process. The panel also concluded (¶4.405) that the EC moratorium was not an SPS measure in itself because it fell outside of the definition of that term in Annex A(1). Thus, the panel concluded that the EC had not acted inconsistently with Article 5.1. However, the panel concluded (¶4.218) that the moratorium on approvals did lead to "undue delay" inconsistent with SPS Agreement Annex C(1)(a) and Article 8.

On the issue of the safeguards, the panel held that the EC member state measures at issue (various actions by France, Austria, Greece, Germany, Luxembourg, and Italy) were SPS measures under Annex A(1) and Article 1.1. The EC sought to justify these measures as "provisional" and permitted under Article 5.7. The panel, as a threshold matter, considered the relationship between Article 5.7 and 5.1 and concluded (¶7.3004) that, as with Article 3.3 and 3.1, Article 5.7 is not an exception to Article 5.1, but rather a "qualified right." This finding had two main effects; first, the panel had to determine as an initial matter whether there was a violation of Article 5.1. Second, the burden of proof of an Article 5.7 violation falls on the complainants. For each of the safeguard measures, the panel concluded (¶7.3036-7.3213) that there was no risk assessment as required by Article

5.1 (and as defined in Annex A(4)). Then, turning to Article 5.7, the panel found (¶7.3218) that this Article contains four requirements, all of which must be met to invoke its protection: (1) The measure must be imposed where relevant scientific information is insufficient; (2) the measure must be imposed on the basis of pertinent information; (3) the party imposing the measure must seek additional information necessary for a more objective assessment of risk; and (4) the measure must be subject to review again within a reasonable period of time. The panel concluded (¶7.3371) that, since the EC had in fact performed risk assessments in all of the safeguard cases, the complainants had established a presumption that the first requirement of Article 5.7 was not met, and the EC had failed to rebut this presumption.

The panel's decision was not appealed and was adopted on November 21, 2006.

V. Waste Minimization and Disposal

Does GATT Article XX permit restrictions on imported goods due to concerns about reducing waste? On the one hand, it may be argued that waste movement is simply commerce and that shipments of waste should be allowed to move freely in national and international commerce from one country to another for disposal or burial. On the other hand, the so-called "proximity principle" holds that waste should be required to be disposed of close to its source of generation.[4] In international trade there is the further value of protecting developing countries against becoming a dumping ground for hazardous waste generated in the developed world. To this end, the Basel Convention on the Control of Transboundary Movements of Hazardous Wastes and Their Disposal, Mar. 22, 1989, UN Doc. EP/IG.80/3, reprinted in 28 ILM 649 (1989), adopts controls on the export of waste.

The issue of import bans of waste returns us to consider the exception under GATT Article XX(b) for measures "necessary to protect human, animal or plant life or health." In both *Brazil—Retreaded Tyres* and *China—Publications and Audiovisual Products* in the following section, the Appellate Body had to find whether the "necessity" requirements of Article XX(b) and XX(a) were satisfied. The Appellate Body found that this required a three-step analysis:

(1) Identify the objective or the value sought to be protected;
(2) Determine whether the measure in question contributes to the objective;
(3) Determine whether a less trade restrictive alternative measure that achieves the desired level of protection is reasonably available.

The cases in this section and the following section explore the meaning of these elements.

---

4. This was the rationale of the Belgium waste case decided by the European Court of Justice, *Commission v. Belgium* [1992] ECR I-4431.

Brazil—Measures Affecting Imports of Retreaded Tyres
Report of the Appellate Body, adopted on December 3, 2007
WT/DS332/AB/R

[The European Communities challenged a law enacted by Brazil that banned the importation of retreaded tyres. The EC argued that the ban was inconsistent with GATT Article XI:1, which requires the general elimination of quotas. The EC also argued that certain fines on the importation of retreaded tyres, and on the marketing, transportation, and storage of imported retreaded tyres violated GATT Article XI:1 or, alternatively, GATT Article III:4, the National Treatment Principle, which prohibits internal regulations that discriminate against imported products. The EC further argued that certain state laws that prohibited the marketing and disposal of retreaded tyres also violated GATT Article III:4. Finally, the EC challenged the exemption from the import ban of tyres from countries of MERCOSUR (or the Southern Common Market), a free trade area consisting of several South American countries. Brazil did not contest that its import ban violated Article XI:1 or Article III:4. Rather, Brazil argued that the import ban was justified as an exception under Article XX(b) as a measure "necessary to protect human, animal, or plant life or health." Brazil also argued that the MERCOSUR exemption was justified under GATT Article XX(d) and GATT Article XXIV permitting free trade areas. The panel found that the Brazilian measure met the requirements of Article XX(b), but rejected the measure as a violation of the chapeau of Article XX(b). Brazil appealed this decision to the Appellate Body. The portion of the Appellate Body's opinion reproduced below focuses on its analysis of Article XX(b).]

BACKGROUND AND THE MEASURE AT ISSUE

FACTUAL BACKGROUND

118. Tyres are an integral component in passenger cars, lorries, and airplanes and, as such, their use is widespread in modern society. New passenger cars are typically sold with new tyres. When tyres need to be replaced, consumers in some countries may have a choice between new tyres or "retreaded" tyres. This dispute concerns the latter category of tyres. Retreaded tyres are used tyres that have been reconditioned for further use by stripping the worn tread from the skeleton (casing) and replacing it with new material in the form of a new tread, and sometimes with new material also covering parts or all of the sidewalls. Retreaded tyres can be produced through different methods, one of which is called "remoulding".

119. At the end of their useful life, tyres become waste, the accumulation of which is associated with risks to human, animal, and plant life and health. Specific risks to human life and health include:

(i) the transmission of dengue, yellow fever and malaria through mosquitoes which use tyres as breeding grounds; and (ii) the exposure of human beings to toxic emissions caused by tyre fires which may cause loss of short-term memory, learning disabilities, immune system suppression, cardiovascular problems, but also cancer, premature mortality, reduced lung function, suppression of the immune system, respiratory effects, heart and chest problems.

Risks to animal and plant life and health include: "(i) the exposure of animals and plants to toxic emissions caused by tyre fires; and (ii) the transmission of a mosquito-borne disease (dengue) to animals."

120. Governments take actions to minimize the adverse effects of waste tyres. Policies to address "waste" include preventive measures aiming at reducing the generation of additional waste tyres, as well as remedial measures aimed at managing and disposing of tyres that can no longer be used or retreaded, such as landfilling, stockpiling, the incineration of waste tyres, and material recycling.

121. The Panel observed that the parties to this dispute have not suggested that retreaded tyres used on vehicles pose any particular risks compared to new tyres, provided that they comply with appropriate safety standards. Various international standards exist in relation to retreaded tyres, including, for example, the norm stipulating that passenger car tyres may be retreaded only once. One important difference between new and retreaded tyres is that the latter have a shorter lifespan and therefore reach the stage of being waste earlier.

THE PANEL'S ANALYSIS OF THE NECESSITY OF THE IMPORT BAN

THE PANEL'S NECESSITY ANALYSIS UNDER ARTICLE XX(B) OF THE GATT 1994

133. The first legal issue raised by the European Communities' appeal relates to the Panel's finding that the Import Ban is "necessary" within the meaning of Article XX(b) of the GATT 1994. The European Communities challenges three specific aspects of the Panel's analysis under Article XX(b). First, the European Communities contends that the Panel applied an "erroneous legal standard" in assessing the contribution of the Import Ban to the realization of the ends pursued by it, and that it did not properly weigh this contribution in its analysis of the necessity of the Import Ban. Secondly, the European Communities submits that the Panel did not define correctly the alternatives to the Import Ban and erred in excluding possible alternatives proposed by the European Communities. Thirdly, the European Communities argues that, in its analysis under Article XX(b), the Panel did not carry out a proper, if any, weighing and balancing of the relevant factors. We will examine these contentions of the European Communities in turn.

143. In *US—Gambling*, the Appellate Body addressed the "necessity" test in the context of Article XIV of the GATS. The Appellate Body stated that the weighing and balancing process inherent in the necessity analysis "begins with an assessment of the 'relative importance' of the interests or values furthered by the challenged measure", and also involves an assessment of other factors, which will usually include "the contribution of the measure to the realization of the ends pursued by it" and "the restrictive impact of the measure on international commerce".

144. It is against this background that we must determine whether the Panel erred in assessing the contribution of the Import Ban to the realization of the objective pursued by it, and in the manner in which it weighed this contribution in its analysis of the necessity of the Import Ban. We begin by identifying the objective pursued by the Import Ban. The Panel found that the objective of the Import Ban is the reduction of the "exposure to the risks to human, animal or plant life or health arising from the accumulation of waste tyres", and noted that "few interests are more 'vital' and 'important' than protecting human beings from health risks,

and that protecting the environment is no less important." The Panel also observed that "Brazil's chosen level of protection is the reduction of the risks of waste tyre accumulation to the maximum extent possible." Regarding the trade restrictiveness of the measure, the Panel noted that it is "as trade-restrictive as can be, as far as retreaded tyres from non-MERCOSUR countries are concerned, since it aims to halt completely their entry into Brazil."

148. The Panel analyzed the contribution of the Import Ban to the achievement of its objective in a coherent sequence. It examined first the impact of the replacement of imported retreaded tyres with *new tyres* on the reduction of waste. Secondly, the Panel sought to determine whether imported retreaded tyres would be replaced with *domestically retreaded tyres*, which led it to examine whether domestic used tyres can be and are being retreaded in Brazil. Thirdly, it considered whether the reduction in the number of waste tyres would contribute to a reduction of the risks to human, animal, and plant life and health.

150. As the Panel recognized, an import ban is "by design as trade-restrictive as can be". We agree with the Panel that there may be circumstances where such a measure can nevertheless be necessary, within the meaning of Article XX(b). We also recall that, in *Korea — Various Measures on Beef,* the Appellate Body indicated that "the word 'necessary' is not limited to that which is 'indispensable'". Having said that, when a measure produces restrictive effects on international trade as severe as those resulting from an import ban, it appears to us that it would be difficult for a panel to find that measure necessary unless it is satisfied that the measure is apt to make a material contribution to the achievement of its objective. Thus, we disagree with Brazil's suggestion that, because it aims to reduce risk exposure to the maximum extent possible, an import ban that brings a marginal or insignificant contribution can nevertheless be considered necessary.

153. In the light of the evidence adduced by the parties, the Panel was of the view that the Import Ban would lead to imported retreaded tyres being replaced with retreaded tyres made from local casings, or with new tyres that are retreadable. As concerns new tyres, the Panel observed, and we agree, that retreaded tyres "have by definition a shorter lifespan than new tyres" and that, accordingly, the Import Ban "may lead to a reduction in the total number of waste tyres because imported retreaded tyres may be substituted for by new tyres which have a longer lifespan." As concerns tyres retreaded in Brazil from local casings, the Panel was satisfied that Brazil had the production capacity to retread domestic used tyres and that "at least some domestic used tyres are being retreaded in Brazil." The Panel also agreed that Brazil has taken a series of measures to facilitate the access of domestic retreaders to good-quality used tyres, and that new tyres sold in Brazil are high-quality tyres that comply with international standards and have the potential to be retreaded. The Panel's conclusion with which we agree was that, "if the domestic retreading industry retreads more domestic used tyres, the overall number of waste tyres will be reduced by giving a second life to some used tyres, which otherwise would have become waste immediately after their first and only life." For these reasons, the Panel found that a reduction of waste tyres would result from the Import Ban and that, therefore, the Import Ban would contribute to reducing exposure to the risks associated with the accumulation of waste tyres. As the Panel's analysis was qualitative, the Panel did not seek to estimate, in quantitative terms, the reduction of waste tyres that would result from the Import Ban, or the time horizon of such a reduction. Such estimates would have been very useful and, undoubtedly, would have strengthened the foundation of the Panel's findings.

Having said that, it does not appear to us erroneous to conclude, on the basis of the hypotheses made, tested, and accepted by the Panel, that fewer waste tyres will be generated with the Import Ban than otherwise.

154. Moreover, we wish to underscore that the Import Ban must be viewed in the broader context of the comprehensive strategy designed and implemented by Brazil to deal with waste tyres. This comprehensive strategy includes not only the Import Ban but also the import ban on used tyres, as well as the collection and disposal scheme adopted by CONAMA Resolution 258/1999, as amended in 2002, which makes it mandatory for domestic manufacturers and importers of new tyres to provide for the safe disposal of waste tyres in specified proportions. For its part, CONAMA Resolution 258/1999, as amended in 2002, aims to reduce the exposure to risks arising from the accumulation of waste tyres by forcing manufacturers and importers of new tyres to collect and dispose of waste tyres at a ratio of five waste tyres for every four new tyres. This measure also encourages Brazilian retreaders to retread more domestic used tyres by exempting domestic retreaders from disposal obligations as long as they process tyres consumed within Brazil. Thus, the CONAMA scheme provides additional support for and is consistent with the design of Brazil's strategy for reducing the number of waste tyres. The two mutually enforcing pillars of Brazil's overall strategy—the Import Ban and the import ban on used tyres—imply that the demand for retreaded tyres in Brazil must be met by the domestic retreaders, and that these retreaders, in principle, can use only domestic used tyres for raw material. Over time, this comprehensive regulatory scheme is apt to induce sustainable changes in the practices and behaviour of the domestic retreaders, as well as other actors, and result in an increase in the number of retreadable tyres in Brazil and a higher rate of retreading of domestic casings in Brazil. Thus, the Import Ban appears to us as one of the key elements of the comprehensive strategy designed by Brazil to deal with waste tyres, along with the import ban on used tyres and the collection and disposal scheme established by CONAMA Resolution 258/1999, as amended in 2002.

155. As we explained above, we agree with the Panel's reasoning suggesting that fewer waste tyres will be generated with the Import Ban in place. In addition, Brazil has developed and implemented a comprehensive strategy to deal with waste tyres. As a key element of this strategy, the Import Ban is likely to bring a material contribution to the achievement of its objective of reducing the exposure to risks arising from the accumulation of waste tyres. On the basis of these considerations, we are of the view that the Panel did not err in finding that the Import Ban contributes to the achievement of its objective.

THE PANEL'S ANALYSIS OF POSSIBLE ALTERNATIVES TO THE IMPORT BAN

156. In order to determine whether a measure is "necessary" within the meaning of Article XX(b) of the GATT 1994, a panel must assess all the relevant factors, particularly the extent of the contribution to the achievement of a measure's objective and its trade restrictiveness, in the light of the importance of the interests or values at stake. If this analysis yields a preliminary conclusion that the measure is necessary, this result must be confirmed by comparing the measure with its possible alternatives, which may be less trade restrictive while providing an equivalent contribution to the achievement of the objective pursued. It rests upon the

complaining Member to identify possible alternatives to the measure at issue that the responding Member could have taken.[5] We recall that, in order to qualify as an alternative, a measure proposed by the complaining Member must be not only less trade restrictive than the measure at issue, but should also "preserve for the responding Member its right to achieve its desired level of protection with respect to the objective pursued".[6] If the complaining Member has put forward a possible alternative measure, the responding Member may seek to show that the proposed measure does not allow it to achieve the level of protection it has chosen and, therefore, is not a genuine alternative. The responding Member may also seek to demonstrate that the proposed alternative is not, in fact, "reasonably available".[7] If the responding Member demonstrates that the measure proposed by the complaining Member is not a genuine alternative or is not "reasonably available", taking into account the interests or values being pursued and the responding Member's desired level of protection, it follows that the measure at issue is necessary.

157. Before the Panel, the European Communities put forward two types of possible alternative measures or practices: (i) measures to reduce the number of waste tyres accumulating in Brazil; and (ii) measures or practices to improve the management of waste tyres in Brazil. The Panel examined the alternative measures proposed by the European Communities in some detail, and in each case found that the proposed measure did not constitute a reasonably available alternative to the Import Ban. Among the reasons that the Panel gave for its rejections were that the proposed alternatives were already in place, would not allow Brazil to achieve its chosen level of protection, or would carry their own risks and hazards.

174. In evaluating whether the measures or practices proposed by the European Communities were "alternatives", the Panel sought to determine whether they would achieve Brazil's policy objective and chosen level of protection[8], that is to say, reducing the "exposure to the risks to human, animal or plant life or health arising from the accumulation of waste tyres"[9] to the maximum extent possible.[10] In this respect, we believe, like the Panel, that non-generation measures are more apt to achieve this objective because they prevent the accumulation of waste tyres, while waste management measures dispose of waste tyres only once they have accumulated. Furthermore, we note that, in comparing a proposed alternative to the Import Ban, the Panel took into account specific risks attached to the proposed alternative, such as the risk of leaching of toxic substances that might be associated to landfilling[11], or the risk of toxic emissions that might arise from the incineration of waste tyres.[12] In our view, the Panel did not err in so doing. Indeed, we do not see how a panel could undertake a meaningful comparison of the measure at issue with a possible alternative while disregarding the risks arising out of the implementation of the possible alternative. In this case, the Panel examined as proposed alternatives landfilling, stockpiling, and waste tyre incineration, and considered that, even if these disposal methods were performed under controlled

---

5. Appellate Body Report, *US—Gambling*, para. 311.

6. *Ibid.*, para. 308.

7. *Ibid.*, para. 311.

8. Panel Report, para. 7.157.

9. *Ibid.*, para. 7.102.

10. *Ibid.*, para. 7.108.

11. *Ibid.*, para. 7.183.

12. *Ibid.*, para. 7.194.

conditions, they nevertheless pose risks to human health similar or additional to those Brazil seeks to reduce through the Import Ban. Because these practices carry their own risks, and these risks do not arise from non-generation measures such as the Import Ban, we believe, like the Panel, that these practices are not reasonably available alternatives.

175. With respect to material recycling, we share the Panel's view that this practice is not as effective as the Import Ban in reducing the exposure to the risks arising from the accumulation of waste tyres. Material recycling applications are costly, and hence capable of disposing of only a limited number of waste tyres. We also note that some of them might require advanced technologies and know-how that are not readily available on a large scale. Accordingly, we are of the view that the Panel did not err in concluding that material recycling is not a reasonably available alternative to the Import Ban.

THE PANEL'S INTERPRETATION AND APPLICATION OF THE CHAPEAU OF ARTICLE XX OF THE GATT 1994

A. THE MERCOSUR EXEMPTION AND THE CHAPEAU OF ARTICLE XX OF THE GATT 1994

213. After finding that the Import Ban was provisionally justified under Article XX(b) of the GATT 1994[13], the Panel examined whether the application of the Import Ban by Brazil satisfied the requirements of the chapeau of Article XX.

215. The focus of the chapeau, by its express terms, is on the application of a measure already found to be inconsistent with an obligation of the GATT 1994 but falling within one of the paragraphs of Article XX. The chapeau's requirements are two-fold. First, a measure provisionally justified under one of the paragraphs of Article XX must not be applied in a manner that would constitute "arbitrary or unjustifiable discrimination" between countries where the same conditions prevail. Secondly, this measure must not be applied in a manner that would constitute "a disguised restriction on international trade". Through these requirements, the chapeau serves to ensure that Members' rights to avail themselves of exceptions are exercised in good faith to protect interests considered legitimate under Article XX, not as a means to circumvent one Member's obligations towards other WTO Members.

[The Appellate Body, after analyzing the chapeau, ruled that the MERCOSUR exemption and the imports of used tyres under court injunctions have resulted in the import ban being applied in a manner that constitutes arbitrary and unjustifiable discrimination and in a manner that constitutes a disguised restriction on international trade. The Appellate Body therefore ruled that the import ban was not justified under Article XX.]

NOTES AND QUESTIONS

1. In the *Brazil—Retreaded Tyres* case the measure was inconsistent with the chapeau of Article XX. How easily might Brazil cure this violation?

---

13. Panel Report, para. 7.215.

2. The *Brazil—Retreaded Tyres* case involved waste import restrictions. Can the Appellate Body's reasoning be applied to validate waste export restrictions as are mandated under the Basel Convention on the Movement of Transboundary Wastes?

3. On what basis would the Appellate Body approve recycling regulations that apply to imported products?

VI.   *Culture and Trade*

Can WTO members restrict imports of goods on the basis of cultural concerns? Many governments and individuals are concerned about the dangers of impoverishment of local culture and of the cultural dominance of the most successful international producer of cultural goods, the United States. At the conclusion of the Uruguay Round of international trade negotiations, the United States congratulated itself that it had prevented the insertion of a cultural exception into the Agreement Establishing the World Trade Organization.[14] The GATT has no general exception for culture, although Article XX(f) permits trade restrictions "imposed for the protection of national treasures of artistic or archaeological value."

GATT Article XX(a) also permits trade restrictions "necessary to protect public morals." No country ever attempted to use this provision to justify trade restrictions on imported goods based upon culture, until the principal case below.

China—Measures Affecting Trading Rights and Distribution Services for Certain Publications and Audiovisual Entertainment Products
Report of the Appellate Body, adopted January 19, 2010
WT/DS363/AB/R

[The United States brought a complaint concerning China's state system that exerted stringent control over the importation of reading material (books, newspapers, periodicals, electronic publications), audiovisual materials (audio and videocassettes, video compact discs, digital video discs), sound recordings, and films for theatrical release. China argued that these restrictions were necessary to protect its population from materials that were inappropriate or offensive to China's social values and morals. The legal issues were many and complex in this case, but the excerpt below focuses on the Appellate Body's interpretation of Article XX(a), which permits trade restrictions that are "necessary to protect public morals."

China's Protocol of Accession, the agreement with other WTO members granting China entry into the WTO in 2000, contained a number of commitments that China was required to make as a condition of admission to the WTO. Since China has a communist system and an authoritarian state-controlled system, the WTO required China to liberalize certain aspects of its system. Prior to entry into the WTO, China granted trading privileges (including the right to import goods) only

---

14. *See* Michael J. Hahn, *A Clash of Cultures? The UNESCO Diversity Convention and International Trade Law*, 9 J. of Int'l Econ. L. 515, 516 (2006).

to state-owned enterprises, i.e., entities that were essentially administrative units of the state. Article 5.1 of the Protocol of Accession required China to grant all enterprises the right to trade in goods (including the right to import) as well as the right to distribute goods internally in China within three years of China's accession to the WTO, with certain limited exceptions not applicable to this case. In particular, Article 5.1 required China to grant these trading and distribution rights to foreign invested enterprises, i.e., subsidiaries established in China and owned by foreign multinational companies. The obligation created by Article 5.1 of China's Protocol of Accession is a WTO obligation on par with an obligation in any of the WTO agreements; China's compliance with Article 5.1 was mandatory.

China refused, however, to comply with Article 5.1 of the Protocol of Accession but continued to maintain a system of restricted import and distribution rights for the products that are the subject of this dispute; China continued to recognize import privileges only in state owned enterprises long after it was required to grant import and distribution rights to all enterprises. According to China, such a system was necessary to protect its own culture from the invasion of products that were inconsistent (or even offensive) to China's cultural mores and values. China asserted that its refusal to comply with Article 5.1 was justified under GATT Article XX(a).

The panel rejected China's defense and China appealed to the Appellate Body, which rendered the opinion below.]

THE "NECESSITY" TEST UNDER ARTICLE XX(a) OF THE GATT 1994

234. The Panel found that China had not demonstrated that any of the provisions that China sought to justify are "necessary to protect public morals" within the meaning of Article XX(a) of the GATT 1994. On appeal, China challenges this conclusion. More specifically, China contends that the Panel erred in finding: (i) that the State-ownership requirement in Article 42(2) of the *Publications Regulation* makes no material contribution to the protection of public morals in China; (ii) that the provisions excluding foreign-invested enterprises from engaging in the importation of the relevant products make no material contribution to the protection of public morals in China; (iii) that the restrictive effect of the provisions on "those wishing to engage in importing" is relevant for assessing the necessity of such provisions under Article XX(a); and (iv) that at least one of the alternative measures proposed by the United States (that is, giving the Chinese Government sole responsibility for conducting content review) was an alternative "reasonably available" to China. In addition, China requests the Appellate Body to complete the analysis and find its measures to be "necessary" to protect public morals within the meaning of Article XX(a) and consistent with the chapeau of Article XX of the GATT 1994.

THE PANEL'S ANALYTICAL APPROACH TO THE "NECESSITY" TEST UNDER ARTICLE XX(a)

239. The Appellate Body has previously considered the proper approach to take in analyzing the "necessity" of a measure in several appeals, in particular:

Korea—Various Measures on Beef (in the context of Article XX(d) of the GATT 1994); *US—Gambling* (in the context of Article XIV(a) of the GATS); and in *Brazil—Retreaded Tyres* (in the context of Article XX(b) of the GATT 1994). In each of these cases, the Appellate Body explained that an assessment of "necessity" involves "weighing and balancing" a number of distinct factors relating both to the measure sought to be justified as "necessary" and to possible alternative measures that may be reasonably available to the responding Member to achieve its desired objective.

242. We do not see that the Appellate Body's approach to the "necessity" analysis in *Brazil—Retreaded Tyres* differs from that in *US—Gambling*, which in turn referred to *Korea—Various Measures on Beef*. In each case, a sequential process of weighing and balancing a series of factors was involved. *US—Gambling* sets out a sequence by using the phrases: "The process *begins with* an assessment of the 'relative importance' of the interests or values furthered by the challenged measure"; "*Having ascertained* the importance of the particular interests at stake, a panel should *then* turn to the other factors that are to be 'weighed and balanced'"; and "A comparison between the challenged measure and possible alternatives should *then* be undertaken". The description of this sequence in *Brazil—Retreaded Tyres* mentions, first, the relevant factors to be weighed and balanced for the measure sought to be justified, and continues that the result of this analysis "must be confirmed by comparing the measure with possible alternatives, which may be less trade restrictive while providing an equivalent contribution to the achievement of the objective". Although the language used is not identical, both reports articulate the same approach and, like the Appellate Body report in *Korea—Various Measures on Beef*, emphasize the need to identify relevant factors and undertake a weighing and balancing process including, where relevant, with respect to proposed alternative measures that may be less trade restrictive while making an equivalent contribution to the relevant objective. These three reports also all recognize that a comprehensive analysis of the "necessity" of a measure is a sequential process. As such, the process must logically begin with a first step, proceed through a number of additional steps, and yield a final conclusion.

[In the excerpted part of the opinion below, the Appellate Body focuses on the second and third elements in the necessity analysis: the contribution of the measure to the interest at stake and whether a less trade restrictive measure was reasonably available.]

THE CONTRIBUTION OF CHINA'S MEASURES TO THE PROTECTION OF PUBLIC MORALS IN CHINA

250. In this subsection, we address claims by China that the Panel erred in finding that the State-ownership requirement and the provisions excluding foreign-invested enterprises from being approved or designated import entities are not "necessary" to protect public morals in China; as well as the claim by the United States that the Panel erred in finding that the State plan requirement can be characterized as "necessary", in the absence of reasonably available alternatives, to protect public morals in China. All these claims of error relate to the Panel's analysis of the *contribution* made by China's measures to the protection of public morals in China.

THE STATE-OWNERSHIP REQUIREMENT

255. China appeals the Panel's finding regarding the "necessity" of the State-ownership requirement. We recall that this requirement, set out in Article 42(2), in conjunction with Article 41, of the Publications Regulation, requires that an enterprise be wholly State-owned in order to be eligible for approval as a publications import entity. After having identified various factors relevant to its analysis of the necessity of this requirement, the Panel weighed and balanced them as follows:

> [W]e note, first of all, that the protection of public morals is a highly important governmental interest and that China has adopted a high level of protection of public morals within its territory. This said, . . . we have not been persuaded that the requirement in question makes a material contribution to the protection of public morals. Also, while it is unclear from the evidence on record to what extent, if any, the requirement in question limits imports of relevant products, it is clear that it completely excludes particular types of enterprise in China from the right to engage in importing. Weighing these factors, we reach the conclusion that China has not demonstrated that the requirement in question is "necessary" to protect public morals in China.

256. China requests the Appellate Body to reverse this finding.

257. First, China asserts that it explained to the Panel that the Chinese Government could not require enterprises with private investment in China to bear the substantial cost of performing the policy function of content review, but could require only those enterprises in which the State owns all of the equity to bear the cost of carrying out content review. China alleges that the Panel mistakenly reduced this argument to a mere "cost analysis" and failed to recognize that China's argument in fact related to the balance between the performance of a public policy function (content review) and the cost associated with performing this public policy function. Secondly, China alleges that the Panel misrepresented China's argument that only wholly State-owned enterprises are capable of satisfying the requirement in Article 42(4) of the *Publications Regulation* that publication import entities must have a suitable organization and qualified personnel. China alleges that the Panel erred in evaluating this argument exclusively under the prism of "cost", when its argument was not only about cost but also about the capacity to perform content review in a manner that preserves China's desired level of protection.

263. Overall, however, we do not see that the Panel failed to consider the public policy component of China's argument. While the Panel's analysis focuses on the cost component, this alone does not establish that the Panel ignored the public policy component of China's argument. As we see it, in assessing China's argument, the Panel decided to consider first whether content review was indeed costly, as China asserted. The Panel requested China to provide an estimate of such costs to import entities. China replied that it was unable to do so. China explained, however, that the cost of content review consists of: (i) human resources cost; (ii) cost of equipment, facilities, and premises used for content review; and (iii) losses incurred from compensation for customers in case of failure of ordered publications to pass content review. Having noted that it had been presented with only very limited evidence in this regard, the Panel found that China had not demonstrated that the cost associated with content review would be so high that it would be unreasonable to impose it on private enterprises, or that only wholly State-owned enterprises

"are able, or should be expected, to bear the cost associated with content review". The Panel also observed that "it is not apparent that wholly state-owned enterprises would be inherently more careful in conducting content review than privately owned ones." Moreover, the two-pronged nature of China's argument is properly reflected in the Panel's statement that, "[i]n China's view, privately-owned enterprises cannot be expected to pay for performing a public interest function." This demonstrates that the Panel did not consider the cost element of China's argument in isolation, but rather in relation to the public policy function. Thus, while the Panel could have analyzed the public policy component of China's argument in more depth, we acknowledge that the Panel was constrained by the fact that only limited evidence had been submitted by China in relation to that argument.

269. We therefore *find* that the Panel did not err, in paragraphs 7.860 and 7.863 of the Panel Report, in its finding regarding the contribution to the protection of public morals in China made by the State-ownership requirement in Article 42(2) of the *Publications Regulation* and we *reject* China's claim that the Panel failed to make an objective assessment of the matter before it, in violation of Article 11 of the DSU.

THE EXCLUSION OF FOREIGN-INVESTED ENTERPRISES

270. China appeals the Panel's finding that China has not demonstrated that the provisions prohibiting foreign-invested enterprises from engaging in the importation of the products at issue are "necessary" to protect public morals in China.

271. The Panel found that the effect of Articles X:2 and X:3 of the List of Prohibited Foreign Investment Industries in the *Catalogue*, in conjunction with Articles 3 and 4 of the *Foreign Investment Regulation*, is to prohibit any foreign-invested enterprise in China from engaging in the importation of books, newspapers, periodicals, electronic publications, or audiovisual products (including sound recordings and films for theatrical release). The Panel also found that Article 4 of the *Several Opinions* directs relevant agencies to ensure, through promulgation of appropriate rules, that no foreign-invested enterprise in China can lawfully import books, newspapers, periodicals, films for theatrical release, other audiovisual products (including sound recordings), or electronic publications. Furthermore, the Panel found that the legal effect of Article 21 of the *Audiovisual (Sub-)Distribution Rule* is that Chinese-foreign contractual joint ventures for the sub-distribution of audiovisual products do not have, and cannot obtain, the right to import audiovisual products. The Panel considered that these provisions excluding foreign-invested enterprises from engaging in importing are intended to reflect the fact that other measures stipulate that only wholly State-owned enterprises are permitted to import the relevant products.

272. China contends that the Panel relied on its finding concerning the State-ownership requirement to conclude that the provisions excluding foreign-invested enterprises from engaging in importing do not contribute to the protection of public morals in China. China argues that, because the Panel's finding concerning the State-ownership requirement is erroneous, "by necessary implication", the Panel's finding in respect of the provisions excluding foreign-invested enterprises from importing is also in error.

273. In addition, China submits that foreign-invested enterprises may not have the requisite understanding and knowledge of the applicable standards of

Chinese public morals and would not be capable of efficiently communicating with the administrative authorities, and that the Panel's finding on the exclusion of foreign-invested enterprises contradicts the finding made elsewhere by the Panel that requiring qualified review personnel contributes materially to the protection of public morals in China.

275. At the outset, we note that the Panel's finding concerning the exclusion of foreign-invested enterprises was based on the same reasoning as its finding relating to the State-ownership requirement. The Panel referred back to its previous finding that it was not persuaded that requiring publication import entities to be wholly State-owned contributes to the protection of public morals in China because they are the only enterprises in China that are able, or should be expected, to bear the cost associated with content review. Having considered that the provisions prohibiting foreign-invested enterprises from engaging in the importation of the products at issue reflect the same prohibition as the State-ownership requirement, "by necessary implication", the Panel was also not persuaded that the provisions prohibiting foreign-invested enterprises from being approved or designated import entities of the relevant products contribute to the protection of public morals in China.

276. We also observe that China's appeal of the Panel's finding relating to the provisions excluding foreign-invested enterprises from engaging in the importation of the relevant products relies upon the same reasons as those advanced by China with respect to the Panel's finding on the State-ownership requirement. We consider that the exclusion of foreign-invested enterprises and the requirement that import entities be wholly State-owned overlap to a large degree, in that both preclude foreign-invested enterprises from engaging in importing. Because we have found above that the Panel committed no error in its finding regarding the contribution to the protection of public morals in China made by the State-ownership requirement, we also reject, for the same reasons, China's claim that the Panel erred in finding that China has not demonstrated that the provisions contribute to the protection of public morals in China.

278. We therefore *find* that the Panel did not err, in paragraphs 7.865 and 7.868 of the Panel Report, in its finding regarding the contribution made by the provisions excluding foreign-invested enterprises from engaging in the importation of the relevant products and we *reject* China's claim that the Panel failed to make an objective assessment of the matter before it in violation of Article 11 of the DSU.

THE STATE PLAN REQUIREMENT

279. The United States requests the Appellate Body to reverse, or to "declare moot and of no legal effect" the Panel's intermediate finding regarding the "necessity" within the meaning of Article XX(a) of the GATT 1994 of the requirement of conformity with China's State plan for the total number, structure, and distribution of publication import entities contained in Article 42 of the *Publications Regulation* (the "State plan requirement"). The Panel found that this requirement can make a material contribution to the protection of public morals. Weighing this contribution together with the other relevant factors, the Panel took account:

> . . . first of all, of the fact that the protection of public morals is a highly important governmental interest and that China has adopted a high level of protection of public

morals within its territory. We must take account, in addition, of the fact that the requirement of conformity with the State plan is apt to make a material contribution to the protection of public morals; that it is unclear to what extent, if any, it limits overall imports of relevant products, but that it is nonetheless likely to minimize unnecessary delays in importing; and that it does not *a priori* exclude particular types of enterprise in China from establishing an import entity. Weighing these factors, we conclude that, in the absence of reasonably available alternatives, the State plan requirement in Article 42 of the *Publications Regulation* can be characterized as "necessary" to protect public morals in China.

281. Article 42 of the *Publications Regulation* sets out eight requirements for the approval of publication import entities. The last of these is that publication import entities may only be approved if they are in conformity with the State plan for the number, structure, and geographical coverage of publication import entities.

282. China did not provide the State plan or specific information about its content to the Panel. In response to a request by the Panel to provide the "State's plans", China stated that "[t]he plans concern the quantity, geographical and product coverage of publication import entities. However, such plans are not available in written form." China did, however, refer to the "State's plans" as prescribing development consistent with the selection of a limited number of import entities with extensive geographic coverage. China explained to the Panel that the requirement to have a small number of companies with extensive geographic coverage ensures that import entities, through branches, have premises in a large number of customs areas, so that no entry gate into the Chinese market is overlooked. In the same section of its first written submission—although without referring explicitly to the State plan—China explained that, "for the content review to be efficient and smooth", it is necessary that only a limited number of entities be authorized to engage in the importation of the relevant products. China further asserted that limiting the number of importation entities "enables the administrative authorities to have efficient control over whether those entities comply with the rules and procedures on inappropriate content."

291. We understand the Panel to have reached its finding regarding the contribution to the protection of public morals made by the State plan requirement on the basis of an assumption that the State plan requirement imposed a limitation on the number of import entities and on the basis of two inferences it drew from this assumption, namely: (i) that a limitation on the number of publication import entities would make it easier for the GAPP [General Administration of Press and Publication] to interact with these entities and to ensure consistency of the review work; and (ii) that a limitation on the number of import entities would allow the GAPP to devote more time to conduct annual inspections of compliance with the content review requirements.

292. We note that the Panel did not cite any evidence in support of its assumption that the State plan requirement imposed a limitation on the number of import entities. We also note that the Panel did not explain why the contribution made by the presumed limitation in the State plan requirement would be a "material" one. We further note that, while China asserted before the Panel that the State plan requirement constitutes a limitation on the number of import entities, China did not point the Panel to evidence supporting that assertion or evidence providing information about the operation of the State plan, or the nature of the limitation contained in the State plan.

296. In our view, the evidence in the Panel record does not establish that any State plan contains a limitation on the number of publication import entities, or that any such limitation would allow the GAPP to devote more time to conduct its annual inspections of the entities' compliance with content review requirements. The Panel exhibit that China relies upon as supporting the latter argument does not explain the scope of annual inspections carried out by the GAPP, or specify the parameters of the verification carried out by the GAPP. Rather, it simply stipulates what kind of documentation an import entity must submit to the authorities in the context of the annual inspection of compliance with the content review requirements. In any event, because we have found that the Panel wrongly assumed that the State plan requirement imposes a limitation on the number of import entities, the inferences that the Panel drew from this assumption have no basis.

297. For all these reasons, we *find* that the Panel erred, in paragraph 7.836 of the Panel Report, in finding that the State plan requirement in Article 42 of the *Publications Regulation* is apt to make a material contribution to the protection of public morals and that, in the absence of a reasonably available alternative, it can be characterized as "necessary" to protect public morals in China.

REASONABLY AVAILABLE ALTERNATIVE MEASURES

312. We turn next to China's appeal with respect to the Panel's analysis of whether a less restrictive measure is reasonably available to China as an alternative means of realizing its objective of protecting public morals. To recall, the Panel found that the suitable organization and qualified personnel requirement and the State plan requirement are "necessary" to protect public morals in China, in the absence of reasonably available alternatives. In order to reach a final determination as to whether or not China had demonstrated the "necessity" of these two requirements, the Panel turned to consider alternative measures proposed by the United States and, in particular, the proposal that the Chinese Government be given sole responsibility for conducting content review. The Panel considered that this proposal is an alternative that would be significantly less restrictive and would make a contribution to the protection of public morals in China that is at least equivalent to the contribution made by the suitable organization and qualified personnel requirement and the State plan requirement. The Panel then examined whether the proposed alternative is reasonably available to China and concluded that China had not demonstrated that this alternative is not "reasonably available".

313. China appeals this finding and submits that the proposed alternative—that the Chinese Government be given sole responsibility for conducting content review—is not "reasonably available", because it is merely theoretical in nature and would impose an undue and excessive burden on China. China alleges that the Panel erred in law and failed to properly address arguments it presented for purposes of demonstrating that the proposed alternative is not "reasonably available".

322. China's main arguments on appeal allege that the Panel erred in law and failed to properly address arguments presented by China in finding that the proposed alternative—that the Chinese Government be given sole responsibility for conducting content review—is reasonably available to China. China contends that this proposed alternative would impose an undue financial and administrative burden on China. China emphasizes that, in the current system, importation entities

participate in the content review process, and that, in particular with respect to reading materials, these importation entities carry most of the burden of content review. The alternative considered by the Panel would require China to engage in "tremendous restructuring" and create a new, multi-level structure for content review within the Government. China points, in addition, to the large quantities of imported reading materials and to time constraints, especially for newspapers and periodicals, which mean that the content review mechanism must have a wide geographic coverage, sufficient manpower, and a capacity to respond quickly. To expect the Chinese Government to assume sole responsibility for the conduct of content review would require the training and assignment of a large number of qualified content reviewers to numerous locations. China adds that the Panel erred in failing to find that "substantial technical difficulties" demonstrate that the proposed alternative is not reasonably available to China. The Panel simply assumed that time-sensitive publications could be submitted electronically to the Chinese Government for content review, when in fact the Government would have to implement a completely upgraded electronic communications system to perform efficiently such an electronic review. China also contends that, if content review were performed at a single central location, according to the proposed alternative, this would make it impossible to "double check" content at the customs level, as is done under the current system.

327. We are not persuaded that the Panel erred in the above analysis. The Panel did not find that the proposed alternative measure involves *no* cost or burden to China. As the Appellate Body report in *US—Gambling* makes clear, an alternative measure should not be found not to be reasonably available merely because it involves *some* change or administrative cost. Changing an existing measure may involve cost and a Member cannot demonstrate that no reasonably available alternative exists merely by showing that no cheaper alternative exists. Rather, in order to establish that an alternative measure is not "reasonably available", the respondent must establish that the alternative measure would impose an *undue* burden on it, and it must support such an assertion with sufficient evidence.

328. In the present case, China did not provide evidence to the Panel substantiating the likely nature or magnitude of the costs that would be associated with the proposed alternative, as compared to the current system. Nor has China, in its appeal, pointed to specific evidence in the Panel record that would allow us to conclude that the Panel erred in failing to attribute sufficient significance to the evidence of financial and administrative burden that may attach to the proposed alternative measure. Instead, China simply argues that the proposal would involve "tremendous restructuring" and would "obviously put on China an excessively heavy financial and administrative burden". However, as we see it, adopting any alternative measure will, by definition, involve some change, and this alone does not suffice to demonstrate that the alternative would impose an undue burden.

332. Accordingly, having reviewed the Panel's analysis of the limited evidence before it, as well as the additional arguments made by China on appeal, we *find* that the Panel did not err, in paragraph 7.908 of the Panel Report, in finding that at least one of the alternative measures proposed by the United States is an alternative "reasonably available" to China.

335. Finally, it may be useful to indicate what we are *not* saying in reaching the above conclusion. We are *not* holding that China is under an obligation to ensure that the Chinese Government assumes sole responsibility for conducting content review. Rather, we are agreeing with the Panel that the United States has

demonstrated that the proposed alternative would be less restrictive and would make a contribution that is at least equivalent to the contribution made by the measures at issue to securing China's desired level of protection of public morals. This does not mean that having the Chinese Government assume sole responsibility for conducting content review is the *only* alternative available to China, nor that China *must* adopt such a scheme. It does mean that China has not successfully justified under Article XX(a) of the GATT 1994 the provisions and requirements found to be inconsistent with China's trading rights commitments under its Accession Protocol and Working Party Report.

NOTES AND QUESTIONS

1. The *China—Publications and Audiovisual Products* case is the first extensive Appellate Body interpretation of GATT Article XX(a). Based on this decision, do you see any possibility that this article can allow countries to limit imports on the basis of cultural concerns?

2. Do you think that China will really allow foreign enterprises to conduct content review and play a role in the imports of media products? Or will China find some other way to deny foreign enterprises this role?

3. Is the diversity of the world's cultures really threatened by international trade and globalization? What are the motivations of the people on both sides of the debate? What are the reasons for the worldwide popularity of American popular culture? Are not free trade and stronger intellectual property rights as advanced by the WTO beneficial in most respects to those who worry about the disappearance of cultural diversity? Is there any need for a cultural exception in the WTO rules?

4. Article 137 of the Treaty on the Functioning of the European Union requires respect for cultural diversity and mandates action on the part of the EU to improve the knowledge and dissemination of European culture. An important part of this regime is the EU Broadcasting Directive, Audiovisual Media Without Frontiers, EC Directive 89/552 and its latest amendment, EC Directive 2007/65 of December 11, 2007. This Directive permits member states of the EU to impose quotas for media content on broadcasters and other media providers in favor of European productions. The purpose of this Directive is to encourage and promote European productions. Is this good policy? Note that the quotas are not placed on imports of products so this Directive is not inconsistent with the GATT. Instead the quotas are placed on service providers. In Chapter 11, we cover the GATS, and we will see that this agreement does not require service liberalization beyond the commitments made by each WTO member. The only first-world WTO members that have entered into substantially free audiovisual and broadcasting commitments are the United States and New Zealand.

5. How can a WTO member advance its cultural interests under WTO rules? On the export side GATT Article XX(f) allows export controls on certain kinds of cultural goods. Beyond this, a country that wants to export its cultural products and services will be interested in reducing import barriers in other countries. This is why tariffs for most cultural products, such as books, are low. On the import side, GATT rules do not permit quotas or discriminatory taxation of foreign cultural products. We have already explored an exception to this rule, GATT Article IV, which permits screen quotas for films. But over the years this quota system

has been relaxed in many countries. There are two methods a WTO member may employ to protect its cultural industries: (1) Under the GATS, market access and National Treatment for service industries are granted only to the extent that pertinent commitments have been made by the individual WTO member. A member can therefore refrain from commitments in important cultural services sectors (such as musical performances). If a member has made no commitment then it can close that services sector completely from foreign competition. (2) A WTO member may subsidize its own cultural industries to give them an advantage over foreign cultural products. Although the WTO Subsidies and Countervailing Measures Agreement regulates subsidies, as we will see in Chapter 10, the SCM Agreement outlaws subsidies only when and to the extent they materially impede the trade interests of other WTO members. In most cases of cultural subsidies this will be difficult or impossible to show.

VII.   *Climate Change, Multilateral Environmental Agreements and Trade*

According to the United Nations Intergovernmental Panel on Climate Change (IPCC), which is composed of 450 scientists from 130 countries, average temperatures in the Northern hemisphere during the second half of the twentieth century were likely the highest in at least the last 1,300 years. Sea level has risen since 1993 at an average rate of 3.1 mm per year, and global greenhouse gas emissions (gases such as carbon dioxide that trap heat in the earth's atmosphere) increased by 70 percent between 1970 and 2004. The IPCC predicts a rise in average temperature of 2-6°C during the present century if action is not taken to curb greenhouse gas emissions. Scientists predict that such a rise would cause widespread damage, an increase in sea level of over 1 meter, and unacceptably rapid changes in ecosystems, temperature, and rainfall patterns all over the earth.[15]

The world community has taken concrete (if insufficient) steps to move toward a low-carbon economy. The United Nations Framework Convention on Climate Change (UNFCC) (1992) accepted by 192 parties, established a process to control greenhouse gas emissions on a global basis. Each year a Conference of the Parties (COP) meets to consider new measures. The most important step taken in this process was the conclusion of the Kyoto Protocol in 1997, which requires thirty-six developed countries to reduce their greenhouse gas emissions from 1990 levels by a specified percentage on or before the end of 2012. If all reduction targets are met, the result would be a total reduction of 5.2 percent below 1990 levels for the participating countries. However, the United States, one of the largest emitters of greenhouse gases, did not ratify the Kyoto Protocol, and many of the states that accepted Kyoto will not meet their reduction targets. In addition, greenhouse gas emissions from developing countries, which had no specific reduction obligation under Kyoto, have snowballed. As a result, greenhouse gas emissions continue to increase, and the concentration of carbon dioxide in the atmosphere averages 380 parts per million (ppm) and is increasing at the rate of about 2 ppm per year. In

---

15. *See* IPCC Fourth Assessment Report (2007) available at http://www.ipcc.ch.

2009 the COP could not agree on a treaty to deal with the problem after the Kyoto Protocol target dates are reached at the end of 2012, but several leaders, including U.S. President Barack Obama, adopted a non-binding political agreement, the Copenhagen Accord, which invited all nations to pledge voluntary reductions of greenhouse gases by 2020. Virtually all of the states that are parties to the UNFCC have submitted reduction pledges to this Accord. Moreover, the COP still has the goal of negotiating a binding greenhouse gas reduction agreement for the target years, 2020 and 2050.

So far no conflict has arisen between the rules of the WTO and the regime of the UNFCC and the Kyoto Protocol. As of this writing it is uncertain whether there will be a new climate change agreement and, if so, whether any provision of such a new agreement would implicate international trade.

The relationship between climate change law and the multilateral trading system is one aspect of a larger problem: the relationship between the WTO and Multilateral Environmental Agreements (MEAs). At this writing there are about 240 MEAs dealing with various environmental issues currently in force. About thirty-eight of these MEAs restrict or impact trade in some way. These MEAs are negotiated outside of the WTO system but many countries belong both to MEAs and the WTO.

Generally there are two categories of trade restrictions to be found in MEAs: First, some MEAs prohibit or restrict trade in products because of the characteristics of the products themselves. For example, the Basel Convention on the Control of Movements of Hazardous Wastes and Their Disposal (in force 1992 with 175 parties) regulates trade in hazardous waste products. Second, some MEAs adopt trade restrictions in order to provide an incentive to join the conventional regime or to sanction violators. For example, the Montreal Protocol on the Protection of the Ozone Layer (in force 1988) has a non-compliance procedure that may impose trade sanctions against violators.

The issue that arises is what happens when an MEA authorizes a country to act in a way that violates a WTO agreement. For example, suppose that an MEA authorizes a country to impose a trade ban. The country is a member of both the MEA and the WTO. Such a trade ban might violate GATT Article XI prohibiting quotas on imports or exports. Can the member imposing the ban justify the ban on the grounds that it was authorized by the MEA? No WTO case has challenged MEAs or declared the trade provisions of an MEA in violation of WTO rules. But the possibility exists of a conflict between MEAs and the rules of the WTO. This possibility was recognized when the WTO was established in 1995 and a special body, the Committee on Trade and the Environment (CTE) was created within the WTO to deal with trade and environment issues. In 2001, the Doha Ministerial Conference agreed to negotiate on the relationship between WTO rules and MEAs, particularly those that contain specific trade obligations. To this end WTO committees and MEA secretariats share information and consult regularly. The idea prevails that it is essential that the trade and environment regimes develop coherently. However, at this writing no agreement has been reached on any specific matter concerning trade and MEAs.

In this section, however, we will explore the possibility that MEAs could present conflicts with the WTO law of international trade, and some of the probable effects of such conflicts. We will also examine various alternatives on how to make MEAs and the WTO agreements compatible. We set the stage by reading a paper on the problem by an official of UNCTAD.

Specific Trade Obligations in Multilateral Environmental Agreements and Their Relationship with the Rules of the Multilateral Trading System
Ulrich Hoffman, Economic Affairs Officer, UNCTAD Secretariat
August 2003

RESULTS OF THE CTE DISCUSSION ON THE MEA-WTO RELATIONSHIP

Proposals made in the CTE on clarifying the relationship between trade measures in MEAs and WTO rules:

PRE DOHA PROPOSALS

Since the creation of the Committee on Trade and the Environment (CTE) in 1995, WTO members have tabled a whole range of proposals on how to address the WTO/MEA relationship. Some have argued that the problem was only theoretical, since no single dispute over trade measures in an MEA had actually come to the WTO for settlement and, therefore, there was no need, at that stage, to change WTO rules to accommodate MEAs. This was defined as the "status quo" approach and it appears that the vast majority of WTO members, including many developing countries, favour this position.

Another group of countries supported what was called a "soft accommodation" approach aimed at increasing the compatibility of environmental agreement with WTO rules. According to this position, there is no need to amend WTO rules to take MEAs into account, but cases of conflict can be addressed by, for instance, waiving, on a case-by-case basis, WTO obligations in order to cover specific trade measures taken pursuant to an MEA, or by developing guidelines for WTO dispute settlement bodies or for MEA negotiators to assist them in the selection of WTO-consistent trade measures to be included in the agreement.

A small group of countries, namely the European Community and Switzerland, supported a "full scale accommodation" approach, whereby WTO rules should be changed to explicitly allow for the use of trade measures by members pursuant to MEAs, so as to give environmental policy makers the certainty and predictability that their regimes would not be overturned in the WTO.

Finally, according to a fourth approach, the burden of accommodation should shift to the MEAs themselves. MEA provisions should be modified on the basis of certain criteria with a view to enhancing clarity and making sure that trade measures are not more trade-restrictive than required to achieve MEA objectives and thus be WTO compatible. This position enjoyed considerable support among developing countries.

POST DOHA PROPOSALS

A large number of proposals supported the idea of a "bottom-up" approach, proposed by Australia, which consisted of three phases: (i) identification of specific trade obligations and WTO rules that are relevant to these obligations; (ii) exchange of experience on these provisions, including information exchange with

MEA secretariats (in this phase it will be important to identify any real issues/problems encountered in implementing specific trade obligations as opposed to discussing theoretical or hypothetical scenarios); and (iii) discussion of matters arising from the work undertaken in phases one and two, and focus on the outcome of the negotiations. Based on this approach, it was proposed to review at more length specific trade obligations in three MEAs: the Convention on International Trade in Endangered Species of Wild Fauna and Flora (CITES), the Montreal Protocol on Substances that Deplete the Ozone Layer (Montreal Protocol), and the Basel Convention on the Control of Transboundary Movement of Hazardous Wastes (Basel Convention).

A second group of proposals favoured a "top-down" approach, advocated by the EU and Switzerland. This would include discussions on (i) issues of scope and definition of specific trade obligations; (ii) the development of certain principles to address the WTO-MEA relationship; (iii) dialogue with MEAs; and (iv) the development of options or solutions. Some delegations suggested that the two approaches were not mutually exclusive and could be pursued in parallel.

A BRIEF ANALYSIS OF SPECIFIC TRADE OBLIGATIONS, FLEXIBILITY MECHANISMS AND SUPPORTIVE MEASURES IN THREE MEAS (CITES, THE MONTREAL PROTOCOL, AND THE BASEL CONVENTION)

[This part focuses on the Specific Trade Obligations (STOs) contained in three major environmental treaties and their possible conflict with the WTO.]

1. CITIES

The key objective of the Convention is to alleviate stress on endangered species arising from one source, namely demand pressures transmitted through international trade. CITES is not supposed to deal with other pressures on endangering species such as (i) loss of natural habitats (from e.g. land conversion); (ii) introduction of new species; (iii) over-exploitation of species caused by domestic commercial and subsistence use; and (iv) pollution and global environment change.

A significant problem for CITES is that generally the direct role of trade in species extinction is less pronounced than the other factors, particularly habitat loss and domestic commercial as well as subsistence use. Therefore, it is often difficult to establish a direct causal link between species extinction and international trade. This results in real or potential conflicts between the environment and trade communities of CITES in deciding on the listing and/or down-listing of species in the Convention.

CITES has a number of trade measures that could qualify as STOs:

- Art. II(4) prohibits trade in specimens of species listen in Appendices I, II, and III, except in accordance with the Convention.
- Art. III regulates all trade in specimens of species listed in Appendix I.
- Art. IV(1)-(6) regulates all trade in specimens of species listen in Appendix II.
- Art. V regulates all trade in specimens of species listen in Appendix III.

- Art. VI (1)-(6) governs permits and certificates related to trade.
- Art. VIII (1)(a and b) and (6) that contain measures to enforce the Convention to prohibit trade.

In addition, as already mentioned above, Article XIV (1) of the Convention stipulates that it "shall in no way affect the right of Parties to adopt (a) stricter domestic measures regarding the conditions for trade, taking, possession or transport of specimens of species included in Appendices I, II, and III, or the complete prohibition thereof; or (b) domestic measures restricting or prohibiting trade, taking, possession or transport of species not included in Appendix I, II or III." This provision leaves considerable discretion to Parties in implementing the trade provisions of the Convention.

CITES has a number of flexibility elements that can be applied to enhance the effectiveness and efficiency of trade measures:

- The down-listing of species from Appendix I to Appendix II is based on consensus or a two-third majority vote.
- (Not in the Convention, but recently developed) national export quotas for a limited amount of trade of Appendix I-listed species (this allows a distinction between national populations that are more sustainably managed than others).
- Limited flexibility for international trade in Appendix I species through an exception, called ranching—CITES-registered farms receive treatment of Appendix II-listed species for international trade (ranching has also led to some general down-listing of species).
- The possibility for a party to make a reservation to a decision on listing of a particular species. The party will then be considered as non-party for this species, but can trade with other non-parties or parties that also made a reservation (for instance, between Thailand and Japan for the Clouded Monitor lizard).
- Treatment of non-parties as parties and therefore lifting of trade restriction if non-Parties have (i) a similar administrative infrastructure, and (ii) requires a CITES comparable permit and certification system.
- The option under Art. 14 of CITES to allow importing or exporting parties to take stricter domestic measures on any species.
- The option of a "zero export quota" for species recently down-listed from Appendix I to Appendix II.

A potential area of tension with WTO rules is the practice to use trade measures against non-complying Parties as enforcement instrument by, for instance, temporarily suspending all trade in CITES-listed species of specific parties that fail to demonstrate within a certain time period that they adopted all necessary measures to adequately implement the Convention. Although there is no specific Article in the Convention on compliance or non-compliance, CITES measures to ensure compliance derive from a set of procedures and mechanisms approved by the parties. Decisions 11.15 of COP XI in April 2000, for instance, stated that the secretariat brought to the attention of parties that four countries (Fiji, Turkey, Viet Nam and Yemen) had high volumes of international trade in CITES-listed species and that their national legislation was believed not to meet the implementation requirements of CITES. It was proposed that these countries should be given till 31 October 2001 to (i) adopt adequate legislation; or (ii) request technical assistance from the secretariat to prepare such legislation and (iii) should report on related progress to the secretariat no later than 30 April 2001. Decision 11.16 of COP XI asked all parties to suspend trade in all CITES-listed species with the four countries in question as from 31 October 2001, if, in spite of assistance, these countries would not adopt the required legislation. A total of 37 countries have been subject to such approach and 17 countries have faced general CITES or species-specific trade bans. The most prominent cases among developing country parties concerned Bolivia, Paraguay, UAE and Thailand.

2.   THE MONTREAL PROTOCOL

The Montreal Protocol is an international legal instrument of the Vienna Convention for the Protection of the Ozone Layer of 1985. It consists of five separate treaties (the Montreal Protocol, that entered into force in 1988, the London Agreement of 1992, the Copenhagen Amendment of 1994, the Montreal Amendment of 1999 and the Beijing Amendment of 2002). In the Montreal Protocol, trade measures are supplementary to the phase-out schedules of ozone-depleting substances (ODS).

The Vienna Convention and the Montreal Protocol only explicitly require bans on trade of ODS and ODS-containing products between parties and nonparties to the treaties. There are however some other measures that also concern trade among parties:

- Implicit control of trade between parties through the formula for calculating ODS consumption: production + import – export (export and import of used/recycled ODS are not included in consumption as recovery obviates the need for new ODS).
- A recently agreed licensing system for ODS trade among parties to combat illegal ODS shipments.
- A recently adopted export ban on used and recycled ODS for parties in non-compliance.
- Voluntary notification by a Party of ODS-containing products it does not want to import.
- Decision XIV/7 of MoP 2002 introduced a reporting provision for proven cases of illegal trade.

Similar to CITES, the Montreal Protocol is equipped with an enforcement mechanism that provides an institutional and legal basis to order trade sanctions against violators. For instance, in Annex IV of the Montreal Protocol, entitled "Non-compliance Procedure", an Implementation Committee was established in order to supervise the national implementation of the Protocol. According to paragraph 9 of the Annex, the Committee shall report to the MOP of the Protocol, including any recommendations it considers appropriate. Then, based on the report, the Parties may decide upon and call for necessary measures to enforce full compliance with the Protocol. To avoid controversy and confine the extent and content of the measures the Parties may take, Annex V of the Protocol sets up a list of measures in a straightforward manner. Apart from non-coercive and inventive means, in paragraph C of the Annex, suspension of trade is clearly specified. This provision has however not yet been invoked.

3.   THE BASEL CONVENTION

The Basel Convention regulates international trade in hazardous waste. The Convention aims at (i) reducing the generation and transboundary movement of hazardous wastes in terms of their volume and hazardousness; (ii) disposing hazardous wastes as close as possible to their source of generations; (iii) preventing illegal traffic; and (iv) prohibiting shipments of hazardous wastes to countries that lack the legal, administrative and technical capacity to manage them in an environmentally sound manner.

The Convention initially confined the regulations of international trade in hazardous waste to a "Prior Information and Consent" (PIC) approach. Subsequently, the [parties] adopted the so-called Basel Ban Amendment that supplements, on the one hand, and significantly revises, on the other hand, the original PIC approach. According to the Ban Amendment, all international shipments of hazardous waste for final disposal and re-use, material recovery or recycling are banned from Annex VII countries (i.e. members of OECD, EC and Liechtenstein) to all other countries.

The original Convention contains the following trade measure that might eventually be considered STOs:

- Arts. 3(1) and 3(2) require reporting on national definitions of hazardous wastes and requirements concerning transboundary movements;
- Arts. 4(1), 4(2)(e), 4(2)(f), 4(2)(g), 4(6), 4(7), 4(8), 4(9) and 4(10) set out specific obligations regarding the transboundary movement of hazardous waste;
- Arts. 6(1), 6(2), 6(3), 6(4), 6(5), 6(9) and 6(10) outline the modalities for transboundary movement of hazardous wastes (some of these modalities may not qualify as STO);
- Art. 8 governs the duty to reimport;
- Art. 9(2) sets out obligations for the repatriation of illegal waste;
- Arts. 13(2), 13(3)(a) and 13(4) elaborate on procedures for the transmission of information.

It is important to note that the Basel Convention has succeeded in significantly reducing waste trafficking from developed countries notably to the less and least developed countries. Although precise data in this respect is scarce, reported cases of waste trafficking have recently become very rare. Also, the Convention has pioneered a Protocol on Liability and Compensation for Damage Resulting from Transboundary Movements of Hazardous Wastes and their Disposal.

The Convention, however, has also a number of conceptual and definitional deficiencies:

- The key underpinning of the Convention and the Ban Amendment is the concept of Environmentally Sound Management of Hazardous Waste (ESM). Existence or lack of ESM in a target country is the lynchpin for allowing or preventing hazardous waste exports to this country. However, the Convention has not yet developed any practical mechanism for implementing ESM, based on clear, science-based criteria. Because the concept of and requirements for ESM are so pervasive in the Convention, it is likely that shipments of Basel wastes to facilities without ESM are a priori illegal. However, the Convention does not specify the manner or the extent to which the state of export must verify ESM. Furthermore, the Convention takes for granted that "all" developing countries will never achieve ESM although today some have already done so.

- The term hazardous waste is not clearly defined in the Convention. It concerns categories of waste in Annex I that need to exhibit one of 13 hazardous characteristics in Annex III, without surpassing any threshold or requiring a risk assessment. This shortcoming has partly been overcome by creating Annex VIII, which contains a list of specific wastes that, from a multilateral point of view, are considered hazardous under the Convention. Some ambiguity however remains. This not only leads to considerable discrepancies between existing lists, but also creates uncertainty for trade flows.

- The BC defines disposal of hazardous waste as including both "final disposal" and "re-use, recovery, and recycling" of material contained in the waste. Unlike CITES, this affects a number of commercially important secondary materials in international trade such as lead and zinc scrap as well as precious and non-ferrous metals contained in waste electrical and electronic assemblies.

- The BC implicitly assumes that there is a propensity for developed countries to dump hazardous waste in developing countries. The actual demand of developing countries, in particular in rapidly industrializing countries with high material intensity of economic growth, for recoverable material is insufficiently recognized. Art. 4.9 (b) of the original Convention allows movements of hazardous waste if required as commodity input. The Ban Amendment, however, overruled this provision. Most of the hazardous waste trade between developed and developing countries, as well as among developing countries is destined for material recovery/recycling and is overwhelmingly demand-, rather than supply-induced.

Although the Ban Amendment is not yet in force, shortly after its adoption, the European Community has revised its regulation on exports and imports of hazardous waste with a view to implementing the Ban Amendment. Therefore, interested developing countries, such as India, Malaysia, the Philippines, or Thailand, have been unable to import hazardous waste destined for recovery operations in accordance with Article 4.9(b) of the Convention.

NOTES AND QUESTIONS

1. What is the answer to reconciling MEAs with the rules of the multilateral trading system? With respect to specific trade obligations in MEAs, why not list these and immunize them from WTO attack? But if this is done, what should be done about non-parties to the MEA who are members of the WTO? Does the immunity apply with respect to non-parties? What about taking disputes concerning MEAs out of the WTO dispute settlement system altogether and creating a separate

consultative mechanism to deal with them? Or should such disputes be relegated solely to the dispute settlement system of the particular MEA in question?

2. *Conflicts of Norms.* The proliferation of international regimes and dispute settlement systems in international law has led to a certain fragmentation of the international social world. Each international regime has specialized and relatively autonomous rules and rule-complexes, legal institutions, and spheres of legal practice. This situation may lead to conflicts of international norms and perhaps even conflicting decisions of international tribunals. International law employs four major methods of resolving conflicts of norms:

- The principle of mutual respect and support
- The principle of lex specialis
- Article 31(3) of the Vienna Convention on the Law of Treaties (VCLT) (1969), which provides that in interpreting a treaty there "shall be taken into account . . . any subsequent agreement between the parties, subsequent practice which establishes agreement between the parties . . . , and any relevant rules of international law applicable in relations between the parties."
- Article 30 of the VCLT, which sets out a partial lex posteriori rule, which provides in general that in the event of a conflict between the provisions of an earlier treaty and a later treaty, the latter will govern.

NOTE ON CLIMATE CHANGE AND TRADE

We do not know at this writing whether there will be a new multilateral treaty on climate change or whether such treaty will contain trade restrictions. But since climate change is such an important problem and since trade restrictions are much discussed as part of the solution, we consider some hypothetical scenarios and apply WTO law as an exercise in possible future outcomes.

As of this writing, no agreement has been reached by WTO Doha negotiators on the relationship between MEAs and WTO law. Products, such as iron and steel, cement, fertilizer, chemicals, and a wide variety of consumer products move freely in international trade, and yet there are no applicable standards for how they are produced in terms of their carbon footprint — the amount of carbon-based energy that goes into their production. Many countries that are concerned with reducing carbon emissions reason that they may take great efforts to develop standards for producing a wide variety of products using the minimum amount of carbon-based energy, but if they do so, their national carbon standards for products will be overwhelmed by imports. And since low-carbon production will be more expensive than products made without such mandates, imported products will take market share away from domestic low-carbon products.

PROBLEM 7-10

Suppose therefore that Country M, a WTO member, has enacted regulations for a wide variety of products requiring their production using minimum carbon-based energy. Country M has informed all of its trading partners of the new standards and set a date by which imports that are not certified as meeting the same low-carbon standards (as applicable to domestic Country M products) will be banned. Review the *EC—Asbestos* case. In that case the Appellate Body accepted the argument that asbestos-containing products were not "like" products to the competing non-asbestos products.

(1) Will the Appellate Body permit the exclusion of imported products that do not meet the low-carbon standards, as consistent with the GATT because they are not like products to the low-carbon domestic products? In any case, can Country M rely upon the WTO TBT Agreement to enforce its low-carbon regulations against imports? Does the TBT Agreement apply? Consider also the applicability of TBT Article 2.

(2) Suppose Country M decides not to set unilateral low-carbon standards for products but instead takes up the matter at the Organization of Economic Cooperation and Development (OECD), a group of leading developed nations, of which it is a powerful member. An OECD committee of experts is appointed to draft low-carbon standards for a wide variety of products that move in international trade. If Country M enforces the resultant OECD standards on all imported products, will this comply with TBT Article 2? Consider also TBT Articles 9 and 12. Should the international standards-setting body be drawn from a broader-based organization such as UNCTAD? If a committee of experts from UNCTAD drafted the international standards, would this satisfy TBT Article 2?

PROBLEM 7-11

Suppose that a new climate change agreement authorizes parties that pledge significant reductions of greenhouse gases to enact certain controls on imported products. The purpose of the new controls is to counteract two kinds of adverse consequences that will otherwise stem from domestic greenhouse gas reductions. Since domestic producers of products would have to switch to low-carbon production methods, they will face problems of "competitiveness" and "leakage." Competitiveness is a problem because the domestic industries will face competition from imports from countries that do not have stringent controls on greenhouse gases. Leakage is a problem because domestic reduction will be offset by foreign emission increases, perhaps in part because of a shift of production from countries that have stringent carbon emission controls to countries with less stringent controls. Suppose Country N, a WTO member that is party to the new climate change agreement, has decided to enact a "cap and trade" program to control domestic carbon emissions. A cap and trade program imposes a nationwide cap on emissions from covered entities. The cap is enforced by a law that makes it illegal to emit greenhouse gases without a permit in the form of an Emission Allowance. Emission Allowances equal to the cap are distributed (either free or for value) to the covered entities, who in turn can either use them or sell them to other covered entities who seek to emit more than the Emission Allowances they own. In order to deal with the competitiveness and leakage problems, Country P, as authorized by the new climate change agreement, enacts an International Emission Allowance program (IEA) to cover imported products. As of the date the new system of cap and trade goes into effect, importers of designated products would have to purchase an IEA to compensate for the negative greenhouse gas impact of their products. Imports from countries with greenhouse gas restrictions comparable to those of Country

N are exempt, but all other importers, including those from several WTO member states, must purchase IEAs.

(1) Is the IEA program consistent with the GATT? Consider Articles I, III, XI, and XIII.

(2) Will the IEA program qualify for a GATT Article XX exception? The main candidates are Article XX(b) and (g). But will the IEA program run afoul of the chapeau of Article XX?

If your conclusion is that the IEA program is inconsistent with WTO rules, but is authorized under the new climate change agreement, we have a conflict of norms between two international law regimes. How can this conflict be resolved? Consider VCLT Article 30.

PROBLEM 7-12

Suppose Country O decides to forego an IEA program because of concerns that it would be inconsistent with WTO law, but instead enacts a tax on the carbon and greenhouse gas inputs of all domestically produced products. This tax is set at 100 percent *ad valorem* of the value of greenhouse gas inputs of each product. This tax is also collected on imported products that must also pay the 100 percent rate. In order to facilitate collection of the tax, Country O will use border tax adjustment (BTA). By using BTA the tax will be collected at the border by Country O customs officials in addition to the applicable GATT bound tariff with respect to WTO members. BTA therefore applies the carbon tax on the destination principle; i.e., the tax is paid and collected in the country in which the product is sold. Thus, with respect to exports leaving Country O, BTA gives exporters a tax refund equal to any carbon tax they have paid on the product being exported. Country O is careful so that the carbon tax paid by importers is exactly equal to the tax paid by domestic producers on products sold domestically. The revenue from the carbon tax is so great that Country O is able to make drastic reductions in corporate and personal income tax rates. Several questions have arisen:

(1) Does this tax and BTA scheme violate the GATT? Consider GATT Article II:2(a). Consider also the Note to GATT Article XVI, Ad Article XVI. In addition, the main guide to BTA is the *1970 Report of the GATT Working Party on Border Tax Adjustments*, GATT B.I.S.D. (18th Supp.) 97, L/3646, adopted on December 2, 1970, at ¶9. The Working Party reported broad consensus that the scope of border tax adjustment was limited to indirect taxes (i.e., taxes levied on products, such as excise duties, sales taxes, value added taxes, and cascade taxes), and there can be no BTA for direct taxes, income taxes, or payroll taxes that are levied on individuals and corporations. However, the Working Party reported divergence of views on "taxes occultes," such as taxes on advertising, energy, machinery, and transport. What does this mean for BTA on carbon inputs by Country O? Is this fatal? Consider the *U.S.—Superfund* case that we read in Chapter 2 of this book. The taxes in that case involved petroleum products, certain basic feedstock chemicals, and downstream products derived from these chemicals. Certainly taxes on inputs to products, even when those inputs are greatly modified in the final product, are indirect taxes eligible for BTA. The only difference with respect to Country O's BTA is that the energy inputs are physically consumed and are not physically incorporated in the final product. But *U.S.—Superfund* did not mention physical incorporation as a requirement or concern. In *U.S.—Superfund* the GATT panel

also made clear that the purpose of the tax—environmental purposes—is irrelevant: "Whether a tax is levied on a product for general revenue purposes or to encourage rational use of environmental resources, is therefore not relevant for the determination of border tax adjustment."[16] Consider again the wording of GATT Article II:2(a)—do the words "from which" suggest that any input, even one that is consumed in the course of production of the product, is eligible for BTA? Do these words exclude BTA for such inputs? This question has never been decided by any panel, or the Appellate Body, or by any official WTO or GATT pronouncement. What do you think?

(2) What about the export side? Is BTA available for exported products? For the answer to this question we must consider the WTO SCM Agreement, Annex I. Note paragraph (h) of Annex I: the excessive rebate of taxes is a prohibited subsidy; but the converse of this is that a rebate of indirect taxes, that is not excessive, is not a subsidy. Furthermore, note the "provided" clause of this subparagraph and its reference to "inputs that are consumed in the production of the exported product." At the end of paragraph (h) the statement is made: "This item shall be interpreted in accordance with the guidelines . . . in Annex II." Turning to Annex II we read footnote 61, a definition of inputs consumed in the production process—"energy, fuels and oil used in the production process . . . ." Thus the debate over BTA for inputs consumed in the production process was resolved in favor of BTA for such inputs. Would a concern for legal symmetry mean that BTA is also available on the import side for inputs consumed in the production process? Is Country O's BTA and carbon tax regime consistent with the GATT?

What about BTA for Country N's IEA program discussed in Problem 7-11? A first problem is that a cap and trade is not a tax but is rather a hybrid system that combines traditional government regulation with economic incentives and a trading scheme to give the program flexibility. Most of the revenue from trading goes not to government as would a tax, but rather accrues to private companies. In the GATT case, *EEC—Measures on Animal Feed Proteins*, GATT B.I.S.D. (25th Supp.) 49, Report of the GATT Panel, adopted on March 14, 1978, an EC regulation required both producers and importers of vegetable proteins to purchase and denature skimmed milk powder from the EC's stocks. This measure was for the purpose of getting rid of surpluses generated by the EC's Common Agricultural Policy by forcing producers and importers to buy them. The EC regulation required importers to post a security deposit for the required purchases. The EC defended the security deposit as a permissible BTA under GATT Article II:2(a). The panel rejected this argument, stating that the security deposit was only an enforcement mechanism for the purchase requirement. This case seems to indicate that an IRA program would not qualify as a BTA. For more discussion of these issues, see the report prepared by the WTO Secretariat, *WTO-UNEP, Trade and Climate Change* (2009) and Hufbauer, Charnovitz, and Kim, *Global Warming and the World Trading System* (Peterson Institute for International Economics, 2009).

---

16. *United States—Superfund*, GATT B.I.S.D. (34th Supp.) 136, Report of the GATT Panel, adopted on June 17, 1987, at ¶5.2.4.

VIII.   Workers' Rights

The issue of whether workers' rights should be included within the WTO is a very controversial subject. The proponents of workers' rights argue that in many countries workers have few rights and are exploited by governments and private businesses, which are also the main beneficiaries of the WTO. Including workers' rights in the WTO will lead to the adoption of worldwide standards that will protect workers. Opponents argue that the WTO cannot be expected to solve all of the world's problems. The WTO would collapse under the enormous burden created by the social, political, and moral responsibilities of protecting workers' rights around the world.

Ironically, workers' rights featured prominently in the Havana Charter of 1948, which was signed by fifty-four countries, including the United States, for the purpose of creating the International Trade Organization. Chapter II of the Havana Charter[17] is entitled "Employment and Economic Activity"; Article 3 of this Chapter concerns "Maintenance of Domestic Employment"; and Article 7 of this Chapter addresses "Fair Labour Standards" as follows:

> The Members recognize that measures relating to employment must take fully into account the rights of workers under inter-governmental declarations, conventions and agreements. The Members realize that unfair labour conditions, particularly in production for export, create difficulties in international trade, and, accordingly, each Member shall take whatever action may be appropriate and feasible to eliminate such conditions within its territory.

The ITO, as we have seen (in Chapter 1), failed to win approval, and only the GATT, which had no provisions on workers comparable to the Havana Charter, became the de facto "charter" for the multilateral trading system. When the WTO was created, there was no general will to revive workers' rights.

Many attempts to introduce workers' rights into the GATT and the WTO have been made, but, because of the controversial nature of the subject matter, none has succeeded. While GATT Article XX(e) allows for import restrictions on goods produced by forced labor, the underlying rationale for this exception is an economic one based on the cost advantages created by forced and prison labor. After the WTO was established in 1995, renewed interest in workers' rights led the first WTO Ministerial Conference in Singapore in December 1996 to adopt the following five point declaration:

- We renew our commitment to the observance of internationally recognized core labor standards.
- The International Labor Organization (ILO) is the competent body to set and deal with these standards, and we affirm our support for its work in promoting them.
- We believe that economic growth and development fostered by increased trade and further trade liberalization contribute to the promotion of these standards.

---

17. Available at http://www.wto.org/English/docs_e/legal_e/havana_e.pdf.

- We reject the use of labour standards for protectionist purposes, and agree that the comparative advantage of countries, particularly low-wage developing countries, must in no way be put into question.
- In this regard, we note that the WTO and ILO Secretariats will continue their existing collaboration.[18]

The most important result of the Singapore Declaration was to remove workers' rights from the formal purview of the WTO and to shift primary responsibility of developing international rules on workers' rights to the International Labor Organization, a non-governmental organization. In recognition of its important new role, the ILO issued a Declaration in 1998 that defined four fundamental rights for workers:

1. Freedom of association and the effective recognition of the right of collective bargaining;
2. The elimination of all forms of forced or compulsory labor;
3. The effective abolition of child labor; and
4. The elimination of discrimination in respect of employment and occupation.[19]

While the ILO has taken an active role in promoting workers' rights, the most important consequence of removing workers' rights from the formal framework of the WTO is that the issue of workers' rights cannot serve as a basis for justifying trade restrictions. Labor standards will continue to be linked with trade, but only in certain peripheral ways. Labor standards are relevant to the cost of goods that qualify for preferential tariff treatment under the Generalized System of Preferences, and regional agreements such as the North American Free Trade Agreement. Private businesses may also adopt the voluntary codes of conduct promulgated by the ILO and other organizations.

PROBLEM 7-13

You are a policy official with the WTO. One concern that has not been addressed so far concerning workers' rights is that inclusion of this subject in the WTO might open the door to including other social issues as well. Given the importance of international trade to economic development in all countries, it is possible to make a link between trade and just about any social issue. Your concern is that the WTO will become a mechanism to solve all of the world's social evils. Why might this be undesirable?

---

18. WTO, Ministerial Conference, Singapore, 9-13 December 1996, *Singapore Ministerial Declaration*, WT/MIN(96)/DEC, December 18, 1996, ¶4.

19. *ILO Declaration on Fundamental Principles and Rights at Work and Its Follow-Up*, June 18, 1998, reprinted in 37 I.L.M. 1233 (1998).

PROBLEM 7-14

Suppose that goods are produced in state-controlled factories in an authoritarian nation located in Southeast Asia. Workers labor under oppressive conditions with few or no rights, so the costs of labor are very low. The United States considers these conditions to be an illegal "subsidy" (i.e., a financial benefit conferred on the factory by the government, in the form of very low labor costs) and would like to impose a countervailing duty (i.e., an extra tariff) on goods imported from that country, in order to offset the subsidy. Is this possible under the WTO?

PROBLEM 7-15

France is considering a ban of imports of all clothing from Country M because the goods are manufactured by underaged workers in deplorable working conditions. The bulk of the proceeds from the imports are used by M's government to fund its tough prison system in which prison inmates are required to work in an agricultural support program that helps farmers grow crops for domestic consumption. Is the ban lawful under GATT Article XX?

PROBLEM 7-16

A specialized agency of the United Nations is considering the proposal of an international convention that will become an annex to the WTO. The proposed convention contains the following basic principles:

(1) All products must be manufactured in accordance with a set of stringent environmental standards designed to deal with critical problems, such as control of greenhouse gas emissions leading to global warming, destruction of natural habitats for animals and vegetation, and extinction of species.
(2) All products must be manufactured in accordance with certain labor policies involving working conditions, sanitation at the workplace, maximum hours of work per day and per week, minimum wages, insurance, health care, and pensions. Workers are entitled to form labor unions.
(3) All products must be certified by a government entity authorized by the UN. Any uncertified products can be the subject of an import trade ban.

Which countries are likely to support this proposal: (1) a group of advanced developed nations or (2) a group of developing countries? Why?

NOTE ON HUMAN RIGHTS AND INTERNATIONAL TRADE

The great majority of WTO members oppose any general linkage between WTO law and human rights. Some particular actions have occurred, however, such as a WTO waiver adopted in 2003 limiting trade in so-called conflict diamonds

(diamonds sold to finance African wars).[20] However, some influential voices have called upon the WTO to adopt an explicit Declaration on Human Rights and International Trade.[21] For comprehensive discussion of these matters, see Thomas Cottier, Joost Pauwelyn, and Elisabeth Burgi (eds.), *Human Rights and International Trade* (Oxford University Press 2005); and Frederick M. Abbott, Christine Breining-Kaufmann, and Thomas Cottier (eds.), *International Trade and Human Rights: Foundations and Conceptual Issues* (University of Michigan Press 2006).

In a famous exchange of views, Ernst-Ulrich Petersmann published several articles[22] calling for "constitutional" reform of international trade law so as to integrate human rights norms into the law of the multilateral trading system. A prominent human rights expert, Philip Alston penned a vigorous response and dissent, stating that such a reform would be a radical change, that it would be dangerous to permit trade panels to interpret human rights instruments, and that to do so would threaten the integrity of international human rights law.[23] Who has the better argument?

---

20. *Waiver Concerning Kimberley Process Certification Scheme for Rough Diamonds*, WT/L/518, WTO Decision of May 15, 2003.

21. A proposed draft Declaration is contained in the *Sixth Report of the International Trade Law Committee of the International Law Association*, Report of the 70th ILA Conference, 2004, at 543 ff. and 554 ff.

22. Ernst-Ulrich Petersmann, *The WTO and Human Rights*, 2000 J. of Int'l Econ. L. 19 (2000); Ernst-Ulrich Petersmann, *Time for a United Nations Global Compact for Integrating Human Rights Law into the Law of Worldwide Organizations: Lessons from European Integration*, 13 Eur. J. Int'l L. 621 (2002).

23. Philip Alston, *Resisting the Merger and Acquisition of Human Rights by Trade Law: A Reply to Petersmann*, 13 Eur. J. Int'l L. 815 (2002).

8 Safeguards

I. Introduction

This Chapter covers "safeguards": measures that a WTO member has the right to impose on a temporary basis if a domestic industry is injured, or threatened with serious injury, because of a surge in imports. The basic idea behind safeguards is that free trade may expose domestic industries to sudden and unexpected increases in competition that may cause serious injury. Such injury can occur even though no unfair trade practices are involved. Safeguards are related to the topic of general exceptions covered in Chapter 7 because safeguards can also be considered to be an exception to trade in the sense that safeguards are considered to be legitimate restrictions on free trade, justified by policy reasons.

Safeguards usually take the form of tariffs, quotas, or tariff-rate quotas. While these measures are generally considered to be trade barriers to be reduced or eliminated, the same measures are justified if used temporarily as safeguards.

In this Chapter, we cover GATT Articles XII, XIII, XIV, XV, XVIII Section B, and XIX. We also cover the important WTO Agreement on Safeguards, which supplements GATT Article XIX.

What are the policy justifications for safeguards? The most common are:

- Safeguards serve as a type of political safety valve against the harmful effects of free trade. Critics of free trade often argue that free trade harms domestic economies. The availability of safeguards to rein in the more drastic effects of free trade, at least in the short term, allows law and policy makers the room to pursue a longer-term free trade strategy. Without safeguards, the public might object to the pursuit of free trade.
- Safeguards are sometimes considered "just compensation" for firms and workers that are harmed by trade liberalization. Under this view, domestic firms and workers that suffer income and job loss have a just claim against the government for compensation.
- Safeguards provide a transition period or breathing room for firms that are suddenly faced with foreign competition through trade liberalization. During this period, law and policy makers can make adjustments on a macro- or micro-economic level to allow these firms to compete effectively or to shift workers and resources from non-competitive firms in an orderly fashion.

We turn first to the treatment of safeguards under the WTO and how these obligations are implemented into U.S. law.

II. Safeguards Under the WTO

Read Article XIX and the WTO Agreement on Safeguards in the Documents Supplement.

The WTO regime establishes general provisions on safeguards and on methods of invoking safeguards in various economic sectors under specialized agreements. As with many other principles of the WTO, safeguards were first recognized under the GATT but now have also been extended to other areas, such as agriculture (Article 5 of the Agreement on Agriculture) and services (Article X of the General Agreement on Trade in Services). Exceptions permitted under TRIPS Articles 17 (copyrights), 30 (patents), and 13 (trademarks) might also be able to serve a similar safeguards function.

The principal safeguards provision is contained in Article XIX of the GATT 1994. Article XIX is the so-called escape clause, allowing members relief from their WTO commitments for the trade in goods. GATT Article XIX:1(a) provides in relevant part:

> If, as a result of unforeseen developments and of the effect of the obligations incurred by a contracting party under this Agreement . . . , any product is being imported into the territory of that contracting party in such increased quantities . . . as to cause or threaten serious injury to domestic producers in that territory of like or directly competitive products, the contracting party shall be free . . . to suspend the obligation in whole or in part or to withdraw or modify the concession.

Under Article XIX, three conditions must exist before a member can escape its WTO obligations: (1) There must be an importation of a product in increased quantities; (2) the increase must be the result of unforeseen developments and must result from the WTO obligations (trade concessions) of the country seeking to invoke the escape clause; and (3) the increase in imports must cause or threaten to cause serious injury to domestic producers of like or directly competitive products. If all of these conditions exist, the WTO member is permitted to disregard its GATT commitments for the imported products in question. The member may subject the imports to increased tariffs, quotas, or tariff-rate quotas.

The WTO Safeguards Agreement amplifies the requirements of GATT Article XIX. A member may apply a safeguard measure to a product only if such products are being imported into its territory in such quantities (absolute or relative to domestic production) so as to cause or threaten to cause serious injury to the domestic producers of like or directly competitive products (Article 2). If a safeguard measure is challenged at the WTO, the complaining party has the burden of proof to make out a prima facie case that the measure is not consistent with Article XIX or the WTO Safeguards Agreement. *See Korea—Definitive Safeguard Measure on Imports of Certain Dairy Products*, WT/DS98/AB/R, Report of the Appellate Body, adopted on January 12, 2000, ¶¶142-150. A safeguard measure may be applied only after an appropriate investigation (Article 3) and a determination of serious injury or a threat thereof (Article 4).

Article 5 of the Safeguards Agreement concerns the characteristics of the safeguard measure itself. The measure may impose higher tariffs or quotas or a combination thereof, but only to the extent necessary to prevent or remedy the serious injury and to facilitate adjustment. If a quota is used, the measure must not reduce the quantity of imports below the level equal to the average of imports in the last three representative years, unless "clear justification" is given (Article 5.1). As a general rule quotas are to be allocated by an agreement with and among supplying countries. However, where this is not possible, the allocation should be according to proportions supplied in a previous representative period (Article 5.2(a)). In exceptional circumstances a quota may be imposed in a discriminatory fashion against imports from certain members whose imports have increased "in disproportionate percentage" in relation to the total increase in imports (Article 5.2(b)).

Article 5.2(b) of the Safeguards Agreement is an exception from the GATT Article XIII, which generally forbids discriminatory quotas. Article XIII applies outside the safeguards area to invalidate any discriminatory application of a quota. For example, in *European Communities—Regime for the Importation, Sale, and Distribution of Bananas, Second Recourse to Article 21.5 of the DSU by Ecuador/Recourse to Article 21.5 of the DSU by the United States,* WT/DS27/AB/R, Report of the Appellate Body, adopted on December 11, 2008 (Ecuador case) and December 22, 2008 (U.S. case), the Appellate Body ruled that an EC regulation reserving a duty-free tariff quota to bananas of Asian-Pacific origin was inconsistent with GATT Article XIII:1 and 2.

Article 6 of the Safeguards Agreement allows provisional safeguard measures under certain circumstances. Article 7 limits most safeguards to four years. Article 8 sets the procedure for supplying countries to seek trade compensation, but the right of suspension in compensation may not be exercised for three years. Article 9 enacts special protections for developing countries both with respect to applying safeguards and to gaining exemptions from the application of safeguards by other members.

Article 10 requires the termination of existing safeguard measures, and Article 11 prohibits new voluntary export restraints and requires those existing to be phased out by 1999.

Articles 12 and 13 concern consultation among members and surveillance by the WTO Committee on Safeguards. Article 14 makes safeguard measures subject to the WTO dispute settlement system.

The WTO Safeguards Agreement is intended to amplify Article XIX, but if there is a conflict between the Safeguards Agreement and Article XIX, the Safeguards Agreement will prevail. *See General Interpretive Note to Annex 1A, Multilateral Agreements on Trade in Goods of the WTO Agreement,* reprinted in The Results of the Uruguay Round of Multilateral Trade Agreements: The Legal Texts 20 (WTO 1999).

PROBLEM 8-1

An unexpected winter freeze destroys the bulk of the citrus crop in the United States. Some of the crop has been saved through extraordinary measures and will be available in supermarkets but must be sold at higher prices. In the meanwhile, citrus fruit from South America is being imported by U.S. supermarkets to satisfy the demands of consumers for fresh orange and grapefruit juice. The U.S. citrus industry seeks immediate escape clause relief in the form of a quantitative restriction on imports from South America, or it will face massive losses that will have repercussions for the entire U.S. economy. What is the analysis that must be conducted under GATT Article XIX and Article 4 of the Safeguards Agreement?

PROBLEM 8-2

The U.S. industry for handheld organizers has been growing at a rate of 8 percent during the past five years and now accounts for 60 percent of all handheld organizers in the United States. Foreign imports from China, Taiwan, and Japan now account for 30 percent. The U.S. industry is considering an escape clause proceeding against the Asian imports but has been advised that it will be impossible to prevail because the U.S. industry has a majority share of the market and because it has been growing steadily for the past five years. Do you agree? Can you think of any additional facts or circumstances that might support the case for the U.S. industry? *See* Article 4.1(a) and 4.2(a) of the Safeguards Agreement.

PROBLEM 8-3

Country A, in Europe, is concerned that its automotive industry has suffered sharp declines in all sectors, but especially for passenger vehicles, mini-vans, and large sport utility vehicles (SUVs). Assume that, as a result of an escape clause investigation, Country A finds that the large influx of imported passenger vehicles from Japan and Korea has caused serious injury to the domestic automobile industry.

Country A declares that safeguards are necessary and imposes a 35 percent tariff on all passenger cars, mini-vans, and SUVs from Japan and Korea. Has Country A acted in accordance with the WTO? *See* Articles 4.2(b) and 5.1 of the Safeguards Agreement.

III. Safeguards Under U.S. Law

Read Sections 201-210 of the Trade Act of 1974 in the Documents Supplement.

The United States has implemented GATT Article XIX, the escape clause, and the relevant provisions of the WTO Safeguards Agreement, into federal law through Sections 201 *et seq.* of the Trade Act of 1974, as amended. Compare the provisions of Section 201 with the safeguard requirements under the WTO agreements. What are the significant differences? Should U.S. law be amended to comport with the WTO law?

In most cases, the first step in a Section 201 escape clause case is the filing of a petition with the International Trade Commission (ITC) by an entity, such as a trade association or union, which is representative of an industry. *See* 19 U.S.C. §2252(a). A copy of the petition is forwarded to the United States Trade Representative (USTR) and any federal agencies directly concerned. *Id.* at §2252(a)(3). Upon the request of the President, the USTR, Congress, or on its own initiative, the ITC can decide to make an investigation into whether an "article is being imported into the United States in such increased quantities as to be a substantial cause of serious injury, or the threat thereof, to the domestic industry producing an article like or directly competitive with the imported article." *See* 19 U.S.C. §2251(a). The ITC must submit its report with its findings and recommendations to the President within 180 days from the date of the filing of the petition. *See id.* at §2252(f)(1). If the ITC makes a finding that imports are the substantial cause of a serious injury or threat of a serious injury to the relevant domestic industry, the President is authorized to make a "positive adjustment to import competition." *See* 19 U.S.C. §2253(a). An affirmative finding under Section 201 is required before any presidential action can be taken. The President is not bound to act at all or if he chooses to act, he is not required to follow the recommendations of the ITC.

The President is authorized to take any of the following actions:

(A) proclaim an increase in, or the imposition of, any duty on the imported article;

(B) proclaim a tariff-rate quota on the article;

(C) proclaim a modification or imposition of any quantitative restriction on the importation of the article into the United States;

(D) implement one or more appropriate adjustment measures, including the provision of trade adjustment assistance;

(E) negotiate, conclude, and carry out agreements with foreign countries limiting the export from foreign countries and the import into the United States of such article;

(F) proclaim procedures necessary to allocate among importers by the auction of import licenses quantities of the article that are permitted to be imported into the United States;

(G) initiate international negotiations to address the underlying cause of the increase in imports of the article or otherwise to alleviate the injury or threat thereof;

(H) submit to Congress legislative proposals to facilitate the efforts of the domestic industry to make a positive adjustment to import competition;

(I) take any other action which may be taken by the President under the authority of law and which the President considers appropriate and feasible; and

(J) take any combination of actions listed in subparagraphs (A) through (I).

19 U.S.C. §2253(a)(3).

Although it is usually clear when the ITC makes a positive injury determination, this is not always the case when the commissioners are unable to agree on key issues. Consider the following case.

Corus Group PLC v. International Trade Commission
United States Court of Appeals, Federal Circuit, 2003
352 F.3d 1351

DYK, Circuit Judge.

[Appellants, a group of foreign steel companies and their U.S. subsidiaries, appealed from a decision of the United States Court of International Trade rejecting their challenge to the President's imposition of a tariff on imported tin mill products pursuant to a finding of serious injury to a domestic industry by the ITC.

The defendants were President George W. Bush; Robert C. Bonner, Commissioner of the now United States Bureau of Customs and Border Patrol; and the ITC (collectively, the government). The appellants argued that the President acted beyond his delegated authority. Under the Trade Act of 1974, 19 U.S.C. §§2101-2495 (2000), the President is allowed to take action if a majority of the six-member ITC finds that the injury requirement has been met. The President is also allowed to treat a tie vote of the ITC (i.e., a split of three-and-three on whether the injury requirement has been met) as an affirmative finding of injury. In this case, the President considered the ITC to be evenly divided on the injury requirement, but the appellants argued that the ITC was not evenly divided. The appellants also argued that the ITC did not sufficiently explain its decision as required by 19 U.S.C. §2252(f)(1) (2000).

At the request of the USTR and Congress, the ITC began a Section 201 escape clause investigation concerning certain steel imports. Of the six commissioners (Bragg, Devaney, Hillman, Koplan, Miller, and Okun), four (Koplan, Okun, Hillman, and Miller) found for the purposes of the investigation that two domestic steel industries were involved: (1) carbon flat rolled steel and (2) tin mill steel products. Three (Koplan, Okun, and Hillman) of the four commissioners found that the domestic tin mill industry did not suffer a serious injury. The fourth commissioner (Miller) found that the tin mill industry did suffer a serious injury.

Two other commissioners (Bragg and Devaney) took a different approach in determining the domestic industry. Rather than separating the domestic steel industry into two separate industries as was done by the four-commissioner majority, the two commissioners found one domestic industry for carbon flat rolled steel, which included tin mill products. These two commissioners found that the domestic industry, carbon flat rolled steel (which included tin mill products), had suffered a serious injury.

Based on the voting by the commissioners, the President found that three commissioners (Miller, Bragg, and Devaney) found an injury to tin mill products and that the commission vote was evenly divided 3-3 on tin mill. Miller had found an injury to tin mill as a distinct industry and Bragg and Devaney had found an injury to carbon flat rolled steel, which included tin mill. On March 5, 2002, the President issued the "Steel Products Proclamation," under which he imposed tariffs on both carbon flat rolled steel and tin mill products over a three-year period of 30 percent in the first year, 24 percent in the second year, and 18 percent in the third year.

The appellants challenged the action of the President with respect to tin mill products. They argued that the President improperly considered the ITC's vote with respect to tin mill products as a tie and that the two commissioners (Bragg and Devaney) that considered tin mill to be part of carbon rolled steel did not explain their decision that the domestic tin mill industry suffered a serious injury. The CIT rejected both claims. The opinion on appeal follows.]

III.

The appellants' first contention on the merits is that the Commission determination was not a 3-3 tie as to tin-mill products as the Commission reported it to be. The Commission reported as follows:

> Chairman Koplan, Vice Chairman Okun, and Commissioner Hillman determine that
> carbon and alloy tin mill products are not being imported into the United States in
> such increased quantities as to be a substantial cause of serious injury to the domestic
> industry; Commissioners Bragg, Miller, and Devaney make an affirmative determina-
> tion regarding imports of carbon and alloy tin mill products.

The appellants contend that Commissioners Bragg and Devaney's votes cannot be counted as affirmative injury determinations as to tin mill products because they did not analyze tin mill products as a separate category. Therefore, appellants argue, the Commission's vote should properly have been reported to the President as a 3-1 determination of no serious injury. There is no merit to this argument.

Commissioners Bragg and Devaney each specifically voted affirmatively with regard to tin mill products. On October 22, 2001, the commissioners recorded their votes at a public hearing. Commissioner Devaney voted as follows: "I find one domestic industry producing all flat products. In this investigation, I am voting in the affirmative with respect to slab, plate, hot-rolled products, cold-rolled products, GOES, corrosion-resistant products, *and tin mill products.*" Commissioner Bragg voted as follows:

> In this investigation, I find that there are 13 domestic like products and 13 corre-
> sponding domestic industries. I find domestic like product number one includes
> carbon and alloy flat products consisting of slabs, cut-to-length plate, hot-rolled, cold-
> rolled, grain-oriented electrical steel, coated products, *and tin mill products.* I vote in
> the affirmative with respect to domestic like product number one.

Moreover, neither commissioner objected when the Commission tallied their votes as affirmative with regard to tin mill products. The Commission tallied three votes, Commissioners Devaney, Bragg, and Miller, as affirmative with regard to tin mill products. It is, therefore, clear that Commissioners Bragg and Devaney intended their votes with regard to tin mill products to be affirmative. Having reached this conclusion, we are not "compelled . . . to probe the mental processes" of the commissioners any further to determine whether their votes were properly counted as affirmative despite those commissioners' different underlying reasoning. Accordingly, the Commission did not err in counting the votes as to tin mill products as a 3-3 tie.

IV.

The more difficult question is whether the Commission determination must be set aside because the Commission failed to adequately explain the basis for the decision of the three commissioners who found serious injury with respect to tin mill products.

The statute requires that "the Commission shall submit to the President a report on each investigation undertaken. . . ." 19 U.S.C. §2252(f)(1) (2000). Subsection 2252(f) provides in detail what the Commission report must contain. *Id.* §2252(f)(2). The Commission report must provide "an explanation of the basis for each recommendation" to the President, *id.* §2252(f)(2)(B), and must include the findings required by subsection 2252(c)(2), *Id.* §2252(f)(2)(D).

The majority opinion in *Maple Leaf* did not address these statutory provisions or delineate what kind of explanation the statute requires from the Commission. The government candidly urges that the statute does not require any rational explanation from the Commission concerning its determinations of serious injury. Once the commissioners have voted, says the government, the inquiry is at an end, even if the statutory report is "totally inconsistent" or "completely irrational." We cannot agree that the statute was designed to leave the Commission so completely unfettered by normal requirements of administrative law.

In a concurring opinion in *Maple Leaf*, Judge Cowen concluded that "[b]efore the [Commission] can be deemed to have complied with this statute, it is . . . necessary . . . that its Report fairly apprise the President, interested parties, and the public of the reasoning underlying its recommendation." *Maple Leaf*, 762 F.2d at 90. We have not had occasion since *Maple Leaf* to determine whether Judge Cowen's view was correct. We now hold that it was because the statute specifically requires that the commissioners provide an explanation. In requiring an explanation the statute implicitly requires that the report to the President provide an internally *consistent* explanation for the conclusions reached.

V.

Our decisions establish that in reviewing a Commission determination, each of the various separate opinions making up the majority decision is subject to judicial scrutiny under the applicable statutory standard. If any opinion necessary to the majority, or in this case the three-vote plurality, fails to satisfy the statutory standard, the decision must be set aside.

However, under our decision in *United States Steel Group*, it is not necessary that separate opinions comprising a majority (or here a plurality), agreeing on a single result, adopt identical or even consistent reasoning in reaching that particular result. In that case, the appellants challenged the Commission's determination that domestic industry was not injured by the importation of hot and cold-rolled steel, contending that two of the commissioners who constituted the majority adopted different tests from the other commissioners to determine material injury—a "one-step test" rather than a "two-step test." We rejected the appellants' argument (there under the APA) that the commissioners composing a majority must employ a single methodology. We determined that "[t]he statute on its face compels no such uniform methodology, and we are not persuaded that we should create one, even were we so empowered." We then observed the complexity of factors that Congress had directed the commissioners to consider in determining material injury, and concluded, "[t]he invitation to employ such diversity in methodologies is inherent in the statutes themselves, given the variety of the considerations to be undertaken and the lack of any Congressionally mandated procedure or methodology for assessment of the statutory tests." *Id.* Hence, "[s]o long as the Commission's analysis does not violate any statute and is not otherwise arbitrary and capricious," *id.*, the various commissioners composing a majority need not rely on identical or consistent methodologies in explaining their conclusions. Thus, here the three-member plurality of the Commission agreed that both the articles included in the broader category of carbon and alloy products and in the narrower category of tin mill products caused serious injury. Commissioner Miller treated the two categories separately. Commissioners Bragg and Devaney treated them together. This inconsistency is not a ground for setting aside the decision.

VI.

Nonetheless, it is necessary that each commissioner's separate opinion be *internally* consistent, and that each opinion adequately explain the commissioner's vote. Here the appellants argue that the opinions of Commissioners Bragg and Devaney also do not satisfy that requirement. On the one hand these commissioners reasoned that tin mill is not a separate category. This view was rejected by a majority of the Commission. Yet, these two Commissioners voted to treat the import of tin mill as a cause of serious injury. Appellants argue that the reasoning of Commissioners Bragg and Devaney (analyzing tin mill as part of a larger category) and their votes (treating tin mill separately) are not consistent and that this inconsistency is potentially significant. Appellants point out that tin mill products comprise only a small percent of the total larger domestic industry. (Appellants' Br. at 40 (stating that "tin mill products represent only 1.7 percent of total flat-rolled product consumption and 2.7 percent of total flat-rolled imports")). Thus, it does not necessarily follow that because the importation of all carbon and alloy flat products causes serious injury to the domestic market, the importation of tin mill products, standing alone, would cause serious injury.

But we think the claimed inconsistency in the opinions of Commissioners Bragg and Devaney is more theoretical than real. They simply voted to treat tin mill as part of a larger category and viewed their votes as to serious injury as a reaffirmation of this position. It is not immediately apparent here that finding that articles A and B combined (here carbon and alloy products and tin mill combined) causes serious injury has different consequences than finding that articles A and B treated separately cause serious injury. To be sure, it is possible that there would be different consequences from a combined finding of serious injury with respect to carbon and alloy products including tin mill than separate findings as to tin mill and other carbon and alloy products, in which event the reasoning of Commissioners Bragg and Devaney might be at variance with their votes. But appellants have not argued that point here. We decline to speculate as to whether such a showing, if made, would invalidate the President's order.

In short, we conclude that appellants have failed to establish that the opinions of Commissioners Bragg and Devaney do not provide adequate explanation or are internally inconsistent.

Affirmed.

PROBLEM 8-4

Due to its depressed state, the U.S. furniture industry files a petition with the ITC seeking relief under the escape clause from imports of cheap furniture from Thailand and Indonesia. After an investigation, however, the ITC finds that imports from Thailand and Indonesia are not a substantial cause of serious injury to the U.S. furniture industry. The negative finding means that the President is not authorized to impose sanctions under Section 201.

Many industry groups are disappointed and hold a weekend meeting with the USTR to discuss the next steps. The USTR holds several closed-door meetings with trade officials from Thailand and Indonesia. Observers stated that the atmosphere was very tense and intimidating. At the end of the meetings, the USTR cheerfully announces that Thailand and Indonesia have voluntarily entered into "Friendship Agreements" to reduce their imports of furniture to the United States by 50 percent and holds up signed copies of the agreements. Standing by are trade officials from Thailand and Indonesia looking very glum. Are these agreements legal? What issues are presented? See *Consumers Union* below.

Consumers Union of the United States, Inc. v. Kissinger
United States Court of Appeals, District of Columbia, 1974
506 F.2d 136

McGowan, Circuit Judge:

[A consumer group challenged actions by the executive in obtaining agreements from Japan and the EC to voluntarily restrict trade as inconsistent with the U.S. Constitution because "such actions" were taken without following the procedures set forth in the Trade Expansion Act of 1962. The district court rejected this challenge and the group appealed to the Court of Appeals, which affirmed the district court based on the opinion below.]

I.

Steel imports into the United States increased more than tenfold over the period 1958-68, with the great bulk of imports coming from Japan and the countries of the European Communities. The effect of this development on the domestic steel industry, which is deemed to be of great importance to the nation's security as well as to its peacetime economy, became a matter of widespread concern. In 1968 bills with substantial backing were introduced in Congress to impose mandatory import quotas on steel.

The Executive Branch regarded the problem created by steel imports as temporary in nature and thus amenable to a short-term solution. It concluded, moreover, that unilaterally imposed mandatory quotas would pose a danger of retaliation under the General Agreement on Trade and Tariffs, prove inflexible and difficult to terminate, and have a seriously adverse impact on the foreign relations of the United States. Import limiting agreements negotiated with other governments were likewise rejected on the State Department's advice that negotiated official restrictions, if achievable, would have political consequences for the foreign governments that would also affect our external affairs adversely. Accordingly, the Executive Branch concluded in 1968 that voluntary import restraint undertakings by foreign producers offered the best hope of alleviating the domestic industry's temporary problems at the least cost to United States foreign, economic and trade policies.

After an initial showing of interest by the foreign producer associations, State Department officials entered into discussions that lasted from June to December, 1968, and resulted in letters being sent to the Secretary in which the Japanese and

European producer associations stated their intentions to limit steel shipments to the United States to specified maximum tonnages for each of the years 1969, 1970, and 1971. During 1970, domestic industry and union representatives urged the State Department to seek renewal of the restraints beyond 1971 to provide greater time within which to achieve needed changes, and the House Ways and Means Committee issued a report to like effect. When various executive organs, such as the President's Council of Economic Advisors, had made the same recommendation, the President directed the Secretary to seek extensions of the limitation representations. Such extensions, covering 1972 through 1974, were forthcoming in letters dated early in May, 1972, and announced by the President on May 6.

The two 1972 letters are substantially alike. Each states the signatories' intention to limit exports of steel products to the United States both in aggregate tonnage and, within such limits, in terms of product mix. Each represents that the signatories 'hold themselves (itself) ready to consult with representatives of the United States Government on any problem or question that may arise with respect to this voluntary restraint undertaking' and expect the United States Government so to hold itself ready. In addition, each states that its undertaking is based on the assumptions that (1) the effect will not be to place the signatories at a disadvantage relative to each other, (2) the United States will take no unilateral actions to restrict exports by the signatories to the United States, and (3) the representations do not violate United States or international laws.

II.

The violation of law alleged in the amended complaint was that the State Department officials had acted to regulate foreign commerce within the meaning of Article 1, Section 8, Clause 3 of the Constitution, and of the laws relating to the regulation of foreign trade set forth in Title 19 of the U.S. Code, including Sections 301 and 352 of the Trade Expansion Act of 1962. The foreign producer defendants were said to be violating the same laws to the extent that they took steps to effectuate the limitations sought by the defendant State Department officials acting in excess of their authority. The relief sought was a declaration that the actions of the State Department officials in seeking the export limitations were *ultra vires*, and an injunction against the defendants from furthering the 1972 letters of intent in any way.

We turn, then, to the District Court's declaration that, in respect of the actions of the Executive culminating in the undertakings stated in the letters of intent, 'the Executive is not preempted and that there is no requirement that all such undertakings be first processed under the Trade Expansion Act of 1962.' That statute, as its name suggests, had as its principal purpose the stimulation of the economic growth of the United States and the maintenance and enlargement of foreign markets for its products.

This was to be achieved through trade agreements reached by the President with foreign countries. Title II of the Act provided that, for a period of five years (1962-67), the President was authorized to enter into such agreements whenever he determined that any existing tariff duties or other import restrictions of either the United States or any foreign country were unduly burdening and restricting the foreign trade of the United States. Upon reaching any such trade agreement, the President was delegated the unmistakably legislative power to modify or continue existing tariffs or other import restrictions, to continue existing duty-free or excise treatment, or to impose additional import restrictions, as he determined to be necessary or appropriate to the carrying out of the agreement. 19 U.S.C. §1821. In connection with the first two of these powers, the Tariff Commission was given an advisory function, which included public hearings; and public hearings were also directed to be held, by an agency designated by the President, in connection with any proposed trade agreement. 19 U.S.C. §§1841, 1843.

Title III of the Trade Expansion Act of 1962, recognizing that domestic interests of various kinds may be adversely affected by concessions granted under trade agreements, authorizes the making of compensating adjustments of various kinds. Section 301 (19 U.S.C. §1901) provides that the Tariff Commission shall undertake investigations of injuries allegedly being done to domestic businesses or workers by such things as increased imports flowing from a trade agreement. After holding public hearings, the Tariff Commission shall make a report to the President. If it affirmatively finds injury to domestic industry, the President may under Section 351 increase or impose tariff duties or other import restrictions, 19 U.S.C. §1981, or alternatively he may under Section 352 negotiate agreements with foreign governments limiting the export from such countries to the United States of the article causing the injury. 19 U.S.C. §1981. If this latter option is taken, the Act provides that the President is authorized to issue regulations governing the entry or withdrawal from warehouse of the article covered by the agreement.

What is clear from the foregoing is a purpose on the part of Congress to delegate legislative power to the President for use by him in certain defined circumstances and in furtherance of certain stated purposes. Without such a delegation, the President could not increase or decrease tariffs, issue commands to the customs service to refuse or delay entry of goods into the country, or impose mandatory import quotas. To make use of such delegated power, the President would of course be required to proceed strictly in accordance with the procedures specified in the statutes conferring the delegation. Where, as here, he does not pretend to the possession of such power, no such conformity is required.

The steel import restraints do not purport to be enforceable, either as contracts or as governmental actions with the force of law; and the Executive has no sanctions to invoke in order to compel observance by the foreign producers of their self-denying representations. They are a statement of intent on the part of the foreign producer associations. The signatories' expectations, not unreasonably in light of the reception given their undertakings by the Executive, are that the Executive will consult with them over mutual concerns about the steel import situation, and that it will not have sudden recourse to the unilateral steps available to it under the Trade Expansion Act to impose legal restrictions on importation. The president is not bound in any way to refrain from taking such steps if he later deems them to be in the national interest, or if consultation proves unavailing to meet unforeseen difficulties; and certainly the Congress is not inhibited from enacting any legislation it desires to regulate by law the importation of steel.

The formality and specificity with which the undertakings are expressed does not alter their essentially precatory nature insofar as the Executive Branch is concerned. In effect the President has said that he will not initiate steps to limit steel imports by law if the volume of such imports remains within tolerable bounds.

Communicating, through the Secretary of State, what levels he considers tolerable merely enables the foreign producers to conform their actions accordingly, and to avoid the risk of guessing at what is acceptable. Regardless of whether the producers run afoul of the antitrust laws in the manner of their response, nothing in the process leading up to the voluntary undertakings or the process of consultation under them differentiates what the Executive has done here from what all Presidents, and to a lesser extent all high executive officers, do when they admonish an industry with the express or implicit warning that action, within either their existing powers or enlarged powers to be sought, will be taken if a desired course is not followed voluntarily.

The question of congressional preemption is simply not pertinent to executive action of this sort. Congress acts by making laws binding, if valid, on their objects and the President, whose duty it is faithfully to execute the laws. From the comprehensive pattern of its legislation regulating trade and governing the circumstances under and procedures by which the President is authorized to act to limit imports, it appears quite likely that Congress has by statute occupied the field of *enforceable* import restrictions, if it did not, indeed, have exclusive possession thereof by the terms of Article I of the Constitution. There is no potential for conflict, however, between exclusive congressional regulation of foreign commerce—regulation enforced ultimately by halting violative importations at the border—and assurances of voluntary restraint given to the Executive. Nor is there any warrant for creating such a conflict by straining to endow the voluntary undertakings with legally binding effect, contrary to the manifest understanding of all concerned and, indeed, to the manner in which departures from them have been treated.

LEVENTHAL, Circuit Judge, dissenting:

In my view, this case is controlled by Congress's exercise of its plenary authority over the regulation of foreign commerce through passage, over the past forty years, of legislation establishing a comprehensive scheme occupying the field of import restraints. I think the executive negotiation and acceptance of these undertakings are activity in a field that has been preempted by Congress, and can only be engaged in by following the procedures set forth in the Congressional enactments.

———————————

The power of the President to negotiate and enter into "Voluntary Restraint Agreements" (VRAs) is a critical part of U.S. foreign trade strategy. The President cannot impose trade sanctions under Section 201 unless the ITC finds that all conditions of Section 201 have been met. In the absence of such a finding, however, the President can still negotiate a non-binding agreement with foreign countries to voluntarily restrict exports under a VRA. A VRA can have the same effect as a quota. An example of a VRA is set forth in the case study below.

Case Study One
The U.S. Auto Safeguards of 1981

We set forth below the famous (or infamous) *U.S. Auto Safeguards of 1981* case involving imports of Japanese automobiles below.

PROBLEM 8-5

The U.S. rubber tire manufacturing industry brings a Section 201 petition alleging serious injury. An investigation by the ITC determines that imports are among several causes that have contributed to a serious injury in the U.S. industry. The ITC identified five major causes that have led to injury to the U.S. industry and quantified the contribution of each factor as follows:

(1) Influx of cheap imports (35 percent)
(2) Lack of real growth in wages in the U.S. economy (15 percent)
(3) Growth in unemployment across all industrial sectors (25 percent)
(4) Decline in overall industrial productivity and competitiveness on a global basis (10 percent)
(5) Inflation (15 percent)

The first factor above relates directly to imports, whereas the next several factors relate to general economic conditions that have forced consumers to reduce their purchases of the products at issue. Under the analysis above, imports are a more significant cause of injury than any single other cause taken alone.

You are a commissioner and are now asked, on the basis of this information, to determine whether imports have caused a serious injury to industry. What preliminary issue must you resolve before you can make your determination? What result would you reach based upon the views of the ITC in the *U.S. Auto Safeguards of 1981* case below? What do you think will be the response of U.S. industry to the position of the ITC?

PROBLEM 8-6

The *U.S. Auto Safeguards of 1981* case resulted in a VRA under which Japan agreed to limit its exports to the United States rather than face the imposition of safeguards or trade restrictions. You are an international trade law expert and policy analyst and are asked to evaluate the advantages and disadvantages of a VRA, as compared to tariffs or quotas imposed as safeguards:

(1) From Japan's perspective, what is the advantage of a VRA over being subject to trade restrictions by the United States? What is likely to be the reaction of the Japanese public to U.S.-imposed trade restrictions? What about a VRA?

(2) What was the only public record of the VRA in the case? What public records would be involved if safeguards were imposed? Compared to safeguards, a VRA is much more informal and private. Is this a benefit to the Japanese government?

(3) What are the disadvantages of the informal and private nature of a VRA to (a) the Japanese public; (b) the U.S. public; and (c) the multilateral trading system as a whole? Why might the WTO object to VRAs? Which countries are likely to use VRAs?

(4) Imagine yourself present and behind closed doors when the United States is holding informal talks with Japan concerning the VRA. At the time, there was legislation pending in the United States (the Danforth-Bentsen Bill) that would have imposed strict limits on imports of Japanese cars. Do you think that the VRA was really voluntary?

Report to the President on Certain Motor Vehicles and Certain Chassis and Bodies Thereof
United States International Trade Commission
Investigation No. TA-201-44
USITC Publication 1110
December 3, 1980

[On June 30, 1980, a group of labor unions, led by the United Automobile Workers, filed a petition for relief under Section 201. The petition alleged that automobile trucks, on-the-highway passenger automobiles, and bodies (including cabs) for automobile trucks were being imported into the United States in such increased quantities as to be a substantial cause of serious injury, or the threat thereof, to the domestic industries producing articles like, or directly competitive with, the imported articles. After an investigation, a majority of the ITC found that the petition had not met the requirements of Section 201 and that relief was not warranted.]

Views of Chairman Bill Alberger

[This part of Commissioner Alberger's opinion below focuses on the passenger and light truck industries. With regard to medium and heavy trucks, Alberger found that imports had not increased, which mandated a negative determination.]

SUBSTANTIAL CAUSE

While I find the domestic industries producing passenger automobiles and light trucks to be suffering serious injury within the meaning of [§2252(b)(1)], I do not find that increased imports are a substantial cause of such injury. I have found the decline in demand for new automobiles and light trucks owing to the general recessionary conditions in the United States economy to be a far greater cause of the domestic industries' plight than the increase in imports. While I also believe that the rapid change in product mix necessitated by the shift of consumer preference away from large, less fuel efficient vehicles, is an important cause of the present injury, I do not view this factor to be a more important cause than increased imports.

THE DECLINE IN OVERALL DEMAND

It has been argued that the downturn in demand is itself a result of several factors, and that to consider demand in the aggregate is to cumulate artificially what are clearly separate causal elements in a manner inconsistent with the purposes or legislative history of [§2251]. Among the separate and identifiable causes mentioned are inflation, unemployment, rising interest rates, and higher energy costs. Undoubtedly, all of these factors played a part in bringing about the present recession in new vehicle sales. Supporters of the petition contend that none of these factors alone played as great a role in bringing about the injury as increasing imports.

All of these contentions seek to isolate and weigh separately the various components of a general economic downturn. In reality, most of the factors mentioned above have worked in unison to bring about what is commonly termed a "recession." Inflation in new vehicle prices coupled with higher credit rates have acted together to drive up the total costs of new motor vehicles. Interest rates have played a particularly important part in the volume of auto sales, because these are long-term consumer durable purchases where credit financing is the norm. Not only have transaction prices for new vehicles and monthly payments for loans increased, but credit has become "tighter," and the refusal rate on auto credit applications has grown. Unemployment and general inflation have acted to reduce the real disposable income of the average consumer, and a normal reaction has been to delay many long-term capital outlays.

All of these phenomena are part and parcel of a generalized recession. But to say [that recessions] are comprised of a multitude of causes is not to say that reduced demand in a recession cannot be cited as a single cause for purposes of [§2251]. The reason for such a policy is readily apparent; if decline in demand for the product is a consequence of a general economic downturn, then the inevitable recovery from the recession will restore health to the industry. Cyclical downturns in the economy are to be expected, and must not force a reliance on unnecessary import remedies. The problem which auto producers confront is one which confronts many sectors of the economy and it cannot be solved by import relief. [I]t is possible for imports to be a "substantial cause" of serious injury [during a recession] only where the absolute or relative increase is of sufficient magnitude to outweigh or equal the effects of the recession itself.

Views of Commissioner Paula Stern

[Commissioner Stern found that although there was serious injury in the domestic passenger car industry, increased imports were not a substantial cause thereof. She agreed with Alberger that the decline in demand and the shift in demand were more important causes than increasing imports. Stern stated that serious injury to the U.S. auto industry will continue but that reform and transformation of the domestic auto industry, not the requested import relief, were necessary for the auto industry to recover. This portion of her findings is set forth below.]

SERIOUS INJURY WILL CONTINUE, IMPORTS NOT A SUBSTANTIAL CAUSE

The unusual problems suffered by this industry in terms of sales, profits and employment will likely continue. However, imports are not threatening to become a substantial cause of any future injury. [While] the plans underway for restructuring the industry [will] address many of the industry's problems continuing difficulties in the cost and availability of consumer credit and unavoidable time lags in the introduction of new fuel-efficient models may retard the industry's recovery. The continued incidence of high capital expenditures will restrain improvements in profits while rapid productivity improvements will prevent employment from ever recovering to former levels. However, in the long-term prospects for the domestic industry as a whole are good as it increasingly focuses on a world rather than national market.

No tangible link between [the auto-makers' ambitious transformation] plans and any requested import relief has been established. [Also] ignoring the huge cost of any remedy to the public [t]he UAW and Ford have professed an interest in encouraging foreign auto producers to locate facilities in the United States. Volkswagen and Honda are well down this path. Furthermore, there are good reasons to believe that relief would be inimical to the interests of most other US producers, because they have already become so highly integrated on an international scale. General Motors has begun a serious program of worldwide expansion. American Motors is dependent on completion of major financing plans with Renault. [Both of these projects] could be seriously jeopardized by import relief.

Dissenting Views of Commissioners George M. Moore and Catherine Bedell

[Commissioners Moore and Bedell disagreed with the majority and found that imports were a substantial cause of injury to the domestic industry. They believed that it was improper to aggregate all of the economic factors and that each isolated factor should have been compared with imports. Otherwise, there would be few, if any, positive injury determinations in times of recession. They also believed that of all of the factors, imports were the most important cause of injury to the domestic automobile industry.]

The United States-Japan Voluntary Restraint Agreement of 1981

The decision of the ITC above did not authorize President Regan to exercise authority under Section 201 to impose safeguards on imports. However, the Reagan Administration negotiated a voluntary restraint agreement with Japan to limit the import of Japanese vehicles into the United States to 1.6 million units, down from 1.8 million in 1980. The agreement progressively liberalized permitted Japanese imports, and in the last year of the agreement, 1985, imports of 2.2 million units were allowed.

NOTES AND QUESTIONS

1. An agreement by a group of private companies to limit and share markets constitutes a per se violation of U.S. antitrust law. On the other hand, if the private companies do not actually agree among themselves but act under compulsion by a foreign sovereign government, then the conduct of these companies will be immune under U.S. antitrust law. This is known as the doctrine of foreign compulsion. See Mitsuo Matsushita and Lawrence Repeta, *Restricting the Supply of Japanese Automobiles: Sovereign Compulsion or Sovereign Collusion?* 14 Case W. Res. J. Int'l L. 47, 58 (1982). Japan carefully structured its program so that the Japanese automobile companies were receiving instructions from the government in order to create a defense based upon the foreign compulsion doctrine to a U.S. antitrust lawsuit.

2. Even after the VRA expired in 1985, the Japanese government continued to restrain exports of autos to the United States and limited exports to 2.3 million units. By limiting exports to the United States while demand for Japanese cars was

very high, Japanese automakers could charge much higher prices. Only in the early 1990s, when Japanese exports were consistently lower than the permitted quota, did Japan end the restraint.

3. What were the economic effects of the VRA? A U.S. Federal Trade Commission staff study[1] estimated that the restraints were costing consumers at least $1.1 billion annually in higher prices, and the economy as a whole was penalized at least $994 million annually in efficiency losses. Japanese automakers gained additional profits estimated to be $824 million, while U.S. automakers gained about $115 million in additional profits. In terms of jobs preserved by the VRA, each job saved was estimated to have cost consumers $113,622, and the annual efficiency cost to the economy for each saved job was $80,682. Was the VRA nevertheless beneficial to the United States?

4. From the 1970s to the 1990s, VRAs were used freely, not only by the United States but by many countries to limit imports, in response to domestic political and economic pressures. Under the WTO, VRAs are now unlawful. Article 11 of the Agreement on Safeguards provides that members "shall not seek, take, or maintain" VRAs.

Case Study Two
The U.S. Steel Safeguards Case of 2002

In early March 2002, President George W. Bush announced the imposition of safeguard measures against ten kinds of steel imports because of the depressed state of the U.S. steel industry. This case was highly unusual because the safeguard measures were imposed on top of existing anti-dumping duties that had already been imposed. At the time that the safeguards were imposed, imports of steel were declining sharply because the anti-dumping duties were having their intended effect. In addition, safeguards were imposed on virtually all steel products. Many countries were genuinely shocked by the severity and scope of the U.S. safeguards. As a result, a number of countries around the world immediately raised their tariffs on steel based on the expectation that their steel imports would increase because of steel diverted from the U.S. market. A number of countries then immediately challenged the U.S. safeguard measures before the WTO.

PROBLEM 8-7

You are a policy analyst for a think tank and watchdog over government action. Upon reviewing the materials below concerning the *U.S. Steel Safeguards of 2002* case and the WTO decision, you wonder if the U.S. government acted for political reasons in this case. For example, when the WTO rejected the U.S.-imposed safeguards as unlawful, President George W. Bush formally rescinded the steel products safeguard measures on December 8, 2003 (*see* Presidential Proclamation No. 7741, 68 Fed. Reg. 68481-84 (Dec. 8, 2003)) less than a month after the decision

---

1. David G. Tarr and Morris E. Morkre, *Aggregate Costs to the United States of Tariffs and Quotas on Imports: General Tariff Cuts and Removal of Quotas on Automobiles, Steel, Sugar, and Textiles* (Federal Trade Commission 1984).

was handed down by the WTO Appellate Body, and even before the formal adoption by the Dispute Settlement Body of the Appellate Body's Report on December 10, 2003. Under the WTO Dispute Settlement Understanding, the losing party in a WTO case has a reasonable period of time (usually fifteen months) to comply with an adopted decision. You wonder why the President acted so quickly. You also know that the U.S. Commerce Department lawyers involved in the *U.S. Steel Safeguards Case of 2002* are smart and knowledgeable about WTO law and that the U.S. imposed safeguards based upon a very weak case. You are asked to write a memorandum addressing the following issues:

(1) Did the United States impose safeguards for political reasons? If so, what were these reasons?

(2) Did the United States use the WTO dispute settlement process for political reasons? How?

(3) Who would gain from the imposition of safeguards that are then swiftly and decisively rejected by the WTO? Did anyone lose? Who?

PROBLEM 8-8

Country Y initiates an escape clause investigation into whether the importation of textiles from Countries A, B, C, and D is the cause of a serious injury to Country Y's domestic textiles industry. Country Y completes the investigation and finds that the imports are the cause of a serious injury and that safeguards are justified under GATT Article XIX and the WTO Safeguards Agreement. Country Y then imposes safeguards in the form of higher tariffs on imports from Countries A and B. Country C's trade minister engages in frantic negotiations with Country Y's foreign trade secretary. As a result of solemn promises by Country C's trade minister to voluntarily impose restrictions on exports, Y decides not to impose safeguards on textiles from Country C. Country Y decides also to exclude safeguards on textiles from Country D because the two countries have a long and amicable relationship and are sure they can work things out.

Are Y's actions consistent with its WTO obligations? What issues are presented? If Y wanted to impose safeguards on imports from Country A and B only, what was Y required to do? *See* Articles 2.1 and 2.2 of the Safeguards Agreement and the case below.

United States—Definitive Safeguard Measures on Imports of Certain Steel Products
Report of the Appellate Body, adopted on December 10, 2003
WT/DS248, 249, 251, 252, 253, 254, 258, 259/AB/R

[Brazil, China, the European Communities, Japan, Korea, New Zealand, Norway, and Switzerland brought a complaint challenging the U.S. steel safeguard measures imposed by President Bush. The panel found that the U.S. safeguard measures were not consistent with Article XIX of the GATT and various provisions of the Safeguards Agreement. The United States appealed various aspects of the panel decision to the Appellate Body. The Appellate Body began its discussion below with a general discussion of the standard of review. The panel held below that the standard of review was not a *de novo* review of the findings of the ITC. Rather, the panel's task was to determine whether the United States had demonstrated in a published report, through a "reasoned and adequate explanation," that unforeseen developments and tariff concessions had led to increased imports causing, or threatening to cause, serious injury to the relevant domestic industry. The Appellate Body found no error in the panel's approach. The Appellate Body then applied this standard—whether the United States had provided a "reasoned and adequate explanation"—to justify its safeguard measures. A second preliminary issue was whether it was necessary to demonstrate, with respect to each safeguard measure, that the increase in imports subject to the safeguard was due to an unforeseen development. In the panel, the United States had argued that the Asian and Russian financial crises together with the strong U.S. dollar resulted in increased imports to the United States. These conditions led to the increase of imports of a broad category of products, including the specific products that were subject to the ten safeguard measures. The Appellate Body rejected the U.S. position. The Appellate Body ruled that under GATT Article XIX, the United States was required to demonstrate, with respect to each of the ten safeguard measures, how an "unforeseen development" led to an increase in imports of the product that is subject to the safeguard measure. The Appellate Body then proceeded to review, with respect to each of the ten safeguard measures, whether increased imports were due to an unforeseen development.

The excerpted portions of the opinion below focus on (1) whether imports were increasing so as to justify safeguards and (2) whether the United States was allowed to exclude Canada, Mexico, Jordan, and Israel from the safeguards imposed.]

366. The United States argues that the Panel's conclusion that the USITC failed to provide a reasoned and adequate explanation of how the facts supported its finding that CCFRS [cold carbon flat rolled steel] was being imported "in such increased quantities" within the meaning of Article XIX:1(a) and Article 2.1 "rests in large measure on the Panel's determination that the ITC 'did not seem to focus on, or at least account' for the fact that there was a decrease in imports, on both an absolute and a relative basis, from interim 2000 to interim 2001." According to the United States, the Panel gave the change between interim periods "dispositive weight", although the actual requirement in Article XIX:1(a) and Article 2.1—as acknowledged by the Panel—is that "[any product] is being imported . . . in such increased quantities", and that, therefore, the "imports need not be increasing at the time of the determination; what is necessary is that imports *have* increased, if the products continue 'being imported' in (such) increased quantities."

367. We agree with the United States that Article 2.1 does *not* require that imports need to be increasing at the time of the determination. Rather, the plain meaning of the phrase "is being imported in such increased quantities" suggests merely that imports must *have* increased, and that the relevant products continue "being imported" in (such) increased quantities. We also do *not* believe that a decrease in imports at the end of the period of investigation would necessarily prevent an investigating authority from finding that, nevertheless, products continue to be imported "in such increased quantities."[2]

---

2. We note that a decrease at the end of a period of investigation may, for instance, result from the seasonality of the relevant product, the timing of shipments, or importer concerns about the investigation. As we have said, the text of Article 2.1 does not necessarily prevent, in our view, a finding of "increased imports" in the face of such a decline.

368. We do not agree, however, with the United States' assertion that the Panel's conclusion that there were no "increased imports" of CCFRS, for purposes of Article 2.1, is a result of the Panel giving "dispositive weight" to the decrease in imports that took place from interim 2000 to interim 2001. As we understand it, the Panel's conclusion was based on the Panel's finding that the USITC had not provided *a reasoned and adequate explanation* of how the facts supported its determination that CCFRS "is being imported in . . . such increased quantities". The reason why the Panel did not find the USITC's *explanation* to be "reasoned and adequate" was the magnitude of the decrease that occurred between interim 2000 and interim 2001 (from 11.5 to 6.9 million short tons). In the words of the Panel, the USITC "did not seem to focus on, or at least account for, [that decrease] . . . in concluding that imports are 'still significantly higher . . . than at the beginning of the period'." In the absence of a reasoned and adequate explanation in the USITC report relating to the decrease in imports that occurred at the end of the period of investigation, the USITC could not be said to have adequately explained the existence of "such increased quantities" within the meaning of Article 2.1.

371. With respect to the timing of the "increased imports" of CCFRS, the Panel found that:

> It may well be that the increase occurring until 1998 could have qualified at the time as an increase satisfying the criteria of Article 2.1 of the Agreement on Safeguards, but the Panel need not express itself on that point because that increase, in itself, *was no longer recent enough at the time of the determination*. In other words, the increase occurring until 1998, *taken by itself and with the decrease thereafter*, is not a sufficient factual basis for supporting a determination in October 2001 that CCFRS "is being imported in . . . increased quantities." [emphasis added]

372. The United States argues that the Panel erred in concluding that the increase in imports that occurred in 1998 "'was no longer recent enough at the time of the determination' to support a finding of increased imports" although "the Panel itself recognized that there are no absolute standards as regards *how* sudden, recent, and significant the increase must be in order to qualify as an 'increase' in the sense of Article 2.1."

373. Based on our review of the Panel's reasoning—in particular, the Panel's conclusions in paragraphs 10.167-10.171 of the Panel Reports, where the Panel states that "[a] *concrete* evaluation is called for" and that "the inquiry is not whether imports have increased 'recently and suddenly' *in the abstract*"—we do not understand the Panel to have meant, as the United States appears to suggest, that an increase in 1998 would not, *under any conditions*, have been recent enough to support a finding of increased imports. Instead, the Panel proceeds to explain that "[i]n other words, the increase occurring until 1998, *taken by itself and with the decrease thereafter*, is not a sufficient factual basis for supporting a determination in October 2001 that CCFRS 'is being imported in . . . increased quantities'."

374. In our view, what is called for in every case is an *explanation* of how the *trend* in imports supports the competent authority's finding that the requirement of "such increased quantities" within the meaning of Articles XIX:1(a) and 2.1 has been fulfilled. It is this *explanation* concerning the *trend* in imports—over the entire period of investigation—that allows a competent authority to *demonstrate* that "a product is being imported in such increased quantities."

376. Therefore, we *uphold* the Panel's conclusion, in paragraph 10.186 and the relevant section of paragraph 11.2 of the Panel Reports, that the application

of the safeguard measure on CCFRS is inconsistent with Articles 2.1 and 3.1 of the *Agreement on Safeguards*, because the United States failed to provide a reasoned and adequate explanation of how the facts support its determination with respect to "increased imports" of that product.

[Using a similar analysis, the Appellate Body then upheld the Panel's finding that the ITC did not provide an adequate and reasoned explanation of how the facts support its determination with respect to increased imports of Stainless Rod Steel and Hot-Rolled Bar.]

PARALLELISM

433. We start by recalling that the United States excluded imports from Canada and Mexico, as well as from Israel and Jordan, from the scope of application of these safeguard measures. The Panel found that these safeguard measures were inconsistent with Articles 2.1 and 4.2 of the *Agreement on Safeguards* because the United States did not, with respect to any of the product categories at issue, establish explicitly that imports from the sources included in the application of these measures, *alone*, satisfied the conditions for the application of a safeguard measure. The United States challenges these findings of the Panel.

438. On appeal, the United States explicitly acknowledges that it "does not dispute that the ITC's parallelism analysis *did not satisfy the standards articulated by the Panel*." However, the United States considers this to be "irrelevant," because it contends that these requirements are not contained in the *Agreement on Safeguards*.

439. We begin our analysis by reviewing the relevant treaty provisions. The word "parallelism" is not in the text of the *Agreement on Safeguards*; rather, the requirement that is described as "parallelism" is found in the "parallel" language used in the first and second paragraphs of Article 2 of the *Agreement on Safeguards*. Article 2 of the *Agreement on Safeguards* stipulates:

Conditions

1. A Member may apply a safeguard measure to a product only if that Member has determined, pursuant to the provisions set out below, that such product is being imported into its territory in such increased quantities, absolute or relative to domestic production, and under such conditions as to cause or threaten to cause serious injury to the domestic industry that produces like or directly competitive products.
2. Safeguard measures shall be applied to a *product being imported* irrespective of its source. [emphasis added]

440. In *US—Wheat Gluten*, we said that:

The same phrase—"product . . . being imported"—appears in *both* . . . paragraphs of Article 2. In view of the identity of the language in the two provisions, and in the absence of any contrary indication in the context, we believe that it is appropriate to ascribe the *same* meaning to this phrase in both Articles 2.1 and 2.2. To include imports from all sources in the determination that increased imports are causing serious injury, and then to exclude imports from one source from the application of the measure, would be to give the phrase "product being imported" a *different* meaning in Articles 2.1 and 2.2 of the *Agreement on Safeguards*. In Article 2.1, the phrase would embrace imports from *all* sources whereas, in Article 2.2, it would exclude imports from certain sources. This would be incongruous and unwarranted. In the usual course, *therefore, the imports included in the determinations made under Articles 2.1 and 4.2 should correspond to the imports included in the application of the measure, under Article 2.2.* (original emphasis; emphasis added to last sentence)

441. Thus, where, for purposes of applying a safeguard measure, a Member has conducted an investigation considering imports from *all* sources (that is, *including* any members of a free-trade area), that Member may not, subsequently, without any further analysis, exclude imports from free-trade area partners from the application of the resulting safeguard measure.

443. In considering the investigation by the competent authority in the case before us, we note that the USITC relied on data for imports from *all* sources. The USITC report states that "[i]n determining whether imports have increased, the Commission considers imports from all sources." We observe also that, in the examination of whether increased imports were a cause of serious injury, the USITC also relied on data for all imports for each product category. It is undisputed by the United States that, in its investigation, the USITC considered imports from *all sources — including* imports from Canada, Israel, Jordan, and Mexico. Nevertheless, imports from Canada, Israel, Jordan, and Mexico were *excluded* from the application of the safeguard measures at issue. Therefore, there is, in these measures, a gap between the imports that were taken into account in the investigation performed by the USITC and the imports falling within the scope of the measures as applied.

444. It was thus incumbent on the USITC, in fulfilling the obligations of the United States under Article 2 of the *Agreement on Safeguards*, to justify this gap by establishing explicitly, in its report, that imports from sources covered by the measures — that is, imports from sources *other than* the excluded countries of Canada, Israel, Jordan, and Mexico — satisfy, *alone*, and in and of themselves, the conditions for the application of a safeguard measure, as set out in Article 2.1 and elaborated in Article 4.2 of the *Agreement on Safeguards*. Further, and as we have already explained, to provide such a justification, the USITC was obliged by the *Agreement on Safeguards* to provide a reasoned and adequate explanation of how the facts supported its determination that imports from sources *other than* Canada, Israel, Jordan, and Mexico satisfy, *alone*, and in and of themselves, the conditions for the application of a safeguard measure.

446. The United States claims that the Panel erred in concluding that the competent authorities are required to account for the fact that excluded imports may have some injurious impact on the domestic industry. The United States submits that, in so far as the Panel indicated that parallelism requires authorities to focus separately on imports from sources that are not excluded from the measure, the Panel's statements "accurately reflect[ ] what the Appellate Body said in [US —]Line Pipe." However, the United States asserts that the Panel went "further" and established a requirement for a separate analysis of imports from sources not subject to the safeguards measure, according to which the competent authority must "affirmatively account for the effect of such imports." The United States contends that the requirement articulated by the Panel has no basis in the text of the *Agreement on Safeguards*.

447. The United States relies on statements made by the USITC in both its original report and the Second Supplementary Report, as establishing that the imports from sources covered by the safeguard measures applied by the United States, *alone,* satisfy the conditions for the application of those measures. The United States acknowledges that, in doing so, the USITC did not "account for the fact that excluded imports may have some injurious impact on the domestic industry," as the Panel required. The United States argues, however, that the Panel, by requiring the competent authority to "account for the fact that excluded imports may have some injurious impact on the domestic industry," "insert[ed] . . . an extra analytical step with respect to parallelism." The United States maintains that nothing in the *Agreement on Safeguards* requires a distinct or explicit analysis of imports from sources *not* subject to the measure.

448. We note, first, that the United States agrees that the "Appellate Body has read th[e] language ['such product . . . being imported' in Article 2.1] to refer to only *imports from sources which are subject to a safeguards measure.*" The United States also agrees that Article 2.1, as read by the Appellate Body, requires the competent authority to "establish explicitly that increased imports from [sources included in the safeguard measure] alone" satisfy the conditions for a safeguard measure. The United States does not contest these requirements in this appeal.

449. Secondly, as we have indicated previously, in *US—Line Pipe,* the conditions set forth in Article 2.1 are further elaborated in Article 4.2. Article 4.2(b) requires that a determination that increased imports have caused or are threatening to cause serious injury to the domestic industry, as required by Article 4.2(a), can be made only where an investigation by a competent authority demonstrates the existence of a "causal link" between "increased imports" and either serious injury or the threat of serious injury. Article 4.2(b), last sentence, stipulates also, for the purposes of determining the existence of such a "causal link," that "[w]hen factors other than increased imports are causing injury to the domestic industry at the same time, such injury shall not be attributed to increased imports." This obligation is sometimes described as the "non-attribution requirement."

450. As a result, the phrase "increased imports" in Articles 4.2(a) and 4.2(b) must, in our view, be read as referring to the same set of imports envisaged in Article 2.1, that is, *to imports included in the safeguard measure.* Consequently, imports *excluded* from the application of the safeguard measure must be considered a factor "other than increased imports" within the meaning of Article 4.2(b). The possible injurious effects that these excluded imports may have on the domestic industry must not be attributed to imports included in the safeguard measure pursuant to Article 4.2(b). The requirement articulated by the Panel "to account for the fact that excluded imports may have some injurious impact on the domestic industry" is, therefore, not, as the United States argues, an "extra analytical step" that the Panel added to the analysis of imports from all sources. To the contrary, this requirement necessarily follows from the obligation in Article 4.2(b) for the competent authority to ensure that the effects of factors other than increased imports—a set of factors that subsumes *imports excluded from the safeguard measure*—are not attributed to imports included in the measure, in establishing a causal link between imports included in the measure and serious injury or threat thereof.

[The Appellate Body recommended that the United States withdraw its safeguards.]

NOTES AND QUESTIONS

1. According to the WTO, a total of 234 Article XIX safeguard measures were initiated by WTO members during the period from January 1, 1995 to April 30, 2012. The largest number were instituted by India (twenty-eight) followed by Indonesia (eighteen), and then Jordan and Turkey (sixteen each). The United States has initiated ten actions.

2. In the *U.S.—Steel Safeguards* case, the United States did not impose safeguards (tariffs) on steel imports from Canada, Mexico, Israel, Jordan, or developing countries. The safeguards appear to have been targeted at Brazil, China, the European Union, and a few other countries. Why? Are political and economic rivalries relevant?

3. What are the options for a WTO member state adversely affected by a safeguard decision? There appear to be four choices:

- Consultation as provided in GATT Article XXII and Article 4 of the DSU
- Adoption of a safeguard measure in response (tit for tat)
- Review of safeguard legality under the DSU procedure
- Unilateral suspension of equivalent obligations (countermeasures)

4. Consider the remedy mandated by the Appellate Body in the *U.S.—Steel Safeguards* case. The U.S. withdrawal of the steel safeguards was prospective only. Does this pose a problem in safeguard cases? Should another remedy be mandated? For a reasoned argument that the WTO should institute a compensation remedy for WTO members that are the victims of wrongful safeguard measures, see Michael J. Hahn, *Balancing or Bending? Unilateral Reactions to Safeguard Measures*, 39 J. of World Trade 301 (2005).

5. *The Use of Quotas in Safeguard Measures: The "Selectivity Problem."* When may WTO members apply safeguard measures in the form of a quota, and when may they allocate the quota among supplying countries? May the quota be targeted against only one or a few countries? The answers to these questions are found in the Agreement on Safeguards, Article 5. This is a compromise based on what is termed "quota modulation."

6. *Special Safeguard on Textiles and Clothing from China.* The now-expired WTO Agreement on Textiles and Clothing (ATC) contained a special safeguard for this economic sector. In 2005, after the expiration of the ATC, both the EU and the United States invoked special safeguards on clothing and textile products that were contained in China's Agreement on Accession to the WTO (2000). The safeguards were invoked on the grounds of "market disruption" caused by the surge of textile and clothing imports from China after the end of the ATC. *See also U.S. Association of Importers of Textiles and Apparel v. U.S. Department of Commerce*, 413 F.3d 1344, 1350 (Fed. Cir. 2005) (denying petition by textile importers for preliminary injunction barring U.S. interagency committee from considering requests for safeguard measures, on the grounds that (a) the court lacked jurisdiction based on ripeness grounds; and (b) the importers failed to established a fair chance of success on the merits).

7. *The Special Safeguard in the Agreement on Agriculture.* A special safeguard provision applies in the case of agricultural products. Article 5 of the Agreement on Agriculture allows members to impose a safeguard measure with respect to certain specially designated trade concessions, if imports exceed a certain "trigger level."

Trigger levels will vary, depending upon the level of market access provided. For example, where market access opportunities are 10 percent or less, the base trigger level is 125 percent of the domestic consumption during the preceding three years. *See* Article 5(4)(a). The trigger level is 110 percent where market access opportunities are greater than 10 percent, but less than or equal to 30 percent and is 105 percent where market access is greater than 30 percent. *See* Article 5(4)(b) and (c). How does this provision differ from Article XIX? Is a special safeguard of this type needed in the agriculture sector?

8. *Adjustment Assistance.* An alternative or complement to safeguard relief is governmental financial assistance and retraining of workers displaced by trade concessions and shifting trade policies. U.S. law provides trade adjustment assistance benefits under the Trade Act of 1974. Adjustment assistance has been criticized because it often does not work very well. *See, e.g., Nelson v. United States Secretary of Labor*, 936 F. Supp. 1026, 1028 (CIT 1996) (certification for trade adjustment assistance benefits denied due to failure to file a petition within one year of separation); *Former Employees of BMC Software v. Secretary of Labor*, 454 F. Supp. 2d 1361, 1354 (CIT 2006) (criticizing the Department of Labor for its high rejection rate of certifications for assistance).

NOTE ON IMPORT RESTRICTIONS TO SAFEGUARD BALANCE OF PAYMENTS

Read GATT Articles XII, XIII, XIV, XV, and XVIII Section B in the Documents Supplement.

The GATT contains special articles to permit the use of quotas for the purpose of safeguarding a member's balance of payments obligations. An importing country will be required to pay for the imports in foreign currency or its local currency, but the importing country might find that its currency reserves are low. If the importing country's currency reserves fall to a very low level, the importing country might be unable to meet its other balance of payments obligations, which might precipitate a financial crisis or threaten the country's economic and political stability. GATT Articles XII and XVIII Section B allow countries to impose safeguards in the form of quotas to limit the amount of imports. Limiting imports will relieve the importing country from having to use its currency reserves. These provisions effectively distinguish between developing and developed countries with respect to the standards involved. In the early years of the GATT, both developing and developed members invoked these sections when they experienced balance of payments problems.

Article XV of the GATT, entitled Exchange Agreements, requires WTO members to cooperate with the International Monetary Fund (IMF) on currency exchange questions, and Article XV:2 and 3 require members to seek IMF consultation with respect to problems concerning balance of payments, monetary reserves, and currency exchange arrangements, and to accept IMF determinations in most respects. In addition, GATT 1994 includes an Understanding on the Balance-of-Payments Provisions in the General Agreement on Tariffs and Trade that sets out detailed procedures for invoking GATT Articles XII and XVIII Section B.

Articles XII and XVIII Section B have fallen into disuse because (1) the institution of floating rates of currency exchange makes balance of payments somewhat self-correcting; (2) the WTO has significantly tightened up the requirements for balance of payments safeguards, as discussed in the safeguards cases involving India and Korea in the paragraphs below; and (3) the IMF is given final say under GATT Article XV:2 on all safeguard issues involving foreign exchange. The IMF is under the control of the United States, the EU, and Japan, which together have majority voting power. In the usual case, a developing country with balance of payments problems will get aid in the form of loans or grants from the IMF, but the IMF will not authorize trade restrictions as part of the aid package.

Developing members have invoked Article XVIII Section B in the past, but decisions of the WTO Appellate Body have made the use of Article XVIII Section B considerably less attractive. In *India—Quantitative Restrictions on Imports of Agricultural, Textile and Industrial Products,* WT/DS90/AB/R, Report of the Appellate Body, adopted on August 23, 1999, the Appellate Body found (¶¶110-115) that balance-of-payments trade restrictions may be maintained only if there is a "clear probability" of the occurrence of one of the conditions of GATT Article XVIII:9: (1) a serious decline or (2) a threat of a serious decline in monetary reserves or (3) inadequate monetary reserves. In the absence of these conditions, safeguards must be removed; such safeguards may not be maintained merely because of a "distant possibility" that balance of payments problems may recur.

Even if safeguards are justified under Article XII or XVIII Section B, the safeguards must be progressively removed as the importing country makes progress in addressing its balance of payment issues. This obligation to progressively scale back safeguards, contained in GATT Article XII:2(b) and Article XVIII Section B:11, was interpreted by a GATT panel in *Korea—Restrictions on Imports of Beef,* GATT B.I.S.D. (36th Supp.) 268, Report of the GATT Panel, adopted on November 7, 1989, to require Korea to remove quotas on the import of beef in place due to balance of payment issues since 1967.

Both Article XII and Article XVIII Section B allow the use of only one type of trade restriction to deal with balance of payments problems: quotas. A quota can be used to restrict the quantity of imports that must be paid for by the importing country with its currency reserves. Using the quota can give the importing country some breathing room to replenish its low reserves, but GATT Article XIII imposes certain disciplines on the application of quotas. Quotas must be administered on a non-discriminatory basis and must be allocated among supplier countries based on their expected shares of trade using country-specific quotas coupled with permits or import licenses. Article XIV allows the importing country in a balance of payments situation to deviate temporarily from the non-discrimination rule of Article XIII, but only with the consent of WTO members and then only on a temporary basis for a small part of its external trade, where the benefits to the importing country substantially outweigh any injury to the trade of other members.

Although a country can unilaterally adopt quotas to deal with balance of payments problems, the country must then immediately enter into WTO consultations with other members affected by the trade restrictions. After the consultations, the quotas will be reviewed periodically. If it is determined by the WTO that quotas are being applied inconsistently with the GATT, the WTO may authorize the aggrieved party to retaliate through the suspension or modification of trade concessions. A developing country that is the target of retaliation has the right to withdraw from the GATT on 60 days' notice.

NOTE ON THE RELATIONSHIP OF GATT ARTICLE XV WITH THE ARTICLES OF AGREEMENT OF THE INTERNATIONAL MONETARY FUND

The fundamental rules of international law on exchange rates in international trade and investment are contained in the Articles of Agreement of the International Monetary Fund (IMF). The IMF's Articles of Agreement date from 1944, but in 1978, after the end of fixed currency exchange rates, the second amendment of the Articles of Agreement was adopted to establish the right of members to adopt exchange arrangements of their choice. The second amendment revised IMF Article IV:2(b) to state that "exchange arrangements may include (i) the maintenance by a member of a value for its currency in terms of the special drawing right or another denominator, other than gold, selected by the member, or (ii) cooperative arrangements by which members maintain the value of their currencies in relation to the value of the currency or currencies of other members, or (iii) other exchange arrangements of a member's choice."

However, IMF Article IV:1 contains a code of conduct obligating members in their conduct of exchange rate policies. This article contains four obligations:

> Each member shall:
> (1) Endeavor to direct its economic and financial policies toward the objective of fostering orderly economic growth with reasonable price stability, with due regard to its circumstances;
> (2) Seek to promote stability by fostering orderly underlying economic and financial conditions and a monetary system that does not tend to produce erratic disruptions;
> (3) Avoid manipulating exchange rates or the international monetary system in order to prevent effective balance of payments adjustment or to gain an unfair competitive advantage over other members; and
> (4) Follow exchange rate policies compatible with the undertakings under [IMF Article IV:1].

The IMF has never found a member to be in breach of key obligation 3—exchange rate manipulation.

Consider the obligations of GATT Article XV. Article XV:2 obligates WTO members to consult with the IMF. What is the scope of the obligation to consult?

In *Argentina—Measures Affecting Imports of Footwear, Textiles, Apparel and Other Items*, WT/DS56/AB/R, Report of the Appellate Body, adopted on April 22, 1998, Argentina argued that one of the trade restrictions in question—an import surcharge—was required under its adjustment program approved by the IMF. The Appellate Body ruled that there was no requirement that the panel needed to consult the IMF because GATT Article XV:2 does not mention IMF-sponsored economic adjustment programs, although the panel perhaps should have consulted the IMF under the general right in the Dispute Settlement Understanding (DSU), Article 13 to seek information and advice on technical matters.

In *India—Quantitative Restrictions on Imports of Agricultural, Textile, and Industrial Products*, WT/DS90/R, Panel Report, upheld by WT/DS90/AB/R, Report of the Appellate Body, both adopted on September 22, 1999, the WTO panel invoked Article 13 of the DSU, rather than GATT Article XV:2, to consult with the IMF on balance of payments matters.

In *Dominican Republic—Measures Affecting the Importation and Internal Sale of Cigarettes*, WT/DS302/R, Panel Report, modified, WT/DS302/AB/R, Report of the Appellate Body, both adopted on May 19, 2005, the panel decided to consult under GATT Article XV:2 in order to verify the argument of the Dominican Republic that a foreign exchange fee imposed on imported cigarettes was an exchange restriction consistent with GATT Article XV:9. The IMF's General Counsel replied that the fee was not an approved exchange restriction. The panel accordingly ruled that the exchange fee was "another charge or duty" inconsistent with GATT Article II:1(b).

Note that there is uncertainty over the relationship of the obligation to consult under GATT Article XV:2 and DSU Article 13.

For more analysis of these matters, see Claus D. Zimmermann, *Exchange Rate Misalignment and International Law*, 105 Am. J. Int'l L. 423 (2011).

PROBLEM 8-9

The United States considers bringing a case in the WTO claiming that China's currency is significantly undervalued in relation to the U.S. dollar. The undervaluation is due to interventionist measures used by China to artificially peg China's currency to the U.S. dollar as opposed to allowing it to float under market conditions. The undervaluation makes Chinese goods cheap for U.S. consumers and U.S. goods expensive for Chinese consumers. The result is an increasing U.S. trade deficit with China (for further discussion of this issue see Chapter 1 at pages 43-45). Evaluate the U.S. case on the basis of GATT Article XV:4. Now consider the effect of GATT Article XV:9. Is this a general exception to Article XV:4? If the United States brings the case, what are its chances of winning?

9   *Developing Countries*

I.   *Introduction*

This Chapter examines the integration of developing countries into the WTO. This Chapter is related to Chapter 7 (general exceptions) and Chapter 8 (safeguards) in that developing countries are entitled to many exceptions from obligations under the WTO agreements.

    This Chapter is organized as follows: We cover (1) an overview of developing countries and the history of developing countries within the GATT/WTO; (2) the early GATT provisions for developing countries; (3) the Generalized System of Preferences under the GATT providing special tariff treatment for developing countries; (4) the general system of special and differential treatment within the overall WTO system; and (5) agricultural trade issues of special concern to developing countries.

A.   Overview of Developing Countries

In the past several decades, vast amounts of wealth, far surpassing previous levels in world history, have been created for a relatively small group of nations. The multilateral trading system, which has ignited the globalization of world trade, has played a prominent role in wealth creation for these countries. This process of wealth creation, however, is also widening the gap between this relatively small group, which controls the vast bulk of the world's wealth, and the other nations of the world, which experience far lower standards of living. About one billion people, one-sixth of the world's population, are trying to survive on less than $1 per day. The rising tide of world trade and economic development has not lifted the level for everyone.

    Unless forceful measures are taken, the gap between relatively rich and poor countries is expected to increase. In the next twenty-five years, about two billion people will be added to the world's population; almost all of this population growth will be in poorer countries. The prospect of a widening gap raises complex economic, social, and political issues that could have profound and negative repercussions on a global scale; it also raises the issue of what measures richer countries, which benefit from globalization, should undertake to assist poorer countries in closing this gap.

    Reducing world poverty is a monumental task that developed countries cannot be expected to shoulder entirely. There are many situations, however, in which the developed world and international organizations can help through economic assistance. Three categories of measures are needed in this regard to raise global living standards:

- Increased and more effective use of aid flows to developing countries;
- Debt forgiveness that converts existing loans into grants, in order to relieve the debt burdens of poor countries; and
- Increased trade and investment opportunities for developing countries.

The first two measures concern economic aid and policy measures that are ultimately up to each country with the assistance of international organizations, such as the agencies of the United Nations and the World Bank. The third measure, however, is firmly within the arena of the World Trade Organization. Since increasing trade opportunities is a major focus, the WTO is now called upon to play a major role in improving the lot of developing countries. In trade, developing countries cite three major concerns:

- They are forced to open their economies in ways dictated by developed country standards;
- They face serious trade and competition barriers (such as high tariffs) in developed countries for those goods and services they are in a position to deliver; and
- They lack the expertise, resources, information, and experience to participate effectively in WTO meetings and negotiations.

Each of these concerns has been addressed, with varying degrees of effectiveness, within the WTO. Since developing countries now constitute the majority of WTO members, their needs and demands have moved to center stage. Several categories of such needs are:

- Greater and more meaningful participation in the various rounds of trade negotiations and in decision making;
- Reductions of tariffs and non-tariff trade barriers on products that are, or can be, easily produced in developing countries; this is the impetus behind the demand for reductions in the subsidies that many countries (such as the United States and European Union members) grant to encourage domestic agricultural production;
- Flexibility to deal with foreign direct investment in ways that suit their national interests; this is the reason why most developing countries oppose the negotiation of a Multilateral Agreement on Investment in the WTO;
- Exceptions and special treatment with respect to intellectual property requirements, especially with regard to pharmaceutical patents (covered in Chapter 13); and
- Services trade liberalization under a measured and cautious approach. Developing country members state that negotiations on services trade should be in the larger context of development as a whole, and that liberalization should be done only in accordance with a development planning strategy, not *ad hoc*. Services liberalization decisions should consider not only the contribution to jobs and to growth in GDP, but also public needs, such as health care, water supply, and financial stability. A developing country should accordingly not liberalize its services sectors until it has

developed a proper plan that accords with its development policies and strategies.

B.   What Is a Developing Country?

The WTO recognizes the special needs of developing countries, but the term itself is not defined in the WTO and is commonly used loosely within the WTO and in many other trade and economic areas. The World Bank, however, annually classifies the economies and countries of the world and offers a definition of developing countries that is widely recognized.[1] The World Bank's main criterion for country classification is gross national income (GNI) per capita. The World Bank divides all nations into four groups:

- low income — $1,005 or less;
- lower middle income — $1,006-$3,975;
- upper middle income — $3,976-$12,275; and
- high income — $12,276 or more.

Low-income and middle-income countries (the first three categories above) are typically referred to as developing countries. Countries in the upper-middle-income group are also called "newly industrialized economies" but are still technically qualified as developing countries. Only the last group, high-income economies, which refer primarily to the small group of countries that are members of the Organization for Economic Cooperation and Development (OECD), are not developing countries. The high threshold level for graduating from developing country status — over $12,276 GNI per capita — means that most countries in the world qualify as developing countries.

The World Bank scheme is not official or mandatory, and the WTO does not require its use. Although the World Bank scheme can be used as a guideline, developing country selection is made in the WTO on an *ad hoc* basis primarily through self-selection. Members of the WTO are free to claim developing country status; however, other WTO members are free to contest such claims. Because substantial benefits accompany developing country status and because the definition of "developing country" is unsettled, many nations claim developing country status. To claim a second category, "least developing country" (LDC) status, for which the highest level of preferential treatment is granted, the WTO requires an official determination under the rules of the United Nations.[2]

About two-thirds of the current 155 members of the WTO are considered to be and look upon themselves as developing countries. Self-selection has caused controversy in the WTO, most notably in the case of China, which wanted developing country status, but had to compromise this claim to gain admission. At the end of the Uruguay Round, the United States and the EU declared they would

---

1. World Development Indicators available at http://www.worldbank.org/data/countryclass.

2. The UN Committee for Development Planning makes this determination based on per capita income, population size, quality of life index, and economic diversification. *See* UN Doc. E/1994/22 (1994).

not consider some countries, such as Singapore, South Korea, and Hong Kong, as developing countries for the purposes of WTO preference programs.

In 2009 the leaders of Brazil, Russia, India, China, and South Africa held a summit meeting to announce the formation of a new international economic institution known as the BRICS, from the first letters in the names of the countries involved. These five countries, all developing or newly industrialized countries, represent almost half the world's population and seek a greater voice in global economic affairs. All five have economic growth rates between 4 and 10 percent as of 2012, and together have a GDP of about 14 trillion, roughly the size of the U.S. economy. The BRICS are endeavoring to organize a broader group of nations known as "emerging market countries," developing countries that have economic growth rates significantly higher than the current growth rates of traditional economic powers, the United States, EU, and Japan. The BRICS' voice within the WTO became stronger when the WTO Ministerial Conference accepted Russia as a member in December, 2011. At this writing there is no official WTO recognition of the BRICS or "emerging market countries."

C.   The History of Developing Countries within the GATT/WTO

The GATT was organized primarily by developed countries, and early in its history, developing countries played a marginal role. Of the original twenty-three GATT contracting parties, ten were developing countries and three of these members withdrew from the GATT in its first few years of existence.[3] Developing countries saw themselves as members of a club that they did not really wish to join and to which they were not really invited.

When the GATT was founded, many parts of the developing world had just gained independence after decades of colonial rule. Many developing countries did not have a great deal of trust in their former colonial masters, leading countries within the GATT, and were skeptical of the benefits of joining the GATT. In addition, the entire world had just suffered a destructive war, and many countries were preoccupied by pressing issues at home. Rather than promoting trade with the developed world, many newly independent developing countries emphasized self-sufficiency and isolationism.

During the GATT's early years, developing countries were very critical of what they believed to be unfair rules that did not provide a level playing field. The GATT was founded on the Most Favored Nation (MFN) principle, which meant equal treatment for all nations. The MFN principle meant that GATT contracting parties could not discriminate against other parties, but it also precluded developing countries from receiving preferential treatment. Any preferential treatment provided to developing countries would have to be extended under the MFN principle to all GATT countries. As a practical matter, the MFN principle barred preferential treatment for developing countries, since no country wanted to be obligated to extend the same favorable treatment to everyone else.

---

3. The ten original developing country GATT contracting parties were Brazil, Burma, China, Ceylon, Chile, Cuba, India, Pakistan, Syria, and Lebanon. In the first few years of the GATT, China, Lebanon, and Syria withdrew from the GATT.

Under the GATT, because developing countries did not receive preferential treatment, they were expected to compete on the same terms with developed countries, even though the former group was far behind in all areas of development. Many developing countries also felt a deep resentment toward developed countries, based on a perception that many of the causes of the backwardness of the developing world were due to the decades of domination by developed countries. Developing countries, totally unprepared, were now required to sink or swim on their own in an intensively competitive environment, competing against developed countries under rules that they had established. Developing countries felt that these conditions were unfair; they wanted preferential treatment within the GATT.

In the 1960s, when developing countries were still a minority within the GATT, two events marked a turning point in their treatment. In late 1961, Uruguay filed a complaint against virtually the entire developed-country membership and listed 576 restrictions that allegedly nullified and impaired Uruguayan exports. Although the litigation itself ended inconclusively, the complaint achieved its political purpose, which was to call attention to the poor treatment of developing countries within the GATT. A second major development was the formation of an organization that was seen as a rival to the GATT, the United Nations Conference on Trade and Development (UNCTAD), which became a permanent UN organization in 1964. The formation of UNCTAD reflected the attitude of developing countries that the GATT was not a hospitable forum for their needs.

UNCTAD's formation was perceived as a strong criticism of the GATT. Adding to the GATT's concerns was the association of UNCTAD with Eastern Block countries, which raised the specter that UNCTAD might create a Cold War rivalry with the GATT. At the same time, developing country membership in the GATT was increasing. By May 1970, fifty-two of the seventy-seven GATT contracting parties could be classified as developing countries.

In 1971, a major breakthrough occurred when the GATT adopted waivers for two types of preferences to favor developing countries: (1) a set-aside of the MFN obligation to permit a "generalized system of preferences" and (2) permission for developing countries to exchange tariff preferences among themselves. In 1979, both waivers were made permanent through the Enabling Clause[4] set forth in part below. The Enabling Clause recognized a permanent exception to the MFN principle. The Enabling Clause settled once and for all that developing countries are entitled to special and differential treatment within the GATT/WTO.

The Enabling Clause continues to guide WTO policy:

GATT Contracting Parties, Decision of November 28, 1979 on Differential and More Favourable Treatment, Reciprocity and Fuller Participation of Developing Countries

Following negotiations within the framework of the Multilateral Trade Negotiations, the CONTRACTING PARTIES decide as follows:

1. Notwithstanding the provisions of Article I of the General Agreement, contracting parties may accord differential and more favourable treatment to developing countries, without according such treatment to other contracting parties.

---

4. *Decision of November 28, 1979 on Differential and More Favourable Treatment, Reciprocity and Fuller Participation of Developing Countries*, GATT B.I.S.D. (26th Supp.) 203 (1980).

2. The provisions of paragraph 1 apply to the following:
    (a) Preferential tariff treatment accorded by developed contracting parties
        to products originating in developing countries in accordance with the
        Generalized System of Preferences;
    (b) Differential and more favourable treatment with respect to the provi-
        sions of the General Agreement concerning non-tariff measures gov-
        erned by the provisions of instruments multilaterally negotiated under
        the auspices of the GATT;
    (c) Regional or global arrangements entered into amongst less-developed
        contracting parties for the mutual reduction or elimination of tariffs
        and, in accordance with criteria or conditions which may be prescribed
        by the CONTRACTING PARTIES, for the mutual reduction or elimina-
        tion of non-tariff measures, on products imported from one another;
    (d) Special treatment on the least developed among the developing coun-
        tries in the context of any general or specific measures in favour of
        developing countries.

    . . .

5. The developed countries do not expect reciprocity for commitments made
    by them in trade negotiations to reduce or remove tariffs and other barri-
    ers to the trade of developing countries, i.e., the developed countries do
    not expect the developing countries, in the course of trade negotiations,
    to make contributions which are inconsistent with their individual develop-
    ment, financial and trade needs. Developed contracting parties shall there-
    fore not seek, neither shall less-developed contracting parties be required
    to make, concessions that are inconsistent with the latter's development,
    financial and trade needs.
6. Having regard to the special economic difficulties and the particular
    development, financial and trade needs of the least-developed countries,
    the developed countries shall exercise the utmost restraint in seeking any
    concessions or contributions for commitments made by them to reduce or
    remove tariffs and other barriers to the trade of such countries, and the
    least-developed countries shall not be expected to make concessions or con-
    tributions that are inconsistent with the recognition of their particular situ-
    ation and problems.

The Enabling Clause also contains a so-called graduation clause, which calls
for the eventual end of preferential treatment. Implementation of the graduation
clause, however, is controversial.

The Uruguay Round, begun in 1984, continued the policy of special and differential treatment for developing countries. However, developed countries were
not willing to simply cave in to all of the demands of developing countries, so the
overall results of the Uruguay Round can best be described as mixed. Most WTO
agreements that came out of the Uruguay Round contain special and preferential treatment for developing countries. Some agreements, such as the agreements
on textiles and agriculture, adopt policies long sought by developing countries.
Others agreements, such as TRIPS, GATS, and TRIMS (Trade-Related Investment
Measures) were viewed as concessions by developing countries to serve important
interests of developed countries.

Overall, there can be no doubt that within the WTO there is a new concern
for developing countries. Following the establishment of the WTO in 1995, the first
WTO Ministerial Conference, held in Singapore in 1996, adopted the following
declaration:

Developing Countries

13. The integration of developing countries in the multilateral trading system is important for their economic development and for global trade expansion. In this connection, we recall that the WTO Agreement embodies provisions conferring differential and more favourable treatment for developing countries, including special attention to the particular situation of least-developed countries. In order to assist them in these efforts, we will improve the availability of technical assistance under the agreed guidelines. We have also agreed to recommendations relative to the decision we took at Marrakesh concerning the possible negative effects of the agricultural reform programme on least-developed and net food-importing developing countries.

Least-Developed Countries

14. We remain concerned by the problems of the least-developed countries and have agreed to a Plan of Action, including provision for taking positive measures, for example duty-free access, on an autonomous basis, aimed at improving their overall capacity to respond to the opportunities offered by the trading system.[5]

Several other initiatives have been set in place since the First Ministerial Conference. In 1997, the WTO, the IMF, the World Bank, UNCTAD, and the UN Development program undertook to provide technical and financial trade-related assistance to least developed countries. In 2001, the Doha Ministerial Conference created initiatives to enhance market access for products of special concern to developing countries, such as agriculture and textiles, added new provisions in WTO agreements to benefit developing countries, and called for technical assistance to developing countries to help them implement WTO obligations and to participate more fully in the WTO.

These initiatives appear to be bearing fruit. In 2011 the value share of world trade in goods for developing countries surged to a fifty-year high of 41 percent after stagnating from 1980 to 2000 (the share was 27.4 percent in 1980 and was only 28.8 percent in 1999). Developing countries' share of services trade also increased (due in part to the financial crisis, which affected developed countries more severely than developing countries, particularly in terms of trade in services). Developing countries' share of world trade in services increased from 18.6 percent in 1980 to 30 percent in 2011. Areas of services trade (the world total of about $1 trillion trade in services is about 20 percent of the trade in goods), where developing countries have some degree of comparative advantage, include information and management services, education, tourism, construction and engineering, culture and sport, and transportation.

Many developing countries are now participating fully and effectively in the work of the WTO. In 2001, thirty-two WTO members created an Advisory Center in Geneva and contributed significant funding to aid developing country participation. The WTO Committee on Trade and Development has also been reconstituted. Developing countries are frequent users of the WTO dispute settlement mechanism, and they have won many key cases against developed country members. The 2003 Ministerial Conference in Cancun, Mexico, failed to agree on a final statement, due mainly to opposition from developing countries.

A major gain for developing countries (although more for some than for others) was the successful integration of trade in textiles and clothing into the

---

5. WTO, Ministerial Conference, Singapore, 9-13 December 1996, *Singapore Ministerial Declaration*, WT/MIN(96)/DEC, December 18, 1996, ¶¶13-14.

framework of the GATT through the WTO Agreement on Textiles and Clothing (1994). Many developing countries are now calling for a similar step to be taken in the area of agricultural trade although these efforts have reached an impasse. Developing countries are exerting more influence in ongoing negotiations over everything from intellectual property to safeguards.

Although progress has been made, there continue to be sharp disagreements. Some developed countries view the demands by developing countries to be excessive and unreasonable; many developing countries feel that developed countries have not lived up to their commitments to provide special and preferential treatment.

NOTE ON THE APPLICATION OF SAFEGUARDS AND QUOTAS CONCERNING TEXTILES AND CLOTHING

One of the WTO agreements concluded during the Uruguay Round of trade negotiations and specifically intended to benefit developing countries was the WTO Agreement on Textiles and Clothing (ATC). Inexpensive textiles (or clothing) from developing countries had been outside the scope of the GATT and subject to heavy protectionist measures such as quotas and high tariffs by developed countries; the ATC was a transitional agreement designed to subject textiles to the general discipline of bound tariffs and elimination of quotas of the GATT. The ATC expired on January 1, 2005. At present, textiles and clothing are fully subject to GATT 1994.

Since the ATC expired, international trade in textiles and clothing has been going through fundamental changes. The integration of this sector into GATT 1994 impacted not only the textile industry in importing countries but also the textile industry in exporting countries. Producers with a competitive advantage in world markets were able to gain a larger share of textile exports. Experts predicted that China and India would dominate world trade in textiles and clothing in the immediate aftermath of the ATC.

This is indeed what has happened. After China began to dominate world exports in textiles, the United States and the EU announced the imposition of safeguard quotas on imports of t-shirts, trousers, underwear shirts, fabrics, yarns, and other textile products, limiting the annual growth of imports of different categories of products to 7.5 percent of the volume in 2004. China denounced the imposition of these quotas, and revoked in part, or in full, export duties on eighty-two textile product lines. Late in 2005, the EU and the United States separately negotiated agreements with China to terminate the safeguards in 2008. These agreements did terminate at the end of 2008, and (with some minor exceptions) Chinese textiles trade with the United States and the EU is now governed by the laws, principles and policies of the WTO framework. Political, economic, and legal maneuvering will no doubt continue in coming years, as world trade in textiles adjusts to freer markets and trade.

II.   The GATT and Developing Countries

In this section, we first consider the original provisions of the GATT that are specifically addressed to the needs of developing countries.

Read GATT Article XVIII and Part IV, Articles XXXVI to XXXVIII, in the Documents Supplement.

The original GATT privilege accorded to developing countries is contained in Article XVIII, which permits developing countries to use measures to protect infant industries from foreign competition. Other than Article XVIII, developing countries had no relief from GATT obligations.

In 1965, Part IV of the GATT, consisting of Articles XXXVI, XXXVII, and XXXVIII, was added to address the issues of concern to developing countries. Article XXXVI is a statement of principles and objectives; Article XXXVII deals with commitments of developed countries; and Article XXXVIII calls for joint action. The problems below further explore the application of these provisions.

PROBLEM 9-1

Country P is an island developing country that has a long history of selling ornaments made from shellfish, lava rocks, and other decorative items to tourists who visit its lush tropical location. Country P's tourist memorabilia industry is a source of profit and is part of its vitally important tourism industry. Recently, as a result of P's entry into the GATT/WTO, cheap imports of shellfish ornaments from Malaysia and Thailand are causing serious disruption of Country P's own industry. P has imposed tariffs of 50 percent as a protective measure under GATT Article XVIII. Are these tariffs permissible? *See* GATT Article XVIII:2. Suppose that P also grants subsidies to the domestic industry in order to provide price support. Is this permitted? *See* GATT Article XVIII:C.

PROBLEM 9-2

Country P has begun to export its shellfish ornaments and other tourist paraphernalia to a few of its neighboring countries, including Country J, an advanced industrialized nation. However, Country P finds that the tariffs imposed by Country J on its products create a serious trade barrier. Country J's tariffs are its GATT-bound rates and are applied to P's products under the Most Favored Nation principle contained in GATT Article II. At a summit meeting, Country J's Foreign Trade Minister promised to reduce tariffs for P's products in accordance with Article XXXVII by March 1, 2013. The date has passed, and nothing has been done. Country P is frustrated and is angered by Country J's delays and excuses. Is Country J in violation of Article XXXVII?

NOTES AND QUESTIONS

1. Based upon the problems, how useful are these GATT provisions (Articles XVIII and Part IV) in addressing the interests of developing countries?

2. Assume the perspective of a developing country. Based upon a review of Article XVIII and Part IV, how would you assess the attitude of developed countries toward developing countries in the GATT?

III. Developing Country Preference Systems Under the WTO

As it became clear that the original GATT privilege (Article XVIII) and Part IV of GATT proved inadequate to address the concerns of developing countries, the GATT adopted general waivers of the MFN principle in 1971 for developing countries and embodied these waivers in the 1979 Enabling Clause. The Enabling Clause also authorized a Generalized System of Preferences (GSP), which serves as a foundation for the preferential treatment of developing countries in the WTO. In this section, we first examine the GSP under GATT as implemented by the United States and the EU.

A. The Generalized System of Preferences for the Trade in Goods

From the outset, the GSP in the United States and the EU was very political and extended preferences only to certain countries and to a limited number of products. Moreover, in order to obtain the preferences, beneficiary developing countries had to agree in advance to observe various norms encompassing everything from human rights and workers' rights to combating illegal drugs.

1. The United States

The United States administers four separate GSP trade programs approved by the Congress. The oldest and most important is the Generalized System of Preferences Program, 19 U.S.C. §2461 *et seq.*, under which designated imports from 131 countries and territories enter the United States duty-free, totaling approximately $35 billion per year. The second program is the Caribbean Basin Initiative, 19 USC §2701 *et seq.*, which benefits eighteen countries in Central America and the Caribbean, is intended to facilitate the development and economic diversification of the Caribbean Basin. A third program is the Andean Trade Preference Act, 19 U.S.C. §3201 *et seq.*, covering Bolivia, Colombia, Ecuador, and Peru, which combines trade preferences with anti-drug trafficking requirements. The most recent program, the African Growth and Opportunity Act, 19 U.S.C. §3701 *et seq.*, seeks to expand trade and investment in sub-Saharan African countries. In 2010, over 93 percent of U.S. imports from sub-Saharan African countries entered duty-free. These four programs overlap, and have different but similar requirements and standards. We consider the GSP program more specifically in this Chapter.

The U.S. GSP program is set forth in Title V of the Trade Act of 1974. There are two basic designations that must be under the GSP: (1) A country is designated as a Beneficiary Developing Country (BDC) and (2) an article is designated for duty-free treatment. Designated articles receive duty-free treatment.

PROBLEM 9-3

Mohlen, a German company, imports steel and other raw materials from Brazil, a BDC under the U.S. GSP program. The raw materials are processed by

Mohlen in Germany into brakes for heavy-duty trucks. The brakes are then shipped to the United States. The cost of the imported raw materials from Brazil is over 35 percent of the appraised value of the article. Are the brakes imported from Germany entitled to duty-free treatment? *See* 19 U.S.C. §2463(a) below. What is the purpose of this rule? Suppose that the materials from Brazil transit through Germany, but never enter the German market, and then enter the United States? What is the result?

PROBLEM 9-4

Country A has been designated as a BDC. Apex is a U.S. company based in Delaware and has set up a manufacturing subsidiary in Country A. Apex supplies the subsidiary in Country A with aluminum ingots from the United States. The manufacturing subsidiary in Country A then manufactures the aluminum ingots into aluminum nails that are used in certain types of industrial products. The manufacturing process of the aluminum nails is complex and involves many different steps. Aluminum nails of the type manufactured by the foreign subsidiary of Apex can be found in many hardware stores in the United States.

The subsidiary, however, does not sell the aluminum nails (that it manufactures) to the United States as a discrete item. Rather, once the subsidiary packages the nails with other types of nails, screws, and bolts. These other nails, screws, and bolts are sourced entirely in Country A. The final product or package is referred to as "General Industrial Nails and Accessories" and is then sold to importers in the United States. Assume that the combined package has been designated as an article entitled to GSP preferences. If the cost of the non-BDC aluminum ingots from the United States can be included in the cost of the materials, then the cost of the materials of the combined package satisfies the 35 percent BDC minimum content requirement. Are the imports entitled to duty-free treatment? Suppose that there is a different tariff line for the aluminum nails and the combined package. Is this relevant? Consult the GSP statute and case below.

Generalized System Of Preferences
19 U.S.C. §2462

SEC. 502. DESIGNATION OF BENEFICIARY DEVELOPING
COUNTRIES

(a) Authority to designate countries

(1) Beneficiary developing countries. The President is authorized to designate countries as beneficiary developing countries for purposes of this subchapter.

(2) Least-developed beneficiary developing countries. The President is authorized to designate any beneficiary developing country as a least-developed beneficiary developing country for purposes of this subchapter, based on the considerations in section 501 of this title and subsection (c) of this section.

(b) Countries ineligible for designation

[This provision prohibits the President from giving BDC designations to countries that are communist; that offer preferences to the products of developed countries other than the United States; that have nationalized or expropriated U.S. property or repudiated U.S. contracts; that refuse to recognize arbitral awards in favor of U.S. citizens; that aid or abet terrorism; that have not taken steps to provide internationally recognized rights to workers; or that have not eliminated the worst forms of child labor.]

19 U.S.C. §2463

SEC. 503. DESIGNATION OF ELIGIBLE ARTICLES

(a) Eligible articles.

(1) Designation. [T]he President is authorized to designate articles as eligible articles from all beneficiary developing countries for purposes of this subchapter by Executive order or Presidential proclamation.

(2) Rule of origin.

(A) General rule. The duty-free treatment provided under this subchapter shall apply to any eligible article which is the growth, product, or manufacture of a beneficiary developing country if—

(i) that article is imported directly from a beneficiary developing country into the customs territory of the United States; and

(ii) the sum of—

(I) the cost or value of the materials produced in the beneficiary developing country or any two or more such countries that are members of the same association of countries and are treated as one country under section 507(2), plus

(II) the direct costs of processing operations performed in such beneficiary developing country or such member countries, is not less than 35 percent of the appraised value of such article at the time it is entered.

(B) Exclusions. An article shall not be treated as the growth, product, or manufacture of a beneficiary developing country by virtue of having merely undergone—

(i) simple combining or packaging operations, or

(ii) mere dilution with water or mere dilution with another substance that does not materially alter the characteristics of the article.

(b) Articles that may not be designated as eligible articles. [Certain import-sensitive articles cannot be designated as eligible articles. These include textiles, certain electronic articles, certain steel articles, and certain agricultural products.]

Under the U.S. GSP program, an article is eligible for GSP benefits only if the article originates in an eligible BDC. *See* 9 U.S.C. §2463(a)(2). Rules of origin, which we covered in Chapter 5, are also very important for the GSP system. Articles will be deemed to originate in GSP countries and be eligible for duty-free treatment if they are wholly responsible for the growth, product, or manufacture of a

BDC. *See id.* at §2463(a)(2)(A). This can occur if the article in its entirety originates in the BDC. Examples are a crop grown in a BDC, minerals obtained in a BDC, or an article manufactured from materials and components entirely sourced in the BDC.

What if, as is often the case, the article consists of BDC materials and also non-BDC materials (i.e., materials that originate in a non-BDC country are sent to the BDC for processing with BDC materials into a final product)? An article cannot be deemed to be of BDC origin unless 100 percent of the components of the article originate in the BDC. In the case of an article with some non-BDC components, those components must be substantially transformed so that they can be considered to be of BDC origin. Then all of the components of the product—both BDC materials and non-BDC materials—can be deemed of BDC origin. We first encountered the substantive transformation test in Chapter 5; this test is also applied in *Torrington* below, involving the GSP.

Where non-BDC materials have been substantially transformed into BDC-origin materials, there is an additional minimum local content requirement that must be met before the product is entitled to duty-free treatment under the GSP: The sum of the cost or value of the materials originating in the BDC (and not transformed from non-BDC materials) and the processing operations in the BDC must be at least 35 percent of the appraised value of the article when it is entered into the United States.

In some cases, it will not be possible to meet the minimum local content value unless the cost or value of the non-BDC materials that have undergone a substantial transformation are included. For example, suppose that a product is made in a BDC from 75 percent imported materials from a non-BDC country and 25 percent local materials sourced in the BDC. To qualify for GSP treatment, the first step is to determine whether the article is wholly an article of a BDC country. To meet this requirement the imported materials must be substantially transformed into materials of BDC origin. Assuming that this requirement is met, the article is now 100 percent of BDC origin. The next step is to determine whether the article consists of at least 35 percent minimum local content value. At this point, U.S. courts would consider the article to contain only 25 percent local content and would not qualify for GSP treatment. The only way for this article to qualify for GSP treatment is if it would be possible to include some portion of the 75 percent imported materials that were substantially transformed. For this to be possible the non-BDC materials must undergo a double substantial transformation. See if you can understand why U.S. courts take this position, as explained in the following case.

Torrington Co. v. United States
United States Court of Appeals, Third Circuit, 1985
764 F.2d 1563

Davis, Circuit Judge.

The Government appeals from a decision of the United States Court of International Trade (CIT, Carman, J.), holding that certain industrial sewing-machine needles imported from Portugal by appellee (Torrington) are entitled to enter the United States duty free under the Generalized System of Preferences (GSP). [W]c affirm.

The GSP statute, 19 U.S.C. §§2461-2465 (1982) authorizes the President (subject to certain restrictions) to prepare a list of beneficiary developing countries (BDCs), and to designate products of those countries which are eligible for GSP treatment. A designated product imported from a listed country may enter the United States duty free. One problem with this general program is that it could be used to allow a noneligible country to conduct minimal finishing operations in a BDC, thereby reaping the benefits of the GSP at the expense of American manufacturers, but without the salutary effect of fostering industrialization in the designated country. Congress therefore provided that products from BDCs must meet certain minimum content requirements in order to qualify for duty-free treatment. To this end, 19 U.S.C. §2463 provides: (b) The duty free treatment provided under section 2461 of this title with respect to any eligible article shall apply only—* * * (2) If the sum of (A) the cost or value of the materials produced in the beneficiary developing country . . . plus (B) the direct cost of processing operations performed in such beneficiary developing country . . . is not less than 35 percent of the appraised value of such article at the time of its entry in the customs territory of the United States.

Section 2463(b) also authorizes the Secretary of the Treasury to "prescribe such regulations as may be necessary to carry out this subsection."

Under this latter authority, the Customs Service has promulgated regulations interpreting the operative phrase in §2463(b)(2)(A), *supra*, "materials produced in the beneficiary developing country." 19 C.F.R. §10.177(a) (1984) states that the words produced in the beneficiary developing "country" refer to constituent materials of which the eligible article is composed which are either: (1) Wholly the growth, product or manufacture of the beneficiary developing country; or (2) Substantially transformed in the beneficiary developing country into a new and different article of commerce.

Thus, if the value of the materials described in §10.177(a)(1) and (2) plus the direct cost of processing operations performed in the BDC account for 35% of the appraised value of the merchandise, the merchandise is entitled to enter duty-free under 19 U.S.C. §§2461 and 2463.

The question in this case is whether industrial sewing-machine needles which Torrington imported met these minimum content requirements. In the trial court, the parties stipulated to an agreed statement of facts which formed the basis of the CIT's decision. These facts establish the following:

The sewing machine needles at issue were exported from Portugal to the United States by Torrington Portuguesa, a manufacturing subsidiary of Torrington. The needles are classifiable under item 672.20 of the Tariff Schedules of the United States (TSUS), "Sewing machines and parts thereof." At the time of the exports, Portugal was designated as a BDC and articles classifiable under item 672.20 were eligible products.

Torrington Portuguesa produced the needles from wire manufactured in a non-BDC and brought into Portugal. On this ground the Customs Service denied duty-free treatment to the needles because they did not incorporate any "materials produced" in Portugal, and the direct cost of producing the needles does not account for 35% of their appraised value. In Customs' view the needles failed to meet the minimum content requirements of 19 U.S.C. §2463(b). Torrington agrees that if Customs' decision not to include the non-BDC wire in the calculation is correct, then the needles do not satisfy the 35% BDC content requirement. On the other hand, if the other requirements are met, then the 35% BDC content prerequisite is also satisfied.

The parties also stipulated to the process by which Torrington Portuguesa produced the needles from the non-BDC wire. Initially, the wire runs through a swaging machine, which straightens the wire, cuts it to a particular length, bevels one end of the wire segment and draws out the straightened wire to alter its length and circumference at various points. The result is known in the needle industry as a "swaged needle blank," a "needle blank," or merely a "swage." The next process in the production of needles is "striking." Striking involves pressing an eye into the swage, forming a spot to provide clearance for the thread, and bending the swage at a particular point. At this stage, the articles are known as struck blanks. The struck blank enters a mill flash machine which removes excess material around the eye and forms a groove along the length of the needle which carries the thread while the needle is in use. The merchandise is then pointed (*i.e.*, sharpened) and stamped with a logo or other information. Finally, the needles are hardened, tempered, straightened, buffed, polished, cleaned and plated. Upon completion, the needle has a sharp point at the narrow end, a long groove running down three-quarters of its body ending near the point, and an eye somewhere in the groove with an indentation in the groove near the eye.

Based on these facts, the Court of International Trade held the needles to be entitled to duty-free entry under the GSP. As a preliminary matter, the court ruled that, under Customs' regulations, the non-BDC wire must undergo *two* substantial transformations when it is manufactured into a needle if the value of the wire is to be included in the 35% calculation, and that each of these transformations under 19 C.F.R. §10.177(a)(2) must result in an "article of commerce." The court stated:

> It is not enough to transform substantially the non-BDC constituent materials into the final article, as the material utilized to produce the final article would remain non-BDC material. There must first be a substantial transformation of the non-BDC material into a new and different article of commerce which becomes "materials produced," and these materials produced in the BDC must then be substantially transformed into a new and different article of commerce.

596 F. Supp. at 1086.

The court then turned to the question of whether the production of needles in Portugal satisfied the dual transformation requirement. The court determined that a substantial transformation occurs if a manufacturing process results in an article of commerce which has a distinctive name, character, or use. 596 F. Supp. at 1086 (citing *Texas Instruments, Inc. v. United States*, 681 F.2d 778, 782 (CCPA 1982)). Here, the court held, the swaging process constitutes an initial transformation, and the succeeding processes constitute the second. Thus, the court concluded that the swaged needle blanks are constituent materials of which the needles are made, and their value (which includes the value of the non-BDC wire) should be included in the 35% value added calculation.

THE DUAL TRANSFORMATION REQUIREMENT

Like the CIT, we think that the statutory language of 19 U.S.C. §2463(b) leads to the Government's position. Congress authorized the Customs Service to consider the "cost or value of materials produced" in the BDC. The parties agree that the wire clearly was not a BDC product. As wire, therefore, it may not be considered a BDC material. However, if Torrington Portuguesa transformed the wire into an intermediate article of commerce, then the intermediate product would be an article produced in the BDC, and the value of *that* product (including the contribution of the wire to the value of that intermediate product) would be included.

In the absence of a dual transformation requirement, developed countries could establish a BDC as a base to complete manufacture of goods which have already undergone extensive processing. The single substantial transformation would qualify the resulting article for GSP treatment, with the non-BDC country reaping the benefit of duty-free treatment for goods which it essentially produced. This flouts Congress' expressed intention to confer the benefits of the GSP fully on the BDC and to avoid conferring duty-free status on the products of a "pass-through" operation.

Moreover, Torrington's contentions, if accepted, would tend to render the 35% requirement a nullity. If only a single transformation were necessary, then the "material produced" in the BDC as a result of this transformation would be the imported product itself. Customs would then face the problem of determining how much of the appraised value of the import resulted from materials produced in the BDC, when the only material produced was the import. The result would always be 100% since the product would always be a constituent material of itself. Congress clearly envisaged some way of separating the final product from its constituent materials, and the dual transformation requirement achieves this end.

THE SWAGES — SUBSTANTIAL TRANSFORMATION INTO A NEW AND DIFFERENT ARTICLE OF COMMERCE

In *Texas Instruments*, the Court of Customs and Patent Appeals adopted the rule, well-established in other areas of customs jurisprudence, that a substantial transformation occurs when an article emerges from a manufacturing process with a name, character, or use which differs from those of the original material subjected to the process. 681 F.2d at 782. The CIT determined here that this substantial transformation test was satisfied when Torrington Portuguesa manufactured needle swages from the wire.

The CIT also concluded correctly that the swages were "articles of commerce." By emphasizing that the article must be "of commerce," the Customs regulation imposes the requirement that the "new and different" product be commercially recognizable as a different article, i.e., that the "new and different" article be readily susceptible of trade, and be an item that persons might well wish to buy and acquire for their own purposes of consumption or production. In this instance, we agree with the CIT that the transfer of over four million swaged needle blanks from Torrington Portuguesa to Torrington is an adequate showing that swaged needle blanks are articles of commerce. There is no reason to believe that those articles could and would not be sold to other manufacturers of needles who wanted to purchase them for further manufacture into the final product.

THE NEEDLES — SUBSTANTIAL TRANSFORMATION INTO A
NEW AND DIFFERENT ARTICLE

The Government urges that, even if the production of swages from wire constitutes a substantial transformation, the manufacture of the needles from the swages does not. The Government [argues] that the swages are actually unfinished needles, and do not undergo a substantial transformation into a new article in order to reach their final form.

The swages are bored (to form an eye), the ridge is carved, and the needle is pointed, cleaned, hardened, plated, etc. The swage is also the approximate size necessary to create the final needle, but, they are producers' goods. The final needles are consumers' goods. The production of needles from swages is clearly a significant manufacturing process, and not a mere "pass-through" operation as the Government apparently contends. Portugal certainly reaps the benefit of this manufacturing process; indeed, short of manufacturing the wire itself, Torrington Portuguesa could do no more than it already does in the production of needles. In these circumstances, we think that Congress intended the GSP statute to apply.

AFFIRMED.

NOTES AND QUESTIONS

1. Critics of the GSP program argue that the standards for duty-free admission are overly complex and the program is too political. The President may refuse to designate an otherwise eligible country for GSP treatment or may cut off such a country for non-observance of various conditions, such as terrorism and violations of human or workers' rights. *See* 19 U.S.C. §2462(b)(2) and (d). Judicial review of the President's decision to cut off a beneficiary country or to remove a product from GSP is limited. In *Florsheim Shoe Co. v. United States*, 744 F. 2d 787 (Fed. Cir. 1984), the court ruled against Florsheim, which was seeking to reverse a Presidential Order withdrawing duty-free treatment for leather products from India, stating that "the Executive's decisions in the sphere of international trade are reviewable only to determine whether the President's action falls within his delegated authority, whether the statutory language has been properly construed, and whether the President's action conforms with the relevant procedural requirements." 744 F.2d at 790. The court granted dismissal of Florsheim's complaint. Of course the President and Congress's GSP determinations are not reviewable directly at the WTO. Do you agree that the GSP program is too political or do you defend these provisions?

2. Under the U.S. GSP program, products may be withdrawn from GSP treatment if a GSP-eligible country exports an article in amounts that exceed certain dollar values or in quantities that account for 50 percent or more of the value of total imports of the article into the United States. *See* 19 U.S.C. §2463(c)(2)(A)(i).

3. The U.S. GSP program is sometimes terminated arbitrarily because of political infighting. For example, the GSP program lapsed on December 31, 2010 and was in limbo for several months until Congress acted to reauthorize it on October 21, 2011, retroactive to January 1, 2011. As an importer or exporter, how would this affect your business?

4. Any GSP country that becomes a "high-income" country under the World Bank guidelines must be delisted from GSP eligibility. *See* 19 U.S.C. §2462(e).

2. *The European Union*

The EU has implemented its own GSP program, which is multifaceted and complex. The basis of the EU program stems from a Decision of November 28, 1979 (L/4903) entitled "Differential and More Favourable Treatment, Reciprocity and Fuller Participation of Developing Countries." The most important aspect of this GSP program has been a series of international partnership agreements with a group of seventy-seven developing nations from Africa, the Caribbean, and the Pacific (ACP nations) (mainly former colonies of European states). The first agreements between the EU and the ACP nations were conventions known as Lomé I-IV. These agreements were followed by the current program denominated the Cotonou Agreement (2000). The Cotonou Agreement inaugurates a wide-ranging partnership between the EU and the ACP nations, which rests on three "pillars": political cooperation, economic and trade cooperation, and development strategies.

In addition to the Cotonou Agreement, the EU maintains additional GSP Arrangements with a variety of non-ACP developing countries, among them India. This program was the subject of the case below.

PROBLEM 9-5

Country C brings a complaint before the DSB, arguing that certain aspects of the EU's GSP program violate the GATT. Products from certain developing countries are allowed special preferences if these countries comply with certain labor and environmental standards. Country C does not meet these standards. As a result, while Country C's products do receive some preferential treatment under the EU's GSP, these products do not receive the higher level of preferences given to developing countries that are considered by the EU to meet its labor and environmental standards. Country C argues that this differential treatment of developing countries among themselves is discriminatory and in violation of the MFN principle contained in GATT Article I. Country C's Trade Minister states, "While the Enabling Clause provides an exception to the MFN principle in allowing developing countries to be treated more favorably than developed countries, all developing countries must be treated the same as a group. Any differential treatment among developing countries is discriminatory and violates the MFN principle as qualified by the Enabling Clause." What result under the case below?

PROBLEM 9-6

Assume that Country C can demonstrate before the DSB that it has the same labor and environmental record as Country K, which enjoys the higher level of preferential treatment under the EU's labor and environment program. What result?

European Communities — Conditions for the Granting of Tariff Preferences to Developing Countries
Report of the Appellate Body, adopted on April 20, 2004
WT/DS246/AB/R

[This case involved a challenge by India over the conditions under which the EC gave preferential GSP treatment to its products. The EC had a scheme to benefit developing countries, but some developing countries were entitled to a higher level of benefits than other developing countries. In all, the EU had five preferential programs. India was the beneficiary of a general arrangement, but the EU also had special and additional incentives. One such program was a special arrangement to combat drug production and trafficking (the Drug Arrangements). Under the Drug Arrangements, 12 predetermined countries (Bolivia, Columbia, Costa Rica, Ecuador, El Salvador, Guatemala, Honduras, Nicaragua, Pakistan, Panama, Peru, and Venezuela) were allowed duty free access to the entire EU for certain products while other developing countries, such as India, were allowed only reductions in duties. The purpose of this program was to encourage farmers in these countries to grow crops other than those used to produce illegal drugs. India challenged the Drug Arrangements as discriminatory. The panel found that the Enabling Clause required "non-discriminatory" preferential programs for developing countries, which meant that the identical program had to be applied to all developing countries. The opinion of the Appellate Body below focuses on the meaning of "non-discriminatory" in the context of the Enabling Clause.]

WHETHER THE DRUG ARRANGEMENTS ARE JUSTIFIED UNDER THE ENABLING CLAUSE

142. We proceed to interpret the term "non-discriminatory" as it appears in footnote 3 to paragraph 2(a) of the Enabling Clause.

151. We examine now the ordinary meaning of the term "non-discriminatory" in footnote 3 to paragraph 2(a) of the Enabling Clause. As we observed, footnote 3 requires that GSP schemes under the Enabling Clause be "generalized, non-reciprocal and non discriminatory". Before the Panel, the participants offered competing definitions of the word "discriminate". India suggested that this word means " 'to make or constitute a difference in or between; distinguish' and 'to make a distinction in the treatment of different categories of peoples or things'." The European Communities, however, understood this word to mean " 'to make a distinction in the treatment of different categories of people or things, esp. *unjustly* or *prejudicially* against people on grounds of race, colour, sex, social status, age, etc.' "

153. [T]he ordinary meanings of "discriminate" converge in one important respect: they both suggest that distinguishing among similarly-situated beneficiaries is discriminatory. For example, India suggests that all beneficiaries of a particular Member's GSP scheme are similarly-situated, implicitly arguing that any differential treatment of such beneficiaries constitutes discrimination. The European Communities, however, appears to regard GSP beneficiaries as similarly-situated when they have "similar development needs". Although the European

Communities acknowledges that differentiating between similarly-situated GSP beneficiaries would be inconsistent with footnote 3 of the Enabling Clause, it submits that there is no inconsistency in differentiating between GSP beneficiaries with "different development needs". Thus, based on the ordinary meanings of "discriminate", India and the European Communities effectively appear to agree that, pursuant to the term "non-discriminatory" in footnote 3, similarly-situated GSP beneficiaries should not be treated differently. The participants disagree only as to the basis for determining whether beneficiaries are similarly-situated.

154. Paragraph 2(a), on its face, does not explicitly authorize or prohibit the granting of different tariff preferences to different GSP beneficiaries. It is clear from the ordinary meanings of "non-discriminatory", however, that preference-granting countries must make available identical tariff preferences to all similarly-situated beneficiaries.

155. We continue our interpretive analysis by turning to the immediate context of the term "non-discriminatory". We note first that footnote 3 to paragraph 2(a) stipulates that, in addition to being "non-discriminatory", tariff preferences provided under GSP schemes must be "generalized". According to the ordinary meaning of that term, tariff preferences provided under GSP schemes must be "generalized" in the sense that they "apply more generally; [or] become extended in application". However, this ordinary meaning alone may not reflect the entire significance of the word "generalized" in the context of footnote 3 of the Enabling Clause, particularly because that word resulted from lengthy negotiations leading to the GSP. In this regard, we note the Panel's finding that, by requiring tariff preferences under the GSP to be "generalized", developed and developing countries together sought to eliminate existing "special" preferences that were granted only to certain designated developing countries. Similarly, in response to our questioning at the oral hearing, the participants agreed that one of the objectives of the 1971 Waiver Decision and the Enabling Clause was to eliminate the fragmented system of special preferences that were, in general, based on historical and political ties between developed countries and their former colonies.

156. It does not necessarily follow, however, that "non-discriminatory" should be interpreted to require that preference-granting countries provide "identical" tariff preferences under GSP schemes to "all" developing countries. In concluding otherwise, the Panel assumed that allowing tariff preferences such as the Drug Arrangements would necessarily "result [in] the collapse of the whole GSP system and a return back to special preferences favouring selected developing countries". To us, this conclusion is unwarranted. We observe that the term "generalized" requires that the GSP schemes of preference-granting countries remain generally applicable. Moreover, unlike the Panel, we believe that the Enabling Clause sets out sufficient conditions on the granting of preferences to protect against such an outcome. As we discuss below, provisions such as paragraphs 3(a) and 3(c) of the Enabling Clause impose specific conditions on the granting of different tariff preferences among GSP beneficiaries.

157. As further context for the term "non-discriminatory" in footnote 3, we turn next to paragraph 3(c) of the Enabling Clause, which specifies that "differential and more favourable treatment" provided under the Enabling Clause:

> . . . shall in the case of such treatment accorded by developed contracting parties to developing countries be designed and, if necessary, modified, to respond positively to the development, financial and trade needs of developing countries.

158. At the outset, we note that the use of the word "shall" in paragraph 3(c) suggests that paragraph 3(c) sets out an obligation for developed-country Members in providing preferential treatment under a GSP scheme to "respond positively" to the "needs of developing countries". Having said this, we turn to consider whether the "development, financial and trade needs of developing countries" to which preference-granting countries are required to respond when granting preferences must be understood to cover the "needs" of developing countries *collectively*.

160. Furthermore, as we understand it, the participants in this case agree that developing countries may have "development, financial and trade needs" that are subject to change and that certain development needs may be common to only a certain number of developing countries. We see no reason to disagree. Indeed, paragraph 3(c) contemplates that "differential and more favourable treatment" accorded by developed to developing countries may need to be "modified" in order to "respond positively" to the needs of developing countries. Paragraph 7 of the Enabling Clause supports this view by recording the expectation of "less-developed contracting parties" that their capacity to make contributions or concessions under the GATT will "improve with the progressive development of their economies and improvement in their trade situation". Moreover, the very purpose of the special and differential treatment permitted under the Enabling Clause is to foster economic development of developing countries. It is simply unrealistic to assume that such development will be in lockstep for all developing countries at once, now and for the future.

161. In addition, the Preamble to the *WTO Agreement*, which informs all the covered agreements including the GATT 1994 (and, hence, the Enabling Clause), explicitly recognizes the "need for positive efforts designed to ensure that developing countries, and especially the least developed among them, secure a share in the growth in international trade commensurate with the needs of their economic development". The word "commensurate" in this phrase appears to leave open the possibility that developing countries may have different needs according to their levels of development and particular circumstances. The Preamble to the *WTO Agreement* further recognizes that Members' "respective needs and concerns at different levels of economic development" may vary according to the different stages of development of different Members.

162. In sum, we read paragraph 3(c) as authorizing preference-granting countries to "respond positively" to "needs" that are *not* necessarily common or shared by all developing countries. Responding to the "needs of developing countries" may thus entail treating different developing-country beneficiaries differently.

163. However, paragraph 3(c) does not authorize *any* kind of response to *any* claimed need of developing countries. First, we observe that the types of needs to which a response is envisaged are limited to "development, financial and trade needs". In our view, a "need" cannot be characterized as one of the specified "needs of developing countries" in the sense of paragraph 3(c) based merely on an assertion to that effect by, for instance, a preference-granting country or a beneficiary country. Rather, when a claim of inconsistency with paragraph 3(c) is made, the existence of a "development, financial [or] trade need" must be assessed according to an *objective* standard. Broad-based recognition of a particular need, set out in the *WTO Agreement* or in multilateral instruments adopted by international organizations, could serve as such a standard.

164. Secondly, paragraph 3(c) mandates that the response provided to the needs of developing countries be "positive". "Positive" is defined as "consisting in or

characterized by constructive action or attitudes". This suggests that the response of a preference-granting country must be taken with a view to *improving* the development, financial or trade situation of a beneficiary country, based on the particular need at issue. As such, in our view, the expectation that developed countries will "respond positively" to the "needs of developing countries" suggests that a sufficient nexus should exist between, on the one hand, the preferential treatment provided under the respective measure authorized by paragraph 2, and, on the other hand, the likelihood of alleviating the relevant "development, financial [or] trade need". In the context of a GSP scheme, the particular need at issue must, by its nature, be such that it can be effectively addressed through tariff preferences. Therefore, only if a preference-granting country acts in the "positive" manner suggested, in "respon[se]" to a widely-recognized "development, financial [or] trade need", can such action satisfy the requirements of paragraph 3(c).

165. Accordingly, we are of the view that, by requiring developed countries to "respond positively" to the "needs of developing countries", which are varied and not homogeneous, paragraph 3(c) indicates that a GSP scheme may be "non-discriminatory" even if "identical" tariff treatment is not accorded to "all" GSP beneficiaries. Moreover, paragraph 3(c) suggests that tariff preferences under GSP schemes may be "non-discriminatory" when the relevant tariff preferences are addressed to a particular "development, financial [or] trade need" and are made available to all beneficiaries that share that need.

173. Having examined the text and context of footnote 3 to paragraph 2(a) of the Enabling Clause, and the object and purpose of the *WTO Agreement* and the Enabling Clause, we conclude that the term "non-discriminatory" in footnote 3 does not prohibit developed-country Members from granting different tariffs to products originating in different GSP beneficiaries, provided that such differential tariff treatment meets the remaining conditions in the Enabling Clause. In granting such differential tariff treatment, however, preference-granting countries are required, by virtue of the term "non-discriminatory", to ensure that identical treatment is available to all similarly-situated GSP beneficiaries, that is, to all GSP beneficiaries that have the "development, financial and trade needs" to which the treatment in question is intended to respond.

174. For all of these reasons, we *reverse* the Panel's finding, in paragraphs 7.161 and 7.176 of the Panel Report, that "the term 'non-discriminatory' in footnote 3 [to paragraph 2(a) of the Enabling Clause] requires that identical tariff preferences under GSP schemes be provided to all developing countries without differentiation, except for the implementation of a priori limitations."

CONSISTENCY OF THE DRUG ARRANGEMENTS WITH THE ENABLING CLAUSE

177. We turn next to examine the consistency of the Drug Arrangements with the Enabling Clause. [The Appellate Body limited its discussion to consistency of the Drug Arrangements with paragraph 2(a) and footnote 3.]

180. We found above that the term "non-discriminatory" in footnote 3 to paragraph 2(a) of the Enabling Clause does not prohibit the granting of different tariffs to products originating in different sub-categories of GSP beneficiaries, but that identical tariff treatment must be available to all GSP beneficiaries with the "development, financial [or] trade need" to which the differential treatment is intended

to respond. The need alleged to be addressed by the European Communities' differential tariff treatment is the problem of illicit drug production and trafficking in certain GSP beneficiaries. In the context of this case, therefore, the Drug Arrangements may be found consistent with the "non-discriminatory" requirement in footnote 3 only if the European Communities proves, at a minimum, that the preferences granted under the Drug Arrangements are available to all GSP beneficiaries that are similarly affected by the drug problem. We do not believe this to be the case.

181. By their very terms, the Drug Arrangements are limited to the 12 developing countries designated as beneficiaries in Annex I to the Regulation. Specifically, Article 10.1 of the Regulation states:

> Common Customs Tariff *ad valorem* duties on [covered products] which originate in a country that according to Column I of Annex I benefits from [the Drug Arrangements] shall be entirely suspended.

182. Articles 10 and 25 of the Regulation, which relate specifically to the Drug Arrangements, provide no mechanism under which additional beneficiaries may be added to the list of beneficiaries under the Drug Arrangements as designated in Annex I.

183. What is more, the Drug Arrangements themselves do *not* set out any clear prerequisites—or "objective criteria"—that, if met, would allow for other developing countries "that are similarly affected by the drug problem" to be *included* as beneficiaries under the Drug Arrangements. Indeed, the European Commission's own Explanatory Memorandum notes that "the benefits of the drug regime . . . are given without *any* prerequisite." Similarly, the Regulation offers no criteria according to which a beneficiary could be *removed* specifically from the Drug Arrangements on the basis that it is no longer "similarly affected by the drug problem". Indeed, Article 25.3 expressly states that the evaluation of the effects of the Drug Arrangements described in Articles 25.1(b) and 25.2 "will be without prejudice to the continuation of the [Drug Arrangements] until 2004, and their possible extension thereafter." This implies that, even if the European Commission found that the Drug Arrangements were having no effect whatsoever on a beneficiary's "efforts in combating drug production and trafficking", or that a beneficiary was no longer suffering from the drug problem, beneficiary status would continue.

186. Against this background, we fail to see how the Drug Arrangements can be distinguished from other schemes that the European Communities describes as "confined *ab initio* and permanently to a limited number of developing countries". As we understand it, the European Communities' position is that such schemes would be discriminatory, whereas the Drug Arrangements are not because "all developing countries are potentially beneficiaries" thereof. In seeking a waiver from its obligations under Article I:1 of the GATT 1994 to implement the Drug Arrangements, the European Communities explicitly acknowledged, however, that "[b]ecause the special arrangements *are only available* to imports originating in [the twelve beneficiaries of the Drug Arrangements], a waiver . . . appears necessary". This statement appears to undermine the European Communities' argument that "all developing countries are potentially beneficiaries of the Drug Arrangements" and, therefore, that the Drug Arrangements are "non-discriminatory".

187. We recall our conclusion that the term "non-discriminatory" in footnote 3 of the Enabling Clause requires that identical tariff treatment be available to all similarly-situated GSP beneficiaries. We find that the measure at issue fails to meet this requirement for the following reasons. First, as the European Communities itself acknowledges, according benefits under the Drug Arrangements to countries other than the 12 identified beneficiaries would require an amendment to the Regulation. Such a "closed list" of beneficiaries cannot ensure that the preferences under the Drug Arrangements are available to all GSP beneficiaries suffering from illicit drug production and trafficking.

188. Secondly, the Regulation contains no criteria or standards to provide a basis for distinguishing beneficiaries under the Drug Arrangements from other GSP beneficiaries. Nor did the European Communities point to any such criteria or standards anywhere else, despite the Panel's request to do so. As such, the European Communities cannot justify the Regulation under paragraph 2(a), because it does not provide a basis for establishing whether or not a developing country qualifies for preferences under the Drug Arrangements. Thus, although the European Communities claims that the Drug Arrangements are available to all developing countries that are "similarly affected by the drug problem", because the Regulation does not define the criteria or standards that a developing country must meet to qualify for preferences under the Drug Arrangements, there is no basis to determine whether those criteria or standards are discriminatory or not.

189. For all these reasons, we find that the European Communities has failed to prove that the Drug Arrangements meet the requirement in footnote 3 that they be "non-discriminatory". Accordingly, we *uphold*, for different reasons, the Panel's conclusion, in paragraph 8.1(d) of the Panel Report, that the European Communities "failed to demonstrate that the Drug Arrangements are justified under paragraph 2(a) of the Enabling Clause".

NOTES AND QUESTIONS

1. The panel in this case ruled that preference-granting countries must provide identical tariff preference regimes to all GSP recipient countries to comply with the non-discrimination requirements of the Enabling Clause. How and why did the Appellate body overturn this ruling?

2. In response to the Appellate Body's ruling in the *EC—Tariff Preferences* case the EU adopted a new GSP scheme called GSP plus, which required three conditions to be agreed upon by GSP beneficiary countries, including the condition that to obtain GSP treatment a country had to ratify and implement a list of international conventions that were also part of the previous GSP scheme. *See* Council Regulation 980/2005, Applying a Scheme of Generalised Tariff Preferences, 2005 O.J. (L 169) (EC). In 2008 this was replaced by a new program, Council Regulation 732/2008, Applying a Scheme of Generalised Preferences, 2008 O.J. (L 211) (EC). The EU is currently working on a new GSP program that it intends to implement in 2014. The proposed new program would concentrate GSP in fewer countries and would reinforce conditions requiring respect of core human rights and workers' rights, environmental standards, and good governance. For least developed countries, GSP treatment is to be extended to all products except arms. The new system is intended to be more transparent and predictable to make it more attractive for

EU importers to purchase GSP products from beneficiary countries. *See* http://www.ec.europa.eu/trade/generalised-system-of-preferences.

B. Special and Differential Treatment Under Other WTO Agreements

The vast bulk of WTO agreements now contain special provisions for developing country members. These special and differential (S&D) provisions fall into the six categories set forth below. Under these six categories, there are, as of this writing, 145 separate provisions for S&D treatment contained in the WTO agreements.

(1) *Increasing Trade Opportunities.* Twelve S&D provisions in four WTO agreements mandate action by members to increase trade opportunities for developing countries.

(2) *Safeguards.* Forty-nine S&D provisions in thirteen WTO agreements require members to take or avoid taking actions to safeguard the interests of developing countries.

(3) *Flexibility.* Thirty S&D provisions in nine WTO agreements allow developing countries exemptions from WTO obligations or a reduced level of commitments.

(4) *Transitional Periods.* Eighteen S&D provisions in eight WTO agreements allow developing countries extended periods of time to comply with WTO commitments.

(5) *Technical Assistance.* Fourteen provisions in six WTO agreements require developed countries to provide technical and financial assistance to developing countries.

(6) *Least Developed Countries.* Twenty-two provisions in seven WTO agreements cover one or more of the previous five areas but allow additional preferences only to least developed country members.

The Fourth WTO Ministerial Conference held in Doha in 2001 considered more than 100 issues raised by developing countries. These issues concerned the problems that developing countries were facing in complying with their WTO obligations. The Doha Conference led to the "Doha Implementation Decision," which offered a two-track solution. First, more than forty items were settled immediately; second, the remaining items were to be resolved through continuing negotiations. As of this writing, most of the issues under the second track have been resolved. As an example of how a problem was settled by negotiation, under the Decision on Special Treatment (Document G/SPS/33 of November 2, 2004), importing countries that impose new measures under the Sanitary and Phytosanitary (SPS) Agreement will provide technical assistance to help exporting countries meet new requirements. SPS standards are intended to protect the importing country in the area of food safety, but new measures can act as a trade barrier, as it will take time and resources for exporting countries to learn how to comply with any new measures. In addition, compliance with some new measures may be so burdensome that the new measure serves to discourage trade. Under the Decision, importing countries will offer technical assistance for all countries in connection with compliance with the new measure. For developing countries, the importing country will negotiate special and differential treatment that will be included as an addendum to the original document setting forth the new SPS measures.

The outcome could take a number of forms: The new or proposed measure could be revised for imports from all WTO members; the importing country could provide technical assistance to the exporting developing country to help it meet the new requirements; special treatment could be given to exports from developing countries, such as a longer period to adjust; or the outcome could be a combination of these.

IV. Agricultural Trade Subsidies

Developing countries made agricultural trade subsidies a *cause célèbre* during the Doha Development Round of trade negotiations begun in 2001. A vocal group of developing nations, led by Brazil, charged that domestic and export subsidies in rich countries inhibit developing countries, in both domestic and export sales, and contribute to perpetuating poverty in the developing world. In this context, an export subsidy is a payment by the government to farmers for agricultural products that are exported to other countries. The subsidy provides a cost advantage to the exporter that will be passed on to the consumer in the form of lower prices. Subsidized exports from developed countries reduce demand within developing countries for domestically produced agricultural products that must compete with the cheap imports from developed countries. Countries that import subsidized products from developed countries buy fewer imports from developing countries. The International Research Institute for Policies in the Food Industry, a think tank partial to this view, estimates that subsidies provided by developed countries reduced annual sales by agricultural producers in developing countries by $24 billion.

There is undoubted truth in this view for many developing countries. For example, until recently Burkina Faso in West Africa was dependent on cotton for about 40 percent of its merchandise exports and according to the International Cotton Advisory Committee (a body that advises governments) world prices for upland cotton would have been about 26 percent higher were it not for the $4 billion that the United States gives its cotton farmers and exporters. However, according to the Food and Agriculture Organization of the United Nations, sixty-six low-income countries (countries with a Gross National Income of less than $1,905 per capita) are also net importers of food. *See* http://www.fao.org/country profiles/lifdc.asp.

While developing countries object to agricultural subsidies, developed countries support their use, at least within certain limits, as an important domestic policy measure. Agricultural subsidies provide essential support for important agriculture sectors that could suffer serious economic hardships without them. The refusal by some developed countries, such as the United States and the EU member states, to eliminate all agricultural subsidies is a source of continuing friction within the WTO.

Although countries differ over the desirability of farm subsidies, there is widespread acknowledgment that they distort trade in both domestic and international markets. This was formally recognized in Article 20 of the Uruguay Round Agreement on Agriculture, which calls for "fundamental reform" and "a substantial progressive reduction in support and protection." However, Article 20 recognizes that this reform cannot consist solely of the elimination of subsidies and the inauguration of a free trade regime. Rather, reform must be progressive, and "non-trade concerns" are to be taken into account. But such non-trade concerns are not defined, and there is no timetable for liberalization. These matters are left for the future.

Of course, many people in the industrialized world also believe agricultural subsidies must be cut. Agricultural subsidies within developed countries are the primary source of contention, and agricultural subsidies in the OECD area have dropped to a thirty-year low, amounting to $220.4 billion. However subsidies in developing countries, particularly China have also increased. The leading subsidy providers are China, about $157 billion; the EU, about $101.4 billion; and Japan, about $58.1 billion. The United States subsidizes about $25.5 billion. The OECD estimates that $31 out of every $100 in farm income came from a government, based on the average from thirty countries. In the EU, it was $35; in the United States $21; in Japan $59; and in Australia $4.

Developing countries, however, are not waiting for negotiations over farm subsidies to succeed; they are actively using the WTO dispute settlement system to complain about farm subsidies, based on the standards in existing WTO agreements. The case below marks one of their most important successes.

PROBLEM 9-7

Assume that Country D, a developed country, has made a commitment to limit its subsidies for its exports of milk under the Agreement on Agriculture (AoA). In Section V, Part II, page 135, of its Schedule of Commitments under the AoA, Country D has made both a base quantity commitment of five million tons per year and a base outlay level of $2.5 million of support per year with steady reductions of both the quantity and the base outlay over a five-year period. In an appendix to its Schedule of Commitments, Country D has a paragraph stating as follows: "The export limiting commitments of milk discussed in Section V, Part II, page 135, does not include milk produced in the Western Provinces of our country. For milk produced in the Western Provinces, we will export no more than 2 million tons per year." Pursuant to the AoA, Country D has notified the WTO of its export subsidy limiting commitments set forth in Section V, Part II, page 135, of five million tons per year and $2.5 million in support.

In the past year, Country D has exported seven million tons of milk with a base outlay of $3.4 million. Thailand argues that Country D has violated its commitments under the Agreement on Agriculture. Country D denies that it has violated its commitments.

(1) What are the arguments in favor of Thailand?
(2) What are the arguments in favor of Country D?
(3) Which side do you think has the better argument? Consult the *EC—Sugar* case below.

PROBLEM 9-8

Country E wishes to extend trade preferences in the form of low or zero tariffs for all imports from three countries, all former colonies located in Africa and Asia. Country E's justification for the preferences is that they are compensation for historical wrongs. No other country is eligible for the preferences. Is this program lawful? What steps must Country E take under the WTO to implement the program? Consult the case below.

PROBLEM 9-9

Country H offers a program of trade preferences for all developing countries. All interested countries must enter into an agreement with Country H to receive the preferences. Country H has set a deadline of January 1, 2013 for conclusion of the agreements. No country will be able to receive trade preferences after that date. Is this program lawful? Consult the case below.

European Communities — Export Subsidies on Sugar
Report of the Appellate Body, adopted on May 19, 2005
WT/DS265, 266, 283/AB/R

[Australia, Brazil, and Thailand brought a complaint against the European Communities for failing to meet its commitments under the Agreement on Agriculture (AoA) to reduce its export subsidies for sugar. Under the AoA, the EC had promised to progressively reduce its exports of subsidized sugar from 1.6 million tons in 1986-1990 to 1.27 million tons in 2000, and to reduce the amount of the financial subsidy for sugar from €780 million to €499 million in 2000. The complainants argued that the EC failed to meet its commitments in two ways. First, the EC did not include exports of sugar that originated in ACP (African-Caribbean-Pacific) countries under a preferential arrangement with those countries; in its reduction commitment schedule under the AoA, the EC added Footnote 1, which stated: "Does not include exports of sugar of ACP and Indian origin on which the Community is not making any reduction commitments. The average of export in the period 1986 to 1990 amounted to 1.6 million tonnes." The complainants argued that Footnote 1 excluded ACP origin sugar from the EC's export subsidy reduction commitments in violation of the EC's AoA reduction commitments. Second, the complaints challenged the EC's domestic sugar subsidy program, which was also subject to reduction commitments under the AoA. With respect to domestically produced sugar, the EC divided this sugar into A, B, and C sugar. The EC was allowed to provide export subsidies to A and B sugar in accordance with its reduction commitments under the AoA, but the complaints argued that the EC also provided exports subsidies to C sugar, which would then be in excess of the exports subsidies the EC was allowed to provide under its AoA commitments. The opinion below first turns to the issue of whether Footnote 1 was consistent with the EC's export subsidy reduction commitments under the AoA.]

161. At issue in this dispute is the meaning of Footnote 1, its conformity with the European Communities' obligations under the *Agreement on Agriculture*, and its implications for the European Communities' export subsidy reduction commitments for sugar.

174. We address, first, the question whether a plain reading of Footnote 1 suggests that the European Communities is undertaking a commitment to "limit" its subsidization of "exports of sugar of ACP and Indian origin." On its face, the first sentence does not indicate that the European Communities is undertaking any such commitment. On the contrary, the first sentence suggests two things: first, the budgetary outlay and quantity level commitments specified in the European Communities' Schedule for sugar do not "include" sugar of ACP and Indian origin; and secondly, with respect to exports of sugar of ACP and Indian origin, the European Communities is not undertaking "any reduction commitments" either by way of budgetary outlay or quantity commitment. It is, therefore, to the second sentence of Footnote 1 that we need to turn to see whether it suggests any commitment to "limit" subsidization on the exports of sugar of ACP and Indian origin. A plain reading of the second sentence does not indicate that it "imposes a limit on the volume of sugar [of ACP and Indian origin] which can be exported with a subsidy." The second sentence, in its plain language, only states that the average of exports of sugar of ACP and Indian origin in the period 1986-1990 amounted to 1.6 million tonnes.

181. We next address the question whether the second sentence of Footnote 1, interpreted in its context, contains a commitment on the part of the European Communities to "limit" its subsidization of exports of sugar to the lower of its imports from ACP countries and India or 1.6 million tonnes. The European Communities relies on the following four main arguments in support of its assertion that the second sentence imposes such a limitation. First, Footnote 1 excludes ACP/India sugar from the budgetary outlay and quantity level commitments specified in its Schedule, and, therefore, the base quantity level of 1,612,000 tonnes specified in its Schedule excludes the figure of 1.6 million tonnes contained in the second sentence of Footnote 1. The latter figure thus pertains solely to exports of ACP/India sugar, as the word "export" in the second sentence has the same meaning as the word "exports" in the first sentence of Footnote 1.

182. Secondly, the reference to the period 1986-1990 in the second sentence is "telling," as this is the base period for export subsidy reduction commitments. The reference to "the average of export" in the base period in the second sentence must be given proper meaning in its context. Such a meaning can be given only if the second sentence is regarded as "limiting" subsidization to a maximum of 1.6 million tonnes, the average of the subsidized exports of ACP/India sugar during the period 1986-1990.

183. Thirdly, the "undisputed evidence" with respect to the European Communities' export subsidy practice shows that it has consistently "limited" its subsidization to the actual imports from ACP countries and India or 1.6 million tonnes, whichever was lower.

184. Lastly, other WTO Members, including the Complaining Parties, were fully aware that the European Communities was exporting *additional* quantities of sugar (over and above its scheduled commitments) equivalent to its imports from ACP countries and India, and that it was "limiting" its subsidization of those exports to the actual level of its imports from those countries.

185. The European Communities, therefore, argues that the second sentence of Footnote 1, if interpreted properly in its context, clearly shows that it imposes a "limitation" on exports of sugar equivalent in volume to its imports of sugar from ACP countries and India up to a maximum of 1.6 million tonnes (the average of its base period subsidized exports of such sugar) or its actual imports from

those countries. If the second sentence is read merely as a piece of information, as the Panel and the Complaining Parties do, then, according to the European Communities, it would be tantamount to reading the sentence out of the text and ignoring it entirely.

186. Here again, we are not convinced by the arguments of the European Communities. The fact that the second sentence makes a specific reference to the average of such exports in the base period does not necessarily lead to an inference that there is a commitment in the sentence to "limit" the quantity of subsidization to that level, particularly when the first sentence says that the European Communities is not making "any reduction commitments." Nor does the practice of the European Communities providing subsidies on exports equivalent to its actual imports from ACP countries and India lead to an inference that that practice flows from a commitment contained in the second sentence of Footnote 1. We are also not persuaded by the argument that, because the first sentence excludes any *reduction* commitments and the second sentence refers to the average of the export in the base period (the starting point for any reduction commitment), the second sentence can only imply a commitment to "limit" the subsidization to the base level quantity.

188. For all these reasons, we find that Footnote 1, by its terms, does not contain a commitment on the part of the European Communities to "limit" its subsidization of exports of sugar to a quantity equivalent to its actual imports of sugar from ACP countries and India or 1.6 million tonnes, whichever is lower. Nor do we find that an interpretation of Footnote 1 that takes into account the arguments advanced by the European Communities leads to the conclusion that Footnote 1 contains such a commitment to "limit" subsidization of exports of ACP/India sugar.

1.   ARTICLE 3.3 OF THE AGREEMENT ON AGRICULTURE

189. We have found that Footnote 1 does not contain a commitment "limiting" subsidization of exports of ACP/India equivalent sugar. However, in view of the extensive argumentation advanced by the European Communities, we proceed to an analysis of the conformity of Footnote 1 with the obligations prescribed by Articles 3, 8, and 9 of the *Agreement on Agriculture*. For this analysis, we assume *arguendo* that Footnote 1 does contain the export subsidy commitment claimed by the European Communities, namely, Footnote 1 reflects a commitment on the part of the European Communities to "limit" the export subsidies on ACP/India equivalent sugar. We note that the Panel also conducted a similar analysis.

190. We begin this analysis with respect to the conformity of Footnote 1 with Article 3.3 of the *Agreement on Agriculture*. The European Communities asserts that Article 3.3 does not *require* a Member to schedule both budgetary outlay *and* quantity commitments in respect of export subsidies listed in Article 9.1. According to the European Communities, "[n]owhere in the *Agreement on Agriculture* is there an obligation for Members to schedule commitments in the form of both budgetary outlay and quantity commitments." Neither Article 3.3, nor Article 8 or 9.1, nor indeed the *Agreement on Agriculture* as a whole, addresses this question. The European Communities emphasizes that "Article 3.3 has as its function the prohibition of the provision of export subsidy in excess of *commitment levels*" and that the obligation contained in it is simply "not to exceed . . . 'budgetary outlay and quantity commitments *specified' in a Member's Schedule*." But neither Article 3.3, nor

indeed Article 8 or 9.1, specifies how those commitments must be expressed in a Member's Schedule. According to the European Communities, the use of the word "and" in Article 3.3 "does not imply a commitment that is only valid if it comports both a budgetary and a quantitative aspect. It simply is a conjunctive between the two different forms of commitments . . . . The word 'specified' refers to what is specified in the [Member's] schedule, without requiring that both forms of commitments be specified."

191. In sum, the European Communities contends that "[t]he obligation in Article 3.3 is only to provide Article 9.1-listed subsidies in conformity with *whatever* commitments are found in a Member's schedule." Such commitments may be budgetary outlay or quantity commitment or both, as a Member may choose to specify in its Schedule. According to the European Communities, the question of how commitments should be expressed is "one of scheduling" and is addressed in paragraph 11 of the "Modalities Paper" and not in the *Agreement on Agriculture*.

192. We begin our analysis of this issue by recalling the text of Article 3.3 of the *Agreement on Agriculture*, which reads:

Incorporation of Concessions and Commitments

. . .

3. Subject to the provisions of paragraphs 2(b) and 4 of Article 9, a Member shall not provide export subsidies listed in paragraph 1 of Article 9 in respect of the agricultural products or groups of products specified in Section II of Part IV of its Schedule in excess of the budgetary outlay and quantity commitment levels specified therein and shall not provide such subsidies in respect of any agricultural product not specified in that Section of its Schedule.

193. By its terms, Article 3.3 of the *Agreement on Agriculture* prohibits the granting of export subsidies (listed in Article 9.1) in excess of the budgetary outlay *and* quantity commitment levels specified in a Member's Schedule. Article 3.3 does not, however, explicitly state that export subsidy commitments must be specified in a Member's Schedule in terms of both budgetary outlay *and* quantity commitment levels. At the same time, Article 3.3 does not explicitly state that a Member may specify its commitment level in terms of either of the two forms of commitments. In our view, the use of the conjunctive "and," and the corresponding use of the word "levels" in the plural, suggest that the drafters of the Agreement intended that both types of commitments must be specified in a Member's Schedule in respect of any export subsidy listed in Article 9.1. Had the drafters intended that a Member could specify one or the other of the two forms of commitments, they would have chosen the disjunctive "or" and correspondingly used the word "level" in the singular. Given the choice, Members would choose only one or the other type of commitment, but not both, so as to minimize their obligations. Therefore, it appears to us that the drafters intended to ensure that export subsidy commitments are specified in Members' Schedules in terms of both budgetary outlay and quantity commitments, by using the word "and" as well as the word "levels" in the text of Article 3.3.

194. We find contextual support for the above interpretation in Article 9.2(b)(iv) of the *Agreement on Agriculture*, which provides:

(iv) the Member's budgetary outlays for export subsidies and the quantities benefiting from such subsidies, at the conclusion of the implementation period, are no greater than 64 percent and 79 percent of the 1986-1990 base period levels, respectively.

For developing country Members these percentages shall be 76 and 86 percent, respectively.

This provision prescribes the export subsidy commitment levels to be reached at the conclusion of the implementation period (and to be maintained thereafter), and those commitment levels are expressed in terms of both budgetary outlays and quantities. We do not see how a Member could comply with Article 9.2(b)(iv), or for that matter Article 9.2(a), without having specified its export subsidy commitments in terms of both budgetary outlays and quantities. We also consider it significant that both Article 9.2(b)(iii) and Article 9.2(b)(iv) use the expression "budgetary outlays for export subsidies and the quantities *benefiting from such subsidies*." (emphasis added) This shows the drafters' recognition of the need to address the budgetary outlays and quantities together.

200. For all these reasons, we agree with the Panel that Article 3.3 requires a Member to schedule both budgetary outlay and quantity commitment levels in respect of export subsidies listed in Article 9.1 of the *Agreement of Agriculture*. As Footnote 1 does not contain a budgetary outlay commitment in respect of export subsidies provided to ACP/India equivalent sugar, we hold that it is inconsistent with Article 3.3 of the *Agreement on Agriculture*.

2. ARTICLE 9.1 OF THE AGREEMENT ON AGRICULTURE

201. We now turn to address the question whether Footnote 1 is consistent with Article 9.1 of the *Agreement on Agriculture*.

206. The chapeau of Article 9.1 says that the subsidies listed in that Article "are subject to reduction commitments under this Agreement." The export subsidies given to ACP/India equivalent sugar, which admittedly fall within the ambit of Article 9.1(a), are therefore subject to reduction commitments. Furthermore, as noted by the Panel, the provisions of Article 9.2(b)(iv) apply to Members that take advantage of the flexibility provisions of Article 9.2(b). Article 9.2(b)(iv) specifies the reduction levels to be achieved at the conclusion of the implementation period with respect to both budgetary outlays and quantities. The provisions of Article 9.2(b)(iv) lend contextual support to the view that export subsidies listed in Article 9.1 are subject to reduction commitments. We further note that Article 9.2(a)(i) and (ii) also make it clear that both budgetary outlay and quantity commitments specified in a Member's Schedule for each year of the implementation period are "reduction" commitments. It follows that the export subsidies provided to ACP/India equivalent sugar are subject to reduction commitments in terms of Article 9.1 of the *Agreement on Agriculture*.

210. For all these reasons, we agree with the Panel that Footnote 1 is inconsistent with Article 9.1 of the *Agreement on Agriculture*.

Do Sales of C Beet Involve Export Subsidies within the Meaning of Article 9.1(C)?

[This part of the opinion now turns to the issue of whether the subsidies provided for domestically produced sugar violated the AoA. All export subsidies for domestically produced sugar were subject to the EC's reduction commitments under its AoA Schedule. There was no issue about the EC's reduction of its export subsidies to A and B sugar. The issue concerned whether the EC was also providing an export subsidy to C sugar. If so, then that subsidy would also have to be counted within the EC's reduction commitments, i.e. to 499 million by 2000. If C sugar was not receiving export subsidies then any financial contributions received by C sugar would not count against the ceiling of AoA ceiling of 499. The Appellate Body turned to this issue.]

233. Our analysis begins with the text of Article 9.1(c) of the *Agreement on Agriculture*, which provides:

Export Subsidy Commitments

1. The following export subsidies are subject to reduction commitments under this Agreement:

   . . .

   (c) payments on the export of an agricultural product that are financed by virtue of governmental action, whether or not a charge on the public account is involved, including payments that are financed from the proceeds of a levy imposed on the agricultural product concerned or on an agricultural product from which the exported product is derived[.]

[The Appellate Body focused its analysis on whether support payments for C sugar were "financed by virtue of government action," the first clause in Article 9.1(c) above.]

238. Turning to the specific circumstances of the present dispute, we note that, in its finding that "payments" in the form of sales of C beet below its total cost of production are "financed by virtue of governmental action," the Panel relied on a number of aspects of the EC sugar regime. The Panel considered, *inter alia*, that: the EC sugar regime regulates prices of A and B beet and establishes a framework for the contractual relationships between beet growers and sugar producers with a view to ensuring a stable and adequate income for beet growers; C beet is invariably produced together with A and B beet in one single line of production; a significant percentage of beet growers are likely to finance sales of C beet below the total cost of production as a result of participation in the domestic market by making "highly remunerative" sales of A and B beet; the European Communities "controls virtually every aspect of domestic beet and sugar supply and management," including through financial penalties imposed on sugar producers that divert C sugar into the domestic market; the European Communities' Sugar Management Committee "overviews, supervises and protects the [European Communities'] domestic sugar through, *inter alia*, supply management"; the growing of C beet is not "incidental," but rather an "integral" part of the governmental regulation of the sugar market; and C sugar producers "*have incentives* to produce C sugar so as to maintain their share of the A and B quotas," while C beet growers "have an incentive to supply as much as is requested by C sugar producers with a view to receiving the high prices for A and B beet and their allocated amount of . . . C beet."

239. We agree with the Panel that, in the circumstances of the present case, all of these aspects of the EC sugar regime have a direct bearing on whether below-cost sales of C beet are financed by virtue of governmental action. As a result, we are unable to agree with the European Communities' first argument on appeal,

namely, that the Panel applied a test under which an Article 9.1(c) subsidy was deemed to exist "simply because [governmental] action 'enabled' the beet growers to finance and make payments." Rather, we believe that the Panel relied on aspects of the EC sugar regime that go far beyond merely "enabling" or "permitting" beet growers to make payments to sugar producers. Indeed, in our view, there is a tight nexus between the European Communities' "governmental action" and the financing of payments in the case before us. We have no doubt that, without the highly remunerative prices guaranteed by the EC sugar regime for A and B beet, sales of C beet could not take place profitably at a price below the total cost of production.

249. As a result, we find no fault with the Panel's weighing and appreciation of the evidence and with the Panel's conclusion that the "payments" at issue are "financed by virtue of governmental action" within the meaning of Article 9.1(c) of the *Agreement on Agriculture*.

NOTE ON U.S. — UPLAND COTTON

The *EC—Sugar Subsidies* case is a landmark ruling, but it followed closely the reasoning in a previous case brought by the United States and New Zealand against Canada in *Canada—Measures Affecting the Importation of Milk and the Exportation of Dairy Products*, WT/DS103/R, Report of the Appellate Body, adopted on October 27, 1999. The developing countries attacking the EU subsidies were not really breaking new ground. However, in *United States—Subsidies on Upland Cotton*, WT/DS267/AB/R, Report of the Appellate Body, adopted on March 21, 2005, a complaint brought by Brazil, the developing world opened an entirely new front in the war between developing and developed countries on agricultural subsidies. The *U.S.—Upland Cotton* decision goes to the heart of the subsidization criteria in the AoA, which makes most types of subsidies illegal. The decision also breaks new ground because it indicates that developing countries can use a powerful new weapon, the WTO Subsidies and Countervailing Measures (SCM) Agreement, to strike down farm subsidies. In the classic case of illegal subsidies, a government makes a payment to an exporter contingent upon the export of a product. The subsidized product, once imported into the aggrieved member, enjoys a price advantage over domestically produced goods. The SCM Agreement allows the aggrieved member to have access to a number of remedies when this occurs, including the imposition of a countervailing duty that offsets the amount of the subsidy.

U.S.—Upland Cotton is a formidable decision, well over 250 pages long and full of complexity. Because much of the case concerned the SCM Agreement, which we cover in Chapter 10, we will see this case again in another context. However, we summarize the decision here because it was a major triumph for developing countries.

At Brazil's request, the Appellate Body ruled on three categories of U.S. subsidies for upland cotton. The Appellate Body found that each category violated U.S. WTO obligations. The Appellate Body also clarified the relationship between the subsidies rules in the AoA and the more general regulations on subsidies contained in the SCM Agreement.

The significance of the *U.S.—Upland Cotton* case is as follows: Prior to this case, if a country provided a domestic or export subsidy in violation of its scheduled reduction commitments under the AoA, the country was in violation of the AoA and had to withdraw the subsidy. However, many subsidies were exempt under the

AoA from inclusion in a WTO member's reduction commitments, which meant that a member could make as many of these payments as it wished without violating the AoA. It seemed to be clear that exempted subsidies under the AoA were also protected from action under the SCM, which targets illegal subsidies. What was unclear was what happened if subsidies that were claimed to be exempt under the AoA were ruled by the WTO to be non-exempt after all; i.e., unqualified for the various AoA "boxes" or exemptions. Under the AoA, it was clear that the subsidies had to be withdrawn, but was it also possible that these subsidies, now illegal under the AoA, were then also subject to sanctions under the SCM Agreement?

The purpose of the SCM Agreement is to provide aggrieved countries with remedies against the payment of illegal government subsidies, which is exactly what the non-exempt agricultural subsidies had been determined to be. No one knew, however, whether the SCM Agreement would apply to agricultural subsidies that lost the protection of an exemption under the AoA. This issue was complicated by various provisions in the AoA, which provide that the AoA takes priority over other WTO agreements, including the SCM Agreement. In *U.S. —Upland Cotton*, however, the Appellate Body fired a warning shot over the bow of developed countries, the most frequent users of agricultural subsidies: Subsidies that are not exempt under the AoA are actionable under the SCM Agreement.

The four major rulings are as follows:

(1) *Domestic Support Payments to Producers with Respect to Historic Upland Cotton Base Acres*

The United States made four types of annual payments to producers who are recognized as owning historic upland cotton base acres, lands where cotton was frequently grown in the past. The four types of payments were termed production flexibility contract payments, market loss assistance payments, direct payments, and countercyclical payments measures. These payments were made in the years 1999, 2000, 2001, and 2002 to holders of historic upland cotton base acres, whether or not they actually grew cotton. In fact, the holders of such lands were encouraged to grow other crops, but they were not prohibited from growing cotton.

Under the AoA, the United States had made commitments to limit domestic subsidies to farmers to a specific level each year, its Aggregate Measure of Support (AMS). The payments to holders of upland cotton base acres were, however, according to the United States, exempt from inclusion in its annual AMS limit. The United States placed these subsidies in the "Green Box" of the AoA; i.e., exempt or lawful subsidies. To qualify as Green Box subsidies, the payments had to be "decoupled" from cotton production; i.e., they were paid regardless of any cotton production. The Appellate Body ruled (¶342) that the subsidies in question cannot be considered "Green Box" subsidies under the criteria in Annex 2, paragraph 6 of the AoA. The Appellate Body agreed with the panel that the amounts of the allegedly "decoupled" payments were linked to production of cotton because they were calculated by multiplying a factor specific to the historic number of acres used to plant upland cotton by the producer. The Appellate Body and panel also found that a great proportion of the recipients of payments continued to grow cotton in the year of payment. Because of these facts, the Appellate Body found a link between the support and a specific commodity, upland cotton. These payments were not "decoupled" within the meaning of the AoA and were not exempted subsidies.

See id. at ¶342. Since these payments were ineligible for "Green Box" treatment, they are not sheltered from the reduction commitments for domestic subsidies in the AoA. This meant that the payments were unlawful under the AoA and had to be discontinued in order to bring the United States into conformity with its commitments under the WTO.

The question also arose whether the payments were sheltered from challenge under Article 13 (commonly referred to as the "Peace Clause") of the AoA, which provides that exempted subsidies under the AoA would not be subject to the imposition of countervailing duties under the SCM Agreement. The Peace Clause is designed to ensure that agricultural subsidies exempted under the AoA are not subject to countervailing duties under the SCM.

The Appellate Body ruled (¶391), however, that under Article 13(b)(ii) of the Peace Clause, agricultural subsidies are exempt from countervailing duties unless they "grant support to a specific commodity in excess of that decided during the 1992 marketing year." Such subsidies are not protected by the Peace Clause from the imposition of countervailing duties. The Appellate Body ruled (¶384) that the four types of payment are "support granted to a particular commodity." Furthermore, the Appellate Body found (¶¶391-394) that this support was "in excess of that decided during the 1992 marketing year" in each relevant year of the implementation period. As a result, the United States was not entitled to the exemption provided by Article 13 from actions under GATT Article XVI:1 and the SCM Agreement Articles 5 and 6. The subsidies were unlawful and subject to being countervailed.

The Peace Clause of Article 13 was only in effect during the implementation period from 1995 to 2004. It would have sheltered the offending programs during the years in question if the payments were not support granted to a particular commodity. But the ruling concerning the Green Box is more important than the ruling concerning the Peace Clause because, although the Peace Clause has expired, the Green Box remains in effect. Payments that do not qualify for protection as falling within the Green Box also lose their immunity from the SCM Agreement. Under the SCM Agreement, these subsidies are unlawful and are subject to countervailing duties and other remedies.

Turning to the SCM Agreement, Article 5 concerns what are termed "actionable subsidies." This is the intermediate category of subsidy (yellow light) that is neither flatly prohibited (red light) nor non-actionable or permitted (green light). To be banned, a showing must be made that an actionable subsidy causes adverse effects to the interests of other WTO members. Adverse effects can be shown by injury to the domestic industry of another member, nullification or impairment of a trade benefit, or serious prejudice to the interests of another member. Serious prejudice is defined, *inter alia*, in SCM Article 6.3(c) as "significant price suppression." The Appellate Body found (¶496) that serious prejudice was present in this case because of significant price suppression in the relevant market, which was found to be the worldwide market for upland cotton during the years 1999 to 2002. The remedy for an actionable subsidy that causes serious prejudice is withdrawal of the subsidy or removal of the adverse effects, and if that is not done within a reasonable time, countermeasures can be authorized commensurate with the degree and nature of the adverse effects. *See* SCM Article 7. No finding was made as to a remedy, presumably because the United States had already terminated the subsidy programs.

(2) Import Substitution Subsidies (Step 2 Payments) to Users of U.S. Upland Cotton

The Appellate Body found (¶584) that this type of subsidy infringes Article 3.1(a) of the SCM Agreement, which defines one of the two types of prohibited subsidy as "subsidies contingent . . . on the use of domestic over imported goods." (The rationale for this provision is that a government subsidy for the use of domestic goods over imports harms imports and is a distortion of trade.) SCM Article 3.1 contains an exception: "Except as provided in the Agreement on Agriculture." Article 3.1 is thus consistent with AoA Article 2.1, which makes clear that the AoA prevails over other WTO agreements: "The provisions of the GATT 1994 and of the other Multilateral Trade Agreement in Annex I to the WTO Agreement shall apply subject to the provisions of this Agreement." Interpreting these two provisions together, the Appellate Body ruled (¶333), however, that the AoA prevails over the SCM, "but only to the extent that the former [the AoA] contains an exemption." In other words, the AoA immunizes subsidies from the reach of the SCM only in the case of a "specific provision [in the AoA] dealing with the same subject matter." *Id.* There is no such specific immunity provision in the AoA for subsidies contingent upon the use of domestic over imported goods. Therefore, the upland cotton subsidies violated Article 3.2 of the SCM, which states that "a member shall neither grant nor maintain subsidies referred to in paragraph 1." Because the subsidies were not exempted from the SCM by the AoA, the subsidies were actionable under the SCM.

(3) Export (Step 2) Subsidies

Certain of the so-called step 2 payments were made to exporters of upland cotton. These payments called into play Article 9.1 of the AoA, which subjects export subsidies to reduction commitments. The United States argued that these subsidies were available to users of cotton and not contingent on export. According to the United States, because these were not export subsidies, the payments were not subject to export reduction commitments, and the United States could continue to provide as many of these payments as it wished without violating Article 9.1 of the AoA. The Appellate Body rejoined (¶577) that, to obtain a subsidy, the payee must submit proof of export; therefore, the payments are "tied" to export.

These payments also constituted another class of prohibited subsidy under the SCM Article 3.1(a), a subsidy contingent on export performance, and were thus an infringement of SCM Article 3.2. These infringements were also actionable under the SCM.

(4) Export Credit Guarantees

The Appellate Body, one member dissenting, ruled that export guarantees accorded by the United States on upland cotton exports were not an exempted form of an export subsidy under AoA Article 10.2. The U.S. government agreed to guarantee the exports of upland cotton by purchasing them if U.S. farmers could not find a buyer abroad. Because the export guarantees were considered to be exempted export subsidies under the AoA, the majority of the Appellate Body accordingly ruled (¶674) that U.S. export guarantees are prohibited by SCM Article 3.1 and 3.2 and are actionable subsidies under the SCM.

POSTSCRIPT: THE GROWING CLOUT OF
DEVELOPING COUNTRIES—IMPLICATIONS FOR THE
FUTURE OF THE WTO

Under the prior practice of the GATT, trade deals affecting all GATT-contracting states were made primarily by a few industrialized countries. The United States and European countries played key roles, often holding preliminary meetings, most famously in the GATT Director General's conference room, the "green room." The deals struck at these clubby meetings among a few GATT-contracting states would then be presented to the entire membership for acceptance. In the WTO, developing countries have, for the most part, rejected the "green room" process. In a speech on October 11, 2006, Pascal Lamy, the Director General of the WTO, took note of this fact, stating that "The Doha Round [of trade negotiations] must deliver trade and growth with strong developmental credentials if developing and least-developed countries are to believe that the deal is worth doing."[6] Now that developing countries, including most importantly Brazil, India, and China, are calling the tune, cutting trade deals will be more difficult and will certainly involve different considerations than those under the GATT.

The growing clout of developing country members of the WTO is reflected in the Doha Agenda, the topics of negotiation approved and set by the November 2001 Declaration of the Fourth Ministerial Conference of the WTO. The Declaration's Work Program is an ambitious list of topics of interest to developing countries: market access for agricultural and non-agricultural products; trade facilitation; trade and transfer of technology; reform of the Dispute Settlement Understanding; and special and differential treatment. In addition, the Doha Implementation Program, approved at the same time, covers over 100 issues, many raised by developing countries.

The needs and demands of developing countries shaped the process of negotiations during the Doha Development Round, most notably in the following ways:

- Agricultural trade issues (including domestic and export subsidies by developed countries) dominated the negotiations, despite the fact that the majority of WTO developing country members are net importers of agricultural products.
- Investment and competition policy negotiations, mentioned prominently at the First Ministerial Conference in Singapore, have been blocked. Many developing countries are concerned about the possible negative effects of new competition rules on these topics on the Doha Agenda.
- TRIPS obligations were interpreted to allow compulsory licensing of pharmaceutical products necessary to protect public health and facilitating exports of such products.
- Developing countries were accorded technical assistance and special and differential treatment to meet new sanitary and phytosanitary measures and regulations adopted by developed countries. These include measures

---

6. Keynote speech at the 23rd Assembly of the International Federation of Pharmaceutical Manufacturers & Associations, available at http://www.wto.org, visited January 16, 2007.

to control Ocratoxin A in soluble coffee in EU countries, deviation from international standards on solid wood packing, as well as diseases such as avian flu, mad cow, and foot and mouth.

- Developing countries are increasingly concerned over too-rapid liberalization of services trade as well. Many are now devising a strategy for services trade that will enhance their own potential.

Unfair Trade Remedies: Anti-Dumping and Countervailing Duties

I. Introduction

So far we have considered barriers (Chapters 5-6) and exceptions (Chapters 7-9) to the trade in goods and their discipline under the GATT. This Chapter also deals with restrictions on trade but whereas the topics covered in previous chapters dealt with restrictions on fair trade, this Chapter deals with restrictions on unfair trade. Thus, the measures examined in this Chapter are also considered to be "justified" restrictions on trade so long as the conditions for their application are met.

We analyze remedies for the two most important unfair trade practices, "dumping" and subsidies, which can be defined for our purposes as follows:

- Dumping occurs when a product is sold in the export market at a price that is lower than the price at which it is sold in the home market. For example, if Japan sells a product at $100 in Japan but sells the same product in the U.S. market at $75 then dumping may exist. The United States may then impose an anti-dumping duty equal to the margin of dumping ($25).
- A countervailable subsidy occurs when a government provides a financial contribution contingent upon export of the product. For example, if France provided a government payment of $15 per unit to a producer that then exports the product to the United States, the U.S. Department of Commerce can impose a countervailing duty (an additional tariff) to offset the effect of the subsidy. Alternatively, the United States can bring an action within the WTO to have the subsidy withdrawn.

In the case of dumping, the only action recognized by the WTO is unilateral action by the aggrieved state in imposing anti-dumping duties. In the case of subsidies, the WTO permits the aggrieved state in some cases either to bring a challenge within the WTO dispute settlement system or to take unilateral action under domestic law.

The WTO disciplines the use of these measures through the Antidumping Agreement and the Agreement on Subsidies and Countervailing Measures, both of which amplify GATT Article VI, the original provision permitting the use of these measures. Measures that fail to comply with these agreements are subject to challenge within the WTO dispute settlement system.

Both anti-dumping and countervailing duties are far more popular with governments and domestic producers alike than the safeguards considered in Chapter 8. Trade protection is easier to justify politically on the basis of combating unfairness than on the grounds that domestic industries cannot compete against fairly traded imports. In the case of safeguards, the standards for obtaining relief are higher. The petitioner must demonstrate "serious injury" (or threat thereof) to a domestic industry. In the case of dumping and illegal subsidies, the petitioner needs to demonstrate only "material injury" (or the threat thereof).

In the first sixteen years of the WTO, from 1995 to 2011, a total of 4,010 dumping investigations and 2,601 anti-dumping measures, and 262 investigations and 164 subsidies and countervailing duties, by WTO members were notified to the WTO Secretariat. As these statistics indicate, dumping actions are far more popular than actions against subsidies. Dumping actions have historically resulted in higher duties and created heavier burdens for foreign companies. Subsidies actions must target, in addition to private companies, the practices of foreign governments in providing subsidies.

Historically, the United States has been the most frequent user of these remedies, followed by the European Union. However, other WTO members, including developing countries, are increasingly employing these remedies.

In the United States, two different statutory schemes govern dumping and subsidies, but both schemes are quite similar and are administered by the same two government agencies: The International Trade Administration within the Department of Commerce (Commerce) decides whether dumping or illegal subsidies exist, and the International Trade Commission (ITC), an independent agency (in the sense that it does not report directly to the President), decides the material injury requirement. Both investigations operate in parallel with each other, but a negative determination by either Commerce or the ITC can terminate the entire investigation. The United States is unusual in international law in having a bifurcated process, and some have attributed its existence to the need to create the appearance of greater independence in the ITC.

In this Chapter, we first analyze the law of dumping. We consider (1) its economic and political justifications; (2) the procedural and substantive aspects of anti-dumping actions under U.S. law; and (3) a comparison of U.S. law to international law contained in the GATT and the Antidumping Agreement, as interpreted by the WTO Appellate Body.

PROBLEM 10-1

Anti-dumping cases are highly popular among U.S. industries and far more so than Section 201 escape clause (or safeguard) cases or even countervailing duty actions. Assume that you are an analyst for a group of U.S. multinational enterprises that have business operations in Country D. The industry group suspects that products from Country D are being subsidized and dumped in the United States. The industry group would like you to discuss a number of possible trade remedies that are available. Please discuss the desirability of (1) bringing a Section 201 escape clause case, compared to an anti-dumping action (in particular, compare the relevant standards for relief between the two cases, and the political justification); or (2) bringing an anti-dumping action, as opposed to a countervailing duty action (in particular, discuss the issue of relief and what type of entity is the particular target of these two actions). Is there a sense in which countervailing duty actions are more risky or have a greater tendency to antagonize the parties involved, creating business risks for your clients?

II.   *Dumping and Anti-Dumping Duties*

A.   The Economic and Political Debate

The economic rationale for imposing anti-dumping duties is that dumping is harmful, but not everyone agrees that every practice that qualifies as dumping is harmful, or that anti-dumping duties are the best remedy. We now explore this debate.

The prevailing justification for the use of anti-dumping duties is as follows:

- dumping requires that the exporting market be segregated and that the importing market be open;
- operating from a segregated market can confer on exporters an advantage that is not due to greater efficiency and cannot be matched by their competitors in the importing country;
- these segregated markets provide the dumper with the opportunity to maximize profits or minimize losses and can be highly injurious for the importing country's industry.

A segregated home market is one that cannot be penetrated by imports due to economic or legal reasons. This protection of the home market may allow the exporter to earn monopoly profits at home and use those profits to support selling exports at artificially low prices in the export market. The main concern is that these practices are not based on free market principles but rather distort and undermine the free market. The exporter is selling at lower prices in the export market not because it produces products more efficiently but because it has an alternative source of profits that are not available to domestic competitors.

So far what we have described is not necessarily harmful to consumers in the export market since the only consequence is that they enjoy lower prices for the exports. However, the exporter may use its artificially low-priced exports to drive domestic competitors in the export market out of business, or to discourage the development of a domestic competitor in the export market. Once this occurs, the exporter can raise its prices or lower the quality of its products. Dumping is also viewed as harmful to domestic competitors even when the exporter does not eliminate domestic competition. At a minimum, dumping allows the exporter to obtain a foothold in the export market not because it operates more efficiently but because it uses its monopoly profits in its home market to support lower prices for its products in the export market.

The potentially harmful effects of dumping put strong political pressure on governments to provide an effective trade remedy. In the United States, dumping is found whenever the product is sold at a lower price (in the United States) than in the home market by more than a *de minimis* margin (2 percent). This definition of dumping can capture forms of conduct that are not necessarily supported by improper motivations. Most economists would agree that dumping to drive out local competitors or to gain a foothold in the export market is harmful, but there exist other reasons why an exporter may charge a lower price in the export market that is supported by sound economic reasons. For example, the export market may be subject to market instabilities caused by a shortage of foreign currency to pay for the imports, a general economic recession, or just sudden changes in consumer tastes and demand. Charging a lower price for the export might be necessary to remain competitive in an export market in the face of economic adversity. The broad definition of dumping captures all cases in which a product is sold in the export market at a price that is lower than in the home market, and as such might include instances of rational economic behavior.

Where dumping is found, the remedy in the United States is to impose an anti-dumping duty on top of any existing tariffs. This has two immediate welfare effects: The anti-dumping duty will be passed onto consumers in the form of higher prices, and domestic producers will also raise their prices. Consumers now pay more for all products, both imports and those that are domestically produced. The economic impact on consumers can be so significant that some have argued that the anti-dumping laws should be abolished. *See* Bryan Johnson and Robert O'Quinn, *Abolish America's Costly Anti-dumping Laws*, The Heritage Foundation, *Backgrounder Update* No. 261 (Oct. 3, 1995). According to this study by the Heritage Foundation, the International Trade Commission published a study in 1995 that examined the welfare of anti-dumping and countervailing duties and found that:

- Anti-dumping and countervailing duties caused a net loss of $1.59 billion in U.S. Gross Domestic Product in 1991;
- When these duties were applied to imports, U.S. prices for domestically produced goods that competed with the imports *also* rose. For example, domestic fertilizer prices increased by 19 percent, domestic lamb meat prices went up by 10 percent, and domestic steel pipe and tube prices rose by 10 percent.
- Anti-dumping duties protect domestic industries and workers affected by the imports, but this is paid for by U.S. consumers. For example, in 1987, U.S. consumers paid $138 million more for ball bearings because of anti-dumping laws. The overall cost to the economy was $70 million. This cost is attributed to anti-dumping duties applied to just one product—ball bearings—and such losses may occur in every single case in which anti-dumping duties are applied.

These findings have caused some to argue that the cure is worse than the disease and that the anti-dumping laws should be abolished.

NOTES AND QUESTIONS

1. If anti-dumping duties are so costly to U.S. consumers and the U.S. economy, why are such remedies so popular?

2. *Effectiveness of Anti-Dumping Duties.* Using anti-dumping duties as a remedy for the use of low prices by a foreign exporter, in order to obtain market share in the domestic import market, is only a second best solution. The optimal solution would be to open the foreign producers' home market to eliminate the monopoly profits and to integrate the two markets into a single international market.

However, this option does not appear to be politically feasible and has little international support.

3. *Anti-Dumping and Antitrust Law.* In addition to violating anti-dumping laws, charging lower prices in different country markets can be subject to antitrust laws. For example, if a company charges lower prices in the United States than it charges in its home market, the practice could constitute price discrimination in violation of the U.S. Robinson-Patman Act, Sections 2 (a)-(f) of the Clayton Act, 15 U.S.C. §13 (a)-(f). In contrast to anti-dumping laws, the anti-trust laws have quite precise standards for recovery for predatory pricing. While anti-dumping laws provide relief for artificially low pricing in the export market alone, under the antitrust statutes, "evidence of below cost pricing is not alone sufficient to permit an inference of probable recoupment and injury to competition." *Id.* at 210. Rather, a plaintiff seeking to establish competitive injury from a rival's low prices must first prove that the prices complained of are below an appropriate measure of its rival's costs. *See, e.g., Brooke Ltd. v. Brown & Williamson Tobacco Corp.,* 509 U.S. 209, 222 (1993). Second, the plaintiff must show that the competitor had a reasonable prospect or a dangerous probability of recouping its investment at below-cost prices. *Id.* at 224. In addition, a defendant charged with price discrimination under the Robinson-Patman Act is allowed to assert various defenses, such as "meeting competition" and "cost justification," that are not available in anti-dumping law. Two cases provide a vivid illustration of the differences between these two legal regimes. U.S. color television manufacturers sued the Japanese color television industry for predatory pricing and lost in *Matsushita Electric Industry Co. v. Zenith Radio Corp.,* 475 U.S. 574 (1986); when the same plaintiffs sued the Japanese industry under the U.S. anti-dumping law, they won. *See Color Picture Tubes from Japan,* USITC Pub. 367, Inv. No. 731-TA-367-370 (July 1971) (final administration review).

PROBLEM 10-2

Suppose that Japan is dumping computer displays in the United States. The same displays sell for $200 in Japan but for $115 in the United States. Despite these differentials, however, Japan will not be able to dump unless it also maintains effective trade barriers to prevent imports from freely penetrating its market. Suppose that you are a buyer in the United States and that you have just purchased a large quantity of imported computer displays from Japan for $115 each. What will you do? How will this prevent Japan from dumping? What is necessary for effective dumping?

PROBLEM 10-3

You are a legislative aide to a congressional committee that is investigating why the antitrust laws of the United States are more sophisticated and evenhanded than anti-dumping and countervailing duty laws, which seem very vague and imprecise by comparison. What is your analysis? Hint: U.S. companies actively lobby Congress concerning both antitrust and anti-dumping and countervailing laws. Antitrust laws allow private causes of action by U.S. companies acting as plaintiffs, but these companies can also find themselves as defendants in antitrust lawsuits brought by other private parties or by the U.S. Justice Department. What about in anti-dumping and countervailing duty actions? What is the posture of a U.S. company in these cases? How might this explain why the antitrust laws are far more evenhanded?

B.   The Operation of the U.S. Anti-Dumping Laws: Procedural Aspects

The procedures for initiating and completing a dumping investigation are complex and are outlined in statutory form in the United States Tariff Act of 1930 as amended, §§732-752, 19 U.S.C. §§1673a-1675a.

The basic provision provides as follows:

§1673. *Imposition of antidumping duties*

If—
> (1) the administering authority determines that a class or kind of foreign merchandise is being, or is likely to be, sold in the United States at less than its fair value, and
> (2) the Commission determines that—
>> (A) an industry in the United States—
>>> (i) is materially injured, or
>>> (ii) is threatened with material injury, or
>> (B) the establishment of an industry in the United States is materially retarded, by reason of imports of that merchandise, or by reason of sales (or the likelihood of sales) of that merchandise for importation, then there shall be imposed upon such merchandise an antidumping duty, in addition to any other duty imposed, in an amount equal to the amount by which the normal value exceeds the export price (or the constructed export price) for the merchandise.

Under §1673, two basic determinations, made by two separate agencies, must occur before anti-dumping duties can be imposed. First, the International Trade Administration, part of the Department of Commerce, must determine that dumping exists; i.e., that the import is being sold in the United States at "less than its fair value," which is further defined to mean that the product is being sold in its home market at a higher price than it is being sold in the United States by more than a *de minimis* amount (2 percent). Second, the International Trade Commission must find that the material injury requirement is satisfied.

To initiate an anti-dumping investigation, petitioners must file a petition with both Commerce and the ITC. Petitioners have standing if they represent either companies or workers that produce a majority of the total domestic U.S. production or at least that they have the support of producers or workers who are responsible for a significant percentage of U.S. output. *See* 19 U.S.C. §1673a(c)(4).

Within twenty days of the filing of the petition, Commerce must determine the sufficiency of the petition. This inquiry is usually limited to whether the petitioner is a proper party, has alleged facts upon which relief may be granted, and has provided as much information in support of the petition as can be reasonably expected at this stage. If Commerce rules that the petition is insufficient, it is dismissed. If Commerce finds that the petition is sufficient, the next step is for the ITC to make its initial ruling.

Within forty-five days of the filing of the petition, the ITC must issue a preliminary finding on whether there is a "reasonable indication" that a U.S. industry has suffered a material injury, is threatened with a material injury, or that the establishment of an industry in the United States has been materially retarded. To make this determination, the ITC will engage in its own fact finding by collecting data from various sources, including the use of questionnaires sent to U.S. industry. Hearings are rare at this stage although the ITC may hold informal conferences with the interested parties. If the ITC makes a negative preliminary injury finding, then the investigation is terminated. If the ITC makes an affirmative finding, then it becomes the turn of Commerce to make a preliminary finding on the existing of dumping.

Within 120 days from its finding that the petition was sufficient, Commerce must make a preliminary finding regarding whether there is a "reasonable basis" to believe that dumping exists; i.e., that the imports have sold at less than fair value. Commerce usually commences an investigation before the ITC issues its preliminary ruling so that the investigation is usually conducted on two fronts simultaneously. To make this preliminary ruling, Commerce will gather as much information as possible about pricing patterns of the domestic and foreign industries. Petitioners will provide information about the domestic industry. Commerce will approach the foreign industries directly through the use of detailed questionnaires.

If Commerce makes a preliminary finding of dumping, then Commerce will direct U.S. Customs to suspend liquidation of the imports. Suspension means that final duties will not be determined for the imports but the imports will be allowed to enter the United States if the importer posts a bond equal to the margin of dumping; i.e., the amount by which the imports are undersold. The bond is in the custody of U.S. Customs, which is not now assured of being able to collect any final anti-dumping duties that are due. If Commerce makes a negative preliminary finding (i.e., that no dumping exists), the investigation does not automatically terminate; rather, Commerce must still make a final determination that no dumping exists. If the preliminary finding is negative then the final determination will likely also be negative but this is not always the case. If the final determination by Commerce is negative, then the investigation terminates. In making the final determination, Commerce will also verify information by dispatching its officials to the foreign country to engage in on-site inspections and verification of data submitted in questionnaires. Commerce must make a final determination within seventy-five days of the preliminary determination.

If the final determination of Commerce finds dumping then the ITC must make a final determination of material injury and that the imports caused the injury. At this stage, the ITC will hold formal hearings to allow interested parties to present evidence and witnesses about the state of the domestic industry. If both the preliminary and final determinations by Commerce on dumping are positive, then the ITC has forty-five days to make its final injury determination. If Commerce's preliminary finding is negative but its final finding is positive, then the ITC has seventy-five days to make its final injury determination. The extra time is necessary because if the preliminary finding of Commerce is negative, the ITC usually does not continue to pursue its injury investigations with any rigor.

Once Commerce has determined that a product from a foreign country has been "dumped" (sold at less than fair value in the United States) and the ITC has found that such dumping has "materially injured" (or threatens) a domestic industry, Commerce will issue an anti-dumping order intended to rectify the unfair trade practice. Upon the issuance of such an order, the additional duties specified in the order must be deposited with the United States Customs and Border Protection Agency "pending liquidation." 19 U.S.C. §1673e(a)(3). "Liquidation" means the final computation or ascertainment of duties on entry. *See* 19 CFR §159.1. At this point the additional duty is collected on imports unless the petitioners in the case withdraw their petition or the foreign exporters reach a "suspension" agreement with Commerce to withdraw from the U.S. market or to eliminate the dumping or the material injury.

There are two methods available if a party wishes to challenge an anti-dumping order. First, judicial review of final DOC or ITC determinations is available by filing a petition with the U.S. Court of International Trade. Decisions of the Court of International Trade may be appealed to the U.S. Court of Appeals for the Federal Circuit, and, by petition for certiorari, to the Supreme Court of the United States. Second, if the goods in question originated in Canada or Mexico, the anti-dumping order may be challenged before a NAFTA binational panel, as required under the North American Free Trade Agreement and the NAFTA Implementation Act of 1993, Pub. L. No. 103-182, 107 Stat. 2057. The determination of a NAFTA binational panel may lead to revocation of an anti-dumping order. *See, e.g., Canadian Wheat Board v. United States*, 641 F.3d 1344, 1348-1353 (Fed. Cir. 2011).

Commerce is required to review its own final determination of dumping on an annual basis if requested by an interested party. The purpose of this review is to ensure that the amount required to be deposited with Customs is the amount of the dumping margin and any excess can be returned. A party may also request review of compliance with a suspension agreement. After a dumping order has been in effect for a number of years, a respondent might request review of the order. If the respondent has not engaged in dumping in the past three years and is not likely to engage in dumping in the future, the order can be revoked.

Commerce and the ITC are required by Article 11.3 of the WTO Antidumping Agreement to determine within five years of the issuance of the anti-dumping order whether the order should be continued or terminated.

C.   The Calculation of Anti-Dumping Duties

Read these statutes in the following order:

> Section 731 (19 U.S.C. 1673) ("Imposition of Antidumping Duties") is the basic operative section.
> Section 772 (19 U.S.C. 1677a) sets forth calculation rules for Export Price and Constructed Export Price.
> Section 773 (19 U.S.C. 1677b) sets forth the calculation rules for Normal Value.
> Section 773A (19 U.S.C. 1677b-1) covers currency conversion.
> Section 777A (19 U.S.C. 1677f-1) deals with sampling and averaging methods.
> Section 781 (19 U.S.C. 1677j) deals with prevention of circumvention.

The U.S. Department of Commerce regulations applicable to anti-dumping cases are set forth in 19 C.F.R. Part 351. Many aspects of the Commerce Department's regulations are controversial, but courts on judicial review give the benefit of the doubt to the agency (under the aegis of the Supreme Court's test in *Chevron U.S.A.,*

Inc. v. Natural Resources Defense Council, 467 U.S. 837 (1984)). For the most part, courts accord broad discretion to Commerce in dumping determinations. *See Smith-Corona Group v. United States*, 713 F.2d 1568, 1571 (Fed. Cir. 1983).

PROBLEM 10-4

Akio, an electronics firm, sells merchandise in Japan to consumers at a price of $25 per item. Akio exports the merchandise to Akio USA, with its distribution office located in Texas, at a price of $15 per item. Akio USA sells the item to Bargain Dollar Stores for $28 per item. Assume that the normal value in Japan is $25. Is there dumping? *See* §1677a(a)-(b).

PROBLEM 10-5

Suba is an Indonesia furniture company that sells an item of furniture to consumers in Indonesia at $35 per item. The price of the item in Indonesia includes transportation costs ($10) from the factory in Indonesia to the consumer. Assume that the export price in the United States is $30. Is there dumping? *See* §1677b(a)(6)(B)(i)-(ii).

PROBLEM 10-6

Lucky Computers, a Taiwanese manufacturer of computer parts and peripherals, sells merchandise to the United States at an export price of $75. Taiwan imposes a consumption tax on all computers and peripherals. The export price to the United States includes a consumption tax of $25. Lucky Computers sells these same items in Taiwan at a normal value of $85 dollars, including the consumption tax. At the end of each tax year, the consumption tax is refunded by the Taiwan government for local sales by Lucky Computers. The consumption tax is not refunded for export sales. Is there dumping? *See* §1677b(a)(6)(B)(iii).

PROBLEM 10-7

Mohlen is a German company that sells high-end kitchen equipment to the United States. Mohlen sells stainless stoves with high-intensity burners in Germany for $1,000 per unit. Mohlen sells 100 units of the stove to a customer in Arkansas at a price of $80,000 and 100 units of the stove to a customer in Ohio for $120,000. Is there dumping? See the discussion on zeroing below.

1.   *How Dumping Is Determined*

In order to determine whether dumping exists, Commerce makes a basic comparison between two prices: the normal value (i.e., the price at which the product is sold in its home market) and the export price (i.e., the price at which the like product is sold in the United States). If the normal value is higher than the export price by more than a *de minimis* amount (2 percent) then Commerce will find dumping.

The normal value will be determined on the basis of actual sales in the home market of the foreign exporter. However, using sales in the foreign market may not always be possible; the foreign exporter may not manufacture the product for sale in its home market or sales in the home market are so small that they are unreliable. In this case, Commerce may use sales to a third country as a basis for establishing the normal value; if no sales to a third country exist, Commerce will use a constructed price as the normal value. This constructed price is based upon various costs and factors of production, plus some amount for profit.

The export price is based upon the price that is charged by the foreign exporter in an arm's-length sale to an importer in the United States. If the transaction involves affiliated entities then an arm's-length sale does not exist. For example, an automobile manufacturer in Country A may sell to an affiliate dealer in the United States. In these cases, Commerce will use a "constructed export price," based upon the first arm's-length sales by the dealer in the United States to an unaffiliated consumer.

In making a dumping determination, Commerce will apply the following basic concepts. The price at which the product is sold in its home market is an accurate reflection of its market price (i.e., its normal value). If the price at which the merchandise is sold in the U.S. market is less than the price at which the merchandise is sold in the home market, then dumping is present; if the export price is equal to or greater than the normal value, then no dumping is present.

To make a fair comparison between the normal value and the export price, however, some adjustments to both prices must usually be made. Commerce seeks to make an "apples to apples" comparison for the purposes of fairness and accuracy. Under U.S. law, the imaginary point in time to make the "apples to apples" comparison is ex-factory; i.e., at the factory door of the foreign manufacturer. Imagine two products that have been manufactured and that are now placed at the factory door. One product is destined for a consumer in the home market and the other product is destined for a buyer in the United States. This is the ideal point at which a comparison of the two prices should be made.

Of course, it is usually not possible to find records of such prices at the factory door; even if such prices were found, these prices usually contain costs that are specific to the U.S. market and to the home market. The basic task of Commerce is to strip away all of the costs and charges that can be attributed to the differences surrounding the sales of the products in the two markets, in order to make a true "apples to apples" comparison. What are some of the adjustments that have to be made?

We start with the export price based upon the invoice price to an unaffiliated purchaser; i.e., the actual price on the bill to the U.S. customer. In many cases, the foreign company will have already completed a sale to a U.S. customer before the goods leave the factory. The invoice price will often include movement costs that are charged by the foreign manufacturer to the U.S. buyer, such as international freight and insurance, brokerage and handling, movement costs in the home market (such as transporting the goods to a port for international shipment), and warehousing expenses in the home market in preparation for export. If these costs are included in the export price, they will need to be deducted in order to make the dumping comparison. All of these costs, as well as others allowed under U.S. law, are deducted from the export price.

Adjustments will also have to be made to the invoice price for the home market sales. Often before the goods leave the factory door, they have often already been sold to an unaffiliated customer in the home market. Again, the starting point is the invoice price. From this price, deductions will need to be made for costs if included in the invoice price to the local customer (such as costs of moving the goods from the factory to the customer or the cost of warehousing the goods in preparation for movement to the customer). Direct selling expenses, if included in the invoice price, must also be deducted. These include expenses for advertising, technical service, warranties, royalties, and commissions. Taxes that are included in the export price but not included in normal value (i.e., are not charged or are refunded) must also be deducted from the normal value.

After all of these adjustments have been made, we now arrive at the imaginary point in time when the two sets of goods are placed at the factory door, one set priced at the net normal value and the other at the net export price. We are now in a position to make the comparison to determine whether the normal value is higher than the export price (in order to determine whether dumping is present).

NOTES AND QUESTIONS

1. *Sales Below Cost.* An important part of the Commerce examination is to determine whether there are sales in the home market (or other comparison market) below the cost of production. Sales below the cost of production are those sales that do not permit recovery of all costs within a reasonable period of time. Sales at below cost will lower the normal value and will tend to reduce or eliminate any margin of dumping. However, Commerce considers such sales to be outside the ordinary course of trade and will exclude them from the calculation of the normal value if they are more than 20 percent of home market sales. Otherwise, a foreign producer with monopoly power might engage in strategic below-cost sales in its home market to preclude a finding of dumping in the foreign market. Commerce will make a comparison only of above-cost sales (i.e., sales in the normal course of trade) in the home market with the export price. If no normal values remain, a comparison will be made between sales in a third country and a constructed value of the merchandise with the export price.

2. *Non-Market Economies.* Commerce uses a different method for certain "non-market economies" (NMEs), such as China. Commerce rejects the use of normal values as unreliable because these prices are based upon free market factors. Prices in NMEs are usually determined in whole or in part by the government. Commerce also rejects the use of constructed value for NMEs because the costs of production are also subsidized in part or in whole by the government. Rather, Commerce obtains all of the "factors of production" (i.e., physical inputs, general expenses, profits, shipping, and other expenses) for such merchandise in NMEs. Commerce then values all of the factors of production in a surrogate third country, a market economy at a comparable level of development to the NME. The value of all of the factors of production in the surrogate country, plus adjustments for profit and expenses, is used as the normal value of the merchandise from the NME. A comparison is then made between the normal value and the export price.

In *Zhejiang DunAn Hetian Metal Co. Ltd. v. United States*, 652 F.3d 1333 (Fed Cir. 2011), a Chinese company, DunAn, challenged a Commerce anti-dumping order with respect to the importation of frontseating service valves (FSVs) from

China. (FSVs are used in air conditioning and heating systems to isolate sections of the system during servicing to facilitate repair and refrigerant recharging.) In order to calculate the value of the principal raw material (brass bar) used to manufacture the FSVs, Commerce used a surrogate—import statistics from India—as the best available information for purposes of valuing brass bar. DunAn asked the court to exclude Indian import data on materials coming from Japan and France on the grounds that the materials imported from these countries were not in fact brass bar, and the inclusion of these materials inflated the dumping margins. The Federal Court of Appeals upheld Commerce's use of this surrogate, however, accepting Commerce's explanation that "without clear evidence to the contrary, [Commerce] will not speculate that these materials have been misclassified." 652 F.3d at 1337. With respect to the use of a surrogate price for labor, however, the court faulted Commerce for using a regression analysis to value labor, because this analysis included data from certain market-economy countries that were not economically comparable to China. *See* 652 F.3d at 1349. On remand Commerce recalculated the dumping margin, lowering it from 12.95% to 11.83%. *See Frontseating Service Valves from the People's Republic of China: Notice of Court Decision Not in Harmony with Final Determination and Notice of Amended Final Antidumping Duty Order Pursuant to Court Decision*, 77 Fed. Reg. 5769 (February 6, 2012).

A. DUMPING CALCULATIONS

We now review several examples of dumping calculations. Assume that the invoice prices for arm's-length sales in both the home market and the U.S. market are the same: $120. The first step in the process is to arrive at a "net" ex-factory price for the normal value and for the export price. The normal value without any adjustments is in the first column. The export price without any adjustments is in the second column. Various deductions (in the parentheses) for costs and expenses are made for both prices in order to obtain "net" prices for comparison. See Figure 10-1.

FIGURE 10-1

	Normal Value	Export Price (or Constructed Export Price)
Selling price	120	120
Adjustments:		
Inland freight	(2)	(2)
Ocean freight		(5)
Level of trade	(1)	(2)
Circumstance of sale	(3)	(2)
Quantity of discount	(5)	
Physical differences	(2)	
Import expenses		(5)
Indirect selling expenses	(4)	(4)
Taxes	(12)	(5)
Total	91	95

In this example, the dumping margin is −4. There is no dumping because there are no sales of the merchandise at less than normal value in the United States. Normally, a dumping investigation would need to be terminated at this point. Commerce may of course reject, accept, or modify the proposed adjustments offered by the parties.

In the example above, the price comparison shown is a simple comparison based on two single sales transactions, what is commonly referred to as a transaction-to-transaction comparison. This method can be used if, for example, it is possible to identify a single transaction of a sale of a similar quantity (e.g., 500 units) in the home market and in the U.S. market at or about the same period of time.

In many cases, the period of review will involve hundreds or thousands of sales in the home market and a similar quantity of U.S. sales. Not all of these sales will be at the same price, as prices may vary depending upon the quantities sold and the season in which the sale occurs, so a method of averaging must be used. Whereas Commerce formerly calculated dumping margins by comparing each individual U.S. sale to a weighted average of the normal value, the WTO now requires a comparison of individual prices to individual prices or average prices to average prices. This was considered a welcome change by many countries because the practice of comparing individual export prices to average normal values resulted in much higher dumping margins. (It was possible to select the individual export prices that resulted in the largest margin of dumping and compare it to the average normal value.) Exceptionally, under current U.S. law, the weighted average of normal values may be compared to individual export prices if there is a pattern of export prices that differ significantly among purchasers, regions, or periods of time. These patterns are deemed to be examples of "targeted dumping," justifying a departure from an average-to-average comparison. However, Commerce has been reluctant to apply this exception.

The usual first step in a dumping comparison is for Commerce to engage in a "model-match methodology"; i.e., determine which products sold in the home market should be compared to products sold in the U.S. market over an appropriate period of time, usually three years. To make an "apples to apples" comparison, Commerce strives first to compare the export prices and normal values of identical products. If the identical product is not sold in the home market and the U.S. market, then Commerce will use the most similar home market product with an adjustment in price to account for any differences. Commerce uses a system of product matching based upon the physical characteristics of the imported products. In the example below, Commerce has identified several different models for the purposes of the price comparison (Model A, Model B, etc.).

The benefits of an average-to-average comparison are offset by Commerce's practice of "zeroing"; i.e., the practice of changing negative dumping margins (where no dumping is found because the export price is actually higher than the normal value) to zero when calculating the overall dumping margin for the company. See Figure 10-2.

Commerce will calculate dumping by dividing the total value of all dumped sales in the United States and the total value of all U.S. sales of the product as follows:

146 (dumped sales in U.S.) / 1929 (total U.S. sales) = 7.6% dumping
margin

FIGURE 10-2
Dumping Calculations Based on Weighted Averages and Zeroing

Quantity Sold to United States	Export Price (per unit)	Total Value of United States Sales	Normal Value (per unit)	Actual Amount of Unit Dumping	Commerce-Recognized Unit Dumping	Total Value of Dumping for Product Sales in U.S.
10 (Model A)	23	230	28	+5	5	50
15 (Model B)	25	375	20	−5	0	−75
20 (Model C)	27	540	22	−5	0	−100
18 (Model D)	24	432	23	−1	0	−18
16 (Model E)	22	352	28	+6	6	96
Total		1,929				−47/146

The 7.6 percent dumping margin is based on a weighted average and will now be imposed on all of the products that were the subject of the investigation when the products enter the United States. Commerce will treat all negative dumping margins as zero and will not allow the negative dumping margins to offset the positive dumping margins. It would have been possible in the example above for Commerce to subtract the negative dumping margins from the positive dumping margins in making the calculation. If Commerce were to offset the positive dumping margins by the negative dumping margins, then the total effect of the sales in the United States is a negative dumping margin (−47 in the last column on the right) instead of a positive dumping margin of 146. In other words, there would be no dumping.

What is the U.S. justification for zeroing? It was upheld by the Court of Appeals for the Federal Circuit in *Timken Co. v. United States*, 354 F.3d 1334 (Fed. Cir. 2004):

> We conclude Commerce based its zeroing practice on a reasonable interpretation of the statute. First, while the statutory definitions do not unambiguously preclude the existence of negative dumping margins, they do at a minimum allow for Commerce's construction.
>
> Second, Commerce's methodology for calculating dumping margins makes practical sense. Commerce calculates dumping duties on an entry-by-entry basis. Its practice of zeroing negative dumping margins comports with this approach. [S]uppose a foreign exporter sells the same product to two U.S. customers. The product has a normal value of $0.90, and is sold to the first customer for $1.00 and the second customer for $0.70. Calculated in accordance with [the dumping statute], the dumping margin for the first customer is zeroed (0.90 − 1.00 = −0.10 → 0) and for the second customer is 0.20 (0.90 − 0.70 = 0.20). Assuming sales of 1000 units to each customer, the first customer would not have to pay any dumping duties because it paid a price above normal value, and the second customer would have to pay $200 (1000 transactions × 0.20 dumping margin/transaction = 200) because it paid a price below normal value. This approach makes sense; it neutralizes dumped sales and has no effect on fair-value sales. [If] Commerce could not zero negative transactions, Commerce [would have] to grant the first customer a credit. Commerce could potentially owe the first customer a payment—a result clearly not contemplated by the statutory scheme.

354 F.3d at 1341.

In a later section of this Chapter, we will see that the WTO has consistently rejected the practice of zeroing as a violation of the Antidumping Agreement.

NOTES AND QUESTIONS

1. Do you believe that the U.S. practice of "zeroing" is justified? Why do the United States and the EU engage in "zeroing"?

2. *Anti-Circumvention Measures.* The United States has enacted so-called anti-circumvention measures in §781 (19 U.S.C. §1677j), an amendment added in 1988 to the 1930 Tariff Act. What is the concern with circumvention of dumping orders? A company subject to a dumping order for its products might ship the parts of the product to a third country or even to the United States, where the parts are then assembled into the final product. The company may make minor alterations to the physical characteristics of the product so that it no longer fits the definition of the product on which the anti-dumping duties are levied. Since dumping duties are normally levied against certain goods from certain named exporters or exporters from a certain country, if production is shifted to a different company or to a different country, the imports may escape the anti-dumping order. The U.S. law is designed to bring these types of situations within the scope of the anti-dumping duty order.

Congress did not want the anti-circumvention measures to interfere with real manufacturing operations in the United States. In order for the anti-circumvention measures to apply, three conditions must be met:

(1) The merchandise sold in the United States must be made from parts or components produced in the country subject to the anti-dumping duty order;

(2) The value of the parts or components imported from the country subject to the order must be "a significant portion of the total value of the [completed] merchandise"; and

(3) The process of assembly or completion in the United States must be "minor or insignificant."

If all of these conditions are met, then the product, although physically assembled in the United States, is treated as if it were a dumped import subject to anti-dumping duties.

While Congress wanted to prevent the circumvention of the anti-dumping laws, Congress did not wish to interfere with foreign investment in the United States for the purpose of setting up genuine manufacturing operations. As a result, with respect to the nature of the assembly or completion, Commerce must consider:

(1) The level of investment in the United States;
(2) The level of research and development in the United States;
(3) The nature of the production process in the United States;
(4) The extent of production facilities in the United States; and
(5) Whether the value of the processing performed in the United States represents a small portion of the value of the merchandise.

If genuine investment and genuine production occurs in the United States, then these products are treated as if they are locally produced and are the result of an attempt to circumvent the anti-dumping laws. U.S. law also takes the same approach for assembly and manufacturing operations in third countries: The test is whether the operations are genuine manufacturing or a smokescreen to avoid paying anti-dumping duties in the United States. Products manufactured in a third country as a result of genuine operations are also outside the scope of the anti-circumvention law. The WTO is silent on the validity of anti-circumvention measures, even though the United States continues to apply this law.

PROBLEM 10-8

Ultra Bright produces washing machines in Japan that are exported to the United States and the EU. In both the United States and the EU, dumping investigations have resulted in findings of dumping, and now Ultra Bright must pay punitive anti-dumping duties in addition to the ordinary tariff payable on all imports of washing machines into the United States and the EU. To stay in business and to satisfy the demand for its washing machines in both markets, Ultra Bright has organized joint ventures and constructed factories in Emporia, Kansas, and Frankfurt, Germany. Each joint venture company imports components of the washing machines from Ultra Bright in Japan and assembles the components for sale in the U.S. and EU markets.

In order to prevent circumvention of its anti-dumping duties, authorities in the EU have taken action. Under EU Regulation 2423/88 (O.J. L 209, Aug. 2, 1988), anti-dumping duties may extend to products assembled in the EU if (1) an anti-dumping order on similar products is in effect; (2) assembly in the EU is by a company related to the one subject to the anti-dumping duty; and (3) the value of imported components exceeds by 50 percent the value of all other parts and materials in the assembled product. On the basis of this regulation, the EU has levied anti-dumping duties on the assembled washing machines.

The U.S. Department of Commerce is considering what to do about the similar assembly plant located in Emporia, Kansas. It is aware that in 1990, a GATT dispute settlement panel ruled that the charges imposed by the EU regulation in question on the assembled products were internal taxes, since they were collected on products in commerce within the EU. As internal taxes, they were subject to the National Treatment principle of GATT Article III, and the panel concluded that these charges violated Article III. *See EEC—Regulation on Imports of Parts and Components*, GATT B.I.S.D. (37th Supp.) 132, Report of the GATT Panel, adopted on May 16, 1990. Since this ruling precedes the WTO Antidumping Agreement entered into in 1994, the Department of Commerce is uncertain whether this ruling would be followed in the WTO. The Antidumping Agreement is silent on the matter of circumvention because no agreement could be reached on the matter. Under §781(a), can Commerce avoid the EU's pitfall and still take action? What are the issues involved?

D.   Injury Analysis

If the Commerce Department finds that dumping exists, the International Trade Commission must find that a material injury exists before Commerce can make a final determination of dumping. The definition of material injury is "harm that is not inconsequential, immaterial or unimportant." *See* 19 U.S.C. §1677(7).

PROBLEM 10-9

The U.S. copper industry has filed a petition with the U.S. Commerce Department and the International Trade Commission seeking the imposition of anti-dumping duties against imports of copper from China. In determining whether the U.S. copper industry has suffered an injury, the ITC is examining the following considerations. Imports from China have remained steady during the first two years of the three-year period of investigation; in the third year, imports declined slightly. The U.S. copper industry has underutilized capacity and has increasing inventories of unsold products. The U.S. copper industry has also suffered financial losses in the past three years, with a sharp downturn in the past year, and has laid off a significant portion of its workforce. Demand for copper among industrial users, the largest consumers in the U.S. market, has shifted in the past several years from copper to other metals, including aluminum. The U.S. Defense Department refused to renew contracts with the industry a year ago and has shifted its sourcing of materials composed of other alloys to other U.S. industries, which are now reporting increased profits. There is some talk within the U.S. copper industry that copper imported from China was purchased by U.S. consumers in place of copper from U.S. industries.

Analyze whether you believe that the material injury requirement has been met in this case. Which factors weigh in favor of a finding? Which factors weigh against the finding? What is your overall conclusion? Consult the *Sandvik* and *Nucor* cases below.

1. Material Injury

To determine whether an industry has been materially injured, the ITC normally examines industry trends over a three-year period, ending with the initiation of the investigation. The ITC will consider a wide array of economic factors, none of which is determinative. The ITC will pay special attention to the following non-exhaustive list of factors:

- Domestic consumption
- Domestic production
- Capacity of the domestic industry and capacity utilization
- Shipments and inventories
- Employment levels
- Profitability
- Ability to raise capital
- Expenditure on research and development

The ITC will examine the interplay of these factors. If domestic consumption is rising while domestic production is falling, this is an indication that imports are replacing domestic production, and the ITC will likely find material injury. If domestic consumption is decreasing, then there is a likelihood that other factors are causing the industry's troubles, such as changing consumer tastes and obsolescence. The following cases concern the material injury requirement.

Sandvik AB v. United States
United States Court of International Trade, 1989
721 F. Supp. 1322, aff'd per curiam, 904 F.2d 46 (Fed. Cir. 1990)

CARMAN, Judge:

[The plaintiffs, Sandvik AB, AB Sandvik Steel and Sandvik Steel Company brought a petition in the federal district court to set aside determinations by the United States International Trade Commission and the International Trade Administration that imports of steel products from plaintiffs caused a material injury to the steel industry in the United States. The court confined its discussion to the material injury issue.]

INDICATORS OF MATERIAL INJURY

Plaintiffs contend that the domestic industry did not suffer sharp declines in capacity, production, shipments, employment or net sales and that the industry did not have "generally low profitability" over the period of investigation. However, the data compiled by the ITC suggest otherwise. Capacity by integrated producers declined from 21,300 short tons to 15,300 short tons between 1984 and 1986. *Id.* at 11. Production by integrated producers decreased by 11 per cent from 1984 to 1986. *Id.* Domestic shipments by integrated producers, measured by both quantity and value fell, from 8,010 short tons valued at $67.4 million in 1984 to 6,681 short tons valued at $60.2 million in 1986. *Id.* at 12. The average number of workers engaged in production of seamless stainless steel pipe fell from 407 in 1984 to 234 in 1986. *Id.* at 12, A-28. Net sales of seamless stainless steel pipe and tube declined steadily during the investigative period. *Id.* at 13. There was an increase in profitability in 1986 that was partially attributable to Babcock & Wilcox leaving the industry. *Id.*

This Court holds that the ITC's determination that the domestic seamless stainless steel pipe and tube industry suffered material injury was reasonable, supported by substantial evidence on the record and otherwise in accordance with law.

MATERIAL INJURY CAUSED BY LESS THAN FAIR VALUE IMPORTS FROM SWEDEN

In making its determination that the domestic industry was materially injured by reasons of less than fair value imports from Sweden, the ITC considered the volume of imports, the effect of imports on prices in the United States for the like product, and the impact of such imports on the relevant domestic industry, among other factors in accordance with 19 U.S.C. §1677(7)(B) (1982). The ITC found that the significant volume of seamless pipe and tube from Sweden and the high import penetration throughout the period of investigation, combined with the pattern of underselling of these imports and the revenue lost to the domestic industry, demonstrate that these LTFV imports have caused material injury to the domestic industry. SITC Pub. No. 2033 at 15.

Plaintiffs contend that the ITC's analysis was erroneous for the following reasons: (1) the ITC failed to exclude non-competing imports from its analysis of both import volume and import penetration; (2) the ITC failed to provide substantial analysis for its conclusion that plaintiffs' import volumes and market penetration were "significant"; (3) the ITC ignored evidence in concluding that plaintiffs consistently undersold domestic producers; and (4) there was no substantial evidence of lost sales or lost revenue.

IMPORT VOLUME AND IMPORT PENETRATION

Plaintiffs claim that significant volumes of their imports did not compete with domestic products and therefore should have been excluded from the analysis of import volume and import penetration. Defendant ITC argues that the ITC is directed by statute to examine injury to the domestic industry producing the like product, most specifically "the volume of imports of the merchandise which is the subject of the investigation." 19 U.S.C. §1677(7)(B)(i). Since plaintiffs' merchandise was not excluded from the like product definition, defendant ITC claims this merchandise can not be excluded from the analysis of import volume and import penetration.

This Court agrees that the ITC does not have the authority to exclude merchandise from the like product designation. *See Sprague Electric Co. v. United States,* 84 Cust. Ct. 260, 261-62, C.R.D. 80-6 (1980) (the "Commission has no authority to refine or modify the class or kind of merchandise found to be, or likely to be, sold at [less than fair value]"). The ITA controls the scope of the investigation, while the ITC determines whether there is material injury or the threat of material injury to the domestic industry producing the like product. 19 U.S.C. §§1673, 1673b(a), 1673d. This Court holds that the ITC's determination to include all of the Swedish imports in its analysis of import values was reasonable, supported by substantial evidence on the record and in accordance with law.

Plaintiffs further contend that the ITC only recited the import volumes and market shares when it had a duty to analyze the data to show the impact which the imports had on the domestic industry. Plaintiffs claim that the ITC's recitation of the figures was a defective analysis under the substantial evidence test as discussed in *USX Corp. v. United States,* 11 CIT 82, 655 F. Supp. 487 (1987). Plaintiffs contend that this faulty analysis did not prove that the subject imports were "significant" as required by 19 U.S.C. §1677(7)(C)(i).

Defendant ITC argues that the figures were analyzed and showed a record level of imports in 1984 (60 per cent higher than the previous year) and an import penetration level of 20.4 per cent in 1984, 15 per cent in 1985 and 17.9 percent in 1986. USITC Pub. No. 2033 at 13-14, A-52, A-56. Import volume declined .5 per cent from interim 1986 to interim 1987 which the ITC attributed, at least in part, to the instant investigation. *Id.* at 14.

In *USX,* a challenge to a final negative antidumping duty determination, the Court found the ITC's analysis did not meet the substantial evidence test because although the ITC stated that levels of market penetration remained low and stable, the Commission failed to discuss the significance of this trend or its relationship to the other facts resulting from the investigation. *USX,* 655 F. Supp. at 490. Defendant notes that the instant investigation revealed (along with the import penetration of 15 to 20 percent) a consistent pattern of underselling, declining prices in the United States market and lost revenues. USITC Pub. No. 2033 at 15. Defendant also distinguishes the instant case from *USX* by noting that the instant case concerns import penetration of 15 to 20 percent, while *USX* involved import penetration of approximately only one percent. *Id*. 655 F. Supp. at 489.

This Court agrees that in the instant case, the ITC did not rely on one single factor or "isolated tidbits of data which suggest a result contrary to the clear weight of the evidence" as the Court found in *USX*. *Id*. This Court holds that the ITC's analysis of the impact which import volumes and market shares had on the domestic industry indicated that the volume was significant and that this analysis was reasonable, supported by substantial evidence on the record and otherwise in accordance with law.

UNDERSELLING OF DOMESTIC PRODUCERS

Plaintiffs claim that the ITC relied on seven isolated instances of underselling while ignoring pricing data for products which did not show consistent underselling. These seven instances occurred when lower-priced Sandvik mechanical tubing was purchased instead of a competing domestic product and the purchasers gave plaintiffs' lower prices as one reason, but in most cases not the only reason, for selecting plaintiffs' product. In addition, plaintiffs state that they sometimes undersell domestic products in order to offset the disadvantage they face because of the longer lead time necessitated by shipping from Sweden.

Plaintiffs contend further that there were significant instances of overselling by Sandvik throughout the period of investigation for both hot and cold rolled pipe. Plaintiffs claim that in reality, the investigation revealed a pattern of selling and underselling which the ITC has found in the past not to meet the statutory standard of significant price undercutting. *See Copperweld Corp.*, 682 F. Supp. at 566.

Defendant ITC and defendant-intervenors cite as evidence of underselling: (1) data on bids for seamless SSHPs; (2) information in purchasers' questionnaires and information on lost sales; and (3) quarterly price comparisons.

The data on bids show that seven of the eleven orders of seamless SSHPs were awarded to plaintiffs and that the price of these seven orders was from eight to fifteen per cent below the quoted domestic price. USITC Pub. No. 2033 at 14-15. Plaintiffs claim the data were not supported by substantial evidence because the products were not representative of the range of products made by them, the purchasers were not representative of all domestic purchasers and only the two largest bids were included in the data. Defendant ITC contends that its record demonstrates that it sought pricing data on a wide range of products, purchasers and imported shipments. ITC C. 17 at A-90. Defendant ITC further notes that it is not required to meet "some ambiguous level of scientific reliability" in compiling its record. *Alberta Pork Producers' Mktg. Bd. v. United States*, 11 CIT 563, 669 F. Supp. 445, 463 (1987).

The purchasing questionnaires and lost sales information indicate that plaintiffs' lower prices was an important factor in purchasers' selections. USITC Pub. No. 2033 at A-71-72, A-80-81. Quarterly price comparisons during January 1984 to June 1987 show that "prices of seamless products 2 and 3 (mechanical tubing) . . . generally fell, prices for seamless product 1 (pipe) and seamless product 4 (redraw hollows) initially increased before declining . . ." USITC Pub. No. 2033 at A-65. Plaintiffs contend that pricing information was not based upon representative sales of Sandvik products in the United States although price comparisons were made with specific products.

The Court notes that the ITC is within its discretion in making a reasonable interpretation of the facts it uncovers in an investigation. *Copperweld*, 682 F. Supp. at 577. This Court holds that the ITC's interpretation of data regarding the under-selling of seamless SSHPs was reasonable, supported by substantial evidence on the record and otherwise in accordance with law.

LOST SALES OR LOST REVENUE

Plaintiffs claim the ITC is unable to confirm any instances of lost sales attributable to lower priced Sandvik products. Defendant-intervenors contend that the bid information noted *supra* was evidence of head-to-head competition between plaintiffs and the domestic industry thus demonstrating lost sales. There was also an unconfirmed allegation of lost sales along with an indication of increased purchases from Sweden. USITC Pub. No. 2033 at A-80.

The ITC verified a specific instance of lost revenue where United States producers cut their prices to compete with the subject merchandise. *Id.* at A-82. In addition, certain purchasers stated that domestic producers had to lower the price of their merchandise to compete with the delivered prices of Swedish pipe and tube. *Id.* at A-80, A-82-83.

This Court holds that the ITC's interpretation of data regarding lost sales or lost revenues was reasonable, supported by substantial evidence on the record and otherwise in accordance with law.

2. Causation

In addition to finding a material injury, the ITC must also find that the injury was caused by the dumped imports. In the past, the practice of the ITC has been to first look at whether the domestic industry has suffered an injury and then to determine causation. Since the 1990s, the common approach has been an integrated one of examining causation and injury together. The ITC looks to various factors under the statutory guidelines to determine causation. Among other factors, the ITC considers

(1) Whether the volume of imports, or the increase in volume, is significant during the three-year period of investigation;

(2) Whether the imported products have been underselling the domestic products, i.e., whether the imports have been sold at lower prices;

(3) Whether domestic prices have been either depressed or prevented from increasing in a reasonable economic manner.

If imports have been increasing and prices in the domestic industry have been decreasing or growth in domestic prices has been suppressed, the ITC is more likely to find causation. The standard of causation is rather limited. The ITC need not weigh the impact of other causes of injury. In addition, the imports need not be the only cause of injury or the most significant cause of injury. The ITC need only find that imports are a cause of injury. The ITC is authorized to find causation even if imports are the least significant cause of injury. *See, e.g., Oil Country Tubular Goods from Israel*, USITC Pub. 1840, Inv. Nos. 701-TA-217 and 731-TA-318 (Apr. 1986).

Nucor Corporation v. United States
United States Court of Appeals, Federal Circuit, 2005
414 F.3d 1331

BRYSON, Circuit Judge.

The appellants, United States Steel Corporation and Nucor Corporation, are domestic steel producers. Along with other domestic producers, they petitioned the International Trade Commission to investigate imports of cold-rolled steel products to determine if those imports were causing material injury to the domestic steel industry. *See* 19 U.S.C. §§1671d(b)(1), 1673d(b)(1). Upon completion of its investigations, the Commission issued final determinations that the domestic steel industry was not materially injured by reason of the imports. The appellants and other domestic producers filed an action in the Court of International Trade challenging the Commission's negative material injury determinations. The Court of International Trade sustained the Commission's determinations. *Nucor Corp. v. United States*, 318 F.Supp.2d 1207 (Ct. Int'l Trade 2004). U.S. Steel and Nucor appeal. We affirm.

I.

Section 201 of the Trade Act of 1974, 19 U.S.C. §2251(a), authorizes the President to take appropriate action to protect domestic industries from substantial injury due to increased quantities of imports. In June 2001, the President requested that the Commission conduct a section 201 investigation of steel products imported between January 1997 and June 2001. Following its investigation, the Commission determined that cold-rolled steel products "were being imported into the United States in such increased quantities as to be a substantial cause of serious injury to the domestic industry" and recommended that safeguard tariffs be imposed on steel products. Consequently, in March 2002 the President imposed safeguard tariffs on steel products, including cold-rolled steel products, of 30 percent for the first year, 24 percent for the second year, and 18 percent for the third year.

In September 2001, a number of domestic steel producers petitioned the Commission to conduct the antidumping and countervailing duty investigations that gave rise to this case.

The Commission's responsibility in an antidumping or countervailing duty investigation is to determine if a domestic industry is materially injured or threatened with material injury by reason of imports. The Commission issued final determinations on all of the subject investigations in September and November 2002. In those determinations, the Commission found that the "Section 201 investigation and the President's remedy fundamentally altered the U.S. market for many steel products, including cold-rolled steel." The Commission found that imports of those products declined sharply and that domestic prices increased significantly in the period after the imposition of the section 201 tariffs. The Commission further reported that, according to purchasers, the reduction in imports due to the section 201 tariffs had led to "higher prices, supply shortages, and some broken or renegotiated contracts." Based on the results of its investigation, the Commission concluded that the section 201 relief was the principal reason for the sharp decline in imports near the end of the investigation period. The Commission further found that, as of the conclusion of the antidumping and countervailing duty proceedings, "the domestic cold-rolled steel products industry is neither materially injured nor threatened with material injury by reason of subject imports." Because the Commission determined that the domestic industry was not suffering present material injury or a threat of material injury as a result of the subject imports, no antidumping or countervailing duties were imposed.

II.

U.S. Steel and Nucor argue that the Commission erred by failing to consider the effects of products imported prior to the imposition of section 201 tariffs when it determined that the domestic industry was not suffering current material injury because of imports. In particular, they contend that the requirement in 19 U.S.C. §§1671d(b)(1) and 1673d(b)(1) that the Commission determine whether the domestic industry is suffering material injury "by reason of imports" mandated that the Commission consider the effects of imports throughout the period of investigation and not confine its consideration to the effects of current imports. Because, in the appellants' view, the Commission based its material injury determinations solely on current imports, the appellants argue that the Commission's material injury determination was legally flawed.

Sections 1671d(b)(1) and 1673d(b)(1) state that the Commission must determine whether a domestic industry "is materially injured . . . by reason of imports." They do not specify how the Commission should weigh imports early in the period of investigation as compared to imports closer to the date of decision, nor do they provide any guidance as to the considerations that should influence the weight the Commission assigns to data from different portions of the investigation period. Because the statutes are silent on those issues, and because the Commission, together with the Commerce Department, is charged with the responsibility of administering the antidumping and countervailing duty statutes, the Commission's construction of those statutes is entitled to deference under the principles of *Chevron U.S.A. Inc. v. Natural Res. Def. Council, Inc.*, 467 U.S. 837, 104 S.Ct. 2778, 81 L.Ed.2d 694 (1984).

We agree with the trial court that it was reasonable for the Commission to interpret the statutory language to permit it to accord different weight to imports during different portions of the period of investigation depending on the facts of each case. In particular, the Commission acted reasonably in construing the statutory language to permit it to focus on the most recent imports and pricing data. That construction is reasonable for several reasons. First, the purpose of antidumping and countervailing duty laws is remedial, not punitive or retaliatory and current data typically is the most pertinent in determining whether remedial measures are necessary. Second, section 1677(7)(B)(i) provides that, in making the material injury determination required by sections 1671d(b)(1) and 1673d(b) (1), the Commission shall consider, *inter alia*, the effects of the subject imports on domestic producers. Section 1677(7)(C)(iii) in turn requires the Commission, in determining the impact of the subject imports on domestic producers, to "evaluate all relevant economic factors which have a bearing on the state of the industry in the United States." As the trial court explained, in most cases the most recent imports will have the greatest relevance to the current state of the domestic industry. Third, the Commission has broad discretion with respect to the period of investigation that it selects for purposes of making a material injury determination. As the Court of International Trade has explained, because the statute "does not expressly command the Commission to examine a particular period of time . . . the Commission has discretion to examine a period that most reasonably allows it to determine whether a domestic industry is injured by [less than fair value] imports." *Kenda Rubber Indus. Co. v. United States*, 630 F.Supp. 354, 359 (Ct. Int'l Trade 1986). Since the Commission has broad discretion to choose the most appropriate period of time for its investigation, it would be nonsensical to hold that once the Commission has chosen an investigation period, it is required to give equal weight to imports throughout the period it has selected. For these reasons, both this court and the Court of International Trade have typically upheld the Commission's exercise of its discretion to focus on imports during particular portions of the investigation period, especially imports during the most recent portion of that period.

In this case, the fact that section 201 tariffs were imposed during the period of investigation made the recent data far more probative than earlier data as to whether the industry was suffering present material injury as a result of imports. The Commission found that the section 201 relief "was having a major impact in the U.S. market for cold-rolled steel and was the overwhelming factor in the sharp decline in subject imports during the most recent period examined." Substantial evidence in the record supports that finding, and the appellants do not challenge the trial court's determination in that regard. Because the imposition of section 201 tariffs had such a dramatic impact on the industry, it was reasonable for the Commission to conclude that the most recent data was the most reliable indicator of whether the industry was suffering material injury as a result of the subject imports and whether the imposition of additional duties would be consistent with the remedial purposes of the antidumping and countervailing duty laws.

III.

Nucor argues that the Commission failed to make the statutorily required determination regarding the effect of underselling of domestic products by importers. The statute requires that in considering the effect of imports on prices,

> the Commission shall consider whether—
> (I) there has been significant price underselling by the imported merchandise as compared with the price of domestic like products of the United States, and
> (II) the effect of imports of such merchandise otherwise depresses prices to a significant degree or prevents price increases, which otherwise would have occurred, to a significant degree.

19 U.S.C. §1677(7)(C)(ii).

Nucor contends that the Commission did not properly assess the significance of underselling because it "failed to provide either a concrete conclusion regarding the significance of underselling or any meaningful discussion of several key components required for such a conclusion." In particular, Nucor objects that the Commission never made a determination as to whether the level of underselling during the period of investigation was significant and that it failed to make separate determinations as to underselling and the effect of imports in depressing prices or preventing price increases. Because the Commission did not make separate findings with respect to those issues, Nucor argues that the decision cannot be sustained.

The Commission complied with the statutory requirement that it consider whether there had been underselling during the investigation period and whether that underselling was significant. The Commission found that the underselling margins of 1999 had essentially disappeared by 2002. In particular, the Commission found that the average margin of underselling went from 9.1 percent in 1999 to an average overselling margin of 4.0 percent in 2002, and that for sales to end users the average underselling went from 24.8 percent in 1999 to 1.5 percent in 2002. It is true, as Nucor contends, that the Commission did not state in so many words that the volume of underselling was an insignificant factor in evaluating whether the effect of imports on prices had led to present material injury to the domestic industry. Nonetheless, the trial court found that to be the plain import of the Commission's analysis, and we agree.

AFFIRMED.

NOTES AND QUESTIONS

1. Be sure that you see that in *Nucor*, the United States had already imposed anti-dumping duties on steel imports in 1998 and then imposed additional tariffs in the form of safeguards. We have already studied the safeguards in Chapter 8. The U.S. steel industry wanted the imposition of additional anti-dumping duties and countervailing duties on top of the safeguards that were themselves imposed on top of anti-dumping duties. The U.S. Steel industry wanted three different remedies imposed on imports of steel. Was the ITC correct in considering the impact of the Section 201 relief? Since dumping involves unfair trade, why is the Section 201 impact relevant?

2. *Domestic Industry and Like Products.* The investigation of material injury requires the identification of a domestic industry. The term "industry" is defined merely as "the producers as a whole of a domestic like product." 19 U.S.C. §1677(4)(A). Moreover, in anti-dumping cases there are no strict tests for determining a "like product." In some cases, like products may include substantially similar articles such as components or sub-assemblies. *See, e.g., Cellular Mobile Telephones and Subassemblies from Japan*, USITC, final determination, 50 Fed. Reg. 45447-01 (1985); *High Capacity Pagers from Japan*, USITC Pub. 1410, Inv. No. 731-TA-102 (Oct. 1983). In other cases the term "like product" is very narrowly defined. *See, e.g., Certain Red Raspberries from Canada*, USITC Pub. 1707, Inv. No. 731-TA-196 (June 1985) (defining the "like product" as red raspberries packed in bulk containers for sale to manufacturers, excluding all other types of fresh market and retail packed red raspberries). Because the U.S. domestic industry is defined in terms of like products, there is very little precision in defining such an industry. *See* Diane P. Wood, *"Unfair" Trade Injury: A Competition Based Approach*, 41 Stan. L Rev. 1153, 1175-1179 (1989). The imprecision of the definitions of "like product" and "domestic industry" in a dumping case contrasts sharply with the precision of such inquiries in an antitrust case, where considerations such as cross-elasticity of demand will be carefully analyzed in determining like products and in defining the industry producing the competitive products. Antitrust cases carefully consider the collective, as well as the independent, market power of the firms involved. *See* Wood, *supra*, at 1178-1179.

E.   International Law Discipline on Anti-Dumping Proceedings: The WTO Antidumping Agreement

Read GATT Article VI.

Read the WTO Agreement on the Implementation of Article VI of the General Agreement on Tariffs and Trade 1994 (the Antidumping Agreement).

The rules of the WTO now impose detailed standards on the conduct of dumping investigations and the imposition of anti-dumping duties. GATT Article VI provides:

> The contracting parties recognize that dumping, by which products of one country are introduced into the commerce of another country at less than the normal value of the products, is to be condemned if it causes or threatens material injury to an established industry in the territory of a contracting party or materially retards the establishment of a domestic industry.

Article VI posits the following requirements for a determination of dumping: (1) The export price must be lower than the normal value of the products; (2) the imported products must cause or threaten to cause material injury to a domestic industry or materially retard the establishment of a domestic industry; and (3) there must be a causal relationship between the dumping and the injury. These requirements, in their broad outline, are similar to U.S. law.

Article VI of the GATT is amplified by the Antidumping Agreement, which addresses virtually all of the substantive and procedural issues that may come up in an anti-dumping case. However, the basic concepts and the language in the Antidumping Agreement differ in certain respects from many national anti-dumping laws. Thus, it will come as no surprise that there have been more GATT and WTO disputes over dumping than with regard to any other single trade topic.

The materials below focus on challenges to the anti-dumping laws of the United States and the EU. The United States and the EU have used their anti-dumping laws aggressively to combat perceived unfair trade practices. Other WTO members have brought several challenges to what they believe is overzealous enforcement.

1.   WTO Challenges to U.S. Anti-Dumping Law: Policy Issues

We begin with WTO challenges to U.S. law raising basic issues of jurisdiction: Does the WTO have authority to strike down domestic laws found to be inconsistent with the Antidumping Agreement?

PROBLEM 10-10

Congress is considering passing a new law targeting countries, such as China, that persistently dump products in the U.S. market. The law provides a penalty for any country found to be engaged in a pattern of dumping; e.g., when more than three different products are being dumped within a single calendar year. In this case, all dumped imports will be subject to a 100 percent increase in anti-dumping duties. The purpose of this law is to deter a pattern of dumping. Is this new law consistent with the WTO?

United States—Anti-Dumping Act of 1916
Report of the Appellate Body, adopted on September 26, 2000
WT/DS136, 162/AB/R

[In this case, the Appellate Body struck down a venerable U.S. anti-dumping statute, the Anti-Dumping Act of 1916 (erstwhile 15 U.S.C. §72), which imposed civil and criminal penalties on importers guilty of dumping "with the intent of destroying or injuring an industry in the United States." Injured private parties were allowed to recover treble damages in such cases. The Act had never been applied at the time that the WTO challenge was brought, but it could have been used by the U.S. government to combat predatory pricing and by private parties to sue foreign exporters and domestic importers of competing products. The United States based its defense of the Act on objecting to the WTO's jurisdiction to consider claims against the law "as such." The Appellate Body disagreed.]

76. Our reading of Article 17 as allowing Members to bring claims against anti-dumping legislation as such is supported by Article 18.4 of the *Anti-Dumping Agreement*.

77. Article 18.4 of the *Anti-Dumping Agreement* states:

> Each Member shall take all necessary steps, of a general or particular character, to ensure, not later than the date of entry into force of the WTO Agreement for it, the conformity of its laws, regulations and administrative procedures with the provisions of this Agreement as they may apply for the Member in question.

78. Article 18.4 imposes an affirmative obligation on each Member to bring its legislation into conformity with the provisions of the *Anti-Dumping Agreement* not later than the date of entry into force of the *WTO Agreement* for that Member. Nothing in Article 18.4 or elsewhere in the *Anti-Dumping Agreement* excludes the obligation set out in Article 18.4 from the scope of matters that may be submitted to dispute settlement.

79. If a Member could not bring a claim of inconsistency under the *Anti-Dumping Agreement* against legislation as such until one of the three anti-dumping measures specified in Article 17.4 had been adopted and was also challenged, then examination of the consistency with Article 18.4 of anti-dumping legislation as such would be deferred, and the effectiveness of Article 18.4 would be diminished.

80. Furthermore, we note that Article 18.1 of the *Anti-Dumping Agreement* states:

> No specific action against dumping of exports from another Member can be taken except in accordance with the provisions of GATT 1994, as interpreted by this Agreement.

81. Article 18.1 contains a prohibition on "specific action against dumping" when such action is not taken in accordance with the provisions of the GATT 1994, as interpreted by the *Anti-Dumping Agreement*. Specific action against dumping could

take a wide variety of forms. If specific action against dumping is taken in a form other than a form authorized under Article VI of the GATT 1994, as interpreted by the *Anti-Dumping Agreement*, such action will violate Article 18.1. We find nothing, however, in Article 18.1 or elsewhere in the *Anti-Dumping Agreement*, to suggest that the consistency of such action with Article 18.1 may only be challenged when one of the three measures [e.g., anti-dumping duties, provisional anti-dumping duties, price undertakings, or suspension agreements] specified in Article 17.4 has been adopted. Indeed, such an interpretation must be wrong since it implies that, if a Member's legislation provides for a response to dumping that does *not* consist of one of the three measures listed in Article 17.4, then it would be impossible to test the consistency of that legislation, and of particular responses thereunder, with Article 18.1 of the *Anti-Dumping Agreement*.

82. Therefore, we consider that Articles 18.1 and 18.4 support our conclusion that a Member may challenge the consistency of legislation as such with the provisions of the *Anti-Dumping Agreement*.

[On the merits, the Appellate Body stated as follows:]

118. Article VI of the GATT 1994 must be read together with the provisions of the *Anti-Dumping Agreement*. Article 1 of that Agreement provides:

> An anti-dumping measure shall be applied only under the circumstances provided for in Article VI of GATT 1994 and pursuant to investigations initiated and conducted in accordance with the provisions of this Agreement. The following provisions govern the application of Article VI of GATT 1994 in so far as action is taken under anti-dumping legislation or regulations.

121. We consider that the scope of application of Article VI is clarified, in particular, by Article 18.1 of the *Anti-Dumping Agreement*. Article 18.1 states:

> No *specific action against dumping* of exports from another Member can be taken except in accordance with the provisions of GATT 1994, as interpreted by this Agreement. (emphasis added)

122. In our view, the ordinary meaning of the phrase "specific action against dumping" of exports within the meaning of Article 18.1 is action that is taken in response to situations presenting the constituent elements of "dumping." "Specific action against dumping" of exports must, at a minimum, encompass action that may be taken *only* when the constituent elements of "dumping" are present. Since intent is not a constituent element of "dumping," the *intent* with which action against dumping is taken is not relevant to the determination of whether such action is "specific action against dumping" of exports within the meaning of Article 18.1 of the *Anti-Dumping Agreement*.

137. As we have concluded above, Article VI of the GATT 1994 and the *Anti-Dumping Agreement* apply to "specific action against dumping." Article VI, and, in particular, Article VI:2, read in conjunction with the *Anti-Dumping Agreement*, limit the permissible responses to dumping to definitive anti-dumping duties, provisional measures and price undertakings. Therefore, the 1916 Act is inconsistent with Article VI:2 and the *Anti-Dumping Agreement* to the extent that it provides for "specific action against dumping" in the form of civil and criminal proceedings and penalties.

NOTES AND QUESTIONS

1. In response to the *U.S.—Anti-Dumping Act of 1916* case, the United States repealed the 1916 Act in 2004.

2. In *United States—Continued Dumping and Subsidy Offset Act of 2000*, WT/DS217, 234/AB/R, Report of the Appellate Body, adopted on January 27, 2003, the Appellate Body similarly ruled that the U.S. Continued Dumping and Subsidy Act of 2000 (CDSOA), commonly called the "Offset Act" or the "Byrd Amendment," was inconsistent with GATT Article VI and the Antidumping Agreement. The CDSOA provided that "[d]uties assessed pursuant to a countervailing duty order, an anti-dumping order, or a finding under the Antidumping Act of 1921 shall be distributed on an annual basis to the affected domestic producers for qualifying expenditures. Such distribution shall be known as 'the continued dumping and subsidy offset.'" *Id.* at 242, footnote 170. Thus, under the CDSOA, petitioners in the specified proceedings, and interested parties that supported the anti-dumping petition, would be eligible to receive the duties assessed.

This law was challenged by many WTO members, led by the EC, Japan, and Brazil. The Appellate Body ruling invoked not only the Antidumping Agreement but also the Agreement on Subsidies and Countervailing Measures (SCM Agreement), which we cover in a later part of this Chapter. The Appellate Body found (¶274) that the CDSOA was a specific action related to a dumping or subsidy within the meaning of Article 18.1 of the Antidumping Agreement and Article 32.1 of SCM Agreement. Under Article VI of the GATT, a WTO member is entitled to take the following responses to dumping: definitive anti-dumping duties, preliminary anti-dumping duties, and price undertakings. The SCM Agreement recognizes four responses to a countervailable subsidy: definitive countervailing duties, preliminary countervailing duties, price undertakings, and multilaterally sanctioned countermeasures under the dispute settlement system. The measures contained in the CDSOA did not fall under all of these allowable measures and was therefore found to be inconsistent with the WTO agreements.

In response to the Appellate Body's ruling, on February 8, 2006, President Bush signed the Deficit Reduction Act of 2005, repealing the CDSOA. However, the repeal legislation states that "[a]ll duties on entries of goods made and filed before October 1, 2007 shall be distributed [under the CDSOA]" Pub. L. No. 109-171 Section 1675c. The U.S. Department of Commerce reports that only a few U.S. companies have received substantial CDSOA monies; 80 percent of the disbursements were paid to thirty-nine companies. Is such legislation good policy? For a post-repeal case in which a domestic producer sued for its share of a distribution of anti-dumping duties, and a decision upholding the constitutionality of the Byrd Amendment (Judge Linn dissenting), see *SKF USA v. United States Customs and Border Protection*, 556 F.3d 1337 (Fed. Cir. 2009).

3. Article 9(5) of the European Union's Basic Anti-Dumping Regulation (Council Regulation (EC) No. 384/96, as amended by Council Regulation (EC) No. 1225/2009) states as follows:

An anti-dumping duty shall be imposed in the appropriate amount in each case, on a non-discriminatory basis on imports of a product from all sources found to be dumped and causing injury, except for imports from those sources from which undertakings . . . have been accepted. The Regulation imposing the duty shall specify the duty for each supplier or, if that is impracticable, and in general . . . [in the case of non-market economies] on the supplying country concerned.

Under this Regulation, EU authorities enforced an anti-dumping order on a countrywide basis in several cases involving Chinese imports, on the grounds that China is an NME. The EU Regulation provided that, as a general rule, countrywide anti-dumping orders can be imposed in the case of imports from NMEs unless certain criteria were met for individual treatment. In *European Communities—Definitive Anti-Dumping Measures on Certain Iron or Steel Fasteners from China*, WT/DS397/AB/R, Report of the Appellate Body, adopted on July 28, 2011, although the EU granted requests for individual treatment from all the Chinese companies concerned, China challenged the EU Regulation "as such" as inconsistent with the WTO Antidumping Agreement. The Appellate Body, considering this issue, ruled (¶¶367-370) that the EU presumption in favor of countrywide treatment in cases involving an NME was inconsistent with Articles 6.10 and 9.2 of the WTO Antidumping Agreement, which in fact calls for a presumption in favor of individual treatment. The Appellate Body further ruled that the tests employed by the EU to determine the difference between individual and countrywide treatment in anti-dumping cases were inconsistent with both articles. The tests used by the EU did not sufficiently relate to the structural relationship between the company accused and the state. Under Articles 6.10 and 9.2, to treat the state as the single exporter it is necessary to make findings concerning (1) the existence of structural links between exporters; (2) the existence of corporate and structural links between the state and exporters; and (3) the existence of control or material influence by the state.

4. A feature of EU anti-dumping law is the application of the so-called "lesser duty rule," Article 9.1 of the WTO Antidumping Agreement, which states that the anti-dumping duty can be less than the margin of dumping if adequate to remove the injury to the domestic industry. In *European Union—Anti-Dumping Measures on Certain Footwear from China*, WT/DS405/R, Report of the Panel, adopted on February 22, 2012, China challenged an EU anti-dumping order on the grounds that the EU applied the lesser duty rule on imports from China at a rate higher than the rate of lesser duties established on imports from Vietnam. The panel rejected this challenge, stating (¶7.924) that "Article 9.1 says nothing about how the amount of the lesser duty should be established," suggesting that there is no lower limit on the amount of duty that a member may impose under the rule. The panel also rejected China's argument of discriminatory treatment based upon Article 9.2, stating (¶¶7.930-7.931) that China's argument does not state a claim that falls within the scope of Article 9.2, and that there is no dispute that the EU did collect some duties from all sources. Do you agree with this ruling?

2.   *Procedural Aspects Under the WTO Rules*

In making a determination of whether dumping exists, Commerce will need to compare normal value with the export price. Much of the information necessary for determining the normal value must be obtained through the foreign manufacturer. Commerce will issue detailed questionnaires to the foreign manufacturers asking for information about its pricing and costs structure.

Commerce will verify the information in the questionnaire by sending a team of officials to visit the foreign company on-site to check the answers in the questionnaire against the actual records of the foreign company. The verification process usually takes one to two weeks and involves "spot" checks, where Commerce will ask for actual company records of isolated transactions or specific information reported in the questionnaire. If the verification confirms the accuracy of the information, Commerce is likely to assume that the other information in the questionnaire is accurate as well. If the verification process finds discrepancies, then Commerce may become very suspicious about the accuracy of the other information in the questionnaire.

Providing information in the questionnaire and cooperating in a verification process can be burdensome to the foreign manufacturer. To ensure the foreign manufacturer's cooperation, Commerce has a very powerful tool at its disposal. If the foreign producer fails to provide information or fails to provide complete information, or if the verification process reveals any information to be false, misleading, or incomplete, Commerce will make its determinations on the basis of the "facts available," which are often based on the allegations in the petition filed by the U.S. industry. Of course, the petitioners will present information in the light least favorable to the foreign manufacturer.

Article 6.7 of the WTO Antidumping Agreement reflects U.S. practice by allowing a member to punish a foreign manufacturer that fails to provide information or impedes an investigation by making determinations on the basis of "facts available." The interpretation of Article 6.7 was involved in the following case.

United States—Anti-Dumping Measures on Certain Hot-Rolled Steel Products from Japan
Report of the Appellate Body, adopted on August 23, 2001
WT/DS184/AB/R

[In this case, the Appellate Body addressed the issue of whether the U.S. Department of Commerce (USDOC) violated the Antidumping Agreement in its procedures for investigations of dumping. The USDOC sanctioned two Japanese companies for failing to provide the requested information by making adverse findings on the basis of "facts available." Japan challenged these practices of the USDOC with regard to the two companies under investigation as inconsistent with the Antidumping Agreement. The Appellate Body ruled as follows:]

A. APPLICATION OF FACTS AVAILABLE TO NSC AND NKK

64. USDOC individually investigated three Japanese exporters of hot-rolled steel: NSC, NKK and Kawasaki Steel Corporation ("KSC"). USDOC requested, in its original questionnaire, that the investigated Japanese exporters provide a weight conversion factor for sales made on a so-called theoretical weight basis, so that USDOC could arrive at a single unit of measurement for all transactions. This would allow USDOC to calculate an overall dumping margin for each company.

65. Although both NSC and NKK made a small number of sales on a theoretical weight basis during the period of investigation, neither company provided a weight conversion factor in its questionnaire responses. NSC explained that it had no way of calculating a weight conversion factor, because it did not know the actual weight of the steel products sold on a theoretical weight basis. NKK stated that it was "impracticable or impossible" to calculate the requested

weight conversion factor. However, before the Panel, the United States argued that, before stating that it was "impossible" to provide a weight conversion factor, NSC and NKK both attempted, in their responses to the initial questionnaires, to avoid providing the factor by stating that it was "unnecessary" to provide this information.

66. NSC and NKK both submitted their questionnaire responses, without the weight conversion factors, by the applicable deadlines of 21 December 1998 (original questionnaire) and 25 January 1999 (supplemental questionnaire). In all, the two companies were given 87 days to respond to the questionnaires.

67. In its preliminary dumping determination, issued on 19 February 1999, USDOC applied "facts available" to the small number of NSC and NKK transactions made on a theoretical weight basis because the actual weight conversion factor had not been submitted. As USDOC chose "adverse" facts available, this led to larger dumping margins for NSC and NKK than would have been the case if the weight conversion factors subsequently submitted by those companies had been used.

68. NSC submitted a weight conversion factor on 23 February 1999, 14 days before verification. While preparing for verification, NSC had discovered that information regarding the actual weight of products sold on a theoretical weight basis did, in fact, exist and was kept in a database at a production facility in the south-west of Japan, which is separate from the main sales database, maintained at its Tokyo headquarters. On the same day, and nine days before verification, NKK also submitted a weight conversion factor. According to the Panel, in reviewing USDOC's preliminary determination, NKK discovered that USDOC had accepted KSC's "best estimate" as a surrogate for an actual weight conversion factor. NKK, thereupon, submitted its own "best estimate" weight conversion factor, based on the same method used by KSC.

69. Shortly after the weight conversion factors had been provided, the petitioners submitted letters requesting USDOC to reject the weight conversion factors submitted by NSC and NKK. USDOC conducted verifications during the week of 8 March 1999 at NSC's and NKK's respective Tokyo headquarters. USDOC did not verify the weight conversion factor submitted by NSC. According to the Panel, USDOC verified NKK's weight conversion factor. On 12 April and 15 April 1999, respectively, USDOC wrote to NSC and NKK informing them that the weight conversion factors submitted had been rejected as untimely.

72. We begin with Article 6.1.1, which provides:

> Exporters or foreign producers receiving questionnaires used in an anti-dumping investigation shall be given at least 30 days for reply. Due consideration should be given to any request for an extension of the 30-day period and, upon cause shown, such an extension should be granted whenever practicable.

74. While the United States stresses the significance of the *first* sentence of Article 6.1.1, we believe that importance must also be attached to the *second* sentence of that provision. According to the express wording of the second sentence of Article 6.1.1, investigating authorities must extend the time-limit for responses to questionnaires "upon *cause shown*", where granting such an extension is "*practicable*" (emphasis added). This second sentence, therefore, indicates that the time-limits imposed by investigating authorities for responses to questionnaires are *not* necessarily absolute and immutable.

75. In sum, Article 6.1.1 establishes that investigating authorities may impose time-limits for questionnaire responses, and that in appropriate circumstances these time-limits must be extended. However, Article 6.1.1 does not, on its own, resolve the issue of when investigating authorities are entitled to *reject* information submitted, and instead resort to facts available, as USDOC did in this case. We consider that this issue is to be resolved by reading Article 6.1.1 together with Article 6.8 of the *Anti-Dumping Agreement*, and Annex II of that Agreement, which is incorporated by reference into Article 6.8.

76. Article 6.8 of the *Anti-Dumping Agreement* provides:

> In cases in which any interested party refuses access to, or otherwise does not provide, necessary information within a reasonable period or significantly impedes the investigation, preliminary and final determinations, affirmative or negative, may be made on the basis of the facts available. The provisions of Annex II shall be observed in the application of this paragraph.

77. Article 6.8 identifies the circumstances in which investigating authorities may overcome a lack of information, in the responses of the interested parties, by using "facts" which are otherwise "available" to the investigating authorities. According to Article 6.8, where the interested parties do not "significantly impede" the investigation, recourse may be had to facts available only if an interested party fails to submit necessary information "within a reasonable period". Thus, if information is, in fact, supplied "within a reasonable period", the investigating authorities *cannot* use facts available, but must use the information submitted by the interested party.

78. Article 6.8 requires that the provisions of Annex II of the *Anti-Dumping Agreement* be observed in the use of facts available. Paragraph 1 of Annex II provides, in relevant part, that:

> The authorities should also ensure that the party is aware that if information is *not* supplied *within a reasonable time*, the authorities will be free to make determinations on the basis of the facts available . . . (emphasis added)

84. Our interpretation of these provisions raises a further interpretive question, namely the meaning of a "reasonable period" under Article 6.8 of the *Anti-Dumping Agreement* and a "reasonable time" under paragraph 1 of Annex II. The word "reasonable" implies a degree of flexibility that involves consideration of all of the circumstances of a particular case. What is "reasonable" in one set of circumstances may prove to be less than "reasonable" in different circumstances. This suggests that what constitutes a reasonable period or a reasonable time, under Article 6.8 and Annex II of the *Anti-Dumping Agreement*, should be defined on a case-by-case basis, in the light of the specific circumstances of each investigation.

85. In sum, a "reasonable period" must be interpreted consistently with the notions of flexibility and balance that are inherent in the concept of "reasonableness", and in a manner that allows for account to be taken of the particular circumstances of each case. In considering whether information is submitted within a reasonable period of time, investigating authorities should consider, in the context of a particular case, factors such as: (i) the nature and quantity of the information submitted; (ii) the difficulties encountered by an investigated exporter in obtaining the information; (iii) the verifiability of the information and the ease with

which it can be used by the investigating authorities in making their determination; (iv) whether other interested parties are likely to be prejudiced if the information is used; (v) whether acceptance of the information would compromise the ability of the investigating authorities to conduct the investigation expeditiously; and (vi) the numbers of days by which the investigated exporter missed the applicable time-limit.

88. The approach taken by the United States in this case excludes the very *possibility*, recognized by Articles 6.1.1 and 6.8 and Annex II of the *Anti-Dumping Agreement*, that USDOC might be required, by these provisions, to extend the time-limits and accept the information submitted, as requested by NSC and NKK.

B. APPLICATION OF ADVERSE FACTS AVAILABLE TO KSC

91. During the period of investigation, KSC made a significant proportion of its export sales to the United States to California Steel Industries Inc. ("CSI"), a joint venture company which is owned 50 percent by KSC and 50 percent by a Brazilian company, Companhia Vale de Rio Doce ("CVRD"). In the proceedings before USDOC, CSI participated as one of the group of petitioners for the United States' hot-rolled steel industry.

92. In order to construct an export price for KSC's United States export sales, USDOC requested KSC to provide information concerning the prices at which CSI resold products it had purchased from KSC, as well as information concerning CSI's further manufacturing costs. KSC, or its lawyers, met with a CSI representative, and sent five separate letters to CSI, over a period of thirteen weeks, requesting cooperation and information. Notwithstanding initial indications that it would assist KSC, CSI eventually refused to supply the relevant information or to allow KSC's lawyers to visit CSI for purposes of gathering that information. Prior to submitting its response to the questionnaire, KSC reported to USDOC its difficulties in obtaining information from CSI, met with USDOC to discuss the issue, and requested several times to be excused from responding to the relevant section of the questionnaire. USDOC did not take any steps to assist KSC in overcoming the difficulties it was experiencing in obtaining the information, nor did USDOC request CSI to supply the information to it directly. Rather, USDOC continued to require KSC to provide the requested information.

94. In its final determination, USDOC concluded that "KSC did not act to the best of its ability with respect to the requested CSI data", and that "it cannot be said that KSC was fully cooperative and made every effort to obtain and provide the information". USDOC, therefore, decided to apply "adverse" facts available in determining that portion of KSC's dumping margin attributable to its sales to CSI. The facts available applied by USDOC significantly increased KSC's overall dumping margin.

95. Before the Panel, Japan did not contest the use of *facts available* for KSC's sales to CSI, but objected to USDOC's finding that KSC did not "cooperate" with USDOC, and to USDOC's consequent use of "*adverse*" facts available for such transactions.

98. We begin our examination of this issue with the last sentence of paragraph 7 of Annex II of that Agreement, which provides:

It is clear, however, that if an interested party does not cooperate and thus relevant information is being withheld from the authorities, this situation could lead to a result which is *less favourable to the party than if the party did cooperate.* (emphasis added)

99. Paragraph 7 of Annex II indicates that a lack of "cooperation" by an interested party may, by virtue of the use made of facts available, lead to a result that is "less favourable" to the interested party than would have been the case had that interested party cooperated. We note that the Panel referred to the following dictionary meaning of "cooperate": to "work together for the same purpose or in the same task." This meaning suggests that cooperation is a *process*, involving joint effort, whereby parties work together towards a common goal. In that respect, we note that parties may very well "cooperate" to a high degree, even though the requested information is, ultimately, not obtained. This is because the fact of "cooperating" is in itself not determinative of the end result of the cooperation. Thus, investigating authorities should not arrive at a "less favourable" outcome simply because an interested party fails to furnish requested information if, in fact, the interested party has "cooperated" with the investigating authorities, within the meaning of paragraph 7 of Annex II of the *Anti-Dumping Agreement.*

103. We also observe that Article 6.13 of the *Anti-Dumping Agreement* provides:

The authorities shall take *due account of any difficulties experienced by interested parties,* in particular small companies, in supplying information requested, *and shall provide any assistance practicable.* (emphasis added)

104. Article 6.13 thus underscores that "cooperation" is, indeed, a two-way process involving joint effort. This provision requires investigating authorities to make certain allowances for, or take action to assist, interested parties in supplying information. If the investigating authorities fail to "take due account" of genuine "difficulties" experienced by interested parties, and made known to the investigating authorities, they cannot fault the interested parties concerned for a lack of cooperation.

105. Bearing in mind our interpretation of the requirements of "cooperation", we recall the approach taken by USDOC and made of record in this case. It is uncontested that the information requested by USDOC: was not known to, nor in the possession of, KSC; related to the prices and costs of CSI; resulted from CSI's own operations and not KSC's; and was known only to, and in the possession only of, CSI. We observe, also, that, as set forth above, KSC made several attempts to obtain the requested information from CSI. Indeed, USDOC itself acknowledged that KSC "has provided a great deal of information and has substantially cooperated with respect to other issues" and that, with respect to the missing information, KSC "[has made] some effort to obtain the data and [. . .] CSI's management rebuffed these efforts".

106. KSC also repeatedly reported to USDOC its difficulties in obtaining information from CSI. However, USDOC took no steps to assist KSC to overcome these difficulties, or to make allowances for the resulting deficiencies in the information supplied.

110. We, therefore, uphold the Panel's finding, in paragraph 8.1(a) of its Report, that the United States acted inconsistently with Article 6.8 and Annex II of the *Anti-Dumping Agreement* in applying "adverse" facts available to KSC's sales to CSI.

NOTES AND QUESTIONS

1. *Sunset Reviews.* Article 11.3 of the Antidumping Agreement sets a limit of five years on an anti-dumping order unless it is affirmatively found that dumping and injury are likely to continue. In *United States—Sunset Reviews of Anti-Dumping Measures on Oil Country Tubular Goods from Argentina*, WT/DS268/AB/R, Report of the Appellate Body, adopted on December 17, 2004, the Appellate Body faulted several waiver provisions (the so-called individual deemed waiver and affirmative waiver procedures) of U.S. sunset reviews because they allow an anti-dumping duty to be continued without the specific finding that dumping and an injury are likely to continue in the absence of such an order. Thus, the U.S. law permitted a continuation of an anti-dumping order without sufficient data. The Appellate Body upheld a challenge not only of the law and regulations, but it also upheld a challenge to the U.S. "Sunset Policy Bulletin" (SPB), although this bulletin was a policy measure that was not legally binding. The Appellate Body (¶187) reasoned as follows:

> The issue is not whether the SPB is a legal instrument within the domestic legal system of the United States, but rather, whether the SPB is a measure that may be challenged within the WTO system. The United States has explained that, within the domestic legal system of the United States, the SPB does not bind the USDOC and that the USDOC "is entirely free to depart from [the] SPB at any time". However, it is not for us to opine on matters of United States domestic law. In our view, the SPB has normative value, as it provides administrative guidance and creates expectations among the public and among private actors. It is intended to have general application, as it is to apply to all the sunset reviews conducted in the United States. It is also intended to have prospective application, as it is intended to apply to sunset reviews taking place after its issuance. Thus, we confirm that the SPB, as such, is subject to WTO dispute settlement.

What is the limit of the WTO's jurisdiction? How can a mere practice, an institutional customary methodology, be challenged at the WTO?

2. *Standard of Review.* Article 17.6 of the Antidumping Agreement provides that "[w]here the panel finds that a relevant provision of the Agreement admits of more than one permissible interpretation, the panel shall find the authorities' measure to be in conformity with the Agreement if it rests upon one of those permissible interpretations." This provision is unique to dumping in the WTO agreements. Was this intended to limit international review of national anti-dumping determinations? Why did the Appellate Body not defer to the U.S. Commerce Department in the cases we have examined above on this point of law? The answer may be found in another WTO case that ruled against zeroing, *European Communities—Anti-Dumping Duties on Imports of Cotton-Type Bed Linen from India*, WT/DS141/AB/R, Report of the Appellate Body, adopted on March 1, 2001. The EC argued that zeroing was a permissible interpretation of Article 2.4.2 of the Antidumping Agreement and that the panel should have accepted this interpretation under the deference standard required under Article 17.6. The Appellate Body rejected (¶65) this argument as follows:

> It appears clear to us from the emphatic and unqualified nature of this finding of inconsistency that the Panel did not view the interpretation given by the European Communities of Article 2.4.2 of the *Anti-Dumping Agreement* as a "permissible interpretation" within the meaning of Article 17.6(ii) of the *Anti-Dumping Agreement*. Thus, the

Panel was not faced with a choice among multiple "permissible" interpretations which would have required it, under Article 17.6(ii), to give deference to the interpretation relied upon by the European Communities. Rather, the Panel was faced with a situation in which the interpretation relied upon by the European Communities was, to borrow a word from the European Communities, "impermissible". We do not share the view of the European Communities that the Panel failed to apply the standard of review set out in Article 17.6(ii) of the *Anti-Dumping Agreement*.

This interpretation by the Appellate Body appears to remove the very deference to national authorities Article 17.6 was intended to require. On the other hand, the Appellate Body frequently invokes the concepts of good faith, fundamental fairness, and due process in its judgments as general principles of international law. Is that what is going on here?

3. Dumping Determinations

Our earlier examination of U.S. law noted that the Commerce Department engages in the practice of zeroing; i.e., Commerce will disregard any transactions in which the export price (the U.S. price) is higher than the normal value (the home market price). This practice was challenged in the following case.

United States—Measures Relating to Zeroing and Sunset Reviews
Report of the Appellate Body, adopted on January 23, 2007
WT/DS/322/AB/R

[This case was brought by Japan in order to complain about the calculation of dumping margins by the U.S. Department of Commerce (USDOC) and the methodology called "zeroing." Japan sought a WTO ruling to condemn zeroing in almost every instance where it may be used—original dumping investigations; periodic reviews (required under Section 751(a) of the Tariff Act in order to review the amount of an anti-dumping duty); new shipper reviews (of an exporter who did not export the product during the period of the original investigation); changed circumstance reviews (under Section 751(b) of the Tariff Act) that might excuse a party originally subject to an anti-dumping duty order from continuing to be subject to the order; and anti-dumping orders continued as part of sunset reviews (required at the end of five years under Section 751(c) of the Tariff Act).

As described by the panel in this case, zeroing refers to the usual practice of the USDOC as follows:

- The product under investigation is divided into groups of identical or broadly similar product types;
- After making adjustments within each product type, a weighted average normal value and export price is calculated for each product type, producing multiple values, one for each product type;
- In some instances, the comparison will show that the weighted average export price will be less than the weighted average normal value, supporting a finding of dumping; in other instances, the export price will be higher than the normal value, tending to reduce a finding of dumping or to reduce the size of the dumping margin, if dumping is found;

- Each of the values for the normal value and the export price are then aggregated to produce one single value. Thus, a single normal value, composed of the aggregated values, can now be compared to a single export price, also consisting of the aggregated values, for the product under investigation for each individual exporter;
- In the aggregation process, in all cases in which the weighted average export price was higher than the normal value (i.e., no dumping found), a value of zero was attributed to these cases for the purposes of determining the final normal value and the final export price;
- USDOC then aggregates all of the values that result in positive finding of dumping, i.e., where the export price is lower than the normal value (so the product is being "dumped" in the United States); the USDOC then takes this total sum of all values of positive instances of dumping and divides this sum by the total value of the exports to the U.S. market to arrive at a weighted average margin of dumping.

There are a number of methodologies of zeroing that are used for different types of situations involving dumping: (1) model zeroing refers to the methodology whereby USDOC makes weighted average to weighted average (W-W) comparisons of the export price and the normal value within individual averaging groups, established on the basis of physical characteristics (models), and treats as zero any amounts by which the average export prices exceed the average normal values; (2) simple zeroing refers to the methodology whereby USDOC determines a weighted average margin of dumping based on a comparison of a weighted average of transactions in the home market with a single transaction or several transactions (W-T) in the United States; and (3) simple zeroing also refers to a comparison of single transactions to single transactions (T-T) in which USDOC will disregard (or treat as zero) any comparisons between the normal value and the export price, where the export price is higher than the normal value. All of these methodologies were challenged by Japan before the panel, which upheld the challenge on every zeroing methodology. Set forth below is the portion of the Appellate Body opinion related to zeroing used in the transaction-to-transaction methodology, but the reasoning for rejecting zeroing was similar for the other types of methodologies.]

118. Article 2.4.2 sets out three comparison methodologies that investigating authorities may use to calculate margins of dumping. The *first sentence* of Article 2.4.2 provides for two comparison methodologies (W-W and T-T) involving symmetrical comparisons of normal value and export price. Article 2.4.2 stipulates that these two methodologies "shall normally" be used by investigating authorities to establish margins of dumping. As an exception to the two normal methodologies, the second sentence of Article 2.4.2 sets out a third comparison methodology which involves an asymmetrical comparison between weighted average normal value and prices of individual export transactions. This methodology may be used only if the following two conditions are met: (i) that the authorities find a pattern of export prices that differ significantly among different purchasers, regions, or time periods; and (ii) that an explanation is provided as to why such differences cannot be taken into account appropriately by the use of a W-W or T-T comparison.

The First Sentence of Article 2.4.2 of
the Anti-Dumping Agreement

119. Under the T-T comparison methodology at issue in this appeal, the margin of dumping is established by a comparison between the normal value and the export price in individual transactions. The issue before us is whether zeroing procedures are, as such, inconsistent with the first sentence of Article 2.4.2 in the context of T-T comparisons in original investigations.

120. Recently, in *US—Softwood Lumber V (Article 21.5—Canada)*, the Appellate Body dealt for the first time with a determination of margins of dumping based on T-T comparisons in an original investigation. For the Appellate Body, the reference in the first sentence of Article 2.4.2 to " 'a comparison' in the singular suggest[ed] an overall calculation exercise involving aggregation of these multiple transactions."[1] Therefore, "[t]he transaction-specific results are mere steps in the comparison process" and the "individual transaction comparisons are not the final results of the calculation, but, rather, are inputs for the overall calculation exercise."[2] Thus, the text of Article 2.4.2 indicates that the calculation of a margin of dumping using the T-T comparison methodology is a "multi-step exercise in which the results of transaction-specific comparisons are inputs that are [to be] aggregated in order to establish the margin of dumping of the product under investigation for each exporter or producer."[3] The Appellate Body found that, in aggregating the results of transaction-specific comparisons, "an investigating authority must consider the results of all of the comparisons and may not disregard the results of comparisons in which export prices are above normal value."[4] The Appellate Body concluded, therefore, that zeroing, as applied in the determination made on the basis of the T-T comparison methodology at issue in that case, was inconsistent with Article 2.4.2 of the *Anti-Dumping Agreement.*

121. We see no reason to depart from the Appellate Body's reasoning in *US—Softwood Lumber V (Article 21.5—Canada)*, which is in consonance with the Appellate Body's approach in the earlier case of *US—Softwood Lumber V* and is consistent with the fundamental disciplines that apply under the *Anti-Dumping Agreement* and Articles VI:1 and VI:2 of the GATT 1994, as highlighted above. In the latter case, the Appellate Body held that, "[i]f an investigating authority has chosen to undertake multiple comparisons, the investigating authority necessarily has to take into account the results of *all* those comparisons in order to establish margins of dumping for the product as a whole under Article 2.4.2."[5] The Appellate Body addressed there the issue of model zeroing under the W-W comparison methodology in an original investigation. That methodology involved the division of the product under investigation into sub-groups of identical, or similar, product types. In aggregating the results of the sub-group comparisons to calculate the dumping margin for the product under investigation, the USDOC had treated as zero the results of the sub-groups in which weighted average normal value was equal to or less than the weighted average export price. Thus, zeroing did not occur within the

---

1. Appellate Body Report, *US—Softwood Lumber V (Article 21.5—Canada)*, para. 87.
2. *Ibid.*
3. *Ibid.*
4. *Ibid.*, para. 122.
5. Appellate Body Report, *US—Softwood Lumber V*, para. 98. (original emphasis).

sub-groups but occurred across the sub-groups in the process of aggregating the results of the sub-group comparisons.

122. The Appellate Body held that dumping and margins of dumping can be found to exist only for the product under investigation as a whole, and that they cannot be found to exist for a type, model, or category of that product. The comparisons at the sub-group level are not margins of dumping within the meaning of Article 2.4.2. It is only on the basis of aggregating all these "intermediate values" that an investigating authority can establish margins of dumping for the product under investigation as a whole. The Appellate Body therefore found that the model zeroing was inconsistent with Article 2.4.2 of the *Anti-Dumping Agreement.*

123. We fail to see why, if, for the purpose of establishing a margin of dumping, such a product is dealt with under the T-T comparison methodology in an original investigation, zeroing would be consistent with Article 2.4.2 of the *Anti-Dumping Agreement.* If anything, zeroing under the T-T comparison methodology would inflate the margin of dumping to an even greater extent as compared to model zeroing under the W-W comparison methodology. This is because zeroing under the T-T comparison methodology disregards the result of each comparison involving a transaction in which the export price exceeds the normal value, whereas under the W-W comparison methodology, zeroing occurs, as noted above, only across the sub-groups in the process of aggregation.

124. We do not consider that the absence of the phrase "all comparable export transactions" in the context of the T-T comparison methodology suggests that zeroing should be permissible under that methodology. Because transactions may be divided into groups under the W-W comparison methodology, the phrase "all comparable export transactions" requires that each group include only transactions that are comparable and that no export transaction may be left out when determining margins of dumping under that methodology. Furthermore, the W-W comparison methodology involves the calculation of a weighted average export price. By contrast, under the T-T comparison methodology, all export transactions are taken into account on an individual basis and matched with the most appropriate transactions in the domestic market. Therefore, the phrase "all comparable export transactions" is not pertinent to the T-T comparison methodology. Consequently, no inference may be drawn from the fact that these words do not appear in relation to this methodology.

125. We acknowledge that the W-W and T-T comparison methodologies are distinct and may not produce identical results. However, as the Appellate Body stated in *US—Softwood Lumber V (Article 21.5—Canada),* the W-W and T-T comparison methodologies "fulfil the same function", they are "alternative means for establishing margins of dumping", and "there is no hierarchy between them".[6] It would therefore be "illogical to interpret the [T-T] comparison methodology in a manner that would lead to results that are systematically different from those obtained under the [W-W] methodology".[7] Indeed, if zeroing is prohibited under the W-W comparison methodology and permitted under the T-T comparison methodology, the application of the T-T methodology would lead to results that are systematically different from those obtained through the application of the W-W methodology. Moreover, by systematically disregarding comparison results involving export

6. Appellate Body Report, *US—Softwood Lumber V (Article 21.5—Canada),* para. 93

7. *Ibid. See also* Appellate Body Report, *US—Softwood Lumber V (Article 21.5—Canada),* footnote 238 to para. 141.

transactions occurring at prices above the normal value, the zeroing methodology fails to establish margins of dumping for the product under investigation properly, as required under Article 2.4.2.

127. As we have stated, the *Anti-Dumping Agreement* does not contemplate the determination of dumping or a margin of dumping at the model- or transaction-specific level. The *Anti-Dumping Agreement* contemplates the aggregation of all the comparisons made at the transaction-specific level in order to establish an individual margin of dumping for each exporter or foreign producer examined. As we understand it, the position of the United States is that Article 2.4.2 does not address the issue of aggregation of transaction-specific comparison results, but if aggregation is performed, the results of comparisons where the export transactions occurred above normal value may be disregarded in the calculation of the margin of dumping, because such transactions do not involve dumping.

128. In this respect, we recall that the *Anti-Dumping Agreement* deals with injurious dumping and that the "volume of dumped imports" is a critical factor in injury determination. As we understand it, under United States law, if an exporter or foreign producer is found to be dumping, the USITC may include all imports from that exporter or foreign producer in the volume of dumped imports for purposes of determining injury. If, as a consequence of zeroing, the results of certain comparisons are disregarded only for purposes of calculating margins of dumping, but taken into consideration for determining injury, this would mean that the same transactions are treated as "non-dumped" for one purpose, and as "dumped" for another purpose. This is not in consonance with the need for consistent treatment of a product in an anti-dumping investigation.

CONCLUSION

137. In the light of our analysis of Article 2.4.2 of the *Anti-Dumping Agreement*, we conclude that, in establishing "margins of dumping" under the T-T comparison methodology, an investigating authority must aggregate the results of all the transaction-specific comparisons and cannot disregard the results of comparisons in which export prices are above normal value.

ARTICLE 2.4 OF THE ANTI-DUMPING AGREEMENT

141. Next, we examine whether zeroing is inconsistent with the "fair comparison" requirement in Article 2.4 of the *Anti-Dumping Agreement*.

143. On appeal, Japan submits that the Panel erred in making Article 2.4 subject to the allegedly "more specific" provisions of Article 2.4.2. In Japan's view, this is contrary to the introductory phrase of Article 2.4.2. We agree with Japan that the Panel's reasoning implies that the "fair comparison" requirement in Article 2.4 is dependent on Article 2.4.2. The Panel appears to have considered Article 2.4.2 as *lex specialis*. To the extent that it did, this would not be a correct representation of the relationship between the two provisions. Rather the introductory clause to Article 2.4.2 expressly makes it "[s]ubject to the provisions governing fair comparison" in Article 2.4.[8]

---

8. Appellate Body Report, *US—Softwood Lumber V (Article21.5—Canada)*, para. 133.

144. Japan further argues that, "[u]nder the zeroing procedures, the United States makes an initial comparison for all comparable export transactions, but in aggregating the comparison results into an overall margin, it includes solely the positive comparison results, disregarding negative results."[9] According to Japan, "the 'partial' comparison that occurs pursuant to the zeroing procedures is 'inherently biased' and not 'fair' "[10] in T-T comparisons in original investigations.

145. In contrast, the United States contends that zeroing does not produce an "artificially inflated" magnitude of dumping but, rather, the correct magnitude of the margin of dumping.[11] The United States further submits that the "fair comparison" requirement must be neutrally defined, as the Appellate Body itself has recognized "the 'need' to balance . . . the rights and obligations of respondents with those of other interested parties", including the domestic industry.[12]

146. The Appellate Body has previously made it clear that the use of zeroing under the T-T comparison methodology distorts the prices of certain export transactions because the "prices of [certain] export transactions [made] are artificially reduced."[13] In this way, "the use of zeroing under the [T-T] comparison methodology artificially inflates the magnitude of dumping, resulting in higher margins of dumping and making a positive determination of dumping more likely."[14] The Appellate Body has further stated that "[t]his way of calculating cannot be described as impartial, even-handed, or unbiased."[15] As the Appellate Body has previously found, under the first sentence of Article 2.4.2, "an investigating authority must consider the results of all the comparisons and may not disregard the results of comparisons in which export prices are above normal value."[16] Therefore, we consider that zeroing in T-T comparisons in original investigations is inconsistent with the fair comparison requirement in Article 2.4.

NOTES AND QUESTIONS

The WTO has decided fourteen decisions consistently declaring virtually every instance of zeroing illegal under WTO rules. U.S. courts are not required to follow WTO decisions, but the WTO decisions on zeroing have had an impact in recent U.S. law. In *JTEKT Corp. and NTN Corp. v. United States*, 642 F.3d 1378 (Fed. Cir. 2011), the court vacated and remanded a zeroing determination in connection with an administrative review carried out by Commerce:

We have long held that Commerce's practice of zeroing is a reasonable statutory interpretation entitled to deference. *Dongbu Steel Co. Ltd. v. United States*, 635 F.3d 1363, 1366 (Fed. Cir. 2011). Historically, Commerce used zeroing in both the initial investigation

---

9. Japan's appellant's submission, para. 134.

10. *Ibid.*

11. United States' appellee's submission, para. 51.

12. *Ibid.*, para. 52 (referring to Appellate Body Report, *US—Oil Country Tubular Goods Sunset Reviews*, para. 243).

13. Appellate Body Report, *US—Softwood Lumber V (Article 21.5—Canada)*, para. 139.

14. Appellate Body Report, *US—Softwood Lumber V (Article 21.5—Canada)*, para. 142.

15. *Ibid.*

16. *See, supra*, para. 137. *See also* Appellate Body Report, *US—Softwood Lumber V (Article 21.5—Canada)*, para. 122.

to determine whether dumping occurred, and in the subsequent administrative reviews of its dumping determination. But this practice has changed. In response to pressure from the World Trade Organization (WTO), Commerce changed its practice with respect to investigations and no longer zeroes in that phase. *Id.* at 1367.

While Commerce did point to differences between investigations and administrative reviews, it failed to address the relevant question—why is it a reasonable interpretation of the statute to zero in administrative reviews, but not in investigations? In order to satisfy the requirement set out in *Dongbu*, Commerce must explain why differences between the two phases make it reasonable to continue zeroing in one phase, but not the other.

642 F.2d at 1384-1385.

On February 6, 2012, the United States, the EU and Japan came to an agreement to resolve their disputes over zeroing. The agreement requires the United States to modify its anti-dumping methodologies so as to eliminate zeroing in administrative reviews, new shipper reviews, and sunset reviews, and to change anti-dumping regulations to that effect. The formal notice of this change was published in the Federal Register; *see Antidumping Proceedings: Calculation of the Weighted Average Dumping Margin and Assessment Rate in Certain Antidumping Duty Proceedings, Final Modification,* 77 Fed. Reg. 8101 (February 14, 2012). This final rule went into effect April 16, 2012.

Does this end zeroing? The answer is unclear. Lower courts have indicated that *JTEKT* does not definitively forbid zeroing. *See, e.g., Union Steel v. United States,* 823 F. Supp. 2d 1346, 1359-1360 (CIT 2012) (court takes no position on whether Commerce can use zeroing going forward); *Union Steel v. United States,* Slip Op. 12-24, 2012 WL 611535, at *11 (CIT Feb. 27, 2012) (zeroing is permissible). The U.S. announcement states that Commerce's anti-dumping methodology "will necessarily include any exceptional or alternative comparison methods that are determined appropriate to address case-specific circumstances." 77 Fed. Reg. at 8102. This seems to leave the door open. Article 2.4.2 of the Antidumping Agreement allows for the comparison between weighted averages and individual transactions under appropriate circumstances. Article 2.4.2 permits comparisons with individual transactions to deal with so-called "targeted dumping," a subject that the WTO panels and Appellate Body have not addressed. If the United States engages in zeroing under "exceptional circumstances," will this practice violate the Antidumping Agreement?

4.   The Material Injury Analysis

Under Article 3.2 of the Antidumping Agreement, the material injury requirement will usually be satisfied if three conditions are present:

(1) Imports have increased significantly in the relevant period of investigation;
(2) Domestic products (that are like or identical) are subject to significant price undercutting by the imports; and
(3) Prices of domestic products (that are like or identical) are subject to depression or have not been subject to increases.

In general, the determination of whether a material injury exists and whether imports are a cause of the injury is now an integrated determination; injury and causation are not considered separately.

In assessing the impact of imports on the domestic industry, a WTO member is to consider a number of broad economic factors, including actual and potential decline in sales, profits, capacity, cash flow, inventories, employment, wages, and ability to raise capital to make investments. Under certain circumstances, a WTO member is permitted to cumulatively assess the impact of imports from different sources on the domestic industry. For example, in some instances, the product that is the subject of the dumping investigation may be exported to the WTO member by a number of different countries. The WTO member is permitted, under certain conditions, to assess the impact of all of these imports together on the domestic industry. The member is allowed to impose an anti-dumping duty on imports from all countries that were investigated, even though imports from each country were not individually examined or assessed.

The following case involves a challenge to the cumulation of imports by the EU.

European Communities — Anti-Dumping Duties on Malleable Cast Iron Tube or Pipe Fittings from Brazil
Report of the Appellate Body, adopted on August 18, 2003
WT/DS219/AB/R

[Brazil challenged the imposition of anti-dumping duties by the EC on a number of grounds. The portion of the Appellate Body's opinion below focuses on the material injury requirement contained in the Antidumping Agreement.]

CUMULATION: ARTICLES 3.2 AND 3.3 OF THE ANTI-DUMPING AGREEMENT

103. We next examine Brazil's claim that the European Communities acted inconsistently with Articles 3.2 and 3.3 of the *Anti-Dumping Agreement* by cumulatively assessing the effects of dumped imports from several countries, including Brazil, without analyzing the volume and prices of dumped imports from Brazil individually, pursuant to Article 3.2.

109. The text of Article 3.3 expressly identifies three conditions that must be satisfied before an investigating authority is permitted under the *Anti-Dumping Agreement* to assess cumulatively the effects of imports from several countries. These conditions are:

(a) the dumping margin from each individual country must be more than *de minimis*;

(b) the volume of imports from each individual country must not be negligible; and

(c) cumulation must be appropriate in the light of the conditions of competition
   (i) between the imported products; and
   (ii) between the imported products and the like domestic product.

By the terms of Article 3.3, it is "only if" the above conditions are established that an investigating authority "may" make a cumulative assessment of the effects of dumped imports from several countries.

110. We find no basis in the text of Article 3.3 for Brazil's assertion that a country-specific analysis of the potential negative effects of volumes and prices of dumped imports is a pre-condition for a cumulative assessment of the effects of all dumped imports. Article 3.3 sets out expressly the conditions that must be fulfilled before the investigating authorities may cumulatively assess the effects of dumped imports from more than one country. There is no reference to the country-by-country volume and price analyses that Brazil contends are pre-conditions to cumulation. In fact, Article 3.3 expressly requires an investigating authority to examine country-specific volumes, not in the manner suggested by Brazil, but for purposes of determining whether the "volume of imports from each country is not negligible".

111. Nor do we find a basis for Brazil's argument in Article 3.2 In stipulating how to undertake the analyses of volume and prices, Article 3.2 refers consistently to the "dumped imports". There is no indication in the text of Article 3.2 that the analyses of volume and prices must be performed on a country-by-country basis where an investigation involves imports from several countries.

112. Examining the general structure of Article 3, we note that the requirement to analyze volumes and prices under Article 3.2 stems from Article 3.1, which we have said is "an overarching provision that sets forth a Member's fundamental, substantive obligation" with respect to the determination of injury and that "informs the more detailed obligations in [the] succeeding paragraphs" of that provision. Article 3.1 provides:

> A determination of injury for purposes of Article VI of GATT 1994 shall be based on positive evidence and involve an objective examination of both *(a)* the volume of the dumped imports and the effect of the dumped imports on prices in the domestic market for like products, and *(b)* the consequent impact of these imports on domestic producers of such products.

Here again we find that the text of this provision refers to the "dumped imports" and gives no indication that the analyses of volume and prices of the "dumped imports" must be country-specific in multiple-country investigations. Article 3.4, which contains requirements also stemming from Article 3.1 and that relate to the examination of the impact of the "dumped imports" on the domestic industry, is equally consistent in referring broadly to the "dumped imports". Therefore, in our view, Brazil's argument that country-specific analyses of volumes and prices are a pre-condition for cumulation in multiple-country investigations, has no basis in either the text or the immediate context of Articles 3.2 and 3.3.

118. For these reasons, we uphold the finding of the Panel, in paragraphs 7.234-7.236 of the Panel Report, that the European Communities did not act inconsistently with Articles 3.2 or 3.3 of the *Anti-Dumping Agreement*, even though the European Commission did not analyze the volume and prices of dumped imports from Brazil individually, pursuant to Article 3.2, as a pre-condition to cumulatively assessing the effects of the dumped imports under Article 3.3.

IMPLICIT ANALYSIS OF THE GROWTH FACTOR: ARTICLE 3.4 OF THE ANTI-DUMPING AGREEMENT

151. We turn now to Brazil's claim relating to the European Communities' evaluation of the injury factor "growth" pursuant to Article 3.4 of the *Anti-Dumping Agreement*.

152. Before the Panel, Brazil claimed that the European Communities had not explicitly addressed "growth", one of the injury factors listed in Article 3.4. The European Communities admitted that no separate record was made of the evaluation of actual and potential negative effects on "growth". The European Communities argued, however, that "while no separate record was made of its evaluation of 'growth', its consideration of this factor is implicit in its analysis of the other factors."

156. The participants in this appeal do not dispute that it is mandatory for investigating authorities to evaluate all of the fifteen injury factors listed in Article 3.4 of the *Anti-Dumping Agreement*. One of the fifteen factors expressly listed in Article 3.4 is the "actual and potential negative effects on . . . growth". The issue raised by Brazil in this appeal is whether the requirements of Article 3.4 were satisfied in this case, even though the factor "growth" was evaluated only "implicitly" and no separate record of its evaluation was made.

157. Looking first to the text of Article 3.4, we find that it calls for "an evaluation of all relevant economic factors and indices having a bearing on the state of the industry". The text, however, does not address the *manner* in which the results of the investigating authority's analysis of each injury factor are to be set out in the published documents.

158. The requirements of "positive evidence" and "objective examination" in Article 3.1 of the *Anti-Dumping Agreement* similarly do not regulate the *manner* in which the results of the analysis are to be set out. In *Thailand—H-Beams*, we examined a claim under Article 3.1, relating to the use of a confidential document for purposes of an injury determination under Article 3.4, and found that:

> . . . the requirement in Article 3.1 that an injury determination be based on "positive" evidence and involve an "objective" examination of the required elements of injury does *not* imply that the determination must be based only on reasoning or facts that were disclosed to, or discernible by, the parties to an anti-dumping investigation. (original emphasis)

159. Our conclusion in that case regarding the obligations in Article 3.1 was premised on the notion that the *manner* in which the analysis of the injury factors and the results of the injury determination are to be disclosed to interested parties and set forth in the published documents is a matter regulated by other provisions of the *Anti-Dumping Agreement*. Thus, in that case, we explained that:

> [w]hether evidence or reasoning is disclosed or made discernible to interested parties by the final determination is a matter of *procedure* and *due process*. These matters are very important, but they are comprehensively dealt with in other provisions, notably Articles 6 and 12 of the *Anti-Dumping Agreement*. (original italics; underlining added)

In our view, this same premise also indicates that Articles 3.1 and 3.4 do not regulate the *manner* in which the results of the "evaluation" of each injury factor are to be set out in the published documents.

161. Accordingly, because Articles 3.1 and 3.4 do not regulate the *manner* in which the results of the analysis of each injury factor are to be set out in the published documents, we share the Panel's conclusion that it is not required that in every anti-dumping investigation a separate record be made of the evaluation of each of the injury factors listed in Article 3.4. [W]e believe that, under the particular facts

of this case, it was reasonable for the Panel to have concluded that the European Commission addressed and evaluated the factor "growth".

CAUSALITY: ARTICLE 3.5 OF THE ANTI-DUMPING AGREEMENT

167. We turn now to Brazil's allegations of error under Article 3.5 of the *Anti-Dumping Agreement*. Brazil identifies two errors by the Panel related to the European Commission's causality analysis:

(a) the finding that the relatively higher cost of production of the European Communities' domestic industry did not constitute a "known factor[] other than dumped imports" under Article 3.5; and

(b) the finding that the European Commission's methodology in this investigation of analyzing causal factors other than dumped imports on an *individual* basis, without consideration of the *collective* effects of these factors, did not result in the attribution to dumped imports of injuries caused by other causal factors.

We address each of these alleged errors in turn.

A. "KNOWN FACTORS OTHER THAN THE DUMPED IMPORTS WHICH AT THE SAME TIME ARE INJURING THE DOMESTIC INDUSTRY"

173. The issue before us is whether, under Article 3.5, the alleged higher cost of production of the European Communities industry, raised by the Brazilian exporter solely in the context of the European Commission's dumping and injury determinations, was a "known factor[ ] other than the dumped imports which at the same time [was] injuring the domestic industry", thereby requiring examination by the European Commission.

174. We begin our examination with the text of the provision governing an investigating authority's causality analysis. Article 3.5 of the *Anti-Dumping Agreement* provides:

> The authorities shall also examine any known factors other than the dumped imports which at the same time are injuring the domestic industry, and the injuries caused by these other factors must not be attributed to the dumped imports. (underlining added)

175. Article 3.5 requires that an investigating authority establish a "causal relationship" between dumped imports and the domestic industry's injury. In the course of identifying this causal relationship, investigating authorities are not permitted to attribute to dumped imports injuries caused by other factors. Critical to the effective operation of the non-attribution obligation, and indeed, the entire causality analysis, is the requirement of Article 3.5 to "examine any known factors other than the dumped imports which at the same time are injuring the domestic industry", for it is the "injuries" of those "known factors" that must not be attrib-

uted to dumped imports. In order for this obligation to be triggered, Article 3.5 requires that the factor at issue:

(a) be "known" to the investigating authority;
(b) be a factor "other than dumped imports"; and
(c) be injuring the domestic industry at the same time as the dumped imports.

177. We note that Brazil's claim rests entirely on the assumption that there was a marked difference in the costs of production between the Brazilian exporter and the European Communities producers. Brazil's factual allegation regarding the difference in costs of production, however, was rejected by the European Commission. As the Panel noted, the "European Communities did investigate the alleged differences in cost of production and market perception . . . and made factual findings that the difference in cost of production was minimal and that there was no significant difference in market perception." These factual findings of the European Commission were affirmed by the Panel, and as such, we do not inquire into them on appeal. Having rejected the Brazilian exporter's factual premise in the context of one phase of the investigation, the European Commission, in our view, had no reason to undertake an analysis in a subsequent phase of the investigation that would have been predicated upon the very correctness of the same premise. In other words, once the European Commission had determined that the allegation of the difference in cost of production was unfounded, it had no obligation to examine its effects on the domestic industry under Article 3.5.

179. We therefore uphold the Panel's finding, in paragraph 7.362 of the Panel Report, that the difference in cost of production between the Brazilian exporter and the European Communities industry was not a "known factor[ ] other than the dumped imports which at the same time [was] injuring the domestic industry".

B.   NON-ATTRIBUTION

185. Brazil challenges the European Communities' causality methodology, as applied in this investigation, because it fails to ensure that injury caused by any other factor is not attributed to the dumped imports. According to Brazil, an investigating authority that has separated and distinguished the injurious effects of other causal factors *individually* from the effects of dumped imports has not fully discharged its obligation under the non-attribution language of Article 3.5. The investigating authority must also separate and distinguish the *collective* effects of the other causal factors from the effects of dumped imports by "evaluat[ing] the *collective* effect of those factors on the alleged causal link between the dumped imports and the injury." Only by separating the *collective* effects of these other causal factors from the effects of dumped imports can an investigating authority ensure that factors other than dumped imports are not a sufficient cause to sever the causal link between the dumped imports and injury.

187. The issue before us, therefore, is whether the non-attribution language of Article 3.5 requires an investigating authority, in conducting its causality analysis, to examine the effects of the other causal factors *collectively* after having examined them *individually*.

188. Article 3.5 provides, in relevant part:

> The authorities shall also examine any known factors other than the dumped imports which at the same time are injuring the domestic industry, and *the injuries caused by these other factors must not be attributed to the dumped imports*. (emphasis added)

This obligates investigating authorities in their causality determinations not to attribute to dumped imports the injurious effects of other causal factors, so as to ensure that dumped imports are, in fact, "causing injury" to the domestic industry. In *US—Hot-Rolled Steel* we described the non-attribution obligation as follows:

> . . . In order that investigating authorities, applying Article 3.5, are able to ensure that the injurious effects of the other known factors are not "attributed" to dumped imports, they must appropriately assess the injurious effects of those other factors. Logically, such an assessment must involve *separating and distinguishing the injurious effects of the other factors from the injurious effects of the dumped imports*. (emphasis added)

Non-attribution therefore requires separation and distinguishing of the effects of other causal factors from those of the dumped imports so that injuries caused by the dumped imports and those caused by other factors are not "lumped together" and made "indistinguishable".

189. We underscored in *US—Hot-Rolled Steel*, however, that the *Anti-Dumping Agreement* does not prescribe the *methodology* by which an investigating authority must avoid attributing the injuries of other causal factors to dumped imports:

> We emphasize that the particular methods and approaches by which WTO Members choose to carry out the process of separating and distinguishing the injurious effects of dumped imports from the injurious effects of the other known causal factors are not prescribed by the *Anti-Dumping Agreement*. What the Agreement requires is simply that the obligations in Article 3.5 be respected when a determination of injury is made.

Thus, provided that an investigating authority does not attribute the injuries of other causal factors to dumped imports, it is free to choose the methodology it will use in examining the "causal relationship" between dumped imports and injury.

190. Turning to Brazil's arguments in this appeal, we do not read Article 3.5 as requiring, in each and every case, an examination of the *collective* effects of other causal factors *in addition to* examining those factors' individual effects.

191. [W]e do not find that an examination of *collective* effects is necessarily required by the non-attribution language of the *Anti-Dumping Agreement*. In particular, we are of the view that Article 3.5 does not compel, *in every case*, an assessment of the *collective* effects of other causal factors, because such an assessment is not always necessary to conclude that injuries ascribed to dumped imports are actually caused by those imports and not by other factors.

192. We believe that, depending on the facts at issue, an investigating authority could reasonably conclude, without further inquiry into *collective* effects, that "the injury . . . ascribe[d] to dumped imports is actually caused by those imports, rather than by the other factors." At the same time, we recognize that there may be cases where, because of the specific factual circumstances therein, the failure to undertake an examination of the collective impact of other causal factors would result in the investigating authority improperly attributing the effects of other causal factors

to dumped imports. We are therefore of the view that an investigating authority is not required to examine the collective impact of other causal factors, provided that, under the specific factual circumstances of the case, it fulfils its obligation not to attribute to dumped imports the injuries caused by other causal factors.

193. We now turn to the facts of this case to examine whether the European Communities has failed to discharge its non-attribution obligation under Article 3.5 by not conducting an examination of the collective impact of other factors. We begin by noting that the European Commission in this investigation expressly identified the proper attribution of injuries as one of the purposes of its causality analysis, stating that it "examined whether the material injury suffered by the Community industry has been caused by the dumped imports and whether other factors might have caused or contributed to that injury, in order not to attribute possible injury caused by other factors to the dumped imports." The European Commission first identified other factors that may be causing injury to the domestic industry. In then evaluating each "other factor" individually, the European Commission determined that each factor's contribution to injury was insignificant (or, for one factor, not so much as to break the causal link between dumped imports and injury). As a result, the European Commission concluded that dumped imports were causing material injury to the domestic industry, without consideration of whether the *collective* effects of the other causal factors undermined the causal relationship between dumped imports and injury.

194. On appeal, Brazil does not contest the European Communities' *individual* separating and distinguishing of the effects of other factors. It relies instead on its argument that an investigating authority is also *required* under Article 3.5 to examine other causal factors collectively *in every investigation*. Aside from this legal argument, which we have rejected, Brazil has not identified how, under the facts of this case, the European Commission's failure to examine the collective impact of the other causal factors resulted in this case in the attribution to dumped imports of injuries resulting from those other factors. If Brazil viewed the analysis of the European Commission in this case to have attributed improperly to dumped imports the injuries caused by other factors, Brazil had the opportunity before the Panel to adduce evidence to this effect. As far as we are aware from the Panel Record, Brazil proffered no such evidence.

195. We therefore uphold the Panel's finding that the causality methodology applied by the European Commission in this investigation, which did not include an examination of the *collective* impact of other known causal factors, did not attribute the injuries caused by those other factors to the dumped imports.

NOTES AND QUESTIONS

1. In *United States—Anti-Dumping Measures on Certain Hot-Rolled Steel Products from Japan*, WT/DS184/AB/R, Report of the Appellate Body, adopted on August 23, 2001, Japan challenged the injury analysis of the United States because the ITC, in defining the domestic industry, had excluded so-called captive production entities. This is required under Section 771(7)(C)(iv) of the U.S. Tariff Act, presumably for the reason that domestic producers (whose production is captive because of vertical integration) do not directly compete with importers. The Appellate Body ruled that this provision is not inconsistent with the WTO on its face, but it should be interpreted by the ITC in accordance with the obligation of Article 4.1 of the Anti-

Dumping Act, which requires a consideration of the totality of the relevant domestic industry, not simply on one segment. Moreover, the Appellate Body cautioned that the "positive evidence" and "objective examination" requirements contained in Article 3.1 are not mere truisms but require that the examination process "must conform to principles of good faith and fundamental fairness." *Id.* at ¶¶191-193.

2. *In Mexico—Anti-Dumping Investigation of High Fructose Corn Syrup (HFCS) from the United States, Recourse to Article 21.5 of the DSU by the United States,* WT/DS132/AB/RW, Report of the Appellate Body, adopted on November 21, 2001, the Appellate Body affirmed the panel's determination faulting Mexico's finding of dumping by the United States. The Appellate Body found that Mexican authorities had acted inconsistently with Article 3.7(i) of the Antidumping Agreement in refusing to take account of an agreement, entered into by soft drink bottlers, promising restraint in their use of high fructose corn syrup. The Appellate Body emphasized (¶100) that the determination of a threat of material injury must be based on facts and the threat must be clearly foreseen and imminent. The Appellate Body also ruled (¶112) that Mexico had violated the Antidumping Agreement because Mexico's determination contained no meaningful analysis of the factors indicating injury listed in Article 3.4.

III. *Subsidies and Countervailing Duties*

A. Introduction

This section examines the law of subsidies and countervailing duties in the WTO and in the United States. Under the WTO system, a multilateral avenue *or* a unilateral avenue of relief may be available for subsidies. This practice is different than that for dumping, which permits only a unilateral option of pursuing relief in the country where the products have been dumped.

In the case of subsidies, however, the government of the aggrieved nation can challenge the legality of the act of subsidization itself within the WTO dispute settlement system. If the WTO finds that the subsidy is inconsistent with the WTO, then the offending member will need to bring its measures into compliance with the WTO by withdrawing the subsidy.

If the government of the aggrieved country decides not to pursue a multilateral avenue, then the domestic industry within the aggrieved nation can bring a countervailing duty action under the country's domestic laws. If the country's investigatory authorities find that a subsidy is present and is more than *de minimis* (at least 1 percent *ad valorem* of the import), then the remedy is the imposition of a duty that "countervails" or offsets the financial advantage created by the subsidy. Countervailing duties can only neutralize the advantage that the subsidy provides in the importing country; the unilateral remedy does not directly affect the ability of the foreign government to continue to provide the subsidy, although the countervailing duty provides pressure to remove the subsidy.

The subsidies investigation and the imposition of any countervailing duties by any WTO member must respect the disciplines set forth in the WTO Subsidies and Countervailing Measures (SCM) Agreement. The SCM Agreement explicitly establishes the dual track for attacking subsidies summarized above. However, these two methods cannot be employed simultaneously or cumulatively (*see* footnote 35 to the SCM Agreement). The unilateral approach is possible only when the imports cause injury in the domestic market of the aggrieved nation. In some cases, the subsidized products may not cause injury in a nation's domestic market but only in its exports markets. For example, suppose that Country A subsidizes products for exports to Country C. Country B, which does not import the subsidized products from Country A, also exports its products to Country C. Country B cannot bring a unilateral action against Country A for A's subsidy program because Country B does not import products from Country A (and B's domestic market does not suffer material injury by reason of the imports). However, Country B might find that its exports to Country C are being harmed by the subsidized exports from Country A. In this case, Country B will need to use the multilateral avenue challenging the legality of Country A's subsidy program within the WTO.

In the materials below, we (1) review the basic policy debate underlying subsidies and countervailing duties; (2) examine the use of the multilateral avenue of relief under the WTO system; and (3) discuss the unilateral option under the countervailing duty laws of the United States.

B. The Economic and Political Rationales for Policies in Favor of and Against Subsidies

The economic and policy debate concerning subsidies reflects, to some degree, similar concerns that applied to dumping. Experts disagree on whether different types of subsidies are harmful and whether the remedy of imposing a countervailing duty to offset the subsidy may cause harms.

1. Types of Subsidies

A subsidy is a financial benefit that is given to a business or firm by a government. Subsidies are widely used by governments as instruments of economic, social, and political policy. Subsidies serve a variety of purposes, including benefiting underdeveloped regions, combating pollution, favoring particular constituents or economic sectors, and encouraging the development of new technologies and products. Governmental subsidies also take many forms; they can be direct or indirect, highly specific or extremely diffuse.

Countries have long recognized that some subsidies serve legitimate social and political ends but that other subsidies may cause harm to foreign traders. The legitimate use of subsidies includes raising standards of living for the poor and reversing environmental degradation. Subsidies can help realize public policy objectives that markets by themselves would not serve or pursue with the same intensity, such as public education and health, assistance for displaced workers, and care for elderly. Subsidies are widely used policy instruments that implicate wider considerations than trade policy.

At the same time, some subsidies may harm foreign traders. There is a key distinction between so-called export subsidies and domestic or production subsidies. An export subsidy is one that is paid to a firm with specific reference to the export of a product. In the crudest form of an export subsidy, a government may pay a firm a fee for every product it exports. An export subsidy may support predatory pricing, similar to the type of predatory pricing involved in dumping cases. Due to the cost advantage that the subsidy provides, a foreign company might be able to export its goods at artificially low prices to the importing country. Most observers believe that this type of export subsidy is harmful in international trade.

However, not all subsidies are so-called export subsidies, and the harmful effects of other types of subsidies are often debated. A domestic or production subsidy is one granted to a firm, regardless of exports. This type of subsidy has less of an impact on trade. The impact may be very slight if the percentage of products exported by that firm is small. Even where exports are relatively high in proportion to the total production, however, the economic impact is reduced because the subsidy is spread over the entire amount produced. From a trade perspective, export subsidies are generally of greater concern than domestic or production subsidies. Under the WTO, even though domestic subsidies may have less impact on international trade, these subsidies may, under certain conditions, be subject to sanctions under the WTO system or be subject to unilateral sanctions in the form of countervailing duties.

2.   The Economic Debate over Subsidies

The economic impact of subsidies in general and particular subsidy programs is a matter of great debate. On the one hand, a subsidy can be viewed as an economic "distortion" in international trade. Two distortions are prominent. For the country importing the subsidized product, there is unfair competition of imports with competing products of unsubsidized domestic producers. Even if subsidized products are sold by the subsidizing nation, A, to a third country, Country C, the domestic producers in Country B may be injured because of a loss of export opportunities in Country C. On the other hand, the "distortion" viewpoint of subsidies may be too narrow. From a global perspective or the viewpoint of the subsidizing country, the welfare gains from the subsidy may outweigh the distortion or may actually compensate for other economic distortions. Ending the subsidy may, in some cases, reduce economic welfare. These cost and benefit considerations in subsidy programs can only be dealt with on a case-by-case basis.

There is also controversy among trade theorists over the remedy for subsidization. The unilateral remedy is usually the imposition of a countervailing duty. The economic rationale for a countervailing duty is doubtful at best, even in the case of a distorting subsidy because the effect of a countervailing duty is to make the product more expensive for consumers in the importing country. The best case for a countervailing duty is when the subsidy is being used as an instrument of predatory pricing by the exporting nation. A second economic case for a countervailing duty is where the subsidy is demonstrably causing serious injury to competing domestic producers in the importing country. However, in many cases, neither of these two scenarios is involved. In the absence of either of these scenarios, it may be best for the importing country simply to send a "thank-you" note to the government of the exporting country for the windfall received by its consumers. Nevertheless, even though neither of these two scenarios may be involved, subsidies may be subject to challenge and sanctions under the WTO system.

PROBLEM 10-11

A domestic U.S. industry that is being harmed by subsidized imports can either initiate a countervailing duty action under U.S. law or request the U.S. government to bring a WTO dispute settlement proceeding challenging the subsidies provided by the foreign government. You are a consultant hired by the industry and are asked to analyze: (1) the differences between these two types of remedies, including who is the petitioning party and why this might be relevant; (2) the types of remedies that are available under each type of proceeding; and (3) the relevant timetables involved in obtaining some form of relief. What is your recommendation on which type of proceeding to bring?

NOTES AND QUESTIONS

1. *Subsidies and China.* On March 30, 2007, the Department of Commerce reversed a longstanding policy of refusing to apply countervailing duties to goods from NMEs by imposing preliminary countervailing duties on imports of high-gloss paper from China. *China CVD Fact Sheet*, United States Department of Commerce (March 30, 2007). The prior policy, affirmed by the landmark decision in *Georgetown Steel Corp. v. United States*, 801 F.2d 1308 (Fed. Cir. 1986), was based on the idea that it was inappropriate to impose countervailing duty laws on NMEs. In determining whether a subsidy exists, the basic comparison is between what the government is doing and a market-based benchmark. Is the government providing a benefit to a foreign firm or company beyond what is available in the market in the foreign country? However, if there is no meaningful market-based benchmark in the foreign country, then it becomes impossible to make this comparison. However, the United States reversed this longstanding position based upon changes in China's economy, which now has sophisticated marketing and manufacturing techniques. Although the changed position applies to all NMEs, the greatest impact of this change is on goods from China, which voiced strong objections and vowed to challenge the new policy both in U.S. courts and in the WTO.

In *GPX International Tire Corp. v. United States*, 666 F.3d 732 (Fed. Cir. 2011), the United States Court of Appeals for the Federal Circuit ruled that, consistent with *Georgetown Steel*, Congress, in amending and reenacting the U.S. countervailing duty laws in 1988 and 1994, "adopted the position that countervailing duty law does not apply to NME [non-market economy] countries. Although Commerce has wide discretion in administering countervailing duty law and antidumping law, it cannot exercise this discretion contrary to congressional intent. We affirm the holding of the [Court of International Trade] that countervailing duties cannot be applied to goods from NME countries." 666 F.3d at 735

On March 13, 2012, President Obama signed into law Public Law No. 112-99, entitled, "An Act to Apply the Countervailing Duty Provisions of the Tariff Act of 1930 to Non-Market Economy Countries, and for Other Purposes." This law reverses the decision of the court in the *GPX International Tire* case, and it applies retroactively to November 20, 2006. Thus countervailing duty orders against Chinese companies that were vacated are now reinstated. Will this pass constitutional muster under the Due Process Clause?

2. The issue of double remedies arises in connection with countervailing duty cases and anti-dumping cases. The United States brought four countervailing duty cases and four anti-dumping cases against China, seeking both anti-dumping and countervailing duties against four different varieties of Chinese imports — circular welded carbon-quality steel; new pneumatic off-the-road tires; light-walled rectangular pipe and tube; and laminated woven sacks. The U.S. investigations led to the imposition of both anti-dumping duties calculated under non-market economy

methodology and countervailing duties on the same products. China challenged the imposition of "double remedies" at the WTO. In *United States—Definitive Anti-Dumping and Countervailing Duties on Certain Products from China*, WT/DS379/AB/R, Report of the Appellate Body, adopted on March 25, 2011, the Appellate Body ruled (¶¶605-606) that the United States Department of Commerce, by imposing countervailing duties and anti-dumping duties concurrently on the same products without having assessed whether double remedies arose from such concurrent duties, acted inconsistently with SCM Agreement Article 19.3. *See also* GATT Article VI:5.

The new countervailing duty law and NMEs signed into effect by President Obama (and discussed in note 1 above) provide that if Commerce finds both countervailable subsidies and dumping in a particular case, and if Commerce can reasonably estimate the extent of any double-counting, Commerce must reduce the anti-dumping duties to the extent that the countervailed subsidy has inflated the dumping margin. This methodology applies prospectively and to redeterminations that Commerce is required to make to comply with WTO rules.

C.   Challenging Subsidies at the WTO: The Subsidies and Countervailing Measures Agreement

We turn now to the multilateral avenue of relief: the use of the WTO to challenge the legality of any subsidies or programs within the WTO dispute settlement system.

The SCM Agreement is divided into several parts. Part I, Articles 1 and 2 defining subsidies, apply to both multilateral challenges to subsidies within the WTO and to unilateral actions under domestic law. Part II (prohibited subsidies) and Part III (actionable subsidies) apply to multilateral challenges. Part IV has been repealed. Part V applies to unilateral actions under domestic law.

Read GATT Articles VI and XVI and Article 1 and 2 of the SCM Agreement.

1.   *Defining Subsidies*

Under Article 1 of the SCM Agreement, in order for a measure to be considered a subsidy, the measure must:

(1)   constitute a financial contribution or income support by a government, which
(2)   confers a benefit.

The term "financial contribution" includes direct funds, goods, or services provided by the government or public body to a business or firm. The WTO is not concerned with private action providing financial support. A financial contribution can also take the form of revenue forgone; i.e., monies that would otherwise have been collected (such as taxes) but are forgone by the government in order to provide a benefit to a recipient. A benefit must also exist; in this sense, the subsidizing government is providing an advantage to the recipient that is not otherwise available in the marketplace. The direct grant (or gift) of funds is one example; but a government loan at less than the prevailing market rate of interest or government forgiveness of debt can also constitute a benefit. On the other hand, a government loan at market rates (or above) might be considered to be a financial contribution but one that does not confer a benefit. If that is the case, then no subsidy will exist.

2.   Specificity

Even if there is a finding of a subsidy under Article 1 of the SCM, the subsidy must be specific in order to be actionable. *See* SCM Article 8. Government assistance in itself is common and permissible. Only subsidies that are specific are actionable under the SCM. What is the reason for this rule? A subsidy that is widely available does not usually create the worrisome economic distortion that a specific subsidy causes. Article 2 sets out the principles for determining if a subsidy is specific: (1) enterprise specificity, where a government targets a particular company or companies; (2) industry specificity, where a government targets a particular industrial section; (3) geographical specificity, where a government designates enterprises in a particular geographical area; and (4) prohibited-subsidy specificity, where the government targets goods destined for export, or requires the use of domestic over foreign goods.

3.   General Framework

Read Parts II and III of the SCM Agreement, Articles 3-7.

Articles 1 to 9 of the SCM Agreement define subsidies and provide a three-category classification scheme:

(1) Prohibited subsidies, commonly called "red light subsidies," are the subjects of Articles 3 and 4. These are export subsidies; i.e., a subsidy given by a government on the condition that the subsidized good be exported. A second category of prohibited subsidies are import substitution subsidies; i.e., subsidies contingent upon the use of domestic (over imported) goods. This occurs, for example, when a government provides a subsidy for the purchase of domestic goods for use in domestic manufacture over the use of foreign imports. Red light subsidies are deemed to be specific and are considered illegal per se. There is no need to show injury in case of a red light subsidy; a red light subsidy, once found, must be withdrawn without delay. Annex I contains an illustrative list of export subsidies. Any export subsidy that falls within the Annex is illegal.

(2) Actionable subsidies, commonly called "yellow light subsidies." Under Article 5, these subsidies are actionable if they cause adverse effects ("nullification or impairment" of a GATT benefit, or "serious prejudice") to other countries.

(3) Green light subsidies are defined in Article 8; these subsidies were originally given a "safe harbor" and were protected from challenge but this Article expired in 2000 when members were unable to agree on retaining it. Green light subsidies are of historical interest only.

The distinction between red light and yellow light subsidies is most meaningful in the context of actions within the WTO dispute settlement system. Where an aggrieved industry brings an action under the countervailing duty laws of the United States, so long as the imports are from a WTO country, the petitioner must always establish a material injury (or threat thereof) before a countervailing duty can be imposed.

The SCM Agreement also contains notification and surveillance provisions (Articles 25 and 26) to ensure transparency of subsidies. Special preferential rules also apply to developing countries (Article 27).

4.   *Agricultural Subsidies*

Articles 3 and 5 of the SCM contain exceptions for agricultural subsidies that are the subject of the WTO Agreement on Agriculture. The AoA is deemed to be more specific than the SCM Agreement so the AoA will govern in cases where both agreements arguably apply. Certain types of subsidies are permitted under the AoA, which means that these agricultural subsidies are not subject to challenge under the SCM. This exemption of permitted agricultural subsidies from the SCM is expressly provided in Article 13, the so-called peace clause. However, Article 13 expired in 2004. As of yet, however, no member has challenged permitted agricultural subsidies under the SCM, and the SCM itself (in Articles 3 and 5) acknowledges that certain agricultural subsidies are exempt from challenge under the SCM.

The AoA divides agricultural subsidies into (1) domestic support and (2) export subsidies. Domestic support subsidies are called "amber box" subsidies because the idea is not to abolish them (although that may be the long-term goal), but to reduce them gradually or to "slow down" the use of these subsidies. Developed countries agreed in 1994 to make reduction commitments of these amber box subsidies over a period of time. Countries will reduce their annual domestic support—the "total aggregate measurement of support," or Total AMS (the base year support 1986-1988), by 20 percent over six years starting in 1995. Developing countries agreed to cut by 13 percent over ten years, while least developing countries are exempt. However, so-called green box subsidies (AoA Article 6 and Annex II) are exempt from the reduction commitments. In addition, certain direct payments where farmers agree to limit production (known as "blue box" subsidies under AoA Article 6.5) are also exempt from reduction commitments; and small-scale, so-called *de minimis* support (AoA Article 6.4), is also exempt. This means that a country can provide as many of these exempted green, blue, and other subsidies as it wishes without violating its reduction commitments; i.e., these exempted subsidies are not counted in the total annual domestic support that countries have agreed to limit.

Export subsidies are subject to limits on spending and quantities of product. Developed countries agreed in 1994 to cut export subsidies 36 percent by value, and 21 percent by quantities, of subsidized exports. Developing countries agreed on such cuts of 24 and 14 percent, respectively. At the Hong Kong Ministerial Conference in 2005, the members of the WTO agreed in principle to eliminate all export subsidies on agricultural products by 2013. Any export subsidy that is not exempt under the AoA will be counted against the country's export reduction commitments.

All of the permitted or exempted subsidies (amber, green, blue box, and export subsidies) under the AoA are exempt from challenge as illegal subsidies under SCM, under the general rule that a special agreement (the AoA) takes precedence over a more general agreement (the SCM). However, the so-called peace clause (AoA Article 13) has expired. Whether this changes the general rule is unclear.

We now consider the remedy against red light and yellow light subsidies.

5.   *Prohibited Subsidies*

The following case considers a prohibited export subsidy in connection with a taxation scheme of the United States.

PROBLEM 10-12

Suppose that India has instituted a new loan forgiveness program for recent college graduates. The graduates go to work for India's new information technology industry that manufactures software and other high-technology products for export. The graduates work for two years as "interns" at no cost to their employers. In exchange, the Indian government will forgive all student loans. Is this a countervailable subsidy? Consult the following case.

PROBLEM 10-13

Germany charges a value added tax of 20 percent on auto parts sold in the domestic market. The charge is not collected on parts that are exported to the United States. Parts that are first sold domestically and are then exported are eligible to receive a rebate of the tax paid. Is this tax scheme lawful under the SCM? See the case below.

United States — Tax Treatment for "Foreign Sales Corporations"
Report of the Appellate Body, adopted on March 20, 2000
WT/DS108/AB/R

[The European Community brought this case against the United States in order to challenge the U.S. Foreign Sales Corporation Act, which exempted certain income earned by foreign corporations from U.S. taxes. Under general U.S. tax principles, the U.S. government asserts the right to tax income earned by U.S. residents or citizens anywhere in the world. A U.S. citizen living and working in Country C will have to report income earned in Country C and may have to pay taxes on the income in the United States. Because there is a possibility that such a U.S. citizen will be subject to double taxation (first by the U.S. government on the basis of nationality and a second time by Country C on the basis that the citizen lives and works there) the United States and many countries have entered into tax treaties for the purpose of avoiding double taxation. These treaties provide that such persons are taxed only once, as a matter of fairness. The issue that arises with respect to treaties that avoid double taxation is that the general definition of a subsidy considers a subsidy to exist when a financial contribution is made, which includes not only grants but also the forgoing of revenue otherwise due. A U.S. taxpayer receives a financial contribution if the U.S. government decides not to collect tax from a taxpayer when that tax is otherwise due; the non-collection of the tax might be considered to be a subsidy. In the case of a double taxation treaty, a government may also be deemed to forgo tax revenue that is otherwise due (because it has already been collected by another government). To avoid classifying the forgoing of taxes under double taxation treaties as an illegal subsidy, the SCM made an explicit exception for double taxation treaties. The forgoing of taxes under a double taxation treaty is not considered to be a subsidy under footnote 59 of the SCM.

In this case, certain foreign sales corporations (FSC) that were organized abroad were subject to U.S. income tax in connection with their services provided in the United States to assist in exporting U.S. goods. These FSCs were also potentially subject to tax in the country in which they were organized and located. The United States enacted laws to exempt from U.S. income taxation the income earned by the FSCs from their export sales transactions. The EC argued that this was an illegal subsidy because it provided a financial contribution to the FSCs by the U.S. government. The United States argued that forgoing the collection of taxes from the FSCs was justified as a means for avoiding double taxation. The Appellate Body opinion examining this issue follows below.]

ARTICLE 1.1(a) OF THE SCM AGREEMENT

90. We turn now to the definition of the term "subsidy" and, in particular, to Article 1.1(a)(1)(ii), which provides that there is a "financial contribution" by a government, sufficient to fulfil that element in the definition of a "subsidy," where "government revenue that is *otherwise due* is foregone or not collected." (emphasis added) In our view, the "*foregoing*" of revenue "*otherwise* due" implies that less revenue has been raised by the government than would have been raised in a different situation, or, that is, "otherwise." Moreover, the word "foregone" suggests that the government has given up an entitlement to raise revenue that it could "otherwise" have raised. This cannot, however, be an entitlement in the abstract, because governments, in theory, could tax *all* revenues. There must, therefore, be some defined, normative benchmark against which a comparison can be made between the revenue actually raised and the revenue that would have been raised "otherwise." We, therefore, agree with the Panel that the term "otherwise due" implies some kind of comparison between the revenues due under the contested measure and revenues that would be due in some other situation. We also agree with the Panel that the basis of comparison must be the tax rules applied by the Member in question. To accept the argument of the United States that the comparator in determining what is "otherwise due" should be something other than the prevailing domestic standard of the Member in question would be to imply that WTO obligations somehow compel Members to choose a particular kind of tax system; this is not so. A Member, in principle, has the sovereign authority to tax any particular categories of revenue it wishes. It is also free *not* to tax any particular categories of revenues. But, in both instances, the Member must respect its WTO obligations. What is "otherwise due," therefore, depends on the rules of taxation that each Member, by its own choice, establishes for itself.

91. The Panel found that the term "otherwise due" establishes a "but for" test, in terms of which the appropriate basis of comparison for determining whether revenues are "otherwise due" is "the situation that would prevail but for the measures in question." In the present case, this legal standard provides a sound basis

for comparison because it is not difficult to establish in what way the foreign-source income of an FSC would be taxed "but for" the contested measure. However, we have certain abiding reservations about applying any legal standard, such as this "but for" test, in the place of the actual treaty language. Moreover, we would have particular misgivings about using a "but for" test if its application were limited to situations where there actually existed an alternative measure, under which the revenues in question would be taxed, absent the contested measure. It would, we believe, not be difficult to circumvent such a test by designing a tax regime under which there would be *no* general rule that applied formally to the revenues in question, absent the contested measures. We observe, therefore, that, although the Panel's "but for" test works in this case, it may not work in other cases. We note, however, that, in this dispute, the European Communities does not contest either the Panel's interpretation of the term "otherwise due" or the Panel's application of that term to the facts of this case. The United States also accepts the Panel's interpretation of that term as a general proposition.

92. The United States does, however, argue that the Panel erred because the general interpretation of the term "otherwise due" "must yield" to the standard the United States perceives in footnote 59 of the *SCM Agreement*, which the United States contends, is the "controlling legal provision" for interpretation of the term "otherwise due" with respect to a measure of the kind at issue. In the view of the United States, footnote 59 means that the FSC measure is not a "subsidy" under Article 1.1 of the *SCM Agreement*. Thus, the United States does not read footnote 59 as providing context for the general interpretation of the term "otherwise due"; rather, the United States views footnote 59 as a form of exception to that general interpretation. The United States submits further that this reading of footnote 59 is "confirmed" by the 1981 Council action, which, it will be recalled, the United States contends forms part of the GATT 1994.

93. Article 1.1 sets forth the general definition of the term "subsidy" which applies "for the purpose of this Agreement." This definition, therefore, applies wherever the word "subsidy" occurs throughout the *SCM Agreement* and conditions the application of the provisions of that Agreement regarding *prohibited* subsidies in Part II, *actionable* subsidies in Part III, *non-actionable* subsidies in Part IV and countervailing measures in Part V. By contrast, footnote 59 relates to one item in the Illustrative List of Export Subsidies.

ARTICLE 3.1(A) OF THE SCM AGREEMENT

96. The United States' appeal from the Panel's findings under Article 3.1(a) is limited to its contention that footnote 59, as "confirmed" by the 1981 Council action, means that the FSC measure is not an "export subsidy." Footnote 59 reads:

> The Members recognize that deferral need not amount to an export subsidy where, for example, appropriate interest charges are collected. *The Members reaffirm the principle that prices for goods in transactions between exporting enterprises and foreign buyers under their or under the same control should for tax purposes be the prices which would be charged between independent enterprises acting at arm's length.* Any Member may draw the attention of another Member to administrative or other practices which may contravene this principle and which result in a significant saving of direct taxes in export transactions. In such circumstances the Members shall normally attempt to resolve their differences

using the facilities of existing bilateral tax treaties or other specific international mechanisms, without prejudice to the rights and obligations of Members under GATT 1994, including the right of consultation created in the preceding sentence.

Paragraph (e) is not intended to limit a Member from taking measures to avoid the double taxation of foreign-source income earned by its enterprises or the enterprises of another Member. (emphasis added)

97. We need to examine footnote 59 sentence by sentence. The first sentence of footnote 59 is specifically related to the statement in item (e) of the Illustrative List that the "full or partial exemption remission, or deferral specifically related to exports, of direct taxes" is an export subsidy. The first sentence of footnote 59 qualifies this by stating that "deferral need not amount to an export subsidy where, for example, appropriate interest charges are collected." Since the FSC measure does not involve the *deferral* of direct taxes, we do not believe that this sentence of footnote 59 bears upon the characterization of the FSC measure as constituting, or not, an "export subsidy."

98. The second sentence of footnote 59 "reaffirms" that, in allocating export sales revenues, for tax purposes, between exporting enterprises and controlled foreign buyers, the price for the goods shall be determined according to the "arm's length" principle to which that sentence of the footnote refers. Like the Panel, we are willing to accept, for the sake of argument, the United States' position that it is "implicit" in the requirement to use the arm's length principle that Members of the WTO are not obliged to tax foreign-source income, and also that Members may tax such income less than they tax domestic-source income. We would add that, even in the absence of footnote 59, Members of the WTO are *not* obliged, by WTO rules, to tax *any* categories of income, whether foreign- or domestic-source income. The United States argues that, since there is no requirement to tax export-related foreign-source income, a government cannot be said to have "foregone" revenue if it elects not to tax that income. It seems to us that, taken to its logical conclusion, this argument by the United States would mean that there could *never* be a foregoing of revenue "otherwise due" because, in principle, under WTO law generally, *no* revenues are ever due and *no* revenue would, in this view, ever be "foregone." That cannot be the appropriate implication to draw from the requirement to use the arm's length principle.

100. The third and fourth sentences of footnote 59 set forth rules that relate to remedies. In our view, these rules have no bearing on the substantive obligations of Members under Articles 1.1 and 3.1 of the *SCM Agreement*. So, we turn to the fifth and final sentence of footnote 59. That sentence provides:

Paragraph (e) is not intended to limit a Member from taking measures to avoid the double taxation of foreign-source income earned by its enterprises or the enterprises of another Member.

101. On appeal, the United States maintains that the FSC measure is a measure "to avoid double taxation of foreign-source income" *under footnote 59.* As a consequence, the United States further contends that the FSC measure is excluded from the prohibition against export subsidies in Article 3.1(a) of the *SCM Agreement.* During the oral hearing, we asked the United States to identify where it had asserted before the Panel that the FSC measure is a measure "to avoid double taxation of foreign-source income" under footnote 59. That is, we asked the United

States to tell us specifically where it had invoked the fifth sentence of footnote 59 as a means of justifying the FSC measure. In reply, the United States pointed to its first written submission to the Panel. In that submission, in describing the FSC measure and before setting forth its legal arguments, the United States stated that "the FSC is designed to prevent double taxation of export income earned outside the United States by exempting a portion of the FSC's income from taxation." The United States pointed also to certain general arguments it made before the Panel concerning the fifth sentence of footnote 59. However, the United States did not indicate that, in its substantive arguments to the Panel, it had justified the FSC measure as a measure "to avoid double taxation" under footnote 59. Nor do we find any indication in the Panel Record that the United States ever invoked this justification. We, therefore, conclude that the United States did not assert, far less argue, before the Panel that the FSC measure is a measure "to avoid double taxation of foreign-source income" under footnote 59. Our conclusion is confirmed by the Panel's statement, in footnote 682 of the Panel Report, that the United States had not asserted that the fifth sentence of footnote 59 was "relevant to this dispute". It follows, therefore, that this issue was not properly litigated before the Panel and that the Panel was not asked to examine whether the FSC measure is a measure "to avoid double taxation of foreign-source income" under footnote 59.

121. In light of all the foregoing, we uphold the Panel's conclusion, in paragraph 8.1 of the Panel Report, that the FSC tax exemptions involve subsidies contingent upon export performance that are prohibited under Article 3.1(a) of the *SCM Agreement*.

NOTES AND QUESTIONS

1. The United States, believing that the Appellate Body had pointed the way toward a solution to the FSC problem, promptly enacted the "FSC Repeal and Extraterritorial Income Exclusion Act of 2000" with the idea of reforming the tax exemption law to conform with footnote 59 of the SCM, which exempts double taxation treaties. The United States wanted to make explicit that the purpose of forgoing tax collection from FSCs was to avoid double taxation, as permitted by footnote 59. The EC, however, challenged the new law in an Article 21.5 compliance proceeding, and both the compliance panel, and the Appellate Body found (¶80(c)) that the reform (known as the ETI Act) failed because a measure only passes muster under footnote 59 if it exempts purely foreign-sourced income. The Appellate Body found that "the United States has not met its burden of proving that the ETI measure, viewed as a whole, falls within the justification available under the fifth sentence of footnote 59." The Appellate Body found (¶256(c)) that the ETI exempted some domestic-source income as well as foreign-source income and did not qualify as a measure to avoid double taxation. *U.S. — Treatment for "Foreign Sales Corporations" — Recourse to Article 21.5 of the DSU by the European Communities*, WT/DS108/AB/RW, Report of the Appellate Body, adopted on January 29, 2002. The story will continue in the section on remedies below.

2. *Prohibited Subsidies.* The most common type of prohibited subsidy under Article 3.1 of the SCM Agreement is an export subsidy, which includes any subsidy that is contingent "in law or in fact" upon export performance. But what is "export contingency"? A leading case on this issue is *Canada — Certain Measures Affecting the Automotive Industry*, WT/DS139, 142/AB/R, Report of the Appellate Body, adopted

on June 19, 2000. In this case the Canadian measure at issue was an import duty exemption granted to manufacturers of motor vehicles who met three conditions: (1) production in Canada of motor vehicles of the class imported; (2) production in Canada that accounted for a certain minimum ratio of all vehicles of that class sold in Canada; and (3) the amount of value added in Canada had to be over a specified minimum. The Appellate Body in this case affirmed (¶¶90-94) the finding of the panel that the Canadian import duty exemption was a subsidy under SCM Agreement Article 1.1, since the duty exemptions constituted the forgoing of revenue otherwise due. The Appellate Body also agreed (¶109) with the panel that the Canadian measure was contingent on export performance, and therefore, inconsistent with SCM Agreement Article 3.1(a), since "the more motor vehicles a manufacturer exports, the more motor vehicles that manufacturer is entitled to import duty-free." In reaching this conclusion, the Appellate Body cited the "tied to" test contained in footnote 4 to Article 3.1(a).

3. The panels and the Appellate Body have been quite receptive to broad construction of Articles 1 and 2 as applied to actions against illegal subsidies. All of the following instances were considered to be illegal subsidies. Consider these cases:

- South Korea provides its shipbuilding industry certain special advantages: The Export-Import Bank of Korea provides (1) advance payment refund guarantees to prospective foreign buyers of vessels; and (2) pre-shipment loan programs at below market interest rates. *See Korea—Measures Affecting Trade in Commercial Vessels*, WT/DS273/R, Report of the Panel, adopted on April 11, 2005.
- Brazil provides export credits for Brazilian export transactions relating to regional aircraft. With direct financing, Brazil lends a portion of the funds required for the transaction; with interest equalization, Brazil pays a portion of the interest charges (i.e., 3 percent of a 10 percent charge). *See Brazil—Export Financing Programme for Aircraft*, WT/DS46/AB/R, Report of the Appellate Body, adopted on August 20, 1999.
- Canada provides financing and loan guarantees at below market rates to aid the sale of civil aircraft. The issue was whether there was a "benefit." In this case, the Appellate Body defined (¶153) benefit as advantage, profit, gift, or a favorable or helpful factor or circumstance to the recipient, and some kind of comparison is implied between what the recipient obtains and what is available in the marketplace. A prohibited export subsidy is contingent, in law or in fact, upon export performance. How is this determined? The Appellate Body ruled (¶169) that the essential elements of contingency in fact are: (1) the granting of the subsidy; (2) the subsidy is tied to exports; and (3) the actual or anticipated exportation or export earnings. *See Canada—Measures Affecting the Export of Civilian Aircraft*, WT/DS70/AB/R, Report of the Appellate Body, adopted on August 20, 1999.

4. Many of the subsidies cases brought to the WTO are aspects of bilateral trade "wars": the tax war between the United States and the EU, which was a continuation of a longstanding battle that began over twenty-five years ago in the GATT; the aircraft subsidy war between Canada and Brazil; the shipbuilding subsidy war between South Korea and the EU; and the latest "war"—the accusation by the United States that the EU illegally subsidizes Airbus while the EC accuses the United States of subsidizing Boeing through U.S. Defense Department contracts.

What does this tell you about actions against subsidies? Are these actions a trade tool or a political tool?

5. *Agricultural Subsidies.* Agricultural subsidies are not generally challenged under the SCM but they can be subject to challenge under the Agreement on Agriculture. Recall that under the AoA, members have made commitments to reduce both domestic and export subsidies for agricultural products. If members exceed the level of support in their reduction commitments, then they are in violation of the AoA. However, many subsidies are exempt and do not have to be included in the aggregate amounts used in determining whether members have excluded their annual reduction commitment levels. In most of these cases, the issue concerns whether the agricultural subsidy is entitled to an exemption or whether the subsidy must be counted against the member's reduction commitments; i.e., a certain annual total amount of support. Panels and the Appellate Body have also been receptive to interpreting the AoA to find that agricultural subsidies are not exempt.

- Canada was found to have violated its export reduction commitments under the AoA. Under its revised support scheme for dairy products, Canada designated milk produced in excess of production quota milk as "commercial export milk" (CEM). Canada argued that CEM was not benefited by an export subsidy, and for this reason, all CEM support should be excluded from Canada's export subsidies reduction commitments. The Appellate Body ruled that CEM did receive an export subsidy because (1) the sale of CEM by producers to processors was below the average cost of production, and thus, the sale of CEM at such artificially low prices constitutes payments to the processors; and (2) these payments are financed by government action. The CEM program meets the standard for an export subsidy, and CEM must be counted against Canada's total level of export subsidies reduction commitments. *Canada—Measures Affecting the Importation of Milk and the Exportation of Dairy Products—Second Recourse to Article 21.5 of the DSU by New Zealand and the United States*, WT/DS103, 113/AB/RW2, Report of the Appellate Body, adopted on December 20, 2002.
- Brazil successfully challenged U.S. cotton subsidies that were provided to farmers to limit production of cotton. Payments to limit agricultural production are exempt from inclusion in the U.S.'s reduction commitments on domestic subsidies if they qualify as exempted "green box" subsidies under the AoA. However, the U.S. program made the payments to the farmers on the basis of the number of acres of land that could be used to grow upland cotton, and the farmers received these payments whether they grew cotton, fruits, vegetables, or nothing at all. The Appellate Body found fault with the program because the payments were not directly tied to limiting production of cotton. As a result, they did not qualify as green box subsidies, and the subsidies had to be included in calculation of the reduction commitment levels of the total amount of annual domestic support by the United States. *United States—Subsidies on Upland Cotton*, WT/DS267/AB/R, Report of the Appellate Body, adopted on March 21, 2005.
- The EC was found to have provided non-exempt export subsidies to beet farmers that allowed them to produce profitably, even though the prices at which the beets were sold were below the average total cost of production. The EC payments also helped to cross-subsidize sugar exports. The

Appellate Body found that the EC payments were export subsidies and had to be counted against the EC's total export reduction commitments. This ruling makes clear the connection between domestic subsidies and export subsidies. *European Communities—Export Subsidies on Sugar*, WT/DS265/AB/R, Report of the Appellate Body, adopted on April 28, 2005.

6. Actionable Subsidies

In any action challenging yellow light subsidies, the complaining member must establish not only that a subsidy exists but that the subsidy causes "adverse effects" under SCM Agreement Article 5. In most cases, members attempt to demonstrate "adverse effects" by showing that the imports result in "serious prejudice," one of the standards of Article 5. The meaning of "serious prejudice" and how it is determined is discussed in the case below.

PROBLEM 10-14

You are an analyst for a U.S. consumers group. You are asked to explain (1) why in the *Indonesia—Autos* case below, the U.S. automobile industry decided not to bring a unilateral action against Indonesia under U.S. domestic law for the imposition of countervailing duties; (2) what exactly was the interest of the United States in bringing the WTO action and what was the harm that the United States argued that it was suffering; and (3) if the United States did not export any automobiles to Indonesia, then what was the real concern of the U.S. automobile industry in asking the United States to bring the WTO case? Is it wise as a matter of policy for the WTO to allow the U.S. automobile industry to take this type of action?

Indonesia—Certain Measures Affecting the Automobile Industry
Report of the Panel, adopted on July 23, 1998
WT/DS54, 55, 59, 64/R

[The United States and the European Communities alleged that the 1996 Indonesia National Car Program provided actionable subsidies causing serious prejudice to their interests within the meaning of SCM Agreement Article 5(c). The panel ruled on these issues.]

2.15 Two sets of measures [that may qualify as subsidies] have been identified by all parties under the 1996 National Car programme:

2.16 The first set of measures—the February 1996 Programme—provides for the grant of "pioneer" or National Car company status to Indonesian car companies that meet specified criteria as to ownership of facilities, use of trademarks, and technology. Maintenance of pioneer status is dependent on the National Cars' meeting increasing local content requirements over a three year period. The benefits provided are exemption from luxury tax on sales of National Cars, and exemption from import duties on parts and components.

2.17 The second set of measures—the June 1996 Programme—provides that National Cars manufactured in a foreign country by Indonesian nationals and which fulfil the local content requirements prescribed by the Minister of Industry and Trade, shall be treated the same as National Cars manufactured in Indonesia, i.e. exempt from import duties and luxury tax. In accordance with Decree 142/96, imported National Cars are deemed to comply with the 20 per cent local content requirement for the end of the first production year if the overseas producer manufacturing the National Cars "counter-purchases" Indonesian parts and components that account for at least 25 per cent of the C&F value of the imported cars.

[A third component of the 1996 National Car Program, a series of loans totaling U.S. $690 million to PT Timor Putra Nasional (TPN), the only qualifying pioneer company, to enable TPN to carry out the National Car project, was not challenged under the SCM Agreement.

As a threshold matter, the panel examined whether the duty and sales tax exemptions were specific subsidies. The panel ruled that under Article 1.1(a) the exemptions constitute revenue forgone; and under Article 1.1(b), a benefit is conferred. Since the subsidy is contingent on the use of domestic over imported goods, it was deemed to be specific under Article 2.3. Thus, the panel concluded these were "specific subsidies." Since these were actionable (yellow light), the measures had to be withdrawn. To determine material injury, the panel turned to whether these actionable subsidies met the "serious prejudice" standard under Article 5.]

CLAIMS OF SERIOUS PREJUDICE UNDER PART III OF THE SCM AGREEMENT

14.153 The European Communities and the United States contend that the tariff and luxury sales tax exemptions provided by Indonesia through the National Car programme are specific subsidies which have caused serious prejudice to their interests within the meaning of Article 5(c) of the Agreement on Subsidies and Countervailing Measures ("SCM Agreement"). Specifically, the complainants allege that the effect of alleged subsidies for the national car is (a) to displace or impede imports of like products of the European Communities and the United States into the Indonesian market and (b) a significant price undercutting by the subsidized national car as compared with like EC and US products in the Indonesian market. The European Communities further contend, in the alternative, that the alleged subsidies provided by Indonesia through the National Car programme threaten to cause serious prejudice to EC interests.

LIKE PRODUCT ANALYSIS

14.163 [The United States and the EC claim] that this serious prejudice arises both from displacement or impedance of their exports of passenger cars to Indonesia and through significant price undercutting of their passenger cars by the subsidized Timor in the Indonesian market.

14.164 Article 6.3 provides in relevant parts as follows:

> Serious prejudice in the sense of paragraph (c) may arise in any case where one or several of the following may apply:
> (a) the effect of the subsidy is to displace or impede the exports of a *like product* of another Member into the Market of the subsidizing Member; . . .
> (b) the effect of the subsidy is a significant price undercutting by the subsidized product as compared with the price of a *like product* of another Member in

> the same market or significant price suppression, price depression or lost sales in the same market; . . . (emphasis added).

It is clear from the text of Article 6.3 that any analysis of displacement or impedance or of price undercutting must focus on the effects of the subsidy vis à vis the *like product* to the subsidized product. In this case, the European Communities and the United States have alleged that the subsidies in question are conferred on the Timor. Accordingly, our analysis of the effects of these subsidies must be performed in relation to their effects on products which are "like products" to that passenger car.

14.173 In our view, the analysis as to which cars have "characteristics closely resembling" those of the Timor logically must include as an important element the physical characteristics of the cars in question. This is especially the case because many of the other possible criteria identified by the parties are closely related to the physical characteristics of the cars in question. Thus, factors such as brand loyalty, brand image/reputation, status and resale value reflect, at least in part, an assessment by purchasers of the physical characteristics of the cars being purchased.

14.176 The European Communities contend that we must consider all passenger cars to be "like" because any effort to differentiate between passenger cars with a multitude of differing characteristics would inevitably result in arbitrary divisions. We are aware that there are innumerable differences among passenger cars and that the identification of appropriate dividing lines between them may not be a simple task. However, this does not in our view justify lumping all such products together where the differences among the products are so dramatic.

14.177 One reasonable way for this panel to approach the "like product" issue is to look at the manner in which the automotive industry itself has analyzed market segmentation. The United States and the European Communities have submitted information regarding the market segmentation approach taken by DRI's Global Automotive Group, a company whose clients include all major auto manufacturers, including KIA, PT TPN's national car partner.

14.181 In our view, the DRI market segmentation analysis presented by the European Communities and the United States supports the view that all vehicles in the C1 Segment—including the 306, Optima and Escort—are "like products" to the Timor within the meaning of the SCM Agreement. By contrast, the DRI analysis places the Vectra and the Neon in different market segments (D1 and C2 respectively), and this in our view weakens the complainants' view that these products should be considered to be "like" the Timor.

[The panel also concluded that unassembled cars may be considered "like products" to assembled vehicles.]

DISPLACEMENT AND IMPEDANCE

14.207 Having determined that certain EC and US passenger car models are (or, in the case of the Neon, may be) like products to the Timor, we must next examine whether the complainants have demonstrated that the effect of the subsidies provided pursuant to the National Car programme has been to displace or impede the exports of those models from the Indonesian market.

(a)   *Market Share Data*

(ii) Actual Sales and Market Share Data   14.212 Having determined that the EC and US models in the C1 Segment (and arguably those in the C2 Segment) are "like" the subsidized Timor, we consider it appropriate to analyze market shares for the C Segment. A review of the data provided by Indonesia under the Annex V procedure demonstrates that the Timor quickly gained a very substantial share of the Indonesian C Segment passenger car market upon its introduction. As shown in Table 1, the Timor was not sold in 1995 and thus had a zero share of the C Segment market. In 1996, the year of introduction, the Timor captured a 16.9 per cent share of the Indonesian C Segment, while during the period January-May 1997 (the latest period for which we have been provided with data), that market share had climbed to 42.4 percent. Table 2 breaks this market share data down on a quarterly basis. These data indicate that Timor had no sales until the fourth quarter of 1996. In that quarter, its market share in the C Segment reached 40.9 per cent. It dropped to 38.8 per cent for the first quarter of 1997 but during the partial second quarter for which we have data (April-May) that share had climbed to 47.7 per cent.

14.213 In assessing whether this change in market share in fact amounted to a displacement or impedance of imports of EC and US origin products into Indonesia, our starting point is actual market shares for the three EC models we have found to be like products, and for the one US model which we assume *arguendo* to be a like product, to the Timor. The Neon was never introduced into the Indonesia market (allegedly because of the National Car programme), and the market share of US-origin passenger cars in the C Segment of the Indonesian passenger car market was therefore zero. Because the Escort also was never introduced into the Indonesian market, the EC market share data are based solely on sales of the 306 and the Optima. As shown in Table 1, *infra* at p. 385, the European Communities in 1995 had an Indonesian market share in the C Segment of 2.4 per cent. The EC share climbed to 5.7 per cent in 1996, but dropped to 3.7 per cent for the period for which we have data (January-May 1997). Table 2, *infra* at p. 386, breaks down these data on a quarterly basis. This analysis shows that in the first three quarters of 1996, EC market share in the C Segment ranged from 6.9 to 7.8 percent. In the fourth quarter of 1996 (the quarter in which the Timor first entered the market), EC market share dropped to 3.7 per cent. In the first quarter of 1997, EC market share fell even further to 3.3 per cent, and remained at a relatively low 4.2 per cent in the partial second quarter for which we have data (April-May 1997).

14.214 Focusing on market shares alone, the data before us show a potentially significant correlation between the introduction of the subsidized Timor and the decline in EC market share in the C Segment of the Indonesian market. The quarterly data show that the EC market share for C Segment cars in Indonesia increased substantially during the first three quarters of 1996, but that, in the fourth quarter of 1996, coincident with the introduction of the Timor, the European models' market share dropped to 3.7 per cent, where it remained on average during the first five months of 1997. Thus, there seems to be little question that the EC market share in the C Segment dropped substantially relative to that of the subsidized Timor, and the close correlation in time between the introduction of the Timor and the drop in EC market share suggests a causal link between the two.

14.216 In spite of their declines in market share, the absolute volume of sales of the relevant EC models did not significantly decline after the introduction of the Timor. Rather, sales of C Segment vehicles from the EC were 419 units in 1995 and 1,445 units in 1996. For 1997 we have full data from the Annex V process on the C Segment only for January-May, and this shows EC sales of 611 units, which amounts to 1,466 units on an annualized basis. We also have sales figures for the Optima (257 units) and 306 (656 units) for the period January-August 1997 from the European Communities. These figures, totalled and annualized, show sales of 1,370 units for 1997. On a quarterly basis, sales of the Optima and 306 remained relatively constant during the period from the fourth quarter of 1996 through May 1997 at between 300 and 400 units per quarter.

14.217 The explanation for the loss of market share with no decline in absolute sales volume is that the size of the Indonesian market expanded after the introduction of the Timor. What is particularly relevant here is that the increase in the size of the market was largely attributable to sales of the Timor. In particular, between the third and fourth quarters of 1996, the market for C Segment cars increased by 6,326 units, of which the Timor accounted for 4,278 units (68%). A similar pattern was evident during the first five months of 1997. Thus, relatively stable EC sales volumes in a rapidly expanding market resulted in market share declines but not in declines in absolute volumes.

14.218 We agree with the European Communities that a complainant need not demonstrate a decline in sales in order to demonstrate displacement or impedance. This is inherent in the ordinary meaning of those terms. Thus, displacement relates to a situation where sales volume has declined, while impedance relates to a situation where sales which otherwise would have occurred were impeded. The question before us is therefore whether the market share and sales data above would support a view that, but for the introduction of the subsidized Timor, sales of EC C Segment passenger cars would have been greater than they were.

14.219 In a usual case, a decline in market share in a stable or growing market, corresponding in time with the introduction of a subsidized product, might suggest that sales would have been higher but for the introduction of the subsidized product. This would be particularly the case where, in the period prior to the introduction of the subsidized product, the market share of the non-subsidized product had been rising. In this case, however, Indonesia contends that the introduction of the subsidized Timor was itself responsible for the rapid expansion of the market through the introduction of a new, highly affordable passenger car within the reach of first-time buyers. While the European Communities dismisses this argument as "purely speculative," the sales data in terms of volume of sales discussed above provide some support for this view. Thus, one possible interpretation of the data is that, if the subsidized Timor had not been introduced, the Indonesian C Segment market would have remained relatively stable or in any event would have posted during the last quarter of 1996 and the first eight months of 1997 more gradual increases, comparable to those experienced during the period between the first quarter of 1995 and the second quarter of 1996.

14.220 Assuming that, had the subsidized Timor not been introduced, the Indonesian C Segment market would have remained stable or grown at a more moderate rate during the period for which we have data, the question is whether sales of EC C Segment models in absolute terms would have been higher than those actually achieved. Here, the data are inconclusive. While the European Communities contend that its market share had been steadily increasing and that this trend would have continued but for the introduction of the subsidized Timor, actual sales consisted of only two models, the Optima and 306. As Table 2 shows, quarterly sales data for the Optima do not demonstrate any clear upward trend in the six quarters prior to the introduction of the subsidized Timor. Rather, the increase in EC sales was a result of the introduction of the 306 in the first quarter of 1996. While the European Communities state that 1996 sales of the 306 (1,086 units) were 400 units lower than planned, we have no knowledge of the basis for those sales forecasts. Sales of the 306 for partial year 1997 were at an annualized rate of between 984 units (January-August data) and 1,070 units (January to May data), down slightly from the annualized rate in the first half of 1996 of 1,214 units. Thus, if we assume that in the absence of the Timor the market would have remained stable or continued a more gradual increase through August 1997, and that the 306 would have maintained the market share it had achieved in the first half of 1996, these sales might have been expected to increase at most slightly. Such a conclusion is, in any event, highly speculative based on the facts available.

14.222 In short, the dramatic fall in EC market share in the C Segment is not in this case decisive evidence of displacement or impedance, as the data lend some credence to the Indonesian view that the introduction of the subsidized Timor actually created much of the market growth. Thus, we are required to speculate as to how the market would have performed in the absence of the introduction of the Timor, and as to the share of the market which EC models could have been expected to obtain in that hypothetical situation. It is quite possible that the Indonesian market would have remained stable or increased somewhat in late 1996 and early 1997, even without the introduction of the subsidized Timor, and that EC models would have at least maintained their market share, such that EC sales would have increased slightly. This conclusion is however highly tentative, and does not in our view satisfy the requirement, in the present case, that serious prejudice be demonstrated by positive evidence.

CONCLUSION

14.236 In the view of the Panel, neither the European Communities nor the United States has demonstrated by positive evidence that the effect of subsidies to the Timor pursuant to the National Car programme has been to displace or impede imports of like passenger cars from the Indonesian market within the meaning of Article 6.3(a) of the SCM Agreement.

6.   PRICE UNDERCUTTING

14.237 In addition to arguing that serious prejudice has been caused to their interests through displacement or impedance of their exports to Indonesia, the complainants assert that the subsidized Timor significantly undercuts the prices of EC and US like products in the Indonesian market.

14.238 In determining whether serious prejudice within the meaning of Article 5(c) arises from price undercutting, we must first consider Article 6.3(c) of the SCM Agreement. That provision states that

"serious prejudice in the sense of paragraph 5(c) may arise in any case where one or several of the following apply:

. . .

> (c) the effect of the subsidy is a significant price undercutting by the subsidized product as compared with the price of a like product of another Member in the same market or significant price suppression, price depression or lost sales in the same market; . . .

Further elaboration on the application of Article 6.3(c) is provided in Article 6.5 of the SCM Agreement, which provides as follows:

> For the purpose of paragraph 3(c), price undercutting shall include any case in which such price undercutting has been demonstrated through a comparison of prices of the subsidized product with prices of a non-subsidized like product supplied to the same market. The comparison shall be made at the same level of trade and at comparable times, due account being taken of any other factor affecting price comparability. However, if such a direct comparison is not possible, the existence of price undercutting may be demonstrated on the basis of export unit values.

(a)   United States

[The panel found that the United States did not export any cars to Indonesia that were "like products" to the Timor and so could not have suffered any serious prejudice.]

(b)   European Communities

14.241 We now turn to the EC argument that the prices of the subsidized National Cars significantly undercut the prices of like passengers cars imported from the European Communities. In support of their price undercutting arguments, the European Communities rely on data regarding the list and market prices for passenger cars sold in Indonesia which show that the Timor has both a list and a market price which are much lower than the list and market prices for the 306 and the Optima, which we have determined to be like products (of another Member) to the Timor.

14.242 With respect to list prices, data submitted by Indonesia during the Annex V process show that the Timor had the lowest list price of any passenger car in the Indonesian market except the Mazda MR-90 as of November 1996 and March 1997.

14.254 We note that under Article 6.3(c) serious prejudice may arise only where the price undercutting is "significant." Although the term "significant" is not defined, the inclusion of this qualifier in Article 6.3(c) presumably was intended to ensure that margins of undercutting so small that they could not meaningfully affect suppliers of the imported product whose price was being undercut are not considered to give rise to serious prejudice. This clearly is not an issue here. To the contrary, it is our view that, even taking into account the possible effects of these physical differences on price comparability, the price undercutting by the Timor of the Optima and 306 cannot reasonably be deemed to be other than significant.

14.255 Finally, we note that serious prejudice may arise under Article 6.3(c) only where the price undercutting is "the effect of the subsidy." In this case, we agree with the European Communities that Indonesia, in information that it provided in the Annex V process effectively concedes that the tariff and tax subsidies under the National Car programme are responsible for the significant level of price undercutting.

14.256 For the foregoing reasons, we find that the effect of the subsidies to the Timor pursuant to the National Car programme is to cause serious prejudice to the interests of the European Communities in the sense of Article 5(c) of the SCM Agreement through a significant price undercutting as compared with the price of EC-origin like products in the Indonesian market.

[Having found a specific subsidy and serious prejudice, the panel recommended that Indonesia withdraw the subsidy.]

7.   WTO Remedies for Subsidization

If an illegal subsidy is found, the ultimate goal of the WTO is to have the offending member withdraw the subsidy. If the offending member does not promptly withdraw the subsidy, the WTO can authorize countermeasures against the offending member. The primary purpose of the countermeasures is not to punish the offending member but is to pressure the offending member to withdraw the subsidy or, in some cases, to offset its harmful effects. The use of countermeasures is involved in the following case.

United States—Tax Treatment for "Foreign Sales Corporations"
**Recourse to Arbitration by the United States under Article
22.6 of the DSU and Article 4.11 of the SCM Agreement
Decision of the Arbitrator, adopted on August 30, 2002
WT/DS108/ARB**

[We pick up the story of the tax war between the EC and United States over the treatment of income earned by Foreign Sales Corporations (FSCs) and derived from assisting in the export sales of goods manufactured in the United States. Recall that in the previous proceedings, the Appellate Body held that the U.S. decision to forgo the collection of taxes from FSCs on income earned from assisting in the export sales of U.S. goods was a prohibited subsidy. The Appellate Body indicated that if the FSC tax exemption were a measure to avoid double taxation then it would have been permitted under the SCM, but the Appellate Body rejected an attempt by the United States to characterize the tax exemption as a measure to avoid double taxation. The United States then attempted to meet this criticism by new legislation, the FSC Repeal and Extraterritorial Income Exclusion Act of 2000 (ETI), which was designed explicitly as a measure to avoid double taxation. The EC challenged the ETI, arguing that it was not a true measure to avoid double taxation but a disguised subsidy for FSCs. The Appellate Body agreed that the ETI was not a true measure to avoid double taxation because it exempted from taxation not only foreign-sourced income but also, in some cases, income earned in the United States. Since the ETI failed to justify the exemption of FSCs from taxation, the United States did not bring its inconsistent measures into conformity with the WTO within the prescribed time limits. As a result, the EC requested countermeasures in the form of suspensions of its WTO trade obligations to the United States. The issue before the Appellate Body was the amount of the countermeasures and whether there were limits on how the countermeasures were to be determined.]

2.12 We note that the time-period within which the United States was to have withdrawn the prohibited FSC subsidy in this dispute originally terminated on 1 October 2000. We also recall that the DSB acceded to the United States' request that the DSB modify the time-period in this dispute so as to expire on 1 November 2000. We further note that the United States enacted the ETI Act on 15 November 2000. It was the ETI Act which was reviewed by the Compliance Panel and, on appeal, by the Appellate Body, under Article 21.5 of the *DSU*.

2.15 We therefore decided to assess the proposed suspension of concessions at the time the United States should have withdrawn the prohibited subsidy at issue, in 2000. We consider it relevant, in light of the nature of the countermeasures proposed by the European Communities, to calculate the appropriate countermeasures on a yearly basis. We thus decided to include the whole of the year 2000 in our assessment, taking into account an adjustment for the shift to the ETI Act.

3.1 The United States has argued that the amount of countermeasures proposed by the European Communities is not appropriate because it is disproportionate to the trade impact of the inconsistent measure on the European Communities. It interprets Article 4.10 of the *SCM Agreement* as requiring countermeasures not to be disproportionate to the trade impact of the violating measure on the complaining Member. It also considers that, in this instance, the amount of the subsidy can and should be used as a "proxy" for the trade impact of the measure. The United States estimated the total value of the subsidy at US$4,125 million for the year 2000, and suggested that, allocating to the European Communities its share of that amount, countermeasures in a maximum amount of US$1,110 million would be appropriate.

4.1 We recall that Article 4.10 of the *SCM Agreement* provides as follows:

> "In the event the recommendation of the DSB is not followed within the time-period specified by the panel, which shall commence from the date of adoption of the panel's report or the Appellate Body's report, the DSB shall grant authorization to the complaining Member to take appropriate[17] countermeasures, unless the DSB decides by consensus to reject the request."

4.2 In addition, Article 4.11 of the *SCM Agreement* defines our mandate as follows:

> "In the event a party to the dispute requests arbitration under paragraph 6 of Article 22 of the Dispute Settlement Understanding ("*DSU*"), the arbitrator shall determine whether the countermeasures are appropriate."[18]

4.3 These two provisions complement each other: the arbitrator's mandate in relation to countermeasures concerning prohibited subsidies under Article 4 of the *SCM Agreement* is defined, quite logically, with reference to the notion embodied in the underlying provision in Article 4.10. The expression "appropriate countermeasures" defines what measures can be authorized in case of non-compliance, and our mandate requires us to review whether, in proposing certain measures to take in application of that provision, the prevailing Member has respected the parameters of what is permissible under that provision.

---

17. This expression is not meant to allow countermeasures that are disproportionate in light of the fact that the subsidies dealt with under these provisions are prohibited.

18. This expression is not meant to allow countermeasures that are disproportionate in light of the fact that the subsidies dealt with under these provisions are prohibited.

THE OBJECT AND PURPOSE OF ARTICLE 4.10

5.51 Our understanding of the terms of Article 4.10, including footnote 9, based on an analysis of the relevant terms taken in their context is, in our view, also consistent with the object and purpose of the *SCM Agreement* in relation to Article 4.10, and of the *WTO Agreement,* as they relate to the dispute settlement remedies.

5.52 In our view, the object and purpose of the DSB's mandate to authorize countermeasures under Article 4.10 can first be drawn from the very language of Article 4.10. Article 4.10 requires that the DSB authorize the complaining Member to take appropriate countermeasures in case of non-compliance with the recommendation of the DSB. In other words, countermeasures are taken against non-compliance, and thus its authorization by the DSB is aimed at inducing or securing compliance with the DSB's recommendation. In this context, pursuant to Article 4.7, the DSB may *only* recommend that the subsidizing Member withdraw the subsidy without delay.

5.56 In the case of prohibited subsidies, we are of the view that the fact that a panel determining that a subsidy found to be prohibited can *only* recommend its withdrawal without delay is significant and must be given some meaning when determining the appropriateness of proposed countermeasures. Furthermore, in our view, the legal means prescribed to ultimately restore the "balance of rights and obligations" of Members in relation to prohibited subsidies are specifically provided for under Article 4.7 of the *SCM Agreement*. In a situation where the balance of rights and obligations has been upset through the granting of a prohibited subsidy, panels may only recommend that the subsidizing Member withdraw the subsidy "without delay" in order to restore such balance.

5.57 In light of the above, we believe that countermeasures authorized under Article 4.10 contribute to the purpose of inducing compliance with the DSB's recommendations, consistently with restoring the balance of rights and obligations between the Members. In our view, the terms of Article 4.10 of the *SCM Agreement*, including footnote 9, confirm that, when assessing the scope of what may be deemed "appropriate" countermeasures, we should keep in mind the fact that the subsidy at issue has to be withdrawn and that a countermeasure should contribute to the ultimate objective of withdrawal of the prohibited subsidy without delay.

6.10 The quantitative element of the breach in this case is, in fact, that the United States has spent approximately US$4,000 million yearly in breach of its obligations. To our mind, each dollar is, as it were, as much a breach of the obligations of the United States as any other. Certain dollars do not become any less so—or effectively "quarantined" from their legal status of breach of an obligation—by virtue of some other criteria (such as trade effects). To put it another way, the United States' breach of obligation is not objectively dismissed because some of the products benefiting from the subsidy are, e.g., exported to another trading partner. It is an *erga omnes* obligation owed in is entirety to each and every Member. It cannot be considered to be "allocatable" across the Membership. Otherwise, the Member concerned would be only partially obliged in respect of each and every Member, which is manifestly inconsistent with an *erga omnes per se* obligation. Thus, the United States has breached its obligation to the European Communities in respect of all the money that it has expended, because such expenditure in breach—the expense incurred—is the very essence of the wrongful act.

6.16 As noted above, the quantitative element of the breach in this case is, in fact, that the United States has spent approximately US$4,000 million in breach of its obligations. The European Communities, for its part, is requesting an authorization to take countermeasures in an amount of US$4,043 million.

6.17 The values concerned are not disproportionate. In purely numerical terms, they are in fact in virtual correspondence.

6.23 In this instance, the European Communities has based its proposed amount of countermeasures on the face value of the subsidy, rather than directly on the benefits conferred by it. The United States has not sought to object to the level of countermeasures on these grounds. Taking all of this into account, we, for our part, have certainly found no reason to consider that, to the extent that this aspect is relevant in the first place, it provides any reason to depart from our judgment that the entitlement to the level of countermeasures stemming from the wrongful act as measured by the expense to government is not disproportionate.

6.24 Thus, it is our view, in light of these considerations, that the countermeasures proposed are not disproportionate to the initial wrongful act to which they are intended to respond.

6.27 In the circumstances of this case, the European Communities is the sole complainant seeking to take countermeasures in relation to this particular violating measure. That is also, in our view, a relevant consideration in our analysis. Had there been multiple complainants each seeking to take countermeasures in an amount equal to the value of the subsidy, this would certainly have been a consideration to take into account in evaluating whether such countermeasures might be considered to be not "appropriate" in the circumstances. That is not, however, the situation before us.

[The Arbitrator approved the EC request in full as to the value of the countermeasures allowed to be levied.]

NOTES AND QUESTIONS

1. Do you agree with the Arbitrator's decision and the interpretation of the remedy provision of Article 4 of the SCM Agreement? Specifically, how do you evaluate the argument that trade effects should be the relevant standard for determining the level of the countermeasure? Is the Arbitrator's argument based on Article 4.10 correct? Do you agree that the decision is in accordance with international law norms? One of the criteria for countermeasures under international law is "proportionality." To what should the award be proportional—should it be based on the seriousness of the offense, the injury to the complainant, or the benefit to the recipients? Finally, the Arbitrator makes the point that the EC was the only complainant. But what if other WTO members see an opportunity and join the fray, albeit belatedly, and also seek to impose countermeasures on the United States?

In *Canada—Export Credits and Loan Guarantees for Regional Aircraft, Recourse to Arbitration by Canada under DSU Article 22.6 and SCM Agreement 4.11*, WT/DS222/ARB, Authorization to Suspend Concessions, Report of the Panel, adopted on March 18, 2003, the Arbitral Panel calculated the amount of the subsidy at US$206,497,305 and then, considering that Canada stated that it did not intend to withdraw the subsidy, added an adjustment of 20 percent so that the appropriate countermeasure was ruled to be US$247,797,000. Is this punitive measure appropriate in a subsidies remedy case?

2. In *Australia—Subsidies Provided to Producers and Exporters of Automotive Leather, Recourse by the United States to Article 21.5 of the DSU*, WT/DS126/R/W, Report of the Panel, adopted on February 11, 2000, the panel ruled that, to comply with the requirement of Article 4.7 of the SCM Agreement, a prohibited subsidy must be withdrawn "without delay" and the subsidy must be repaid by the recipient. Is this interpretation correct? Many WTO members, including the United States, the winning party in the dispute, objected to this remedy. Is this remedy practicable or realistic?

NOTE ON THE AIRCRAFT SUBSIDY TRADE WAR BETWEEN THE UNITED STATES AND THE EUROPEAN UNION

In 2004 both the EU and the United States complained at the WTO, accusing each other of illegally subsidizing aircraft production and export sales. This trade war over aircraft subsidies was sparked by the fact that the traditional industry leader, Boeing, lost its industry lead to Airbus, based in Toulouse, France, in 2003. The case against the EU was decided by the Appellate Body in 2011, *European Communities and Certain Member States—Measures Affecting the Trade in Large Civil Aircraft*, WTDS316/AB/R, Report of the Appellate Body, adopted on June 1, 2011. Most importantly, the Appellate Body ruled in this case that certain "launch aid" rendered to Airbus by the EU and member states, as well as certain infrastructure measures and equity infusions, constituted subsidies under SCM Article 1. The Appellate Body also affirmed the panel's findings of serious prejudice under SCM Articles 5(c) and 6.3 because of market displacement and lost export sales for Boeing, and because the panel sufficiently established a genuine and substantial causal link between the subsidies and the displacement and lost sales.

The case against the United States was handed down by the Appellate Body in 2012, *Report of the Appellate Body, United States—Measures Affecting Trade in Large Civil Aircraft*, WT/DS353/AB/R, Report of the Appellate Body, adopted on March 23, 2012. The Appellate Body concluded that NASA procurement contracts and Department of Defense assistance akin to a kind of joint venture provided specific subsidies to Boeing within the meaning of SCM Articles 1 and 2. The Appellate Body also found serious prejudice under SCM Article 5 in that the subsidies contributed in a genuine and substantial way to Boeing's development of new technologies, and (applying a "but for" test of causation) ruled that Airbus had suffered serious prejudice with respect to certain subsidies in violation of SCM Articles 5(c) and 6.3.

How should this trade dispute be resolved? Should both sides be required to end their subsidies or should the WTO establish binding guidelines for government support of the aircraft industry? This problem is becoming more acute as China, Brazil, Russia, and certain other countries emerge as industry competitors.

D.   Countervailing Duty Procedures Under U.S. Law

Read the following provisions of the U.S. Tariff Act of 1930, as amended, in the Documents Supplement:

Section 701 (19 U.S.C. §1671) is the basic operative section imposing countervailing duties.

Sections 771 (5), (5A), (5B), (6), (7), (8), and (9) [19 U.S.C. §§1677 (5), (5A), (5B), (6), (7), and (9)] are definitions respectively of countervailable subsidy (§1677(5)); specificity (§1677(5A)); categories of noncountervailable subsidies (§1677(5B)); net countervailable subsidy (§1677(6)); material injury (§1677(7)); and interested party (§1677(9)).

Section 771B (19 U.S.C. §1677B) deals with calculation of countervailable subsidies on certain processed agricultural products.

We now examine countervailing duties under U.S. law, which is the oldest and most highly developed national law in this area. U.S. law requires the presence of two elements as a prerequisite for levying countervailing duties: (1) the existence of a subsidy and (2) a material injury to a domestic industry (or a threat thereof) caused by the subsidized imports.

Under U.S. law, the determination of whether a subsidy exists closely tracks the WTO standard. A subsidy exists when (1) a financial contribution has been made that (2) confers a benefit on (3) a specific business or firm. The second element is an affirmative determination on the injury requirement. The injury determination in a countervailing duty case is quite similar to the injury determination in anti-dumping cases. Most of the same factors necessary to determining injury to the domestic industry are considered in both types of injury determinations. All subsidies must satisfy the injury requirement under U.S. law before a countervailing duty can be imposed.

As in an anti-dumping case, petitioners must be interested parties in order to have standing to commence a subsidies investigation. *See* 19 U.S.C. §1677(9). An interested party includes a manufacturer, producer, or wholesaler, of a domestic like product, as well as groups of workers representative of affected industries. The petition must be filed with both Commerce and the ITC.

Within twenty days, Commerce must determine the sufficiency of the petition. As in the case of dumping investigations, Commerce is likely to find that the petition is legally sufficient.

Within forty-five days of the filing of the petition, the ITC must make a preliminary finding that there is a "reasonable likelihood" of a material injury or threat thereof or material retardation of the establishment of an industry caused by the subsidized imports. If the ITC makes an affirmative finding then the investigation continues to the next phase that involves two determinations by Commerce.

Within sixty-five days of the filing of the petition, Commerce must make a preliminary determination on whether a subsidy exists and, if so, the amount. Commerce will use information submitted by petitions but will also send questionnaires to the foreign exporters and relevant governments.

If the preliminary determination is positive, then Commerce suspends liquidation of the imports; i.e. suspends final determination of the duties owned. The importer is still allowed to enter the goods into the U.S. market, but must post a bond or make a case deposit equal to the amount of the subsidy that will ultimately be assessed. If the preliminary determination is negative, then the investigation does not end, but continues until Commerce makes a final determination.

Within seventy-five days of its preliminary determination, Commerce must make a final determination on whether a subsidy exists, and the amount of the subsidy. During this seventy-five-day period, Commerce will send its officials to the foreign nation to verify information contained in the questionnaires. If the information is inaccurate or incomplete then Commerce will make its findings on the basis of the facts available; i.e., petitioners' facts. Commerce may also hold hearings at this stage. If Commerce's final determination is negative then the investigation is terminated.

Within forty-five days of a final positive determination by Commerce, the ITC must make a final determination of material injury. This determination is made by the ITC on the basis of evidence submitted by the parties during the earlier stages of the proceeding, an internal ITC report, a hearing at which both parties may make oral and written submissions, and briefs submitted by the parties after the hearing has concluded. The ITC will make its final determination of injury based upon the same factors and the same standard of proof as used in anti-dumping cases. If the ITC makes a negative final determination, the investigation is terminated. If the ITC makes a positive final determination, then a countervailing duty order is issued and the importer must now actually make cash payment of the countervailing duty for all subsequent imports.

Countervailing duties are sometimes assessed against all exporters from the offending country. This practice differs somewhat from the practice concerning anti-dumping duties in which the anti-dumping duty is usually assessed against individual exporters who are selected by the Commerce Department for investigation and are willing to defend the anti-dumping duty investigation. A general rate is then assessed against all of the other exporters in an anti-dumping duty action. In the case of both anti-dumping duties and countervailing duties, however, U.S. law provides a procedure whereby an individual exporter can make a showing before Commerce as to why a different rate should be applied to its products.

As in the case of anti-dumping duties, countervailing duty orders are subject to annual review to determine whether the countervailing duty should be modified to reflect a change in the amount of the margin or whether a party is in compliance with a suspension agreement. Commerce may terminate an investigation or revoke an order if the involved government has stopped subsidizing for three consecutive years or the companies involved have not received any subsidies for five consecutive years. The "sunset" review provision contained in Article 21.3 of the SCM Agreement requires that five years after the issuance of the countervailing duty order, Commerce and the ITC must make an affirmative determination that the subsidy and injury are likely to continue; otherwise, the order must be terminated.

PROBLEM 10-15

Med-Tech, a U.S. company engaged in manufacturing hospital equipment, is experiencing a consistent loss of market share to import competition. Upon investigation, Med-Tech receives information that an import competitor in Country B, a WTO member, is receiving export financing at preferential rates and special tax exemptions. Advise Med-Tech how to file a countervailing duty petition.

- Is Med-Tech an interested party? *See* 19 U.S.C. §1667(9).
- What should the petition contain, and where should it be filed? *See* 19 U.S.C. §1671.

- Is there a countervailable subsidy? *See* 19 U.S.C. §§1677(5)(A)-(B), 1677(5)(D), 1677(5)(E), and 1677(5A).
- What must be done to show material injury? *See* 19 U.S.C. §1667(7).

PROBLEM 10-16

Med-Tech further discovers that its import competitors have received generous research and development support from their governments. In addition, certain of the import competitors from Country A have received special government grants because their manufacturing operations are located in so-called "disadvantaged regions" of their home country. Does Med-Tech have any recourse? *See* 19 U.S.C. §1667(5B).

Med-Tech also discovers that its competitor in Country B is the recipient of government loans that are conditioned on purchasing local products for its manufacturing. What recourse is available? *See* 19 U.S.C. §1667(5A).

PROBLEM 10-17

A U.S. exporter is bidding on a project in Malaysia and is competing against an exporter from Thailand. The company from Thailand offers a bid that is extremely low, possibly below what one would consider the cost of production. The U.S. exporter believes that the reason the company from Thailand is able to bid so low is that it is being assisted by its government with low-cost loans and payment of various export-related expenses. Where can the U.S. exporter file an action?

PROBLEM 10-18

The Indian government buys surplus supplies of cotton and linen fabric in Mumbai. The government is able to negotiate a steep discount because it buys very large quantities of the fabric. The government sells the fabrics at the same price that it paid to manufacturers who makes shirts for export to the United States. Is this a subsidy? *See* 19 U.S.C. §1677(5)(E).

PROBLEM 10-19

Indonesia makes payments to processors who turn cut limber into wood usable for making furniture. The payments result in substantial savings to the processers, which then sell the wood to local furniture manufacturers. The manufacturers use the wood to make furniture that is exported to the United States. The U.S. furniture industry brings a countervailing duty investigation. The furniture manufacturers' defense is that they have received no financial contribution from a government so no subsidy exists. What is the result? *See* 19 U.S.C. §1677-1.

E.   WTO Standards for Countervailing Duty Investigations

Read Articles 10 to 23 of the WTO SCM Agreement.

Read also Articles 24 to 26 of the SCM on institutions and transparency.

The following case involves a review of a U.S. countervailing action by the Appellate Body.

United States — Countervailing Duty Investigation on Dynamic Random Access Memory Semiconductors (DRAMS) from Korea
Report of the Appellate Body, adopted on July 20, 2005
WT/DS296/AB/R

INTRODUCTION

1. The United States and Korea each appeals certain issues of law and legal interpretations developed in the Panel Report, *United States — Countervailing Duty Investigation on Dynamic Random Access Memory Semiconductors (DRAMS) from Korea* (the "Panel Report"). The Panel was established to consider a complaint by Korea against the United States regarding the imposition of countervailing duties ("CVDs") on DRAMS and memory models containing DRAMS from Korea, following an investigation by the United States Department of Commerce (the "USDOC") and the United States International Trade Commission (the "USITC").

2. The CVD investigation was initiated in November 2002, in response to a petition filed by Micron Technology, Inc. ("Micron"). The Korean companies investigated included Hynix Semiconductor, Inc. ("Hynix") and Samsung Electronics Co., Ltd. ("Samsung"). The Government of Korea (the "GOK") participated in the investigation as an interested party.

3. On the basis of subsidy and injury determinations by the USDOC and the USITC, respectively, the USDOC issued a CVD order on 11 August 2003, imposing CVDs of 44.29 per cent on Hynix, which would be paid by importers as cash deposits at the same time as they would normally deposit estimated customs duties.

4. Before the Panel, Korea alleged that the United States acted inconsistently with its obligations under Articles 1, 2, 10, 12, 14, 15, 19, 22, and 32 of the *Agreement on Subsidies and Countervailing Measures* (the "*SCM Agreement*"), as well as under Article VI:3 of the *General Agreement on Tariffs and Trade 1994* (the "GATT 1994").

B.   ARTICLE 1.1(A)(1)(IV) OF THE SCM AGREEMENT

1.   *The Meaning of the Terms Entrusts and Directs*

106. Article 1.1 lays down when a "subsidy" shall be deemed to exist for purposes of the *SCM Agreement*, namely, when (i) there is a "financial contribution by a government or any public body", and (ii) "a benefit is thereby conferred". This part of the appeal is concerned with the "financial contribution" element of the

definition of a "subsidy". Article 1.1(a)(1) of the *SCM Agreement* states that there is a financial contribution by a government or any public body where:

(i) a government practice involves a direct transfer of funds (e.g. grants, loans, and equity infusion), potential direct transfers of funds or liabilities (e.g. loan guarantees);

(ii) government revenue that is otherwise due is foregone or not collected (e.g. fiscal incentives such as tax credits);

(iii) a government provides goods or services other than general infrastructure, or purchases goods;

(iv) a government makes payments to a funding mechanism, or entrusts or directs a private body to carry out one or more of the type of functions illustrated in (i) to (iii) above which would normally be vested in the government and the practice, in no real sense, differs from practices normally followed by governments[.]

107. Article 1.1(a)(1) makes clear that a "financial contribution" by a government or public body is an essential component of a "subsidy" under the *SCM Agreement.* No product may be found to be subsidized under Article 1.1(a)(1), nor may it be countervailed, in the absence of a financial contribution. Furthermore, situations involving exclusively private conduct—that is, conduct that is not in some way attributable to a government or public body—cannot constitute a "financial contribution" for purposes of determining the existence of a subsidy under the *SCM Agreement.*

108. Paragraphs (i) through (iv) of Article 1.1(a)(1) set forth the situations where there is a financial contribution by a government or public body. The situations listed in paragraphs (i) through (iii) refer to a financial contribution that is provided *directly* by the government through the direct transfer of funds, the foregoing of revenue, the provision of goods or services, or the purchase of goods. By virtue of paragraph (iv), a financial contribution may also be provided *indirectly* by a government where it "makes payments to a funding mechanism", or, as alleged in this case, where a government "entrusts or directs a private body to carry out one or more of the type of functions illustrated in (i) to (iii) . . . which would normally be vested in the government and the practice, in no real sense, differs from practices normally followed by governments". Thus, paragraphs (i) through (iii) identify the types of actions that, when taken by private bodies that have been so "entrusted" or "directed" by the government, fall within the scope of paragraph (iv).

110. The term "entrusts" connotes the action of giving responsibility to someone for a task or an object. In the context of paragraph (iv) of Article 1.1(a)(1), the government gives responsibility to a private body "to carry out" one of the types of functions listed in paragraphs (i) through (iii) of Article 1.1(a)(1). As the United States acknowledges, "delegation" (the word used by the Panel) may be a means by which a government gives responsibility to a private body to carry out one of the functions listed in paragraphs (i) through (iii). Delegation is usually achieved by formal means, but delegation also could be informal. Moreover, there may be other means, be they formal or informal, that governments could employ for the same purpose. Therefore, an interpretation of the term "entrusts" that is limited to acts of "delegation" is too narrow.

111. As for the term "directs", we note that some of the definitions—such as "give authoritative instructions to" and "order (a person) *to do*"—suggest that the

person or entity that "directs" has authority over the person or entity that is directed. In contrast, some of the other definitions—such as "inform or guide"—do not necessarily convey this sense of authority. In our view, that the private body under paragraph (iv) is directed "*to carry out*" a function underscores the notion of authority that is included in some of the definitions of the term "direct". This understanding of the term "directs" is reinforced by the Spanish and French versions of the *SCM Agreement*, which use the verbs "ordenar" and "ordonner", respectively. Both of these verbs unambiguously convey a sense of authority exercised over someone. In the context of paragraph (iv), this authority is exercised by a government over a private body. A "command" (the word used by the Panel) is certainly one way in which a government can exercise authority over a private body in the sense foreseen by Article 1.1(a)(1)(iv), but governments are likely to have other means at their disposal to exercise authority over a private body. Some of these means may be more subtle than a "command" or may not involve the same degree of compulsion. Thus, an interpretation of the term "directs" that is limited to acts of "command" is also too narrow.

112. Paragraph (iv) of Article 1.1(a)(1) further states that the private body must have been entrusted or directed to carry out *one of the type of functions* in paragraphs (i) through (iii). We therefore agree with Korea that there must be a demonstrable link between the government and the conduct of the private body.

THE PANEL'S REVIEW OF THE USDOC'S EVIDENCE

A.   INTRODUCTION

127. We consider next the Panel's examination of the evidence underlying the USDOC's finding of entrustment or direction. After providing a general interpretation of Article 1.1(a)(1)(iv) of the *SCM Agreement*, the Panel turned to the evidence relied upon by the USDOC in order to determine whether it was sufficient to support the USDOC's finding of entrustment or direction. Based on its review of the evidence, the Panel concluded that the USDOC "could not properly have found that there was sufficient evidence to support a generalized finding of entrustment or direction with respect to private bodies spanning multiple creditors and multiple transactions over the period of investigation."

B.   THE USDOC'S FINDING OF ENTRUSTMENT OR DIRECTION

131. In its subsidy determination, the USDOC found that numerous financial institutions, both public as well as private bodies, participated in financial transactions related to Hynix. For the purpose of this determination, the USDOC distinguished between public bodies, government-owned and controlled private creditors, and private creditors not owned or controlled by the GOK. The Panel maintained this distinction in its analysis, adopting the categorization of Group A, B, and C creditors put forward by the United States. Accordingly, Hynix's public bodycreditors were referred to as Group A creditors, and included the Korean Development Bank ("KDB"), the Industrial Bank of Korea, and other "specialized" banks. The GOK-owned or -controlled private creditors, which were found by

the USDOC not to be public bodies, were referred to as Group B creditors; these included the Korea Exchange Bank and KFB. Private entities in which the GOK had much smaller, or even non-existent shareholdings, were referred to as Group C creditors; among these creditors were KorAm Bank, Hana Bank, and Kookmin Bank. We use the same categories herein.

135. The USDOC drew three factual inferences from the evidence on the record before it: (i) the GOK maintained a policy of supporting Hynix's financial restructuring and thereby avoiding the firm's collapse; (ii) the GOK exercised the control or influence over Hynix's creditors necessary to implement this policy; and (iii) the GOK at times used this control/influence to "pressure" or coerce Hynix's creditors to continue supporting the financial restructuring of the firm. On the basis of these inferences, the USDOC arrived at a conclusion of entrustment or direction covering virtually all of Hynix's creditors and their participation in any or all of the four financial transactions examined:

> [T]he GOK has entrusted or directed financial institutions to carry out the GOK subsidy program to bail out Hynix. In so doing, the GOK both entrusted and directed various GOK financial institutions. As outlined above, the GOK gave authoritative instructions and directives to financial institutions, and made it well known that it fully backed the bailout program. Moreover, once the Hynix Creditors' Council was formed and had a majority of GOK-owned or controlled banks, the GOK entrusted those banks with continuing the bailout process to its conclusion. Accordingly, we find that the GOK's entrustment or direction to these institutions allowed the GOK to execute its bailout policy program, thus providing a financial contribution to Hynix. . . .

144. Notwithstanding the USDOC's reliance on the *totality* of the evidence, the Panel maintained that "[i]n order to" follow the same approach, it was required to assess the "probative value of each evidentiary factor separately". Accordingly, with respect to each of the factual underpinnings of the USDOC's finding of entrustment or direction, the Panel examined *individually* the pieces of evidence on which the USDOC relied to support the particular premise.

145. We see no error, in principle, in a panel's review of individual pieces of evidence under Article 1.1(a)(1)(iv), even where the investigating authority draws its conclusion from the *totality* of the evidence.

146. We find that the Panel erred, however, in the *manner* in which it reviewed the individual pieces of evidence. We note, first, that the Panel often appeared to examine whether each piece of evidence, viewed *in isolation*, demonstrated entrustment or direction. For example, the USDOC found relevant that the Financial Supervisory Commission (the "FSC") had increased the credit limits placed on banks providing loans to a single borrower so that additional funds could be provided to Hynix. The Panel disagreed:

> Even though the [United States] may be correct in arguing that certain creditors would not have been able to participate in the syndicated loan without the loan limit waiver, we do not consider that the [US]DOC could properly have *inferred from this that creditors were entrusted or directed* to participate in the syndicated loan. . . . The [United States] also argues that entrustment or direction to the banks to assist Hynix would be meaningless if the banks were legally precluded from complying with the GOK's directives. While this may be the case, this does not mean that *there is government entrustment or direction every time that a loan limit waiver is provided.* (emphasis added)

We do not read the USDOC to have inferred *solely from the waiver of loan limits* that entrustment or direction had taken place. Nor do we consider that the USDOC's reliance on this evidence suggests that "there is government entrustment or direction every time that a loan limit waiver is provided", for this would follow only if the USDOC had based its finding of entrustment or direction *exclusively* on the waivers of loan limits.

147. Similarly, the USDOC also relied on documents provided during verification meetings to find that an FSC vice-chairman had attended a meeting of the May 2001 Creditors' Council "to urge creditor banks to execute the resolutions made by creditors". This evidence was relied on by the USDOC in support of its understanding that the GOK had applied pressure on Hynix's creditors to participate in the financial restructuring of the firm. The Panel dismissed the relevance of this evidence:

> [T]he fact that a regulatory authority attends a meeting of creditors at the request of the lead creditor in order to urge—and not instruct—creditor banks to execute resolutions made by creditors would not allow an investigating authority to properly conclude that such *attendance amounted to governmental entrustment or direction* of creditors to participate in the restructuring. (original underlining; italics added)

The USDOC did not advance the view that the attendance of the FSC official, in and of itself, "amounted to" entrustment or direction. In arriving at this conclusion, the Panel essentially faulted the USDOC for drawing a certain inference from a single piece of evidence, where, in fact, the agency did no such thing.

152. In this case, as we observed above, the USDOC relied on the evidence to arrive at certain factual conclusions as an intermediate step in its analysis *before* finding entrustment or direction. These intermediate factual conclusions were: (i) the GOK pursued a policy of preventing the financial collapse of Hynix; (ii) the GOK held control or influence over Hynix's Group B and C creditors; and (iii) the GOK pressured certain of Hynix's Group B and C creditors into participating in the financial restructuring. A proper assessment by the Panel, therefore, would have considered whether the individual piece of evidence being examined could tend to support—not establish in and of itself—the *particular intermediate factual conclusion* that the USDOC was seeking to draw from it. By looking instead to whether such evidence directly supported a finding of entrustment or direction, the Panel determined certain pieces of evidence not to be probative when, in fact, had they been properly viewed in the framework of the USDOC's examination, their relevance would not have been overlooked.

158. In sum, we are of the view that, in analyzing the USDOC's evidence under Article 1.1(a)(1)(iv), the Panel assessed the relevance of many individual pieces of evidence by examining whether *each* of them was sufficient to establish entrustment or direction. In so doing, the Panel failed to appreciate the circumstantial nature of the USDOC's evidence and to consider the relevance of that evidence for the particular inferences the USDOC sought to draw. This error, in turn, contributed to various findings of the Panel dismissing or discounting individual pieces of evidence relied on by the USDOC. Furthermore, in its "global" examination of the evidence, the Panel failed to consider that pieces of evidence, especially circumstantial evidence, might become more significant when viewed in their totality. For these reasons, we *find* that the Panel *erred* in failing to examine the USDOC's evidence in its totality, and requiring, instead, that individual pieces of evidence,

in and of themselves, establish entrustment or direction by the GOK of Hynix's creditors.

[Based upon its analysis of the errors committed by the panel, the Appellate Body set aside the panel's decision.]

PROBLEM 10-20

Titan Steel is a large enterprise in the steel manufacturing business that was formerly owned and operated by the government of Country K, a WTO member. Titan Steel was recently sold by the government to a group of private investors, who are now running the former state-owned enterprise as a private company. Under its new management, Titan Steel now seeks to export to the United States. Competitors in the United States believe that (1) the sale price was extremely low; and (2) Titan Steel still benefits from the generous infusions of government monies that were previously made when it was operated by the government of Country K. Titan Steel claims that it has received no further government infusions since the privatization. What are the issues involved, and what recourse is possible by the affected U.S. companies? See the notes below.

PROBLEM 10-21

A factory in Thailand hires a private trucking company to transport goods at a high expense over rugged hilly terrain to the nearest port for export to the United States. In 2013, the Thai government levels the terrain and builds a road and a bridge. The factory can now ship the goods using its own vans and is able to reap significant savings in transportation costs. The United States brings a countervailing duty action claiming that the works are a subsidy. What is the result? See 19 U.S.C. §1677(5)(D)(iii) and the notes below.

NOTES AND QUESTIONS

1. Commerce's final determination of a countervailable subsidy was reviewed by the U.S. Court of International Trade in *Hynix Semiconductor Inc. v. United States*, 425 F. Supp. 2d 1287 (CIT 2006). The court upheld Commerce's conclusion that the Korean government entrusted or directed financial contributions received by Hynix during its restructuring and that these contributions conferred a countervailable benefit. Commerce applied a three-pronged analysis to its interpretation of 19 U.S.C. §1677(5)(B)(iii). First, Commerce found that the Korean government entrusted or directed certain financial institutions to provide preferential loans and equity infusions to Hynix; second, Commerce determined that the contributions to Hynix did not differ in substance from practices normally followed by governments in conferring a subsidy; and third, Commerce found, by comparing the contributions to Hynix with similar transactions under market conditions, that the contributions conferred a "benefit" to Hynix. *Id.* at 1294-1295.

2. In *AK Steel Corp. v. United States*, 192 F.3d 1367 (Fed. Cir. 1999), the court affirmed, on the basis of a substantial evidence test, a Commerce finding that the Korean government's construction of infrastructure (harbor works, a road, and

a rail spur) was a countervailable subsidy. A major issue was specificity; all governments provide infrastructure as public goods and it would be impossible to consider all infrastructure to be an illegal subsidy. Commerce found that infrastructure projects are general, and not specific (1) if the government does not limit who can move into the area; (2) if the area is used in fact by more than one industry or group; and (3) those that move into the area have equal access to infrastructure improvements. The evidence showed that these tests were not met and that the infrastructure provided to the Korean company was specific. To measure the benefit conferred, Commerce used what the company would have to spend to build the infrastructure if the Korean government had not built it. This measure was affirmed by the Court of Appeals. *Id.* at 1381.

NOTE ON THE PRIVATIZATION OF STATE-OWNED ENTERPRISES

A special issue arises in connection with the privatization of former state-owned enterprises that had in the past received government subsidies: Are goods produced by the state-owned enterprise subject to countervailing duties even though the enterprise has been sold to a private company? U.S. law (19 U.S.C. §1677(5)(F)) provides that, even though there is a "change in ownership" of a foreign state-owned enterprise, the products sold by the new private owner can still be considered to benefit from a countervailable subsidy.

Multiple challenges were made in recent years to the U.S. approach. Commerce's methodology created an "irrebuttable presumption" that the subsidies "passed through" to the new owners and precluded Commerce from considering any evidence to the contrary. This methodology was rejected by both the WTO and a federal appeals court. *See United States—Imposition of Countervailing Duties on Certain Hot-Rolled Lead and Bismuth Carbon Steel Products Originating in the United Kingdom,* WT/DS138/AB/R, Report of the Appellate Body, adopted on June 7, 2000; and *Delverde SRL v. United States,* 202 F.3d 1360, 1369 (Fed. Cir. 2000) (interpreting §1677(5)(F) as preventing the adoption of a per se rule). Following these rebuffs, Commerce issued a new methodology known as the "same person" methodology. Under this approach, Commerce considers whether the post-privatization entity is the "same person" that received the original subsidies, considering such factors as continuity of assets and retention of personnel. If this analysis leads to the conclusion that the "same person" still exists, then Commerce will find that the non-recurring subsidy given to the state-owned enterprise before privatization is passed through to the new private owner.

The "same person" methodology was also successfully challenged in the WTO. The "same person" methodology requires Commerce to conclude that if the same person is found to exist then an irrebuttable presumption arises that a countervailable benefit is passed through to the new owners. *See United States—Countervailing Measures Concerning Certain Products from the European Communities,* WT/DS212/AB/R, Report of the Appellate Body, adopted on January 8, 2003.

This decision, as well as new challenges, caused Commerce to adopt a further change. *See* 68 Fed. Reg. 37125 (June 23, 2003). Commerce's new methodology focuses on whether the privatization was conducted at arm's length and at fair market value. If so, then the previous subsidy did not pass through to the new owner. A WTO compliance panel partially faulted Commerce in applying the new methodology because it did not reexamine two cases and overlooked evidence in a third. *See United States—Countervailing Measures Concerning Certain Products from the European Communities, Recourse to 21.5 of the DSU*, WT/DS212R/W, Report of the Panel, adopted on September 27, 2005. Happy that its methodology has survived at least up to the present, Commerce reexamined all the EC cases and revoked the countervailing duties imposed.

NOTE ON THE U.S.-CANADA SOFTWOOD LUMBER CASE

This dispute between the United States and Canada, which raged in various phases from 1982 to 2006, involved an effort by the United States to impose both anti-dumping and countervailing duties to imports of softwood lumber from Canada. At the heart of the case were so-called upstream subsidies that did not benefit the wood products themselves but that resulted from the artificially low stumpage prices that Canadian provinces charge private companies to cut standing timber on public lands. Due to the low stumpage prices, the private companies can sell the lumber at lower prices to Canadian companies that process the raw timber into construction lumber. In turn, the Canadian companies that produce the construction lumber can charge lower prices when the lumber is exported to the United States. In the latest round of the dispute, when the United States imposed countervailing duties on imports of Canadian softwood lumber, Canada brought multiple challenges both at the WTO and under NAFTA.

In the major WTO case, the Appellate Body agreed with Commerce that "harvesting rights" (low stumpage fees), granted by Canadian provincial governments to private companies to cut timber on public lands, satisfied the "financial contribution" element of a subsidy. However, the Appellate Body faulted Commerce because it never made a finding on whether the benefit of the low stumpage fee was passed through to the companies that processed the cut lumber into construction lumber. *See Final Countervailing Duty Determinations with Respect to Certain Softwood Lumber from Canada*, WT/DS257/AB/R, Report of the Appellate Body, adopted on January 19, 2004.

This long-running dispute was finally settled in 2006 when the two governments signed the U.S.-Canada Softwood Lumber Agreement. Under this agreement, both the United States and Canada will end all litigation over trade in softwood lumber, and unrestricted trade is to be resumed. However, when the lumber market is soft and prices fall below a benchmark price, Canadian exporting provinces must choose either to collect an export tax that ranges from 5 to 15 percent or to limit export volumes. As for the anti-dumping and countervailing duties already collected by the United States, the parties agreed that $500 million would be distributed to the Coalition for Fair Lumber Imports, the main U.S. industry group that led the challenge to softwood lumber imports. In addition, $50 million was distributed to a binational industry council, and $450 million was put into a fund for low-income housing and disaster relief in the United States. This agreement was strongly applauded by the Coalition for Fair Lumber Imports. However, on January 18, 2011, the United States filed a formal petition for arbitration with the Canadian government challenging Canada's current lumber pricing system.

Pursuant to the 2006 Agreement, arbitration is being conducted under the rules of the London Court of International Arbitration. At this writing this arbitration proceeding is pending.

What are the lessons of this dispute? Repeated rulings by WTO bodies and NAFTA panels found the U.S.-imposed duties illegal but the United States ignored these rulings. Was a bilateral deal outside the framework of both the WTO and NAFTA warranted? Is the U.S.-Canada Softwood Lumber Agreement a good precedent for the way such disputes should be handled, instead of resorting to NAFTA or the WTO?

11 *Trade in Services and the GATS*

I. *Introduction*

Chapters 5 through 10 have so far concentrated on the trade in goods. Beginning with this Chapter, we examine the treatment of the other major channels of trade under the WTO: services, foreign investment, and technology. Recall that much of the GATT jurisprudence developed in connection with the trade in goods is immediately applicable to the other channels of trade.

In this Chapter, we address the topic of trade in services as regulated under the General Agreement on Trade in Services (GATS).

The adoption of the GATS in the Uruguay Round reflects the growing importance of services in world trade. In international trade, services trade is about 20 percent of the trade in goods, and this proportion is growing rapidly. Trade in services is especially important to developed countries, which dominate in services trade. For example, in 2010 the United States and the EU accounted for 61 percent of world exports in commercial services.[1] Although the United States maintains a trade deficit in goods ($738 billion in 2011), the United States enjoys a trade surplus in services ($178 billion in 2011).[2] Services are also more important every year for developing countries. The importance of services to the overall GDP of a country is a measure of its stage of economic development. At the domestic level in developed countries, services are the largest component of GDP; this is seldom the case in developing countries.

According to the United Nation's International Labor Organization (ILO), services became the biggest source of employment in the world in 2006, surpassing agriculture and industry for the first time—no doubt in world history. In 2009, 43.1 percent of the world's workers worked in service jobs while 35 percent were employed in agriculture and 21.8 percent in industry.[3] The trend toward more service employment is expected to continue, especially in developing countries. In the near future, the ILO predicts that services will provide more than half of global employment opportunities. *See* International Herald Tribune, *Services Now Biggest Employer*, p. 15 (January 25, 2007).

---

1. *World exports of commercial services by region and selected economy, 2000-2010,* available at http://www.wto.org/english/res_e/statis_e/its2011_e/its11_appendix_e.htm.

2. *Trade in Goods and Services, 1992-present,* available at http://www.bea.gov/international/index.htm.

3. *Global Employment Trends 2011,* available at http://www.ilo.org/wcmsp5/groups/public/@dgreports/@dcomm/@publ/documents/publication/wcms_150440.pdf.

This Chapter is structured as follows: After a brief overview, we cover (1) definitions of services and the modes of supply; (2) general obligations under the GATS; (3) market access commitments; and (4) special agreements governing access to specific service sectors.

II. The Definitions of "Services" and "Modes of Supply"

Read GATS Article I and Article XVIII in the Documents Supplement.

While the GATS bears some similarity to the GATT, there are also important differences between the agreements. The primary concern of the GATT is border measures, such as tariffs and quotas, which create trade barriers. Border measures, however, are ineffective instruments to restrict trade in services. For example, a lawyer or architect who desires to provide international services may do so by way of telephone, fax, or e-mail or he may travel to see his customer, or his customer may come to see him. As a consequence, governments commonly regulate and restrict services trade not by border measures but through internal regulations. The focus of the GATS is on reducing or eliminating the various forms of internal regulations that are used to restrict service trade, not on border controls.

The basic mechanism employed in the GATS to reduce barriers to trade in services is the so-called positive list approach, which is borrowed from the GATT. Under the GATT, members submit a schedule that commits them to stated tariff ceilings; only the tariffs listed in a member's GATT schedule are subject to GATT obligations. GATT members are free to apply any tariffs they wish to unlisted items.

Under GATS, members submit a GATS schedule of specific services sectors that are given market access. A member commits to open its market to foreign competition in only those listed sectors. A member makes no market access commitments with respect to services sectors that are not listed in its GATS schedule. A member is free to deny all access to any sector that is not listed.

The decision to lift trade restrictions on services is an entirely voluntary one that is made by each WTO member during the course of multilateral negotiations with other WTO trading partners. However, there are strong institutional pressures to liberalize trade in the WTO, and a nation that refuses to liberalize will not enjoy the full benefits of the WTO system.

The GATS covers any service in any sector except those supplied in the exercise of government authority. *See* Article I:1-3. Article I:2 identifies four modes of trade in services:

(1) Mode 1 (cross-border): where both provider and user remain in their home territory (e.g., services provided by facsimile, e-mail, phone, or other means of communication);

(2) Mode 2 (consumption abroad): where services are provided to the user who travels to the territory of the provider (e.g., tourism);

(3) Mode 3 (commercial presence): where the provider establishes a commercial presence to provide services in the territory of the user (e.g., a

U.S. bank, insurance, or financial services company establishes a branch or subsidiary in Japan);

(4) Mode 4 (movement of natural persons): where services are provided when a natural person provider temporarily travels to the territory of the user (e.g., an attorney, accountant, interpreter, or teacher travels to another country to consult or lecture).

The GATS applies to any "measure" taken by governmental bodies or non-governmental associations exercising delegated authority affecting any of these modes of trade in services. *See* GATS Article I:3. In general, the GATS does not apply to actions of private entities.

NOTES AND QUESTIONS

1. The discussion above indicates that the definition of services is broad. Why are services defined in categories of transactions rather than through substantive categories? How many substantive categories of services are there?

2. Governmental services (i.e., police, fire, tax, and customs administration) are exempt from the GATS; however, the WTO Government Procurement Agreement may cover some government services. Thus, GATS concepts may be relevant in this case. Article XIII:2 of the GATS requires negotiations on government procurement of services, and these are now ongoing.

3. The broad scope of the GATS outlined above suggests that the concept of services is not sharply differentiated from other trade categories, such as goods, technology, or foreign direct investment. This issue arises because services trade is defined by modes of transactions rather than by what is transacted. One can easily see how a services transaction can also implicate the trade in goods. If a service is supplied in conjunction with a product, are both the GATS and the GATT potentially involved? In *European Communities—Regime for the Importation, Sale and Distribution of Bananas*, WT/DS27/AB/R, Report of the Appellate Body, adopted on September 25, 1997, the Appellate Body employed a two-part test to determine whether a measure is one affecting trade in services. First, are there services, according to the definition and the use of that term in Article I? Second, are there potential effects? The Appellate Body further ruled that some measures could fall under both agreements. *Id.* at ¶222. Thus, the banana import licensing procedures at issue were subject to both the GATS and the GATT. In addition, the operators of companies engaged in the banana wholesale trade were suppliers of wholesale trade services under the GATS. *Id.* at ¶228. Similarly, in *Canada—Certain Measures Affecting the Automotive Industry* WT/DS139, 142/AB/R, Report of the Appellate Body, adopted on June 19, 2000, the Appellate Body found that the GATS applied because Canada's import duty exemption program affected the wholesale services market for automobiles in Canada by reserving access to duty-free goods to a closed category of service suppliers while excluding others. *Id.* at ¶¶176-182.

Despite this overlap between the GATS and the GATT, the Appellate Body in the *EC—Bananas* case pointed out that the analysis under each agreement will be different: "[W]hile the same measure could be scrutinized under both agreements, the specific aspects of that measure examined under each agreement could be different. Under the GATT, the focus is on how the measure affects the goods involved. Under the GATS, the focus is on how the measure affects the supply of the service or the service suppliers involved." *Id.* at ¶221. This can only be determined on a case-by-case basis. The Appellate Body concluded that the panel had failed to examine whether the measure in question, an import duty exemption program, affected wholesale services by reserving access to duty-free goods to a closed category of service suppliers. *Id.* at ¶¶164-167.

III.   GATS Obligations

GATS obligations can be divided into two general categories. First, there are general obligations that apply to all measures affecting services, regardless of whether the services sector is the subject of a market access commitment. Second, there are obligations that apply to measures affecting services sectors that are the subject of selective market access commitments.

A.   General Obligations

All WTO members are bound by the general obligations of the GATS even though the member may have made no market access commitments for the services sector in question.

Article II of the GATS requires MFN treatment. With respect to any measure affecting services, WTO members must accord unconditionally and automatically to any other WTO member treatment no less favorable than is extended to a measure covering the like services and like suppliers from any other country. MFN treatment means that although a WTO member may have no legal obligation to provide access to a services sector because it is not a listed sector, if the member chooses to do so, it must accord the same treatment to every other WTO member.

The issue of "likeness" is relevant to GATS Article II. The definition of "like" services and services suppliers is analogous to, but different from, the issue of "like" products under the GATT. In the GATS context, the concept of likeness appears to depend solely upon whether in fact the same or similar services are provided, regardless of the characteristics of the service suppliers themselves. In *Canada—Certain Measures Affecting the Automobile Industry*, WT/DS139, 142/R, Report of the Panel, adopted on June 19, 2000, the panel ruled (¶¶10.247-10.248) that "to the extent that the services suppliers concerned supply the same services, they should be considered 'like' for purposes of this case." The panel rejected as irrelevant the different characteristics of the suppliers—whether they were manufacturers or non-manufacturers, or whether they had production facilities in Canada. The "likeness" issue also comes up in GATS Article XVII, which is discussed below.

Unlike the MFN principle under the GATT, the MFN principle under GATS is distinctly limited. A WTO member can list exemptions to MFN in the GATS Annex on Article II Exemptions. The exemption would allow a GATS member to refuse to extend similar favorable treatment for services given to one country to another WTO member. In listing exemptions, the member must follow the criteria set forth in Annex II. These exemptions can be maintained for up to ten years and are subject to periodic review and negotiation.

The availability of exemptions to MFN allows WTO members to prevent free riding in services trade. Under the GATT Country A must extend MFN treatment to Country B, a free rider, even though Country B does not extend the same level of benefits to any country and is therefore not required to extend the same level of benefits to Country A in return. Under the GATS, however, a WTO member, such as Country A, can prevent free riding by listing Country B on its list of exemptions in its GATS Schedule.

The GATS also contains these other "general obligations and disciplines":

(1)   All relevant measures must be transparent, which requires their prompt publication (Article III); however, certain confidential information may be withheld (Article III bis).

(2)   All domestic regulations affecting services must be administered in a reasonable, objective, and impartial manner (Article VI:1).

(3)   All members are encouraged to mutually recognize national agreements on services and to harmonize standards of domestic regulation (Article VII).

(4)   Service monopolies and exclusive service providers must not abuse their monopoly position or act inconsistently with a member's commitments (Article VIII).

(5)   Business practices that restrain competition must be addressed through "full and sympathetic consideration" with a "view to eliminating" the practice (Article IX).

(6)   Payments and transfers of capital must be open with respect to a Member's commitments (Article XI).

(7)   Subsidies affecting services are subject to negotiation with a view to eliminating their trade-distorting effects (Article XII).

The GATS also contains a number of qualifications and exemptions to these general obligations. WTO members are allowed to conclude preferential trade agreements creating special privileges that do not need to be extended to all other WTO members under the MFN principle (Article V). Members are allowed to disregard their GATS obligations to apply safeguard measures (Article X) to protect local industries and safeguards to maintain balance of payments obligations (Article XII). Government procurement is exempt from GATS obligations (Article XIII), and general exceptions exist to protect public morals; human, animal, plant life, or health; and to protect against fraud and invasion of privacy (Article XIV). Article XIV bis provides an exemption for certain issues of national security.

The GATS also explicitly calls for progressive liberalization of services trade through future negotiations (Article XIX). Members are expected to progressively liberalize their GATS schedules by making additional commitments (Article XX), but commitments may also be modified and withdrawn (Article XXI). Developing countries are encouraged to participate in trade services liberalization (Article IV).

PROBLEM 11-1

Country I is a WTO member that enters into a bilateral agreement with Country X, a non-WTO member. The bilateral agreement calls for both countries to open up the services trade in maritime, property, and life insurance. The United Kingdom has one of the leading insurance industries in the world. The U.K. now wishes to enter the insurance market in Country I, but the Foreign Trade Minister of Country I states, "Sorry, but we did not include insurance as part of our GATS schedule, so we don't have to give you any access." What result under the MFN principle in GATS Article II? Assume that Country I has made no exemptions to MFN in the Annex to GATS Article II.

PROBLEM 11-2

Country A has made no GATS commitments on environmental services. A's Environmental Protection Bureau (EPB) has hired Waste Solutions, a multinational waste and environmental management company based in the U.K., to clean up its seriously polluted lakes and rivers. A U.S. company now wishes to make a very competitive bid for a second contract for other lakes and rivers that need treatment. The EPB Chief says, "Sorry, but we plan to close the bids to foreign companies." The U.S. company says, "Wait a minute, you can't do that. You just hired a company in the U.K. You need to give us MFN treatment." What result? *See* Article XIII.

What if a private company in Country A had hired Waste Solutions to treat its industrial wastes, then opened bids for additional waste treatment services, but refuses to consider bids from foreign companies? *See* Article I.3(a).

PROBLEM 11-3

Country M is a WTO developing country that has entered into a bilateral investment treaty with the United States. In the agreement, M promised to supply all essential infrastructures to support U.S.-owned subsidiaries set up in M. Total Electric Power (TEP), a privately owned company that has been granted a monopoly over the utilities sector, has been supplying utilities to the U.S. subsidiaries. However, due to insufficient capacity, TEP must engage in periodic "blackouts" in areas outside the major cities in order to maintain a constant supply of utilities to the major cities where all of the U.S. subsidiaries are located. A French company located in a second-tier city in M has found that these blackouts are seriously disrupting its business. The French company argues that these blackouts are unlawful. Assume that M has made no exemptions to its MFN obligations under the GATS. What result? *See* GATS Article VIII:1.

B.   Obligations for Committed Sectors

Under the GATS, a second set of obligations applies specifically to measures affecting services in committed sectors (although note that the general obligations apply to these sectors as well). Services sectors that are committed in a member's GATS schedule enjoy National Treatment (Article XVII) and market access (Article XVI), subject to express limitations and qualifications.

Article XVII, the National Treatment provision, is the core of the GATS. The National Treatment principle under GATS requires a member to accord treatment to foreign services and services suppliers that is no less favorable than the member applies to like domestic services and service suppliers. However, unlike in the case of the GATT, National Treatment is distinctly limited. Under GATS, National Treatment extends only to service sectors inscribed in an individual WTO member's schedule of specific commitments, and even then, National Treatment with respect to these service sectors can be conditioned and qualified. *See* Article XVII. Thus, any obligation to provide National Treatment to a foreign supplier for a services sector can be completely avoided if the WTO member omits the sector from its GATS schedule. This omission will allow the WTO member to freely favor domestic suppliers and to discriminate against foreign suppliers in the service sector. If a member includes a service sector in its GATS schedule, the member is also allowed to qualify or limit National Treatment for that sector.

The same approach applies for market access under Article XVI. A service sector that is committed under a member's GATS schedule enjoys market access except to the extent limited or qualified.

Unless the sector is expressly limited or qualified in a member's GATS schedule, Article XVI on market access prohibits the following measures:

(a) Limits on the number of service suppliers;
(b) Limits on the value of transactions or assets;
(c) Limits on the total quantity of service output;
(d) Limits on the number of natural persons that can be employed;
(e) Limits on the type of legal entity that can be used; and
(f) Limits on participation of foreign capital or investment.

Again, it must be emphasized that two conditions must occur before a member is fully bound not to impose any of the measures contained in (a)-(d). The member must (1) commit to open up a service sector to foreign competition in its GATS schedule and (2) impose no limitations on market access for any of the modes of supply for the service sector. It is quite common, however, for a member to commit to open up a service sector but to impose limits on market access, allowing that member to impose one or more of the restrictions contained in (a)-(e) above.

Under Article XVIII, WTO members may impose additional limitations on committed service sectors other than limitations on market access under Article XVI or limitations on National Treatment under Article XVII. Some examples of such additional limitations are the regulatory principles contained in the reference paper that is part of the WTO Telecoms Agreement. These additional limitations are referred to as commitments or undertakings.

PROBLEM 11-4

Assume that Country E's GATS schedule includes construction and engineering services, with no restrictions on market access. Country E passes a law providing that foreign workers shall not constitute more than 50 percent of the labor used in a construction project and that wages for foreign workers cannot exceed 50 percent of total payroll. Is this restriction lawful? *See* GATS Article XVI.

PROBLEM 11-5

Assume that Country C's GATS schedule includes food and beverage services and that C's schedule contains no limitations on market access or National Treatment. C passes a law that all licenses for all new restaurants, whether owned by local or foreign business operators, must satisfy an economic needs test based on population density for the particular location. Is this restriction lawful? *See* GATS Article XVI.

PROBLEM 11-6

Country Y's GATS schedule includes financial services, including banking and insurance. Under the column headings "conditions and limitations on market access" and "National Treatment" in its GATS schedule, however, Country Y notes that it is "unbound" for mode 3 (commercial presence). This allows Country Y to impose any of the market access limitations prohibited by Article XVI for the commercial presence mode of providing financial services. Country Y is also allowed to discriminate against foreign service suppliers and services.

Country Y's company law provides for three forms of business entities: a publicly traded limited liability corporation, a closed corporation, and a joint venture for all fields of business. Country Y subsequently passes a law that requires all foreign invested insurance companies to take the form of a joint venture in which the foreign investor is partnered with a local insurance company. Is this restriction lawful under Article XVI (market access) and Article XVII (National Treatment)?

NOTES AND QUESTIONS

1. *MFN and National Treatment.* The *EC—Bananas* case, *European Communities—Regime for the Importation, Sale and Distribution of Bananas*, WT/DS27/R, Report of the Panel, and WT/DS27/AB/R, Report of the Appellate Body, adopted on September 25, 1997 (also known as *Bananas III*) was the first case to apply the non-discrimination rules under GATS Article II (MFN) and Article XVII (National Treatment). The Appellate Body's approach to the National Treatment obligation was to consider whether the measures in question adversely modified the conditions of competition for foreign services providers as compared to their domestic counterparts. For the MFN obligation, the Appellate Body considered conditions of competition for some foreign services suppliers as against other foreign services suppliers.

The GATS issues involved the EC licensing scheme for the importation and distribution of bananas. The scheme divided wholesalers of bananas into two categories, A and B. Wholesalers that had previously sold bananas from African, Caribbean, and Pacific (ACP) countries were placed into Category B; ACP countries were entitled to preferential access to the EC market for many of their products under the Lomé Agreement with the EC. Other wholesalers of bananas from so-called dollar zone countries in Central and South America (e.g., Ecuador, Honduras, Guatemala, and Mexico) that did not benefit from preferential access to the EC market were placed in Category A. Under the EC licensing scheme, the two categories were applied to traders regardless of their nationality, but only on the basis of the origin of the bananas they sold, i.e., whether they sold ACP or dollar zone bananas. *See* Report of the Panel at ¶7.324. The import licenses in question were also freely transferable. *Id.* at ¶7.336.

The licensing scheme allocated 66.5 percent of the import licenses for dollar zone bananas to Category A wholesalers. Category B wholesalers were allocated 30 percent of the import licenses for dollar zone bananas, regardless of whether they had previously traded dollar zone bananas (a small number of licenses were reserved for so-called hurricane licenses, for traders adversely affected by tropical storms). Because there were not enough import licenses for all importers of dollar zone bananas, some Category A wholesalers were forced to pay a premium to purchase import licenses from Category B holders.

The Appellate Body ruled that the EC banana licensing procedures are measures that "affect" trade in services and that the wholesale operators were service suppliers under the GATS Article I:2(c). In addition, the Appellate Body agreed (¶¶234-244) with the panel that the allocation to Category B operators of 30 percent of the licenses for importing third-country and non-ACP bananas is discrimination that is inconsistent with GATS Article II:1, which covers both *de jure* and *de facto* discrimination.

With regard to the National Treatment obligation, the Panel ruled that four elements must be present to prove a violation:

(1) A commitment by a member with respect to the relevant services sector or mode of supply;
(2) The existence of a measure that affects the supply of services in that sector or mode of supply;
(3) The measure must apply to both foreign and domestic like services and/ or service suppliers; and
(4) The measure must accord less favorable treatment to foreign services and/or service suppliers.

Id. at ¶7.314.

Establishing the first two elements did not present serious issues; the first was purely factual, and the second was established by the complainants in showing which wholesalers provided the services involved, and how they were affected by the licensing scheme. *See* Report of the Appellate Body at ¶¶227-228.

The third element, the like-supplier issue, was satisfied by the finding that the services provided are "like." This being the case, those providing them are "like" suppliers. *See* Report of the Panel at ¶7.322.

The crux of the case was element four: The Appellate Body noted and upheld the Panel's finding that "given that license transferees are usually Category A operators who are most often service suppliers of foreign origin, and since license sellers are usually Category B operators who are most often service suppliers of EC (or ACP) origin, we conclude that service suppliers of the Complainants' origin [foreign service providers] are subject to less favorable conditions of competition in their ability to compete in the wholesale services market for bananas than service providers of EC (or ACP) origin." *See* Report of the Appellate Body at ¶244.

These rulings are highly controversial. Is the *EC—Bananas* case an example of *de facto* discrimination that violates the GATS Articles II and XVII, or did the Panel and the Appellate Body confuse product discrimination with services discrimination?

On whether there was confusion, note that the nationality of a wholesale trader is irrelevant for the purposes of whether a trader is deemed to be in Category A or B. A wholesale trader of any nationality will be classified under Category A or B, depending upon whether the trader sells bananas from the ACP or from the dollar zone countries. Moreover, most wholesale traders do not have any predisposition in favor of bananas from any particular origin; rather, they seek to maximize their revenues and will sell bananas either from the ACP or dollar zone countries, depending upon which product is favored by the market. As the licensing scheme did not impede wholesale traders from access to Category A or B, it appears that the real issue in this case was the preferential treatment given to bananas from a certain origin, which is a goods issue, not a services issue.

The Appellate Body considered a second case involving distribution services in *Canada—Certain Measures Affecting the Automotive Industry*, WT/DS139, 142/AB/R, Report of the Appellate Body, adopted on June 19, 2000. This case involved an import duty exemption accorded by Canada to manufacturers of autos and auto parts that met certain conditions. These duty exemptions, which were geared to U.S. manufacturers, were challenged by the EU and Japan. The panel, in addition to finding violations of GATT Article I:1, found a violation of GATS Article II:1 (MFN). The Appellate Body reversed the panel's finding with respect to the GATS, not on the merits but because the panel did not follow the correct order of analysis. The correct order of analysis under GATS is (1) a determination whether the measure is covered by the GATS; (2) an interpretation of the legal standards in GATS Article II:1; (3) factual findings as to the treatment of wholesale trade services and service suppliers of motor vehicles of different WTO members commercially present in Canada; and (4) an application of the interpretation of GATS Article II:1 to the facts (¶171). Since the panel failed to assess the relevant facts and failed to interpret GATS Article II:1, the Appellate Body reversed the panel's findings without completing the analysis.

2. *Domestic Regulation.* While measures regulating foreign services and services suppliers are subject to extensive obligations under the GATS, domestic regulation of services is subject to the much less stringent requirement under Article VI, which states that the regulations must be objective and transparent and not more burdensome than necessary. Even regulations that are strictly domestic on their face (i.e., that apply to all service providers whether domestic or foreign and do not single out foreign suppliers) can also affect foreign suppliers of services. For example, a country might issue licensing requirements for all service suppliers. While these measures are not directed at foreign services and service suppliers and might fall outside the scope of GATS Article XVI (market access) and XVII (National Treatment), these regulations can obviously affect foreign suppliers by denying or creating barriers to market entry. How should the WTO deal with the issue of domestic regulation that affects foreign services? Or is the political pressure not to impose overly restrictive regulations on domestic services a sufficient incentive to curb stringent domestic regulation affecting all services, including foreign services?

NOTE ON THE LISTS OF ARTICLE II (MFN) EXEMPTIONS

The MFN obligation in the GATS is unique within the WTO because countries are allowed to designate exemptions from MFN. How do these exemptions work? The lists of exemptions for each member form a part of the Annex on Article II Exemptions.

In contrast to the complex nature of schedules of commitments, these lists are largely self-explanatory and are structured in a straightforward manner. In order to ensure a complete and precise listing of a country's MFN exemptions, each country is required to provide five types of information for each exemption:

- Description of the sector or sectors in which the exemption applies;
- Description of the measure, indicating why it is inconsistent with Article II;
- The country or countries to which the measure applies;
- The intended duration of the exemption; and
- The conditions creating the need for the exemption.

IV.   *Market Access Commitments*

Read GATS Article XVI, Article XX, Article XXI in the Documents Supplement.

The market access commitments under the GATS are specific to each WTO member and are contained in each member's GATS schedules (available at http://www.wto.org). Members must observe market access (Article XVI) and National Treatment disciplines (Article XVII) only for the services sectors listed on their GATS schedules, subject to any limitations or qualifications.

Here, courtesy of the WTO web site, is a sample (fictitious) market access commitment. We quote from the WTO website on how to read the GATS Schedule set forth below:

> [The GATS] is a relatively complex document, more difficult to read than a tariff schedule under GATT. While a tariff schedule, in its simplest form, lists one tariff rate per product, a schedule of commitments contains at least eight entries per sector: the commitments on each market access and national treatment with regard to the four modes of supply.
>
> The services schedule of "Arcadia", an imaginary WTO Member, displays the normal four-column format (Box C). While the first column specifies the sector or sub-sector concerned, the second column sets out any limitations on market access that fall within the six types of restrictions mentioned in Article XVI:2. The third column contains any limitations that Arcadia may want to place, in accordance with Article XVII, on national treatment. A final column provides the opportunity to undertake additional commitments as envisaged in Article XVIII; it is empty in this case.
>
> Any of the entries under market access or national treatment may vary within a spectrum whose opposing ends are full commitments without limitation ("none") and full discretion to apply any measure falling under the relevant Article ("unbound"). The schedule is divided into two parts. While Part I lists "horizontal commitments",

i.e. entries that apply across all sectors that have been scheduled, Part II sets out commitments on a sector-by-sector basis.

Arcadia's horizontal commitments under mode 3, national treatment, reserve the right to deny foreign land ownership. Under mode 4, Arcadia would be able to prevent any foreigner from entering its territory to supply services, except for the specified groups of persons. Within the retailing sector, whose definitional scope is further clarified by reference to the United Nations provisional Central Product Classification (CPC), commitments vary widely across modes. Most liberal are those for mode 2 (consumption abroad) where Arcadia is bound not to take any measure under either Article XVI or XVII that would prevent or discourage its residents from shopping abroad.

Entries into schedules should remain confined to measures incompatible with either the market access or national treatment provisions of the GATS and to any additional commitments a Member may want to undertake under Article XVIII. Schedules would not provide legal cover for measures inconsistent with other provisions of the Agreement, including the MFN requirement under Article II or the obligation under Article VI:1 to reasonable, objective and impartial administration of measures of general application. MFN-inconsistent measures, that have not been included in the relevant list, need to be rescinded and the same applies to any inconsistencies with Article VI.

By now you should see that the listing of a services sector on its GATS schedule by a member does not mean the sector is fully open to foreign competition. Only those services sectors that (1) are listed on a member's GATS schedule and (2) do not contain any limitations (i.e., have the inscription "none") on market access and National Treatment and do not contain inscriptions of any other undertakings under column four are opened to full access within the limits of GATS.

PROBLEM 11-7

Max's Club, based in France, runs a very successful retailing business selling high-end luxury consumer goods in a large warehouse-like setting. Max's Club is seeking to establish stores in Arcadia and would like your advice on its plans. Max's business model in France is based on controlling all aspects of the retail sales operations from wholesale distribution to final sales to the consumer. Max's Club owns one central wholesale distribution facility that is responsible for shipping all of its goods to all of its wholly owned retail establishments throughout France. Max's Club believes that it is very important to follow the same business model in Arcadia.

Max's Club would like to assign its vice president of operations to Arcadia for a five-year assignment and would also like to assign about 250 current employees to its Arcadia stores to work as sales clerks. Max's Club has also discovered that the Arcadian government maintains a program providing low-interest loans to Arcadian businesses for start-up operations. Max's Club is interested in whether these funds might be available as a source of capital. Advise Max's Club on any issues you see with its business plan in light of Arcadia's GATS schedule below.

Box C: Sample Schedule of Commitments: Arcadia

Sector or sub-sector	Limitations on market access	Limitations on national treatment	Additional commitments
I. Horizontal Commitments			
All sectors included in this schedule	4) Unbound, other than for (a) temporary presence, as in intra-corporate transferees, of essential senior executives and specialists and (b) presence for up to 90 days of representatives of a service provider to negotiate sales of services.	3) Authorization is required for acquisition of land by foreigners.	
II. Sector-specific Commitments			
4. Distribution services C. Retailing services (CPC 631, 632)	1) Unbound (except for mail order: none). 2) None. 3) Foreign equity participation limited to 51 percent. 4) Unbound, except as indicated in horizontal section.	1) Unbound (except for mail order: none). 2) None. 3) Investment grants are available only to companies controlled by Arcadian nationals. 4) Unbound.	

PROBLEM 11-8

Country K is a transition economy that is attempting to implement market reforms against the background of a former socialist regime. K has recently joined the WTO, and its GATS schedule includes entertainment services, with no restrictions on market access and National Treatment. Country K's Ministry of Culture has grown alarmed at the popularity of high-budget foreign films that depict extreme and realistic violence that are incompatible with K's traditional values. For this reason, K's Ministry of Culture has enacted a law requiring all foreign films to be shown only after 8 P.M. The Ministry of Culture reasons that at such times, only emancipated adults are likely to view such films. No restrictions apply on the broadcast times of locally produced films. The Ministry of Culture finds that although local films also depict violence, these scenes are not very realistic because the low budgets of local companies do not allow them to use high-technology, digital computer-generated imaging to produce realistic scenes. The Ministry argues that these restrictions are necessary to protect its traditional values. Is this restriction lawful? *See* Article XIV and the *U.S. — Gambling Services* case below.

United States—Measures Affecting the Cross-Border Supply of Gambling and Betting Services
Report of the Appellate Body, adopted on April 20, 2005
WT/DS285/AB/R

[Antigua and Barbuda brought a complaint before the WTO challenging several U.S. laws and regulations that restricted gambling and betting services. The focus of the panel, as well as the Appellate Body, was on three federal laws: the Wire Act, the Travel Act, and the Illegal Gambling Business Act. According to Antigua and Barbuda, these laws had the effect of limiting the cross-border trade in gambling and betting. The WTO panel agreed with the complainants that U.S. restrictions on cross-border gambling and betting services were inconsistent with the U.S. schedule of specific commitments under the GATS as well as under GATS Article XVI relating to market access. The United States appealed the panel's findings to the Appellate Body.

The services in question were supplied through the cross-border supply Mode I, utilizing the internet.

The Appellate Body's opinion, set forth below, dealt with three sets of issues. First, the United States argued that gambling and betting services were excluded from its GATS schedule and, as a result, the United States was entirely free to regulate or limit this sector. This is an issue of treaty interpretation. Second, the United States argued that even if it included gambling and betting services within its GATS schedule, the United States could nevertheless restrict gambling and betting under a general exception set forth in Article XIV(a) of GATS, permitting measures necessary to protect public morals and public order. Crucial to the U.S. position is the meaning of "necessity" under Article XIV. Third, if the U.S. laws at issue could be justified as necessary under Article XIV(a), the chapeau of Article XIV requires that such measures be applied in a manner that does not constitute arbitrary or unjustifiable discrimination or a disguised restriction on the trade in services. This issue turned on whether the measures were applied evenhandedly to both domestic and foreign suppliers of gambling and betting services.]

INTERPRETATION OF THE SPECIFIC COMMITMENTS MADE BY THE UNITED STATES IN ITS GATS SCHEDULE

158. The Panel found, at paragraph 7.2(a) of the Panel Report, that:

. . . the United States' Schedule under the GATS includes specific commitments on gambling and betting services.

The United States appeals this finding. According to the United States, by excluding "sporting" services from the scope of subsector 10.D of its GATS Schedule, it excluded gambling and betting services from the scope of the specific commitments that it undertook therein.

Interpretation of Subsector 10.D According to the General Rule of Interpretation: Article 31 of the Vienna Convention

162. The United States' appeal focuses on the Panel's interpretation of the word "sporting" in subsector 10.D of the United States' GATS Schedule. According to the United States, the ordinary meaning of "sporting" includes gambling and betting and the Panel erred in finding otherwise. We observe first that the interpretative question addressed by the Panel was a broader one, namely "whether the US Schedule includes specific commitments on gambling and betting services notwithstanding the fact that the words 'gambling and betting services' do not appear in the US Schedule." In tackling this question, the Panel turned to Sector 10 of the United States' Schedule to the GATS, which Antigua claimed included a specific commitment on gambling and betting services, and the United States claimed did not. The relevant part of the United States' Schedule provides:

Sector or subsector	Limitations on market access
10. Recreational, Cultural, & Sporting services A. Entertainment services (including theatre, live bands and circus services)	1) None 2) None 3) None 4) Unbound, except as indicated in the horizontal section
B. News agency services	1) None 2) None 3) None 4) Unbound, except as indicated in the horizontal section
C. Libraries, Archives, Museums and other Cultural services	1) None 2) None 3) None 4) Unbound, except as indicated in the horizontal section
D. Other Recreational services (except sporting)	1) None 2) None 3) The number of concessions available for commercial operations in federal, state and local facilities is limited 4) Unbound, except as indicated in the horizontal section

172. We also consider it useful to set out, briefly, the nature of the two documents at issue. On 10 July 1991, the GATT Secretariat circulated document W/120,

entitled "SERVICES SECTORAL CLASSIFICATION LIST". [T]he document consists of a table in two columns. The left column is entitled "SECTORS AND SUBSECTORS" and consists of a list classifying services into 11 broad service sectors, each divided into several subsectors (more than 150 in total). The right column is entitled "CORRESPONDING CPC" and sets out, for nearly every subsector listed in the left-hand column, a CPC number to which that subsector corresponds. It is not disputed that the reference in W/120 to "CPC" is a reference to the United Nations' Provisional Central Product Classification. The CPC is a detailed, multi-level classification of goods and services. The CPC is *exhaustive* (all goods and services are covered) and its categories are *mutually exclusive* (a given good or service may only be classified in *one* CPC category). The CPC consists of "Sections" (10), "Divisions" (69), "Groups" (295), "Classes" (1,050), and "Subclasses" (1,811). Of the 10 "Sections" of the CPC, the first five primarily classify *products*. They are based on the Harmonised Commodity Description and Coding System, and are not referred to in W/120. The second five Sections of the CPC primarily classify *services*, and all of the references in W/120 are to sub-categories of these five Sections.

[The Appellate Body found that an examination of the treaty's context and its object and purpose in accordance with Article 31 of the Vienna Convention failed to clarify the ambiguity surrounding the terms "other recreational services (except sporting)." Under the Vienna Convention, when Article 31 fails to resolve the interpretation issue, the parties are to then use Article 32, which permits the use of supplementary means of interpretation.]

INTERPRETATION OF SUBSECTOR 10.D IN ACCORDANCE WITH SUPPLEMENTARY MEANS OF INTERPRETATION: ARTICLE 32 OF THE VIENNA CONVENTION

196. We observe, as a preliminary matter, that this appeal does *not* raise the question whether W/120 and the 1993 Scheduling Guidelines constitute "supplementary means of interpretation, including the preparatory work of the treaty and the circumstances of its conclusion." Both participants agree that they do, and we see no reason to disagree.

198. Turning to the question of how the subsector 10.D entry "Other recreational services (except sporting)" is to be interpreted in the light of W/120 and the Scheduling Guidelines, we consider it useful to set out the relevant parts of both documents. The relevant section of W/120 is as follows:

Sectors and sub-sectors	*Corresponding CPC*
[. . .]	
10. Recreational, Cultural and sporting services (other than audiovisual services)	
A. Entertainment services (including theatre, live bands and circus services)	9619
B. News agency services	962
C. Libraries, Archives, Museums and other Cultural services	963
D. Sporting and other Recreational services	964
E. Other	

199. Thus, W/120 clearly indicates that its entry 10.D — "Sporting and other recreational services" — corresponds to CPC Group 964. W/120 does not, however, contain any explicit indication of: (i) whether the reference to Group 964 necessarily incorporates a reference to *each and every sub-category* of Group 964 within the CPC; or (ii) how W/120 relates to the GATS Schedules of individual Members.

201. In the CPC, Group 964, which corresponds to subsector 10.D of W/120 (Sporting and other recreational services), is broken down into the following Classes and Sub-classes:

964 Sporting and other recreational services
9641 Sporting services
    96411 Sports event promotion services
    96412 Sports event organization services
    96413 Sports facility operation services
    96419 Other sporting services
9649 Other recreational services
    96491 Recreation park and beach services
    96492 Gambling and betting services
    96499 Other recreational services n.e.c.

Thus, the CPC Class that corresponds to "Sporting services" (9641) does *not* include gambling and betting services. Rather, the Sub-class for gambling and betting services (96492) falls under the Class "Other recreational services" (9649).

204. In our view, the requisite clarity as to the scope of a commitment could not have been achieved through mere omission of CPC codes, particularly where a specific sector of a Member's Schedule, such as sector 10 of the United States' Schedule, follows the structure of W/120 in all other respects, and adopts *precisely* the same terminology as used in W/120. As discussed above, W/120 and the 1993 Scheduling Guidelines were prepared and circulated at the request of parties to the Uruguay Round negotiations for the express purpose of assisting those parties in the preparation of their offers. These documents undoubtedly served, too, to assist parties in reviewing and evaluating the offers made by others. They provided a common language and structure which, although not obligatory, was widely used and relied upon. In such circumstances, and in the light of the specific guidance provided in the 1993 Scheduling Guidelines, it is reasonable to assume that parties to the negotiations examining a sector of a Schedule that tracked so closely the language of the same sector in W/120 would — absent a clear indication to the contrary — have expected the sector to have the same coverage as the corresponding W/120 sector. This is another way of stating that, as the Panel observed, "unless otherwise indicated in the Schedule, Members were assumed to have relied on W/120 and the corresponding CPC references."

208. In our view, therefore, the relevant entry in the United States' Schedule, "Other recreational services (except sporting)," must be interpreted as *excluding* from the scope of its specific commitment services corresponding to CPC class 9641, "Sporting services." For the same reasons, the entry must be read as *including* within the scope of its commitment services corresponding to CPC 9649, "Other recreational services," including Sub-class 96492, "Gambling and betting services."

ARTICLE XVI OF THE GATS: MARKET ACCESS

214. Article XVI of the GATS sets out specific obligations for Members that apply insofar as a Member has undertaken "specific market access commitments" in its Schedule.

221. The chapeau to Article XVI:2, and sub-paragraphs (a) and (c), provide:

In sectors where market-access commitments are undertaken, the measures which a Member shall not maintain or adopt either on the basis of a regional subdivision or on the basis of its entire territory, unless otherwise specified in its Schedule, are defined as:

(a) limitations on the number of service suppliers whether in the form of numerical quotas, monopolies, exclusive service suppliers or the requirements of an economic needs test; . . .

(c) limitations on the total number of service operations or on the total quantity of service output expressed in terms of designated numerical units in the form of quotas or the requirement of an economic needs test;[4]

258. The Panel's explanation of the three federal laws is set out in paragraphs 6.360 to 6.380 of the Panel Report. It is, in our view, useful to set out briefly the relevant part of each statute, as well as the Panel's finding in respect of that statute. The relevant part of the Wire Act states:

Whoever being engaged in the business of betting or wagering knowingly uses a wire communication facility for the transmission in interstate or foreign commerce of bets or wagers or information assisting in the placing of bets or wagers on any sporting event or contest, or for the transmission of a wire communication which entitles the recipient to receive money or credit as a result of bets or wagers, or for information assisting in the placing of bets or wagers shall be fined under this title or imprisoned not more than two years, or both.

259. With respect to this provision, the Panel found that "the Wire Act prohibits the use of at least one or potentially several means of delivery included in mode 1," and that, accordingly, the statute "constitutes a 'zero quota' for, respectively, one, several or all of those means of delivery." The Panel reasoned that the Wire Act prohibits service suppliers from supplying gambling and betting services using remote means of delivery, as well as service operations and service output through such means. Accordingly, the Panel determined that "the Wire Act contains a limitation 'in the form of numerical quotas' within the meaning of Article XVI:2(a) and a limitation 'in the form of a quota' within the meaning of Article XVI:2(c)."

260. As regards the Travel Act, the Panel quoted the following excerpt:

(a) Whoever travels in interstate or foreign commerce or uses the mail or any facility in interstate or foreign commerce, with intent to—
(1) distribute the proceeds of any unlawful activity; or
(2) commit any crime of violence to further any unlawful activity; or
(3) otherwise promote, manage, establish, carry on, or facilitate the promotion, management, establishment, or carrying on, of any unlawful activity, and thereafter performs or attempts to perform—

---

4. Subparagraph 2(c) does not cover measures of a Member which limit inputs for the supply of services.

(A) an act described in paragraph (1) or (3) shall be fined under this title, imprisoned not more than 5 years, or both; or

(B) an act described in paragraph (2) shall be fined under this title, imprisoned for not more than 20 years, or both, and if death results shall be imprisoned for any term of years or for life.

(b) As used in this section (i) "unlawful activity" means (1) any business enterprise involving gambling . . . in violation of the laws of the State in which they are committed or of the United States.

261. The Panel determined that "the Travel Act prohibits gambling activity that entails the supply of gambling and betting services by 'mail or any facility' to the extent that such supply is undertaken by a 'business enterprise involving gambling' that is prohibited under state law and provided that the other requirements in subparagraph (a) of the Travel Act have been met." The Panel further opined that the Travel Act prohibits service suppliers from supplying gambling and betting services through the mail, (and potentially other means of delivery), as well as services operations and service output through the mail (and potentially other means of delivery), in such a way as to amount to a "zero" quota on one or several means of delivery included in mode 1. For these reasons, the Panel found that "the Travel Act contains a limitation 'in the form of numerical quotas' within the meaning of Article XVI:2(a) and a limitation 'in the form of a quota' within the meaning of Article XVI:2(c)."

262. The Panel considered the relevant part of the Illegal Gambling Business Act to be the following:

(a) Whoever conducts, finances, manages, supervises, directs or owns all or part of an illegal gambling business shall be fined under this title or imprisoned not more than five years, or both.

(b) As used in this section—

(1) 'illegal gambling business' means a gambling business which—

(i) is a violation of the law of a State or political subdivision in which it is conducted;

(ii) involves five or more persons who conduct, finance, manage, supervise, direct, or own all or part of such business; and

(iii) has been or remains in substantially continuous operation for a period in excess of thirty days or has a gross revenue of $2,000 in any single day.

(2) 'gambling' includes but is not limited to pool-selling, bookmaking, maintaining slot machines, roulette wheels or dice tables, and conducting lotteries, policy, bolita or numbers games, or selling chances therein.

263. The Panel then determined that because the IGBA "prohibits the conduct, finance, management, supervision, direction or ownership of all or part of a 'gambling business' that violates state law, it effectively prohibits the supply of gambling and betting services through at least one and potentially all means of delivery included in mode 1 by such businesses"; that this prohibition concerned service suppliers, service operations, and service output; and that, accordingly, the IGBA "contains a limitation 'in the form of numerical quotas' within the meaning of Article XVI:2(a) and a limitation 'in the form of a quota' within the meaning of Article XVI:2(c)."

265. We have upheld the Panel's finding that the United States' Schedule to the GATS includes a specific commitment in respect of gambling and betting

services. In that Schedule, the United States has inscribed "None" in the first row of the market access column for subsector 10.D. In these circumstances, and for the reasons given in this section of our Report, we also *uphold* the Panel's ultimate finding, in paragraph 7.2(b)(i) of the Panel Report, that, by maintaining the Wire Act, the Travel Act, and the Illegal Gambling Business Act, the United States acts inconsistently with its obligations under Article XVI:1 and Article XVI:2(a) and (c) of the GATS.

ARTICLE XIV OF THE GATS: GENERAL EXCEPTIONS

266. Finally, we turn to the Panel's analysis of the United States' defence under Article XIV of the GATS. [Article XIV allows a WTO member to adopt measures that restrict or limit trade in services where those "measures are . . . necessary to protect public morals or to maintain public order."]

300. [T]he Panel considered whether the Wire Act, the Travel Act, and the IGBA are "necessary" within the meaning of that provision. The Panel found that the United States had not demonstrated the "necessity" of those measures.

DETERMINING "NECESSITY" UNDER ARTICLE XIV(A)

304. We note, at the outset, that the standard of "necessity" provided for in the general exceptions provision is an *objective* standard. [A] panel must, on the basis of the evidence in the record, independently and objectively assess the "necessity" of the measure before it.

307. A comparison between the challenged measure and possible alternatives should then be undertaken, and the results of such comparison should be considered in the light of the importance of the interests at issue. It is on the basis of this "weighing and balancing" and comparison of measures, taking into account the interests or values at stake, that a panel determines whether a measure is "necessary" or, alternatively, whether another, WTO-consistent measure is "reasonably available."

308. An alternative measure may be found not to be "reasonably available", however, where it is merely theoretical in nature, for instance, where the responding Member is not capable of taking it, or where the measure imposes an undue burden on that Member, such as prohibitive costs or substantial technical difficulties. Moreover, a "reasonably available" alternative measure must be a measure that would preserve for the responding Member its right to achieve its desired level of protection with respect to the objective pursued under paragraph (a) of Article XIV.

317. In our view, the Panel's "necessity" analysis was flawed because it did not focus on an alternative measure that was reasonably available to the United States to achieve the stated objectives regarding the protection of public morals or the maintenance of public order. Engaging in consultations with Antigua, with a view to arriving at a negotiated settlement that achieves the same objectives as the challenged United States' measures, was not an appropriate alternative for the Panel to consider because consultations are by definition a process, the results of which are uncertain and therefore not capable of comparison with the measures at issue in this case.

322. Having reversed this finding, we must consider whether, as the United States contends, the Wire Act, the Travel Act, and the IGBA are properly characterized as "necessary" to achieve the objectives identified by the United States and accepted by the Panel.

325. [W]e understand the Panel to have acknowledged that, *but for* the United States' alleged refusal to accept Antigua's invitation to negotiate, the Panel would have found that the United States had made its *prima facie* case that the Wire Act, the Travel Act, and the IGBA are "necessary," within the meaning of Article XIV(a). We thus agree with the United States that the "sole basis" for the Panel's conclusion to the contrary was its finding relating to the requirement of consultations with Antigua.

326. Turning to the Panel's analysis of alternative measures, we observe that the Panel dismissed, as irrelevant to its analysis, measures that did not take account of the specific concerns associated with *remote* gambling. We found above that the Panel erred in finding that consultations with Antigua constitutes a measure reasonably available to the United States. Antigua raised no other measure that, in the view of the Panel, could be considered an alternative to the prohibitions on remote gambling contained in the Wire Act, the Travel Act, and the IGBA. In our opinion, therefore, the record before us reveals no reasonably available alternative measure proposed by Antigua or examined by the Panel that would establish that the three federal statutes are not "necessary" within the meaning of Article XIV(a). Because the United States made its *prima facie* case of "necessity," and Antigua failed to identify a reasonably available alternative measure, we conclude that the United States demonstrated that its statutes are "necessary," and therefore justified, under paragraph (a) of Article XIV.

327. For all these reasons, we *find* that the Wire Act, the Travel Act, and the IGBA are "measures . . . necessary to protect public morals or to maintain public order," within the meaning of paragraph (a) of Article XIV of the GATS.

THE CHAPEAU OF ARTICLE XIV

339. The chapeau of Article XIV provides:

> Subject to the requirement that such measures are not applied in a manner which would constitute a means of arbitrary or unjustifiable discrimination between countries where like conditions prevail, or a disguised restriction on trade in services, nothing in this Agreement shall be construed to prevent the adoption or enforcement by any Member of measures [of the type specified in the subsequent paragraphs of Article XIV]. . . .

The focus of the chapeau, by its express terms, is on the *application* of a measure already found by the Panel to be inconsistent with one of the obligations under the GATS but falling within one of the paragraphs of Article XIV. By requiring that the measure be *applied* in a manner that does not constitute "arbitrary" or "unjustifiable" discrimination, or a "disguised restriction on trade in services," the chapeau serves to ensure that Members' rights to avail themselves of exceptions are exercised reasonably, so as not to frustrate the rights accorded other Members by the substantive rules of the GATS.

DID THE PANEL FAIL TO TAKE ACCOUNT OF THE "ARBITRARY" OR "UNJUSTIFIABLE" NATURE OF THE DISCRIMINATION REFERRED TO IN THE CHAPEAU?

352. In the course of examining whether the Wire Act, the Travel Act, and the IGBA are applied consistently with the chapeau of Article XIV, the Panel considered whether these laws are enforced in a manner that discriminates between domestic and foreign service suppliers. Antigua identified four United States firms that it claimed engage in the remote supply of gambling services but have not been prosecuted under any of the three federal statutes: Youbet.com, TVG, Capital OTB, and Xpressbet.com. Antigua contrasted this lack of enforcement with the case of an Antiguan service supplier that "had modelled [its] business on that of Capital OTB" but was nevertheless prosecuted and convicted under the Wire Act. In support of its argument that it applies these statutes equally to domestic and foreign service suppliers, the United States submitted statistical evidence to show that most cases prosecuted under these statutes involved gambling and betting services solely within the United States.

356. In our view, the proper significance to be attached to isolated instances of enforcement, or lack thereof, cannot be determined in the absence of evidence allowing such instances to be placed in their proper context. Such evidence might include evidence on the *overall* number of suppliers, and on *patterns* of enforcement, and on the reasons for particular instances of non-enforcement. Indeed, enforcement agencies may refrain from prosecution in many instances for reasons unrelated to discriminatory intent and without discriminatory effect.

357. Faced with the limited evidence the parties put before it with respect to enforcement, the Panel should rather have focused, as a matter of law, on the wording of the measures at issue. These measures, on their face, do *not* discriminate between United States and foreign suppliers of remote gambling services. We therefore *reverse* the Panel's finding, in paragraph 6.589 of the Panel Report, that

> . . . the United States has failed to demonstrate that the manner in which it enforced its prohibition on the remote supply of gambling and betting services against TVG, Capital OTB and Xpressbet.com is consistent with the requirements of the chapeau.

358. The United States and Antigua each alleges that the Panel did not comply with its obligations under Article 11 of the DSU in its analysis under the chapeau of Article XIV. We examine first Antigua's appeal relating to video lottery terminals and Nevada bookmakers, and then consider the United States' appeal concerning the Interstate Horseracing Act.

359. The Panel examined Antigua's allegations that several states in the United States permit video lottery terminals, and that Nevada permits bookmakers to offer their services over the internet and telephone. The Panel rejected both of these allegations. Antigua contends that the Panel made these findings notwithstanding that Antigua had submitted evidence and the United States had submitted none, and that, by so finding, the Panel effectively "reversed" the burden of proof.

360. Antigua is correct that the burden of proof is on the United States, as the responding party invoking the Article XIV defence. Once the United States established its defence with sufficient evidence and arguments, however, it was for Antigua to rebut the United States' defence. In rejecting Antigua's allegations relating to video lottery terminals and Nevada bookmakers, we understand the

Panel to have determined that Antigua failed to rebut the United States' asserted defence under the chapeau, namely that its measures do not discriminate at all. Consequently, we do not read the Panel to have reversed the burden of proof in these two instances, and we dismiss this ground of Antigua's appeal.

361. We now turn to the United States' Article 11 claim relating to the chapeau. The Panel examined the scope of application of the Interstate Horseracing Act ("IHA"). Before the Panel, Antigua relied on the text of the IHA, which provides that "[a]n interstate off-track wager *may be accepted* by an off-track betting system" where consent is obtained from certain organizations. Antigua referred the Panel in particular to the definition given in the statute of "interstate off-track wager":

> [T]he term . . . 'interstate off-track wager' means a legal wager placed or accepted in one State with respect to the outcome of a horserace taking place in another State and includes pari-mutuel wagers, where lawful in each State involved, *placed or transmitted by an individual in one State via telephone or other electronic media and accepted by an off-track betting system in the same or another State,* as well as the combination of any pari-mutuel wagering pools. (emphasis added)

Thus, according to Antigua, the IHA, on its face, authorizes domestic service suppliers, but not foreign service suppliers, to offer remote betting services in relation to certain horse races. To this extent, in Antigua's view, the IHA "exempts" domestic service suppliers from the prohibitions of the Wire Act, the Travel Act, and the IGBA.

362. The United States disagreed, claiming that the IHA—a civil statute—cannot "repeal" the Wire Act, the Travel Act, or the IGBA—which are criminal statutes—*by implication,* that is, merely by virtue of the IHA's adoption *subsequent* to that of the Wire Act, the Travel Act, and the IGBA. Rather, under principles of statutory interpretation in the United States, such a repeal could be effective only if done *explicitly,* which was not the case with the IHA.

363. Thus, the Panel had before it conflicting evidence as to the relationship between the IHA, on the one hand, and the measures at issue, on the other.

364. In our view, this aspect of the United States' appeal essentially challenges the Panel's failure to accord sufficient weight to the evidence submitted by the United States with respect to the relationship under United States law between the IHA and the measures at issue. The Panel had limited evidence before it, as submitted by the parties, on which to base its conclusion. This limitation, however, could not absolve the Panel of its responsibility to arrive at a conclusion as to the relationship between the IHA and the prohibitions in the Wire Act, the Travel Act, and the IGBA. The Panel found that the evidence provided by the United States was not sufficiently persuasive to conclude that, as regards wagering on horseracing, the remote supply of such services by *domestic* firms continues to be prohibited notwithstanding the plain language of the IHA. In this light, we are not persuaded that the Panel failed to make an objective assessment of the facts.

366. In sum, we *find* that none of the challenges under Article 11 of the DSU relating to the chapeau of Article XIV of the GATS has succeeded.

(f) Conclusion Under the Chapeau

367. In paragraph 6.607 of the Panel Report, the Panel expressed its overall conclusion under the chapeau of Article XIV as follows:

. . . the United States has not demonstrated that it does not apply its prohibition on the remote supply of wagering services for horse racing in a manner that does not constitute "arbitrary and unjustifiable discrimination between countries where like conditions prevail" and/or a "disguised restriction on trade" in accordance with the requirements of the chapeau of Article XIV.

368. This conclusion rested on the Panel's findings relating to two instances allegedly revealing that the measures at issue discriminate between domestic and foreign service suppliers, contrary to the defence asserted by the United States under the chapeau. The first instance found by the Panel was based on "inconclusive" evidence of the alleged non-enforcement of the three federal statutes. We have reversed this finding. The second instance found by the Panel was based on "the ambiguity relating to" the scope of application of the IHA and its relationship to the measures at issue. We have upheld this finding.

369. Thus, *our* conclusion—that the Panel did not err in finding that the United States has not shown that its measures satisfy the requirements of the chapeau—relates solely to the possibility that the IHA exempts only *domestic* suppliers of remote betting services for horse racing from the prohibitions in the Wire Act, the Travel Act, and the IGBA. In contrast, the *Panel's* overall conclusion under the chapeau was broader in scope. As a result of our reversal of one of the two findings on which the Panel relied for its conclusion in paragraph 6.607 of the Panel Report, we must *modify* that conclusion. We *find*, rather, that the United States has not demonstrated that—in the light of the existence of the IHA—the Wire Act, the Travel Act, and the IGBA are applied consistently with the requirements of the chapeau. Put another way, we uphold the Panel, but only in part.

OVERALL CONCLUSION ON ARTICLE XIV

370. Our findings under Article XIV lead us to modify the overall conclusions of the Panel in paragraph 7.2(d) of the Panel Report. The Panel found that the United States failed to justify its measures as "necessary" under paragraph (a) of Article XIV, and that it also failed to establish that those measures satisfy the requirements of the chapeau.

371. We have found instead that those measures satisfy the "necessity" requirement. We have also upheld, but only in part, the Panel's finding under the chapeau. We explained that the only inconsistency that the Panel could have found with the requirements of the chapeau stems from the fact that the United States did not demonstrate that the prohibition embodied in the measures at issue applies to both foreign *and* domestic suppliers of remote gambling services, notwithstanding the IHA—which, according to the Panel, "does appear, on its face, to permit" *domestic* service suppliers to supply remote betting services for horse racing. In other words, the United States did not establish that the IHA does not alter the scope of application of the challenged measures, particularly vis-à-vis domestic suppliers of a specific type of remote gambling services. In this respect, we wish to clarify that the Panel did not, and we do not, make a finding as to whether the IHA does, in fact, permit domestic suppliers to provide certain remote betting services that would otherwise be prohibited by the Wire Act, the Travel Act, and/or the IGBA.

372. Therefore, we *modify* the Panel's conclusion in paragraph 7.2(d) of the Panel Report. We *find*, instead, that the United States has demonstrated that the

Wire Act, the Travel Act, and the IGBA fall within the scope of paragraph (a) of Article XIV, but that it has not shown, in the light of the IHA, that the prohibitions embodied in these measures are applied to both foreign and domestic service suppliers of remote betting services for horse racing. For this reason alone, we *find* that the United States has not established that these measures satisfy the requirements of the chapeau.

NOTES AND QUESTIONS

1. Was the decision of the Appellate Body in the *U.S. — Gambling Services* case a victory for the United States? The Appellate Body found (¶369) that "the United States has not demonstrated that [the Interstate Horseracing Act,] the Wire Act, the Travel Act and the [Illegal Gambling Business Act] are applied consistently with the requirements of the [GATS Article XIV] chapeau." In October 2006, the United States passed the Unlawful Internet Gambling Enforcement Act, which expands the 1961 Wire Act's prohibition on the use of wire-based communications to include the Internet. The Act also compels financial institutions to identify and block gambling-related transactions transmitted through their payment systems. The Act grants exemptions for intrastate online bets made on domestic and some overseas horseracing through U.S. sites such as YouBet.com, as well as exemptions for remote gambling conducted by Native American tribal groups. Antigua and Barbuda then brought a compliance proceeding under Article 21.5 of the Dispute Settlement Understanding challenging whether the change in U.S. law brought U.S. law into compliance with its WTO obligations. In the compliance proceeding, the United States argued that there was no explicit finding that its measures did not satisfy the requirements of Article XIV, and it was found only that the United States did not demonstrate an affirmative defense. The United States accordingly stated that it could comply with the WTO findings without taking any new action and that its existing laws prohibit interstate transmission of bets or wagers, including bets on horseracing. The United States cited an ongoing investigation of illegal horserace betting. The compliance panel, however, rejected the U.S. argument and stated that the United States had failed to comply with the WTO rulings. *See* Report of the Panel, *United States — Measures Affecting the Cross-Border Supply of Gambling and Betting Services, Recourse to Article 21.5 by Antigua and Barbuda*, WT/DS285/RW, Report of the Panel, adopted on May 22, 2007.

2. Since the United States had failed to comply with the WTO rulings in the *U.S. — Gambling Services* case, Antigua on June 21, 2007 requested, pursuant to DSU Article 22.2 authorization to suspend concessions or other obligations against the United States in the amount of over $3 billion per year. The United States objected to the level of suspension proposed, and, pursuant to DSU Article 22.6, the matter was referred to arbitration. Since the United States was the objecting party, it had the burden of proof in the resulting proceeding. In *United States — Measures Affecting the Cross-Border Supply of Gambling and Betting Services, Recourse to Arbitration by the United States under DSU Article 22.6*, WT/DS285/ARB, Decision by the Arbitrator, circulated on December 21, 2007, the arbitrators split on the issue of how to calculate the nullification and impairment involved. Two of the arbitrators constructed a "counterfactual" under which it was supposed that the U.S. would provide unrestricted market access for remote gambling and betting on horseracing. The rationale for this was the fact that the DSB's rulings were addressed to discriminatory

treatment of gambling on horseracing. This counterfactual would take into account the U.S. defense based on GATS Article XIV, although this defense ultimately failed to comply with the chapeau of that Article. These arbitrators found (¶¶3.41-3.49) that it was not reasonable on the part of Antigua to assume unrestricted access to all sectors of the U.S. remote gambling market. The third arbitrator (¶¶3.67-3.68), however, was not persuaded that the U.S. had demonstrated that Antigua's proposal was unreasonable. The majority arbitrators then calculated (¶¶3.188-3.189) Antigua's estimated revenue loss from remote gambling on horseracing and, taking into account the possible growth in U.S. demand, arrived at a nullification and impairment figure of US$21 million per year. The arbitrators then decided (¶¶4.117-4.119) to apply DSU Article 22.3 since Antigua is a small, developing country and suspension of concessions under the GATS is not practicable. The arbitrators found accordingly that Antigua under the procedures of DSU Article 22.3 was eligible to suspend obligations under the TRIPS Agreement in the amount of up to $21 million annually.

3. In *China—Measures Affecting Trading Rights and Distribution Services for Certain Publications and Audiovisual Entertainment Products*, WT/DS363/AB/R, Report of the Appellate Body, adopted on January 19, 2010, the Appellate Body was called upon to determine whether "sound recording distribution services" in China's GATS Schedule extends to distribution by electronic means as well as by physical means. After considering the ordinary meaning and context of the words in question and the object and purpose of the GATS, the Appellate Body concluded (¶¶410-416) that China's GATS Schedule includes electronic distribution of sound recordings, and that China's Circular on Internet Culture, Network Music Opinions, and Several Opinions are each inconsistent with China's national treatment commitments under Article XVII of the GATS and that certain provisions of China's Foreign Investment Regulation were also inconsistent with Article XVII of the GATS insofar as these measures prohibit foreign investment entities from engaging in the distribution of sound recording in electronic form.

4. In scheduling GATS commitments, most WTO members use the Services Sectoral Classification List (SSCL) circulated as a note by the WTO Secretariat, WTO Doc MNT.GNS/W120, and widely known as W/120. The SSCL is not mandatory but is used by most members. The SSCL is largely based upon the UN's Central Product Classification (CPC) system of twelve main service sectors:

- Business services, including professional and computer services
- Communication services, including telecommunications
- Construction and engineering services
- Distribution services
- Educational services
- Environmental services
- Financial services, including insurance and banking
- Health-related and social services
- Tourism and travel
- Recreational, cultural, and sporting services
- Transport
- Other services not included elsewhere

The CPC has a coding system out to five digits. The system consists of sections (the first digit), divisions (first and second digits), groups (the first three digits), classes (the first four digits), and subclasses (all five digits taken together). Members make commitments at the two-, three-, four-, and five-digit levels. It is important for a member to have a thorough mastery of the SSCL and the CPC. Mistakes in understanding the CPC can lead to an inadvertent commitment, as in the *U.S. — Gambling Services* case.

V.   *Sectoral Annexes to the GATS*

When the GATS entered into force, three sector-specific negotiations concerning telecommunications, financial services, and maritime transport had not yet been completed. The GATS applied to all services in all sectors, but the negotiators believed that these sectors presented special issues that required separate agreements to be included as annexes to the GATS. These annexes serve as side agreements and the starting point for new negotiations. At present there are completed annexes to the GATS that deal with (1) the movement of natural persons; (2) financial services; (3) telecommunications; and (4) air transport services.

Our focus in this section is the WTO Telecoms Agreement, perhaps the most complex of these sectoral agreements. A study of the Telecoms Agreement will illustrate some of the complex issues involved.

The negotiations on the WTO Telecoms Agreement continued well after the entry into force of the WTO agreements on January 1, 1995. On April 30, 1996, the Council on Trade in Services adopted the Commitments in Basic Telecommunications as well as the Fourth Protocol to the GATS, which stipulated that the WTO Telecoms Agreement would enter into force on January 1, 1998. The final WTO Telecoms Agreement was reached in mid-February 1997. Sixty-nine countries signed the first multilateral treaty on this field.

The WTO Telecoms Agreement actually consists of four separate instruments:

(1)   the GATS;
(2)   the GATS Annex on Telecommunications;
(3)   the Reference Paper;
(4)   the schedules of specific commitments.

The GATS Annex on Telecommunications is an integral part of the GATS by virtue of Article XXIX. The schedules of specific commitments are also part of the GATS by virtue of Article XX:3. The Reference Paper was an agreement that set forth additional regulatory principles that the negotiators believed were necessary to supplement the other agreements. However, the Reference Paper was never adopted by all WTO members. Rather, some countries did, some did not, and other countries adopted parts, but not all, of the Reference Paper. The result is that there are many national reference papers that differ in content and that are based in part or entirely on the Reference Paper. However, if a member has adopted a national reference paper, it becomes part of its specific commitments under the GATS and, for that member, its reference paper is part of the WTO Telecoms Agreement.

The complexity of the WTO Telecoms Agreement can be attributed to the special challenges in the telecommunications field. The typical GATS process of dismantling government-created access barriers might be of little use in the tele-communications field, which is often dominated by private entities that are able to deny access through a variety of means not attributed to government behavior. Privatization of the telecommunications field in many countries has left large private entities to take the place of state monopolies. A foreign supplier of telecommunications services needs to be given an interconnection to the domestic telecommunications network in order to provide telecommunications services, such as long distance phone calls. A private entity, or a group of private entities, might be able to deny market access to foreign competition by refusing to provide an interconnection. Such refusal might consist of charging excessive rates for interconnections or by relegating foreign competitors to smaller networks. As this would be private conduct not government action the conduct would not be subject to GATS. For this reason, the negotiators of the WTO Telecoms Agreement perceived a need to supplement the GATS through access and regulatory principles contained in the Annex and Reference Paper. The extent to which the WTO Telecoms Agreement regulates anti-competitive behavior is the subject of the following problem and case.

PROBLEM 11-9

Pursuant to Country K's recently enacted telecommunications law, the State Monopoly on Telecommunications has been privatized and split into four private companies. Under Country K's telecommunications law, the country has also been divided into four separate regions with each new private company enjoying exclusive rights within each territory. The companies have also established prices, similar within a 5 percent range, for local and long distance telephone services. K has listed telecommunications as a sector open to foreign competition under its GATS schedule with no restrictions on National Treatment or market access. However, K has also made additional commitments under Article XVIII and has adopted a national reference paper that is substantially identical to the GATS Reference Paper.

World Telenet is a U.S.-based, high-speed long distance company seeking to enter the market in Country K. World Telenet charges Country K with violations of the WTO Telecoms Agreement. World Telenet argues that it is being overcharged for access rates and that it cannot obtain meaningful access to K's market for long distance phone calls.

In its defense, Country K argues that these companies have not engaged in any conduct that falls within the scope of the WTO Telecoms Agreement and that even if such conduct did occur, the conduct was required by Country K's own national law, which operates as a complete defense to a violation of GATS. What result? See the case below.

Mexico — Measures Affecting Telecommunications Services
Report of the WTO Panel, adopted on June 1, 2004
WT/DS204/R

[In the 1990s, Sprint, a U.S. telecommunications company, entered into an agreement with Telmex, Mexico's largest telecommunications company, to provide international long distance telephone services between the United States and

Mexico. Other U.S. telecommunications companies, such as AT&T and MCI, were relegated to partnerships with smaller Mexican telecommunications companies and could not enjoy access to Telmex's larger networks. Under all modern telecommunications systems, foreign suppliers of telecommunications services, such as the U.S. companies in this case, had to rely on a domestic telecommunications company such as Telmex for an "interconnection" with Telmex's national networks, in order to complete or "terminate" an international long distance telephone call from the United States to Mexico. As there were two different networks involved, one based in the United States and one based in Mexico, an interconnection between the two networks allowing for the exchange of traffic was necessary before a call from the United States to Mexico could be completed. Mexico's international long distance (ILD) rules required Telmex and other Mexican providers to negotiate a settlement rate for all incoming calls that was charged to the U.S. company for the cost of the interconnection. AT&T believed that the settlement rate was not cost-oriented and that it was being overcharged.

In addition, under the ILD rules, all domestic providers were required to accept incoming calls in proportion to their outgoing calls. This rule meant that in some cases Telmex had to give up incoming calls to other Mexican telecommunications providers or accept incoming calls from other Mexican providers. Rather than actually transferring these calls, however, Telmex and other operators completed these calls but provided financial compensation to other suppliers to which the calls should have been transferred. The United States believed that this was a form of market sharing that, along with price fixing, was used to overcharge foreign companies for access rates. These practices frustrated the entry of U.S. companies into the Mexican market.

The U.S. companies sought the assistance of the USTR, who brought a complaint before the WTO and demanded that Mexico provide access on a non-discriminatory basis to Telmex's networks. Under the GATS, Mexico has undertaken specific commitments for telecommunications service under Articles XVI (market access), XVII (National Treatment), and XVIII (additional commitments). The additional commitments consist of pro-competitive undertakings in the area of telecommunications as specified in Mexico's national reference paper. The United States made two specific claims: (1) Telmex failed to provide an interconnection to U.S. suppliers on a cost-oriented basis in violation of its commitments under §§2.1 and 2.2 of its reference paper; and (2) Telmex engaged in anti-competitive practices, i.e., formed a horizontal price fixing cartel, in violation of §1.1 of Mexico's national reference paper.

In deciding whether the access rates were cost-oriented, the WTO panel had to decide several crucial preliminary issues. Mexico claimed that the interconnection commitment was not even applicable at all because such GATS commitments were applicable only when there was an international trade in services. According to Mexico, for an international trade in services to occur, a single firm must transmit the data from the United States to the end use caller in Mexico. This would require some type of presence in Mexico. In this case, however, the U.S. provider merely "hands off" the transmission in Mexico to a domestic supplier that completes or terminates the call. In other words, Mexico argued that the interconnection commitment covered services in Mode 3 (commercial presence) but not in Mode 1 (cross-border supply). Thus, the panel had to first consider whether a trade in services triggering GATS obligations was involved:]

7.42 More generally, a supplier of services under the GATS is no less a supplier solely because elements of the service are subcontracted to another firm, or are carried out with assets owned by another firm. What counts is the service that the supplier offers and has agreed to supply to a customer. In the case of a basic telecommunications service, whether domestic or international, or supplied cross-border or through commercial presence, the supplier offers its customer the service of completing the customer's communications. Having done so, the supplier is responsible for making any necessary subsidiary arrangements to ensure that the communications are in fact completed. The customer typically pays its supplier the price of the end-to-end service, regardless of whether the supplier contracts with, or uses the assets of, another firm to supply the service.

[The panel then found that interconnection commitments cover Mode 1 as well as Mode 3:]

7.117. In sum the ordinary meaning, in the heading of Section 2 of Mexico's Reference Paper, of the term "interconnection"—that it does not distinguish between domestic and international interconnection, including through accounting rate regimes—is confirmed by an examination of any "special meaning" that the term "interconnection" may have in telecommunications legislation, or by taking into account potential commercial, contractual or technical differences inherent in international interconnection. We find that any "special meaning" of the term "interconnection" in Section 2 of Mexico's Reference Paper does not justify a restricted interpretation of interconnection, or of the term "linking", which would exclude international interconnection, including accounting rate regimes, from the scope of Section 2 of the Reference Paper.

[Having found that the interconnection commitment was applicable, the panel now had to decide whether Telmex was bound by the commitment. Section 2.2 of Mexico's national reference paper required "interconnection with a *major* supplier." The reference paper further defined a major supplier as "a supplier which has the ability to materially affect the terms of participation (having regard to price and supply) in the relevant market." *Id.* Because there was no further definition of "relevant market," the panel had to arrive at a definition, which was essential to determining whether Telmex was a major supplier. The panel accepted the position of the United States that the relevant market was based upon demand substitutability:]

7.152. Is this market for termination the "relevant" market? For the purposes of this case, we accept the evidence put forward by the United States, and uncontested by Mexico, that the notion of demand substitution—simply put, whether a consumer would consider two products as "substitutable"—is central to the process of market definition as it is used by competition authorities. Applying that principle, we find no evidence that a domestic telecommunications service is substitutable for an international one, and that an outgoing call is considered substitutable for an incoming one. One is not a practical alternative to the other. Even if the price difference between domestic and international interconnection would change, such a price change would not make these different services substitutable in the eyes of a consumer. We accept, therefore, that the "relevant market for telecommunications services" for the services at issue—voice, switched data and fax—is the termination of these services in Mexico.

[Based on this definition of the relevant market, the panel had little difficulty in finding that Telmex was a major supplier. Now the panel was ready to determine whether the access rates charged by Telmex were "cost oriented." The panel concluded that the United States had made its case that the rates were not cost oriented:]

7.216. The Panel decided, after having received no evidence from Mexico in response to our questions relating to the United States cost estimates, to base itself on the methodologies presented to the Panel by the United States and not refuted by Mexico. On this basis, we conclude overall that the interconnection rates charged by Telmex to United States suppliers of the services at issue are not "cost-oriented" within the meaning of Section 2.2(b) of Mexico's Reference Paper, since by any of the methodologies presented to the Panel by the United States, they are substantially higher than the costs which are actually incurred in providing the interconnection. Therefore, we find that Mexico has failed to fulfil its commitments under Section 2.2(b) of the Reference Paper by failing to ensure that a major supplier in terms of Section 2.2 of the Reference Paper provides interconnection to United States basic telecom suppliers of the services at issue on a facilities basis under cost-oriented rates.

[The panel then turned to the second issue — whether the practices by Telmex and other Mexican providers were anti-competitive. This part of the opinion is set forth below.]

C.   WHETHER MEXICO HAS MET ITS COMMITMENT UNDER SECTION 1 OF ITS REFERENCE PAPER

7.222 The United States argues that Mexico has not met the requirements of Section 1.1 of its Reference Paper, which provides that "[a]ppropriate measures shall be maintained for the purpose of preventing suppliers who, alone or together, are a major supplier from engaging in or continuing anti-competitive practices." In the absence of a precise definition of "anti-competitive practices", the United States argues that the term encompasses, at a minimum, practices usually proscribed under national law: abuse of dominant position, monopolization, and cartelization. The United States argues that, far from proscribing such behaviour, Mexico maintains measures that *require* Mexican telecommunications operators to adhere to a horizontal price-fixing cartel led by Telmex. This requirement is contained in ILD Rule 13, which obliges the Mexican operator with the most outgoing traffic on a particular international route to negotiate with the suppliers of that country a single settlement rate, which then applies, by virtue of ILD Rule 23, to all other Mexican operators. Anti-competitive practices are also evidenced, according to the United States, by the required "proportionate return" system defined in ILD Rule 2:XIII, by which a Mexican operator is entitled to receive as much incoming traffic as it sends outgoing traffic.

7.223 In response, Mexico argues that its Reference Paper commitments apply only to matters within its border, and not to services supplied under an accounting rate regime. In any case, Mexico contends, it has put in place "appropriate measures" to prevent anti-competitive practices under its general competition laws. As for the ILD Rules they are, according to Mexico, aimed at increasing competition — by stopping new entrants from being undercut on pricing, and by preventing foreign operators from dictating prices to their Mexican affiliates. The United States had not shown that Telmex is a "major supplier" in the relevant market, and behaviour legally required under Mexican law could not be an "anti-competitive practice".

7.224 We examine first the terms of Section 1.1 of Mexico's Reference Paper. It reads:

> "Prevention of anti-competitive practices in telecommunications
>
> Appropriate measures shall be maintained for the purpose of preventing suppliers who, alone or together, are a major supplier from engaging in or continuing anti-competitive practices."

7.225 We note that Section 1.1 contains three key elements: (i) a "major supplier"; (ii) "anti-competitive practices"; and (iii) "appropriate measures" which must be maintained. We examine each of these elements in turn.

1. IS TELMEX A "MAJOR SUPPLIER"?

7.227 In our earlier analysis of the United States claim under Section 2.2 of Mexico's Reference Paper, we found that Telmex is a "major supplier" within the meaning of Mexico's Reference Paper, with respect to the services at issue. We based this finding on the ability of Telmex to affect the terms of participation through use of its position in the relevant market, which we found to be the termination in Mexico of the services at issue. We see no reason to alter our analysis of the same term, with respect to same services, in examining Mexico's commitments under Section 1 of its Reference Paper. We find therefore that Telmex, for the purposes of Section 1 of its Reference Paper, is a "major supplier."

2. WHAT ARE "ANTI-COMPETITIVE PRACTICES"?

7.231 We now examine the term "anti-competitive practices" in the context of the Reference Paper. Examples of "anti-competitive practices" are set out in paragraph 2 of Section 1, which states that such practices "shall include in particular":

(a) "engaging in anti-competitive cross-subsidization;
(b) using information obtained from competitors with anti-competitive results; and
(c) not making available to other services suppliers on a timely basis technical information about essential facilities and commercially relevant information which are necessary for them to provide services."

7.237 An examination of the object and purpose of the Reference Paper commitments made by Members supports our conclusion that the term "anti-competitive practices", in addition to the examples mentioned in Section 1.2, includes horizontal price-fixing and market-sharing agreements by suppliers which, on a national or international level, are generally discouraged or disallowed. An analysis of the Reference Paper commitments shows that Members recognized that the telecommunications sector, in many cases, was characterized by monopolies or market dominance. Removing market access and national treatment barriers was not deemed sufficient to ensure the effective realization of market access commitments in basic telecommunications services. Accordingly many Members agreed to additional commitments to implement a pro-competitive regulatory framework designed to prevent continued monopoly behaviour, particularly by *former* monopoly operators, and abuse of dominance by these or any other major suppliers. Members wished to ensure that market access and national treatment commitments would not be undermined by anti-competitive behaviour by monopolies or dominant suppliers, which are particularly prevalent in the telecommunications sector. Mexico's Reference Paper commitment to the prevention of "anti-competitive practices" by major suppliers has to be read in this light.

7.238 Based on this analysis, we find that the term "anti-competitive practices" in Section 1 of Mexico's Reference Paper includes practices in addition to those listed in Section 1.2, in particular horizontal practices related to price-fixing and market-sharing agreements.

(b) Whether Practices Required Under a Member's Law Can Be "Anti-competitive Practices"

7.239 We now take up the issue of whether acts by a major supplier can be "anti-competitive practices" if they are *required* by a Member's law, and not freely undertaken by a major supplier.

7.244 The Panel is aware that, pursuant to doctrines applicable under the competition laws of some Members, a firm complying with a specific legislative requirement of such a Member (e.g. a trade law authorizing private market-sharing agreements) may be immunized from being found in violation of the general domestic competition law. The reason for these doctrines is that, in most jurisdictions, domestic legislatures have the legislative power to limit the scope of competition legislation. International commitments made under the GATS "for the purpose of preventing suppliers . . . from engaging in or continuing anti-competitive practices"[5] are, however, designed to limit the regulatory powers of WTO Members. Reference Paper commitments undertaken by a Member are international obligations owed to all other Members of the WTO in all areas of the relevant GATS commitments. In accordance with the principle established in Article 27 of the Vienna Convention, a requirement imposed by a Member under its internal law on a major supplier cannot unilaterally erode its international commitments made in its schedule to other WTO Members to prevent major suppliers from "continuing anti-competitive practices". The pro-competitive obligations in Section 1 of the Reference Paper do not reserve any such unilateral right of WTO Members to maintain anti-competitive measures.

(i) Uniform Settlement Rate

7.261 With respect to the uniform settlement rate, we have found that the ILD Rules require Telmex to negotiate a price, that is then approved by Mexican authorities and applied by Telmex and the other Mexican suppliers to the termination of the services at issue. Mexico justifies this uniform pricing scheme as pro-competitive since, according to Mexico, it removes the possibility that Telmex, or Mexican operators which are foreign affiliates, engage in predatory pricing, or are played against each other by major foreign operators. This Mexican argument admits that one purpose of the uniform pricing requirement is to limit

---

5. Section 1.1 of the Reference Paper.

price competition such as "predatory pricing". Yet Mexico gives no evidence that its existing competition laws are inadequate to deal with predatory pricing, or that it has well-founded reasons for believing that predatory pricing or unfair treatment by foreign affiliates would occur in Mexico absent the uniform settlement rate in the ILD Rules. Nor does Mexico show that predatory pricing could not be dealt with by telecommunications regulations in ways other than through uniform pricing.

7.262 We find the United States argument convincing that the removal of price competition by the Mexican authorities, combined with the setting of the uniform price by the major supplier, has effects tantamount to those of a price-fixing cartel. We have previously found that horizontal practices such as price-fixing among competitors are "anti-competitive practices" under Section 1 of Mexico's Reference Paper. We have also found that a GATS obligation "of preventing suppliers . . . from engaging in or continuing anti-competitive practices" cannot be unilaterally abrogated by a national regulation *requiring* such an anti-competitive practice within the meaning of Section 1 of Mexico's Reference Paper (see paragraphs 7.243 to 7.245 above). For the same reasons, anti-competitive price fixing by telecommunications suppliers cannot be unilaterally exempted from the scope of Section 1 by a government requirement imposing such price fixing. We find, therefore, that the uniform settlement rate under the ILD Rules requires practices by a major supplier, Telmex, that are "anti-competitive" within the meaning of Section 1 of Mexico's Reference Paper.

(ii) Proportionate Return

7.263 With respect to the "proportionate return" system, we have found that Telmex and other Mexican operators terminating the services at issue are required under the ILD Rules to give up traffic to, or accept traffic from, one another depending on whether the proportion of incoming traffic surpasses, or falls short of, their proportion of outgoing traffic. We have also found that Mexico permits Mexican suppliers to negotiate financial compensation agreements between themselves instead of actually transferring surplus traffic among themselves. Mexico justifies this system on substantially the same grounds as the uniform settlement system which the proportionate return system supports. For the reasons explained already in paragraph 7.261 above, we are not convinced by Mexico's justification of this restrictive allocation among competing suppliers of incoming traffic calls and market shares.

7.264 We find that the allocation of market share between Mexican suppliers imposed by the Mexican authorities, combined with the authorization of Mexican operators to negotiate financial compensation between them instead of physically transferring surplus traffic, has effects tantamount to those of a market sharing arrangement between suppliers. We have previously found that certain horizontal practices, such as market sharing arrangements, are "anti-competitive practices" in Section 1 of Mexico's Reference Paper. We recall our previous finding that practices of a major supplier, even if they result from a legal requirement, can be anti-competitive practices within the meaning of Section 1 of Mexico's Reference Paper. We find therefore that the proportionate return system under the ILD Rules requires practices by a major supplier, Telmex, that limit rivalry and competition among competing suppliers and are "anti-competitive" within the meaning of Section 1 of Mexico's Reference Paper.

NOTES AND QUESTIONS

1. How did the panel reach its conclusion that Mexico's reference paper included antitrust obligations? Do you agree with how the panel reached this conclusion?

2. The WTO has an ambitious work program under the GATS, which we summarize as follows:

(1)   *Negotiations.* In early 2000, multilateral negotiations began on further liberalizing international trade in services as required by GATS Article XIX. In March 2001, members agreed on the 2001 Guidelines setting forth procedures for how offers and requests for offers will be made and procedures on how the negotiations will be conducted. These negotiations also reinforced some of the basic principles of the GATS, including the "positive list" approach. The Doha Ministerial Conference incorporated these negotiations into a "single undertaking" of the Doha Development Agenda. Since July 2002, a process of multilateral and bilateral negotiations on market access has been underway.

(2)   *New Disciplines.* Negotiations started in 1995 on disciplines that are not currently included in GATS: rules on emergency safeguard measures, government procurement, and subsidies. Work so far has concentrated on safeguards, i.e., temporary restrictions on market access commitments to deal with market disruptions due to foreign competition.

(3)   *Domestic Regulations.* In 1995, work began on establishing harmonized standards on domestic regulations governing entry by foreign service suppliers through the use of qualification requirements, licensing, and technical standards. By December 1998, members had agreed disciplines on domestic regulations for the accountancy sector. Work on other sectoral disciplines is continuing.

(4)   *MFN Exemptions.* All of the existing MFN exemptions inscribed on members' GATS schedules pursuant to GATS Article II are being reviewed to determine whether they should continue.

(5)   *"Autonomous" Liberalization.* Some countries have liberalized services sectors on their own initiative. In March 2001, members agreed that future GATS negotiations should include criteria for taking this "autonomous" or unilateral liberalization into account. These criteria were agreed upon on March 6, 2003.

(6)   *Least-Developed Countries.* GATS mandates that members must provide special treatment to least-developed countries during the negotiations. Discussions began in March 2002. On September 3, 2003, members agreed on the "modalities"—the scope of the treatment and methods to be used.

(7)   *Assessment of Services Trade.* As mandated by Article XIX, members are conducting an overall assessment of the trade in services, including the GATS objective of increasing the participation of developing countries in services trade.

(8) *Air Transport Services.* Members are reviewing whether to include additional air transport services within GATS, which currently applies to these services only in a limited fashion.

(9) *Maritime Transport Services.* Negotiations in this sector have not been fruitful and have been suspended since 1996.

Little progress has been made on these topics and issues.

12 *Foreign Direct Investment and TRIMS*

I. Introduction

In previous chapters, we examined the trade in goods (Chapters 5 through 10) and trade in services (Chapter 11). This Chapter examines the third channel of trade: foreign direct investment (FDI) and its regulation under the multilateral trading system.

Foreign direct investment (FDI) remains the only channel of trade among the four major channels (i.e., goods, services, technology, and FDI) that is not covered by a general agreement under the WTO. The reasons for this omission can be traced to the controversial nature of FDI, as further detailed below. Some limited aspects of FDI are covered by the Agreement on Trade-Related Investment Measures (TRIMS), one of the Uruguay Round agreements, which is the subject of this Chapter. FDI is also affected in peripheral ways by other WTO agreements.

The omission of FDI from the WTO may seem anomalous as it comes at a time when the world is experiencing a period of accelerated growth in FDI that exceeds growth in the other channels of trade. For example, in 2011, FDI rose by 17 percent over the 2010 level to total $1.5 trillion,[1] a growth rate that far exceeds the annual growth rate in the trade in goods (5 percent for exports), services (11 percent),[2] and technology transfer as measured by growth in royalties and licenses fees (11 percent for 2010).[3] Of this amount 50 percent ($753 billion) was invested in industrialized countries, but unprecedented investment flows are being experienced by developing countries. Most investment has its source in developed countries; but in 2005, developing countries invested $328 billion abroad. Ironically, it may be the importance of FDI that has led to the impasse in negotiating a comprehensive agreement.

This Chapter is organized as follows: We (1) examine the controversial history of FDI within the framework of the WTO and other international organizations and (2) provide an overview of TRIMS. For those interested in the more

---

1. *Global Investment Trends Monitor*, No. 8, Jan. 24, 2012, available at http://unctad.org/en/docs/webdiaeia2012d1_en.pdf.

2. Press Release, World Trade Organization, Trade Growth to Slow in 2012 After Strong Deceleration in 2011 (April 12, 2012), available at http://www.wto.org/english/news_e/pres12_e/pr658_e.htm.

3. *World receipts of royalties and licence fees by region, 2009 and 2010,* available at http://www.wto.org/english/res_e/statis_e/its2011_e/its11_trade_category_e.htm.

general topic of the international law of investment, a must-read is Campbell McLachlan, *Investment Treaties and General International Law*, 57 Int'l & Comp. L.Q. 361 (2008).

PROBLEM 12-1

The Trade Minister of Zenda, a developing country, has just been approached by Danko Chemical Industries, which is interested in establishing a $2 billion plant in Zenda and in providing 20,000 new jobs. Danko currently has a substantial plant in Rura, a neighboring country.

Zenda is very interested in this project, but a disgruntled former employer of Danko in Rura has just provided a copy to the press of the following e-mail written by Danko's general manager: "Wow, it looks as if we have reached high toxicity levels from dumping our wastes in the lakes and streams a bit sooner than projected—in seven years instead of ten as we had thought. The local populace is getting really upset, so we'll need to implement our back-up plan and pack up and move now. It's just three years ahead of time, but our stock price has already tripled in the past seven years. Zenda seems very interested, so all is going as planned. Can you draw up the termination notices for the local employees and begin the transfer of all of our bank accounts out of Rura?" Should the Trade Minister of Zenda be concerned? What are these concerns? Zenda has just joined the WTO. Will the WTO protect Zenda from the type of conduct Danko has exhibited in Rura? Consider the discussion in section A below.

A.   FDI and World Trade

To understand why FDI is so controversial, we begin by a review of FDI and its relationship to the other channels of trade.

In Chapter 1, we referred to FDI as the ownership interest of a business entity resident in one nation by a business entity resident in a foreign nation. The most basic example of FDI is when a parent corporation in the United States establishes a wholly or partially owned subsidiary in a foreign country.

To understand the issues surrounding FDI, let us compare the international sale, the most simple form of international trade, with FDI, the most complex. Of course, many things can go wrong in the sales transaction but in the vast bulk of sales transactions, the buyer receives the contracted-for goods and the seller receives its payment. At this point the transaction has been completed and the parties part ways. From the point of view of the nations of the two parties involved, the basic international trade law issue concerns the amount of the tariff or any quantitative restrictions that are imposed on the goods when they cross the border of the buyer's nation. In most cases, these tariffs will be "bound" by the GATT schedules of the nations involved.

While the international sales transaction primarily involves the single trade law issue of border control measures, FDI involves a myriad of trade law issues, some of which involve high risk. Some nations, particularly developing nations, consider FDI to a double-edged sword, promising great benefits but also involving high risks. FDI also involves risks for the foreign investor as well.

We highlight four of the issues involving risks to both sides:

(1) *Expropriation and Nationalization.* From the foreign investor's perspective, a significant risk is that the foreign nation will nationalize or expropriate all of the assets of the foreign investor, including its wholly foreign owned subsidiaries, bank accounts, and capital assets. If a dispute arises with the foreign government, or if a politically unstable country undergoes a change in attitude toward foreign companies, a foreign government could simply issue a decree declaring the immediate confiscation of all of the foreign investor's assets in the foreign country. The foreign investor is usually left without any recourse in these cases. If the foreign investor attempts to seek redress in local courts, such attempts are usually fruitless, and the prospects for any meaningful redress are illusory. Expropriation has occurred with regularity throughout the twentieth century in politically unstable areas of the world such as the Middle East and Central and South America. Historically, foreign investors have considered expropriation to be one of their greatest risks.

(2) *Repatriation of Capital.* Many host countries are concerned that foreign investors do not have a long-term interest in the welfare of the recipient country. A foreign invested enterprise might be operated to earn as much profit as possible in the short term and then, at the first hint of trouble or a downturn in business, the foreign investor will suddenly terminate its operations, close its doors, and repatriate all of its capital. A large capital flight might lead to economic and political instability in a country that is dependent on the foreign subsidiaries to generate jobs and hard currency obtained through the sale of the products abroad. Related concerns are the repatriation of profits: The foreign investor may wish to return profits earned by its foreign subsidiaries to its home country to pay shareholders. The foreign nation may prefer to see the profits reinvested locally or paid out in dividends locally.

(3) *Workers' Rights.* Some foreign nations, especially developing countries, are concerned that foreign investors might exploit the nation's workers by offering low wages, little training, and few benefits. Nations are also concerned about deplorable working conditions and the use of child and forced/slave labor. On the other side, foreign investors wish to benefit from the low costs of doing business in the recipient nation and resist pressure to raise wages or hire more workers than necessary in order to absorb the costs of wages and benefits that would have to otherwise be provided by the foreign government.

(4) *Harm to the Environment.* Some developing countries are concerned that they will become the dumping ground for hazardous wastes generated by the developed world. Multinational companies might decide to locate their most dangerous activities in the developing world in order to avoid the more rigorous environmental regulations of their home countries. There is also a concern that developing countries will be pressured to maintain low standards or to grant exemptions to existing environmental standards to multinational companies as an incentive to invest. Lax environmental standards, government corruption, and indifference create many opportunities for environmental destruction.

A comparison of these FDI issues to the single trade issue of lowering tariffs in the GATT makes it apparent why it will be much harder to reach a general agreement on FDI within the framework of the WTO. Tariffs are basically an issue of economics. By contrast, FDI involves economic, political, social, and moral issues.

Despite the complexities of the issues involved, an effort was made to negotiate a comprehensive agreement on investment in the 1990s. The agreement, to be known as the Multilateral Agreement on Investment (MAI), was to be negotiated and completed under the auspices of the Organization of Economic Cooperation and Development (OECD), based in Paris. Once the MAI was completed, the plan was to incorporate the MAI as one of the covered agreements of the WTO, completing the set of existing agreements on goods, technology, and services. The goal of the MAI was to liberalize the legal environment for FDI, following the same approach used for the other channels of trade by the GATT, GATS, and TRIPS.

As it turned out, assigning the task of negotiating the MAI to the OECD was a strategic error. The OECD is composed of leading industrialized nations, including the United States and the EU. While some non-OECD countries were allowed to be observers, there was (and continues to be) a perception by many developing countries that the OECD is a rich nations' club that has little interest in the welfare of the developing world. The role of the OECD led to a lack of trust in the MAI by developing countries and a host of Non-Government Organizations (NGOs) concerned with social and environmental issues. Due to this opposition and the realization that the widespread adoption of the MAI was not politically feasible, it was abandoned in 1998. In 2001, the WTO agreed at the Doha Ministerial Conference to take up the negotiations on trade and investment beginning in 2003 and established a negotiating group on trade and investment. Shifting the negotiations from the OECD to the WTO itself was intended to appease the concerns of developing countries that they were shut out of the negotiation process. However, by this time, developing country members within the WTO had shifted their attention to several other pressing issues: special and differential treatment across the board for developing and least developed countries, access to medicines and life-saving drugs, and special rules for two areas of great concern for developing countries: agriculture and textiles. At the Cancun meeting in 2004, the WTO officially abandoned the negotiation on trade and investment. The subject of trade and investment is not likely to be revived again in the WTO any time in the near future.

These developments should not be interpreted to indicate that developing countries are not interested in FDI. To the contrary, all countries are interested in attracting FDI and are engaged in an intense and escalating international competition for foreign capital. What the demise of the MAI does indicate is that trade liberalization in FDI is not likely to occur at the multilateral level through the WTO. Rather, trade liberalization in FDI is occurring rapidly at levels below the multilateral level as follows:

(1) *National Level.* Nations are revising their domestic laws to encourage FDI. A recent UNCTAD report indicates that most of the changes in national regimes affecting FDI have a liberalizing effect. *See* World Investment Report xv-xvi (2002).

(2) *Bilateral Level.* Many nations have entered into bilateral investment treaties (BITs) that deal with the major issues outlined above: protection against nationalization and expropriation; protection against sudden capital flight; basic standards of treatment, such as National Treatment and MFN; workers' rights; the environment; and dispute resolution. The

United States has hundreds of BITs and is continually entering into new agreements.

(3) *Regional Level.* The EU has led the movement toward the dismantling of national barriers in FDI within a customs union. A basic goal of the EU is the promotion of the freedom of movement of capital (one of the four basic freedoms to go along with the freedom of movement of goods, services, and persons). NAFTA liberalizes FDI within its three countries, the United States, Canada, and Mexico. Other regional entities are negotiating liberalizing measures related to FDI.

While trade liberalization through regulation of FDI is occurring largely outside of the WTO, it would also be a mistake to believe that the WTO does not affect FDI. To the contrary, the trade liberalization measures contained in the GATT, GATS, and TRIPS have direct effects in promoting and encouraging FDI. For example, the GATT benefits companies engaged in FDI directly because the bulk of all international sales of goods occurs between different affiliates of a multinational company. These international sales are subject to tariffs at the border, so the reduction of tariffs under the GATT provides a direct benefit to multinational companies. U.S.-based MNCs may wish to set up a customer service center overseas in India, which has an abundance of highly educated, low-cost English-speaking workers. These MNCs would be aided greatly in efforts to establish a services subsidiary by the GATS, which provides for trade liberalization for Mode 3; i.e., services delivered through the commercial presence of the provider. MNCs would also greatly benefit from TRIPS, which requires minimal levels of protection for IP rights in every WTO member.

NOTES AND QUESTIONS

1. Why did the MAI fail? Why did developing countries who were members of the WTO refuse to sign the MAI? The failure of the MAI did not deter the great upward swing in FDI during the 1970s and continuing today. Why? Is an MAI really needed?

2. Given the importance of FDI to the world economy, the lack of a general agreement within the WTO on FDI seems like a glaring omission. How can the WTO claim to be the world's most important treaty on international trade without an agreement on FDI? Is the WTO deficient because it does not deal directly with FDI?

II. The Agreement on Trade-Related Investment Measures (TRIMS)

Read the WTO Agreement on Trade-Related Investment Measures (TRIMS) in the Documents Supplement.

The concerns of host nations about FDI raise the possibility that host nations may impose restrictions on FDI to protect themselves from exploitation. The types of restrictions that nations have imposed fall into two general categories: local content and export performance requirements. Local content requirements typically condition some type of preferential treatment on the purchase of locally produced goods that can be used by the foreign invested enterprise (FIE) in its manufacturing process. The FIE is discouraged or prohibited from importing parts from its home country. Typical performance requirements are minimum export targets. Exports are beneficial to the host nation because they generate hard currency and help to improve the host nation's trade balance.

Prior to the Uruguay Round, the only meaningful protection for foreign investors within the GATT system was found in the National Treatment principle contained in Article III of the GATT, which is the focus of the *Canada—FIRA* case below (decided before the WTO was established). During the Uruguay Round, a very limited negotiation led to the adoption of the WTO Agreement on Trade-Related Investment Measures (TRIMS) in 1994. TRIMS has a very narrow focus—it is designed primarily to protect FDI from discriminatory treatment such as local content and performance requirements and helps to supplement the National Treatment principle in GATT Article III and the prohibition against quantitative restrictions (quotas) contained in GATT Article XI. In other words, TRIMS was intended to protect FDI by leveling the playing field. TRIMS was never intended to play a role similar to that of the GATT, GATS, and TRIPS in liberalizing trade.

PROBLEM 12-2

Assume that in order to obtain approval for its wholly owned foreign subsidiary in Chile, Titan USA signs a contract with the Chilean government promising that the subsidiary will purchase at least 50 percent of the raw materials and physical inputs from Chilean sources for its manufacturing. Titan USA also promises that its Chilean subsidiary will import no more than 50 percent of its inputs from abroad. Are these agreements consistent with the GATT? The Chilean government claims that, because no government measures were ever involved, the GATT is inapplicable. These were voluntary agreements, and no one forced Acme USA to sign them. Is this a good argument? See the *Canada—FIRA* case below.

Canada—Administration of the Foreign Investment Review Act
Report of the GATT Panel, adopted on February 7, 1984
B.I.S.D. (30th Supp.) 140

THE FOREIGN INVESTMENT REVIEW ACT

2.2 In December 1973 the Parliament of Canada enacted the Foreign Investment Review Act. According to Section 2(1) of this Act, the Parliament adopted the law "in recognition that the extent to which control of Canadian industry, trade and commerce has become acquired by persons other than Canadians and the effect thereof on the ability of Canadians to maintain effective control over their economic environment is a matter of national concern" and that it was therefore expedient to ensure that acquisitions of control of a Canadian business or establishments of a new business by persons other than Canadians be reviewed and assessed and only be allowed to proceed if the government had determined that they were, or were likely to be, of "significant benefit to Canada".

2.3 Section 2(2) lists five factors to be taken into account in assessing whether a proposed investment is or is likely to be of significant benefit to Canada. These are:

(a)   the effect of the acquisition or establishment on the level and nature of economic activity in Canada, including, without limiting the generality of the foregoing, the effect on employment, on resource processing, on the utilization of parts, components and services produced in Canada, and on exports from Canada;

(b)   the degree and significance of participation by Canadians in the business enterprise or new business and in any industry or industries in Canada of which the business enterprise or new business forms or would form a part;

(c)   the effect of the acquisition or establishment on productivity, industrial efficiency, technological development, product innovation and product variety in Canada;

(d)   the effect of the acquisition or establishment on competition within any industry or industries in Canada; and

(e)   the compatibility of the acquisition or establishment with national industrial and economic policies, taking into consideration industrial and economic policy objectives enunciated by the government or legislature of any province likely to be significantly affected by the acquisition or establishment.

2.4 *Written undertakings given by investors.* The Act provides that investors may submit written undertakings on the conduct of the business they are proposing to acquire or establish, conditional on approval by the Canadian government of the proposed acquisition or establishment. The submission of undertakings is not required under the Act but, as the administration of the Act evolved, they are now routinely submitted in support of nearly all larger investment proposals. Many undertakings are the result of negotiations between the investor and the Canadian government. Undertakings given by investors may deal with any aspect of the conduct of a business, including employment, investment, research and development, participation of Canadian shareholders and managers, productivity improvements as well as practices with respect to purchasing, manufacturing, and exports. There are no pre-set formulas or prescriptions for the undertakings.

2.5 *Purchase undertakings.* Undertakings with respect to the purchase of goods have been given in a variety of forms:

— Some involve best efforts to seek Canadian sources of supply;
— some specify a percentage or amount of purchases of Canadian products;
— some envisage replacement of imports with Canadian-made goods in a specific dollar amount;
— some refer to the purchase of Canadian products, others only to the purchase from Canadian suppliers (whether of domestic or imported goods);
— some involve a commitment to set up a purchasing division in the Canadian Subsidiary; and
— some involve a commitment to consult with federal or provincial industry specialists in drawing up tender lists.

Undertakings on purchases are often but not always conditional on goods being "available", "reasonably available" or "competitively available" in Canada with respect to price, quality, and delivery or other factors specified by the investor.

2.6 *Manufacturing undertakings.* Some firms have given undertakings to manufacture in Canada products or components of a product used or sold by the firm.

2.7 *Export undertakings.* The undertakings involving the export of goods have been given in a variety of forms:

— Some involving development of natural resources are predicated on the development of offshore markets;
— some involve a specific export target, expressed as a percentage of output or sales, often to be achieved within a specified time frame;
— some involve assigning to the Canadian business exclusive rights to export either all its products to certain countries or specified products on a world basis;
— some involve a commitment by the investor to assist the Canadian subsidiary in selling its products in foreign markets; and
— some involve commitments that the Canadian business will not be restricted from seeking out and taking advantage of any export opportunities.

FINDINGS

(A)   GENERAL

5.1 In view of the fact that the [GATT] does not prevent Canada from exercising its sovereign right to regulate foreign direct investments, the Panel examined the purchase and export undertakings by investors subject to the Foreign Investment Review Act of Canada solely in the light of Canada's trade obligations under the [GATT].

(B)   UNDERTAKINGS TO PURCHASE GOODS OF CANADIAN ORIGIN IN PREFERENCE TO IMPORTED GOODS OR IN SPECIFIED AMOUNTS OR PROPORTIONS, OR TO PURCHASE GOODS FROM CANADIAN SOURCES

5.4 *Article III:4.* The Panel first examined whether the purchase undertakings are to be considered "laws, regulations or requirements" within the meaning of Article III:4. As both parties had agreed that the Foreign Investment Review Act and the Foreign Investment Review Regulations—whilst providing for the possibility of written undertakings—did not make their submission obligatory, the question remained whether the undertakings given in individual cases are to be considered "requirements" within the meaning of Article III:4. In this respect the Panel noted that Section 9(c) of the Act refers to "any written undertakings . . . relating to the proposed or actual investment given by any party thereto conditional upon the allowance of the investment" and that Section 21 of the Act states that "where a person who has given a written undertaking . . . fails or refuses to comply with such undertaking" a court order may be made "directing that person to comply with the undertaking". The Panel further noted that written purchase undertakings—leaving aside the manner in which they may have been arrived at (voluntary submission, encouragement, negotiation, etc.)—once they were accepted, became part of the conditions under which the investment proposals were approved, in which case compliance could be legally enforced. The Panel therefore found that the word "requirements" as used in Article III:4 could be considered a proper description of existing undertakings.

5.5 The Panel could not subscribe to the Canadian view that the word "requirements" in Article III:4 should be interpreted as "mandatory rules applying across-the-board" because this latter concept was already more aptly covered by the term "regulations" and the authors of this provision must have had something different in mind when adding the word "requirements". The mere fact that the few disputes that have so far been brought before the CONTRACTING PARTIES regarding the application of Article III:4 have only concerned laws and regulations does not in the view of the Panel justify an assimilation of "requirements" with "regulations". The Panel also considered that, in judging whether a measure is contrary to obligations under Article III:4, it is not relevant whether it applies across-the-board or only in isolated cases. Any interpretation which would exclude case-by-case action would, in the view of the Panel, defeat the purposes of Article III:4.

5.6 The Panel carefully examined the Canadian view that the purchase undertakings should be considered as private contractual obligations of particular foreign investors vis-à-vis the Canadian government. The Panel recognized that investors might have an economic advantage in assuming purchase undertakings, taking into account the other conditions under which the investment was permitted. The Panel felt, however, that even if this was so, private contractual obligations entered into by investors should not adversely affect the rights which contracting parties, including contracting parties not involved in the dispute, possess under Article III:4 of the General Agreement and which they can exercise on behalf of their exporters. This applies in particular to the rights deriving from the national treatment principle, which—as stated in Article III:1—is aimed at preventing the use of internal measures "so as to afford protection to domestic production".

5.7 The Panel then examined the question whether less favourable treatment was accorded to imported products than that accorded to like products of Canadian origin in respect of requirements affecting their purchase. For this purpose the Panel distinguished between undertakings to purchase goods of Canadian origin and undertakings to use Canadian sources or suppliers (irrespective of the origin of the goods), and for both types of undertakings took into account the qualifications "available", "reasonably available", or "competitively available".

5.8 The Panel found that undertakings to purchase *goods of Canadian origin* without any qualification exclude the possibility of purchasing available imported products so that the latter are clearly treated less favourably than domestic products and that such requirements are therefore not consistent with Article III:4. This finding is not modified in cases where undertakings to purchase goods of Canadian origin are subject to the qualification that such goods be "available". It is obvious that if Canadian goods are not available, the question of less favourable treatment of imported goods does not arise.

5.9 When these undertakings are conditional on goods being "competitively available" (as in the majority of cases) the choice between Canadian or imported products may frequently coincide with normal commercial considerations and the latter will not be adversely affected whenever one or the other offer is more competitive. However, it is the Panel's understanding that the qualification "competitively available" is intended to deal with situations where there are Canadian goods available on competitive terms. The Panel considered that in those cases where the imported and domestic product are offered on equivalent terms, adherence to the undertaking would entail giving preference to the domestic product. Whether or not the foreign investor chooses to buy Canadian goods in given practical situations, is not at issue. The purpose of Article III:4 is not to protect the interests of the foreign investor but to ensure that goods originating in any other contracting party benefit from treatment no less favourable than domestic (Canadian) goods, in respect of the requirements that affect their purchase (in Canada). On the basis of these considerations, the Panel found that a requirement to purchase goods of Canadian origin, also when subject to "competitive availability", is contrary to Article III:4. The Panel considered that the alternative qualification "reasonably available" which is used in some cases, is *a fortiori* inconsistent with Article III:4, since the undertaking in these cases implies that preference has to be given to Canadian goods also when these are not available on entirely competitive terms.

5.10 The Panel then turned to the undertakings to buy from *Canadian suppliers.* The Panel did not consider the situation where domestic products are not available, since such a situation is not covered by Article III:4. The Panel understood the choice under this type of requirement to apply on the one hand to imported goods if bought through a Canadian agent or importer and on the other hand to Canadian goods which can be purchased either from a Canadian "middleman" or directly from the Canadian producer. The Panel recognized that these requirements might, in a number of cases, have little or no effect on the choice between imported or domestic products. However, the possibility of purchasing imported products *directly* from the foreign producer would be excluded and as the conditions of purchasing imported products through a Canadian agent or importer would normally be less advantageous, the imported product would therefore have more difficulty in competing with Canadian products (which are not subject to similar requirements affecting their sale) and be treated less favourably. For this reason, the Panel found that the requirements to buy from Canadian suppliers are inconsistent with Article III:4.

5.11 In case undertakings to purchase from Canadian suppliers are subject to a "competitive availability" qualification, as is frequent, the handicap for the imported product is alleviated as it can be obtained directly from the foreign producer if offered under more competitive conditions than via Canadian sources. In those cases in which Canadian sources and a foreign manufacturer offer a product on equivalent terms, adherence to the undertaking would entail giving preference to Canadian sources, which in practice would tend to result in the purchase being made directly from the Canadian producer, thereby excluding the foreign product. The Panel therefore found that requirements to purchase from Canadian suppliers, also when subject to competitive availability, are contrary to Article III:4. As before (paragraph 5.9), the Panel considered that the qualification "reasonably available" is *a fortiori* inconsistent with Article III:4.

PROBLEM 12-3

The Alliance for Safeguarding America's Economy, a nonprofit advocacy group, is concerned about the growing foreign ownership of U.S. corporations.

The Alliance is concerned about the impact of foreign ownership on the economic welfare and national security interests of the United States. The Alliance has proposed the following legislation, applicable to all U.S. companies with a net market value of $10 billion or more, for consideration by Congress:

No company shall be established in the United States and no merger or acquisition involving a United States corporation shall be lawful unless the newly formed or resulting company meets the following conditions:

(1) A majority of the members of the board of directors and the senior management group exercising substantial control of the company are U.S. citizens, permanent residents, or have a habitual residence in the United States;

(2) Equity in the company must be at least 50 percent owned by U.S. citizens or permanent residents;

(3) The company must operate in a field involving advanced technology;

(4) The company shall purchase at least 50 percent of its supplies from U.S. distributors;

(5) The company shall export at least 50 percent of all production.

All companies meeting these conditions will be entitled to favorable tax treatment under applicable taxation laws.

Analyze each of these provisions separately. Are they consistent with the National Treatment principle in Article 2 of TRIMS? Consider also *Canada—FIRA*, and the *Indonesia—Autos* case below.

Indonesia—Certain Measures Affecting the Automobile Industry
Report of the WTO Panel, adopted on July 2, 1998
WT/DS54/R

[This dispute concerned a series of laws maintained by Indonesia with respect to the manufacture and sale of motor vehicles and their component parts. Indonesian laws created the 1993 car program conferring "National Car" status and tax and other advantages to Indonesian companies that produced cars in Indonesia developed with designs and technologies based on national capability and with minimum amounts of local content. A second measure, the June 1996 programme, granted a similar status to cars manufactured in foreign countries that met the same Indonesian design and content standards. The United States, Japan, and the European Communities contested these measures on the grounds that the local content requirements violated the National Treatment obligations contained in Article 2 of TRIMS and Article III.4 of the GATT.]

1. THE RELATIONSHIP BETWEEN THE TRIMS AGREEMENT AND ARTICLE III OF GATT

14.60 Since the complainants have raised claims that the local content requirements of the car programmes violate both the provisions of Article III:4 of

GATT and Article 2 of the TRIMs Agreement, we must consider which claims to examine first.

14.61 In this regard, we note first that on its face the TRIMs Agreement is a fully fledged agreement in the WTO system. The TRIMs Agreement and Article III:4 prohibit local content requirements that are TRIMs and therefore can be said to cover the same subject matter. But when the TRIMs Agreement refers to "the provisions of Article III", it refers to the substantive aspects of Article III; that is to say, conceptually, it is the ten paragraphs of Article III that are referred to in Article 2.1 of the TRIMs Agreement, and not the application of Article III in the WTO context as such. Thus if Article III is not applicable for any reason not related to the disciplines of Article III itself, the provisions of Article III remain applicable for the purpose of the TRIMs Agreement.

14.62 Consequently, since the TRIMs Agreement and Article III remain two legally distinct and independent sets of provisions of the WTO Agreement, we find that even if either of the two sets of provisions were not applicable the other one would remain applicable. And to the extent that complainants have raised separate and distinct claims under Article III:4 of GATT and the TRIMs Agreement, each claim must be addressed separately.

14.63 As to which claims, those under Article III:4 of GATT or Article 2 of the TRIMs Agreement, to examine first, we consider that we should first examine the claims under the TRIMs Agreement since the TRIMs Agreement is more specific than Article III:4 as far as the claims under consideration are concerned.

2. THE APPLICATION OF THE TRIMS AGREEMENT

14.64 Article 2.1 of the TRIMs Agreement provides that

" . . . no Member shall apply any TRIM that is inconsistent with the provisions of Article III or Article XI of GATT 1994."

By its terms, Article 2.1 requires two elements to be shown to establish a violation thereof: first, the existence of a TRIM; second, that TRIM is inconsistent with Article III or Article XI of GATT. No claims have been raised with reference to a violation of Article XI of GATT.

14.65 Article 2.1 of the TRIMs Agreement refers to Article III generally. It is our view that the complainants have limited their TRIMs inconsistency claims to the aspects of the Indonesian car programmes that would violate the provisions of the TRIMs Agreement which prohibit any advantage conditional on meeting local content requirements. In other words, while the complainants have claimed that some other aspects of the same car programmes also violate the provisions of Article III:2 of GATT, they have not claimed that the tax discrimination aspects of the measures *per se* violate the TRIMs Agreement. Therefore, we will examine under the TRIMs Agreement, only the consistency of the local content requirements made effective through the custom duty and tax benefits of these car programmes. Later, we shall examine the consistency of the tax discrimination aspects *per se* of these car programmes with the provisions of Article III:2 of GATT.

14.66 We note also that Article 2.2 of the TRIMs Agreement provides:

"2.2 An Illustrative List of TRIMs that are inconsistent with the obligations of national treatment provided for in paragraph 4 of Article III of GATT 1994 . . . is contained in the Annex to this Agreement."

14.67 The United States and the European Communities claim that any measure that falls within the description of Item 1(a) of the Illustrative List of the TRIMs Agreement constitutes *per se* a TRIM inconsistent with Article 2 of the TRIMs Agreement. For the United States, if any Member, in whatever context, requires the purchase by an enterprise of a domestic product in order to obtain an advantage, that requirement by definition has investment consequences for such an enterprise, bringing the measure within the coverage of the TRIMs Agreement and confirming its violation thereof. The United States adds that, even if the identification of a relationship to investment were necessary to prove an inconsistency with the TRIMs Agreement, the Indonesian measures under examination fulfil such a condition, because the measures necessitate an investment in Indonesia (as a producer of motor vehicles or motor vehicle parts and components) to qualify for the various tax and customs duty incentives.

14.69 The European Communities and Japan submit as well that the central aspect of the various measures included in the Indonesian car programmes is to develop domestic manufacturing capability of automobiles and automotive parts and components, and that they thereby qualify as "investment" measures. For these complainants, the Indonesian car programmes are "trade related" because they encourage the use of domestic over imported parts and thereby affect trade.

14.70 Indonesia argues that, while its subsidies may at times indirectly affect investment decisions of the recipient of the subsidy or other parties, these decisions are not the object, but rather the unintended result, of the subsidy. Indonesia adds that many subsidies will result indirectly in increased investment. Indonesia adds that these subsidies have not been adopted as investment regulations. Therefore, for Indonesia, the measures under examination are not trade-related investment measures. Indonesia also supports the argument put forward by India, a third party, that the TRIMs Agreement is basically designed to govern and provide a level playing field for foreign investment, and that therefore measures relating to internal taxes or subsidies cannot be construed to be trade-related investment measures.

14.71 We note that the arguments presented by the parties reflect different views on whether any requirement by an enterprise to purchase or use a domestic product in order to obtain an advantage, by definition falls within the Illustrative List or whether the TRIMs Agreement requires a separate analysis of the nature of a measure as a trade-related investment measure before proceeding to an examination of whether the measure is covered by the Illustrative List. However, if we were to consider that the measures in dispute in this case are in any event trade-related investment measures, it would not be necessary to decide this basic issue of interpretation. We note in this regard that the United States and the European Communities have also argued in the alternative that, even if it is necessary to show a relationship of a measure to investment, any such requirement would be satisfied in the case under consideration.

14.72 Therefore, we will first determine whether the Indonesian measures are TRIMs. To this end, we address initially the issue of whether the measures at issue are "investment measures". Next, we consider whether they are "trade-related". Finally, we shall examine whether any measure found to be a TRIM is inconsistent with the provisions of Article III and thus violates the TRIMs Agreement.

(A)   ARE THE INDONESIAN MEASURES "INVESTMENT MEASURES"?

14.73 We note that the use of the broad term "investment measures" indicates that the TRIMs Agreement is not limited to measures taken specifically in regard to *foreign* investment. Contrary to India's argument, we find that nothing in the TRIMs Agreement suggests that the nationality of the ownership of enterprises subject to a particular measure is an element in deciding whether that measure is covered by the Agreement. We therefore find without textual support in the TRIMs Agreement the argument that since the TRIMs Agreement is basically designed to govern and provide a level playing field for foreign investment, measures relating to internal taxes or subsides cannot be construed to be a trade-related investment measure. We recall in this context that internal tax advantages or subsidies are only one of many types of advantages which may be tied to a local content requirement which is a principal focus of the TRIMs Agreement. The TRIMs Agreement is not concerned with subsidies and internal taxes as such but rather with local content requirements, compliance with which may be encouraged through providing any type of advantage. Nor, in any case, do we see why an internal measure would necessarily not govern the treatment of foreign investment.

14.74 We next consider whether the Indonesian measures are investment measures. In this regard, we consider the following extracts (emphases added) from the official Indonesian legislation relevant and instructive.

14.75 With regard to the 1993 car programme, we note:

— The "considerations section" of the Decree of the Ministry of Industry announcing the 1993 car programme states:

"a. that within the framework of *supporting and promoting the development of the automotive industry and/or the component industry* in the future, it is deemed necessary to regulate the local content levels of domestically produced motor vehicles or components in connection with the grant of incentives in the imposition of import duty rates;
b. that in order to *further strengthen domestic industrial development* by taking into account the trend of technological advance and the increase of the capability and mastering of industrial design and engineering, it is necessary to improve the relevant existing regulations already laid down;"[4]

— The "considerations section" of the 1995 amendment to the 1993 car programme states:

"That *in the framework of further promoting of the development of the motor vehicles industry and/or domestically produced components*, it is considered necessary to amend . . . "[5]

14.76 With regard to the February 1996 car programme, we note the following:

---

4. Decree of the Ministry of Industry No. 114/M/S/6/1993, 9 June 1993.
5. Decree of the Ministry of Industry No. 108/M/S/5/1995, on the amendment of the attachment I to Decree of the Ministry of Industry No. 114/M/S/6/1993, 23 May 1995.

— The title of the Presidential Instruction for the National Car programme (No.2) is "The *Development* of the National Automobile Industry".[6]

— Paragraph a) of the "Considering" section of the Government Regulation No.20 states:

> "that in the effort *to promote the growth of the domestic automotive industry*, it is deemed necessary to enact regulations concerning the Sales Tax on Luxury Goods upon the delivery of domestically produced motor vehicles".[7]

— In addition, the State Minister for Mobilization of Investment Funds/ Chairman of the Investment Coordinating Board issued a decree entitled "Investment Regulations within the Framework of the Realisation of the Establishment of the National Automobile Industry"[8] which emphasized that the new measures were intended to promote investment, stating in its fifth considering:

> "5. that it is therefore necessary to issue *a decree for the regulation of investment* in the national automobile industry."

— Article 2 of that same Investment Regulation by the Minister of State for Mobilization of Investment Funds/Chairman of the Investment Coordinating Board provides:

> "In order *to realise the development of the national automobile industry* as meant in Article 1:
>
> 1. . . .
> 2. *In the endeavour to realise the development of such national car industry, the investment approval will be issued to the automobile industry sector with tax facilities in accordance with legal provisions enacted specifically for such purpose.*"

— The Decision relating to the investment facilities regarding the Determination of PT. Timor Putra National to Establish and Produce a National Car, entitled "Decision of the State Minister for the Mobilization of Investment Funds/Chairman of the Capital Investment Co-ordinating Board" states:

> "1. That *in implementing a national car industry it is deemed necessary to determine investment approval* for a car industry which will build and produce a national car.
> 2. That in the framework of investment for the car industry, PT. Timor Putra National has submitted an application and working program to build a national car industry and *has obtained domestic investment approval* (PMDN) NO.607/PMDN/1995, dated 9 November 1995".[9]

---

6. Instruction of the President of the Republic of Indonesia No.2 of 1996, 19 February 1996.

7. Government Regulation No.20 of 1996, 19 February 1996.

8. Decree of the State Minister for Mobilisation of Investment Funds/Chairman of the Investment Coordinating Board No. 01/SK/1996, 27 February 1996.

9. Decision of the State Minister For the Mobilization of Investment Funds/Chairman of the Capital Investment Co-ordinating Board Number 02/SK/1996, 5 March 1996.

[The Panel then also reviewed similar official statements concerning the 1996 car programme.]

14.78 We note also that Indonesia indicates[10] that the objectives of the National Car programme include the following:

— To improve the competitiveness of local companies and strengthen overall industrial development;
— To develop the capacity of multiple-source auto parts and components;
— To encourage the development of the automotive industry and the automotive component industry;
— To bring about major structural changes in the Indonesian automobile industry;
— To encourage the transfer of technology and contribute to large-scale job creation;
— To encourage car companies to increase their local content, resulting in a rapid growth of investment in the automobile industry.

14.79 Indonesia has also stated that PT TPN is a "domestic capital investment company".[11]

14.80 On the basis of our reading of these measures applied by Indonesia under the 1993 and the 1996 car programmes, which have investment objectives and investment features and which refer to investment programmes, we find that these measures are aimed at encouraging the development of a local manufacturing capability for finished motor vehicles and parts and components in Indonesia. Inherent to this objective is that these measures necessarily have a significant impact on investment in these sectors. For this reason, we consider that these measures fall within any reasonable interpretation of the term "investment measures".

14.81 With respect to the arguments of Indonesia that the measures at issue are not investment measures because the Indonesian Government does not regard the programmes as investment programmes and because the measures have not been adopted by the authorities responsible for investment policy, we believe that there is nothing in the text of the TRIMs Agreement to suggest that a measure is not an investment measure simply on the grounds that a Member does not characterize the measure as such, or on the grounds that the measure is not explicitly adopted as an investment regulation.

(B)   ARE THE INDONESIAN MEASURES "TRADE-RELATED"?

14.82 We now have to determine whether these investment measures are "trade-related". We consider that, if these measures are local content requirements, they would necessarily be "trade-related" because such requirements, by definition, always favour the use of domestic products over imported products, and therefore affect trade.

---

10. See paragraph 6.51 of the Descriptive Part.
11. See paragraph 6.50 of the Descriptive Part.

(C)   ILLUSTRATIVE LIST OF THE TRIMS AGREEMENT

14.83 An examination of whether these measures are covered by Item (1) of the Illustrative List of TRIMs annexed to the TRIMs Agreement, which refers amongst other situations to measures with local content requirements, will not only indicate whether they are trade-related but also whether they are inconsistent with Article III:4 and thus in violation of Article 2.1 of the TRIMs Agreement.

14.84 The Annex to the TRIMs Agreement reads as follows:

Annex Illustrative List

1. TRIMs that are inconsistent with the obligation of national treatment provided for in paragraph 4 of Article III of GATT 1994 include those which are mandatory or enforceable under domestic law or under administrative rulings, or compliance with which is necessary to obtain an advantage, and which require:

    (a)   the purchase or use by an enterprise of products of domestic origin or from any domestic source, whether specified in terms of particular products, in terms of volume or value of products, or in terms of a proportion of volume or value of its local production;"

14.85 We note that all the various decrees and regulations implementing the Indonesian car programmes operate in the same manner. They provide for tax advantages on finished motor vehicles using a certain percentage value of local content and additional customs duty advantages on imports of parts and components to be used in finished motor vehicles using a certain percentage value of local content. We also note that under the June 1996 car programme, the local content envisaged in the February 1996 car programme could be performed through an undertaking by the foreign producer of National Cars to counter-purchase Indonesian parts and components.

14.86 For instance, the Decision to issue the Decree of the Minister of Industry Concerning The Determination of Local Content Levels of Domestically Made Motor Vehicles or Components attached to the Decree of the Ministry of Industry announcing the 1993[12] car programme states in its Article 2:

"(1) The Automotive Industry and/or the Components Industry *may obtain certain Incentives* within the framework of importing needed Components, Sub-Components, basic materials and semi-Finished Goods, originating in one source as well as various sources (multi sourcing), *if the production has reached/can achieve certain Local Content levels.* (. . .)

(3) The *Local Content levels* of domestically made Motor Vehicles and/or Components which are *eligible for Incentives*, including their Incentive rates, shall be those listed in Attachment I to this decree." (emphasis added)

The Instruction of the President of the Republic of Indonesia No.2 of 1996 of the National Car programme (dated 19 February 1998) states in its "INSTRUCT . . . SECONDLY":

"WITHIN the framework of establishment of the National Car Industry:"

---

12. Decree of the Ministry of Industry No. 114/M/S/6/1993, 9 June 1993.

1. The Minister of Industry and Trade will foster, guide and grant facilities in accordance with provisions of laws in effect such that the national car industry:
   a. uses a brand name of its own;
   b. *uses components produced domestically as much as possible*;
   c. is able to export its products." (emphasis added)

More specifically Regulation No. 20/1996 established the following sales tax structure where passenger cars of more than 1600cc and jeeps with local content of less than 60% would pay 35% tax; passenger cars of less than 1600cc, jeeps with local content of more than 60%, and light commercial vehicles (other than jeeps using gas) would pay 20% tax; and National Cars would pay 0% tax.[13] We recall that one of the requirements for designation as a "National Car" is that the local content rate must be 20% at the end of the first year, 40% at the end of the second year and 60% at the end of the third year.[14]

14.87 We also note with reference to the June 1996 car programme, that the Decree of the President of the Republic of Indonesia Number 42 of 1996[15] on the production of National Cars provides in Article 1:

"National Cars which are made overseas by Indonesian workers and fulfil the local content stipulated by the Minister of Industry and Trade will be treated equally to those made in Indonesia."

The Decree of the Minister of Industry and Trade adopted pursuant to this Presidential Decree 42 states in Articles 1, 2 and 3:

"Article 1

Within the framework of preparations, the production of national cars can be carried out overseas for a one-time maximum period of 1 (one) year on the condition that Indonesian made parts and components are used.

Article 2

The procurement of Indonesian made parts and components shall be performed through a system of counter purchase of parts and components of motor vehicles by the overseas company carrying out the production and reexporting of national cars to Indonesia.

Article 3

The value of the Counter purchase referred to in Article 2 shall be fixed at the minimum of 25% (twenty-five percent) of the import value of the national cars assembled abroad (C&F value)".

---

13. See paragraphs 2.28 *et seq.* of the Descriptive Part. Regulation No. 36/1996 increased the tax incentive available by providing that passenger cars and light commercial vehicles with a local content in excess of 60% would pay 0% tax. See paragraphs 2.36 *et seq.* of the Descriptive Part.

14. See paragraphs 2.24 *et seq.* of the Descriptive Part.

15. The Decree of the Minister of Industry and Trade No. 142/MPP/Kep/6/1996 Regarding the Production of the National Car, 5 June 1996.

14.88 We believe that under these measures compliance with the provisions for the purchase and use of particular products of domestic origin is necessary to obtain the tax and customs duty benefits on these car programmes, as referred to in Item 1(a) of the Illustrative List of TRIMs.

14.89 We need now to decide whether these tax and customs duty benefits are "advantages" in the meaning of the chapeau of paragraph 1 of that Illustrative List. In the context of the claims under Article III:4 of GATT, Indonesia has argued that the reduced customs duties are not internal regulations and as such cannot be covered by the wording of Article III:4. We do not consider that the matter before us in connection with Indonesia's obligations under the TRIMs Agreement is the customs duty relief as such but rather the internal regulations, i.e. the provisions on purchase and use of domestic products, compliance with which is necessary to obtain an advantage, which advantage here is the customs duty relief. The lower duty rates are clearly "advantages" in the meaning of the chapeau of the Illustrative List to the TRIMs Agreement and as such, we find that the Indonesian measures fall within the scope of the Item 1 of the Illustrative List of TRIMs.

14.90 Indonesia also argues that the local content requirements of its car programmes do not constitute classic local content requirements within the meaning of the *FIRA* panel (which involved a binding contract between the investor and the Government of Canada) because they leave companies free to decide from which source to purchase parts and components. We note that the Indonesian producers or assemblers of motor vehicles (or motor vehicle parts) must satisfy the local content targets of the relevant measures in order to take advantage of the customs duty and tax benefits offered by the Government. The wording of the Illustrative List of the TRIMs Agreement makes it clear that a simple advantage conditional on the use of domestic goods is considered to be a violation of Article 2 of the TRIMs Agreement even if the local content requirement is not binding as such.

14.91 We thus find that the tax and tariff benefits contingent on meeting local requirements under these car programmes constitute "advantages". Given this and our earlier analysis of whether these local content requirements are TRIMs and covered by the Illustrative List annexed to the TRIMs Agreement, we further find that they are in violation of Article 2.1 of the TRIMs Agreement.

NOTES AND QUESTIONS

1. As interpreted by GATT panels and the WTO Appellate Body, are GATT Articles III:4 and XI:1 broad enough to encompass investment measures? If so, why is TRIMS needed? What is added by TRIMS? Is the illustrative list in the Annex an important contribution?

2. Is there any possibility of conflict between GATT and TRIMS? If so, which agreement will prevail?

PROBLEM 12-4

Assume that China has just concluded a BIT, giving Germany exclusive privileges and preferential tax treatment to make FDI in heavy trucks, the last automotive sector that has not been exploited. Heavy trucks are in high demand to service China's booming construction industry, but the supply of high-quality vehicles is inadequate. Germany's auto industry was the first to recognize this opportunity and was able to beat Japan and the United States in obtaining a BIT. Germany's auto industry is thrilled and is in the process of setting up five new manufacturing facilities outside of Beijing and Shanghai. You represent the Detroit Auto Industry and demand similar treatment from China under the MFN principle. What result under TRIMS?

PROBLEM 12-5

Upon reading the BIT between China and Germany closely, you see that the agreement also allows Germany to set up service and repair centers for all types of cars and financial services companies that will help to provide financing to customers for the purchase of all new trucks and passenger cars. The Detroit Auto Industry is very interested in setting up business operations in these areas to service the China market because it already has manufacturing facilities in China for passenger cars. What result under TRIMS? *See also* GATS Article II. What difference, if any, is there between this problem and Problem 12-4?

NOTE ON THE ROLE OF THE WTO IN INTERNATIONAL INVESTMENT LAW

The WTO is unlikely to expand the small role it plays in international investment law. Very few WTO complaints have been made concerning the TRIMS Agreement. International investment law is likely to remain primarily within the scope of BIT and regional free trade agreements such as NAFTA. International dispute settlement under these agreements is very lively. NAFTA Chapter 11's investor protection dispute settlement mechanism has spawned many cases against Mexico, Canada, and the United States.[16] Investor-state arbitrations before the International Convention on the Settlement of Investment Disputes Between States and Nationals of Other States (in force 1966) now involve 143 states-parties, almost all of whom are WTO members. This lively field of law is beyond the scope of this book but is covered in Chapter 6 of Chow and Schoenbaum, *International Business Transactions: Problems, Cases, and Materials* (2d ed. 2010).

---

16. For a listing and reports, see http://www.international.gc.ca/trade.

13 *Intellectual Property and TRIPS*

I. Introduction

This Chapter focuses on the last of the four channels of trade—technology or intellectual property (IP)—and its treatment under TRIPS. We will focus on the impact of four major categories of IP rights on international trade:

- Copyrights, which protect original expression fixed in a tangible medium;
- Patents, which protect inventions that are novel, non-obvious, and useful;
- Trademarks, which designate the origin of goods and services; and
- Geographical indications, which identify goods by the name of a place or location where the goods are produced.

In this Chapter, we (1) discuss the role of IP in international trade and the treatment of IP in the WTO; (2) examine the most important substantive areas of IP within the TRIPS framework; and (3) analyze the enforcement of international IP rights under TRIPS and U.S. law. We consider only IP in international trade, not IP as such. For a full treatment of international IP, see Daniel Chow and Edward Lee, *International Intellectual Property: Problems, Cases, and Materials* (2d ed. West 2012).

A. Intellectual Property and International Trade

To appreciate the fundamental role of IP in international trade, it is necessary to understand the link between technology and competitiveness in the modern world. Technology increases efficiency in industrial productivity, which is necessary for economic growth and development. A country's level of competitiveness and comparative advantage in the world economy is tied directly to its status as an innovator of advanced technology. Innovator countries, such as the United States, Germany, and Japan, find that there is great demand for their products and services. In general, the higher the level of technology embedded in a product or service, the more competitive the product or service becomes in other countries. Innovator countries, however, are less likely to engage in international trade if a recipient country does not afford adequate protection for IP rights. Thus, IP plays a role either to encourage or to discourage international trade.

Intellectual property rights are created by national laws and, as a result, are territorial in nature. In the absence of an international treaty, it is necessary for an IP owner to follow the separate requirements and procedures of each country in order to obtain rights. For example, an owner of a patent registered in the United States acquires an IP right in the United States, but not in other countries.[1] To receive patent protection in Japan, the U.S. owner must file a separate patent application in Japan under Japanese law. The U.S. patent owner will have to repeat this process in every country to acquire patent protection. The same territorial limitations generally apply to other forms of IP as well. Enforcement in the country granting IP rights is also essential. Thus, the IP law regime of the recipient or importing country is very important for international trade, as discussed in the following examples.

Let us begin with the trade in goods. Assume that Acme USA, a manufacturer in the United States, wishes to sell computer chips to a buyer in Country Z. Acme has registered U.S. trademarks that protect the famous brand name of the product, as well as U.S. patents that protect its technology. If Acme wishes to sell the product to Country Z, Acme must first make sure that it obtains registrations for its trademarks and patents in Country Z. If Acme does not obtain trademarks and patents in Z, then copycats in Z can make unauthorized copies of the product with legal impunity, as Acme's U.S. trademarks and patents do not have any extraterritorial effect in Z and offer Acme no protection there. Even if Acme registers its trademarks and patents in Country Z, Acme may find that Z does not effectively enforce its laws against counterfeiting and piracy. Acme may be very reluctant to sell its products to a buyer in Z if Z has weak laws protecting IP rights.

A provider of services will have the same concerns. If Acme provides consulting services to a manufacturer in Country Z, Acme might be exposing trade secrets, confidential business information, and valuable know-how to theft and misappropriation in Z. Or Acme might have a valuable business method that is protected by a patent in the United States. Country Z might not recognize patents for business methods at all, or patent rights (even if granted) might not be rigorously enforced.

In technology transfer, a third channel of trade, the protection of IP, becomes a primary consideration. In a typical international technology transfer arrangement, the owner of IP in one country will license or assign the rights to the IP to a party in a second country. The first step in this transaction is for the IP owner to obtain all IP rights in the country where the license or assignment agreement will be executed. Let us assume that Acme wishes to transfer its advanced technology for a computer chip, protected in a patent, to a licensee in Country Z in order to allow the licensee to manufacture the chip locally. Acme will first apply for a patent registration in Country Z and, once the registration is obtained in Acme's name, license the patent rights to the licensee in a separate licensing agreement. Since Acme is giving the licensee access to its proprietary technology, there is always the risk that the technology will be misappropriated or stolen. Acme will want assurances that under Z's legal system, Acme can enforce its patent rights and the patent licensing agreement against the licensee and third parties.

Concerns regarding the protection of IP arise with even greater force in foreign direct investment (FDI), the fourth channel of trade, because FDI is often the

---

1. An international treaty, the Patent Cooperation Treaty, discussed in a later section, creates a process in which a single international application can result in the granting of national registrations in designated countries.

most effective means of technology transfer in the world today. Let us assume now that Acme USA decides to establish Acme-China, Ltd., a wholly or partially owned subsidiary in China. In addition to establishing the physical plant of the subsidiary, Acme USA must also transfer the know-how and technology that is necessary to manufacture the computer chips to Acme-China. In general, the U.S. parent company will obtain patents, copyrights, and trademarks in its own name in China and then license the rights to the subsidiary. The reason for this arrangement is that the parent company wishes to remain the owner of all of Acme's IP rights anywhere in the world. From the standpoint of China (the recipient country) FDI provides access to advanced technology that can be absorbed and that can be used to improve China's own industries. The recipient of advanced technology through FDI may be able to close the gap with developed countries. In fact, China has become, through this process of technology absorption, a global industrial power.

From Acme USA's standpoint, however, FDI also carries significant risks. Not only is Acme USA transferring its most advanced technology to China, but the operations of the subsidiary also create many opportunities for theft and misappropriation that are difficult to control and can result in piracy of Acme's products. In fact, theft of IP rights is one of the most contentious trade issues between the United States and China and is increasingly the subject of disputes brought within the WTO.

These considerations indicate that countries with a strong IP legal regime provide an attractive destination for FDI. By contrast, weak IP legal regimes may create a deterrent to FDI.

B. Intellectual Property and the WTO

The importance of protecting IP in trade led the United States and other innovator countries to include IP in the Uruguay Round of trade negotiations. Whether IP should be covered under the WTO was a controversial issue, pitting developed countries against developing countries. Developed countries like the United States sought strong IP protection, while developing countries were concerned that IP laws would be used to deny them access to advanced technology.

The international aspects of IP have long been the focus of the World Intellectual Property Organization (WIPO), a special agency of the United Nations that administers some twenty-four international IP conventions. Many developing countries fought to keep IP outside of the WTO and within WIPO, a largely toothless organization with no enforcement powers. By contrast, the WTO held out the prospect of a much more effective system of compliance backed by a formal dispute settlement mechanism.

A second concern for developing countries was that while IP was a single, isolated issue under WIPO, under the WTO, IP became linked with other trade issues. A country's failure to meet its IP obligations might lead to retaliation against the offending country in another sector of trade, such as an increase in tariffs on imported goods from the offending country. The offending country's other trade benefits, such as MFN tariffs and technical assistance, might also be suspended. The link between IP and other trade issues in the WTO was made explicit by the requirement that all WTO members must accept all WTO agreements (except those designated "plurilateral") including TRIPS, and cannot pick and choose among agreements "à la carte."

TRIPS continues to provoke sharp debate in many quarters. Defenders argue that IP encourages invention and innovation. IP protection also requires inventions to be disclosed, which helps technology dissemination and leads to further technological progress. Some developing countries, led by Brazil and India, seek to weaken certain IP rights guaranteed by TRIPS, working not only through the WTO but also through UNCTAD, which has long been a principal developing country forum. Disputes over IP are not entirely along developed and developing country lines, however; some of the sharpest disputes also exist between the United States and the EU, two leading competitors in IP innovation.

C.   TRIPS: An Overview

Read the Agreement on TRIPS in the Documents Supplement.

At the outset, it is useful to have an overview of TRIPS, which is constructed very logically and systematically.

Part I deals with "General Provisions and Basic Principles." The obligations of National Treatment and MFN treatment are central to Part I. What is the relationship between TRIPS and the principal existing international IP conventions? In 1995 the WTO and WIPO entered into a formal cooperative agreement (reprinted at 34 ILM 681). There is now a common register of IP laws and regulations, and the two organizations cooperate, especially with respect to the notification of new laws and regulations and the provision of technical assistance.

Part II concerns the definitions and minimum international standards for seven different types of IP rights: copyright; trademarks; geographical indications; industrial designs; patents; layout-designs of integrated circuits; and trade secrets. All WTO members agree to comply with these minimums, but they are free (and sometimes pressured) to exceed them. Some of these concepts are distinctive to civil law jurisdictions and were not at first familiar to American IP lawyers. TRIPS does not require standardization of national IP laws on all issues; for example, the United States employs a first-to-use criterion for trademarks, while the rest of the world uses a first-to-file standard for trademarks. This difference is not resolved by TRIPS.

Part III contains the minimum civil, criminal, and administrative procedures that every WTO member must maintain to protect and enforce IP rights. These procedures are patterned after U.S. law. We will consider some of these in more detail below.

Part IV concerns the institutional facilities that WTO members must maintain to allow the acquisition of IP rights within their territories.

Part V on dispute settlement provides for transparency and makes certain disputes concerning IP rights subject to the WTO dispute settlement procedures.

Part VI deals with transitional arrangements, particularly for developing country members of the WTO that did not previously have laws protecting certain types of IP. These arrangements allow developing countries and least developed countries additional time to enact IP laws. (Other WTO members are obligated to comply with TRIPS within one year from the date that the WTO was established on January 1, 1995 or, if they became WTO members after that date, from the date that they joined.) The time periods under this Part are now largely passed; however, the Doha Ministerial Declaration of 2001 extended the time for compliance by least developed country members under Article 66 with respect to pharmaceutical patents to 2016. On November 30, 2005, WTO members extended the general deadline under Article 66 to July 1, 2013.

Part VII establishes a Council for TRIPS within the WTO to facilitate consultations and to cooperate with WIPO. Article 71 provides a procedure for amendment.

It is noteworthy that TRIPS contains relatively few "special and differential" treatment provisions to benefit developing countries.

D. TRIPS, Civil Society, and Developing Countries

Developing countries and non-governmental organizations (NGOs) call for significant changes in TRIPS. Only one such change has been accepted as of this writing, the Doha Declaration and TRIPS amendment provision on *Access to Medicines*, which we cover in this Chapter. Some of the other significant civil society problems of TRIPS, as pointed out by NGOs and developing countries, are as follows.

1. Are the distinctions in TRIPS Article 27.3(b) concerning patentability sufficiently clear? This provision allows members to exclude from patentability (1) "plants and animals, *other than* microorganisms" and (2) "essentially biological processes . . . *other than* non-biological and microbiological processes." Many developing countries wish for cultural or religious reasons to exclude certain animals and plants from patentability. This provision allows them to exclude essentially biological processes and plants and animals from patentability. What does this mean?

2. Are there any moral or ethical considerations with respect to Article 27.3(b)? At the Tenth Conference of the Parties (COP-10) of the United Nations Convention on Biological Diversity in Nagoya, Japan in October 2010, Bolivia argued that patenting life forms is immoral and violates the values that traditional peoples hold sacred, and extends capitalism by assuring the domination of a handful of rich-country multinational corporations. Is this a valid concern?

3. As to the patentability of plants, which of the following are patentable under TRIPS: seeds; plant cells and plants themselves; plant varieties and parent lines; hybrids; procedures to obtain hybrids; a DNA sequence that is the code for certain plant proteins; isolated or purified plant proteins; plasmids and transformed ion vectors containing a particular gene sequence? All of these are patentable under U.S. law. *See J.E.M. Ag Supply v. Pioneer Hi-Bred International, Inc.*, 534 U.S. 134, 138-141 (2001).

4. Does TRIPS protect so-called farmers' rights, the rights of traditional farmers to continue to save and exchange seeds from crops they have harvested, a practice that is very important in many countries? Does Article 30 cover farmers' rights?

5. Is there any protection in TRIPS for what is termed "traditional knowledge"? Article 8(j) of the United Nations Convention on Biological Diversity (1992) requires the protection of traditional knowledge and culture. Traditional knowledge has no accepted precise definition, but generally consists of tradition-based inventions, practices, designs, literary, artistic, and informational creations by regional- and local-based

communities. See the *Informational Note on Traditional Knowledge* (2002) prepared by the International Bureau of WIPO, http://www.wipo.int. Do the patent provisions of TRIPS protect against so-called bio-piracy—a patent application that attempts to patent a practice that falls into the category of traditional knowledge (for example, a variety of rice developed by traditional farmers in country X)?

6. Must patents of genetic resources disclose their sources? The Doha Declaration of 2001 (¶19) called for negotiation in the WTO on the relationship between TRIPS and traditional knowledge and folklore. A coalition of WTO members, Brazil, India, Bolivia, Colombia, Cuba, the Dominican Republic, Ecuador, Peru, Thailand, and an African group have called for the amendment of TRIPS to require patent applicants to disclose the country of origin of genetic resources and traditional knowledge used in inventions and to present evidence that they received prior informed consent (based on benefit-sharing) if traditional knowledge or genetic materials from developing countries is involved in the patent application. *See* WTO, Council for Trade-Related Aspects of Intellectual Property Rights, *The Protection of Traditional Knowledge and Folklore, Summary of Issues Raised*, IP/C/W/370/Rev.1, March 6, 2006.

7. A related but broader issue is the relationship between TRIPS and the UN Convention on Biological Diversity (CBD) (1992). Virtually all WTO members (but not the United States) are also parties to the CBD. In general, the CBD authorizes developing countries to regulate access to the genetic materials within their territories and to protect their traditional knowledge, folklore, and culture. The Doha Declaration of 2001 called for negotiations on the relationship between TRIPS and CBD. So far no agreement has been reached. As yet no WTO dispute has raised the issue of a conflict between these two treaties. For discussion of the proposals of WTO members, see WTO, Council for Trade-Related Aspects of Intellectual Property Rights, *The Relationship between the TRIPS Agreement and the Convention on Biological Diversity, Summary of Issues Raised and Points Made*, IP/C/W/368/Rev.1, February 8, 2006. For the views of the parties to the CBD, see the *Nagoya Protocol on Access to Genetic Resources and the Fair and Equitable Sharing of Benefits Arising from their Utilization to the Convention on Biological Diversity, Text and Annex* (2011).

No final answers have been settled by WTO members on any of these issues. The debate is likely to rage for many years to come.

We now turn to some of the trade issues with respect to the principal forms of IP. In the sections below, we focus on copyright, patent, trademarks, and geographical indications.

II.   Copyright

Copyrights, which are addressed in Articles 9 to 14 of TRIPS, protect creative expression in a fixed or tangible medium. The expression must be original—it must originate with the author and cannot be copied from another source. The most important right granted to the author or owner of the copyright is to prevent others from making unauthorized copies of the protected work. Examples of copyrighted works are audio-visual works such as books, movies, music, and computer programs. Business and entertainment software, an important multi-billon dollar global industry, is protected primarily by copyright, although other IP rights might also apply.

Article 9 of TRIPS incorporates Articles 1-21 of the Berne Convention for the Protection of Literary and Artistic Works, which was originally signed in Paris in 1883 (most recently revised in Paris in 1971) and is the most important international treaty dealing with copyright prior to TRIPS. The Berne Convention establishes a very important mechanism for the acquisition of copyrights in foreign countries. Under the Berne Convention, if an author is a national of a Berne country or a work is first published in a Berne country, a copyright automatically inheres in the work upon its creation, assuming that it is original. *See* Berne Convention Article 3. No formalities, such as filing or registration, must be required—the copyright is automatic and inheres in the work upon its creation. Under the National Treatment provision of Article 5 of the Berne Convention, the work is then automatically entitled to the same rights given to nationals of every other Berne country. The combined effect of Articles 3 and 5 is that any work that is entitled to protection under the Berne Convention gives its author a copyright under the domestic law of every other Berne country. An author has a "basket" of national copyrights under the laws of each Berne country. For example, A writes a book in the United States. The book is original and a copyright in the work arises under U.S. copyright law. Under Berne, A then automatically has a German copyright under German law (which may vary somewhat from U.S. law), a French copyright under French law, a Chinese copyright under Chinese law, and so forth for each Berne country. Without the Berne Convention, an author might have to publish or register the work in a foreign country in order to obtain protection.

Because these Berne articles were incorporated into TRIPS through Article 9, this same mechanism for the acquisition of international copyrights now applies to and for all WTO members, regardless of whether the member is also a Berne Convention signatory. This is an important advantage for all WTO members.

The following case illustrates how the National Treatment principle operates to extend copyright protection to foreign nationals and how copyright is important to promote trade. Although this case involves an application of the National Treatment principle in European Community law, the case also shows how the National Treatment obligation applies to copyright and how the same principle applies in Berne/TRIPS to provide a basket of national copyrights throughout the WTO.

Phil Collins v. Imtrat Handelsgesellschaft GmbH
European Court of Justice, October 20, 1993
[1993] ECR I-5145, C-92/92

[This case was referred to the ECJ by a German court, concerning interpretation of the National Treatment provision contained in Article 7 of the ECC Treaty.]

3. The questions were raised in proceedings between Phil Collins, singer and composer of British nationality, and a phonogram distributor, Imtrat

Handelsgesellschaft GmbH ('Imtrat') relating to the marketing, in Germany, of a compact disk containing the recording, made without the singer's consent, of a concert given in the United States.

4. According to Paragraphs 96(1) and 125(1) of the German Copyright Act of 9 September 1965 (Urheberrechtsgesetz, hereinafter 'the UrhG') performing artists who have German nationality enjoy the protection granted by Paragraphs 73 to 84 of the UrhG in respect of all their performances. In particular, they may prohibit the distribution of those performances which are reproduced without their permission, irrespective of the place of performance. In contrast, the effect of the provisions of Paragraph 125(2) to (6) of the UrhG, relating to foreign performers, as interpreted by the Bundesgerichtshof [Federal Supreme Court] and the Bundesverfassungsgericht (Federal Constitutional Court), is that those performers cannot avail themselves of the provisions of Paragraph 96(1), where the performance was given outside Germany.

5. Phil Collins applied to the Landgericht Muenchen I for an interim injunction prohibiting the marketing of the compact disk in question. It questioned, however, the conformity of those national provisions with the principle of non-discrimination laid down by the first paragraph of Article 7 of the Treaty.

6. In those circumstances, the Landgericht Muenchen I stayed the proceedings and referred the following questions to the Court for a preliminary ruling:

'1. Is copyright law subject to the prohibition of discrimination laid down in the first Paragraph of Article 7 of the EEC Treaty?

2. If so: does that have the (directly applicable) effect that a Member State which accords protection to its nationals for all their artistic performances, irrespective of the place of performance, also has to accord that protection to nationals of other Member States, or is it compatible with the first paragraph of Article 7 to attach further conditions (i.e. Paragraph 125(2) to (6) of the German Urheberrechtsgesetz of 9 September 1965) to the grant of protection to nationals of other Member States?'

15. [These] questions concern the first paragraph of Article 7 of the Treaty which lays down the general principle of non-discrimination on the grounds of nationality. As is expressly provided in that paragraph, the prohibition of discrimination contained in it applies only within the scope of application of the Treaty.

16. The questions referred to the Court must accordingly be regarded as seeking, essentially, to ascertain:

— whether copyright and related rights fall within the scope of application of the Treaty within the meaning of the first paragraph of Article 7, and consequently, if the general principle of non-discrimination laid down by that article applies to those rights;

— if so, whether the first paragraph of Article 7 of the Treaty precludes the legislation of a Member State from denying to authors or performers from other Member States, and those claiming under them, the right, accorded by that legislation to the nationals of that State, to prohibit the marketing, in its national territory, of a phonogram manufactured without their consent, where the performance was given outside its national territory.

THE APPLICATION OF THE PROVISIONS OF THE TREATY
TO COPYRIGHT AND RELATED RIGHTS

17. The Commission, the German Government, the United Kingdom, Phil Collins and EMI Electrola maintain that copyright and related rights, inasmuch as they constitute, in particular, economic rights which determine the conditions in which an artist's works and performances may be exploited in return for payment, fall within the scope of application of the Treaty.

18. Imtrat maintains, to the contrary, that the conditions for the grant of copyright and related rights, which concern the existence, and not the exercise, of those rights, do not, according to Article 222 of the Treaty and well-established case law of the Court, fall within the scope of application of the Treaty. Taking up the findings of the Bundesgerichtshof on that point, Patricia and Mr. Kraul [the defendants] submit in particular that at the material time in the main proceedings copyright and related rights were not, in the absence of Community rules or harmonization measures, governed by Community law.

19. As Community law now stands, and in the absence of Community provisions harmonizing national laws, it is for the Member States to establish the conditions and detailed rules for the protection of literary and artistic property, subject to observance of the applicable international conventions.

20. Copyright and related rights are economic in nature, in that they confer the right to exploit commercially the marketing of the protected work, particularly in the form of licences granted in return for payment of royalties.

21. Whilst the commercial exploitation of copyright is a source of remuneration for the owner, it also constitutes a form of control of marketing, exercisable by the owner, the copyright management societies and the grantees of licences. From this point of view, the commercial exploitation of copyright raises the same problems as does the commercial exploitation of any other industrial and commercial property right.

22. Like the other industrial and commercial property rights, the exclusive rights conferred by literary and artistic property are by their nature such as to affect trade in goods and services and also competitive relationships within the Community. For that reason, and as the Court has consistently held, those rights, although governed by national legislation, are subject to the requirements of the Treaty and therefore fall within its scope of application.

23. Thus they are subject, for example, to the provisions of Articles 30 and 36 of the Treaty relating to the free movement of goods. According to the case-law of the Court, musical works are incorporated into phonograms which constitute goods the trade in which, within the Community, is governed by the above provisions.

24. Furthermore, the activities of copyright management societies are subject to the provisions of Articles 59 and 66 of the Treaty relating to the freedom to provide services. [T]hose activities should not be conducted in such a way as to impede the free movement of services, and particularly the exploitation of performers' rights, to the extent of partitioning the common market.

25. Finally, the exclusive rights conferred by literary and artistic property are subject to the provisions of the Treaty relating to competition.

27. It follows that copyright and related rights, which by reason in particular of their effects on intra-Community trade in goods and services, fall within the scope of application of the Treaty, are necessarily subject to the general principle

of non-discrimination laid down by the first paragraph of Article 7 of the Treaty, without there even being any need to connect them with the specific provisions of Articles 30, 36, 59, and 66 of the Treaty.

28. Accordingly, it should be stated in reply to the question put to the Court that copyright and related rights fall within the scope of application of the Treaty within the meaning of the first paragraph of Article 7; the general principle of non-discrimination laid down by that article therefore applies to those rights.

DISCRIMINATION WITHIN THE MEANING OF THE FIRST PARAGRAPH OF ARTICLE 7 OF THE TREATY

29. Imtrat and Patricia maintain that the differentiation which is made between German nationals and nationals of the other Member States in the cases referred to it by the national courts is objectively justified by the disparities which exist between national laws and by the fact that not all Member States have yet acceded to the Rome Convention [for the Protection of Performers, Producers of Phonograms and Broadcasting Organizations]. That differentiation is not, in those circumstances, contrary to the first paragraph of Article 7 of the Treaty.

30. It is undisputed that Article 7 is not concerned with any disparities in treatment or the distortions which may result, for the persons and undertakings subject to the jurisdiction of the Community, from divergences existing between the laws of the various Member States, so long as those laws affect all persons subject to them, in accordance with objective criteria and without regard to their nationality.

31. Thus, contrary to what Imtrat and Patricia maintain, neither the disparities between the national laws relating to the protection of copyright and related rights nor the fact that not all Member States have yet acceded to the Rome Convention can justify a breach of the principle of non-discrimination laid down by the first paragraph of Article 7 of the Treaty.

32. In prohibiting 'any discrimination on the grounds of nationality,' Article 7 of the Treaty requires, on the contrary, that persons in a situation governed by Community law be placed on a completely equal footing with nationals of the Member State concerned. In so far as that principle is applicable, it therefore precludes a Member State from making the grant of an exclusive right subject to the requirement that the person concerned be a national of that State.

33. Accordingly, it should be stated in reply to the question put to the Court that the first paragraph of Article 7 of the Treaty must be interpreted as precluding legislation of a Member State from denying, in certain circumstances, to authors and performers from other Member States, and those claiming under them, the right, accorded by that legislation the nationals of that State, to prohibit the marketing, in its national territory of a phonogram manufactured without their consent, where the performance was given outside its national territory.

NOTES AND QUESTIONS

1. Why was Collins not entitled to copyright protection under the German Copyright Act? If Collins had been a German national would he have received protection under the German Copyright Act? Why did the ECJ believe that it was necessary to extend the same treatment given to German nationals to Phil Collins?

2. In addition to adopting the bulk of the substantive provisions of Berne, TRIPS adopted important new substantive provisions of its own in Articles 10-14.

- Article 10 provides that computer programs are protected by copyright, ending a long debate over whether computer programs should be protected by copyright or patent. (Some aspects of computer programs may also be entitled to patent protection.)
- Article 11 applies to rental rights for computer software and movies.
- Article 12 provides that the term of copyright protection is the life of the author plus fifty years.
- Article 13 recognizes limited exceptions to copyright.
- Article 14 covers the rights of performers to their live performances, the rights of producers of phonograms, and the rights of broadcasting companies. These rights were traditionally in a gray area of copyright law.

3. Read Article 13 on "Limitations and Exceptions." Is Article 13 too broad or too narrow? It is commonly interpreted to contain three criteria; what are they? Section 110 (5) of the U.S. Copyright Act provides two important limitations to copyright: (1) a so-called homestyle exception that allows unrestricted private home use of copyrighted material; and (2) a small business exception to exempt from copyright liability anyone who turns on a radio or television in certain types of public establishments, such as bars, restaurants, and retail stores. Recorded music, such as CDs or cassette tapes, is not within this exception. In *United States—Section 110(5) of the U.S. Copyright Act*, WT/DS160/R, Report of the Panel, adopted on June 15, 2000, a WTO panel upheld the homestyle exception but ruled that, given the large number of establishments that may benefit from a business exemption, this does not qualify as a "certain special case" under Article 13. *Id.* at ¶6.272. The United States did not appeal from this decision, but has not amended the applicable provision of U.S. law, which is styled "the Sonny Bono Fairness in Music Act of 1998." The EC invoked sanctions against the United States, and a panel of WTO arbitrators ruled that the level of EC benefits being nullified or impaired under this provision is equal to 1.2 million euros per year. *See United States—Section 110(5) of the U.S. Copyright Act*, WT/DS160/ARB25/1, Report of the Appellate Body, adopted on November 9, 2001, at ¶5.1.

4. Does copyright protection extend to works that are censored or prohibited by law in the territory of a WTO member? This question arose in the case of *China—Measures Affecting the Protection and Enforcement of Intellectual Property Rights*, WT/DS362/R, Report of the Panel, adopted on March 20, 2009. The panel answered yes, because TRIPS Article 9.1 incorporates the Berne Convention, which allows censorship (Article 17), but requires that copyright be available for such works (Article 5(1)).

5. Developing countries criticize the TRIPS copyright system as too broad, and advocate that TRIPS be amended to include a defined list of public interest exceptions, an international fair use provision, and a library exception. *See* Ruth L. Okediji, *The International Copyright System: Limitations, Exceptions and Public Interest Considerations for Developing Countries* 10-16 (UNCTAD, International Centre for Trade and Sustainable Development, Issue Paper 17, 2006).

III. *Patents*

A. Introduction

Patents, addressed in Articles 27-34 of TRIPS, are a set of exclusive rights protecting inventions that exhibit novelty, non-obviousness, and utility.[2] The hallmark of a patent is novelty; the invention must be new and cannot be contained in, or anticipated by, the existing state of the art. An invention must also be non-obvious (display sufficient inventiveness) and must also be useful or capable of industrial application. Examples of patented inventions are pharmaceuticals, chemical compounds, and machines. Patents may also be available for certain processes and methods, including both scientific and business methods.

Article 2 of TRIPS incorporates Articles 1-12 and Article 19 of the International Convention for the Protection of Intellectual Property, which was originally signed in Paris in 1883 and most recently revised in Stockholm in 1967. This treaty, commonly known as the Paris Convention, was the most important international treaty relating to patents and trademarks prior to TRIPS. Unlike the treatment of copyright under the Berne Convention, the Paris Convention does not contain any minimum substantive standards for patent. Rather, the Paris Convention merely provides for National Treatment and a right of priority; i.e., a period of one year in which an inventor will be protected against certain events that might otherwise defeat the patent. Because of the importance of patents, countries could not agree on a uniform set of standards and so a compromise was reached in which the Paris Convention allowed each nation to decide its own substantive standards subject to National Treatment and priority rights. Under the Paris Convention, it was up to each country as to how much (or little) patent protection to provide and whether certain types of inventions, such as pharmaceuticals, were eligible for patents at all.

Unlike the case of copyright where formalities cannot be required, all modern patent systems require the filing of a patent application that is subject to a review and approval process that can vary greatly among national legal systems. The requirement of formalities prevents a broad application of the National Treatment principle to patents that, in the Berne/TRIPS context, allowed a copyright owner to automatically acquire a basket of national copyrights in all Berne/WTO countries as the result of the acquisition of a single copyright in a Berne/WTO country. Rather, in the absence of an international treaty such as the Patent Cooperation Treaty (PCT), an inventor must file a patent application in each country in which the inventor seeks a patent. Signed in 1970 as a special agreement among parties to the Paris Convention, the PCT has helped to alleviate the burdens of separate filings by allowing for a system in which a single international application process can result in separate national patents in each country designated in the application. However, even in the case of a PCT application, the national patent office of each country has the final authority to decide whether to grant or refuse the patent.

---

2. TRIPS uses a different terminology, preferring the terms "inventive step" and "capable of industrial application" over "non-obvious" and "useful." But under TRIPS, "inventive step" and "capable of industrial application" set forth in Article 27 are synonymous with the terms "non-obvious" and "useful," respectively. *See* TRIPS Article 27 n.5.

Countries believed that the decision to grant a patent was too important to remove from the final authority of each nation.

The United States, the EU, Japan, and other developed countries wanted to ensure that the deficiencies of the Paris Convention were corrected in the WTO. During the Uruguay Round, the United States led the push for the adoption of a set of minimum substantive standards for patents in TRIPS. The initiative to impose minimum standards caused great concern for developing countries because they believed that the real goal of developed countries was to deny access to advanced technology. Prior to TRIPS, nothing prevented a country from refusing to grant patents and obtaining free access to advanced technology. For example, a U.S. patent for a drug, while providing patent protection in the United States, would provide no protection for the drug in a foreign country because, as we saw earlier, all IP laws are limited by the principle of territoriality. The U.S. patent owner would need to obtain a patent registration in the foreign country to receive protection there. Prior to the Uruguay Round, however, some countries (such as India) refused to recognize patents for pharmaceuticals. Anyone could lawfully copy the U.S. drug in India for local use or even for export abroad. This provided India with free access to valuable technology. If countries were required to recognize patents for pharmaceuticals, then the U.S. drug company could obtain a patent under the laws of India. Indian companies, once free to copy the U.S. drug with impunity, would now have to negotiate a license and pay fees in order to lawfully copy the drug. For some countries (such as India) whether to join the WTO posed a serious dilemma. The WTO promised significant trade benefits, but at the price of having to adopt Western-style IP laws that could deny access to technology.

In the end, the United States and other developed countries had their way. Minimum substantive standards for patents were incorporated into TRIPS.

Read TRIPS Articles 27 to 34.

PROBLEM 13-1

Prior to joining the WTO, Country W had the following law: "No patents or any other forms of intellectual property providing private rights shall be available for any pharmaceuticals." Why would Country W have such a law? Under such a law, would unauthorized copying of pharmaceuticals patented in the United States be permitted in Country W? Now that Country W has joined the WTO (and assuming that Country W is not entitled to a delay in implementing its WTO obligations), must Country W amend its laws? *See* TRIPS Article 27.

NOTES AND QUESTIONS

What is the minimum acceptable term of a patent? *See* Article 33. In *Canada—Term of Patent Protection*, WT/DS170/AB/R, Report of the Appellate Body, adopted on September 8, 2000, the United States brought a challenge to Canada's Patent Act, which specified two lengths of patent term: (1) a term of twenty years from the filing date for patents filed on or after October 1, 1989 and (2) a term of seventeen years from the date of issue with respect to patent applications filed before October 1, 1989 (so-called Old Act patents). Canada relied on the provisions of Article 70.1 to argue that the new term of TRIPS did not apply to Old Act patents. The Appellate Body disagreed, interpreting Article 70.1 to apply to acts related to the patent, not to the patent itself. The Appellate Body further ruled that Article 70.2 applies to Old Act patents, and thus Canada must apply the new term in Article 33. *Id.* at ¶102(a).

PROBLEM 13-2

Country Q has the following law: "All patents registered by foreign nationals in Q must be used to manufacture products in Q within the first three years of registration. If local manufacture does not occur within three years, the patent shall be forfeited and transferred to a local company." Country Q has now joined the WTO. Is Country Q's patent law consistent with TRIPS? *See* TRIPS Article 27.

PROBLEM 13-3

Country N has the following law: "All patents for pharmaceuticals shall be entitled to a twenty-year term starting from the date of invention, which shall be established to the satisfaction of the National Patent Office. If the National Patent Office is not satisfied that the applicant has demonstrated the date of invention, the date of invention shall be deemed to be the date five years before the filing date." Is this law consistent with TRIPS? *See* Article 33.

B.   TRIPS, Pharmaceutical Patents, and Access to Medicines

Soon after TRIPS was established, multinational pharmaceutical companies came under intense criticism for using their patent rights to charge monopoly prices that had the effect of denying access to life-saving medicines in poor countries. The access to medicines debate is one of the most controversial issues in the WTO. On one side, pharmaceutical companies claim that it costs around $1.78 billion (approximately $873 million out-of-pocket) to successfully bring a new drug to the market. Drug companies argue that unless they can recoup those costs through sales, they will be unable to develop new life-saving medicines and everyone will be worse off. To do so, strong patent protection for the drugs is indispensable. On the other side, developing countries cannot pay the monopoly prices that pharmaceutical companies charge for their drugs. Developing countries claim that there should be public policy limits on patent protection because many of these drugs are life-saving medicines essential to public health.

Although TRIPS contains several "public health" exceptions (*see* Article 27.2 and 27.3), partisans of developing countries argued that these were not broad enough to cope with emergency health situations in many countries, especially with respect to HIV-AIDS, tuberculosis, and malaria. They advocated greater use of compulsory licensing, a mechanism for allowing a third party to use the patent, if certain conditions are present, without the patent owner's consent.

From the point of view of the patent owner, however, a compulsory license can be highly risky. In any technology licensing arrangement, there is a risk that the licensee will misuse or steal the licensed technology. For this reason, IP owners are very cautious in entering into licensing agreements and will exercise due diligence in selecting suitable licensees. Most owners of technology are highly opposed to being forced to work with a licensee not of their own choosing.

While patent owners may object to compulsory licenses, their use has proven quite effective in practice to address health needs. A prominent example of an effective strategy to combat a public health crisis based upon a compulsory license is Brazil's highly successful national program to combat AIDS. Brazil has been able to reduce the mortality rate of the approximately 540,000 people infected with HIV by about one-half. Critical to the success of the Brazilian AIDS program is the following compulsory licensing provision:

Brazil Industrial Property Law, Article 68

Compulsory License

68. A patent shall be subject to compulsory licensing if the owner exercises his rights therein an abusive manner or if he uses it to abuse economic power under the terms of an administrative or judicial decision.

(1) The following may also be grounds for compulsory licensing:

I. failure to work the subject matter of a patent on the territory of Brazil, failure to manufacture or incomplete manufacture of the product or failure to completely use a patented process, except for failure to work due to lack of economic viability, in which case importing shall be admitted; or

II. marketing that does not satisfy the needs of the market. . . .

(3) If a compulsory license is granted on the grounds of abuse of economic power, a period of time, limited to that laid down in Article 74, shall be secured to a licensee who proposes to manufacture locally, to import the subject matter of the license, provided it has been placed on the market directly by the patent owner or with his consent. . . .

(5) A compulsory license under paragraph (1) may only be requested on expiry of three years after grant of the patent.

Multinational pharmaceutical companies find this law and similar laws in other countries to be highly objectionable. TRIPS deals with compulsory licensing in Article 31.

Read TRIPS Article 31 carefully.

Note the many strict conditions surrounding compulsory licensing under TRIPS, and consider the following problems:

PROBLEM 13-4

You are counsel to a coalition of U.S. pharmaceutical companies that objects to Brazil's compulsory licensing law. The coalition is considering whether to seek the help of the USTR in bringing a WTO challenge to the Brazilian law. The coalition asks you to analyze whether Article 68 of the Brazilian Industrial Property Law is consistent with TRIPS Article 31. What is your reply?

PROBLEM 13-5

You are an advisor to Country K, a country with a national health crisis. Country K is one of the poorest and least developed countries in the world and depends almost entirely on agriculture and tourism for its revenues; Country K has difficulty in providing the infrastructure and resources to support even basic industry on a long-term basis. Education is very poor by international standards. You've been asked by the government of K to explain what appears to be a puzzle: The Brazilian national program to combat AIDS has been very successful in obtaining access to medicines even though Brazil has only issued a few compulsory licenses—how has Brazil used the compulsory license provision? Review the discussion above on how multinational companies view compulsory licenses. Brazil is an emerging economy with some surprising successes in industry and has ambitions of joining the first rank of industrial countries. Can Country K use the same strategy pioneered by Brazil?

1. The Doha Declaration

In 2000, the United States filed a dispute settlement proceeding at the WTO to challenge the Brazilian compulsory licensing law. Several U.S. pharmaceutical companies and other multinationals also filed a lawsuit in South Africa to challenge a similar compulsory licensing scheme, the South African Medical and Related Substances Control Act of 1997. These challenges initially received the strong support of the U.S. government despite intense international criticism by many developing countries and NGOs interested in human rights and public health. The latter group was concerned that these challenges would undermine successful health programs in Brazil and South Africa that might serve as models for other countries. In the face of intense political pressure, the U.S. government withdrew its support for the U.S. pharmaceutical companies. Without this support, the U.S. drug industry quickly withdrew its lawsuit in South Africa, and the United States also withdrew its complaint at the WTO against Brazil.

At the 2001 Doha Ministerial Conference, developing countries and their allies obtained the following Declaration:

DOHA WTO Ministerial Conference 2001:
TRIPS and Public Health
WT/MIN(01)/DEC/2 (November 20, 2001)

1. We recognize the gravity of the public health problems afflicting many developing and least-developed countries, especially those resulting from HIV/AIDS, tuberculosis, malaria and other epidemics.

2. We stress the need for the WTO Agreement on Trade-Related Aspects of Intellectual Property Rights (TRIPS Agreement) to be part of the wider national and international action to address these problems.

3. We recognize that intellectual property protection is important for the development of new medicines. We also recognize the concerns about its effects on prices.

4. We agree that the TRIPS Agreement does not and should not prevent members from taking measures to protect public health. Accordingly, while reiterating our commitment to the TRIPS Agreement, we affirm that the Agreement

can and should be interpreted and implemented in a manner supportive of WTO members' right to protect public health and, in particular, to promote access to medicines for all. In this connection, we reaffirm the right of WTO members to use, to the full, the provisions in the TRIPS Agreement, which provide flexibility for this purpose.

5. Accordingly and in the light of paragraph 4 above, while maintaining our commitments in the TRIPS Agreement, we recognize that these flexibilities include:

a. In applying the customary rules of interpretation of public international law, each provision of the TRIPS Agreement shall be read in the light of the object and purpose of the Agreement as expressed, in particular, in its objectives and principles.

b. Each member has the right to grant compulsory licences and the freedom to determine the grounds upon which such licences are granted.

c. Each member has the right to determine what constitutes a national emergency or other circumstances of extreme urgency, it being understood that public health crises, including those relating to HIV/AIDS, tuberculosis, malaria and other epidemics, can represent a national emergency or other circumstances of extreme urgency.

d. The effect of the provisions in the TRIPS Agreement that are relevant to the exhaustion of intellectual property rights is to leave each member free to establish its own regime for such exhaustion without challenge, subject to the MFN and national treatment provisions of Articles 3 and 4.

6. We recognize that WTO members with insufficient or no manufacturing capacities in the pharmaceutical sector could face difficulties in making effective use of compulsory licensing under the TRIPS Agreement. We instruct the Council for TRIPS to find an expeditious solution to this problem and to report to the General Council before the end of 2002.

7. We reaffirm the commitment of developed-country members to provide incentives to their enterprises and institutions to promote and encourage technology transfer to least-developed country members pursuant to Article 66.2. We also agree that the least-developed country members will not be obliged, with respect to pharmaceutical products, to implement or apply Sections 5 and 7 of Part II of the TRIPS Agreement or to enforce rights provided for under these Sections until 1 January 2016, without prejudice to the right of least-developed country members to seek other extensions of the transition periods as provided for in Article 66.1 of the TRIPS Agreement. We instruct the Council for TRIPS to take the necessary action to give effect to this pursuant to Article 66.1 of the TRIPS Agreement.

PROBLEM 13-6

Although the United States withdrew its WTO complaint against Brazil in 2001, a group of pharmaceutical companies is thinking of renewing a challenge to the Brazilian compulsory licensing law. However, the group is aware that the Doha Declaration is a new development that may change the odds of a successful challenge. The group has come to your law firm to seek an opinion on whether the Brazilian compulsory licensing law is consistent with TRIPS Article 31 in light of the Doha Declaration. What is your analysis?

2. *The Implementation Decision*

Paragraph 6 of the Doha Declaration recognized the special situation of least developed countries. In order to make use of a compulsory license, a nation must have reached a certain minimal level of development. Manufacturing of pharmaceuticals requires an industrial infrastructure (e.g., utilities, telecommunications, and transportation) and human capital (e.g., engineers, scientists, business managers, and lawyers) that some of the least developed countries of the world do not have. To assist these countries, the WTO issued the following:

Implementation of Paragraph 6 of the Doha Declaration on the TRIPS Agreement and Public Health
Decision of the WTO General Council, August 30, 2003
WT/L/520

The General Council . . . *[d]ecides* as follows:

1. For the purposes of this Decision:

(a) "pharmaceutical product" means any patented product, or product manufactured through a patented process, of the pharmaceutical sector needed to address the public health problems as recognized in paragraph 1 of the Declaration.

(b) "eligible importing Member" means any least-developed country Member, and any other Member that has made a notification to the Council for TRIPS of its intention to use the system as an importer, it being understood that a Member may notify at any time that it will use the system in whole or in a limited way, for example only in the case of a national emergency or other circumstances of extreme urgency or in cases of public non-commercial use.

(c) "exporting Member" means a Member using the system set out in this Decision to produce pharmaceutical products for, and export them to, an eligible importing Member.

2. The obligations of an exporting Member under Article 31(f) of the TRIPS Agreement shall be waived with respect to the grant by it of a compulsory licence to the extent necessary for the purposes of production of a pharmaceutical product(s) and its export to an eligible importing Member(s) in accordance with the terms set out below in this paragraph:

(a) the eligible importing Member(s) has made a notification to the Council for TRIPS, that:

(i) specifies the names and expected quantities of the product(s) needed;

(ii) confirms that the eligible importing Member in question, other than a least developed country Member, has established that it has insufficient or no manufacturing capacities in the pharmaceutical sector for the product(s) in question in one of the ways set out in the Annex to this Decision; and

(iii) confirms that, where a pharmaceutical product is patented in its territory, it has granted or intends to grant a compulsory licence in accordance with Article 31 of the TRIPS Agreement and the provisions of this Decision;

(b) the compulsory licence issued by the exporting Member under this Decision shall contain the following conditions:

(i) only the amount necessary to meet the needs of the eligible importing Member(s) may be manufactured under the licence and the entirety of this production shall be exported to the Member(s) which has notified its needs to the Council for TRIPS;

(ii) products produced under the licence shall be clearly identified as being produced under the system set out in this Decision through specific labeling or marking. Suppliers should distinguish such products through special packaging and/or special colouring/shaping of the products themselves, provided that such distinction is feasible and does not have a significant impact on price; and

(iii) before shipment begins, the licensee shall post on a website the following information:

- the quantities being supplied to each destination as referred to in indent (i) above; and
- the distinguishing features of the product(s) referred to in indent (ii) above;

(c) the exporting Member shall notify the Council for TRIPS of the grant of the licence, including the conditions attached to it. The information provided shall include the name and address of the licensee, the product(s) for which the licence has been granted, the quantity(ies) for which it has been granted, the country(ies) to which the product(s) is (are) to be supplied and the duration of the licence.

5. Members shall ensure the availability of effective legal means to prevent the importation into, and sale in, their territories of products produced under the system set out in this Decision and diverted to their markets inconsistently with its provisions, using the means already required to be available under the TRIPS Agreement.

NOTES AND QUESTIONS

1. How will the Implementation Decision help least developed countries obtain needed medicines? How might the system lead to a black market in patented drugs? If you represented a multinational pharmaceutical company, would you feel confident that the system set up by the Implementation Decision will not be abused?

2. Has the tide of international public opinion shifted too far against pharmaceutical companies? Do they have any legitimate concerns? Are there any circumstances in which a compulsory license cannot be justified?

3. Do you think that the Doha Declaration and the Implementation Decision will result in a rash of compulsory licenses and exports under compulsory licenses to least developed countries? Or will multinational companies respond by cutting their prices to avoid being forced to give their technology to third parties? Are the Doha Declaration and Implementation Decision really political tools that are being given to the developing world to force a reduction in drug prices?

4. If pharmaceutical companies are forced to cut their prices in the developing world, will pharmaceutical companies simply sit by and accept lower profits, or will

they attempt to recoup their losses elsewhere? If so, where and in what countries? Who pays in the end? Is this a good result?

5. The TRIPS Council has completed work on an amendment to Article 31 to make this Implementation Decision permanent. The amendment will become effective when it is approved by two-thirds of the WTO membership.

IV.   *Trademarks and Geographical Indications*

A.   Trademarks

A trademark is any sign or combination of signs that is capable of distinguishing goods or services from those of another. *See* TRIPS Article 15. While novelty is the hallmark of patent and originality is the hallmark of copyright, distinctiveness is the hallmark of trademark law. Trademarks are also sometimes referred to as brands. Examples of trademarks are the many brand names for consumer goods and services (Coca-Cola, for example, one of the most recognized and valuable trademarks in the world).

Article 2 of TRIPS incorporates the bulk of the trademark provisions of the Paris Convention. As in the case of patents, the Paris Convention requires National Treatment and priority rights (six months in the case of trademarks) but does not contain minimum substantive standards for trademarks. These standards are now contained in TRIPS, which adds important new articles concerning protectable subject matter (Article 15), rights conferred (Article 16), requirement of use (Article 19), and the prohibition of compulsory licensing (Article 21). Like patents, trademarks are subject to formalities. All trademarks, like patents, must be separately registered in each nation where rights are sought, unless the owner proceeds through a special international registration system created under two multilateral treaties, the Madrid Agreement[3] and the Madrid Protocol.[4]

The following case examines the application to a trademark dispute of the National Treatment Principle contained in TRIPS Article 4, and the Most Favored Nation Principle set forth in TRIPS Article 4.

United States — Section 211 Omnibus Appropriations Act of 1998
Report of the WTO Appellate Body, adopted on February 1, 2002
WT/DS176/AB/R

[This dispute involved Section 211 of the U.S. Omnibus Appropriations Act of 1998, which was a rider attached to the major appropriations law in that year to deal with a trademark dispute between Bacardi & Co. Limited, the maker of Bacardi rum, and Pernod Ricard, S.A., a French company. Beginning in 1993, Pernod was involved in a joint venture known as Havana Club Holding, with Cubaexport,

---

3. Madrid Agreement Concerning the International Registration of Marks, April 14, 1891.

4. Protocol Relating to the Madrid Agreement Concerning the International Registration of Marks, June 27, 1989.

a Cuban government trading agency, to make and sell Havana Club label rum. Havana Club Rum was first marketed in pre-Castro Cuba by the Arechabala family. When Castro came to power, he nationalized the Arechabala business and confiscated its assets. The business assets were transferred to Cubaexport, which continued to operate the business and became the owner of the trademark in Cuba.

In 1963, the United States imposed a trade embargo on Cuba pursuant to the Trading with the Enemy Act of 1917, ch. 106, §5(b), 40 Stat. 415. The Cuban Embargo Regulations, promulgated by the Treasury Department and administered by the Office of Foreign Assets Control, prevented the Pernod-Cubaexport joint venture from selling its products in the United States. The Regulations generally prohibit all persons subject to U.S. jurisdiction from engaging in any transaction involving property in which Cuba or a Cuban national has an interest. Transactions are permitted only under a general or specific license authorized by the U.S. government.

The surviving members of the Arechabala family living in Spain allowed the trademark to lapse, and the last rights in the United States lapsed in 1973. In 1974, Cubaexport applied for and received the trademark from the U.S. Patent and Trademark Office. The United States was legally bound to allow the trademark registration by Cubaexport under the Inter-American Trademark Convention. In 1994, Bacardi attempted to register the mark in the United States, but its application was denied. When Bacardi began to market "Havana Club Rum" in spite of the denial, Havana Club Holding filed suit in a federal district court to restrain the use of the mark. *See Havana Club Holding v. Galleon S.A.*, 203 F.3d 116 (2d Cir. 2000). In 1997, Bacardi also bought the mark from the Arechabala family. After intense lobbying by Bacardi, Congress passed Section 211 as follows:

Section 211

(a) (1) Notwithstanding any other provision of law, no transaction or payment shall be authorized or approved pursuant to section 515.527 of title 31, Code of Federal Regulations . . . with respect to a mark, trade name, or commercial name that is the same or substantially similar to a mark, trade name or commercial name that was used in connection with a business or assets that were confiscated unless the original owner of the mark, trade name, or commercial name, or the bona fide successor-in-interest has expressly consented.

(2) No U.S. Court shall recognize, enforce or otherwise validate any assertion of rights by a designated national based on common law rights or registration obtained under such section 515.527 of such a confiscated mark, trade name, or commercial name.

(b) No U.S. Court shall recognize, enforce or otherwise validate any assertion of treaty rights by a designated national or its successor-in-interest under Section 44(b) or (e) of the Trademark Act of 1946 for a mark, trade name, or commercial name that is the same as or substantially similar to a mark, trade name, or commercial name that was used in connection with a business or assets that were confiscated unless the original owner or such mark, trade name, or commercial name, or the bona fide successor-in-interest has expressly consented.

Section 515.527, referred to above in Section 211, created a general license allowing a Cuban national to pay the fee for a trademark registration in the U.S. Patent and Trademark Office. This allows Cuban nationals to obtain U.S. registrations for their trademarks, which would otherwise be prohibited under the Cuban Embargo Regulations. After lobbying by Bacardi, however, Section 211(a)(1) was added to prohibit the use of the general license to register a trademark in cases where the business assets used in connection with the trademark in Cuba had been confiscated, unless the original trademark owner has consented. The effect of Section 211 would be to prevent the Cuban government from confiscating the business assets and trademark of a Cuban national, transferring the business and trademark to a state-owned company, and then registering the trademark in the United States. These were exactly the factual circumstances surrounding the Havana Club Rum trademark. Under Section 211(a)(1)(2), a designated nation (obviously referring to Cuba or a Cuban national) seeking to enforce a U.S. trademark similar to a trademark that had been confiscated in Cuba would have to first demonstrate to a U.S. court that it had not obtained the U.S. registration in violation of Section 211(a)(1). Otherwise, the court would have to refuse enforcement.

Cuba is a member of the WTO (and was a founding member of the GATT) and has been a party to the Paris Convention since 1917. Despite this, the United States maintains a trade embargo against Cuba under GATT Article XXI, but this embargo was not at issue in this case.

The EC challenged the consistency of Section 211 with TRIPS as well as the Paris Convention. The portion of the Appellate Body opinion below focuses on whether Section 211 violates the National Treatment principle and the Most Favored Nation principle.]

IX.   ARTICLE 2(1) OF THE PARIS CONVENTION (1967) AND ARTICLE 3.1 OF THE TRIPS AGREEMENT

233. We turn now to the issue of national treatment. In this appeal we have been asked to address, for the first time, this fundamental principle of the world trading system as it relates to intellectual property. There are two separate national treatment provisions that cover trademarks as well as other intellectual property rights covered by the *TRIPS Agreement*. The European Communities claims, on appeal, that Sections 211(a)(2) and (b) violate both.

234. One national treatment provision at issue in this appeal is Article 2(1) of the Paris Convention (1967), which states:

> Nationals of any country of the Union shall, as regards the protection of industrial property, enjoy in all the other countries of the Union the advantages that their respective laws now grant, or may hereafter grant, to nationals; all without prejudice to the rights specially provided for by this Convention. Consequently, they shall have the same protection as the latter, and the same legal remedy against any infringement of their rights, provided that the conditions and formalities imposed upon nationals are complied with.

239. In addition to Article 2(1) of the Paris Convention (1967), there is also another national treatment provision in the *TRIPS Agreement*. The other national treatment provision at issue in this appeal is Article 3.1 of the *TRIPS Agreement*, which states in relevant part:

> Each Member shall accord to the nationals of other Members treatment no less favourable than that it accords to its own nationals with regard to the protection of intellectual property . . .

275. On appeal, the European Communities argues that the Panel erred in its conclusion about discrimination among original owners. The European Communities maintains that, on their face, both Sections 211(a)(2) and 211(b) violate the national treatment obligation under the *TRIPS Agreement* and the Paris Convention (1967) because they provide less favourable treatment to Cuban nationals who are original owners than to United States nationals who are original owners.

276. Specifically, the European Communities asks us to consider the following particular set of circumstances that exists under the statute. There are two separate owners who acquired rights, either at common law or based on registration, in two separate United States trademarks, before the Cuban confiscation occurred. Each of these two United States trademarks is the same, or substantially similar to, the signs or combination of signs of which a trademark registered in Cuba is composed. That same or similar Cuban trademark was used in connection with a business or assets that were confiscated in Cuba. Neither of the two original owners of the two United States trademarks was the owner of that same or similar trademark that was registered in Cuba. Those two original owners each seek to assert rights in the United States in their two respective United States trademarks. The situation of these two original owners of these two United States trademarks is identical in every relevant respect, but one. That one difference is this: one original owner is a national of Cuba, and the other original owner is a national of the United States.

277. The European Communities asks us to consider this specific situation involving these two original owners, one from Cuba and one from the United States. The European Communities argues that, on the face of the statute, in this situation, the original owner who is a Cuban national is subject to Sections 211(a)(2) and (b), and the original owner who is a United States national is not. This alone, as the European Communities sees it, is sufficient for us to find that Sections 211(a)(2) and (b) violate the national treatment obligation of the United States.

278. Like the European Communities, we see this situation as critical to our determination of whether the treatment of original owners under Section 211 is consistent with the national treatment obligation of the United States under Article 2(1) of the Paris Convention (1967) and Article 3.1 of the *TRIPS Agreement*.

279. The situation highlighted by the European Communities on appeal exists because Sections 211(a)(2) and (b) apply to "designated nationals". A "designated national" is defined in Section 515.305 of Title 31 CFR as "Cuba and any national thereof including any person who is a specially designated national." Thus, Sections 211(a)(2) and (b) apply to original owners that are Cuban nationals. Original owners that are United States nationals are not covered by the definition of "designated national" and, thus, are not subject to the limitations of Sections 211(a)(2) and (b).

280. Thus, in our view, the European Communities is correct on this issue. Sections 211(a)(2) and (b) are discriminatory *on their face*.

281. We conclude, therefore, that the European Communities has established a *prima facie* case that Sections 211(a)(2) and (b) discriminate between Cuban nationals and United States nationals, both of whom are original owners of trademarks registered in the United States which are composed of the same or substantially similar signs as a Cuban trademark used in connection with a business or assets that were confiscated in Cuba.

X.   Article 4 of the **TRIPS** Agreement

297. Like the national treatment obligation, the obligation to provide most-favoured-nation treatment has long been one of the cornerstones of the world trading system. For more than fifty years, the obligation to provide most-favoured-nation treatment in Article I of the GATT 1994 has been both central and essential to assuring the success of a global rules-based system for trade in goods. Unlike the national treatment principle, there is no provision in the Paris Convention (1967) that establishes a most-favoured-nation obligation with respect to rights in trademarks or other industrial property. However, the framers of the *TRIPS Agreement* decided to extend the most-favoured-nation obligation to the protection of intellectual property rights covered by that Agreement. As a cornerstone of the world trading system, the most-favoured-nation obligation must be accorded the same significance with respect to intellectual property rights under the *TRIPS Agreement* that it has long been accorded with respect to trade in goods under the GATT. It is, in a word, fundamental.

305. The allegations submitted by the European Communities on most-favoured-nation treatment of original owners are similar to those described in the previous section on national treatment. As it did with respect to national treatment, the European Communities supports its claim under Article 4 of the *TRIPS Agreement* by focusing on a particular set of circumstances that exists under the statute, *on its face*, involving original owners.

306. Like the situation posed by the European Communities earlier, the one set forth in the most-favoured-nation treatment involves two separate owners who acquired rights, either at common law or based on registration, in two separate United States trademarks, before the Cuban confiscation occurred. Each of these two United States trademarks is the same, or substantially similar to, signs or a combination of signs of which a trademark registered in Cuba is composed. That same or similar Cuban trademark was used in connection with a business or assets that were confiscated in Cuba. Neither of the two original owners of the two United States trademarks was the owner of that same or similar trademark that was registered in Cuba. Those two original owners each now seek to assert rights in the United States in their two respective United States trademarks. The situation of these two original owners of these two United States trademarks is identical in every relevant respect, but one. That one difference is this: one original owner is a national of Cuba, and the other original owner is a national of a country other than Cuba or the United States. We will refer, for the sake of convenience, to this other original owner as "a non-Cuban foreign national".

307. Pointing to this particular situation, the European Communities argues that, on the face of the statute, the original owner who is a Cuban national is subject to Sections 211(a)(2) and (b), and the original owner who is a non-Cuban foreign national is not. This alone, as the European Communities sees it, is sufficient for us to find that Sections 211(a)(2) and (b) violate the most-favoured-nation obligation of the United States.

308. We agree with the European Communities that the situation it describes on appeal is within the scope of the statute *on its face*. As we explained earlier, the term "designated national" as defined in Section 515.305 of 31 CFR and Section 211(d)(1) includes non-Cuban foreign nationals only when they are successors-in-interest to Cuba or a Cuban national. Non-Cuban foreign nationals who are original owners are not covered by the definition of "designated national" and are thereby not subject to Sections 211(a)(2) and (b).

309. Therefore, here too, as with national treatment, the European Communities has established a *prima facie* case that Sections 211(a)(2) and (b) are discriminatory on their face, as between a Cuban national and a non-Cuban foreign national both of whom are original owners of United States trademarks composed of the same or substantially similar signs as a trademark used in connection with a business or assets that were confiscated in Cuba.

NOTES AND QUESTIONS

1. What is the crux of the violations found by the Appellate Body? To understand the argument, note that a Cuban national would be required to undertake an additional step under Section 211(a)(2) to obtain enforcement of a trademark in a U.S. court, a step that a U.S. national or a national of another WTO member (other than Cuba) would not be required to undertake. This extra step would be required if the U.S. trademark is similar to a trademark that was confiscated in Cuba. What is this extra step?

2. Note that TRIPS allows the Appellate Body to rule also on matters pertaining to the WIPO conventions. Is it useful to allow the WTO to exercise this power? How does being subject to review by the WTO affect the stature of the WIPO?

B.   Geographical Indications

Geographical indications (GIs) identify goods as originating in a territory, region, or locality where a certain quality, reputation, or other characteristic of the good is attributable to its origin. *See* TRIPS Article 22. GIs are very important for wines, cheeses, foods, and other goods that are associated with a certain geographical region. Examples are Bordeaux, Chardonnay, and Champagne, all wines that are associated with territories in France.

GIs are given protection under Articles 22 and 23 of TRIPS and are very important in the EU, the world's leading proponent for the protection of GIs. GIs are not treated as a separate type of IP right in the United States but are subsumed under trademark law. The following problems and case illustrate some important issues concerning GIs in the EU.

PROBLEM 13-7

Harry's Buckeye Delicatessen in Columbus, Ohio, places the following advertisement in a local newspaper: "Enjoy our own delicious homemade Peking Duck with a glass of our finest Bordeaux-style wine, made from grapes grown right here in Ohio." Assume that these products are protected by GIs in their country of origin. Is the advertisement consistent with TRIPS? *See* TRIPS Articles 22 and 23. What is the difference between these two items?

PROBLEM 13-8

Larry's Food Pit Stop in California purchases wine in large barrels from the Normandy region of France. Larry's then sells the wine in large one-gallon containers and in smaller half-bottle carafes with a convenient twist-off top, with the label "Normandy Wine—Genuine Product of France." Assume that France has a GI for the wine. The French Wine Association says, "Incredible! Only you Americans would think of something like this. It's outrageous, and we want this stopped." What's the French Wine Association's worry? What result? See the case below.

PROBLEM 13-9

Carlo is a skilled food artisan from the Parma region of Italy. For most of his adult life, Carlo has worked in preparing and slicing ham under the watchful eye of the Consorzio del Prosciutto di Parma, a professional association of producers of Parma ham, in the Parma region of Italy. Not only did Carlo earn several certifications for his excellent skills, he was also promoted to vice-director of the Consorzio for food preparation. Recently, Carlo moved to the United Kingdom to go to business school. He also now works part time as a chef at Tilberry's, a combination high-end restaurant and gourmet food shop. Tilberry's imports Parma ham from Italy in bricks. In the restaurant portion of Tilberry's, Carlo brings the brick to the table and slices the ham for salads and appetizers right in front of customers who marvel at his amazing skills. He also slices the ham in the delicatessen area of the restaurant at the request of consumers who wish to buy the ham to take home and enjoy it there. At the end of each day, he slices and packages the remaining portions of any unfinished bricks and labels them, "Authentic Parma Ham from Italy—Expertly Sliced in the U.K." The packages are then placed for sale in a refrigerated display case attractively decorated with Italian flags. The Consorzio claims that its rights in the GI for Parma ham have been violated. What is your analysis? Discuss the claims against both Tilberry's and Carlo. Consider the case below.

Consorzio del Prosciutto di Parma v. Asda Stores, Ltd.
European Court of Justice, 2003
[2003] ECR I-5121

[The House of Lords referred a question to the ECJ concerning the protection of geographical indications and protected designations of origin (PDOs) under Council Regulation (EEC) No. 2081/92 of July 14, 1992, as amended.]

2 That question was raised in proceedings between Consorzio del Prosciutto di Parma ('the Consorzio'), an association of producers of Parma ham, established in Italy, and Salumificio S. Rita SpA ('Salumificio'), a company also established in Italy, a producer of Parma ham and a member of the Consorzio, of the one part, and Asda Stores Ltd ('Asda'), a company established in the United Kingdom, an operator of supermarkets, and Hygrade Foods Ltd ('Hygrade'), also established in the United Kingdom, an importer of Parma ham, of the other part, concerning the marketing in the United Kingdom under the protected designation of origin 'Prosciutto di Parma' ('the PDO "Prosciutto di Parma"') of Parma ham sliced and packaged in that Member State.

LEGAL BACKGROUND

NATIONAL LEGISLATION

3 Article 1 of Legge No 26, tutela della denominazione di origine 'Prosciutto di Parma' (Law No 26 on protection of the designation of origin 'Prosciutto di Parma') of 13 February 1990 reserves the designation 'Prosciutto di Parma' ('Parma ham') exclusively to ham marked with a distinguishing mark allowing it to be identified at any time, obtained from fresh legs of pigs raised and slaughtered in mainland Italy, produced in accordance with provisions laid down in the law, and aged in the typical production area for a minimum period laid down in the law.

4 Article 2 of the Law of 13 February 1990 defines the typical production area as the relevant part of the province of Parma. Article 3 sets out the specific characteristics of Parma ham, including its weight, colour, aroma and flavour.

5 Article 6 of the law provides that:

— after the mark has been applied, Parma ham may be marketed boned and in pieces of varying shape and weight or sliced and suitably packaged;
— if it is not possible to keep the mark on the product, the mark is to be indelibly stamped so that it cannot be removed from the packaging, under the supervision of the competent body and in accordance with the method determined by the implementing regulation;
— in that case, the packaging operations are to be carried out in the typical production area as referred to in Article 2.

6 Article 11 provides that the competent ministers may make use of the assistance of an association of producers for purposes of supervision and control.

7 Article 25 of Decreto No 253, No 26 (Decree No 253 implementing Law No 26 of 13 February 1990) of 15 February 1993 (GURI No 173 of 26 July 1993, p. 4, 'the Decree of 15 February 1993') prescribes that the slicing and packaging of Parma ham must take place at plants in the typical production area which are approved by the Consorzio.

8 Article 26 of that decree requires the slicing and packaging of the product to be carried out in the presence of representatives of the Consorzio.

9 The Decree of 15 February 1993 also contains provisions on packaging and labelling.

10 Under a decree of 12 April 1994, the Consorzio was given the task of monitoring the application of the provisions concerning the 'Prosciutto di Parma' designation of origin.

COMMUNITY LAW

11 Article 29 EC states:

'Quantitative restrictions on exports, and all measures having equivalent effect, shall be prohibited between Member States.'

12 Under Article 30 EC, Article 29 EC does not preclude prohibitions or restrictions on exports justified inter alia on grounds of the protection of industrial and commercial property.

[After citing and quoting the EC legislation, the Court explained the procedure for registering a "protected designation of origin" (PDO).]

15 Articles 5 to 7 lay down an ordinary procedure for registration of a PDO. In that procedure, an application is to be made to the Commission through the intermediary of a Member State (Article 5(4) and (5)). The application is to include the specification in accordance with Article 4 (Article 5(3)). The Commission is to verify that the application includes all the particulars provided for in Article 4 (Article 6(1)). If it reaches a positive conclusion, it is to publish in the Official Journal of the European Communities among other things the name of the product, the main points of the application and the references to national provisions governing the preparation, production or manufacture of the product (Article 6(2)). Any Member State or any legitimately concerned natural or legal person may object to the registration, in which case the objection is to be examined in accordance with a specified procedure (Article 7). If there is no objection, the Commission is to register the designation and publish it in the Official Journal of the European Communities (Article 6(3) and (4)).

THE MAIN PROCEEDINGS

22 Asda operates a chain of supermarkets in the United Kingdom. It sells among other things ham bearing the description 'Parma ham', purchased presliced from Hygrade, which itself purchases the ham boned but not sliced from an Italian producer who is a member of the Consorzio. The ham is sliced and hermetically sealed by Hygrade in packets each containing five slices.

23 The packets bear the wording 'ASDA A taste of Italy PARMA HAM Genuine Italian Parma Ham'.

24 The back of the packets states 'PARMA HAM All authentic Asda continental meats are made by traditional methods to guarantee their authentic flavour and quality' and 'Produced in Italy, packed in the UK for Asda Stores Limited'.

25 On 14 November 1997 the Consorzio brought proceedings by writ in the United Kingdom against Asda and Hygrade seeking various injunctions against them, essentially requiring them to cease their activities, on the ground that they were contrary to the rules applicable to Parma ham.

26 On 17 November 1997 it issued a notice of motion seeking the injunctions claimed in its writ and statement of claim.

27 Asda and Hygrade opposed the applications, arguing in particular that Regulation No 2081/92 and/or Regulation No 1107/96 did not confer on the Consorzio the rights it alleged.

28 The applications were dismissed.

29 The Consorzio appealed to the Court of Appeal (England and Wales). Salumificio was granted leave to intervene in the proceedings. The appeal was dismissed on 1 December 1998.

30 The Consorzio and Salumificio thereupon appealed to the House of Lords.

31 Since the House of Lords considered that the outcome of the case depended on the interpretation of Regulation No 2081/92 and Regulation No 1107/96, it

decided to stay the proceedings and refer the following question to the Court for a preliminary ruling:

> 'As a matter of Community law, does Council Regulation (EEC) No 2081/92 read with Commission Regulation (EC) No 1107/96 and the specification for the PDO "Prosciutto di Parma" create a valid Community right, directly enforceable in the court of a Member State, to restrain the retail sale as "Parma ham" of sliced and packaged ham derived from hams duly exported from Parma in compliance with the conditions of the PDO but which have not been thereafter sliced, packaged and labelled in accordance with the specification?'

33 It should . . . be observed that the main proceedings concern slicing and packaging operations carried out at a stage other than that of retail sale and restaurant sale, for which it is common ground that the condition that those operations must be carried out in the region of production does not apply.

34 Consequently, where reference is made in the present judgment to the condition of slicing and packaging in the region of production, that relates only to slicing and packaging operations carried out at a stage other than that of retail sale and restaurant sale.

65 The specification of the PDO 'Prosciutto di Parma,' by requiring the slicing and packaging to be carried out in the region of production, is intended to allow the persons entitled to use the PDO to keep under their control one of the ways in which the product appears on the market. The condition it lays down aims better to safeguard the quality and authenticity of the product, and consequently the reputation of the PDO, for which those who are entitled to use it assume full and collective responsibility.

66 Against that background, a condition such as at issue must be regarded as compatible with Community law despite its restrictive effects on trade if it is shown that it is necessary and proportionate and capable of upholding the reputation of the PDO 'Prosciutto di Parma'.

67 Parma ham is consumed mainly in slices and the operations leading to that presentation are all designed to obtain in particular a specific flavour, colour and texture which will be appreciated by consumers.

68 The slicing and packaging of the ham thus constitute important operations which may harm the quality and hence the reputation of the PDO if they are carried out in conditions that result in a product not possessing the organoleptic qualities expected. Those operations may also compromise the guarantee of the product's authenticity, because they necessarily involve removal of the mark of origin of the whole hams used.

69 By the rules it lays down and the requirements of the national provisions to which it refers, the specification of the PDO 'Prosciutto di Parma' establishes a set of detailed and strict rules regulating the three stages which lead to the placing on the market of prepackaged sliced ham. The first stage consists of boning the ham, making bricks, and refrigerating and freezing them for slicing. The second stage corresponds to the slicing operations. The third stage is the packaging of the sliced ham, under vacuum or protected atmosphere.

71 First, after checking the authenticity of the hams used, a selection must be made from them. Only hams which satisfy additional, more restrictive conditions, relating in particular to weight, length of aging, water content, internal humidity rate and lack of visible faults, may be sliced and packaged. Further selections are made at the various stages of the process, if anomalies in the product which

cannot be detected before boning or slicing appear, such as dots resulting from micro-haemorrhages, areas of blankness in the muscle or the presence of excess intra-muscular fat.

72 Second, all operators in the region of production who intend to slice and package Parma ham must be approved by the inspection structure, which also approves the suppliers of packaging.

73 Third, representatives of the inspection structure must be present at each of the three stages in the process. They monitor permanently compliance with all the requirements of the specification, including the marking of the product at each stage. When the operations are completed, they certify the number of packages produced.

74 During the various stages there are technical operations and strict checks relating to authenticity, quality, hygiene and labelling. Some of these require specialist assessments, in particular during the stages of refrigeration and freezing of the bricks.

75 In this context, it must be accepted that checks performed outside the region of production would provide fewer guarantees of the quality and authenticity of the product than checks carried out in the region of production in accordance with the procedure laid down in the specification. First, checks performed in accordance with that procedure are thorough and systematic in nature and are done by experts who have specialised knowledge of the characteristics of Parma ham. Second, it is hardly conceivable that representatives of the persons entitled to use the PDO could effectively introduce such checks in other Member States.

76 The risk to the quality and authenticity of the product finally offered to consumers is consequently greater where it has been sliced and packaged outside the region of production than when that has been done within the region.

77 That conclusion is not affected by the fact, pointed out in the present case, that the ham may be sliced, at least under certain conditions, by retailers and restaurateurs outside the region of production. That operation must in principle be performed in front of the consumer, or at least the consumer can require that it is, in order to verify in particular that the ham used bears the mark of origin. Above all, slicing and packaging operations carried out upstream of the retail sale or restaurant stage constitute, because of the quantities of products concerned, a much more real risk to the reputation of a PDO, where there is inadequate control of the authenticity and quality of the product, than operations carried out by retailers and restaurateurs.

78 Consequently, the condition of slicing and packaging in the region of production, whose aim is to preserve the reputation of Parma ham by strengthening control over its particular characteristics and its quality, may be regarded as justified as a measure protecting the PDO which may be used by all the operators concerned and is of decisive importance to them (see, to that effect, *Belgium v Spain*, paragraph 75).

79 The resulting restriction may be regarded as necessary for attaining the objective pursued, in that there are no alternative less restrictive measures capable of attaining it.

80 The PDO 'Prosciutto di Parma' would not receive comparable protection from an obligation imposed on operators established outside the region of production to inform consumers, by means of appropriate labelling, that the slicing and packaging has taken place outside that region. Any deterioration in the quality or authenticity of ham sliced and packaged outside the region of production, resulting from materialisation of the risks associated with slicing and packaging, might harm the reputation of all ham marketed under the PDO 'Prosciutto di Parma',

including that sliced and packaged in the region of production under the control of the group of producers entitled to use the PDO.

[The ECJ went on to rule that because Italy used the simplified registration procedure, notice was given to business operators only that the name "Prosciutto di Parma" is a PDO and no notice was given of the conditions that slicing and packaging operations had to occur in the region of production. Accordingly, business operators cannot be held legally responsible for the conditions related to slicing and packaging in Italy.]

THE COURT hereby rules:

1. Council Regulation (EEC) No 2081/92 of 14 July 1992 on the protection of geographical indications and designations of origin for agricultural products and foodstuffs must be interpreted as not precluding the use of a protected designation of origin from being subject to the condition that operations such as the slicing and packaging of the product take place in the region of production, where such a condition is laid down in the specification.

2. Where the use of the protected designation of origin 'Prosciutto di Parma' for ham marketed in slices is made subject to the condition that slicing and packaging operations be carried out in the region of production, this constitutes a measure having equivalent effect to a quantitative restriction on exports within the meaning of Article 29 EC, but may be regarded as justified, and hence compatible with that provision.

3. However, the condition in question cannot be relied on against economic operators, as it was not brought to their attention by adequate publicity in Community legislation.

NOTES AND QUESTIONS

The United States and the EU, the two leading technology innovators in the world, have sharp disputes over IP. The United States is not very enthusiastic about GIs. The United States believes that IP laws are intended to protect technology. Are GIs based upon technology? Are the differences between the United States and the EU on GIs based on a "new world" versus an "old world" split? The United States and Australia filed a broad-based challenge to the EC regulations concerning GI and PDOs in 2003. The WTO panel rejected most of the challenges but did rule that the EC regulations denied National Treatment in violation of TRIPS Article 3.1 with respect to GI application procedures, objection procedures, the availability of protection, and inspection structures. Application procedures, inspection, and the availability of protection under the regulations also violated the GATT National Treatment provision, Article III:4. The panel's decision was not appealed. *European Communities—Protection of Trademarks and Geographical Indications for Agricultural Products and Foodstuffs*, WT/DS174, 290/R, Report of the Appellate Body, adopted on April 20, 2005.

PROBLEM 13-10

Burt's Farm Fresh Foods based in Parma, Ohio, near Cleveland, advertises that it sells the finest "Parma ham." In fact, the ham is produced in farms located in Parma, Ohio. The Consorzio seeks to ban the use of the term by Burt's. Burt, Jr. says, "Hey, we've been selling Parma ham since 1955 when my father, Burt Sr., first opened the store." What result? *See* TRIPS Article 24(5).

V.   Enforcement Under TRIPS

Read Part III, "Enforcement of Intellectual Property Rights," of TRIPS, Articles 41-61 in the Documents Supplement.

TRIPS breaks new ground in international IP protection with its provisions requiring WTO members to enforce IP rights. When TRIPS was negotiated during the Uruguay Round, commercial piracy was a serious business problem, but the magnitude of the problem has skyrocketed in the past decade since the WTO was established. For this reason, effective enforcement of IP is more important than ever in international business. Because the enforcement provisions of TRIPS were negotiated with commercial piracy in mind, we begin with a brief overview of the commercial piracy problem.

A.   Commercial Piracy

According to the Global IP Center, worldwide annual losses attributable to counterfeiting and commercial piracy have now reached the staggering sum of $650 billion, which is more than the GDP of many countries. *See* http://www.theglobalipcenter .com/facts (citing Frontier Economics, *Estimating the Global Economic and Social Impacts of Counterfeiting and Piracy*, February 2011). Many multinational companies now consider commercial piracy to be their most serious global business problem.

Commercial piracy refers primarily to copyright piracy (i.e., the unauthorized making of identical or substantially similar copies of copyright-protected works) and to trademark counterfeiting (i.e., the unauthorized use of an identical or substantially similar trademark on identical or similar goods). Copyright piracy and trademark counterfeiting are the primary focus of the enforcement provisions in TRIPS. In the area of copyright piracy, the most serious piracy problems are in motion pictures, music, books, and business and entertainment software. In 2011 the commercial value of pirated PC software reached as high as $63.4 billion. *See* Business Software Alliance, *Shadow Market—2011 BSA Global Software Piracy Study*, 1 (9th ed. May 2012). According to one study, the U.S. economy loses approximately $16 billion in lost earnings, and $3 billion in lost tax revenue, due to copyright piracy. *See* Stephen E. Siwek, *The True Cost of Copyright Industry Piracy to the U.S. Economy*, Institute for Policy Innovation, Policy Report #189, 6 (October 2007). Of that $16 billion, approximately $12.5 billion is lost due to sound recording piracy (such as music records). *See* Stephen E. Siwek, *The True Cost of Sound Recording Piracy to the U.S. Economy*, Institute for Policy Innovation, Policy Report #188, 12 (August 2007).

Although the losses from copyright piracy are significant, most multinational companies consider the trademark counterfeiting problem to be much more serious and attribute the bulk of the $650 billion annual losses to counterfeiting. While copyright piracy is primarily limited to a few categories of audio-visual media and software products, counterfeiting can occur in an almost unlimited variety of products. Watches, clothing, shoes, and handbags are well-known targets of counterfeiters, but there are also counterfeit drugs, liquor, chemical fertilizers, airplane parts, and even entire automobiles. Large criminal syndicates, with an organization similar to those of large corporations, engage in a global trade in counterfeit products. Figure 13-1 shows recent data for seizures of pirated and infringing goods at U.S. ports of entry:

FIGURE 13-1
Department of Homeland Security
U.S. Customs and Border Protection and U.S. Immigration and Customs
Enforcement FY 2011 Top Source Countries for
IPR Seizures

Country	Domestic Value	Percentage of Total
China	$109,996,380	62%
Hong Kong	$ 32,155,987	18%
India	$ 4,535,478	3%
Pakistan	$ 3,954,932	2%
Taiwan	$ 2,287,596	1%
Switzerland	$ 1,407,426	1%
Malaysia	$ 1,285,547	1%
South Korea	$ 714,426	Less than 1%
United Kingdom	$ 714,424	Less than 1%
Mexico	$ 654,941	Less than 1%
All Other Countries	$ 20,626,201	12%
Total FY 04 Domestic Value	$178,322,633	
Number of Seizures	24,792	

Source: U.S. Customs and Border Protection Office of International Trade, *Intellectual Property Rights—Fiscal Year 2011 Seizure Statistics* (2012), available at http://www.cbp.gov. Figures for trading partners are based on country of origin and/or country of export as listed in the seizure report.

The United States inspects only a tiny percentage of all containers at U.S. ports of entry. These statistics represent the value of the goods that are actually seized, so they can only be a fraction of the total volume of pirated and infringing goods that enter the United States and an even smaller percentage of the global trade in counterfeit goods.

According to Figure 13-1, China (62 percent) accounts for the largest volume by far of pirated and infringing goods seized by U.S. officials. Because many pirated goods are also transshipped from China through Hong Kong (18 percent) and other countries before their final destination, many experts believe that China accounts for up to, if not more than, 80 percent of all the pirated and counterfeit goods in the world. China's role in piracy is further explored in the materials below.

Statement of Professor Daniel Chow before
the Senate Government Oversight and
Management Subcommittee
April 20, 2004

In terms of size, scope, and magnitude, trademark counterfeiting in China is considered by many to be the most serious counterfeiting problem in world history. A recent study by the PRC State Council Research and Development Center reported that in 2001 the PRC economy was flooded with between $19-$24 billion worth of counterfeit goods. Brand owners in China estimate that 15 to 20% of all well-known brands in China are counterfeit and estimate their losses to be in the tens of billions of dollars per year. Counterfeiting is estimated to now account for approximately 8% of China's gross domestic product.

China has also become the platform for the export of counterfeit products to other countries in Asia, Europe, and the United States. In 2003, China accounted for 66% or over $62 million of the $94 million of all counterfeit and infringing goods seized by the U.S. Customs Service at ports of entry into the United States. An ominous development is that beginning in 2004, exports of counterfeits from China to the United States and other parts of the world may begin to increase significantly for the foreseeable future.

There are several explanations for the unprecedented size and scope of counterfeiting in China:

(1) *Foreign Direct Investment and Advanced Technology.* In recent years, China's economy has enjoyed unprecedented growth for an economy of its size with growth rates of 9.8% from 1980-92 and at 9% more recently. According to some estimates, China is on track to have the world's largest economy in the first decades of the twenty first century. This is a remarkable achievement for a nation that was mired in backwardness and poverty just several decades ago.

This economic growth has been fueled in large part by foreign direct investment from multinational enterprises. In the 1990s, China emerged as the world's second largest recipient of foreign direct investment behind only the United States and in 2002, China surpassed the United States to become the world's largest recipient of foreign direct investment with $50 billion of foreign capital inflows. FDI is the best means in the world today for the transfer of advanced technology, intellectual property, and other forms of valuable information. In many cases today the intellectual property component of a FDI in the form of patents, copyrights, and trademarks is the most important component of the foreign investment. For example, the value of the Coca-Cola trademark in China is worth many more times to that company than the millions of dollars in capital that it has invested in China. The same is true for the patents and copyrights owned by pharmaceutical companies and software companies doing business in China today. However, while MNEs are creating a transfer of technology through FDI that is being absorbed into China's legitimate economy through joint ventures and wholly foreign owned enterprises, some of this intellectual property is also being diverted into China's illegitimate economy as pirates steal this technology to engage in counterfeiting and other forms of commercial piracy. It is no coincidence that China, the world's largest recipient of FDI, advanced technology, and intellectual property also has the world's most serious commercial piracy problem.

(2) *State Support of Counterfeiting and Local Protectionism.* No problem of this size and scope could exist without the direct or indirect involvement of the state. In China, the national government in Beijing appears to be sincere in its recognition of the importance of protecting intellectual property rights, but national level authorities are policy and law-making bodies whereas enforcement occurs on the ground at the local level. At this level, local governments are either directly or indirectly involved in supporting the trade in counterfeit goods. Counterfeiting has become so important that this illegal trade now supports entire local economies and a crackdown on counterfeiting would result in a shutdown of the local

economy with all of the attendant costs of unemployment, dislocation, social turmoil, and chaos. Because the costs of a crackdown at the local level can be so severe, counterfeiting is heavily defended at local levels.

(3) *Ineffective Legal Enforcement and Lack of Deterrence.* China has a developing legal system that is weak in many respects by comparison to legal systems in advanced industrialized countries such as the United States. While China's intellectual property laws are now considered by most observers to be in compliance with the standards set by TRIPS, enforcement of these laws remains inadequate and fails to create sufficient deterrence to counterfeiting.

The combination of these factors—the world's largest influx of foreign direct investment and widespread access to advanced technology, direct or indirect government involvement and support of the counterfeit trade, and a weak legal system that does not create sufficient deterrence for counterfeiters in a very lucrative trade—has resulted in a counterfeiting and commercial piracy problem that is unprecedented in world history.

Oral Testimony of Professor Daniel Chow before the United States-China Economic and Security Review Commission
June 8, 2006

The problem right now is that [counterfeiting] has become so big, so integrated, and [that] it's such an important part of the economy. There are millions, or perhaps tens of millions of people, and hundreds of cities, like Yiwu [that] depend upon the trade in counterfeit goods.

So what happens if you have a national crackdown? You have a severe economic and social problem. It's going to involve a huge expenditure of resources and political capital, and it is something that the Chinese government is not going to do unless it has to do. That's what you have on one side.

What do you have on the other side? You have multinational companies in China who are reluctant to do anything to offend the Chinese government. They're afraid of retaliation against their businesses so they often praise the Chinese government. When President Hu visited Microsoft several weeks ago, Chairman Bill Gates thanked him for the improvement in their protection of intellectual property.

That very same week I was talking to somebody from Microsoft in China and she told me how she's tearing her hair out because they're losing $10 billion a year. So [China's] getting a mixed message; these companies are being politically correct to perhaps the most politically incorrect country in the world.

What's the Chinese government going to do? It's going to do what it is doing now, which is it's going to appease the multinationals by making what, in essence, in my opinion, are cosmetic changes that do not address the serious fundamental issues of the dependence of local economies on the illegal trade in counterfeit goods, the existence of organized crime, the existence of local protectionism and corruption at the local level.

Unless, I think, these root causes are really squarely addressed, we're not going to see in my opinion any significant improvement in the problem in counterfeit goods in the near future.

NOTE ON TRADE SANCTIONS UNDER U.S. SPECIAL 301

Special 301 of the U.S. Trade Act of 1974 provides the United States Trade Representative with authority to identify foreign countries that deny adequate and effective protection of IP rights or fair and equitable market access to U.S. persons that rely on IP protection.

Read Special 301, Sections 306-307 (19 U.S.C. §§2416-2417) of the U.S. Trade Act of 1974, in the Documents Supplement.

There are several categories that the USTR uses to evaluate foreign countries: priority foreign country (PFC), priority watch list, watch list, and special mention. If a country is identified as a PFC, the USTR must open a Section 301 investigation, which may lead to some form of trade sanctions. Countries that are not classified as PFCs but fall in the other categories are not subject to a mandatory Special 301 action but are on notice that they are at risk of being elevated to PFC status. In 2005, the United States invoked sanctions under this provision against Ukraine, a designated PFC (not a member of the WTO) because that country failed to take needed action to enforce IP laws. The sanctions included $75 million in retaliatory tariffs and removal from the U.S. list of beneficiary countries under the Generalized System of Preferences (see Chapter 9).

In 2004, the USTR designated China as a priority watch list country. Other countries on the priority watch list in 2012 are Algeria, Argentina, Canada, Chile, India, Indonesia, Israel, Pakistan, Russia, Thailand, Ukraine, and Venezuela. The watch list includes twenty-six additional countries (excluding Paraguay, which is currently being monitored under Section 306). No country is currently a PFC. Is it surprising that China is not a PFC, a designation that would mandate a Section 301 investigation? For an update on designations under Special 301, consult the USTR web site, http://www.ustr.gov.

To what extent can trade sanctions be invoked against WTO members under this law? Recall the discussion of Section 301 in Chapter 1, and the USTR's representation to the WTO that the United States would not invoke unilateral sanctions against a WTO member under Section 301.

PROBLEM 13-11

At a meeting with a group of glum representatives from multinational companies doing business in China, the Chinese Minister of Trade says, "We are being unfairly criticized for our record on intellectual property rights. In the past five years, we have nearly doubled the number of enforcement actions to over 40,000 trademark enforcement cases per year. That's a pretty good record, so you guys have nothing to complain about." The Minister then hands out copies of the table below to the group to back up her point. In fact, the Minister is correct, as the following actual statistics from China's State Administration of Industry and Commerce (AIC) demonstrate. You've been asked by the companies to analyze this data. Is there anything to complain about?

AIC Trademark Enforcement Activity, 2000-2010 (condensed version)

Year	Cases	Average Fine	Average Compensation	Criminal Prosecutions
2000	22,001	$ 794	—	45 total or 1 in 489 cases
2001	22,813	$1,154	—	86 total or 1 in 265
2004	40,171	$ 834	—	96 total or 1 in 418
2009	51,044	$1,252	$3,124	92 total or 1 in 554
2010	56,034	$1,294	$3,953	175 total or 1 in 320

Source: State Administration of Industry and Commerce Annual Statistics.

B. TRIPS Enforcement Obligations

Commercial piracy presents a daunting challenge to IP owners. The drafters of TRIPS sought to address some of these concerns through the enforcement provisions (Articles 41-61) in Part III of TRIPS.

1. General Obligations

Read the "General Obligations" enforcement provision, TRIPS Article 41, and consider the following problem:

PROBLEM 13-12

You are counsel to a group of developing and least developed countries in Asia and Africa and are asked to explain to the TRIPS Council why Article 41 creates a heavy burden on your clients. In making the argument, your clients have asked you to keep the following points in mind:

- What assumptions about the development of a country's legal system underlie Article 41(4)? Do all countries have courts that review administrative decisions? If a country currently does not allow for judicial review of administrative action, will Article 41(4) create burdens on some countries?
- What assumptions about a country's constitutional and legal system underlie Article 41? For example, do all countries respect court decisions as being more authoritative than an administrative decision or police action? Some countries have military governments. How would they respond to the concept of judicial review?
- What assumptions about judges, lawyers, and law enforcement officials underlie Article 41? Do all persons who fall into these groups in all countries have training in copyright, patent, trademark, and other areas of IP? Are these areas in which special training is required for lawyers and judges? What burdens are created?
- What type of legal system is Article 41 based upon? What country or countries currently have these types of legal systems? Is it appropriate or fair to impose these requirements on your clients?

2. *Criminal Enforcement*

Read TRIPS Article 61, which requires criminal enforcement against certain types of intellectual property violations that occur on a "commercial scale." In the following case, the United States argued that China's criminal laws relating to counterfeiting failed to satisfy Article 61.

China — Measures Affecting the Protection and Enforcement of Intellectual Property Rights
Report of the Panel, adopted on January 26, 2009
WT/DS362/R

[In August 2007, the United States brought several challenges of China's laws relating to intellectual property. In the portion excerpted below, the WTO Panel considers the U.S. claim that China's thresholds for criminal procedures and penalties are inconsistent with Article 61 of TRIPS.]

C. CRIMINAL THRESHOLDS

1. DESCRIPTION OF THE MEASURES AT ISSUE

[Articles 213-218 of China's Criminal Law make it a crime to use counterfeit trademarks, sell counterfeit trademark goods, or engage in criminal copyright infringement, provided that such conduct reaches a certain "serious" or "large" level. The Supreme People's Court and the Supreme People's Procuratorate have further defined these provisions with certain quantitative thresholds triggered, e.g., by the monetary value of the illegal sales or gains. —*Ed.*]

7.400 [For example], Article 1 of Judicial Interpretation No. 19 [2004] interprets the phrase "the circumstances are serious" in Article 213 of the Criminal Law and may be translated as follows:

"Whoever, without permission from the owner of a registered trademark, uses a trademark which is identical with the registered trademark on the same kind of commodities, in any of the following circumstances which shall be deemed as 'the circumstances are serious' under Article 213 of the Criminal Law, shall be sentenced to fixed-term imprisonment of not more than three years or criminal detention for the crime of counterfeiting registered trademark, and shall also, or shall only, be fined:

(1) the *illegal business operation volume* of not less than 50,000 Yuan[5] or the *amount of illegal gains* of not less than 30,000 Yuan;

(2) in the case of counterfeiting two or more registered trademarks, the *illegal business operation volume* of not less than 30,000 Yuan or the *amount of illegal gains* of not less than 20,000 Yuan;

(3) other serious circumstances." (emphasis added)

7.409 [Likewise,] Article 5 of Judicial Interpretation No. 19 [2004] interpreted the phrases "the amount of illegal gains is relatively large" and "there are

---

5. This corresponds to US$6,250 at average market exchange rates (¥8.013/US$ for 2004-2007).

other serious circumstances" under Article 217 of the Criminal Law and may be translated as follows:

> "Whoever, for the purpose of making profits, commits any of the acts of infringement of copyright under Article 217 of the Criminal Law, with the *amount of illegal gains* of not less than 30,000 Yuan which shall be deemed as 'the amount of illegal gains is relatively large'; in any of the following circumstances which shall be deemed as 'there are other serious circumstances,' shall be sentenced to fixed-term imprisonment of not more than three years or criminal detention for the crime of infringement of copyright, and shall also, or shall only, be fined:
>
> (1) the *illegal business operation volume* of not less than 50,000 Yuan;
> (2) reproducing [/] distributing, without permission of the copyright owner, a written work, musical work, cinematographic work, television or other video works, computer software and other works of not less than 1,000[6] in total;
> (3) other serious circumstances." (emphasis added)

7.479 [T]he Panel concludes that, whilst the structure of the thresholds and the method of calculation of some of them can take account of various circumstances, acts of trademark and copyright infringement falling below *all* the applicable thresholds are not subject to criminal procedures and penalties. The Panel will now consider whether any of those acts of infringement constitute "wilful trademark counterfeiting or copyright piracy on a commercial scale" within the meaning of Article 61 of the TRIPS Agreement.

3. CLAIM UNDER THE FIRST SENTENCE OF ARTICLE 61 OF THE TRIPS AGREEMENT

7.502 This claim is brought under the first sentence of Article 61 of the TRIPS Agreement.

[The Panel reviews the various parts of TRIPS Article 61, and focused on the language in Article 61 which requires that members must "provide for criminal procedures and penalties for willful trademark and copyright piracy on a commercial scale." The United States argued that China's laws were in violation of Article 61 because they did not provide for criminal sanctions for certain acts of piracy on a commercial scale. According to the Panel, the key issue is the meaning of "commercial scale." The Panel analyzes this issue below.]

(i) *"On a Commercial Scale"*

7.540 [The Panel rejected the argument by the United States that "on a commercial scale" should be interpreted to mean any commercial activity.] The provisions of the Paris Convention (1967) incorporated by Article 2.1 of the TRIPS Agreement include uses of the word "commercial" in the phrase "industrial or commercial establishment" (in the singular or plural) and in the phrases "industrial or commercial matters" and "industrial or commercial activities."[7] The provisions of

---

6. The number "1000" has been superseded by "500."
7. Article 10*bis* of the Paris Convention (1967).

the Berne Convention (1971) incorporated by Article 9.1 of the TRIPS Agreement include the phrase "any commercial purpose."[8]

7.541 The context shows that the negotiators chose to qualify certain activities, such as rental, exploitation and use, as "commercial." They also chose to qualify various nouns, such as "terms," "value," "nature" and "interests," as "commercial" or "non-commercial." In a similar way, they could have agreed that the obligation in the first sentence of Article 61 would apply to cases of wilful and "commercial" trademark counterfeiting or copyright piracy. This would have included all commercial activity. Indeed, the records of the negotiation of the TRIPS Agreement show that this formulation was in fact suggested (by the United States) at an early stage.[9]

7.543 Instead, the negotiators agreed in Article 61 to use the distinct phrase "on a commercial scale." This indicates that the word "scale" was a deliberate choice and must be given due interpretative weight. "Scale" denotes a relative size, and reflects the intention of the negotiators that the limitation on the obligation in the first sentence of the Article depended on the *size* of acts of counterfeiting and piracy. Therefore, whilst "commercial" is a qualitative term, it would be an error to read it solely in those terms. In context it must indicate a quantity.

7.577 The Panel . . . finds that a "commercial scale" is the magnitude or extent of typical or usual commercial activity. Therefore, counterfeiting or piracy "on a commercial scale" refers to counterfeiting or piracy carried on at the magnitude or extent of typical or usual commercial activity with respect to a given product in a given market. The magnitude or extent of typical or usual commercial activity with respect to a given product in a given market forms a benchmark by which to assess the obligation in the first sentence of Article 61. It follows that what constitutes a commercial scale for counterfeiting or piracy of a particular product in a particular market will depend on the magnitude or extent that is typical or usual with respect to such a product in such a market, which may be small or large. The magnitude or extent of typical or usual commercial activity relates, in the longer term, to profitability.

(ix) Conformity of the Measures at Issue with Respect to the Level of the Thresholds

7.609 The Panel has reviewed the measures [at issue] and agrees that, on their face, they do exclude certain commercial activity from criminal procedures and penalties. For example, some of the criminal thresholds are set in terms that refer expressly to commercial activity, such as "illegal business operation volume," which is defined in terms of "manufacture, storage, transportation, or sales" of infringing products, and "illegal gains" which is defined in terms of profit. However, based solely on the measures on their face, the Panel cannot distinguish between acts that, in China's marketplace, are on a commercial scale, and those that are not.

---

8. Articles II(9)(a)(iv) and IV(4)(c)(iii) of the Appendix to the Berne Convention (1971).

9. The United States suggested in October 1988 a provision applying to trademark counterfeiting and copyright infringement that were "wilful and commercial" (see document MTN.GNG/NG11/W/14/Rev.1). This suggestion was not taken up. A later US proposal, like certain other proposals, used the phrase "on a commercial scale" (see document MTN.GNG/NG11/W/70).

7.610 Certain thresholds are set in monetary terms, ranging from ¥20,000 profit to ¥50,000 turnover or sales. The measures, on their face, do not indicate what these amounts represent as compared to a relevant commercial benchmark in China. Each of these amounts represents a range of volumes of goods, which vary according to price. Another factor to take into account is the period of time over which infringements can be cumulated to satisfy these thresholds. One threshold is set not in monetary terms but rather at 500 ("copies" for the sake of simplicity). Whilst it is reasonably clear to the Panel how many goods that comprises with respect to certain traditional media, this is not, on its face, related to any relevant market benchmark in China either.

7.611 The Panel has noted the United States' repeated assertions that certain amounts constitute counterfeiting or piracy on a commercial scale. The most recurrent example concerns 499 copyright-infringing "copies," although it is not related to the same product in all examples or, sometimes, to any product. The only facts in these examples are amounts equal to, or slightly less than, those in the measures themselves. Those amounts, in combination with the monetary thresholds and the factors used in the thresholds, demonstrate the class of acts for which China does not provide criminal procedures and penalties to be applied. Those numbers and factors do not, in themselves, demonstrate what constitutes a commercial scale for any product or in any market in China.

7.614 . . . [T]he United States did not provide data regarding products and markets or other factors that would demonstrate what constituted "a commercial scale" in the specific situation of China's marketplace.

7.615 In its rebuttal of China's assertion regarding the scale of commerce in China, the United States noted that the "commercial scale" standard was a relative one. It commented on the Economic Census statistics submitted by China but at the same time dismissed their relevance as they are aggregate statistics related to undefined average economic units. It also recalled an earlier assertion that the Chinese market, including the market for many copyright and trademark-bearing goods, is fragmented and characterized by a profusion of small manufacturers, middlemen, distributors, and small outlets at the retail level.

7.616 The Panel has reviewed the evidence in support of this assertion. The evidence comprises a quote from a short article from a US newspaper, the *San Francisco Chronicle*, titled "*30,000-Store Wholesale Mall Keeps China Competitive*" regarding the number of stores in a particular mall in Yiwu and the physical dimensions of some stalls; a statistic quoted from an extract from a management consultant report titled "*The 2005 Global Retail Development Index*" that the top ten retailers in China hold less than 2 per cent of the market, and another statistic that the top 100 retailers have less than 6.4 per cent; and a quote from an article in *Time* magazine titled "*In China, There's Priceless, and for Everything Else, There's Cash*" that a shopping mall in Luohu spans six floors of small stores.

7.617 The Panel finds that, even if these sources were suitable for the purpose of demonstration of contested facts in this proceeding, the information that was provided was too little and too random to demonstrate a level that constitutes a commercial scale for any product in China.

7.627 The United States also submitted other press articles to illustrate points in its first written submission, particularly regarding the calculation of certain thresholds. The Panel has reviewed the press articles and notes that none of them are corroborated, nor do they refer to events or statements that would not require corroboration. Whilst the publications are reputable, most of these particular articles are brief and are quoted either for general statements or random pieces of information. Most are anecdotal in tone, some repeating casual remarks about prices of fake goods, anonymous statements or speculation. They have titles including *"Fake Pens Write Their Own Ticket,"* *"Chasing copycats in a tiger economy,"* *"Hollywood takes on fake Chinese DVDs,"* *"Film not out yet on DVD? You can find it in China"* and *"Inside China's teeming world of fake goods."* Most of the press articles are printed in US or other foreign English-language media that are not claimed to be authoritative sources of information on prices and markets in China. There are four press articles from Chinese sources, one from Xinhua News Agency and three from the English-language *China Daily.* Two are quoted simply to demonstrate the existence of certain goods in China; another quotes a vague statement from unnamed "market insiders" on how illegal publishers tend to work; and the other quotes an "insider" for the maximum and minimum prices of a range of pirated and genuine goods. One other alleged "recent news account" is not attributed to any source at all.

7.629 The Panel emphasizes that, in the absence of more reliable and relevant data, it has reviewed the evidence in the press articles with respect to a central point in this claim that is highly contested. The credibility and weight of that evidence are therefore critical to the Panel's task. For the reasons set out above, the Panel does not ascribe any weight to the evidence in the press articles and finds that, even if it did, the information that these press articles contain is inadequate to demonstrate what is typical or usual in China for the purposes of the relevant treaty obligation.

7.669 In light of the Panel's findings . . . above, the Panel concludes that the United States has not established that the criminal thresholds are inconsistent with China's obligations under the first sentence of Article 61 of the TRIPS Agreement.

NOTES AND QUESTIONS

1. Why did the United States lose on the point that China failed to provide criminal penalties for piracy on a "commercial scale"? Was the evidence on "commercial scale" presented by the United States credible? MNCs have been quite reluctant to come forward and to provide detailed information about their losses. Why? *See* United States International Trade Commission, hearing transcript, 38-41, June 15-16, 2010 (testimony of Daniel Chow, Ohio State University).

2. China has a worldwide reputation as a leading producer of counterfeit goods. Does the result of the WTO's decision surprise you? Will this decision embolden China in being more lax on enforcement?

3. Can you make an argument that this case does not end the controversy but that the WTO has given the United States a roadmap on how to successfully bring this case? There is no bar to refiling this case in the WTO. If the United States wants to refile this case, how should the United States deal with the evidentiary issue? What role must MNCs play? If the United States prepares the case properly, should the United States refile this case? If it does, will the outcome be different?

PROBLEM 13-13

Kurata, a powerful criminal organization, manufactures and sells unauthorized copies of drugs in Country T. Estimates are that the annual revenues from the trade in Country T alone easily exceed $1 billion. When Sogi, the kingpin of Kurata, is caught in a big drug sting, he is given a civil fine. Afterwards Sogi returns to his mountainside luxury villa, and the case against him is closed. Country T's laws do not provide criminal penalties in this type of case. Titan Drugs, a multinational pharmaceutical company with registrations for all its IP rights pertaining to its pharmaceuticals in Country T, is outraged. Titan's CEO says, "This is a blatant violation of TRIPS Article 61!" Is he correct?

NOTES AND QUESTIONS

1. The United States imposes criminal penalties for trafficking in counterfeit goods and services (*see* 18 U.S.C. §2320) and for willful copyright infringements (*see* 17 U.S.C. §506 (criminal offenses)). The United States has also enacted the Economic Espionage Act of 1996, 18 U.S.C.A. §§1831-1839, which imposes criminal liability for the theft or misappropriation of trade secrets for the benefit of foreign governments and certain other entities. Of these laws, which are required by TRIPS?

2. Article 61 requires criminal liability for trademark counterfeiting and copyright piracy only if the activity is willful and on a commercial scale. Why does TRIPS reserve special treatment for trademark counterfeiting and copyright piracy as opposed to other types of IP offenses, such as patent infringements and theft of trade secrets and business know-how? Why are counterfeiting and copyright piracy considered so egregious that criminal punishment is warranted? In the area of patent infringements, it might be possible to argue that there is a policy justification for infringements of pharmaceutical patents to provide access to medicines. Is there also a policy justification for willful trademark counterfeiting and copyright piracy on a commercial scale?

3.   Civil and Administrative Enforcement

Articles 42-50 of TRIPS, the provisions dealing with civil and administrative enforcement, require features that are usually associated with mature and sophisticated legal systems such as that of the United States. WTO members are required to provide for injunctions against infringing activity (Article 44), compensatory damages and attorney's fees (Article 45), and disposal of infringing goods outside the channels of commerce (Article 46). Rights holders are entitled to certain evidentiary presumptions against offenders who are unable to produce evidence (Article 43) and to obtain information from the infringer concerning third parties and the distribution of infringing goods and services (Article 47).

Like many of the other provisions in TRIPS, Article 50, which requires provisional measures, is based upon U.S. law and practice. Article 50(2) incorporates a feature of U.S. procedure that IP owners in the United States believe is critical to a successful strategy of civil enforcement: *ex parte* injunctive relief. Under U.S. federal practice, a plaintiff is allowed to apply for a temporary restraining order (TRO) before a federal district court on an *ex parte* basis. (If the district court decides to issue a TRO, a copy of the order is sent to the U.S. Attorney's Office, which can choose to bring a federal criminal prosecution.) Accompanied by a federal marshal, the plaintiff then serves the TRO, usually with a seizure order, on the defendant. Service of the TRO also notices a preliminary hearing within fifteen days in accordance with Rule 65(a) of the Federal Rules of Civil Procedure. At the preliminary hearing, the plaintiff can then seek a preliminary injunction pending the final outcome of the case, which might include a permanent injunction prohibiting the defendant from engaging in any further infringing activity. In most cases involving counterfeiting or copyright piracy where the defendant's liability is clear, the case is finally resolved at the preliminary hearing where a consent decree is issued if the defendant appears, or a default judgment if the defendant has fled.

NOTES AND QUESTIONS

1. The United States insisted that TRIPS require provisional measures to be available on an *ex parte* basis and has challenged laws that provide for injunctive relief, but not on an *ex parte* basis. Why is *ex parte* relief so important?

2. The EU has issued a directive requiring all member states to permit injunctive relief to "be taken without the defendant having been heard." Article 9(4), Corrigendum to Directive 2004/48/EC of the European Parliament and of the Council of April 29, 2004 on the Enforcement of Intellectual Property Rights, 2004 O.J. (L 157).

4. Border Controls

Read TRIPS Articles 51 to 60 on border enforcement of IP rights.

a. BORDER CONTROLS UNDER TRIPS

A previous section examined the U.S. challenge to China's criminal laws under Article 61. In the same case, the United States also challenged China's compliance with the border controls required by TRIPS.

PROBLEM 13-14

Chinese authorities seize 20,000 bottles of counterfeit shampoo intended for export. The counterfeit shampoo consists of plastic bottles of shampoo with a glued-on label bearing the trademark "Raven Hair Shampoo." Once the label is removed the bottles are nondescript generic bottles used by many different brand owners to sell their shampoo. Pursuant to Chinese law, the authorities remove the labels and sell the shampoo to the highest bidder at a public auction where there is high interest. You are the brand owner of the infringed trademark. What is your concern with this procedure? Is it lawful under Chinese law? Is it lawful under TRIPS?

China—Measures Affecting the Protection and Enforcement of Intellectual Property Rights
Report of the Panel, adopted on January 26, 2009
WT/DS362/R

B. CUSTOMS MEASURES

1. DESCRIPTION OF THE MEASURES AT ISSUE

7.193 This Section of the Panel's findings concerns three of China's Customs measures. The Regulations on Customs Protection of Intellectual Property Rights

("Customs IPR Regulations") were enacted by the Standing Committee of the State Council in November 2003 and entered into force in March 2004. Article 27 provides for the confiscation of goods determined to have infringed an intellectual property right and, in the third paragraph, sets out different options for the disposal or destruction of such goods. The parties agreed to translate the relevant text as follows:

> "Where the confiscated goods which infringe on intellectual property rights can be used for the social public welfare undertakings, Customs shall hand such goods over to relevant public welfare bodies for the use in social public welfare undertakings. Where the holder of the intellectual property rights intends to buy them, Customs can assign them to the holder of the intellectual property rights with compensation. Where the confiscated goods infringing on intellectual property rights cannot be used for social public welfare undertakings and the holder of the intellectual property rights has no intention to buy them, Customs can, after eradicating the infringing features, auction them off according to law. Where the infringing features are impossible to eradicate, Customs shall destroy the goods."

[The other measures are implementing regulations and are similar in substance to the basic law above.]

[The United States challenged China's law on various grounds. The panel rejected the U.S. argument "that Customs lacks authority to donate goods to social welfare bodies in such a manner as to avoid any harm to the right holder caused by lower quality goods," allegedly in violation of TRIPS Articles 59 and 46. The panel found that that one of the social welfare bodies, the Red Cross, distributed donated goods in disaster relief projects so it could not be assumed that the recipients are misled as to the origin of the goods or that the recipients are potential consumers of the genuine goods. The panel also noted that China had a Customs-Red Cross Memorandum that imposed restrictions on the donated goods to prevent their return into the stream of commerce. Accordingly, the Panel rejected the U.S. challenge to China's donation of confiscated goods to the Red Cross. The Panel considered the U.S.'s other challenge below.]

2. CLAIM UNDER ARTICLE 59 OF THE TRIPS AGREEMENT

(a) *Main Arguments of the Parties*

[Auction and authority to order the destruction of infringing goods]

7.197 The United States claims that the competent Chinese authorities lack the scope of authority to order the destruction or disposal of infringing goods required by Article 59 of the TRIPS Agreement. The measures at issue create a "compulsory scheme" so that the Chinese customs authorities cannot exercise their discretion to destroy the goods and must give priority to disposal options that allow infringing goods to enter the channels of commerce or otherwise cause harm to the right holder. *Donation to social welfare bodies* can be harmful to a right holder and nothing appears to prevent such bodies from selling the infringing goods; *sale to the right holder* harms the right holder in the amount that the right holder pays for the infringing goods; and *auction* does not constitute disposal outside the channels of commerce and, absent his consent, may harm the right holder. Where any of these three options is available, the authorities are not authorized to order *destruction* of the infringing goods.

7.329 The [United States'] claim is that the measures, on their face, treat auction (and the other disposal methods) as "compulsory prerequisites" to destruction and create a "compulsory sequence of steps" that renders auction mandatory in certain circumstances. China responds that the Regulations express a "preference" for certain disposition methods and that the Implementing Measures confirm this prioritization. China argues that the measures vest Customs with "considerable discretion" to determine what method is appropriate and that Customs has the legal authority to order any of the four disposition methods.

7.330 The Panel begins by examining the measures on their face. The Customs IPR Regulations set out four disposition methods in Article 27, of which auction is the third. With respect to auction, Article 27 provides as follows:

"Where the confiscated goods infringing on intellectual property rights cannot be used for social public welfare undertakings and the holder of the intellectual property rights has no intention to buy them, Customs *can*, after eradicating the infringing features, auction them off according to law." (emphasis added)

7.331 This phrase provides for the auction of infringing goods. It is conditional on the non-application of the first two methods, i.e. donation to social welfare bodies and sale to the right holder. This phrase uses a modal verb translated as "can" (or "may"). This indicates that the Customs IPR Regulations impose no obligation to auction infringing goods even where the first two disposition methods are not applied.

7.333 The succeeding phrase on destruction provides that "[w]here the infringing features are impossible to eradicate, Customs shall destroy the goods." This indicates that the provision that Customs shall destroy the goods is conditional upon whether "the infringing features are impossible to eradicate". That condition, on its face, does not imply that there is any lack of authority to destroy the goods where the infringing features are *not* impossible to eradicate.

7.335 The United States submits that if none of the first three options is viable, "Customs *may, then and only*, proceed to the third item: destruction of the goods" (emphasis added). However, in the Panel's view, this misreads the text which provides that if none of the first three options is viable, Customs shall destroy the goods. It does not state that Customs *shall not* destroy the goods in other situations.

7.343 Accordingly, the Panel finds that the United States has not established that the Customs measures on their face oblige Customs to order the auction of infringing goods.

7.355 The Panel recalls its findings . . . and concludes that the United States has not established that the Customs measures are inconsistent with Article 59 of the TRIPS Agreement, as it incorporates the principles set out in the *first* sentence of Article 46 of the TRIPS Agreement [i.e., "In order to create an effective deterrent to infringement, the judicial authorities shall have the authority to order that goods that they have found to be infringing be, without compensation of any sort, disposed of outside the channels of commerce in such a manner as to avoid any harm caused to the right holder, or, unless this would be contrary to existing constitutional requirements, destroyed."].

(x)   *Auction and "Simple Removal of the Trademark Unlawfully Affixed"*

7.356 The Panel recalls its finding that "the principles set out in Article 46" as incorporated by Article 59 of the TRIPS Agreement include the *fourth* sentence of Article 46. That sentence provides as follows:

"In regard to counterfeit trademark goods, the simple removal of the trademark unlawfully affixed shall not be sufficient, other than in exceptional cases, to permit release of the goods into the channels of commerce."

7.365 It seems clear from this provision that the eradication of infringing features is a condition attached to auction of goods confiscated by Customs. Article 27 of the Customs IPR Regulations is implemented and confirmed by Article 30(2) of the Implementing Measures and is expressly confirmed by the first operative paragraph of Public Notice No. 16/2007 which provides, relevantly, as follows:

"Where the confiscated infringing goods are auctioned by Customs, Customs shall completely eradicate all infringing features on the goods and the packaging thereof strictly pursuant to Article 27 of the Regulations, including eradicating the features infringing trademarks, copyright, patent and other intellectual property rights."

7.366 It is undisputed that in all cases in which Customs auctions goods that it has confiscated under the measures at issue, Customs first removes the infringing features.

7.379 The Panel notes that the fourth sentence of Article 46, by its specific terms, is not limited to an action to render goods non-infringing, which the simple removal of the trademark would achieve. Rather, the fourth sentence of Article 46 imposes an additional requirement beyond rendering the goods non-infringing in order to deter further acts of infringement with those goods. Therefore, it is insufficient, other than in exceptional cases, to show that goods that have already been found to be counterfeit are later unmarked. The release into the channels of commerce of such goods, while they may no longer infringe upon the exclusive rights in Article 16 of the TRIPS Agreement, will not comply with the requirement in the fourth sentence of Article 46, as incorporated by Article 59.

7.385 [T]he Panel considers that, in regard to counterfeit trademark goods, China's Customs measures provide that the simple removal of the trademark unlawfully affixed is sufficient to permit release of the goods into the channels of commerce. Therefore, the Panel considers that, in regard to counterfeit trademark goods, China's Customs measures provide that the simple removal of the trademark unlawfully affixed is sufficient to permit release of the goods into the channels of commerce in more than just "exceptional cases". [T]he Customs measures are inconsistent with Article 59 of the TRIPS Agreement, as it incorporates the principle set out in the *fourth* sentence of Article 46 of the TRIPS Agreement.

NOTES AND QUESTIONS

1. Can you explain the U.S. argument that Chinese authorities did not have the unrestricted power to destroy infringing goods as required by Article 59 of TRIPS? Why did the panel find China's procedure (in eradicating the trademark on counterfeit goods and then selling the goods) to be inconsistent with Articles 59 and 46 of TRIPS?

2. One of the major concerns of the United States was that the current methods of disposal of counterfeit goods would result in the goods re-entering the market. Can you explain the United States' argument? Are you persuaded by China's argument that the goods will not re-enter the market for sale?

3. Considering how this case was resolved, which country prevailed on the most important issues: the United States or China?

b. BORDER CONTROLS UNDER U.S. LAW AND EU LAW

U.S. law provides for a simple set of procedures for trademark and copyright owners to enlist the aid of Customs in controlling the entry of counterfeit, pirated, and infringing goods (i.e., goods that are partial copies of trademarks and copyrights). These laws are contained in various titles of the U.S. Code: Titles 15 (Trademarks), 17 (Copyright), 18 (Criminal provisions), and 19 (Customs). The U.S. Customs Service has implemented a set of procedures that trademark and copyright owners can invoke to enforce these laws. These procedures are set forth in 19 C.F.R. Chapter 1, subparts C and D. These procedures are available for trademarks and copyrights only. A different set of laws apply to patents, which we examine in the next section.

The owner of a trademark registered with the U.S. Patent and Trademark Office can record the trademark with Customs under procedures set forth in 19 C.F.R. §§133.1-133.4. Once a trademark is recorded, Customs will seize and forfeit goods bearing a counterfeit or substantially similar trademark. Customs will also detain trademarks that partially copy or infringe, but do not counterfeit, a recorded mark. Under its own independent authority, Customs will seize and confiscate *counterfeit* goods with unrecorded marks, but Customs will not detain *infringing* goods unless the mark is recorded. Copyright owners must first register their copyrights with the U.S. Copyright Office and then record the copyright with Customs. Once the copyright is recorded, U.S. Customs will seize pirated goods and will also detain infringing goods that are not identical copies. Customs will also seize *pirated* goods, regardless of whether the copyright is recorded, but will not detain *infringing* goods unless the copyright is recorded.

In sum, all counterfeit trademarked goods and pirated copyright goods are subject to seizure by Customs, but infringing goods are subject to seizure only if the trademark or copyright is first registered with the U.S. Patent and Trademark Office or the U.S. Copyright Office, and then separately recorded with Customs.

Customs will also seize, under certain circumstances, gray market goods or parallel imports that involve a trademark or copyright that has been recorded. Gray market goods are genuine goods that are intended to be sold in a foreign market but that are diverted for sale in the home market of the IP owner. For example, a U.S. company manufactures a trademarked good for sale in Germany but an unauthorized U.S. discounter may buy the goods in Germany and import them into the United States. The IP owner can ban the importation of gray market goods in some, but not all, cases. Customs has a procedure that allows an importer to request a ruling on whether the importation of certain goods would be subject to seizure because they violate recorded trademarks or copyrights.

NOTES AND QUESTIONS

1. Although the recordation procedures for copyright and trademark are simple, you should not assume that using border seizures alone is an effective strategy to stop the influx of counterfeit and pirated goods. Customs randomly inspects only a small percentage of all containers that enter the United States. In most cases,

the IP owner must also provide detailed intelligence before an illegal shipment is seized. How is this information obtained?

2. In accordance with Article 51, the EU requires its member states to implement border controls that permit the seizure and forfeiture of counterfeit trademarked goods and pirated copyright goods. *See* Council Regulation No. 1383/2003, 2003 O.J. (L 196) (EC); *see also* Corrigendum to Directive 2004/48/EC of the European Parliament and of the Council of April 29, 2004 on the Enforcement of Intellectual Property Rights, 2004 O.J. (L 157).

c. SECTION 337 EXCLUSION ORDERS

Section 337 of the U.S. Tariff Act allows IP owners to bar the entry of imported goods that infringe IP rights. Although Section 337 is available for all IP rights, the bulk of cases involve patents because of the availability of the simple customs recordation procedures for trademarks and copyrights. Patent infringements are usually much more complex determinations than copyright or trademark infringements so the simple customs recordation procedures are not available for patents. Instead, patent owners usually resort to Section 337. TRIPS mandates border control measures for trademarks and copyrights only; not for patents. For this reason, we have elected to treat Section 337 separately as a type of national remedy.

Read Section 337 (19 U.S.C. §1337) in the Documents Supplement.

Under Section 337, the complainant must initiate an investigation before the International Trade Commission (ITC), which has the power to hold hearings before issuing a final determination. The ITC's determination is subject to review by the President and can be appealed to the Court of Appeals for the Federal Circuit. The ITC's final determination can include a limited exclusion order (excluding goods manufactured by the parties to the ITC proceeding) or a general exclusion order (excluding all infringing goods from any source). The ITC can also order the named respondents to cease and desist from any further infringing activity. Exclusion orders are enforced by U.S. Customs at the border. Decisions by the ITC are reached expeditiously, usually within fifteen months of the institution of the investigation.

In the 1980s, the EC brought a complaint at the GATT that the then-existing version of Section 337 violated GATT Article III:4, the National Treatment provision. A GATT panel agreed, finding that the availability to complainants in Section 337 of a choice of forum (the ITC or a federal district court), as well as certain of the procedural advantages of Section 337 that are available to challenge imported products of non-U.S. origin, are not available to challenge imports of U.S. origin. (The U.S. origin products were first sold abroad, and an unauthorized party seeks to re-import them into the United States.) *See United States — Section 337 of the Tariff Act of 1930*, GATT B.I.S.D. (36th Supp.) 345, Report of the GATT Panel, adopted on November 7, 1989. After this case, the U.S. Congress refashioned Section 337 in 1994. In the case that follows, we see that Section 337 is increasingly being used by non-U.S.-based multinational companies to enforce international IP rights.

The following case provides a good example of the issues that can arise in a Section 337 patent case involving gray market goods.

Fuji Photo Film Co., Ltd. v. International Trade Commission
United States Court of Appeals, Federal Circuit, 2007
474 F.3d 1281

DYK, Circuit Judge.

[Fuji Photo Film Co., Ltd. (Fuji) sold lens-fitted film packages (LFFPs), which are disposable one-time use cameras. A consumer who uses the LFFP, which is preloaded with film, gives the LFFP to a film processor and receives back only the photographs and the negatives, but not the LFFP itself. Jazz Photo Corp. (Jazz) obtained empty LFFP shells sold in the United States and abroad and refurbished them by reloading the film and resealing the LFFP shells. Jazz then sold the refurbished LFFPs to U.S. consumers. Fuji was the owner of numerous U.S. patents in the LFFP and sought to bar entry of the imports of the LFFPs under Section 337. Whether Fuji could assert its patent rights to exclude the refurbished LFFPs depended on the resolution of two issues: (1) whether Fuji's rights in the LFFPs were "exhausted" and (2) whether the refurbishment constituted a permissible repair or impermissible reconstruction.

Under exhaustion doctrine, Fuji's patent rights will be deemed to be terminated in a particular product if Fuji has received the full benefits of the patent in that product such as through a sale; if Fuji's patent rights are exhausted, Fuji has no right to control the resale or distribution of the product that is the subject of the exhausted patent and, as a result, cannot bar the importation of the product into the United States. On the other hand, if Fuji's patent rights in a product are not exhausted, Fuji can assert the patent right as a basis to bar the entry of the imports. In a prior case, the Federal Circuit Court of Appeals held that Fuji's patent rights are exhausted only if the first sale of the product occurred in the United States. *See Fuji Photo Film Co. v. International Trade Commission*, 386 F.3d 1095 (Fed. Cir. 2004). This ruling meant that Fuji could not bar the importation of LFFPs that were first sold in the United States and then sent abroad for refurbishment. However, Fuji's patent rights were not exhausted in LFFPs that were first sold abroad (i.e., where the first sale did not occur in the United States). For these LFFPs, Fuji could bar their importation into the United States. As some of the LFFPs were first sold in the United States and some were first sold abroad, Fuji could, under the exhaustion doctrine, prevent the entry of some, but not all, of the LFFPs.

A second issue concerned whether the refurbishment was a permissible repair or prohibited reconstruction. Even if the first sale of the LFFP occurred in the United States and exhausted Fuji's patent rights, a third party is not allowed to create a new product or reconstruct the LFFP because this would violate Fuji's patent rights, which include the right to make the product. Because reconstruction is deemed to be the making of a new product, reconstruction would violate Fuji's patent rights regardless of whether the rights in the particular LFFP were exhausted by a first sale in the United States. As a result, it was crucial to determine whether the refurbishment constituted a repair or a reconstruction. If the refurbishment was a prohibited reconstruction, then Fuji could exclude the entry of all reconstructed LFFPs on the basis of its patent rights, even if the LFFPs had been first sold in the United States and then sent abroad for refurbishment. In its investigation under Section 337, the International Trade Commission found that some of the

LFFPs had been illegally reconstructed. The ITC set forth in detail the acts that constituted impermissible reconstruction.

The ITC then imposed a general exclusion order prohibiting the entry of the LFFPs deemed to infringe Fuji's patents and a cease and desist order barring Jazz and certain of Jazz's directors and officers from importing the cameras and from engaging in other infringing activity. This present appeal was brought by Fuji and by Jack Benun, one of Jazz's principals, concerning civil penalties assessed against Benun for violating the cease and desist order.]

The present litigation arises out of an enforcement proceeding instituted by the Commission on September 24, 2002, to investigate Fuji's allegation that Jazz, Benun, and Jazz's then-president and Chief Executive Officer Anthony Cossentino violated the cease and desist order by importing and selling infringing LFFPs during the period after the decision [in *Jazz Photo Corp. v. Int'l Trade Comm'n*, 264 F.3d 1094 (Fed. Cir. 2001) (*Jazz I*)]. On April 6, 2004, the ALJ issued his initial determination. He first concluded that Jazz imported and sold 27 million LFFPs covered by at least one claim of Fuji's asserted patents from August 21, 2001, to December 12, 2003. Relying on *Jazz I*, he then set forth a two-part test defining permissible repair: 1) proof that the cameras were first sold in the U.S. so as to exhaust U.S. patent rights; 2) proof that the cameras were repaired rather than reconstructed.

Since Jazz's refurbishment of LFFPs apparently occurred entirely abroad, there were evidentiary problems in determining whether the patent rights were exhausted, i.e., whether the cameras were first sold in the United States. Ultimately, the ALJ concluded that 40% (10,783,092) of the LFFPs were first sold abroad and therefore infringed because they failed the first prong of the permissible repair defense; he also concluded that 60% (16,174,638) were first sold in the United States and satisfied the exhaustion prong.

Overall, the ALJ found that 1,740,750 of the 27 million LFFPs imported and sold during the relevant period were permissibly repaired (742,500 through the nineteen step process and 998,250 by receiving half backs). By contrast, the ALJ found that Jazz had failed to carry its burden to show permissible repair for all 15,957,730 LFFPs sold in 2001 and 2002 because they either had unexhausted patent rights or there was insufficient evidence of the processes used. In addition, he found that Jazz had not shown permissible repair for 9,259,250 LFFPs sold in 2003 (4,400,000 with unexhausted patent rights; 3,861,000 for which there was insufficient evidence of the processes used; and 998,250 which received full backs).

The ALJ then imposed a civil penalty of $13,675,000 on Jazz. He also imposed a $154,000 penalty on Cossentino and held Benun, as the more culpable of the two, jointly and severally liable for the entire $13 million penalty imposed on Jazz. In doing so, he rejected Benun and Cossentino's argument that they were not personally bound by the order and that the penalty violated their due process rights.

On July 27, 2004, the Commission declined to review the ALJ's violation determinations, but determined to review the ALJ's penalty determination. On review, the Commission accepted the ALJ's penalty findings as to Jazz and Benun, but reduced Cossentino's penalty to $119,750.

Fuji, Jazz, Benun, and Cossentino all timely appealed to this court. Jazz and Cossentino reached a settlement with the Commission and withdrew their appeals.

DISCUSSION

I.

[On appeal, Fuji argued that the Commission erred in concluding that some of the LFFPs at issue in the case were permissibly repaired. The court of appeals held, however, that Fuji lacked standing to bring this appeal, reasoning that any additional civil penalties collected would go to the United States, not Fuji. The court also noted that although private plaintiffs may have standing in some cases where increased civil penalties would discourage future violations, there was no threat of ongoing violations because Jazz had filed for bankruptcy and had ceased business operations before this appeal.]

II.

We turn to Benun's appeal. Benun first argues that the Commission lacked the authority to impose civil penalties on him because it lacked the authority to issue a cease and desist order against him. *See* 19 U.S.C. §1337(f)(1)-(2). According to Benun, 19 U.S.C. §1337(f)(2) only allows the imposition of civil penalties on a person to whom a cease and desist order has been duly issued. Further, he argues, a cease and desist order can only be issued to a "person violating [Section 1337], or believed to be violating section 1337." Benun asserts that he was never found to be personally violating section 1337 by engaging in infringing conduct. Thus, he claims, a cease and desist order could not be legitimately issued against him, and the award of civil penalties should be reversed.

Benun is mistaken as to the scope of the Commission's authority. The Commission plainly had authority to issue an order against Jazz when the Commission found it was infringing Fuji's patents, and it could properly enjoin Jazz's officers, employees, and agents from causing Jazz to engage in future violations. In *Wilson v. United States*, 221 U.S. 361, 31 S. Ct. 538, 55 L. Ed. 771 (1911), the Supreme Court explicitly noted:

> A command to the corporation is in effect a command to those who are officially responsible for the conduct of its affairs. If they, apprised of the writ directed to the corporation, prevent compliance or fail to take appropriate action within their power for the performance of the corporate duty, they, no less than the corporation itself, are guilty of disobedience and may be punished for contempt.

Id. at 376, 31 S. Ct. 538.

Benun contends that this rule is inapplicable in the context of administrative orders because there is no administrative equivalent for Federal Rule of Civil Procedure 65(d), which binds corporate officers to injunctions issued to their corporations. However, in *Federal Trade Commission v. Standard Education Society*, 302 U.S. 112, 58 S. Ct. 113, 82 L. Ed. 141 (1937), the Federal Trade Commission ("FTC") brought an administrative complaint against two related corporations and three individuals who were the managers and sole stockholders of the corporations and issued a cease and desist order against all of the respondents. The validity of the order was challenged on the grounds that the FTC did not have the power to reach the individual corporate officers. On appeal, the Supreme Court reiterated the rule announced in *Wilson* and concluded that individuals "who are in charge and control of the affairs of respondent corporation[ ] would be bound by a cease and desist order rendered [by the FTC] against the corporation[ ]." *Id.* at 119, 58 S. Ct. at 113. Moreover, in cases under the Federal Trade Commission Act, 15 U.S.C. §45(b), courts of appeals have consistently upheld the inclusion of corporate officers in FTC cease and desist orders even when, as here, the administrative complaint and proceedings were directed solely to the corporation and there was no specific statutory authority for the issuance of orders to corporate officers.

In this case the Commission found that Benun, as Jazz's "principal consultant" and COO, was a decision maker and part of the management team. Benun does not challenge this finding on appeal. Under these circumstances the Commission could legitimately issue a cease and desist order against him.

III.

Benun argues alternatively that Jazz did not violate the cease and desist order because Jazz's activities constituted permissible repair. Repair is an affirmative defense to a claim of infringement, and Benun, as the party raising the affirmative defense, had the burden of establishing this defense by a preponderance of the evidence. The repair issue is a legal question based on underlying facts. We review the Commission's legal determinations without deference and its factual determinations for substantial evidence.

A.

The affirmative defense of repair only applies to products whose patent rights have been exhausted through a first sale in the United States. The Commission concluded that 40% of the LFFPs in issue were first sold abroad and had unexhausted patent rights. This conclusion was supported by substantial evidence. It was based on studies conducted by Fuji's expert that used the identifying numbers printed on the LFFPs and Fuji's production and shipping databases to determine where samples of Fuji-type LFFPs with Jazz packaging (i.e., ones that were refurbished by Jazz) were first sold.

Benun urges that the Commission's decision in this respect was not supported by substantial evidence, primarily arguing that Jazz's so-called informed compliance program required a finding in Jazz's favor. Benun asserts that this program tracked shells from collection through the refurbishment process to sale and insured that only shells collected from the United States were refurbished for sale here. The Commission rejected this argument for two reasons. First, it concluded that the program was too disorganized and incomplete to provide credible evidence that Jazz only refurbished shells collected from the United States. Second, the Commission concluded that at most the program could insure that Jazz only refurbished LFFPs *collected* from the United States, not LFFPs that were first *sold* here.

Responding to the second ground, Benun urges that proof that Jazz limited its activities to shells collected in the United States was sufficient to prove exhaustion because Fuji "infected the pool" of camera shells collected in the United States by taking actions that made it difficult for Jazz and Benun to insure that these shells were from LFFPs first sold here. These actions allegedly included allowing Kodak to import cameras with Japanese writing on them for sale in the United States; allowing Kodak to import spent shells into the United States for recycling; and allowing tourists to bring cameras first sold abroad into the United States for personal use. Under these circumstances, Benun argues that a presumption should arise that shells collected in the United States were first sold here. However, the Commission found that the number of shells falling into these categories was insignificant, and that finding was supported by substantial evidence. Moreover, there was evidence that Jazz treated substantial numbers of its own shells collected in the United States (the "reloaded reloads") as having been sold in the United States even though it knew that 90% of these shells were first sold abroad (before the first refurbishment).

In any event, the Commission's first ground—that the program was too incomplete and disorganized to be credible—was supported by substantial evidence. Since there was no suggestion that the incomplete and disorganized nature of the program was due to Fuji's actions, this ground alone was sufficient to justify a conclusion that Benun had not carried his burden to prove exhaustion.

NOTES AND QUESTIONS

Section 337 actions are gaining popularity: In 2009 (calendar year, not fiscal year), there were thirty-one complaints; in 2010, there were fifty-six complaints; and in 2011, there were sixty-nine complaints. Due to the expense and time involved, however, it is unlikely that Section 337 actions will equal the number of recordations of trademarks and copyrights with the Customs Service; thus customs seizure may be the preferred remedy for infringing trademarks and copyright, while Section 337 is used primarily with respect to patents.

14 *Export Controls*

The GATT and the WTO have been traditionally concerned with import controls applied to goods at the border because these controls can create barriers to trade and the reduction and dismantling of such controls has occupied the GATT/WTO for much of its existence. In this Chapter, we examine export controls, which are not extensively addressed in the GATT or the WTO because such controls are not usually used for protectionist reasons. However, the United States has the most ambitious, complex, and controversial export control regime in the world that must be understood by any serious student of trade law. In this Chapter, we first examine (1) WTO provisions applicable to exports and (2) the export controls of the United States that can potentially apply to all four channels of trade: goods, services, investment, and technology.

Governments impose export controls for both economic and non-economic reasons. For developing countries export controls in the form of taxes raise revenue; they may also be employed to diversify exports from overreliance on primary commodities to promote more processed goods. Export controls may be used to control domestic price fluctuations, to relieve shortages, or to influence world prices for certain key commodities such as oil, coffee, and cocoa. Governments also cite non-economic reasons for export controls: environmental protection and national security. The United States imposes export controls not only for economic reasons, but also for political and foreign policy purposes. We will examine some of these political objectives in a following section.

What is the economic impact of using export controls? In general terms export controls distort market prices and impose a net-welfare loss on the economy that employs them. An export tax imposed on a product, for example, will increase the price of the product on the world market, causing foreign consumers of the product to turn to alternative suppliers of the product. Domestic producers of the product will then shift some portion of their production formerly produced for export to the domestic market, resulting in lower domestic prices for the product in question. In the extreme case of an export ban, all production will be shifted to the domestic market, producing what amounts to a subsidy to purchasers (such as domestic processing industries) of the product.

If, however, the export control is placed upon a product that accounts for a significant portion of the world supply, international consumers may not be able to purchase the quantities needed, and the world price will rise dramatically and shortages may develop. Foreign importers must pay more and will try to develop alternative or substitute sources of supply. In the short run there will be a net income transfer from the importing to the exporting countries. But in the longer run the export control may lead to domestic inefficiencies in the export-controlling country because the domestic price is artificially low, and foreign importers will turn to substitute sources so the export-controlling country may lose future market share.

The WTO tracks export controls of members through its Trade Policy Review (TPR) mechanism. Of the 131 WTO members that have undergone TPR since the beginning of the WTO in 1995, 72 (55 percent) were identified as having imposed export taxes: 90 percent of these 72 members impose export duties on agricultural products; 44 percent impose duties on raw materials; and 26 percent impose duties on other commodities such as manufactured goods. Export taxes are most often imposed on sugar, coffee, cocoa, forestry and fisher products, mineral and metal products, and leather, skin, and hides. In addition, virtually all WTO members have some form of quantitative restriction on the export of specific types of products. In contrast to export taxes, which are usually imposed for economic reasons, quantitative restrictions or bans on the export of products are usually imposed for non-economic reasons, for national security, to protect the environment, to conserve goods related to culture and heritage, and to conserve and protect food supplies.[1]

I.   WTO Export Rules

A.   General Considerations

The GATT and WTO have not historically focused on export controls, but with globalization, increases in world population, and growing demand for natural resources, food and commodities, export restrictions increasingly come into play. The WTO rules on exports are growing in importance.

Due to the preoccupation of the GATT and the WTO with import problems, few cases involving export controls have arisen, and aspects of the WTO rules on exports are unclear or disputed. In this section we read the WTO Appellate Body's opinion in the first major case squarely confronting export controls, *China—Measures Related to the Exportation of Various Raw Materials*, WT/DS394, 395, 398/AB/R, Report of the Appellate Body, adopted February 22, 2012.[2] To set the stage, we provide a short summary of the basic WTO export rules.

Note that the GATT Article II concerning Schedules of Trade Concession of WTO members is limited to import charges and regulations; export charges and regulations are not mentioned. However, Article I—MFN treatment—covers both import and export requirements. GATT Article XXVIII bis also authorizes negotiations among WTO members not only over imports but over exports. Thus, many

---

1. Information on export controls may be found on the WTO web site, http://www.wto.org and are summarized in Kim, *Recent Trends in Export Control Restrictions*, OECD Trade Policy Working Papers, No. 101 (OECD Publishing 2010).

2. Previous cases concerning export restraints include, *inter alia*, Report of the Panel. Japan—Trade in Semi-conductors, L/6309-35S/116 (May 4, 1988); Report of the Panel, Argentina—Measures Affecting the Export of Bovine Hides and the Import of Finished Leather, WT/DS155/R, Report of the Panel, adopted on February 16, 2001; and Report of the Panel, United States—Measures that Utilized Export Limits As Subsidies (DS 194), GATT Doc. C.P. 2/SR 11 (1948).

commentators state that MFN treatment is required with respect to export concession agreements so that if two or more WTO members agree to reduce or eliminate
export duties among themselves, this benefit must be extended to all WTO members in accordance with the MFN principle. *See* Mitsuo Matsushita, 3 *Trade, Law and
Development* 267, 272-274 (2011).

Other GATT articles explicitly stating export rules are Article VIII, which lays
down limits with respect to export fees and formalities; Article X, which requires
publication and impartial and objective administration of export trade regulations; Article XIII requires export restrictions on products to be imposed on a
non-discriminatory basis upon WTO members; and Article XVII requires state-
trading enterprises to act without discrimination and in accord with commercial
considerations with respect to exports as well as imports.

The most important GATT provision covering exports as well as imports is
Article XI, which we already studied in Chapter 6. Article XI prohibits quantitative restrictions and other "prohibitions and restrictions other than duties, taxes
or other charges," not only on imports but also on exports. However, there are a
number of exceptions to this prohibition: two of these are contained in Article
XI:2(a) and (b) and ten others are contained in GATT Article XX(a) to (j). Note
that export duties or taxes are expressly permitted under Article XI. The interplay
between Article XI and Article XX is the subject of the following case.

We must mention here Article 12 of the WTO Agreement on Agriculture,
which is an elaboration on GATT Article XI and requires "any [WTO] Member
[who] institutes [an] export prohibition or restriction on foodstuffs in accordance
with paragraph 2(a) of Article XI of GATT 1994," must (a) give "due consideration"
to the effects on importing members' food security concerns and give notice in writing, providing, upon request, necessary information. Many WTO members have
recently invoked AoA Article 12, including Argentina, India, Indonesia, Ukraine,
Egypt, Kazakhstan, Serbia, Tanzania, China, Nepal, Pakistan, Bangladesh, Brazil,
Vietnam, Bolivia, and Russia. We provide one example: In 2010, India, fearing a
spike in domestic cotton prices that would hurt its textile industry, imposed a temporary ban on cotton exports. This contributed to high demand for cotton that
pushed world prices up to their highest point since the American Civil War, according to The Economist.[3] This spike in prices, coming on the heels of years of declines,
caught everyone by surprise. The Gap announced profit warnings, and the agricultural divisions of two trading companies, Glencore and the Noble Group took
large losses. Many countries, including India and China, stockpiled vast quantities
of cotton. Then prices for cotton collapsed in mid-2011. As The Economist has documented, "a vicious circle of price rises, stockpiling and export bans does not make
sense in the medium term for any commodity, whether cotton, onions or iron ore.
It erodes confidence in supply chains, and may dent overall production. Behaviour
that may be rational for individual actors can cause chaos if everyone copies it."[4]

Some WTO members, such as Japan, have called for new and stronger prohibitions on export controls.[5]

---

3. The Economist, March 10, 2012, at 78.

4. *Ibid.*

5. The METI Report, Japan, 2010 Report on Compliance by Major Trading Partners
with Trade Agreements, 23-26; 327-354 (Tokyo: Japanese Ministry of Trade, Economy and
Industry, 2011).

China — Measures Related to the Exportation of
Various Raw Materials
Report of the Appellate Body, adopted February 22, 2012
WT/DS394, 395, 398/AB/R

[This case involved a complaint brought against China by the United States, the European Union and Mexico with regard to Chinese export restrictions on a variety of natural resources, including forms of bauxite, coke, fluorspar, magnesium, manganese, silicon carbide, silicon metal, yellow phosphorous and zinc. These materials are required for the production of high-technology products. The complainants believed that export restrictions kept the cost of the raw materials high in the rest of the world but low in China, creating a competitive advantage. Four types of Chinese export restraints were at issue: (1) export duties; (2) export quotas; (3) export licensing; and (4) minimum export price requirements. The complaining parties cited forty different Chinese measures that allegedly were inconsistent with Chinese obligations under either the GATT or the Chinese Protocol of Accession to the WTO.

As to the various export duties, although permitted by the GATT Article XI:1, the Panel ruled (¶4) that certain export duties violated China's obligations under China's Accession Protocol. Paragraph 11.3 of this Protocol states that China shall eliminate all export taxes and charges except for those specifically listed in Annex 6 of the Protocol or applied in conformity with GATT Article VIII. Annex 6 lists eighty-four different products for which export charges up to certain amounts are permitted. Considering these provisions, the Panel found that (¶4) except for yellow phosphorous, the export charges on the commodities in question were inconsistent with Paragraph 11.3 of the Accession Protocol. The Panel also concluded (¶7.105) that China did not consult with affected WTO members prior to the imposition of export charges in violation of Annex 6 of the Accession Protocol. On appeal, China argued that the export charges were validated by GATT Article VIII. The Appellate Body rejected (¶290) this appeal, stating that the export duties are outside the scope of Article VIII. The Appellate Body also agreed (¶291) with the panel that ruled that since the language in Paragraph 11.3 of the Accession Protocol leaves out any reference to GATT Article XX, "this suggests that China may not have recourse to Article XX to justify a breach of its commitment to eliminate export duties." However the Appellate Body ruled (¶287) in China's favor that since the raw materials at issue are not listed in Annex 6, the consultation requirements in the Note to Annex 6 are not applicable so China did not breach any consultation duty.

As to China's export licensing requirements, the Panel observed (¶¶7.893-7.913) that export licensing falls within the scope of GATT Article XI:1, and the WTO Import Licensing Agreement does not concern exports so is of limited value in interpreting Article XI:1. GATT Article XI:1 does not prohibit all licensing of exports but only that which has a limiting or restrictive effect. The Panel also found (¶¶7.921-7.950) that China's export licensing system does have a restrictive effect because the open-ended discretion in its administration causes uncertainty which amounts to a restriction on exportation that is inconsistent with Article XI:1. On appeal, the Appellate Body declared (¶¶234-235) the Panel's ruling on this issue to be "moot and of no legal effect" because these claims were not within the Panel's terms of reference.

As to China's minimum export prices requirements, the Panel, citing the *Japan — Semi-Conductors* case, ruled (¶7.1082) that requiring enterprises to set minimum export prices or to face penalties constitutes restricting the exportation of products in violation of GATT Article XI:1. On appeal, the Appellate Body ruled (¶¶234-235) that the panel's ruling on this issue was "moot and of no legal effect" because these claims were not within the panel's terms of reference.

The main remaining issues concerned China's export quotas, the subject to the portion of the opinion reproduced below. GATT Article XI prohibits export quotas but Article XI:2(a) creates an exception permitting quotas when the quota is temporary and the exporter is facing a crucial shortage of the products exported. China relied on Article XI:2(a) to justify its export quota before the Panel but its argument was rejected. China also attempted to justify its export quota on the basis of Article XX(g). Article XX is the general exceptions provision, creating an exception to all GATT obligations if certain conditions are met. China asserted Article XX(g), which permits trade restrictions "relating to the conservation of exhaustible natural resources if such measures are made effective in conjunction with restrictions on domestic production or consumption." This argument was also rejected by the Panel. China appealed on both of these points to the Appellate Body, which issued the opinion below.]

B.   ARTICLE XI:2(a) OF THE GATT 1994

318. Article XI of the GATT 1994 provides, in relevant part:

General Elimination of Quantitative Restrictions

1. No prohibitions or restrictions other than duties, taxes or other charges, whether made effective through quotas, import or export licenses or other measures, shall be instituted or maintained by any contracting party on the importation of any product of the territory of any other contracting party or on the exportation or sale for export of any product destined for the territory of any other contracting party.
2. The provisions of paragraph 1 of this Article shall not extend to the following:
   (a) Export prohibitions or restrictions temporarily applied to prevent or relieve critical shortages of foodstuffs or other products essential to the exporting contracting party[.]

322. [W]e note that Article XI:2(a) permits such measures to be "temporarily applied to prevent or relieve critical shortages of foodstuffs or other products essential to the exporting Member." We examine the meaning of each of these concepts — "temporarily applied," "to prevent or relieve critical shortages," and "foodstuffs or other products essential" — in turn below.

323. First, we note that the term "temporarily" in Article XI:2(a) of the GATT 1994 is employed as an adverb to qualify the term "applied." The word "temporary" is defined as "[l]asting or meant to last for a limited time only; not permanent; made or arranged to supply a passing need." Thus, when employed in connection with the word "applied," it describes a measure applied for a limited time, a measure taken to bridge a "passing need." As we see it, the definitional element of "supply[ing] a passing need" suggests that Article XI:2(a) refers to measures that are applied in the interim.

324. Turning next to consider the meaning of the term "critical shortage," we note that the noun "shortage" is defined as "[d]efficiency in quantity; an amount lacking" and is qualified by the adjective "critical," which, in turn, is defined as "[o]f, pertaining to, or constituting a crisis; of decisive importance, crucial; involving risk or suspense." The term "crisis" describes "[a] turning-point, a vitally important or decisive stage; a time of trouble, danger or suspense in politics, commerce, etc." Taken together, "critical shortage" thus refers to those deficiencies in quantity that are crucial, that amount to a situation of decisive importance, or that reach a vitally important or decisive stage, or a turning point.

325. We consider that context lends further support to this reading of the term "critical shortage." In particular, the words "general or local short supply" in Article XX(j) of the GATT 1994 provide relevant context for the interpretation of the term "critical shortage" in Article XI:2(a). We note that the term "in short supply" is defined as "available only in limited quantity, scarce." Thus, its meaning is similar to that of a "shortage," which is defined as "[d]efficiency in quantity; an amount lacking." Contrary to Article XI:2(a), however, Article XX(j) does not include the word "critical," or another adjective further qualifying the short supply. We must give meaning to this difference in the wording of these provisions. To us, it suggests that the kinds of shortages that fall within Article XI:2(a) are more narrowly circumscribed than those falling within the scope of Article XX(j).

326. For Article XI:2(a) to apply, the shortage, in turn, must relate to "foodstuffs or other products essential to the exporting Member." Foodstuff is defined as "an item of food, a substance used as food." The term "essential" is defined as "[a]bsolutely indispensable or necessary." Accordingly, Article XI:2(a) refers to critical shortages of foodstuffs or otherwise absolutely indispensable or necessary products. By including, in particular, the word "foodstuffs," Article XI:2(a) provides a measure of what might be considered a product "essential to the exporting Member" but it does not limit the scope of other essential products to only foodstuffs.

327. Article XI:2(a) allows Members to apply prohibitions or restrictions temporarily in order to "prevent or relieve" such critical shortages. The word "prevent" is defined as "[p]rovide beforehand against the occurrence of (something); make impracticable or impossible by anticipatory action; stop from happening." The word "relieve" means "[r]aise out of some trouble, difficulty or danger; bring or provide aid or assistance to." We therefore read Article XI:2(a) as providing a basis for measures adopted to alleviate or reduce an existing critical shortage, as well as for preventive or anticipatory measures adopted to pre-empt an imminent critical shortage.

C.   THE PANEL'S EVALUATION OF CHINA'S EXPORT QUOTA ON REFRACTORY-GRADE BAUXITE

329. China argues that the Panel erred in finding that China had not demonstrated that its export quota on refractory-grade bauxite was "temporarily applied," within the meaning of Article XI:2(a) of the GATT 1994, to either prevent or relieve a "critical shortage." With respect to the Panel's interpretation of the term "temporarily," China supports the Panel's finding that the word "temporarily" "suggest[s] a fixed time-limit for the application of a measure." China, however, alleges that the Panel subsequently "adjusted" its interpretation of the term "temporarily" to exclude the "long-term" application of export restrictions. China argues that the

term "temporarily" does not mark a "bright line" moment in time after which an export restriction has necessarily been maintained for too long. Instead, Article XI:2(a) requires that the duration of a restriction be limited and bound in relation to the achievement of the stated goal. Furthermore, China argues that the Panel erroneously found that Article XI:2(a) and Article XX(g) are mutually exclusive, and that this finding was a significant motivating factor for the Panel's erroneous interpretation of the term "temporarily" in Article XI:2(a). China submits that the two provisions are not mutually exclusive, and instead apply cumulatively.

330. We note that the Panel found that the word "temporarily" suggests "a fixed time-limit for the application of a measure," and also expressed the view that a "restriction or ban applied under Article XI:2(a) must be of a limited duration and not indefinite." We have set out above our interpretation of the term "temporarily" as employed in Article XI:2(a). In our view, a measure applied "temporarily" in the sense of Article XI:2(a) is a measure applied in the interim, to provide relief in extraordinary conditions in order to bridge a passing need. It must be finite, that is, applied for a limited time. Accordingly, we agree with the Panel that a restriction or prohibition in the sense of Article XI:2(a) must be of a limited duration and not indefinite.

331. The Panel further interpreted the term "limited time" to refer to a "fixed time-limit" for the application of the measure. To the extent that the Panel was referring to a time-limit fixed in advance, we disagree that "temporary" must always connote a time-limit fixed in advance. Instead, we consider that Article XI:2(a) describes measures applied for a limited duration, adopted in order to bridge a passing need, irrespective of whether or not the temporal scope of the measure is fixed in advance.

332. China alleges that the Panel erred in reading the term "temporarily" to exclude the "long-term" application of export restrictions. In particular, China refers to the Panel's statements that Article XI:2(a) cannot be interpreted "to permit the long-term application of . . . export restrictions," or to "permit long-term measures to be imposed." We consider that the terms "long-term application" and "long-term measures" provide little value in elucidating the meaning of the term "temporary," because what is "long-term" in a given case depends on the facts of the particular case. Moreover, the terms "long-term" and "short-term" describe a different concept that the term "temporary," employed in Article XI:2(a). Viewed in the context of the Panel's entire analysis, it is clear, however, that the Panel used these words to refer back to its earlier interpretation of the term "temporarily applied" as meaning a "restriction or prohibition for a limited time." Because the Panel merely referred to its earlier interpretation of the term "temporarily applied" and did not provide additional reasoning, the Panel cannot be viewed as having "adjusted" its interpretation of the term "temporarily" to exclude the "long-term" application of export restrictions.

335. Turning then to the Panel's application of the term "temporarily applied" in the present case, China alleges that the Panel failed to take into consideration the fact that China's export restrictions on refractory-grade bauxite are subject to annual review. China faults the Panel for "simply assum[ing]" that China's restriction on exports of refractory-grade bauxite will be maintained indefinitely. China submits that, at the close of each year, the factual circumstances are assessed in the light of the legal standard set forth in Article XI:2(a) to establish whether the export restriction should be maintained. We note that China has made parallel claims, under Article XI:2(a), alleging an error of application, and under Article

11 of the DSU, alleging that the Panel failed to make an objective assessment of the facts. We consider China's allegation that the Panel "simply assumed" something to be more in the nature of a claim made under Article 11 of the DSU, and therefore address it below at the end of our analysis in this section.

336. China further argues that the Panel erred in its interpretation and application of Article XI:2(a) by presuming that export restrictions "imposed to address a limited reserve of an exhaustible natural resource" cannot be "temporary" and that a shortage of an exhaustible non-renewable resource cannot be "critical." The Panel reasoned that, "if there is no possibility for an existing shortage ever to cease to exist, it will not be possible to 'relieve or prevent' it through an export restriction applied on a temporary basis." The Panel further stated that, "[i]f a measure were imposed to address a limited reserve of an exhaustible natural resource, such measure would be imposed until the point when the resource is fully depleted." The Panel added that "[t]his temporal focus seems consistent with the notion of 'critical,' defined as 'of the nature of, or constituting, a crisis.'"

337. We do not agree with China that these statements by the Panel indicate that the Panel presumed that a shortage of an exhaustible non-renewable resource cannot be "critical" within the meaning of Article XI:2(a). The Panel noted instead, correctly in our view, that the reach of Article XI:2(a) is not the same as that of Article XX(g), adding that these provisions are "intended to address different situations and thus must mean different things." Articles XI:2(a) and XX(g) have different functions and contain different obligations. Article XI:2(a) addresses measures taken to prevent or relieve "critical shortages" of foodstuffs or other essential products. Article XX(g), on the other hand, addresses measures relating to the conservation of exhaustible natural resources. We do not exclude that a measure falling within the ambit of Article XI:2(a) could relate to the same product as a measure relating to the conservation of an exhaustible natural resource. It would seem that Article XI:2(a) measures could be imposed, for example, if a natural disaster caused a "critical shortage" of an exhaustible natural resource, which, at the same time, constituted a foodstuff or other essential product. Moreover, because the reach of Article XI:2(a) is different from that of Article XX(g), an Article XI:2(a) measure might operate simultaneously with a conservation measure complying with the requirements of Article XX(g).

344. For the above reasons, we *uphold* the Panel's conclusion that China did not demonstrate that its export quota on refractory-grade bauxite was "temporarily applied," within the meaning of Article XI:2(a) of the GATT 1994, to either prevent or relieve a "critical shortage," and we dismiss China's allegation that the Panel acted inconsistently with its duty to conduct an objective assessment of the matter as required by Article 11 of the DSU.

B. ANALYSIS

353. Article XX of the GATT 1994 provides, in relevant part:

General Exceptions

Subject to the requirement that such measures are not applied in a manner which would constitute a means of arbitrary or unjustifiable discrimination between countries where the same conditions prevail, or a disguised restriction on international trade, nothing in this Agreement shall be construed to prevent the adoption or enforcement by any contracting party of measures:

. . .

(g) relating to the conservation of exhaustible natural resources if such measures are made effective in conjunction with restrictions on domestic production or consumption[.]

355. In order to fall within the ambit of subparagraph (g) of Article XX, a measure must "relat[e] to the conservation of exhaustible natural resources." The term "relat[e] to" is defined as "hav[ing] some connection with, be[ing] connected to." The Appellate Body has found that, for a measure to relate to conservation in the sense of Article XX(g), there must be "a close and genuine relationship of ends and means." The word "conservation," in turn, means "the preservation of the environment, especially of natural resources."

356. Article XX(g) further requires that conservation measures be "made effective in conjunction with restrictions on domestic production or consumption." The word "effective" as relating to a legal instrument is defined as "in operation at a given time." We consider that the term "made effective," when used in connection with a legal instrument, describes measures brought into operation, adopted, or applied. The term "in conjunction" is defined as "together, jointly, (with)." Accordingly, the trade restriction must operate jointly with the restrictions on domestic production or consumption. Article XX(g) thus permits trade measures relating to the conservation of exhaustible natural resources when such trade measures work together with restrictions on domestic production or consumption, which operate so as to conserve an exhaustible natural resource. By its terms, Article XX(g) does not contain an additional requirement that the conservation measure be primarily aimed at making effective the restrictions on domestic production or consumption.

357. The Appellate body addressed Article XX(g) in *US—Gasoline*. The Appellate Body noted Venezuela's and Brazil's argument that, to be deemed as "made effective in conjunction with restrictions on domestic production or consumption," a measure must be "primarily aimed at" both conservation of exhaustible natural resources and making effective certain restrictions on domestic production and consumption. The Appellate Body, however, found that:

. . . "made effective" when used in connection with a measure—a governmental act or regulation—may be seen to refer to such measure being "operative," as "in force," or as having "come into effect." Similarly, the phrase "in conjunction with" may be read quite plainly as "together with" or "jointly with." Taken together, the second clause of Article XX(g) appears to us to refer to governmental measures like the baseline establishment rules being promulgated or brought into effect together with restrictions on domestic production or consumption of natural resources. Put in a slightly different manner, we believe that the clause "if such measures are made effective in conjunction with restrictions on domestic production or consumption" is appropriately read as a requirement that the measures concerned impose restrictions, not just in respect of imported gasoline but also with respect to domestic gasoline. The clause is a requirement of even-handedness in the imposition of restrictions, in the name of conservation, upon the production or consumption of exhaustible natural resources.

358. Accordingly, in assessing whether the baseline establishment rules at issue in *US—Gasoline* were "made effective in conjunction with" restrictions on domestic production or consumption, the Appellate Body relied on the fact that those rules were promulgated or brought into effect "together with" restrictions on domestic production or consumption of natural resources. However, even though Brazil and Venezuela had presented arguments suggesting that it was necessary that the purpose of the baseline establishment rules be to ensure the effectiveness of restrictions on domestic production, the Appellate Body did *not* consider this to be necessary. In particular, the Appellate Body did not consider that, in order to be justified under Article XX(g), measures "relating to the conservation of exhaustible natural resources" must be primarily aimed at rendering effective restrictions on domestic production or consumption. Instead, the Appellate Body read the terms "in conjunction with," "quite plainly," as "together with" or "jointly with," and found no additional requirement that the conservation measure be primarily aimed at making effective certain restrictions on domestic production or consumption.

359. The Panel in the present case appears to have considered that, in order to prove that a measure is "made effective in conjunction with" restrictions on domestic production or consumption in the sense of Article XX(g), it must be established, first, that the measure is applied jointly with restrictions on domestic production or consumption, and, second, that the purpose of the challenged measure is to make effective restrictions on domestic production or consumption. In particular, the Panel's use of the words "not only . . . but, in addition," as well as the reference at the end of the sentence to the GATT panel report in *Canada-Herring and Salmon*, indicate that the Panel did in fact consider that two separate conditions have to be met for a measure to be considered "made effective in conjunction with" in the sense of Article XX(g).

360. We see nothing in the text of Article XX(g) to suggest that, in addition to being "made effective in conjunction with restrictions on domestic production or consumption," a trade restriction must be aimed at ensuring the effectiveness of domestic restrictions, as the Panel found. Instead, we have found above that Article XX(g) permits trade measures relating to the conservation of exhaustible natural resources if such trade measures work together with restrictions on domestic production or consumption, which operate so as to conserve an exhaustible natural resource.

361. Based on the foregoing, we *find* that the Panel erred in interpreting the phrase "made effective in conjunction with" in Article XX(g) of the GATT 1994 to require a separate showing that the purpose of the challenged measure must be to make effective restrictions on domestic production or consumption.

[The Appellate Body upheld the recommendation of the panel that China should bring its export measures into conformity with its WTO obligations.]

NOTES AND QUESTIONS

1. The Appellate Body's opinion in this case is considerably less extensive than the panel's decision. Note that many of the panel's findings were declared moot and of no legal effect on technical grounds by the Appellate Body. These technical grounds aside, was the panel correct?

2. The *China—Raw Materials* case is the first Appellate Body interpretation of GATT Article XI:2(a). Do you agree with the interpretation and the Appellate Body's characterization of the relation between this Article and GATT Article XX(g)?

3. Although Article XX(b) or (g) were declared not applicable in this case, on a different set of facts these exemptions may justify export controls in the future. What facts would give rise to the applicability of these provisions? If one or both of these provisions were to apply, how should a WTO member allocate export quotas of a resource between domestic and foreign purchasers and among competing foreign purchasers? Note the difference between these two provisions: Article XX(b) lacks the "evenhandedness" requirement of Article XX(g).

4. What was the difference between the panel and the Appellate Body concerning the interpretation of the "made effective in conjunction with restrictions on domestic production or consumption" requirement of Article XX(g)?

5. Future shortages of resources or commodities may provoke greater use of export controls by WTO members. In March 2012, the United States and Japan filed complaints at the WTO against China to contest Chinese restrictions on the export of some fifteen kinds of rare-earth metals that are crucial in the production of a wide range of products, including missiles, car batteries, cell phones, and a variety of magnets. China currently produces over 90 percent of such rare-earth metals and has orchestrated export restrictions ranging from bans on quotas to prohibitive export duties.

B.   Article XXI and National Security Exceptions

GATT Article XXI provides "Security Exceptions" to the WTO rules as follows:

> Nothing in this Agreement shall be construed
>
> (a) to require any contracting party to furnish any information the disclosure of which it considers contrary to its essential security interests; or
>
> (b) to prevent any contracting party from taking any action which it considers necessary for the protection of its essential security interests
>
> > (i) relating to fissionable materials or the materials from which they are derived;
> >
> > (ii) relating to the traffic in arms, ammunition and implements of war and to such traffic in other goods and materials as is carried on directly or indirectly for the purpose of supplying a military establishment;
> >
> > (iii) taken in time of war or other emergency in international relations; or
>
> (c) to prevent any contracting party from taking any action in pursuance of its obligations under the United Nations Charter for the maintenance of international peace and security.

These security exceptions are also contained in GATS Article IV, TRIPS Article 73, and certain other WTO agreements. Although Article XXI has been invoked several times, there is no definitive interpretation of its scope, no doubt because of the sensitive nature of its subject matter. Article XXI was first invoked in 1949 by the United States to justify export restraints against Czechoslovakia. The United States took the position that a nation should be able to unilaterally invoke Article XXI as a carte blanche exception to any of its GATT obligations, while the Czech government argued that Article XXI should be interpreted narrowly. A GATT panel agreed with the United States and set the tone for the subsequent interpretation of Article XXI by noting that "since the question clearly concerned Article XXI, the U.S. action would seem to be justified because every country must have the last resort relating to its own security."[6] This very broad interpretation of the scope of Article XXI set the stage for a difference of opinion that is still unresolved: Should a WTO member's interpretation of its own security needs be beyond question, or should WTO panels and the Appellate Body have jurisdiction to interpret Article XXI to rein in excessive security claims?

The most open ended of the security exceptions, Article XXI:b(iii), states that a WTO member is not prevented from "taking any action which it considers necessary for the protection of its essential security interests . . . taken in time of war or other emergency in international relations." This provision provides the legal basis for export controls. However, Article XXI:b(iii) has not been the subject of extensive GATT/WTO litigation, so there is little guidance on the meaning of some of its terms. The leading GATT cases involving this provision concerned U.S. sanctions during the 1980s in retaliation for Nicaragua's support for subversive activities in Central America and against its military build-up. However, both cases were decided inconclusively.[7] Although there is scant WTO jurisprudence concerning the meaning of Article XXI:b(iii), this Article is the basis on which the United States justifies its trade embargo with Cuba, as well as other trade restrictions imposed out of foreign policy considerations.

NOTE ON MULTILATERAL EXPORT CONTROLS

The United States together with thirty-nine additional countries, including all NATO members, Japan, Australia, New Zealand, and the Russian Federation, participate in a multilateral export control regime known as the Wassenaar Arrangement on Export Controls for Conventional Arms and Dual Use Goods and Technology.[8] The purpose of this arrangement is to enhance regional and global security by a coordinated effort to control trade in arms and in dual use goods and technology. The Wassenaar Arrangement's secretariat, which is located in Vienna, administers export control lists for all its members. These are divided into lists for dual use items, sensitive items, and very sensitive items. The implementation of controls depends, however, on the national laws and export controls of the member nations. The Wassenaar Arrangement convenes meetings of the parties and fosters exchanges of information. Particular attention is placed on missile proliferation controls and chemical and biological weapons technology controls. Decision making in the Arrangement depends on consensus of the members. The Wassenaar Arrangement finds justification under GATT Article XXI:b(ii).

---

6. *Summary Record of the Twenty-Second Meeting,* GATT B.I.S.D. (2d Supp.) 28 (1948).

7. *See United States—Import of Sugar from Nicaragua,* GATT B.I.S.D. (31st Supp.) 67 (1984); *United States—Trade Measures Affecting Nicaragua,* Report of the Panel, GATT Doc. L/6053 (1986).

8. *See* http://www.wassenaar.org.

II. *U.S. Export Controls*

A. Introduction

The United States has an extensive and controversial export control regime that is designed to serve both U.S. national security and foreign policy interests. In this section, we consider the following three major U.S. export control regimes:

- regulation of the export of goods and technology;
- trade embargoes and other trade restrictions on foreign countries; and
- anti-boycott legislation designed to protect countries friendly to the United States from the effects of an unsanctioned economic boycott.

These export controls concern not only goods and technology but also impose certain restrictions on persons and business enterprises.

Authority for the U.S. export control regime is contained in a series of statutes passed by the U.S. Congress pursuant to its constitutional power to regulate foreign commerce. U.S. Const., art. I, §8, cl. 3. (See Chapter 3 of this book examining congressional power over foreign trade.) The laws relating to exports of goods and technology are contained in the Arms Export Control Act (AECA), 22 U.S.C. §2778 *et seq.* dealing with "munitions," (i.e., products and technology that have a military use) and in the Export Administration Act of 1979 (EAA), 50 U.S.C. §2401 *et seq.* dealing with products and technology that have a "dual use," (i.e., both commercial and military uses) and with all other products and technology that do not have military uses. Two additional grants of authority over exports are contained in the International Emergency Economic Powers Act, 50 U.S.C. §1701 *et seq.* and the Trading with the Enemy Act, 50 U.S.C. §1 *et seq.*

Congress has delegated authority to the President under the AECA and the EAA, and the President in turn has delegated the authority to implement each of these acts. For the EAA, the President has delegated authority to the Secretary of Commerce, who has issued the Export Administration Regulations (EAR), 15 C.F.R. §§730-734, which provide detailed rules and procedures applicable to exports of goods. The EAR is administered by the Bureau of Industry and Security (BIS) of the Department of Commerce. For the AECA, the President has delegated authority to the Secretary of State, who has issued the International Traffic in Arms Regulations, 22 C.F.R. §§120-130, which are administered by the Directorate of Defense Trade Controls. The IEEPA and the TWEA provide authority for trade embargoes, other trade restrictions, and anti-boycott legislation that we will also be considering below. The IEEPA is also important because, when the EAA expires, as it periodically does, the IEEPA is used to maintain the existing statutory scheme until a new version of the EAA is enacted by the Congress.

In addition, the U.S. Census Bureau requires the filing of the Shipper's Export Declaration (SED) for most exports. The SED contains general information concerning the parties to the transaction, the products, and the authorization, if required, for the shipment. The SED is the mechanism used to compile official export trade statistics and to enforce the export trade laws of the United States.

Another important federal regime that relates to exports is the Foreign Corrupt Practices Act, 15 U.S.C. §78dd-1 *et seq.* (FCPA). Under the anti-bribery provisions of the FCPA, certain payments made directly or indirectly by a U.S. person or entity to a foreign government official are illegal, even though the payment occurs entirely outside of the United States. The FCPA imposes significant civil and criminal penalties for any violations. Given the prevalence of bribery of government officials in many parts of the world, no company in the United States can afford to ignore the FCPA and must have internal policies to deal with these issues. While the FCPA applies to the sale of goods, issues concerning government corruption and bribery arise most frequently in connection with foreign direct investment; i.e., a company might be pressured to make a bribe in connection with obtaining government approval for a project or a business contract. For this reason, we treat the FCPA extensively in Chapter 6 of our companion book, Chow and Schoenbaum, *International Business Transactions: Problems, Cases, and Materials* (Aspen 2d 2010).

B.   Export Controls Under the EAA and the EAR

Most export transactions in the United States proceed under the EAA and the EAR, so our treatment of export controls will focus on this regime. Under the EAR, most exports do not need authorization; i.e., a license from the BIS. However, some exports do require a license, and the exporter must understand and comply with the procedures for obtaining a license that must be reported on the SED. The Export Administration Regulations are easily available at http://www.bis.doc.gov/policiesandregulations/ear/index.htm; the Export Administration Regulations Database is http://www.gpo.gov/bis/ear/ear_data.html.

Exports of munitions are subject to a separate regime of controls under the International Traffic in Arms Regulations (ITAR), which are administered by the State Department. We do not extensively consider the ITAR, which has its own regulations. (The overall approach of the ITAR is similar to the EAR, although the specific content differs.)

In these materials, we proceed step by step through the export transaction, and we will also introduce some problems to help you work through the procedures. We begin with some basic considerations:

(1)   *What Is an Export?* An export occurs when any "item" is sent from the United States to a foreign destination. An "item" refers to commodities (physical objects), software, and technology, including information. How the item is transported outside the United States does not matter. An item can be carried on an airplane or contained in an automobile that crosses national borders. The item can be sent via mail, fax, e-mail, or telephone. An item that is uploaded to or downloaded from an Internet site may be considered an export. The transaction does not have to be commercial in nature; i.e., no money needs to change hands. Mailing a necktie to a friend in Italy qualifies as an export transaction. An export occurs even if an item leaves the United States on a temporary basis and then returns; i.e., if the friend in Italy travels to the United States and returns the tie. Two special rules concerning exports should be emphasized. A "deemed export" refers to the release of information technology, subject to the EAR, to a foreign national in the United States. This transaction is deemed to be an export to the home country of the foreign national, even though the foreign national is still in the United States. An export also includes a "reexport" of an item. For example, suppose

that an item is exported from the United States to Spain. The item is then exported from Spain to India. This "reexport" is subject to the EAR, even though the exporter is a foreign national and the export occurs in a foreign country. The item is of U.S. origin and is considered by the Commerce Department to be under the jurisdiction of the EAR. The BIS will sometimes issue an export license on condition that no reexport in a foreign country will occur absent express permission from BIS.

(2) *When Is an Export License Needed from the Bureau of Industry and Security (Department of Commerce)?* Under the EAR, certain items cannot be lawfully exported without a license from the BIS. In determining whether a license from BIS is required, four questions must be considered:

- What is being exported?
- Where is the destination of the export?
- Who will receive the item?
- What use will be made of the item?

We examine each of these questions below.

1.   What Is Being Exported?

The first step in determining whether an export license is required is determining whether the item in question is subject to the jurisdiction of the Commerce Department and EAR, since all such items must be classified under the Commerce Control List (CCL). All items in the United States are subject to the jurisdiction of the EAR, except for publicly available technology and software (excluding encrypted items) and those items subject to the exclusive jurisdiction of other federal entities, such as the State Department (weapons and munitions), Energy Department (special fission materials), and the Nuclear Regulatory Commission (nuclear reactors). Certain items outside of the United States may also be subject to the EAR. Items of U.S. origin, wherever located, are subject to the EAR. Certain foreign-made items are subject to the EAR if the item exceeds certain *de minimis* levels of U.S. content (Part 734 Supplement 2), or if the foreign produced item is the direct product of U.S. technology or software.

For items that are subject to the EAR, the next step is to determine the correct Export Control Classification Number (ECCN). The ECCN is a code (e.g., 3A001) that describes a particular item and the controls imposed on that item. All ECCNs are listed in the CCL set forth in Supplement 1 to Part 774.

The CCL is divided into ten broad categories:

0	Nuclear materials, facilities, and equipment (and miscellaneous items)
1	Materials, chemicals, microorganisms and toxins
2	Materials processing
3	Electronics
4	Computers
5	Telecommunications and information security
6	Sensors and lasers
7	Navigation and avionics
8	Marine
9	Propulsion systems, space vehicles, and related equipment

Each category is further subdivided into five product groups:

A   Systems, equipment, and components
B   Test, inspection, and production equipment
C   Material
D   Software
E   Technology

Each ECCN consists of five characters: a number, a letter, and then three more numbers. Returning to our earlier example, 3A001, the first number tells us that the item falls into CCL category 3 (electronics) and product group A (equipment). The third character, or second number, identifies the reason for the control in accordance with the following scheme:

0   National security
1   Missile technology
2   Nuclear nonproliferation
3   Chemical and biological weapons
9   Anti-terrorism, crime control, regional stability,
        short supply, and UN sanctions

In our example, 3A001, the third character "0" indicates that the reason for control is national security. The final two numbers indicate the order of the entry within the category. In many cases, the classification of the ECCN is highly technical, and while the exporter is allowed to determine the classification on its own, the exporter is also allowed to seek advice from the manufacturer. Note that the exporter is strictly liable for any errors for purposes of the EAR, even if the error does not involve willfulness or negligence. An exporter is allowed to submit information and obtain a formal classification ruling from the BIS.

Each ECCN is followed by a description of the item. Then next to the ECCN are all the reasons that the entry is controlled, with a reference for each reason to the Commerce Country Chart (CCC) that must be reviewed to determine licensing requirements for the particular destination. The complete list of reasons for control are:

AT   Anti-terrorism
CB   Chemical and biological weapons
CC   Crime control
EI   Encryption items
FC   Firearms convention
MT   Missile technology
NS   National security
NP   Nuclear nonproliferation
RS   Regional stability
SS   Short supply
XP   Computers
SI   Significant items

What if the exporter determines that an item is subject to the EAR, but there is no applicable ECCN? Any item subject to the EAR that is not listed on the CCL and does not have an ECCN is classified as EAR99. EAR99 items usually consist of low-technology consumer goods and do not require a license. However, if the EAR99 item is destined for an embargoed country, to an end user of concern, or in support of a prohibited end use, a license may be required (or may be refused) by the BIS.

2. Where Is the Destination of the Export?

Once an ECCN has been determined, it is necessary to cross reference the ECCN with the CCC before it can be determined whether a license is required. The ECCNs and the CCC, taken together, define the export controls to which the item is subject, based on the technical features of the product and the country of destination.

The CCC is divided into four groups as follows:

- Group A: Regime Members
- Group B: Less Restricted
- Group C: (Reserved Category)
- Group D: Countries of Concern
- Group E: Terrorism Supporting Countries

In general, members of Group A are subject to the fewest levels of restrictions with the level of restrictions rising with each ascending group. As of this writing, there are forty-four members of Group A, including Canada, Denmark, France, Germany, and Japan. Most of these countries are members of various cooperative export control groups that establish voluntary rules that deal with the proliferation of dangerous items, such as missile technology. Country Group B is the largest category with about 168 countries. The principal exclusions from Country Group B are embargoed countries and some current or former communist countries. Country Group D includes countries "of concern." These are countries that pose special national security concerns, although these concerns do not necessarily involve a direct threat to the United States. Among the countries on this list are China, Burma, Egypt, India, Israel, Russia, Taiwan, and Vietnam. The most restricted group, Group E, has five countries: Cuba, Iran, North Korea, Sudan, and Syria, all considered to be terrorist-supporting countries. Cuba is also the subject of a unilateral and complete trade embargo with few exceptions.

For each reason for control in an entry, there is a reference to a CCC. The CCC is divided into rows, with each Country listed by alphabetical order, and the columns in the Chart are reasons for control. An "X" in any cell (the intersection of the row and the column) means that a license is required. For example, "AT 1" means the column bearing the heading in the CCC, which appears in Supplement 1 to Part 738 of the EAR. If an "X" appears in this cell, a license is required.

3. Who Will Receive the Item?

Even where an ECCN indicates that no license is required or an EAR99 designation applies, the item may still be subject to a license requirement based upon the identity of the person or organization that is receiving the item.

The U.S. government maintains the following lists of prohibited persons or entities:

(1) Entity List, EAR Part 744 Supplement 4: A list of organizations identified by BIS as engaging in activities related to the proliferation of weapons of mass destruction.

(2) Specially Designated Nationals (SDNs) and Blocked Persons, EAR Part 764 Supplement 3: A list maintained by the Treasury Department's Office of Foreign Assets Control comprising persons or individuals who are known to represent countries subject to trade embargoes and trade restrictions or known to be involved in terrorism or drug trafficking.

(3) Unverified List: A list of firms for which BIS was unable to do a complete end use check investigation. Exporters must demonstrate that they have exercised a duty to inquire about these firms before making an export to them.

(4) Denied Persons: A list maintained by BIS of persons who are denied export privileges. Some of these persons live in the United States. It is unlawful to sell a product to a person on this list who wishes to export it. If the denied person is outside the United States, it is unlawful to assist this person in exporting an item from the United States.

4. What Use Will Be Made of the Item?

Some end uses are prohibited altogether, while others require a license. For example, it is not permitted to export any item to an entity that is engaged in the proliferation of weapons of mass destruction, even if the item itself is innocuous, such as a pencil or a light bulb. Some of these entities may also be on one of the prohibited lists discussed above, while other persons or entities may not be on a prohibited list but are nevertheless engaged in prohibited uses.

NOTES AND QUESTIONS

1. *License and Exceptions.* If a license is required, the exporter must apply to the BIS for an export license. If the application is approved, the BIS will issue a license number, with an expiration date (usually two years from date of issuance), that must be used on all export documents, such as the Shipper's Export Declaration. However, the majority of U.S. exports do not require a license. Either the item is designated as an EAR99 because it is not on the CCL, or there is no "X" in the box in the CCC. In each of these situations, the exporter should enter "NLR" on the Shipper's Export Declaration.

2. *Exceptions.* If a license is required, an exception may be applicable. There are three common exceptions (and many others):

- Shipments of Limited Value (LVS): This exception covers exports having limited net value. The limit is set forth in each individual ECCN. LVS is available only for destinations in Country Group B, discussed above.
- Shipments to Country Group B (GBS): This exception covers exceptions for commodities (not software or technology) where authorized by the individual ECCN. There are no limitations on value or frequency for a GBS exception.

- Civil End Users and End Uses (CIV): This exception covers exports and reexports to civil end users for civil end uses in Country Group D (except for North Korea). Items exported under license exception CIV cannot be later transferred to military end users, for military end uses, or for EAR-prohibited proliferation activities.

3. The BIS recently tightened its export requirements for items that are exported to China and might have both a civil and military end use. The BIS issued a new control based upon knowledge of a military end use on exports and reexports of items on the CCC that previously did not require a license. The new rules also increase levels of scrutiny for items that are on the CCL and controlled for reasons of national security, chemical and biological weapons proliferation, nuclear nonproliferation, and missile technology for export to China. *See* 15 C.F.R. §§742-744, 748, 750, and 758.

PROBLEM 14-1

Smith, an engineer at Super Dynamics, a manufacturer of high-speed turbine engines, e-mails a draft of a research memorandum to a friend from graduate school who is now working in France for a French company. After the friend reads the paper, Smith calls the friend in France to chat about the findings and recommendations of the paper for about fifteen minutes. Smith later posts the paper on a web site. Nelson downloads the paper in the Philippines but never reads it. Have there been any export transactions subject to EAR?

PROBLEM 14-2

During a state visit to the United States, the President of Country T visits the Seattle headquarters of New Age Software, a cutting-edge technology company, which is about to launch a new computer operating system. During the visit, Sora, an official from the President's entourage, runs into an old friend, Jones, the senior vice president of product development at New Age, who spent time in his youth as a Peace Corps volunteer in Country T. Sora and Jones go to Jones's office to reminisce. Jones also brags to Sora about some breakthrough features of New Age's operating system, sells Sora some of New Age's software at a substantial discount, and gives Sora a gift of a bag of gourmet coffee beans. Sora is now back in Country T. Have there been any exports subject to the EAR? If so, how many?

PROBLEM 14-3

Ajax Cement Co. has been contacted by a buyer in Syria interested in purchasing a large quantity of reinforced concrete blocks for building bridges and underground tunnels. Ajax Cement Co. advises the wholesale purchaser that Syria is in Country Group E, the most restricted country group. The buyer says, "No problem. Just send the concrete to my cousin in France." Ajax applies for a license to export the product to France. What issues are presented?

PROBLEM 14-4

Your client, General Business Machines (GBM), is interested in selling its products abroad. GBM would like to know whether it needs to obtain licenses, whether any exceptions apply, and whether there are any "red flags" that are raised for the following items:

(1) a polygraph machine to Kenya for use at a private company;
(2) a polygraph machine to Japan for use in a university;
(3) a polygraph machine to a distributor in Italy with clients in the Middle East and Africa;
(4) a quantity of microprocessors that are capable of operating under extreme cold to be sent to South Korea;
(5) a quantity of microprocessors that are capable of operating under extreme cold to be sent to Jordan. Jordan is in Country Group B.

To answer this problem, consider the following materials from the EAR and then consider the CCC.

Excerpts from U.S. Export Administration Regulations
Export Control Classification Numbers (ECCN)

3A981 Polygraphs (except biomedical recorders designed for use in medical facilities for monitoring biological and neurophysical responses); fingerprint analyzers, cameras and equipment; automated fingerprint and identification retrieval systems; psychological stress analysis equipment; electronic monitoring restraint devices; and specially designed parts and accessories.

License Requirements
Reason for Control: CC

Control(s)	**Country Chart**
CC applies to entire entry	CC Column 1

License Exceptions

> LVS: N/A
> GBS: N/A
> CIV: N/A

List of Items Controlled
> Unit: Equipment in number
> Related Controls: N/A
> Related Definitions: N/A

The List of items controlled is contained in the ECCN heading.

3A001 Electronic components, as follows (see List of Items Controlled).

License Requirements
Reason for Control: NS, MT, NP, AT

Control(s)	Country Chart
NS applies to entire entry	NS Column 2
AT applies to entire entry	AT Column 1

License Exceptions

LVS: N/A for MT or NP
         Yes for:
         $1,500: 3A001.c
         $3,000: 3A001.b.1, b.2, b.3, .d, .e and .f
         $5,000: 3A001.a (except a.1.a and a.5.a when
                 controlled for MT), and .b.4 to b.7
GBS: Yes for 3A001.a.1.b, a.2 to a.12 (except .a.5.a when
                 controlled for MT), b.2, and b.8 (except for TWTAs
                 exceeding 18 GHz).
CIV: Yes for 3A001.a.3.b, a.3.c, a.4, a.7, and a.11.

List of Items Controlled

Unit: Number
a.2. "Microprocessor microcircuits", "microcomputer microcircuits", microcontroller microcircuits * * *
   a.2.a. Rated for operation at an ambient temperature
            above 398 K (125°C);
   a.2.b. Rated for operation at an ambient temperature
            below 218 K (-55°C); *or*
   a.2.c. Rated for operation over the entire ambient
            temperature range from 218 K (-55°C)
            to 398 K (125°C).

Supplement No. 1 to part 738
Commerce Country Chart Reason for Control

	CB1	CB2	CB3	NP1	NP2	NS	NS2	MT1	RS1	RS2	FC1	CC1	CC2	CC3	AT1	AT2
Ireland	X					X		X	X	X		X		X		
Israel	X	X	X	X	X	X	X	X	X	X		X		X		
Italy	X					X		X	X							
Jamaica	X	X		X		X	X	X	X	X	X	X		X		
Japan	X					X		X	X							
Jordan	X	X	X	X		X	X	X	X	X		X		X		
Kazakhstan	X	X	X			X	X	X	X	X		X	X			
Kenya	X	X		X		X	X	X	X	X		X		X		
Kiribati	X	X		X		X	X	X	X	X		X		X		
Korea, North	X	X	X	X	X	X	X	X	X	X		X	X	X	X	X
Korea, South	X	X				X	X	X	X	X		X		X		
Kuwait	X	X	X	X		X	X	X	X	X		X				
Kyrgyzstan	X	X	X	X		X	X	X	X	X		X	X			
Laos	X	X		X		X	X	X	X	X		X	X			
Latvia	X					X		X	X							
Lebanon	X	X	X	X		X	X	X	X	X		X		X		

III.   *U.S.-Imposed Embargoes and Trade Restrictions on Foreign Countries*

A.   Introduction

In addition to the controls imposed on the export of goods by the EAR, the United States has a separate regime that imposes restrictions on trading with specific countries.[9] These restrictions are based upon the International Emergency Economic Powers Act (IEEPA), 50 U.S.C. §1701 *et seq.*, and the Trading with the Enemy Act, 50 U.S.C. §1 *et seq.* (TWEA). Additional statutory authority is found in the Antiterrorism and Effective Death Penalty Act, 8 U.S.C. §219, 18 U.S.C. §2332d, and 18 U.S.C. §2339b, the Foreign Narcotics Kingpin Designation Act, Pub. L. No.106-120, Tit. VIII Stat. 1606, 1626-1636, and the Syria Accountability and Lebanese Sovereignty Restoration Act, Pub. L. No. 108-175. Various executive orders relating to these acts and delegating authority for their enforcement and implementation can be found in 31 C.F.R., Chapter V.

The Office of Foreign Assets Control (OFAC) of the U.S. Department of the Treasury has been delegated authority to implement these trade sanctions through its own regulations. There are several important distinctions between the regimes administered by OFAC and the BIS. The regime of trade sanctions imposed under the IEEPA and the TWEA uses the comprehensive economic force of the United States against targeted countries or groups for foreign policy goals, whereas the EAR imposes restrictions aimed at controlling the dissemination of dual use products and technology to end users around the world. Thus, BIS focuses on products and products classification, while the expertise of OFAC is in financial transactions. OFAC accomplishes its objectives by blocking assets and imposing restrictions on trade and financial transactions. Finally, the jurisdiction of the EAR is based upon the product and U.S. persons, whereas the jurisdiction of OFAC covers all U.S. persons and citizens. Note that there will be cases in which there will be overlap between both of these two export regimes; i.e., exports that are permitted under the EAR may be banned under a trade embargo, or the same transaction may be banned under both regimes.

OFAC maintains current sanctions programs against the following countries or groups: Balkans, Belarus, Burma (Myanmar), Ivory Coast, Cuba, Congo, Iran, Iraq, Liberia, North Korea, Sudan, Syria, and Zimbabwe. The United States currently has three comprehensive sanctions programs against Cuba, Iran, and Sudan. Each regime targets a particular government and also persons that are deemed to be instrumentalities of that government and called "Specially Designated Nationals" (SDNs). SDNs may or may not be based in the targeted country; many are not. OFAC maintains a current list of over 3,000 SDNs located all over the globe. SDNs are not limited to persons.

In addition to country-based controls, OFAC also maintains separate control regimes against certain prohibited activities. These activity-based regimes are:

---

9. For a skeptical evaluation of the effectiveness of such regimes, see Gary Clyde Hufbauer, Jeffrey J. Schott, Kimberly Ann Elliott, and Barbara Oegg, *Economic Sanctions Reconsidered: Historical and Current Policy* (Peterson Institute 3d 2007).

Diamond Trading, Narcotics Trafficking, Non-Proliferation of Weapons of Mass Destruction, and Terrorism. Persons or entities involved in these activities are SDNs.

All U.S. citizens, wherever located, all U.S. companies, and all persons in the United States (collectively, U.S. persons) are prohibited from engaging in transactions involving "property" in which a targeted country, government, or SDN has any "interest." The range of prohibited activities include exports, imports, trade, investment, financing, technology transfer, and assisting in or participating in such activities. All of these regimes block or freeze the property of any targeted entities when such property comes within the jurisdiction of the United States or the possession or control of a U.S. person. Two of the OFAC regimes based on the TWEA (Cuba and North Korea) apply not only to U.S. persons but also to foreign entities that are "owned or controlled by" a U.S. person. The OFAC regulations do not define what constitutes ownership, but OFAC takes the position that any entity that is wholly or majority owned by a U.S. person is covered. Control exists when a U.S. person has authority to control the board of directors of a foreign company or has managerial control of a foreign company. In the case of two countries, Cuba and North Korea, the United States maintains a comprehensive embargo: All economic transactions with Cuba and North Korea are banned with only a few exceptions, such as humanitarian aid. *See, e.g., Empresa Cubana del Tabac v. Culbro Corp.*, 399 F.3d 462 (2d Cir. 2005) (Cuban embargo regulations prevent Cuban entities from obtaining U.S. trademark rights).

All of these regimes prohibit evasion by a covered U.S. person. The concept of evasion is broad: It prohibits efforts to restructure a transaction that is subject to control for the purpose of evading U.S. jurisdiction. For example, a covered person cannot restructure a transaction to evade U.S. controls by assigning responsibility for the transaction to a non-covered person, such as a non-U.S. affiliate company, entity, or individual.

Any U.S. person seeking to engage in transactions with a targeted country, government, or SDN must apply to OFAC for a license. OFAC will issue licenses based on some limited exceptions, such as for agricultural goods or humanitarian items. Violations of the OFAC sanctions programs can result in criminal and civil penalties. The civil penalties vary, depending upon the substantive law that has been violated. The highest civil penalty is $1.07 million for each violation under the Foreign Narcotics Kingpin Designation Act.

PROBLEM 14-5

While on a trip to England, James visits an Oriental rug emporium in London, where he purchases a beautiful Persian rug made in Iran (Persia was the former name of Iran). He wishes to ship the rug back to the United States. Is this allowed?

PROBLEM 14-6

Linda is a U.S. citizen who has worked in the U.S. pharmaceutical industry for several years. Recently, Linda was hired by SwissPharma, a multinational pharmaceutical company based in Geneva. Linda has moved to Switzerland to work as a regional sales manager for SwissPharma covering the Middle East,

Africa, and Asia. Recently, SwissPharma has been approached by the African Trading Company, based in Sudan, for the purchase of various drugs and chemical supplies. As Linda is the regional sales manager for the Middle East and Africa, Linda has to approve the sale. Are there any issues under OFAC regulations?

PROBLEM 14-7

On a trip to Cuba to attend a scholarly conference, Raymond, a famous professor of art history, is introduced to several local scholars and artists. One of the artists, Alphonse, is a well-known local artist who has long admired Raymond and offers to paint his portrait as a gift. Alphonse's works are well known in Cuba and parts of South America. Raymond is delighted. Should he accept the gift?

PROBLEM 14-8

A company based in Syria has approached a representative of Uniforms 'R Us (URS), a clothing manufacturer based in the United States, for the sale of work clothes and uniforms for oil workers. Under the relevant OFAC regime, Syria is a targeted country, so URS cannot complete this sale. However, the OFAC regime targeting Syria does not reach foreign subsidiaries of URS that are lawfully organized and are considered legal persons of a foreign country. URS knows that it cannot sell the uniforms to Syria but would like to tell the Syrian representative to contact its affiliate in France to purchase the clothes. Is this lawful under the OFAC regulations?

IV.   Anti-Boycott Regulations

The United States maintains two anti-boycott regimes designed to prevent U.S. persons (including companies) from participating in boycotts directed against countries viewed as friendly to the United States. Although the anti-boycott laws are framed in general terms, they are enforced only against U.S. persons involved in the economic boycott of Israel maintained by Arab states. In the materials below, we focus on the anti-boycott law set forth in the EAR. *See* EAR Part 760. The EAR anti-boycott law is administered aggressively by the Commerce Department's Office of Anti-boycott Compliance (OAC). The U.S. Treasury Department also maintains an anti-boycott regime that penalizes taxpayers who cooperate with an unsanctioned foreign boycott by denying certain tax benefits.

The Commerce Department's anti-boycott law has jurisdiction when a U.S. person or U.S. company is involved and the activity takes place in interstate or foreign commerce. A U.S. person includes a "controlled in fact" foreign affiliate, which refers to the authority of a domestic concern to establish the general policies or control the day-to-day management of a foreign affiliate.

The following actions are prohibited under the Commerce Department's anti-boycott law:

- refusing to do business with Israel, Israeli companies, or Israeli persons or with "blacklisted" companies;
- providing boycott-related information, such as information about business relationships with Israel, Israeli companies, Israeli citizens, or blacklisted companies;
- discriminating against any U.S. person on the basis of race, religion, sex, or national origin;
- evasion.

Id. at Part 760.2(a), (b), (d), and 760.4.

A person or entity covered by the anti-boycott law must report each request to take any action to further the boycott. The request, whether oral or written, must be reported, regardless of whether the request concerns an action that is permitted or prohibited or whether the person or entity complies with the request. Failure to comply with the anti-boycott law will subject the offender to criminal and civil penalties. The maximum civil fine is $10,000 per violation.

PROBLEM 14-9

Ajax Co., a U.S. company based in Maryland, is interested in selling goods to a wholesale distributor in Kuwait. At a lunch meeting, the Kuwaiti representative says to Jones, the Ajax general manager, "Oh, by the way, you don't do any business with Israel or Israeli companies, right?" Ajax has never in fact done business with Israel, but Jones is a bit taken aback by the question and gives an evasive response. Later when Jones gets back to his office, he receives an e-mail message from his Kuwaiti lunch companion saying, "We'd be delighted to go through with the deal, but would you please kindly furnish us a letter with the information that I requested at lunch?" The next day Jones sends a letter by overnight mail with the following statement: "We have done business with companies located in the following countries or territories: Canada, Mexico, Brazil, Germany, the U.K., China, Japan, and Hong Kong." This information is entirely accurate. Has Ajax violated the anti-boycott law? If so, what is the maximum civil penalty that would be involved? What if Jones had never in fact read the anti-boycott law?

United States v. Meyer
United States Court of Appeals, First Circuit, 1988
864 F.2d 214

Coffin, Circuit Judge.

Appellant Robert Meyer is a Massachusetts lawyer charged with violating anti-boycott regulations issued under the Export Administration Act, 50 U.S.C. App. §§2401-2420 (1969) (as amended), by completing, and failing to inform the Commerce Department about, a Saudi Arabia trademark registration form that asked whether his client had a business relationship with Israel. Appellant refused to pay a $5,000 civil fine, and the government then brought this suit to collect the penalty. The district court upheld the assessment, and we affirm.

We begin by relating the particulars of Meyer's alleged violation. In December 1977, in the course of assisting a client who sought to register a trademark in Saudi

Arabia, Meyer received an Authorization of Agent form from a Saudi Arabian firm that processed applications for trademark registration in that country. The form included a section characterized in the cover letter as a "Creed Declaration." In relevant part, it stated:

I/We also hereby solemnly declare that this company has no relations with Israel, which would contradict the following boycott principles:

1. Establishment of a branch of the factory in Israel.
2. Establishment of assembling factory in Israel or presence of an agent who assembles the products of the company in Israel.
3. The availability of general agents or central offices for the Middle East in Israel.
4. Granting the right to use the company's name by Israeli companies.
5. Participation in Israeli factories or companies.
6. Rendering technical assistance to Israeli companies.
7. In case one of the promoters is an Israeli national.

In January 1978, Meyer mailed the completed form to the Saudi Arabian Embassy in Washington, D.C. The next month, in response to a request from the Embassy, Meyer attempted to obtain State Department notarization of the form through a Virginia associate. The State Department responded to the associate's request by explaining that it could not authenticate documents "relating to the Arab boycott of Israel," and it further stated that the law "prohibit[s] U.S. persons from providing certain boycott information." The Virginia lawyer later wrote to Meyer that he authenticated the form through the U.S. Arab Chamber of Commerce, "[a]fter failing to obtain authentication by the State Department because of the Arab boycott."

In April, Meyer wrote a letter to his client in which he described his efforts to obtain authentication of the form, explaining that one problem he encountered was "that the Department of State would not apply its Certificate because of the boycott provisions [and] that Saudi Arabia would not waive the boycott provisions." In September 1978, Meyer sent a copy of the completed form to the Saudi Arabian firm that had sent it to him.

Meyer received a letter from the firm in November, explaining that the form he submitted was unacceptable because it was not authenticated by the State Department. The letter added, however, that the Creed Declaration was no longer required, and it suggested that the change was made because Saudi Arabia recognized "that the United States State Department will not legalize any document which contains the Boycott provisions." A new form, without the declaration, was enclosed. Meyer sent the new form to his client, but he never received a reply from her. He therefore closed his file on this matter.

The statute under which Meyer was charged authorized the President to issue regulations prohibiting the furnishing of information about whether any person has a business relationship with a boycotted country when the information is given "with intent to comply with, further, or support" an unsanctioned foreign boycott. 50 U.S.C. App. §2403-1a(a)(1)(D). This intent requirement was repeated, and elaborated on, in the regulations enacted under the statute. *See* 15 C.F.R. §§369.1(e), 369.2(d)(1), (5). The regulations also required certain persons receiving requests for such information to file a report with the Department of Commerce. 15 C.F.R. §369.4.

Meyer's primary argument is that he lacked the requisite intent to violate the statute and regulations. He claims that his sole purpose in transmitting the form containing the Creed Declaration was to secure a trademark registration for his client, and that nothing he did "either furnished any information or in any way had anything to do with any boycott." The purpose of the Declaration, he asserts, was "not to derive information or knowledge, but merely to exclude [those] unworthy" to obtain a trademark registration.

We disagree that Meyer's actions fell outside of the regulatory prohibition. Although an individual does not violate section 369.2(d) if he takes a prohibited action *inadvertently, see* 15 C.F.R. §369.1(e)(3), the regulations expressly state that an individual who does an act "[knowing] that such action was required or requested for boycott reasons" will be deemed to have acted "with intent to comply with an unsanctioned foreign boycott." *Id.* at §369.1(e)(6). The regulations spell out the significance of the intent requirement:

> (4) Intent in this context means the reason or purpose for one's behavior. It does not mean that one has to agree with the boycott in question or desire that it succeed or that it be furthered or supported. But it does mean that the reason why a particular prohibited action was taken must be established.
>
> (5) Reason or purpose can be proved by circumstantial evidence. For example, if a person receives a request to supply certain boycott information, the furnishing of which is prohibited by this Part, and he knowingly supplies that information in response, he clearly intends to comply with that boycott request. It is irrelevant that he may disagree with or object to the boycott itself. Information will be deemed to be furnished with the requisite intent if the person furnishing the information knows that it was sought for boycott purposes.

15 C.F.R. §369.1(e)(4), (5).

Included in the regulations are "Examples of 'Intent,'" one of which resembles the circumstances of this case:

> (viii) A, a U.S. chemical manufacturer, receives a "boycott questionnaire" from boycotting country Y asking, among other things, whether A has any plants located in boycotted country X. A, which has never supported Y's boycott of X, responds to Y's questionnaire, indicating affirmatively that it does have plants in X and that it intends to continue to have plants in X.
>
> A's responding to Y's questionnaire is deemed to be action with intent to comply with Y's boycott, because A knows that the questionnaire is boycott-related. It is irrelevant that A does not also wish to support Y's boycott.

In addition, an example in the section of the regulations discussing what it means to furnish information about business relationships is strikingly similar to this case, and illustrates that appellant's completion of the Creed Declaration was prohibited.

> (xvii) U.S. company A, a manufacturer of certain patented products, desires to register its patents in boycotting country Y. A receives a power of attorney form required to register its patents. The form contains a question regarding A's business relationships with or in boycotted country X. A has no business relationships with X and knows or has reason to know that the information is sought for boycott reasons.

> A may not answer the question, because A would be furnishing information about its business relationships with or in a boycotted country.

15 C.F.R. §369.2(d).

There is no doubt that Meyer knew that the Creed Declaration was boycott-related. The document expressly asked for a declaration that the company had no relationship with Israel that would "contradict . . . boycott principles." If he somehow failed to notice the language on the form when he received it, his Virginia associate's letter explaining the State Department's refusal to authenticate the form certainly brought the boycott issue directly to his attention. Indeed, when appellant wrote to his client in April 1978, he referred to the "boycott provisions" in the document.

In light of Meyer's obvious awareness of the Creed Declaration, appellant can not contend that he inadvertently violated the regulations when he arranged for completion of the form and transmitted it, thus fulfilling Saudi Arabia's boycott requirements. Instead, appellant emphasizes the district court's finding "that at no time did he consciously intend to violate the laws of the United States or any applicable regulations established by the commerce department." We find no fault with this conclusion, but—as the district court recognized—it does not help appellant. The maxim that ignorance of the law is no excuse is fully applicable here. Appellant sent the application form to Saudi Arabian officials with full awareness that it contained a signed declaration that his client did no business with Israel. In so doing, he intentionally complied with Saudi Arabia's boycott of Israel. That he had no intent to break the law does not erase the fact that he did so.

As to the reporting requirement, the Administrative Law Judge found a violation in Meyer's failure to report the original receipt of the form in December 1977. At that time, the reporting regulation applied to exporters and related service organizations. According to the regulation, "related service organization[s]" include, but are not limited to, banks, insurers, freight forwarders, and shipping companies. 15 C.F.R. §369.4. The ALJ concluded that the language is broad enough to include a lawyer assisting a client in registering a trademark, and we agree. Appellant's client sought trademark protection in Saudi Arabia in preparation for selling products there, and appellant's function was, in essence, to facilitate the export of his client's goods by arranging for the registration of the company's trademark. This was sufficient to bring him within the regulation.

Appellant also claims that he received inadequate notice of the regulations. He particularly criticizes the State Department for failing to warn him, through his Virginia associate, that he would be subject to sanctions if he pursued his attempt to file the application for a trademark registration. The government properly published these regulations in the Federal Register in January 1978, however, and appellant has suggested no reason why the government had any obligation to provide particularized notice to him. In fact, the State Department's response when it declined to authenticate the application form arguably put appellant on notice that he should look into the law "prohibit[ing] U.S. persons from providing certain boycott information."

Finally, we find no merit in appellant's argument that applications for trademark registration are not covered by the statute and regulations at issue here.

AFFIRMED.

NOTES AND QUESTIONS

1. How does answering a boycott-related questionnaire support the boycott of Israel? How does the failure to report a request for boycott-related information support the boycott?

2. In *United States v. Meyer*, was the Virginia lawyer also guilty of an anti-boycott law violation?

Table of Cases

Principal cases are indicated by italicized case names and page references.

Index